WHO'S WHO
OF BRITISH
MEMBERS OF PARLIAMENT

Volume
III
1919-1945

Who's Who
of British
Members of Parliament

VOLUME

III

1919–1945

A Biographical Dictionary
of the House of Commons

Based on annual volumes of
'Dod's Parliamentary Companion' and other sources

MICHAEL STENTON
Peterhouse, Cambridge

and
STEPHEN LEES
University of Cambridge Library

THE HARVESTER PRESS, SUSSEX

HUMANITIES PRESS, NEW JERSEY

First published in Great Britain in 1979 by
THE HARVESTER PRESS LIMITED
Publisher: John Spiers
17 Ship Street,
Brighton, Sussex
and in the USA by
Humanities Press Inc.,
Atlantic Highlands, NJ 07716

Who's Who of British Members of Parliament Volume 3
© 1979 The Harvester Press Limited

British Library Cataloguing in Publication Data
Who's who of British Members of Parliament.
  Vol. 3 : 1919-1945
  1. Great Britain. Parliament. House of Commons—Biography
  I. Stenton, Michael   II. Lees, Stephen
  328.41 '07' 30922   JN672

  ISBN 0-85527-325-9

Humanities Press Inc.
ISBN 0-391-00768-8

Photosetting by Thomson Press (India) Ltd., New Delhi and
printed in Great Britain by
Redwood Burn Limited, Trowbridge and Esher

Contents

Preface by Michael Stenton

Rather than reiterate the observations which I made in the the Prefaces to Volumes I and II I refer the reader back to these and will concentrate my remarks on the nature of the present volume. Difficult editorial choices have had to be made and must be understood by anyone needing to know the exact status of an entry. In earlier volumes it was almost invariably the case that the structure of each entry was as follows:

i.   an extract from *Dod's Parliamentary Companion*,
ii. an account of the Member's electoral history,
iii. details of his post-Parliamentary career,
iv. date of death.

Where possible glaring errors in (i) were corrected, although to nothing like the extent that would have been necessary had a completely revised version of Dod been intended. The second section (ii) was sometimes taken from Dod, but, equally often, was drawn from other sources and made complete. The rest of the entry was, where possible, provided by the editors. But in the present volume the editors have interfered more extensively than before with the substance of the original Dod entry. This is largely due to the unfortunate reticence of the Labour members of the 1918-45 period about themselves and their origins. It must not be thought for one moment that this reserve reflected any embarrassment at the lack of the titled forbears, public schools, mothers, fathers, dates of birth, and good West End addresses which are to be found so frequently in the biographies of their political opponents. On the contrary, their reticence has a more militant aspect since it implied that all that the student of politics needed to know was a man's name, his allegiance and his principles. It has, of course, proved difficult for the editors of this volume to treat this egalitarian brevity with all the respect that it might, in its original context, have deserved. If in this volume almost all Members have parents and birthdays at the beginning of each entry it is not always because Dod discovered them. In short, we have in this instance set aside our rule not to tamper with Dod's text except under grave provocation. If the spirit of the original has been slightly diminished, it has been done in the name of equality. After this confession may we affirm all the more forcefully that the political meat of our entries is still reproduced from Dod *verbatim*. Scholars may agree or disagree with what they find here, but it is contemporary and it is evidence. Of course, the needs of scholarship vary: some will need the hand-book others will need to refer to the originals.

What we offer here supplements Dod without entirely supplanting it. This is not simply because many of our entries are more substantial than Dod's slimmer but authentic originals, it is also because it has only been possible to reprint one of the very many Dod entries which, over the course of a long career, might accumulate in respect of any single MP. The earlier entries are often less informative than the later ones, which is only to be expected, but the changes sometimes register definite shifts in political position. More perversely, there are a fair number of earlier entries which are actually longer and more revealing than for the same MP ten or twenty years later! But in this matter editorial rigour has prevailed, and we have stuck to our practice of using the last and latest Dod reference as the basis of our biographical paragraph. Any earlier version, without substantial revision, could be grossly misleading; with such revision it would cease to resemble Dod at all. Such is the slippery slope which has always lain before us: one alteration implies another until the text disappears in the revision. That, whatever the inelegancies of our editorial logic, is a fate we have evaded wherever humanly possible.

Perhaps concrete illustration of the fluctuating utility of Dod's witness would be useful. Firstly we may note a case of marginal and merely cosmetic revisions. Anthony Eden crops up in the 2nd 1924 edition as a 'Captain' at the head of the entry but with no further reference to his military career. His mother is specified as Sybil Lady Eden. In 1925 service in 'France and Flanders' gets a mention. In 1929 we find 'Brig.-Maj. 1915-19' for the first time, but no mention of Lady Sybil. Such minor variations may offer little reward to textual scholarship. Somewhat more useful may be the case of Daniel Hopkin who is reasonably forthcoming in 1931:

> S. of David Hopkin, Farm Labourer. B. July 11, 1887; ed. at Council Sch. and at South Wales Training Coll. Carmarthen, and at St Catherine's Coll. Cambridge. Exhibition, M.A., LL.B; m. 1920 Ednee Stella d. of J. Viterbo. Served with B.E.F. 1914-18.'

But in 1940 Hopkin is the son of a nameless 'Glamorgan farm worker' without council school, award, degree, wife or war service. This is the sort of change which might conceivably be of some importance to the biographer of Daniel Hopkin or to the student of fashion and style in the self-advertisement of politicians. More intriguing still is the change in David Kirkwood's entries. In 1923 his status as a socialist militant was set out thus: 'Was chief steward of the Beadmore Works in the early period of the war, and a member of the Clyde Workers Committee which organised a series of strikes. Deported in 1916.' This passage is to be found in every edition up until 1936 when we find 'Treasurer of the Clyde Workers' Committee. Deported in 1916.' The martyrdom is intact and a position of financial responsibility has been added, but the strikes have disappeared. Prima facie judgments are, of course, not in order.

The lesson one must learn is that some entries are more objective than others and that it is not always immediately possible to see how interesting points have been suppressed or omitted. Dod supplies the need for a means of rapid reference to absolute essentials very well indeed, but beyond that the historian cannot expect complete satisfaction because the entries are not history but pieces of contemporary political utterence.

*   *   *

Charles Roger Phipps Dod (1793-1855) was the son of a county Leitrim vicar whose family were of Shropshire origin. He entered the King's Inns, Dublin, in 1816, but soon abandoned his legal studies, became a journalist and gravitated to London. Like several others, he saw in the Great Reform Act a peg on which to hang a new political handbook and launched the *Parliamentary Pocket Companion* in 1833. He was in a strong position in doing this, for Dod was one of the small group of men who lifted *The Times* to its unique position in the history of journalism. During the editorial reigns, first of Thomas Barnes and then, after 1841, of the legendary Delane, Charles Dod served and then succeeded John Tyas as head of the Press Gallery staff at the time when *The Times* was establishing its tradition of comprehensive and reliable Parliamentary reporting. Such a tradition was long thwarted by over-crowding and poor acoustics in the Gallery: problems which Fleet Street overcame only when the place was burnt down in 1834; but the new Gallery contained nineteen press boxes (*The Times* was allotted three of the best, while *Hansard* made do with one) providing facilities for Dod to organise his team of scribes systematically. With his own pen, Dod produced the daily summaries which readers were reasonably expected to prefer to the prestigious and exhaustive but practically unreadable full reports. Charles Dod (or 'Dodd' before 1847) was also an obituary writer whose use of the columns of *The Times* was considered rather too free and pointed by his superiors.[1]

Dod also produced a *Peerage, Baronetage and Knightage* annually from 1841 and a volume of *Electoral Facts* in 1853. His son, Roger Phipps Dod, later a captain in the Shropshire yeomanry, took over most of the work of producing both the *Peerage* and the retitled *Parliamentary Companion* in 1843. This task he continued after his father's death in 1855 until his own, as a result of a shooting accident, ten years later. *Dod's Parliamentary Companion* then assumed the name under which it has flourished ever since.

There are other nineteenth century annual publications which supplement without supplanting *Dod* as a guide to Parliament. *Vacher's Parliamentary*

Companion runs, like *Dod*, from 1833 to the present and provides lists of Members, constituencies, election results and office holders, but it lacks the element of political description. Debrett's *Illustrated House of Commons*, begun in 1867, offers a paragraph on each MP and every member of the judicial bench, but sadly its claim to distinction rests upon the heraldic shields it bestows wherever possible: there are no portraits. One of Charles Dod's most distinguished successors as head of *The Times's* parliamentary staff was Charles Ross, who edited *Ross's Parliamentary Record* from 1875: a periodical cast in the form of a dictionary of Parliamentary business—bills, summaries of debates, major division lists, dates and names of resolutions—which reverted to its original name of the *Parliamentary Record* in 1880. Other relevant publications of this type are listed extensively in H.J. Hanham *Bibliography of British History 1851-1914* (1976) in section II under 'Parliament' and 'The Electoral System'.

M.S.

1. Mowbray Morris to John Walter 1856, Vol. ii, *History of The Times* (1935-52), pp. 592-4.

Acknowledgements

We are indebted to Mr. D.L. Clarke, Librarian of the British Library of Political and Economic Science, for permission to consult the unpublished files relating to C. Cook, *Sources in British Political History 1900-51* and to Angela Raspin for providing access to them. Mr. J. Lonsdale, Librarian of *The Times* kindly provided information about certain recalcitrant editions of that newspaper and we gratefully acknowledge help received from Henry Pelling, Brendan Bradshaw and Tom Dunne. The Editors would again like to thank Mavis Thomas for her skill and accuracy in the preparation of the manuscript of this third volume.

Advice to Readers

This is the third volume of four, which taken together will supply biographies of every Member of Parliament to have sat in the House of Commons between 1832-1979. Volume I comprises more than 3050 lives for the years 1832-1885 inclusive. Volume II covers the years 1886-1918. Volume III covers 1919-1945 and Volume IV will cover the period from 1945 to the dissolution of Parliament which was elected in October 1974.

The foundation of the whole set of reference works is the long run of *Dod's Parliamentary Companion*, published annually (sometimes twice a year) since 1832 and still continuing. The fullest and best entry for each MP has been taken from this source, and supplemented where possible with important additional information. Yet the personal and idiosyncratic style of Charles Dod's original entries has been maintained, with minor adjustment where events he mentions in the present tense have been rendered into the past. The biographies have then been organised into these new volumes, for ease of reference.

The following notes on the location of each biography in particular volumes, party labels, supplementary data which has been specially researched, changes of names and further guidance on supplementary sources will assist the user:

WHICH VOLUME IS AN MP IN?

The biography of an MP is printed in the volume whose dates cover the *end of his career in Parliament*, rather than his year of initial entry. All those who sat both before and after 1918 have been included in Volume III and there are a handful of entries which appear in both Volumes II and III as an extra help to the reader.

The index of names clearly indicates with a dagger those members whose full entries appear both in Volume II and Volume III, and with an asterisk those members who continued to sit after 1945 and whose entries appear in Volume IV.

WHICH VOLUME OF 'DOD' IS THE PRINCIPAL SOURCE FOR EACH LIFE?

In the majority of cases the very last entry has been used. After certain general elections Dod ran a second edition. Unless otherwise specified the first edition of Dod is the one which has been used. The year of Dod which has been used as the source has been clearly indicated in square brackets at the end of each entry.

PARTY LABELS

Those given by Charles Dod are used.

SUPPLEMENTARY DATA ADDED

Each entry essentially follows that of Dod but a number of consistent changes have been made to ensure that all the information appears in the same order. Some variations used by Dod have been retained; Brecknockshire and Breconshire are used interchangeably, as also are Salop and Shropshire.

The consistent order that we have followed is: name, address, clubs, details of parentage, birth, marriage, education, career prior to entering Parliament, political principles or affiliations, views on controversial or important questions, full Parliamentary career including every occasion when a person unsuccessfully contested a seat, reason for finally leaving Parliament, subsequent career when known, and the date of death when this can be traced. It was found that Dod was less concerned in giving full information about the occasions when MPs were unsuccessful candidates and a considerable amount of checking and adding of details has been necessary. Neither could Dod include any information about contested seats after an MP had finally left Parliament. This information has been fully researched and added to the relevant entries. Usually this additional information appears after the details of the parliamentary career, except for details about birth-date, parentage, education, and marriage—all of which have been inserted into the main body of the entry.

There were a number of successful candidates who entered and left Parliament between editions and no entries are to be found in Dod. In those cases we have provided all the information about the Parliamentary career, together with full details about any other seats contested either before or after they sat. We have added further information when this has been available. Entries are included for the Sinn Feiners who were elected for Irish constituencies in 1918 although they never took their seats at Westminster.

If an MP is still alive at the time of writing this volume it has been indicated by a star at the end of the entry. When neither a star nor a date of death is given this shows that we have not been able to establish whether the subject of the entry is still alive.

CHANGES OF NAMES
Many individuals changed their family names during this period and there are sometimes discrepancies between the names recorded in standard reference books and those which appeared in *Dod's Parliamentary Companion*. As a general rule we have followed the *Parliamentary Companion* and where necessary cross references are given in the text and in the name index.

OTHER CONVENTIONS FOLLOWED
'Returned in 1922' etc., means elected at the general election in that year. 'Retired in 1929' etc., means that the sitting MP failed to contest his seat. There is no implication that the man took a sober decision to end his political career. Where the word is not used it is because there is something standing in the text constituting the formal cause of the MPs departure from the House of Commons: electoral defeat, a peerage, a government appointment, etc. To 'contest' a seat, or to be 'a candidate', is, by gentlemanly omission, not to be elected.

SUPPLEMENTARY SOURCES
After the convenience of *Dod* the way is hard. In this book attempts have been made, usually with success, to trace those MPs who left the House of Commons, inherited a Peerage from some distant relative and died in obscurity, were raised to the Bench in the Scottish Court of Session and adopted an unfamiliar judicial title, or emigrated and changed their names. Peerages and Baronetages are very useful in tracing such people and some even thornier problems have been solved by using L.G.Pine, *New Extinct Peerage 1884-1971* (London, 1972). For example there is no entry in *Who was Who* under Sir William Brass, who sat for Clitheroe until June 1945, and attempts to trace his career after leaving the House are doomed to failure unless it is realised that by August 1945 the Barony of Chattisham had been created for him and then extinguished by his death.

Works providing information about MPs while they still remained in Parliament include *Debrett's Illustrated House of Commons and the Judicial Bench*, an annual publication from 1867 to 1931, and *The Times Guide to the House of Commons*, published after most general elections this century. Information on their subsequent careers can usually be found in *Who's Who*, *Who Was Who* and *Kelly's Handbook...*, but there remains a small band of MPs who are not included in these works or whose entries are very brief. *The Dictionary of National Biography* only contains entries for the more prominent but is a valuable source of information on such topics as Sir Hamar Greenwood's baptismal Christian names. Most former MPs, but by no means all, received an obituary notice in *The Times* on their death and all the obituaries which could be traced have been used as a source of information for this volume. (A few obituaries which are listed in *The Official Index to The Times* were published only in the later editions of a particular day's issue of *The Times*, editions which have not been published on microfilm and not preserved by libraries, not even by the library of *The Times* itself, some of whose copies were destroyed during the war.) These obituaries proved to be valuable, not only because they include details not readily available elsewhere, but also because they reveal mistakes in the more usual sources. For example *Who was Who* provides incorrect dates of death for Pierce McCann, Ronald McNeill (Lord Cushendun), Liam Mellowes, Robert Smillie and Penry Williams. Obituary notices in other newspapers, national, regional and local, were also used and although the lack of an index to most of them limited their value, they were useful for checking, clarifying and supplementing information retrieved from other sources.

Official material of relevance includes the official return of election expenses, published as a Parliamentary Paper after each general election except 1918, *The Journal of the House of Commons* (which is useful for checking new writs), *London Gazette* (for the dates of appointments to offices of profit under the Crown) and the lists of members contained in *Hansard*.

Other works have been valuable in confirming or contradicting dubious statements in *Dod*, notably F.W.S. Craig, *British Parliamentary Election Results*, *Vacher's Parliamentary Companion* (published at frequent intervals, usually monthly or quarterly, since 1832), *Whitaker's Almanack* (annually since 1869), D. Butler and A. Sloman, *British Political Facts 1900-1975* (4th edition, London, 1975), C. Cook and B. Keith, *British Historical Facts 1830-1900* (London, 1975), and W.P.W. Phillimore, *An Index to Changes of Name ... 1760-1901* (London, 1905). J.A. Venn, *Alumni Cantabrigienses 1752-1900* (Cambridge, 1940-54) contains an entry for Cambridge men who matriculated before 1900 but J. Foster, *Alumni Oxonienses 1715-1886* was published in 1888 and so contains little of value for this volume. Registers of other universities, colleges and schools have often been useful, as have membership lists of learned societies and professional bodies.

The Irish members present problems all their own since they appear only haphazardly in the usual biographical sources and there is often conflicting information about those who do appear. Most of the Irish in this volume are the Sinn Feiners elected in 1918 (who never took their seats at Westminster) and efforts have been made in compiling their entries to give full details of their subsequent careers in the Governments and Parliamentary of the Irish Free State and the Republic of Ireland. The main sources are the Irish equivalents of *Dod* and *The Times Guide to the House of Commons*, namely *Oireachtas Companion and Saorstat Guide* (1928-30), *Free State Parliamentary Companion* (1932) and *Irish Parliamentary Handbook* (1939-45). Other important sources are the lists of members and ministers contained in *Minutes of the Proceedings of the First Parliament of the Republic of Ireland 1919-21*, *Private Sessions of the Second Dail ... 1921-22* and *The Official Reports of Parliamentary Debates* for the Seanad and the Dail. Useful biographical information has also been gleaned from *Burke's Irish Family Records* (London, 1976) and from

J.S. Crone, *A Concise Dictionary of Irish Biography* (Dublin, 1937). Valuable sources for those whose careers led them to Stormont and the Parliament and Government of Northern Ireland are *The Official Reports of Parliamentary Debates* for the Northern Ireland Senate and House of Commons. *Debrett's Illustrated House of Commons* ... until its demise in 1931 also included sections on the Parliaments and Governments of both parts of Ireland.

All Labour MPs will eventually be included in J.M. Bellamy and J. Saville, *Dictionary of Labour Biography* (London, 1972-), the first 4 volumes of which have been used for this work, and in the forthcoming Harvester Press publication J.O. Baylen and N.J. Gossman, *The Biographical Dictionary of Modern British Radicals since 1770*. Useful information has been found in *The Labour Who's Who*, issued in 1924 and 1927, and S.V. Bracher, *The Herald Book of Labour Members* (London, 1923). Other valuable sources are the 'Deaths' sections of *Reports of the Annual Conference of the Labour Party*, which revealed hitherto unsuspected errors in *Who was Who* (such as the dates of death of Jack Lees Robert Spence) as well as providing the only clues for the deaths of Michael Brothers and Alfred Davies.

Volumes 3 & 4 of C. Cook, *Sources of British Political History 1900-51* (London, 1977) list the papers of members who sat between those dates and C. Hazlehurst and C. Woodland, *A Guide to the Papers of British Cabinet Ministers 1900-51* (London, 1974) is also extremely useful. For other members it is necessary to have recourse to the National Register of Archives.

A special effort has been made to provide accurate information about all Government posts held by MPs, although the details of a few minor appointments remain surprisingly obscure, especially in the kaleidoscopic changes among the lower ranks during the first half of 1919. D. Butler and A. Sloman, *British Political Facts 1900-1975* (4th edition, London, 1975) is much the best source of information and can be supplemented by the lists of ministers in *Hansard* and *Vacher's Parliamentary Companion* as well as by the announcement of appointments in *London Gazette* and in the newspapers of the day.

When the printed sources were known to differ an attempt has been made to resolve the discrepancies, if necessary by consulting the indexes of births and deaths at the Office of Population Censuses and Surveys. For example the date of birth of J.A.St. G.F. Despencer-Robertson is given by *Dod* as 1890 and by *Debrett's Illustrated House of Commons* ... and *Who was Who* as 1893; suspicion was aroused by the fact that he was at Eton from 1900 to 1905 and at Oxford from 1905 to 1909 and a search for the original evidence revealed that his birth was registered as early as 1886. Death certificates were also consulted for, among others, G.F. Sawyer and T.T. Broad, whose deaths seem not to be recorded in the printed sources.

This volume contains 46 entries for MPs whose deaths have not been traced—over half of them Irish. The editors would be grateful for any further information about these members and for corrections or significant additions to any of the entries in this volume and its two predecessors.

ABBREVIATIONS

The following abbreviations are used in this book: B means born; Bart. Baronet; bro. brother; Capt. Captain; Co. county; Col. Colonel; Coll. College; d. daughter; Dept. Deputy; educ. educated; eld. eldest; Gen. General; Gov. Governor; Hon. Honourable; jun. junior; Lieut. Lieutenant; Maj. Major; m. married; Nr. near; PC. Privy Councillor; Pres. President; Rt. Right; Sec. Secretary; sen. senior; s. son; Visct. Viscount.

Who's Who of British
Members of Parliament, 1919-1945

ABRAHAM, Rt. Hon. William. Bryn-y-Bedw, Pentre, South Wales. Westminster Palace Hotel, Victoria Street, London. S. of Thomas Abraham, a working Collier and Copper-Smelter. B. at Cwmavon, Glamorgan, 1842; m. 1860, Sarah Williams (she died 1900). Educ. at Cwmavon National School. Popularly known as 'Mabon' which was his bardic pen-name. Worked in the mines at ten years of age. From 1873 was a Miners' Agent, and was Vice-President of the Monmouthshire and South Wales Conciliation Board; President of the South Wales Miners' Federation; Treasurer of the Miners' Federation of Great Britain 1907. PC. 1911. A Labour Member. Sat for the Rhondda division of Glamorganshire from 1885-1918. Elected for Rhondda W. in December 1918 and sat until he resigned in 1920. Died 14 May 1922. [1920]

ACKROYD, Thomas Raven. 41 Clarendon Road, Chorlton-on-Medlock, Manchester. National Liberal. S. of William and Elizabeth Ackroyd. B. at Manchester 7 August 1861; m. 1893. Educ. at Chancery Lane Wesleyan School, Manchester Mechanical School, and Owens Coll. A Bank Manager. A Liberal. Elected for the Moss Side division of Manchester in December 1923 and sat until he was defeated in October 1924. Contested the seat unsuccessfully in 1922 and again in 1929. Member of Manchester City Council from 1923, Alderman from 1939. Died 26 April 1946. [1924 2nd ed.]

ACLAND, Rt. Hon. Sir Francis Dyke, Bart. 14 Weatherby Gardens, London. Killerton, Exeter. Brooks's. S. of the Rt. Hon. Sir Arthur Dyke Acland, 13th Bart., of Columb John. B. 7 March 1874; m. 1st, 31 August 1905, Margaret, d. of Charles James Cropper, Esq., of Ellergreen, Kendal (she died 12 December 1933); secondly, 10 December 1937, Constance, d. of J. Dudley, Esq., of Oxford. Educ. at Rugby, and Balliol Coll., Oxford. Succeeded his father in 1926. A Forestry Commissioner; Chairman of the Dental Board; Chairman of Education Committee and Housing Sub-Committee of Devon County Council, of

National Allotments Society, and of the National Mark Honey Trade Committee. PC. 1915. Financial Secretary to the War Office and member of the Army Council 1908-10 and 1911; Parliamentary Under-Secretary for Foreign Affairs 1911-15; Financial Secretary to the Treasury February-June 1915; Parliamentary Secretary to Board of Agriculture and Fisheries 1915-16. An Opposition Liberal Member. Sat for the Richmond division of the N. Riding of Yorkshire from January 1906 until January 1910 when he was defeated. Sat for the Camborne division of Cornwall from December 1910-November 1922 when he unsuccessfully contested Tiverton. Elected for the Tiverton division of Devon in June and December 1923, but was defeated there in October 1924. Unsuccessfully contested Hexham in May 1929. Elected for Cornwall N. in July 1932 and sat until his death on 9 June 1939. Assistant Director of Secondary Education for the W. Riding of Yorkshire 1903-06. Parliamentary Private Secretary to the Rt. Hon. R. B. Haldane, Secretary of State for War, 1906-08. Died 9 June 1939. [1939]

ACLAND, Sir Richard Thomas Dyke, Bart. Continued in House after 1945: full entry in Volume IV.

ACLAND-TROYTE, Lieut.-Col. Sir Gilbert John Acland, C.M.G., D.S.O. See TROYTE, Lieut.-Col. Sir Gilbert John Acland, C.M.G., D.S.O.

ADAIR, Rear-Admiral Thomas Benjamin Stratton. 43 St. George's Road, London. United Service. S. of Gen. Sir Charles William Adair, K.C.B., Royal Marines. B. 6 November 1861. Educ. for the Royal Navy. Joined H.M.S. *Britannia* as a cadet August 1874; specialised in gunnery. Assistant to Director of Naval Ordnance 1894-95. Captain 1899. From 1904 to 1906 commanded H.M.S. *Montagu* but after it was grounded on Lundy Island on 30 May 1906 he was court-martialled, severely reprimanded and deprived of his command. Retired from the navy in 1907 and granted the rank of Rear-Admiral 1908. Member of the Ordnance Committee 1900-02. Served as

Lieut. of *Orion* in Egypt 1882-83. Manager of the Ordnance Factory of William Beardmore and Company Limited, Glasgow 1907-18. A Coalition Unionist, interested in naval and industrial matters. Elected for the Shettleston division of Glasgow in December 1918 and sat until he retired in 1922. Died 12 August 1928.   [1922]

ADAMS, David. Jesmond Cottage, Newcastle-upon-Tyne. S. of John Adams, Esq., Merchant, of Newcastle-upon-Tyne. B. 27 June 1871; m. 7 September 1897, Elizabeth d. of Capt. John Patterson. Educ. at Science and Art Schools, Newcastle, Rutherford Coll., and Armstrong Coll., Newcastle. A Shipowner and Engineer. Director of D. Adams and Company Limited, Shipowners, of Newcastle-upon-Tyne, and Anglo-Scottish Trading Company Limited, Newcastle-upon-Tyne. Sheriff of Newcastle 1922-23; Lord Mayor 1930-31. A Labour Member. Unsuccessfully contested Newcastle W. in 1918. Elected for Newcastle W. in November 1922, and was defeated there in December 1923. Unsuccessfully contested York in 1924, and Barrow-in-Furness in 1931. Elected for the Consett division of Durham in November 1935 and sat until his death on 16 August 1943. Elected to Newcastle City Council in 1902. Died 16 August 1943.   [1943]

ADAMS, David Morgan. 8 Southill Street, Poplar, London. S. of D.M. Adams, Esq., of Ystradowen, Glamorgan. B. 23 February 1875; m. 1900, Ada (she died 1941). Served with 69th Welch Regiment in India for over 37 years; in Lightship, Trinity House Service; Docks, Port of London Authority; Trades Union Official, Transport and General Workers' Union from 1920; member of Poplar Board of Guardians 1912-30, of Metropolitan Asylums Board 1928-30, of London County Council from 1930, and of Poplar Borough Council from 1918; Mayor 1934-35. A Labour Member. Sat for S. Poplar from 1931 until his death on 19 May 1942.   [1942]

ADAMS, Maj. Samuel Vyvyan Trerice. 3 Gloucester Gate, London. S. of the Rev. Canon S.T. Adams, Rural Dean of Cambridge. B. 22 April 1900; m. 9 October 1925, Mary Grace, d. of Edward Bloxham Campin, Esq. Educ. at Haileybury (senior scholar) and at King's Coll., Cambridge (senior exhibitioner); President of Union, Winchester Prizeman. Barrister-at-Law, Inner Temple 1927; President Hardwicke Society 1932; joined the army April 1940; Maj. December 1940; D.A.A.G. August 1941. A Unionist. Elected for Leeds W. in October 1931 and again in November 1935 and sat until he was defeated in July 1945. Unsuccessfully contested Fulham E. in February 1950. Died 13 August 1951.   [1945]

ADAMSON, Jennie Laurel. Continued in House after 1945: full entry in Volume IV.

ADAMSON, Rt. Hon. William. Victoria Street, Dumfermline. S. of James Adamson, Esq., Miner. B. 2 April 1863; m. 1887, Christine, d. of David Marshall, Esq. Educ. at village dame school. Worked as a Miner for 27 years. Was Assistant Secretary of Fife, Kinross and Clackmannan Miners' Association 1902-1908, when he was appointed Gen. Secretary. Chairman Parliamentary Labour Party 24 October 1917; leader of that party in the House of Commons 1918-21; PC. 1918; Secretary for Scotland January-November 1924; Trustee of Scottish National Library 1925; LL.D. St. Andrew's and Glasgow Universities; Secretary of State for Scotland June 1929-August 1931. A Labour Member. Unsuccessfully contested W. Fife in January 1910. Elected for W. Fife in December 1910 and sat until he was defeated in October 1931; defeated again for W. Fife in November 1935. Died 23 February 1936.   [1931 2nd ed.]

ADAMSON, William Murdoch. 20 Woodcombe Crescent, Forest Hill, London. B. in 1881 at Kilmarnock; m. 1902, Jennie Laurel Johnston, subsequently MP for Dartford and Bexley. National Officer Transport and General Workers' Union; a Lord Commissioner of The Treasury and Government Whip March 1941-October 1944. A Labour Member. Sat for the Cannock division of Staffordshire from November 1922-October 1931 when he was defeated. Re-elected for Cannock in November 1935 and sat until he retired in June 1945. Died 25 October 1945. [1945]

ADDISON, Rt. Hon. Christopher. Peterley Farm, Nr. Great Missenden, Buckinghamshire. S. of Robert Addison, Esq., of Hogsthorpe, Lincolnshire. B. 19 June 1869; m. 1st, 1902, Isobel, d. of Archibald Grey, Esq. (she died 1934); secondly, 1937, Dorothy, d. of J.P. Low, Esq. Educ. at Trinity Coll., Harrogate, and St. Bartholomew's Hospital. M.B., B.S. London, F.R.C.S. England; Lecturer on Anatomy at St. Bartholomew's Hospital; Hunterian Professor and Examiner in Antomy to the Universities of Cambridge and London; Chairman of Board of Intermediate Medical Studies of the University of London; Secretary of Anatomical Society and Editor of Quarterly Medical Journal. Parliamentary Secretary to Board of Education August 1914-May 1915; Parliamentary Secretary to Ministry of Munitions May 1915-December 1916. Minister of Munitions December 1916-July 1917, of Reconstruction July 1917 to January 1919; President of Local Government Board January 1919; First Minister of Health June 1919-April 1921; Minister without Portfolio April-July 1921; Parliamentary Secretary Ministry of Agriculture June 1929; Minister of Agriculture June 1930-August 1931; PC. 1916. Elected as a Liberal for the Hoxton division of Shoreditch in January 1910 and for Shoreditch in December 1918, defeated in November 1922. Unsuccessfully contested Hammersmith S. for Labour in October 1924. Returned for the Swindon division of Wiltshire in May 1929, defeated in October 1931, re-elected at a by-election on 25 October 1934, but again defeated in November 1935. A Liberal Member 1910-22 and a Labour Member 1929-31 and 1934-35. Leader of the House of Lords August 1945-October 1951. Secretary of State for Dominions August 1945-July 1947; Secretary of State for Commonwealth Relations July 1947-October 1947; Lord Privy Seal October 1947-March 1951; Paymaster General July 1948-April 1949; Lord President March-

October 1951. Leader of the Labour Party in the House of Lords 1940-51. Created Baron Addison 1937, Viscount Addison 1945. K.G. 1946. Died 11 December 1951. [1931 2nd ed.]

ADKINS, Sir William Ryland Dent. 5 Paper Buildings, Temple, London. Springfield, Northampton. Reform, Bath, and Eighty. S. of W. Adkins, Esq., of Northamptonshire. B. 11 May 1862. Educ. at Mill Hill School, University Coll., London, B.A., and Balliol Coll., Oxford. A Barrister, called 1890 Inner Temple; K.C. 1920; Recorder of Nottingham 1911; Recorder of Birmingham November 1920; F.S.A.; Dept.-Lieut. for Northamptonshire; J.P. for Northamptonshire and Northampton and Chairman of Northamptonshire County Council; Chairman of Council of County Councils Association; Knighted 1911. A Liberal. Elected for the Middleton division of Lancashire in 1906 and sat until 1918. Sat for the Middleton and Prestwich division of Lancashire from 1918 and sat until he was defeated in 1923. Again defeated in 1924. Member of the Committee of the Congregational Union. Member of Speaker's Conference on Electoral Reform 1917. Died 30 January 1925. [1923]

AGG-GARDNER, Rt. Hon. Sir James Tynte. Queen's Hotel, Cheltenham. Carlton, St. James's, Windham, and Garrick. S. of James Agg-Gardner, Esq., of Cheltenham, and Eulalie Emily, d. of R. Hopkyns Northey, Esq., of Oving House, Buckinghamshire. B. 25 November 1846 at Cheltenham. Unmarried. Educ. at Harrow, and Trinity Coll., Cambridge. Called to the bar at the Inner Temple 1873. J.P. for Cheltenham; Lord of the Manor of Cheltenham. Elected first Freeman of the Borough in 1896. Knighted 1916. PC. 1924. A Conservative. Unsuccessfully contested Cheltenham in 1868, 1880 and 1906. Sat for Cheltenham from 1874-80, 1885-95, and 1900-06. Re-elected for Cheltenham in April 1911 and sat until his death on 9 August 1928. Chairman of House of Commons Kitchen Committee 1917-28. Was twice Mayor Cheltenham. Died 9 August 1928. [1928]

3

AGNEW, Peter Garnett. Continued in House after 1945: full entry in Volume IV.

AINSWORTH, Lieut.-Col. Charles. Holcombe, Lancashire. Carlton. S. of Hargreaves Ainsworth, Esq., of Windermere and Margaret, d. of Thomas Forrest, Esq., of Hoole. B. 25 February 1874; m. 1902, Clara H., d. of H.R. Middlemost, Esq., of Huddersfield. Lieut.-Col. Lancashire Fusiliers; served in Egypt 1914; Turkey 1915. A Conservative. Sat for Bury from December 1918, when he defeated the 'Coupon' Liberal candidate, until he retired in 1935. Member of Church Assembly 1919-29. Brevet-Col. 1932. Died 10 April 1956.   [1935]

AITCHISON, Rt. Hon. Craigie Mason. 12 India Street, Edinburgh. S. of the Rev. James Aitchison, of Falkirk, and Elizabeth Craigie. B. 26 January 1882; m. 1919, Charlotte Forbes, d. of James Jones, Esq., of Torwood Hall, Larbet. Educ. at Falkirk High School, and University of Edinburgh; Vans Dunlop Scholar, Mental Philosophy; Muirhead Prizeman, Civil Law; M.A., LL.B. Edinburgh. An Advocate of the Scottish bar 1907; K.C. 1923; PC. 1929. Lord Advocate for Scotland from June 1929 to August 1931 and in the National Government from September 1931 to October 1933. Unsuccessfully contested Clackmannan and E.Stirling as a Liberal in November 1922 and December 1923. A Labour Member until 1931 and then a National Labour Member. Unsuccessfully contested Hartlepool in October 1924 and Glasgow central in May 1929. Elected for the Kilmarnock division of Ayr and Buteshire in November 1929 and sat until October 1933 when he was appointed Lord Justice Clerk, with the judicial title of Lord Aitchison. Died 2 May 1941.   [1933]

ALBERY, Sir Irving James, M.C. 3 Parkside, Knightsbridge, London. The Manor House, Farningham, Kent. Carlton, and Gresham. S. of James Albery, dramatic Author, and Mary Moore, who m. secondly, Sir Charles Wyndham. B. 12 May 1879; m. 1906, Jill Mary, d. of Henry Arthur Jones, Esq., dramatic Author (she died 1967).

Educ. at Uppingham School, and University of Freiburg. Member of London Stock Exchange 1902-64; senior partner of Messrs. I. Albery and Company. Served in South African War and in Egypt and France 1914-18. M.C. Knight Bach. 1936. A Conservative. Unsuccessfully contested Bow and Bromley in December. 1923. Elected for the Gravesend division of Kent in October 1924 and sat until he was defeated in July 1945. Died 14 November 1967.   [1945]

ALDEN, Percy. 33 Bloomsbury Square, London. B. 6 June 1865 at Oxford; m. 1899, Dr. Margaret Pearse. Educ. at Balliol Coll., Oxford; M.A. A Journalist and Lecturer. Warden of Mansfield House University Settlement 1891-1901. Honorary Secretary of the Council for the Study of International Relations, and British Institute of Social Service. Councillor of West Ham 1892-1901; Dept. Mayor 1898. Wrote *Unemployed; a National Question, Housing, The Unemployable and the Unemployed*. Editor of Social Service Handbooks. Sat for the Tottenham division of Middlesex from 1906 until defeated at Tottenham N. November 1918. Unsuccessfully contested Luton as Labour candidate in November 1922. Elected for Tottenham S. in December 1923 and sat until he was defeated in October 1924. A Liberal Member until 1918 and a Labour Member from 1923 to 1924. Knighted in 1933. Died as a result of enemy action in June 1944.   [1924 2nd ed.]

ALEXANDER, Rt. Hon. Albert Victor, C.H. Continued in House after 1945; full entry in Volume IV.

ALEXANDER, Ernest Edward. Era Lodge, Lyttelton Road, Leyton, London. Naze Park, Walton-on-Naze. S. of Edward Reuben Alexander, Esq., of Leytonstone. B. 28 June 1872; m. 3 October 1896, Emmeline, d. of Joseph Conquest, Esq., of Bow. Educ. at Stationers Co.'s Foundation School. A Master Printer. Member of Leyton Urban District Council from 1901-04, of Essex County Council from 1918, and of Walton-on-Naze Urban District Council 1926. A conservative. Unsuccessfully contested Leyton E. in December 1918. Elected for Leyton E. in November 1922, defeated December 1923. Elected again for Leyton E. in October 1924 and sat until he was defeated in May 1929. Died 29 September 1946.   [1929]

ALEXANDER, Lieut.-Col. Maurice, K.C., C.M.G. House of Commons, London. Empire, and Canada. S. of Lewis George Alexander, Esq., J.P. B. 24 December 1889. Educ. at McGill University. Called to the Quebec bar 1910; K.C. 1922. Member of the firm of Davidson, Wainwright, Alexander and Elder, Barristers, Montreal. Commissioned in the 1st Regiment Grenadier Guards, Canada 1911; served with the Expeditionary Force in the Great War; C.M.G. 1917. After the Armistice became Secretary at the British Embassy, Washington. A National Liberal. Elected for S.E. Southwark in November 1922 and sat until he was defeated in December 1923. Unsuccessfully contested Norfolk N. as a Liberal in October 1924 and Newcastle-on-Tyne E. as a Labour candidate in October 1931. Died 16 July 1945.   [1923]

ALEXANDER, Brigadier-Gen. Sir William, K.B.E., C.B., C.M.G., D.S.O. 43 Hertford Street, London. Marlston House, Nr. Newbury. Carlton, and R.A.F. Western, and Conservative, Glasgow. S. of Thomas Alexander, Esq., of Brentham Park, Stirling, and Isabella Hill, d. of James Goldie, Esq. B. 4 May 1874; m. 1st, 28 June 1911, Beatrice Evelyn, d. of John Ritchie, Esq., of Bingham, Paramatta, New South Wales (she died 4 December 1928); secondly, 21 January 1930, Ruby May, his deceased wife's sister (she died (1951). Educ. at Kelvinside Academy, Glasgow University, and Göttingen. Director of Companies. Director of Administration of Explosive Factories, Ministry of Munitions 1916-17; Controller of Aircraft Supply and Production Ministry of Munitions 1917-19; Director-Gen. of Purchases Ministry of Munitions 1919-20; member of Air Council 1919. A Conservative. Elected for central Glasgow in December 1923 and sat until he retired in June 1945. D.S.O. 1916, K.B.E. 1920. Died 29 December 1954.   [1945]

ALLEN, Col. John Sandeman, O.B.E., M.C., T.D. Lissant Mount, Fairview Road, Oxton, Birkenhead. Constitutional, and St. Stephens. S. of Sir John Sandeman Allen, MP for West Derby. B. 30 May 1892; m. 18 January 1916, Eudora Mary, d. of A.H. Heal, Esq., of Birkenhead. Educ. at Birkenhead School, and in France and Germany. With Booth S.S. Company Limited; Underwriting Member of Lloyd's. Consul for Belgium in Liverpool. Commanded Lancashire and Cheshire Hy. Bde. R.A. (T.A.) and 106th Lancashire Yeomanry, R.A.; T.A. Served in France and Belgium 1914-19; Commanded a Defence Training Regiment 1940, R.A. 1941, an A.A. Regiment 1942. Served overseas from August 1942 (1939-43 Star). Member of Walton-on-Thames Urban District Council; member of Birkenhead Chamber of Commerce; member of Empire Parliamentary Delegation to East Africa 1934 and of Scientific Delegation to West Africa 1938. A Conservative. Elected for Birkenhead W. in October 1931 and sat until 1945 when he unsuccessfully contested Norfolk S. O.B.E. 1938. Died 29 September 1949.   [1945]

ALLEN, Sir John Sandeman. 196 Ashley Gardens, London. 17B Devonshire Road, Prince's Park, Liverpool. Carlton, Thatched House, Exchange, University, and Constitutional. S. of J.S. Allen, Esq., of Liverpool. B. 26 September 1865; m. 1st, 3 October 1888, Amy, d. of J.H. Spencer, Esq., of Eastbourne; secondly, 11 December 1920, Margaret, d. of David Roberts, Esq., of Beddington. Educ. at Brighton, Collegiate School, Edinburgh, and in France and Germany. Chairman of Liverpool Underwriters' Association 1919-20, of Chamber of Commerce 1923-26, of Technical and Commercial Education Committee 1924-27 and of Savings Committee 1922-27; also of W. Lancashire Mental Welfare Association 1923-27; J.P. for Liverpool. Vice President of Royal Empire Society, Chairman 1928-30, of Joint East African Board, of Transport Group, International Chambers of Commerce, and of Federation of Chambers of Commerce of British Empire. Chairman Association British Chambers of Commerce and of Coastal Trade Development Council;

President of International Parliamentary Commercial Conference; Treasurer of Mercantile Marine Service Association. Knight Bach. 1928. A Conservative. Elected for the W. Derby division of Liverpool in October 1924 and sat until his death on 3 June 1935. [1935]

ALLEN, Ronald Wilberforce. Homeleigh, Walton-on-Thames. National Liberal. S. of the Rev. William Henry Allen, Wesleyan Minister. B. 24 November 1889 at Stamford Hill, London. Unmarried. Educ. at Scarborough Coll., University of London, King's Coll.; B.A. 1910. A Solicitor, admitted 1913; Senior Partner of Wilberforce, Allen and Bryant, 188 Strand, London. Member St. Albans Town Council 1920-23. Sub-Lieut. R.N.V.R. during the war. Lecturer on Literary and economic subjects; contributor to various papers and magazines. A Liberal. Unsuccessfully contested E. Leicester March 1922 and S. Leicester November 1922. Elected for the S. division of Leicester December 1923 and sat until he was defeated in October 1924. Unsuccessfully contested Banbury in May 1929 and Penryn and Falmouth in November 1935. Knighted 1932. Author of *Methodism and Modern World Problems.* Died 10 August 1936. [1924 2nd ed.]

ALLEN, William, K.C. 16 Park Square, London. B. 1870: m. 1st, 1893, Janette, d. of John Hall, Esq.; secondly, 1929, Mrs. Oliver Riley. Educ. at Emmanuel Coll., Cambridge. J.P. for Staffordshire; Barrister-at-Law 1905; K.C. 1930; Recorder of Ludlow from 1928-32. Recorder of Newcastle-under-Lyme from 1932-45. Parliamentary Charity Commissioner 1935. Member of Tithe Commission from 1937. Sat for Newcastle-under-Lyme as a Liberal from 1892-1900 when he was defeated. Unsuccessfully contested the Burslem division of Stoke-upon-Trent in October 1924 as a Constitutionalist with Conservative and Liberal support. Elected for the Burslem division in October 1931 as a supporter of the National Government and sat until he was defeated in November 1935 standing as a National Liberal. Died 11 September 1945. [1935]

ALLEN, William Edward David. 23 Buckingham Gate, London. Carlton, Buckinghamshire, and Union (Belfast). S. of William Edward Allen, Esq., of Commonwood House, Chipperfield, Hertfordshire. B. 6 January 1901; m. 1st, 6 December 1922, Lady Phyllis King, d. of Lionel, 3rd Earl of Lovelace (divorced 1932); secondly, 1943, Nathalie, d. of Maxime Kossovsky (she died 1966); thirdly, 1969, Anne, d. of P. Pentland, Esq., of Heyfield, Australia. Educ. at Eton. Chairman of David Allen and Sons Limited, and of David Allen Advertising Agency Limited; Director of David Allen and Sons' Billposting Limited; Member of the Ulster Unionist Council from 1923; F.R.G.S. An Ulster Unionist. Unsuccessfully contested Tyrone and Fermanagh in November 1922. Elected for Belfast W. in May 1929 and sat until he retired in October 1931. Resigned from the Ulster Unionist Party in March 1931 and joined Sir Oswald Mosley's New Party, but resigned after the 1931 election. Capt. Life Guards 1940-42. Press Attaché in Beirut, Baghdad and Ankara 1943-45. O.B.E. 1948. Fellow of Society of Antiquaries. Author of *Caucasian Battlefields, The Ukraine, The Turks in Europe* and other works. Died 18 September 1973. [1931 2nd ed.]

ALLEN, Lieut.-Col. Sir William James, K.B.E., D.S.O. 6 Cleaver Park, Belfast. S. of Joseph Allen, Esq. B. 15 October 1866; m. 1st, 18 March 1892, Maria, d. of John Ross, Esq. (she died 14 November 1937); secondly, 1938, Lillah Ierne, d. of R. Hill Forsythe, Esq., of Lurgan. Educ. at Lurgan Coll. Honorary Secretary Ulster Unionist Council. Raised and served with Pioneer Battalion Royal Irish Rifles in France and Belgium, which regiment he commanded in 1918. Had Croix de Chevalier of Legion of Honour; D.S.O. 1918; K.B.E. 1921, on King's visit to open 1st Parliament of Northern Ireland. Dept.-Lieut. for Armagh. A Conservative. Elected for N. Armagh November 1917 and December 1918. Sat for Co. Armagh from November 1922 until his death on 20 December 1947 as a result of a road accident. [1948]

ALPASS, Joseph Herbert. Continued in House after 1945: full entry in Volume IV.

ALSTEAD, Robert. 19 Upper Dicconson Street, Wigan. S. of John and Hannah Alstead. B. at Appley Bridge, Wigan 23 October 1873; m. 1896, Sarah, d. of Samuel Deakin, Esq., of Wigan. Educ. at National Schools, Wigan, and Wigan Technical Coll. Started work as newspaper boy at the age of ten; later a Woollen Manufacturer. Member of Wigan County Borough Council from 1913-1929; Gov. of Wigan Coll. and of Wigan Grammar School. Chairman Advisory Committee, Wigan Area, Ministry of Labour. A Liberal. Unsuccessfully contested Wigan in 1918 and Altrincham in 1922. Sat for the Altrincham division of Cheshire from December 1923 until he was defeated in October 1924; again defeated in May 1929. Mayor of Wigan from 1926-27. O.B.E. 1939. Died 9 September 1946.
[1924 2nd ed.]

AMERY, Lieut.-Col. Rt. Hon. Leopold Charles Maurice Stennett. 112 Eaton Square, London. Athenaeum, Alpine, Beefsteak, and Carlton. S. of Charles F. Amery, Esq., of Middle Coombe, Lustleigh, South Devon. B. 22 November 1873; m. 16 November 1910, Florence, d. of John Hamar Greenwood, Esq., of Whitby, Canada. Educ. at Harrow, and Balliol Coll., Oxford; Fellow of All Souls, Oxford, Honorary D.C.L. Honorary Fellow of Balliol 1946. Barrister-at-Law, Inner Temple 1902. On editorial staff of *The Times* 1899-1909. Served in Flanders, Salonika, and the Near East 1914-16; Capt. 14th 1st Birmingham Battalian Royal Warwickshire Regiment 1914; Lieut.-Col. on Gen. Staff 1917; on the staff of the Interallied War Council at Versailles and Assistant Secretary to the War Cabinet and Imperial War Cabinet 1917-18. Under-Secretary for the Colonies January 1919-April 1921. Parliamentary and Financial Secretary to the Admiralty April 1921-October 1922. PC. 1922. First Lord of the Admiralty October 1922-January 1924. Secretary of State for the Colonies November 1924-June 1929; and for Dominion Affairs July 1925-June 1929. Secretary of State for India and for Burma May 1940-July 1945.

A Conservative. Unsuccessfully contested E. Wolverhampton in 1906, 1908 and January 1910. Unsuccessfully contested Bow and Bromley in December 1910. Elected for S. Birmingham in May 1911 and for the Sparkbrook division of Birmingham in December 1918. Sat until he was defeated in July 1945. Companion of Honour 1945. Died 16 September 1955.   [1945]

AMMON, Charles George. 70 Ferndene Road, London. Authors'. S. of Charles George Ammon, Esq. B. 22 April 1873; m. 1898, Ada Ellen, d. of David May, Esq. (she died 1958). Educ. at elementary schools. Employed in the Post Office Service and was Organizing Secretary of the Union of Post Office Workers. Alderman of Camberwell 1934-53, Mayor 1950-51. Dept.-Lieut., and J.P. for London 1920; member of London County Council for N. Camberwell 1919-25 and 1934-46. Chairman of Parliamentary Committee London County Council. Leader of the Labour Party, London County Council 1922; Labour Whip, House of Commons November 1922. Parliamentary Secretary to the Admiralty January-November 1924 and June 1929-August 1931. Member of W. African Commission 1938-39, of Select Committee on National Expenditure 1939; Chairman of Parliamentary mission to Newfoundland 1943 and of London County Council 1941. A Labour Member. Unsuccessfully contested N. Camberwell in December 1918. Sat for N. Camberwell from Febuary 1922-October 1931 when he was defeated; re-elected for N. Camberwell in November 1935 and sat until he was created Baron Ammon in 1944. Chairman of National Dock Labour Corporation 1944-50. PC 1945. Capt. of Gentlemen-at-Arms and Chief Government Whip in House of Lords August 1945-July 1949 when he resigned at the Prime Minister's request after a disagreement over the national dock strike. National President of the Brotherhood Movement 1929 and 1945. A Dept. Speaker of the House of Lords. Methodist local preacher. President of U.K. Band of Hope Union. Died 2 April 1960.   [1944]

ANDERSON, Sir Alan Garrett, G.B.E.
7 Palace Green, London. Notgrove Manor, Cheltenham. Brooks's, City of London, City Carlton, and R.Y.S. S. of James G.S. Anderson, Esq., and Dr. Elizabeth Garrett Anderson. B. 9 March 1877; m. 9 June 1903, Muriel Ivy, d. of G.W. Duncan, Esq. Educ. at Elstree School, Eton, and Trinity Coll., Oxford; Honorary Fellow, Oxford. A Director of Anderson, Green and Company Limited, Ship Owners, Managers of the Orient Line; a Director of the Bank of England, of the L.M. and S. Railway and of the Suez Canal Company; a Lieut. of the City of London. Commander of the Crown of Italy, Officer of the French Legion of Honour, Commander of Order of White Rose of Finland. Honorary Capt. R.N.R., Honorary Col. 7th Gloucestershire Regiment. A Conservative. Returned unopposed for the City of London in June and November 1935 and sat until he resigned in January 1940. President of Chamber of Shipping 1924-25. High Sheriff of County of London 1922. K.B.E. 1917, G.B.E. 1934. Controller of Railways, Ministry of War Transport 1941-45. Died 4 May 1952.

[1940]

ANDERSON, Frank. Continued in House after 1945: full entry in Volume IV.

ANDERSON, Hugh Alfred. House of Commons, London. Ferndene, Coleraine. B. 26 November 1867. Educ. at Coleraine Academical Institution and Trinity Coll., Dublin. A Solicitor in Coleraine and Secretary to the North Derry Unionist Association. A Unionist. Elected for N. Londonderry in December 1918 and sat until he resigned in February 1919. Died 16 June 1933. [1919]

ANDERSON, Rt. Hon. Sir John, G.C.B., G.C.I.E., G.C.S.I. Continued in House after 1945: full entry in Volume IV.

ANGELL, Sir Ralph Norman. 4 King's Bench Walk, Temple, London. Northey Island, off Maldon, Essex. S. of Thomas Angell Lane, Esq., of Mansion House, Holbeach. B. 26 December 1872. Educ. privately and at Lycée de St. Omer, France, and Geneva, Switzerland. A Journalist and author; on staff of *Eclair*, Paris 1898-1904; Gen. Manager Paris *Daily Mail* 1904-14. Editor Foreign Affairs, Knight Bach. 1931. A Labour Member. Unsuccessfully contested the Rushcliffe division of Nottinghamshire in November 1922 and Rossendale in December 1923. Elected for Bradford N. in May 1929 and sat until he retired in October 1931. Unsuccessfully contested London University in November 1935. Founder member of the Union of Democratic Control 1914. Nobel Peace Prize 1933. Member of Council of Royal Institute of International Affairs 1928-42. Adopted the surname Angell in lieu of Lane by deed-poll. Died 7 October 1967. [1931 2nd ed.]

ANSTRUTHER-GRAY, William John. Continued in House after 1945; full entry in Volume IV.

APPLIN, Lieut.-Col. Reginald Vincent Kempenfelt, D.S.O. Fortescue Lodge, Chaseside, Enfield. Junior United Service. S. of Capt. Vincent J. Applin, Esq. B. 11 April 1869; m. 1st, April 1902, Beatrix Caroline, d. of George Bather, Esq., of Wroxeter (she died 4 March 1933); secondly 1935, Daisy B. Rogers, née Fifield. Educ. at Sherborne School, and Newton Coll. Commanded 14th Hussars 1919-22. District Commissioner Bloemfontein 1901. Police Magistrate and J.P., Labuan 1896-98. Served in S. African War and in France 1914-18. D.S.O. 1902. A Conservative. Unsuccessfully contested Dartford for the National Party (The 'National Party' was a group of dissident Tory imperialists formed in 1917 by H. Page Croft) in April 1920, and the Abbey division of Westminster for the Anti-Waste League in August 1921. Elected for the Enfield division of Middlesex in October 1924. Unsuccessfully contested the same division in May 1929. Re-elected for the Enfield division of Middlesex in October 1931 and sat until he retired in 1935. Emigrated to South Africa in 1935. O.B.E. 1919. Died 3 April 1957 in South Africa. [1935]

APSLEY, Lieut.-Col. Allen Algernon Bathurst, The Lord, D.S.O., M.C. Petty France, Badminton, Gloucestershire. S. of 7th Earl Bathurst who died 1943. B. 3 August 1895; m. 27 February 1924, Violet, d. of Col. Bertram Meeking. Educ. at Eton, and Christ Church, Oxford. President of U.K. Pilots' Association 1925; Dept.-Lieut., and J.P. for Gloucestershire, and Dept.-Lieut. for Bristol. Brevet Maj. Royal Gloucestershire Hussars Yeomanry 21st Armoured Car Company. Parliamentary Private Secretary to Lieut.-Col. Buckley when Parliamentary Secretary Overseas Trade Department 1922, to Lieut.-Col. Moore-Brabazon when Parliamentary Secretary Ministry of Transport 1925-28, and to the Rt. Hon. Sir Thomas Inskip when Minister for Co-ordination of Defence 1936-February 1939. A National Conservative. Sat for Southampton from 1922-29 when he retired. Elected for Bristol Central in October 1931 and again in November 1935. Sat until he was killed on active service in an air accident in the Middle East on 17 December 1942. M.C. 1917; D.S.O. 1918. Director of *Morning Post*, with which his family had a connection for over 100 years, but resigned in 1935 after a disagreement with the editor. Died 17 December 1942. [1943]

APSLEY, Violet Emily Mildred Bathurst, The Lady. 25 Berkeley Square, London. Petty France, Badminton, Gloucestershire. B. 1895. D. of Capt. Bertram Charles Christopher Spencer Meeking, of Richings Park, Buckinghamshire. m. 27 February 1924, Lord Apsley, D.S.O., M.C., Conservative MP for Southampton from 1923-29 and for Bristol Central from 1931-42, who was killed on Active Service December 1942, s. of 7th Earl Bathurst. Lady of the Rectory Manor of Iver; National Chairman Women's Section British Legion. A Conservative. Elected for Bristol central in February 1943 and sat until she was defeated in July 1945. Unsuccessfully contested Bristol N.E. in February 1950. Member of Sodbury Rural District Council from 1941-43. Director of Western Airways 1936-55. C.B.E. 1952. Died 19 January 1966. [1945]

ARCHDALE, Rt. Hon. Edward Mervyn. Riversdale, Ballinamallard, Co. Fermanagh. Kildare Street Club, Dublin. Constitutional. Ulster, Belfast. S. of Nicholas Montgomery Archdale, Dept.-Lieut., J.P., and Adelaide Archdale. B. at Rossfad, Co. Fermanagh 1853; m. 1880, Alicia Bland, d. of Quintin Fleming, Esq., of Liverpool (she died 1924). Educ. at Knight's Naval School, Southsea. Entered the Royal Navy in the *Britannia* in 1866; retired as Lieut. 1880. Dept.-Lieut., and J.P. for Co. Fermanagh, High Sheriff 1884. Chairman Standing Committee Ulster Unionist Council from its formation in 1904. Commodore Enniskillen Yacht Club; President Co. Fermanagh Golf Club. PC. (Ireland) 1921. Minister for Agriculture and Commerce Northern Ireland 1921-25. A Unionist. Sat for N. Fermanagh from 1898 to 1903 when he resigned. Re-elected for N. Fermanagh in October 1916 and again December 1918. Sat until he retired in 1922. Sat for Fermanagh and Tyrone, Northern Ireland Parliament from 1921 and for Enniskillen from 1929-38. Northern Ireland Minister of Agriculture from 1925-33. Honorary LL.D. Queen's University, Belfast. Created Bart. 1928. Died 2 November 1943. [1922]

ARCHER-SHEE, Lieut.-Col. Martin, C.M.G., D.S.O. Ashurst Lodge, Sunninghill, Berkshire. Carlton, Naval & Military, and Cavalry. S. of Martin Archer-Shee and Elizabeth Pell, of New York. B. 5 May 1873; m. 1905, Frances, d. of Alfred Pell, Esq., of New York; 4 sons, 3 daughters. Educ. at the Oratory School, H.M.S. *Britannia*, and Sandhurst. Served in the Royal Navy as midshipman 1888-90 and entered the army in 19th Hussars 1893, Brevet-Maj. 1902, resigned 1905; Maj. Reserve of Officers 1906. Lieut.-Col. 1915. Served in South African War 1899-1902 (Siege of Ladysmith), D.S.O. 1900, and mentioned three times in despatches, wounded, and with Expeditionary Force 1914-18; 19th Hussars; wounded; despatches four times; C.M.G. 1919; commanded 12th Gloucester Regiment 1915-17; 2/4 York and Lancashire 1917; 10th K.O.S.B. 1918. A Conservative. Elected for Finsbury Central in January and December 1910 and for

9

Finsbury in December 1918. Sat until he was defeated in December 1923. Unsuccessfully contested Peckham division of Camberwell in October 1924. He was a Roman Catholic opponent of Home Rule who abandoned the Lloyd George coalition in July 1921 because of the Irish Truce. Knighted 1923. Died 6 January 1935.
[1923]

ARMITAGE, Robert. Farnley Hall, Leeds. 14 Whitehall Court, London. Bath, National, and Reform. S. of William James Armitage, Esq., of Farnley, Leeds, and Emily, d. of William Nicholson, Esq., of Roundhay. B. 22 February 1866 at Farnley; m. 1st, 1891, Caroline Katherine, d. of Dudley H. Ryder, Esq., of Hemel Hempstead (she died 1933); secondly, 1936, Mary, widow of the Rev. E.B. Russell. Educ. at Westminster, and Trinity Coll., Cambridge. Called to the bar at the Inner Temple 1889. Chairman of Farnley Iron Company Limited, Leeds, and of Brown Bayley's Steel Works Limited, Sheffield. Lord Mayor of Leeds 1904-05. A Liberal. Sat for Leeds central from 1906 until he was defeated in November 1922. Died 10 February 1944.   [1922]

ARMSTRONG, Henry Bruce. Deans Hill, Armagh. Carlton. S. of William Jones Wright Armstrong, J.P., Dept.-Lieut. for Co. Armagh, High Sheriff 1840, and Frances Elizabeth, widow of Sir Michael McCreagh, K.C.H., and d. of Capt. Christopher Wilson, 22nd Regiment. B. 27 July 1844 at Hull House, Shoulden, Kent; m. 1883, Margaret, d. of William Leader, Esq., of Rosnalee, Co. Cork (she died 1936). Educ. at Armagh Royal School, and Trinity Coll., Cambridge. Barrister-at-Law 1868; J.P., Dept.-Lieut. for Co. Armagh 1873 and 1880; Vice-Lieut. 1920; High Sheriff Armagh 1875; Longford 1894; Senator Queen's University, Belfast 1920; County Councillor Armagh 1899-1920; Chairman 1909-1920; Senator Northern Ireland July 1921-37. Travelled extensively in the East and Far East. A Conservative Unionist. Returned unopposed for mid Armagh in June 1921 and sat until he retired in October 1922. Lord-Lieut. of Armagh 1924-39. PC. (Northern Ireland) 1932. Died 4 December 1943.   [1922]

ARNOLD, Sydney. Westbourne, Hale, Cheshire. Reform, and National Liberal. S. of W.A. Arnold, Esq., of Hale, Cheshire. B. 13 January 1878 at Altrincham. Educ. at Manchester Grammar School. Unmarried. A Stockbroker in Manchester; Honorary Treasurer of N.W. Counties Branch of Free Trade Union from 1910. A Liberal. Unsuccessfully contested the Holderness division of the E. Riding of Yorkshire in December 1910. Elected for the Holmfirth division of the W. Riding of Yorkshire in June 1912, and for the Penistone division of the W. Riding of Yorkshire in December 1918. Sat until he resigned in 1921. Member of the Labour Party from 1922 until he resigned in 1938. Created Baron Arnold in 1924. Under Secretary for the Colonies from January-November 1924. Paymaster General June 1929-March 1931, when he resigned through ill-health. Died 3 August 1945.
[1921]

ARNOTT, John. House of Commons, London. S. of Henry and Mary Arnott. B. 1871 at Kincardine-on-Forth, Fifeshire. Educ. at Ruskin Coll., Oxford. A Blacksmith. Lord Mayor of Leeds from from 1925-26. A Labour Member. Unsuccessfully contested Leeds W. in December 1918, Kingston-upon-Hull S.W. in November 1922, December 1923 and October 1924. Elected for Kingston-upon-Hull S.W. in May 1929 and sat until he was defeated in October 1931. Again defeated in November 1935. Died 20 February 1942.   [1931 2nd ed].

ASHLEY, Lieut.-Col. Rt. Hon. Wilfrid William. Gayfere House, Wood Street, London. Broadlands, Romsey, Hampshire. Classiebaum Castle, Sligo. Carlton, and Brooks's. S. of the Rt. Hon. E. Ashley and Sybella Charlotte, d. of Sir W. Farquhar, 3rd Bart. B. 13 September 1867; m. 1st, 4 January 1901, Maud, only child of Rt. Hon. Sir E. Cassel (she died 1911); secondly, 29 August 1914, Muriel, d. of Walter Spencer, Esq., of Fownhope Court, Hereford. Educ. at Harrow, and Magdalen Coll., Oxford. Lieut. Grenadier Guards 1889-1898; Maj. 3rd Hampshire Regiment; 1898-1901 Lieut.-Col. commanding 20th King's Liverpool Regiment. Chairman of the Anti-Socialist Union. A Unionist Whip 1911-13. Parliamentary Secretary Ministry of Transport and Office of Works October 1922-October 1923. Under-Secretary for War October 1923-January 1924. Minister of Transport November 1924-June 1929. Dept.-Lieut. and J.P. for Hampshire. Alderman of Hampshire County Council. PC. 1924. A Conservative. Sat for the Blackpool division of N. Lancashire from 1906-18, for the Fylde division of Lancashire from 1918-22, and for the New Forest and Christchurch division of Hampshire from 1922 until he was created Baron Mount Temple in January 1932. High Steward of Romsey. Died 3 July 1939.   [1932]

ASHMEAD-BARTLETT, Capt. Ellis, C.B.E. 2 Down Street, London. Carlton. S. of Sir Ellis Ashmead-Bartlett. B. 11 February 1881; m. 14 August 1919, Maria Alexandrina de Exi Elizalde of Buenos Aires. Educ. at Marlborough. A Barrister-at-Law, Inner Temple. Served in the Dardanelles Expedition and in France 1916-19. C.B.E. 1920. A Conservative. Unsuccessfully contested Normanton in January 1910, Poplar in December 1910, and Hammersmith N. in December 1923. Elected for Hammersmith N. in October 1924 and sat until he resigned in 1926. War correspondent in the Russo-Japanese War 1904, in Morocco 1907-09, in Tripoli 1910 and in the Balkan War 1912-13. Author of *The Uncensored Dardanelles*. Died in Lisbon 4 May 1931.   [1926]

ASKE, Sir Robert William, Bart., K.C. 4 Elm Court, Temple, London. Clevehurst, St. Georges Avenue, Weybridge, Surrey. Reform, and National Liberal. S. of Edward Aske, Esq. B. 29 December 1872; m. 1st, 17 February 1899, Edith, d. of Charles Macgregor, Esq. (she died 20 January 1900); secondly, 2 June 1909, Edith, d. of W.H. Cockerline, Esq. (she died 22 June 1918). Barrister-at-Law, Middle Temple 1914; LL.D. London; Gold Medallist in Laws; J.P. and three times Dept. Sheriff of Kingston-upon-Hull; Lieut.-Col. (R.) 5th East Yorkshire (T.F.); T.D.; Knighted 1911, created Bart. 1922. Unsuccessfully contested central Hull in January and December 1910 and July 1911. Elected for Newcastle E. in December 1923, defeated October 1924. Re-elected in May 1929 and sat until he retired in June 1945. A Liberal Member until 1931, thereafter a Liberal Nationalist. K.C. 1934. Died 10 March 1954.   [1945]

ASQUITH, Rt. Hon. Herbert Henry. 44 Bedford Square, London. The Wharf, Sutton Courtne. Athenaeum, and Reform. 2nd s. of J.Dixon Asquith, of Croft House, Morley, Yorkshire, by Emily, d. of W. Willans, Esq., of Huddersfield. B. at Morley 1852; m. 1st, 1877, Helen Kelsall, d. of Frederick Melland, Esq., of Manchester (she died 1891); secondly, 1894, Margaret, d. of Sir Charles Tennant, Bart. Educ. at the City of London School, and Balliol Coll., Oxford, of which he was a scholar and Fellow; B.A., first class classics, and Craven Scholarship. Called to the bar at Lincoln's Inn 1876; Q.C. 1890; bencher 1894. Was Home Secretary 1892-95; Chancellor of the Exchequer December 1905 to April 1908, when he was appointed Prime Minister and First Lord of the Treasury; resigned 5 December 1916. Secretary of State for War April to August 1914; Honorary D.C.L. Oxford and Durham; Honorary LL.D. Cambridge, Edinburgh, Glasgow, Leeds, Bristol, St. Andrews, and McGill Universities; Lord Rector of Glasgow University 1906, and Aberdeen University 1909; Honorary Fellow of Balliol Coll. 1908; F.R.S.; Elder Brother of Trinity House 1909; awarded special war medals by the King January 1920. A Liberal. Sat for E. Fife from 1886 to December 1918 when he was defeated. Elected for Paisley February 1920, November 1922 and again in December 1923, defeated in October 1924. Leader of Liberal Party April 1908-October 1926. K.G. 1925. Created Earl of Oxford and Asquith 1925. Unsuccessful candidate for election as Chancellor of Oxford University 1925. Author of *Memories and Reflections, The Genesis of the War*, and *Fifty Years of Parliament*. Died 15 February 1928.
          [1924 2nd ed.]

ASSHETON, Rt. Hon. Ralph. Continued in House after 1945: full entry in Volume IV.

ASTBURY, Lieut.-Commander Frederick Wolfe. Newlands, Prestwich, Lancashire. St. Stephen's. S. of Frederick James Astbury, Esq., J.P. B. 1872; m. 1903, Beatrice, d. of C.W. Bayley, Esq. Educ. privately. J.P. for Lancashire 1911; member of Prestwich District Council 1909, and Lancashire County Council 1910. Director of Manchester Chamber of Commerce. Joined R.N. 1915. A Conservative. Elected for W. Salford in 1918 when he defeated the 'Coupon' Liberal candidate, and 1922, defeated there in December 1923. Re-elected for W. Salford in 1924, and sat until defeated in May 1929. Again returned in October 1931 and sat until he retired in October 1935. Resigned the Conservative whip in May 1935. Died 28 December 1954. [1935]

ASTOR, Lieut.-Col. Hon. John Jacob. 18 Carlton House Terrace, London. Hever Castle, Kent. Marlborough, Carlton, Beefsteak, and Turf. S. of the 1st Visct. Astor. B. 20 May 1886; m. 28 August 1916, Lady Violet Mary Elliot, d. of 4th Earl of Minto and widow of Maj. Lord Charles Mercer Nairne (she died 1965). Educ. at Eton, and New Coll., Oxford. Served with 1st Life Guards 1906-19; Aide-de-Camp Viceroy of India 1911-14; France 1914-18; Chevalier Legion of Honour; Commanded Household Siege Battery 1918; Maj. 1919; Honorary Col. Kent and Sussex Heavy Brigade, R.A.; Honorary Col. 42nd Battalion Royal Tank Regiment; Lieut.-Col. Home Guard 1941; a Lieut. of City of London; President of Kent Council and of Fleet Street Branch of British Legion; Honorary Secretary King's Roll National Council; Chairman of Westminster Employment Committee from 1924. J.P. for Kent; Alderman London County Council 1922-25; member of Post Office Advisory Council; member of Broadcasting Commissions 1923 and 1935; President of Dover Coll.; Honorary Freeman of Dover; Chairman of *The Times* Publishing Company 1922-29; President of Press Club and of Council of Empire Press Union; Chairman of Fourth and Fifth Imperial Press Conferences. A Director of G.W. Railway, of Hambro's Bank Limited, and of Barclay's Bank Limited, Dept. Chairman of Phoenix Assurance Company; President of M.C.C. 1937-38; Chairman of Hurlingham Club and of Middlesex Hospital; Dept.-Lieut. for Kent; F.R.C.M. A Conservative. Unsuccessfully contested Dover in January 1921. Sat for the Dover division of Kent from November 1922 until he retired in June 1945. Unseated for having voted on 4 March 1924 without taking the oath but was re-elected unopposed on 12 March 1924. Created Baron Astor of Hever 1956. Died 20 July 1971. [1945]

ASTOR, Nancy Witcher Astor, The Viscountess, C.H. 9 Babmaes Street, London. 4 St. James's Square, London. B. 1879. D. of C.D. Langhorne, Esq., of Virginia. M. 1st, 1897, R.G. Shaw, Esq. (divorced 1903); secondly, 3 May 1906, Waldorf, 2nd Visct. Astor (he died 1952). A Conservative, and the first woman to take a seat in the Imperial Parliament. Sat for the Sutton division of Plymouth from 1919 until she retired in June 1945. Companion of Honour 1937. Died 2 May 1964. [1945]

ASTOR, Hon. Waldorf. Cliveden, Taplow, Buckinghamshire. 4 St. James's Square, London. Carlton, Turf, and Marlborough. S. of Visct. Astor of Hever Castle, Kent. B. 19 May 1879; m. 1906, Nancy, d. of C.D. Langhorne, Esq., of Mirador, Greenwood, Virginia. Educ. at Eton, and New Coll., Oxford. A member of the Inner Temple; a Gov. of Guy's Hospital and of the Peabody Trust; Chairman of Treasury Committee on Tuberculosis. Chairman of the State Medical Research Committee, Parliamentary Secretary to the Prime Minister January 1917; Parliamentary Secretary to the Ministry of Food July 1918 to January 1919. A Unionist. Unsuccessfully contested Plymouth in January 1910. Elected for Plymouth in December 1910 and for the Sutton division of Plymouth in December 1918. Sat until he succeeded to the Peerage as 2nd Viscount Astor in October 1919. Parliamentary Secretary to Local Government Board January-June 1919, to Ministry of Health June 1919-April 1921. Lord Mayor of Plymouth from 1939-44. Chairman of Royal Institute of International Affairs 1935-49. Proprietor

of the *Observer*. Died 30 September 1952.
[1919]

ASTOR, Hon. William Waldorf. Continued in House after 1945: full entry in Volume IV.

ATHOLL, Katharine Marjory Stewart Murray, Duchess of, D.B.E. 98 Elm Park Gardens, London. Blair Castle, Blair Atholl. Eastwood, Dunkeld. Ladies' Carlton. D. of Sir James Ramsay, 10th Bart., of Bamff. B. 6 November 1874; m. 20 July 1899, John, 8th Duke of Atholl, K.T. (he died 1942). Educ. at Wimbledon High School, and Royal Coll. of Music; Honorary D.C.L. Oxford, McGill, Glasgow, Manchester, Leeds, Durham and Columbia Universities. Member of Departmental Committee on Highlands and Island Medical Services 1912, and of Perthshire Education Authority 1919-24; and of Central Agricultural Wages Committee for Scotland 1918-20; Chairman of Scottish Board of Health's Consultative Committee on Highlands and Islands 1920-24. Member of Departmental Committee on Scottish Tinkers 1917-18, and of Royal Common Civil Service 1929-31. Parliamentary Secretary Board of Education November 1924-June 1929 when she was the first woman to hold office in a Conservative government. J.P. A Conservative. Sat for the Kinross and Western division of Perth and Kinross from December 1923 until she resigned in November 1938. The Conservative Whip was withdrawn from her May-September 1935. In April 1938 she resigned the Whip, sitting as an Independent until November 1938, when she resigned her seat and contested the by-election as an Independent but was defeated by the Conservative candidate. D.B.E. 1918. Chairman of British League for European Freedom 1944-60. Died 21 October 1960. [1938]

ATKEY, Albert Reuben. The Park, Nottingham. 30 Burleigh Mansions, St. Martin's Lane, London. Royal Automobile. S. of Charles and Emma Atkey. B. at Nottingham 1 July 1867; m. 1st, March 1890, Euphemia Althea, d. of Robert Hawksley, Esq. (she died 1941); secondly

1942, Mrs. Lilian Stembridge of Leeds. Educ. at the Huntingdon Street Board School, Nottingham, and University Coll., Nottingham. Managing Director of a large provincial motor garage business. Nottingham City Councillor 1908, Sheriff of Nottingham 1911, Chairman of Nottingham Water Committee and Trent Navigation Committee. J.P. of the City of Nottingham. A Unionist. Elected for central Nottingham in December 1918 and sat until he was defeated in November 1922; again defeated December 1923. Knighted 1935. Lord Mayor of Nottingham 1929-30, Alderman from 1928. President of British Waterworks Association. Died 9 November 1947.
[1922]

ATKINSON, Cyril. 74 Oakwood Court, London. 12 King's Bench Walk, Temple London. S. of Leonard William Atkinson, Esq., of Manchester. B. 9 May 1874; m. 1st, 26 September 1900, Kathleen, d. of Michael Longridge, Esq. (she died 1947); secondly, 1948, Florence Morton, widow of Michael Henderson, Esq. LL.D. London. A Barrister-at-Law, Lincoln's Inn 1897; K.C. 1913; bencher 1920. A Conservative. Sat for the Altrincham division of Cheshire from October 1924 until he was appointed a High Court Judge in 1933. Knighted 1933. Judge of King's Bench Division 1933-48. Treasuer of Lincoln's Inn 1942. Member of Church Assembly 1950-55. Died 29 January 1967.
[1933]

ATTLEE, Rt. Hon. Clement Richard. Continued in House after 1945: full entry in Volume IV.

AUSTIN, Sir Herbert, K.B.E. Lickey Grange, Bromsgrove. Junior Carlton, St. Stephens, Royal Automobile, 1900, Motor, British Empire, Motor Yacht, Midland Automobile, and Birmingham Conservative. S. of Charles Steven Austin, Esq., of Wentworth, Yorkshire. B. at Bovingdon, Buckinghamshire 8 November 1866; m. 1887, Miss Helen Dron, of Melbourne, Australia. Educ. at Rotherham Grammar School, and Brampton Coll. At the age of 22 joined Mr. F.Y. Wolseley, bro. of Lord Wolseley, in the Wolseley Sheep Shearing

Machine Company, Australia, Returned to England, assisted in founding the Wolseley Tool and Motor Car Company, of which he became Chief Engineer and General Manager; one of the founders of the Society of Motor Manufacturers and Traders, President 1934. Severed his connection with the Wolseley Company in 1905 and founded the Austin Motor Company Limited, of Northfield, Birmingham. K.B.E. 1917. A Conservative. Elected for the King's Norton division of Birmingham in 1918, and sat until defeated in October 1924. President of Institution of Automobile Engineers 1930. Created Baron Austin 1936. Died 23 May 1941.   [1924 2nd ed.]

AYLES, Walter Henry. Continued in House after 1945: full entry in Volume IV.

BAGLEY, Capt. Edward Albert Ashton. Constitutional. S. of Thomas Ashton Bagley, Esq., of Coningsby, Lincolnshire. B. 1876. Well known as the Organizing Secretary of the Lancashire and North-Western Counties Division of the Tariff Reform League until the war. Joined the army early in 1915, and served three years in Egypt and Palestine as R.A.S.C. officer. Published various articles and pamphlets on economic and labour questions. A Unionist. Unsuccessfully contested Leicester in January 1910 and Radcliffe-cum-Farnworth in December 1910. Elected for the Farnworth division of Lancashire in December 1918 and sat until he was defeated in November 1922. Died 5 November 1961.
                              [1922]

BAILEY, Eric Alfred George Shackleton. The School House, Lancaster. St. Stephen's, and Constitutional. S. of the Rev. H.S. Bailey, D.D., Headmaster of Lancaster Grammar School. B. 28 July 1905. Educ. at Grammar School, Lancaster, Rossall, and at Worcester Coll., Oxford. Barrister-at-Law, Inner Temple 1928. A Conservative. Elected for the Gorton division of Manchester in October 1931 and sat until he was defeated in November 1935. Emigrated to Australia.*   [1935]

BAILLIE, Sir Adrian William Maxwell, Bart. 25 Grosvenor Square, London. Leeds Castle, Maidstone. Polkemmet, Whitburn, West Lothian. S. of Sir Robert Baillie, 4th Bart, succeeded his bro. in 1914. B. 5 May 1898; m. 4 November 1931, Olive Cecilia, d. of 1st Baron Queenborough. Educ. at Eton. Lieut. Scots Greys R. of O.; 2nd Sec. Diplomatic Service Washington 1924-28. Dept.-Lieut., and J.P. for Linlithgow. A Conservative. Unsuccessfully contested Linlithgowshire in May 1929. Sat for Linlithgowshire from October 1931-November 1935 when he was defeated. Elected for the Tonbridge division of Kent in March 1937 and sat until he retired in June 1945. Died 8 January 1947.   [1945]

BAILLIE-HAMILTON, Hon. Charles William. 67 Tufton Street, London. S. of George, Lord Binning, and grand-s. of George, 11th Earl of Haddington. B. 22 May 1900; m. 17 July 1929, Wanda, d. of Norman Holden, Esq., of Norton Priory, Chichester (divorced 1932). Educ. at Eton, and University Coll., Oxford. Granted precedence of younger s. of an Earl in 1918. A Conservative. Unsuccessfully contested Peebles and S. Midlothian in October 1924. Elected for Bath in March 1929 and sat until he retired in October 1931. Private Secretary to the Rt. Hon. Stanley Baldwin, Prime Minister, 1924-29. Died 24 April 1939.
                              [1931 2nd ed.]

BAIRD, Rt. Hon. Sir John Lawrence, Bart., C.M.G., D.S.O. Urie, Stonehaven. Carlton, and Turf. S. of Sir Alexander Baird, 1st Bart., of Urie, and Annette, d. of 1st Baron Haldon. B. 27 April 1874; m. 1905, Lady Ethel Keith-Falconer, d. of 10th Earl of Kintore. Educ. at Eton, and Christ Church, Oxford. Secretary in the Diplomatic Service at Cairo, Paris and Buenos Aires 1898-1908; Attaché at Vienna 1896; Acting Agent and Consul-Gen. in Abyssinia 1903; Political Officer attached to Abyssinian Force in Somaliland 1903. C.M.G. 1904. Served with Expeditionary Force 1914-15; D.S.O. 1915; J.P. and Dept.-Lieut. for Kincardineshire. J.P. for Warwickshire; Maj. Scottish Horse. Parliamentary Private Secretary to Mr. Bonar

Law 1911-16; Under-Secretary of State for Air Ministry December 1916 to January 1919; Under-Secretary of State, Home Office July 1919 to October 1922. Minister of Transport and First Commissioner of Works October 1922-January 1924. PC. 1922. A Conservative. Sat for the Rugby division of Warwickshire from January 1910 to November 1922, and for Ayr Burghs from November 1922 until May 1925 when he was created Baron Stonehaven. In 1919 he acted as an unofficial Government spokesman, in January as an Additional Parliamentary Secretary at the Ministry of Munitions, in February as Assistant to Visct. Astor, Parliamentary Secretary to Local Government Board, and from February to May as Parliamentary Secretary designate to the proposed Ministry of Ways and Communications, although he was not appointed to this ministry when it was created in May 1919 as the Ministry of Transport. Succeeded as Bart. 1920. G.C.M.G. 1925. Gov.-Gen. of Australia 1925-30. Chairman of the Conservative Party 1931-36. Created Visct. Stonehaven 1938. Died 20 August 1941.
[1925]

BAKER, John. 88 Hertford Road, East Finchley, London. 78 Swinton Street, London. National Labour. S. of John Baker, Esq., Brick-maker. B. 8 April 1867; m. H. Jennie Elcum. Educ. at Board School. F.F.I., F.R.S.S. A Locomotive Driver. Gen. Secretary Amalgamated Society of Enginemen and Cranemen 1907; member of Stockton Town Council 1906-10. Labour Advisory Commissioner Ministry of Munitions, and of Food Commission of Board of Trade Advisory Commission 1924. Member of Sir Arthur Balfour's Commission of Enquiry into Industry and Trade 1924, and of Fuel and Power Commission 1926. A Labour Member. Unsuccessfully contested Kidderminister in 1918, and the Bilston division of Wolverhampton in 1922 and 1923. Elected for the Bilston division of Wolverhampton in October 1924 and sat until he was defeated in October 1931. Died 3 May 1939. [1931 2nd ed.]

BAKER, Walter John. 43 Cromwell Road, London. B. 1876. Head of the Research Department, and Assistant Gen. Secretary Union of Post Office Workers. A Labour Member. Unsuccessfully contested the Harborough division of Leicestershire in 1918 and 1922. Sat for Bristol E. from December 1923 until he died on 2 December 1930. Before his election was a member of the House of Commons telegraph staff. Member of the Institute of Public Administration. Died 2 December 1930. [1929 2nd ed.]

BALDWIN, Oliver Ridsdale. See CORVEDALE, Oliver Ridsdale Baldwin, Visct. Continued in House after 1945: full entry in Volume IV.

BALDWIN, Rt. Hon. Stanley, F.R.S. 10 Downing Street, London. Astley Hall, Nr. Stourport. Athenaeum, Carlton, United University, and Travellers'. S. of Alfred Baldwin, Esq., for 16 years MP for the Bewdley division of Worcestershire, of Wilden House, Stourport. B. 3 August 1867; m. 12 September 1892, Lucy, O.B.E., d. of E.L.J. Ridsdale, Esq., of Rottingdean (she died 1945). Educ. at Harrow, and Trinity Coll., Cambridge. Parliamentary Private Secretary to Mr. Bonar Law, Chancellor of the Exchequer December 1916; Junior Lord of the Treasury January 1917; Joint Financial Secretary to the Treasury June 1917; President of the Board of Trade April 1921 to October 1922; Chancellor of the Exchequer October 1922-August 1923; Prime Minister and First Lord of the Treasury May 1923 to January 1924, November 1924-June 1929, and from June 1935-May 1937; Lord President of the Council August 1931-June 1935, and Lord Privy Seal September 1932-January 1934; PC. 1920. Lord Rector of Edinburgh University 1923, and of Glasgow University 1928. Honorary LL.D. Cambridge, St. Andrews and Durham Universities 1923; Honorary D.C.L. Oxford and Durham 1925; F.R.S. 1927; Honorary LL.D. Birmingham and Edinburgh Universities 1927, London and Belfast 1933, Liverpool 1934; Chancellor of St. Andrews University from 1929, and of Cambridge University from 1930. Elder Brother of Trinity House. Grand Master of Primrose League from 1925. A Trustee of the British Museum 1927. Gov. of Charterhouse 1933.

Member of the Institut de France. Honorary Bencher, Inner Temple 1936. Member of Imperial War Graves Commission 1936. A Conservative. Unsuccessfully contested Kidderminster in 1906. Sat for the Bewdley division of Worcestershire from February 1908 to June 1937 when he was created Earl Baldwin of Bewdley. Leader of Opposition 1924 and 1929-31. Leader of Conservative Party 1923-37. K.G. 1937. Died 14 December 1947.   [1937]

BALDWIN-WEBB, Col. James. Olton, Warwickshire. Carlton, and Constitutional. S. of James Bertram Webb, Esq., and Elizabeth, d. of C.H. Baldwin, Esq. B. 5 February 1894. Educ. privately. Managing Director of Baldwins (Birmingham) Limited. Member of Birmingham City Council from 1925; served overseas 1914-18. Served in France during World War 1 and subsequently served in the Territorial Army; promoted Col. 1932. Dept.-Lieut. for Staffordshire. A Conservative. Elected for The Wrekin division of Shropshire in October 1931 and again in November 1935. The by-election was not held in The Wrekin until 26 September 1941 subsequent to him being presumed drowned as a result of enemy action on 17 September 1940.   [1940]

BALFOUR, Rt. Hon. Sir Arthur James, K.G., O.M. 4 Carlton Gardens, London. Whittingehame, Prestonkirk, N.B. Carlton, Athenaeum, Travellers', and others. S. of James Maitland Balfour, Esq., of Whittingehame, Haddingtonshire, by Lady Blanche Cecil, d. of the 2nd Marq. of Salisbury. B. 1848. Educ. at Eton, and Trinity Coll., Cambridge. In the early part of his parliamentary career he acted with Lord R. Churchill as one of the so-called "Fourth Party." Was Private Secretary to the Marq. of Salisbury as Foreign Secretary 1878-80, and during the special mission of Lord Beaconsfield and Lord Salisbury to Berlin 1878; a PC. and President of Local Government Board 1885; Secretary for Scotland 1886-87; Chief Secretary for Ireland 1887-91; First Lord of the Treasury and Leader of the House of Commons 1891-92 and 1895-1905; Prime Minister July 1902 to December 1905; Lord Privy Seal 1902-03; First Lord of

the Admiralty May 1915 to December 1916; Secretary of State for Foreign Affairs December 1916 to October 1919; Lord President of the Council from October 1919 to October 1922; member of the Peace Conference, Paris 1919. Undertook a special mission to the United States in 1917. Delegate to Washington Peace Conference 1921. Lord Rector of St. Andrews University 1886, of Glasgow University 1890, Chancellor of the University of Edinburgh from 1891; Chancellor of Cambridge University from October 1919. Leader of the Unionist Party in the House of Commons 1891-1911. Order of Merit 1916. F.R.S., Honorary LL.D. Edinburgh, St. Andrews, Glasgow, Dublin, Manchester, Liverpool, Birmingham, Sheffield Bristol; Honorary D.C.L. Oxford, Durham, and Columbia University, New York. President of British Association 1904. Elder Brother of Trinity House. Dept.-Lieut. for East Lothian. Author of *A Defence of Philosophic Doubt* 1879, *Essays and Addresses* 1883, *The Foundations of Belief* 1895, *Reflections Suggested by the New Theory of Matter, Decadence, Speeches (1880-1905) on Fiscal Reform* 1906, *Criticism and Beauty* (Romanes Lecture) 1910, *Theism and Humanism* (Gifford Lectures) 1914, etc. A Unionist. Sat for Hertford from 1874 to 1885, and Manchester E. from 1885 to 1906 when he was defeated. Elected for the City of London in February 1906 and sat until he was created Earl of Balfour in May 1922. K.G. March 1922. Lord President of Council April 1925-June 1929. Died 19 March 1930.   [1922]

BALFOUR, George. 66 Queen Street, London. Elmstead Lodge, Chislehurst. Foss House, Perthshire. Carlton, St. Stephen's, and City of London. S. of William Balfour, Esq. B. 1872; m. 1901, Margaret Malloch, d. of David Mathers, Esq., of Dundee. Educ. at Portsmouth, Dundee Technical Institute, and University Coll. M.I.Mech.E. and M.I.E.E., and other scientific institutions. J.P. for the City of Dundee. Founder and head of Messrs. Balfour, Beatty and Company, London; Chairman of the Power Securities Corporation, and Director of various companies. A Conservative. Unsuccessfully contested the Govan division of

Lanarkshire in December 1910 and December 1911. Sat for Hampstead from December 1918 until he died on 26 September 1941. [1941]

BALFOUR, Capt. Rt. Hon. Harold Harington, M.C. Carlton, Royal Aero, and R.A.F. S. of Col. N.H. Balfour. B. 1 November 1897; m. 1st, 15 December 1921, Diana, d. of Sir Robert Harvey, 2nd Bart., of Langley Park (divorced 1946); secondly, 1947, Mary Ainslie, d. of Baron Profumo. Educ. at Chilverton Elms, Dover, and at R.N.C. Osborne. Served with 60th Rifles, R.F.C. and R.A.F. 1914-1923. Parliamentary Under-Secretary of State for Air May 1938-November 1944; Minister Resident in West Africa November 1944-July 1945; PC. 1941. A Conservative. Unsuccessfully contested the Stratford division of West Ham in October 1924. Sat for the Isle of Thanet division of Kent from May 1929 until he retired in June 1945. Created Baron Balfour of Inchrye 1945. President of Federation of Chambers of Commerce of the British Empire 1946-49. President of Commonwealth and Empire Industries Association 1956-60. Member of Board of British European Airways 1955-56. Chairman of B.E.A. Helicopters Limited 1964-66. Author of *An Airman Marches* and *Wings over Westminster.** *[1945]

BALFOUR, Sir Robert, Bart. 7 Gracechurch Street, London. 7 Prince's Gate, London. Langham Hall, Essex. Reform, City of London, Ranelagh, and Bath. B. 1844; m. Josephine Maria, d. of James Beazley, Esq., of Liverpool. Educ. at Madras Coll., St. Andrews. A partner in Balfour, Williamson and Company, Merchants, Liverpool and London. Created Bart. 1911. A Liberal. Sat for the Partick division of Lanarkshire from 1906 to 1918 and for the Partick division of Glasgow from 1918 until he retired in 1922. Died 4 November 1929. [1922]

BALNIEL, David Robert Alexander Lindsay, Lord. 1 Bryanston Place, London. Travellers'. S. of David, 27th Earl of Crawford and Balcarres, K.T. B. 20 November 1900; m. 9 December 1925, Mary, d. of the Rt. Hon. Lord Richard Cavendish. Educ. at Eton, and Magdalen Coll., Oxford. Parliamentary Private Secretary to Minister of Agriculture November 1924, and to the Rt. Hon. Sir E. Hilton Young, Secretary to Overseas Trade Department August-October 1931, and when Minister of Health November 1931-June 1935. Member of Standing Commission on Museums and Galleries 1937. A Conservative. Unsuccessfully contested Wigan in 1923. Elected for the Lonsdale division of Lancashire in October 1924 and sat until he succeeded to the Peerage as Earl of Crawford and Balcarres in 1940. Styled Lord Balniel 1913-40. G.B.E. 1951; K.T. 1955. Rector of St. Andrews University 1952-55. Dept. Gov. of Royal Bank of Scotland 1962-75; Trustee of British Museum 1940-73; Trustee of National Gallery 1935-41, 1945-52, 1953-60, Chairman 1938-39 and 1946-48; Trustee of National Galleries of Scotland 1944-75, Chairman 1944-74; Chairman of Royal Fine Art Commission 1943-57; Chairman of National Trust 1945-65. Died 13 December 1975. [1940]

BANBURY, Rt. Hon. Sir Frederick George, Bart. 41 Lowndes Street, London. Warneford Place, Highworth, Wiltshire. Carlton. Eld. s. of Frederick Banbury, Esq., of Shirley House, Surrey. B. 2 December 1850 in London; m. 1873, Elizabeth Rosa, 2nd d. of Thomas Barbot Beale, Esq., of Brettenham Park, Suffolk (she died in 1930). Educ. at Winchester, and abroad. Became a partner in the firm of F. Banbury and Sons, Stockbrokers, 23 Old Broad Street, 1873, and head of the firm in 1879, retired 1906. Was Chairman of the Great Northern Railway; Chairman of Select Committee on National Expenditure 1920; created Bart. in 1902; PC. 1916. One of the Temporary Chairmen of Committees; Chairman of the Estimates Committee. A Conservative. Sat for Peckham from 1892 until January 1906, when he was defeated at the general election. Elected for the City of London in June 1906 and sat until January 1924 when he was created Baron Banbury of Southam. Chairman of R.S.P.C.A. Died 13 August 1936. [1924]

BANFIELD, John William. 3 Rosedew Road, London. S. of Frederick Charles Banfield, Esq., of Burton-on-Trent. B. 1875; m. 1897, Anne Elizabeth, d. of John Newman, Esq., of Worcester. Gen. Secretary National Union of Operative Bakers and Confectioners until 1940. A Labour Member. Unsuccessfully contested the Aston division of Birmingham in December 1918 and W. Fulham in May 1930 and again in October 1931. Elected for Wednesbury in July 1932 and again in November 1935 and sat until he died on 25 May 1945.   [1945]

BANKS, Sir Reginald Mitchell, K.C. 24 Kensington Gore, London. 1 Temple Gardens, London. Carlton, and Oxford and Cambridge. S. of Sir William Mitchell Banks, M.D., LL.D., F.R.C.S., and Elizabeth Rathbone Elliott. B. 1880; m. 1st, 1905, Leone, d. of M.T. Harries, Esq., of Manchester (she died 1924); secondly, 1926, Eve, widow of Edward Epstein, Esq., of Louisville, Kentucky. Educ. at Rugby and Christ Church, Oxford. A Barrister-at-Law, Inner Temple 1905; K.C. 1923; Bencher 1930; Recorder of Wigan 1928-34. Served in India and Mesopotamia 1914-17. Knight Bach. 1928. A Conservative. Sat for the Swindon division of Wiltshire from November 1922 to May 1929, when he was defeated. Re-elected for Swindon in October 1931 and sat until 1934 when he was appointed a County Court Judge for Hull and district. Author of *The Conservative Outlook*. Died 9 July 1940.   [1934]

BANNER, Sir John Sutherland Harmood. See HARMOOD-BANNER, Sir John Sutherland.

BANTON, George Stapleford, Westfield, Leicester. B. 1856 at Melton Mowbray. A Coal Merchant. Alderman of Leicester City Council; Chairman of Leicester Tramways Committee. J.P. for Leicester. One of the Pioneers of the I.L.P. A Labour Member. Unsuccessfully contested E. Leicester in December 1918. Sat for E. Leicester from March to November 1922 when he was defeated. Re-elected for the same seat in December 1923 and sat until he was defeated in October 1924. Mayor of Leicester 1925-26. Died 19 April 1932.   [1924 2nd ed.]

BARCLAY, Robert Noton. Mobberley Hall, Cheshire. National Liberal. S. of Robert and Mary Ann Noton Barclay. B. 11 May 1872; m. 23 June 1898, Helena Margaret, d. of John K. Bythell, Esq., Managing Director of Manchester Ship Canal. Educ. at Uppingham, and Victoria University, Manchester. Member of Manchester City Council from 1917; Director of Manchester Chamber of Commerce (President 1914-16); J.P. for Manchester. A Liberal. Elected for the Exchange division of Manchester in December 1923 and sat until he was defeated in October 1924. Again defeated May 1929. Lord Mayor of Manchester 1929-30; Knighted 1936; Chairman of District Bank 1936-46; High Sheriff of Cheshire 1937-38. Died 24 November 1957.   [1924 2nd ed.]

BARCLAY-HARVEY, Sir Charles Malcolm. Dinnet, Aberdeenshire. Carlton, Marlborough, and St. James's. New, Edinburgh. S. of James Charles Barclay-Harvey, Esq., of Dinnet, Aberdeenshire. B. 2 March 1890; m. 1st, 7 February 1912, Margaret Joan, d. of H.D. Beresford Heywood, Esq., of Pontesford, Shropshire (she died 1 December 1935); secondly, 23 March 1938, Lady Muriel Bertie, d. of 12th Earl of Lindsey and widow of Capt. H. Liddell-Granger. Educ. at Eton, and Christ Church, Oxford. Parliamentary Private Secretary to Sir John Gilmour 1924-29 and to Sir Godfrey Collins 1932-36 when Secretaries of State for Scotland. Knight Bach. 1936. A Conservative. Elected for the Kincardine and Western division of Aberdeen and Knicardine in December 1923 and sat until defeated in May 1929. Re-elected for the same seat in October 1931. Sat until March 1939 when he was appointed Gov. of South Australia, retired 1944. Member of Aberdeenshire County Council 1945-55. J.P. for Aberdeenshire from 1922, Dept.-Lieut. from 1945. Died 17 November 1969.   [1939]

BARKER, George. 116 Alexander Road, Abertillery, Monmouthshire. S. of William and Elizabeth Barker. B. at Hanley 13 March 1858; m. 1884, Margaret, d. of Edward and Sarah Sadler. Educ. at Norwood National School. Advisory Agent to Monmouthshire and Western Valleys District, South Wales Miners' Federation. J.P. for Co. Monmouth. Served seven years in the Buffs; medal and clasp Zulu War 1879. A Labour Member. Elected for the Abertillery division of Monmouthshire in December 1920. Sat until he retired in May 1929. Member of Executive of Miners' Federation of Great Britain 1911-21. Died 28 October 1936. [1929]

BARKER, Maj. Robert Hewitt. Junior Army and Navy, and Royal Automobile. B. 1887; m. 1916, Violet, d. of C. Gartside, Esq., of Ashton-under-Lyne. Educ. at Bedford School. Formerly a Lancashire County Rugby forward. Joined the 6th Lancashire Fusiliers; served in Egypt, Gallipoli, and France, gaining the rank of Maj. Invalided home in the summer of 1918. An Independent Member. Elected for the Sowerby division of the W. Riding of Yorkshire in December 1918 and sat until he retired in October 1922. Died 14 February 1961. [1922]

BARLOW, Rt. Hon. Sir Clement Anderson, K.B.E. 34, 35 New Bond Street, London. 34 Chapel Street, London. Carlton. S. of the Very Rev. W.H. Barlow, Dean of Peterborough. B. 1868; m. 1934, Miss D.L. Reed, of Sandwich. Educ. at Repton School, and King's Coll., Cambridge; 1st cl. Law Senior Whewell School and Yorke Prize Essayist, M.A., LL.D. A Barrister-at-Law (Studentship of the Inns of Court, Scholar of the Middle Temple). Official Principal to Archdeacons of London, Hampstead, and St. Albans; a partner in the firm of Sotheby, Wilkinson and Hodge; member of London County Council 1907-10, and Vice-Chairman of Parliamentary Committee, Member of Canterbury House of Laymen. Honorary Secretary of Cambridge House. Raised Salford Brigade Lancashire Fusiliers 1914-15. Member of the Committee on Modern Foreign Languages 1916-17. Chairman of the Select Committee on Pensions 1919, and Acting Chairman of the inter-Departmental Committee dealing with the tuberculous soldier 1919. K.B.E. 1918. Senior Government Delegate at the Inter-National Labour Conferences, Genoa 1920, and Geneva 1921. Parliamentary Secretary to the Ministry of Labour April 1920 to October 1922. Minister of Labour October 1922 to January 1924. PC. 1922. A Conservative. Unsuccessfully contested S. Salford January 1910. Elected for S. Salford in December 1910 and sat until defeated there in December 1923. Created Bart. 1924. Chairman of Royal Commission on Location of Industry 1937-40. Adopted the surname of Montague-Barlow in lieu of Barlow in 1946. Chairman of House of Laity, Church Assembly 1945-46. F.S.A. Died 31 May 1951. [1923]

BARNES, Alfred John. Continued in House after 1945: full entry in Volume IV.

BARNES, Rt. Hon. George Nicoll. 76 Herne Hill, London. B. 1859 at Lochee, Forfar; m. 1882, Jessie, d. of T. Langlands, Esq., of Dundee. Educ. at elementary schools. Apprenticed to an Engineer at Dundee; Assistant Secretary to Amalgamated Society of Engineers 1892-96, and Gen. Secretary from 1896-1908; President of National Committee of Organized Labour on Old Age Pensions; member of Mosley Commission to America 1902. Vice-Chairman of the Labour Party in House of Commons 1908-10, and Chairman 1910-11. Chief of Organizing Department of Independent Labour Party in 1909. Chairman of Co-operative Printing Society, London. PC. 1916. C.H. 1920. Honorary D.C.L. Oxford 1920; Honorary LL.D. Cambridge 1920. Pensions Minister December 1916-August 1917; member (without portfolio) of War Cabinet August 1917 to October 1919, and of the reconstructed Cabinet October 1919 to January 1920. A Labour Member but resigned from the Labour Party in 1918. Unsuccessfully contested Rochdale in 1895. Sat for Blackfriars division of Glasgow 1906-18, and for the Gorbals division of Glasgow from December 1918 until he retired in October 1922. Leader of the National Democratic Party from 1918. Author of *From Workshop to War Cabinet* (1924) and other works. Died 21 April 1940.   [1922]

BARNES, Maj. Harry. 3 Plowden Buildings, Middle Temple, London. 6 Mitre Court Chambers, Temple, London. Low House, Edmondbyers, Shotley Bridge, Co. Durham. National Liberal. S. of Harry Barnes, Esq. B. 5 December 1870 at Ryde, Isle of Wight; m. 1896, Elizabeth Mary, d. of Thomas Scott, Esq., of Sunderland. Educ. at the British School, Sunderland. Architect, Surveyor, Arbitrator, and Valuer. Fellow of the Royal Institute of British Architects; Fellow of the Surveyors' Institution. District Valuer Newcastle-upon-Tyne 1916-18; County Adjutant Northumberland Volunteer Force 1916-March 1918; Commanding Officer 2nd Volunteer Battalion Northumberland Fusiliers with rank of Maj. March 1918. A Liberal. Elected for Newcastle E. in December 1918 and sat until he was defeated in November 1922. Unsuccessfully contested Newcastle E. in January 1923, Tynemouth in December 1923 and October 1924, and Halifax in July 1928. Voted for a capital levy in 1919. Joined Labour Party in 1931. Alderman of London County Council 1923-25 and Labour Member of the Council for E. Fulham 1934-35. Fellow of Royal Statistical Society. Member of Town Planning Institute and Royal Sanitary Institute. Died 12 October 1935.   [1922]

BARNETT, Maj. Sir Richard Whieldon. Park Lodge, Park Village West, London. Carlton, and St. Stephen's. Eld. s. of Richard Barnett, Esq., M.D. Edinburgh, of Ardmore, Holywood, Co. Down, and Adela Sarah, only d. of the Rev. Edward Whieldon, of Hales Hall, Staffordshire, and grand-d. of Thomas Whieldon, Esq., of Fenton Grove, Staffordshire, the eminent Potter, who was High Sheriff of Staffordshire in 1787. B. 6 December 1863; m. 1892, Maud Emmeline, d. of William Cawsey, Esq., of Sidmouth, Devon (she died 1920). Educ. privately, and at Wadham Coll., Oxford; Classical Exhibitioner 1883, B.A. 1887, M.A. 1889, B.C.L. 1889. Barrister-at-Law Middle Temple 1889. Capt. 1st Oxford University V.B. Oxfordshire L.I. 1887-88. Capt. and Instructor of Musketry, 8th V.B.

King's R. Rifles, The Rangers, 1889-97; attached to the Gen. Staff 1914; Staff Officer for Musketry 36th Ulster division 1914-15, 40th division 1915-16; Brevet Maj. 1919. President of British Controlled Oilfields Limited, and a Director of other petroleum undertakings. A member of the Council of the Institution of Petroleum Technologists, and of the National Rifle Association. Member of Chairmen's Panel for Grand Committees from 1923. Created Knight 1925. Member of Court of Assistants Worshipful Company of Turners. President of Commercial Company of House of Commons 1924. A Conservative. Elected for W. St. Pancras in October 1916, and for S.W. St. Pancras in December 1918. Sat until he retired in May 1929. Chairman of Executive Committee of British Chess Federation. Died 17 October 1930.   [1929]

BARNSTON, Sir Harry, Bart. Crewe Hill, Farndon, Cheshire. Carlton, and Bath. S. of Maj. William Barnston, 55th Foot, and Mary Emma, d. of Col. King, K.H. of 16th Lancers. B. 12 December 1870. Unmarried. Educ. at private schools, and at Christ Church, Oxford; M.A. Was called to the bar at the Inner Temple 1898. Chairman of Tarvin Board of Guardians, at one time Capt. Cheshire Yeomanry; rejoined 1914 and saw active service abroad. J.P. and Dept.-Lieut. for Cheshire. Parliamentary Private Secretary to Sir A. Griffith-Boscawen 1919; Comptroller of the Household and Government Whip April 1921 to January 1924, and November 1924-January 1928. Created Bart. 1924. A Conservative. Unsuccessfully contested Stockport in 1906. Sat for the Eddisbury division of Cheshire from January 1910 until he died on 22 February 1929.   [1929]

BARR, Rev. James. 75 Clonston Street, Glasgow. S. of Allan Barr, Esq., of Beanscroft, Ayrshire. B. 26 July 1862; m. 1890, Martha, d. of A.H. Stephen, Esq., of Kilmarnock. Educ. at Waterside School, Fenwick, at Kilmarnock Academy, and at Glasgow University, 1st class honours in Mental Philosophy, and at Glasgow Free Church Coll. A United Free Church Minister. Member of Glasgow School Board

1903-14, and of Royal Commission on Housing for Scotland 1914-17. Chairman of Select Committee on Capital Punishment 1929-30. Chairman of Parliamentary Labour Party 1931. Moderator of United Free Church of Scotland 1929-30 and 1943-44. A Labour Member. Elected for the Motherwell division of Lanarkshire in October 1924 and sat until defeated in October 1931. Unsuccessfully contested the Kilmarnock division of Ayrshire in November 1933. Elected for the Coatbridge division of Lanarkshire in November 1935 and sat until he retired in June 1945. Died 24 February 1949. [1945]

BARRAND, Arthur Rhys. Oak Lodge, Bycullah Road, Enfield. National Liberal. S. of J.A. and M.E. Barrand. B. 28 October 1861 at Stoke Newington; m. Emily Brydon, d. of Henry Fletcher Schofield, Esq., of Manchester. Educ. at the Birkbeck School, Kingsland, and Finsbury Technical Coll. An Actuary June 1895; Barrister-at-Law Middle Temple June 1906. Author of various contributions on legal and actuarial subjects; Joint Editor of the last edition of Bunyon's *Law of Life Assurance*. A Liberal Coalition Member. Elected for the Pudsey and Otley division of the W. Riding of Yorkshire in December 1918 and sat until he was defeated in November 1922. Director of Prudential Insurance Company. Died 3 August 1941. [1922]

BARRIE, Sir Charles Coupar, K.B.E. 54a Parliament Street, London. Tullybelton, Bankfoot, Perthshire. Bath, and Reform. S. of Sir Charles Barrie, Dept.-Lieut., J.P., and Lord Provost of Dundee. B. 1875; m. 1926, Ethel, d. of Sir James Broom. Educ. at Blairlodge School, Polmont. A Shipowner and Merchant at Dundee. Served at the Admiralty and Ministry of Shipping 1916-18. Minister of Munitions representative at Peace Conference; member of Supreme Economic Council; Chairman of Disposals Board and of Advisory Committee to Department of Overseas Trade and Post Office; Chairman of the Navy, Army and Air Force Institutes 1921; Dept.-Lieut., and J.P. A Liberal National. Elected for Elgin Burghs in October 1918; sat for

Banffshire from December 1918-October 1924 when he was defeated and for Southampton from October 1931 until he resigned in January 1940. Created Baron Abertay June 1940. Died 6 December 1940. [1940]

BARRIE, Rt. Hon. Hugh Thom. The Manor House, Coleraine. Carlton, Constitutional, and St. Stephen's. B. 1860 at Glasgow; m. 1892, Katherine, eld. d. of the Rev. W.H. Quarry. A Merchant; Dept.-Lieut. and J.P. for Co. Londonderry. Vice-President of the Department of Agriculture and Technical Instruction, Ireland January 1919 to November 1921. PC. (Ireland) 1920. A Coalition Unionist. Sat for N. Londonderry from 1906 to December 1918 when he retired. Re-elected for N. Londonderry in March 1919 and sat until he died on 18 April 1922. High Sheriff of Londonderry in 1918. Senator in Northern Ireland Parliament 1921-22. Died 18 April 1922. [1922]

BARSTOW, Percy Gott. Continued in House after 1945: full entry in Volume IV.

BARTLETT, Charles Vernon Oldfield. Continued in House after 1945: full entry in Volume IV.

BARTLEY-DENNISS, Sir Edmund Robert Bartley. Belmont, Uxbridge, Middlesex. 1 Essex Court, Temple, London. Carlton, St. Stephen's, 1900, and Cecil. S. of Edumund P. Denniss, Esq., (s. of Col. G.H. Denniss, 43rd Regiment), and Caroline Christiana, d. of Lieut.-Gen. Sir Robert Bartley, K.C.B. B. 9 April 1854 in London; m. 1877, Margaret Ellen, d. of George Barlow, Esq., J.P., of Oldham (she died 1930). Educ. at Christ's Hospital, Wrens, and Hertford Coll., Oxford; Scholarship in Natural Science at Sidney Sussex Coll., Cambridge. A Barrister, called at the Middle Temple 1879. A member of Hendon District Council for 15 years and Chairman for three years, and was a member of Middlesex County Council for Harrow. Member of the Council of the London Chamber of Commerce, and of the London Court of Arbitration. Vice-Chairman of Grand

Council of the Primrose League. Honorary Treasurer of the Air League of the British Empire. A Unionist. Unsuccessfully contested Oldham in December 1910. Elected for Oldham in November 1911, and re-elected until he retired in October 1922. K.C. 1922. Knighted in 1922, when he adopted the surname of Bartley-Denniss in lieu of Denniss. Died 20 March 1931.

[1922]

BARTON, Sir Andrew William. Wyberslegh Hall, Disley, Cheshire. National Liberal. S. of Robert Barton, Esq., of Hamilton, N.B. B. 5 August 1862 at Hamilton; m. 1895, Jessie, d. of James Boyd, Esq., of Manchester (she died 1915); secondly, January 1918, Olive Ruth Bryson, Matron of Balmoral Red Cross Hospital, Llandudno, d. of Oliver Bryson, Esq., of Lyford, Co. Donegal (she died 1956). Educ. at Glasgow High School, Athenaeum, and University. J.P. for Lancashire. Knighted 1917. A Liberal. Elected for Oldham in January 1910 and sat until November 1922 when he unsuccessfully contested the Exchange division of Manchester. Member of Manchester City Council 1906-09. Fellow of Royal Society of Arts. Died 9 July 1957.

[1922]

BARTON, Capt. Basil Kelsey, M.C. Welton Lodge, Welton, Yorkshire. S. of Maj. Bernard Barton. B. 1879. Educ. at Oundle. A Solicitor. A Conservative. Elected for the Central division of Kingston-upon-Hull in October 1931 and sat until he was defeated in November 1935. Died 2 July 1958.

[1935]

BARTON, Robert Childers. Glendalough House, Annamoe, Co. Wicklow. S. of Charles William Barton, Esq. B. 1881; m. 1950, Rachel Warren Lothrop, d. of Fiske Warren, of Boston, Massachusetts (she died 1973). Educ. at Rugby, and Christ Church, Oxford. Chairman of Wicklow County Council 1920. Escaped from Mountjoy Gaol March 1919. Re-arrested February 1920 and sentenced to three years penal servitude under the Defence of the Realm Act. A Sinn Feiner. Elected for W. Wicklow in December 1918 but did not take his seat.

Member of Dail for W. Wicklow to 1921, for Kildare and Wicklow 1921-23 as an Anti-Treaty Member. Minister for Economic Affairs 1921-22. Signatory of 1921 Treaty but later opposed it. Chairman of Agricultural Credit Corporation 1934-54, of Turf Development Board 1935-60. Died 10 August 1975.

[1922]

BATEMAN, Arthur Leonard. 215 Queen's Road, Peckham, London. Bartholomew, and City Livery. S. of Arthur Bateman, Esq. B. 22 August 1879. Educ. privately. A Sack and Basket Manufacturer. Member of Camberwell Borough Council 1922-31; Mayor of Camberwell 1929-30; member of London County Council 1931-34. A Freeman and Liveryman of the City of London. A Conservative. Elected for N. Camberwell in October 1931 and sat until he retired in October 1935. Unsuccessfully contested S. Tottenham in July 1945. Member of Warwick Borough Council 1946-51. Died 8 May 1957.

[1935]

BATEY, Joseph. 21 The Avenue, Durham. S. of Isaac Batey, Esq. B. 1867; m. 1888, Martha Irving. Member of the Town Council and Board of Guardians South Shields. J.P. A Checkweighman, later an official of the Durham Miners' Association. A Labour Member. Unsuccessfully contested the Spennymoor division of Durham in 1918. Elected for the Spennymoor division in November 1922 and sat until he resigned in 1942. Died 21 February 1949.

[1942]

BAXTER, Arthur Beverley. Continued in House after 1945: full entry in Volume IV.

BEAMISH, Rear-Admiral Tufton Percy Hamilton, C.B. Chelworth, Chelwood Gate, Haywards Heath, Sussex. Carlton, United Service, and Royal Automobile. S. of Rear-Admiral H.H. Beamish, C.B. B. 26 July 1874; m. 8 October 1914, Margaret, d. of Henry Simon, Esq., of Didsbury. Joined R.N. 1888, retired 1922. Served in East Africa 1896, in Benin Expedition 1897, in the Falkland Island Action 1914, at the Battle of Jutland 1916. At the Admiralty as Assistant to Chief of Staff 1912; Naval Assistant to First Sea Lord August-

November 1914; Dept.-Lieut. for Sussex. A Conservative. Sat for the Lewes division of Sussex from July 1924-31 when he retired; re-elected for Lewes in June 1936 and sat until he retired in June 1945. C.B. 1917. Died 2 May 1951. [1945]

BEASLEY, Pierce. B. 1883. A Dublin Journalist, known as a writer in Gaelic League and Sinn Fein papers. Was sentenced to penal servitude for the part he played in the rebellion of Easter 1916. Escaped from Strangeways Gaol October 1919. A Sinn Feiner. Was returned unopposed for E. Kerry in December 1918 but did not take his seat. Member of Dail for E. Kerry to 1921 and for Kerry and W. Limerick as a Pro-Treaty Member 1921-23. [1922]

BEATTIE, Francis. Auchans, Dundonald, Ayrshire. Carlton, Caledonian and Western. New, Art, and Conservative, Glasgow. S. of William Beattie, Esq., J.P., of Dineiddwg, Stirlingshire. B. 1885; m. 1922, Sarah Edith, d. of Henry Lewis-Thomas, Esq. Educ. at Whitehill School, Glasgow, Blairlodge, Stirlingshire, and the University of Glasgow. Chairman of William Beattie Limited, and various other Bread Bakeries in Scotland. Dept. Director of Emergency Bread Supplies and Trade Adviser on Bread Supplies for Scotland, Ministry of Food to 1942; member of Sea-Fish Commission 1933-36, of Market Supply Committee (Agricultural Marketing Act 1933) 1937-39, and of other Government Committees; of Committee of Enquiry on Rating and Valuation in Scotland 1943. Deacon Convener of the Trades of Glasgow 1933-35; Freeman and Liveryman of the City of London; Gov. of Royal Mechanical Coll., Glasgow; member of Board of Management of the Western Infirmary, Glasgow; Gen. Commissioner of Income Tax for Lower Ward of Lanark; Trustee of Savings Bank of Glasgow; Director of Merchants' House, Glasgow; member of Executive Committee of Scottish Development Council, of T.A. and A.F. Association of Glasgow, of Board of Trade local Price Regulation Committee for S.W. District of Scotland. Maj. 9th H.L.I., served in France 1914-18. Dept.-Lieut., and J.P. for Glasgow. A National Unionist Member.

Member for the Cathcart division of Glasgow from April 1942 until his death in a road accident on 28 December 1945. [1946]

BEATTIE, John. Continued in House after 1945: full entry in Volume IV.

BEAUCHAMP, Sir Brograve Campbell, Bart. House of the Pines, Virginia Avenue, Virginia Water. S. of Sir Edward Beauchamp, 1st Bart. B. 5 May 1897; m. 8 October 1923, Lady Evelyn Herbert, d. of George, 5th Earl of Carnarvon. Educ. at Eton. Lieut. 1st Life Guards. Parliamentary Private Secretary to Sir John Reith, Minister of Transport August.-October 1940. Parliamentary Private Secretary to Richard Law, Esq., Parliamentary Under-Secretary of State for Foreign Affairs 1942-43. A Conservative. Unsuccessfully contested Lowestoft November 1922. Sat for Walthamstow E. from October 1931 until he retired in June 1945. Succeeded as Bart. 1925. Died 25 August 1976. [1945]

BEAUCHAMP, Sir Edward, Bart. 26 Grosvenor Place, London. S. of the Rev. W.H. Beauchamp and Augusta, d. of Dr. T. Arnold, and grand-s. of Sir William Beauchamp-Proctor, Bart. B. 12 April 1849 at Chedgrave, Norfolk; m. 1st, 1875, Frances May, d. of his Hon. James Stephen, County Court Judge (she died 1886); secondly, 1890, Betty Campbell, d. of Archibald Woods, Esq., of Columbus, U.S.A. Educ. privately, and in the Royal Navy. An Underwriter, and a member of Lloyd's from 1873, of which he was Chairman 1905 and 1913. Created Bart. 1911. A Liberal. Sat for the Lowestoft division of Suffolk from 1906 to January 1910 when he was defeated. Re-elected for that division in December 1910 and sat until he retired in October 1922. Died in Lahore on 1 February 1925. [1922]

BEAUMONT, Hubert. Continued in House after 1945: full entry in Volume IV.

BEAUMONT, Michael Wentworth. Wotton House, Aylesbury. Brooks's, Bucks, and Carlton. S. of Hon. Hubert Beaumont, MP, and Elisa, d. of M.P. Grace, Esq., of

23

Battle Abbey, and grand-s. of Wentworth, 1st Baron Allendale. B. 8 February 1903; m. 1st, 24 February 1924, Hon. Faith Muriel Pease, d. of Baron Gainford (she died 16 February 1935); secondly, 30 December 1935, Doreen Christian, d. of Sir Herbert Davis-Goff, of Glenville, Waterford. Educ. at Eton, Oundle, and Royal Military Coll., Sandhurst. 2nd Lieut. Coldstream Guards 1923-24; 2nd Lieut. 99 (Bucks and Berks Yeomanry) Field Brigade R.A. (T.A.) 1925; Lieut. 1927, Capt. 1932. County Councillor 1925-34, J.P. for Buckinghamshire 1927 and Dept.-Lieut. 1938. Parliamentary Private Secretary to H. Ramsbotham when Parliamentary Secretary to Board of Education November 1931-December 1932. A Conservative. Unsuccessfully contested the Forest of Dean in October 1924, and July 1925. Elected for the Aylesbury division of Buckinghamshire in May 1929 and sat until he resigned in May 1938. Died 19 December 1958.   [1938]

BEAUMONT, Hon. Ralph Edward Blackett. Plas Llwyngwern, Machynlleth, Montgomeryshire. S. of 1st Visct. Allendale. B. 12 February 1901; m. 22 March 1926, Helena Mary Christine, d. of Brigadier-Gen. Wray, C.B., C.M.G., M.V.O. (she died 1962). Educ. at Eton, and at Christ Church, Oxford. J.P. for Montgomery. Parliamentary Private Secretary to Rt. Hon. George Tryon, Postmaster-Gen. March 1936-February 1940, and to Rt. Hon. Sir James Grigg when Secretary of State for War May 1942-July 1945. Member of Governing Body of Church in Wales. A Unionist. Unsuccessfully contested the Cannock division of Staffordshire in May 1929. Elected for Portsmouth central in October 1931. Sat until he was defeated in July 1945. Vice-Lieut. of Montgomeryshire 1962-74; High Sheriff 1957; Dept.-Lieut. 1961; C.B.E. 1967. Died 18 September 1977.   [1945]

BEAUMONT-THOMAS, Maj. Lionel, M.C. See THOMAS, Maj. Lionel Beaumont, M.C.

BECK, Sir Arthur Cecil Tyrrell. 26 St. James's Street, London. Brooks's, Marlborough, Reform, and National Liberal. S. of Arthur William Beck, Esq. B. 3 December 1876 in S. Africa; m. 1922, Lillian, d. of A.K. Rickards, Esq., of Monmouthshire. Educ. at Haileybury, and Jesus Coll., Cambridge. A Barrister, Lincoln's Inn 1898, but did not practise. A J.P. for Huntingdonshire and Bedfordshire and Mayor of St. Ives, Huntingdonshire 1905-06. Parliamentary Private Secretary to Mr. Illingworth, Chief Liberal Whip 1914; Junior Lord of the Treasury February to May 1915; Vice-Chamberlain of the Household May 1915 to December 1917. Parliamentary Secretary and Controller of Finance to the Ministry of National Service June 1917 to January 1919; Parliamentary Secretary to the Ministry of National Service and Reconstruction January-December 1919. A Liberal Whip 1906-17; Treasurer of Eastern Countries Liberal Federation; Secretary, and later Chairman of Liberal Insurance Committee. Member of Royal Commission on Civil Service 1912-15; Honorary Secretary Central Land and Housing Council and of Munitions Parliamentary Committee; Member of the National War Savings Committee; Member of Executive Committee of Navy League; Honorary Lieut. in R.N.V.R. 1914. Knighted 1920. A Liberal Member until August 1921 when he joined Horatio Bottomley's Independent Parliamentary Group. Sat for the Wisbech division of Cambridgeshire from 1906 to January 1910, when he unsuccessfully contested the Chippenham division of Wiltshire. Sat for the Saffron Walden division of Essex from December 1910 until he retired in October 1922. Died 22 March 1932.   [1922]

BECKER, Harry Thomas Alfred. Constitutional, Eccentric, and Royal Automobile. S. of Sir Frederick Becker. B. at Wandsworth 16 June 1892; m. 1st, 1912, Anne, d. of William Lochhead Lipton, Esq; secondly, 1926, Mabel, d. of William Parnham, Esq., thirdly, 1939, Dorothy, d. of John Henry Newman, Esq. (divorced 1952); fourthly, 1952, Mary Beth, d. of Clyde and Mae Browder, of Tennessee. Educ. at Colet Court, and Uppingham. Served in the war 1915-18. A Conservative. Unsuccessfully contested W. Bermondsey in 1918 as ex-soldier candidate. Elected for Richmond in November 1922 and sat until he retired in October 1924. Elected in 1922 as an Independent Conservative, supported by the Anti-Waste League, defeating the official Conservative candidate. Naturalized citizen of U.S.A. 1955.* [1924 2nd ed.]

BECKETT, John Warburten. 139 High Street, London. 17 Cliffords Inn, London. 1917. S. of William Beckett, Esq., of Thurlwood, Cheshire. B. 11 October 1894; m. 1st, 2 April 1918, Helen, d. of John Shaw, Esq., of Cricklewood; secondly, 28 June 1930, Kyrle, d. of J. Bellew and widow of Arthur Bourchier, Esq. Educ. at Council School, Latymer Secondary School, and the Polytechnic. Shop Assistant 1909-10; Advertising Expert 1912-14 and 1917-19; Journalist 1919-24; Chairman of National Union of Ex-Servicemen 1918-19; member of Hackney Borough Council 1919-22. Served in army 1914-17. A Labour Member. Unsuccessfully contested N. Newcastle in 1923. Elected for Gateshead in October 1924 and for the Peckham division of Camberwell in May 1929. Sat until he was defeated in November 1931. Joined ILP in 1931 and was opposed at the 1931 election by an official Labour candidate. Director of Publications for British Union of Fascists and was imprisoned under the Defence of the Realm Act. A co-founder with the Duke of Bedford of the British People's Party in 1938. Died December 1964. [1931 2nd ed.]

BECKETT, Hon. Sir William Gervase, Bart. 1a Cavendish Square, London. Kirkdale Manor, Nawton, Yorkshire. Carlton, Bachelors', and R.Y.S. S. of William Beckett, Esq., MP, and bro. of Ernest, 2nd Baron Grimthorpe; granted the precedence of the son of a Baron in 1905. B. 14 January 1866; m. 1st, 1896, Hon. Mabel Duncombe, d. of Visct. Helmsley and grand-daughter of 1st Earl of Feversham (she died 1913); secondly, 1 November 1917, Lady Marjorie Greville, d. of 5th Earl of Warwick and widow of 2nd Earl of Feversham. Educ. at Eton. Partner in Beckett's Bank, Leeds; Director of the Westminster Bank Limited and of the *Yorkshire Post*. Proprietor of the *Saturday Review*. A Conservative. Unsuccess-

fully contested the Whitby division of Yorkshire in June 1905. Sat for Whitby from 1906-18; for the Scarborough and Whitby division of Yorkshire from 1918-22 when he retired. Elected for N. Leeds in December 1923 and sat until he retired in May 1929. Created Bart. 1921. Capt. Yorkshire Hussars, Imperial Yeomanry. Assistant Military Secretary, Northern Command 1914-16. Assistant Director of War Trade Department 1918-19. Died 24 August 1937. [1929]

BEECH, Maj. Francis William 26 Spencer Gardens, Well Hall Road, Eltham, London. S. of Zachariah and Emma Beech. B. 5 June 1885; m. 1st, 1914, Florence Hannah Mary Jenkins (she died 1963); secondly, 1963, Phyllis Alexandra Cooper. Educ. at Long Ashton, Bristol and Lewis School, Pengam. Solicitor 1911. Served in army from 1915, Maj. and Staff Paymaster, R.A.P.C. A Conservative. Elected for Woolwich W. in November 1943 and sat until he was defeated in July 1945. Alderman, Woolwich Borough Council; Mayor 1955-56. Dept. Chairman of L.C.C. from 1952-53. J.P. for County of London. Freeman, City of London. C.B.E. 1952. Died 21 February 1969. [1945]

BEECHMAN, Nevil Alexander. Continued in House after 1945: full entry in Volume IV.

BEIT, Sir Alfred Lane, Bart. Holmer Ridings, Holmer Green, High Wycombe. 41 Threadneedle Street, London. S. of Sir Otto Beit, 1st Bart., K.C.M.G. B. 19 January 1903; m. 20 April 1939, Clementine, d. of Maj. Hon. Clement Mitford and Lady Helen Nutting. Educ. at Eton, and at Christ Church, Oxford. Private Secretary to Sir Arthur Steel-Maitland, Bart. 1928-29. Succeeded as Bart. 1930. Squadron Leader R.A.F.V.R. September 1939. Parliamentary Private Secretary to Rt. Hon. Oliver Stanley, Secretary of State for the Colonies November 1944. A Conservative. Unsuccessfully contested S.E. St. Pancras in May 1929. Elected for S.E. St. Pancras in October 1931 and sat until he was defeated in July 1945.* [1945]

BELL, Maj. Sir Arthur Clive Morrison, Bart. See MORRISON-BELL, Maj. Sir Arthur Clive, Bart.

BELL, James. 116 Belgrave Road, Oldham. S. of John Bell, Esq., a Miner. B. 1872 at Darlington; m. 1895, Elizabeth Hannah, d. of Cowling and Charlotte Heaton. Educ. in elementary schools. A Trade Union Secretary 1905. J.P. for Oldham, and Chairman of the Oldham Insurance Committee. A Labour Member. Elected for the Ormskirk division of Lancashire in December 1918 and sat until he was defeated in November 1922. Unsuccessfully contested Rossendale in October 1924, Bury in May 1929 and October 1931, and Blackburn in November 1935. Died 28 December 1955. [1922]

BELL, Joseph Nicholas. 90 Friern Park, Finchley, London. Automobile, Newcastle-on-Tyne. S. of Nicholas Bell, Esq., Farmer, of Hightoun. B. at Islington 7 March 1864; m. 1896, Florence Nightingale, d. of Thomas Harrison, Esq., of Newcastle-on-Tyne. Educ. at Low Row Board School, and Gilsland School. A Farmer in youth, and Labourer; Trade Union Secretary 1888 National Amalgamated Union of Labour. Member Management Committee General Federation of Trade Unions. J.P. 1897. Vice-President General Council Trade Union Congress 1921. A Labour Member. Unsuccessfully contested Leith Burghs at a by-election in February 1914. Elected for Newcastle-on-Tyne E. in November 1922 and died on 17 December 1922. [1923]

BELL, Ronald McMillan. Continued in House after 1945: full entry in Volume IV.

BELL, Col. William Cory Heward, D.S.O. Winford Manor, Somerset. Springherne, Ross-on-Wye. Carlton, and Junior United Service. S. of W. Heward Bell, Esq. B. in London 25 October 1875; m. 1903, Violet Mary, d. of Capt. J.D. Bowly, R.E. (she died 1950). Educ. at Westminster, and Royal Military Academy. Joined Royal Field Artillery 1895; Capt. 1901; retired 1911. Served in South African War, Queen's Medal, 4 clasps. Rejoined August 1914; served continuously on the Western front with the 1st Divisional Artillery from November 1914 till the cessation of hostilities. Twice mentioned in despatches; awarded the D.S.O. 1 January 1917. French Croix de Guerre 1918. A Conservative. Elected for the Devizes division of Wiltshire in December 1918. Sat until he was defeated in December 1923. Member of Wiltshire County Council 1931-46; High Sheriff of Wiltshire 1932; Dept.-Lieut. and J.P. for Wiltshire. Died 6 February 1961. [1923]

BELLAIRS, Carlyon Wilfroy. 10 Eaton Place, London. Gore Court, Maidstone. Carlton. S. of Lieut.-Gen. Sir William Bellairs, K.C.M.G. B. 15 March 1871 at Gibraltar; m. 1911, Charlotte, d. of Col. H.L. Pierson, of Long Island, U.S.A. (she died 1939). Educ. in H.M.S. *Britannia*, and Royal Naval Coll. Joined Royal Navy 1885; Lieut. 1891; retired 1902; was specially promoted to Lieut. having obtained 1st class certificates in all subjects. Lecturer for War course for Senior Naval Officers 1902-05. Member of London County Council 1913-15. A Conservative. Sat for King's Lynn as a Liberal from 1906-09, and as a Unionist from 1909-10. Unsuccessfully contested W. Salford in January 1910 and the Walthamstow division of Essex in December 1910. Elected for Maidstone in February 1915 and for the Maidstone division of Kent in 1918. Sat until he retired in October 1931. Declined a Baronetcy in 1927. Died in Barbados 22 August 1955. [1931 2nd ed.]

BELLAMY, Albert, C.B.E. Fox Street, Stockport. S. of James Bellamy, Esq., of Stockport. B. 1870; m. d. of John Fisher, Esq., of Halifax. Educ. at Manchester Elementary School. President of A.S.R.S. 1911-13, and of N.U.R. 1913-17. Parliamentary Private Secretary to the Rt. Hon. F.O. Roberts, Minister of Pensions June 1929. A Labour Member. Unsuccessfully contested Wakefield in 1918 and 1922. Elected for Ashton-under-Lyne in October 1928. Sat until he died on 26 March 1931. C.B.E. 1917. J.P. for Stockport and President of Stockport Trades Council. Died 26 March 1931.

[1931 2nd ed]

BELLENGER, Frederick John. Continued in House after 1945: full entry in Volume IV.

BENN, Sir Arthur Shirley, Bart., K.B.E. 18 Bolton Gardens, London. Carlton. S. of the Rev. J.W. Benn, Rector of Carrigaline and Douglas, Co. Cork. B. 20 December 1858; m. 1888, Alys Marie, d. of F.A. Lüling, Esq., of Springhill, Alabama (she died 4 June 1932). Educ. at Clifton Coll., and abroad. A Student of the Inner Temple. Managing Director of Hunter, Benn and Company, and British Vice-Consul at Mobile, Alabama, U.S.A. 1898-1902; member of London County Council 1907-11, and Chairman of Highways Committee 1909-10; member of London T.F.A. K.B.E. 1918. Created Bart. 1926. President Association of British Chambers of Commerce 1921-23. Chairman of National Unionist Association 1921; President Federation of Chambers of Commerce of B.E. 1931-34, and of the Knights of the Round Table Club. A Conservative. Unsuccessfully contested Battersea in 1906 and January 1910. Elected for Plymouth in December 1910, and for the Drake division of Plymouth in December 1918 and again in November 1922. Sat until defeated in 1929. Elected for the Park division of Sheffield in October 1931 and sat until he was defeated in November 1935. Director of International Chamber of Commerce from 1927. Created Baron Glenravel 1936. Died 13 June 1937. [1935]

BENN, Capt. Sir Ion Hamilton, Bart., C.B., D.S.O. 17 Collingham Gardens, London. Brooks's, Carlton, and Royal Thames Yacht. S. of the Rev. J.W. Benn, Rectory of Carrigaline and Douglas, Co. Cork, and Maria Louisa, d. of Gen. C. Hamilton, C.B. B. 31 March 1863 at Douglas, Co. Cork; m. 1st, 1885, Frances, d. of N. Bridges, Esq., M.A., of Wallington Manor, Surrey (she died 1948); secondly, 1950, Katherine Winifred, d. of Brockwill Grier, Esq., of Montreal. A Director of Price and Pierce Limited, London, and Price Brothers Limited, Quebec. Mayor of Greenwich 1901-02; Member of the Metropolitan Water Board 1903-06; London County Council 1907-10; Director of the Port of London Authority 1909-61. Honorary Col. 20th Battalion London Regiment. Temporary Lieut.-Commander R.N.R. 1914. Temporary Commander R.N.V.R. 1915; mentioned in despatches. D.S.O. 20 July 1917 for work done in bombardment of Zeebrugge and Ostend in May and June 1917; mentioned in despatches 21 July 1918; promoted Acting-Capt. 23 April 1918; mentioned in despatches, C.B. 28 August 1918. Created Bart. 1920. A Unionist. Unsuccessfully contested Greenwich in 1906. First elected for Greenwich in January 1910 and sat until he retired in October 1922. T.D. 1926. Member of Thames Conservancy Board 1937-46. Died 12 August 1961. [1922]

BENN, Capt. Rt. Hon. William Wedgwood, D.S.O. 40 Millbank, London. S. of Sir John Benn, 1st Bart., of Old Knoll. B. 10 May 1877; m. 17 November 1920, Margaret, d. of Daniel Holmes, Esq., at one time MP for Govan. Educ. at Lycee Condorcet, Paris, and at University Coll., London; B.A. 1898, Fellow 1916. Served with Yeomanry and R.N.A.S. in Egypt, Gallipoli, Italy and Mediterranean 1914-18. Rejoined R.A.F. May 1940. Had D.F.C., French Legion of Honour, Croix de Guerre, also Italian Military Cross and Medal for Valour. Chairman of National Relief Fund 1914. A Junior Lord of the Treasury and Liberal Whip 1910-15; Secretary of State for India June 1929-August 1931; PC. 1929. A Labour Member. Sat as Liberal MP for the St. Georges division of Tower Hamlets from 1906-18, and for Leith, as a Liberal MP from December 1918 until March 1927, when he resigned to join the Labour Party. Sat for Aberdeen N. from August 1928 until October 1931, when he was defeated. Unsuccessfully contested Dudley in November 1935. Elected for the Gorton division of Manchester in February 1937 and sat until he was created Visct. Stansgate in 1942. Vice President of Allied Control Commission for Italy 1943-44. Secretary of State for Air August 1945-October 1946. D.S.O. 1916. Died 17 November 1960. [1942]

BENNETT, Sir Albert James, Bart.
Gloucester House, Park Lane, London.
Kirklington Hall, Southwell, Nottingham-
shire. Carlton, Brooks's, and Bath. S. of
Edward and Eliza Bennett. B. 17 September
1872; m. 1st, 15 December 1896, Caroline
Carleton, d. of Jacob Backus, Esq (divorced
1938); secondly, 1938, Leopoldine, d. of
Leopold Armata, Esq., of Vienna. Educ.
privately. Had large interests in South
America, and was a Director of several
Industrial Companies. Member of the
Mechanical Transport Board, War Office,
and the Leather Control Board; Controller
for South and Central America Ministry of
Information 1914-19. M.F.H. (the Rufford)
1920-22. J.P. for Nottinghamshire.
Chairman Nottingham Conservative
Association; Assistant Treasurer of the
Conservative Party. Created Bart. 1929.
Unsuccessfully contested Chippenham as a
Liberal in 1918. Sat as Liberal MP for the
Mansfield division of Nottinghamshire from
November 1922-November 1923 when he
was defeated. Elected for Nottingham
Central as a Conservative in October 1924
and sat until he resigned in 1930. Chairman
of Estimates Committee 1927-29. Died
14 December 1945.   [1929 2nd ed.]

**BENNETT, Air Vice-Marshal Donald
Clifford Tyndall.** Royal Aero. S. of George
Thomas Bennett, Esq., of Brisbane, Queensland. B. 14 September 1910; m. 1935, Elsa,
d. of Charles Gubler, Esq., of Zurich. Served
with R.A.F. and Royal Australian Air Force
1939-45; commanded Pathfinder force of
Bomber Command 1942-45. D.S.O. 1942;
C.B.E. 1943; C.B. 1944. Air Vice-Marshal
1943. A Liberal. Elected for W. Middlesbrough in May 1945 and sat until he was
defeated in July 1945. Unsuccessfully contested N. Croydon in March 1948 and N.
Norwich in February 1950 as a Liberal.
Unsuccessfully contested Nuneaton in
March 1967 as an Independent with the
support of the National Party. Managing
Director and Chief Executive of British
South American Airways Corporation 1946-
48. Chairman of Executive Committee of
United Nations Association of Great
Britain 1946-49. President of Radar Associa-
tion of Great Britain 1946-49. President of

Radar Association 1952-55. Fellow of Royal
Aeronautical Society. Chairman of Political
Freedom Movement and National Council
of Anti-Common Market Organisations.
Chairman and Managing Director of Dart
Aircraft Limited, Fairtravel Limited and
Fairthorpe Limited. Author of *Complete Air
Navigator*, *Air Mariner*, *Freedom from War*,
Pathfinder and *Let us Try Democracy*.★

BENNETT, Sir Ernest Nathaniel.
22 Egerton Terrace, London. Cwmllecoe-
diog, Machynlleth. Reform, Bath, and Fly-
fishers'. S. of Canon Bennett of Rede,
Suffolk. B. 12 December 1868; m. 4 October
1915, Marguerite, d. of H.G. Kleinwort,
Esq., of Wierton Place, Maidstone. Educ. at
Durham School, and at Hertford Coll.,
Oxford. Fellow of Hertford Coll.; J.P. for
Oxfordshire. Capt. 4th Oxford and Bucks
L.I.; served in South African War 1900-02,
and in France, etc. 1914-18. Parliamentary
Private Secretary to Lord Strachie when
President of Board of Agriculture 1909;
Knight Bach. 1930; Assistant Postmaster-
Gen. October 1932-December 1935.
Member of Lothian (Indian Franchise)
Commission 1932; British Delegate
Assembly, League of Nations 1933; Member
of Select Committee on National Expendi-
ture 1939. A Nationalist. Sat as a Liberal
for the Woodstock division of Oxfordshire
from 1906-January 1910 when he was
defeated; again defeated in December 1910.
Unsuccessfully contested the Westbury divi-
sion of Wiltshire in December 1918, Banbury
in November 1922 and December 1923, and
St. Pancras S.W. in October 1924 as a
Labour candidate. Elected for Cardiff
central in May 1929, re-elected as National
Labour in October 1931 and sat until he
retired in June 1945. Press correspondent in
Crete 1897 and Sudan 1898. Served with the
Turkish army 1911-12. Joined the Labour
Party in 1916. Died 2 February 1947.[1945]

BENNETT, Sir Peter Frederick Blaker.
Continued in House after 1945: full entry
in Volume IV.

BENNETT, Sir Thomas Jewell. 38 Hans
Place, London. Harwarton, Speldhurst,
Kent. Carlton, and Oriental. S. of J.T.

Bennett, Esq. B. 1852 at Wisbech, Cambridgeshire; m. 1917, Elena, d. of Thomas Brooke-Jones, Esq., of Ferrol, Spain. A Journalist, for seventeen years in India; Editor until 1901 of *The Times of India*, Bombay, and partowner. Wrote largely on India and other Eastern questions. Knighted 1921. C.I.E. 1903. J.P. for Kent. A Conservative. Unsuccessfully contested the Brigg division of Lincolnshire in December 1910. Elected for the Sevenoaks division of Kent in December 1918 and again in November 1922. Sat until he was defeated in December 1923. Member of National Assembly of Church of England. Died 16 January 1925.
[1923]

BENNETT, William. 77a Lavender Hill, London. 187 Windsor Road, Torquay. National Liberal. S. of Samuel Bennett, Esq., Accountant, of Oakhill, Somerset. B. 7 April 1873; m. 1899, d. of A.J. Murrin, Esq. Educ. at Bath Grammar School, and Metropolitan Coll. of Pharmacy. Passed examination as Pharmacist 1896. A Labour Member. Unsuccessfully contested Guildford in 1918, 1922 and 1923. Elected for Battersea S. in February and May 1929 and sat until he was defeated in October 1931. Unsuccessfully contested Hitchin in June 1933, Harborough in November 1933 and Cardiff E. in November 1935. Alderman, London County Council from 1934-37. Died 4 November 1937. [1931 2nd ed.]

BENSON, George. Continued in House after 1945: full entry in Volume IV.

BENTHAM, Dr. Ethel. 110 Beaufort Street, London. D. of William Bentham, Esq., J.P., of Co. Dublin. B. 5 January 1861. Unmarried. Educ. at Alexandra School and Coll., Dublin, London School of Medicine (Royal Free Hospital), Rotunda Hospital, Dublin, and Paris and Brussels. Member of Kensington Borough Council 1913-26; member Metropolitan Asylums Board. A Labour Member. Unsuccessfully contested E. Islington in November 1922, December 1923 and October 1924. Elected for E. Islington in May 1929 and sat until she died on 19 January 1931. Joined Labour Party in 1902. Worked in general practice in Newcastle-on-Tyne for 13 years. Member of the Society of Friends from 1920. Member of the National Executive of the Labour Party 1918-20, 1921-26 and 1928-31. Died 19 January 1931. [1929 2nd ed.]

BENTINCK, Lord Henry Cavendish. See CAVENDISH-BENTINCK, Lord Henry.

BERKELEY, Capt. Reginald Cheyne, M.C. 4 Carlisle Mansions, London. Bucks, Savage, and Royal Automobile. S. of Humphry George Berkeley, Esq., and Agnes Mary Cheyne. B. 1890; m. 1st, 1914, Gwendoline Louise Judith, d. of Alfred Cock, Esq., Q.C.; secondly, 1926, Mrs. Hildegarde Digby. Educ. at Bedford Modern School, and University of New Zealand. A Barrister-at-Law, Middle Temple and New Zealand. Served in the Great War with the Rifle Brigade; twice wounded; M.C. Appointed to Gen. Staff 1918; Brigade-Maj. 2nd Infantry Brigade. Demobilized in 1919 and joined Staff of League of Nations Union. On staff of League of Nations Secretariat 1921-22. Published *French Leave*, *Eight o'Clock*, *The Oilskin Pocket* (with James Dixon), and *Decorations and Absurdities* (with Bohun Lynch). A Liberal. Elected for Nottingham central in November 1922. Retired in October 1924. Unsuccessfully contested Aberdeen N. in May 1929, Nottingham central in May 1930 and Aberdeenshire central in October 1931. Died in Hollywood 30 March 1935.
[1924 2nd ed.]

BERNAYS, Robert Hamilton. 18 Allington Court, Allington Street, London. Reform. S. of the Rev. S.F.L. Bernays, Rector of Finchley. B. 6 May 1902; m. 25 April 1942, Nancy, Senior Commissioner A.T.S., and d. of G.B. Bitton, Esq., of Shortwood Lodge, Pucklechurch, Bristol. Educ. at Rossall School, and Worcester Coll., Oxford. *News Chronicle* Leader Writer 1925-29, Special Correspondent India 1930-31, Germany 1933; member of Makerere Education Commission to Uganda 1937; Parliamentary Private Secretary to Sir Robert Hamilton when Parliamentary Under-Secretary of State for the Colonies

November 1931; Parliamentary Secretary Ministry of Health May 1937-July 1939; Parliamentary Secretary Ministry of Transport July 1939-May 1940. Dept.-Regional Commissioner Southern Counties June 1940-April 1942. Joined R.E. 1942. Unsuccessfully contested Rugby in June 1929. Elected as a Liberal in 1931 and became a Liberal National in September 1936, although he had remained on the Government benches in November 1933 when the Liberals went in Opposition. Elected for Bristol N. in October 1931 and sat until he was killed along with J.D. Campbell, MP for Antrim, when their aircraft was lost on 23 January 1945.

[1945]

BERRY, Hon. (Geoffrey) Lionel. The Priory, Pembury, Kent. Carlton, Guards', and Bath. Eld. s. of Lord Kemsley. B. 29 June 1909; m. 21 June 1933, Lady Helene Candida Hay, d. of 11th Marq. of Tweeddale. Educ. at Marlborough, and Magdalen Coll., Oxford. Dept. Chairman of Kemsley Newspapers Limited 1938-59. A Grenadier Guardsmen. A Conservative. Returned unopposed for the Buckingham division of Buckinghamshire in August 1943 and sat until he was defeated in July 1945. Master of Spectacle Makers' Company 1949-51 and 1959-61. Member of Northamptonshire County Council 1964-70. Dept.-Lieut. for Leicestershire, High Sheriff 1967. Succeeded to Peerage as Visct. Kemsley 1968. Fellow of Royal Society of Arts. Knight of Order of St. John of Jerusalem.* [1945]

BERRY, Sir George Andreas. 9 Falkland House, London. North Berwick. St. Stephen's, and University (Edinburgh). S. of Walter Berry, Esq., of Glenstriven, Argyllshire. B. 6 October 1853; m. 24 May 1883, Agnes Jean, d. of Sir W. Muir, K.C.S.I. (she died 2 July 1929). Educ. at Marlborough, and Edinburgh University; M.B., LL.D. A Conservative. Elected for Scottish Universities in November 1922. Returned unopposed for Scottish Universities in December 1923. Sat until he retired in October 1931. Knighted 1916. President of Royal Coll. of Surgeons, Edinburgh. President of Ophthalmological Society of

United Kingdom. Knight Grand Cross of the Order of the Dannebrog (Denmark). Died 18 June 1940. [1931 2nd ed.]

BERRY, Maj. Hon. (John) Seymour. Audleys Wood, Basingstoke. White's, and Buck's. Eld. s. of Visct. Camrose. B. 12 July 1909. Educ. at Eton and Christ Church, Oxford. Capt. City of London Light A.A. Brigade R.A. (T.A.); Maj. 1941. A Director of *The Daily Telegraph*, Amalgamated Press Limited. A Conservative. Elected for the Hitchin division of Hertfordshire in March 1941 and sat until he was defeated in July 1945. Succeeded to the Peerage as Visct. Camrose 1954. Younger Brother of Trinity House. Vice-Chairman of Amalgamated Press Limited 1942-59. Chairman of *The Daily Telegraph* until 1968, Dept.-Chairman from 1968.* [1945]

BETHEL, Albert. The Gables, Knott End, Fleetwood. B. 1874. Member of the firm of Messrs. J. Bethel and Sons, Albert Mills, Eccles. Alderman of Eccles Corporation. A Conservative. Elected for Eccles in October 1924 and sat until he was defeated in May 1929. Died 26 July 1935. [1922]

BETHELL, Sir John Henry, Bart. Bushey House, Bushey, Hertfordshire. Reform, and National Liberal. S. of George Bethell, Esq., of Woodford, Essex. B. 1861; m. 1895, Florence, d. of James W. Wyles, Esq. A Director of Barclays Bank Limited, Royal Exchange Assurance Corporation, and Warwick Estates Company Limited. J.P. for Essex. Knighted 1906. Created Bart. 1911. A Liberal. Unsuccessfully contested Romford division of Essex in 1894 and 1895, and West Ham N. in 1900. Elected for the Romford division of Essex in 1906, January 1910 and December 1910 and for East Ham N. in December 1918. Sat until he retired in October 1922. Created Baron Bethell 1922. Chairman of Frederick Hotels Limited and British Land Company Limited. Mayor of West Ham twice. Mayor of East Ham twice. Died 27 May 1945. [1922]

BETTERTON, Rt. Hon. Sir Henry Bucknall, Bart., C.B.E. 166 Ashley Gardens, London. Fedsden, Roydon, Ware.

Carlton. Eld. s. of Henry Inman Betterton, Esq., J.P., of Woodville, Leicestershire. B. at Woodville 1872; m. 1st, 1912, Violet, widow of Capt. Hervey Greathed, 8th Hussars, and youngest d. of J.S. Gilliat, Esq., of Chorleywood Cedars, MP (she died 1947); secondly, 1948, Inez, d. of Alfred Lubbock, Esq. Educ. at Rugby, and Christ Church, Oxford. A Barrister-at-Law, Inner Temple 1896. PC. 1931. Parliamentary Secretary Ministry of Labour March 1923-January 1924, and November 1924-June 1929. Minister of Labour from August 1931-June 1934. Created Bart. 1929. A Conservative. Elected for the Rushcliffe division of Nottinghamshire in December 1918 and sat until June 1934 when he was appointed Chairman of the Unemployment Assistance Board. Retired 1941. Created Baron Rushcliffe 1935. Member of Political Honours Scrutiny Committee. O.B.E. 1918. C.B.E. 1920. Died 18 November 1949. [1934]

BEVAN, Aneurin. Continued in House after 1945: full entry in Volume IV.

BEVAN, Stuart James, K.C. 2 Plowden Buildings, Temple, London. Carlton, Oxford & Cambridge, and Beefsteak. S. of William James Bevan, Esq., Merchant of S. Kensington. B. 1872; m. 1900, Sylvia, d. of George Grossmith, Esq. Educ. at St. Pauls School, and Trinity Coll., Cambridge. A Barrister-at-Law, Middle Temple 1895; Recorder of Bristol 1932-35. A Conservative. Elected for Holborn in June 1928 and sat until his death on 25 October 1935, the day Parliament was dissolved. [1935]

BEVERIDGE, Sir William Henry, K.C.B. Master's Lodgings, University College, Oxford. Reform. S. of Henry Beveridge, Esq., of Pitfold, Shottermill. B. 5 March 1879; m. 15 December 1942, Jessy, d. of William Phillip, Esq., of Dundee, and widow of D.B. Mair, Esq. (she died 1959). Educ. at Charterhouse, and Balliol Coll., Oxford, M.A. and B.C.L. 1902, Honorary Fellow 1939, D.Sc. London, Honorary LL.D. Aberdeen, Chicago, and Paris, Columbia Honorary D.Litt. McGill, Honorary D.Litt. Hum. Pennsylvania, Master of University Coll., Oxford 1937. Director of Labour Exchanges Board of Trade 1909, Assistant Secretary Employment Department 1913; Assistant Gen. Secretary Ministry of Munitions 1915; 2nd Secretary Ministry of Food 1916; Permanent Secretary 1919; member of Royal Commission on Coalmining Industry 1925; Director of London School of Economics 1919-37; member of Senate of London University 1919; Vice-Chancellor 1926-28, F.B.A. 1937. Chairman of Unemployment Insurance Statutory Committee; President of Royal Economic Society 1940, of Royal Statistical Society 1941 and of Social Security League 1943; Chairman of Interdepartmental Committee on Social Insurance and allied Services 1941-42. C.B. 1916. K.C.B. 1919. A Liberal. Elected for the Berwick-on-Tweed division of Northumberland in October 1944 and sat until he was defeated in July 1945. Author of the *Report of the Committee on Social Insurance and Allied Services* (the 'Beveridge Report') published 1 December 1942. Master of University Coll., Oxford 1937-45. Created Baron Beveridge 1946. Chairman of Aycliffe Development Corporation 1947-53 and Peterlee Development Corporation 1949-51. F.B.A. 1937. Died 16 March 1963. [1945]

BEVIN, Rt. Hon. Ernest. Continued in House after 1945: full entry in Volume IV.

BIGLAND, Alfred. Wexford Lodge, Birkenhead. Carlton, Constitutional, and 1900. S. of Edwin Bigland, Esq., of Birkenhead, and Adelaide Merryweather. B. 15 March 1855; m. 1878, Emily Jane, d. of H.B. Arkle, Esq. (she died 1931). Educ. at the Friend's School, Sidcot, Somerset. Chairman of Bigland Sons and Jeffreys Limited. A member of Birkenhead School Board 1893-1902, and from 1902 of the Education Committee and a member of the Town Council 1907-13. Wrote *England's Future under Tariff Reform* and *The Call of Empire*. Raised Bantam Battalion Cheshire Regiment during the war. Appointed Assitant Director in Propellant Supplies Branch of the Ministry of Munitions January 1916. Controller of Oils and Fats Ministry of Food February 1917. A Coalition Unionist. Unsuccessfully contested Birkenhead in

January 1910. Elected for Birkenhead in December 1910, and for the E. division of Birkenhead in December 1918. Sat until he was defeated in November 1922. Died 7 February 1936. [1922]

BILLING, Noel Pemberton. Royal Corinthian, and Royal Aero. S. of Charles Eardley Billing, Esq., of Birmingham, Iron Founder, and Annie Emilia Claridge, of Coventry. B. at Hampstead 1881; m. 1903, Lilian Maude, d. of Theodore Schweitzer, Esq., of Bristol (she died 1923). Fought in the Boer War 1899-1901. R.N.A.S. 1914-16; retired Squadron Commander. Author of *Endowment by Increment*. Contributor to *Nineteenth Century*, *Fortnightly Review*, and other periodicals on social and industrial problems. Founder and Editor of *Aerocraft* 1908-10. Founder and first President of the "Vigilantes", a society with "the object of promoting purity in public life." An Independent, supported a strong air policy. Unsuccessfully contested Mile End in January 1916. Elected for the Hertford division of Hertfordshire on 9 March 1916 and sat until he resigned in 1921. Unsuccessfully contested Hertford in 1929, Hornsey in May 1941, Dudley in July 1941, The Wrekin in September 1941 and Hampstead in November 1941. Died 11 November 1948. [1921]

BIRCHALL, Sir John Dearman. Cotswold Farm, Cirencester. S. of John Dearman Birchall Esq. B. 26 September 1875; m. 1900, Adela, d. of Philip James Digby Wykeham, Esq., of Tythrop House, Oxfordshire. Educ. at Eton, and New Coll., Oxford; B.A., Hons. in History. Maj. Gloucestershire Yeomanry. Served in France 1918; T.D. Dept.-Lieut., and J.P. for Gloucestershire. Alderman Gloucestershire County Council. Member of National Assembly. Second Church Estates Commissioner (unpaid) 1923 and 1924-29. Knight Bach. 1929. A Conservative. Unsuccessfully contested N. Leeds in 1906 and January and December 1910. Elected for N.E. Leeds in December 1918 and sat until he resigned in 1940. Member of Church of England Central Board of Finance. Died 6 January 1941. [1940]

BIRD, Sir Alfred Frederick. Tudor Grange, Solihull, Warwickshire. Weardale, Newbridge, Wolverhampton. Artillery Mansions, London. Carlton, Junior Carlton, and Royal Automobile. S. of Alfred Bird, Esq., F.C.S. of Birmingham. B. 27 July 1849 in Birmingham; m. 1875, Eleanor Frances, d. of R. Lloyd Evans, Esq. Educ. at King Edward's School, Birmingham. Chairman of Alfred Bird and Sons Limited, Manufacturing Chemists, Deritend, Birmingham. Dept.-Lieut. and J.P. for Warwickshire. Member of the Alpine Club, and a member of Automobile Club of France. Knighted 1920. Created Bart. 1922. A Coalition Unionist. Unsuccessfully contested Wednesbury in 1906. Elected for Wolverhampton W. in January 1910 and sat until he died on 7 February 1922, as the result of a road accident. [1922]

BIRD, Ernest Roy. The Beacon, Penn, Buckinghamshire. 11 Serjeant's Inn, London. Carlton, Constitutional, and Gresham. S. of Ernest Bird, Esq., Solicitor, of Kensington. B. 13 October 1883; m. 18 May 1909, d. of G.H. Greenland, Esq. Educ. at St. Paul's School. A Solicitor. Chairman of Kettners Limited. A Conservative. Unsuccessfully contested N. Lambeth in 1922 and 1923. Elected for the Skipton division of the W. Riding of Yorkshire in October 1924 and sat until he died in Johannesburg on 27 September 1933. [1933]

BIRD, Sir Robert Bland, Bart. 90 Eaton Place, London. The White House, Solihull, Warwickshire. Carlton. S. of Sir Alfred Bird, Bart., MP. B. 20 September 1876; m. 23 July 1904, Edith Wilmshurst, d. of Stephen William Challen, Totehill, Esq., of Solihull. Educ. at King Edward VI School, Birmingham. Chairman of Alfred Bird and Sons Limited, Birmingham. A Conservative. Sat for W. Wolverhampton from March 1922-May 1929, when he was defeated. Re-elected for W. Wolverhampton in October 1931. Sat until he retired in June 1945. Succeeded as Bart. 1922. K.B.E. 1954 Died 20 November 1960. [1945]

BIRD, Sir William Barrott Montfort. The Grosvenor Hotel, Victoria, London.

Eartham House, Nr. Chichester. Carlton, and Windham. S. of William Frederic Wratislaw Bird, Esq., Solicitor, of Grays Inn, and Fanny, d. of William Bateman, Esq. B. at 5 King's Road, Bedford Row, London 11 July 1855; m. 1895, Margaret, d. of William Spencer, Esq. (she died 1933). Educ. at Bruce Castle School. Admitted a Solicitor in 1880; retired from practice. High Sheriff of Sussex 1912-13. Master of Salters' Company 1919-20; twice Master of the Company of Makers of Cards. Travelled extensively and in most countries of the world. A Conservative. Returned unopposed for the Chichester division of Sussex in April 1921. Elected for the Chichester division of Sussex again in November 1922 and sat until he was defeated in December 1923. Knighted 1920. Died 13 November 1950. [1923]

BIRKETT, William Norman, K.C. 3 Temple Gardens, London. S. of Thomas and Agnes Birkett, of Ulverston, Lancashire. B. 6 September 1883; m. 1920, Ruth, d. of Frans Emil and Anna Nilsson. Educ. at Barrow-in-Furness, and Emanuel Coll., Cambridge, Honorary Fellow 1946. Barrister-at-Law, Inner Temple 1913, Northern Circuit. President of Cambridge University Union 1910. A Liberal. Unsuccessfully contested the King's Norton division of Birmingham in 1918. Elected for E. Nottingham in December 1923, defeated October 1924. Re-elected for E. Nottingham in May 1929 and sat until he was defeated in October 1931. K.C. 1924. Judge of King's Bench Division 1941-50. Knighted 1941. PC. 1947. Lord Justice of Appeal 1950-57. Created Baron Birkett 1958. Chairman of Court of London University 1946-62. Died 10 February 1962.
[1931 2nd ed.]

BLACK, John Wycliffe. The Elms, Stonesgate, Leicester. National Liberal. S. of Robert and Sarah Anne Black. B. in London 21 July 1862; m. Eunice, d. of James Marsden, Esq., J.P., of Wigan. Educ. at Western (London) and Bishop Stortford Grammar Schools. A Boot Manufacturer for 33 years. Member and Chairman of Wigston Urban District Council; member and Alderman of County Council for 16 years. A Liberal. Unsuccessfully contested the Harborough division of Leicester in 1922. First elected for the Harborough division in December 1923 and sat until he was defeated in October 1924. Died 18 June 1951. [1924 2nd ed.]

BLADES, Sir George Rowland, Bart., G.B.E. Fairmile Hatch, Cobham, Surrey. 17 Abchurch Lane, London. The Rookery, Seaview, Isle of Wight. Carlton, and St. Stephen's. S. of Rowland Hill Blades, Esq. B. 15 April 1868; m. 17 January 1907, Margaret, d. of Arthur Reiner, Esq., of Sutton. Educ. at King's Coll. School. Chairman Blades, East and Blades Limited. Member of Common Council of City of London from 1913. Alderman for Bassishaw Ward of the City 1920-48. J.P. for Counties of London and Surrey. Sen. Sheriff of London 1917-18. Lord Mayor of London 1926-27. Created Knight Bach. 1918, created Bart. 1922. Honorary Col. 54th (London) Anti-Aircraft Brigade R.G.A.; member of city of London T.A.A.; President of Surrey Provincial Division National Unionist Association; Almoner of Christs Hospital; Court of Guy's Hospital; Council of London Chamber of Commerce; Committee of City of London Savings Association. A Conservative. Sat for the Epsom division of Surrey from December 1918 until June 1928 when he was created Baron Ebbisham. F.S.A., G.B.E. 1927. President of Institute of Printers 1905. President of Federation of British Industries 1928-29. Treasurer of Conservative Party 1931-33. President of National Union of Conservative Associations 1936. Died 24 May 1953. [1928]

BLAIR, Sir Reginald. Carlton. S. of George MacLellan Blair, Esq., of Glasgow, and Jean, d. of James Scott, Esq. B. 8 November 1881; m. 10 June 1905, Mabel, d. of G.B. Wieland, Esq. (she died October 1936). Educ. at Kelvinside, and University of Glasgow. Member of Institute of Accountants and Actuaries in Scotland; Chairman of London Municipal Society 1919-29, later Trustee. Home Secretary's Nominee and later Chairman Race Course Control Board. Served in France and Middle East

33

1914-16. Dept.-Lieut., and J.P. for Middlesex and J.P. for Buckinghamshire. Knight Bach. 1921. A Conservative. Sat for Bow and Bromley from 1912-22 when he retired. Unsuccessfully contested Kennington in 1923. Elected for the Hendon division of Middlesex in November 1935 and sat until he retired in June 1945. Created Bart. 1945. Chairman of Racecourse Betting Control Board. Died 18 September 1962.   [1945]

BLAKE, Sir Francis Douglas, Bart. Tillmouth Park, Cornhill-on-Tweed. United University. S. of Capt. Francis Blake, Northumberland Light Infantry (Militia) and Mary, d. of the Rev. Roddam Douglas, Vicar of Tremdon, Co. Durham. B. at Carlisle 27 February 1856; m. 1886, Selina Colquhoun, eld. d. of James Cleland Burns, Esq., of Glenlee, Hamilton, N.B. (she died 1915). Educ. at Berwick Grammar School, Cheltenham, and University Coll., Oxford. A Barrister, called at the Inner Temple 1881. A Dept.-Lieut. and J.P. for Northumberland; Chairman of the Northumberland County Council and Chairman Territorial Force Association; Chairman of Quarter Sessions 1917; Honorary Col. Northumberland Cyclist Battalion. A Coalition Liberal. Unsuccessfully contested Tynemouth borough in 1895 and 1900. Elected for the Berwick-on-Tweed division of Northumberland in August 1916 and sat until he retired in October 1922. Created Bart. 1907. C.B. 1919. Died 5 February 1940.   [1922]

BLAKER, Sir Reginald, Bart. 3 Temple Gardens, London. Knowles, Ardingly, Sussex. S. of Sir John George Blaker, 1st Bart. B. 27 April 1900; m. 1930, Sheila, d. of Dr. Alexander Cran, of Guildford. Educ. at Charterhouse. Coldstream Guards S.R. Maj. R.A. (T.A.) (T.D.). Barrister-at-Law, Inner Temple 1921. A Conservative. Elected for the Spelthorne division of Middlesex in October 1931. Sat until he retired in June 1945. Succeeded as Bart. in 1926. Died 3 January 1975.   [1945]

BLANE, Thomas Andrew. 28 Billiter Street, London. B. 1881. Built up an influential position in the shipping world.

Member of the Court of Common Council City of London 1914-21, Alderman 1921-22, and other public bodies. A Coalition Unionist. Elected for S. Leicester in December 1918 and sat until he retired in October 1922. Director of Anglo-European Steamship Coal and Pitwood Company Limited. Died 19 August 1940.   [1922]

BLINDELL, Sir James. Knebworth, Park Drive, Grimsby. National Liberal. S. of of Richard Blindell, Esq. B. 1884 at Hitchin; m. 1904, Eliza, d. of Louis Good, Esq., of Grimsby. Educ. at St. Mary's School, Hitchin. Managing Director of Blindells Limited, Boot Factors of Grimsby. A junior Lord of the Treasury and Government Whip, October 1932-May 1937; Knight Bach. 1936. A Liberal National. Elected for the Holland-with-Boston division of Lincolnshire in March 1929 as a Liberal; re-elected in May 1929 and, as a Liberal Nation, in October 1931. Sat until his death in a road accident on 10 May 1937. Assistant Whip 1931-32 and Chief Whip of the Liberal National Party 1932-37. Member of Grimsby Town Council from 1919, Alderman from 1932. J.P. for Grimsby. Died 10 May 1937.   [1937]

BLUNDELL, Francis Nicholas. 26 Hans Road, London. Crosby Hall, Blundellsands, Liverpool. Arthur's, and 1900. S. of Francis Nicholas Blundell, Esq., and the novelist M.E. Francis. B. 16 October 1880; m. 25 July 1918, Theresa Victoria, d. of Wilfred Ward, Esq., of Northwood Park, Isle of Wight. Educ. at Stonyhurst, The Oratory School, Birmingham, and Merton Coll., Oxford; B.A. 1904. A Landowner and Farmer. Capt. Lancashire Hussars Yeomanry; served in France etc. 1914-19 (despatches); Chamberlain of Sword and Cloak to Pope Pius XI. Dept.-Lieut., J.P., County Councillor for Lancashire. Chairman of Catholic Education Council. A Conservative. Elected for the Ormskirk division of Lancashire in November 1922 and sat until he was defeated in May 1929. Director of National Poultry Scheme from 1934. Charter-Mayor-elect of Crosby at the time of his death. Died 28 October 1936.   [1922]

BLYTHE, Ernest. S. of James Blythe, Esq., of Lisburn, Co. Antrim. B. 13 April 1889; m. 1919, Miss Annie McHugh. Sentenced to 12 months imprisonment at Mountjoy 1919; discharged through illness owing to hunger strike. A Sinn Feiner. Elected for Monaghan N. in December 1918 but did not take his seat. A Journalist and Author. Member of Dail for N. Monaghan to 1921, for Monaghan 1921-33. Pro-Treaty, later Cumann na nGaedheal Member. Minister for Trade 1921-22, for Local Government 1922-23, for Finance 1923-32, for Posts and Telegraphs 1927-32. Vice-President of Executive Council 1927-32. Member of Senate 1934-36. Managing Director of Abbey Theatre 1941-67. A Protestant. Member of Radio Eireann Authority 1961-65. Died 23 February 1975.
[1922]

BOLAND, Harry. 15 The Crescent, Clontarf, Dublin. A Merchant Tailor. A Sinn Feiner. Elected for S. Roscommon in December 1918 but did not take his seat. Member of Dail for S. Roscommon to 1921 and Anti-Treaty Member for S. Roscommon and S. Mayo 1921-22. Private Secretary and Press Agent to Eamonn de Valera. Died 1 August 1922 after being shot by the National Forces while resisting arrest.
[1922]

BOLES, Dennis Coleridge. Continued in House after 1945: full entry in Volume IV.

BOLES, Lieut.-Col. Dennis Fortescue, C.B.E. Watts House, Bishop's Lydeard, Taunton. Carlton, Junion United Service, Ranelagh, Arthur's, and Royal Automobile. S. of the Rev. J.T. Boles, of Ryll Court, Exmouth. B. 1861; m. 1894, Beatrice, d. of John Lysaght, Esq., of Hengrave Hall, Suffolk. Educ. at Bradfield Coll., and Exeter Coll., Oxford. Lieut.-Col. commanding 3rd Battalion Devonshire Regiment, C.B.E. 1919. Dept.-Lieut. and J.P. for Somerset. A Coalition Unionist. Elected for W. Somerset in July 1911, and for the Taunton division of Somerset in December 1918. Sat until he resigned in 1921. Created Bart. 1922. High Sheriff of Somerset in 1923. Died 26 July 1935. [1921]

BONDFIELD, Rt. Hon. Margaret Grace. 28 Tavistock Square, London. D. of William and Ann Bondfield, of Furnham, Somerset. B. 1873. Chief Woman Officer of National Union of General and Municipal Workers; Assistant Secretary National Federation of Women Workers 1916-21; a British Representative at Labour Convention at Washington 1919, and at Geneva 1921, 1923, 1926 and 1927; Government Delegate 1924 and 1930; President of Trades Union Congress General Council 1923. Parliamentary Secretary Ministry of Labour January-October 1924; Minister of Labour June 1929-August 1931; PC. 1929. A Labour Member. Unsuccessfully contested Northampton in 1920 and 1922. Elected for Northampton in December 1923; but defeated again in October 1924. Elected for Wallsend July 1926 and again in May 1929; defeated in 1931 and 1935. The first woman Cabinet Minister. Companion of Honour 1948. Vice President of National Council of Social Service. Died 16 June 1953.
[1931 2nd ed.]

BONWICK, Alfred James. 12 Cursitor Street, London. Oakhill House, Horsham, Sussex. Reform, Devonshire, National Liberal, Eighty, and Aldwych. S. of James Bonwick, Esq., and Elizabeth Fowler. B. in London 1 November 1883; m. 20 November 1909, Florence Elizabeth, youngest d. of Maj. W. Robinson. A Director of newspaper and printing companies. A Liberal. Elected for the Chippenham division of Wiltshire in November 1922. Defeated in October 1924. A Liberal Whip 1924. Died 4 September 1949. [1924 2nd ed.]

BOOTHBY, Robert John Graham. Continued in House after 1945: full entry in Volume IV.

BORODALE, David Field Beatty, Visct. 17 Grosvenor Square, London. S. of Admiral of the Fleet, Earl Beatty. B. 22 February 1905. m. 1st, 1937, Dorothy Power Sands (divorced 1945); secondly, 1946, Mrs. Dorothy Rita Bragg (divorced 1950); thirdly, 1951, Mrs. Adelle O'Connor (divorced 1958); fourthly, 1959, Diane, d. of Mrs. Duncan Kirk. Educ. at R.N. Coll.,

Dartmouth. Joined R.N. and retired as Lieut. in 1929. A Conservative. Elected for the Peckham division of Camberwell in October 1931. Sat until he succeeded to the Peerage as Earl Beatty in March 1936. Styled Visct. Borodale 1919-36. Under Secretary of State for Air May-July 1945. D.S.C. 1942. Chairman of Navy League 1937-41, President 1941-44. Member of London County Council 1937-46. Served in Royal Navy 1939-45, Commander. Died 10 June 1972. [1936]

BORWICK, Maj. George Oldroyd, D.S.O. 17a South Audley Street, London. Cavalry, and Bath. S. of Joseph Cooksey Borwick, Esq., and Elizabeth Borwick, née Oldroyd. B. at Leytonstone 7 March 1879; m. 1915, Hon. Mary Cavendish, d. of 4th Baron Waterpark. Educ. at Harrow, and Trinity Coll., Oxford. A Baking Powder Manufacturer. Served in the Surrey Yeomanry (Maj.) throughout the war; D.S.O. and Legion of Honour; mentioned in despatches (thrice). A Conservative and Unionist. Unsuccessfully contested Poplar in 1906 and Limehouse in January 1910. Elected for N. Croydon in December 1918 and sat until he retired in October 1922. Died 27 June 1964. [1922]

BOSCAWEN, Rt. Hon. Sir Arthur Sackville Trevor Griffith. See GRIFFITH-BOSCAWEN, Rt. Hon. Sir Arthur Sackville Trevor.

BOSSOM, Alfred Charles. Continued in House after 1945: full entry in Volume IV.

BOTTOMLEY, Horatio William. 26 King Street, St. James's, London. The Dicker, Sussex. S. of William King Bottomley, Esq., and nephew of George Jacob Holyoake, Esq. B. in London 23 March 1860; m. 1880, Elise, d. of Samuel Norton, Esq. Educ. at Mason's Coll., Birmingham. A well-known Journalist; founder of the *Financial News*, and proprietor of the *Sun;* founder, editor, and principal proprietor of *John Bull*; author of *Bottomley's Book.* Proprietor and editor of *Sunday Illustrated;* proprietor and editor of *The Sunday Evening Telegram.* An Independent Member and Chairman of the Independent Parliamentary Group. Unsuccessfully contested the Hornsey division of Middlessex in 1887, and S. Hackney in 1900. Sat for S. Hackney as a Liberal from 1906 to 1911 when the South Hackney Liberal Association withdrew their support; retained his seat until 1912 when he resigned as a result of his bankruptcy. Re-elected for S. Hackney in December 1918 and sat until 1 August 1922 when he was expelled from the House of Commons, having been charged with fraudulent conversion, found guilty on 23 counts and sentenced to 7 years penal servitude. Released from prison in 1927. Died 26 May 1933. [1922]

BOULTON, Sir William Whytehead, Bart. Braxted Park, Witham, Essex. Carlton. S. of William Whytehead Boulton, Esq., of Beverley. B. 1873; m. 23 April 1903, Rosalind Mary, d. of Sir John Milburn, 1st Bart. Maj. 7th Volunteer Battalion Essex Regiment and Lieut. Royal Horse Guards (Blue) Reserve Regiment; Dept.-Lieut. for Essex; Lord of the Manor of Great Braxted and Kelvedon Hall; Chairman of Maldon division Conservative Association; a Lord Commissioner of the Treasury and Government Whip February 1940-March 1942. Vice-Chamberlain of H.M. Household March 1942 July 1944; created Bart. 1944. A National Conservative. Elected for the central division of Sheffield in October 1931. Sat until he retired in June 1945. Died 9 January 1949. [1945]

BOURNE, Rt. Hon. Robert Croft. Fyfield Manor, Abingdon. Carlton. S. of Col. G.C. Bourne, F.R.S. B. 15 July 1888; m. 7 July 1917, Lady Hester Margaret Cairns, d. of Wilfrid, 4th Earl Cairns. Educ. at Eton, and New Coll., Oxford; M.A. 1918. A Barrister-at-Law, Lincoln's Inn 1913. County Councillor and J.P. for Herefordshire. Temporary Chairman of Committees 1928; Dept. Chairman of Committees of Ways and Means 1931-38. PC. 1935. A Conservative. Unsuccessfully contested Oxford city in 1923. Sat for Oxford city from June 1924 until his death on 7 August 1938. A distinguished oarsman.

Served with Hereford Regiment, Capt. 1917. Member of Thames Conservancy 1927. Died 7 August 1938. [1938]

BOWATER, Sir Thomas Vansittart, Bart. 53 Hans Mansions, Hans Road, London. Constitutional, Royal Automobile, and Ranelagh. S. of William Vansittart Bowater, Esq., of Bury Hall, Lower Edmonton, London. B. 20 October 1862; m. 1st, 1887, Emily Margaret, d. of John Spencer, Esq., of Croydon (she died 1924); secondly, 12 August 1925, Alice Mary, widow of A. Coysgarne Sim, Esq., of Harrow Weald Park. Educ. at Manchester, and Stourbridge. Lieut. City of London; Sheriff 1905; Alderman 1907-38; Lord Mayor 1913-14; Honorary Freeman City of Manchester; Gov. of the Royal Hospitals. Created Knight 1906; Bart. 1914. A Conservative. Unsuccessfully contested the City of London as an Independent Conservative in May 1922. Sat for the City of London from February 1924 until his death on 28 March 1938. Chairman of Bowater's, Paper Manufacturers until 1927. Died 28 March 1938. [1938]

BOWDLER, William Audley. National Liberal. S. of William Henry Bowdler, Esq., J.P., and Elizabeth Ann Richard. B. 7 September 1884 at Kirkham, Lancashire; m. 22 August 1918, Marguerite, d. of G.W. Parkes, Esq., of St. Annes-on-the-Sea. Educ. at Kirkham Grammar School, and Rossall. A Scientist and for some time Chemical Manufacturer; Director of Messrs. Small and Parkes, Limited, Hendham Vale, Manchester. Joined T.F. August 1912; served through war in France and India. Wounded at Somme 1916. A Liberal. Elected for the Holderness division of Yorkshire in November 1922 and sat until he was defeated in December 1923. Died 20 February 1969. [1923]

BOWEN, John William. 26 Kelmscott Road, Wandsworth Common, London. Parliamentary Labour. S. of John Bowen, Esq., Railwayman. B. 8 May 1876; m. 27 October 1903, Eva, d. of Robert Sanger, Esq. (she died 1953). Educ. at Gowerton, Glamorganshire. Gen. Secretary Union of Post Office Workers; President Post Office Employees' Approved Society; Chairman Workers' Travel Association; Fellow Faculty Insurance; member Gen. Council T.U.C.; member Committee on National Debt and Taxation 1924-25. A Labour Member. Unsuccessfully contested Newport in December 1918, October and November 1922, December 1923, and October 1924. Elected for the Crewe division of Cheshire in May 1929 and sat until he was defeated in October 1931; again defeated in November 1935. C.B.E. 1939. Member of London County Council from 1940-61, Alderman 1951-61, Chairman 1949-52. Knighted 1953. Died 1 April 1965. [1931 2nd ed.]

BOWER, Norman Adolph Henry. Continued in House after 1945: full entry in Volume IV.

BOWER, Commander Robert Tatton, R.N. 3 Oakhill Road, Putney, London. United Service, and R.Y.S. S. of Sir Robert Bower, K.B.E., C.M.G., Chief Constable of the N. Riding of Yorkshire. B. at Bray, Co. Wicklow, 9 June 1894; m. 26 September 1922, Hon. Henrietta Strickland, d. of 1st Baron Strickland. Educ. at Cheam School, and Royal Naval Coll. Served at sea 1914-18; with R.A.F. Coastal Command and at sea 1939-40; R.N. and R.A.F. Staff Colleges. A Unionist. Elected for the Cleveland division of the N. Riding of Yorkshire in October 1931. Sat until he was defeated in July 1945. Chairman of Executive of Society for Individual Freedom 1950-53. Died 5 July 1975. [1945]

BOWERMAN, Rt. Hon. Charles William. 4 Battledean Road, Highbury, London. S. of Charles Bowerman, Esq., of Honiton. B. 22 January 1851; m. 1876, Louisa, d. of W. Peach, Esq. Apprenticed as a Compositor. Was Gen. Secretary and later Parliamentary Secretary of the London Society of Compositors; President of Trades Union Congress 1901; an Alderman of London County Council 1901-06; Secretary of Trades Union Congress 1911-23; Member Board of Trade Arbitration Court. PC. 1916. J.P. for County of London 1919. Junior Whip to Labour Party 1916. A

37

Labour Member. Sat for Deptford from 1906 until he was defeated in October 1931. President of National Printing and Kindred Trades Employees' Federation. Died 11 June 1947. [1931 2nd ed.]

BOWLES, Francis George. Continued in House after 1945: full entry in Volume IV.

BOWLES, Col. Henry Ferryman. Forty Hall, Enfield. Woughton, Bletchley, Buckinghamshire. Carlton, and Conservative. Eld. s. of H.C.B. Bowles, Esq., J.P., and Dept.-Lieut. of Waltham Cross. B. 19 December 1858 at Enfield; m. 1889, Florence, d. of J.L. Broughton, Esq., of Tunstall Hall, Market Drayton (she died 1935). Educ. at Harrow, and Jesus Coll., Cambridge. Commandant Middlesex Volunteers; Honorary Col. 7th Battalion Middlesex Regiment from 1904. Chairman Edmonton Petty Sessions; Councillor and then Alderman Middlesex County Council 1889-1943. Dept.-Lieut. for Middlesex; Patron of the living of Woughton. A Conservative. Sat for the Enfield division of Middlesex from 1889-1906 when he was defeated; re-elected for that division in December 1918 and sat until he retired in October 1922. Barrister-at-Law, Inner Temple 1883. Created Bart. 1926. High Sheriff of Middlesex 1928-29. Died 14 October 1943. [1922]

BOWYER, Sir George Edward Wentworth, Bart., M.C. Denham Lodge, Weston Underwood, Olney, Buckinghamshire. Carlton, and International Sportsman's. S. of Lieut.-Col. W.G. Bowyer, R.E. B. 16 January 1886; m. 27 February 1919, Hon. Daphne Mitford, d. of Alegernon, 1st Baron Redesdale, G.C.V.O., K.C.B. Educ. at Eton, and New Coll., Oxford. A Barrister-at-Law, Inner Temple 1910. Capt. Oxford and Bucks Light Infantry; M.C. President of Urban District Councils Association 1923-25 and from 1929; Parliamentary Private Secretary to Sir P. Cunliffe-Lister, President of Board of Trade 1921-24. Vice-Chairman of Conservative and Unionist Party Organization 1930-December 1935. Conservative Party Whip 1925-35. Comptroller of the Household June-December 1935. Junior Lord of the Treasury December 1927-June 1929. Created Knight Bach. 1929; Bart. 1933. Heir Presumptive to the Baronetcy of Bowyer of Denham. A Conservative. Elected for the Buckingham division of Buckinghamshire in December 1918 and sat until he was created Baron Denham in 1937. Parliamentary Secretary to Ministry of Agriculture September 1939-May 1940. Conservative Whip in House of Lords 1945-47. Died 30 November 1948. [1937]

BOYCE, Sir Harold Leslie, K.B.E. Rhossili, Brunswick Road, Gloucester. Hillfield, Eldersfield, Gloucester. Carlton, Constitutional, City Livery, Royal Automobile, United Wards, Walbrook Ward, and Gloucester. S. of Charles Boyce, Esq., of Sydney. B. 9 July 1895; m. 16 July 1926, Maybery, d. of E.P. Bevan, Esq., of Melbourne. Educ. at Sydney Grammar School, and Balliol Coll., Oxford, M.A. Barrister-at-Law, Inner Temple 1922; Substitute Delegate and Legal Adviser, Australian Delegation to Third Assembly League of Nations, and Adviser and Technical Expert before Permanent Mandates Committee at Geneva 1922. Director of Sharpness Docks, of Gloucester Foundry Limited, Gloucester and Birmingham Navigation Company, of Wagon Repairs Limited, of Gloucester Newspapers Limited, of Cheltenham and District Gas Company, of Severn Valley Gas Corporation Limited, and of Gas Consolidation Limited; Chairman and Managing Director of Gloucester Railway Carriage and Wagon Company Limited; Chairman of S.P.B.A. Supplies Limited; Vice-Chairman of Gloucester Gas Company; Alderman of the City of London for Ward of Walbrook, one of H.M.'s Lieuts. and J.P.; Commissioner of Central Criminal Court; Gov. of Royal Hospitals; Liveryman of the Loriners and Carpenters Companies; High Sheriff of Gloucester 1941-42; member of Grand Council of Primrose League; O. St. J., F.R.G.S. Served with Australian Forces in France, Egypt and Gallipoli 1914-18; member of Empire Parliamentary Delegation to N. Rhodesia 1930; K.B.E. 1944. A Conservative. Elected for Gloucester in May 1929 and sat until he was defeated in

July 1945. Created Bart. 1952. Sheriff of City of London 1947-48, Lord Mayor 1951-52. Died 30 May 1955. [1945]

BOYD-CARPENTER, Maj. Sir Archibald Boyd. River House, Walton-on-Thames, Surrey. Carlton, Garrick, Beefsteak, St. Stephen's, and Pratt's. S. of Bishop Boyd-Carpenter. B. 26 March 1873; m. Annie d. of T. Dugdale, Esq., of Blackburn and Harrogate. Educ. at Harrow, and Balliol Coll., Oxford, Secretary and President of Union. Maj. R. of O., H.L.I.; served in South African War 1900-02, and in France 1915-18; D.A.D. War Office. J.P. for Harrogate; Mayor 1909-11; County Councillor 1910-19. Parliamentary Secretary Ministry of Labour November 1922-March 1923; Financial Secretary to the Treasury March-May 1923; Paymaster Gen. May 1923-January 1924; Financial Secretary to Admiralty July 1923-January 1924. Created Knight Bach. 1926. A Conservative. Unsuccessfully contested the Colne Valley division of the W. Riding of Yorkshire in January and December 1910. Sat for N. Bradford from December 1918-23, but was defeated there in December 1923. Elected for Coventry in 1924. Unsuccessfully contested Coventry in May 1929. Elected for the Chertsey division of Surrey in October 1931. Sat until he died on 27 May 1937. [1937]

BOYD-ORR, Sir. John. Continued in House after 1945: full entry in Volume IV.

BRABNER, Commander Rupert Arnold, D.S.O., D.S.C., R.N.V.R. 55 Bishopsgate, London. Admiralty, Rex House, Regent Street, London. Grigsby Farm, Smarden, Kent. Carlton, and Royal Aero. S. of William Wilberforce Brabner, Esq., of Loughton, Essex. B. 29 October 1911; m. 1944, Mrs. Phyllis Myfanwy Berner, d. of W.E. Molins, Esq., of Bexley. Educ. at Felsted School, and St. Catharine's Coll., Cambridge. A Banker. Member of London County Council 1937-February 1945; R.N.V.R. Joined Fleet Air Arm 1939; served at sea; Technical Assistant to 5th Sea Lord June 1943-July 1944. D.S.O. 1942, D.S.C. 1943. Assistant Government Whip July 1944. Parliamentary Under-Secretary of State for Air November 1944. A Conservative. Elected for Hythe in July 1939 and sat until his death on 27 March 1945, when his aircraft was lost near the Azores. [1945]

BRACE, Rt. Hon. William. Devonfield, Newport, Monmouthshire. B. 1865 at Risca; m. 1891, Nellie, d. of William Humphreys, Esq. Educ. at Risca Board School. Started work in the Risca Collieries at the age of 12, and became a Miners' Agent and President of South Wales Miners' Federation. Member of Royal Commission on Coal Supplies; Vice-Chairman of Labour Party 1911. Parliamentary Under-Secretary to Home Department May 1915 to January 1919. PC. 1916. Contributed weekly articles to newspapers on labour topics. A Labour Member. Elected for S. Glamorgan in 1906, and for the Abertillery division of Monmouthshire in December 1918. Sat until he was appointed Chief Labour Adviser to the Department of Mines in 1920. Retired 1927. Died 12 October. 1947. [1920]

BRACKEN, Rt. Hon. Brendan. Continued in House after 1945: full entry in Volume IV.

BRACKENBURY, Capt. Henry Langton. Thorpe Hall, Louth, Lincolnshire. Oxford and Cambridge, and Carlton. S. of Maj. Henry Brackenbury, H.M. Bodyguard. B. at Colchester 26 April 1868; m. 1898, Florence, d. of Edgar Mills, Esq., of Menlo Park, California. Educ. at Corpus Christi Coll., Oxford. A Barrister, Inner Temple 1902; J.P. for the Co. of Lindsey; High Steward of Louth. Capt. 3rd Lincolnshire Regiment. A Coalition Unionist. Sat for the Louth division of Lincolnshire from January 1910 to December 1910, when he was defeated. Re-elected for Louth in December 1918 and sat until he died on 28 April. 1920. [1920]

BRAITHWAITE, Sir Albert Newby. Continued in House after 1945: full entry in Volume IV.

BRAITHWAITE, Joseph Gurney.
Continued in House after 1945: full entry
in Volume IV.

BRAMSDON, Sir Thomas Arthur.
Grosvenor Hotel, London. 34 Elm Grove,
Southsea, Hampshire. National Liberal.
S. of John Bramsdon, Esq., of Portsmouth.
B. 27 February 1857; m. 1880, Mary Anna
Adelaide, only d. of Capt. Charles Augustus
Reid, 20th Bengal Infantry (she died 1928).
Educ. at Esplanade House, Portsmouth.
A Solicitor, admitted 1878. Corner for
Portsmouth from 1884-1935; Chairman of
School Board 1892-98; President of Ports-
mouth Liberal Association; member of
Home Office Committee on Working of
Coroners Law, Anaesthetics, and the
Inebriates Acts. Introduced the Bill which
became the Oaths Acts 1909, and the Bill
which became the forerunner of the
Children's Act 1908. Chairman of Select
Committee on Business Premises 1921.
Member of Central Committee of the
N.S.P.C.C. Active on various war organiza-
tions. Grand senior deacon of English
Freemasons. A Liberal. Represented Portsmouth May to October 1900 when he was
defeated and from 1906-January 1910, when
he was defeated by Lord Charles Beresford.
Sat for Central Portsmouth from 1918-22
when he was defeated. Re-elected for Central
Portsmouth in December 1923 and sat until
he retired in October 1924. J.P. for Portsmouth. Knighted 1909. Died 29 September
1935.   [1924 2nd ed.]

BRASS, Sir William. The Old Rectory,
Chattisham, Ipswich. Carlton, and Travel-
lers'. S. of William Brass, Esq., and Catherine
Elizabeth Price. B. in London 11 February
1886. Unmarried. Educ. at Eton, and Trinity
Coll., Cambridge. Served with Surrey
Yeomanry and Flying Corps. In France,
etc. 1915-18. Chairman of St. John's
Hospital, Lewisham and of British Film
Institute; Director of Guardian Assurance
Company Limited. Parliamentary Private
Secretary to Rt. Hon. Neville Chamberlain,
December 1922-January 1924 and December
1924-27; to Rt. Hon. L.S. Amery when Do-
minions and Colonial Secretary 1927-28,
to the Rt. Hon. John Moore-Brabazon

when Minister of Transport October 1940,
and when Minister of Aircraft Production
May 1941-February 1942; Member of Em-
pire Parliamentary Delegation to South
Africa 1924, and to Canada 1943. Knight
Bach. 1929. A Conservative. Elected for the
Clitheroe division of Lancashire in
November 1922 and sat until he retired in
June 1945. Created Baron Chattisham June
1945. Died 24 August 1945.   [1945]

**BRASSEY, Sir Henry Leonard
Campbell, Bart.** 42 Upper Grosvenor
Street, London. Apethorpe Hall, Peter-
borough. Carlton, and Turf. S. of H.A.
Brassey, Esq., MP. of Preston Hall, Aylesford.
B. 7 March 1870; m. 30 June 1894, Lady
Violet Gordon Lennox, d. of 7th Duke
of Richmond and Gordon (she died 1946).
Educ. at Eton, and Christ Church, Oxford.
Served in Royal Sussex Militia 1888-92,
and W. Kent Yeomanry; retired as Maj.
1905; Maj. Northamptonshire Yeomanry
1914. A member of the Jockey Club.
Dept.-Lieut. for Northamptonshire 1922.
Created Bart. 1922. A Conservative. Unsuccessfully contested E. Cambridgeshire
in 1903 and Grantham 1906. Member for
Northamptonshire N. from January 1910-18,
and for the Peterborough division of
Northamptonshire from December 1918
until he was defeated in May 1929. Created
Baron Brassey of Apethorpe 1938. J.P. for
Kent and Northamptonshire. High Sheriff
of Northamptonshire 1907. Died 22 October
1958.   [1929]

BREESE, Maj. Charles Edward. Morva
Lodge, Portmadoc. S. of a Clerk of the
Peace for Merionethshire. B. 1867; m. 1894,
Janet, youngest d. of the Rev. Paul Methuen
Stedman, of Suffolk. Educ. at Shrewsbury
School. A Solicitor and Liberal Churchman.
Member of Carnarvonshire County Council.
Interested in the Wales slate industry.
Chairman of the Executive Committee
Cambrian Archaeological Association.
Served for three years with the Army in the
European War. A Coalition Liberal. Elected
for Carnarvonshire in December 1918 and
sat until he was defeated in November 1922.
Died 15 August 1932.   [1922]

BRIANT, Frank. Alford House, 6-14 Lambeth Walk, London. National Liberal. B. 1863. Unmarried. At one time in the Civil Service. Member of Lambeth Board of Guardians 1898-1925; Chairman 1910-25; member of London County Council 1905-19 and 1931-34. Honorary Superintendent Alford House Institute for Working Men and Lads from 1885. Chairman of Lambeth Borough Council 1899-1919. A Congregationalist. A Liberal. Sat for N. Lambeth from December 1918-May 1929, when he was defeated. Re-elected for N. Lambeth in October 1931 and sat until his death on 1 September 1934. [1934]

BRIDGEMAN, Rt. Hon. William Clive. Admiralty House, Whitehall, London. Leigh Manor, Ministerley, Shropshire. Carlton. S. of the Rev. the Hon. J. Bridgeman (s. of 2nd Earl of Bradford) and Marianne Caroline, d. of Ven. Archdeacon Clive. B. 31 December 1864; m. 30 April 1895, Caroline Beatrix, D.B.E. 1924, d. of Hon. Cecil T. Parker. Educ. at Eton, and Classical Scholar of Trinity Coll., Cambridge; M.A. Member of London School Board 1897-1904, and London County Council 1904; Assistant Private Secretary to Lord Knutsford at Colonial Office 1889-92, and Sir M. Hicks-Beach, Chancellor of the Exchequer 1895-99; appointed a Unionist Whip 1911; Junior Lord of the Treasury May 1915 to December 1916; Assistant Director of the War Trade Department 1915 to December 1916; Parliamentary Secretary to the Ministry of Labour December 1916 to January 1919; Parliamentary Secretary to the Board of Trade January 1919; Secretary for Mines August 1920 to October 1922. Secretary of State Home Department October 1922-January 24. First Lord of the Admiralty 1924-29. Ecclesiastical Commissioner May 1923. PC. 1920; J.P. and Dept.-Lieut. for Shropshire; Chairman of Governing Body of Shrewsbury School. Elder Brother of Trinity House 1928. A Conservative. Unsuccessfully contested N. Worcestershire in 1892, mid Derbyshire 1895, and the Oswestry division of Shropshire in 1904. Sat for the Oswestry division from 1906 until he retired in May 1929. Created Visct. Bridgeman 1929. President of M.C.C. 1931. Chairman of

B.B.C. 1935. Died 14 August. 1935. [1929]

BRIGGS, William James Harold. Broadford, Chobham, Surrey. Carlton, Royal Automobile, and Flyfisher's. S. of William Briggs, Esq., J.P., of Manchester. B. 1870; m. 2 August 1893, Jessie May, d. of Ambrose Veevers, Esq. Educ. at Seafield, Lytham, and privately. A Conservative. Elected for the Blackley division of Manchester in December 1918; sat until defeated in December 1923. Elected again for the Blackley division in October 1924 and sat until he was defeated in May 1929. Member of Surrey County Council from 1930. Died 6 May 1945. [1929]

BRISCOE, Capt. Richard George, M.C. Longstowe Hall, Cambridge. Carlton. S. of W.A. Briscoe, Esq., of Longstowe Hall, Cambridgeshire. B. 1893. Educ. at Eton, and Magdalen Coll., Oxford. Lieut. Grenadier Guards. Honorary Attaché British Embassy, Berlin 1923. H.M. Lieut. for Cambridgeshire 1943-57. Parliamentary Private Secretary to Rt. Hon. Walter Guinness when Financial Secretary to the Treasury November 1924-November 1925, and when Minister for Agriculture 1925-June 1929, to Capt. H. Crookshank when Under-Secretary Home Office October 1934, when Secretary for Mines June 1935-April 1939, when Financial Secretary to the Treasury April 1939, and when Postmaster-Gen. December 1942. A Conservative. Elected for Cambridgeshire in December 1923 and sat until he retired in June 1945. Died 11 December 1957. [1945]

BRITTAIN, Sir Harry Ernest, K.B.E., C.M.G. 2 Cowley Street, London. 13 King's Bench Walk, Temple, London. Carlton, Bath, Royal Thames Yacht, Pilgrims', and American. S. of W.H. Brittain, Esq., of Storth Oaks, near Sheffield. B. 24 December 1873; m. 1st, 4 November 1905, Alida, d. of Sir Robert Harvey, of Dundridge, Totnes (she died 1943); secondly, 1961, Muriel Leslie, d. of H.L. Dixton, Esq. Educ. at Repton, and Worcester Coll., Oxford; M.A. Lieut. 4th West York Volunteer Artillery; Barrister-at-Law, Inner Temple 1897. Active head of the Pilgrims' Club from its foundation in 1902 until 1919 when he was appointed Vice-President. Trustee of Washington Manor House, Sulgrave. Was on the staff of the *Standard* and *Evening Standard* 1902; Director of *The Sphere* and *Tatler* 1906-08. Member Executive Empire Parliamentary Association. Originator and organizer of the First Imperial Press Conference 1909, and elected Honorary Life Member of the Empire Press Union; Chairman of Arrangements Committee for Second Conference in Canada 1920, and for Third Conference in Australia 1925; Honorary LL.D. McGill University. President British International Association of Journalists 1920-22. Chairman Press Hospitality Committee British Empire Exhibition and member of Executive and Publicity Council. Travelled extensively. Engaged in special work throughout the U.S.A. 1915. Director of Intelligence, National Service Department. Founder and Chairman of the American Officers' Club 1917. A Founder and member of Executive of Anti-Socialist Union. Member Committee British Olympic Association. Chairman of Middlesex division of Conservative Association 1925. Director several business concerns. Cross of Officer of the Order of the Crown of Belgium, Commander of Order of the Crown of Roumania and of the White Lion of Czechoslovakia. A Conservative. Sat for the Acton division of Middlesex from December 1918 until he was defeated in May 1929. K.B.E. 1918; C.M.G. 1924. Died 9 July 1974 at the age of 100.   [1929]

BRITTON, George Bryant. Lodge Side, Kingswood, Bristol. National Liberal. B. 1863; m. 1902, Annie, d. of John Henshaw, Esq. A Boot and Shoe Manufacturer at Bristol. At one time a leader of the South East Liberal Association; member of the Bristol City Council; interested in welfare movements. Lord Mayor of Bristol 1920-21. J.P. for Bristol. A Coalition Liberal. Elected for Bristol E. in December 1918 and sat until he retired in October 1922. Died 11 July 1929.   [1922]

BROAD, Francis Alfred. Sweet Briar, Hertford Road, Great Amwell, Ware, Hertfordshire. S. of William John Broad,

Esq. B. 15 March 1874; m. November 1900, Eliza, d. of Thomas Macer, Esq., of Wormley, Hertfordshire. A Scientific Instrument Maker (operative). J.P. for Middlesex. A Labour Member. Unsuccessfully contested Edmonton in 1918. Returned for Edmonton from November 1922 until he was defeated October 1931. Re-elected for Edmonton in November 1935 and sat until he retired in June 1945. Died 3 January 1956.   [1945]

BROAD, Thomas Tucker. Truas, Tintagel, Cornwall. National Liberal. B. 1863. Educ. at New and University Colls., London. A Congregational Minister 1892; engaged in Y.M.C.A. work during the war; a member of the Sheffield Board of Guardians. A Liberal. Elected for the Clay Cross division of Derbyshire in December 1918 and sat until he was defeated in November 1922. Unsuccessfully contested Leyton E. in December 1923. Died 26 January 1935.   [1922]

BROADBENT, Col. John. Northwood, Ashton-under-Lyne. Bella Vista, Castleton, Derbyshire. S. of Timothy Broadbent, Esq., Jeweller, of Ashton-under-Lyne. B. 4 September 1872; m. 22 December 1897, Mary Hannah, d. of Jonas Marland, Esq., of Pawtucket, U.S.A. Educ. at Stamford Academy, Ashton-under-Lyne. Mayor of Ashton-under-Lyne 1923-25; J.P. for Ashton and Derbyshire. A Conservative. Unsuccessfully contested Ashton-under-Lyne in May 1929. Elected for the seat in April and again in October 1931. Sat until he was defeated in November 1935. Commanded 9th Battalion, Manchester Regiment 1914-18. Died 9 June 1938.   [1935]

BROADBRIDGE, Sir George Thomas, Bart., K.C.V.O. 27 Old Bond Street, London. Wargrave Place, Wargrave, Berkshire. Carlton. S. of Henry Broadbridge, Esq., of Brighton. B. 13 February 1869; m. 1st, 1894, Fanny Kathleen, d. of Richard Brigden, Esq., of Brighton (she died 8 March 1928); secondly, 1929, Clara Maud, d. of John Swansbourne, Esq., of Bognor (she died 1949). Educ. at Brighton. Created Bart. in 1937; Knight Bach. 1929; K.C.V.O.

1937; F.I.C.S., F.R.G.S. Master of the Worshipful Company of Gardeners 1934; a Lieut. of the City of London; Sheriff 1933-34; Lord Mayor 1936-37. Alderman of the City of London for Ward of Candlewick from 1930; Master of the Worshipful Company of Lorimers. A Conservative. Elected for the City of London in April 1938 and sat until August 1945 when he was created Baron Broadbridge. Died 16 April 1952.   [1945]

BROCKLEBANK, Sir Clement Edmund Royds. Winsley, Bradford-on-Avon. Athenaeum, and Carlton. S. of Thomas Brocklebank, Esq., of Wateringbury Place, Kent. B. 28 August 1882; m. 1927, Grace, d. of A.J. Wise, Esq., of Wold House, Nafferton, Yorkshire. Educ. at Eton, Magdalen Coll., Oxford, and Cuddesdon Theological Coll. Parliamentary Private Secretary to Sir Vivian Henderson when Parliamentary Under-Secretary of State for Home Office November 1927-May 1929, to Sir Edward Hilton Young when Minister of Health December 1934, to Rt. Hon. Malcolm Macdonald, when Secretary of State for the Colonies June 1935, for the Dominions November 1935, for the Colonies May 1938, and when Minister of Health May 1940-February 1941, to the Rt. Hon. Sir John Anderson when Lord President of the Council March 1941, and when Chancellor of the Exchequer September 1943. Knight Bach. 1937. A Conservative. Unsuccessfully contested Smethwick in 1923. Sat for E. Nottingham October 1924-May 1929. Unsuccessfully contested Birkenhead E. in May 1929. Elected for the Fairfield division of Liverpool in October 1931. Sat until he was defeated in July 1945. Trained for the clergy at Cuddesdon Theological Coll. Ordained deacon 1907, priest 1908; Curate of St. Matthews, Westminister 1907-15, of Holy Redeemer, Clerkenwell 1916; Chaplain of Westminster Hospital 1916-18; Vicar of Holy Redeemer, Clerkenwell 1918-20. Died 24 August 1949.   [1945]

BROCKWAY, Archibald Fenner. Continued in House after 1945: full entry in Volume IV.

BROMFIELD, William. Foxlowe, Leek, Staffordshire. B. 24 January 1868 in Manchester. An expert organizer who devoted his energies to the interests of the operatives in the silk and other textile trades of Leek and neighbourhood. A Labour Member. Sat for the Leek division of Staffordshire from December 1918-October 1931 when he was defeated. Re-elected for the Leek division in November 1935 and sat until he retired in June 1945. Gen. Secretary of Amalgamated Society of Textile Workers and Kindred Trades 1919-42. Died 3 June 1950.   [1945]

BROMLEY, John. 9 Arkwright Road, London. B. 1876 at Hadnall, Shropshire. Gen. Secretary of Associated Society of Locomotive Engineers and Firemen from 1914-36. A Labour Member. Unsuccessfully contested N.E. Leeds in 1918, and Barrow-in-Furness in November 1922 and December 1923. Elected for Barrow-in-Furness in October 1924. Sat until he retired in October 1931. Member of General Council of T.U.C. 1921-36. President of T.U.C. 1932. Died 7 September 1945.   [1931 2nd ed.]

BROOKE, Brigadier-Gen. Christopher Robert Ingham, C.M.G., D.S.O. 60 Frenchgate, Richmond, Yorkshire. Carlton, and Naval & Military. Royal Norfolk and Suffolk Yacht. S. of Ven. Archdeacon Brooke, of Halifax. B. 4 July 1869; m. 1899, Irene, d. of Lieut.-Col. A.B. Coddington, R.E. (she died 22 September 1925). Educ. at Winchester. Joined K.O.Y.L.I. 1890; retired 1920. Served in South African War 1899-1901, and in France etc., 1915-18. A Conservative. Elected for the Pontefract division of the W. Riding of Yorkshire in October 1924 and sat until he was defeated in May 1929. D.S.O. 1915; C.M.G. 1917. Died in South Africa 27 December 1948.   [1922]

BROOKE, Henry. Continued in House after 1945: full entry in Volume IV.

BROOKE, Willie. 177 Gladstone Street, Bradford. S. of Frederick Brooke, Esq., Woolsorter. B. 18 December 1895. Educ. at Carlton Street Secondary School,

Bradford, and at London Labour Coll. Connected with Trade Union Administration. Official of the Amalgamated Society of Dyers. Councillor, City of Bradford from 1925. A Labour Member. Sat for Dumbartonshire from May 1929-October 1931 when he was defeated. Elected for Batley and Morley in November 1935 and sat until his death on 21 January 1939. [1939]

BROOKS, Thomas Judson. Continued in House after 1945: full entry in Volume IV.

BROTHERS, Michael. 33 Markham Street, Blackburn. S. of Michael Brothers, Esq., of Blackburn. B. 1870. Studied at Technical Schools, and won first honours in in the London and City Guilds Examination. A Cotton Trade Union Leader; member of National Executive of Labour Party 1930-39. A Labour Member. Unsuccessfully contested Duddleston division of Birmingham in November 1922. Elected for Bolton in May 1929 and sat until he was defeated in October 1931. Member of Blackburn Borough Council 1928-32. J.P. for Blackburn from 1935. Died 1952. [1931 2nd ed.]

BROTHERTON, Col. Sir Edward Allen, Bart. Roundhay Hall and Kirkham Abbey, Yorkshire. Carlton, and Bath. S. of Theophilus Brotherton, Esq., of Manchester. B. at Ardwick Green, Manchester 1856. Educ. at the Victoria University. A Chemical Manufacturer. A Coalition Unionist with "strong peace" views. Sat for Wakefield from March 1902-December 1910 when he was defeated. Re-elected for Wakefield in December 1918 and sat until he retired in October 1922. Created Bart. 1918; Baron Brotherton 1929. Mayor of Wakefield 1902-03; Lord Mayor of Leeds 1913-14. Benefactor of Leeds University. J.P. and Dept.-Lieut. for the W. Riding of Yorkshire. Honorary Col. 15th W. Yorks, which he raised. F.S.A. Died 21 October 1930. [1922]

BROTHERTON, John. House of Commons, London. S. of Francis and Sarah Brotherton. B. 7 March 1867; m. 1897, Haidee Wigglesworth. Worked in a flaxmill as a halftimer at the age of 10. An Engineer, and long prominent in matters affecting the engineering industry. A Labour Member. Unsuccessfully contested Gateshead in December 1918. Elected for Gateshead in November 1922 and sat until he was defeated in December 1923. Member of Leeds City Council 1927-30 and 1932-41. Died 8 March 1941. [1923]

BROUN-LINDSAY, Maj. George Humphrey Maurice, D.S.O. 51 Cadogan Place, London. Boodle's. S. of Alfred Lindsay, Esq. B. 23 October 1888; m. 1921, Edith Christian Broun Baird, of Wellwood, Ayrshire. Educ. at Cheltenham, and Royal Military Coll., Sandhurst. Joined K.O.S.B. 1909, retired 1921. Served in France and Italy 1914-18. Assumed the additional surname of Broun in 1921. Parliamentary Private Secretary to Douglas Hacking when Under-Secretary for Home Department, February-November 1927, and when Under-Secretary for Overseas Trade Department from November 1927. A Conservative. Elected for the Partick division of Glasgow in October 1924 and sat until he was defeated in May 1929. J.P. for East Lothian and Vice-Lieut. from 1949. Knighted 1947. D.S.O. 1919. Died 23 June 1964. [1929]

BROWN, Rt. Hon. Alfred Ernest, M.C. 4 Exeter Mansions, Shaftesbury Avenue, London. National Liberal. Scottish Liberal. S. of William Henry Brown, Esq., of Torquay. B. 27 August 1881; m. 8 June 1907, Eva, d. of B.B. Narracott, Esq., of Torquay. Educ. at Torquay. A Lecturer. Enlisted in the Sportsmen's Battalion 1914; Lieut. Somerset L.I. 1916. M.C. and Italian Silver Star for Valour. Chairman of Select Committee on House of Commons Procedure 1931-32. Parliamentary Secretary Ministry of Health November 1931-September 1932; Secretary of Mines October 1932-June 1935; Minister of Labour June 1935-May 1940; Secretary of State for Scotland May 1940-February 1941; Minister of Health February 1941-November 1943; Chancellor of the Duchy of Lancaster November 1943-May 1945; Chairman of European Council U.N.R.R.A. 1944. PC. 1935. Unsuccessfully contested Salisbury in 1918 and 1922, and Mitchan in March 1923. Sat for Rugby from December 1923 until October 1924 when he was defeated. Elected for Leith in March 1927 and sat until he was defeated in July 1945. A Liberal until 1931, thereafter a Liberal National. Leader of the Liberal National Group 1940-45. Minister of Aircraft Production May-July 1945. Companion of Honour 1945. Baptist lay preacher. Died 16 February 1962.   [1945]

BROWN, Charles. George V. Villas, Garden Lane, Sutton-in-Ashfield, Nottinghamshire. S. of William Brown, Esq., of Cromford, Derbyshire. B. 1884; m. 1910, d. of Matthew Brailsford, Esq., of Mansfield. Educ. at Cromford Board School, and at Private School. Member of Sutton-in-Ashfield Urban District Council 1925 and of Nottinghamshire County Council 1928. Was a Hosiery Worker at Sutton-in-Ashfield and an Educational Organizer of National Council of Labour Colleges. A Labour Member. Elected for the Mansfield division of Nottinghamshire in May 1929 and sat until his death on 22 December 1940.
                [1941]

BROWN, Rt. Hon. Douglas Clifton. See CLIFTON BROWN. Rt. Hon. Douglas. Continued in House after 1945: full entry in Volume IV.

BROWN, Brigadier-Gen. Howard Clifton. Holmbush, Faygate, Sussex. Cavalry. S. of Col. J. Clifton Brown, MP, of Holmbush, Faygate. B. 3 April 1868; m. 14 July 1903, Eirene, d. of Sir Henry Hodges. Educ. at Eton, and Trinity Coll., Cambridge. Served in South African War 1900-1901, with 12th Lancers; commanded the regiment 1908-12, and the South Eastern Brigade 1914-18. Dept.-Lieut. and J.P. for Sussex. A Conservative. Returned unopposed for the Newbury division of Berkshire June 1922, defeated in December 1923. Re-elected for the Newbury division in October 1924 and sat until he retired in June 1945. Died 11 September 1946.
                [1945]

BROWN, Rt. Hon. James, O.B.E. 51 Western Avenue, Annbank by Ayr. S. of

James Brown, Esq., of Newton-on-Ayr. B. 16 December 1862 at Whitletts, Ayr; m. 1888, Catherine, d. of Matthew Steele, Esq., of Kilbarchan. Educ. at Annbank Public School. A Miner from 12 years of age to 41; from then Miners' Agent in Ayrshire; Secretary Ayrshire Miners 1909. Dept.-Lieut. and J.P. for Ayrshire. LL.D. Glasgow. O.B.E. 1917. Lord High Commissioner to the General Assembly of Church of Scotland 1924, 1930 and 1931. PC. 1930. A Labour Member. Unsuccessfully contested N. Ayrshire in 1906 and January 1910. Returned for S. Ayrshire from December 1918 until defeated in October 1931. Re-elected for S. Ayrshire in November 1935 and sat until his death on 21 March 1939.   [1939]

BROWN, John Wesley. House of Commons, London. S. of James Brown, Esq., of Middlesbrough. B. 1873. Chairman of Hanson, Brown and Company Limited, General Merchants and Shipbrokers, Middlesbrough and Newcastle-on-Tyne. Director of various local companies. One of the founders of the Chartered Institute of Shipbrokers. A Conservative. Elected for E. Middlesbrough in November 1922 and sat until he retired in November 1923. Unsuccessfully contested the seat in May 1929. J.P. for Middlesbrough; Mayor of Middlesbrough 1932-33. Vice-Consul for the Argentine Republic. Died 8 November 1944.   [1923]

BROWN, Thomas James. Continued in House after 1945: full entry in Volume IV.

BROWN, Rt. Hon. Thomas Watters, K.C. Kintore, Donaghadee, Co. Down. S. of James A. Brown, Esq., of Newtownards, and Marianne Watters. B. 1879 at Newtownards, Co. Down; m. 1913, Mary, d. of William Hadden, Esq., of Cookstown, Co. Tyrone. Educ. at Campbell Coll., Belfast and Queen's University, Belfast. Called to the bar in 1907. K.C. (Ireland) February 1918; called to the English bar in November 1919. Solicitor-Gen. for Ireland June 1921 to August 1921; Attorney-Gen. for Ireland August to November 1921. A Unionist. Elected for N. Down in December 1918 and sat until January 1922 when he was appointed a Judge of the High Court of Northern Ireland. Dept.-Lieut. Co. Down 1937. Died 7 October 1944.   [1922]

BROWN, William John. Continued in House after 1945: full entry in Volume IV.

BROWNE, Alexander Crawford. 18 Windsor Park, Belfast. Constitutional. Reform (Belfast). M. Dorothy Evelyn, d. of J.C.M.Dawson, Esq., of Belfast. Educ. at the Methodist Coll., Belfast. J.P. for Co. Down. Trustee of the Methodist Church in Ireland. A Conservative. Elected for Belfast W. in October 1931 and sat until he died on 11 December 1942.   [1943]

BRUFORD, Robert. House of Commons, London. S. of Robert Bruford, Esq., J.P. B. June 1868; m. Frances, d. of Edward Jeffries, Esq. Educ. at Fullands School, Taunton. A well-known Agriculturist; Chairman of the Taunton branch of the National Farmers Union and of its County Executive. Chairman of the Taunton Board of Guardians and Rural District Council. A Conservative. Elected for the Wells division of Somerset in November 1922 and sat until he was defeated in December 1923. Member of Somerset County Council from 1907 and Alderman from 1928. Chairman of Mental Hospitals Association 1929-31. Chairman of Council of Agriculture for England 1937-38. Died 29 December 1939.   [1923]

BRUGHA, Cathal. See BURGESS, Charles.

BRUNNER, Sir John Fowler Leece, Bart. 43 Harrington Gardens, London. Sandiway House, Northwich. Reform, National Liberal, and Automobile. S. of the Rt. Hon. Sir John Tomlinson Brunner, Bart., MP, and Salome, d. of James Davies, Esq., of Liverpool. B. at Widnes 24 May 1865; m. 17 April 1894, Lucy, d. of Octavius Vaughan Morgan, Esq., MP for Battersea. Educ. at Cheltenham, Polytechnic School, Zurich, and Trinity Hall, Cambridge. A Director of Brunner, Mond and Company and of I.C.I. until 1927; member of the Central Appeal Tribunal during the war.

A Liberal. Unsuccessfully contested the Hyde division of Cheshire in 1900. Sat for the Leigh division of Lancashire from 1906-January 1910 and the Northwich division of Cheshire from January 1910-18 when he was defeated. Unsuccessfully contested Southport in 1922. Elected for Southport in December 1923 and sat until he was defeated in October 1924. Unsuccessfully contested Cheltenham in September 1928. Member of Cheshire County Council 1892-95. Succeeded as Bart. 1919. Chairman of Madeley Collieries Limited and Park Hall Colliery Limited. Died 16 January 1929.   [1924 2nd ed.]

BRUTON, Sir James. Wotton Hill, Gloucester. Carlton, and Constitutional. S. of Henry Bruton, Esq., J.P. B. at Newent, Gloucestershire 6 February 1848; m. 1880, Rosa Gertrude, d. of John Michael Butt, Esq., J.P., of Gloucester. Educ. at Crypt Grammar School, Gloucester. A Miller and Corn Merchant. Mayor of Gloucester nine times. J.P. for City of Gloucester. Honorary Lieut.-Col. 3rd Battalion Gloucestershire Volunteer Regiment; Honorary Freeman City of Gloucester 1918. First High Sheriff of Greater Gloucester 1900. A Conservative. Elected for Gloucester in December 1918. Sat until he retired in November 1923. Chairman of Gloucester and Sharpness Canal Company Limited and of James Reynolds and Company Limited, Millers. Knighted 1916. Died 26 February 1933.   [1923]

BUCHAN, John, C.H. St. Stephen's House, London. Elsfield Manor, Oxford. Athenaeum, St. Stephen's and Alpine. New, Edinburgh. S. of the Rev. John Buchan. B. 26 August 1875; m. 15 July 1907, Susan Charlotte, d. of Hon. Norman Grosvenor. Educ. at the University of Glasgow, and Brasenose Coll., Oxford; M.A., Scholar 1st Class Lit. Hum., Stanhope Hist. Essay, Newdigate Prize, President of Union. A Barrister-at-Law, Middle Temple 1901; Private Secretary to Lord Milner when High Commissioner for South Africa 1901-03; Temporary Lieut.-Col. on H.Q. Staff in France 1916-17; Director of Information 1917-18; J.P. for Oxfordshire and Dept.-

Lieut., and J.P. for Peebles-shire; Honorary D.C.L. Oxford; Honorary Fellow of Brasenose 1934; Honorary LL.D. Glasgow and St. Andrews. A Director of Reuters. A Trustee of National Library of Scotland and of the Pilgrim Trust. Lord High Commissioner to the General Assembly of Church of Scotland 1933 and 1934. An Historian and Novelist. Companion of Honour 1932. Officer of the Crown of Belgium and of the Crown of Italy. A A Conservative. Sat for the Scottish Universities from April 1927 until May 1935 when he was appointed Gov. Gen. of Canada. Created Baron Tweedsmuir 1935. PC. 1937. Chancellor of Edinburgh University 1937-40. Died 11 February 1940. [1935]

BUCHANAN, Lieut.-Col. Arthur Louis Hamilton, O.B.E. Drumpellier, Coatbridge, Lanarkshire. Carlton, and Naval and Military. New, Edinburgh. S. of David William Ramsay Buchanan, Esq., of Drumpellier and Corsewall, and Lady Katherine, d. of the 3rd Earl of Donoughmore. B. at Richmond, Surrey 1866; m. 1903, Adeline, eld. d. of Richard Musgrave Harvey, Esq. Educ. at Newton Coll., Devon. Served 25 years in Gordon Highlanders (S.A. War); B.E.F. 1914 to end of the war; Commanded Base Depot in France. J.P. and Dept.-Lieut. for Lanarkshire. A Coalition Unionist. Elected for the Coatbridge division of Lanarkshire in December 1918 and sat until he was defeated in November 1922. O.B.E. 1919. Died 15 February 1925. [1922]

BUCHANAN, George. Continued in House after 1945: full entry in Volume IV.

BUCHAN-HEPBURN, Patrick George Thomas. Continued in House after 1945: full entry in Volume IV.

BUCKINGHAM, Sir Henry Cecil, C.B.E. 27 Hans Place, London. Seale Lodge, Farnham, Surrey. Carlton. S. of Joseph Hicks Buckingham, Esq., of Truro. B. in London 2 May 1867; m. 3 February 1906, Madeline, d. of William Bull, Esq., of Hove, Sussex. Educ. at Harrow. Arbitrator City of London Court of Arbitration; member of Advisory Committee of the City of London 1916-18. Sheriff of London 1910-11; member of many Government Committees 1914-18. Master of the Skinners' Company 1918-19. Chairman of Income Taxpayers' Society. Had the 1911 coronation medal. Knighted 1911. C.B.E. 1920. A Conservative. Elected for the Guildford division of Surrey in November 1922 and sat until his death on 1 August 1931. [1931 2nd ed.]

BUCKLE, John. 13 Eighteenth Avenue, New Wortley, Leeds. B. 1867. Was travelling organizer of the Boot and Shoe Operatives Society. Leader of Labour group on Leeds City Council and first Labour Alderman of Leeds. J.P. for Leeds. A Labour Member. Elected for Eccles in November 1922. Sat until he was defeated in October 1924. Died 8 November 1925. [1924 2nd ed.]

BUCKLEY, Lieut.-Col. Albert, D.S.O. The Withens, Blundellsands, Lancashire. 88 Cadogan Place, London. Conservative, Liverpool. S. of William Buckley, Esq., J.P., of Blundellsands. B. at Blundellsands 10 April 1877; m. 1919. Elsie Juanita, 2nd d. of J.E. Fisher, Esq., of Liverpool. Educ. at Merchant Taylors School, Great Crosby, and Aldenham School, Elstree, Hertfordshire. A Wool-Broker. Lieut.-Col. 5th Battalion King's Liverpool Regiment. Served in South Africa 1901-02, and in France 1915 to the close of the war; D.S.O. and Bar; twice mentioned in despatches; wounded. Parliamentary Private Secretary to the Rt. Hon. F.G. Kellaway 1920-21. Junior Lord of the Treasury October 1922 to March 1923. Assistant Whip (unpaid) April 1921 to October 1922. A Conservative. Elected for the Waterloo division of Lancashire in December 1918 and sat until he retired in November 1923. Secretary for Overseas Trade Department from March to November 1923, when, as a Free Trader, he resigned in disagreement with the Government's Protectionist policy. Chairman of Liverpool Chamber of Commerce 1924-28. Member of Mersey Docks and Harbour Board 1928-51. Died 13 November 1965. [1923]

BUCKLEY, Daniel. See BUCKLEY, Donald.

BUCKLEY, Donald. Maynooth, Co. Kildare. B. 1866. Educ. at National School Maynooth, and Belvedere and Marist Colleges, Dublin. A Shopkeeper. A Sinn Feiner. Elected for N. Kildare in December 1918 but did not take his seat. Member of Dail for N. Kildare to 1921 and for Kildare and Wicklow 1921-22, as an Anti-Treaty Member. Fianna Fail Member of Dail for Kildare 1927-32. Chairman of Kildare County Council. Gov.-Gen. (Seanascal) of Irish Free State 1932-37.   [1922]

BUDSLEY, Donald. See BUCKLEY, Donald.

BULL, Bartle Brennan. Trevor House, Belgrave Place, London. 1 Garden Court, Temple, London. Carlton, and Boodle's. S. of William Perkins Bull, Esq., K.C., LL.D., of Canada. B. 1 April 1902; m. 7 November 1931, Rosemary, d. of Jacob Baur, Esq., of Chicago (divorced 1949). Educ. at Eton, and Magdalen Coll., Oxford, M.A. Barrister-at-Law, Inner Temple 1928. Parliamentary Private Secretary to Capt. Rt. Hon. Euan Wallace when Financial Secretary to the Treasury May 1938 and when Minister of Transport April 1939-May 1940, to Maj. Rt. Hon. G. Lloyd George, Minister of Fuel and Power June 1944. Lieut. Coldstream Guards September 1939. A Conservative. Elected for the Enfield division of Middlesex in November 1935 and sat until he was defeated in July 1945. Died 17 October 1950.   [1945]

BULL, Rt. Hon. Sir William James, Bart. Vencourt, Hammersmith, London. 474 Uxbridge Road, London. Carlton, Constitutional, Junior Constitutional, and 1900. S. of Henry Bull, Esq., Solicitor, and Cecilia, d. of J.P. Howard, Esq., of Whitehed Wood, Shirley, Hampshire. B. 29 September 1863; m. 5 January 1904, Lilian, d. of Gabriel Brandon, Esq., of Worthing. Educ. at St. Mary's Academy. A Solicitor, head of the firm of Bull and Bull, Lincoln's Inn; Director of Siemens; a Gov. of the Latymer Charities, Honorary Solicitor to the Royal Life Saving Society, and Trustee Royal Humane Society; Member of Speaker's Reform Bill Conference 1916; Maltravers Herald Extraordinary 1922; Chairman of London Unionist MPs., and Knight Principal of the Imperial Society of Knights; on the Board of W. London Hospital. Member London County Council 1892-1901. Chairman Petitions Committee; Knight Bach. 1905. J.P., PC. 1918. Created Bart. 1922. A Conservative. First elected for Hammersmith in 1900 and sat until 1918. Sat for the S. division of Hammersmith from December 1918 until he retired in May 1929. Parliamentary Private Secretary to Rt. Hon. Walter Long 1903-21. First Honorary Freeman of the Borough of Hammersmith 1930. Died 23 January 1931.   [1929]

BULLOCK, Harold Malcolm. Continued in House after 1945: full entry in Volume IV.

BULMER-THOMAS, Ivor. See THOMAS, Ivor. Continued in House after 1945: full entry in Volume IV.

BURDEN, Thomas William. Continued in House afte 1945: full entry in Volume IV.

BURDETT-COUTTS, Rt. Hon. William Lehman Ashmead-Bartlett. 1 Stratton Street, London. Holly Lodge, Highgate, London. Carlton. 2nd s. of Ellis Bartlett, Esq., of Plymouth, New England, by Sophia, d. of John King Ashmead, Esq., of Philadelphia. His grand-parents on both sides were British subjects. B. in 1851 in U.S.A.; m. 1881, Baroness Burdett-Coutts (she died 1906), and assumed by Royal Licence the surname of Burdett-Coutts. Educ. privately; gained the first scholarship at Keble Coll., Oxford, M.A. In Turkey 1877-78 during the Russo-Turkish war, as Special Commissioner (voluntary) of the Baroness's Turkish Compassionate Fund; Star and Second Class of Medjidiyeh. Gov. of Christ's Hospital; twice Master of the Turners' Company, and one of the Founders of the British East Africa Possessions; he carried the Hampstead Heath Act 1885; Police Enfranchisement, and Metropolitan

Management Amendment Acts 1887; and Advertisement Rating Act 1889; Chairman Governing Body of Burdett-Coutts Schools, Westminster. Founded with the Baroness, the Westminster Technical Institute. Took a prominent part in reconstruction the City of Westminster under the Local Government Act 1899. In South African War 1900, was *The Times* correspondent on Sick and Wounded, his lectures and subsequent action in the House of Commons resulted in a drastic reform of the Army Medical Service. Author of *Lest We Forget* 1900, a record of his work in this matter. From 1902 advocated reform in English railways, resulting in Railway Accounts and Returns Act 1910. Successfully led opposition to Proportional Representation 1917-18. In May 1920 issued Statement of Reasons and led debate in support of Imperial War Graves Commission's policy of "equality" of treatment, and confirmed *nem. con.* by House of Commons; received resolution of thanks from Commission. PC. 1921. A Unionist. Sat for Westminster from November 1885 to December 1918; elected unopposed for the Abbey division of Westminster in December 1918 and sat until his death on 28 July 1921. [1921]

BURDON, Col. Rowland. Castle Eden, Co. Durham. Arthur's, and Carlton. S. of the Rev. John Burdon, of Castle Eden. B. 19 June 1857; m. 1887, Mary Arundell, 2nd d. of Wyndham Slade, Esq., of Mountys Court, Taunton. Educ. at Repton, and University Coll., Oxford. Lieut.-Col. and Honorary Col. Commanding 1st Volunteer Battalion Durham Light Infantry. J.P., Dept.-Lieut., and V.D. A Coalition Unionist. Unsuccessfully contested S.E. Durham in December 1910. Elected for the Sedgefield division of Durham in December 1918 and sat until he retired in October 1922. Died 1 August 1944. [1922]

BURGESS, Charles. 5 Fitzwilliam Terrace, Upper Rathmines, Dublin. B. at Clontarf 8 July 1874. Educ. at Belvedere Coll. A candle manufacturer. A Sinn Fein Member. Returned for Waterford Co. in December 1918 but did not take his seat and died on 7 July 1922, after being shot by the National forces. Member of Dail for Co. Waterford to 1921 and for E. Tipperary and City and County of Waterford 1921-22 as an Anti-Treaty Member. Chairman of Dail in January 1919. President of the Ministry January-April 1919. Minister of Defence 1921-22. Died 7 July 1922. [1922]

BURGESS, Frederick George. 205 Euston Road, London. B. 1871. A Railway man until 1919. Political Agent, Writer, Lecturer and Cartoonist. Held many positions in the N.U.R. as Delegate and Representative; member of many Government Committees 1915-18. A Labour Member. Unsuccessfully contested Maidstone in 1918. Elected for York in May 1929 and sat until he was defeated in October 1931. Unsuccessfully contested Accrington in November 1935. Died 31 March 1951. [1931 2nd ed.]

BURGESS, Stanley. House of Commons, London. S. of Richard John Burgess, Esq., of Ipswich. B. 1889 at Ipswich; m. 1914, Ida, d. of Thomas Nicholson, Esq., of Holmesfield, Derbyshire. One of the officials of the Amalgamated Engineering Union. A Labour Member. Unsuccessfully contested Leith in December 1918. Elected for Rochdale in November 1922 and sat until he was defeated in December 1923. [1923]

BURGHLEY, David George Brownlow Cecil, The Lord. Pilsgate House, Stamford. S. of 5th Marq. of Exeter. B. 9 February 1905; m. 1st, 10 January 1929, Lady Mary Scott, d. of 7th Duke of Buccleuch, K.T. (divorced 1946); secondly, 1946, Diana Mary, widow of Col. D. Forbes and d. of Hon. Arnold Henderson. Educ. at Eton, and Magdalene Coll., Cambridge. Lieut. Grenadier Guards 1927-29, R. of O. Honorary Col. 5th Battalion Northants Regiment. Dept.-Lieut. for Northamptonshire 1937-46 and for Huntingdon and Peterborough from 1965, and a J.P. for the Soke of Peterborough. Chairman of Junior Imperial League 1933-37, President 1939; member of International Olympic Committee from 1933 and of Propaganda Committee of National Fitness Council; President of Amateur Athletic Association 1936-76. A Director of Army and Navy Stores Limited, of London and N.E. Railway, of National Provincial Bank, and of Firestone Tyre Company, and of Land Improvement Company. Chairman of London Board of London and Lancashire Insurance Company Limited. Parliamentary Private Secretary to Visct. Hailsham for World Conference 1932, and to Col. J.J. Llewellin when Parliamentary Secretary Ministry of Supply September 1939-May 1940. Lieut.-Col. Assistant Divisional Tank Supply 1941-42. Controller of American Supplies and Repairs Ministry of Aircraft Production July 1942. A Conservative. Elected for the Peterborough division of Northamptonshire in October 1931 and sat until August 1943 when he was appointed Gov. of Bermuda. Gov. of Bermuda 1943-45. K.C.M.G. 1943. Styled Lord Burghley 1905-56. Succeeded as Marq. of Exeter in 1956. Rector of St. Andrews University 1949-52. President of International Amateur Athletic Federation 1946-76. Chairman of British Olympic Association 1936-66, President 1966-77. Hereditary Grand Almoner. Lord Paramount of Soke of Peterborough. Mayor of Stamford 1961. Winner of Olympic gold medal, 400 metres hurdles 1928.* [1943]

BURGIN, Rt. Hon. Edward Leslie. 2 Whitehall Court, London. Aplins Close, Harpenden, Hertfordshire. Reform, National Liberal, Whitefriars, and Eighty. S. of Edward Lambert Burgin, Esq., Solicitor. B. 13 July 1887; m. 30 May 1912, Dorothy, d. of Charles Cooper, Esq., of Finchley. Educ. at Christ's Coll., Finchley, London University, Lausanne, and in Paris. Solicitor 1909; Scott Scholar University Scholarship; Principal and Director of Studies, Law Society; LL.D. London 1913; Member of Senate London University; Charity Commission 1931-32. Parliamentary Secretary Board of Trade September 1932; Minister of Transport May 1937; Minister without Portfolio April 1939; Minister of Supply July 1939-May 1940. Intelligence Officer on Gen. Staff in Italy 1918. Croce di Guerra. PC. 1937. A Liberal until 1931, thereafter a Liberal Nationalist. Unsuccessfully contested Hornsey in November 1921, and at the general elections of 1922, 1923 and 1924. Unsuccessfully contested the N. division of East Ham in April 1926. Elected for the Luton division of Bedfordshire in May 1929 and sat until he retired in June 1945. Died 16 August 1945. [1945]

BURGOYNE, Lieut.-Col. Sir Alan Hughes. Whitehall Court, London. Finchers House, Amersham, Buckinghamshire. Carlton, Conservative, and Royal Thames Yacht. S. of Peter Bond Burgoyne, Esq., of Broadlands, Ascot. B. 30 September 1880; m. 7 March 1906, Irene Victoria Eason, d. of Ebenezer Macdonald, Esq., of the Isles, of Sydney, N.S.W. Educ. at Kelly Coll., at Liege and Montpellier Universities, and at Queen's Coll., Oxford. Director of P.B. Burgoyne, Colonial Merchants. Served in France, Palestine and N.W. Frontier of India 1914-18; Controller of Priority Department Ministry of Munitions 1918-19; Secretary Parliamentary Air Commission 1918-20. F.R.G.S., C.Inst.M.E., J.P. for Buckinghamshire; Knight. Bach. 1922. A Conservative. Unsuccessfully contested Kings Lynn in 1906. Member for N. Kensington from January 1910 to October 1922 when he retired. Unsuccessfully contested Aylesbury division of Buckinghamshire in December 1923; elected for the division in October 1924 and sat until his death on 26 April 1929. Author of a collection of poetry and volumes on submarines and naval history. Founder and Editor of *Navy League Annual*. Supporter of the National Party 1917-18. Died 26 April 1929. [1929]

BURKE, James Aloysius. Rockforest, Roscrea, Co. Tipperary. S. of Tobias Henry Burke, Esq. B. 1893; m. 1929, Zenaide, d. of Capt. Alexis Bashkiraff, of Russia. Educ. at Clongowes Wood, and Trinity Coll., Dublin. A Sinn Fein Member. Returned unopposed for mid Tipperary in December 1918 but did not take his seat. Member of Dail for mid Tipperary to 1921 and for Co. Tipperary 1921-38. Pro-Treaty, later Cumann na nGaedheal and Fine Gael Member. Minister for Local Government and Public Health 1923-27. Parliamentary Secretary to Minister of Finance 1927-32. [1922]

BURKE, Wilfrid Andrew. Continued in House after 1945: full entry in Volume IV.

BURMAN, John Bedford. Tibbington House, Edgbaston, Birmingham. Carlton, and Constitutional. S. of William Burman, Esq., of Edgbaston. B. 6 October 1867; m. 1906, Elizabeth Vernon, d. of C.H. Pugh, Esq., of Penns, Warwickshire (she died 1936). Member of Birmingham city council from 1908; Alderman 1921; J.P. Chairman Electric Supply Company, Vice-President Birmingham Chamber of Commerce. Chairman of Burman and Sons Limited, and of Burman, Cooper and Company Limited. Introduced Money-lenders Act. 1927. A Conservative. Elected for the Duddeston division of Birmingham in December 1923 and October 1924. Sat until he was defeated in May 1929. After leaving school worked as a journalist on *Birmingham Mail*, *Birmingham Gazette* and *The Sportsman*. Lord Mayor of Birmingham 1931-32. Knighted 1936. High Sheriff of Warwickshire 1940-41. Died 4 March 1941. [1929]

BURN, Col. Charles Rosdew. 10 Hill Street, Berkeley Square, London. Fyvie Castle, Aberdeenshire. Carlton, Naval & Military, New Edinburgh, Royal Northern, Aberdeen, and Hurlingham. S. of Gen. Robert Burn, Commandant Royal Artillery, of Jessfield, Modlothian, and Caroline, d. of Maj. Little. B. 20 February 1859 at Pinner; m. 1891, Hon. Ethel Louise Forbes-Leith; (O.B.E., Lady of Grace of St. John of Jerusalem, twice mentioned in despatches in the Great War), only d. of Lord Leith of Fyvie. Educ. at Cheltenham Coll., and Royal Military Coll., Sandhurst. Entered the army 1878, and served with 8th Hussars and Royal Dragoons. Aide-de-Camp to H.M. King George V. A member of H.M. Royal Body Guard and Royal Body Guard for Scotland (Scottish Archers). Was Aide-de-Camp to Viceroy of India 1883-85 and 1887-88, and to the Duke of Connaught 1891-96. Served in Hazara campaign 1888, and in South African War 1900-01, and was mentioned in despatches. O.B.E. (Military); Officer of Legion of Honour; Officer of Crown of Belgium; served in European War 15 August 1914 to 5 February 1919. Twice mentioned in despatches. A Conservative. Unsuccessfully contested E. Aberdeenshire January 1910. First elected for the Torquay division of Devonshire in December 1910 and sat until he retired in November 1923. Created Bart. 1923. Adopted the surname of Forbes-Leith of Fyvie in lieu of Burn in 1925. Died 2 November 1930. [1923]

BURN, Thomas Henry. 18 Ratcliffe Street, Belfast. S. of Thomas Hy. and Agnes Burn. B. at Belfast 19 January 1875. Educ. at the Belfast National School. A Lithographic Printer, Secretary of the Belfast Branch of the Lithographic Printing Society. A Unionist Labour Member. Elected for the St. Anne's division of Belfast in December 1918, and sat until he retired in October 1922. Sat for W. Belfast in the Parliament of Northern Ireland from May 1921 to March 1925. Assistant Parliamentary Secretary to Northern Ireland Ministry of Finance 1921-25. [1922]

BURNETT, John George. Powis House, Aberdeen. S. of George Burnett, Esq., Lyon King of Arms. B. 30 March 1876; m. 13 November 1901, Helen, d. of Capt. Duncan M. Irvine (she died 1944). Educ. at Glenalmond and at Magdalen Coll., Oxford. Barrister-at-Law, Inner Temple 1930; L.R.A.M. and A.R.C.M.; J.P. for Aberdeen; member of Aberdeen School Board 1906-11, and of Town Council 1928-31. Secretary War Pensions Committee 1915-20. A Unionist. Elected for Aberdeen N. in October 1931 and sat until he was defeated in November 1935. County Army Welfare Officer for Aberdeen and Kincardine 1940-47. Died 20 January 1962. [1935]

BURNEY, Commander Charles Dennistoun. 20 Carlton House Terrace, London. Upham House, Upham, Hampshire. Marlborough, and Ranelagh. S. of of Admiral of the Fleet Sir Cecil Burney, Bart., G.C.B., G.C.M.G. B. 28 December 1888; m. 15 March 1921, Gladys, d. of George Henry High, Esq., of Lake Shore Drive, Chicago. Educ. privately, and in

H.M.S. *Britannia*. Joined R.N. 1905; in command of H.M.S. *Velox* 1914. Appointed H.M.S. *Vernon* 1915, and invented two devices known as the explosive paravane and protector paravane, which were fitted throughout the British and Allied Navies and Mercantile Marine with satisfactory results in destroying submarines and protecting vessels from mines. Prominently associated with Imperial airship project. A Conservative. Sat for the Uxbridge division of Middlesex from November 1922 until he retired in May 1929. Succeeded as Bart. 1929. Died in Hamilton, Bermuda 11 November 1968. [1929]

BURNIE, Maj. James. 9 Breeze Hill, Bootle. S. of Joseph Burnie, Esq., Contractor and Refrigerator Builder. B. at Bootle 10 May 1882; m. 21 July 1910, Ruth, eld. d. of G. Thornton, Esq. (she died 1939). Educ. at St. John's, Bootle, and Merchant Taylors, Great Crosby. A Contractor and Refrigerator Builder (Bell and Burnie Limited). M.C. 1918; Maj. T.A. Reserve. A Liberal. Elected for Bootle in November 1922. Sat until he was defeated in October 1924. Unsuccessfully contested Bootle in November 1935 and Crosby in February 1950. Mayor of Bootle 1936-37. Died 15 May 1975. [1924 2nd ed.]

BURTON, Col, Henry Walter, O.B.E. Church Hill, Wickford, Essex. Carlton, St. Stephen's, and Royal Automobile. S. of the Rev. William Henry Burton, of Stoke Newington. B. December 1876; m. March 1898, Constance Mary, d. of Edward Desmoulins, Esq. (she died 10 August 1935). Educ. at Goudhurst. Served in Matabele War 1896, in South African War 1889-1901, in France 1915-18. With German occupation 1919-20; British Representative on Inter-allied Navigation Commission 1919-20. L.D.V. May 1940; Commanding 1st Essex Battalion Home Guard 1940-43. Member of Committee of British Beet Society. A Conservative. Returned for the Sudbury division of W. Suffolk in October 1924 and sat until he was defeated in July 1945. O.B.E. 1919. Chairman of Grosvenor House Limited. Died 23 November 1947. [1945]

BURY, Lieut.-Col. Charles Kenneth Howard. See HOWARD-BURY, Lieut.-Col. Charles Kenneth.

BUTCHER, Herbert Walter. Continued in House after 1945: full entry in Volume IV.

BUTCHER, Sir John George, Bart. 32 Elvaston Place, London. Riccall Hall, Yorkshire. Danesfort, Killarney. Carlton. S. of the Most Rev. Samuel Butcher, Lord Bishop of Meath, and Mary Leahy, of South Hill, Killarney. B. 15 November 1851 at Killarney; m. 1898, Alice Mary, d. of E.L. Brandeth, Esq., J.P. Educ. at Marlborough Coll., and Trinity Coll., Cambridge; Bell University Scholar, 8th Classic, and 8th Wrangler, and was a Fellow of his Coll. 1875. A Barrister, called 1878 at Lincoln's Inn; a Q.C. 1897. Bencher of Lincoln's Inn 1902, Treasurer 1926. J.P. for the E. Riding of Yorkshire. Received Honorary Freedom of York 1906; created Bart. 1918. A Conservative. Sat for York from 1892 to 1906, when he was defeated. Re-elected for York from January 1910. Sat until he retired in November 1923. Created Baron Danesfort 1924. Vice Chairman of R.S.P.C.A. Died 30 June 1935. [1923]

BUTLER, Sir George Geoffrey Gilbert, K.B.E. 2 Ryder Street, London. Corpus Christi College, Cambridge. Carlton, and United University. S. of Spencer Perceval Butler, Esq., Conveyancing Counsel to the High Court. B. 15 August 1887; m. 8 November 1916, Elisabeth Levering, eld. d. of J. Levering Jones, Esq., of Philadelphia. Educ. at Clifton, and Trinity Coll., Cambridge. Fellow of Corpus Christi Coll., Cambridge from 1910 and president from 1928; in the Foreign Office from 1915-19. C.B.E. 1918: K.B.E. 1919. Parliamentary Private Secretary to Sir S. Hoare November 1924. J.P. for Cambridgeshire. A Conservative. Elected for Cambridge University in December 1923. Sat until his death on 2 May 1929. [1929]

BUTLER, Hugh Myddleton. House of Commons, London. S. of Ambrose and Isabella Butler of Leeds. B. 3 May 1857; m. 1881, Annette, d. of Edward Scofield,

Esq. (she died 1932). Educ. at Leeds Grammar School and Yorkshire Coll., Leeds. A Director of the Kirksall Forge Company. Chairman of the North Leeds Conservative Association 1902-43. A Conservative. Elected for N. Leeds in November 1922 and sat until he retired in November 1923. Died 10 October 1943. [1923]

BUTLER, James Ramsay Montagu. House of Commons, London. 3rd s. of Dr. Henry Montagu Butler, Master of Trinity. B. 1889. Unmarried. Fellow of Trinity Coll., Cambridge from 1913. Served in the war with the Scottish Horse; twice mentioned in despatches. O.B.E. 1919; M.V.O. 1920. Chief Historian for the Military Histories of Second World War. Knighted 1958. Vice Master of Trinity Coll., Cambridge 1955-60. Regius Professor of Modern History, University of Cambridge 1947-54. Author of *The Passing of the Great Reform Bill*, *History of England 1815-1918*, and other historical works. An Independent Liberal. Elected for Cambridge University November 1922 and sat until he was defeated in December 1923; again defeated in October 1924. Died 2 March 1975. [1923]

BUTLER, Rt. Hon. Richard Austen. Continued in House after 1945: full entry in Volume IV.

BUTT, Sir Alfred, Bart. 17 Waterloo Place, London. Crosways, Newmarket. Carlton. S. of F. Butt, Esq. B. 20 March 1878; m. 1st, 16 April 1902, Georgina, d. of Frederick Say, Esq., of Norwich (she died 1960); secondly, 1960, Wilhelmina Wahl. During the war rendered service at the Ministry of Food. Knight Bach. 1918; Bart. 1929. A Conservative. Elected for the Balham and Tooting division of Wandsworth in November 1922 and sat until he resigned in 1936, after the budget leak involving J.H. Thomas and himself. Entered theatre management in 1898 and was Managing Director of the Palace, Drury Lane, Empire, Adelphi and Gaiety Theatres, London. Died 8 December 1962. [1936]

BUTTON, Howard Stransom. The Cedar House, Hillingdon, Middlesex. St. Stephen's, and City Carlton. S. of Alfred Button and Mary Jane, d. of John Stransom, Esq., of Uxbridge. B. at Uxbridge 14 February 1873; m. 7 September 1898, d. of Mr. E. Pike, of Ticehurst, Sussex. Educ. at University Coll. School. A Produce Merchant. Member of Middlesex County Council from March 1919. J.P. for Middlesex 1921. A Conservative. Elected for the Wrekin division of Shropshire in November 1922 and sat until he retired in November 1923. Knighted 1936. Chairman of Middlesex County Council 1933-36. High Sheriff of Middlesex 1937-38. Alderman of City of London 1938-43, Sheriff 1941-42. Died 18 August. 1943. [1923]

BUXTON, Charles Roden. 6 Erskine Hill, Golder's Green, London. 1917, and National Labour. 3rd s. of Sir T.F. Buxton, 3rd Bart. B. 27 November 1875; m. 11 August 1904, Dorothy Frances, d. of Arthur Trevor Jebb, Esq. Educ. at Harrow, and Trinity Coll., Cambridge; M.A. Barrister-at-Law, Inner Temple 1902. Private Secretary to his father when Gov. of S. Australia, 1897-98; Principal of Morley Coll. 1902-10; 2nd Lieut. in Royal First Devon Yeomanry. A Labour Member. Unsuccessfully contested E. Hertfordshire in 1906, and Ashburton division of Devon in 1908. Sat as a Liberal for the Ashburton division from January-Decembry 1910 when he was defeated. Unsuccessfully contested Accrington for Labour in December 1918. Elected for Accrington in November 1922, defeated December 1923 and October 1924. Elected for the Elland division of the W. Riding of Yorkshire in May 1929 and sat until he was defeated in October 1931; again defeated in Elland in November 1935. Treasurer of ILP 1924-27. Editor of *Independent Review* 1906-07, *Albany Review* 1907-08. Died 16 December 1942. [1931 2nd ed.]

BUXTON, Rt. Hon. Noel Edward. 12 Rutland Gate, London. Colne Cottage, Cromer. Reform. 2nd s. of Sir T. Fowell Buxton, 3rd Bart. B. 9 January 1869; m. 30 April 1914, Lucy Edith, d. of Maj. Pelham Burn. Educ. at Harrow, and Trinity Coll., Cambridge, (Hons. Hist., M.A.).

53

Was Aide-de-Camp to his father when Gov. of South Australia 1895-98. A member of Whitechapel Board of Guardians. Chairman of the Balkan Committee. Minister of Agriculture January-October 1924; President of the Board of Agriculture and Fisheries June 1929-30; PC. 1924. Unsuccessfully contested Ipswich as a Liberal in 1900. Sat as a Liberal MP for the Whitby division of the N. Riding of Yorkshire from June 1905-January 1906, when he was defeated, and for N. Norfolk from January 1910-December 1918, when he was again defeated. Elected as a Labour Member for N. Norfolk in 1922 and sat until he was created Baron Noel-Buxton in June 1930. Joint Chairman of the Anti-Slavery and Aborigines Protection Society. President of Save the Children Fund and Miners Welfare Fund. Died 12 September 1948   [1929 2nd ed.]

CADOGAN, Maj, Hon. Sir Edward Cecil George, K.B.E., C.B. Warren Farm, Lewknor, Oxfordshire. Carlton. S. of 5th Earl Cadogan. B. 15 November 1880. Educ. at Balliol Coll., Oxford. A Barrister-at-Law, Inner Temple 1905. Maj. Suffolk Yeomanry; served overseas 1914-18. Secretary to Sir James Lowther, later Visct. Ullswater, when Speaker of the House of Commons 1911-21; Dept.-Lieut. and J.P. for London; Vice-Lieut. 1945-58; member of Indian Statutory Commission 1927-30. A Conservative. Unsuccessfully contested Kings Lynn in January 1910. Sat for Reading from 1922-23 when he was defeated, and for the Finchley division of Middlesex from 1924-35, when he retired. Sat for Bolton from September 1940 until he retired in June 1945. K.B.E. 1939. Dept.-Chairman of Great Western Railway. Died 13 September 1962.   [1945]

CAINE, Derwent Hall. See HALL CAINE, Derwent.

CAINE, Gordon Ralph Hall. See HALL CAINE, Gordon Ralph.

CAIRNS, John. The Drive, Gosforth, Newcastle-on-Tyne. B. 1859 at Choppington, Northumberland; m. 1901, Annie Dixon.

Financial Secretary of the Northumberland Miners' Association; Secretary on the men's side of the Joint Committee in the Northumberland Coal Trade; President of the Northumberland Aged Mine Workers' Homes Association; J.P. for Newcastle-on-Tyne. Author of *Money, Economics of Industry*, etc. Member of Primitive Methodist Church. M.B.E. 1918. A Labour Member. Elected for Morpeth in December 1918 and sat until he died on 23 May 1923.
                           [1923]

CAMERON, Alexander Gordon. 28 Crowhurst Road, London. S. of Donald Cameron, Esq. B. at Oban 1876. A Joiner in Glasgow. A Trade Union Official; an Appointee of Government in 1917 to enquire into Industrial and Social Conditions of Scottish Workers. A Labour Member. Unsuccessfully contested the Kirkdale division of Liverpool in January and July 1910, Jarrow in December 1910, and Woolwich W. in December 1918. Elected for the Widnes division of Lancashire in May 1929 and sat until he was defeated in October 1931; again defeated in November 1935. Chairman of National Executive of Labour Party 1920-21. Died 30 May 1944.
                           [1931 2nd ed.]

CAMPBELL, Sir Edward Taswell, Bart. 52 Westmorland Road, Bromley, Kent. Carlton, I Zingari and M.C.C. S. of Col. Frederick Campbell, C.B., and grand-s. of Sir John Campbell, Bart., of Airds, Argyllshire. B. 9 April 1879; m. 28 January 1904, Edith, L.(G.) St.J., d. of A.J. Warren, Esq. Educ. at Dulwich Coll., later Gov. An East India Merchant. H.B.M. Vice-Consul in Java 1914-20. Chairman Anglo-Netherlands Society, of James Allens' Girls School, Dulwich, and of Royal Normal Coll. for the Blind. K.(G.) St. J.; Member of London County Council 1922-25. Parliamentary Private Secretary to the Rt. Hon. Sir Kingsley Wood when Postmaster-Gen., November 1931, when Minister of Health June 1935, when Secretary of State for Air May 1938, when Lord Privy Seal April 1940, when Chancellor of the Exchequer May 1940-September 1943, and to the Rt. Hon. H.U. Willink when

Minister of Health November 1943. Created Knight Bach. 1933; Bart. 1939; J.P. for Kent. Commissioner of Staff of Metropolitan Special Constabulary. A Conservative. Unsuccessfully contested N.W. Camberwell in Elected for N.W. Camberwell in October 1924, defeated May 1929. Sat for Bromley from September. 1930 until his death on 17 July 1945, after the completion of polling for the General Election but before the result was announced. He was subsequently returned at the head of the poll and a by-election was held. [1945]

CAMPBELL, Vice-Admiral Gordon, V.C., D.S.O. House of Commons, London. Bath. S. of Col. F. Campbell, C.B. B. 6 January 1886; m. 14 January 1911, Mary Jeanne, d. of J.H.V. S. David, Esq. Educ. at Dulwich Coll., and in H.M.S. *Britannia*. Joined R.N. 1900, retired as Rear-Admiral 1928, Vice-Admiral 1932. A Nationalist. Elected for Burnley in October 1931 and sat until he was defeated in November 1935. D.S.O. 1916; V.C. 1917. Died 3 October 1953. [1935]

CAMPBELL, John Dermot. 59 Somerton Road, Belfast. S. of R. Garrett Campbell, Esq., C.B.E. B. 20 January 1898; m. 12 February 1930, Josephine Patricia, d. of Sir Joseph McConnell, Bart., MP. Educ. at Wellington, and Royal Military Academy, Woolwich. A Flax Spinner. Dept.-Lieut. for Belfast. Dept. Flax Controller for Northern Ireland from 1940. A Unionist. Elected for Antrim in February 1943 and sat until he was killed along with R.H. Bernays, MP for Bristol N., when their aircraft was lost on 23 January 1945. Served in Palestine with Royal Artillery 1918-19. Member of N. Ireland Parliament for the Carrick division of County Antrim 1943-45. Died 23 January 1945. [1945]

CAMPBELL, John Gordon Drummond. Tankenville, Kingston Hill. Athenaeum. S. of Col. Archibald Neil Campbell. B. at Dumdum, India 15 February 1864; m. 1908, Blanche, d. of Canon A.V. Thornton. Educ. at Charterhouse, and Corpus Christi Coll., Oxford. A Barrister, Lincoln's Inn 1890. H.M. Inspector of Schools 1892-1909.

Author of *Siam in the 20th Century*, and joint author of *William Haig Brown of Charterhouse*. A Coalition Unionist. Unsuccessfully contested the Mansfield division of Nottinghamshire in January 1910, and the Eccles division of Lancashire in December 1910. Elected for Kingston-on-Thames in December 1918 and sat until he retired in October 1922. Educational adviser to the King of Siam 1899-1901. Died 11 January 1935. [1922]

CAMPBELL-JOHNSTON, Malcolm. 18/19 Salisbury Place, Gloucester Place, London. Constitutional. S. of R.A. Campbell-Johnston, Esq., of Crowthorne, Wellington Coll. B. 14 April 1871; m. 1922, May Isabel Fisk, widow, d. of Belle Gray Taylor, of New York. Educ. at Marlborough, and abroad. Barrister-at-Law 1893; Transvaal bar 1902. Member London County Council 1922-34 and 1937-38; served with B.E.F. 1914-18. A Conservative. Unsuccessfully contested the Osgoldcross division of the W. Riding of Yorkshire in December 1910. Elected for East Ham S. in October 1931 and sat until he was defeated in November 1935. Died 12 March 1938. [1935]

CAMPION, William Robert. Danny, Hurstpierpoint, Sussex. Wellington. S. of Col. W.H. Campion, C.B., of Danny Park, Hassocks, Sussex, and Hon. Gertrude Brand, d. of 1st Visct. Hampden. B. 3 July 1870 in London; m. 1894, Katharine Mary, d. of the Rev. the Hon. William Byron. Educ. at Eton, and New Coll., Oxford. A J.P. for Sussex, and Honorary Lieut.-Col. 4th Battalion Royal Sussex Regiment. D.S.O. 1917. Dept.-Lieut. for Sussex. A Conservative. Unsuccessfully contested N. Worcestershire in 1906 and January 1910. First elected for the Lewes division of Sussex in June 1910 and sat until June 1924 when he was appointed Gov. of Western Australia. Retired 1931. K.C.M.G. 1924. Died 2 January 1951. [1924 2nd ed.]

CAPE, Thomas. 91 Harrington Road. Workington. S. of William Cape, Esq., Coal-Miner. B. 5 October 1868 at Cockermouth; m. 1890, Dinah, d. of Jonathan and Eleanor Hodgson, of Cockermouth. Educ.

55

at the endowed school, Great Broughton. Became a Coal-Miner when 13 years of age. Agent for Cumberland Miners' Association from 1916. A Labour Member. Sat for the Workington division of Cumberland from 1918 until he retired in June 1945. M.B.E. 1917; J.P. for Workington. Primitive Methodist local preacher. Died 6 November 1947.

[1945]

CAPORN, Arthur Cecil. 54 South Croxted Road, Dulwich, London. S. of Arthur Leeson Caporn, Esq., of Radcliffe-on-Trent and South Africa. B. 16 April 1884; m. May 1912, Dorothy Frances, d. of Richard Marriott, Esq., of The Park, Nottingham. Educ. at South African Coll. School, privately, and at Trinity Hall, Cambridge. Barrister-at-Law, Middle Temple 1907. A National Conservative. Elected for Nottingham W. in October 1931 and sat until he was defeated in November 1935. County Court Judge 1939-53. Died 25 November 1953. [1935]

CAREW, Charles Robert Sydenham. Warnicombe, Tiverton, Devon. Carlton, and Windham. S. of the Rev. R.B. Carew. B. 7 June 1853 at Collipriest, Tiverton, Devon; m. 1891, Muriel, eld. d. of Sir John Heathcote-Amory, Bart. (she died 4 March 1939). Educ. at Blundell's School, and St. John's Coll., Cambridge; B.A. J.P. for Devon. A Unionist. Elected for the Tiverton division of Devon in December 1915 and sat until he retired in October 1922. Died 23 March 1939. [1922]

CARLILE, Sir Edward Hildred, Bart. Ponsbourne Park, Nr. Hertford. Carlton. S. of Edward Carlile, Esq., of Richmond, Surrey. B. 10 July 1852 at Brixton; m. 1876, Isabella, d. of C. Hanbury, Esq., of Little Berkamsted, Hertfordshire (she died 1924). Educ. privately in England and Switzerland. A Capt. 2nd W. Yorkshire Yeomanry, and Lieut.-Col. 2nd Volunteer Battalion West Riding Regiment; Honorary Col. of the Battalion from 1906, T.D. 1912. A J.P. and Dept.-Lieut. for Hertfordshire and J.P. for the W. Riding of Yorkshire. Knighted 1911; created Bart. 1917. A Unionist. Unsuccessfully contested Huddersfield in 1900. First

elected for the St. Albans division of Hertfordshire in 1906 and sat until he resigned in 1919. Unsuccessfully contested Hertford in June 1921. C.B.E. 1919. High Sheriff of Hertfordshire 1922. Benefactor of Bedford Coll., London. Died 26 September 1942.

[1919]

CARR, William Theodore. Greystead, Carlisle. National. S. of Thomas William Carr, Biscuit Manufacturer. B. at Carlisle 30 July 1866; m. 1893, Edith, d. of Lieut.-Col. F.F.T. Hobbs, A.P.D. Educ. at the Old Hall School, Wellington, Shropshire, and Owens Coll., Manchester. A Biscuit Manufacturer and Flour Miller; Chairman and Managing Director of Carr and Company Limited, Carlisle, and Carr's Flour Mills, Carlisle. J.P. for the County of Cumberland 1903. A Coalition Liberal. Elected for Carlisle in December 1918 and sat until he was defeated in November 1922. C.B.E. 1920. Died 31 January 1931. [1922]

CARSON, Rt. Hon. Sir Edward Henry. 5 Eaton Place, London. Orion Bungalow, Birchington, Thanet. Carlton, and Garrick. S. of E.H. Carson, Esq., C.E., at one time Vice-President of the Royal Institute of Irish Architects. B. 1854; m. 1st, 1879, Sarah, d. of H. Persee Kirwan, Esq. (she died 1913); secondly, 1914, Ruby, d. of Col. Frewen. Educ. at Dublin University, M.A. Called to the Irish bar 1877, and to the Middle Temple 1893; Q.C. (Ireland) 1889. Was Solicitor-Gen. for Ireland from June to August 1892; Q.C. (England) 1894; PC. (Ireland) 1896; PC. 1905; Solicitor-Gen. 1900-05; Attorney-Gen. May to October 1915; First Lord of the Admiralty December 1916 to July 1917. Member of the War Cabinet without Portfolio July 1917 to January 1918. Bencher of the King's Inns and of the Middle Temple. Leader of the Irish Unionist Party from 1910-1921. A Unionist. Sat for Dublin University from 1892 to 1918. Elected for the Duncairn division of Belfast in December 1918 and sat until May 1921 when he was appointed Lord of Appeal in Ordinary; retired 1929. Knighted 1900. Created Baron Carson (Law life peerage) 1921. Died 22 October 1935.

[1921]

CARTER, Rei Alfred Deakin, O.B.E. Rushford, Rushford Park, Levenshulme, Manchester. S. of Joseph Carter, Esq., of Manchester. B. 1856; m. 1881, Annie, d. of W.H. Woodworth, Esq., of Southport (she died 1894). Alderman of Manchester City Council 1908-38 and prominent in the public life of Manchester. O.B.E. 1920 J.P. for Lancashire. Honorary Treasurer of the Lancashire Division of the National Unionist Association. Chairman Manchester Branch British Empire Union. A Coalition Unionist. Elected for the Withington division of Manchester in December 1918 and sat until he retired in October 1922. Died 4 Februry 1938. [1922]

CARTER, William. (I). 119 Foxhall Road, Sherwood Rise, Nottingham. S. of Thomas Carter, Esq., Brick Maker, of Mansfield. B. 12 June 1862. Was a Checkweighman at a local colliery. Member of Mansfield Town Council; member of the Local Appeal Tribunal; an official of the Nottinghamshire Miners' Association; member of the Executive of the Miners' Federation of Great Britain. J.P. for Nottinghamshire. A Labour Member. Elected for the Mansfield division of Nottinghamshire in December 1918 and sat until he was defeated in November 1922. Gen. Secretary of Nottinghamshire Miners' Association 1926-32. Died 29 February 1932. [1922]

CARTER, William. (II). 34 Lady Margaret Road, London. S. of James Burton Carter, Esq., of Sommercoats, Derbyshire. B. 12 August 1867; m. 30 December 1920, d. of Matthew Turnbull, Esq. Educ. at Annesley National School. N.U.R. organiser 1910-27; member of Metropolitan Water Board 1928; Manager of London County Council Schools from 1920; J.P. for London from 1925. Mayor of St. Pancras 1919-20. A Labour Member. Unsuccessfully contested E. Leyton in 1918 and 1922. Elected for St. Pancras S.W. in May 1929 and sat until he was defeated in October 1931. Died 18 August 1940. [1931 2nd ed.]

CARTLAND, John Ronald Hamilton. Poolbrook, Malvern. S. of Maj. Bertram Cartland. B. 3 January 1907 at Pershore.

Educ. at Charterhouse. A Unionist. Elected for the King's Norton division of Birmingham in November 1935 and sat until he was killed in action in May 1940. His death was not confirmed until January 1941 and the by-election was held on 8 May 1941. [1941]

CARVER, Col. William Henton. The Croft, North Cave, E. Yorkshire. Carlton, and Conservative. Yorkshire. S. of Benjamin Carver, Esq., of Polefield, Prestwich. B. 27 May 1868; m. 1st, 16 October 1895, Florence Rosalie, d. of Edward Philip Maxsted, Esq., of The Cliff, Hessle (she died 5 February 1937); secondly; 1955, Veronica, d. of the Rev. Charles Moor, of Kensington. Educ. at Uppingham. President of Hull Chamber of Commerce 1925-26; Dept.-Lieut., J.P., and County Alderman for the E. Riding of Yorkshire. A Director of London and North Eastern Railway Company and of Wilson's Brewery, Manchester. Maj. 3rd K.O.Y.L.I. and 10th Service Battalion E. Yorkshire Regiment. Served in France etc. 1914-19. Honorary Col. East Yorkshire Regiment. A Conservative. Elected for the Howdenshire division of the E. Riding of Yorkshire in November 1926 and sat until he retired in June 1945. Died 28 January 1961. [1945]

CARY, Robert Archibald. Continued in House after 1945: full entry in Volume IV.

CASEY, Thomas Worrall. 101 Burngreave Road, Sheffield. S. of William and Jemima Ann Casey. B. 13 October 1869 at Intake, Sheffield; m. 1st, 1894; secondly, Gladys. General Secretary of the Winding and General Engineers' Society, and took an active part in Sheffield Labour Politics. J.P. for Sheffield. A Coalition Liberal. Elected for the Attercliffe division of Sheffield in December 1918 and sat until he was defeated in November 1922. Unsuccessfully contested Ilkeston in December 1923 and Gloucester in May 1929 as a Liberal, and Rotherham in November 1935 as a Liberal National. Methodist local preacher for 60 years. Member of Mexborough Urban District Council for 6 years. Died 29 November 1949. [1922]

57

CASSELLS, Thomas. Thornlea, Ladiesmill, Falkirk. S. of John Cassells, Esq., Solicitor, of Hamilton. B. 7 August 1902; m. 2 February 1928, Margaret Adams Dick, d. of John Cassells, Esq., Chief Magistrate of Hamilton. Educ. at Hamilton Academy, and at the Universities of Edinburgh and Glasgow; McRarlane's Scholarship in Law, Glasgow University. Admitted a Solicitor in 1926. Councillor of Falkirk Burghs from 1928, and Dean of Guild; member of Stirling County Council and Asylum Board; Solicitor to Scottish Trade Union; Specialist in Law of Workmen's Compensation and Employers' Liability. He travelled extensively. A Labour Member. Unsuccessfully contested Dumbartonshire in November 1935. Elected for Dumbartonshire in March 1936 and sat until 1941 when he was appointed Sheriff Substitute of Inverness, Elgin and Nairn. Died 16 June 1944.   [1941]

CASSELS, James Dale, K.C. 28 Wimbledon Park Road, London. 3 Hare Court, Temple, London. Forest Row, Sussex. S. of Robert Cassels, Esq., Civil Servant. B. 22 March 1877; m. 1st, 1900, Alice Jessie, d. of Josiah Stone, Esq. (she died 1904); secondly, 26 August 1906, Bertha Frances, d. of Alfred Terry, Esq., Civil Servant (she died 1957); thirdly, 1958, Mrs. Deodora Croft, O.B.E., widow of Col. C.M. Croft. Educ. at Westminster City School. Barrister-at-Law, Middle Temple 1908; K.C. February 1923. Bencher 1929. Member of the Bar Council. Recorder of Guildford 1927-29, for Brighton from 1929 to 1939. Served with R.A.S.C. in France and Germany 1916-19; Capt. General List. A Conservative. Sat for Leyton W. November 1922-May 1929, when he was defeated. Elected for Camberwell N.W. in October 1931 and sat until he retired in October 1935. A Journalist until 1911, a Sub-editor on *Morning Post.* Knighted 1939. Judge of King's (later Queen's) Bench Division 1939-61. Treasurer of Middle Temple 1947. Died 7 February 1972.   [1935]

CASTLEREAGH, Edward Charles Stewart Robert Vane-Tempest-Stewart, Visct. 101 Park Street, London. Ramsbeck, Ullswater, Penrith. Brown House, Worplesdon Hill, Woking. Carlton, Turf, and White's. S. of Charles, 7th Marq. of Londonderry, K.G. B. 18 November 1902; m. 31 October 1931, Romaine, d. of Maj. Boyce Combe (she died 1951) Educ. at Eton, and Christ Church, Oxford, B.A. Assistant Managing Director Londonderry Collieries; J.P. for Durham and Co. Down and Dept.-Lieut. Co. Down. Honorary Attaché British Embassy, Rome 1924-25. A Conservative. Unsuccessfully contested Darlington in May 1929. Returned unopposed for Co. Down in October 1931, re-elected November 1935 and sat until he retired in June 1945. Styled Visct. Castlereagh 1915-49. Succeeded his father as Marq. or Londonderry in 1949. Member of Church Assembly 1950-55. Died 17 October 1955.   [1945]

CASTLE STEWART, Arthur Stuart, Earl (Irish Peerage). 2 Hare Court, Temple, London. Old Lodge, Nutley, Uckfield. Stuart Hall, Stewartstown, Co. Tyrone. Carlton. 3rd s. of 6th Earl Castle Stewart. B. 6 August 1889; m. 16 December 1920, Eleanor Mary, d. of S.R.G. Guggenheim, Esq., of New York. Educ. at Charterhouse, and Trinity Coll., Cambridge. Succeeded his father in 1921. Served in France 1914-18. A Conservative. Elected for the Harborough division of Leicestershire in May 1929 and again in October 1931. Sat until he resigned in 1933. M.C. 1918. Styled Visct. Stuart from the death of his eld. bro. in 1915 until his father's death in 1921. Called to the bar, Inner Temple 1943. J.P. for Sussex. Died 5 November 1961.   [1933]

CAUTLEY, Sir Henry Strother, Bart., K.C. 4 Brick Court, Temple, London. 33 Montagu Square, London. Buxhalls, Lindfield, Sussex. Carlton, and Oxford & Cambridge. S. of Henry Cautley, Esq., of Bramley, near Leeds, and Mary Ellen, d. of Thomas Strother, Esq., of Killinghall, Yorkshire. B. 9 December 1863; m. 1 October 1902, Alice Bohun, d. of B.H.C. Fox, Esq., J.P., of Woodhouse Eaves, Leicestershire. Educ. at Charterhouse; Scholar, King's Coll., Cambridge, Scholar and first class Math. Tripos 1884. A Barrister-at-Law, Middle Temple 1886. Bencher 1925. Practised in London and on the N.E. Circuit, and was Author of two law works. Recorder of Sunderland 1918-35. Chairman of East Sussex Quarter Sessions from 1927 and member of East Sussex County Council 1927. K.C. 1919. Created Bart. 1924. A Conservative. Unsuccessfully contested Dewsbury in 1892 and 1895. Sat for E. Leeds from 1900 to 1906, when he was defeated. Sat for the East Grinstead division of Sussex from January 1910 until June 1936 when he was created Baron Cautley. Died 21 September 1946.   [1936]

CAVENDISH-BENTINCK, Lord Henry.
16 Queen Anne's Gate, London. Underley Hall, Kirkby Lonsdale. Carlton, and Brooks's. S. of Lieut.-Gen. A. Cavendish-Bentinck. B. 28 May 1863; m. 27 January 1892, Lady Olivia Taylour, d. of the Earl of Bective. Educ. at Eton, and Christ Church, Oxford. Was raised to the rank of a Duke's son in 1880 after his half bro. had succeeded as 6th Duke of Portland. Lieut.-Col. Derbyshire Yeomanry; served in South Africa 1900 and Gallipoli 1915. Lord-Lieut. and Alderman County of Westmorland. Member of London County Council for W. Marylebone from 1907-10. A Conservative. Unsuccessfully contested N.W. Norfolk in 1885. Sat for N.W. Norfolk from 1886-92, when he was defeated. Sat for S. Nottingham from 1895-1906, when he was again defeated. Elected for S. Nottingham in January 1910 and sat until he was defeated in May 1929. Died 6 October 1931.   [1929]

CAYZER, Sir Charles William, Bart.
86 Eaton Square, London. Kinpurnie Castle, Angus. Carlton, and Cavalry. S. of Sir Charles Cayzer, 2nd Bart., of Gartmore. B. 6 January 1896; m. 1 October 1919, Beatrice Eileen, d. of James Meakin, Esq., of Westwood Manor, Staffordshire, and of the Countess Sondes. Educ. at Repton, Oriel Coll., Oxford, and Royal Military Coll., Sandhurst. A Director of Cayzer, Irvine and Company Limited. Lieut. 19th Royal Hussars 1915-19; served in France 1916-18. Succeeded as Bart. 1917. Member of Royal Company of Archers. Additional Private Secretary (unpaid) to the Rt. Hon. Robert Munro, Secretary for Scotland 1920-21. A Conservative. Sat for the City of Chester division of Cheshire from November 1922 until he died on 18 February 1940.   [1940]

CAYZER, Maj. Sir Herbert Robin, Bart.
2 St. Mary Axe, London. Tylney Hall, Nr. Basingstoke. Lanfine, Ayrshire. Cavalry, and Carlton. S. of Sir Charles Cayzer, 1st Bart., of Gartmore. B. 23 July 1881; m. 18 January 1911, Freda Penelope, d. of Col. W.H. Rathbone, R.E. Educ. at Rugby. Vice-Chairman and later Chairman of Clan Line Steamers and of Cayzer, Irvine and Company Limited; Director of the Houston Line Limited, Scottish Shire Line Limited, English Coaling Company Limited, London, General Shipowners Association, the Liverpool Steamship Owners Association, and the Glasgow Shipowners Association. 2nd in Command Q.O.R. Glasgow Yeomanry 1914; commanded 24th Division Mt. Troops in France. J.P. for the County and City of Glasgow and for Hampshire; Dept.-Lieut. for Hampshire and for Sussex. Created Bart. 1924. Member of Council Chamber of Shipping. A Conservative. Elected for Portsmouth S. in December 1918 and November 1922, and resigned that seat in December 1922. Re-elected for Portsmouth S. in August 1923 and sat until June 1939 when he was created Baron Rotherwick. President of Chamber of Shipping 1941-42, of Institute of Marine Engineers 1949-50. Died 16 March 1958.   [1939]

CAZALET, Col. Victor Alexander, M.C.
Great Swifts, Cranbrook, Kent. Brooks's, Bath, and M.C.C. S. of William Cazalet, Esq., and Maud, d. of Sir John Heron-Maxwell, 7th Bart., of Springhall. B. 27 December 1896. Educ. at Eton, and Christ Church, Oxford. Capt. Household Cavalry and Household Battalion. Served in France 1916-18 and afterwards on Staff of Supreme War Council, Versailles; also on Staff in Siberia 1919. Liaison officer with Polish Forces 1940-43. Private Secretary to Sir Philip Cunliffe-Lister when President of the Board of Trade 1922-23, and his Parliamentary Private Secretary 1924-27; Parliamentary Private Secretary to the Rt. Hon. J.H. Thomas, Secretary of State for the Dominions 1931. A Conservative. Unsuccessfully contested Chippenham division of

59

Wiltshire in December 1923. Elected for the Chippenham division in October 1924 and sat until he was killed on active service in an air crash while travelling with Gen. Sikorski on 4 July 1943.   [1943]

CAZALET-KEIR, Thelma. See KEIR, Thelma Cazalet.

CECIL, Rt. Hon. Lord Edgar Algernon Robert. See CECIL, Rt. Hon. Lord Robert.

CECIL, Rt. Hon. Sir Evelyn, G.B.E. 2 Cadogan Square, London. Lytchett Heath, Poole. Athenaeum, and Carlton. S. of Lord Eustace Cecil and grand-s. of the 2nd Marq. of Salisbury. B. 30 May 1865; m. 16 February 1898, Hon. Alicia Amherst, C.B.E., d. of 1st Lord Amherst of Hackney. Educ. at Eton, and New Coll., Oxford, B.A. 1887, M.A. 1890. Barrister-at Law, Inner Temple 1889, and joined the Western Circuit. Called to N.S.W. bar (*Hon. Causa*) 1926. Was Assistant Private Secretary to Lord Salisbury as Prime Minister 1891-92 and 1895-1902, and a member of the London School Board from 1894 to 1899. Was the last Englishman to confer with Presidents Kruger and Steyn before the South African War 1899. Chairman of Select Committee Foreign Steamship Subsidies and their effect on British Trade 1901-02, and of Eastern Mail Committee 1904. Member of permanent Commission of International Railway Congress from 1905; Executive committee 1920. Delegate at Washington 1905, Berne 1910, Rome 1922, London 1925. Member of Public Retrenchment Committee 1915 and of Second Chamber Conference 1918. Knight of Justice of St. John of Jerusalem and Secretary-Gen. of the Order 1915-21, and Vice-Chairman of the Joint War Committee with British Red Cross Society. Chairman of Selected Committee on the Telephone Service 1921-22. Member of Royal Commission on Honours 1922 and of Privy Council Honours Committee 1923-24. Introduced and was Chairman of Select Committee on the Judicial Proceedings (Regulation of Reports) Bill 1923, re-introduced 1924-25, passed 1926. PC. 1917. G.B.E. 1922. Author of a history of *Primogeniture* 1894, *On the Eve of the War* 1900.

etc. A Conservative. Sat for the Hertford division of Hertfordshire from 1898 to 1900, and for Aston Manor from 1900 to 1918. Sat for the Aston division of Birmingham from December 1918 until he retired in May 1929. Created Baron Rockley 1934. Chairman of Royal Commission on Safety and Health in Coal Mines 1935-38. Died 1 April 1941.   [1929]

CECIL, Rt. Hon. Lord Hugh Richard Heathcote. 21 Arlington Street, London. Hatfield House, Hertfordshire. Carlton, and Junior Carlton. S. of the 3rd Marq. of Salisbury. B. 14 October 1869. Educ. at Eton, and University Coll., Oxford; M.A. 1894; Fellow of Hertford Coll., Oxford from 1891. D.C.L. (Oxon); LL.D. Edinburgh and Cambridge. Private Secretary to his father when Secretary of State for Foreign Affairs; member of the Mesopotamia Commission 1916. Lieut. Royal Flying Corps 1915. PC. 1918. A Conservative. Sat for Greenwich from 1895 to 1906, when he was defeated standing as a Free Trader. Sat for Oxford University from January 1910 until January 1937 when he was appointed Provost of Eton; retired 1944. Created Baron Quickswood 1941. Died 10 December 1956.

[1936]

CECIL, Rt. Hon. Lord Robert. 15 Grosvenor Crescent, London. Gale, Chelwood Gate, East Grinstead, Sussex. Carlton, and St. Stephen's. 3rd s. of 3rd Marq. of Salisbury. B. 1864 in London; m. 1889, Lady Eleanor Lambton, d. of 2nd Earl of Durham. Educ. at Eton, and University Coll., Oxford. A Barrister; called at the Middle Temple 1887; Q.C. 1899; Chancellor and Vicar-Gen. of York from 1915. Under-Secretary and Assistant Secretary for Foreign Affairs May 1915 to November 1918; Minister of Blockade, February 1916 to July 1918. Chancellor of Birmingham University 1918; Honorary LL.D. Liverpool University 1920. Honorary D.C.L. Edinburgh University 1921. British delegate to League of Nations Commission Peace Conference 1919. Chief British representative on Supreme Economic Council 1919. Appointed as one of South Africa's representatives at first and second Assembly meeting of League of Nations, Geneva. PC.

1915. Author of *Principles of Commercial Law, Essays of Lord Salisbury*, 2 volumes, etc. An Independent Conservative and Free Trader. Sat for E. Marylebone from 1906 to January 1910, when he unsuccessfully contested Blackburn. Defeated in the Wisbech division of Cambridgeshire in December 1910. First elected for the Hitchin division of Hertfordshire in November 1911 and sat until he retired in 1923. Created Visct. Cecil of Chelwood 1923. Lord Privy Seal May 1923-January 1924. Chancellor of Duchy of Lancaster November 1924-August 1927, when he resigned over the disarmament issue. President of League of Nations Union 1923-45. Rector of Aberdeen University 1924-27. Nobel Peace Prize 1937. Companion of Honour 1956. Died 24 November 1958. [1923]

CHADWICK, Sir Robert Burton. 41 Bramham Gardens, London. 31 St. Mary Axe, London. Carlton, Royal Thames Yacht, and 1900. S. of Joseph Chadwick, Esq., of Liverpool. B. 20 June 1869; m. 1st, 8 February 1903, Catherine Barbara, d. of Thomas Williams, Esq (she died 1935); secondly, 1936, Norah Irene, d. of A.J. Gibbs, Esq. Educ. at Birkenhead. Head of the firm of Joseph Chadwick and Sons, Liverpool and London; and Chadwick, Weir and Company, Buenos Ayres. Was Director-Gen. of Stores and Transport, Ministry of Munitions; member of Disposals Board and numerous Government Committees; member of the Mersey Docks and Harbour Board; Chairman of the Liverpool Shipowners Association, etc. Spent ten years at sea in early life. Served in the South African War 1900-01, Duke of Lancaster's Yeomanry. Royal Humane Society's Medal for Saving Life at Sea. Knighted 1920. Capt. R.N.R. Parliamentary Secretary to Board of Trade November 1924-January 1928. A Conservative. Elected for Barrow-in-Furness in December 1918 and for Wallasey in November 1922. Sat until he retired in October 1931. Created Bart. 1935. Assumed the surname of Burton-Chadwick in lieu of Chadwick in 1936. Representative of the Ministry of War Transport in Argentina, Uruguay and Chile 1939-46. Died 21 May 1951. [1931 2nd ed.]

CHALLEN, Charles. Continued in House after 1945 : full entry in Volume IV.

CHALMERS, John Rutherford. See RUTHERFORD, John Rutherford.

CHAMBERLAIN, Rt. Hon. Arthur Neville, F.R.S. 10 Downing Street, London. Westbourne, Edgbaston, Birmingham. Carlton. S. of the Rt. Hon. Joseph Chamberlain and Florence, d. of Timothy Kenrick, Esq. B. 18 March 1869 at Birmingham; m. 5 January 1911, Annie Vere, d. of Maj. W.U. Cole and Mrs. Herbert Studd. Educ. at Rugby, and Mason Coll., Birmingham. Honorary LL.D., Birmingham, Bristol, Cambridge and Leeds; Honorary D.C.L. Oxford; Honorary D.Litt., Reading: Elected to Birmingham City Council in 1911; Lord Mayor 1915-16. Director-Gen. of National Service December 1916-August 1917. Postmaster-Gen. October 1922-March 1923. Paymaster-Gen. February-March 1923. Minister of Health March-August 1923, November 1924-June 1929, and August-November 1931 in National Government. Chancellor of the Exchequer August 1923 to January 1924, and November 1931-May 1937; Prime Minister and First Lord of the Treasury May 1937-May 1940; Chairman of Conservative Party June 1930-April 1931, and Leader of the Conservative Party May 1937-October 1940. Lord President of the Council May-October 1940. PC. 1922. F.R.S. 1938. A Conservative. MP for the Ladywood division of Birmingham from December 1918-May 1929, and for the Edgbaston division of Birmingham from May 1929 until his death on 9 November 1940. [1940]

CHAMBERLAIN, Rt. Hon. Sir Joseph Austen, K.G. 24 Egerton Terrace, London. Carlton, and United University. Eld. s. of the Rt. Hon. Joseph Chamberlain, MP, and Harriet, d. of Archibald Kenrick, Esq., of Birmingham. B. 16 October 1863; m. 21 July 1906, Ivy Muriel, G.B.E., d. of Col. H.L. Dundas. Educ. at Rugby, and Trinity Coll., Cambridge, M.A.; studied at the Ecole des Sciences Politiques, Paris, and at Berlin; D.C.L. Oxford, Honorary LL.D. Birmingham, Cambridge, Sheffield, Glasgow 1926, Toronto 1928, and Lyons 1936. Civil Lord of the Admiralty 1895-1900; Financial Secretary to the Treasury 1900-02. PC. 1902. Postmaster-Gen. 1902-03, and Chancellor of the Exchequer October 1903 to December 1905. Secretary of State for India May 1915 to July 1917 when he resigned. Member of War Cabinet without Portfolio from April 1918 to January 1919; Chancellor of Exchequer January 1919 to March 1921, and Lord Privy Seal and Leader of the Commons March 1921 to October 1922. Secretary of State for Foreign Affairs and Dept. Leader of the House of Commons November 1924-June 1929. First Lord of the Admiralty in National Government August-October 1931. Chairman of Royal Commission on Indian Finance and Currency 1913. K.G. 1925. A Conservative. Sat for E. Worcestershire from March 1892 to July 1914, and for W. Birmingham from July 1914 until his death on 16 March 1937. Leader of the Conservative Party in the House of Commons March 1921-October 1922. Rector of Glasgow University 1925-28. Chancellor of Reading University 1935-37. Died 16 March 1937.   [1937]

CHANNON, Henry. Continued in House after 1945: full entry in Volume IV.

CHAPMAN, Allan. Carlton, and Pratt's. New Edinburgh. S. of H. Williams Chapman, Esq. B. 1897; m. Beatrice, d. of Edward Cox, Esq., of Cardean. Educ. at Queens' Coll., Cambridge. R.F.C. and R.A.F. Parliamentary Private Secretary to Rt. Hon. Walter Elliot when Secretary of State for Scotland February 1938 and when Minister of Health May-November 1938, to the Rt. Hon. Sir John Anderson, Lord Privy Seal November 1938, when Secretary of State Home Affairs and Minister for Home Security September 1939-October 1940, and when Lord President of the Council October 1940-March 1941; Assistant Postmaster-Gen. March 1941. Joint Parliamentary Under-Secretary of State for Scotland March 1942-July 1945. A Conservative. Elected for the Rutherglen division of Lanarkshire in November 1935 and sat until he was defeated in July 1945. Died 7 January 1966.   [1945]

CHAPMAN, Col. Robert, C.M.G., D.S.O. Undercliff, Cleadon, Nr. Sunderland. Constitutional. County, Durham. Union, Newcastle-upon-Tyne. S. of Henry Chapman, Esq., of Westoe Village, South Shields. B. 3 March 1880; m. 10 November 1909, Hélène Paris d. of James George Mac-Gowan, Esq., of Paris. Educ. at South Shields High School, and at University of London; B.A. Fellow of Institute of Chartered Accountants; Col. R.A., T.F. 2nd Lieut. 3rd Durham Artillery Volunteers 1900. Served in France 3 years. Commanded 4th Durham Howitzer Battalion and 250th Brigade R.F.A. D.S.O. 1916; C.M.G. 1918. Chevalier of Legion of Honour. Mayor of South Shields 1931 and member of Borough Council 1921-52. A National Conservative. Elected for the Houghton-le-Spring division of Durham in October 1931 and sat until he was defeated in November 1935. Army Welfare Officer for County Durham 1939-52. Church Commissioner and Member of Church Assembly. High Sheriff of County Durham 1940-41 and Vice-Lieut. 1946-58. Knighted 1950; Created Bart. 1958. Died 31 July 1963.   [1935]

CHAPMAN, Sir Samuel. House of Commons, London. B. 1860. Chairman of Messrs. Scott, Son and Company, London, Edinburgh and Glasgow. J.P. for the Co. of Perth; member of Perthshire Education Authority; Chairman Political Committee Scottish Conservative Club. Knighted in 1920 for services in connection with the Perth and Perthshire Prisoners of War Fund. A Conservative. Unsuccessfully contested Perth city in 1906 and January 1910 and Greenock in December 1910 and 1918. Sat for Edinburgh S. from November 1922 until he retired in June 1945. Died 29 April 1947.   [1945]

CHAPPLE, Dr. William Allan. 1 Horseferry Road, London. National Liberal. S. of J.C. Chapple, Esq. B. in New Zealand 1864; m. 1891, Sarah, only d. of Thomas Turnbull, Esq., F.R.I.B.A. Educ. at Otago University. M.D., Ch.B., M.R.C.S., D.P.H. Author of *The Fertility of the Unfit*, *The Evils of Alcohol*, *The Art of Physical Development*, *Fiji—Its Problems and Resources*. A Liberal. Sat for Stirlingshire from January 1910-18 when he unsuccessfully contested Stirlingshire E. and Clackmannan. Elected for Dumfriesshire in November 1922 and again in December 1923 but was defeated there in October 1924. Member of the New Zealand House of Representatives for Tuapeka for a few months in 1908. Died 19 October 1936.   [1924 2nd ed.]

CHARLETON, Henry Charles. 15 St. Andrews Drive, Stanmore. S. of Henry Charleton, Esq., Engine-driver. B. at Kentish Town, 1 March 1870; m. 11 July 1897, Louisa Jane, d. of Charles Alcock, Esq., of Kentish Town. Educ. at Mansfield Place Board School, and Working Men's Coll., St. Pancras. Engine-driver, Midland Railway. Executive member N.U.R. 1917-19 and 1923. Member Locomotive Conciliation Board 1907-21; Chairman Sectional Council (Locomotive) M.R. 1921-23. J.P. for London; Alderman London County Council 1934-36. A Gov. of Queen Mary's (Roehampton) Hospital and of Working Men's Coll. Parliamentary Private Secretary to Arthur Ponsonby, Under-Secretary for Dominions June 1929. Labour (English) Whip 1935. A Labour Member. Elected for S. Leeds in November 1922 and sat until he was defeated in October 1931. Re-elected for S. Leeds in November 1935 and sat until he retired in June 1945. Chairman of Estimates Committee 1929-30. Junior Lord of the Treasury March-August 1931. Died 8 October 1959.   [1945]

CHARTERIS, Brigadier-Gen. John Waterside, Ecclefechan. United Service. S. of Professor Matthew Charteris, of Glasgow University. B. 8 January 1877; m. 2 October 1913, Noel, d. of C.D. Hodgson, Esq., of The Hallams, Shanley Green. Educ. at Merchiston School and Royal Military Academy, Woolwich. Joined R.E. 1896; retired 1922. A Conservative. Unsuccessfully contested Dumfriesshire in December 1923. Elected for Dumfriesshire in October 1924 and sat until he was defeated in May 1929. D.S.O. 1915; C.M.G. 1919. Died 4 February 1946.   [1929]

CHATER, Daniel. Continued in House after 1945: full entry in Volume IV

CHATFEILD-CLARKE, Sir Edgar. Oakfield, Wootton, Isle of Wight. Reform. S. of Thomas Chatfeild-Clarke, Esq., F.R.I.B.A., J.P., of Oakfield, Wootton, Isle of Wight, and Ellen, d. of J.S. Nettlefold, Esq., of Birmingham. B. 17 February 1863. Unmarried. Educ. at King's Coll. School, and in Dresden. A J.P. for Hampshire, and Dept.-Lieut. and County Councillor for the Isle of Wight. Member of Isle of Wight Education Standing Committee and Advisory Committee on appointment of Magistrates. A Liberal. Elected for the Isle of Wight in November 1922 and sat until he retired in November 1923. Knighted 1913. Died 16 April 1925.   [1923]

CHETWYND TALBOT, Gustavus Arthur. See TALBOT, Gustavus Arthur.

CHEYNE, Sir William Watson, Bart., C.B., K.C.M.G. House of Commons, London. Leagarth, Fetlar, Shetland. S. of Andrew Cheyne and Eliza M.B. Watson. B. 14 December 1852 at Hobart Town, Tasmania; m. 1st, 1887, Mary, d. of the Rev. C. Servante (she died 1894) ; secondly, 1894, Margaret, d. of George Smith, Esq., S.S.C. (she died 1922). Educ. at Aberdeen Grammar School, and University, and Edinburgh University. A Surgeon, began study at Edinburgh 1871; Assistant Surgeon to King's College Hospital, London 1879; Surgeon to that hospital 1886. Professor of Surgery 1890; of Clinical Surgery 1901; M.B., C.M., F.R.C.S., F.R.S., D.Sc. (Oxford), LL.D. (Edinburgh). President of the Royal College of Surgeons 1914-17. Consulting Surgeon to the British Army in South African campaign; Surgeon-Gen., later Surgeon Rear-Admiral R.N. Held many other appointments. Author of many papers and books, chiefly on bacteriology and surgical matters. A Coalition Member (Conservative). Elected for Edinburgh and St. Andrews Universities in August 1917, and for the Scottish Universities in December 1918. Sat until he retired in October 1922. C.B. 1900; created Bart. 1908; K.C.M.G. 1916. Lord-Lieut. of

Orkney and Shetland 1919-30. Died 19 April 1932. [1922]

CHICHESTER, Lieut.-Col. Robert Peel Dawson Spencer. Moyola Park, Castle Dawson, Ireland. Guards, Carlton, and Junior United Service. S. of the Rt. Hon. Lord S. Chichester, 3rd s. of 4th Marq. of Donegall, and Mary, only child of Col. Dawson, MP. B. 13 August 1873 at Castle Dawson, Ireland; m. 1901, Dehra Kerr-Fisher, (later Dame Dehra Parker), MP for Co. Londonderry and Londonderry City in N. Ireland Parliament, and only child of James Kerr-Fisher, Esq., of the Manor House, Kilrea, Co. Londonderry and Chicago, U.S.A. Educ. at Eton. Lieut.-Col. (retired) 14th Royal Irish Rifles and 6th Middlesex Regiment; Maj. 8th Irish Guards. J.P. County Antrim, County Londonderry and County Donegal. A Unionist. Returned unopposed for S. Londonderry in August 1921 and sat until he died on 10 December 1921. [1922]

CHILCOTT, Lieut.-Commander Sir Harry Warden Stanley. 36 St. James's Street, London. The Salterns, Warsash, Hampshire. Carlton. S. of W.W. Chilcott, Esq., of Chilcott, Somerset. B. 11 March 1871. Unmarried. Director of the General Oil Conservancy Limited, and various other companies in the City of London. Served in France with R.N.A.S. 1915-17. Undertook special foreign missions for the Government 1917-22. Foreign Political Secretary Law Officers of the Crown 1918-22. Member of Sub-committee dealing with the Punishment for Breaches of the Laws of War. J.P. for Hampshire. Knighted 1922. A Conservative. Member for the Walton division of Liverpool from December 1918 until he retired in May 1929. Died 8 March 1942. [1929]

CHILD, Col. Sir Smith Hill, Bart., C.B., C.M.G., D.S.O., M.V.O. Stallington Hall, Staffordshire. 2 Ryder Street, London. Guards, and Turf. S. of John George and Helen Child. B. 19 September 1880 at Hopesay, Shropshire; m. 1925, Barbara, d. of Ernest Villiers, Esq. Educ. at Eton, and Christ Church, Oxford. 3rd Royal Scots (M.) 1899-1900; Irish Guards 1901-1909; R.F.A. (T.) 1910. Served in the South African and European wars; Col. Commanding Royal Artillery 46th North Midland Division (T.). A Coalition Unionist. Elected for the Stone division of Staffordshire in December 1918 and sat until he retired in October 1922. Succeeded as Bart. 1896. Gentleman Usher to King George V 1927; Dept.-Master of the Household 1929-36; Master of the Household 1936-41. Extra Equerry to King George VI as to Queen Elizabeth II 1937-58. Died 11 November 1958. [1922]

CHORLTON, Alan Ernest Leofric, C.B.E. 55 Lower Belgrave Street, London. Junior Carlton, and St. Stephen's. S. of Thomas Chorlton, Esq., of Audenshaw, Lancashire. B. 24 February 1874; m. 1st, 1907, Louise, d. of W. De'Ady, Esq. (she died 1932); secondly, 1939, Ivy Mary, d. of Albert Curling, Esq. Educ. at Manchester Technical School, and University. President I.Mch.E., M.Inst.C.E., M.Inst.E.E.; Fellow Royal Aeronautical Society. C.B.E. 1917. A National Conservative. Unsuccessfully contested the Platting division of Manchester in May 1929. Elected for the Platting division in October 1931, and for Bury in November 1935. Sat until he retired in June 1945. Died 6 October 1946. [1945]

CHOTZNER, Alfred James. 3 Courtenay Terrace, Hove, Sussex. Carlton, Union, Oriental, and Ranelagh. S. of Dr. J. Chotzner, of Belfast. B. 28 March 1873; m. 1st, 1906, Ethel Kathleen Lan, d. of I. Davis, Esq. (she died 1924); secondly, 1930, Beatrice Violet, d. of J.P. Lash, Esq. Educ. at Harrow, and St. John's Coll., Cambridge, B.A. 1895. Entered I.C.S. 1895; District and Sessions Judge, East Bengal and Assam 1909; Judge of the High Court of Calcutta 1924-28, when he retired. A Conservative. Elected for the Upton division of West Ham in October 1931 and sat until he resigned in 1934. Died 12 February 1958. [1934]

CHRISTIE, James Archibald. Framingham Manor, Norfolk. S. of J.H.B. Christie, Esq. B. 1873; m. 1909, Mabel, d. of Canon

Sedgwick (she died 1939). Educ. at Charterhouse, and Magdalen Coll., Oxford. A Barrister-at-Law. J.P. for Norfolk. Alderman, Norfolk County Council. A Conservative. Elected for S. Norfolk in October 1924 and sat until he retired in June 1945. Died 16 October 1958. [1945]

CHURCH, Maj. Archibald George, D.S.O., M.C. 25 Victoria Street, London. University of London, 1917, and National Labour. S. of Thomas Church, Esq., Compositor. B. 7 September 1886; m. 1st 21 December 1912, Gladys, d. of Albert Hunter, Esq; secondly, 1945, Katherine Mary Strange, d. of T.S. Wickham, Esq. Educ. at Elementary and Secondary Schools, and at University Coll., London; B.Sc. A Schoolmaster 1909-14; author and writer. Served with Siege Artillery, Air Force, Field Artillery and Infantry 1914-19; M.C. 1918; D.S.O. 1920; retired as Maj.; Order of St. Vladimir. Secretary Association of Scientific Workers 1920-31; Parliamentary Private Secretary to the Rt. Hon. Sidney Webb 1924. Member East African Parliamentary Commission 1924; Commission on Education in the Colonies 1925; of Industrial Health Research Board, and of Essex Agricultural Commission. Joint Secretary Co-ordinating Committee for Government Joint Industrial Councils; member League of Nations Union Council. Parliamentary Private Secretary to Rt. Hon. Tom Shaw, Secretary of State for War June 1929-January 1931. A Labour Member. Unsuccessfully contested the Spelthorne division of Middlesex in November 1922. Elected for E. Leyton in December 1923, defeated in October 1924. Elected for Wandsworth Central in May 1929 and sat until October 1931 when he unsuccessfully contested London University as a National Labour candidate. Unsuccessfully contested E. Bristol in November 1935 and Derby in July 1936 for the National Labour Party and S. Tottenham as an Independent National in July 1945. Secretary of British Science Guide 1931-33. Chairman of Raven Oil Company 1937-51. Died 23 August 1954. [1931 2nd ed.]

CHURCHILL, Randolph Federick Edward Spencer, M.B.E. Ickleford House, Hitchin. S. of The Rt. Hon. Winston Spencer Churchill, MP. B. 28 May 1911; m. 1st, October 1939, Hon. Pamela Digby, d. of 11th Baron Digby (divorced 1946); secondly, 1948, June, d. of Rex Osborne, Esq., of Malmesbury (divorced 1961). Lieut. 4th Hussars Supp. R. of O. A Conservative. Unsuccessfully contested the Wavertree division of Liverpool as an Independent Conservative in February 1935, and as a Conservative the W. Toxteth division of Liverpool in November 1935, and Ross and Cromarty division of Inverness-shire and Ross and Cromarty in 1936. Returned unopposed for Preston in September 1940 and sat until he was defeated in July 1945. M.B.E. 1944. Unsuccessfully contested the Devonport division of Plymouth in February 1950 and October 1951. Styled 'The Honourable' after his mother's elevation to the Peerage in 1965. Died 6 June 1968. [1945]

CHURCHILL, Rt. Hon. Sir Winston Leonard Spencer, K.G., O.M., C.H., F.R.S. 28 Hyde Park Gate, London. Chartwell, Westerham. Carlton, and Turf. S. of Rt. Hon. Lord Randolph Churchill, MP. B. 30 November 1874; m. 12 September 1908, Clementine, G.B.E., d. of Col. Sir Henry Hozier, K.C.B. Educ. at Harrow, and Sandhurst. Joined 4th Hussars 1895; served with Spanish forces in Cuba, with the Malakand field force, the Tirah Expedition, the Nile, in South African War, and with Royal Scots Fusiliers in France 1916. Under-Secretary of State for the Colonies 1905-08, President of the Board of Trade 1908-10, Home Secretary 1910-11, First Lord of the Admiralty 1911-15, Chancellor of Duchy of Lancaster 1915, Minister of Munitions 1917-19, Secretary of State for War and for Air 1919-21, Secretary of State for the Colonies 1921-22. Chancellor of the Exchequer November 1924-June 1929. First Lord of the Admiralty and Member of War Cabinet September 1939-May 1940. Prime Minister and Minister for Defence and First Lord of the Treasury May 1940-July 1945; Lord Warden of the Cinque Ports 1941-65. Grand Master of the Primrose League 1943. Prime Minister and First Lord of the

Treasury 1951-55, Minister of Defence 1951-52. PC. 1907. K.G. 1953; C.H. 1922; O.M. 1946. Unsuccessfully contested Oldham as a Conservative in July 1899 and elected there in 1900. Joined the Liberal Party in 1904 and sat until January 1906 when he was elected for N.W. Manchester. Unsuccessfully contested N.W. Manchester in April 1908, on his appointment as President of Board of Trade, but elected for Dundee in May 1908 and sat until he was defeated in November 1922. Unsuccessfully contested W. Leicester as a Liberal in December 1923 and the Abbey division of Westminster as a Constitutionalist, in opposition to Conservative and Liberal candidates, in March 1924. Elected for the Epping division of Essex in October 1924 as a Constitutionalist, with Liberal but not Conservative opposition, took the Conservative Whip and sat until July 1945 when he was elected for Woodford. Sat for Woodford until he retired in 1964. Leader of the Conservative Party October 1940-April 1955. Father of the House of Commons 1959-64. Died 24 January 1965.   [1964]

CHURCHMAN, Lieut.-Col. Sir Arthur Charles, Bart. 20 Prince's Gate, London. Abbey Oaks, Sproughton, Suffolk. Carlton, Junior Carlton, St. Stephen's, 1900, and Royal Automobile. S. of H.C. Churchman, Esq., of Ipswich. B. at Ipswich 7 September 1867; m. 1891, Edith, d. of J.A. Harvey, Esq. Educ. at Ipswich School, and privately. A Director and Dept. Chairman of the British American Tobacco Company Limited (resigned 11 July 1923). Mayor of Ipswich 1901; J.P. for Suffolk 1903; Lieut.-Col. Essex and Suffolk R.G.A. 1908-11; Lieut.-Col. 2-6 Battalion Suffolk Regiment 1914-17; Controller Mineral Oil Production Department 1917-18. Created Bart. 1917. A Conservative. Unsuccessfully contested Ipswich in January and December 1910. Sat for the Woodbridge division of Suffolk from July 1920 until he retired in May 1929. Created Baron Woodbridge 1932. Dept.-Lieut. of Suffolk, High Sheriff 1931-32. Died in South Africa 3 February 1949.
[1929]

CHUTER EDE, Rt. Hon. James. See EDE, Rt. Hon. James Chuter. Continued in House after 1945: full entry in Volume IV.

CLANCY, John Joseph. Courtown, Co. Sligo. Was arrested in May 1918 and interned in Usk prison. Released, then sentenced to three months imprisonment for unlawful assembly in April 1919. A Sinn Fein Member. Elected for N. Sligo in December 1918 but did not take his seat. Member of Dail for N. Sligo to 1921. Chairman of Sligo County Council. [1922]

CLARKE, Andrew Bathgate. 64 Campsie Road, Musselburgh, Midlothian. S. of John Clark, Esq., Butcher, of Edinburgh. B. 5 February 1868. Secretary of the Mid and East Lothian Miners Association 1919; prominent in the coal strike of 1921. A Labour Member. Unsuccessfully contested N. Midlothian in November 1922. Elected for N. Midlothian in December 1923 and sat until he was defeated in October 1924; re-elected in January 1929 and sat until he was defeated in May 1929. Once again defeated in 1931. President of Scottish Miners' Association 1932-40. Member of Musselburgh Town Council. J.P. for Midlothian. Died 1 February 1940.

[1924 2nd ed.]

CLARKE, Frank Edward. Canmore, 33 Park Crescent, Erith, Kent. St. Andrew's. S. of Herbert William Clarke, Esq., of Erith, Kent, Merchant and Accountant. B. 21 November 1886; m. 18 April 1914, Hilda Mary, d. of Harold Strickland, Esq., of Dartford. Educ. at Dartford Grammar School, and at the University of London. An Industrialist. Managing Director of Herbert W. Clarke and Sons (Erith) Limited; a Freeman of the Port of London; J.P., and County Councillor for Kent, Alderman 1938; Chairman of Erith Urban District Council Finance Committee. Commissioner of Boy Scout Movement for 21 years. Commodore of Erith Yacht Club. A Unionist. Elected for the Dartford division of Kent in October 1931 and again in November 1935. Sat until his death on 12 July 1938.   [1938]

CLARKE, John Smith. House of Commons, London. B. 1885. An Author, Journalist, and Lecturer. Member of Glasgow City Council 1926-56; J.P. for Glasgow; Fellow of Society of Antiquaries. Scotland's contributor to *Forward* and other periodicals. A Trustee of the National Gallery from 1930. Also a circus trainer and performer. A Labour Member. Elected for the Maryhill division of Glasgow in May 1929 and sat until he was defeated in October 1931. Died 30 January 1959.
[1931 2nd ed.]

CLARKE, Ralph Stephenson. Continued in House after 1945: full entry in Volume IV.

CLARRY, Sir Reginald George. 5 Chandos Court, Caxton Street, London. Carlton, and Royal Automobile. S. of George Clarry, Esq., F.C.I.S. B. 24 July 1882; m. 1906, Laura Marian, d. of Edmund Sapey, Esq. Educ. at Marling School, Stroud, and Cardiff University. A Civil Engineer, specialising in Carbonisation of Coal. A Director of several companies; Managing Director Duffryn Steel and Tin Plate Works, Morriston. F.C.I.S.; Knight Bach. 1936. A Conservative. Sat for Newport, Monmouthshire from October 1922 until 1929, when he was defeated. Returned for Newport in 1931 and sat until his death on 17 January 1945. [1945]

CLAY, Lieut.-Col. Rt. Hon. Herbert Henry Spender. See SPENDER-CLAY, Lieut.-Col. Rt. Hon. Herbert Henry.

CLAYTON, Sir George Christopher, C.B.E. 61 St. James's Court, Buckingham Gate, London. Crabwall Hall, Chester. Conservative. S. of John Shaw Clayton, Esq., of Standfield, Wavertree, Liverpool. B. 11 July 1869; m. 1896, Mabel, d. of David Grainger, Esq., of Culmore, Liverpool. Educ. at Harrow, and at the Universities of Liverpool and Heidelberg. A Director of Imperial Chemical Industries; Chairman of Liverpool Gas Company. J.P., Ph.D., F.R.I.C. C.B.E. 1919. Created Knight Bach. 1933. A Conservative. Sat for the Widnes division of Lancashire from

November 1922-May 1929 when he was defeated. Elected for the Wirral division of Cheshire in October 1931 and sat until he retired in October 1935. Died 28 July 1945.
[1935]

CLEARY, Joseph Jackson. 45 Kremlin Drive, Old Swan, Liverpool. 18 Cathcart Hill, Tufnell Park, London. S. of Joseph Cleary, Esq., J.P., of Liverpool. B. 26 October 1902; m. 1945, Ethel McColl. Educ. at Holy Trinity Church of England School, Anfield, and Skerry's Coll., Liverpoll. Member of Liverpool City Council from 1927, Alderman 1941, Lord Mayor 1949-50. A Labour Member. Unsuccessfully contested the E. Toxteth division of Liverpool in March and May 1929 and the W. Derby division of Liverpool in October 1931. Elected for the Wavertree division of Liverpool in February 1935 and sat until he was defeated in November 1935. Unsuccessfully contested the Walton division of Liverpool in May 1955. J.P. for Liverpool. Knighted 1965. Dept. Chairman of Mersey Docks and Harbour Board 1969-70.*

CLIFTON BROWN, Rt. Hon. Douglas. Continued in House after 1945: full entry in Volume IV.

CLIFTON BROWN, Brigadier-Gen. Howard. See BROWN, Brigadier-Gen. Howard Clifton.

CLIMIE, Robert. 25 Armour Street, Kilmarnock. B. 1868; m. 1890, Jane Mickle. A member of the Amalgamated Engineering Union; member of Kilmarnock Town Council from 1905; a Magistrate for Kilmarnock. A Labour Member. Unsuccessfully contested the Kilmarnock division of Ayr and Bute in November 1922. Elected for Kilmarnock in December 1923, defeated defeated there in October 1924. Re-elected in May 1929 and sat until his death on 3 October 1929. [1929 2nd ed.]

CLOUGH, Sir Robert. Oakworth Court, Nr. Keighley. Constitutional, and 1900. S. of County Alderman Thomas Clough, J.P. B. at Steeten, near Keighley 10 February 1873; m. 1st, 1896, Edith Mary, d. of P.W.

Musgrave, J.P., of Otley (she died 1908); secondly, 1909 Alice, d. of James Mathers, Esq., of Leeds. Educ. at Giggleswick Grammar School, and Stuttgart. Governing Director of Keighley Gas and Oil Engine Company Limited, Imperial Works, Keighley. Mayor of Keighley 1907-08. Knighted 1921. A Democratic Unionist and strong believer in Imperial Preference. Elected for the Keighley division of the W. Riding of Yorkshire in December 1918 and sat until he retired in October 1922. Unsuccessfully contested the Shipley division of the W. Riding of Yorkshire as a Conservative in May 1929. Died 27 September 1965.

[1922]

CLOWES, Samuel. 5a Hill Street, Hanley. S. of James Clowes, Esq., of Milton, Stoke-on-Trent. B. 1864. President of the National Council of Pottery Industry; Secretary of National Society of Pottery Workers 1916-28; President of N.S. Royal Infirmary. Member of City Council, Stoke-on-Trent, Alderman 1927. J.P. for Stoke-on-Trent. A Labour Member. Elected for the Hanley division of Stoke-on-Trent in October 1924 and sat until his death on 25 March 1928.

[1928]

CLUSE, William Sampson. Continued in House after 1945: full entry in Volume IV.

CLYDE, Rt. Hon. James Avon. 27 Moray Place, Edinburgh. Briglands, Fossoway, Kinross-shire. 59 Pall Mall, London. Carlton. S. of Dr. J. Clyde, Classical Master Edinburgh Academy, and Elizabeth Rigg, of Whitehaven. B. 14 November 1863 in Dollar; m. 1895, Anna Margaret, d. of P.W. Latham, Esq., M.D., of Cambridge. Educ. at Edinburgh Academy and University; M.A., LL.B., LL.D. Was called to the Scottish bar 1887; K.C. 1901; and Solicitor-Gen. for Scotland October-December 1905. Dean of Faculty of Advocates from 1915 to 1918. Lord-Advocate from December 1916 to March 1920. Honorary Bencher, Gray's Inn 1919. PC. 1916. A J.P. and Dept.-Lieut. for Co. of Kinross. Lord-Lieut. of Kinross 1937-44. Member of the Dardanelles Commission 1916; Chairman of Advisory Committee on Egyptian Judicial Reform. A Unionist. Unsuccessfully contested Clackmannan and Kinross in 1906. Sat for Edinburgh W. from 1909 to 1918. Elected for Edinburgh N. in December 1918 and sat until March 1920 when he was appointed Lord President of the Court of Session, with the Judicial title of Lord Clyde; retired 1935. Chairman of Trustees of National Library of Scotland 1936-44. Chairman of Royal Commission on Court of Session and Office of Sheriff Principal 1926-27. Died 16 June 1944.

[1920]

CLYDESDALE, Douglas Douglas-Hamilton, Marq. of Douglas and, A.F.C. 107 Eaton Square, London. Dungavel Strathaven, Lanarkshire. Bath, and Royal Aero. New, Edinburgh. Western, Glasgow. S. of Douglas, 13th Duke of Hamilton and Brandon. B. 3 February 1903; m. 2 December 1937, Lady Elizabeth Percy, d. of Alan, 8th Duke of Northumberland, K.G. Educ. at Eton, and Balliol Coll., Oxford. F.R.G.S.; member of King's Body Guard for Scotland (Royal Company of Archers); Honorary Col. 7th Battalion H.L.I.; Wing-Commander Aux. Air Force; Chief Pilot Mount Everest Flight Expedition 1933. A Conservative. Unsuccessfully contested the Goran division of Glasgow in May 1929. Sat for Renfrew E. from November 1930 until March 1940 when he succeeded to the Peerage as Duke of Hamilton and Brandon. Styled Marq. of Douglas and Clydesdale, but usually referred to as Marq. of Clydesdale 1903-40. Rudolf Hess, the German Dept.-Fuehrer, attempted to make contact with the Duke on arriving in Scotland 10 May 1941, in the belief that together they could persuade the British Government to initiate peace negotiations. The Duke was, at that time, an officer in the R.A.F. and scarcely knew Hess at all. President of British Airline Pilot's Association from 1937. Lord Steward of the Royal Household 1940-64. Chancellor of St. Andrews University 1948-73. President of Air League 1959-68. High Commissioner of Church of Scotland 1953-55 and 1958. Died 30 March 1973. [1940]

CLYNES, Rt. Hon. John Robert. 41 St. John's Avenue, Putney, London. S. of of Patrick Clynes, Esq., of Oldham. B. 27 March 1869; m. 13 September 1893, Mary, d. of Owen Harper, Esq. Educ. at elementary schools. Worked in a Cotton Factory. President National Union of General and Municipal Workers. Parliamentary Secretary Ministry of Food July 1917-July 1918; Food Controller July 1918 to January 1919. Vice-Chairman of Labour Party in House of Commons 1910-11 and 1918-21. Chairman of Labour Party in House of Commons 1921-22; Dept. Leader of Labour Party 1923-31. PC. 1918; Honorary D.C.L. Durham and Oxford 1919; J.P. for Oldham; Lord Privy Seal and Dept. Leader of the House of Commons January-October 1924; Secretary of State for Home Affairs June 1929-August 1931. A Labour Member. Sat for N.E. Manchester from 1906-18, and for the Platting division of Manchester from December 1918-October 1931 when he was defeated. Re-elected for the Platting division in November 1935 and sat until he retired in June 1945. Died 23 October 1949. [1945]

COATES, Sir Edward Feetham, Bart. Tayles Hill, Ewell. Helperby Hall, Yorkshire. Queen Anne's Lodge, St. James's Park, London. Carlton, Junior United Service, Yorkshire, and R.Y.S. Eld. s. of James Coates, Esq., J.P., and Dept.-Lieut. of Helperby Hall, Yorkshire, and Elizabeth, d. of William Sayer, Esq., of Yarm, Yorkshire. B. 1853; m. 1878, Edith, d. of Capt. P. Woolley, of Bolney, Sussex. Educ. at Marlborough Coll. A Stockbroker. Lieut. of City of London; Dept.-Lieut., J.P. and County Alderman for Surrey, and J.P. and Dept.-Lieut. for the N. Riding of Yorkshire; Chairman of the Surrey County Council from 1905-09. On the Roll for High Sheriff 1905; member of Committee of Surrey Territorial Force Association; Trustee of Crystal Palace. Maj. in the 3rd Battalion (M.) West Riding Regiment. Trustee of National Portrait Gallery. Patron of 1 living. Created Bart. 1911. A Unionist. Unsuccessfully contested the Elland division of the W. Riding of Yorkshire in 1900. Sat for Lewisham from December 1903 to 1918.

Returned unopposed for the W. division of Lewisham in December 1918 and sat until his death on 14 August 1921. [1921]

COATES, Lieut.-Col. Norman. Bray Court, Berkshire. Bath. S. of Thomas Coates, Esq., Landowner. B. at Durham 27 April 1890; m. 27 December 1913, Mary Gladys, only d. of Hubert G. Poole, Esq., of Truro. Educ. at Durham School, and King's Coll., London. Gazetted to the Welsh Regiment 1911; served throughout the European War; wounded at Suvla Bay; D.A.A.G. to Lord Allenby, 1917; D.A.A.G. and O.M.G. to Cavalry Corps, E.E.F. 1917; A.A.G., Gen. Headquarters 1918; Military Secretary to Lord Allenby 1919; Tribunal Secretary to Chief of Imperial General Staff, War Office 1920; Commandant, United Service Coll., Bray 1921. M.C.; Brevet Maj.; order of St. Anne 1915; mentioned in despatches. A Conservative. Elected for the Isle of Ely in November 1922 and sat until he retired in November 1923. Dept. Director of Prisoners of War Department at War Office 1940-41. [1923]

COATS, Sir Stuart Auchincloss, Bart. 10 Charles Street, Berkeley Sqare, London. Ballathie, Stanley, Perthshire. Carlton, Bachelors', and St. James's. S. of Sir James and Sarah Auchincloss Coats. B. at Paisley 1868; m. at Paisley 1891, Jane Muir, d. of Thomas Greenlees, Esq., of Paisley, Renfrewshire (she died 1958). Educ. in the United States of America. Private Chamberlain of Sword and Cape to four successive Popes from 1905. Commander of the Order of the Crown of Italy. A partner of J. and P. Coats, President and Director of the Canada Thread Company, Vice-President and Director of the Conant Thread Company, and Coats Thread Company, and the Spool Cotton Company. Chairman of the Committee of Management of the Italian Hospital. A Conservative. Unsuccessfully contested Morpeth borough in 1906 and Deptford in January 1910 and December 1910. Elected for the Wimbledon division of Surrey in April 1916 and for E. Surrey in December 1918. Sat until he retired in October 1922. Succeeded as Bart. 1913. Died in Paris 15 July 1959. [1922]

COBB, Sir Cyril Stephen, K.B.E., M.V.O.
5 Cornwall Terrace, Regent's Park, London. Carlton, Constitutional, New University, and Bath. S. of James Francis Cobb, Esq., Banker of Margate. B. at Margate 6 October 1861. Educ. at Newton Abbot Coll., South Devon, and Merton Coll., Oxford. A Barrister-at-Law, Middle Temple 1887. Member London County Council 1905-34, Vice-Chairman 1910-11, Chairman 1913-14; Chairman Education Committee 1911-13 and 1917-21; Chairman of the Asylum and Mental Deficiency Committee 1914-17; member of the Public Works Reorganization Committee, India 1916-17. K.B.E. 1918. A Conservative. Sat for W. Fulham from December 1918-May 1929, when he was defeated. Re-elected for W. Fulham in May 1930 and sat until his death on 8 March 1938. [1938]

COBB, Capt. Edward Charles, D.S.O.
17 Ashley Gardens, Rother Hill, Midhurst, Sussex. Carlton, and M.C. S. of George Cobb, Esq., of Lively Island, Falkland Islands. B. 4 September 1891; m. 28 November 1918, Gladys Ryder, d. of H.J. King, Esq., of Poles, Ware, Hertfordshire. Educ. at St. Paul's School, and at Royal Military Coll., Sandhurst. 2nd Lieut. Northamptonshire Regiment 1911. Served in Cameroons, E.F. and B.E.F. 1914-16, retired 1924. Member of London County Council 1925-34; Chairman of Education Committee 1932-34. J.P. for Sussex. A National Unionist. Elected for Preston in November 1936 and sat until July 1945 when he unsuccessfully contested the Eton and Slough division of Buckinghamshire; again defeated in Eton and Slough in February 1950. D.S.O. 1916. Parliamentary Private Secretary to H. Balfour 1938-39, to Rt. Hon. O. Stanley 1939-40 and to Rt. Hon. L.S. Amery 1940-41. Died 14 May 1957. [1945]

COCHRANE, Commander Hon. Archibald Douglas, R.N., D.S.O. 24 Onslow Square, London. Carlton. S. of Thomas, 1st Baron Cochrane of Cults. B. 8 January 1885; m. 6 January 1926, Hon. Dorothy Cornwallis, d. of Fiennes, 1st Baron Cornwallis, of Linton. Joined R.N. 1901. Com-manded Submarine during German War. Parliamentary Private Secretary to Maj. Walter Elliot when Parliamentary Under-Secretary of State for Scotland 1924-29. A Conservative. Sat for E. Fife from October 1924 to May 1929 when he was defeated. Elected for Dumbartonshire in March 1932 and again in November 1935. Sat until February 1936 when he was appointed Gov. of Burma. D.S.O. 1915. Gov. of Burma 1936-41. Rejoined the navy 1941. Died 16 April 1958. [1936]

COCKERILL, Brigadier-Gen. Sir George Kynaston, C.B. 19 Knightsbridge, London. Carlton. S. of Robert William Cockerill, Esq., and Clara Sandys, d. of Maj.-Gen. Charles Pooley. B. 13 August 1867; m. 2 January 1900, Mildred, d. of Frederick W. Jowers, Esq., of Wivelsfield, Sussex (she died 1935). Educ. at Cheltenham, and Sandhurst. 2nd Queen's Regiment 1888; specially promoted Maj. Royal Fusiliers 1908; Lieut.-Col. 1914. Saw much service in India from 1888 to 1898; despatches and two medals; D.A.A.G. South Africa 1900-02; despatches, Queen's and King's Medals, and Bt.-Maj. Maj. General Staff, War Office 1902-07. British technical delegate, Hague Conference 1907. Retired 1910. Gold Medallist and Macgregor Memorial Silver Medallist of R.U.S.I. of India. Director of Special Intelligence, General Staff, War Office 1914-18, organizing British Military Intelligence Services. Brevet-Col. 1917. Commander of the Legion of Honour, Crown of Belgium and Crown of Italy; Star of the Sacred Treasure of Japan; Grand Cross of St. Stanilas of Russia; C.B. 1916; Knight Bach. 1926. A Conservative. Unsuccessfully contested the Thornbury division of Gloucestershire in December 1910. Returned unopposed for the Reigate division of Surrey in December 1918, November 1922 and December 1923. Elected again for the Reigate division of Surrey in October 1924. Sat until he retired in October 1931. Fellow of Royal Geographical Society, Zoological Society and Royal Horticultural Society. Died 19 April 1957. [1931 2nd ed.]

COCKS, Frederick Seymour. Continued in House after 1945: full entry in Volume IV.

COHEN, Maj. Jack Benn Brunel. 15 Devonshire Street, London. Carlton, and Bath. S. of Alderman Louis S. Cohen, J.P., of Liverpool, and May, d. of the Rt. Hon. L.W. Levy, of Sydney, N.S.W. B. 5 October 1886; m. 22 April 1914, Vera, d. of Sir Stuart Samuel, Bart., of Maresfield. Educ. at Cheltenham. Maj. 5th Battalion King's (Liverpool) Regiment T.F.; served in France, etc. 1914-17 when he lost both legs. Honorary Treasurer of the British Legion. A Conservative. Sat for the Fairfield division of Liverpool from December 1918, when he defeated the 'Coupon' Liberal candidate, until he retired in October 1931. Treasurer of British Legion 1921-30 and 1932-46, Vice-Chairman 1930-32. Knighted 1943; K.B.E. 1948. Vice-Chairman of Remploy Limited 1950-55, Chairman 1955-56. Died 11 May 1965. [1931 2nd ed.]

COLEGATE, William Arthur. Continued in House after 1945: full entry in Volume IV.

COLFOX, Maj. Sir (William) Philip, Bart., M.C. Symondsbury Manor, Bridport. Army & Navy. S. of Col. T.A. Colfox, of Coneygar, Bridport. B. 25 Febuary 1888; m. 1920, Mary Frances, d. of Col. J.B.S. Bullen, of Catherston, Charmouth. Educ. at Eton, and Royal Military Academy, Woolwich. Joined R.F.A. 1908; Maj. 1918. Served in France and Flanders 1914-17. J.P. for Dorset. Parliamentary Private Secretary to Maj. G. Tryon when Parliamentary Secretary Ministry of Pensions 1920-21, and to Hon. E.F. Wood when Under Secretary Colonial Office 1921-22; Assistant Whip (unpaid) 1922-23. Created Bart 1939. A Conservative. Sat for N. Dorset from December 1918 to November 1922. Member for W. Dorset from November 1922 until he resigned in 1941. High Sheriff of Dorset 1946-47, Dept.-Lieut. from 1945. Died 8 November 1966. [1941]

COLIVET, Michael Patrick. Castleview Gardens, Limerick. B. May 1884; m. 1st, 1912, Anna Hartigan, of Limerick (she died 1921); secondly, 1928, Una Garvey, of Kilrue, Co. Galway. Educ. at St. Joseph's Seminary, Galway. Manager of Shannon Foundry, Limerick 1910-22. A Sinn Fein Member. Was returned unopposed for Limerick city in December 1918, while interned in England but did not take his seat. Member of the Dail for Limerick until 1921 and for Limerick City and E. Limerick 1921-23 as an Anti-Treaty Member. Chairman of Irish Housing Board 1932-45. Gen. Housing Inspector, Local Government Department 1945-55. Died 4 May 1955. [1922]

COLLIE, Sir Robert John. 22 Porchester Terrace, London. Reform, and Ranelagh. S. of James Collie, Esq., of Pitfodels, Aberdeenshire, and Christina Gorham. B. 15 August 1860 in Aberdeen; m. 1st, 1886, Jessie, d. of John Edgar, Esq., of Mid-Locharwoods, Dumfriesshire (she died 1928); secondly, 1928, Lady Arrol, d. of James Robertson, Esq., and widow of Sir William Arrol. Educ. at Aberdeen University. A Consulting Physician, M.B., C.M. 1882; M.D. 1884. Knighted 1912; C.M.G. 1918; Dept.-Lieut. and J.P. for County of London. Lieut.-Col. R.A.M.C.; Medical Examiner to the London County Council and Chief Medical Officer to the Metropolitan Water Board. Made many contributions to medical literature. A National Liberal. Elected for the Partick division of Glasgow in November 1922 and sat until he retired in November 1923. Died 4 April 1935. [1923]

COLLINDRIDGE, Frank. Continued in House after 1945: full entry in Volume IV.

COLLINS, Cornelius. A Clerk in Dublin Post Office. A Sinn Fein Member. Returned unopposed for W. Limerick in December 1918 but did not take his seat. Member of Dail for W. Limerick to 1921 and for Kerry and W. Limerick 1921-23 as an Anti-Treaty Member. [1922]

COLLINS, Rt. Hon. Sir Godfrey Pattison, K.B.E., C.M.G. 4 Smith Square, London. Reform and Ranelagh. S. of A.G.

Collins, Esq., Publisher, of Glasgow. B. 26 June 1875; m. 26 April 1900, Faith, d. of J.C. Aitken Henderson, Esq. Educ. at Temple Grove, East Sheen, and H.M.S. Britannia. Joined Royal Navy 1888, retired 1893. Managing Director of W. Collins, Sons and Company Limited, Publishers, Glasgow and London. Parliamentary Private Secretary to Col. Seely, Secretary for War 1910-14, and to Mr. Gulland, Chief Liberal Whip 1915-16. Member of War Office Supplies Committee 1912-13; Maj.-Inspector Q.M.G. Services War Office Staff 1915; served in Egypt, Gallipoli, and Mesopotamia 1915-16; Lieut.-Col. September 1916; C.M.G. 1917. Junior Lord of the Treasury August 1919 to Feburary 1920 when he resigned and withdrew his support from the Coalition; Chief Liberal Whip 1924-26; Secretary of State for Scotland September 1932-October 1936. PC. 1932; K.B.E. (Military) 1919. Parliamentary Charity Commissioner November 1920. A Liberal until 1931, thereafter a Liberal National. Sat for Greenock from January 1910 until his death on 13 October 1936. [1936]

COLLINS, Michael. Woodfield, Clonakilty, Co. Cork. S. of Michael Collins, Esq. B. 1890 at Clonakilty, Co. Cork. Entered Civil Service as a Clerk at the age of 15 and later worked as a Bank Clerk in London. Returned to Ireland in 1916 and was taken prisoner at the Post Office in Dublin during the Easter Rising. A Sinn Fein Member. Returned unopposed for S. Cork in December 1918 but did not take his seat. Member of N. Ireland Parliament for Armagh 1921-22. Member of Dail for S. Cork until 1922, as a Pro-Treaty Member. Finance Minister in the Provisional Government 1921-22 and Chairman from January 1922. Commander in Chief of the army July-August 1922. Killed at Bealnabla, Co. Cork on 22 August 1922 after being ambushed by the Irish Irregulars. [1922]

COLLINS, Patrick. Lime Tree House, Bloxwich. National Liberal. S. of John and Norah Collins. B. at Chester 5 April 1859; m. 1st, 1880, Flora, d. of James Ross, Esq., of Wrexham (she died 1932); secondly,

1935, Clara Mullett. Educ. at St. Werburghs, Chester. A theatre and cinema proprietor and outdoor amusement caterer. Councillor for Walsall from 1918, Alderman 1930; President of Showmen's Guild. A Liberal. Elected for Walsall in November 1922 and sat until he was defeated in October 1924. Died 8 December 1943.

[1924 2nd ed.]

COLLISON, Levi. Tulketh Mount, Ashton-on-Ribble, Preston. National Liberal. S. of S. Collison, Esq., of Preston. B. at Preston 1875; m. 1899, Agnes, d. of Alfred Spencer, Esq., of Westerton, Lincolnshire. Educ. privately. An Art Publisher, and interested in the cotton trade. Founder and Chairman of Collison's Limited, and Director of several printing companies. J.P. for Lincolnshire. A Liberal. Unsuccessfully contested the Penrith and Cockermouth division of Cumberland in May 1921. Elected for Penrith and Cockermouth in November 1922 and sat until he was defeated in December 1923. Died 22 October 1965.

[1923]

COLMAN, Nigel Claudian Dalziel. 49 Grosvenor Square, London. Carlton, and Royal Automobile. S. of Frederick Edward Colman, Esq., Dept.-Lieut., and Chairman of J. and J. Colman Limited, and of Helen, d. of Davison Octavius Dalziel, Esq. B. 1886; m. 1952, Nona Ann, d. of E.H.M. Willan, Esq. Member of London County Council for Brixton 1925-28; Chairman of Central Council of National Union of C. and U. Associations 1939; Chairman of National Union of C. and U. Associations Metropolitan Area 1934-36. A Conservative. Elected for the Brixton division of Lambeth in June 1927 and sat until he was defeated in July 1945. Chairman of National Union of Conservative Associations 1939 and of its Executive Committee 1945-51. Created Bart. 1952. President of London Conservative Union 1952-59. President of National Horse Association 1935-45. Chairman of British Horse Society 1952-55. Director of Reckitt and Colman Limited and of J. and J. Colman Limited. Died 7 March 1966.

[1945]

COLVILLE, Col. Rt. Hon. David John, T.D. 56 Eaton Square, London. Braidwood House, Braidwood, Lanarkshire. Carlton. New (Edinburgh). S. of John Colville, Esq., MP, of Cleland, Lanarkshire. B. 13 February 1894; m. 6 October 1915, Agnes Anne, d. of Sir William Bilsland, Bart. Educ. at Charterhouse, and Trinity Coll., Cambridge. Served with 6th Cameronians (Scottish Rifles), T.A. Director of Steel and Engineering Companies including Messrs. David Colville and Sons Limited. Dept.-Lieut., and J.P. for Lanark. PC. 1936. Parliamentary Private Secretary to A.N. Skelton when Parliamentary Under-Secretary of State for Scotland August-October 1931; Secretary of Overseas Trade Department November 1931-November 35; Parliamentary Under-Secretary of State for Scotland November 1935-October 36; Financial Secretary to the Treasury October 1936-May 1938. Secretary of State for Scotland May 1938-May 1940. Col. General Staff July 1940. A Conservative. Unsuccessfully contested Motherwell as a National Liberal in November 1922, and the N. Midlothian division of Midlothian and Peebles in January 1929. Elected for this division in May 1929 and sat until January 1943 when he was appointed Gov. of Bombay; retired 1948. Lord-Lieut. of Lanarkshire 1952-54. Created Baron Clydesmuir 1947. Gov. of B.B.C. from 1950. Died 31 October 1954. [1943]

COLVIN, Brigadier-Gen. Richard Beale, C.B.(Mil.), C.B.(Civil). Monkhams, Waltham Abbey, Essex. Arthur's, and 1900. S. of B.B. Colvin, Esq., of Pishiobury and Monkhams, Essex, and Emma Elizabeth, d. of D. Britten, Esq., of Kenswick, Worcestershire. B. 4 August 1856 at Pishiobury, Sawbridgeworth, Hertfordshire; m. 1895, Lady Gwendoline A.A.B. Rous, youngest d. of the 2nd Earl of Stradbroke. Educ. at Eton, and Trinity Coll., Cambridge. Raised and commanded 20th Battalion I.Y. 1900; raised and commanded Essex Yeomanry 1902-11; commanded 2nd London Mounted Brigade 1915-16. County Commandant Essex Volunteers 1916-17; Honorary Brigadier-Gen. 1917. Chairman of the Essex Territorial Force Association from 1908. J.P. and Dept.-Lieut. for Essex. Knight of Grace of St. John of Jerusalem; Master of the East Essex Foxhounds 1885-90 and of the Essex and Suffolk Foxhounds 1891-94. A Conservative. Elected for the Epping division of Essex in June 1917 and sat until he retired in November 1923. High Sheriff of Essex 1890 and Lord-Lieut. of Essex 1929-36. Died 17 January 1936. [1923]

COMPTON, Joseph. 139 Tottenham Court Road, London. B. in Northern Ireland 21 April 1881; m. 1902, Catherine, d. of George Condie, Esq. Educ. at board school. A Trade Union Official; Assistant Gen. Secretary National Union of Vehicle Builders. A Labour Member. Unsuccessfully contested Swindon in 1918 and 1922. Sat for the Gorton division of Manchester from December 1923-October 1931, when he was defeated. Re-elected for the Gorton division of Manchester in November 1935 and sat until his death on 18 January 1937. Member of Manchester City Council 1919-25. Chairman of House of Commons Kitchen Committee 1929-31. Chairman of National Executive of Labour Party 1933. Died 18 January 1937. [1937]

COMPTON-RICKETT, Rt. Hon. Sir Joseph Compton. Wingfield, Bournemouth. Reform, and National Liberal. Eld. s. of Joseph Rickett, Esq., of East Hoathly, Sussex, and Cordelia, d. of Edmund Dunn, Esq. B. in London 1847; m. 1868, Catharine, d. of the Rev. H.J. Gamble, of Upper Clapton. Educ. at King Edward VI Grammar School, Bath, and privately. Chairman of Rickett, Cockerell and Company Limited, and other companies. Chairman of Congregational Union of England and Wales 1907-08; President National Council for Evangelical Free Churches 1915-16. Dept.-Lieut. for the N. Riding of Yorkshire. Author of several books including *Origins and Faith*, *The Christ that is to be*, and *The Quickening of Caliban*. Knighted 1907; PC. 1911. Paymaster-Gen. from December 1916-July 1919; Charity Commissioner 1917. Assumed additional name of Compton by Royal Licence in 1908. A Liberal. Represented Scarborough from

1895-1906; and the Osgoldcross division of the W. Riding of Yorkshire from 1906 to 1918. Elected for the Pontefract division of the W. Riding of Yorkshire in December 1918 and sat until his death on 30 July 1919. [1919]

COMYNS CARR, Arthur Strettell. 5 Palace Mansions, Palace Street, London. National Liberal. S. of Joseph William Comyns Carr, Esq., dramatic author, by his marriage with Alice Laura Vansittart Strettel, novelist. B. at St. Marylebone 19 September 1882; m. 19 October 1907, Cicely Oriana Raikes Bromage, d. of R.R. Bromage, Esq (she died 1935). Educ. at Winchester, and Trinity Coll., Oxford. Barrister-at-Law, Gray's Inn 1908. Joint author of text book on National Insurance; member of Land Inquiry Committee (London) 1912; and Land Acquisition Committee. A Liberal. Unsuccessfully contested S.W. St. Pancras in 1918 and 1922. Elected for E. Islington in December 1923 and sat until he was defeated in October 1924. Unsuccessfully contested Ilford in February 1928 and May 1929, Epping in October 1931, E. Nottingham in November 1935, Shrewsbury in July 1945, City of London in October 1945 and Berwick-upon-Tweed in February 1950. K.C. 1924; Knighted 1949. Treasurer of Gray's Inn 1950. Chairman of Foreign Compensation Commission 1950-58. President of Liberal Party 1959. President of Institute of Industrial Administration. President of Association of Approved Societies. Died 20 April 1965. [1924 2nd ed.]

CONANT, Roger John Edward. Continued in House after 1945: full entry in Volume IV.

CONNOLLY, Martin Henry. 208 Hampstead Road, Newcastle-on-Tyne. S. of John Connolly, Esq., of Newcastle. B. 1874; m. 1st, 1898, Mary, d. of William Young, Esq. (she died 1926); secondly, 1929, Hannah Margaret, d. of Mark Coxon, Esq., and widow of John Whitelaw, Esq., of Byker. Member of the General Council of Boiler Makers' Society. Member of City Council of Newcastle. A Labour Member. Unsuccess-

fully contested Middlesborough E. in 1922 and 1923. Elected for Newcastle-upon-Tyne E. in October 1924 and sat until he was defeated in May 1929. Died 8 August 1945. [1922]

CONWAY, Sir (William) Martin. 47 Romney Street, London. Allington Castle, Maidstone. Athenaeum, and Burlington Fine Arts. S. of Canon William Conway, of Westminster. B. at Rochester 12 April 1856; m. 1st, 1884, Katrina, d. of C. Lambard, Esq., of Maine, U.S.A. (she died 1933); secondly, 1934, Iva, widow of Reginald Lawson, Esq., of Saltwood Castle. Educ. at Repton, and Trinity Coll., Cambridge. University Extension Lecturer 1882-85; Professor of Art University Coll., Liverpool 1885-88. Honorary Secretary Art Congress 1888-90. Slade Professor of Fine Arts, Cambridge 1901-04; Hon. Litt.D., Durham and Manchester. Travelled much, climbed the great heights in the Himalayas and the Andes, and wrote much on art, travel, exploration, etc. Director-Gen. of the Imperial War Museum 1917; Trustee of the National Portrait Gallery. Knight Bach. 1895. A Conservative. Unsuccessfully contested Bath as a Liberal in 1895. Sat for the Combined English Universities from December until he retired in October 1931. Created Baron Conway of Allington 1931. Vice-President of Society of Antiquaries and of Royal Geographical Society. President of Kent Archaeological Society. Died 19 April 1937. [1931 2nd ed.]

COOK, Lieut.-Col. Sir Thomas Russell Albert Mason. Sennowe Park, Guist, Norfolk. Carlton. Norfolk. S. of Thomas Cook, Esq., Director of Tourist Agency. B. 12 June 1902; m. 13 February 1926, Gweneth Margaret, d. of Spencer Evan Jones, Esq., of Banwell Abbey, Somerset. Educ. at Eton, and Worcester Coll., Oxford. Member of Norfolk County Council 1928-44; Chairman of Anglo-Brazilian Society and of the Luxembourg Society. County Commissioner St. John Ambulance Brigade; served with 5th Battalion Royal Norfolk Regiment 1920-25; Staff Capt. 18th division 1939; G.H.Q. France 1940; Liaison Officer to Allied Forces War Office 1941; J.P. for Norfolk

1934. O.St. J.; Order of Civic Cross (Belgium), of the White Lion (Czechoslovakia) of Christ (Portugal), Gold Cross King George 1st (Greece), St. Gediminus (Lithuania), Commissioner of the Oaken Crown of Luxembourg. Commander of the Southern Cross (Brazil), of the Order of St. Sava (Yogoslavia) and of St. Olav (Norway). Proprietor of *Norfolk Chronicle* 1935-55. Created Knight Bach. 1937. A Conservative. Unsuccessfully contested N. Norfolk in 1924, 1929 and 1930. Elected for N. Norfolk in October 1931 and sat until he was defeated in July 1945. Master of Worshipful Company of Glaziers 1960. Died 12 August 1970.

[1945]

COOKE, James Douglas. Mill Cottage, Broadbridge Heath, Horsham. Carlton. S. of John Cooke, Esq., of Christchurch, New Zealand. B. 19 June 1879; m. 10 April 1907, d. of Gen. James Burston, of Melbourne. Educ. at Melbourne University, and London Hospital, M.B., B.S. 1901, F.R.C.S. 1905. Maj. R.A.M.C. 1915-19, served in France 1916-19. A Conservative. Unsuccessfully contested the Peckham division of Camberwell in May 1929. Elected for S. Hammersmith in October 1931 and sat until he was defeated in July 1945. Knighted 1945. Died 13 July 1949. [1945]

COOPER, Rt. Hon. Alfred Duff, D.S.O. H.B.M. Embassy, Paris. Bachelors', White's, and Beefsteak. S. of Sir Alfred Cooper, and Lady Agnes Cooper, sister of 1st Duke of Fife, K.T. B. 22 February 1890; m. 2 June 1919, Lady Diana Manners, d. of the 8th Duke of Rutland. Educ. at Eton, and New Coll., Oxford. In the Foreign Office 1913. Served overseas with Grenadier Guards 1914-18. D.S.O. 1919. Financial Secretary to the War Office January 1928-June 1929 and August 1931-June 1934; Financial Secretary to the Treasury June 1934-November 1935; Secretary of State for War November 1935-May 1937. First Lord of the Admiralty May 1937-October 1938 when he resigned over the Munich agreement; Minister of Information May 1940-July 1941; Chancellor of Duchy of Lancaster July 1941-November 1943; Resident Minister at Singapore for Far Eastern Affairs December

1941-November 1943; Representative of H.M. Government in the U.K. with the French Commission of National Liberation in Algiers with the rank of Ambassador November 1943; H.M. Ambassador in Paris October 1944-1947. PC. 1935. A Conservative. Elected for Oldham in October 1924. Defeated at Oldham in May 1929. Sat for the St. George's division of Westminster from March 1931 until he retired in June 1945. Created Visct. Norwich 1952. Died 1 January 1954. [1945]

COOPER, Sir Richard Ashmole, Bart. 6 Carlton Gardens, London. Carlton, Portland, Automobile, St, Stephen's, Ranelagh, and Sports. S. of Sir R.P. Cooper, 1st Bart., and Elizabeth, d. of Elias Ashmole Ashmall, Esq. B. 11 August 1874 at Shenstone, Lichfield; m. 1900, d. of the Rev. E. Priestland. Educ. at Clifton Coll. Succeeded as 2nd Bart. 1913. A member of the firm of William Cooper and Nephews, Chemical Manufacturers. Chairman of Berkhamsted Urban District Council; a member of Hertfordshire County Council. A Unionist. Elected for Walsall in January 1910 and sat until he retired in October 1922. Supporter of the National Party 1917-22 and elected as its candidate in 1918 although without Conservative opposition. Died 5 March 1946. [1922]

COOPER, Rt. Hon. Thomas Mackay, K.C., O.B.E. Dover House, Whitehall, London. 16 Hermitage Drive, Edinburgh. Carlton. S. of John Cooper, Esq., City Engineer, Edinburgh. B. 24 September 1892. Unmarried. Educ. at George Watson's Coll. and at the University of Edinburgh. Admitted to the Scottish bar 1915, K.C. 1927; O.B.E. 1919. Solicitor-Gen. for Scotland May-October 1935; Lord Advocate October 1935-June 1941. PC. 1935. A National Conservative. Elected for Edinburgh W. in May and November 1935. Sat until June 1941 when he was appointed Lord Justice Clerk, with the Judicial title of Lord Cooper. Lord Justice Clerk 1941-47. Lord Justice General and Lord President of the Court of Session 1947-54. Created Baron Cooper of Culross 1954. President of Scottish History Society 1945-49. F.S.A. (Scot.),

F.R.S.E., F.R.A.S. Died 15 July 1955.
[1941]

COOTE, Capt. Colin Reith, D.S.O. 4 Wilfred Street, London. Eld. s. of Howard Coote, Esq., Lord-Lieut. of Huntingdonshire, of Stukeley Hall, Huntingdonshire. B. 1893. Educ. at Rugby School, and Balliol Coll., Oxford; took 2nd in Greats. At the outbreak of war enlisted as a private. Received a commission in the Gloucester Regiment and was wounded on the Somme. A Liberal. Elected for the Wisbech division of Cambridgeshire in December 1917. Returned unopposed for the Isle of Ely in December 1918 and sat until he was defeated in November 1922. D.S.O. 1918. Dept. Editor of *Daily Telegraph* 1945-50, Editor 1950-64. Knighted 1962. Author.*
[1922]

COOTE, William. "Aberfoyle", Maryville Park, Belfast. Clogher, Co. Tyrone. Constitutional. S. of William Coote and Sarah Coote. B. 1863 at Ballyjamesduff, Co. Cavan, of Hugenot extraction; m. 1889, Letitia, d. of James Allan, Esq., of Castleblayney, Co. Monaghan (she died 1923). Educ. at grammar and private classical schools. A Woollen Manufacturer in 1909 and a Hosiery Manufacturer in 1915. District Councillor for County Tyrone 1899; County Councillor for County Tyrone 1902; J.P. for County Tyrone 1901. A democratic Conservative and Unionist. Elected for S. Tyrone in February 1916 and sat until he retired in October 1922. Dept.-Lieut. for County Tyrone. Member of the Northern Ireland Parliament for Fermanagh and Tyrone 1921-24. Died 14 December 1924.
[1922]

COPE, Maj. Sir William, Bart., T.D. Cornborough, Porthcawl, Glamorgan. Oxford & Cambridge, Carlton, and 1900. S. of Matthew Cope, Esq., J.P., of St. Mellons, near Cardiff. B. at Roath, Cardiff 18 August 1870; m. 1900, Helen, younger d. of Maj. A. Shuldham, Dept.-Lieut., of Flowerfield, Co. Londonderry. Educ. at Repton, and Clare Coll., Cambridge, B.A. 1891, M.A. 1893. Barrister-at-Law Inner Temple 1895. Glamorgan Yeomanry 2nd Lieut. 1901, Maj. 1914. J.P. for Glamorgan 1914. Cambridge "blue" Rugby Football 1891; Welsh International Rugby Football 1896. Lord Commissioner of the Treasury (unpaid) March 1923 to January 1924, and November 1924-January 1928; Comptroller of H.Ms. Household from January 1928 to June 1929, and Welsh Whip from 1923 to 1929. Created Bart. 1928. A Conservative. Sat for the Llandaff and Barry division of Glamorganshire from December 1918 until he was defeated in May 1929. K.C. 1933. Dept.-Lieut. for Glamorgan, High Sheriff 1932-33. Created Baron Cope 1945. Died 15 July 1946.
[1929]

COPELAND, Ida. High Chase, Colwich, Stafford. D. of C. Fenzi and Mrs. Leonard Cunliffe. B. circa 1875; m. 1915, Ronald Copeland, Esq. (he died 1958). Fellow of Royal Society of Arts. A Conservative. Elected for the Stoke division of Stoke-on-Trent in October 1931 and sat until she was defeated in November 1935. Died 29 June 1964.
[1935]

CORNWALL, Rt. Hon. Sir Edwin Andrew, Bart. 155 Fenchurch Street, London. Heath Royal, Putney Heath, London. Holcombe Burnell, Nr. Exeter, Devon. Reform, Municipal and County, and National Liberal. S. of Andrew Cornwall, Esq., of Lapford, Devon. B. 1863; m. 1883, Ellen Mary, d. of John Day, Esq., of Oxford (she died 1929). A member of London County Council for Bethnal Green 1892-1910; Vice-Chairman 1903-05; Chairman 1905-06. Knighted 1905; Bart. 1918; PC. 1921. Member of Thames Conservancy Board 1899-1909. A member of Port of London Authority from 1908-19. First Mayor of Fulham 1900. A Dept.-Lieut. and J.P. for London. Officer of the Legion of Honour. Vice-Chairman Territorial Force Association of County of London 1907-14. Comptroller of the Household December 1916 to February 1919; Chairman of the National Insurance Joint Commission and Insurance Minister in the House of Commons December 1916 to February 1919. Dept.-Chairman of Committee of Ways and Means February 1919 to October 1922. A Liberal. Unsuccessfully contested

Fulham 1895 and 1900. Elected for N.E. Bethnal Green in 1906 and sat until he retired in October 1922. Died 27 February 1953. [1922]

CORVEDALE, Oliver Ridsdale Baldwin, Visct. Continued in House after 1945: full entry in Volume IV.

CORY, Sir Clifford John, Bart. 98 Mount Street, London. Llantarnam Abbey, Monmouthshire. Reform, Devonshire, National Liberal, Royal Automobile, Hurlingham, Ranelagh, and Roehampton. S. of John Cory, Esq., J.P., and Dept.-Lieut., of Duffryn, near Cardiff, and Anna Maria, d. of John Beynon, Esq., of Newport, Monmouthshire. B. 1859 at Cardiff; m. 1893, Jane Ann, d. of Albert A. Lethbridge, Esq. Educ. privately, and abroad. Chairman of Cory Brothers and Company Limited, Colliery Owners and Coal Exporters, South Wales. Member of Glamorgan County Council 1892-1910, and of the S. Wales Conciliation Board; Chairman S. Wales and Monmouthshire School of Mines. J.P. and Dept.-Lieut. for Glamorgan; J.P. for Monmouthshire; High Sheriff 1906; created Bart. 1907. Commander of the Order of Leopold II. A Liberal. Unsuccessfully contested S. Monmouthshire in 1895 and the Tonbridge division of Kent in 1900. Sat for the St. Ives division of Cornwall from 1906-22 when he was defeated. Re-elected for the St. Ives division of Cornwall in December 1923 and sat until he was defeated in October 1924. Died 3 February. 1941. [1924 2nd ed.]

CORY, Sir James Herbert, Bart. Coryton, Whitchurch, Glamorgan. Mount Stuart, Cardiff. Carlton, Junior Carlton, and St. Stephen's. S. of John Cory, Esq., Shipowner. B. 7 February 1857 at Padstow, Cornwall; m. 1st, 1879, Elizabeth Hoskin Wills (she died 1898); secondly, 1910, Elizabeth Walker, of Irvine, Ayrshire. Educ. at Tregoney, Cornwall. Director of John Cory and Sons Limited, Shipowners, Cardiff, etc.; Bute Shipbuilding, Engineering and Dry Dock Company, and other companies. Dept.-Lieut. and J.P. for Glamorgan; High Sheriff 1913. A Conservative. Elected for

Cardiff District in November 1915 and for Cardiff S. December 1918 and sat until he was defeated in December 1923. Created Bart. 1919. Died 7 February 1933. [1923]

COSGRAVE, William Thomas. 174 St. James's Street, Dublin. S. of Thomas Cosgrave, Esq. B. in Dublin 1880; m. 1919, Louise, d. of Alderman Flanagan of Dublin (she died 1959). Educ. at University Coll., Dublin. Was prominent in Dublin as a member of the City Corporation 1909-22 being Chairman of its Finance Committee 1916-22. Treasurer of Sinn Fein. Was sentenced to death for his part in the Irish Rebellion during Easter 1916. The sentence was commuted to penal servitude for life, but he was afterwards released. Rearrested March 1920. A Sinn Fein Member. Elected for Kilkenny city August 1917. Returned unopposed for N. Kilkenny in December 1918 but did not take his seat. Member of Dail for N. Kilkenny to 1921, for Carlow and Kilkenny 1921-27, for Cork City 1927-44. Leader of Opposition 1932-44. Pro-Treaty, later Cumann na nGaedheal and Fine Gael Member. Minister of Local Government 1917-21 and January-August 1922. President of Dail 1922, President of Executive Council of Irish Free State 1922-32. Minister of Finance 1922-23. Minister of Defence in 1924. Died 16 November 1965. [1922]

COSTELLO, Leonard Wilfred James. 46 Redcliffe Square, South Kensington, London. Peak Cottage, Sidmouth. National Liberal, Eighty, Roehampton, Devonshire, and Exeter (Liberal). S. of James Edward and Alice Eliza Costello. B. in London 25 August 1881; m. 1st, 27 July 1907, Winifred Avery, d. of Thomas Belgrave, Esq. (she died 1950); secondly, 1952, Joan Barbara Alice Piper, d. of George Earle Hewitt, Esq. Educ. at Dulwich Coll., and Peterhouse, Cambridge; M.A., LL.B. A Barrister-at-Law, Inner Temple, called 24 June 1903. Lecturer in common law, University Coll., Nottingham 1906-08 and London County Council 1909-10. Wrote on the Law relating to Engineering, the Profiteering Act 1919; and numerous articles on Insurance, etc. A Liberal. Unsuccessfully

77

contested the Strand division in January 1910, and Exeter in 1918 and 1922. Elected for Huntingdonshire in December 1923 and sat until he was defeated in October 1924. Knighted 1935. C.B.E. 1946. Served with R.A.S.C. 1916-18. Judge of High Court of Calcutta 1926-40. High Sheriff of Devon 1945-46. Dept. Chairman of Devon Quarter Sessions 1940-47, Chairman 1947-56. J.P. for Devon. Died 2 December 1972.

[1924 2nd ed.]

COTTS, Sir William Dingwall Mitchell, Bart., K.B.E. 24 Hans Place, London. Coldharbour Wood, East Liss, Hampshire. National Liberal, Royal Societies', Thatched House, and Royal Automobile. S. of William Cotts, Esq., of Sanquhar, Dumfriesshire. B. 15 July 1871 at Tynron, Co. Dumfriesshire; m. 1901, Agnes, 2nd d. of Robert Sloane, Esq., of Sanquhar. Educ. privately, and at Wallace Hall Academy. A Merchant, Colliery Proprietor and Shipowner. Created Bart. 1921. A National Liberal. Unsuccessfully contested the Western Isles division of Inverness and Ross and Cromarty in 1918. Elected for the Western Isles division of Inverness and Ross and Cromarty in November 1922 and sat until he retired in November 1923. K.B.E. 1919. J.P. for County of London. Died 20 January 1932.

[1923]

COUPER, James Brown. 2 Derby Crescent, Glasgow. Carlton, Royal Automobile, Royal Thames Yacht, St. Stephen's, 1900, Conservative, and New. Royal Clyde Yacht, and Royal Scottish Automobile, Glasgow. S. of John Stewart Couper, Esq., Shipowner, of Glasgow. B. 1870. Educ. at Glasgow High School. A Shipowner; Member of the Baltic Shipping Exchange, of the Glasgow Royal Exchange, Trades' House, Merchants' House, and Chamber of Commerce, Glasgow. Dept.-Lieut., J.P. for the County and City of Glasgow. Member of Interallied Parliamentary Mission to Washington and Ottawa 1925, and of Empire Parliamentary Delegation to Australia 1926. A Conservative. Unsuccessfully contested the St. Rollox division of Glasgow in 1922 and the Maryhill division of Glasgow in 1923. Elected for the Maryhill division of Glasgow in October

1924 and sat until he was defeated in May 1929. Died 14 October 1946. [1929]

COURTAULD, Maj. John Sewell. Burton Park, Petworth. Carlton, and Turf. S. of Sidney Courtauld, Esq., of Bocking Place, Braintree. B. 26 August 1880; m. 1907, Henrietta Barbara, d. of Sir Arthur Holland. Educ. at Rugby, and King's Coll., Cambridge. Served on the Western Front, in Greece and Palestine. Maj. 1917; M.C. A Conservative. Elected for the Chichester division of West Sussex in October 1924 and sat until he died on 20 April 1942.

[1942]

COURTHOPE, Col. Rt. Hon. Sir George Loyd, Bart. Artillery Mansions, Victoria Street, London. Whiligh, Sussex. Carlton, Farmers, Bath, and National. S. of George J. Courthope, Esq., of Whiligh, Sussex. B. 12 June 1877; m. 1st, 14 June 1899, Hilda, d. of Maj.-Gen. H. Pelham Close (she died 11 November 1940); secondly, 5 September 1944, Margaret, d. of Frederick Barry, Esq. Educ. at Eton, and Christ Church, Oxford, Honorary M.A. Barrister-at-Law, Inner Temple 1901. Commanded 5th Battalion (Cinque Ports) Royal Sussex Regiment and Kent and Sussex Territorial Infantry Brigade; Chairman of Prayer Book Copyright Company, Central Chamber of Agriculture 1909, United Club 1908-09, Dept. Commission on Swine Fever 1910. Vice-President of Land Agents' Society and of National Rifle Association; President Sugar Beet Council 1913, of English Forestry Association 1916-21, of Royal English Arboricultural Society 1918-20; Assistant Controller of Timber Supplies 1917-19. Chairman English Consultative Committee under the Forestry Acts 1919-27; President of Central Landowners' Association; a Forestry Commissioner; member of Central Board of Finance of Church of England. Served in France with 1st division B.E.F. 1915; M.C., T.D. D.L., J.P. for Sussex. Chairman of Brewers Society 1937-38; President Royal Agricultural Society 1944. Represented the Forestry Commission in House of Commons, and Chichester Diocese in National Church Assembly; Ecclesiastical Commissioner; member of Council of

Surveyors Institution, Chairman of Unionist Agricultural Committee. A Liveryman of the City of London and Prime Warden of the Goldsmiths' Company. Director of Southern Railway and other companies. Created Bart. 1925. PC. 1937. A Conservative. Sat for the Rye division of Sussex from 1906 until he retired in June 1945. Created Baron Courthope 1945. Died 2 September 1955. [1945]

COVE, William George. Continued in House after 1945: full entry in Volume IV.

COWAN, Dugald McCoig. 7 Novar Drive, Glasgow. S. of John Cowan, Esq., of Glasgow. B. 1865. Unmarried. Educ. at the Glasgow University, M.A.; LL.D Aberdeen. He was Head Master of North Kelvinside Higher Grade School, Glasgow from 1896 to 1919, and took a leading part in the Educational Institute of Scotland and other educational bodies. A Liberal. Sat for the Scottish Universities from December 1918 until his death on 30 December 1933. [1934]

COWAN, Sir William Henry. 215 Ashley Gardens, London. The Crow's Nest, Fairwarp, Uckfield, Sussex. Carlton, Constitutional, and Royal Automobile. S. of William Cowan, Esq., of Edinburgh. B. 22 May 1862; m. 2 August 1899, Winifrede, d. of Daniel Smith, Esq., of Edinburgh. Educ. at Merchiston Castle, and at Collegiate School, and University of Edinburgh. Knight Bach. 1917. Chairman of Parkinson and W. and B. Cowan, Limited, and its subsidiaries. Sat as a Liberal for the Guildford division of Surrey 1906 January 10, and for E. Aberdeenshire from January 1910-22 when he was defeated. Joined Conservative Party in 1923. Elected as a conservative for N. Islington in December 1923. Sat until he retired in May 1929. J.P. for Sussex. Died 11 January 1932. [1929]

COX, Capt. Horace Brimson Trevor. Roche Old Court, Winterslow, Wiltshire. Bachelors', and Guards. S. of C. Horace Cox, Esq., of Roche Old Court, Winterslow. B. 14 June 1908; m. 1957, Gwenda Mary, d. of Alfred Ellis, Esq., of Woodford. Educ.

at Eton, and abroad, studied Commercial and Political Conditions in Germany 1927-29 and in America 1929-30, and Canada and in the Near East, Egypt and Palestine 1934. Capt. Welsh Guards (S.R.). Served with B.E.F. in France December 1939-June 1940 and on General Staff 1940-44. Parliamentary Private Secretary to Rt. Hon. Sir Ronald Cross, Bart., when Parliamentary Secretary Board of Trade May 1938 and when Minister of Economic Warfare September 1939-May 1940 and to Rt. Hon. H.V. Willink when Minister of Health 1945. A Conservative. Unsuccessfully contested N.E. Derbyshire in November 1935. Elected for the Stalybridge and Hyde division of Cheshire in April 1937 and sat until he was defeated in July 1945. Unsuccessfully contested Birkenhead in February 1950 and, as an Independent Conservative, Salisbury in February 1965. Joined Labour Party March 1966. Honorary Treasurer of Russian Relief Association 1945-47. Member of Executive Committee of Country Landowners' Association 1964-68. Assumed the surname Trevor Cox in lieu of Cox.* [1945]

COZENS-HARDY, Hon. William Hepburn. 1 Halkin Place, London. Travellers', and Athenaeum. S. of Lord Cozens-Hardy. B. in London 25 March 1868; m. 1895, Constance Gertrude Lilian d. of Col. Sir William Everett, K.C.M.G. Educ. at New Coll., Oxford. Called to the bar, Lincoln's Inn 1893. K.C. 1912. Commander R.N.V.R.; 1914-18 on Admiralty War Staff. J.P. for Norfolk. A Liberal Coalitionist. Elected for S. Norfolk in December 1918 and sat until he succeeded to the Peerage as Baron Cozens-Hardy in June 1920. Died, as the result of a road accident at Buchhof in Bavaria, 25 May 1924. [1920]

CRADDOCK, Sir Reginald Henry, G.C.I.E., K.C.S.I. 3 Whitehall Court, London. East India Service, and Ranelagh. S. of Surgeon-Maj. William Craddock. B. 11 March 1864; m. 6 March 1888, Frances Henrietta, C.B.E., d. of Gen. H.R. Browne, C.B. (she died 19 December 1932). Educ. at Wellington, and Keble Coll., Oxford; Honorary Fellow 1931. Joined

I.C.S. 1884; Commissioner Nagpur division 1901-07; Chief Commissioner Central Provinces 1907-12; member of Viceroy's Council 1912-17; Lieut.-Gov. of Burma 1917-22; 1st Chancellor of Rangoon University 1920; retired from I.C.S. 1923; member of Royal Commission on I.C.S. 1923-24. A Conservative. Sat for the Combined English Universities from October 1931 until his death on 10 February 1937. [1937]

CRAIG, Capt. Rt. Hon. Charles Curtis. 29 Brompton Square, London. Carlton, and Royal Yacht Squadron. 5th s. of James Craig, Esq., J.P., of Craigavon. B. 18 February 1869; m. 1897, Lillian Bowring, d. of J. Wimble, Esq., of Ditton Hill, Surrey (she died 1954). Educ. at Clifton Coll. Capt. 11th Battalion Royal Irish Rifles. Served in France 1914-16. Chevalier of the Legion of Honour. Dept.-Lieut. for Co. Down. Parliamentary Secretary Ministry of Pensions 1923-24; PC. (N. Ireland) 1922. A Conservative. Sat for S. Antrim from February 1903 to 1922. Sat for Antrim Co. from November 1922 until he retired in May 1929. Died 28 January 1960. [1929]

CRAIG, Sir Ernest, Bart. Milton House, Alsager, Cheshire. S. of William Young Craig, Esq. B. 1859; m. 24 August 1887, Anna, d. of James McKay, Esq., of Pittsburgh. Educ. at Sandbach Grammar School, Canton Schule of Zurich, and at College of Physical Science, Newcastle-on-Tyne. A Mining Engineer with large interests in New Mexico. Had charge of Labour questions in Iron and Steel Production Department of Ministry of Munitions 1916-18. Parliamentary Private Secretary to Sir Laming Worthington Evans 1917-18. Member of Mission to U.S.A. 1918. Created Bart. 1927. A Conservative. Unsuccessfully contested the Crewe division of Cheshire in December 1910. Represented Crewe from 1912-18 when he retired, and from October 1924 until he retired in May 1929. Died 9 April 1933. [1929]

CRAIG, Lieut.-Col. Sir James, Bart. Craigavon, Co. Down. Cleve Court, Streatley-on-Thames, Berkshire. 6 Victoria Square, London. Carlton, and Constitu-

tional. S. of James Craig, Esq., of Craigavon, Co. Down. B. 8 January 1871; m. 1905, Cecil Mary Nowell Dering, d. of Sir Daniel Tupper, M.V.O. Served in South Africa 1900-02; Dept.-Lieut. for Co. Down; Treasurer of the Household December 1916 to January 1918. Parliamentary Secretary to Ministry of Pensions January 1919 to April 1920; Parliamentary and Financial Secretary to the Admiralty April 1920-June 1921. Created Bart. in 1918. A Unionist. Unsuccessfully contested Fermanagh N. in March 1903. Sat for E. Down 1906-18 and for mid Down from 1918 until he resigned in June 1921. PC. (Ireland) 1921 and PC. (Northern Ireland) 1922. Honorary LL.D. Queen's University, Belfast 1922. Honorary D.C.L. Oxford 1926. Created Visct. Craigavon 1927. Sat in the Parliament of Northern Ireland for Co. Down 1921-29 and for N. Down 1929-40. Prime Minister of Northern Ireland from June 1921 until his death on 24 November 1940. [1921

CRAIG, Norman Carlyle. 1 Harley Street, London. Fairfield House, St. Peter's, Thanet. 10 King's Bench Walk, Temple, London. Carlton, Royal Thames Yacht, and St. Stephen's. S. of William Simpson Craig, Esq., M.D., of Ham Common, Surrey. B. 15 November 1868; m. 9 November 1918, Dorothy, widow of Lieut. A.W. Stone, R.N.V.R., and d. of Mr. and Mrs. E.S. Eccles, of Hoylake. Educ. at Bedford and Peterhouse, Cambridge; Class. Sch. and Prizeman, M.A. Was called to the bar 1892; K.C. 1909; bencher of the Inner Temple 1919. Sub-Lieut. R.N.R. September 1914; Lieut. Commander R.N.V.R. April 1915. A Unionist. Elected for the Isle of Thanet division of Kent in January 1910 and sat until his death on 14 October 1919. [1919]

CRAIK, Rt. Hon. Sir Henry, Bart., K.C.B. 5a Dean's Yard, London. Athenaeum. S. of the Very Rev. James Craik, D.D., of Glasgow, and Margaret, d. of W. Grieve, Esq., of Leith. B. 18 October 1846 at Glasgow; m. 1873, Fanny Esther, d. of Charles Duffield, Esq., of Manchester (she died 13 December 1923). Educ. at High School, and the University, Glasgow, and Balliol Coll., Oxford; M.A. Was an Examiner in Education Department 1870; Senior Examiner 1878. Secretary of Scottish Education Department 1885-1904. C.B. 1887. K.C.B. 1897. PC. 1918. Created Bart. 1926. LL.D. Glasgow and St. Andrews. J.P. for London. Author of *Life of Swift*, *The State and Education*, *Century of Scottish History*, *Life of Clarendon*, and other works. A Conservative. Sat for Glasgow and Aberdeen Universities from 1906 to 1918, and for the Scottish Universities from December 1918 until his death on 16 March 1927.   [1927]

CRANBORNE, Rt. Hon. Robert Arthur James Gascoyne Cecil, Visct. 25 Charles Street, London. S. of James, 4th Marq. of Salisbury, K.C.B. B. 27 April 1893; m. 8 December 1915, Elizabeth, d. of the Rt. Hon. Lord Richard Cavendish. Educ. at Eton, and Christ Church, Oxford. A Parliamentry Under-Secretary of State for Foreign Affairs August 1935-February 1938, when he resigned. Paymaster-Gen. May-October 1940; Secretary of State for the Dominions October 1940-February 1942. A Conservative. Elected for Dorset S. in May 1929 and sat until January 1941 when he was called up to the House of Lords as Baron Cecil of Essendon. Styled Visct. Cranborne 1903-47. PC. 1940. Secretary of State for Colonies February-November 1942. Lord Privy Seal November 1942-September 1943 and October 1951-May 1952. Secretary of State for Dominions September 1943-July 1945. Leader of the House of Lords February 1942-July 1945 and October 1951-March 1957. Secretary of State for Commonwealth Relations March-November 1952. Lord President of the Council November 1952-March 1957. Leader of the Conservative Party in the House of Lords February 1942-March 1957, when he resigned over the release of Archbishop Makarios. K.G. 1946, Chancellor of Order of Garter 1960-72. Succeeded his father as Marq. of Salisbury 1947. High Steward of Hertford 1947-72. Chancellor of Liverpool University 1951-71. Chairman of Royal Commission on Historical Monuments 1957-72. Died 23 February 1972.   [1941]

CRAVEN-ELLIS, William Craven. Round Hill, Bramshaw, Lyndhurst. Home Farm, Beaulieu, Hampshire. Royal Southampton Yacht. S. of Thomas Ellis, Esq., of Manchester. Grand-s. of William Craven, founder of Craven Brothers, Machine Tool Makers. B. 1880; m. 1906, Grace, d. of William Henry Stanley, Esq., of Liverpool. Educ. at Manchester Grammar School. Assumed the additional surname of Craven by deed Poll 1931. Served 1914-19. Lieut. T.A. Reserve 1915. Senior partner of Ellis and Sons, Valuers and Surveyors, of Manchester and Liverpool; Chairman and Managing Director and Director of many companies covering Finance, Investments Estate development, Property management, Land Machine Tool Manufacture. A Nationalist. Unsuccessfully contested Barnsley as a Conservative in 1923 and 1929. Sat for Southampton from October 1931 until he was defeated in July 1945. Unsuccessfully contested Southampton Itchen as an Independent Nationalist in February 1950. Chairman of House of Commons Monetary Committee 1934-44. Master of Worshipful Company of Glovers 1943-44. Died 17 December 1959.   [1945]

CRAWFORD, Col, Rt. Hon. Robert Gordon Sharman. See SHARMAN-CRAWFORD, Col. Rt. Hon. Robert Gordon.

CRAWFURD, Horace Evelyn. 63a Ebury Street, London. National Liberal. S of John William Crawfurd, Esq. B. 13 January 1881. Educ. at Merchant Taylor's School, and at St. John's Coll., Oxford; Fellow. Lecturer at Liverpool University 1904-10. R.N.A.S. and R.F.C. A Liberal. Unsuccessfully contested W. Walthamstow in 1922 and 1923. Elected for W. Walthamstow in October 1924 and sat until he was defeated in May 1929. Unsuccessfully contested E. Islington in February 1931 and W. Leicester in November 1935. Chairman of National Federation of Scrap Iron Steel and Metal Merchants 1939-53. President of National Road Haulage Association. Died 14 March 1958.   [1929]

CRICHTON-STUART, Lord Colum Edmund. Ardencraig, Rothesay, Isle of Bute. Travellers'. 3rd s. of 3rd Marq. of Bute. B. 3 April 1886; m. 14 February 1940, Elizabeth Caroline, d. of Sir Edward Stanley Hope, K.C.B., and widow of 6th Marq. of Lansdowne. Educ. at Harrow, and Christ Church, Oxford, B.A. 2nd Lieut. Scots Guards S.R.; Attache in H.M. Diplomatic Service 1910; 3rd Secretary 1913; 2nd Secre-1919, retired 1919; J.P. for Buteshire. A Conservative. Unsuccessfully contested Cardiff E. in 1918. Sat for the Northwich division of Cheshire from November 1922 until he retired in June 1945. Lord-Lieut. of Bute 1953-57. Died 18 August 1957. [1945]

CRIPPS, Rt. Hon. Sir Richard Stafford. Continued in House after 1945: full entry in Volume IV.

CRITCHLEY, Alexander. Ambassadors' Hotel, Upper Woburn Place, London. Aigburth Road, Liverpool. S. of William Edwin Critchley, Esq. B. 17 December 1893; m. 1925, Lucy Lindsay. Educ. at Liverpool University. Member of Liverpool City Council. An Accountant. A Conservative. Elected for the Edge Hill division of Liverpool in November 1935 and sat until he retired in June 1945. Died 4 September 1974. [1945]

CRITCHLEY, Brigadier-Gen. Alfred Cecil. House of Commons, London. S. of Oswald Asheton Critchley, Esq. B. 1890, near Calgary, Canada; m. 1st, 1916, Maryon, d. of John Galt, Esq.; secondly, 1927, Joan, d. of Reginald Foster, Esq.; thirdly, 1938, Diana Fishwick. Educ. at St. Bees, and Royal Military Coll., Kingston, Canada. Served with 7th Canadian Infantry Brigade. D.S.O. 1916; C.M.G. 1919. A National Conservative. Unsuccessfully contested the Gorton division of Manchester in May 1929 and E. Islington in February 1931. Elected for the Twickenham division of Middlesex in June 1934 and sat until he retired in October 1935. C.B.E. 1943. Director-Gen. of B.O.A.C. 1943-46. Chairman of Skyways Limited 1946-54. Died 9 February 1963. [1935]

CRITTALL, Valentine George. New House, Chelmsford. S. of Francis Henry Crittall, Esq., Manufacturer. B. at Braintree 28 June 1884; m. 1st, 28 June 1916, Clive Lillian, d. of Charles Lunday MacDermott, Esq. (she died 1932); secondly, 1933, Mrs. Lydia Keed, d. of J.J. Revy, Esq. (she died 1947); thirdly, 1955, Mrs. Phyllis Dorothy Parker, d. of C. Cloutman, Esq. Educ. at Uppingham. Managing Director of a company making metal window frames. A Labour Member. Elected for the Maldon division of Essex in December 1923 and sat until he was defeated in October 1924. Parliamentary Private Secretary to Lord Thomson, Secretary of State for Air in 1924. J.P. for Essex. Knighted 1930. Director of Bank of England 1948-55. Created Baron Braintree 1948. Died 21 May 1961. [1924 2nd ed.]

CROFT, Brigadier-Gen. Sir Henry Page, Bart., C.M.G. 69 Cadogan Gardens, London. Knole, Bournemouth. Carlton. S. of Richard Benyon Croft, Esq., R.N., of Fanhams Hall, Hertfordshire. B. 22 June 1881; m. 10 July 1907, Hon. Nancy Borwick, d. of 1st Baron Borwick. Educ. at Shrewsbury, Eton, and Trinity Hall, Cambridge. Managing Director of Henry Page and Company Limited, Maltsters, Ware. Lieut.-Col. Commanding 1st Battalion Hertfordshire Regiment 1920-24; temporary Brigadier-Gen. 1916, and Hon. Brigadier-Gen. 1917; Brevet-Col. 1924. Served in France 1914-16. T.D. Dept.-Lieut. for Hertfordshire 1917. Created Bart. 1924. Chairman of Executive Committee of Empire Industries Association. Chancellor of the Primrose League 1928-29. A Conservative. Unsuccessfully contested Lincoln in 1906. Elected for Christchurch in January 1910 and December 1910, and for Bournemouth in December 1918. Sat until 1940 when he was created Baron Croft. Principal organiser of the National Party 1917-22 and elected in 1918 as a National Party candidate although without Conservative opposition. Under-Secretary of State for War May 1940-July 1945. Chairman of Organisation Committee of Tariff Reform League 1913-17. Died 7 December 1947. [1940]

CROOK, Charles Williamson 15 Manor Road, Sidcup. S. of William Crook, Esq., of Preston. B. 1862; m. 1900, Grace, d. of Benjamin Swinfer, Esq., of Hackney. Educ. at Barrow-in-Furness, Alston Coll., near Preston, and St. John's Coll., Battersea. Headmaster of Wood Green Central County Secondary School; President of the National Union of Teachers 1916-17; a member of the Burnham Committees. Member of the Senate of London University, and of the Royal Commission of the Position of Natural Science in Great Britain. A Conservative. Elected for East Ham N. in November 1922 and sat until he was defeated in December 1923. Again elected for East Ham N. in October 1924 and sat until his death on 29 March 1926.   [1926]

CROOKE, Sir (John) Smedley. Hopwood Alvechurch. Plas Merian, Aberdovey, Merioneth. Constitutional. S. of Charles Crooke, Esq., of Walsall. B. 1861 at Matlock, Derbyshire; m. 30 April 1895, Pattie, d. of the Rev. William Edwards, of Kilsby, Northamptonshire. Educ. at Aldridge Grammer School and Shoal Hill Coll., Cannock. Member of Bromsgrove Board of Guardians and Rural District Council, and of Worcester County Council and T.F.A. Fellow of Guild of Church Musicians and of Victoria Coll. of Music. Member National Executive Council of British Legion. J.P. for Birmingham; President of Birmingham County Council of British Legion; Knight Bach. January 1938. A Conservative. Sat for the Deritend division of Birmingham from November 1922-May 1929, when he was defeated. Re-elected for the Deritend division in October 1931. Sat until he retired in June 1945. Died 13 October 1951.   [1945]

CROOKS, Rt. Hon. William. 81 Gough Street, Poplar, London. S. of George Crooks, Esq. B. 1852 at Poplar; m. 1st, 1871, d. of Thomas South, Esq., of Hull (she died 1892); secondly, 1893, d. of John Lake, Esq., of Gloucester. Educ. at George Green School, and partly at Poplar Poor Law School. Started work when only 9 years of age, and was apprenticed to a Cooper in 1866. Was a member of the London County Council 1892-1910; a member of Metropolitan Asylums Board; Chairman of Poplar Board of Guardians 1898-1906, and Mayor of Poplar 1901. PC. 1916. A Labour Member. Sat for Woolwich from 1903 to January 1910, when he was defeated. Re-elected for Woolwich in December 1910 and sat until December 1918, when he was elected for Woolwich E. Sat until he resigned in February 1921. Died 5 June 1921.   [1921]

CROOKSHANK, Col. Chichester de Windt. 2 Ryder Street, London. Johnstounburn, Humbie, East Lothian. Carlton, and Bath. New, Edinburgh. S. of Col. A.C.W. Crookshank, C.B. B. 18 October 1868; m. 1910, Mary, d. of Andrew Usher, Esq., of Johnstounburn. Educ. at Brackenbury's School, Wimbledon, and Royal Military Academy, Woolwich. Joined R.E. 1887; Lieut.-Col. R. of O. 1916; Brevet-Col. 1924. Served in Miranzai Expedition 1891, in South African War 1900-02, in Natal Native Rebellion 1906, in France, etc. 1914-18; member of H.M.'s Body Guard, Honorary Corps of Gentlemen at Arms 1920, and of King's Body Guard for Scotland, Royal Company of Archers 1929; K.(G.) St.J. J.P. for East Lothian 1928. A Conservative. Unsuccessfully contested Great Yarmouth in 1922, and Berwick and Haddington in 1923. Elected for Berwick and Haddington in October 1924 and sat until he retired in May 1929. Elected for Bootle in October 1931 and sat until he retired in October 1935. F.S.A. Member of Haddington District Council 1940-48. Died 23 October 1958.   [1935]

CROOKSHANK, Rt. Hon. Harry Frederick Comfort. Continued in House after 1945: full entry in Volume IV.

CROOM-JOHNSON, Reginald Powell. 3 Cresswell Gradens, London. 1 Hare Court, Temple, London. Carlton, and Garrick. S. of Oliver Croom-Johnson, Esq. B. 27 July 1879; m. 9 September 1909, Ruby, d. of E.E. Hobbs, Esq., of Clifton. Educ. at Bristol Cathedral School, and London University. LL.B. Solicitor 1901. A Barrister-at-Law, Inner Temple 1907; K.C. 1927; Bencher 1935. Recorder of Bath from 1928. Assisted in raising the Old Boys' Corps

August 1914; later joined K.O.Y.L.I.; attached to Judge Advocate General's Department for special service connected with Mesopotamia Commission 1917. Author of Legal and other works. A Conservative. Elected for the Bridgwater division of Somerset in May 1929 and sat until he was appointed a High Court Judge in 1938. Knighted 1938. Judge of King's Bench Division 1938-54. J.P. and Dept.-Chairman of Quarter Sessions, Somerset. Died 29 December 1957. [1938]

CROSS, Rt. Hon. Sir Ronald Hibbert, Bart. Continued in House after 1945: full entry in Volume IV.

CROSSLEY, Anthony Crommelin. 26 Mallord Street, London. Travellers', Beefsteak, and Flyfishers'. S. of Sir Kenneth Crossley, 2nd Bart. B. 13 August 1903; m. 7 February 1927, Clare, d. of Brigadier-Gen. Alan Thomson, D.S.O., Royal Engineers, of Craig Hall, Aberdeenshire. Educ. at Eton, and Magdalen Coll., Oxford. Parliamentary Private Secretary to Col. C.M. Headlam 1932-34, and to Capt. A.U. Hudson, Parliamentary Secretaries Minister of Transport November 1935. A Conservative. Elected for Oldham in October 1931, and for the Stretford division of Lancashire in November 1935. Sat until his death in an air crash off the coast of Denmark on 15 August 1939. [1939]

CROWDER, John Frederick Ellenborough. Continued in House after 1945: full entry in Volume IV.

CROWLEY, Dr. John. Ballycastle, Ballina, Co. Mayo. Educ. at Queen's Coll., Cork. A Sinn Fein Member. Elected for N. Mayo in December 1918 but did not take his seat. Member of Dail for N. Mayo to 1921, for N. and W. Mayo 1921-23, for N. Mayo 1923-27. An Anti-Treaty Member, joined Fianna Fail in 1926. Dispensary Medical Officer at Ballycastle. Licentiate of Royal Coll. of Surgeons and Royal Coll. of Physicians. Died 17 February 1934. [1922]

CROWLEY, N. James. Listowel, Co. Kerry. A Sinn Fein Member. Returned unopposed for N. Kerry in December 1918 but did not take his seat. Member of Dail for N. Kerry to 1921, for Kerry and W. Limerick 1921-23, for Kerry 1923-32. Pro-Treaty, later Cumann na nGaedheal Member. Member of Royal Coll. of Veterinary Surgeons from 1906. Died 21 January 1946. [1922]

CRUDDAS, Col. Bernard, D.S.O. Middleton Hall, Morpeth. Naval & Military. S. of John Cruddas, Esq., of Stoke Bishop, Bristol. B. 1 January 1882; m. 22 October 1908, Dorothy, d. of George Wilkinson, Esq., of Newcastle-upon-Tyne. Educ. at Waynflete, Winchester, and Royal Military Coll., Sandhurst. J.P. and Dept.-Lieut. for Northumberland. Joined Northumberland Fusiliers 1900, retired 1923. A National Conservative. Unsuccessfully contested the Wansbeck division of Northumberland in May 1929. Elected for the Wansbeck division of Northumberland in October 1931 and again in November 1935. Sat until he resigned in 1940. D.S.O. 1918. High Sheriff of Northumberland 1942. Died 23 December 1959. [1940]

CULVERWELL, Cyril Tom. 44 Prince's Gardens, London. S. of Thomas James Holmes Culverwell, Esq., of Litfield House, Clifton, Bristol, and Louisa, d. of Joseph Tinn, Esq., of Frenchay, Bristol. B. 22 October 1895; m. 5 February 1919, Christabel, d. of Dr. William Fitzwilliam Carter, of Bristol. Educ. at Clifton Coll., and Queens' Coll., Cambridge. A Conservative. Elected for Bristol W. in February 1928 and sat until he retired in June 1945. Member of Bristol City Council 1924-30. Died 29 October 1963. [1945]

CUNDIFF, Frederick William. Continued in House after 1945: full entry in Volume IV.

CUNLIFFE, Sir Joseph Herbert, K.C. 15 Old Square, Lincoln's Inn, London. Hou Hatch, South Weald, Essex. S. of Thomas Cunliffe, Esq., J.P., Newspaper Proprietor, of Bolton. B. 1 July 1867; m. 1st, 1894, Mary, d. of Edward Balshaw, Esq., of Heaton, Bolton (she died 1930);

secondly, 1932, Maud, d. of Joseph Clegg, Esq., of High Crompton (she died 1954). Educ. at Bolton Grammar School. Barrister-at-Law Middle Temple and Lincoln's Inn 1896; K.C. 1912. H.M. Attorney Gen. of Duchy of Lancaster from 1921-1946; Bencher, Lincoln's Inn 1919; member of the Gen. Council of the bar 1914-46 and of the Council of Legal Education 1920-45. Knighted 1926. Chairman of Lord Chancellor's Commission on County Courts 1917-19 and Home Office Commission on Supervision of Charities 1925-27. A Conservative. Elected for Bolton in December 1923 and again October 1924. Sat until he retired in May 1929. Chairman of Gen. Council of the Bar 1932-46. Treasurer of Lincoln's Inn 1941. Chairman of Essex Quarter Sessions 1937-46. K.B.E. 1946. Died 9 April 1963. [1929]

CUNLIFFE-LISTER, Rt. Hon.Sir Philip, G.B.E., M.C. 7 Lygon Place, London. Swinton, Masham, Yorkshire. Carlton. S. of Yarburgh George Lloyd-Greame, Esq., of Sewerby House, Bridlington. B. 1 May 1884; m. 5 September 1912, Mary Constance, d. of the Rev. Ingram Boynton, Rector of Barmston, Driffield. Educ. at Winchester, and at University Coll., Oxford. Barrister-at-Law, Inner Temple 1908. Served in France 1915-16; Joint Secretary Ministry of National Service 1917-18; K.B.E. 1920. G.B.E. 1929. Assumed the surname of Cunliffe-Lister in lieu of Lloyd-Greame in 1924. Parliamentary Secretary Board of Trade 1920-21; Secretary of Overseas Trade Department 1921-22; PC. 1922; President of Board of Trade October 1922-January 1924, November 1924-June 1929, and August-October 1931; Secretary of State for the Colonies November 1931-June 1935. A Conservative. Sat for the Hendon division of Middlesex from December 1918 until he retired in October 1935. Created Visct. Swinton 1935 and Earl of Swinton 1955. Secretary of State for Air June 1935-May 1938, when he resigned. Appointed Chairman of the new Home Defence (Security) Executive in May 1940; this was often called the 'Swinton Committee' and, although formed to identify 'fifth column' enemies, handled wider security issues. Companion of Honour 1943. Chairman of United Kingdom Commercial Corporation 1940-42. Minister resident in W. Africa June 1942-October 1944. Minister of Civil Aviation October 1944-July 1945. President of National Union of Conservative and Unionist Associations 1949. Chancellor of Duchy of Lancaster and Minister of Materials October 1951-November 1952. Secretary of State for Commonwealth Relations November 1952-April 1955. Dept.-Leader of House of Lords 1951-55. Dept.-Lieut. for the N. Riding of Yorkshire. Died 27 July 1972. [1935]

CUNNINGHAM, Patrick. Continued in House after 1945: full entry in Volume IV.

CUNNINGHAM-REID, Capt. Alec Stratford, D.F.C. 32 Gloucester Place, London. Marlborough, Carlton, and Bath. S. of the Rev. Arthur Cunningham-Reid. B. 20 April 1895; m. 1st, 12 May 1927, Hon. Ruth Mary Ashley, d. of Rt. Hon. Lord Mount Temple (from whom he obtained a divorce 1939); secondly, 1944, Angela Williams (divorced 1949); thirdly, Hélène Taylor-Smith. Educ. at University Coll. School, and Clare Coll., Cambridge. Served in France 1914-18; Sappers then R.F.C. Parliamentary Private Secretary (unpaid) to Sir John Baird, Bart., First Commissioner of Works 1922, to Lieut.-Col. Rt. Hon. Wilfrid Ashley, Minister of Transport 1924-29. Elected for Warrington in November 1922, unsuccessfully contested Warrington in December 1923. Sat for Warrington again from October 1924-May 1929 when he unsuccessfully contested Southampton. Elected for St. Marylebone in April 1932 and sat until he was defeated in July 1945. A Conservative until May 1942 when the Whip was withdrawn; thereafter sat as an Independent Conservative and contested St. Marylebone in 1945 but was defeated by the official Conservative candidate. Died 26 March 1977. [1945]

CURRY, Aaron Charlton. Weetwood, Whickham, Newcastle-upon-Tyne. 8 Ellison Place, Newcastle-upon-Tyne. S. of Thomas Curry, Esq., Colliery Engineman, of Newcastle-upon-Tyne. B. 17 August 1887; m.

14 August 1913, Jane Cranston, d. of George Wilson, Esq., of Newcastle-upon-Tyne. Educ. at elementary schools. A Corporate Accountant. Member of Whickham Urban District Council 1931-37. A Liberal. Unsuccessfully contested the Houghton-le-Spring division of Durham in 1923 and 1924, Wallsend in July 1926, and the Bishop Auckland division of Durham on 7 February 1929 and again on 30 May 1929. Elected for the Bishop Auckland division in October 1931 as a Liberal National, but rejoined the Liberals in 1933 and sat until he was defeated in November 1935. Lord Mayor of Newcastle-on-Tyne 1949-50, and 1956-57. Member of Newcastle City Council 1941-57, Alderman 1951-57. Died 6 January 1957.
[1935]

CURTIS-BENNETT, Sir Henry Honywood. 89 Piccadilly, London. Boreham Lodge, Chelmsford. Garrick, Beefsteak, Royal Automobile, and National Sporting. S. of Sir Henry Curtis-Bennett, Metropolitan Magistrate. B. 31 July 1879; m. 4 April 1903, Elsie Eleanor, d. of A.A. Dangar, Esq., of Baroona, New South Wales. Educ. at Radley Coll., and Trinity Coll., Cambridge. A Barrister-at-Law, Middle Temple 1902; K.C. 1919; Knight 1922. Served with Secret Service 1916-19. A Conservative. Elected for the Chelmsford division of Essex in October 1924 and sat until he resigned in 1926. Dept.-Chairman of Essex Quarter Sessions 1923-35, Chairman 1935-36. Recorder of Colchester 1929-36. Chairman of County of London Sessions 1936. Died 2 November 1936. [1926]

CURZON, Francis Richard Henry Penn Curzon, Visct., C.B.E. 35 Curzon Street, London. Carlton, Turf, Marlborough, and 1900. S. of 4th Earl Howe, G.C.V.O. B. May 1884; m. 1st, 28 October 1907, Mary d. of Col. Montagu Curzon (divorced 1937); secondly, 1937, Joyce Mary McLean, d. of C.M. Jack, Esq., of Johannesburg (divorced 1943); thirdly, 1944, Sybil Shafto, d. of Francis Johnson, Esq. Educ. at Eton, and Christ Church, Oxford. Capt. R.N.V.R. from 1921; V.D. 1921; Lieut. 1906; Sub-Lieut. 1904. Commanded the "Howe" Battalion 2nd Royal Naval Brigade in Belgium and Antwerp, 1914; served in H.M.S. *Queen Elizabeth* December 1914; Aide-de-Camp 1925. A Junior Lord of the Treasury (unpaid) from November 1924 to January 1924. London Whip, Central Conservative and Unionist Central Office. A Conservative. Sat for Battersea S. from December 1918 until he succeeded to the Peerage as Earl Howe in January 1929. Styled Visct. Curzon 1900-29. C.B.E. 1924; PC. 1929. Chairman of British Racing Drivers' Club 1928-64. Died 26 July 1964.
[1929]

CUSACK, Dr. Bryan. Turloughmore, Co. Galway. Educ. at Galway Coll. Was interned in Birmingham prison. A Sinn Fein Member. Elected for N. Galway in December 1918 but did not take his seat. Member of Dail for N. Galway to 1921, for Co. Galway 1921-23 as an Anti-Treaty Member. [1922]

DAGGAR, George. Continued in House after 1945: fully entry in Volume IV.

DALKEITH, Walter John Montagu-Douglas-Scott, Earl of. 2 Grosvenor Place, London. Eildon Hall, St. Boswells. Carlton. Eld. s. of the 7th Duke of Buccleuch and and Queensbury. B. 30 December 1894; m. 21 April 1921, Esther Mary, d. of Maj. William Lascelles, Coldstream Guards. Educ. at Eton, and Christ Church, Oxford. Capt. Grenadier Guards, R. of O. Lieut.-Col. Commanding 4th K.O.S.B.'s. J.P. for Dumfriesshire; J.P. and H.M. Lieut. Roxburghshire 1932-73. Aide-de-Camp to Gov.-Gen. of Canada 1920. A Conservative. Elected for Roxburgh and Selkirk in 1923 and sat until he succeeded to the Peerage as Duke of Buccleuch and Queensberry on 19 October 1935. Styled Lord Whitchester 1894-1914 and Earl of Dalkeith 1914-35. PC. 1937. Lord Steward of the King's Household 1937-40. K.T. 1949. Lord Clerk Register and Keeper of the Signet 1956-73. Died 4 October 1973.
[1935]

DALLAS, George. 92 Great Russell Street, London. Parliamentary Labour. S. of George Dallas, Esq., of Glasgow. B. 6 August 1878; m. 1920, Mary, d. of William Brown, Esq.

Educ. at Elementary School, Technical Coll., and at London School of Economics. Chief Organiser of Agricultural Workers' Union; member of Royal Commission on Agriculture 1919-20; member of Council of Agriculture for England, and Chairman of Labour Party Advisory Commission of Agriculture and Rural Problems. Parliamentry Private Secretary to the Rt. Hon. C. Addison, Parliamentary Secretary to Ministry of Agriculture June 1929. A Labour Member. Unsuccessfully contested the Maldon division of Essex in December 1918 and November 1922, Roxburgh and Selkirk in December 1923 and October 1924. Elected for the Wellingborough division of Northamptonshire in May 1929 and sat until he was defeated in October 1931; again defeated in November 1935. Chairman of National Executive of Labour Party 1939. Chairman of Timber Control Board 1939-45. C.B.E. 1946. J.P. for Northamptonshire. Died 4 January 1961.

[1931 2nd ed.]

DALRYMPLE-WHITE, Lieut.-Col. Sir Godfrey Dalrymple, Bart. 95 Eaton Square, London. Carlton, Guards', and Bachelors'. S. of Gen. Sir Henry Dalrymple White, K.C.B. B. 6 July 1866; m. 3 June 1912, Hon. Catherine Cary, d. of 12th Visct. Falkland. Educ. at Brighton, Wellington Coll., and Sandhurst. Joined Grenadier Guards 1885; Lieut.-Col. commanding Reserve Battalion August 1914 to February 1916. Served on the staff in France February 1916 to August 1918 Aide-de-Camp to Gen. Sir John Ross in Canada 1892-93, and to Gen. Sir H. Trotter, Home District 1899-1900; served in South African War 1900-02. F.R.G.S. and F.Z.S. Created Bart. 1926. A Conservative. Unsuccessfully contested the Devizes division of Wiltshire in 1906. Elected for the Southport division of Lancashire in January and December 1910, and for Southport borough in December 1918. Sat until he retired in November 1923; re-elected for Southport in October 1924 and sat until he retired in October 1931. Assumed the surname of Dalrymple-White in lieu of White in 1926. Died 1 April 1954. [1931 2nd ed.]

DALTON, Rt. Hon. Edward Hugh John Neale. Continued in House after 1945: full entry in Volume IV.

DALTON, Florence Ruth. 5 Carlisle Mansions, Westminster. D. of Thomas Hamilton Fox, Esq. B. 1890; m. 1914, Edward Hugh John Neale Dalton, MP for Peckham 1924-29 and for Biship Auckland 1929-32, 1935-59, created Baron Dalton 1960 (he died 1962). Educ. at Chantry Mount School, Bishops Stortford, and London School of Economics. Assistant Secretary, Workers' Educational Association 1918-19. Member of London County Council 1925-31, Alderman 1936-42. A Labour Member. Elected for the Bishop Auckland division of Durham (for which constituency her husband, then MP for Peckham, was the prospective candidate) in February 1929 and sat until she retired in May 1929, when her husband was elected. Member of Arts Council 1957-62. Died 15 March 1966.

DALZIEL, Sir Davison Alexander, Bart. 18 Grosvenor Place, London. Carlton, and Junior Carlton. S. of Davison Octavian Dalziel, Esq. B. 17 October 1852; m. 29 January 1876, Harriet, d. of J. Dunning, Esq. Chairman of the Pullman Car Company Limited; Chairman of the Board and Chairman of Managing Committee of the International Sleeping Car Company. Created Bart. 1919. First introduced motor cabs into London; Proprietor of the *Evening Standard* and of the *Pall Mall Gazette*. Officier of the Legion of Honour; Commander of the Order of the Crown of Italy. A Conservative. Unsuccessfully contested the Brixton division of Lambeth in 1906. Sat for the Brixton division of Lambeth from January 1910-December 1923 when he was defeated. Re-elected for the Brixton division in October 1924 and sat until June 1927 when he was created Baron Dalziel of Wooler. Died 18 April 1928. [1927]

DALZIEL, Rt. Hon. Sir James Henry, Bart. Reform, and National Liberal. S. of James Dalziel, Esq. B. at Borgue, Kirkudbrightshire 1868; m. 1928, Amy Thackery, widow of Donald Macrae, Esq. (she died 26 June 1935). Educ. at Borgue Academy, Shrewsbury High School, and King's Coll., London. A Newspaper Proprietor (Reynolds' News). Knighted 1908; PC. 1912. Created Bart. 1918. A Liberal, who held advanced views on all political and social questions. Sat for Kirkcaldy Burghs from 1892 until he resigned in February 1921. Created Baron Dalziel of Kirkcaldy June 1921. Died 15 July 1935. [1921]

DARBISHIRE, Charles William. Queen Anne's Mansions, London. Elms Cross, Bradford-on-Avon. Reform, National Liberal, City of London, and Queen's. S. of Col. C.H. Darbishire, J.P., and Dept.-Lieut., of Plas Mawr, Penmaenmawr. B. in London 17 June 1875; m. 28 June 1905, Frances Middleton Davidson, d. of D. Davidson, Esq., Sheriff, Inverness-shire, Fort William, Scotland. Educ. at Giggleswick School. An East India Merchant. Managing Director of Paterson, Simons and Company Limited, London and Straits Settlements. Held many public offices in Singapore 1910-19. Wrote on "Commerce and Currency" in *One Hundred Years of Singapore*. A Liberal. Elected for the Westbury division of Wiltshire in November 1922 and again in December 1923. Sat until he was defeated in October 1924. Served with Singapore Volunteer Rifles 1914-19. Died in Singapore 5 June 1925. [1924 2nd ed.]

DAVIDSON, Frances Joan Davidson, Viscountess. Continued in House after 1945: full entry in Volume IV.

DAVIDSON, Rt. Hon. Sir John Colin Campbell, G.C.V.O., C.H., C.B. 16 Great College Street, London. Carlton, New University, United University, and Pratt's. S. of Sir James Mackenzie Davidson, M.B., C.M. B. 23 February 1889; m. 10 April 1919, Hon. Joan Dickinson, d. of the Rt. Hon. Lord Dickinson, K.B.E. (she was created Baroness Northchurch 1964). Educ. at Westminster, and Pembroke Coll., Cambridge. A Barrister-at-Law, Middle Temple. Private Secretary to Lord Crewe when Secretary of State for the Colonies 1910,

to the Rt. Hon. L. Harcourt 1910-15, to the Rt. Hon. A. Bonar Law 1915-16, to the Chancellor of the Exchequer 1916-20; Parliamentary Private Secretary to Leader of House of Commons November 1920-March 1921, to the Rt. Hon. S. Baldwin when President of the Board of Trade 1921-22, to the Rt. Hon. A. Bonar Law 1922-23. Chancellor of Duchy of Lancaster 1923-24; Parliamentary and Financial Secretary to the Admiralty November 1924 to December 1926. Chairman of Conservative and Unionist Organization November 1926-May 1930. Chancellor of Duchy of Lancaster November 1931-May 1937. PC. 1928. A Conservative. Returned unopposed for the Hemel Hempstead division of Hertfordshire in November 1920; elected for the same seat in 1922, but was defeated there in December 1923. Re-elected for the Hemel Hempstead division of Hertfordshire in October 1924 and sat until June 1937 when he was created Visct. Davidson. Companion of Honour 1923. G.C.V.O. 1935. Controller of Production at Ministry of Information 1940-41. President of Hispanic and Luso-Brazilian Councils, and of Anglo-Argentine Society. Died 11 December 1970. [1937]

DAVIDSON, Maj.-Gen. Sir John Humphrey, K.C.M.G., C.B., D.S.O. 9 King William Street, London. Cams Hall Farm, Fareham, Hamshire. Bath. S. of George Walter Davidson, Esq. B. 24 July 1876; m. 12 December 1905, Margaret, d. of John Peter Grant, Esq., of Rothiemurchus. Educ. at Harrow, and Sandhurst. Joined 60th Rifles 1896. Served in the South African War 1899-1902, and in France 1914-18; Maj.-Gen. 1917. Eleven times mentioned in despatches and awarded French, Belgian, and American decorations. K.C.M.G. 1919. A Conservative. Sat for the Fareham division of Hampshire from July 1918 until he resigned in February 1931. D.S.O. 1900; C.B. 1917. Col.-Commandant of King's Royal Rifle Corps 1937-45. Chairman of Union Bank of Australia 1937-49. Died Died 11 December 1954. [1931 2nd ed.]

DAVIDSON, John James. 22 Sunart Road, Glasgow. S. of John Davidson, Esq.,

Tailor, of Inverness. B. 13 December 1899; m. 1923, Mary, d. of William Stevenson, Esq. Educ. at elementary school, Glasgow. A Stereotyper. Served overseas with Royal Scots Fusiliers, H.L.I. Member of Management Committee of Glasgow I.L.P.; Chairman of Glasgow Labour Party 1933-35. Parliamentary Private Secretary to Joseph Westwood, Parliamentary Under-Secretary of State for Scotland 1941. A Labour Member. Sat for the Maryhill division of Glasgow from November 1935 until he retired in June 1945. [1945]

DAVIES, Alfred. Moorfield Terrace, Hollingworth, Nr. Manchester. B. at Stockport 1871. An Operative Spinner at Hollingworth. Member of the Executive of the Hyde Operative Cotton Spinners' Association. A Labour Member. Elected for the Clitheroe division of Lancashire in December 1918 and sat until he was defeated in November 1922; again defeated in December 1923. Died December 1940. [1922]

DAVIES, Alfred Thomas, C.B.E. The Eagles, West Hill, Highgate, London. 4 Haymarket, London. Bullockdown Cottage, Beachey Head, Eastbourne. Constitutional. S. of John Thomas Davies, Esq., of Llanarthney, Carmarthenshire. B. 17 July 1881 m. 1912, Joanna Elizabeth, d. of John Lewis, Esq., of Llanelly. Educ. at the London Polytechnic. Honorary Secretary and Organizer in London of the Welsh Prisoners of War Fund; Organizer of the All Welsh service in Westminster Abbey June 1918. Director *Pall Mall Gazette*, Director Austin Motor Company. Life Gov. of Middlesex and St. Bartholomew's Hospitals. A Conservative. Elected for Lincoln in December 1918. Sat until he retired in October 1924. C.B.E. 1920; Knighted 1931. Member of St. Pancras Borough Council 1913-19, Mayor 1931-32. Member of London County Council 1931-37. Died 16 November 1941. [1924 2nd ed.]

DAVIES, Dr. Arthur Vernon, O.B.E. The Dell, Working. St. Stephen's. S. of Edwin Edgar Davies, Esq., of Bridgend, Glamorgan. B. 10 June 1872; m. Annie, d. of J. Brooke Unwin, Esq., M.D., of Dunchurch. Educ. at Owens Coll., Manchester. Practised at Crompton, Lancashire; certifying Surgeon 1900-22; Medical Officer of Health and Infant M.O. 1919-22. M.O. and Public Vaccinator Oldham Union; Knight of Grace of Order of St. John of Jerusalem in England. A Conservative. Elected for the Royton division of Lancashire in October 1924. Sat until he retired in October 1931. Died 4 August 1942. [1931 2nd ed.]

DAVIES, David. 6 Iddesleigh Mansions, London. Plas Dinam, Llandinam, Montgomeryshire. Reform, and Bath. S. of Edward Davies, Esq., of Plas Dinam, Llandinam. B. 11 May 1880; m. 1st, 1910, Amy, d. of L.T. Penman, Esq., of Broadwood Park, Lanchester (she died 1918); secondly, 9 December 1922, Henrietta Margaret, d. of James Grant Fergusson, Esq., of Baledmund, Pitlochry. Educ. at Merchiston School, Edinburgh, and King's Coll., Cambridge; M.A., LL.D. Wales, F.R.G.S. A member of the Councils of each of the three Welsh University Colleges, the Normal Coll., Bangor, and of the Court of the University of Wales; President of Aberystwyth University Coll.; Life President of King Edward VII Welsh National Memorial Association; Director of Great Western Railway Company and of the Midland Bank; Chairman of Ocean and Wilsons Limited and Welsh Town Planning and Housing Trust. President of the Railway Benevolent Association 1919; a J.P. for Montgomeryshire and Honorary Almoner Order of St. John of Jerusalem for Wales 1918. Vice-President of League of Nations Union. A Liberal until November 1926 when he resigned the Whip; sat as an Independent 1926-29. Sat for Montgomeryshire from 1906 until he retired in May 1929. Parliamentary Private Secretary to Rt. Hon. D. Lloyd George when Minister of Munitions and Prime Minister 1916-17. President of National Library of Wales 1927-44. Created Baron Davies 1932. Died 16 June 1944. [1929]

DAVIES, David Lewis. House of Commons, London. B. 1873. Miner's agent for the Pontypridd district and election agent for the Pontypridd constituency. A Labour

Member. Unsuccessfully contested Pontypridd division of Glamorganshire in December 1918. Elected for the Pontypridd division of Glamorganshire in March and October 1931, and was returned again unopposed in November 1935. Sat until his death on 25 November 1937. [1938]

DAVIES, David Richard Seaborne. 8 Gayton Crescent, Hampstead, London. Y Garn, Pwllheli, Caernarvonshire. S. of David Seaborne Davies, Esq., of Pwllheli. B. 26 June 1904. Educ. at Pwllheli Grammar School, University Coll. of Wales, Aberystwyth, and St. John's Coll., Cambridge. Lecturer and Reader in English Law at London School of Economics 1929-45. Seconded to Nationality Division of Home Office 1941-45. A Liberal. Elected for the Caernarvon Boroughs in April 1945 and sat until he was defeated in July 1945. Professor of Common Law and Dean of the Faculty of Law, University of Liverpool 1946-71, Public Orator 1950-55, Pro-Vice Chancellor 1956-60, Warden of Derby Hall 1947-71. Member of Standing Committee on Criminal Law Revision 1959-72. President of Society of Public Teachers of Law 1960-61. President of National Eisteddfod of Wales 1955, 1973 and 1975. High Sheriff of Caernarvonshire 1967-68.*

DAVIES, Sir David Sanders. Plas-y-Castell, Denbigh. Reform. S. of John Owen Davies, Esq. B. May 1852 at Llansadrwn, Carmarthenshire; m. 1886, Jane Emily, d. of Thomas Gee, Esq., of Denbigh. Educ. at Llandovery. A Merchant, Director of Pugh, Davies and Company Limited, Manchester. Was active in County Council and educational work in Denbighshire. J.P. for Manchester 1895, and for Denbighshire 1906. High Sheriff for Denbighshire 1915. Knighted 1918. A Coalition Liberal. Elected for the Denbigh division of Denbighshire in December 1918 and sat until he retired in October 1922. Died 28 February 1934. [1922]

DAVIES, Edward Clement. Continued in House after 1945: full entry in Volume IV.

DAVIES, Ellis William. Craig Wen, Carnarvon. Reform, and National Liberal. S. of David Davies, Esq., of Bethesda. B. 12 April 1871; m. 1901, Minnie, d. of Richard Hughes, Esq., of Portmadoc (she died 1931). Educ. at Liverpool Coll. Admitted Solicitor 1899. 1st Cl. Honours, Law Society Prize. Alderman of Carnarvon County Council; Gov. of N. Wales University Coll., Bangor; Director of Selfridge and Company Limited, and of the National Press of Wales. Member of Lord Faversham's Commission on Landed Estates, of Lloyd George's Land Inquiry, of the Speaker's Franchise Conference, of Lord Bryce's Second Chamber Conference 1917, and of the Chairmen's Panel. A Liberal. Sat for the Eifion division of Carnarvonshire from June 1906 to November 1918. Unsuccessfully contested Carnarvonshire in December 1918. Sat for the Denbigh division of Denbighshire from December 1923 until he retired in May 1929. Joined Labour Party in 1934 but resigned because he disagreed with its foreign policy in February 1939 and joined the Liberal National Party. Chairman of Carnarvon County Council 1939. Died 28 April 1939. [1929]

DAVIES, Evan. Caerwent, Libanus Road, Ebbw Vale, Monmouthshire. S. of Evan Davies, Esq., of Beaufort. B. 1875. Worked in a mine at 12 years of age. A Miner; Agent to the Ebbw Vale District of Miners. J.P. for Monmouthshire 1916. A Labour Member. Sat for the Ebbw Vale division of Monmouthshire from July 1920 until he retired in May 1929. Died 22 December 1960. [1929]

DAVIES, Maj. Sir George Frederick, C.V.O. Leigh House, Chard. Oxford & Cambridge, and Carlton. S. of Theo. H. Davies, Esq., of Ravensdale, Tunbridge Wells. B. at Honolulu 19 April 1875; m. 28 June 1900, Mary Ellen, d. of Col. John Birney, R.E., of Redcastle, N.B. Educ. at Uppingham, and King's Coll., Cambridge, M.A. J.P. and County Alderman for Somerset. Served with 5th Battalion Gloucestershire Regiment in France 1914-19. Knight Bach. 1936. Assistant Government Whip November 1931-October 1932; Lord Commissioner of the Treasury October 1932-December 1935; Vice-Chamberlain of H.M.s Household December 1935-May 1937; Comptroller May-October 1937. A Conservative. Sat for the Yeovil division of Somerset from October 1923 until he retired in June 1945. Vice-Consul at Honolulu before First World War. C.V.O. 1937. Died 21 June 1950.   [1945]

DAVIES, George Maitland Lloyd. Maenau Hall, Nr. Llanrwst. S. of John Davies, Esq., Merchant, of Liverpool, and Given, d. of the Rev. John Jones, of Talysarn. B. at Liverpool 30 April 1880; m. 1916, Leslie Eleanor, d. of M. Holroyd Smith, Esq. Educ. at the Liverpool Institute High School. Manager Bank of Liverpool at Wrexham until 1912; Secretary Welsh Town Planning and Housing Trust Limited, Cardiff till 1915. Assistant Secretary Fellowship of Reconciliation until 1916. Imprisoned at Wormwood Scrubbs, Knutsford, Dartmoor and Birmingham 1917-19 for "peace propaganda". Wrote for the *Socialist Review*. A "Christian Pacifist" and took the Labour whip in February 1940. Elected for the University of Wales in December 1923 and sat until he was defeated in October 1924. Servant of Fellowship of Reconciliation from 1916. Minister of Presbyterian Church of Wales. Committed suicide 16 December 1949.   [1924 2nd ed.]

DAVIES, John Cledwyn. House of Commons, London. B. 1869. A Barrister-at-Law, Middle Temple; Headmaster of Holywell Secondary School. Director of Education for Denbighshire and after his retirement Member of Denbighshire County Council. A National Liberal. Elected for the Denbigh division of Denbighshire in November 1922 and sat until he retired in November 1923. Unsuccessfully contested Denbigh as a Liberal in November 1935. Died 31 December 1952.   [1923]

DAVIES, Sir Joseph, K.B.E. 29 Chester Terrace, London. Bath, Reform, and National Liberal. S. of Thomas Seth Davies, Esq., of St. Issells, Pembrokeshire. B. 11 December 1866 at Newport, Monmouthshire; m. 1894, Blanche, d. of John Heron

Wilson, Esq., Shipowner, of Cardiff. Educ. at Bristol Grammar School. Director Cambrian Railways; Chairman Status Investment Trust; Chairman Agwi Petroleum Corporation Limited. Secretary in Prime Minister's Secretariat 1916-18. Accompanied Labour Mission to U.S.A. 1917. J.P. for the County of Glamorgan. K.B.E. January 1918. Editor *South Wales Coal Annual* 1903-17. Author of *Railway Rates and Charges of United Kingdom*. A Coalition Liberal. Unsuccessfully contested Hereford city as a Liberal in December 1910. Elected for the Crewe division of Cheshire in December 1918 and sat until he was defeated in November 1922. Died 3 December 1954.   [1922]

DAVIES, Matthew Lewis Vaughan. See VAUGHAN DAVIES, Matthew Lewis.

DAVIES, Rhys John. Continued in House after 1945: full entry in Volume IV.

DAVIES, Stephen Owen. Continued in House after 1945: full entry in Volume IV.

DAVIES, Sir Thomas. 12 Gloucester Street, Cirencester. Constitutional. S. of William Davies, Esq., of Glamorgan. B. 15 August 1858; m. 1881, Kate, d. of William Vokes, Esq. Educ. privately. A Schoolmaster, 1877. Unionist Agent for Cirencester division from 1885 to 1918. Chairman of Gloucestershire L.E.A. 1919-21. Created Knight Bach. 1924. A Conservative. Sat for the Cirencester and Tewkesbury division of Gloucestershire from December 1918 until he retired in May 1929. County Councillor for Gloucestershire 1899-1910, County Alderman 1910-21. Died 17 November 1939.   [1929]

DAVIES, Sir William Howell. 3 Whitehall Court, London. Down House, Stoke Bishop, Bristol. Reform, and National Liberal. S. of Thomas Davies, Esq. B. 13 December 1851 at Narberth, Pembroke; m. 1882, Ada Mary, d. of Obed. Hosegood, Esq., J.P., Bristol. Educ. privately. A Tanner and Leather Merchant at Bristol. A member of Bristol City Council from 1885; Mayor 1895-96; Alderman 1897; Chairman of Finance Committee 1902-29; Chairman of the Docks Committee 1899-1908. Knighted 1908. A Liberal. Unsuccessfully Contested S. Bristol in 1900. First elected for S. Bristol in 1906 and sat until he retired in October 1922. Died 26 October 1932.   [1922]

DAVISON, John Emanuel. 32 Cottingham Street, Attercliffe, Sheffield. S. of John Davison, Esq., of Sheffield. B. at Smethwick 28 November 1870. Educ. at a Sheffield elementary school. An official of the Ironfounders' Society. Member of Trade Union Advisory Committee to Ministry of Munitions; Vice-Chamberlain of the Household February-November 1924. A Labour Whip 1924-25. A Labour Member. Sat for Smethwick from December 1918 until he resigned in December 1926. Died 2 March 1927.   [1926]

DAVISON, Sir William Henry, K.B.E. 14 Kensington Park Gardens, London Carlton, Athenaeum, and Oxford & Cambridge. S. of Richard Davison, Esq., of Ballymena, Co. Antrim. B. 1872; m. 1st, 4 June 1898, Beatrice Mary, d. of Sir Owen Roberts (m. dissolved in 1928); secondly, 6 June 1929, Constance, d. of Maj. Charles Marriott, 6th Dragoon Guards. Educ. at Shrewsbury, and Keble Coll., Oxford; M.A. 1898. Barrister-at-Law, Inner Temple 1895. K.B.E. 1918. Mayor of Kensington 1913-19. Raised and equipped the 22nd Battalion Royal Fusiliers in September 1914. Dept.-Lieut. and J.P. for London. Fellow of Society of Antiquaries, and Vice-President Royal Society of Arts. Treasurer of Whitechapel Arts Gallery; Gov. of the Foundling Hospital; Chairman of Income Tax Payers Society; Master of the Worshipful Company of Cloth Workers 1941-43; a Freeman of the City of London. President of Kensington Chamber of Commerce; Chairman of Improved Industrial Dwellings Company Limited, of E. Surrey Water Company and Water Companies Association of Great Britain, of British Mutual Banking Company Limited, of N.S.W. Land and Agency Company Limited and of Met. Division National Union of Conservative Associations 1928-30; Co-opted member of London Education Committee 1908-10. A Conservative. MP

for S. Kensington from 1918 until August 1945 when he was created Baron Broughshane. Died 19 January 1953.   [1945]

DAWES, James Arthur. 71 Kennington Park Road, London. Ravensbury, Dartmouth, South Devon. Oxford & Cambridge. S. of Richard Dawes, Esq., of Castle Hill, Ealing. B. 16 June 1866 at Blackheath; m. 1920, Mrs. Violet Garner, d. of Mr. and Mrs. Pridmore of Penge. Educ. at Harrow, and University Coll., Oxford; M.A., B.C.L. Solicitor 1891. Mayor of Southwark 1900, 1913 and 1914; a member of Metropolitan Water Board 1900, and of the London County Council 1906-19. Chairman of London Insurance Committee 1912-14. A J.P. for Co. of London. Commander (acting) R.N.V.R. 1918. Mayor of Dartmouth November 1921. A Liberal. Elected for the Walworth division of Newington in January 1910 and sat until elected for S.E. Southwark in December 1918. Sat until his death on 14 November 1921.   [1921]

DAWSON, Sir Philip. Maybourne, Laurie Park, Sydenham, London. Carlton, and St. Stephen's. B. 6 October 1866; m. 12 January 1898, Lucy Hume, d. of the Rev. A.B. Simpson, Rector of Fittleworth and Prebendary of Chichester. Educ. Privately, and at Ghent and Liège Universities. A Consulting Engineer. Member of Electrification of Railways Advisory Committee, Ministry of Transport, and of the Water Power Resources Committee, Board of Trade. Knight Bach. 1920. A Conservative. Sat for W. Lewisham from September 1921 until his death in Berlin on 24 September 1938. Member of the Institutions of Civil, Mechanical and Electrical Engineers. Member of London County Council for W. Lewisham. Chairman of Anglo-Italian Parliamentary Committee. President of Institute of Fuel 1937-38. Died 24 September 1938.   [1938]

DAY, Harry. Mapleton House, Coventry Street, London. Eccentric, and Royal Automobile. S. of D.J. Day, Esq. B. 16 September 1880; m. 26 June 1901, Kathleen Amelia Rea. Educ. at Hanway School, Stepney Board School, and Tivoli House Academy.

J.P. for London; member London County Council. Owner of several theatres and music halls. Chairman of Mutual Property Insurance Company and of Metropolitan Reinsurance Company. A Labour Member. Unsuccessfully contested Kingston-upon-Thames in November 1922 and Central division of Southwark in December 1923. Elected for Central division of Southwark in October 1924 and May 1929, defeated October 1931. Re-elected for the Central division of Southwark in November 1935 and sat until his death in Quebec on 16 September 1939. [1939]

DEAN, Arthur Wellesley. The Hall, Carlton Scroop, Grantham. Constitutional. S. of Seth Ellis Dean, Esq., of Dowsby Hall, Lincolnshire. B. 27 August 1857; m. 1889, Katherine, d. of John Stewart, Esq., of Murtle, Aberdeenshire. Educ. at Trent Coll., Derbyshire. Member of Kesteven County Council from 1896-1922. J.P. A Conservative. Unsuccessfully contested the Holland with Boston division of Lincolnshire in December 1923. Elected for the Holland with Boston division in July 1924 and again in October 1924. Sat until his death on 7 February 1929. [1929]

DEAN, Lieut.-Commander Percy Thompson, V.C. 5 Victoria Street, London. B. 1877; m. 1927, Mrs. M.R. Hardicker, widow of J.O. Hardicker, Esq. A State Merchant and Cotton Spinner; member of the Blackburn Town Council. Joined the R.N.V.R., for the part he played in Zeebrugge exploit April 1918 was awarded the V.C. Parliamentary Private Secretary (unpaid) to Sir James Craig when Parliamentary Secretary to Ministry of Pensions 1919-20. A Coalition Unionist. Elected for Blackburn in December 1918 and sat until he retired in October 1922. Died 20 March 1939. [1922]

DEANS, Richard Storry. 3 Elm Courte, Temple, London. Carlton. S. of Rev. Joseph Deans. B. 1868; m. 1st, Margaret, d. of John Lang, Esq. (she died 1915); secondly, Ethel, d. of J. Lawson, Esq., of Sheffield. Educ. at London University. Barrister-at-Law, Gray's Inn 1893, Bencher 1927; LL.D.;

Author of various works on legal subjects. Editor *Macdonell's Law of Master and Servant*. Recorder of Rotherham from 1928 to 1932. A Conservative. Elected for the Park division of Sheffield in December 1923 and sat until he was defeated in May 1929. Recorder of Newcastle-on-Tyne 1932-38. Treasurer of Gray's Inn 1938. Died 31 August 1938. [1929]

de CHAIR, Somerset Struben. Continued in House after 1945: full entry in Volume IV.

DEELEY, Sir Harry Mallaby, Bart. See MALLABY-DEELEY, Sir Harry Mallaby, Bart.

de ERESBY, Lord Willoughby. See WILLOUGHBY DE ERESBY, Gilbert James Heathcote-Drummond-Willoughby, Lord. Continued in House after 1945: full entry in Volume IV.

DE FRECE, Col. Sir Walter. Sefton Park, Stoke Poges, Buckinghamshire. Western House, Kings Road, Hove. Carlton, Constitutional, and Royal Temple Yacht. S. of Henry de Frece, Esq., of Liverpool and Brighton. B. 7 October 1870; m. 16 August 1890, 'Vesta Tilley' Matilda Alice, d. of Henry Powlers, Esq., of Worcester. Educ. at the Royal Institute, Liverpool, and at Brussels. Honorary Col. 9th Battalion Manchester Regiment; a Trustee of the King's Fund for Disabled Soldiers and Sailors; Dept.-Lieut. for Berkshire. Knight Bach. 1919. Chairman of Parliamentary Entertainment Commission. A Conservative. Sat for Ashton-under-Lyne from January 1920-October 24, and for Blackpool from October 1924 until he retired in October 1931. Died in Monaco 7 January 1935. [1931 2nd ed.]

DE LA BÈRE, Rupert. Continued in House after 1945: full entry in Volume IV.

DE MARKIEVICZ, Constance Georgine, Countess. See MARKIEVICZ, Constance Georgine, Countess de.

DENISON, Hon. William Gervase. See BECKETT, Hon. Sir William Gervase, Bart.

93

DENISON-PENDER, Capt. John Cuthbert Denison 65 Eaton Place, London. Lower Hare Park, Six Mile Bottom, Newmarket. Carlton, Bath, Marlborough, Wellington, and Garrick. Eld. s. of Sir John Denison-Pender, K.C.M.G. B. 1882; m. 1906, Irene, only child of Ernest de la Rue (she died 1943). Educ. at Eton. A Director of Eastern Telegraph Company, Eastern and South African Telegraph Company, West African Telegraph Company, and Northern Assurance Company. Member of London County Council from 1910-1919. During the war served in France 1914-17 and War Office 1918, with the Red Cross and army. A Coalition Unionist. Elected for the Newmarket division of Cambridgeshire in May 1913, and for the Balham and Tooting division of Wandsworth in December 1918. Sat until he retired in October 1922. Managing Director of Cable and Wireless Limited 1929-45. Created Baron Pender 1937. Died 4 December 1949. [1922]

DENMAN, Hon. Richard Douglas. Staffield Hall, Kirkoswald, Carlisle. S. of Richard Denman, Esq., grand-s. of 2nd Baron Denman. B. 24 August 1876; m. 10 June 1914, May, d. of James Spencer, Esq. Educ. at Westminster School, and Balliol Coll., Oxford, B.A., Stanhope Prize Essay 1898. Served in France with R.F.A. 1916-17. Parliamentary Private Secretary to Rt. Hon. S. Buxton when President of Board of Trade 1910, Rt. Hon. R.E. Prothero when President of Board of Agriculture 1917, and to Rt. Hon. H.A.L. Fisher when President of Board of Education 1918. 2nd Church Estates Commissioner 1931-43. Treasurer of Queen Anne's Bounty 1939-44. Chairman of National Labour Organisation 1943. Sat for Carlisle as a Liberal from January 1910-December 1918 when he retired. Unsuccessfully contested Newcastle-on-Tyne W. in November 1922 and Carlisle in December 1923 as a Liberal. Joined the Labour Party in 1924. Sat for Leeds Central from May 1929 until he retired in June 1945. A Labour Member 1929-31 and a National Labour Member 1931-45. Created Bart. 1945. Died 22 December 1957. [1945]

DENNIS, John William. 19 St. James's Square, London. Nocton Hall, Nr. Lincoln. Carlton, Constitutional, St. Stephen's, and Hurlingham. Eld. s. of William Dennis, Esq., J.P., of Kirton, Lincolnshire. B. 16 May 1865; m. 1st, 1915, Evangeline, d. of Dr. Armstrong of New York (she died 1919); secondly, 1922, Hilda Mary Clavering, d. of C.L. Tredcroft, Esq., and widow of 8th Earl De La Warr. Educ. at Kirton Grammar School, and King's Coll., London. Was in the Civil Service 1883-91; founded the London Branch of W. Dennis and Sons 1891. Member of the Tariff Commission 1904-21; Mayor of Westminster 1907-08. Officer of the Legion of Honour. Potato Controller (unpaid) in the Ministry of Food 1917. A Coalition Unionist. Elected for the Deritend division of Birmingham in December 1918 and sat until he retired in October 1922. Died 4 August 1949. [1922]

DENNISON, Robert. Chippenham, Bosworth Road, New Barnet. S. of William Dennison, Esq., of Glasgow. B. 14 December 1879; m. 1903, Frances, d. of C. Jenkinson, Esq., of Darlington. Educ. at Elementary School and Science School, Glasgow. A Trade Union Officer, Iron and Steel Trades Confederation 1912; Town Councillor Stockton-on-Tees 1912-17. J.P. for Stockton, Hertfordshire and Middlesex. Councillor East Barnet Urban District Council. A Labour Member. Unsuccessfully contested Walsall in 1922, and Cleveland in 1923. Elected for the King's Norton division Birmingham in October 1924 and sat until he was defeated in May 1929. Died 10 November 1951. [1929]

DENNISS, Sir Edmund Robert Bartley. See BARTLEY-DENNISS, Sir Edmund Robert Bartley.

DENVILLE, Alfred Arthur Hinchcliffe. Weathertrees, South Hill Avenue, Harrow. Constitutional. S. of Charles D'Enville, Esq., of Nottingham. B. 27 January 1876; m. 26 August 1895, Kate, d. of George Saville, Esq., of Portsmouth. Educ. at Ushaw Coll. A Theatrical Manager and Producer. Founder and Honorary Secretary of Denville Hall, Haven of Rest for Aged

Members of Theatrical Profession. Recruiting Officer and Organizer of Charitable Schemes 1914-18. Propaganda Agent. A Conservative. Unsuccessfully contested the Hanley division of Stoke-on-Trent in 1928. Elected for Newcastle-upon-Tyne central in October 1931. Sat until he was defeated in July 1945. Died 23 March 1955. [1945]

de ROISTE, Liam. Employed by the Cork County Committee of Technical Instruction as an Itinerant Teacher. A Sinn Fein Member. Elected for Cork City in December 1918 but did not take his seat. Member of Dail for Cork City to 1923 as a Pro-Treaty Member. Died 15 May 1959.
[1922]

de ROTHSCHILD, James Armand Edmond. See ROTHSCHILD, James Armand Edmond de.

de ROTHSCHILD, Lionel Nathan. See ROTHSCHILD, Lionel Nathan de.

DESPENCER ROBERTSON, Maj. James Archibald St. George Fitzwarenne, O.B.E. Sydenham House, Lewdown, Devon. Carlton. S. of Sir Helenus Robertson, and Kate Ann, d. of Thomas Morris-Bankes, Esq. B. 7 November 1886. Unmarried. Educ. at Eton, and New Coll., Oxford. Parliamentary Private Secretary to the Rt. Hon. C.C. Craig when Parliamentary Secretary to Ministry of Pensions 1923. Served with Royal Welch Fusiliers 1914-19. O.B.E. 1919. 2nd-Lieut. Emergency Reserve September 1939. Acting Lieut.-Col. 1941. Assumed the additional surname of Despencer in 1916. A Conservative. Sat for W. Islington from 1922 until 1923 when he was defeated. Unsuccessfully contested W. Islington again in 1924 and 1929. Elected for the Salisbury division of Wiltshire in March and October 1931 and again in November 1935. Sat until his death on 5 May 1942.
[1942]

de VALERA, Eamonn. Kinlan Road, Kilincarrig, Greystones, Co. Wicklow. S. of Vivian de Valera. B. in New York 14 October 1882; m. 1910, Sinead ni Fhlannagain (she died 1975). Educ. at National University of Ireland. Some of his earlier years were spent at Bruree, Co. Limerick. A Professor of Mathematics, and was a mathematical teacher at Rockwell Coll., and Blackrock Coll. Chancellor of the National University of Ireland 1921-45. A Sinn Feiner, who was sentenced to death for the part he took in the rising in Ireland during Easter week 1916. This was commuted to penal servitude for life, and he was in prison when adopted as candidate. He was released and was elected for E. Clare in July 1917. Was re-arrested in May 1918 and still interned when again returned unopposed for E. Clare in December 1918. Escaped from prison February 1919. Later engaged actively in Sinn Fein propagandism in U.S.A. Also returned for E. Mayo in December 1918 but did not take his seat. Unsuccessfully contested S. Down and the Falls division of Belfast in December 1918. Member of Northern Ireland Parliament for Down 1921-29, and for Down S. 1933-38. Member of Dail for E. Clare and for E. Mayo to 1921, for Co. Clare 1921-59. President of Sinn Fein 1917-26. An Anti-Treaty Member, Founder of Fianna Fail 1926, President of Fianna Fail 1926-59. President of Dail to 1922, President of Executive Council of Dail 1932-37, Taoiseach (Prime Minister) 1937-48, 1951-54, 1957-59, Minister for External Affairs 1932-48, Minister of Education 1939-40. Leader of Opposition 1927-32, 1948-51, 1954-57. President of Irish Republic 1959-73. Died 29 August 1975. [1922]

DEVLIN, Joseph. 3 College Square, North Belfast. S. of Charles Devlin, Esq., of Belfast. B. 1872. Unmarried. Educ. at Christian Brothers' School, Belfast. Gen. Secretary of United Irish League. An Irish Nationalist Member. Sat for N. Kilkenny from February 1902 to January 1906 when he was elected for N. Kilkenny and for W. Belfast. He chose to represent W. Belfast and sat until December 1918 when he was elected for the Falls division of Belfast. He sat until November 1922 when he unsuccessfully contested the Exchange division of Liverpool. Member of N. Ireland Parliament for Belfast W. 1921-29 and Belfast central 1929-34. Returned unopposed for Fermanagh and Tyrone in May 1929 and sat until he died on 18 January 1934. [1934]

95

DEWHURST, Commander Harry. Dale Ford, Sandiway, Cheshire. 105 Ashley Gardens, London. Orleans, Automobile, and Carlton. S. of George B. Dewhurst, Esq. B. at St. Asaph, N. Wales 27 February 1866; m. 1890, Ethel Norris, d. of B. Davies, Esq., of Adlington, Lancashire. Educ. at Winchester, and Repton. A member of the firm of George and R. Dewhurst, Cotton Spinners and Manufacturers; J.P. for Cheshire; member of the Cheshire Hunt. Served as a remount officer in England and France, and as King's Messenger for the Admiralty. A Coalition Unionist. Elected for the Northwich division of Cheshire in December 1918 and sat until he retired in October 1922. Died 27 June 1931.   [1922]

DICKIE, Capt. John Purcell. 15 Pollards Hill South, Norbury, London. S. of James Dickie, Esq., Naval Architect. B. 14 July 1874; m. 1926, Isabel, d. of T.A. Edmeades, Esq., of Melbourne (she died 1954). Educ. at Union British School, South Shields. An Engineer. Served in France 1914-18; Capt. R.E. A Liberal Nationalist. Unsuccessfully contested Gateshead in November 1922. Elected for Gateshead as a Liberal in December 1923, defeated October 1924. Unsuccessfully contested Darlington in 1926 and the Consett division of Durham in May 1929. Elected again for the Consett division of Durham in October 1931 as a Liberal National and sat until he was defeated in November 1935.   [1935]

DICKSON, Thomas Scott. County Houses, Hamilton Road, Larkhall. B. 1 November 1885. Worked in the local quarries. A Reporter on *The Scotsman*; later sub-editor of *Forward*, organ of the Socialist movement in Scotland. Member of Lanarkshire County Council. Parliamentary Private Secretary to T. Johnston when Parliamentary Under-Secretary for Scotland June 1929. A Labour Member. Unsuccessfully contested the Lanark division of Lanarkshire in 1922. Elected for the Lanark division in December 1923; defeated in October 1924. Re-elected for the Lanark division in May 1929 and sat until he retired in October 1931. President of National Union of Journalists 1925-26. Died 25 January 1935.   [1931 2nd ed.]

96

DIGBY, Kenelm Simon Digby Wingfield. Continued in House after 1945: full entry in Volume IV.

DIXEY, Arthur Carlyne Niven. 21 Grosvenor Street, London. S. of the Rev. A. Niven and Catherine Dixey. B. 1889; m. 1st, 1915, Helen, d. of Dr. William Loynd (she died 1945); secondly, 1949, Valerie, d. of E.C. Cole, Esq. Educ. at Manchester Grammar School. Admitted Solicitor 1913. A Conservative. Elected for the Penrith and Cockermouth division of Cumberland in December 1923 and sat until he retired in October 1935. Died 25 May 1954.   [1935]

DIXON, Charles Harvey. Gunthorpe, Oakham. Carlton, and Junior Carlton. S. of Henry Dixon, Esq. B. 1862, at Watlington, Oxfordshire; m. 1890, Miss J.P. Robinson, of Esher. Educ. privately. A Conservative. Unsuccessfully contested the Harborough division of Leicestershire in October 1900, June 1904 and January 1906. Sat for Boston, Lincolnshire from January 1910 until he retired in November 1918. Elected for the Rutland and Stamford division of Lincolnshire in November 1922 and sat until his death on 22 September 1923.   [1923]

DIXON, Capt. Rt. Hon. Herbert, O.B.E. Ballyalloy, Nr. Comber, Co. Down. Draycot, Cerne, Chippenham, Wiltshire. Carlton, Constitutional, and Cavalry. S. of the Rt. Hon. Sir Daniel Dixon, 1st Bart. B. 23 January 1880; m. 25 November 1905, Hon. Ina Bingham, d. of John, 5th Baron Clanmorris. Educ. at Rugby, and Sandhurst. Capt. Reserve of Officers 6th Inniskilling Dragoons. Served in South African War with the Inniskillings and in Remounts 1914-18; mentioned in despatches, and O.B.E. 1919. PC. (N. Ireland) 1923. Chief Unionist whip and Parliamentary (Patronage) Secretary to the Ministry of Finance of Northern Ireland 1921-42. A Conservative. Sat for the Pottinger division of Belfast from December 1918 to November 1922 and for E. Belfast from November 1922 until 1939 when he was created Baron Glentoran. In the Northern Ireland Parliament sat for E. Belfast from 1921 to 1929 and for the Bloomfield division of Belfast from 1929 to 1950. Northern Ireland Minister of Agriculture 1941-43. High Sheriff of Co. Kildare 1916. Succeeded his bro. as Bart. 10 May 1950. Died 20 July 1950. [1939]

DOBBIE, William. Continued in House after 1945: full entry in Volume IV.

DOCKRELL, Sir Maurice Edward. Camolin, Monkstown, Co. Dublin. United Service, Dublin. S. of Thomas Dockrell, Esq., J.P. B. in Dublin 21 December 1850; m. 1875, Margaret, d. of George W. Shannon, Esq., Solicitor of Dublin (she died 1926). Educ. at Portora Royal School, Enniskillen, and Trinity Coll., Dublin. Dept.-Lieut. and J.P. for Dublin. Knighted by King Edward VII 1905. Chairman of Dockrell and Sons Limited, Merchants, Dublin. Chairman of Dublin Recruiting Committee 1914-18. Member of the Irish Liquor Commission 1917, and of the Irish Recuiting Council 1918. A Unionist supporter of the Coalition Government, apart from its Irish policy of Home Rule. Unsuccessfully contested St. Patrick's division of Dublin in 1885. Elected for the Rathmines division of Dublin Co. in 1918 and sat until he retired in October 1922. Died 5 August 1929. [1922]

DODD, John Samuel. Sutton Grange, Macclesfield. Lyon Work, Oldham. Reform, and Junior Army & Navy. S. of William Dodd, Esq., J.P., of Keldwith, Windermere. B. 13 October 1904; m. 1937, Margaret McDougall, d. of William Hamilton, Esq., of Glasgow. Educ. at Uppingham, Rouen, and Christ's Coll., Cambridge, M.A., M.I. Mech.E. Chairman of several companies; Dept. President Association of British Chambers of Commerce. Member of Council Empire Cotton Growing Corporation. Underwriting member of Lloyds; member of Central National Service Committee for Great Britain 1939; Honorary Adviser on Tank Production, Ministry of Supply 1940-41. Maj. 47th Royal Tank Regiment. A Liberal National. Unsuccessfully contested Oldham as a Liberal in May 1929. Elected for Oldham in November 1935 and sat until he was defeated in July 1945. Knighted

1947. Fellow of Royal Geographical and Royal Philatelic Societies. Chairman of Executive Committee of National Liberal Council 1947-49. Died 3 September 1973. [1945]

DODDS, Stephen Roxby. Langdale, Heswall, Cheshire. National Liberal. S. of Thomas Liddell Dodds, Esq., J.P. B. at Birkenhead 29 January 1881; m. 1921, Edith May, d. of Johnston Bell, Esq., of Heswall, Cheshire. Educ. at Rydal School, Colwyn Bay, and Trinity Hall, Cambridge. A Solicitor, admitted 1906. A Liberal. Unsuccessfully contested the Wirral division of Cheshire in November 1922. Elected for the Wirral division of Cheshire in December 1923 and sat until he was defeated in October 1924; again defeated in May 1929. President of Liverpool Law Society 1939-40. Vice-Chairman of Methodist Insurance Company Limited. Died 10 September 1943. [1924 2nd ed.]

DOLAN, James Nicholas. Manorhamilton, Co. Leitrim. B. at Manorhamilton 1884; m. 1914, d. of John O'Reilly, Esq., of Ardagh. A Sinn Fein Member. Was interned in Gloucester prison at the time of his election for Co. Leitrim in December 1918 and did not take his seat. Member of Dail for Leitrim to 1921, for Leitrim and N. Roscommon 1921-23, for Leitrim and Sligo 1923-32, and 1933-37, when he unsuccessfully contested Leitrim as an Independent. Pro-Treaty, later Cumann na nGaedheal Member. Chief Whip of Cumann na nGaedheal 1924-27. Dept. Speaker of Dail in 1927. Parliamentary Secretary to Minister of Industry and Commerce 1927-32. [1922]

DOLAND, Lieut.-Col. George Frederick, O.B.E. House of Commons, London. Constitutional. S. of George Richard Doland, Esq. B.1 May 1872; m. Minnie Mary, O.St.J., d. of George Richardson, Esq., of Balham. Educ. privately. Served 1914-19 as O.C. Co. of London R.A.S.C. Motor Transport Volunteers. O.B.E. 1919. Mayor of Wandsworth 1928-29 and 1933-34; member of London County Council from 1933. Governing Director of companies; Dept.-Lieut., and J.P. for London. A Conservative.

Elected for the Balham and Tooting division of Wandsworth in July 1936 and sat until he retired in June 1945. Died 26 November 1946. [1945]

DONALD, Thompson. 129 Leighton Road, London. A Shipwright who was employed by a Belfast firm. Honorary Secretary of the Ulster Unionist Labour Association; member of the Unionist Labour deputation which visited London to urge the case against Home Rule. A Unionist Labour Member. Elected for the Victoria division of Belfast in December 1918 and sat until he retired in October 1922. Member of Northern Ireland Parliament for Belfast E. 1921-25. [1922]

DONNELLY, Patrick. 70 Hill Street, Newry. B. 1878. Educ. at Queen's Coll., Belfast. A Solicitor at Newry. A Nationalist. Elected for S. Armagh in February 1918 and sat until he retired in October 1922. Died 13 August 1947. [1922]

DONNER, Patrick William. Continued in House after 1945: full entry in Volume IV.

DORAN, Edward. 63 Beverstone Road, Thornton Heath, Surrey. B. at Failsworth 1885. A Conservative. Unsuccessfully contested the Silvertown division of West Ham in October 1924. Elected for Tottenham N. in October 1931 and sat until he was defeated in November 1935. Died 15 December 1945. [1935]

DORMAN-SMITH, Col. Rt. Hon. Sir Reginald Hugh. 63 Lansdowne House, Berkeley Square, London. Stodham Park, Liss. S. of Maj. E.P. Dorman Smith, of Bellamont Forest, Co. Cavan. B. 1899; m. 2 March 1921, Doreen Agnes, d. of Sir John Watson, 2nd Bart., of Earnock. Educ. at Harrow, and Royal Military Coll., Sandhurst. 15th Sikhs (I.A.) and 5th Queens Royal Regiment (T.A.). J.P. and member of Surrey County Council; President National Farmers' Union 1936-37. Knight Bach. 1937. PC. 1939; Minister of Agriculture and Fisheries January 1939-May 1940. A Conservative. Elected for the Petersfield division of Hampshire in November 1935 and sat until

February 1941 when he was appointed Gov. of Burma. Rejoined the army 1940. G.B.E. 1941. Gov. of Burma 1941-46. J.P. for Hampshire, High Sheriff 1952. Died 20 March 1977. [1941]

DOUGLAS, Francis Campbell Ross. Continued in House after 1945: full entry in Volume IV.

DOUGLAS AND CLYDESDALE, Douglas Douglas-Hamilton, Marq. of See CLYDESDALE, Douglas Douglas-Hamilton, Marq. of Douglas and

DOUGLAS-HOME, Rt. Hon. Sir Alexander Frederick, K.T. Continued in House after 1945: full entry in Volume IV.

DOWER, Alan Vincent Gandar. Continued in House after 1945: full entry in Volume IV.

DOYLE, Sir Nicholas Grattan. See GRATTAN-DOYLE, Sir Nicholas Grattan.

DREWE, Cedric. Continued in House after 1945: full entry in Volume IV.

DRIBERG, Thomas Edward Neil. Continued in House after 1945: full entry in Volume IV.

DRUMMOND-WOLFF, Henry Maxence Cavendish. 113 Eaton Square, London. Hoddington House, Upton Grey, Basingstoke. Oak Haven, Newport, Rhode Island, U.S.A. Carlton. S. of Cecil Drummond-Wolff, Esq., of Caplanne, Billère, Pau, and grand-s. of Sir Henry Drummond-Wolff, G.C.B., G.C.M.G. B. 16 July 1899; m. 14 June 1933, Margaret, d. of Gibson Fahnestock, Esq., of Newport, Rhode Island, U.S.A. Educ. at Radley, and Royal Military Coll., Sandhurst. Served With R.F.C. 1917, retired from R.A.F. 1919. Member of Grand Council of Primrose League 1934-35. A Conservative. Unsuccessfully contested Rotherham in February 1933. Elected for the Basingstoke division of Hampshire in March 1934 and sat until he retired in October 1935. President of Committee of

Empire Economic Union 1952. Author of several works on the Empire and Commonwealth.* [1935]

DUCKWORTH, George Arthur Victor. 43 Catherine Place, London. Travellers', and Garrick. S. of Maj. A.C. Duckworth of Orchardleigh Park, Somerset. B. 3 January 1901; m. 1st, 27 March 1927, Alice, d. of John Henry Hammond, Esq., of New York (divorced 1945); secondly, 1945, Elizabeth, d. of Alfred Ehrenfeld, Esq., of Forest Green; thirdly, 1968, Mary, d. of Ven. E. Hope and widow of Capt. K. Buxton. Educ. at Eton, and Trinity Coll., Cambridge. Parliamentary Private Secretary to Geoffrey Shakespeare when Parliamentary Secretary Ministry of Health 1932-36, when Parliamentary Secretary Board of Education September 1936, and when Financial Secretary to the Admiralty May 1937-1939. A Conservative. Elected for the Shrewsbury division of Shropshire in May 1929 and sat until he retired in June 1945. Member of Somerset County Council 1949-64. J.P. for Somerset.* [1945]

DUCKWORTH, John. The Knolle, Wilpshire, Blackburn. S. of George Duckworth, Esq. B. 1 November 1863; m. 1890, Ruth, d. of William Sutcliffe, Esq. Member of the firm of Duckworth and Eddleston, Cotton Manufacturers, of Blackburn. J.P. for Blackburn. A Liberal. Elected for Blackburn in December 1923. Sat until he retired in May 1929. Died 22 January 1946. [1929]

DUCKWORTH, William Rostron. Lansdowne, Knowle, Warwickshire. 9 St. James's Square, Manchester. Constitutional. S. of William Duckworth, Esq., of Burnley. B. 24 November 1879; m. 18 September 1937, Catherine, d. of James Austin, Esq., and widow of Sir Francis Reynolds of Abberley, Worcestershire. Educ. at Farnworth and Bury Grammar Schools, and privately. A Chartered Accountant; member of the Institute 1902-08; Alderman of Blackpool County Borough Council; member of Education Committee; J.P., Dept. Mayor 1933-34 and 1935-36; Mayor 1938-39; Chairman of Waller and Hartley Limited, of Blackpool, and of many other Limited Companies. F.R.G.S. 1933; Vice-President Association of Education Committees and Fishery Member Lancashire and Western Sea Fisheries Commission 1937; member of Court of Governors Manchester University 1936 and of Administrative Council of Empire Cotton Growing Corporation 1938. Trustee Preston Savings Bank. A Conservative. Elected for the Moss Side division of Manchester in November 1935 and sat until he was defeated in July 1945. Vice-President of National Federation of Property Owners 1943-52. Died 14 July 1952. [1945]

DU CROS, Sir Arthur Philip; Bart. Craigweil House, Aldwick, Sussex. La Fiorentina, Cap St. Jean, Alpes Maritimes. Carlton, and Junior Carlton. Travellers' (Paris). S. of Harvey du Cros, Esq., at one time MP for Hastings, and Annie, d. of John Roy, Esq., of Durrow, Queen's Co. B. 1871; m. 1st, 1895, Maude, d. of William Goodling, Esq., of Coventry, two sons, two daughters (divorced 1923); secondly, 1928, Florence May, d. of J.W. King, Esq., of Walton, Buckinghamshire (she died 1951); thirdly, Mary Louise Joan Beaumont. Educ. for the Civil Service, into which he passed in 1886. President and Life Director of the Dunlop Rubber Company Limited, and Chairman of the Parent Tyre Company Limited. J.P. for Middlesex. Honorary Col. 8th Battalion Royal Warwickshire Regiment. Associate of the National Gallery of British Art. Created Bart. in 1916. A Unionist. Unsuccessfully contested Bow and Bromley in 1906. Sat for Hastings from March 1908 to December 1918. Elected for the Clapham division of Wandsworth in December 1918 and sat until he resigned in May 1922. Died 28 October 1955. [1922]

DUDGEON, Maj. Cecil Randolph. Cargen Holm, Troqueer, Galloway. National Liberal. S. of Col. R.F. Dudgeon. B. 7 November 1885; m. 1909, Grizel, d. of H.J. Younger, Esq., Dept.-Lieut. (marriage dissolved 1930). Educ. privately. Chairman of the Galloway Education Authority. Member of Stewartry of Kirkcudbright County Council from 1911, and Chairman of Education Authority 1922. Served with

King's Own Scottish Borderers in France 1914-18. A Liberal. Elected for Galloway November 1922, returned unopposed in December 1923; contested the same division in October 1924 and November 1925, and re-elected for Galloway in May 1929. Sat until October 1931 when he unsuccessfully contested Galloway as the candidate of Sir Oswald Mosley's New Party. C.B.E. 1951. Chief Food Officer for Scotland 1950-52. Died 4 November 1970. [1931 2nd ed.]

DUFFY, George Gavan. 39 Mespil Road, Dublin. S. of Sir George Charles Gavan Duffy, Prime Minister of Victoria. B. 21 October 1882 in Australia; m. 1908, Margaret, d. of A.M. Sullivan, Esq., MP. Educ. in France, and at Stonyhurst. A Solicitor, at one time in practise in London. A member of the Irish Bar, prepared the defence in the Sir Roger Casement case. A Sinn Fein Member. Elected for Dublin Co. S. in December 1918 but did not take his seat. Member of Dail for Dublin Co. S. to 1921, for Dublin Co. 1921-23 initially as a Pro-Treaty Member, but later as an opponent of the Treaty. Minister for Foreign Affairs in the Provisional Government 1922. Called to Inner Bar 1929. High Court Judge from 1936 and President of the High Court of Ireland from 1946. Died 10 June 1951. [1922]

DUFFY, Thomas Gavan. Miners' Hall, Cleator Moor, Cumberland. S. of Bernard Duffy, Esq., Merchant Dealer. B. in Dublin 25 September 1867; m. 1897, Mary, d. of Robert Gowland, Esq., Farmer, of Yorkshire. Educ. at Christian Brothers School, Dublin, and St. Francis Xavier's, Liverpool. A Journalist; Author; Lecturer; Trade Union Official. Gen. Secretary Cumberland Iron Ore Miners 1908-31. Author of *The Fight for the Schools*, and *Victims of Commerce*. A Labour Member. Unsuccessfully contested the Whitehaven division of Cumberland in 1918. Elected for the Whitehaven division of Cumberland in November 1922. Sat until he was defeated in October 1924. Member of Cumberland County Council. Died 4 August 1932. [1924 2nd ed.]

DUGDALE, John. Continued in House after 1945: full entry in Volume IV.

DUGDALE, Sir Thomas Lionel, Bart. Continued in House after 1945: full entry in Volume IV.

DUGGAN, Edmund John. 26 Upper St. Brigid's Road, Drumcondra, Dublin. B. at Longwood, Co. Meath in about 1873. A Solicitor. A Sinn Fein Member who was, with two other Members arrested in the course of a raid in Dublin November 1920. Elected for S. Meath in December 1918 but did not take his seat. One of the 5 Irish signatories of the 1921 Anglo-Irish Treaty. Member of Dail for S. Meath to 1921, for Louth and Meath 1921-23, for Meath 1923-33. Pro-Treaty, later Cumann na nGaedheal Member. Minister for Home Affairs in 1922; Parliamentary Secretary to the Executive Council 1922-26; Parliamentary Secretary to Minister of Finance 1926-27; Parliamentary Secretary to the President and to Minister of Defence 1927-32. Senator, Irish Free State 1933-36. Chairman of Dun Laoghaire Borough Council 1934-35. Died 6 June 1936. [1922]

DUGGAN, Hubert John. 112B, Gloucester Place, London. White's, and Bucks. S. of Alfred Duggan, Esq., and Grace Hinds, subsequently The Marchioness Curzon of Kedleston. B. 24 July 1904; m. 1928, Joan, d. of Sir James Dunn (divorced 1930). Educ. at Eton. Life Guards 1924-28 and 1939-43, Capt. 1940. Parliamentary Private Secretary to Capt. Euan Wallace, Civil Lord of the Admiralty November 1931-November 1935. A Conservative. Unsuccessfully contested East Ham S. in May 1929. Elected for the Acton division of Middlesex in October 1931. Sat until he died on 25 October 1943. [1943]

DUKES, Charles. 27 Cornwall Street, Warrington. B. at Stourbridge 1881. An organizer of National Union of General and Municipal Workers; Gen. Secretary 1934-46; associated with Trade Union Movement for many years. A Labour Member. Elected for Warrington in December 1923, defeated October 1924. Re-elected for Warrington in

May 1929 and sat until he was defeated in October 1931. C.B.E. 1942. Director of Bank of England 1947-48. Created Baron Dukeston 1947. President of T.U.C. 1945-46, member of General Council 1934-47. Died 14 May 1948. [1931 2nd ed.]

DUNCAN, Rt. Hon. Sir Andrew Rae, G.B.E. Continued in House after 1945: full entry in Volume IV.

DUNCAN, Charles. 14 Forres Garden, Golder's Green, London. S. of Alexander Duncan, Esq., a Pilot. B. 8 June 1865 at Middlesbrough; m. 1890, Lydia Copeland. An Engineer; Gen. Secretary of the Workers Union from 1899 to 1929; member of Middlesbrough Town Council 1895-1900. Was a Whip and Secretary to the Labour Party. A Labour Member. Sat for Barrow-in-Furness from 1906-18, but was defeated there in December 1918. Unsuccessfully contested The Wrekin division of Shropshire in February and November 1920. Elected for the Clay Cross division of Derbyshire in November 1922 and sat until his death on 6 July 1933. [1933]

DUNCAN, James Alexander Lawson. Continued in House after 1945: full entry in Volume IV.

DUNCANNON, Vere Brabazon Ponson-by, Visct. C.M.G. 22 Portland Place, London. Garryhill, Bagnalstown, Co. Carlow. Carlton, and Marlborough. Eld. s. of 8th Earl of Bessborough. B. in London 27 October 1880; m. 1912, Roberte, d. of Baron de Neuflize. Educ. at Harrow, and Trinity Coll., Cambridge; B.A. Was called to the bar at the Inner Temple 1903. Member of London County Council 1907-10. Served in Gallipoli and France 1915-17. A Unionist. Unsuccessfully contested Carmarthen Boroughs in 1906. Sat for Cheltenham from January to December 1910 when he was defeated, for Dover from June 1913 to December 1918, and for the Dover division of Kent from December 1918 until December 1920 when he succeeded to the Irish Peerage as Earl of Bessborough and the U.K. Peerage as Baron Duncannon. Styled Visct. Duncannon 1906-20. Suppor-

ter of the National Party 1917-18. Gov.-Gen. of Canada 1931-35. PC. 1931. Created Earl of Bessborough in the U.K. Peerage 1937. Died 10 March 1956. [1920]

DUNGLASS, Alexander Frederick Douglas-Home. See DOUGLAS-HOME, Rt. Hon. Sir Alexander Frederick, K.T. Continued in House after 1945: full entry in Volume IV.

DUNN, Edward. Greenwood, 52 Blyth Road, Maltby, Rotherham. S. of Henry Dunn, Esq., Coalminer, of Dudley. B. 21 December 1880; m. 26 December 1914, Maggie, d. of Thomas Buckley, Esq. Educ. at Kiveton Park School. A Coalminer. Member of Executive Committee of Miners Federation of Great Britain 1930-36, of West Riding County Council 1919-45, Alderman 1922, Leader of Labour group 1933-36. Parliamentary Private Secretary to Maj. Arthur Henderson, Joint Under-Secretary of State for War July-December 1942. A Labour Member. Elected for the Rother Valley division of the W. Riding of Yorkshire in November 1935 and sat until his death on 8 April 1945. Chairman of Maltby Parish Council 1916-24 and of Malty Urban District Council 1924-45. Dept. Regional Commissioner for North-Eastern Civil Defence Region 1941-45. Died 8 April 1945. [1945]

DUNN, John Freeman. Poyning's, Sheldon Avenue, Highgate, London. National Liberal, and Eighty. S. of George Freeman Dunn, Esq. B. 12 April 1874 at Basingstoke; m. February 1914, Constance, d. of David Mark Henderson, Esq., of Victory House, Hove. Educ. at Queen Mary's School, Basingstoke. Managing Director of the British American Trading Company Limited (Merchant Banking and Investment Company); was for 15 years Manager of the Hove and Brighton branches of the Midland Bank. A Barrister-at-Law; Gray's Inn 1909. Associate of the Institute of Bankers (Gilbart Prizeman). A Liberal. Elected for the Hemel Hempstead division of Hertfordshire in December 1923 and sat until he was defeated in October 1924. Unsuccessfully contested the Faversham division of Kent in January 1928 and the Chichester division of W. Sussex in May May 1929. Died 7 December 1954.

[1924 2nd ed.]

DUNNE, Philip Russell Rendel. 11 Arlington Street, London. S. of E.M. Dunne, Esq., MP of Gatley Park, Hereford-shire. B. 28 February 1904; m. 1st, 1930, Margaret Ann, d. of Thomas Walker, Esq., of Troon; secondly, 1945, Audrey, widow of Bernard Rubin, Esq., and d. of C.R. Simp-son, Esq., of Ramsey, Huntingdonshire. Educ. at Eton, and Royal Military Coll., Sandhurst. Joined the Royal Horse Guards. A Conservative. Elected for the Stalybridge and Hyde division of Cheshire in November 1935 and sat until he resigned in 1937. Member of the Jockey Club. M.C. 1943. Died 13 April 1965. [1937]

DUNNICO, Rev. Herbert. 74 Wellesley Road, Ilford, Essex. King's Buildings, Dean Stanley Street, London. S. of James Dunnico and Mary Owen, of Newtown, Monmouth-shire. B. 2 December 1876; m. 1903, Emma, d. of Robert Rathbone, Esq. (she died 1952). Educ. at Nottingham University, Rawdon Theological Institute, and Midland Bap-tist Coll. Entered the Baptist Ministry 1902. Secretary Peace Society 1915. President Liverpool Free Church Council 1914. District Moderator Lancashire and Ches-hire Association of Baptist Churches 1915-16. Town Councillor, Ilford and County Councillor, Essex; J.P. for Essex; Chief Magistrate and Returning Officer of Parlia-mentary Borough of Ilford 1925-26; F.R.C.I.; President Empire Publicity Advisory Council; Vice-President and Director of Bureau International De la Paix; Dept.-Chairman of House of Commons Committee of Ways and Means 1929-31. A Labour Member. Unsuccessfully contested Ilford in December 1918. Sat for the Consett division of Durham from November 1922 until he was defeated in October 1931. Un-successfully contested Wednesbury as National Labour candidate in November 1935. Knighted 1938. Honorary Warden of Browning Settlement, Southwark 1932-53. Died 2 October 1953. [1931 2nd ed.]

DU PRE, William Baring. Wilton Park, Beaconsfield. Carlton, and United Service. Eld. s. of James Du Pre and Lily, d. of T. Stokoe, Esq., and great-nephew of Caledon George Du Pre, Dept.-Lieut. and MP for Buckinghamshire. B. 1875; m. 1st, 1903, Youri Wynyard, d. of Capt. H. Townley Wright, R.N. (she died 1942); secondly, 1945, Beryl, widow of Hon. Robert Dudley Ryder. Educ. at Winchester Coll., and Royal Military Coll., Sandhurst. Held a commission in the King's Royal Rifles; served in South Africa with 13th Imperial Yeomanry 1900; medal and three clasps. Lieut.-Col. Commanding the Leicestershire Royal Horse Artillery (T.F.); served in European war 1914-18; J.P. and Dept. Lieut. for Buckinghamshire; High Sheriff 1911. A Conservative. Unsuccessfully contes-ted the Loughborough division of Leicester-shire in 1906. Sat for the Wycombe division of Buckinghamshire from February 1914 until he was defeated in December 1923. Died 23 August 1946. [1923]

EADY, George Hathaway. Victoria Park, Shipley, Yorkshire. Constitutional. S. of John Amos Eady, Esq., of Market Rasen. B. 1865; m. 1896, d. of J. Mitchell, Esq., of Halifax. Educ. at Hartshead. A Spinner and Manufacturer of Dress Clothes. Member of Bradford City Council. J.P. for Yorkshire. A Conservative. Elected for Bradford Central in October 1931 and sat until he was defeated in November 1935. Died 1 September 1941. [1935]

EALES, John Frederick, K.C. 3 Brick Court, Temple, London. Sandiford, North-wood, Middlesex. St. Stephen's. S. of William Eales, Esq., of Luton. B. 1881; m. 1905, Emily, d. of Frederick Randall, Esq., of Luton. Admitted a Solicitor 1904; Barrister-at-Law, Middle Temple 1910, and joined the Midland Circuit; K.C. 1929. Recorder of Coventry 1928-34, Recorder of Nottingham August 1934-August 1936. A Conservative. Elected for the Erdington division of Birmingham in October 1931. Sat until his death on 6 August 1936

[1936]

EASTWOOD, John Francis, O.B.E., K.C.
1 Garden Court, Temple, London. Bachelors', and M.C.C. S. of John Edmund Eastwood, Esq., of Enton, Witley. B. 13 October 1887; m. 1st, Alice Leonora Zacyntha, d. of Col. L.R.C. Boyle (she died 1933); secondly, 8 August 1934, Dorothea, d. of Rupert Butler, Esq., of Kings Hall, Milton, Marlborough. Educ. at Eton, and Trinity Coll., Cambridge. A Barrister-at-Law 1911. Served with Grenadier Guards 1914-18, Court Martial Officer for London 1918-20; Legal Officer, Ireland 1920-22; Recorder of Tenterden 1935-40. A Conservative. Elected for the Kettering division of Northamptonshire in October 1931. Sat until 1940 when he was appointed a Metropolitan Police Magistrate. K.C. 1937. Died 30 January 1952. [1940]

ECCLES, David McAdam. Continued in House after 1945: full entry in Volume IV.

ECKERSLEY, Peter Thorp. Midways, Ashley, Alterincham, Cheshire. Carlton, M.C.C., and Royal Aero. S. of William Eckersley, Esq. B. 2 July 1904; m. 1930, Audrey, d. of J.L. Hyde Johnson, Esq. Educ. at Rugby, and Trinity Coll., Cambridge. A Director of Limited Companies 1925. A National Conservative. Unsuccessfully contested Leigh in October 1931. Sat for the Exchange division of Manchester from November 1935 until he was killed on active service on 13 August 1940. Capt. of Lancashire County Cricket Club 1929-35. Lieut. in the Air division of R.N.V.R. Died 13 August 1940. [1940]

EDE, Rt. Hon. James Churter. Continued in House after 1945: full entry in Volume IV.

EDEN, Rt. Hon. Robert Anthony. Continued in House after 1945: full entry in Volume IV.

EDGAR, Clifford Blackburn. Wedderlie, Richmond, Surrey. Royal Societies, British Empire, St. Stephen's, Constitutional and University of London. S. of John Edgar, Esq., of Richmond Hill. B. 1857; m. 1883, Mary, d. of George Fowden, Esq. (she died 1929). Educ. at the University of Manchester: B.Sc., and the University of London: Mus. Bac. An original Director of the Niger Company, and Vice-Chairman from 1910. Director of the Bank of British West Africa. Alderman, Dept.-Lieut. and J.P. for Surrey; Chairman of the County Council from 1917-22. Senator of the University of London from 1905; Chairman of the University Finance Committee 1910 to 1920. Thrice Mayor of Richmond. Vice-Chairman of the Surrey Territorial Force Association 1907-20. Master of the Worshipful Company of Musicians 1913-14. A Conservative. Elected for Richmond in December 1918 and sat until he was defeated in November 1922. Died 20 March 1931. [1922]

EDGE, Sir William, Bart. Riversleigh, Lytham, Lancashire. Reform. S. of Sir Knowles Edge. B. 21 November 1880; m. 9 August 1904, Ada, d. of I. Ickringill, Esq., of Keighley. Educ. at Bolton Grammar School. Barrister-at-Law, Middle Temple; Staff Capt. at War Office; J.P. for Lancashire. Parliamentary Private Secretary to Sir Auckland Geddes when Minister of National Service 1917-19, to Sir Robert Horne when Minister of Labour 1919. Lord Commissioner of the Treasury August 1919-July 22, when he resigned. National Liberal Whip 1922-23; Liberal Whip 1929-30; Parliamentary Charity Commissioner October 1932-March 1935. Knight Bach. 1922; created Bart. 1937. A Liberal until 1931, thereafter a Liberal Nationalist. Sat for Bolton from 1916-23. Unsuccessfully contested Bolton in December 1923. Elected for the Bosworth division of Leicestershire in May 1927 and sat until he retired in June 1945. Died 18 December 1948. [1945]

EDMONDS, Garnham. House of Commons, London. B. 1866. A prominent worker in his constituency. Was a member of the London County Council 1910-22; Mayor of Bethnal Green in 1908; J.P. A Liberal. Elected for N.E. Bethnal Green in November 1922 and sat until he was defeated in December 1923; again defeated in October 1924. Died 9 April 1946. [1923]

EDMONDSON, Maj. Sir Albert James.
1 Gloucester Gate, London. The Manor
House, Sandford St. Martin, Oxfordshire.
Carlton. S. of James Edmondson, Esq., of
Weston, Hertfordshire. B. 29 June 1887; m.
1911, Elsie, d. of J.G. Freeman, Esq. (she
died 1946). Educ. at University Coll. School.
Joined Honorary Artillery Company
(R.H.A.) 1910; served in France, etc. 1914-
18. Staff appointment Eastern Command
1918. Member of Oxfordshire County
Council 1922-37; Dept.-Lieut. 1943. Parlia-
mentary Private Secretary to Parliamentary
Secretary Ministry of Pensions 1925-June
1929, and to Minister of Pensions November
1931. Private Secretary to Chief Civil
Commissioner 1926; Assistant Government
Whip 1937. Lord Commissioner of the
Treasury April 1939. Vice-Chamberlain of
H.M.'s Household November 1939, Treasur-
er March 1942-July 1945. Knight Bach.
1934. A Conservative. Elected for the
Banbury division of Oxfordshire in
November 1922 and sat until he retired in
June 1945. Created Baron Sandford 1945.
Chairman of Carlton Club 1946-56. High
Steward of Banbury 1947. Died 16 May
1959. [1945]

EDMUNDS, James Ewart. Highfield,
Rhiwbina Hill, Cardiff. S. of Edmund
Edmunds and Annie Louise, d. of J. Lucas,
Esq., Schoolmaster and Schoolmistress of
Gilwen, Breconshire. B. 5 May 1882; m.
31 October 1920, Keturah, d. of Edmund
Morgan, Esq., of Taffs Well. Educ. at
Howard Gardens Secondary School, and
University Coll., Cardiff. A Certificated
Teacher 1903-20, Cardiff L.E.A. Member
of Cardiff Board of Guardians 1913-25;
J.P. for Cardiff 1926. A Labour Member.
Unsuccessfully contested Cardiff Central in
December 1918, November 1922 and
December 1923. Elected for Cardiff E. in
May 1929 and sat until he was defeated in
October 1931. Secretary of Cardiff Trades
Council 1911-22, President 1924-28. New-
port District Secretary of Transport and
General Workers' Union. Died 1962.
[1931 2nd ed.]

**EDNAM, William Humble Eric Ward,
Visct., M.C.** 38 Green Street, London. S. of
2nd Earl of Dudley. B. 30 January 1894; m.
1st, 1919, Lady Rosemary Millicent
Leveson-Gower, d. of 4th Duke of Suther-
land (she died 1930); secondly, 1943, Laura,
Viscountess Long (divorced 1954); thirdly,
1961, Princess Grace Radziwill. Educ. at
Eton, and Christ Church, Oxford. Lieut.
Worcestershire Yeomanry 1912-14; Lieut.
and Capt. 10th Hussars 1914-20; served with
B.E.F. 1914-18; Brigade Maj. of the 23rd
Brigade 1918-19; Staff Capt. 1st Cavalry
Brigade 1919-20. Served in Ireland 1920.
Parliamentary Private Secretary to Earl
Winterton 1922-24. Styled Visct. Ednam
1894-1932. M.C. A Conservative. Sat for
Hornsey from November 1921 until he
retired in October 1924. Elected for Wednes-
bury in October 1931 and sat until he
succeeded to the Peerage as Earl of Dudley
in June 1932. Chairman of British Iron and
Steel Corporation. President of Society of
British Gas Industries 1926-27; of British
Iron and Steel Federation 1935-36; British
Iron and Steel Institute 1938-40 and Federa-
tion of Chambers of Commerce of the
British Empire 1937-45. Died in Paris
26 December 1969. [1932]

EDWARDS, Alfred. Continued in House
after 1945: full entry in Volume IV.

EDWARDS, Allen Clement. 5 Paper
Buildings, Temple, London. National
Liberal. S. of George B. Edwards, Esq. B.
1869 at Knighton; m. 1st, Fanny Emerson
(she died 1920); secondly, 1922, Alice May,
d. of Walter Edwin Parker, Esq. Educ. at
Knighton National School. A Barrister,
called at the Middle Temple 1899 and was
specially interested in trade union cases.
Wrote works on social and labour questions.
Chairman National Democratic Party 1919-
20. A Liberal. Unsuccessfully contested
Tottenham in 1895 and Denbigh district in
1900. Sat for Denbigh district from 1906 to
January 1910 when he was defeated. Elected
for E. Glamorganshire in December 1910 as
a Liberal and sat until December 1918 when,
standing as a pro-Coalition National Democratic Party candidate, he was elected for
East Ham S. Sat until November 1922 when
he was defeated standing as a N.D.P.
candidate with unofficial Conservative

support. Died 23 June 1938.   [1922]

EDWARDS, Rt. Hon. Sir Charles.
Continued in House after 1945: full entry in
Volume IV.

EDWARDS, Ebenezer. House of
Commons, London. B. 1884 at Chevington,
Northumberland. A Coal Miner. Represen-
ted Northumberland Miners' Association on
the Miners' Federation of Great Britain. A
Labour Member. Unsuccessfully contested
the Wansbeck division of Northumberland in
May and December 1918. Elected for
Morpeth in May 1929 and sat until he was
defeated in October 1931. Universally
known as 'Ebby' Edwards. Secretary of
Miners' Federation of Great Britain 1932-46.
President of T.U.C. 1944. Labour Relations
Officer of National Coal Board 1946-53.
Died 6 July 1961.   [1931 2nd ed.]

EDWARDS, George, O.B.E. 7 Lichfield
Street, Fakenham, Norfolk. B. 1850 in
Norfolk; m. 1872, Charlotte Corke (she
died 1912). Commenced farm work at the
age of six. President of the National Agricul-
tural Labourers Union; member of Norfolk
County Council from 1906; elected an
Alderman 1918. O.B.E. 1919 for platform
work during the war. A Labour Member.
Unsuccessfully contested S. Norfolk in
December 1918. Sat for S. Norfolk from
July 1920 to November 1922 when he was
defeated. Re-elected for S. Norfolk in
December 1923 and sat until he was defeated
in October 1924. Secretary of National
Union of Land Workers 1906-13. President
of National Council of Agriculture 1924.
Knighted 1930. Primitive Methodist lay
preacher for 60 years. Died 6 December
1933.   [1924 2nd ed.]

EDWARDS, Lieut.-Col. John. Rhydding,
Neath, South Wales. S. of the Rev. James
Edwards, one of the leaders of Welsh
Nonconformity. B. at Llanbadarn, Aberyst-
wyth 1882; m. 1932, Gwen, d. of J. Davies
Bryan, Esq. Educ. at the British and Inter-
mediate Schools, Neath, University Coll. of
Wales, Aberystwyth: Scholar; B.A. London
University. Rugby footballer (London Welsh
and Middlesex County). A Schoolmaster;

member of the National Union of Teachers.
Served in the army from September 1914 (Infantry); ranks to Lieut.-Col.; D.S.O. 1918,
twice mentioned in despatches. In France 3
years. Took an active interest in New School
Welsh Drama in authorship and acting.
A Liberal-Labour Coalition Member.
Elected for the Aberavon division of Glamorganshire in December 1918 and sat until
he was defeated in November 1922 standing
as a National Liberal. Unsuccessfully contested University of Wales as an Independent
Liberal in December 1923. Barrister-at-Law,
Gray's Inn 1921. High Sheriff of Cardiganshire 1942. Died 23 May 1960.   [1922]

EDWARDS, John Hugh. Silver Lodge,
Purley. Authors'. S. of Councillor John
Edwards, of Aberystwyth. B. 1871. Educ.
at Aberystwyth Grammar School, and University Coll. of Wales. A member of Court
of Governors of University Coll. of Wales,
and National Museum and National Library
of Wales; member of Aberystwyth Town
Council from 1914. J.P. for Surrey 1920.
Author of *From Village Green to Downing
Street*, the Life of Mr. Lloyd George, MP,
and *Short History of the Welsh People*. A
Liberal. Sat for mid Glamorganshire from
December 1910-18, and for the Neath
division of Glamorganshire from 1918-22
when he was defeated. Elected for Accrington in December 1923 and again in October
1924 and sat until he was defeated in May
1929. Elected as a Constitutionalist in
1924 with Liberal and Conservative support
but took the Liberal Whip during the
1924-29 Parliament. President of Guildford
and District Free Church Federal Council.
Died 14 June 1945.   [1929]

EDWARDS, Ness. Continued in House
after 1945: full entry in Volume IV.

EDWARDS, Walter James. Continued in
House after 1945: full entry in Volume IV.

EGAN, William Henry. 49 Hamilton
Square, Birkenhead. B. 14 February 1869.
Member of Birkenhead Town Council 1911-
43; J.P. 1918; Secretary of the local Trades
Council. A Labour Member. Unsuccessfully
contested W. Birkenhead in 1918 and 1922,

elected for W. Birkenhead in December 1923, contested the same division in October 1924. Re-elected for W. Birkenhead in May 1929 and sat until he was defeated in October 1931. Mayor of Birkenhead 1939-40 and 1941-42. A Roman Catholic. Died 10 September 1943. [1931 2nd ed.]

ELLIOT, Rt. Hon. Walter Elliot. Continued in House after 1945: full entry in Volume IV.

ELLIOTT, Sir George Samuel. Borough Hall, Islington. B. 1847 in Islington; m. Elizabeth Frances, d. of Robert Hellier, Esq., of Devonshire. Member of the old Islington Vestry, and 13 times Mayor of the Borough of Islington. Poor Law Guardian, and member of Metropolitan Asylums Board and London County Council. Raised two Battalions during the war and actively supported various local war charities. A Coalition Unionist. Elected for W. Islington in December 1918 and sat until he retired in October 1922. Knighted 1917. Died 4 May 1925. [1922]

ELLIS, Sir (Robert) Geoffrey, Bart. Connaught House, 163-4 Strand, London. Long Ashes, Netherside, Skipton, Yorkshire. Moat House, Melbourn via Royston, Hertfordshire. Carlton, and Athenaeum. S. of W.H. Ellis, Esq., of Shipley Hall, Yorkshire. B. 4 September 1874. Unmarried. Educ. at Peterhouse, Cambridge, M.A., Nat. Sc. Tripos. Barrister-at-Law, Inner Temple 1901; partner in Beckett and Company, Bankers, of Leeds, until amalgamation with the Westminster Bank 1920. Dept.-Lieut., and J.P. for the W. Riding of Yorkshire. Created Bart. 1932. A Conservative. Unsuccessfully contested the Holmfirth division of Yorkshire in January 1910 and June 1912. Elected for Wakefield in November 1922. Unsuccessfully contested Wakefield in December 1923; re-elected in October 1924, defeated May 1929. Sat for the Winchester division of Hampshire from October 1931-October 1935. Elected for the Ecclesall division of Sheffield in November 1935 and sat until he retired in June 1945. Counsel to the Crown in Peerage and honours claims 1922-54. Chairman of W. Riding Quarter

Sessions 1938-42. Died 28 July 1956. [1945]

ELLIS, William Craven See CRAVEN-ELLIS, William Craven.

ELLIS-GRIFFITH, Rt. Hon. Sir Ellis Jones, Bart., K.C. Buckingham Palace Mansions, London. 3 King's Bench Walk, Temple, London. Towyn Capel, Holyhead. S. of T.M. Griffith of Brynsiencyn, Anglesey. B. 1860; m. 1892, Mary, d. of the Rev. R. Owen, of Mold. Educ. at the University Coll. of Wales, and Downing Coll., Cambridge. A Barrister-at-Law, Middle Temple 1887. Recorder of Birkenhead 1907-12. K.C. 1910. Under-Secretary Home Department 1912-15. PC. 1914. Created Bart. 1918. A Liberal. Unsuccessfully contested the W. Toxteth division of Liverpool in 1892. Sat for Anglesey from 1895-1918 when he was defeated. Unsuccessfully contested the University of Wales in November 1922. Elected for the Carmarthen division of Carmarthenshire in December 1923 and sat until he resigned in July 1924. Fellow of Downing Coll., Cambridge 1888-92. Adopted the surname of Ellis-Griffith in lieu of Griffith in 1918. Died 30 November 1926. [1924 2nd ed.]

ELLISTON, Capt. Sir George Sampson, M.C. Heathcroft, Hampstead Way, London. Athenaeum, and Savage. Union, Blackburn. S. of W.A. Elliston, Esq., M.D., of Stoke Hall, Ipswich. B. 27 July 1875; M. 1904, Alice Louise, d. of Joseph Causton, Esq. Educ. at Ipswich, Framlingham, and St. Catharine's Coll., Cambridge, M.A. Served with B.E.F. 1915-19. Barrister-at-Law, Lincoln's Inn 1901. Member of the Corporation of the City of London (Chief Commoner 1943), and of the Metropolitan Water Board. Dept.-Lieut., and J.P. for the Co. of London. Knight Bach. 1944. A Conservative. Elected for Blackburn in October 1931 and again in November 1935. Sat until he retired in June 1945. Vice-President of Royal Sanitary Institute. Died 21 February 1954. [1945]

ELMLEY, William Lygon, Visct. 5 Connaught Place, London. The Lighthouse,

Winterton, Great Yarmouth. Beefsteak, Reform, and National Liberal. S. of William, 7th Earl Beauchamp, K.G. B. 3 July 1903; m. 16 June 1936, Else, d. of Fru J.B. Schrive, of Copenhagen, and widow of Direktor Dornonville de la Cour. Educ. at Eton, and Magdalen Coll., Oxford. Assistant Whip August-October 1931. Parliamentary Private Secretary to Leslie Hore-Belisha, when Parliamentary Secretary to Board of Trade 1931-32, when Financial Secretary to the Treasury October 1932-July 1934, when Minister of Transport July 1934-May 1937, and when Secretary of State for War May 1937. A Liberal until 1931, thereafter Liberal National. Elected for Norfolk E. in May 1929 and sat until 1938 when he succeeded to the Peerage as Earl Beauchamp. Styled Visct. Elmley 1903-38. Dept.-Lieut. and J.P. for Worcestershire. Member of Worcestershire County Council 1940-52. Served with Royal Army Ordnance Corps and in Italy, Capt. 1945.* [1939]

ELVEDEN, Rupert Edward Cecil Lee Guinness, Visct. C.B., C.M.G. 11 St. James's Square, London. Pyrford Court, Nr. Woking. Oakleigh, Southend-on-Sea. Carlton, Garrick, and Beefsteak. Leander. Eld. s. of Earl of Iveagh. B. 29 March 1874 in London; m. 1903, Lady Gwendolen Onslow, d. of 4th Earl of Onslow (she died 1966). Educ. at Eton, and Trinity Coll., Cambridge. Served in South African War 1900. Commander of London division R.N.V.R.; Capt.1919. Member of London School Board and of London County Council from 1904-10; C.M.G. 1901; C.B.1911. A Conservative. Unsuccessfully contested the Haggerston division of Shoreditch in 1906. Sat for the Haggerston division from August 1908-January 1910, when he was defeated. Again defeated in December 1910. Sat for S.E. Essex from March 1912 until he was elected for Southend-on-Sea in December 1918. Sat until 1927 when he succeeded to the Peerage as Earl of Iveagh. Styled Visct. Elveden from 1919, when his father was created 1st Earl of Iveagh, until he succeeded to the Earldom in 1927. Chairman of Arthur Guinness Son and Company Limited 1927-62. Chancellor of Dublin University 1927-63. K.G. 1955; F.R.S. 1964.

Dept.-Lieut. for Suffolk and Surrey and a Lieut. of City of London. Died 14 September 1967. [1927]

EMERY, James Frederick. Beech House, Bolton Road, Pendleton, Salford. S. of W.J. Emery, Esq., of Wigan. B. 17 December 1886; m. 1912, Florence Beatrice, d. of R.F Gradwell, Esq., of Preston (she died 1963). Educ. at University of Manchester. Member of Salford City Council 1923-35; Chairman of W. Salford Conservative Association 1922-35. J.P. for Salford 1927. Mayor of Salford 1932-33. Director of Companies. A Conservative. Elected for Salford W. in November 1935 and sat until he was defeated in July 1945. Knighted 1957.* [1945]

EMLYN-JONES, John Emlyn. 40 Cyncoed Road, Cardiff. National Liberal. S. of Evan Jones, Esq., Coal Factor. B. in Cardiff 22 January 1889; m. 31 March 1915, Rhoda, eld. d. of Capt. and Mrs. Richard Care, Cardiff. Educ. at Cardiff High School, and in France, Spain and Italy. A Shipowner, Merchant and Exporter. A Liberal. Unsuccessfully contested N. Dorset in 1918. Elected for N. Dorset in November 1922. Sat until he was defeated in October 1924. Unsuccessfully contested E. Cardiff in May 1929 and October 1931 and Flintshire in November 1935. J.P. for Cardiff. Killed in an air crash at Nice 3 March 1952. [1924 2nd ed.]

EMMOTT, Charles Ernest George Campbell. 39 Smith Street, London. Carlton. S. of Charles Emmott, Esq., of Oldham, and Lady Constance Campbell, d. of 8th Duke of Argyll. B. 12 November 1898. Educ. at Lancing, and Christ Church, Oxford, M.A., Class. Scholar. Barrister-at-Law, Middle Temple 1924. A Conservative. Unsuccessfully contested Preston in May 1929. Elected for the Springburn division of Glasgow in October 1931 and for E. Surrey in November 1935. Sat until he retired in June 1945. Chairman of British-Italian Society. Died 14 April 1953. [1945]

EMRYS-EVANS, Paul Vychan. Peatswood, Market Drayton, Shropshire. Travellers'. S. of John Emrys-Evans, Esq., C.M.G. B. 1 April 1894; m. 1928, Evelyn Dorothy, d. of Col. Francis Randle Twemlow, D.S.O., of Peatswood, Market Drayton (she died 1962). Educ. at Harrow, and King's Coll., Cambridge, M.A. Lieut. Suffolk Regiment; served in France 1916. Attached to Foreign Office 1917, at Embassy, Washington 1918-19, Foreign Office 1919-23. Parliamentary Under-Secretary of State for the Dominions March 1942-July 1945. A Conservative. Unsuccessfully contested Leicester W. in May 1929. Elected for Derbyshire S. in October 1931. Sat until he was defeated in July 1945. Director of British South Africa Company, President 1962. Chairman of Charter Consolidated Limited 1965-66. Died at Nice 26 October 1967.   [1945]

ENGLAND, Col. Abraham, C.M.G., D.S.O., T.D. Halkyn Castle, Nr. Holywell, North Wales. National Liberal, and Manchester Reform. B. 3 January 1867; m. 1894, Lucie, d. of William Dunkerley, Esq. Educ. privately. Served in France, Belgium, Egypt and Gallipoli 1915-18. Honorary Col. 42nd T.F. Division; member of E. Lancashire T.F.A. A Wholesale Clothier in Manchester. A Liberal. Unsuccessfully contested Heywood and Radcliffe division of Lancashire in 1921. Sat for the Heywood and Radcliffe division of Lancashire from November 1922 until he retired in October 1931. Elected as a Constitutionalist in 1924, with Liberal and Conservative support, but accepted the Liberal Whip during the 1924-29 Parliament. Elected as a Liberal in 1929, although without Conservative opposition and in 1931 supported the Liberal National group. President of Manchester Reform Club 1934. Dept.-Lieut. for Lancashire. Died 4 January 1949.   [1931 2nd ed.]

ENTWISTLE, Sir Cyril Fullard, K.C., M.C. Limefield, Broadway, Hale, Cheshire. 3 Temple Gardens, Temple, London. S. of J. Entwistle, Esq., of Bolton and St. Annes, Cotton Manufacturer. B. 23 September 1887; m. 1940, Ethel M. Towlson, of Hale, Cheshire. Educ. at Bolton Grammar School, and Victoria University of Manchester, LL.B., 1st Class Honours, 1908, Dauntsey

Legal and Graduate Scholar; 1st Class Honours Solicitors' Final 1909, Clement's Inn and Daniel Reardon Prizeman, Travers Smith Scholar. Admitted a Solicitor 1910. Barrister-at-Law, Inner Temple 1919; K.C. 1931. 1st Commander R.G.A. April 1915; Maj. R.G.A. 1917. Commanded 235 Siege Battery R.G.A. Dept.-Chairman of Ways and Means January-October 1924. Member of Chairman's Panel from 1931 and a member appointed under Parliament Act to advise on money bills. Knight Bach. 1937. A Conservative. Sat as Liberal Member for S.W. Hull from December 1918 until 1924 when he was defeated. Unsuccessfully contested Bolton as a Conservative in May 1929. Elected for Bolton as a Conservative in October 1931 and sat until he was defeated in July 1945. Joined the Conservative Party 1926. Died 9 July 1974.   [1945]

ERRINGTON, Eric. Continued in House after 1945: full entry in Volume IV.

ERSKINE, James Malcolm Monteith. 7 Eccleston Square, London. Carlton, and Junior Carlton. S. of Capt. David Holland Erskine, H.B.M. Consul at Madeira, and grand-s. of Sir David Erskine, 1st Bart., of Cambo. B. 18 July 1863; m. 7 September 1898, Cicely Grace, d. of the Rev. Charles Penrose Quicke, of Newton St. Cyres. Educ. at Wellington Coll. J.P. for Sussex. Member of the Rural District Council, Thakeham. Chairman of Clan Erskine Society Committee. A Conservative. Elected for the St. George's division of Westminster from June 1921 as a candidate of the Anti-Waste League, defeating the official Conservative candidate; re-elected in November 1922 as the candidate of the St. George's Independent Conservative Association, with the support of the Anti-Waste League, again defeating the official Conservative candidate. Re-elected as the official Conservative candidate without opposition in December 1923 and October 1924 and sat until he retired in May 1929. Knighted 1929. Died 5 November 1944.   [1929]

ERSKINE, John Francis Ashley Erskine, The Lord, G.C.S.I., G.C.I.E. 6 St. James's Square, London. Carlton.

S. of Walter, 12th Earl of Mar and Kellie. B. 26 April 1895; m. 2 December 1919, Lady Marjorie Hervey, d. of Frederick, 4th Marq. of Bristol. Educ. at Eton, and Christ Church, Oxford. Scots Guards and Argylle and Sutherland Highlanders. Assistant Private Secretary to Lord Long 1920-21. Parliamentary Private Secretary to Sir W. Joynson-Hicks 1922-23, January 1924, and November 1924-June 1929. Assistant Whip in National Government November 1931. Gov. of Madras 1934-40. A Conservative. Elected for the Weston-super-Mare division of Somerset in November 1922, and was defeated there in December 1923. Sat for the same division from October 1924 to June 1934 when he was appointed Gov. of Madras. Returned unopposed for Brighton in May 1940 and sat until he resigned in 1941. Died 3 May 1953, during his father's lifetime. [1941]

ERSKINE-BOLST, Capt. Clifford Charles Alan Lawrence. Fountain Court, Buckingham Palace Road, London. Carlton, Ranelagh, Junior Naval & Military, St. Stephen's, and Royal Automobile. S. of Charles Young Erskine-Bolst, Esq. B. 1878; m. March 1920, Blanche Fletcher Ryer, d. of Senator Maguire, of Massachusetts, U.S.A., and widow of Fletcher Ryer, Esq., of California, U.S.A. Educ. at Blair Lodge, Polmont, Perthshire. Capt. Black Watch. F.R.G.S. J.P. A Freeman of the City of London. A Conservative. Elected for S. Hackney in August and November 1922, defeated there in 1923. Elected for Blackpool in October 1931 and sat until he retired in October 1935. Died 11 January 1946. [1935]

ERSKINE-HILL, Sir Alexander Galloway Erskine, Bart. 39 Heriot Row, Edinburgh. Quothquhan Lodge, Biggar, Lanarkshire. Carlton. S. of Robert Alexander Hill, Esq., of Coneyhill House, Bridge of Allan. B. 3 April 1894; m. 3 December 1915, Christian, d. of John Colville, Esq., MP, of Cleland, Lanarkshire. Educ. at Rugby, and Trinity Coll., Cambridge. Advocate Scottish bar, called 1920, and Barrister-at-Law, Inner Temple 1919. K.C. 1935. A Director of L.N.E.R. Standing Junior

Counsel Scottish Department of Agriculture 1932; Advocate Depute to the Lord Advocate 1932-35. Served overseas 1914-18; Honorary Col. 1939. Chairman of Conservative Members '1922' Committee 1940-44. A Conservative. Unsuccessfully contested N. Lanarkshire as a Liberal in 1918. Elected for Edinburgh N. in November 1935 and sat until he was defeated in July 1945. Created Bart. 1945. Assumed the surname Erskine-Hill in lieu of Hill 1943. Died 6 June 1947. [1945]

ESSENHIGH, Reginald Clare. 2 Harcourt Buildings, Temple, London. Birdhurst, Holmwood Gardens, Wallington, Surrey. S. of Henry Streeter Essenhigh, Esq. B. 7 September 1890; m. 22 August 1924, Helen, d. of John Hogg, Esq., of Cambuslang, Lanarkshire. Educ. at Blue Coat, Warrington Secondary Schools, and at Royal Coll. of Art. Barrister-at-Law, Gray's Inn 1922, Northern Circuit. Capt. Manchester Regiment; served in France and Belgium 1914-19, retired. A Unionist. Unsuccessfully contested the Newton division of Lancashire in May 1929. Elected for the Newton division of Lancashire in October 1931 and sat until he was defeated in November 1935. County Court Judge 1936-55. Died 1 November 1955. [1935]

ETCHINGHAM, John R. Courtown Harbour, Gorey, Co. Wexford. Was arrested in May 1918 and interned in Lincoln prison. A Sinn Fein Member. Elected for Wicklow E. in December 1918 but did not take his seat. Member of Dail for E. Wicklow to 1921, for Wexford 1921-22, as an Anti-Treaty Member. Secretary for Fisheries 1921-22. Chairman of Wexford County Council. [1922]

ETHERTON, Ralph Humphrey. Goldsmith Building, Temple, London. Carlton, Junior Carlton, Pratts, and Crockfords. S. of Louis Etherton, Esq. B. 11 February 1904; m. 1944, Johanne Patricia, d. of Gerald Cloherty, Esq., of Galway. Educ. at Charterhouse, and Trinity Hall, Cambridge, M.A. Barrister-at-Law 1926, Inner Temple and Northern Circuit. Served with R.A.F.V.R. Flight-Lieut. 1940-42. Member of Parliamentary Delegation to Australia and New Zealand 1944. A National Conservative. Unsuccessfully contested the Everton division of Liverpool in November 1935. Elected for the Stretford division of Lancashire in December 1939 and sat until he was defeated in July 1945. ★ [1945]

EVANS, David Owen. Grosvenor House, Park Lane, London. Rhydclomennod, Llangranog, Llandyssul, Cardiganshire. Reform, National Liberal, and Eighty. S. of William Evans, Esq., Farmer. B. 1876; m. 1899, Kate, d. of David Morgan, Esq., of Aberffrwd. Educ. at Llandovery School, and Royal Coll. of Science, London. A Barrister-at-Law, Gray's Inn. Vice-President International National Nickel Company of Canada; Delegate Director of Mond Nickel Company; Director of Henry Gardner and Company Limited. A Liberal. Elected for Cardiganshire in September 1932 and again in November 1935. Sat until his death on 11 June 1945. His knighthood was announced in the Dissolution honours list of 7 June but he died before the award was conferred. [1945]

EVANS, Ernest. 22 Pelham Crescent, London. 2 Mitre Court Buildings, Temple, London. Huanfa, Ceibach, Newquay, Cardiganshire. National Liberal. S. of Evan Evans, Esq., Clerk to the Cardiganshire County Council. B. 1885; m. 1925, Constance Anne, d. of Thomas Lloyd, Esq., of Hadley Wood. Educ. at Llandovery Coll., University Coll. of Wales, Aberystwyth and Trinity Hall, Cambridge; B.A., LL.B. A Barrister-at-Law, on the S. Wales Circuit 1910; K.C. 1937; Dept.-Chairman and later Chairman Cardigan Quarter Sessions. Private Secretary to the Rt. Hon. D. Lloyd George 1918-20. An Opposition Liberal Member. Sat for Cardiganshire from 1921-December 1923, when he was defeated. Elected for the University of Wales in October 1924 and sat until 1942 when he was appointed County Court Judge; retired 1957. Chairman of Anglesey Quarter Sessions. Died 18 January 1965. [1942]

EVANS, Col. Sir Henry Arthur. Claridges Hotel, Brook Street, London. Carlton, Marl-

borough, and Guards. County, Cardiff. S. of Arthur S. Evans, Esq., of Snaresbrook. B. 24 September 1898; m. 29 March 1920, Mary Stewart, d. of John Claflin, Esq., of Morristown (divorced 1929 but remarried 1949). Served in Egypt and France 1914-20, transferred Regular Army Reserve Welsh Guards 1920; served in France December 1939-40, commanding 8th Group Pioneer Corps, Havre Defence Force and Havre Garrison (rear Headquarters) (despatches); Lieut.-Col. Regular Army Reserve; Honorary Col. R.A.T.A. Chairman Parliamentary Select Committee of Private Bills 1942-44, of British Group Interparliamentary Union from 1939 (President ad interim 1943). Chairman Welsh Parliamentary Party 1938-39 and 1942-43; Treasurer of Conservative and Unionist Members Committee 1942; member of Executive of Empire Parliamentary Association, of British American Parliamentary Committee and Comité Exécutif et du Counseil Union Interparlementaire. Vice-Chairman Wales and Monmouthshire Conservative and Unionist Council, and of Anglo-Brazilian Society 1943. Dept.-Chairman and Director of a group of Public Companies. Member of Court of Governors of Welsh University, National Museum of Wales and Welsh National Library. Member .of Honorary Society of Cymmrodorion Parliamentary Mission to U.S.A. Congress 1943. Secretary to Empire Parliamentary Delegation to West Indies and Bermuda 1926. Aide-de-Camp to Private Secretary to Admiral of the Fleet, Earl Jellicoe, G.C.B., O.M., G.C.V.O., on his Canadian Tour 1931. Member of Speaker's Conference in Electoral Reform 1944. Knight Bach. 1944. A National Liberal until July 1923, thereafter a Conservative. Elected for Leicester E. in 1922. Unsuccessfully contested Leicester E. in December 1923. Sat for Cardiff S. from October 1924-May 1929 when he retired; re-elected in October 1931 and again in November 1935. Sat until he was defeated in July 1945. Died in Paris 25 September 1958. [1945]

EVANS, Herbert. St. Alban's Avenue, Bedford Park, London. Collieston-by-Ellon, Aberdeenshire. Royal Societies, and National Labour. S. of John Evans, Esq. B. at Burton-on-Trent 1868; m. Jennie, d. of Robert Mitchell, Esq., of Aberdeen. Educ. at Regent Street Polytechnic. H.M. Inspector, Home Office 1894. National Health Insurance Commission 1911. Served with Middlesex Regiment 1914-16, Maj. Principal Private Secretary to Minister of Pensions 1916-18. Inspector Gen., Ministry of Pensions 1918-27. C.B.E. 1920. Editor of *Social Worker's Armoury* on behalf of National Brotherhood Council. Prospective Parliamentary candidate for Grimsby 1928. A Labour Member. Unsuccessfully contested the Maldon division of Essex in May 1929. Elected for Gateshead in June 1931 and sat until his death on 7 October 1931, the day before the dissolution of Parliament.

EVANS, Capt. Richard Thomas. 20 Palace Road, Llandaff, Glamorganshire. National Liberal. B. 1890; m. 1918, Edith, d. of Morgan Rhys Williams, Esq. Educ. at the University of Wales. A Lecturer in Economics and Political Science University Coll. of S. Wales. Capt. S. Wales Borderers. Served in France 1914-18. A Liberal. Unsuccessfully contested the Llanelly division of Carmarthenshire in December 1923, October 1924 and May 1929. Elected for Carmarthen division of Carmarthenshire in October 1931 and sat until he was defeated in November 1935. Died 20 July 1946. [1935]

EVANS, Rt. Hon. Sir Worthington Laming, Bart. See WORTHINGTON-EVANS, Rt. Hon. Sir Worthington Laming, Bart.

EVERARD, Sir (William) Lindsay. Ratcliffe Hall, Leicestershire. Carlton, and Guards'. S. of T.W. Everard, Esq., of Bradgate Park, Leicester. B. 1891; m. 1918, Ione, d. of Capt. M.B. Armstrong, of Moyaliffe Castle, Co. Tipperary. Educ. at Harrow, and Trinity Coll., Cambridge. Served with Leicestershire Yeomanry and 1st Life Guards 1914-18. Honorary Air Commodore 605 Co. of Warwick (Fighter Squadron) A.A.F. A Company Director and Agriculturist. Dept.-Lieut., and J.P. for Leicestershire, High Sheriff 1924-25.

Knight Bach. 1939. A Conservative. Elected for the Melton division of Leicestershire in October 1924 and sat until he retired in June 1945. Pioneer of private aviation. Vice-President of Royal Aero Club. Chairman of Directors of Everards Brewery Limited, Leicester and John Sarson and Son Limited. Died 11 March 1949. [1945]

EYRES-MONSELL, Rt. Hon. Sir Bolton Meredith, G.B.E. Admiralty House, Whitehall, London. Dumbleton Hall, Evesham. Carlton, and Army & Navy. S. of Lieut.-Col. Bolton J. Monsell. B. 1881; m. 1st, 1904, Caroline Mary, d. of William Henry Eyres, Esq., of Dumbleton Hall, Evesham, and assumed the additional name of Eyres (divorced 1950): secondly, 1950, Mrs. Essex Leila Hilary Drury, grand-d. of Earl of Ypres. Educ. at Stubbington House, Fareham, and H.M.S. *Britannia*. Joined the Royal Navy 1895, retired 1906; rejoined and served at sea 1915-16; Unionist Whip 1911-15; liaison officer between Army and Navy in Egypt; in command of H.M.S. *Glowworm* 1916; Commander 1918. Treasurer of the Household February 1919; Civil Lord of the Admiralty April 1921 to October 1922; Parliamentary and Financial Secretary to the Admiralty October 1922; Parliamentary Secretary to the Treasury July 1923 to Janauary 1924, November 1924-June 1929 and August-November 1931; First Lord of the Admiralty November 1931-June 1936. Chief Conservative Whip 1923-31. G.B.E. 1929. PC. 1923. A Conservative. Sat for the Evesham division of Worcestershire from January 1910 until he retired in October 1935. Created Visct. Monsell 1935. High Steward of Evesham. Director of British Airways 1937. Commissioner for Civil Defence, South Eastern Region 1941-45. Died 21 March 1969. [1935]

FAHY, Francis Patrick. 17 Norfolk Road, Philsboro, Dublin. S. of John Fahy, Esq., of Kilchreest, Co. Galway. B. 1880 in Galway; m. 1908, Anna, d. of D. Barton, Esq., of Tralee. Educ. at Mungret Coll., Limerick, and Royal University of Ireland. Was a teacher of Irish, Latin, and Science at St. Vincent's Coll., Castlenock when arrested in May 1918. A Sinn Fein Member.

interned in Reading prison at the time of his election for S. Galway in December 1918 and did not take his seat. Member of Dail for S. Galway to 1921, for Co. Galway 1921-37, for E. Galway 1937-48, for S. Galway 1948-53. An Anti-Treaty Member, joined Fianna Fail 1926. Speaker of Dail 1932-51. Died 12 July 1953.   [1922]

FAIRBAIRN, Richard Robert. Barbourne, Worcester. National Liberal. S. of Richard R. Fairbairn, Esq., Labour Leader. B. in London 27 May 1867; m. 1892, Louisa, d. of Thomas Beechey, Esq., Merchant Tailor in the City of London. Educ. at the Ryerson Public School, Toronto, Canada. Tramways Manager in Worcester, Birmingham and London 1890-1908; Secretary Worcester Liberal Association from 1908; J.P. for Worcester 1907; Member Lord Chancellor's Advisory Committee; City Councillor from 1899. Severn Commissioner, etc. Road Transport Officer for Midland division, Ministry of Food during the war. A Liberal. Unsuccessfully contested Worcester in December 1910 and December 1918. Elected for Worcester in November 1922 and sat until he was defeated in December 1923. Unsuccessfully contested Worcester in October 1924, May 1929, October 1931 and November 1935. Died October 1941.   [1923]

FAIRFAX, Capt. James Griffyth. 80 Ashley Gardens, London. Athenaeum, Bath, United, 1900, and Hurlingham. Norfolk, Norwich. S. of C.B. Fairfax, Esq., of Sydney, N.S.W. B. 15 July 1886; m. 11 October 1922, Rosetta Mary, d. of Capt. Sir John Glover, G.C.M.G., R.N. Educ. at Winchester, and at New Coll., Oxford, 3rd cl. Honours Mods., 1st cl. English Lit., B.A. Barrister-at-Law, Inner Temple 1912, N.S.W. 1920. Author and Journalist. Capt. R.A.S.C. Served in Mesopotamia, etc. 1914-19 A Conservative. Elected for Norwich in October 1924 and sat until he was defeated in May 1929. Member of Executive Council of Association of Chambers of Commerce 1928-45. Died 27 January 1976.   [1929]

FALCON, Capt. Michael. 3 Cadogan Terrace, London. S. of Michael Falcon, Esq.,

J.P. of Horstead House, Norwich. B. 1888; m. 1920, Kathleen, only d. of Capt. Gascoigne, Seaforth Highlanders, and Mrs. Gascoigne, of Devizes. Educ. at Harrow, and Pembroke Coll., Cambridge. Was Capt. of Cambridge University cricket eleven and Norfolk Co. eleven. Played for the Gentlemen of England. A Barrister-at-Law, Inner Temple 1911. B.A., LL.B. Capt. in the Norfolk (T.) Artillery, served in France, Egypt, and Palestine. A Conservative. Elected for E. Norfolk in December 1918 and sat until he was defeated in December 1923. High Sheriff of Norfolk 1943-44. Died 27 February 1976.   [1923]

FALCONER, James. Empire House, Kingsway, London. Devonshire. S. of Donald Falconer, Esq., of Milton of Conon, Forfarshire. B. 1856 at Carmyllie, Forfarshire; m. Ada, d. of Robert Kennedy, Esq., C.E. Educ. at Arbroath High School, and Edinburgh University. A Writer to the Signet 1884; practised in Edinburgh. A Liberal. First elected for Forfarshire in February 1909. Re-elected for Forfarshire in January and December 1910, defeated there in 1918. Again elected for Forfarshire in November 1922 and sat until he was defeated in October 1924. Founder of Scottish Rural Workers Society. Died 21 April 1931.   [1924 2nd ed.]

FALLE, Sir Bertram Godfray, Bart. 13 Eaton Place, London. New University, and Coaching. S. of J.G. Falle, Esq., a Judge of the Royal Court of Jersey, and Mary, d. of F. Godfray, Esq., Barrister, of Bagatelle, Jersey. B. 21 November 1859; m. 18 July 1906, Mary, d. of Russell Sturgis, Esq., and widow of Lieut.-Col. L. Seymour, Grenadier Guards (she died 1942). Educ. privately, and at Victoria Coll., Jersey, Pembroke Coll., Cambridge, and Paris University. Travelled extensively in the East and West. A Barrister-at-Law, Inner Temple 1885. Was an Enroller of Deeds at H.M. Office of Works and English Judge of Native Tribunal at Cairo 1901-03. Maj. R.F.A., served in France, etc. 1914-18. Created Bart. 1916. A Conservative. Unsuccessfully contested E. Somerset in 1906 as a Liberal Unionist. Sat for Portsmouth from January 1910-18, and for Portsmouth N. from 1918 until January 1934 when he was created Baron Portsea. Died 1 November 1948. [1934]

FALLS, Maj. Sir Charles Fausset. Little Derryinch, Enniskillen. Constitutional. Kildare Street, Dublin. S. of Henry Falls, Esq., of Fallsbrook, Co. Tyrone. B. 1 January 1860; m. March 1887, Clare, d. of William Bentham, Esq. (she died 1929). Educ. in H.M.S. *Conway*, and at Trinity Coll., Dublin. Served with Inniskilling Fusiliers, Ulster division in France 1914-19. Dept.-Lieut. for Co. Fermanagh. Knight Bach. 1923. A Conservative. Unsuccessfully contested Fermanagh and Tyrone in 1923. Elected for Fermanagh and Tyrone in October 1924 and sat until he retired in May 1929. Died 20 September 1936. [1929]

FANSHAWE, Commander Guy Dalrymple, R.N. 12a St. James's Court, Buckingham Gate, London. Dalveagh, Aberfoyle, Perthshire. Carlton, and United Service. S. of Admiral of the Fleet Sir Arthur Fanshawe, G.C.B., G.C.V.O. B. 30 March 1882; m. 16 August 1910, Louisa Charlotte, d. of Col. Hon. Sir Harry Crichton, K.C.B. (she died 1948). Educ. at Twyford School, at Winchester, and in H.M.S. *Britannia*. Joined R.N. 1896. Served in China 1900 and during war 1914-18. Member of Interallied Naval Comn. of Control, Berlin 1919-23. A Conservative. Elected for the W. Stirlingshire division of Stirlingshire and Clackmannan in October 1924 and sat until he was defeated in May 1929. Parliamentary Private Secretary to Rt. Hon. L.S. Amery 1928-29. Vice-President of Royal National Lifeboat Institution. Died 19 June 1962. [1929]

FARQUHARSON, Maj. Alexander Charles. 48 St. George's Road. London. 1 Carlton Terrace, Spennymore, Co. Durham. National Liberal, Leeds County, and Liberal. S. of James Farquharson, Esq., of Cove, Aberdeen. B. 1864; m. 1903, Elizabeth, d. of Edward Blockley, Esq., of Kew Gardens. Educ. at Peterhead Academy, and Glasgow University. A medical man who before the war was in practice at

Spennymore, Co. Durham. Capt. R.A.M.C., Headquarters Staff 63rd division; Dept.-Assistant Director of Medical Services in the Northern Command 1916-18. A Coalition Liberal. Elected for N. Leeds in December 1918 and sat until he retired in October 1922. D.P.H. University of Cambridge. Barrister-at-Law, Middle Temple 1917. Died 27 May 1951. [1922]

FAWKES, Maj. Frederick Hawksworth. Farnley Hall, Nr. Otley. S. of the Rev. Frederick Fawkes. B. 1870. Educ. at Eton, and Trinity Hall, Cambridge. Chairman of the W. Riding Agricultural Committee; representative for the W. Riding on the National Agricultural Council; member of the Council of the Yorkshire Agricultural Society. A member of the same family as Guy Fawkes. A Conservative. Elected for the Pudsey and Otley division of Yorkshire in November 1922 and sat until he retired in November 1923. Member of W. Riding County Council 1908-34; High Sheriff of W. Riding 1932. Died 1 February 1936. [1923]

FELL, Sir Arthur. Lauriston House, Wimbledon Common, London. Carlton. S. of Alfred Fell, Esq., Merchant, and Fanny, d. of Henry Seymour, Esq. B. 7 August 1850 at Nelson, New Zealand; m. 1st, 1877, Annie, d. of Baron von Rosenberg of Dresden; secondly, 1900, Matilda, d. of Dr. Wortabet, of Edinburgh. Educ. at King's Coll. School, and St. John's Coll., Oxford: M.A. Admitted a Solicitor 1874; retired 1906. F.S.S., F.R.C.I. Chairman House of Commons Channel Tunnel Committee. Author of numerous pamphlets on economic subjects, *The Channel Tunnel and Food Supplies in Time of War*, etc. Knighted 1918. A Conservative. First elected for Great Yarmouth in 1906 and sat until he retired in October 1922. Died 29 December 1934. [1922]

FENBY, Thomas Davis. 13 St. John Street, Bridlington. S. of George William Fenby, Esq., of Bridlington. B. 1875; m. 1900, Elizabeth Ann, d. of Henry Adamson, Esq., of Helperthorpe. Educ. at Bridlington School. Mayor of Bridlington 1922-23.

Member of the County Council for the E. Riding of the Yorkshire from 1910, Alderman from 1923. A Liberal Whip from 1926. A Liberal. Unsuccessfully contested Howdenshire in 1918, and the Buckrose division of Yorkshire in 1922 and 1923. Elected for Bradford E. in October 1924 and sat until he was defeated in May 1929; again defeated in November 1935. Chairman of E. Riding Quarter Sessions. Died 4 August 1956.   [1929]

FERGUSON, Hugh. Motherwell, Lanarkshire. B. 1863. In early life was a Soldier; active in recruiting during the war. An Orangeman, Auctioneer, Baillie of the Burgh. A Conservative. Unsuccessfully contested the Motherwell division of Lanarkshire in 1918 and 1922. Elected for the Motherwell division of Lanarkshire in December 1923 and sat until he was defeated in October 1924. Convicted at Hamilton Sheriff Court on 30 May 1933 of receiving 70 cast-iron plates and 8 cwt. of railway chairs knowing them to be stolen.
                                      [1924 2nd ed.]

FERGUSON, Sir John, K.B.E. 125 Sloane Street, London. Great Bounds, Bidborough, Kent. Carlton, Pilgrims, Royal Automobile, and Ranelagh. New, Edinburgh. S. of George Ferguson, Esq., of Rosslyn. B. 19 May 1870; m. 5 September 1903, Adelaide Helen, d. of Col. C. Telfer Smollett, of Bonhill, Dumbartonshire. Educ. at Gordons Coll., Aberdeen. A Banker, President of English Institute of Bankers 1926-27. Assistant to Surveyor-Gen. of Supply, War Office 1917-19. K.B.E. 1918. A Conservative. Unsuccessfully contested Hammersmith S. in May 1929. Elected for the Twickenham division of Middlesex in August 1929 and again in October 1931. Sat until his death on 17 July 1932. [1932]

FERMOR-HESKETH, Maj. Thomas. 7 Rutland Gate, London. Eaton Neston, Towcester, Northamptonshire. Rufford Hall, Nr. Ormskirk, Lancashire. Carlton, and Arthur's. Eld. s. of Sir T.G. Fermor-Hesketh, 8th Bart. B. at Rufford Hall, near Ormskirk, Lancashire 17 November 1881; m. 9 September 1909, Florence

Louise Breckinridge, d. of J.W. Breckinridge, Esq., of San Francisco, and grand-d. of Gen. J.C. Breckinridge, Vice-President of the U.S.A. Educ. at Eton, Sandhurst Royal Military Coll., and Trinity Coll., Cambridge; B.A. 1909. President of University Engineering Society. For some time Advisory Engineer to Lancashire War Agricultural Committee. Farmed some 3,500 acres, owning about 8,000 acres. J.P. for Lancashire 1910. J.P. for Co. of Northampton 1922. A Conservative. Unsuccessfully contested the Ormskirk division of Lancashire as Conservative Unionist in 1918. Elected for the Enfield division of Middlesex in November 1922 and sat until he was defeated in December 1923. High Sheriff of Northamptonshire 1932. Succeeded as Bart. 1924. Created Baron Hesketh 1935. Died 20 July 1944.   [1923]

FERMOY, Edmund Maurice Roche, 4th Baron (Irish Peerage). Park House, Sandringham. B. 15 May 1885, succeeded his father as 4th Baron in the Peerage of Ireland 1920; m. 17 September 1931, Ruth Sylvia, d. of W.S. Gill, Esq., C.B., of Dalhebity, Bieldside, Aberdeenshire. Educ. at St. Paul's School, U.S.A., and Harvard University. Flying Officer R.A.F. 1941. A Conservative. Unsuccessfully contested the Horncastle division of Lincolnshire in November 1922. Sat for the King's Lynn division of Norfolk from October 1924 to October 1935 when he retired. Re-elected for the King's Lynn division of Norfolk in February 1943 and sat until he retired in June 1945. Mayor of King's Lynn 1931-32. Died 8 July 1955.   [1945]

FIELDEN, Edward Brocklehurst. 19 Great College Street, London. Court of Hill, Ludlow. Dobroyd Castle, Todmorden. Carlton, and Conservative. S. of Joshua Fielden, Esq., MP, of Nutfield Priory. B. 10 June 1857; m. 1st, 1884, Mary, d. of Thomas Knowles, Esq., MP, of Darn Hall, Cheshire (she died 1902); secondly, 18 April 1906, Mysie, M.B.E. 1918, d. of William Theed, Esq. (she died 10 March 1942). Chairman of Lancashire and Yorkshire Railway 1910-23; Dept.-Chairman L.M. and S. Railway from 1923. J.P. for Oxfordshire and Shropshire. High Sheriff of Shropshire 1911. Engineer to Thames Valley Drainage Commission 1881-94. Chairman of Finance Committee Shropshire County Council from 1920. A Conservative. Sat for the Middleton division of Lancashire from 1900-06 when he retired. Sat for the Exchange division of Manchester from October 1924 until October 1935 when he retired. Died 31 March 1942.   [1935]

FILDES, Sir Henry. 3 Whitehall Court, London. Endon House, Kerridge, Macclesfield. Reform, and White's. S. of Henry Fildes, Esq., of Stockport. B. 12 May 1870; m. 25 April 1899, Janita Olive, d. of A.P. Garland, Esq., of Blackburn. Educ. at Partwood School, and Harris Institute, Preston. J.P. for Stockport 1915. Maj. Cheshire R.A.S.C. (M.T.). Knight Bach. 1932. A Liberal Nationalist. Elected for Stockport as a Coalition Liberal in March 1920 and sat until he was defeated in December 1923; again defeated in September 1925 and in May 1929. Elected as a Liberal Nationalist for Dumfriesshire in September and in November 1935 and sat until he retired in June 1945. Died 12 July 1948.   [1945]

FINBURGH, Samuel. Lyndhurst, Broughton Park, Manchester. Constitutional. Athenaeum, Manchester. S. of the Rev. Mark Finburgh. B. 1867; m. 1891, Clara, d. of B. Kostoris, Esq., of Manchester. Educ. at Hope Place Schools and Institute, Liverpool. J.P. for Salford. A Cotton Manufacturer; representative for Manchester on Board of Deputies of British Jews; President of North Salford Conservative Association. A Conservative. Unsuccessfully contested N. Salford in 1922 and 1923. Elected for N. Salford in October 1924 and sat until he retired in May 1929. Mayor of Salford 1929-30. President of the Council of Manchester and Salford Jews 1934-35. Died 26 April 1935.
          [1929]

FINDLAY, Sir John Edmund Ritchie, Bart. Aberlour House, Aberlour, Banffshire. Carlton, and Bath. S. of Sir John Findlay, Bart., K.B.E. B. 2 June 1902; m. 1st, 9 February 1927, Margaret Jean, d. of Norval Bantock Graham, Esq., of Wolverhampton (whom he divorced in 1943); secondly, 1947, Mrs. Laura Elsom, d. of Percival Hawley, Esq. Educ. at Harrow, and Balliol Coll., Oxford. Director of *The Scotsman* 1930-53. A Unionist. Elected for Banff in November 1935 and sat until he retired in June 1945. Succeeded as Bart. 1930. Died 6 September 1962.   [1945]

FINNEY, Samuel. Miners' Hall, Burslem, Stoke-on-Trent. S. of Francis John and Martha Finney. B. at Talk-o'-th'-Hill, N. Staffordshire 1857; m. 1884, the only d. of James and Harriet Bagnell, of Ellesmere, Shropshire. Educ. at the local Primitive Methodist day school. A Miner. Commenced work at Talk-o'-th'-Hill at the age of 10. Appointed Miners' Checkweighman February 1881; President of the N. Staffs. Miners' Federation 1888 to 1912; Secretary and Agent to the same Federation from 1912. Elected a member of Burslem Town Council 1903; a member of the County Borough Council of Stoke-on-Trent from its formation. Alderman and J.P. A Labour Member. Unsuccessfully contested Hanley in July 1912. Elected for N.W. Staffordshire in January 1916 and for the Burslem division of Stoke-on-Trent in December 1918. Sat until he retired in October 1922. Died 14 April 1935.   [1922]

FINNEY, Victor Harold. 1 Dinsdale Road, Roker, Sunderland. S. of John T. Finney, Esq., of Sunderland. B. 1897; m. 1928, Aileen Rose, d. of J. Whiteley-Gallagher, Esq., of Co. Cork. A Sunderland man who was studying at Armstrong Coll. when the war broke out. Joined the army as a gunner; served four years at the front; returned and resumed his studies, passing with honours in history and economics. A Liberal. Unsuccessfully contested the Hexham division of Northumberland in 1922. Elected for the Hexham division of Northumberland in December 1923 and sat until he was defeated in October 1924. Executive with Rank Organisation 1943-66. Died 10 April 1970.
          [1924 2nd ed.]

FISHER, Rt. Hon. Herbert Albert Laurens. 28 Ashley Gardens, London. Rock Cottage, Thursley, Godalming.

Athenaeum. S. of Herbert William Fisher, Esq. B. 21 March 1865; m. 6 July 1899, Lettice, d. of Sir Courtenay Ilbert, G.C.B. Educ. at Winchester, New Coll., Oxford, Paris, and Göttingen. Vice-Chancellor of Sheffield University 1912-16, and Fellow and Tutor of New Coll., Oxford 1888-1912; Fellow of the British Academy in 1907, President 1928-32; Trustee of the British Museum. Delivered the South African Lectures in 1908; the Lowell Lectures, Boston in 1909, and was Chichele Lecturer in Foreign History, Oxford University in 1911-12; Honorary LL.D. Edinburgh 1913, Honorary Litt.D.Sheffield University 1918; Honorary LL.D. Cambridge 1920; a member of the Royal Commission on the Public Services in India 1912-15, and of the Government Committee on German Outrages in 1915. F.R.S. 1920. Wrote *The Mediaeval Empire*, 1898, *A Political History of England*, 1906, *Bonapartism*, 1908, *The Republican Tradition in Europe*, 1911, *Political Unions*, 1911, *Napoleon Bonaparte*, 1913, and *Studies in History and Politics*, 1920. President of the Board of Education December 1916 to October 1922. PC. 1916. A Liberal. Elected for the Hallam division of Sheffield as a member of Mr. Lloyd George's War Ministry in December 1916. and for the Combined English Universities in December 1918. Sat until he resigned in 1926. Warden of New Coll., Oxford 1925-40. Gov. of B.B.C. 1935-39. O.M. 1937. Died 18 April 1940. [1926]

FISON, Frank Guy Clavering. Crepping Hall, Suffolk. Junior Carlton. S. of James O. Fison, Esq., of Stutton Hall, Suffolk. B. 11 December 1892; m. 22 February 1922, Evelyn, d. of L. Bland, Esq., of Copdock, Suffolk. Educ. at Charterhouse, and Christ Church, Oxford. Chairman of Fison, Packard and Prentice Limited, and of Chemical Union Limited. Served with Suffolk Regiment 1914-18 in France, etc. A Conservative. Elected for the Woodbridge division of Suffolk in May 1929 and sat until he retired in October 1931. Unsuccessfully contested Ipswich in July 1945. Knighted 1957. J.P. for E. Suffolk. Dept.-Lieut. for Suffolk, High Sheriff 1942.★ [1931 2nd ed.]

FITZGERALD, Thomas Desmond. B. 1889. A native of Kerry. Sent to an English prison after the rebellion; amnestied, but in 1918 was interned in Gloucester Gaol. A Sinn Fein Member. Elected for the the Pembroke division of Dublin Co. in December 1918 but did not take his seat. Minister for Publicity 1921-22, Minister for External Affairs 1922-27, Minister for Defence 1927-32. Member of Dail for Pembroke division of Dublin Co. to 1921, for Dublin Co. 1921-32, for Carlow and Kilkenny 1932-37, as a Pro-Treaty Member, later as a Member of Cumann na nGaedheal and Fine Gael. Member of the Senate 1938-43. A Poet and Dramatist. Died 9 April 1947. [1922]

FITZROY, Capt. Rt. Hon. Edward Algernon. Speaker's House, Palace of Westminster, London. Kenricks, Hambleden, Henley-on-Thames. Guards', and Brooks's. S. of 3rd Baron Southampton. B. 24 July 1869; m. 19 November 1891, Muriel, d. of Col. the Hon. A.C.H. Douglas-Pennant. Educ. at Eton, and Royal Military Coll., Sandhurst. D.C.L. Cambridge, LL.D. Oxford 1934. A Dept.-Lieut., J.P., and County Councillor for Northamptonshire. Capt. 1st Life Guards; Page of Honour to H.M. Queen Victoria. Served in France 1914-16. Dept.-Chairman of Ways and Means, House of Commons November 1922-November 1923 and November 1924-June 1928; PC. 1924. A Conservative. Sat for Northamptonshire S. from 1900 to 1906, when he retired, and from January 1910 to December 1918. Sat for the Daventry division of Northamptonshire from December 1918 until his death on 3 March 1943. Speaker of the House of Commons June 1928-March 1943. Supporter of the National Party 1917-18. His widow was created Viscountess Daventry in 1943. Died 3 March 1943. [1943]

FLANAGAN, William Henry. Ollerenshaw Hall, Whaley Bridge. Constitutional, London and Manchester. S. of William Flanagan, Esq., of Manchester. B. 8 April 1871; m. 12 July 1899, Lilian, d. of Edwin James Ashley, Esq. Educ. at St. Margaret's, Whalley Range, and Manchester School of

Technology. Chairman and Managing Director of Imperial Patent Wadding Company Limited; Proprietor of Bates Brothers. A Conservative. Unsuccessfully contested the Clayton division of Manchester in February 1922. Sat for the Clayton division of Manchester from November 1922 until defeated in December 1923. Unsuccessfully contested the Clayton division in May 1929. Re-elected in October 1931 and sat until he retired in October 1935. Member of Buxton Town Council until 1922. Died 21 June 1944. [1935]

FLANNERY, Sir James Fortescue, Bart. Wethersfield Manor, Essex. 5 Somers Place, Hyde Park, London. Carlton, Reform, National Sporting, and Savage. S. of Capt. John Flannery and Elizabeth, d. of James Kerr, Esq., of Stranraer. B. 16 December 1851 in Liverpool; m. 1882, Edith, d. of Osborn Jenkyn, Esq., of Ealing Common (she died 1936). Educ. at the Liverpool School of Science. A Consulting Engineer, Member Institute of Consulting Engineers; President Institute Marine Engineers 1897. President Association of Consulting Marine Engineers 1920. Was Inspecting Engineer under Sir E.J. Reed, K.C.B. Chief Constructor of the Navy; Admiralty Assessor to the Dockyard Committee for seettling Labour disputes in the engineering trades in 1895, and British Commissioner Brussels International Exhibition 1897 and Milan Exhibition 1906. Chairman of Flannery, Baggalay and Johnson Limited, Marine Engineers, London, Liverpool, and Rotterdam. A Director of Barclay's Bank. H.M. Lieut. for City of London, a J.P. for Counties of London, Essex, Kent, and Surrey. Knighted 1899. Created Bart. 1904. A Unionist. Sat for the Shipley division of Yorkshire from 1895-1906, when he unsuccessfully contested Cardiff. First elected for the Maldon division of Essex in January 1910 and sat until he retired in October 1922. Died 5 October 1943. [1922]

FLEMING, David Pinkerton, K.C., M.C. 40 Heriot Row, Edinburgh. S. of John Fleming, Esq., Writer, of Glasgow. B. 1877; m. 1913, Joan, d. of James Swan, Esq. Educ. at Glasgow High School, and at Universities of Edinburgh and Glasgow. A Barrister-at-Law Scotland 1902; served in France and Belgium 1915-18. M.C. A Conservative. Unsuccessfully contested Dumbartonshire in December 1923. Elected for Dumbartonshire in October 1924 and sat until January 1926 when he was appointed a Judge of the Court of Session, with the judicial title of Lord Fleming. Solicitor-Gen. for Scotland November 1922-April 1923 and November 1924-December 1925. K.C. 1921. Chairman of Committee on Public Schools 1942-43. Died 20 October 1944. [1925]

FLEMING, Edward Lascelles. Continued in House after 1945: full entry in Volume IV.

FLETCHER, Reginald Thomas Herbert. 2 Camp View, Wimbledon, London. Fivewents Way, Crowborough. S. of Nicholas Fletcher, Esq., of Rampholme, Windermere. B. 27 March 1885; m. 1909, Elspeth, d. of the Rev. H.J. Lomax, of Abbotswood, Buxted. Educ. at Shirley House, Blackheath. Parliamentary Private Secretary to The Rt. Hon. A.V. Alexander, First Lord of the Admiralty May 1940-December 1941. Unsuccessfully contested the Basingstoke division of Hampshire as a Liberal in November 1922. Sat as Liberal MP for Basingstoke from 1923 until 1924, when he was defeated. Unsuccessfully contested the Tavistock division of Devon as a Liberal in October 1928. Joined the Labour Party in 1929. Elected as a Labour Member for the Nuneaton division of Warwickshire in November 1935 and sat until 1942 when he was created Baron Winster. Minister of Civil Aviation August 1945-October 1946. PC. 1945; K.C.M.G. 1948. Gov. of Cyprus 1946-49. Died 7 June 1961. [1942]

FLINT, Abraham John. 4 Brick Court, Temple, London. Southover, Rosemary Hill Road, Little Aston, Sutton Coldfield, Warwickshire. S. of Abram Reginald Flint, Esq., Solicitor, of Derby. B. 1903; m. 1930, Eleanor Mary, d. of J.J. Jones, Esq., of Loughborough. Educ. at Oundle. A Barrister-at-Law, Inner Temple 1929. A National Labour Member. Elected for the Ilkeston division of Derbyshire in October 1931 by a majority of 2 votes and sat until he retired in October 1935. County Court Judge 1957-71. Dept.-Lieut. for Nottinghamshire. Died 23 January 1971. [1935]

FOOT, Dingle Mackintosh. Continued in House after 1945 : full entry in Volume IV.

FOOT, Isaac. Pencrebar, Callington, Cornwall. Reform, and National Liberal. S. of Isaac Foot, Esq., of Plymouth, Builder. B. 23 February 1880; m. 1st, 24 October 1904, Eva, d. of Angus Mackintosh, Esq., M.D., of Chesterfield (she died 1946); secondly, 1951, Catherine Elizabeth Taylor, d. of Frederick Dawe, Esq., of Liskeard. Educ. at Plymouth Public School, and Hoe Grammar School. Admitted Solicitor 1902. Member of Plymouth City Council; Dept. Mayor of Plymouth 1920-21; Lord Mayor 1945-46. Member of Indian Round Table Conference 1930-31, and of Burma Round Table Conference 1931. Secretary for Mines August 1931-September 1932. A Liberal. Unsuccessfully contested the Totnes division of Devon in January 1910, the Bodmin division of Cornwall in December 1910 and December 1918, and the Sutton division of Plymouth in November 1919. Elected for the Bodmin division of Cornwall in February and November 1922, and sat until defeated there in October 1924. Re-elected for Bodmin in May 1929; returned unopposed October 1931 and sat until he was defeated in November 1935. Unsuccessfully contested the St. Ives division of Cornwall in June 1937 and the Tavistock division of Devon in July 1945. PC. 1937. Vice-President of Methodist Conference 1937-38. President Liberal Party 1947. Fellow of Royal Society of Literature. President of Cromwell Association. J.P. for Cornwall, Dept.-Chairman of Cornwall Quarter Sessions 1945-53, Chairman 1953-55. Died 13 December 1960. [1935]

FORD, Sir Patrick Johnstone, Bart. 7 Moray Place, Edinburgh. Westerdunes, North Berwick. Carlton. New, Edinburgh S. of James Ford Esq., of Edinburgh. B. 5 March 1880; m. 1905, Jessie Hamilton, d. of Henry Field, Esq. Educ. at Edinburgh Academy, New Coll., Oxford, M.A.; and Edinburgh University, LL.B. Knight 1926. Advocate 1907. Lord Commissioner of the Treasury May-December 1923. Created Bart. 1929. A Conservative. As a Liberal Unionist unsuccessfully contested E. Edinburgh in 1909 and January 1910, and Inverness Burghs in December 1910. Sat for N. Edinburgh from April 1920 until December 1923 when he was defeated. Re-elected for N. Edinburgh in October 1924 and sat until he retired in October 1935. F.R.S.A. 1939. Served with Cameron Highlanders 1914-15. Died 28 September 1945. [1935]

FOREMAN, Sir Henry, O.B.E. 2 Prince of Wales Terrace, Kensington, London. 2 Eastern Terrace, King's Cliff, Brighton. Carlton, Constitutional, and Automobile. S. of George Foreman, Esq., of Kensington, London. B. 1852; m. 1st, 1873, d. of W. Howe, Esq., of Bayswater, London (she died 1893); secondly, 1901, Lucy d. of A.J. Randall, Esq. Mayor of Hammersmith 1913-20; Alderman 1919-24. Honorary Col. and Founder 20th London Cadet Corps. Commander and Honorary Commandant Hammersmith division of the Red Cross Society; presented to War Office, Ravenscourt Park Hospital for Officers; raised 140th Heavy Battery, R.G.A., and 40th Division Ammunition Column during European war. O.B.E. (Civil) 1918; Knighted 1921. A Conservative. Elected for Hammersmith N. in December 1918 and sat until he retired in November 1923. Died 11 April 1924. [1923]

FORESTIER-WALKER, Sir Charles Leolin, Bart., K.B.E. Park House, Rhiwderin, Monmouth. Carlton, and Wellington. S. of Sir George Forestier-Walker, 2nd Bart., of Castleton, J.P. and Hon. Fanny Morgan, d. of 1st Baron Tredegar. B. 6 May 1866; m. 26 June 1894, Alice, d. of John Blandy-Jenkins, Esq. Educ. at the Royal Academy, Gosport. Chairman of Cordes (Dos Works) Limited, Ironworks, Newport, and of Thomas Spittle Limited, Newport. Dept.-Lieut. and J.P. for Monmouth. Chairman of the St. Mellons District Council and the Graig Parish Council. Member of Forestry Commission 1919-29; a Commissioner (unpaid) on the Board of Control 1920-30. A Welsh Church Commissioner (unpaid) 1921. Chairman of Monmouthshire County Council 1923-34. K.(G.) St. J., K.B.E. 1925; created Bart. 1929. A Conservative. Unsuccessfully contested S. Monmouthshire in January and December 1910. Elected for the Monmouth division of Monmouthshire in December 1918 and sat until his death on 13 May 1934.   [1934]

FORGAN, Dr. Robert. House of Commons, London. S. of the Rev. Dr. Forgan, Convener of U.F. Church of Scotland Foreign Missions Commission. B. 1891; m. 1st, 1916, Winifred Mary, d. of Robert Cran, Esq., of Ballater; secondly, 1938, Winifred Jan, d. of Henry Rees, Esq., of Kenton. Educ. at Aberdeen Grammar School and University, and Cambridge University. Served in R.A.M.C. 1914-18; M.C. Specialist M.O. Lanarkshire 1921-29; member of Glasgow Town Council from 1926 to 1929. A Labour Member until February 1931 when he joined the New Party. Elected for W. Renfrew in May 1929 and sat until he was defeated in October 1931, standing as a candidate of Sir Oswald Mosley's New Party. Director of Organisation and later Dept.-Leader of British Union of Fascists from 1932; resigned in 1934. Died 8 January 1976.   [1931 2nd ed.]

FORREST, Walter. 4 Avenue Road, London. Thatched House. S. of Sir William Croft Forrest. B. 28 July 1869; m. 1st, 1899, Kate, d. of James Shillings, Esq. (she died 1913); secondly, 23 September 1915, Mary, d. of J.W. Crabbe, Esq., of Cambridge, widow of J.W. McDuff. Member of the County Council for the W. Riding of Yorkshire 1905-19 and of Pudsey Town Council 1900-19. A Liberal. Sat for Pontefract from September 1919 until he was defeated in November 1922. Unsuccessfully contested Batley and Morley in December 1923. First elected for Batley and Morley in October 1924 and sat until he was defeated in May 1929. Mayor of Pudsey 1909-12. Joined the Conservative Party in 1931, and subsequent to the formation of the Liberal National Party, became Treasurer

of the London Liberal National Party and a member of the Executive of the Liberal National Council. Knighted 1935. Died 18 July 1939.   [1929]

FORSTER, Rt. Hon. Henry William. Exbury, Southampton. 41 Hans Place, London. Carlton, Wellington, and R.Y.S. S. of Maj. John Forster, of 6th Dragoon Guards, and Emily, d. of John Ashton Case, Esq., of Thingwell Hall, and Ince Hall, Lancashire. B. 1866 at Southend Hall, Kent; m. 1890, the Hon. Rachel Cecily, d. of 1st Lord Montagu of Beaulieu. Educ. at Eton, and New Coll., Oxford. Was a Junior Lord of the Treasury 1902-05, and one of the Conservative Whips 1902-11. Financial Secretary to the War Office from May 1915 to December 1919. PC. 1917. A Unionist. Represented the Sevenoaks division of Kent from 1892 to 1918. Elected for the Bromley division of Kent in December 1918 and sat until he was created Baron Forster in December 1919. Gov.-Gen. of Australia 1920-25. G.C.M.G. 1920. Died 15 January 1936.   [1919]

FOSTER, Sir Harry Seymour. 34 St. James' Court, Buckingham Gate, London. Homelands, Henley-on-Thames. Carlton, City Carlton, Eccentric, and Royal Automobile. S. of S.G. Foster, Esq. B. 29 April 1855; m. 6 June 1878, Amy, d. of John Sparks, Esq. Educ. at Heath Mount, Hampstead, at Dane Hill, Margate, and City of London Schools. A Chartered Accountant 1876-85. Consul-Gen. for Persia from 1894-1923. Member of London School Board from 1885-91; Member London County Council from 1889-92, Sheriff of London 1891-92, a Lieut. of the City of London; Dept.-Lieut., J.P. for Suffolk. F.G.S., F.R.G.S., F.S.S. Knight Bach. 1918. A Conservative. Sat for the Lowestoft division of Suffolk 1892-1900 when he retired and again from January 1910, until defeated in December 1910. Elected for Portsmouth central in October 1924 and sat until he retired in May 1929. Died 20 June 1938.   [1929]

FOSTER, William. Continued in House after 1945: full entry in Volume IV.

FOX, Sir Gifford Wheaton Grey, Bart. Continued in House after 1945: full entry in Volume IV.

FOX, Henry Wilson. See WILSON-FOX, Henry.

FOXCROFT, Capt. Charles Talbot. Hinton Charterhouse, Bath. Carlton, and Windham. S. of Edward Talbot Day Foxcroft, Esq., Dept.-Lieut., and J.P. of Hinton Charterhouse. B. 1868. Unmarried. Educ. at Eton, Magdalen Coll., Oxford, and Cirencester Agricultural Coll. Capt 2/4th Somersets 1914-16. Assistant Adjutant 2nd Volunteer Battalion P.A.S.L.I. 1917-19. Dept.-Lieut. and J.P. for Somerset, Commander of the Order of the Crown of Italy. Parliamentary Private Secretary to Lord Wolmer when Assistant Postmaster-Gen. December 1924. A Conservative. Unsuccessfully contested the Frome division of Somerset in 1906 and again in January and December 1910. Sat for Bath from October 1918 to December 1923, when he was defeated. Re-elected for Bath in October 1924 and sat until his death on 11 February 1929. [1929]

FRANCE, Gerald Ashburner. Newbiggen Hall, Newcastle-on-Tyne. Reform, and National Liberal. S. of James Ashburner France, Esq., and Martha, d. of Richard Appleton, Esq., of Yarm, Yorkshire. B. 4 August 1870 at Stockton-on-Tees; m. 1898, Hilda, d. of Thomas H. Bainbridge, Esq., of Eshott, Northumberland. Educ. privately. A partner in the firm of J.A. France and Son, Importers and Agents, London and Newcastle-on-Tyne. J.P. and County Alderman and Chairman of Insurance Committee for Northumberland; Chairman of Newcastle Gladstone Club from 1903. Lieut. R.N.V.R. February 1915. Parliamentary Private Secretary to Mr. Runciman when President of the Board of Trade 1916. A Liberal. Sat for the Morley division of Yorkshire from January 1910 to December 1918. Elected for Batley and Morley in December 1918 and sat until he retired in October 1922. Died 11 February 1935. [1922]

FRANKEL, Daniel. Paris Gardens, Kingsbury Road, London. S. of Harris Frankel, Esq., of Mile End. B. 18 August 1900; m. 1921, Lily, d. of Joseph Marks, Esq., of Stepney. Member of Stepney Borough Council, Mayor 1929. Member of London County Council 1931-46. A Labour Member. Elected for the Mile End division of Stepney in November 1935 and sat until he was defeated by the Communist candidate in July 1945.* [1945]

FRANKLIN, Leonard Benjamin, O.B.E. 32 Hyde Park Gardens, London. The Grange, Gouldhurst, Kent. Reform, National Liberal, Eighty, and Cobden. 3rd s. of Ellis A. Franklin, Esq., Banker, of 35 Porchester Terrace, and Adelaide, sister of the 1st Baron Swaythling. B. in London 15 November 1862; m. 11 January 1888, Laura Agnes, d. of William Ladenburg, Esq., of London, one s. and three daughters. Educ. at King's Coll., London, and Athenée Royale, Brussels. A Barrister-at-Law, Inner Temple and Lincoln's Inn; also a Banker. A Liberal. Unsuccessfully contested N. Paddington in December 1910 and 1918, and S.E. St. Pancras in 1922. Elected for Central Hackney in December 1923 and sat until he was defeated in October 1924. Unsuccessfully contested Central Hackney in May 1929 and October 1931. O.B.E. 1919. Senior Partner in A. Keyser and Company, Bankers, 1929-44. Knighted 1932. Died 11 December 1944. [1924 2nd ed.]

FRASER, Maj. Sir Keith Alexander, Bart. 59 Sloane Street, London. Carlton Curlieu, Leicestershire. Inverinate, N.B. S. of Lieut.-Gen. J. Keith Fraser, C.M.G. B. 24 December 1867; m. 1910, Lady Coventry, 2nd d. of Lord and Lady Coventry. Educ. at Eton. Entered the army, 7th Hussars 1888; retired 1903. A Conservative. Unsuccessfully contested Caithness in 1906 and the Bosworth division of Leicestershire in January 1910. Elected for the Harborough division of Leicestershire in December 1918 and sat until he was defeated in December 1923. Succeeded his uncle as Bart. 1898. Maj. 3rd County of London Yeomanry 1914. Dept.-Lieut. for Leicestershire and J.P. for Ross and Cromarty. Died 21 September 1935. [1923]

FRASER, Thomas. Continued in House after 1945: full entry in Volume IV.

FRASER, Sir William Jocelyn Ian. Continued in House after 1945: full entry in Volume IV.

FREEMAN, Peter. Continued in House after 1945: full entry in Volume IV.

FREMANTLE, Sir Francis Edward, O.B.E., T.D. Bedwell Park, Hatfield, Hertfordshire. Carlton. S. of the Very Rev. the Hon. William Henry Fremantle, Dean of Ripon, and Isabella, d. of Sir Culling Eardley, 3rd Bart. B. 29 May 1872; m. 22 July 1905, Dorothy, d. of H.J. Chinnery, Esq., J.P., of Fringford Manor, Bicester. Educ. at Eton, (K.S.), and Balliol Coll., Oxford. M.A., M.D., M.Ch., F.R.C.S., F.R.C.P., D.P.H. County Medical Officer of Health for Hertfordshire 1902-16 (later Consulting Medical Officer of Health); President of Incorporated Society of Medical Officers of Health 1920-21; President Epidemiological Section, Royal Society of Medicine 1928-30. Served in South African War with R.A.M.C.; Plague Medical Officer Punjab 1903-04; War Correspondent in Manchuria during Russo-Japanese War; served in Gallipoli, Egypt, and Mesopotamia 1914-18 as Lieut.-Col. R.A.-M.C. (T.A.). Dept.-Lieut., and J.P. for Hertfordshire; member London County Council 1919-22; Chairman of Health and Housing Committees of Parliament and Medical Committee and of Publications and Debates Reports Select Committees. Member of Industrial Health Research Board 1929-34, of Church Assembly from 1930, of Ecclesiastical Committee from 1924; member of Central Housing of Nursing and of Rent Restriction Acts Committees 1922, 1931 and 1937, of C. Medical War Committee and of B.M.A. Planing Commission; Gov. of Guy's and of St. Bartholomews Hospitals. Trustee of Sutton Dwellings. Chairman of Herts Pharmaceuticals Limited. Director of Rickmansworth and Uxbridge Water Company and of St.

Albans Water Company. Created Knight Bach. 1932. A Conservative. Sat for the St. Albans division of Hertfordshire from December 1919 until his death on 26 August 1943. [1943]

FULLER, Capt. Albert George Hubert. 41 Rutland Gate, London. Junior Army & Navy, and Royal United Service Institution. B. 10 December 1894; m. 1st 10 December 1927, Lilian Margaret Couper, d. of D.C. Thomson, Esq., of Broughty Ferry (she died 1955); secondly, 1960, Mary Morel. Capt. Indian Army, retired 1931. A Conservative. Elected for the Ardwick division of Manchester in October 1931 and sat until he was defeated in November 1935. Commanded 7th Queen's Own Royal West Kent Regiment 1936-39. J.P. for Kent. 1950. Member of Sevenoaks Rural District Council 1947-56. Died 27 July 1969. [1935]

FURNESS, George James. House of Commons, London. S. of George Furness, Esq., of Willesden, Contractor in England, Russia and Italy. B. 1868; m. 1898, Mabel Mary, d. of Inspector-Gen. James Eames, R.N. Educ. at King William's Coll., Isle of Man. Graduated as a Civil Engineer at the Crystal Palace School; associated with his father in foreign railway constructional work. Member of Middlesex County Council for 18 years. A Conservative. Elected for Willesden W. in November 1922 and sat until he was defeated in December 1923. High Sheriff of Middlesex 1936. Died 11 June 1936. [1923]

FURNESS, Stephen Noel. 11 North Street, London. Otterington Hall, Northallerton. Brooks's. S. of Sir Stephen Furness, MP. B. 18 December 1902. Educ. at Charterhouse, and Oriel Coll., Oxford, M.A. Barrister-at-Law, Middle Temple 1927. Parliamentary Private Secretary to Rt. Hon. Sir John Simon when Home Secretary November 1936-May 1937; Assistant Whip May 1937; Lord Commissioner of the Treasury May 1938-May 1940. 2nd Lieut. 1st Battalion London Irish Rifles. Maj. 1941. Unsuccessfully contested Hartlepools as a Liberal in May 1929. Elected for

Sunderland in November 1935 as a Liberal National and sat until he was defeated in July 1945. Chairman of Furness Shipbuilding Company Limited. Died 14 April 1974.
[1945]

FYFE, Rt. Hon. Sir David Patrick Maxwell. See MAXWELL FYFE, Rt. Hon. Sir David Patrick. Continued in House after 1945: full entry in Volume IV.

GADIE, Lieut.-Col. Anthony. Oakwood, Toller Lane, Bradford. Thorpe's Chambers, Hu.tlegate, Bradford. Constitutional. S. of Thomas M. Gadie, Esq. B. 7 September 1868; m. 19 April 1894, Eliza, d. of J.B. Gadie, Esq. Educ. at St. Peters School, Bradford. Was a Builder and Contractor; served with R.F.A. 1914-18; an Auctioneer and Valuer; Lord Mayor of Bradford 1920-21; member of City Council from 1900 Alderman from 1907; J.P., T.D. 1914; Chairman of Bradford Conservative Association 1924-47. A Conservative. Elected for the central division of Bradford in October 1924 and sat until he was defeated in May 1929. Knighted 1935. Freeman of City of Bradford 1944. Died 24 August 1948.
[1929]

GALBRAITH, James Francis Wallace, K.C. 3 New Square, London. Monkswood, Kenley. Constitutional, United University, United, and 1900. 2nd s. of Hugh James and K.A. Galbraith. B. 1872. Unmarried. Educ. at Blackheath Proprietary School, and Oriel Coll., Oxford. A Barrister-at-Law, Lincoln's Inn 1895; K.C. 1919; bencher 1922; Honorary Treasurer of General Council of the Bar. A Conservative. Unsuccessfully contested Halifax in January and December 1910. Elected for E. Surrey in November 1922 and sat until he retired in October 1935. County Court Judge 1935-45. Died 29 January 1945.
[1935]

GALBRAITH, Samuel, O.B.E. 8 The Avenue, Durham. S. of Samuel Galbraith, Esq. B. 4 July 1853 at Ballydrain, Comber, Ireland; m. d. of Henry Petty, Esq. A self-educated man. Was Miners' Agent 1900-15; member of Durham County Council from 1888, and Alderman from 1900; J.P.

for Co. Durham. O.B.E. 1917. A Liberal and Labour Member but was opposed by an official Labour candidate in 1918. Sat for mid Durham from April 1915 to November 1918. Elected for the Spennymoor division of Durham in December 1918 and sat until he retired in October 1922. Died 10 April 1936.
[1922]

GALBRAITH, Thomas Dunlop. Continued in House after 1945: full entry in Volume IV.

GALLACHER, William. Continued in House after 1945: full entry in Volume IV.

GALLIGAN, Peter Paul. Drumnalaragh, Bellanagh, Co. Cavan. A Draper's Assistant. A Sinn Fein Member. Returned unopposed for W. Cavan in December 1918 but did not take his seat. Member of Dail for W. Cavan to 1921, for Cavan 1921-22. In January 1922 voted in favour of the Treaty but also in favour of De Valera's re-election as President of Dail.
[1922]

GAMMANS, Leonard David. Continued in House after 1945: full entry in Volume IV.

GANDAR DOWER, Alan Vincent. See DOWER, Alan Vincent Gandar. Continued in House after 1945: full entry in Volume IV.

GANGE, Edwin Stanley. Stoke Bishop, Bristol. Mendip Lodge, Hutton, Somerset. National. S. of the Rev. E.G. Gange, of Broadmead, Bristol. B. at Bristol 1871; m. 1895, Alice, d. of Henry Denning, Esq. Educ. at private schools in Bristol. A Merchant. J.P. for the City and County of Bristol 1916. Member of Bristol Town Council. A Liberal Coalitionist. Elected for N. Bristol in December 1918 and sat until he retired in October 1922. Sheriff of Bristol 1931-32. Died 29 February 1944.
[1922]

GANZONI, Capt. Sir Francis John Childs, Bart. 7 Prince's Gardens, London. Stoke Park, Ipswich. Carlton, St. Stephen's, and Boodle's. S. of Julius Charles Ganzoni, Esq. B. 19 January 1882; m. 31 May 1930, Gwendolen, d. of Arthur Turner, Esq., of Ipswich. Educ. at Tonbridge School, and

Christ Church, Oxford, B.A. 1904, M.A. 1908. A Barrister-at-Law, Inner Temple 1906. F.R.G.S. Capt. 4th Battalion Suffolk Regiment. Served with B.E.F. 1914-18. Knighted 1921. Created Bart. 1929. Parliamentary Private Secretary to the Rt. Hon. Sir William Mitchell-Thomson, Postmaster-Gen. 1924-29. A Temporary Chairman of Committee of the Whole House 1933-35; Chairman of Private Bill Committee from 1923; Chairman of Kitchen Committee from 1931. A Conservative. Sat for Ipswich from May 1914 until defeated in December 1923. Re-elected for Ipswich in October 1924 and sat until he was created Baron Belstead in January 1938. Chairman of Private Bills Committee of House of Lords 1940-58. J.P. and Dept.-Lieut. for Suffolk. Army Welfare Officer for Ipswich 1939-42, for Suffolk 1942-49, with rank of Lieut.-Col. Died 15 August 1958.   [1938]

GARDINER, James. Dargill, Crieff. Reform, National Liberal. Edinburgh Liberal, and Glasgow Liberal. S. of John C. Gardiner, Esq., and Harriett Ann Boune Gardiner. B. near Crieff 1860; m. 1st, 1887, Elizabeth Maude, d. of John D. Christie, Esq. (she died 1921); secondly, 1 September 1922, Elizabeth Christie, d. of Daniel Christie, of Bengal and Drummond Carnoch, Comrie. Educ. at Morison's Academy, Crieff, and privately. A J.P. for Perthshire; well known in Church and social work; Honorary President National Farmers Union of Scotland; a recognised authority on Agriculture, including Research and Plant Raising; member of the Council of National Institute of Agricultural Botany; Fellow of the Council of Agriculture for Scotland; served on National Potato Advisory Committee and Scottish Potato Allocation Authority; well known as a potato raiser; successful shorthorn breeder. A Liberal. Elected for Kinross and Western division of Perth and Kinross in December 1918; returned unopposed again in November 1922 and sat until he retired in November 1923. Died 31 December 1924.   [1923]

GARDNER, Benjamin Walter. Wood cutters Lodge, Over Worton, Middle Barton, Oxford. S. of W.B. Gardner, Esq., of Halstead, Essex. B. 1865; m. 1890. Educ. at Elementary School. A founder of the West Ham I.L.P. A Labour Member. Unsuccessfully contested the Upton division of West Ham in November 1918 and again in November 1922. Elected for the Upton division of West Ham in December 1923, defeated October 1924; re-elected in May 1929, defeated October 1931. Again re-elected for the Upton division of West Ham in May 1934 and sat until he retired in June 1945. Died 13 January 1948.   [1945]

GARDNER, Ernest. Spencers, Maidenhead. 3rd s. of J.G. Gardner, Esq., of Havering, Essex, and Elizabeth, d. of P. Silvester, Esq., of Shelhaven, Essex. B. 1846; m. 1st, 1878, Mary, only d. of William Peto, Esq., of Cookham (she died 1903); secondly, 1910, Amy, d. of Lieut.-Gen. J.W. Laurie, C.B. Educ. at Orsett House, Essex. A J.P., and Alderman of the County Council for Berkshire, a member of the Draper's Company, and Master of the Company 1901-02. Mayor of Maidenhead 1892-93. A Conservative. Returned unopposed for the Wokingham division of Berkshire in July 1901 and sat until December 1918. Elected for the Windsor division of Berkshire in December 1918 and sat until he retired in November 1922. Knighted 1923. Died 7 August 1925.   [1922]

GARDNER, James Patrick. 14 Leysfield Road, Shepherd's Bush, London. Hammersmith Labour. S. of A. Gardner, Esq., of Belfast. B. 5 March 1883; m. October 1902, Mary Catherine, d. of J. Kelly, Esq. Educ. at Christian Brothers School, Belfast. An Architectural Sculptor. J.P. for London; member of Hammersmith Borough Council 1919-22 and 1928. A Labour Member. Unsuccessfully contested Hammersmith N. in 1922. Elected for Hammersmith N. in December 1923, defeated October 1924. Re-elected for Hammersmith N. in May 1926 and sat until he was defeated in October 1931. Died 25 July 1937.   [1931 2nd ed.]

GARDNER, Rt. Hon. Sir James Tynte Agg. See AGG-GARDNER, Rt. Hon. Sir James Tynte.

GARLAND, Charles Samuel. House of Commons, London. S. of Charles Garland, Esq., of Stourbridge. B. 23 June 1887; m. 1912, Constance Marion Avis, d. of Alfred Rye, Esq. Educ. at Camberwell Grammar School and Royal Coll. of Science. Well known for political work in Dulwich, Streatham and Central Wandsworth. A Chemical Engineer; Vice-Chairman of the Society of Chemical Industry; Chairman of the Joint Industrial Council of the Gas Mantle Industry. A Conservative. Elected for S. Islington in November 1922 and sat until he was defeated in December 1923. Fellow of Royal Institute of Chemistry. Member of Institution of Chemical Engineers, President 1941-42. President of British Association of Chemists 1925-26. Member of Clean Air Council 1957-60. President of National Union of Manufacturers 1956-58, Honorary Treasurer 1925-51. Died 6 December 1960. [1923]

GARRO-JONES, George Morgan. Dale, Crowborough, Sussex. Royal Air Force. S. of the Rev. David Garro-Jones, Congregational Minister. B. 1894; m. 1940, Elizabeth, d. of C.E. Churchill, Esq. Educ. at Caterham School. Barrister-at-Law, Gray's Inn 1923. Editor of *The Daily Dispatch*. Private Secretary to Lord Greenwood at Home Office, Department of Overseas Trade, and when Chief Secretary for Ireland 1920. Served with Denbighshire Yeomanry 1913-14, and in France with Infantry and R.F.C. 1915-17. Honorary Capt. R.A.F.; Advisory Office to U.S. Air Service 1917-18; member of Empire Parliamentary Delegation to West Africa 1928. Parliamentary Secretary Ministry of Production August 1942-May 1945. Dept. Chairman of Radio Board. Unsuccessfully contested N.E. Bethnal Green as a National Liberal in 1922 and S. Hackney as a Liberal in 1923. Sat as Liberal MP for South Hackney from 1924-29, when he retired. Elected as a Labour Member for N. Aberdeen in November 1935 and sat until he retired in June 1945. Joined Labour Party 1929, but resigned in 1952 and rejoined the Liberal Party in 1958. Chairman of Television Advisory Committee 1946-49. Created Baron Trefgarne 1947. Chairman of Colonial Development Corporation 1947-50. Adopted surname of Trefgarne in lieu of Garro-Jones in 1954. Died 27 September 1960. [1945]

GATES, Ernest Everard. Continued in House after 1945: full entry in Volume IV.

GATES, Percy George. 66 Philbeach Gardens, London. Carlton, and Conservative. S. of Philip Gates, Esq., K.C., Judge of County Courts, and Anna Maria Harblin. B. in London 9 June 1863; m. 6 December 1888, Mabel, d. of the Rev. G.D.W. Dickson, Vicar of St. James the Less, Westminster. Educ. at Wellington Coll., Berkshire. A Solicitor and Parliamentary Agent from 1886 to 1908. Director of Hoare and Company Limited. Chairman of Brewers Society 1920-21. Mayor of Kensington 1904-05; member of London County Council 1911-19. A Conservative. Elected for N. Kensington in November 1922 and sat until he was defeated in May 1929. Director of Charrington and Company. Died 31 March 1940. [1929]

GAULT, Lieut.-Col. Andrew Hamilton, D.S.O. Hatch Court, Taunton. St. Hilaire, P.Q., Canada. Carlton, and Bath. S. of A.F. Gault, Esq., of Montreal. B. 18 August 1882; m. 1st, 1904, Marguerite, d. of Hon. George Stephens (divorced); secondly, 1922, Dorothy Blanche, d. of C.J. Shuckburgh, Esq., of Hatch Court, Taunton. Educ. at Bishop's Coll. School, Lennoxville, and at McGill University. Served with Canadian Mounted Rifles in South African War, and with Princess Patricia's Canadian L.I. in France 1914-18, which regiment he raised and equipped. Consul-Gen. for Sweden in Canada 1909-11; President of Gault Brothers and Company, and Gault Realities Limited, and Director of other Canadian Companies; member of Council of Montreal Board of Trade 1911-13. Order of the Crown of Belgium and of St. Anne of Russia with crossed swords (3rd class). Freeman of Borough of Taunton 1932. A Conservative. Unsuccessfully contested the Taunton division of Somerset in December 1923. Elected for Taunton in October 1924 and sat until he retired in October 1935. D.S.O. 1915. Recalled to active list 1940, Brigadier 1942.

Died in Montreal 28 November 1958.

[1935]

GAUNT, Vice-Admiral Sir Guy Reginald Archer, K.C.M.G., C.B. Albany, London. Gaunt's Wood, Nr Leek, Staffordshire. United Service, Garrick, Royal Automobile, and Royal Thames Yacht. S. of Judge Gaunt, of Leek, Staffordshire, and Melbourne. B. 25 May 1870; m. 1st, 23 November 1904, Margaret, d. of Sir Thomas Wardle (divorced 1928); secondly, 1932, Sybil, d. of A. Grant-White, Esq., and widow of W. Joseph, Esq. Educ. at Melbourne Grammar School. Joined the R.N. 1895; retired 1918, Vice-Admiral 1924, Admiral 1928. C.M.G. 1916; K.C.M.G. 1918; C.B. 1918. Naval attaché in Washington 1914-18. A Conservative. Unsuccessfully contested the Leek division of Staffordshire as a Coalition Liberal in December 1918. Sat for the Buckrose division of Yorkshire from November 1922 until he resigned in 1926. Died 18 May 1953. [1926]

GAVAN DUFFY, George. See DUFFY, George Gavan.

GAVAN-DUFFY, Thomas. See DUFFY, Thomas Gavan.

GEDDES, Rt. Hon. Sir Auckland Campbell, K.C.B. Athenaeum, and Union. S. of Auckland Campbell Geddes, Esq., of Edinburgh, Civil Engineer, and Christian Helen Anderson, d. of the Rev. Alexander Anderson, D.D., of Chanonry, Old Aberdeen. B. in London 21 June 1879; m. September 1906, Isabella Gamble, 3rd d. of W.A. Ross, Esq., of Staten Island, New York. Educ. at George Watson's Coll., Edinburgh, and Edinburgh University; M.B., Ch.B. (Hons.) 1903, M.D. (Gold Medal) 1908. Professor of Anatomy, McGill University, Montreal; Professor of Anatomy, Royal Coll. of Surgeons, Dublin, and Assistant Professor of Anatomy, University of Edinburgh. Served in South African War, Lieut. H.L.I.; served in the European War 1914-16. Brevet Lieut.-Col. (Honorary Brigadier-Gen.) T.F.; Director of Recruiting, War Office 1916 and 1917; Minister of National Service August 1917 to January 1919; also President of Local Government Board October 1918-January 1919; Minister of National Service and Reconstruction January 1919 to May 1919; President of the Board of Trade May 1919-March 1920. PC. 1917. A Unionist. Elected for the Basingstoke division of Hampshire in October 1917 and again in December 1918. Sat until March 1920 when he was appointed Ambassador to the United States. Ambassador to the United States from 1920-23. C.B. 1917; K.C.B. 1917; G.C.M.G. 1922. Chairman of Rio Tinto Company and of Rhokana Corporation. Created Baron Geddes 1942. Regional Civil Defence Commissioner 1939-42. Died 8 January 1954. [1920]

GEDDES, Maj.-Gen. Rt. Hon. Sir Eric Campbell, G.C.B., G.B.E. 12a Manchester Square, London. Marlborough, and Windham. S. of Auckland Geddes, Esq., of Edinburgh, and Christina Helen, d. of the Rev. Alexander Anderson, D.D. of Chanonry, Old Aberdeen. B. 26 September 1875; m. 2 November 1900, Gwendolen, d. of the Rev. Arthur Stokes; 3 sons. Educ. at Merchiston and Oxford Military Coll. Dept. Gen. Manager of N. Eastern Railway 1911-19. Dept. Director of Munitions 1915-16; Director Gen. of Military Railways, War Office, and Director Gen. of Transportation on the staff of the Field-Marshal C.-in-C. in France, and Inspector-Gen. of Transportation for all theatres of war; Honorary Maj.-Gen. 1916-17; Controller on the Board of Admiralty, with temporary rank of Honorary Vice-Admiral May-July 1917; First Lord of the Admiralty July 1917-January 1918. Imperial War Cabinet. Appointed Representative War Cabinet in charge of all questions of demobilization and rehabilitation of Industry December 1918; Minister with Portfolio January-May 1919; first Minister of Transport May 1919 to October 1921. Chairman of the Committee appointed to advise the Chancellor of the Exchequer on National Expenditure 1921. Knighted 1916. PC. 1917; K.C.B. (Mil.) 1917; G.B.E. 1917; G.C.B. (Civ.) 1919; LL.D. (Honorary) University of Sheffield 1920; Legion of Honour; Order of Leopold; Croix de Guerre Belge. A Conservative. Elected for Cambridge Borough in

1917 and sat until he resigned in February 1922. President of the Federation of British Industries 1923-24. Chairman of Dunlop Rubber Company. Chairman of Imperial Airways Limited. Died 22 June 1937.

[1922]

GEE, Capt. Robert, V.C., M.C. 110 Sutton Court, London. S. of Robert Gee, Esq., of Leicester. B. 7 May 1876; m. 1902, Elizabeth, d. of Peter Dixon, Esq. Educ. at Countesthorpe Cottage Homes. Joined Royal Fusiliers 1892, served in the ranks for 22 years, received a Commission August 1915; served on Staff of 29th division in France. Law Student, Gray's Inn 1918. A Conservative. Unsuccessfully contested the Consett division of Durham in 1918 as the candidate of the pro-Coalition National Democratic Party. Sat for E. Woolwich from 1921-22. Unsuccessfully contested E. Woolwich in November 1922, E. Newcastle in January 1923, and the Bishop Auckland division of Durham in December 1923. Elected for the Bosworth division of Leicestershire in October 1924 and sat until he resigned in 1927, after emigrating to Australia. V.C. 1918. Commissioner of Declarations, Western Australia 1953. Died in Perth, Western Australia 2 August 1960.

[1927]

GIBBINS, Joseph. Continued in House after 1945: full entry in Volume IV.

GIBBONS, Lieut.-Col. William Ernest, O.B.E. Beam House, Tettenhall, Wolverhampton. Constitutional. S. of W.P. Gibbons, Esq., J.P., of Wombourne, Staffordshire. B. 24 April 1898; m. 1st, 5 April 1922, Alma, d. of George Pfister, Esq., of Schaffhausen, Switzerland (she died 1955); secondly, 1964, Verity Anne Parson. Educ. at Bromsgrove School. Director of Gibbons (Dudley) Limited, Manufacturers, and of Gibbons Brothers Limited, Engineers. Served in France with S. Staffordshire Regiment 1917-18 and 1940; Commandant of Infantry School, Northern Ireland from 1942. A National Conservative. Elected for the Bilston division of Wolverhampton in September 1944 and sat until he was defeated in July 1945. O.B.E. 1944. Dept.-Lieut. and J.P. for

Staffordshire. Died 15 August 1976.

[1945]

GIBBS, Col. Rt. Hon. George Abraham. 22 Belgrave Square, London. Tyntesfield, Bristol. Carlton, and Arthur's. Eld. s. of Antony Gibbs, Esq., of Tyntesfield, and Janet Louisa, d. of John L. Merivale, Esq., Senior Registrar, Court of Chancery. B. 6 July 1873; m. 1st, 26 November 1901, Hon. Victoria Floria Florence de Burgh Long, C.B.E., d. of Walter, Visct. Long of Wraxall (she died 1920); secondly, 21 July 1927, Hon. Ursula (former Maid of Honour), d. of Hon. Sir Arthur Lawley, G.S.C.I., G.C.I.E., K.C.M.G. (later 6th Baron Wenlock). Educ. at Eton, and Christ Church, Oxford. Lieut.-Col. on the Territorial Reserve of Officers; Lieut.-Col. commanding North Somerset Yeomanry January 1909-January 1914; from November 1914 to 1917 commanded 2/1st North Somerset Yeomanry. T.D. Served in South Africa 1900. A J.P. and Dept.-Lieut. for Somerset. Conservative Whip in the House of Commons 1917-28; Treasurer of H.M's. Household from 1921-January 1924, and November 1924-January 1928. PC. 1923. A Conservative. Sat for Bristol W. from 1906 until January 1928 when he was created Baron Wraxall. President of Somerset Society 1912-22. Died 28 October 1931.

[1928]

GIBSON, Sir (Charles) Granville. Oakwood Hall, Roundhay, Leeds. Constitutional. S. of Simeon Gibson, Esq. B. 8 November 1880. Educ. at Central High School, and University of Leeds. A Leather Manufacturer and Tanner. Chairman of Leather Producers' Association 1921-24; President Light Leather Tanners' and Curriers' Federation 1923-24; Member of Court, Leeds University 1925-39; Chairman Department for Leather Industries, Leeds University 1925-39, and President of Leeds Chamber of Commerce January 1939-41. Member Leeds City Council for 12 years; Lord Mayor of Leeds 1924-25. President of Association of British Chambers of Commerce 1938-39. Chairman of Executive Council Federation of Chambers of Commerce of B.E. 1938-40; member of

British National Commission of International Chambers of Commerce, and of British Mission to South America 1940-41. Knight Bach. 1937. Unsuccessfully contested Leeds S. as a Liberal December 1923. Elected as a Conservative for the Pudsey and Otley division of the W. Riding of Yorkshire in May 1929 and sat until he retired in June 1945. Died 17 July 1948.   [1945]

GIBSON, Herbert Mellor. House of Commons, London. B. 22 February 1896. A Director of Manchester and Salford Equitable Co-operative Society. A Labour Member. Elected for the Mossley division of Lancashire in May 1929 and sat until he was defeated in October 1931; again defeated in November 1935. J.P. for Manchester. Director of Co-operative Wholesale Society Limited from 1936. Director of Colonial Development Corporation from 1948. Died 27 March 1954.   [1931 2nd ed.]

GIBSON, Robert, K.C. 2 Essex Court, Temple, London. 42 Heriot Row, Edinburgh. Dinnet, Balerno, Midlothian. S. of Robert Gibson, Esq., of Cadzow Lodge, Hamilton. B. 20 April 1886; m. 1913, Elizabeth, d. of William Atkinson, Esq., of Prestwick (she died 1959). Educ. at Hamilton Academy, at the University of Glasgow and in London. At Glasgow was Cunningham Gold Medallist in Mathematics, Donaldson Scholar in Chemistry, Metcalfe Bursar in Science, Stewart Bursar in Law, M.A. (Hons.), B.Sc., LL.B.; Secretary, then President of Glasgow University Students' Representative Council. Lecturer on Applied Science and Electrical Engineering. Joined R.G.A. 1915, retired as Capt. 1919. Called to the Scottish bar 1918, K.C. 1931. Senior Advocate Depute 1929-31. Member of Scottish Churchmen's Commission U.S.A. and Canada 1923; Chairman of Scottish Council of Labour Party 1932-34. A Labour Member. Unsuccessfully contested Roxburgh and Selkirk in May 1929, Edinburgh N. in October 1931, Scottish Universities in March 1934, and Dundee in November 1935. Elected for Greenock in November 1936 and sat until June 1941 when he was appointed Chairman of the Scottish Land Court, with the judicial title

of Lord Gibson; retired in March 1965. Fellow of Royal Society of Edinburgh. Died 9 April 1965.   [1941]

GILBERT, James Daniel. 21 Kennington Terrace, London. National Liberal. S. of James Gilbert, Esq., of Newington. B. in W. Newington in 1864; m. 1st, Lucy (she died 1921); secondly, 1926, Jessie, d. of W. Bromley, Esq. Educ. privately. Honorary Secretary of the W. Newington Liberal Association 1885-98. Member of the London County Council from 1898 to 1928. Chairman of the London County Council Committees - Corporate Property 1899-1900; Fire Brigade 1900-02; Rivers 1903-06; Gen. Purposes 1906-07. Was Chief Progressive Whip 1901-07. Proposed the resolution for the Circular Overbridge and Embankment trams; promoted Steamboats Bill and organized first services; suggested the site for the new county hall at Westminster Bridge. Member of Thames Conservancy from 1901 to 1938, Chairman 1937-38; Land Tax Commissioner 1907; member of the Port of London Authority from 1913 to 1939; Chairman of Stores Committee from 1919 to 1934, and of River Committee 1934-39; Dept.-Lieut. and J.P. for London. Member of County of London Territorial Association; a member of the Select Committees on Transport 1918 and London Traffic 1919. Chairman London Liberal Group 1919 and 1922; Chairman Standing Committees, House of Commons, 1923. Travelled in India, Burmah, Australia, New Zealand, Canada, United States, Egypt, Morocco, Russia, etc. Member of the Executive Committees National Liberal Federation 1906-18, and London Liberal Federation 1902-21. Wrote *Two and a Half years' Record of the Moderate Party* 1909, and *The Record of the Second Moderate Council* 1912. A Liberal. Sat for W. Newington from January 1916 to November 1918. Sat for Southwark Central from December 1918 until he was defeated in October 1924. Died 16 September 1941.   [1924 2nd ed.]

GILL, Thomas Harry. 25 Euston Road, London. 89 Lindley Street, York. S. of William Gill, Esq., Station Master, N.E. Railway. B. at Hutton Cranswick 5

December 1885; m. secondly, 1930, Leila Gladys, d. of C.A. Elliott, Esq. Educ. at Driffield Grammar School. National President Railway Clerks' Association from 1919; member of Railway National Wages Board; President York Co-operative Society 1916; J.P. for York. A Labour Member. Unsuccessfully contested York in December 1918 and November 1922, and Blackburn in October 1924. Elected for Blackburn May 1929 and sat until he was defeated in October 1931. Member of Board of Co-operative Wholesale Society from 1932 to to 1951, President 1948. President of International Cooperative Alliance 1948-55. Knighted 1950. Died 20 May 1955.

[1931 2nd ed.]

GILLETT, Sir George Masterman. 24 Redington Road, London. S. of George Gillett, Esq., Banker. B. in London September 1870; m. 1898, Edith Mary, d. of Dr. John Dixon. Educ. at the Society of Friends Boarding School, Scarborough, and Paris. A Discount-Banker 1894. Member of Finsbury Borough Council 1900-06; London County Councillor 1910-22; Alderman 1922-24. J.P. for the County of London. Member of House of Commons Appeal Tribunal Military Service Act. 1916-18. Secretary of Overseas Trade Department June 1929-August 1931; Parliamentary Secretary to Ministry of Transport August-October 1931. Knight Bach. 1931. A Labour Member until August 1931, thereafter a National Labour Member. Unsuccessfully contested Finsbury in 1922. Elected for Finsbury in December 1923 and sat until he was defeated in November 1935. Commissioner for the Special Areas of England and Wales 1936-39. Died 10 August 1939.

[1935]

GILLIS, William. Hoyland Common, Yorkshire. S. of William Gillis, Esq., and Ruth Bagnell. B. 10 November 1859 on board ship in the Black Sea. Brought up at Gressenhall, Norfolk. Chairman of Hoyland Nether Urban District Council; member of the W. Riding County Council, and numerous other bodies. A Labour Member. Nominated by the Yorkshire Miners' Association, was elected for the Penistone

division of the W. Riding of Yorkshire in March 1921 and sat until he was defeated in November 1922. On the staff of Yorkshire Miners' Association 1922-29. J.P. for W. Riding of Yorkshire. Died 18 September 1929.

[1922]

GILMOUR, Lieut.-Col. Rt. Hon. Sir John, Bart., G.C.V.O., D.S.O. 6 Cadogan Square, London. Montrave, Leven, Fife. Carlton. S. of Sir John Gilmour, 1st Bart. B. 27 May 1876; m. 1st, 9 April 1902, Mary Louise, d. of E.T. Lambert, Esq., of Telham Court, Sussex (she died 1919); secondly, 17 April 1920, Violet Agnes, d. of E.T. Lambert, Esq. Educ. at Glenalmond Coll., Edinburgh University, and Trinity Hall, Cambridge; Honorary LL.D. Glasgow, Edinburgh, and St. Andrews. Honorary Capt. in the army, and Lieut.-Col. Fife and Forfar Yeomanry; Honorary Col. (F. and F.T.) 20th Armoured Car Company; served in South African War 1900-02 and in Gallipoli, Egypt and Palestine 1915-18. Was a member of Fife County Council 1901-10 and of the Royal Commission on Horse Breeding 1910; Director of Highland Agricultural Society; and Caledonian Railway Company. Unionist Whip 1913-15 and 1919. Junior Lord of the Treasury April 1921 to October 1922 and December 1923 to January 1924. Scottish Whip December 1923. Secretary for Scotland November 1924-July 26, Secretary of State for Scotland July 1926-June 1929. Minister of Agriculture and Fisheries August 1931-September 1932; Secretary of State for Home Affairs September 1932-June 1935. Minister of Shipping October 1939-March 1940. Lord Rector of Edinburgh University 1926-30. PC. 1922. Lord High Commissioner to the General Assembly of the Church of Scotland 1938-39. Vice-Lieut. Fife 1936; Brigadier Royal Company of Archers. D.S.O. 1918. Succeeded as Bart. 1920. G.C.V.O. 1935. A Conservative. Unsuccessfully contested E. Fife in 1906. Sat for E. Renfrewshire from January 1910-18, and for the Pollok division of Glasgow from December 1918 until his death on 30 March 1940.

[1940]

GINNELL, Laurence. 143 Leinster Road, Rathmines, Dublin. S. of Laurence Ginnell,

Esq., and Mary Monaghan. B. 1854 at Delvin, Westmeath; m. 1902, Alice, d. of J. King, Esq., J.P., of Kilbride. Self-educated. A Barrister, called at the Middle Temple 1893 and at the Irish bar 1906; one of the founders of the Irish Literary Society. Author of *The Brehon Laws, The Doubtful Grant of Ireland, Land and Liberty*, etc. Several times arrested; released from Mountjoy Gaol September 1919. Re-arrested and released April 1920. A Sinn Fein Member. Unsuccessfully contested N. Westmeath in 1900. Elected for N. Westmeath in 1906 and for Westmeath Co. in December 1918 but did not take his seat after 1918. Sat as a Nationalist from 1906 but was expelled from the Party in 1909, defeated the official Nationalist candidate in January 1910, and associated himself with Sinn Fein from 1916. Member of Dail for Westmeath to 1921, for Longford and Westmeath as an Anti-Treaty Member 1921-23. Envoy of the self-styled Irish Republic in the United States 1922-23. Died in Washington 17 April 1923.

[1922]

GLANVILLE, Harold James. 18 Slaithwaite Road, Lewisham, London. National Liberal. S. of James Glanville, Esq., Chartered Account, of London. B. 5 June 1854; m. 1881, Hannah Elizabeth d. of James Abbott, Esq., of Bermondsey (she died 1891); secondly, 1918, Bertha, widow of P.B. Nimmo, Esq., of Brockley, London. Educ. at Deptford Grammar School. A Merchant. A member of Bermondsey Vestry, of the London County Council 1898-1910, and of the Metropolitan Water Board. A J.P. for the Co. of London. A Liberal. Unsuccessfully contested Rotherhithe in 1892. Sat for Bermondsey from January 1910 to December 1918 and for W. Bermondsey from December 1918 until he retired in October 1922. Died 27 September 1930. [1922]

GLANVILLE, James Edward. Continued in House after 1945: full entry in Volume IV.

GLASSEY, Alec Ewart. The Homestead, Penn Hill Avenue, Parkstone, Dorset. S. of the Rev. W. Glassey, Congregational Minister of Normanton. B. 29 December 1887; m. 14 September 1910, Mary Eleanor, d. of G.H. Longbottom, Esq., of Sheffield. Educ. at Penistone Grammar School. President of E. Dorset Liberal Association, and Vice-President of Western Liberal Federation. English Whip 1930-31. A Liberal. Unsuccessfully contested E. Dorset in October 1924. Elected for E. Dorset May 1929 and sat until he was defeated in October 1931. Junior Lord of Treasury September-November 1931. Chairman of Congregational Union of England and Wales 1941-42, Chief Commissioner of Reconstruction 1942-57, Co-Treasurer 1953-57. Chairman of Commonwealth Missionary Society 1945-47 and 1961-62. J.P. for Poole. Died 26 June 1970. [1931 2nd ed.]

GLEDHILL, Gilbert. Heatherlea, Elmfield Terrace, Halifax. Constitutional. S. of George Henry Gledhill, Esq., of Halifax. B. 22 May 1889; m. 21 October 1920, Philippa Amy, d. of Ralph S. Holmes, Esq., of Berwick-on-Tweed. Educ. at Perse School, Cambridge, and Bradford and Bridlington Grammar Schools. A Sales Director. Served in 5th Cheshire Regiment overseas with B.E.F. 1915-17, with Ministry of Munitions 1917, with Aircraft Production Department 1918-19. A Conservative. Unsuccessfully contested Halifax in May 1929. Elected for Halifax in October 1931 and sat until he was defeated in July 1945. Died 2 September 1946. [1945]

GLOSSOP, Clifford William Hudson. Continued in House after 1945: full entry in Volume IV.

GLUCKSTEIN, Col. Louis Halle. 39 Elm Tree Road, London. Carlton. S. of Joseph Gluckstein, Esq., O.B.E. B. 23 February 1897; m. 7 April 1925, Doreen, d. of A.F. Klean, Esq. Educ. at St. Paul's School, and Scholar of Lincoln Coll., Oxford. Barrister-at-Law, Lincoln's Inn 1922. Served as Lieut. Suffolk Regiment with B.E.F. 1915-18 (despatches). Capt. (T.A.) September 1939, France 1940 (despatches). Maj. 1941; Lieut.-Col. 1943; Col. 1944. A Conservative. Unsuccessfully contested Nottingham E. in May 1929. Elected for Nottingham E. in October 1931 and sat until he was defeated in

July 1945. Unsuccessfully contested Nottingham E. in February 1950 and Holborn and St. Pancras S. in October 1951. K.C. 1945. Knighted 1953. C.B.E. 1964. Honorary Fellow of Lincoln Coll., Oxford 1968. Bencher of Lincoln's Inn 1952, Treasurer 1970. Dept.-Lieut. for County of London 1952-77. Member of London County Council 1955-64 and of Greater London Council 1964-73, Chairman 1968-69. Chairman of Army Kinema Corporation 1956-68 and of Services Kinema Corporation from 1969. *   [1945]

GLYN, Sir Ralph George Campbell, Bart. Continued in House after 1945: full entry in Volume IV.

GOFF, Sir Park, K.C. 18a St. James's Court, Buckingham Gate, London. Carlton, Junior Carlton, Constitutional, St. Stephen's, Marlborough, Oxford & Cambridge, and Royal Automobile. S. of Col. Bruce Goff, Dept.-Lieut., and J.P. B. 12 February 1871. Unmarried. Educ. at Marlborough, and Trinity Coll., Oxford; M.A., B.C.L., F.R.G.S., F.R.A.S. Barrister-at-Law, Inner Temple 1895, K.C. 1925. Gold Staff Officer at the Coronation of King Edward VII and King George V. Honorary King's Messenger 1914-18. Parliamentary Private Secretary (unpaid) to the First Lord of the Admiralty February 1919. Knight Bach. 1918. Honorary Registrar of the Imperial Society of Knights Bachelor. Member of the British Council of the Olympic Games from 1920; Chairman 1923-24, of Private Bill Committee 1920-23, and 1925-26, and of United Club. Member of Select Committee on London Traffic 1919, of Paris Parliament Commercial Conference 1920, of Lisbon and of Stockholm Inter-Parliament Conference 1921, of Police and Traffic Select Committee 1921, of Inter-Parliament Conference Bordeaux 1922, Copenhagen 1923; appointed by the Speaker President of Parliament Mission to Esthonia, Latvia and Lithuania 1923. Member of Inter-Parliament Conference Washington and Ottawa 1925, of Select Committee on Procedure 1927, of International Commercial Conference Union of South Africa 1927; President of the Men of Sussex Society 1930-

33. A Conservative. Unsuccessfully contested N.E. Lanarkshire in 1911. Sat for the Cleveland division of Yorkshire from December 1918-23 when he was defeated and from 1924 until 1929 when he was defeated. Elected for the Chatham division of Rochester in October 1931 and sat until he retired in October 1935. Created Bart. 1936. Founder and first President of the Anglo-Baltic States Society. Fellow of the Royal Geographical and Royal Astronomical Societies. Died at Cannes 14 April 1939.
[1935]

GOLDIE, Sir Noel Barré. 18 Lower Sloane Street, London. 3 Dr. Johnsons Buildings, Temple, London. Talbot Lodge, Clarence Road, St. Albans. Oxford & Cambridge, and Hurlingham. S. of John Henry Goldie, Esq., of Southfields, Lillington, Leamington. B. 26 December 1882; m. 10 August 1911, Effie Agnes Graham, d. of Charles Graham Rowe, Esq., of Alscott, Aigburth, Liverpool. Educ. at Rugby, and Trinity Coll., Cambridge, B.A., LL.B. 1904. Barrister-at-Law, Inner Temple 1905; K.C. 1928; Bencher 1935; Recorder of Burnley 1929-35, of Manchester 1935-56; member of Bar Council 1932-46; Chairman of United Club 1935-37. Served in France and Belgium 1914-18 as Staff Capt., R.A. A Conservative. Unsuccessfully contested Warrington in May 1929. Elected for Warrington in October 1931 and sat until he was defeated in July 1945. Knighted 1945. Commissioner of Assize on S.E. Circuit from 1947. Divorce Commissioner 1947-48. Died 4 June 1964.   [1945]

GOODMAN, Col. Albert William. Old Dean Hall, Camberley. Carlton, and Constitutional. S. of William Goodman, Esq., of Melbourne. B. 1880; m. 1904, d. of Mark Solomon, Esq., of Sydney. Educ. in Melbourne. Honorary Col. 27 (London) A.A. 5/2 Battalion R.E. (T.A.). Resident in India 1904-24. A Real Estate Dealer. A Conservative. Unsuccessfully contested the Bow and Bromley division of Poplar in May 1929. Elected for Islington N. in October 1931 and sat until his death on 22 August 1937.   [1937]

GORDON, Lieut.-Col. Alexander Theodore. Newton, Insch, Aberdeenshire. S. of Alexander Morison Gordon, Dept.-Lieut. and J.P. of Newton, Insch. B. 11 May 1881. Educ. at Trinity Coll., Glenalmond, and in France. Joined Gordon Highlanders 1899; served in South African War 1900-02; Queen's Medal, 3 clasps; King's Medal, 2 clasps. Served with Gordon Highlanders and A.S.C. in European War. Area Administrative Officer (Scotland) for War Office 1916-19. A Coalition Unionist. Elected for the central division of Aberdeen and Kincardineshire in December 1918 and sat until his death on 6 March 1919.

[1919]

GORMAN, William. 11 Monument Road, Wigan. Manchester Reform. S. of William Gorman, Esq., Iron Merchant. B. at Wigan 15 October 1891. Unmarried. Educ. at Wigan Grammar School. Barrister-at-Law, Middle Temple 1921, Bencher 1938, Treasurer 1959. A Liberal. Unsuccessfully contested the Royton division of Lancashire in November 1922. Elected for the Royton division of Lancashire in December 1923 and sat until he was defeated in October 1924. Served with Royal Artillery 1914-18, with R.A.F.V.E. 1939-45. Assistant Judge Advocate Gen. 1942-44. Recorder of Wigan 1934-48, of Liverpool 1948-50. K.C. 1932. Knighted 1950. Judge of King's (Queen's) Bench Division from 1950. Honorary Freeman of Wigan. 1954. Died 21 December 1964. [1924 2nd ed.]

GOSSLING, Archibald George. 147 Buchanan Gardens, London. S. of Harry Russell Turner Gossling, Esq. B. 1878; m. 1903, Anne Elizabeth Tweed. A Joiner. Member of National Housing and Town Planning Commission, and National Federation of Building Trades' Operatives. A Labour Member. Unsuccessfully contested the Yardley division of Birmingham in November 1922, December 1923 and October 1924. Elected for the Yardley division of Birmingham in May 1929 and sat until he was defeated in October 1931. Managing Director of East Anglian Trustee Savings Bank, Wymondham. Died 19 May 1950. [1931 2nd ed.]

GOSLING, Harry, C.H. Good Fetch, Waldegrave Road, Strawberry Hill, Middlesex. B. 1861. President of Transport and General Workers Union 1921-24; member of the Port of London Authority, the Imperial War Graves Commission and Labour Member for twenty-five years of the London County Council. Had a lifelong association with the river workers of the Metropolis. J.P. C.H. 1917. Minister of Transport January-November 1924 and Paymaster-Gen. May-November 1924. A Labour Member. Unsuccessfully contested Lambeth N. in December 1910. Uxbridge in 1918 and the Kennington division of Lambeth in 1922. Sat for the Whitechapel and St. George's division of Stepney from February 1923 until his death on 24 October 1930. Gen. Secretary of Amalgamated Society of Watermen, Lightermen and Bargemen 1893-1921. Chairman of Parliamentary Committee of T.U.C. 1916. Died 24 October 1930. [1929 2nd ed.]

GOULD, Frederick. 6 North Road, Midsomer Norton. S. of Joshua Gould, Esq., Coal Miner. B. 28 June 1879; m. 25 December 1903, Emma, d. of David Gay, Esq., of Midsomer Norton. Educ. at Midsomer Norton National Church of England School. Member of Midsomer Norton Urban District Council for 12 years; Chairman for 5 years. A Boot Operative for 20 years; Political Agent for 10 years. Parliamentary Private Secretary to W.R. Smith, Parliamentary Secretary to the Board of Trade 1930. J.P. A Labour Member. Elected for the Frome division of Somerset in December 1923, unsuccessfully contested the same division in October 1924. Re-elected for the Frome division of Somerset in May 1929 and sat until he was defeated in October 1931. Unsuccessfully contested Leicester E. in November 1935. O.B.E. 1941. Alderman, Somerset County Council. Died 23 February 1971. [1931 2nd ed.]

GOULD, James Childs. 2 Millbank House, Westminster, London. Ty-to-Maen, St. Mellons, Monmouthshire. Carlton, Devonshire, St. Stephen's, Constitutional, Unionist, and Junior Constitutional. S. of Richard Gould, Esq., of Huish, Devon. B. at

Penarth, Glamorganshire 1882; m. 1905, May Flagg, of Grand Manan, N.B., Canada. Educ. at the Higher Grade School, Cardiff. A Shipowner, Shipbuilder, Engine Builder, Coal Exporter, Merchant, etc. Member of Cardiff City Council 1916-19; first Independent Chairman of the Cardiff Maritime Board 1919; member of Council of several Hospitals and of the Pensions Committee (Wales) etc. Chairman of ten limited companies and Director of numerous others. A Conservative. Elected for Central Cardiff in December 1918 and sat until he retired in October 1924. Died 2 July 1944.

[1924 2nd ed.]

GOULDING, Rt. Hon. Sir Edward Alfred, Bart. Wargrave Hall, Berkshire. Carlton, Marlborough, and Constitutional. S. of William Goulding, Esq., former MP for Cork. B. 1862. Unmarried. Educ. at Clifton Coll., and St. John's Coll., Cambridge. A Barrister, called at the Inner Temple 1887. A member of London County Council 1895-1901; Parliamentary Private Secretary (unpaid) to Mr. H. Chaplin, when President of Local Government Board 1895-98. Chairman of Tariff Reform League Organization Department 1904-12. A J.P. for London and Berkshire; Dept.-Lieut. for Co. Cork. Created Bart. 1915; PC. 1918. A Conservative. Sat for the Devizes division of Wiltshire from 1895-1906. Unsuccessfully contested central Finsbury in 1906, and was elected for Worcester in February 1908. Sat until he retired in October 1922. Chairman of Rolls-Royce Limited and of Central London Electricity Distribution Committee (1934) Limited. Created Baron Wargrave 1922. Died 17 July 1936.

[1922]

GOWER, Sir Robert Vaughan, K.C.V.O., O.B.E. Sandown Court, Tunbridge Wells. Carlton, Junior Carlton, and City Livery. S. of J.R. Gower, Esq., J.P., of Tunbridge Wells. B. 10 November 1880; m. 1st, 29 June 1907, Dorothy, d. of H.M. Wills, Esq. (she died 3 November 1936); secondly, 12 April 1944, Vera, d. of Dr. C.H. Thomas, of Kilmartin, Argyll, and widow of Ronald Angus Daniel, Esq. Created Knight Bach. 1919. C.St.J., Honorary D.C.L.,

LL.D., F.S.A., F.S.G., F.R.G.S., J.P.; Chairman of Bench from 1933. Representative Joint War Commission Royal Red Cross and Order of St. John No. 12 Region. Alderman Tunbridge Wells 1914-34; Mayor 1917-19; Honorary Freeman 1924; member Kent County Council 1910-25; Military Appeal Representative, Kent Tribunals 1916-17; member of Local Government Board Commission on One Man Trades 1917-18, of Ministry of Health Department Committee on Municipal and Local Officers' Superannuation 1926. Chairman of Conservative and Unionist Association, Tunbridge Wells from 1921., R.S.P.C.A. from 1928 to 1951 and of National Canine Defence League from 1921. President of Property Owners' Protection Association. Honorary Col. 88th City of London A.A. Regiment R.A., T.A. Honorary Air Commodore 129 Squad Air Defence Cadet Corps. President 129 Squad Air Training Corps. Chairman of Naval Dockyards Members Committee of House of Commons from 1929, of Committee of Members representing Defence and Evacuation areas, House of Commons and of Animal Welfare Group of House of Commons from 1925. Chevalier of French Legion of Honour, Commander of Order of Merit of Hungary, with Star, of the Crown of Italy, Grand Officer of the Order of the Nile. Officer of the Order of the Crown of Belgium. A Conservative. Elected for central Hackney in October 1924 and for the Gillingham division of Rochester in May 1929. Sat until he retired in June 1945. K.C.V.O. 1935. M.B.E. 1918; O.B.E. 1919. President of R.S.P.C.A. 1951. Died 6 March 1953. [1945]

GRACE, John. Whitby Hall, Wirral, Chester. 1 Brick Court, Temple, London. Conservative. S. of Thomas Wilkinson Grace, Esq., Solicitor, of Whitby Old Hall, Chester. B. 16 November 1886; m. 1929, Ione, d. of Dr. Samuel Rideal, D.Sc., J.P., of Guildford (divorced 1932) Educ. at Wyllies, Cuckfield, Sussex. Barrister-at-Law, Middle Temple 1923; served in France, etc. 1914-17. A Conservative. Elected for the Wirral division of Cheshire in October 1924 and sat until he retired in October 1931.

[1931 2nd ed.]

GRAHAM, Capt. Alan Crosland. 24 Trevor Place, London. Carlton. S. of Sir Crosland Graham. B. 2 August 1896; m. 1st, 21 November 1939, Marion, d. of M.C. Du Plessis, Esq., of Cape Town (divorced 1948); secondly, 1953, Marie Antoinette Louise Pavluc. Educ. at Rugby, and Trinity Coll., Oxford, B.A., Hons. in History 1921. F.S.A. Private Secretary to 1st Earl Balfour 1925-29, to Visct. Hailsham when Minister for War 1931-35; attended Ottawa conference 1932 and Economic Conference (London) 1933. 2nd Lieut. Q.O. Cameron Highlanders, served in France 1916-17 and in Russia 1918-19. 3rd Class Order of St. Anne with Crossed Swords. A Conservative. Unsuccessfully contested the Denbigh division of Denbighshire in May 1929 and the Darwen division of Lancashire in October 1931. Elected for the Wirral division of Cheshire in November 1935 and sat until he retired in June 1945. Died 10 May 1964. [1945]

GRAHAM, Duncan Macgregor. Gowrie House, Bothwell Road, Hamilton, Scotland. S. of Malcolm Graham, Esq., Miner. B. at Airdrie March 1867; m. 1st, 1897, Isabella Miller, d. of Thomas Gillies, Esq., Miner (she died January 1914); secondly, Isabella, d. of William Moore, Esq., of Newarthill. Educ. at Whiterigg, Lochside, and Longrigg Public Elementary Schools. A Miner 1878, Checkweigher 1892; Political Organizer, Scottish Miners' Federation 1908-18; Gen. Secretary Lanarkshire Miners' County Union 1918-23. A Labour Member. Sat for the Hamilton division of Lanarkshire from December 1918 until his death on 19 October 1942. [1942]

GRAHAM, Sir Frederick Fergus, Bart. Continued in House after 1945: full entry in in Volume IV.

GRAHAM, Robinson. 44 Raglan Road, Burnley. S. of David Graham, Esq., of Burnley. B. 1878; m. 1904, Rhoda, d. of Edward Harrison, Esq., of Padiham. Assistant Secretary of the Burnley Weavers' Association, Secretary 1941-47. A Labour Member. Elected for Nelson and Colne in June 1920 and sat until he retired in October 1922. [1922]

GRAHAM, Rt. Hon. William. 29 Sunningfields Road, Hendon, London. Eld. s. of George Graham, Esq., of Edinburgh. B. at Peebles 29 July 1887; m. 1919, Ethel Margaret, only d. of H.B. Dobson, Esq., of Harrogate, Yorkshire, J.P., for Edinburgh. Educ. at Peebles Public School, George Heriot's School, Edinburgh, and Edinburgh University; M.A. with Hons. in Economic Science 1915, LL.B. 1917, and Hon. LL.D. 1927, Edinburgh University. A Journalist from 1905. Labour member of Edinburgh Town Council 1913-19; Chairman of Edinburgh Disablement Committee, and member of many public bodies in that city. Financial Secretary to the Treasury January-November 1924 and Junior Lord of the Treasury February-November 1924; President of the Board of Trade June 1929-August 1931. PC. 1924. A Labour Member. Sat for the Central division of Edinburgh from December 1918 until he was defeated in October 1931. Chairman of Public Accounts Committee 1924-29. Adviser to Messrs. Schwab and Snelling, Stockbrokers 1931-32. Died 8 January 1932. [1931 2nd ed.]

GRAHAM-LITTLE, Sir Ernest Gordon Graham. Continued in House after 1945: full entry in Volume IV.

GRANT, Sir James Augustus, Bart. Househill, Nairn. Carlton, and Boodle's. S. of Col. J.A. Grant, C.B., C.S.I. B. 8 March 1867; m. 1896, Nina Frances, d. of A.C. Kennard, Esq. Educ. at Edinburgh and at Christ Church, Oxford. J.P. for Cumberland. Member County Council of Nairn 1907. Created Bart. 1926. A Conservative. Unsuccessfully contested Elgin Burghs in 1892, Banffshire 1893, 1895, and 1906. Sat for the Egremont division of Cumberland from January 1910-18. Sat for Whitehaven division of Cumberland from 1918-22 when he was defeated. Sat for the Southern division of Derbyshire from October 1924 until he was defeated in May 1929. Registrar of Royal Coll. of Art 1899-1904. Died 29 July 1932. [1929]

GRANT-FERRIS, Robert Grant. Continued in House after 1945: full entry in Volume IV.

GRANVILLE, Edgar Louis. Continued in House after 1945: full entry in Volume IV.

GRATTAN-DOYLE, Sir Nicholas Grattan. Highfield, Hadley Wood, Hertfordshire. Carlton, Royal Automobile, and 1900. S. of John Doyle, Esq., of Ballyroe House, Co. Wexford. B. 18 August 1862; m. 1st, 1899, Kathryn Deering Nevins, of New Jersey (she died 1902); secondly, 1907, Gwendoline Fane Mackusick, of Lyttel Hall, Surrey. Educ. privately, and at St. Aidans Academy, Enniscorthy. Dept.Lieut., and J.P. for Co. Durham. J.P. for Hertfordshire and Middlesex. Dept. Director Education and Propaganda, Ministry of Food 1918; Freeman of the City of London. Knight Bach. February 1924. Unsuccessfully contested Gateshead as a Liberal Unionist in January 1910. Sat as a Conservative for Newcastle-on-Tyne N. from December 1918 until he resigned in April 1940. Director of Northern Newspapers Limited. Adopted the surname of Grattan-Doyle in lieu of Doyle 1925. Died 14 July 1941. [1940]

GRAVES, Frances Marjorie. 10 Barton Street, London. Ladies' Carlton. D. of William Graves, Esq., of Allerton, Liverpool. B. 17 September 1884. Educ. privately, and at Chateau de Dieudonne, France. Member of Holborn Borough Council from 1928-1934. Representative for London on Executive of National Union of Conservative and Unionist Associations. A Conservative. Elected for S. Hackney in October 1931 and sat until she was defeated in November 1935. Member of Dorset County Council. Died 17 November 1961. [1935]

GRAY, Ernest. Hillworth, 104 Tulse Hill, London. Carlton, and Junior Constitutional. B. 1857; m. Florence Caroline, d. of J. Garside, Esq. Educ. at St. John's Coll., Battersea. Educational Secretary National Union of Teachers. Maj. 6th Essex Regiment. Member London County Council from 1907-1925; Vice-Chairman London County Council 1915-16. Joint Editor with Sir J. Yoxall of *The Red Code, Companion to the Code*, and *Education Handbook*. A Coalition Unionist. Sat for West Ham N. from 1895-

1906 when he was defeated. Unsuccessfully contested West Ham N. again in January 1910 and Accrington in December 1910. Elected for Accrington in December 1918 and sat until he was defeated in November 1922. President of National Union of Teachers 1894. Knighted 1925. Died 6 May 1932. [1922]

GRAY, Frank. Shipton Manor, Oxfordshire. Reform, National Liberal, and Eighty. S. of Sir Walter Gray. B. at Oxford 1880; m. 1914, d. of Henry John Panton, Esq., of Wareham, Dorset. Educ. at Rugby. Admitted a Solicitor after passing with honours 1903; retired 1916. Held a number of legal appointments in Oxford before retirement. Author of *The Confessions of a Private*. Liberal Whip 1924. A Liberal. Unsuccessfully contested Watford in 1918. Elected for Oxford City in November 1922 and December 1923 but in May 1924 on petition this last election was declared void and he was unseated. Unsuccessfully contested Portsmouth central in October 1924. Served as a Private in the Oxfordshire and Buckinghamshire L.I. and Royal Berkshire Regiment. County Councillor and J.P. for Oxfordshire. Died 2 March 1935. [1924]

GRAY, Harold William Stannus. House of Commons, London. S. of Maj. George Gray. B. at Graymount, Co. Antrim 16 August 1867; m. 1894, Rowena, d. of T.R. Stannus, Esq. Educ. at Eton, and Magdalene Coll., Cambridge. Served with the Red Cross in France for several years; a well-known Cambridgeshire Farmer and Sportsman. A Conservative. Elected for Cambridgeshire in November 1922 and sat until he retired in November 1923. High Sheriff of Co. Antrim 1895 and of Cambridgeshire and Huntingdonshire 1939. K.B.E. 1938. Member of Cambridgeshire County Council. Died 23 May 1951. [1923]

GRAY, Milner. Belmont, New Bedford Road, Luton. National Liberal, and Eighty. S. of Archibald Campbell Gray, Esq., Baptist Minister, and Jimima, d. of Dr. Milner, of Edinburgh. B. 11 May 1871; m. June 1902, Elizabeth, d. of Mark S. Luck, Esq. Educ.

privately. A Hat Manufacturer. Alderman of Bedford County Council. A Liberal. Unsuccessfully contested the Wellingborough division of Northamptonshire in December 1918, St. Albans division of Hertfordshire in December 1919, Bedford division of Bedfordshire in December 1923 and October 1924. Elected for mid Bedfordshire in May 1929 and sat until he was defeated in October 1931. Unsuccessfully contested mid Bedfordshire in November 1935 and W. Derbyshire in June 1938. Parliamentary Secretary to Ministry of Labour September-November 1931. C.B.E. 1937. Chairman of Liberal Party Organisation 1934-40. Died 10 April 1943. [1931 2nd ed.]

GRAYSON, Lieut.-Col. Sir Henry Mulleneux, K.B.E. 100 Lancaster Gate, Hyde Park, London. Ravens Point, Holyhead. Union. S. of Henry Holdrege Grayson, J.P. B. at Liverpool 26 June 1865; m. 1st, 1891, Dora Beatrice, d. of Frederick Harrington, Esq. (divorced 1927); secondly, 1927, Louise Mary, widow of R.H. Earle, Esq. Educ. at Winchester Coll. High Sheriff of Anglesey 1917-18. Director of Ship Repairs, Admiralty 1917-19. Commander of the Order of the Crown of Italy; Officer of the Legion of Honour; K.B.E. 1920; and Commander of the Order of Leopold II. A Coalition Unionist. Elected for Birkenhead W. in December 1918 and sat until he retired in October 1922. Created Bart. 1922. Member of firm of H. and C. Grayson, Shipbuilders and Ship-repairers. Member of Institute of Naval Architects 1896. Died 27 October 1951. [1922]

GREAVES-LORD, Sir Walter Greaves, K.C. 1 Garden Court, Temple, London. Windy Gap, Seaford, Sussex. East Hill, Sanderstead. Carlton, and St. Stephen's. S. of Simeon Lord, of Ince, and Hannah, d. of John Elliott, Esq., of Dunstable. B. 21 September 1878; m. 12 August 1903, Caroline Ethel, d. of Sir Albert Stephenson. Educ. at Wigan Grammar School, Southport College, and University Coll., Liverpool. LL.B. Liverpool and Victoria Universities. A Barrister-at-Law, Gray's Inn 1900; K.C. 1919; Bencher 1920; Treasurer 1933. Vice-Chairman of Bar Council 1932; Recorder of Manchester 1925-35; Chancellor of Primrose League 1926-27. A Freeman of the City of London and of the Feltmakers' Company. Knight Bach. 1927. A Conservative. Unsuccessfully contested the Ince division of Lancashire in January and December 1910. Sat for the Norwood division of Lambeth from November 1922 until February 1935 when he was appointed a High Court Judge. Judge of the King's Bench Division 1935-40. Assumed the surname of Greaves-Lord in lieu of Lord in 1910. Died 18 June 1942. [1935]

GREEN, Albert. The Knoll, Normanton, Derby. St.Stephen's. S. of Joseph Green, Esq., Manufacturer of Derby. B. at Derby 3 November 1874; m. 1900, a d. of Godfrey Turner, Esq. Educ. at Derby Elementary Schools and Technical Coll. Became a Manufacturer on the death of his father in 1902. Entered Derby Town Council August 1911; Mayor November 1915: J.P. for Derby December 1918. A Democratic Conservative. Elected for Derby in December 1918 and sat until he was defeated in November 1922. Died 25 September 1941. [1922]

GREEN, Joseph Frederick. 32 Upper Mall, Hammersmith, London. S. of Joseph Edwin Green, Esq., J.P. B. 5 July 1855 in London; m. a d. of W. Claydon, Esq. Educ. at Islington Proprietary School, University of Oxford (St. Mary Hall), and King's Coll., London. A descendant of John Green, Esq., MP for Essex, and Speaker of the House of Commons 1461. Secretary to the International Arbitration and Peace Association 1886 to 1917. Chairman of the Executive of the National Democratic Party. A Coalition National Democratic and Labour Party Member. Elected for W. Leicester in 1918 and sat until he was defeated in November 1922. Parliamentary Private Secretary to Sir Eric Geddes, Minister of Transport 1920-21. Secretary of the Conservative Members' '1922' Committee. On staff of Conservative Research Department. Ordained deacon 1880 and priest 1881. Curate of St. Mary's, Tothill Fields, Westminster 1880-86. President of the Johnson Society, Lichfield 1921-22.

Chairman of Society for the Protection of Ancient Buildings. Chairman of English Positivist Committee 1923-31. Died 1 May 1932. [1922]

GREEN, Walter Henry. 64 Southwood Road, London. S. of Thomas William Green, Esq., of Deptford. B. March 1878; m. 1905, Grace, d. of James Puddefoot, Esq. Educ. at London County Council Elementary School. An Engineer. Political Secretary 1921; County Alderman London County Council 1928-36; Chairman Parliamentary Committee London County Council 1934-37; Mayor of Deptford 1920-21; member of Deptford Borough Council from 1909-1956, of National Executive of Labour Party, Chairman 1941-42; J.P. for London. A Labour Member. Elected for Deptford in November 1935 and sat until he retired in June 1945. Member of Metropolitan Water Board 1946-53. C.B.E. 1949. Died 13 April 1958. [1945]

GREENALL, Thomas. Dingsdale, Folly Lane, Swinton, Manchester. S. of Thomas Greenall, Esq., Coal Miner. B. 5 May 1857 at Tarbuck, Lancashire; m. 1879, Sarah, d. of William Saunders, Esq. Started work at 9 years of age. For 20 years worked in coal mine; for 23 years was a Miners' Agent. President of the Lancashire and Cheshire Miners' Federation. Vice-President Lancashire, Cheshire and North Staffordshire Miners' Wages Board. Member of the Executive Committee of the Miners' Federation of Great Britain. J.P. of the borough of Salford. A Labour Member. Unsuccessfully Contested Leigh in January 1910 and Farnworth in 1918. Sat for the Farnworth division of Lancashire from November 1922 until he retired in May 1929. Died 22 December 1937. [1929]

GREENE, Sir Walter Raymond, Bart., D.S.O. 31 St. James's Place, London. Burrough House, Burrough-on-the-Hill Melton Mowbray. Carlton, and Turf. Eld. s. of Sir E. Walter Greene, Bart., MP for Bury St. Edmunds. B. 4 August 1869 at Bury St. Edmunds. Unmarried. Educ. at Eton, and Oriel Coll., Oxford. Lieut.-Col. Loyal Suffolk Hussars; served in South African War 1900 and with British Expeditionary Force 1914-15 as Capt. 9th Lancers; D.S.O. 1915; Lieut.-Col. commanding 2/3rd County of London Yeomanry. J.P. for Suffolk; a member of London County Council for N. Hackney 1907-10. Chairman of the Housing of the Working Classes Committee 1909-10. A Conservative. Sat for the Chesterton division of Cambridgeshire from 1895-1906, when he was defeated. First elected for Hackney N. in January 1910 and sat until he was defeated in December 1923. Succeeded as Bart. 1920. Died 24 August 1947. [1923]

GREENE, William Pomeroy Crawford. 5 West Eaton Place, London. Carlton, and Cavalry. S. of Hon. George Henry Greene, Member of Legislative Council of New South Wales, and Ellen Elizabeth, d. of Lieut.-Col. Andrew Crawford, I.S.C. B. 28 June 1884, at Iandra, New South Wales. Educ. at Haileybury, and Trinity Coll., Cambridge, M.A. A Landowner. King Edward's Horse, 11th Australian Light Horse, and Capt. 13th Hussars; served in France and Mesopotamia 1914-19; J.P. for New South Wales. A Conservative. Sat for Worcester from December 1923 until he retired in June 1945. Died 10 May 1959. [1945]

GREENWELL, Col. Thomas George. West House, Cleadon, Co. Durham. Carlton, and Lansdowne. S. of T.W. Greenwell, Esq., of Sunderland. B. 18 December 1894; m. 9 April 1918, Mabel Winifred, d. of T.H. Catcheside, Esq., J.P., of Newcastle-upon-Tyne. Educ. at Gresham's School, Holt, and Kings Coll., Durham University. Joined R.A. 1914; served overseas with R.G.A. and R.F.C. 1915-17 and with 55th (Medium) and 63rd A.A. Regiments R.A. to 1938. Rejoined 1939, formed 123rd (Light) A.A. Battery 1940. T.D. 1944. Managing Director of T.W. Greenwell, Ship Repairers of Sunderland until 1960, and of Wear Arc Welding Company; Director of Lloyds British Testing Company Limited, Dudley; Chairman N.E. Coast Ship Repairers Association 1937-40 and of Dry Dock Owners and Repairers Central Council 1938-40; a Commissioner of the

River Wear Commission; member of Executive Committee of Shipbuilding Employers Federation. A Conservative. Elected for Hartlepools in June 1943 and sat until he was defeated in July 1945. Unsuccessfully contested Hartlepools in February 1950. High Sheriff of Co. Durham 1951-52. J.P. and Dept.-Lieut. for Co. Durham. Died 15 November 1967. [1945]

GREENWOOD, Rt. Hon. Arthur. Continued in House after 1945: full entry in Volume IV.

GREENWOOD, Rt. Hon. Sir Hamar, Bart., K.C. 13 Chester Terrace, London. Carlton, British Empire, and 1900. S. of John Hamar Greenwood, Esq., Barrister-at-Law, of Whitby, Ontario. B. 7 February 1870 (his birth was registered in the name Thomas Hubbard Greenwood but he was known by, and used the name Hamar Greenwood); m. 23 May 1911, Margery, D.B.E., d. of Walter Spencer, Esq., of Fownhope Court, Herefordshire. Educ. at Whitby, and at Toronto University; B.A. Barrister-at-Law, Grays Inn 1906, Australia and Canada. Bencher 1917, K.C. 1919. Lieut.-Col. 10th South Wales Borderers 1915-16, Canadian Mil. 1886-1900, King Edward's Horse 1901-13. Under Secretary of State for the Home Department January-July 1919; Secretary for Overseas Trade Department of Board of Trade July 1919-April 1920; Chief Secretary for Ireland April 1920-October 1922. PC. 1920 and PC. (Ireland) 1920; created Bart. 1915. Sat as Liberal Member for York from January 1906 to January 1910, when he was defeated, and for Sunderland from December 1910 to November 1922 when he was again defeated. Unsuccessfully contested Sunderland as a Liberal in December 1923. Elected for Walthamstow E. in October 1924 as a Constitutionalist, with the support of the Conservative, but was opposed by a Liberal candidate and took the Conservative Whip when Parliament met. Sat until he retired in May 1929. Created Baron Greenwood 1929 and Visct. Greenwood 1937. Treasurer of Gray's Inn 1930. Honorary Treasurer of Conservative Party 1933-38. President of British Iron and Steel Federation 1938-39.

President of Pilgrims Society 1948. Chairman of Dorman Long and Company Limited. Died 10 September 1948. [1929]

GREENWOOD, Thomas Hubbard. See GREENWOOD, Rt. Hon. Sir Hamar, Bart.

GREENWOOD, William. 35 Belgrave Road, Oldham. S. of Edmund Greenwood, Esq., Cotton Mill Manager, of Rochdale. B. at Rochdale 25 February 1875; m. 1900, Elizabeth Marion, d. of Thomas Shirley Whittaker, Esq., of Marple, Cheshire (she died 1923). Educ. at elementary schools in Rochdale, Shawforth, and Royton, Stockport Technical School, and Manchester University. Long engaged in Cotton Spinning and Chairman of a number of companies. A Conservative. Sat for Stockport from March 1920 until his death on 12 August 1925. [1925]

GREER, Harry. 65 Sloane Street, London. S. of William Greer, Esq., of Dundalk. B. 18 September 1876; m. 1906, Marguerite Charlotte, d. of Louis Roche, Esq. Largely interested in Colonial and Far East trade and development. A Managing Director of the Mercantile Marine Finance Corporation Limited. Travelled extensively. A Coalition Unionist. Elected for the Clapham division of Battersea and Clapham in June 1918, and for the Wells division of Somerset in December 1918. Sat until he retired in October 1922. Knighted 1922. Chairman of Lord Roberts Memorial Workshops and of Baird Television Limited. Died 20 March 1947. [1922]

GREGORY, Henry Holman. 37 St. James's Place, London. Garrick, Reform, and Albemarle. S. of H.T. Gregory, Esq., Solicitor, of Bath. B. 30 June 1864; m. 1st, 1891, Ada, d. of Mark Whitwell, Esq., J.P. (she died 1930); secondly, 1935, Nannette Evelyn, d. of C.E. O'Leary, Esq. Admitted a Solicitor of the Supreme Court 1886; called to the bar at the Middle Temple 1897; K.C. 1910. Recorder of Bath from 1916-1924; Bencher of the Middle Temple 1920. A Coalition Liberal. Elected for Derbyshire S. in December 1918 and sat until he retired in October 1922. Recorder of Bristol 1924-29. Judge of the City of London Court 1929-32, Common Serjeant 1932-34 and Recorder of City of London 1934-37. Knighted 1935. Chairman of Royal Commission on Unemployment Insurance 1930-32. Died 9 May 1947.   [1922]

GREIG, Col. Sir James William, C.B., K.C. 3 New Square, Lincoln's Inn, London. 41 Carlisle Mansions, Carlisle Place, Westminster, London. Caledonian. S. of John Borthwick Greig, Esq., W.S. and Parliamentary Agent, and Mary, d. of William Grant, Esq., of Madeira. B. 31 January 1859; m. Jeannie, d. of Capt. E. Brown of Salem, U.S.A. (she died 1931). Educ. at University Coll. School, and University Coll., London, B.A., LL.B.; and at Sorbonne and Collège de France, Paris. Called at Lincoln's Inn 1882; K.C. 1913; Bencher of Lincoln's Inn 1917. Honorary Col. and Lieut.-Col. commanding 14th (County of London) Battalion (London Scottish) 1904-11, raised and commanded 2nd and 3rd Battalions C.B. 1911. V.D. Parliamentary Private Secretary (unpaid) to Secretary for Scotland 1917-22; Knighted 1921. A Liberal. Elected for Renfrewshire W. in January 1910. Sat until he was defeated in November 1922. Unsuccessfully contested Berwick and Haddington in May 1929. Died 10 June 1934.   [1922]

GRENFELL, David Rhys. Continued in House after 1945: full entry in Volume IV.

GRENFELL, Edward Charles. 4 Cavendish Square, London. Carlton, Brooks's, White's, and Beefsteak. S. of Henry Riversdale Grenfell, Esq., MP and Alethea, eld. d. of H. Adeane, Esq., MP. B. 29 May 1870; m. 16 August 1913, Florence, d. of George Henderson, Esq. Educ. at Harrow, and Trinity Coll., Cambridge. A Partner in the firm of Morgan, Grenfell and Company, Bankers. A Director of Bank of England 1905-40. A Conservative. Sat for the City of London from May 1922 until June 1935 when he was created Baron St. Just. Lieut. of City of London. Died 26 November 1941.   [1935]

GRETTON, Col. Rt. Hon. John. 35 Belgrave Square, London. Stapleford Park, Melton Mowbray. Carlton, and R.Y.S. S. of John Gretton, Esq., of Stapleford Park, Melton Mowbray and Burton-on-Trent. B. 1 September 1867; m. 24 April 1900, Hon. Maud Helen de Moleyns, d. of 4th Lord Ventry (she died 29 July 1934). Educ. at Harrow. J.P. for Derbyshire and Dept.-Lieut., and J.P. for Leicestershire. Chairman of Bass, Ratcliffe and Gretton, Burton-on-Trent. PC. 1926. A Conservative. Sat for S. Derbyshire from 1895 until 1906, when he was defeated in the general election. Sat for Rutland from June 1907 to November 1918, and for the Burton division of Staffordshire from December 1918 until he resigned in 1943. C.B.E. 1919. Created Baron Gretton 1944. Died 2 June 1947.   [1943]

GRETTON, Hon. John Frederic. 4 Eaton House, Upper Grosvenor Street, London. Needwood, Burton-on-Trent. Carlton, Buck's, and R.Y.S. S. of The Rt. Hon. Lord Gretton, Conservative MP for the Burton division of Staffordshire 1918-43, and the Hon. Maud Helen de Moleyns, d. of 4th Lord Ventry. B. 15 August 1902; m. 6 May 1930, Margaret, d. of Capt. H. Loeffler. Educ. at Eton. A Director of Bass, Ratcliffe, Gretton, Worthington and Company Limited. A Conservative. Elected for the Burton division of Staffordshire in July 1943 and sat until he was defeated in July 1945. Succeeded to the Peerage as Baron Gretton in 1947. O.B.E. 1950.*
          [1945]

GREY, George Charles. 1a Cheltenham Terrace, London. Guards', Boodle's, and National Liberal. S. of Maj.-Gen. W.H. Grey. B. 2 December 1918. Educ. at Winchester, and Hertford Coll., Oxford. Lieut. Grenadier Guards 1938. A Liberal. Returned unopposed for the Berwick-on-Tweed division of Northumberland in August 1941 and sat until he was killed in action near Caumont 30 July 1944.   [1944]

GRIDLEY, Sir Arnold Babb, K.B.E. Continued in House after 1945: full entry in Volume IV.

GRIFFITH, Arthur. 122 St. Lawrence Road, Clontarf, Dublin. S. of Arthur Griffith, Esq., Printer. B. in Dublin 1872. Educ. at Christian Brothers School, Dublin. A Journalist. Known as a leader of the Sinn Fein movement, of which he was Vice-President. Editor of *Sinn Fein* 1906-15, the organ of the party of that name. Was interned in England. After his release on the amnesty following the rebellion in Dublin, he revived the paper under the title of *Nationality* in 1916. Was again interned in 1918. Released; re-arrested in 1920. A Sinn Fein Member. Elected for Cavan E. in June 1918 on the death of Mr. Samuel Young. Returned for E. Cavan and N.W. Tyrone in December 1918 but did not take his seat for either constituency. Member of Northern Ireland Parliament for Fermanagh and Tyrone 1921-22. Member of Dail for E. Cavan to 1921, for Cavan 1921-22, as a Pro-Treaty Member. Secretary for Foreign Affairs 1921-22. President of Dail Eireann January-August 1922. Died 12 August 1922. [1922]

GRIFFITH, Rt. Hon. Sir Ellis Jones, Bart., K.C. See ELLIS-GRIFFITH, Rt. Hon. Sir Ellis Jones, Bart., K.C.

GRIFFITH, Frank Kingsley, M.C. 3 Hare Court, Temple, London. Chilton, 8 Durham Avenue, Bromley, Kent. National Liberal. S. of Col. Frank Griffith, V.D., and Florence, d. of James Hudson, Esq. B. 23 December 1889; m. 1st, 26 September 1924, Eleanor, d. of Sir Robert Bruce, C.B. (she died 1954); secondly, 1955, Margaret Winifred, widow of H. Louch, Esq. Educ. at Marlborough, and Balliol Coll., Oxford. A Barrister-at-Law, Inner Temple 1915, N.E. Circuit. Master of the Worshipful Company of Plasterers 1927. Capt. 3rd Lincolnshire Regiment, served in France 1914-18. Recorder of Richmond 1932-40; Parliamentary Private Secretary to the Rt. Hon. Sir Herbert Samuel, Secretary of State, Home Office November 1931-October 1932. An Opposition Liberal. Unsuccessfully contested Bromley in 1922, 1923 and 1924. Elected for Middlesbrough W. in March 1928 and sat until 1940 when he was appointed a County Court Judge. County Court Judge from 1940-56. Chairman of

E. Riding of Yorkshire Quarter Sessions 1947-56. Died 25 September 1962. [1940]

GRIFFITH- BOSCAWEN, Rt. Hon. Sir Arthur Sackville Trevor. 29 Palace Gate, London. Carlton, Constitutional, Athenaeum, and Royal Automobile. S. of Capt. Griffith-Boscawen and Helen Sophia, d. of Admiral Duff. B. 18 October 1865 at Trevalyn Hall, Wrexham; m. 1st, 1892, Edith, d. of S. Williams, Esq., of Boones, Edenbridge (she died 7 July 1919); secondly, 1921, Phyllis, eld. d. of W. Denham, Esq., of Rawdon Hall, Holyport, Berkshire. Educ. at Rugby, and Queen's Coll., Oxford, 1st class classics 1888, 2nd History 1889, President of Union 1888. Col. 3rd Battalion Queen's Own (Royal W. Kent Regiment), and commanded a Battalion of the Hampshire Regiment in France 1916 (twice mentioned in despatches). A J.P. for Kent and Berkshire. Private Secretary to Sir M. Hicks-Beach, when Chancellor of the Exchequer 1895-1900. Parliamentary Charity Commissioner 1900-06; Parliamentary Secretary to the Ministry of Pensions December 1916 to January 1919; Parliamentary Secretary to the Board of Agriculture and Minister of Fisheries January 1919. Minister of Agriculture and Fisheries February 1921-October 1922. Honorary Secretary of Church Parliamentary Committee; member of the London County Council 1910-13. Knighted 1911. PC. 1920. A Unionist. Sat for Tunbridge division of Kent from 1892 to 1906, when he was defeated. Unsuccessfully contested E. Denbighshire in August 1906, and Dudley in January 1910. Sat for Dudley from December 1910 until March 1921 when he failed to secure re-election after his appointment as Minister of Agriculture. Elected for the Taunton division of Somerset in April 1921 and sat until he was defeated in November 1922. Unsuccessfully contested the Mitcham division of Surrey in March 1923. Minister of Health October 1922-March 1923 when he resigned after his defeat at the Mitcham by-election. Chairman of Welsh Church Commissioners 1923-45. Chairman of Royal Commission on Transport 1928-31. Chairman of Transport Advisory Council 1936-45. Died 1 June 1946. [1922]

GRIFFITHS, George Arthur. 14 Park View, Royston, Nr. Barnsley. S. of William Griffiths, Esq., of Buckley, N. Wales. B. 7 May 1878; m. September 1902, June, d. of John Cadman, Esq., of Beverley, Shropshire. Educ. at Buckley National School. A miner from the age of 12. Member of Royston U.D.C. from 1910 to 1941. Parliamentary Private Secretary to Wilfred Paling, Parliamentary Secretary Ministry of Pensions April 1941 and when Minister of Pensions August 1945. A Labour Member. Sat for the Hemsworth division of Yorkshire from 1934 until his death on 15 December 1945. Member of W. Riding County Council 1925-45. J.P. for W. Riding. Member of Salvation Army. Died 15 December 1945.

[1946]

GRIFFITHS, James. Continued in House after 1945: full entry in Volume IV.

GRIFFITHS, Sir John Norton, Bart., K.C.B., D.S.O. See NORTON-GRIFFITHS, Sir John Norton, Bart., K.C.B., D.S.O.

GRIFFITHS, Thomas. 45 Lewis Road, Neath. S. of Thomas and Mary Griffiths. B. at Neath 1867; m. 1891, Mary Elizabeth, d. of Dr. David Morgan, Architect, of Neath. Educ. in a voluntary school, and trained in industrial, economic, and sociological subjects at Ruskin Coll., Oxford. Appointed Organizer of British Steel Smelters, etc., Association 1899; Divisional Officer, Iron and Steel Trades' Confederation 1916. Member of the Neath Town Council; Chairman of Managers' Education Committee; member of Advisory Committee of Labour Exchange and Sectional Insurance Committee. Labour Whip 1919-25. Treasurer of Household January-November 1924. A Labour Member. Sat for the Pontypool division of Monmouthshire from December 1918 until he retired in October 1935. Died 4 February 1955.

[1935]

GRIGG, Lieut.-Col. Rt. Hon. Sir Edward William Macleay, K.C.M.G., K.C.V.O., D.S.O., M.C. 15 Westminster Gardens, London. Tormarton Court, Badminton.

Guards', Beefsteak, and Oxford & Cambridge. S. of Henry Grigg, Esq., C.I.E., Madras C.S. B. 8 September 1879; m. 31 January 1923, Hon. Joan Dickson-Poynder, d. of Lord Islington. Educ. at Winchester, and New Coll., Oxford. Joined Grenadier Guards 1915; served overseas 1915-19; A.A.G. War Office 1919; Military Secretary to H.R.H. The Prince of Wales on Canadian and Australasian visits 1919 and 1920. Private Secretary to Rt. Hon. D. Lloyd George 1921-22. Secretary of Rhodes Trust 1922-25; Gov. and C. in C. Kenya Colony 1925-30; Chairman of Milk Commission 1932; Parliamentary Secretary Ministry of Information September 1939. Financial Secretary to the War Office April 1940. Joint Parliamentary Under-Secretary of State to the War Office May 1940-March 1942. Minister Resident in Middle East November 1944-July 1945. PC. November 1944. A National Conservative. Sat as a Liberal Member for Oldham from 1922-25. Elected for the Altrincham division of Cheshire as a National Conservative in June 1933 and sat until he retired in June 1945. Secretary to the Editor of *The Times* 1903; Assistant Editor of *Outlook* 1905-06; Head of the Colonial Department of *The Times* 1908-13; Joint Editor of *Round Table* 1913-14. M.C. 1917; D.S.O. 1918. Created Baron Altrincham 1945. Editor of *English Review*, later *National and English Review* from 1948 to 1955. Dept.-Lieut. of Gloucestershire from 1950. Died 1 December 1955.

[1945]

GRIGG, Rt. Hon Sir Percy James, K.C.B., K.C.S.I. 3 Whitehall Court, London. Athenaeum, and Oriental. S. of Frank Alfred Grigg, Esq., of Exmouth. B. 16 December 1890; m. 30 July 1919, Gertrude Charlotte, d. of the Rev. G.F. Hough, of Worcester. Educ. at Bournemouth, and St. John's Coll., Cambridge, Honorary Fellow 1943. Joined the Treasury 1913; served overseas 1915-18. Private Secretary to successive Chancellors of the Exchequer 1921-30; Chairman of Board of Customs and Excise 1930-31 and of Board of Inland Revenue 1931-33; Finance Member Government of India 1934-39; Permanent Under-Secretary of State for War 1939-42;

Secretary of State for War February 1942-July 1945. PC. 1942. A National Conservative. Elected for Cardiff E. in April 1942 and sat until he was defeated in July 1945. British Executive Director of International Bank for Reconstruction and Development (World Bank) 1946-47. Chairman of Committee on Departmental Records 1954. Chairman of Bass Ratcliff and Gretton 1959-61, and of Bass, Mitchells and Butlers 1961-64. Died 5 May 1964. [1945]

GRIGGS, Sir William Peter. The Drive, Ilford, Essex. S. of John and Martha Griggs. B. at South Hackney 1 November 1853; m. Georgina, d. of Thomas Hodges, Esq., of Kensington. Educ. privately. Governing Director of the South Essex Recorders Limited, and W.P. Griggs and Company Limited. Knighted 1916. Member of Ilford District Council from 1899, Chairman 1910. Member of Essex County Council from 1901, Alderman. J.P. for Essex. A Coalition Unionist. Unsuccessfully contested the Romford division of Essex in December 1910. Elected for Ilford in December 1918 and sat until his death on 11 August 1920. [1920]

GRIMSTON, Hon. John. Continued in House after 1945: full entry in Volume IV.

GRIMSTON, Robert Villiers. Continued in House after 1945: full entry in Volume IV.

GRITTEN, William George Howard. Carlton, Pratt's, and 1900. S. of William and Annie Howard Gritten. B. 1870; m. 1918, Helena Blanche Paget, widow of Commander Webb. Educ. at Brasenose Coll., Oxford; Classical Scholar and Exhibitioner, Hons. Lit. Hum., M.A. A Barrister-at-Law, Inner Temple 1899, and on the Northern Circuit and Central Criminal Court. F.R.G.S. and Writer. A Conservative. Unsuccessfully contested The Hartlepools in January, June, and December 1910. Elected for The Hartlepools in December 1918 when he defeated the Coupon Liberal candidate, but was defeated there in November 1922 and again in December 1923. Re-elected for The Hartlepools in May 1929 and sat until his death on 5 April 1943. [1943]

GROTRIAN, Herbert Brent. Knolls, Leighton Buzzard. Carlton, and United University. S. of Frederick Brent Grotrian, Esq., MP., of Ingmanthorpe, Yorkshire. B. 29 March 1870; m. 1902, Mary Lilian, d. of Robert Adams, Esq., of Hamilton, Ontario. Educ. at Rossall School, and at Trinity Coll., Oxford, M.A., B.C.L. 1892. Barrister-at-Law, Inner Temple 1894; K.C. 1925; Recorder of Scarborough from 1918 to 1946, J.P. for Hertfordshire and Bedfordshire. A Conservative. Unsuccessfully contested the S.W. division of Kingston-upon-Hull in 1922 and 1923. Elected for S.W. Kingston-upon-Hull in October 1924 and sat until he was defeated in May 1929. High Sheriff of Bedfordshire 1931, Dept.-Lieut. 1938-49. Chairman of Bedfordshire Quarter Sessions 1939-51. Died 28 October 1951. [1929]

GROVES, Thomas Edward. 42 Chobham Road, London. B. at Stratford 1884. Educ. at an Elementary School, Carpenters' Company Institute, and Ruskin Coll., Oxford. Member of West Ham Borough Council from 1919. Alderman, J.P. and Mayor of West Ham. Parliamentary representative National Union of Vehicle Builders. President of West Ham Society for the Welfare of the Blind, of Amusement Caterers Association of Great Britain and Ireland; Chairman of British Bank of Commerce, of Aero Welders Limited, Surrey and of Box and Company, Builders, Shipston-on-Stour. A Nurseryman and Fruit Farmer. Barrister-at-Law, Gray's Inn. An English Whip from 1931 to 1944. A Labour Member. Sat for the Stratford division of West Ham from November 1922 until he was defeated in July 1945. In 1944 he failed to be readopted by the West Ham Labour Party and in 1945 he unsuccessfully contested the seat as an Independent in opposition to the official Labour candidate and so was expelled from the Labour Party. Died 29 May 1958. [1945]

GRUFFYDD, William John. Continued in House after 1945: full entry in Volume IV.

GRUNDY, Thomas Walter. 15 Godstone Road, Rotherham. B. 1864; m. 1885, Eliza Metcalfe. A Coal Miner, and Checkweigher. Member of Rotherham School Board 1893; Rotherham Borough Council 1900; Mayor 1915-16. Member of the Yorkshire Miners' Association. A Labour Member. Sat for the Rother Valley division of the W. Riding of Yorkshire from December 1918 until he retired in October 1935. Died 28 January 1942. [1935]

GUEST, Col. Hon. Christian Henry Charles. 3 Queen Anne Street, London. S. of Ivor, 1st Baron Wimborne. B. 15 February 1874; m. 12 July 1911, Hon. Frances Henrietta Lyttelton, d. of Charles, 8th Visct. Cobham (she died 20 January 1918). Educ. at Eton. Col. 1st Royal Dragoons; served in South African War 1900-02 and overseas 1915, 1917-18. G.S.O. War Office 1914-15. Parliamentary Private Secretary to Rt. Hon. Charles Hobhouse, Chancellor of Duchy of Lancaster and Postmaster-Gen. 1911-15. Sat for E. Dorset from June to December 1910, for Pembroke Boroughs from December 1910-18, when he unsuccessfully contested Wandsworth central, and for N. Bristol from 1922-23, when he was defeated. Elected for the Drake division of Plymouth in June 1937 and sat until he was defeated in July 1945. Sat as a Liberal until 1923 but joined the Conservative Party in 1930 and sat as a Conservative from 1937 to 1945. Died 9 October 1957. [1945]

GUEST, Capt. Rt. Hon. Frederick Edward, C.B.E., D.S.O. 19 Berkeley Street, London. S. of 1st Baron Wimborne. B. 14 June 1875; m. 29 June 1905, Amy, d. of Henry Phipps, Esq., of U.S.A. Educ. at Winchester. Assistant Private Secretary to Mr. Winston Churchill 1907-10; Junior Lord of the Treasury 1911-12; Treasurer of the Household 1912-15; Joint Patronage Secretary to the Treasury and Chief Government Whip March 1917 to April 1921. Secretary of State for Air April 1921-October 1922. Capt. 1st Life Guards, Reserve of Officers; served in White Nile 1900; South African War 1901-02; in France as Aide-de-Camp to Field Marshal Sir John French 1914-16; D.S.O. 1917; Legion of Honour 1915; C.B.E. (Military) 1919; East Africa 1916-17. PC. 1920. Unsuccessfully contested the Kingswinford division of Staffordshire in January 1906, the Cockermouth division of Cumberland in August 1906 and the Brigg division of Lincolnshire in February 1907. Elected for E. Dorset in January 1910, but was unseated on petition in May 1910. Re-elected for E. Dorset in December 1910 and December 1918, then defeated in November 1922. Elected for the Stroud division of Gloucestershire in December 1923, and for Bristol N. in October 1924, where he was defeated in May 1929 standing as an Independent Liberal with unofficial Conservative support. Elected for the Drake division of Plymouth in October 1931 and sat until his death on 28 April 1937. Sat as a Liberal until 1929 but joined the Conservative Party in 1930 and sat as a Conservative from 1931 to 1937. Died 28 April 1937 [1937]

GUEST, Hon. Ivor Grosvenor. Wimborne House, Arlington Street, London. Turf, White's, Beefsteak, Bucks, and Orleans. S. of Visct. Wimborne. B. 21 February 1903; m. 1938, Lady Mabel Fox-Strangways, d. of 6th Earl of Ilchester. Educ. at Eton, and Trinity Coll., Cambridge. A Company Director. A National Conservative. Elected for Brecon and Radnor in November 1935 and sat until he succeeded to the Peerage as Visct. Wimborne in 1939. O.B.E. 1953. Served with Northamptonshire Yeomanry 1939-43. Parliamentary Private Secretary to Lord Sherwood, Under Secretary for Air 1943-45. Died 7 January 1967. [1939]

GUEST, John. The Elders, South Hindley, Barnsley. S. of George Guest, Esq. B. 1867. Vice-President of Yorkshire Miners' Association. County Alderman and J.P. for the W. Riding of Yorkshire. A Wesleyan Methodist. A Labour Member. Sat for the Hemsworth division of the W. Riding of Yorkshire from December 1918 until his death on 6 October 1931. [1931 2nd ed.]

GUEST, Hon. Oscar Montague. Wycliffe House, Hay, Hereford. S. of Ivor,

1st Baron Wimborne. B. 24 August 1888; m. 19 January 1924, Kathleen Susan, d. of Graham Paterson and Lady Rowena Paterson. Educ. at Harrow, and Trinity Coll., Cambridge. A Director of Companies. Parliamentary Private Secretary to F.G. Keilaway when Postmaster-Gen. from 1921-22. Sat for the Loughborough division of Leicestershire as a Coalition Liberal from 1918-22 when he retired. Elected for Camberwell N.W. in November 1935 as a Conservative and sat until July 1945 when he unsuccessfully contested Brecon and Radnor. Prospective candidate for Hornchurch until 1949. Served with the Lothian and Border Horse and with R.F.C. 1914-18. Died 8 May 1958.   [1945]

GUINNESS, Hon. Rupert Edward Cecil Lee. See ELVEDEN, Rupert Edward Cecil Lee Guinness. Visct.

GUINNESS, Thomas Loel Evelyn Bulkeley. 27 Chester Street, London. S. of Benjamin Guinness, Esq. B. 1906; m. 1st, 4 July 1927, Hon. Joan Barbara Yarde-Buller, d. of John, 3rd Baron Churston (marriage dissolved in 1936 and she m. secondly, Prince Aly Khan); secondly, 24 November 1936, Lady Isabel Manners, d. of John, 9th Duke of Rutland (marriage dissolved 1951); thirdly, 1951, Gloria, d. of Raphael Rubio, of Mexico. Parliamentary Private Secretary to Sir Philip Sassoon, Bart., Under-Secretary of State for Air November 1932-May 1937. Wing Commander A.A.F. (R. of O.) September 1939. A Conservative. Unsuccessfully contested the Whitechapel and St. Georges division of Stepney in May 1929 and December 1930. Elected for Bath in October 1931 and sat until he retired in June 1945. O.B.E. 1942.*   [1945]

GUINNESS, Lieut.-Col. Rt. Hon. Walter Edward, D.S.O. 10 Grosvenor Place, London. Knockmaroon, Castleknock, Co. Dublin. The Manor House, Bury St. Edmunds. Carlton, and Bachelors'. 3rd s. of the Earl of Iveagh. B. 29 March 1880; m. 24 June 1903, Lady Evelyn Erskine, d. of the 14th Earl of Buchan (she died 1939). Educ. at Eton. Lieut.-Col. Loyal Suffolk

Hussars Imperial Yeomanry; served as Capt. in South African War 1900-01, and in France, etc. 1914-18, D.S.O. 1917 and bar 1918. A member of London County Council for N. Paddington 1907-10. Chairman of Housing of Working Classes Committee 1908. Under-Secretary of State for War October 1922. Financial Secretary to the Treasury October 1923-January 1924, and November 1924-November 1925; Minister of Agriculture and Fisheries November 1925-June 1929. PC. 1924. A Conservative. Unsuccessfully contested N.W. Suffolk in 1906. Sat for the Bury St. Edmunds division of Suffolk from August 1907 until he retired in October 1931. Created Baron Moyne 1932. Chairman of Royal Commission on University of Durham 1934, of Committee on Cinematograph Films 1936, and of West Indies Royal Commission 1938-39. Parliamentary Secretary to Ministry of Agriculture and Fisheries May 1940-February 1941. Secretary of State for Colonies and Leader of the House of Lords February 1941-February 1942. Dept. Minister resident in the Middle East August 1942-January 1944. Minister resident in the Middle East from January 1944 until 6 November 1944 when he was assassinated in Cairo by members of the Fighters for the Freedom of Israel Organization - the 'Stern Gang.'   [1931 2nd ed.]

GUNSTON, Maj. Sir Derrick Wellesley, Bart., M.C. 24 Princes Court, Knightsbridge, London. South End, Wickwar, Gloucestershire. Carlton, Bath, and R.Y.S. S. of Maj. B.H. Gunston. B. 26 February 1891; m. 18 October 1917, Evelyn, d. of Howard St. George. Educ. at Harrow, and Trinity Coll., Cambridge. Capt. Irish Guards, R. of O. Served in France 1915-19. Parliamentary Private Secretary to Rt. Hon. Sir Kingsley Wood when Parliamentary Secretary to Ministry of Health 1926-June 1929, to Rt. Hon. Neville Chamberlain, when Minister of Health August-October 1931, and when Chancellor of the Exchequer November 1931-January 1936. Parliamentary Private Secretary to Sir Edward Grigg, Joint Parliamentary Under-Secretary of State for War May 1940-February 1942. Created Bart. 1938. A Conservative. Elected for the Thornbury division of Gloucestershire in October 1924 and sat until he was defeated in July 1945. * [1945]

GUTHRIE, Thomas Maule. Rose Hill, Brechin. S. of James Guthrie, Esq., of Pitforthie, Banker, of Brechin. 1927, Ella Kate, d. of W.G. Leete, Esq., of Liverpool. Educ. at Brechin High School, Montrose Academy, and Edinburgh University. A Solicitor and Agent for Royal Bank, Brechin; partner in Messrs. David Guthrie and Sons and other industrial concerns. Provost of Brechin 1902-08; Town Clerk of Brechin 1908-20. Served throughout the European war with the Black Watch, and later on Upper Nile. A Liberal. Returned for Moray and Nairn in June 1922 as a Coalition Liberal and again in November 1922 as a National Liberal and sat until he was defeated in December 1923. Died 30 March 1943. [1923]

GUY, James Campbell Morrison, M.C. 21 Drummond Place, Edinburgh. St. Andrews, and Royal Automobile. S. of John C. Guy, Esq., Advocate, Sheriff Substitute at Edinburgh. B. 12 June 1894; m. 15 September 1926, Deirdre, d. of W.A. Mackinnell, Esq., of Kirkcudbright. Educ. at Edinburgh Academy and University. Advocate 1921. Served with R.N.V.R. and R.M. 1914-18. A Unionist. Elected for Edinburgh Central in October 1931 and again in November 1935. Sat until he resigned in November 1941. Advocate Depute in Sheriff Court 1932. [1941]

GUY, William Henry. Continued in House after 1945: full entry in Volume IV.

GWYNNE, Rupert Sackville. 47 Catherine Street, London. Wootton Manor, Polegate, Sussex. Carlton, and Bachelors'. S. of James Eglinton Gwynne, Esq., of Folkington Manor, Polegate, and Mary, d. of William Purvis, Esq. B. 2 August 1873; m. 1905, Hon. Stella Ridley, d. of 1st Visct. Ridley. Educ. at Shrewsbury School, and Pembroke Coll., Cambridge; B.A. Was called to the bar at the Inner Temple 1898. J.P. and County Councillor for E. Sussex, and Chairman of Eastbourne Rural District Council. Financial Secretary to War Office March 1923 to January 1924. A Conservative. Elected for the Eastbourne division of Sussex in January 1910 and sat until he retired on 9 October 1924. Died 12 October 1924. [1924 2nd ed.]

HACKING, Maj. Rt. Hon. Sir Douglas Hewitt, Bart., O.B.E. Mannings Hill Cottage, Cranleigh. Carlton. S. of J. Hacking, Esq., of Clayton-le-Moors. B. 4 August 1884; m. 1909, Margery Allen, d. of H.H. Bolton, Esq., of Newchurch-in-Rossendale. Educ. at Giggleswick School, and Manchester University. Chairman Rishton Council; Commission in East Lancashire Regiment August 1914. Served 2 years in France. Member of Empire Parliamentary Delegation to South Africa 1924. Parliamentary Private Secretary to Sir James Craig, Ministry of Pensions 1920, Admiralty 1920-21, and to Sir L. Worthington Evans, Bart., Secretary of State for War 1921-22. Vice-Chamberlain of the Household 1922-January 1924 and November 1924-December 1925; Conservative Whip 1922-25; Under-Secretary of State for Home Department and Representative of the Office of Works in the House of Commons December 1925-November 1927. Secretary to Department Overseas Trade November 1927-June 1929; Parliamentary Under-Secretary of State for Home Department February 1933-June 1934; Financial Secretary to War Office June 1934-November 1935, Under-Secretary of State for Dominions November 1935-March 1936. Government Delegate to International Assembly of League of Nations, Geneva 1933. Chairman of Conservative Party Organisation March 1936-March 1942. Chancellor of Primrose League 1931. Lay member of Gen. Medical Council from 1932. Vice-President Hotels and Restaurants Association 1927-33, and from 1944. President of Residential Hotels Association 1931-33; Vice-Chairman National Union of Conservative and Unionist Associations 1930-33; Chairman of Lancashire, Cheshire and Westmorland Provincial Area thereof 1932-34, of Home Office Committee on Compensation for Silicosis 1926, and of Technical Committee on Taxi Cabs 1927-

35. Chairman of War Office Committee on Redistribution of Royal Ordnance Factories 1934. Member of Surrey Territorial Association 1943. Dept.-Lieut. for Surrey 1940. Governor of Cranleigh School. Founded Travel Association of Great Britain and Ireland 1928. Created Bart. 1938. PC. 1929. A Conservative. Sat for the Chorley division of Lancashire from December 1918 until he retired in June 1945. Created Baron Hacking 1945. Died 29 July 1950. [1945]

HADEN-GUEST, Leslie Haden. Continued in House after 1945: full entry in Volume IV.

HAILWOOD, Augustine. Struan, Lindow Common, Wilmslow. Constitutional. Constitutional, Manchester. S. of James and Elizabeth Hailwood. B. in Manchester 1875; m. Mary Hilda, 6th d. of Francis Amiel, Esq., of Birkdale. Educ. at the Xaverian Coll., Manchester. A Wholesale Baker. Member of the Manchester City Council 1909-11; J.P. for Manchester 1917. A Gov. of St. Bede's Coll., Manchester A Coalition Unionist. Elected for the Ardwick division of Manchester in December 1918 and sat until he was defeated in November 1922. Unsuccessfully contested Ardwick again in December 1923. Died 1 December 1939. [1922]

HALES, Harold Keates. Selahdale, 6 West Heath Avenue, Golders Green, London. S. of Lewis George Hales, Esq., of Higher Ardwick, Manchester. B. 22 April 1868; m. March 1915, Ethel, d. of Joseph King, Esq. Educ. at Chorlton High School, Manchester, and Burslem, Staffordshire. Member of Stoke-on-Trent Federated Council November 1910; served with R.N. Gallipoli 1915. A Conservative. Elected for the Hanley division of Stoke-on-Trent in October 1931 and sat until he was defeated in November 1935. Founder of the firm of Hales Brothers, Shippers and Merchants 1929. Died 7 November 1942 as the result of a boating accident on the Thames near Shepperton; his body was recovered from the River Wey at Weybridge on 8 December 1942. [1935]

HALL, Sir Douglas Bernard, Bart. 10 Cadogan Gardens, London. The Castle Priory, Wallingford, Berkshire. Carlton, Boodle's, and White's. S. of Bernard Hall, Esq., J.P., of Petworth, and Margaret, d. of William Calrow, Esq., Dept.-Lieut., J.P. B. 1866; m. 1890, Caroline, d. of T.J. Montgomery, Esq., of Larchmont Manor, New York State, U.S.A. Educ. at Charterhouse, and Christ Church, Oxford. A J.P. for W. Sussex, a member of the County Licensing Committee, High Sheriff 1907 and Lord of the Manor and patron of the livings of Burton and Barlavington in Sussex. Temporary Capt. R.E. A Unionist. Unsuccessfully contested Penryn and Falmouth in 1906. Elected for the Isle of Wight in January 1910. Sat until he retired in October 1922. Served with B.E.F. from 1914 and later with High Explosives Department, Ministry of Munitions. Created Bart. 1919. Died 30 June 1923. [1922]

HALL, Frederick. 26 Victoria Road, Barnsley. B. 1855 in Staffordshire; m. 1878, Ann Maria, d. of William Edwards, Esq., (she died 1929). Worked in a Rotherham Colliery. Was appointed local Secretary Aldwarke Branch of Yorkshire Miners' Association in 1878, and was Agent of the Association for the whole of Yorkshire 1904-18. Member of the W. Riding of Yorkshire County Council for twelve years. J.P. for the W. Riding of Yorkshire. Appointed a Labour Whip January 1919. Lord Commissioner of the Treasury January-October 1924. Member of United Methodist Church. Member of Rawmarsh School Board and Urban District Council. A Labour Member. Sat for the Normanton division of the W. Riding of Yorkshire from November 1905 until his death on 18 April 1933. [1933]

HALL, Lieut.-Col. Sir Frederick, Bart., K.B.E., D.S.O. 30 Hyde Park Gardens, London. Carlton, and Constitutional. S. of Herbert Hall, Esq. B. 7 October 1864; m. 16 April 1892, Annie Ellen, d. of Dr. Henry Hall (she died 19 February 1929). Director of Gardner, Mountain and Company, of County of London Electric Supply Company Limited, of the South London

Electric Supply Corporation Limited, and of the South Metropolitan Electric Supply Company Limited. A Member of Lloyd's and the Baltic; Chairman and Managing Director of the Mercantile Marine Finance Corporation Limited; a member of the London County Council from 1907-13; member of the County of London Territorial Association. Lieut.-Col. R.F.A. K.B.E. 1918. D.S.O. 1918. Created Bart. 1923. A Conservative. Sat for the Dulwich division of Camberwell from December 1910 until his death on 28 April 1932. [1932]

HALL, Rt. Hon. George Henry. Continued in House after 1945: full entry in Volume IV.

HALL, James Henry. Cooden, 101 Fyfield Road, Walthamstow. S. of James Hall, Esq. B. 24 March 1877; m. Theresa Ellen, d. of G. Coleman, Esq., of Leyton. Employed as a foreman by the Port of London Authority. Alderman of Stepney Borough Council from 1934. A Labour Member. Elected for the Whitechapel and St. George's division of Stepney in December 1930, and was defeated there in October 1931. Re-elected for the Whitechapel and St. George's division of Stepney in November 1935 and sat until his death on 6 June 1942. [1942]

HALL, Capt. Walter D'Arcy. Hay, Breconshire. S. of Thomas Skarratt Hall, Esq., of Weeting Hall, Brandon. B. 10 August 1891; m. 1st, 1920, Ann Madelaine, d. of Col. Charles Brook, of Kenmount, Annan (divorced); secondly, 1957, Ruth Penelope Owen. Educ. at Eton, and Royal Military Coll., Sandhurst. Joined 20th Hussars 1911. Served in France 1914-19. M.C. and bar. French Croix de Guerre. A Conservative. Elected for Brecon and Radnor in October 1924, but defeated there in May 1929. Re-elected for Brecon and Radnor in October 1931 and sat until he retired in October 1935. Parliamentary Private Secretary to H.D. King when Financial Secretary to War Office.* [1935]

HALL, William George Glenvil. Continued in House after 1945: full entry in Volume IV.

HALL, Admiral Sir William Reginald, K.C.M.G., C.B. 63 Cadogan Gardens, London. Garrick, and Beefsteak. S. of Capt. William Henry Hall, R.N. B. 28 June 1870; m. 28 June 1894, Ethel Wotton, d. of Sir William Abney, K.C.B. (she died 1932). Educ. at private school, H.M.S. *Britannia*, and R.N. Coll., Greenwich. Joined R.N. 1883. Admiral 1926. Inspecting Capt. of Mechanical Training Establishments 1906-07; Naval Assistant to Comptroller of Navy 1911-13. Commanded the *Cornwall*, *Natal*, and *Queen Mary*, taking part in the last-named in the battle of Heligoland Bight. Director of Naval Intelligence 1914-19. Principal Agent of Unionist Party 1923-24. A Conservative. Sat for the W. Derby division of Liverpool from February 1919-December 1923. Unsuccessfully contested W. Derby in December 1923. Sat for the Eastbourne division of Sussex from June 1925 until he retired in May 1929. C.B. 1915. Rear-Admiral 1917; Vice-Admiral 1922; Admiral 1926. Died 22 October 1943. [1929]

HALLAS, Eldred. King's Heath, Birmingham. S. of Edward and Sarah Hallas. B. at Stainland, Yorkshire 1870; m. 1892, Clara, d. of Arthur Bottomley, Esq., of Bradford. Educ. in elementary schools and evening classes. A Trade Union Secretary, writer, etc. City Councillor of Birmingham for 7 years from November 1911. Author of *Josie, The Upward Way*, etc. Elected for the Duddeston division of Birmingham in December 1918 and sat until he retired in October 1922. Elected in 1918 as a member of the pro-Coalition National Democratic Party with Conservative support but took the Labour Whip from October 1919. Lecturer at the Ethical Church 1906. Founder of Birmingham and District Municipal Employees' Association 1910. President of Birmingham and W. District Branch of National Union of General and Municipal Workers 1922-26. Died 13 June 1926. [1922]

HALL CAINE, Derwent. 66 Great Queen Street, London. Heath End House, Hampstead Heath. Royal Automobile, and National Labour. S. of Sir Hall Caine, C.H. B. 12 September 1891. Educ. at Isle of Man, and Eastbourne. Managing Director of "The Readers' Library" Publishing Company Limited. A Labour Member until August 1931 when he joined the National Labour group. Unsuccessfully contested Reading in November 1922, the Clitheroe division of Lancashire in October 1924. Elected for the Everton division of Liverpool in May 1929 and sat until October 1931 when he unsuccessfully contested the seat as a supporter of the National Government but was defeated by the Conservative candidate. Knighted 1933. Created Bart. 1937. Died 2 December 1971.

[1931 2nd ed.]

HALL CAINE, Gordon Ralph, C.B.E. Woolley Firs, Maidenhead, Berkshire. Greeba Castle, Isle of Man. Carlton. S. of Sir Hall Caine, K.B.E. B. 16 August 1884; m. 1st, 1913, Lillian, d. of J.L. Digges, Esq. (she died 1948); secondly, 1949, Dorothy Sara, d. of J.T. Hornsby-Sample. Educ. at King William's Coll., Isle of Man. Director of many Public Companies. Served on Government Committees 1914-19; Dept. Controller of Paper 1918-19. Officer of the Legion of Honour. C.B.E. 1920. A Conservative although he did not receive official Conservative support at the 1922 election. Sat for E. Dorset from November 1922 to May 1929, when he was defeated. Re-elected for E. Dorset in October 1931 and again in November 1935 and sat until he retired in June 1945. Died 5 March 1962. [1945]

HALLS, Walter. 43 Henry Road, West Bridgeford, Nottingham. S. of William Halls, Esq., Farm Shepherd, of Gaulby, Leicestershire. B. at Tugby, Leicestershire 16 June 1871; m. 1892. Jane, d. of John Hanes, Esq., village Postmaster of Sharnford. Leicestershire. Educ. at Tugby and Gaulby elementary schools. Elected Organiser of the National Union of Railwaymen December 1909. A Labour Member. Unsuccessfully contested Northampton in 1918. Elected for the Heywood and Radcliffe division of Lancashire in June 1921 and sat until he was defeated in November 1922. Unsuccessfully contested the Heywood and Radcliffe division of Lancashire in December 1923 and Derby in October 1931. Lord Mayor of Nottingham 1940-41. Died 20 October 1953. [1922]

HALSTEAD, Maj. David. Highfield, Haslingden, Lancashire. S. of Richard Halstead, Esq., Cotton Manufacturer, and Susannah, d. of John Anderton, Esq., of Haslingden. B. at Haslingden 16 March 1861; m. 1st, 1883, Esther, d. of William Lindsay, Esq., Ironfounder, of Haslingden (she died 1 September 1920); Secondly, 1923, Louisa, d. of William Duckworth, Esq., of Haslingden. Educ. at Haslingden National Schools, and Stanley Street Academy, Accrington. A Cotton Spinner and Manufacturer and Bleacher. Mayor of Haslingden 1917-19. Maj. 5th East Lancashire Regiment; T.D., J.P. 1920 and Dept.-Lieut. 1921. Author of *The Annals of Haslingden, A History of St. James Parish Church, Haslingden*. Vice-President of the Lancashire Authors Association. A Conservative. Elected for Rossendale in November 1922 and sat until he retired in November 1923. President of Lancashire and Cheshire Antiquarian Society 1924. Fellow of Society of Antiquaries. Died 10 July 1937. [1923]

HAMBRO, Angus Valdemar. Milton Abbas, Blandford. Carlton. S. of Sir Everard Hambro, K.C.V.O. B. 8 July 1883; m. 1st, 1 July 1907, Rosamond Maud, d. of Maj. Robert Kearsley, of Stapeley, Nantwich (she died 18 January 1914); Secondly, 29 April 1916, Vanda, d. of St. John Charlton, Esq., of Malpas. Educ. at Eton. Capt. Dorset Yeomanry (T.A. Reserve). Parliamentary Private Secretary to Secretary of State for Air 1918. A National Conservative. Sat for S. Dorset from January 1910 to October 1922 when he retired. Elected for N. Dorset in July 1937 and sat until he retired in June 1945. Dept.-Lieut. for Dorset, High Sheriff 1934-35. County Councillor and J.P. for Dorset. President of English Golf Union 1946. Died 19 November 1957. [1945]

HAMILTON, Maj. Sir Collingwood George Clements. Cransford Hall, Saxmundham. Carlton. S. of the Ven. George Hans Hamilton, Archdeacon of Northumberland and Canon of Durham, and Lady Louisa, sister of Robert 4th Earl of Leitrim. B. 1 November 1877; m. 6 May 1906, Eleanor, d. of Henry Simon, Esq., of Didsbury. Educ. at Aysgarth, and at Charterhouse. An Electrical Engineer. J.P. for Cheshire and Suffolk 1927. Knight Bach. 1922. Lieut. 5th Cheshire Regiment 1914; Maj. Queen's Westminsters; served in France with R.F.C. 1917. Director of Enrolment for National Service 1916; Controller of Contract Claims, Ministry of Munitions 1918. Director of Commercial Companies. Parliamentary Private Secretary to Sir Laming Worthington-Evans when Minister of Pensions 1919-20. Chairman of Officers' Pension Warrant Committee 1919, and of War Office Committee to report Combination of Pay Department and Records Department 1920. A Conservative. Sat for the Altrincham division of Cheshire from 1913-23. Unsuccessfully contested the Altrincham division of Cheshire in December 1923, and also Lincoln in October 1924. Elected for Ilford in February 1928 and sat until he resigned in 1937. Created Bart. 1937. Died 12 January 1947.   [1937]

HAMILTON, Mary Agnes. 12 York Buildings, London. D. of Professor Robert Adamson, of Glasgow. B. 8 July 1882; m. 1905, C.J. Hamilton, Esq. Educ. at Glasgow High School, and Newnham Coll., Cambridge. A Journalist. Member of Balfour Commission on British Trade and Industry 1924-29. Member of Royal Commission on Civil Service 1929-31. A Labour Member. Unsuccessfully contested the Chatham division of Rochester in December 1923 and Blackburn in October 1924. Elected for Blackburn in May 1929 and sat until she was defeated in October 1931. Gov. of B.B.C. 1933-37. Alderman of London County Council 1937-40. C.B.E. 1949. Author of biographies of Ramsay Macdonald, Arthur Henderson, Margaret Bonfield, Sidney and Beatrice Webb, Mary Macarthur, and numerous other works including several novels. Died 10 February 1966.   [1931 2nd ed.]

HAMILTON, Sir Robert William. 161 Oakwood Court, London. Reform. S. of Sir R.G.C. Hamilton, K.C.B. B. 26 August 1867; m. 17 December 1925, Gertrude Mary Sutherland, d. of John Williamson, Esq., of Kirkwall. Educ. at St. Paul's School, and Trinity Hall, Cambridge. Barrister-at-Law, Inner Temple 1895. In the Colonial Service 1895-1920; Principal Judge and Chief Justice, East Africa Protectorate 1905-20. Knight Bach. 1918. Parliamentary Under-Secretary of State for the Colonies August 1931-September 1932. Scottish Liberal Whip May 1934-October 1935. A Liberal. Sat for Orkney and Shetland from November 1922 until he was defeated in November 1935. Fellow of Royal Geographical Society and of Society of Antiquaries of Scotland. Died 15 July 1944.   [1935]

HAMMERSLEY, Samuel Schofield. 19 Chesham Street, London. Saxons, Buxted, Sussex. Carlton, Brooks's, Clarendon, and Constitutional. Manchester. S. of John Schofield Hammersley, Esq., Cotton Spinner, of Oldham. B. 1892; m. 1919, Kate, d. of W. Wakley, Esq., of Guernsey. Educ. at King's Coll., Cambridge. Served with E. Lancashire Regiment in Gallipoli, and with Tank Corps in France 1915-18. Capt. R. of O. Managing Director of S. Noton Limited. Parliamentary Private Secretary to A.M. Samuel, Financial Secretary to the Treasury 1927-June 1929. A Conservative. Unsuccessfully contested Stockport in December 1923. Sat for Stockport from October 1924 until 1935 when he retired. Elected for Willesden E. in July 1938 and sat until he was defeated in July 1945; defeated again at Willesden E. in February 1950. Executive Chairman of Anglo-Israel Association 1951-63. Died 28 March 1965.   [1945]

HANBURY, Sir Cecil. 41 Smith Square, London. Kingston, Maurward, Dorchester. Athenaeum, and Travellers'. S. of Sir Thomas Hanbury, K.C.V.O. B. 10 March 1871; m. 25 June 1913, Effield Dorothy Cecil, d. of J.F. Symons-Jeune, of Wallingford Park, Oxford. Educ. at Fettes Coll., Edinburgh, and Trinity Coll., Cambridge.

Knight Bach. 1935. Partner in Ward, Hanbury and Company, Merchants of London and Shanghai. Grand Officer of the Italian Order of the Crown and strong supporter of Mussolini and the Abyssinian campaign. Fellow of the Linnean Society. A Conservative. Unsuccessfully contested N. Dorset in 1922 and 1923. Elected for N. Dorset in October 1924 and sat until his death on 10 June 1937. [1937]

HANCOCK, John George. Miners' Offices, Old Basford, Nottingham. S. of Joseph Hancock, Esq., Coal Miner. B. 15 October 1857 at Pinxton, Derbyshire; m. 1882, Mary Hoten. Educ. at Pinxton and Selston Village Schools. A Miners' Agent for Nottingham from 1892, and a member of Nottingham Town Council. J.P. for Nottinghamshire. Sat for mid Derbyshire from July 1909-1918. Sat for the Belper division of Derbyshire from December 1918 until he was defeated in December 1923. A Liberal and Labour Member until April 1915 when the Labour Whip was withdrawn from him; thereafter a Liberal Member. Secretary of the Nottinghamshire Miners' Association from 1897 to 1921. Treasurer of Nottinghamshire and District Miners' Industrial Union 1927-37. Methodist local preacher. Died 19 July 1940. [1923]

HANLEY, Denis Augustine. 97 Cadogan Gardens, London. Eythorpe Cottage, Stone, Aylesbury. Carlton, and Constitutional. S. of Edmund Hanley, Esq., of Kintbury, Berkshire. B. 26 July 1903; m. 1935, Kathleen Mary, d. of J.P. Eyre, Esq. Educ. at Downside School, and at Trinity Coll., Cambridge. A Conservative. Elected for Deptford in October 1931 and sat until he retired in October 1935. Served in Royal Naval Scientific Service 1938-54. * [1935]

HANNA, George Boyle. 15 Rosetta Avenue, Belfast. Constitutional, London. Ulster Reform, Belfast. S. of Robert Hanna, Esq., Auctioneer of Ballymena. B. at Ballymena 17 December 1877; m. 1903, Sunnie, d. of Redmond Mack, Esq., of Lisburn. Educ. at Gracehill and Ballymena

Academies, and privately. A Solicitor 1901-20; later a Barrister-at-Law; called to the Irish bar November 1920. Member of Antrim County Council from 1908-21, and Finance and Law Committee from 1914. An Independent Unionist. Elected for E. Antrim in May 1919 when he defeated the official Unionist candidate, and sat until he retired in October 1922. K.C. 1933. Member of N. Ireland Parliament for Co. Antrim 1921-29 and for Larne 1929-37. Parliamentary Secretary to N. Ireland Ministry of Home Affairs 1925-37. County Court Judge for Tyrone and Chairman of Quarter Sessions 1937-38. Died 30 October 1938. [1922]

HANNAH, Ian Campbell. Whim, West Linton, Peeblesshire. Sandyfields House, Sedgley, Dudley, Worcestershire. S. of John Hannah, Esq., Dean of Chichester. B. 16 December 1874; m. 1904, Edith Browning, d. of Dr. J.H. Brand. Educ. at Winchester, and Trinity Coll., Cambridge. Master of English School, Tientsin 1897-99; Assistant at Michaelhouse, Natal 1910; President of King's Coll., Nova Scotia 1904-06; Professor of Church Hist. Oberlin Coll. 1915-25; Fellow of Society of Antiquaries; J.P. for Peeblesshire; Extra Mural Lecturer Cambridge University. Unsuccessfully contested Sunderland as a Liberal in 1924. Elected as a National Conservative for the Bilston division of Wolverhampton in November 1935 and sat until his death on 7 July 1944. [1944]

HANNON, Sir Patrick Joseph Henry. Continued in House after 1945: full entry in Volume IV.

HANSON, Sir Charles Augustin, Bart. Fowey Hall, Cornwall. Carlton. S. of Joseph and Mary A. Hanson. B. at Fowey 1846; m. 1868, Martha Sabina, d. of James Appelbe, Esq., of Halton, Canada. Educ. locally. Emigrated to Canada, where he was a Wesleyan Minister; returned to England 1890. Chairman of Gresham Life Assurance Society. J.P. for Cornwall. High Sheriff of Cornwall and Sheriff of London. Alderman of the City of London 1909-21. Lord Mayor of London 1917-18. Dept.-Lieut.

for Cornwall. Created Bart. in 1918. J.P. for Co. of London 1919. A Unionist. Elected for the Bodmin division of Cornwall in August 1916 and sat until his death on 17 January. 1922. [1922]

HARBISON, Thomas James Stanislaus. Lay, Cookstown, Co. Tyrone. S. of John Harbison, Esq., of Cookstown, Co. Tyrone. B. 1864; m. 1st, 1892, Elizabeth, d. of Nathaniel Maguire, Esq.; secondly, 1920, Annie, d. of John Beverdige, Esq. Educ. at Cookstown Academy, and St. Malachy's Coll., Belfast. Admitted a Solicitor 1891. Member of Tyrone County Council 1911. A Nationalist. Elected for E. Tyrone in April 1918, for N.E. Tyrone in December 1918 and for Fermanagh and Tyrone in November 1922 and December 1923. Sat until he retired in October 1924. Returned unopposed for Fermanagh and Tyrone in May 1929 and sat until his death on 22 November 1930. Member of Northern Ireland Parliament for Fermanagh and Tyrone 1921-29. Died 22 November 1930. [1929 2nd ed.]

HARBORD, Sir Arthur, C.B.E. 60 St. Peter's Road, Great Yarmouth. National Liberal. S. of Robert Harbord, Esq. B. 1865; m. Charlotte Nellie, d. of J.M. Belward, Esq. Educ. at British School, and Winchester House School, Great Yarmouth. Member of Yarmouth Town Council from 1898; Alderman from 1916; Mayor 1917-19, 1923-24, and 1934-35. C.B.E. 1935. Knight Bach. 1939. A Liberal until 1931, thereafter a Liberal Nationalist. Elected for Great Yarmouth in November 1922 and sat until he was defeated in October 1924; re-elected for Great Yarmouth in May 1929 and sat until his death on 24 February 1941. [1941]

HARDIE, Agnes Agnew. 44 Hillside Court, London. D. of John Pettigrew, Esq. B. in about 1874; m. 1909, George Hardie, Esq., Member for the Springburn division of Glasgow who died 26 July 1937. Pioneer member and organiser of Shop Assistants' Union. Women's organiser for Labour Party in Scotland 1918-23. A Labour Member. Elected for the Springburn division of Glasgow in September 1937 and sat until she retired in June 1945. Died 24 March 1951. [1945]

HARDIE, David. 18 Albany Drive, Rutherglen, Lanarkshire. S. of David Hardie, Esq., of Grangemouth, Stirlingshire. Younger bro. of James Keir Hardie. B. in about 1860; m. Annie Paton. J.P. for Lanarkshire. Member of Rutherglen Burgh Council from 1910, Provost from 1937. A Labour Member. Elected for the Rutherglen division of Lanarkshire in May 1931 and sat until he was defeated in October 1931. Unsuccessfully contested the Rutherglen division of Lanarkshire in November 1935. Died 8 April 1939.

HARDIE, George Downie Blyth Crookston. 88 Erskine Hill, London. S. of David Hardie and Mary Keir. Younger bro. of Keir Hardie. B. in about 1874; m. 1909, Agnes Agnew Pettigrew, d. of John Pettigrew, Esq. An Engineer. A Labour Member. Unsuccessfully contested the Springburn division of Glasgow in 1918. Sat for the Springburn division of Glasgow from November 1922-October 1931 when he was defeated, and was re-elected there in November 1935. Sat until his death on 26 July 1937. [1937]

HARLAND, Albert. 10 Psalter Lane, Sheffield. 4 Esplanade, Scarborough. S. of the Rev. A.A. Harland, of Harefield, Middlesex. B. 6 September 1869. Educ. at Temple Grove, East Sheen, Rugby, and Corpus Christi Coll., Cambridge. A Snuff Manufacturer. Member of Sheffield County Borough Council from 1902-11, 1923-24 and 1929-36. J.P. A Conservative. Elected for the Ecclesall division of Sheffield in December 1923 and sat until May 1929 when he unsuccessfully contested the Hillsborough division of Sheffield. Died 25 February 1957. [1929]

HARLAND, Henry Peirson. Otterspool, Aldenham, Watford. Union. S. of the Rev. A. Harland, Vicar of Harefield. B. 1876; m. 1917, Helen Reilly, d. of John Barbour, Esq., and widow of Thomas Andrews, Esq. Educ. at Rugby School. Director of Harland and

Wolff Limited, Shipbuilders and Engineers, of Short and Harland Limited, and of the Ocean Transport Company Limited; Chairman of Heaton Tabb and Company Limited. On Staff of Chinese Engineering Company, Tientsin; on Staff of Lord Perrie as Controller of Merchant Shipping 1914-18. M.Inst. C.E., M.I.M.E., M.I.N.A.; member of the Court of the Worshipful Company of Shipwrights, of Gen. Committee of Lloyds Register and of Consultative Committee of Shipbuilders and Engineers conferring with Marine Department of Board of Trade. President and Chairman of Aldenham Conservative Association and Vice-Chairman of Watford Conservative Association. A Unionist. Returned Unopposed for Belfast E. in February 1940 and sat until he retired in June 1945. Died 11 August 1945. [1945]

HARMOOD-BANNER, Sir John Suther-land. Aston Hall, Preston Brook, Cheshire. Carlton. S. of Harmood Walcot Banner, Esq., Accountant. B. 8 September 1847 at Liverpool; m. 1st, 1876, Elizabeth, d. of Thomas Knowles, Esq., of Darnhall Hall, Cheshire, MP for Wigan (she died 1903); secondly, 1908, Ella, d. of J.E.H. Linford, Esq. Educ. at Radley Coll. A Chartered Accountant, member of the firm of Harmood-Banner and Son, of Liverpool; a J.P. and Dept.-Lieut. for Cheshire; High Sheriff 1902; a member of the Liverpool City Council from 1894; and was Chairman of the Finance Committee. Lord Mayor 1912-13. President of the Institute of Chartered Accountants 1904-05, and of the Association of Municipal Corporations 1907. Knighted 1913. A Conservative. Elected for the Everton division of Liverpool in February 1905 and sat until he retired in October 1924. Created Bart. 1924. Adopted the surname Harmood-Banner in lieu of Banner in 1876. Died 24 February 1927. [1924 2nd ed.]

HARMSWORTH, Cecil Bisshopp. 28 Montagu Square, London. Reform, and National Liberal. 3rd s. of Alfred Harmsworth, Esq., Barrister-at-Law, and Geraldine Mary, d. of William Maffett, Esq., of Dublin. B. 28 September 1869 at Hampstead; m. 1897, Emilie Alberta, d. of William Hamilton Maffett, Esq. (she died 1942). Educ. at Trinity Coll., Dublin; sen. moderator in Modern Literature, Stewart Scholar in Literature B.A. 1891, M.A. 1911. Parliamentary Under-Secretary to the Home Office February to May 1915. Parliamentary Private Secretary (unpaid) to Mr. Runciman and Mr. McKenna. A member of the Prime Minister's Secretariat 1917-19. Under-Secretary, Foreign Affairs January 1919-October 1922. Author of *Pleasure and Problem in South Africa.* A Liberal. Unsuccessfully contested the Droitwich division of Worcestershire in 1900, and N.E. Lanarkshire in 1901. Sat for the Droitwich division of Worcestershire from 1906 to January 1910, when he was defeated. Elected for the Luton division of Bedfordshire in July 1911 and December 1918 and sat until he retired in October 1922. Created Baron Harmsworth 1939. Died 13 August 1948. [1922]

HARMSWORTH, Hon. Esmond Cecil. 27 Abingdon Street, London. S. of Lord Rothermere. B. 29 May 1898; m. 1st, 12 January 1920, Margaret Hunam, d. of William Redhead, Esq., and Janet, Lady Lacon (divorced 1938); secondly, 1945, Ann Geraldine Mary, d. of Hon. Guy Charteris and widow of 3rd Baron O'Neill (divorced 1952); thirdly, 1966, Mrs. Mary Ohrstrom, d. of Kenneth Murchison, Esq., of Dallas. Educ. at Eton. Capt. Royal Marine Artillery. A Conservative. Sat for the Isle of Thanet division of Kent from November 1919 until he retired in May 1929. Succeeded to the Peerage as Visct. Rothermere 1940. Chairman of Associated Newspapers Limited 1932-71, President from 1971. Chairman of Newspaper Proprietors Association 1934-61. Chancellor of Newfoundland University 1952-61. Died 12 July 1978. * [1929]

HARMSWORTH, Sir Robert Leicester, Bart. Moray Lodge, Campden Hill, London. Reform. 4th s. of Alfred Harmsworth, Esq., Barrister-at-Law, of the Middle Temple, and Geraldine Mary, d. of William Maffett, Barrister-at-Law, Dublin. B. 1870; m. 1892, Anne, d. of T. Scott, Esq., of

Wandsworth, and Cornard, Suffolk. Educ. at Marylebone Grammar School. Created Bart. 1918. A Liberal. Elected for Caithness in 1900 and for Caithness and Sutherland in December 1918 and sat until he was defeated in November 1922. Chairman of the companies owning the *Western Morning News*, *Western Times* and *The Field*. Died 19 January 1937. [1922]

HARNEY, Edward Augustine St. Aubyn, K.C. 28 Morpeth Mansions, London. S. of Richard Harney, Esq., J.P., of Kiloteran House, Co. Waterford, and Ann M. King, of Co. Tipperary. B. in Dublin 1865; m. 1st, 1897, Clarissa Margaret Benington, d. of R.C. Benington, Esq., M.D. (marriage dissolved in 1922); secondly, 1927, Kathleen, d. of J. Anderson, Esq., of South Shields. Educ. at Clongowes Wood Coll., Ireland (Jesuits), and Trinity Coll., Dublin. Called to the Irish bar 1892, to the Australian bar 1899; K.C. Australia 1905, to the English bar (Gray's Inn) 1906; K.C. England 1920. Member of Australian Senate from 1901-03. Author of essays on *Imperialism in Australia* and *Emigration*. A Liberal. Sat for South Shields from November 1922 until he retired on 10 May 1929. Died 17 May 1929. [1929]

HARRIS, Sir Henry Percy, K.B.E. 98 Gloucester Terrace, London. Cherry Croft, Forest Row, Sussex. Carlton, and Oxford & Cambridge. S. of Sir George David Harris, London County Councillor, and Eliza Margaret, d. of Henry Adderley, Esq. B. 8 September 1856; m. 1st, 1908, Ethel Alice, d. of E. Chivers Bower, Esq., of Broxholme, Scarborough (she died 1933). secondly, 1934, Eva Margaret, d. of A.E. Stearns, Esq. Educ. at Eton, and Christ Church, Oxford. Called to the bar at Lincoln's Inn 1881. Member of London County Council from 1892-1910; Leader of Moderate Party 1904-06; Dept.-Chairman 1898 and Chairman 1907-08. J.P. and Dept.-Lieut. for London. Chairman of London War Pensions Committee. K.B.E. 1917. A Unionist. Elected for S. Paddington in January 1910 and sat until he retired in October 1922. Died 23 August 1941. [1922]

HARRIS, John Hobbis. Denison House, Vauxhall Bridge Road, London. The Glen, Crawley, Sussex. National Liberal. S. of John H. and Elizabeth Harris. B. at Wantage, Berkshire 29 July 1874; m. 6 May 1898, Alice, 2nd d. of Alfred Seeley, Esq., of Frome, Somerset. Educ. at King Alfred's School, Wantage, and privately. Author, traveller and Organizing Secretary to the Anti-Slavery and Aborigines Protection Society. Chairman Finance Committee London Liberal Federation; President Dulwich Liberal Association; member of Committee League of Nations Union, Balkans Committee, and National Liberal Club Committee. Author of *Dawn and Darkest Africa, Chartered Millions, Africa-Slave or Free*, and numerous pamphlets. A Liberal. Unsuccessfully contested N.W. Camberwell in 1922. Elected for N. Hackney in December 1923 and sat until he was defeated in October 1924. Unsuccessfully contested N. Hackney in May 1929 and the Westbury division of Wiltshire in October 1931. Knighted 1933. Died 30 April 1940. [1924 2nd ed.]

HARRIS, Rt. Hon. Sir Percy Alfred, Bart. Morton House, Chiswick Mall, London. Reform, Eighty, and National Liberal. S. of W. Harris, Esq., Merchant, of New Zealand. B. in London 6 March 1876; m. April 1901, Frieda, 2nd d. of J. Astley Bloxam, Esq., F.R.C.S., Senior Surgeon Charing Cross Hospital. Educ. at Harrow, and Trinity Hall, Cambridge. A Barrister-at-Law, Middle Temple 1899. Had interests in New Zealand. Member London County Council from 1907-34 and 1946-52, Chief Progressive Whip 1909-14; Dept. Chairman London County Council 1916; Dept.-Lieut. Co. of London. Honorary Secretary Central Association Volunteer Regiments and V.T.C. 1914-18; Assistant Director Volunteer Services, War Office 1916-18. Created Bart. 1932. Chief Whip of Liberal Parliamentary Party November 1935-July 1945, Dept. Leader 1940-45. PC. 1940. A Liberal. Unsuccessfully contested the Ashford division of Kent in 1906, and Harrow in January 1910. Sat for the Harborough division of Leicestershire from 1916-18. Unsuccessfully contested the Harborough division of

Leicestershire in 1918. Sat for S.W Bethnal Green from November 1922 until he was defeated in July 1945. Unsuccessfully contested Bethnal Green in February 1950. Died 28 June 1952. [1945]

HARRISON, Francis Capel. 6 Charles Street, Mayfair, London. Darningham Hall, Aldborough. Authors'. S. of Edward Francis and Lilian Harrison. B. at Calcutta, 21 June 1863. Unmarried. Educ. at Rugby and Balliol Coll., Oxford. In the Indian Civil Service, retired as Comptroller and Auditor-Gen. of India 1911. Chairman Finance Committee London County Council. C.S.I. 1909. Wrote various papers on currency. A Conservative. Elected for the Kennington division of Lambeth in November 1922 and sat until he retired in November 1923. Died 10 September 1938. [1923]

HARRISON, Gerald Joseph Cuthbert. 63 Tufton Street, London. Junior Carlton. S. of John Robinson, Esq., of Scalesceugh, by Carlisle, and of Croft House, Helensburgh. B. 20 August 1895; m. 23 April 1924, Isobel, d. of James Schmidt, Esq., of Pooley Bridge, Cumberland. Educ. at Charterhouse, and at Exeter Coll., Oxford. Capt. R.A., T.F. 1914; served in Egypt, Palestine and Syria 1916-19. Parliamentary Private Secretary to the Rt. Hon. W.C. Bridgeman, 1st Lord of the Admiralty from 1926-1929. A Conservative. Elected for the Bodmin division of Cornwall in October 1924 and sat until he was defeated in May 1929. High Sheriff of Cumberland 1945-46, Dept.-Lieut. 1953-54. Died 6 December 1954. [1929]

HARTINGTON, Edward William Spencer Cavendish, Marq. of. 85 Eaton Square, London. Churchdale Hall, Ashford, Bakewell. Eld. s. of 9th Duke of Devonshire. B. 6 May 1895; m. 21 April 1917, Lady Mary Cecil, d. of 4th Marq. of Salisbury. Educ. at Eton, and Trinity Coll., Cambridge. Served in France 1915-18, Lieut.-Col. commanding 24th Derbyshire Yeomanry Armoured Car Company. Member of British Delegation, Peace Conference, Paris 1919; Under-Secretary of State for Dominions March 1936-May 1940; Dept.-Lieut. for Derbyshire, Lord-Lieut. 1838-50. A Conservative. Unsuccessfully contested N.E. Derbyshire in December 1918 and W. Derbyshire in November 1922. Sat for W. Derbyshire from December 1923 until May 1938 when he succeeded to the Peerage as 10th Duke of Devonshire. Styled Marq. of Hartington from 1908-38. Under-Secretary of State for India and Burma May 1940-January 1943. Under-Secretary of State for Colonies January 1943-July 1945. M.B.E. 1919; K.G. 1941. Mayor of Buxton 1919-20. High Steward of Cambridge University 1938-50, Chancellor of Leeds University 1939-50. Died 26 November 1950. [1938]

HARTLAND, George Albert. Avondale Hotel, Tavistock Place, London. St. Giles, Norwich. Conservative, and 1900. S. of John Francis Hartland, Esq., M.D., of Aglish, Co. Waterford. B. 14 July 1884. Educ. at St. Francis Xavier's Coll., Liverpool. A Journalist, and Insurance Manager. A Conservative. Elected for Norwich in October 1931 and sat until he retired in October 1935. Died 18 July 1944. [1935]

HARTSHORN, Rt. Hon. Vernon, O.B.E. Hill Crest, Maesteg, Glamorgan. S. of Theophilus Hartshorn, Esq. B. 1872. President of the South Wales Miners' Federation and member of the National Executive of the Miners' Federation of Great Britain. Member of the Coal Controller's Advisory Committee, and of the Coal Trade Organization Committee. Postmaster-Gen. from January-October 1924. Lord Privy Seal June 1930-March 1931. O.B.E. 1918; PC. 1924. A Labour Member. Unsuccessfully contested Mid Glamorgan in March and December 1910. Sat for the Ogmore division of Glamorgan from December 1918 until his death on 13 March 1931. [1931 2nd ed.]

HARVEY, Sir George. 96 Jermyn Street, London. Throsenby, West Kingston, Angmering-on-Sea. S. of John Harvey, Esq., of Scarborough. B. 1870; m. 1894, Sarah, d. of J. Kenward, Esq. Was connected with the Connaught Rooms Limited, and The Cafe Royal Limited. Mayor of Holborn

1920-24; member London County Council 1922-24. Knight Bach. 1936. A Conservative. Elected for the Kennington division of Lambeth in October 1924, and defeated there in May 1929. Re-elected for the Kennington division of Lambeth in October 1931 and again in November 1935. Sat until his death on 27 March 1939.

[1939]

HARVEY, Maj. Samuel Emile. 53 Rutland Gate, London. Dunbridge, Totnes, Devon. Carlton, Cavalry, and Junior Carlton. S. of Sir Robert Harvey, of Dunbridge, Totnes. B. 7 December 1885; m. 8 January 1912, Elizabeth Sybil, d. of R.R. Lockett, Esq., of Liverpool. Educ. at Eton. Served with 1st King's Dragoon Guards November 1905-22. A Conservative. Elected for the Totnes division of Devon in November 1922, but defeated there in December 1923. Re-elected for the Totnes division of Devon in October 1924 and sat until he retired in October 1935. Knighted 1935. J.P. and Dept.-Lieut. for Devon. High Sheriff 1941. Died 9 November 1959.

[1935]

HARVEY, Thomas Edmund. Rydal House, Grosvenor Road, Leeds. Barmoor, Hutton-le-Hole, Yorkshire. S. of William Harvey, Esq., of Leeds. B. 4 January 1875; m. 1911, Alice Irene, d. of Professor Silvanus Thompson, F.R.S. Educ. at Bootham School, York, Yorkshire Coll., and Christ Church, Oxford, M.A., and at Universities of Paris and Berlin. Assistant in British Museum 1900-04; Dept. Warden and Warden of Toynbee Hall 1904-11; member London County Council 1994-07. Parliamentary Private Secretary to Ellis Griffith 1912-13, and to Rt. Hon. Charles Masterman when Financial Secretary to the Treasury 1913-14. Sat for W. Leeds as a Liberal Member from January 1910 until November 1918 when he retired. Unsuccessfully contested Dewsbury in November 1922. Elected for Dewsbury in December 1923, defeated October 1924. Unsuccessfully contested N. Leeds in May 1929. Elected for Combined English Universities as an Independent Progressive Member in March 1937 and sat until he retired in June 1945.

Member of Stepney Borough Council 1909-11. Member of Society of Friends. Master of the Guild of St. George 1934-51. Chairman of National Loan Collection Trust. Died 3 May 1955.

[1954]

HARVIE-WATT, Sir George Steven, Bart. Continued in House after 1945: full entry in Volume IV.

HASLAM, Henry Cobden. 30 Eaton Square, London. Delamere, Skegness, Lincolnshire. Constitutional. S. of Henry Haslam Esq. B. 1870; m. 1899, Julie Henriette Francoise, d. of Edward Dupont, Esq. Educ. at Dover Coll., Gonville and Caius Coll., Cambridge, Sc.D. 1914. Engaged for many years in scientific research at Medical Schools, Cambridge University. Author of numerous Scientific Works. A Conservative. Elected for the Horncastle division of Lincolnshire in October 1924 and sat until he retired in June 1945. M.R.C.S. and L.R.C.P. 1896, St. Thomas' Hospital. Died 7 February 1948.

[1945]

HASLAM, Sir John. 17 Morshead Mansions, London. S. of John Haslam, Esq., of Bromley Cross, Bolton. B. 27 February 1878; m. 4 August 1902, Edith Mary, d. of Alfred Booth, Esq., of Bradshaw, Bolton. Educ. at Chethams Coll., Manchester. Chairman of Organisation Committee of National Federation of Grocers' Associations 1911-23. Member of National Church Assembly 1919-40. J.P. for Bolton; Knight Bach. 1927. A Conservative. Unsuccessfully contested the Westhoughton division of Lancashire in December 1923 and October 1924 and Rochdale in May 1929. Elected for Bolton in October 1931 and sat until his death on 21 May 1940.

[1940]

HASLAM, Lewis. 8 Wilton Crescent, London. Reform, Bath, Ranelagh, and National Liberal. S. of John Haslam, Esq., J.P., of Gilnow House, Bolton, and Jane, d. of Joshua Crook, Esq., of White Bank, Bolton. B. 25 April 1856 at Bolton; m. 1893, Helen Norma, d. of Henry Dixon, Esq., of Watlington, Oxfordshire. Educ. privately, at University Coll. School, and University

Coll., London. J.P. for Lancashire. Officer Order of the Crown of Belgium. A Liberal. Unsuccessfully contested the Westhoughton division of Lancashire in 1892, and the Stamford division of Lincolnshire in 1900. Sat for Monmouth District from 1906-18. Elected for Newport in December 1918 and sat until his death on 12 September 1922.

[1922]

HASTINGS, Sir Patrick Gardiner, K.C. 5 Paper Buildings, Temple, London. S. of Gardiner Hastings, Esq. B. 1880; m. 1906, Mary Ellenore, d. of Col. Grundy. Educ. at Charterhouse. A Mining Engineer and Journalist. A Barrister-at-Law, Middle Temple 1904; K.C. 1919; Bencher. Saw service in the South African War. Created Knight 1924. Attorney-Gen. January-October 1924. A Labour Member. Sat for Wallsend from November 1922 until he resigned in 1926. Retired from the bar 1948. Author of a number of plays, including *Scotch Mist* and *The Blind Goddess*, and film scripts. Died 26 February 1952.   [1926]

HASTINGS, Somerville. Continued in House after 1945: full entry in Volume IV.

HAWKE, John Anthony, K.C. 1 Essex Court, Temple, London. Carlton, and Garrick. S. of Edward Henry Hawke, Esq., J.P., and Emily Catherine Wooldridge. B. 7 June 1869; m. 1894, Winifred, d. of N.H. Stevens, Esq., M.D. Educ. at Merchant Taylors' School, and St. John's Coll., Oxford, Honorary Fellow 1931. A Barrister-at-Law, Middle Temple 1892; K.C. 1913; Bencher 1923. Attorney-Gen. to H.R.H. the Prince of Wales 1923. Recorder of Plymouth 1912. A Conservative. Elected for the St. Ives division of Cornwall in November 1922. Unsuccessfully contested the same division in December 1923. Re-elected for the St. Ives division of Cornwall in October 1924 and sat until 1928 when he was appointed a High Court Judge. Knighted 1928. Treasurer of Middle Temple 1937. Vice-Chairman of Bar Council 1924-28. Judge of the King's Bench Division 1928-41. Died 30 October 1941.   [1928]

HAY, Capt. John Primrose. 12 Miller Street, Shawlands, Glasgow. S. of William Hay, Esq., Master Saddler, of Coatbridge. B. at Coatbridge 4 April 1878; m. in Shanghai Cathedral 1909, Jeanie Scott Bell, of Glasgow. Educ. at Glasgow Free Church Training Coll., and Glasgow University. Lecturer in mathematics, Manchuria Christian Coll., 1906-15. Commissioned in R.G.A. September 1915; served in France till April 1919. A Labour Member. Elected for the Cathcart division of Glasgow in November 1922 and sat until he was defeated in December 1923. Defeated again in Cathcart in 1924 and May 1929. Died 5 December 1949.   [1923]

HAY, Maj. Thomas William. Fulmer Place, Fulmer, Buckinghamshire. Cavalry, and Pratt's. S. of Admiral of the Fleet Lord John Hay, MP and Lady John Hay. B. at Fulmer, Buckinghamshire 25 August 1882. Unmarried, Educ. at Clifton Coll. Maj. in the Leicestershire Yeomanry. A Conservative. Elected for S. Norfolk in November 1922 and sat until he was defeated in December 1923. Served in R.A.F.V.R., Squadron Leader 1941. Died 10 July 1956.

[1923]

HAYCOCK, Alexander Wilkinson Frederick. House of Commons, London. S. of J.L. Haycock, Esq. B. in Canada 28 December 1882. Educ. at Cataraqui School, at Kingston Collegiate Institute, and at Queen's University, Toronto. A Labour Member. Unsuccessfully contested the Winchester division of Hampshire in November 1922. Sat for Salford W. from December 1923-October 1924, when he was defeated. Re-elected for Salford W. in May 1929 and sat until he was again defeated in October 1931. Unsuccessfully contested Salford W. in November 1935 and the Bucklow division of Cheshire in July 1945. Barrister-at-Law, Gray's Inn 1939. Died 15 December 1970.   [1931 2nd ed.]

HAYDAY, Arthur. 28 Stamford Road, West Bridgford, Nottingham. S. of Thomas Bloomfield Hayday, Esq. B. 24 October 1869 at the Tidal Basin, West Ham; m. twice. Educ. at the St. Luke's National

School, Tidal Basin. A Chemical Worker; Trimmer and Stoker in the merchant service; Permanent Official National Union of General Workers 37 years; represented I.L.O. Section of League of Nations at S. American States Conference, Santiago 1935-36; Councillor and Alderman of West Ham 1896-1910. British Trade Union Representative at American Labour Convention 1917; Parliamentary Private Secretary to Rt. Hon. J.R. Clynes January-October 1924 and 1929-31. A Labour Member. Sat for W. Nottingham from December 1918-October 1931 when he was defeated; re-elected for W. Nottingham in November 1935 and sat until he retired in June 1945. President of T.U.C. 1930-31. Died 28 February 1956. [1945]

HAYES, Hugh. Lurgan, Co. Down. M. 1st, Frances Lyness, of Waringstown; Secondly, widow of Dr. Hugh Atkinson, of London. A Solicitor, admitted 1882. A Presbyterian. A Unionist. Elected for W. Down in February 1922 and sat until he retired in October 1922. Died 5 September 1928.

HAYES, John. Skibbereen, Co. Cork. Was very active in propaganda work for the new movement in Ireland. Arrested in raid on Sinn Fein offices, Dublin November 1919 and sentenced to three months imprisonment. Re-arrested m. 1920. A Sinn Fein Member. Returned unopposed for W. Cork in December 1918 but did not take his seat. Member of Dail for W. Cork to 1923, as a Pro-Treaty Member. Editor of *Southern Star* published in Skibbereen. [1922]

HAYES, John Henry. 57 Clapton Common, London. S. of Police-Inspector J.W. Hayes. B. at Wolverhampton 14 October 1889; m. 19 July 1913, Ethel, 2nd d. of St. Thomas Stroudley, School-master, of Albrighton. Educ. at St. Mark's, and Science and Technical Schools, Wolverhampton. A Sergeant in the Metropolitan Police 1909-19. Parliamentary Private Secretary to F.O. Roberts, Minister of Pensions January-October 1924. A Labour Whip from 1925-31. Vice-Chamberlain of the Royal Household June 1929-August 1931. A Labour Member. Unsuccessfully contested the Edge Hill division of Liverpool in November 1922. Sat for the Edge Hill division from March 1923 until he was defeated in October 1931; again defeated in November 1935. Member of editorial board of *Police Review*. Secretary of British Optical Association. Died 25 April 1941. [1931 2nd ed.]

HAYES, Dr. Richard Francis Thomond House, South Circular Road, Dublin. Educ. at Catholic University, Dublin. A member of the Sinn Fein Executive, sentenced to 20 years penal servitude in connection with fighting in the Swords district of N. County Dublin 1916; released; re-arrested in Dublin May 1918; interned in Reading prison. A Sinn Fein Member. Elected for E. Limerick in December 1918 but did not take his seat. Member of Dail for E. Limerick to 1923, for Co. Limerick 1923-24. A Pro-Treaty, later Cumann na nGaedheal Member. Author of *Biographical Dictionary of Irishmen in France, Ireland and Irishmen in the French Revolution, Irish Swordsmen of France, Old Irish Links with France* and *The Last Invasion of Ireland*. [1922]

HAYWARD, Evan. 38 Hyde Park Gate, London. National Liberal. S. of Robert Hayward, Esq., of Fishponds, Gloucestershire. B. 2 April 1876; m. 1913, Elizabeth Marion Bergfeldt, of Boston, U.S.A. Educ. at British School, and Katherine, Lady Berkeley's Grammar School, Wotton-under-Edge. A Solicitor, admitted 1900 and practised in London and West Hartlepool. A Liberal. Elected for S.E. Durham in January 1910 and for the Seaham division of Durham Co. in December 1918. Sat until he was defeated in November 1922. Served in Worcester Regiment, Maj. Died 30 January 1958. [1922]

HEADLAM, Rt. Hon. Sir Cuthbert Morley, Bart. Continued in House after 1945: full entry in Volume IV.

HEALY, Cahir. Continued in House after 1945: full entry in Volume IV.

HEATHCOTE-DRUMMOND-WILL-OUGHBY, Hon. Claud. See WILL-OUGHBY, Hon. Claud Heathcote-Drummond-.

HEILGERS, Maj. Frank Frederick Alexander. Wyken Hall, Bardwell, Suffolk. Carlton, Travellers', and Boodle's. S. of A.F. Heilgers, Esq., of Wannock, Polegate. B. 25 June 1892. Unmarried. Educ. at Harrow, and Magdalen Coll., Oxford, M.A. A Farmer. J.P. for Suffolk; Alderman W. Suffolk County Council; Parliamentary Private Secretary to the Rt. Hon. Walter Elliot when Minister of Agriculture December 1935-October 1936, and to the Rt. Hon. H. Ramsbotham, Minister of Pensions May 1937-June 1939, and when 1st Commissioner of Works June 1939-February 1940. Served in Gallipoli, Egypt and Palestine 1915-19. Rejoined the army September 1939. A Conservative. Elected for the Bury St. Edmunds division of Suffolk in October 1931, was returned unopposed for the Bury St. Edmunds division of Suffolk in November 1935. Sat until his death in a railway accident on 16 January 1944. [1944]

HELMORE, Air Commodore William, C.B.E. Shotover, Coombe Lane, Kingston Hill. Athenaeum, and Royal Air Force. S. of William Reynolds Helmore, Esq., Solicitor. B. 1 March 1894; m. 5 September 1939, Enid Sylvia, d. of Henry Edward Capes, Esq., J.P., of Stowcroft, Chislehurst. Educ. at Blundells School, Royal Military Academy, Woolwich, and Christ's Coll., Cambridge, Ph.D., M.Sc. Served with R.F.C. in France 1916 and later with R.A.F. Retired 1937, but returned to the active list 1939. R.A.F. War Commentator 1941-43. Assistant Scientific Adviser to Chief of Air Staff 1939; Technical Adviser Ministry of Aircraft Production 1941-45. A Conservative. Elected for the Watford division of Hertfordshire in February 1943 and sat until he was defeated in July 1945. C.B.E. 1942. Technical Director of Castrol. Director-Gen. of Aluminium Association 1946. Fellow of Chemical Society and of Royal Aeronautical Society. Member of Brabazon Committee on Civil Aviation 1943-45. Chairman of Civil Aviation Committee on Certification of Aircraft 1947-48. Died 18 January 1964. [1945]

HELY-HUTCHINSON, Maurice Robert, M.C. 16 Cadogan Square, London. Carlton, Beefsteak, and City University. S. of the Rt. Hon. Sir Walter Hely-Hutchinson, G.C.M.G. B. 22 May 1887; m. 11 August 1920, Melita, d. of Admiral Sir Colin Keppel, K.C.I.E., K.C.V.O., C.B., D.S.O. Educ. at Eton, and Balliol Coll., Oxford. Lieut. Irish Guards 1915-18. A Merchant Banker. Member of Milk Marketing Board from 1933-45. A Conservative. Elected for Hastings in November 1937 and sat until he retired in June 1945. M.C. 1917. Chairman of Tanganyika Concessions Limited. Died 11 February 1961. [1945]

HAMMERDE, Edward George, K.C. 9 Chelsea Manor Studios, Flood Street, Chelsea. S. of James George Hemmerde, Esq., Manager of the Imperial Ottoman Bank. B. 13 November 1871 at Peckham; m. 30 September 1903, Lucy Elinor Colley, d. of Charles Courtney Colley, Esq., of Streatham (divorced 1922). Educ. at Winchester, and University Coll., Oxford. Barrister-at-Law, Inner Temple 1897. K.C. 1908. Recorder of Liverpool from 1909-48. Wrote the following plays, *A Butterfly on the Wheel*, *The Crucible* in collaboration with Francis Neilson, MP, and alone *Proud Maisie*, *A Cardinal's Romance*, and *A Maid of Honour*. A Labour Member. Unsuccessfully contested Winchester in 1900, Shrewsbury in January 1906. Represented E. Denbighshire from August 1906-December 1910. Unsuccessfully contested Portsmouth in December 1910. Sat for N.W. Norfolk from 1912-18, when he retired, all as a Liberal. Elected for the Crewe division of Cheshire in November 1922 and December 1923 and sat until he was defeated in October 1924. Died 24 May 1948. [1924 2nd ed.]

HENDERSON, Arthur. Continued in House after 1945: full entry in Volume IV.

HENDERSON, Rt. Hon. Arthur. Transport House, Smith Square, London. S. of

David Henderson, Esq. B. 1863; m. 1888, Eleanor, d. of W. Watson, Esq., of Forest Row. Educ. at St. Mary's School, Newcastle-on-Tyne. Appenticed to Robert Stephenson and Company and held several official positions in connection with Trade Union Societies. Secretary of the N.E. Coast Conciliation Board from 1894. A member of Newcastle City Council and Durham County Council and Darlington Borough Council; Mayor 1903. Chairman of the Labour Party in the House of Commons 1908-10 and 1914-17. President of Board of Education 1915-16. Paymaster-Gen. and Labour Adviser to H.M. Government August-December 1916. Member of War Cabinet, without portfolio December 1916-August 1917, when he resigned. Secretary of State for Home Affairs January-November 1924; Secretary of State for Foreign Affairs June 1929-August 1931. Member of Railway Commission 1911. J.P. for Durham. Chief Labour Whip 1914, 1921-24 and 1925-27. PC. 1915. Chairman of Disarmament Conference Geneva from 1931. Secretary of National Executive of Labour Party 1912-35. Treasurer of Labour Representation Committee 1904-06 and of National Executive of Labour Party 1906-12. Leader of Labour Party and Leader of Opposition August-October 1931. Nobel Peace Prize 1934. A Labour Member. Sat for the Barnard Castle division of Durham from July 1903-December 1918. Unsuccessfully contested East Ham S. in December 1918. Sat for the Widnes division of Lancashire from August 1919 until 1922 when he was defeated. Elected for Newcastle E. in January 1923; defeated in December 1923. Elected for Burnley in February and October 1924 and in May 1929. Unsuccessfully contested Burnley in October 1931. Sat for the Claycross division of Derbyshire from September 1933 until his death on 20 October 1935.
[1935]

HENDERSON, John James Craik. 190 St. Vincent Street, Glasgow. Carlton. S. of Robert Jenkinson Henderson, Esq. B. 21 December 1890; m. 27 September 1917, Ivie Hester Mary, d. of H.L. Hertslet, M.V.O., of the Lord Chamberlain's Department. Educ. at George Watson's Coll., Edinburgh, and University of Glasgow. Senior partner of Miller Thompson, Henderson and Company, Solicitors, of Glasgow. Professor of Mercantile Law, University of Glasgow 1929-40. Capt. Royal Scots, served 1914-19. Director of Law Union and Rock Insurance Company, of James Howden and Company Limited, and other companies; Chairman of Hillhead Unionist Association. A Conservative. Elected for N.E. Leeds in March 1940 and sat until he was defeated in July 1945. Knighted 1953. Died 3 December 1971.
[1945]

HENDERSON, Joseph. Continued in House after 1945: full entry in Volume IV.

HENDERSON, Capt, Robert Ronald. House of Commons, London. S. of J. Henderson, Esq., Dept.-Lieut., and J.P. B. 1876; m. 20 July 1909, Margaret, d. of Sir George Dashwood, 6th Bart., of Kirtlington. Capt. 3rd Hussars; served in India, in South African War 1899-1901, and in France 1914-18. J.P. for Buckinghamshire and Oxfordshire. A Conservative. Unsuccessfully contested the Gainsborough division of Lincolnshire in January 1910. Elected for the Henley division of Oxfordshire in October 1924 and sat until his death on 16 January 1932.
[1932]

HENDERSON, Thomas. Drumayne, Govan, Glasgow. B. at Burntisland, Fife, 1867. Worked as a Ship's Carpenter on the Clyde and in Belfast. A member of the Board of Management of a Glasgow Co-operative Society; member of Glasgow Town Council 1919-22. A Labour Whip from 1925-1931. Comptroller of the Royal Household June 1929-August 1931. A Labour Member. Sat for the Tradeston division of Glasgow from November 1922 until October 1931, when he was defeated; re-elected for the Tradeston division in November 1935 and sat until he retired in June 1945. C.B.E. 1931. Died 28 January 1960.
[1945]

HENDERSON, Sir Thomas. 7 Nottingham Place. Langlands, Hawick. S. of James Henderson, Esq., J.P., and Elizabeth J. Cruickshank. B. at Hawick 15 July 1874;

m. 1900, Helen Scott, d. of James Thyne, Esq., of Edinburgh. Educ. at Hawick, and Blairlodge School. A Hosiery Manufacturer (Innes, Hendersons Limited). J.P. and Honorary Sheriff Substitute for Roxburghshire. Held various local offices. Knighted 1919. A National Liberal. Elected for Roxburgh and Selkirk in November 1922 and sat until he was defeated in December 1923. Died 3 May 1951.   [1923]

HENDERSON, Col. Sir Vivian Leonard, M.C. 17 Kidderpore Gardens, London. Carlton. S. of Francis Henderson, Esq., J.P., and Alice, d. of Sir C.F. Hamond, MP. B. 6 October 1884; m. 1913, Eileen Marjorie, d. of Brigadier-Gen. G.W. Dowell, C.M.G., C.B.E. Educ. at Uppingham, and Sandhurst. Joined Loyal North Lancashire Regiment 1904; Lieut. Reserve of Officers 1911; Capt. S.R. 1914; Lieut.-Col Commanding 3rd Loyal North Lancashire Regiment 1921. Aide-de-Camp and P.S. to Sir Cavendish Boyle, Gov. of Mauritius 1909-11. Served in France etc. 1914-18, M.C. 1914. Dept.-Lieut. for London 1937. J.P. for London 1934. Parliamentary Private Secretary to Sir James Craig, Parliamentary Secretary to Ministry of Pensions 1919-20; member of Central Advisory Pensions Council. Member of Royal Commission on Fire Prevention 1921. Honorary Secretary King's Roll National Council 1923-27. Chairman of Estimates Committee 1926 and 1927 and from 1931-35. Under-Secretary of State for the Home Department November 1927-June 1929. Knight Bach. 1927. A Conservative. Sat for the Tradeston division of Glasgow from December 1918 until 1922, when he was defeated. Unsuccessfully contested Bootle in 1923, and was elected there in 1924 and defeated May 1929. Elected for the Chelmsford division of Essex in October 1931 and sat until he retired in October 1935. Chairman of Domestic Proceedings Court Hampstead Petty Sessions 1937-59. Chairman of Fire Service Research Trust 1940-60. Died 3 February 1965.   [1935]

HENDERSON, William Watson. 81 Carlisle Mansions, Carlisle Place, London. S. of the Rt. Hon. Arthur Henderson, MP, Secretary of State for Foreign Affairs 1929-31. B. 8 August 1891. Educ. at Queen Elizabeth Grammar School, Darlington. A Journalist from 1912. Secretary Joint Press and Publicity Department Trade Union Congress and Labour Party 1921-45. Editor of *The Labour Magazine*. Parliamentary Private Secretary to the Rt. Hon. Wedgwood Benn, Secretary of State for India, December 1929. A Labour Member. Elected for the Enfield division of Middlesex in December 1923, defeated October 1924. Re-elected for the Enfield division of Middlesex in May 1929 and sat until he retired in October 1931. Private Secretary to Rt. Hon. John Hodge when Minister of Labour 1917. Created Baron Henderson 1945. Lord in Waiting to the King and Government Whip in the House of Lords October 1945-June 1948, and Additional member of the Air Council 1945-47. Under-Secretary of State for Foreign Affairs June 1948-October 1951. PC. 1950. Chairman of Alliance Building Society 1966-72, Director 1955-75. Representative of the Labour Peers on the Executive Committee of Parliamentary Labour Party 1952-55.*

[1931 2nd ed.]

HENDERSON-STEWART, Sir James Henderson, Bart. Continued in House after 1945: full entry in Volume IV.

HENEAGE, Lieut.-Col. Sir Arthur Pelham, D.S.O. Walesby Hall, Market Rasen, Lincolnshire. Cavalry. S. of Capt. F.W. Heneage, R.E. B. 1881; m. 1912, Anne, d. of Brigadier-Gen. N.D. Findlay, C.B. Educ. at Eton, and Royal Military Academy, Woolwich. Lieut.-Col. R.H.A. and R.F.A.; served in France, etc. 1914-18; member of Inter-allied Commission of Control, Berlin. Vice-President Urban District Councils Association 1925-45 and of Rural District Councils Association 1931-45. Dept.-Lieut. for Lincolnshire. J.P. for Parts of Lindsey. Chairman of Central Chamber of Agriculture 1928. President of Catchment Boards Association; Honorary Col. 53rd (City of London) Anti-Aircraft Battalion R.A. (T.) Parliamentary Private Secretary to P.J. Pybus, Esq., Minister of Transport November 1931-February 1933 and to Sir

Walter Womersley, Assistant Postmaster-Gen. 1936 to September 1939 and when Minister of Pensions September 1939-June 1945. Member of Central Advisory Water Committee Ministry of Health and Central Advisory Committee Ministry of Pensions. A Conservative. Elected for the Louth division of Lincolnshire in October 1924 and sat until he retired in June 1945. Knighted January 1945. D.S.O. 1917. Member of Lindsey County Council. High Sheriff of Lincolnshire 1947. Died 22 November 1971. [1945]

HENN, Sir Sydney Herbert Holcroft, K.B.E. 6 Evelyn Gardens, London. Windham, City of London, and Royal Automobile. S. of the Rev. John Henn, Hon. Canon of Manchester. B. at Manchester 4 December 1861; m. 8 September 1892, Frances Amie Edith, d. of Frederick B. Shanklin, Esq. Educ. at Marlborough, and Manchester Grammar School. A Merchant, with the firm of Duncan, Fox and Company, from January 1881 to December 1913. Director of Army Priority at War Office 1917-19. Member of Disposal Board Ministry of Munitions 1919-21. K.B.E. 1918. A Conservative. Sat for Blackburn from November 1922 until he was defeated in May 1929. Died 21 October 1936. [1929]

HENNESSY, Maj. Sir George Richard James, Bart., O.B.E. 32 Belgrave Square, London. Grayshott Hall, Grayshott, Hampshire. Carlton, and Marlborough. S. of Richard Hennessy, Esq. B. 23 March 1877; m. 14 December 1898, Ethel Mary, d. of C. Wynter, Esq. (she died 1951). Educ. at Eton. Served in South African War 1900-01, and in France 1915-18 with K.R.R.C. Member of Hampshire County Council 1910-19. J.P., High Sheriff 1911. O.B.E. (mil.) 1918. Parliamentary Private Secretary (unpaid) to T. Macnamara, Minister of Labour 1921-22; Junior Lord of the Treasury December 1922-January 1924, and November 1924-December 1925. Vice-Chamberlain of H.M's. Household December 1925-January 1928; Treasurer of H.M's. Household January 1928-June 1929 and September-November 1931; and Dept. Chief Whip from January 1928-

November 1931. Created Bart. 1927. A Conservative. Sat for the Winchester division of Hampshire from December 1918 until he retired in October 1931. Vice-Chairman of Conservative Party Organisation 1931-41. Created Baron Windlesham 1937. Died 8 October 1953. [1931 2nd ed.]

HENNIKER-HUGHAN, Vice-Admiral Sir Arthur John, Bart. Airds, Parton, Kirkcudbrightshire. Naval & Military. S. of Sir Brydges Henniker, 4th Bart., of Newton Hall. Succeeded his bro. in 1908. B. 24 January 1866; m. 26 January 1904, Inger, d. of Graham Hutchison, Esq., of Balmaghie, Castle Douglas (she died 1923). Assumed the additional surname of Hughan in 1896. Entered Royal Navy 1879. Capt. of *Ajax* 1914-16. C.B. 1919. Rear-Admiral 1916; retired 1919. Vice-Admiral 1920, Admiral 1925. Administrative Superintendent of Devonport Dockyard 1916-1919. A Conservative. Elected for Galloway in October 1924 and sat until his death on 4 October 1925. [1925]

HENRY, Sir Charles Solomon, Bart. 5 Carlton Gardens, London. Parkwood, Henley-on-Thames. Brooklands, Wellington, Shropshire. Devonshire, National Liberal, Royal Automobile, British Empire, Eighty, and Portland. S. of I.S. Henry, Esq., of Adelaide, South Australia. B. 1860 at Adelaide; m. 1892, Julia, d. of Leonard Lewisohn, Esq., of New York. Educ. at Marylebone and All Souls Grammar School (in connection with King's Coll.) and the University of Göttingen. The founder and Managing Director of C.S. Henry and Company Limited, Merchants, London. Created Bart. 1911. J.P. for Berkshire. A Coalition Liberal. Unsuccessfully contested the Chelmsford division of Essex in 1900. Elected for the Wellington division of Shropshire in 1906 and sat until 1918. Returned unopposed for The Wrekin division of Shropshire in December 1918 and sat until his death on 27 December 1919. [1920]

HENRY, Rt. Hon. Denis Stanislans, K.C. 28 Fitzwilliam Square, Dublin. Carlton, Constitutional, and Ulster. S. of James and

Ellen Kelly Henry. B. at Cahore, Draperstown, Co. Derry 1864; m. 1910, Violet, d. of the Rt. Hon. Hugh Holmes. Educ. at Mount St. Mary's Coll., Chesterfield, and Queen's Coll., Belfast. Barrister (Ireland) 1885; Q.C. 1896; Bencher, King's Inns 1898. Solicitor-Gen. for Ireland 1918-19; Attorney-Gen. for Ireland 1919-21; PC. (Ireland) 1919. A Commissioner of Charitable Donations and Bequests, Ireland; Chairman of the Dublin Riots Commission. J.P. and Dept.-Lieut. for Londonderry. A Unionist. Unsuccessfully contested N. Tyrone in 1906 and 1907. Elected for S. Londonderry in May 1916 and sat until August 1921 when he was appointed Lord Chief Justice of N. Ireland. A Roman Catholic. Created Bart. 1922. Senator, Queen's University, Belfast. Died 1 October 1925. [1921]

HEPWORTH, Joseph. Woodlawn, Apperley Bridge, Bradford. S. of Elijah Hepworth, Esq., of Bradford. B. in about 1876. Managing Director of Hepworth and Grandage, Engineers. Vice-President of Institute of British Foundrymen. A Conservative. Elected for Bradford E. in October 1931 and sat until his death on 11 May 1945. [1945]

HERBERT, Sir Alan Patrick. Continued in House after 1945: full entry in Volume IV.

HERBERT, Hon. Aubrey Nigel Henry Molyneux. 28 Bruton Street, London. Pixton Park, Dulverton. St. James, Bath, and Travellers'. S. of 4th Earl of Carnarvon. B. 1880; m. 1910, Hon. Mary Gertrude Vesey, d. of 4th Visct de Vesci. Educ. at Eton, and Balliol Coll., Oxford, B.A. Honorary Attaché in the Diplomatic Service Tokyo 1902, Constantinople 1904. Lieut. Royal North Devon Yeomanry; resigned 1903. Served with Expeditionary Force in France 1914; Capt. Special Reserve Irish Guards (wounded); served in Egypt and Gallipoli 1915, and Mesopotamia and Salonika 1916. Gen. Staff Officer with temporary rank of Lieut.-Col. 1918. Private Secretary to Mr. Duke when Chief Secretary for Ireland. Fellow of Royal Geographical Society. A Conservative. Unsuccessfully

contested S. Somerset in January and December 1910. Elected for the same constituency in November 1911. Returned for the Yeovil division of Somerset in December 1918 and sat until his death on 26 September 1923. [1923]

HERBERT, Rt. Hon. Sir Dennis Henry, K.B.E. Clarendon Lodge, Watford. Carlton, and City of London. S. of the Rev. Henry Herbert, Rector of Hemingford Abbots, Huntingdonshire. B. 25 February 1869; m. 1903, Mary Graeme, d. of Valentine Graeme Bell, Esq., C.M.G. Educ. at King's School, Ely, and Wadham Coll., Oxford, Honorary Fellow 1933. Admitted a Solicitor 1895. Member of Council of the Law Society, President 1941-42. Member of the Hertfordshire County Council from 1912. County Alderman 1933, Dept.-Lieut., and J.P. for Hertfordshire. K.B.E. 1929. Dept.-Chairman of Ways and Means, House of Commons June 1928-June 1929. Chairman of Ways and Means and Dept. Speaker September 1931-December 1942. PC. 1933. A Conservative. Sat for the Watford division of Hertfordshire from 1918 until January 1943 when he was created Baron Hemingford. Chairman of Equity and Law Life Assurance Society 1931-40. Died 10 December 1947. [1943]

HERBERT, George. House of Commons, London. Heworth Cottage, York. S. of William Herbert, Esq., of York. B. 1892; m. 1916, Elsie, d. of G.E.Barton, Esq., of York (she died 1952). Served in Army 1914-19 and 1939-44, Maj. M.B.E. 1917. A Conservative. Elected for Rotherham in October 1931 and sat until he resigned in February 1933. Food Controller, Gibraltar. Author of works on trade and land settlement.* [1933]

HERBERT, Lieut.-Col. John Arthur. 14 Montagu Square, London. Llanover, Abergavenny. Carlton, Turf, and Bucks. S. of Sir Arthur Herbert, G.C.V.O., of Coldbrook, Abergavenny. B. 1895; m. 11 June 1924, Lady Mary Fox-Strangways, d. of Giles, 6th Earl of Ilchester. Educ. at Wellington, and Harvard, U.S.A. Joined Royal Horse Guards 1915; served in France and Flanders 1916-18; Maj. 1930, retired 1934. Lieut.-Col. 2nd Battalion Monmouthshire Regiment (T.A.) 1939. Aide-de-Camp to Viceroy of India 1926-28; Dept.-Lieut., J.P., and County Councillor for Monmouth; Parliamentary Private Secretary to Lord Stanley, when Parliamentary Secretary to the Admiralty April 1936, and when Parliamentary Under-Secretary for India May 1937. A Conservative. Elected for the Monmouth division of Monmouthshire in June 1934 and sat until June 1939 when he was appointed Gov. of Bengal; retired October 1943. Assistant Government Whip (unpaid) 1937-39. Died 11 December 1943.   [1939]

HERBERT, Sir Sidney, Bart. 32 Hill Street, London. Boyton Manor, Wiltshire. Carlton, and Turf. S. of Hon. Sir Michael Herbert. B. 29 July 1890. Unmarried. Educ. at Eton, and Balliol Coll., Oxford. Served with Royal Horse Guards in France 1915-18. Private Secretary to the Secretary of State for War 1919-20. Parliamentary Private Secretary to the President of the Board of Education November 1922 to August 1923, and to the Prime Minister August 1923-January 1924 and November 1924-27. Created Bart 1936. A Conservative. Sat for the Scarborough and Whitby division of the N. Riding of Yorkshire from November 1922 until April 1931, when he resigned. Sat for the Abbey division of Westminster from July 1932 until his death at Cannes on 22 March 1939.   [1939]

HERRIOTTS, John. 31 Eden Terrace, Ferryhill, Co. Durham. S. of Joseph Herriotts, Esq., Miner. B. 13 September 1874 at Tredegar, Monmouthshire; m. 1900, Frances Ann Ingman. A Checkweighman at Windlestone Colliery. J.P. for Co. Durham. Member of the Durham County Council 1907-10. A Labour Member. Unsuccessfully contested the Sedgefield division of Durham Co. in 1918. Elected for the Sedgefield division in November 1922, defeated December 1923 and October 1924. Re-elected in May 1929 and sat until he was defeated in October 1931. Member of Sedgefield Rural District Council 1934-35. Died 27 June 1935.   [1931 2nd ed.]

HEWART, Rt. Hon. Sir Gordon, K.C. Garden Hill, Totteridge, Hertfordshire. 2 Harcourt Buildings, Temple, London. Reform, Garrick, and National Liberal. S. of G. Hewart, Esq., of Bury. B. 7 January 1870 at Bury, Lancashire; m. 1st, 1892, Sara Wood, d. of J. Hacking Riley, Esq., of Bury (she died 1933); secondly, 1934, Jean, d. of J.R. Stewart, Esq., of New Zealand. Educ. at Bury Grammar School, Manchester Grammar School, and University Coll., Oxford, (Scholar 1887, B.A. 1891, M.A. 1893). Was called to the bar at the Inner Temple 1902; member of the Northern Circuit; K.C. 1912. Solicitor-Gen. December 1916 to January 1919; Attorney-Gen. January 1919 to March 1922. Member of Cabinet 1921-22. Knighted in 1916. Bencher of the Inner Temple 1917. PC. 1918. J.P. for the Co. of Hertford. A Liberal. Unsuccessfully contested N.W. Manchester in 1912. Elected for Leicester in June 1913, and for E. Leicester in December 1918 and sat until March 1922 when he was appointed Lord Chief Justice and Created Baron Hewart. Lord Chief Justice 1922-40. President of Classical Association 1926, and of English Association 1929. President of War Compensation Court 1922-29. Created Visct. Hewart 1940. Honorary Fellow of University Coll., Oxford. Died 5 May 1943.   [1922]

HEWETT, Sir John Prescott, G.C.S.I. 8 Cumberland Mansions, Bryanston Square, London. Carlton, Arthur's, Oriental, and Garrick. S. of the Rev. John Hewett and Anna Louisa Lyster Hamner. B. 25 August 1854 at Barham, Kent; m. December 1879, Ethel Charlotte, d. of H.B. Webster, Esq., of Bengal Civil Service. Educ. at Winchester Coll., and Balliol Coll., Oxford. Entered the Bengal Civil Service 13 December 1877; retired 15 September 1912. Secretary to Government Home Department 1889; Chief Commissioner, Central Provinces 1902; member of Council for India 1904; Lieut.-Gov. of United Provinces 1907-12. President of the Coronation Durbar Committee Delhi 1911. K.B.E. 1917. A Conservative. Elected for the Luton division of Bedfordshire in November 1922 and sat until he was defeated in December 1923. Died 27 September 1941.   [1923]

HEWLETT, Thomas Henry. Dunham Knoll, Altrincham, Cheshire. Constitutional. Clarendon, Manchester. S. of Alderman Thomas R. Hewlett, of Manchester. B. 23 November 1882; m. 5 August 1931, Joan Margaret, d. of J.H.S. Allen, Esq. Educ. at Manchester. Chairman and Managing Director of Anchor Chemical Company Limited, Clayton, Manchester, and of Joseph Anderson and Sons Limited, Clayton, Manchester; J.P. for Manchester. Acting Chairman of Manchester Conservative and Unionist Association; President of Clayton Conservative Club and of Windsor Institute (Pendleton Ragged School); Honorary Treasurer of Manchester and Salford Street Children's Mission. Controller of Dyestuffs, Board of Trade November 1941, An Underwriting Member of Lloyds; a Director of The District Bank Limited. A Conservative. Unsuccessfully contested the Clayton division of Manchester in October 1935. Returned unopposed for the Exchange division of Manchester in September 1940 and sat until he was defeated in July 1945. Died 25 May 1956.   [1945]

HICKMAN, Brigadier-Gen. Thomas Edgecomb, D.S.O., C.B. Wergs Hall, Wolverhampton. Kildonan Lodge, Kildonan, Sutherland. Carlton, St. Stephen's Naval & Military, Prince's, and Hurlingham. S. of Sir Alfred Hickman, MP, 1st Bart. B. 25 July 1859; m. 1907, Elizabeth Maud, d. of Surgeon-Maj. J.A. Smith, D.S.O., of Kimberley. Educ. at Cheltenham Coll. Joined the Worcester Regiment 1881, Maj. 1896; Col. 1900; served in Egyptian Camel Corps 1884-85 and took part in several engagements in Egypt during 1887-96; D.S.O. 1889. Dongola Expedition 1896, and the Soudan Campaign 1898; Gov. of Dongola Province 1899. Was on special service in S. African War 1900-01 (mentioned in despatches); C.B. 1900; Brigadier-Gen. in command of Middleburg District, Cape Colony 1902-08. Was Brigadier-Gen. with Expeditionary Force in France; mentioned in despatches, later retired. M.F.H., Albrighton Hunt; Dept.-Lieut. for Staffordshire. A Unionist. Elected for S. Wolverhampton in January and December 1910 and for the Bilston division of Wolverhamp-

ton in 1918. Sat until he retired in October 1922. Director of Stewarts and Lloyds Limited. Died 23 October 1930. [1922]

HICKS, Ernest George. Continued in House after 1945: full entry in Volume IV.

HIGGINS, Kevin Christopher. See O'HIGGINS, Kevin Christopher.

HIGGS, Walter Frank. Nuthurst Grange, Hockley Heath, Warwickshire. Carlton, and Constitutional. Union, Birmingham. S. of Charles Higgs, Esq., of Kidderminster. B. 7 April 1886; m. 1921, Cecilia Elizabeth, d. of J.S. Yeoman, Esq. Educ. at Birmingham Technical School. An Electrical Motor Manufacturer. Founder and Chairman of Higgs Motors Limited, Witton, Birmingham; served with G.E.C. Limited, B.T.H. Limited and E.C.C. Limited; M.I.E.E., member of Birmingham City Council 1934-37. Life Gov. of University of Birmingham. A National Conservative. Elected for W. Birmingham in April 1937 and sat until he was defeated in July 1945. President of Birmingham Chamber of Commerce 1948. Died 8 August 1961.   [1945]

HIGHAM, Sir Charles Frederick. Fairfield, Kingsbury, Middlesex. Savoy Court. Carlton, and Constitutional. S. of Charles and Emily Higham. B. at Walthamstow 17 January 1876; m. 1st, 1911, Jessie Stuart, d. of John Munro, Esq., of Elgin (she died 1925); secondly, 1925, Mrs. Eloise Ellis, d. of J.C. Rowe, Esq., of Buffalo, N.Y. (divorced 1930); thirdly, 1930, Josephine Janet, d. of H.A. Webb, Esq., of Cheltenham (divorced 1934); fourthly, 1936, Mrs. Ruth Agnes Marian Neligan, d. of Maj. R. Dawes-Smith. Educ. at St. Albans. Was engaged all his life in advertising. Assisted the Government throughout the war by writing the Appeals for Men and Money (Honorary); Assistant Organizer of the Victory War Loan Campaign; member Coalition Publicity Committee; Advertising Adviser to the Treasury, the Admiralty, Navy and Army Canteen Board, etc. Author of *Scientific Distribution*. Knighted 1921. A Coalition Unionist. Elected for S. Islington in December 1918 and sat until he retired in

October 1922. Died 24 December 1938.
[1922]

HILDER, Col. Frank. Huskards, Ingatestone, Essex. Carlton, and Junior United Service. S. of Edward Martin Hilder, Esq. B. 3 October 1864; m. 1895, Evelyn Mary, 2nd d. of Lieut.-Col. Wilding Wood (she died 1939). Educ. privately. Member of the London Stock Exchange. Territorial Commission 1901, Essex Imperial Yeomanry; Maj. Essex R.H.A. 1908-14; Maj. 2nd King Edward's Horse 1914-15; Lieut.-Col. 2/3 S. Mid. F.A. Brigade 1915-16; O.C. Res. Battery R.F.A., Ripon November 1906-May 1917. O.C. 21st Corps Ammunition Dumps June 1917; Egypt Expeditionary Forces. Dept.-Lieut. of Essex and J.P. 1906. A Conservative. First elected for S.E. Essex in December 1918 and sat until he was defeated in December 1923. High Sheriff of Essex 1935-36. Died 23 April 1951. [1923]

HILEY, Sir Ernest Varvill, K.B.E. 74 Onslow Gardens, London. Carlton, and Conservative. S. of Charles Hiley and Elizabeth C. Varvill. B. 11 October 1868 at Yeadon, Yorkshire; m. 1908, Edith Caroline, widow of Walter Whetstone, Esq., and d. of Charles Henry Beckingham. Educ. privately. A Solicitor in 1891. Dept. Town Clerk Birmingham 1894; Town Clerk of Leicester 1902; Town Clerk of Birmingham 1908; Dept.-Director General of National Service 1917. A Conservative. Elected for the Duddeston division of Birmingham in November 1922 and sat until he retired in November 1923. K.B.E. 1918. Chairman of Glover and Main Limited. Member of Royal Commission on Lunacy and Mental Disorder 1924-26. Member of Royal Commission on Transport 1928. Died 19 July 1949. [1923]

HILL, Sir Alexander Galloway Erskine, Bart. See ERSKINE-HILL, Sir Alexander Galloway Erskine, Bart.

HILL, Alfred. House of Commons, London. B. 1867. Educ. at the Vicarage School, Welwyn, Hertfordshire. In early life worked in the boot and shoe trade as a Clicker; for many years a Trade Union Treasurer and Secretary. Member of the Executive Committee of the National Union of Boot and Shoe Operatives. Member of the Leicester Council. A Labour Member. Elected for Leicester W. in November 1922 and sat until he retired in November 1923. Died 14 July 1945. [1923]

HILL, Professor Archibald Vivian, F.R.S. 16 Bishopswood Road, Highgate, London. Athenaeum. S. of Jonathan Hill, Esq., of Bristol. B. 26 September 1886; m. 1913, Margaret Neville, d. of Dr. J. N. Keynes (she died 1970). Educ. at Blundell's School, and Trinity Coll., Cambridge, Sc.D., Honorary LL.D. Edinburgh, D.Sc. Manchester, Oxford, Pennsylvania, Bristol and Algiers; M.D. Louvain; F.R.S. 1918; Nobel Prize, Physiology 1922. Honorary Fellow of Trinity, Cambridge 1941, of Kings 1927; Professor of Physiology, Manchester 1920, and University Coll., London 1923; Foulerton Research Professor, Royal Society 1926-51; Secretary of Royal Society 1935; Capt. Cambridgeshire Regiment T.A. 1914-19; Director of A.A. Exp. Section Ministry of Munitions 1916-19. After 1939 he was Chairman of Scientific Research Committee, Central Register Ministry of Labour and National Service, and of Executive Committee of National Physical Laboratory; member of War Cabinet Scientific Advisory Committee, of Advisory Council Department of Scientific and Industrial Research, and of Colonial Research Committee Association. Member of Ordnance Board. An Independent Conservative. Elected for Cambridge University in February 1940 and sat until he retired in June 1945. O.B.E. (Mil.) 1918. Companion of Honour 1946. Trustee of British Museum 1947-63. President of British Association 1952. Died 3 June 1977. [1945]

HILLARY, Albert Ernest. 92 Fenchurch Street, London. National Liberal, and Carlyle. S. of John Hillary, Esq., of Tow Law, Co. Durham. B. in Durham 1868; m. 1897, Annie Maud Mary, d. of W. Bartleet, Esq., of Sparkhill (she died 1945). Was in business in New Zealand; later became Managing Director of Carsons Limited, Chocolate Makers, of Glasgow. Section leader in Special Police dealing with air raids during the war. A Liberal. Unsuccessfully contested Barnard Castle in 1918. Elected for the Harwich division of Essex in November 1922. Sat until he was defeated in October 1924. Died 10 February 1954.   [1924 2nd ed.]

HILLMAN, Dr. George Brown, M.B.E. Artillery Mansions, Victoria Street, London. Southfield House, Wakefield. S. of the Rev. S.D. Hillman, Independent Minister, of Ilkley, Yorkshire. B. 1867; m. 1895, Christina Gordon, d. of John Henderson, Esq., of Bradford. Educ. at Ilkley High School, and Leeds University, Med. Department. Mayor of Wakefield 1927-28; J.P. Chairman of the W. Riding of Yorkshire Local Medical Panel Committee from 1918. Honorary Capt. R.A.M.C. Officer-in-Charge of Military Hospital, Malta. A National Conservative. Unsuccessfully contested the Normanton division of the W. Riding of Yorkshire in May 1923. Elected for Wakefield in October 1931 and sat until his death on 19 March 1932.   [1932]

HILLS, Adam. S. of Adam and Ellen Hills. B. 10 August 1880; m. 1906, Isabella Lillie Buck. Member of National Union of Railwaymen; member of Newcastle City Council from 1934. A Labour Member. Elected for the Pontefract division of the W. Riding of Yorkshire in November 1935 and sat until his death in June 1941. [1941]

HILLS, Maj. Rt. Hon. John Waller. 26 Chester Terrace, London. Hills Court, Ash, Canterbury. S. of H.A. Hills, Esq., of Highhead Castle, Cumberland, and Anna, d. of the Rt. Hon. Sir William Grove. B. 1867; m. 1st, 1897, Stella, d. of H. Duckworth, Esq. (she died 1897); secondly, 13 June 1931, Mary Grace, d. of Leon Ashton, Esq. Educ. at Eton, and Balliol Coll., Oxford. Admitted a Solicitor 1897. Served with Durham Light Infantry in France etc. 1914-16. Financial Secretary to the Treasury October 1922-March 1923, when he resigned after his defeat in the Edge Hill by-election. J.P. for Cumberland. PC. 1929. A Conservative. Sat for Durham City from 1906-18 and for the Durham

division of Co. Durham from 1918 until 1922 when he was defeated. Unsuccessfully contested the Edge Hill division of Liverpool in March 1923. Elected for the Ripon division of the W. Riding of Yorkshire in December 1925 and sat until his death on 24 December 1938. He would have been created a Bart. in the New Year Honours List of 1939 but as he had died the previous week the Baronetcy was created in favour of his son.   [1939]

HILL-WOOD, Sir Samuel Hill, Bart. 52 Eaton Place, London. Moorfield, Glossop, Derbyshire. Carlton, and Bachelors' S. of Samuel Wood, Esq., of Moorfield, Glossop. B. 12 March 1872; m. 21 April 1899, Hon. Decima Bateman-Hanbury, d. of 2nd Baron Bateman. Educ. at Eton. Dept.-Lieut., and J.P. for Derbyshire and Herefordshire. Assumed surname of Hill-Wood in 1910. Created Bart. 1921. A Conservative. Unsuccessfully contested the High Peak division of Derbyshire in January 1910. Elected for the High Peak division of Derbyshire in December 1910 and sat until he retired in May 1929. Capt. of Derbyshire County Cricket Club 1899-1901. Died 4 January 1949.   [1929]

HILTON, Cecil. Oakwood, Fairhaven Road, St. Anne's-on-Sea. Constitutional, Manchester and Bolton. S. of Joseph Hilton, Esq. B. 1884; m. 1909, Alice, d. of Henry Felton, Esq., of Oldham. Educ. at Elementary School, and Continuation Classes. A Director of Cotton Mills in Accrington, Middleton, and Oldham. A Conservative. Unsuccessfully contested Bolton in December 1923. Elected for Bolton in October 1924 and sat until he was defeated in May 1929. Died 19 June 1931.   [1929]

HINCHINGBROOKE, Alexander Victor Edward Paulet Montagu, Visct. Continued in House after 1945: full entry in Volume IV.

HINDLE, Frederick. Astley Bank, Darwen, Lancashire. S. of Frederick George Hindle, Esq., Solicitor, MP for Darwen division of Lancashire, January 1910. B. 28 July 1877 at Darwen; m. 1928, Alys, d. of

James Lawrence, Esq., of Chorley. Educ. at Charterhouse, Owens Coll., and Victoria University, Manchester. A Solicitor, admitted 1899. Lieut. Army Service 1914-18; 1914 Star; Chevalier Legion of Honour; French Croix de Guerre with two palms. A Liberal. Unsuccessfully contested Darwen in 1918 and 1922. Elected for the Darwen division of Lancashire in December 1923 and sat until he was defeated in October 1924. Mayor of Darwen 1912-13. Alderman, Lancashire County Council. Knighted 1943. Dept.-Commissioner for Civil Defence, N.W. Region 1941-45. Chairman of Blackburn and E. Lancashire Hospital Management Committee 1948-53. Died 23 April 1953.
[1924 2nd ed.]

HINDS, John. 71 Ashley Gardens, London. Neuadd-deg, Carmarthen. Reform, and National Liberal. S. of William Hinds, Esq., of Cwnin Farm, Carmarthen, and Mary, d. of David Jones, Esq., of Penronw. B. 26 July 1862 at Cwnin Farm, Carmarthen; m. 1893, Lizzie, d. of Robert Powell, Esq., of Cefntrefna, Llandovery. Educ. at Carmarthen Grammar School. Chairman and Founder of Hinds and Company, Blackheath, and Chairman of Drapers' and General Fire Corporation. President of Baptist Union of Wales. Chairman of Welsh Liberal Parliamentary Party 1922-23. Lord-Lieut. of the County of Carmarthen 1917-28. A Liberal. Sat for W. Carmarthenshire from December 1910 to November 1918. Sat for the Carmarthen division of Carmarthenshire from December 1918 until he retired in November 1923. Elected as a Coalition Liberal in 1918 and a National Liberal in 1922 but joined the Asquithian Liberals in 1923. Mayor of Carmarthen 1925-26. President of London Welsh Literary Union. Died 23 July 1928.
[1923]

HIRST, George Henry. Darfield, Nr. Barnsley. B. at Elsecar, near Barnsley 17 May 1868. A Checkweighman at the Dearne Valley Colliery; member of the Joint Board, and delegate to Council of the Yorkshire Miners' Association. Chairman of Darfield Urban District Council. J.P. for W. Riding of Yorkshire. A Labour Member. Sat for the Wentworth division of the W.Riding of Yorkshire from December 1918 until his death on 13 November 1933. [1933]

HIRST, William. 13 Nurser Place, Bradford. B. 1873. Member of Bradford City Council; President of Bradford Co-operative Society. J.P. for Bradford. A Labour Member. Unsuccessfully contested S. Bradford in 1918, 1922 and 1923. Elected for S. Bradford in October 1924 and sat until he was defeated in October 1931. Unsuccessfully contested S. Bradford in November 1935. Died 5 May 1946. [1931 2nd ed.]

HOARE, Rt. Hon. Sir Samuel John Gurney, Bart., G.C.S.I., G.B.E., C.M.G. Templewood, Northrepps, Cromer. Carlton. S. of Sir Samuel Hoare, 1st, Bart. B. 24 February 1880; m. 16 October 1909, Lady Maud Lygon, D.B.E., d. of 6th Earl Beauchamp. Educ. at Harrow, and New Coll., Oxford; Honorary Fellow; 1st Class Hon. Mods., 1st Class Mod. Hist.; LL.D. Cambridge, D.C.L. Oxford. Capt. Norfolk Yeomanry; Lieut.-Col. Gen. Staff, First Grade; Honorary Col. 47th Division (2nd London) R.A.S.C.; member London County Council 1907-10; Chairman of Fire Brigade; Assistant Private Secretary to the Rt. Hon. A. Lyttelton, when Secretary for the Colonies 1903-05. Succeeded as Bart. 1915; political work in Italy 1916; C.M.G. 1917. Secretary of State for Air October 1922-January 1924, November 1924-June 1929, and April-May 1940; for India August 1931-June 1935, for Foreign Affairs June-December 1935; First Lord of the Admiralty June 1936-May 1937; Secretary of State Home Office May 1937-September 1939; Lord Privy Seal (until April) and Member of War Cabinet September 1939-May 1940. Ambassador to Spain May 1940-December 1944. Member of Royal Commission on Civil Service and on Honours and of Joint Select Committee on Indian Constitution 1933; Chairman of Irish Refugees Committee; Dept.-Lieut., and J.P. for Norfolk; Air Commodore of 604 R.A.A.F. Squadron; member of County of London T.F.A.; Elder Brother of Trinity House 1936-59; Chancellor of Reading University 1937-59. Awarded Grand Cross of several

Foreign Orders. PC. 1922. President of Howard League for Penal Reform 1947. Chairman of Magistrates Association 1947-52. President of Lawn Tennis Association 1932-58. President of National Skating Association 1945-57. A Conservative. Unsuccessfully contested Ipswich in 1906. Sat for Chelsea from January 1910 until he was created Visct. Templewood in July 1944. Died 7 May 1959. [1944]

HOBHOUSE, Arthur Lawrence. Hadspen House, Castle Cary, Somerset. Athenaeum, and National Liberal. S. of the Rt. Hon. Henry Hobhouse, MP from 1885-1906; Chairman of Somerset County Council. B. at Kensington 15 February 1886; m. 1919, Konrodin d. of the Rt. Hon. F. Huth Jackson. Educ. at Eton, St. Andrews University, and Trinity Coll., Cambridge. A Solicitor from February 1911 until 1914. J.P. for Somerset 1921. A Liberal. Unsuccessfully contested the Wells division of Somerset in 1922. Elected for the Wells division of Somerset in December 1923 and sat until he was defeated in October 1924. Defeated again in 1929. Served with B.E.F. 1914 and later with the Claims Commission. Knighted 1942. Member of Somerset County Council from 1925, Alderman from 1934, Chairman 1940-47. Chairman of National Parks Committee 1945-47. Chairman of County Councils Association 1946-50, President 1951-53. Honorary F.R.I.B.A. 1948. Pro-Chancellor of Bristol University 1947-65. Died 20 January 1965. [1924 2nd ed.]

HODGE, Lieut.-Col. James Philp. 11 King's Bench Walk, Temple, London. Garrick, Walton Heath Golf. Union Interalliée (Paris). 2nd s. of Archibald Hodge, Esq., of Hoole Park, Chester, a Fifeshire Miner. B. 1879; m. 1917, Anna Fortunée. 2nd d. of Michel Venture, Esq., Shipowner of Marseilles (she died 1944). Educ. at Chester Cathedral Choir School. Practised as a Chartered Accountant in Chester at the age of 21. Relinquished this profession for that of the bar; called by the Inner Temple 1917, and was on the Northern Circuit. Served prior to the war as Private in Inns of Court O.T.C.; obtained commission

in A.P.D. and went to France in 1914. Served also in Salonika and in Egypt, being subsequently appointed Inspector of Pay Offices with rank of Lieut.-Col. A Liberal. Elected for Preston in November 1922 and sat until he was defeated in October 1924. Died 12 July 1946. [1924 2nd ed.]

HODGE, Rt. Hon. John. 37 Shooters Hill Road, Blackheath, London. S. of William Hodge, Esq., Ironworks Dept. Manager. B. at Muirkirk 29 October 1855; m. 1885, Mary, d. of J. Forsyth, Esq., Engineer, of Motherwell (she died 1931). Educ. at Ironworks School, Motherwell, and Hutchesontown Grammar School, Glasgow. President of the Iron and Steel Trades' Confederation until 1931; President of Glasgow Trades Council 1891; International Conference Zurich 1893; a member of Manchester City Council 1897-1901; member of Industrial Council. Acting-Chairman of Labour Party 1915. Member of the Mesopotamia Commission 1918. Minister of Labour December 1916 to August 1917. PC. 1916. Minister of Pensions August 1917 to January 1919. A Labour Member. Unsuccessfully contested the Gower division of Glamorganshire in 1900 and Preston in 1903. Sat for the Gorton division of Lancashire from 1906 to 1918 and for the Gorton division of Manchester from 1918 until he retired in November 1923. President of T.U.C. 1892. Author of *Workman's Cottage to Windsor Castle* 1931. Died 10 August 1937. [1923]

HODGES, Frank. Thornfield, Trafalgar Road, Twickenham. S. of Thomas and Louisa Hodges. B. at Woolaston, Gloucestershire 30 April 1887; m. Henrietta, d. of John Carter Esq., of Abertillery. Started work at 14 in a Welsh mine; obtained a Miners' Federation Scholarship at Ruskin Coll. in 1909; helped to found the Central Labour Coll. Was Secretary of the Miners' Federation 1918-24. Author of *Nationalization of the Mines*. Civil Lord of the Admiralty January-November 1924. A Labour Member. Elected for the Lichfield division of Staffordshire in December 1923 and sat until he was defeated in October 1924. Secretary of International Miners Federation 1925-27. Member of

Central Electricity Board 1927-47. Died 3 June 1947. [1924 2nd ed.]

HOFFMAN, Philip Christopher. 38 Oakwood Road, London. S. of James Hoffman, Esq. B. 26 June 1878; m. 13 October 1913, Annie Mary, d. of Samuel Morgan, Esq., of Treorchy, Glamorgan. Educ. at Cooper's School, Stepney, and Warehousemen, Clerks' and Drapers' School, Purley, Surrey. Associated with the Drapery Trade and an Authority on Shop Life and Conditions; Regional Organiser of Shop Workers' Union. Dept.-Chairman of London County Council Advisory Committee on Distributive Training. A Labour Member. Unsuccessfully contested Essex S.E. in November 1922. Elected for Essex S.E. in December 1923 and defeated in October 1924. Elected for Sheffield Central in May 1929 and sat until he was defeated in October 1931. Defeated again in November 1935. Died 20 April 1959.

[1931 2nd ed.]

HOGBIN, Henry Cairn. Highlands, Thornbury Road, Osterley Park. S. of Thomas Parker Hogbin, Esq., of Tilmanston, Kent. B. 16 November 1880; m. 1st, 1905, Winifred Maggie, d. of A.C. Brown, Esq., of Hounslow (she died 1940); secondly, 1955, Jessie McKenzie Sutherland. A member of the firm of Lawe's Chemical Company. An organizer of agricultural production for the Ministry of Food during the war. A Liberal. Unsuccessfully contested Battersea N. in 1922. Elected for Battersea N. in December 1923 and sat until he was defeated in October 1924, standing as a Constitutionalist with Liberal and Conservative support. Unsuccessfully contested the Stourbridge division of Worcestershire as a Conservative in February 1927. J.P. for Middlesex 1928. Died 13 June 1966.

[1924 2nd ed.]

HOGG, Rt. Hon. Sir Douglas McGarel, K.C. 57 Portland Place, London. Carters Corner Place, Hailsham, Sussex. Carlton, and Athenaeum. S. of Quintin Hogg and Alice Anna, d. of William Graham, Esq. B. 28 February 1872; m. 1st, 14 August 1905, Elizabeth, d. of James Trimble Brown,

Esq., and widow of Hon. Archibald Majoribanks (she died 10 May 1925); secondly, 1929, Mildred, d. of Rev. E.P. Dew and widow of Hon. Clive Lawrence. Educ. at Cheam, and Eton (Capt. of Oppidans). A Barrister-at-Law, Lincolns Inn 1902; K.C. 1917; Bencher 1920. Attorney-Gen. to the Prince of Wales 1920-22; PC. and Knight 1922. Attorney-Gen. October 1922-January 1924 and November 1924-March 1928. Served in South African War. A Conservative. Sat for St. Marylebone from November 1922 until March 1928 when he was appointed Lord Chancellor and created Baron Hailsham. Created Visct. Hailsham 1929. Leader of the Conservative Party in the House of Lords 1930-35. Lord Chancellor March 1928-June 1929 and June 1935-March 1938. Secretary of State for War and Leader of the House of Lords November 1931-June 1935. Lord President March-October 1938. President of M.C.C. 1933. Died 16 August 1950. [1928]

HOGG, Hon. Quintin McGarel. Continued in House after 1945: full entry in Volume IV.

HOGGE, James Myles. Press Club, Fleet Street, London. S. of Robert Hogge, Esq. B. 1873 at Edinburgh; m. 1905, Florence, d. of R. Hopkins, Esq., of Malton, Yorkshire. Educ. at Normal School, University, and New Coll., Edinburgh. Assistant Minister at College Street United Free Church, Edinburgh. A Journalist and social investigator; member of City Council of York. Was President of Students' Representative Council, Edinburgh; President National Federation of Discharged and Demobilized Sailors and Soldiers 1919-20. Author of *Facts of Gambling, Scotland Insured, Pensions, Allowances, and Civil Liabilities, Licensing in Scandinavia,* etc. One of the Editors of *Scottish Students' Song Book, British Students' Song Book,* and *War Pensions and Allowances.* Joint Chief Whip of Non-Coalition Liberals 1919-23. An Advanced Radical and Scottish Home Ruler. Unsuccessfully contested the Camlachie division of Glasgow in December 1910. Elected for E. Edinburgh in February 1912 and sat until he was defeated in October 1924. Parliamentary Adviser to National

Association of Schoolmasters and to Association of Ex-Service Civil Servants. Died 27 October 1928. [1924 2nd ed.]

HOHLER, Sir Gerald Fitzroy, K.C. 34 Moore Street, London. 3 Harcourt Buildings, Temple, London. Carlton, and New University. S. of Henry Booth Hohler, Esq., J.P., and Dept.-Lieut. B. 1862. Unmarried. Educ. at Eton, and Trinity Coll., Cambridge. Barrister-at-Law, Inner Temple 1888; K.C. 1906; bencher 1915, and practised on the S.E. Circuit. Created Knight 1924. A Conservative. Sat for Chatham from January 1910-18. Sat for the Gillingham division of Rochester from December 1918 until he retired in May 1929. J.P. for Kent. Died 30 January 1934. [1929]

HOLBROOK, Col. Sir Arthur Richard, K.B.E., V.D. 19 Porchester Square, London. Carlton, Constitutional, Savage, Unionist, 1900, Cecil, and United. S. of Richard Holbrook, Esq., of Southsea, Newspaper Proprietor. B. 28 April 1850; m. 16 April 1878, Amelia Mary, d. of Alexander Parks, Esq., of Constantinople (she died 1944). Educ. at Portsea Diocesan School. A Newspaper Proprietor in Portsmouth. Dept.-Lieut. for Hampshire. Chairman Portsmouth Conservative Association 1885-98; President Portsmouth Divisional Council Primrose League, and Representative for Hampshire on Grand Council; Commanded 3rd (Duke of Connaught's Own) V.B. Hampshire Regiment 1898-1904; Commanded R.A.S.C. Salisbury Plain District August 1914 to August 1919; Military Member for Hampshire T.F.A.; member of Council of National Rifle Association; President Portsmouth Chamber of Commerce 1902-07; President Newspaper Society 1913-14; member of Admiralty, War Office, and Press Committees; Fellow Institute of Journalists. F.R.S.A. Prov.-Grand Master of Mark Masons of Hampshire and Isle of Wight. K.B.E. 1918. V.D. 1892. A Conservative. Sat for the Basingstoke division of Hampshire from 1920-23. Unsuccessfully contested the seat in December 1923. Re-elected for the Basingstoke division of Hampshire in October 1924 and sat until

he retired in May 1929. President of London Hampshire Society 1930-35. Died 24 December 1946. [1929]

HOLDSWORTH, Sir Herbert. 108 Leeds Road, Eccleshill, Bradford. National Liberal. S. of Samuel Holdsworth, Esq., of Liversedge, Yorkshire. B. 1890; m. 24 June 1914, Beatrice, d. of William Lee, Esq. Educ. at Batley Grammar School. A Rag Merchant. Assistant Government and Chief Party Whip May 1940-December 1942. Knight Bach. 1944. A Liberal until 1938, thereafter a Liberal National. Unsuccessfully contested the Rothwell division of Yorkshire in May 1929. Elected for Bradford S. in October 1931 as an Opposition Liberal and sat until he retired in June 1945. Died 8 July 1949. [1945]

HOLLAND, Alfred. Lansbury, Stretton Road, Morton, Alfreton, Derbyshire. S. of Alfred H. Holland, Esq., Coal Miner, of Tibshelf, Derbyshire. B. 29 January 1900; m. 16 April 1921, Ivy Annie, d. of Thomas Etches, Esq., of Hillside Farm, Stretton, Derbyshire. Educ. at Christ Church School. Employee of Tibshelf Co-Operative Society Limited; member of Derbyshire County Council 1931; Vice-President Clay Cross Division Labour Party; Branch Secretary National Union of Distributive and Allied Workers; Methodist Lay Preacher and Church Secretary. A Labour Member. Elected for the Clay Cross division of Derbyshire in November 1935 and sat until his death on 30 August 1936. [1936]

HOLLAND, Lieut.-Gen Sir Arthur Edward Aveling, K.C.B., K.C.M.G., D.S.O., M.V.O. 45 Carlisle Mansions, London. Hanslope Lodge, Stony Stratford, Buckinghamshire. Naval & Military. S. of Maj.-Gen. Arthur Butcher, of Danesfort, Co. Kerry. B. 13 April 1862; m. 25 July 1906, Mary, d. of L.D. Hall, Esq. Educ. at Royal Military Academy, Woolwich. Assumed the surname of Holland in lieu of Butcher in 1910. Joined R.A. 1880, Lieut.-Gen. 1919; served in Burma 1886-89, in South African War 1899-1901, in France 1914-19. Lieut.-Gen. Commanding 1st Army Corps. Commandant Royal Military Academy, Woolwich 1912-

14. D.A.A.G., R.A. Madras 1895-98; Assistant Military Secretary to Gov. of Malta 1903-05, at War Office 1910-12; K.C.B. 1918, K.C.M.G. 1919. A Conservative. Elected for Northampton in October 1924 and sat until his death on 7 December 1927.   [1928]

HOLLINS, Arthur. Eastbourne Villa, 2 Eastbourne Road, Hanley, Stoke-on-Trent. S. of William Hollins, Esq., of Burslem. B. 19 September 1876; m. 4 August 1900, Ann, d. of George Sturgess, Esq., of Wolstanton. Educ. at St. Paul's Church School, and Wedgwood Institute, Burslem. Gen. Secretary National Society of Pottery Workers 1910-47. J.P., and Alderman of City Council, Stoke-on-Trent. Lord Mayor 1933-34. F.R.S.A. A Labour Member. Sat for the Hanley division of Stoke-on-Trent from April 1928-October 1931 when he was defeated; re-elected for the Hanley division of Stoke-on-Trent in November 1935 and sat until he retired in June 1945. C.B.E. 1949. Died 22 April 1962.   [1945]

HOLLINS, James Henry. B. 1877. A Labour Member. Elected for the Silvertown division of West Ham in February 1940 and sat until he retired in June 1945. Member of West Ham Borough Council 1913-45, Alderman from 1925, Mayor 1929-30. J.P. for West Ham 1920-46. Died 22 September 1954.   [1945]

HOLMES, Sir Joseph Stanley. Continued in House after 1945: full entry in Volume IV.

HOLT, Capt. Herbert Paton, M.C. 20 Cadogan Gardens, London. Lackham House, Lacock, Wiltshire. Cavalry, St. Stephen's, and White's. S. of Sir Herbert Holt, of Montreal. B. 10 December 1890; m. 1st, 21 June 1922, Aileen Elizabeth, d. of G.L. Cains, Esq., of Montreal (she died 1945); secondly, 1946, Opal Eree M'ilhenny, d. of C.A. McCauley, Esq., of Meadville, U.S.A. Educ. at St. Albans School, and Royal Military Coll., Canada. Joined 3rd Dragoon Guards 1910, retired 1920. Director of Messrs. Andrew Holt and Company. A Conservative. Elected for the Upton division of West Ham in October 1924 and

sat until he retired in May 1929. High Sheriff of Wiltshire 1935-36. Served as Maj. in Pioneer Corps in France 1939-40. Died 1 June 1971.   [1929]

HOMAN, Cornelius William James. 13 Fortis Court, Muswell Hill, London. Avenue House, Netley Abbey, Hampshire. Constitutional, Royal Automobile, and St. Stephen's. S. of Capt. W.H. Homan, Esq. B. 17 August 1900; m. 1st, 1924, Olive Victoria, d. of John Mitchell, Esq., of Falmouth; secondly, 1934, Lilian Ada Baldwin. A Financial Expert. Served in France, etc. 1915-17. Member of London, Manchester, Birmingham, and Sheffield Chambers of Commerce. A Freeman of City of London, and of the Worshipful Company of Gardeners; a Liveryman of the City of London; F.R.G.S., F.R.C.I. A Conservative. Elected for Ashton-under-Lyne in October 1924 and sat until October 1928 when his seat was declared vacant after he had been adjudicated a bankrupt.*   [1928]

HOOD, Sir Joseph, Bart. Greycourt, Wimbledon Common, London. Ivanhoe, Frinton-on-Sea, Essex. Carlton, Constitutional, and St. Stephen's. S. of John and Eliza Hood. B. 31 March 1863 at Ashby-de-la-Zouch, Leicestershire; m. 1st, 1900, Katherine, d. of Martin Kenny, Esq., of Ballindaggin, Co. Wexford (she died 1913); secondly, 1915, Marie Josephine, d. of Archibald Robinson, Esq., J.P. of Dublin. Educ. at the Ashby-de-la-Zouch Grammar School. A Solicitor, admitted 1890. Created Bart. 1922. A Conservative. Elected for Wimbledon in December 1918. Sat until he retired in October 1924. Dept.-Chairman of British-American Tobacco Company Limited until 1921. Mayor of Wimbledon 1930-31. Died 10 January 1931.

[1924 2nd ed.]

HOPE, Capt. Hon. Arthur Oswald James, M.C. 10 Cleveland Gardens, London. Guards', Pratt's, and Turf. S. of the Rt. Hon. Lord Rankeillour. B. 7 May 1897; m. 2 June 1919, Grizel, d. of Brigadier-Gen. Sir Robert Gordon Gilmour, Bart., C.B., C.V.O., D.S.O., of The Inch, Liberton.

Educ. at Oratory School, and Royal Military Coll., Sandhurst. Capt. Coldstream Guards 1917. Served in France 1915-18 and Turkey 1922. Awarded Croix de Guerre (France). Parliamentary Private Secretary to Col. Lane Fox 1924-27; Assistant Whip April-December 1935; a Junior Lord of the Treasury December 1935-May 1937; Vice-Chamberlain of H.M. Household May-October 1937, Treasurer October 1937-April 1939. A Conservative. Sat for the Nuneaton division of Warwickshire from October 1924-until May 1929 when he was defeated. Elected for the Aston division of Birmingham in October 1931 and sat until he resigned in April 1939, on appointment as Gov.-designate of Madras. Gov. of Madras March 1940-February 1946. G.C.I.E. 1939. Succeeded to the Peerage as Baron Rankeillour 1949. Died 26 May 1958.   [1939]

HOPE, Sir Harry. Kinnettles, Forfar. Carlton. New, Edinburgh. S. of James Hope, Esq., of Eastbarns, Dunbar. B. 24 September 1865; m. 4 February 1897, Margaret, d. of Robert Holmes-Kerr, Esq., Underbank, Ayrshire (she died 1948). Educ. at Collegiate School, and University of Edinburgh. Capt. Haddington and Berwick Art. Mil. J.P. Haddington; President Scottish Chamber of Agriculture. Visited Australia and New Zealand and wrote on agricultural resources there; member of Agricultural Commission on the Dominion of Canada 1908 to report on agricultural resources of the Dominion; member of Food Production and other Commissions 1915. Knight Bach. 1920. A Conservative. Unsuccessfully contested Elgin and Nairn in 1906. MP for Buteshire from January 1910-18, for W. Stirlingshire from 1918-22, unsuccessfully contested the same seat in November 1922 and December 1923. Elected for Forfarshire in October 1924. Sat until he retired in October 1931. Created Bart. 1932. Convenor of Angus County Council from 1937. Dept.-Lieut. of Angus 1936, Vice-Lieut. 1938. President of County Councils Association of Scotland 1940-42. Died 29 December 1959.
[1931 2nd ed.]

HOPE, Rt. Hon. James Fitzalan. Heron's Ghyll, Uckfield, Sussex. Carlton. S. of J.R. Hope-Scott (formerly Hope), Esq., Q.C., of Abbotsford, N.B., and Lady Victoria Howard, d. of 14th Duke of Norfolk. B. 11 December 1870; m. 1st, 15 November 1892, Mabel, d. of Francis Riddell, Esq., of Cheeseburn Grange, Northumberland (she died 1938); secondly, 1941, Lady Beatrice Kerr-Clark, d. of 9th Earl of Drogheda and widow of S.R. Kerr-Clark. Educ. at Oratory School, Birmingham, and Christ Church, Oxford. Assistant Honorary Secretary Conservative Central Office; Private Secretary to Duke of Norfolk when Postmaster-Gen. 1896-1900, and subsequently to Marq. of Londonderry 1900-05, to Mr. Gerald Balfour when President of Board of Trade, and to Mr. A. Lyttelton when Colonial Secretary. Treasurer of the Household May 1915 to December 1916; Lord of the Treasury December 1916 to February 1919; Financial Secretary to the Ministry of Supply February 1919-April 1921. Dept. Speaker and Chairman of Committee of Ways and Means 1921-23 and from December 1924, to May 1929. J.P. for Sussex. Author of *History of 1900 Parliament*. PC. 1922. A Conservative. Unsuccessfully contested the Elland division of Yorkshire in 1892, Pontefract 1895, and the Brightside division of Sheffield in 1897. Sat for the Brightside division of Sheffield from 1900-06, when he was defeated. Sat for the central division of Sheffield from April 1908 until May 1929 when he unsuccessfully contested E. Walthamstow. Created Baron Rankeillour 1932. Died 14 February 1949.   [1929]

HOPE, Col. Sir John Augustus, Bart., O.B.E. Pinkie House, Musselburgh, Midlothian. Naval & Military, and Carlton. S. of the Rev. C.A. Hope, Hon. Canon of Ripon and Julia Sophia, d. of John Watson Barton, Esq., of Stapleton Park, Yorkshire; succeeded his uncle, Sir Alexander Hope, Bart., of Craighall, as 16th Bart., 7 March 1918. B. 7 July 1869 at Edinburgh; m. 1910, Hon. Mary Bruce, eld. d. of Lord Balfour of Burleigh. Educ. at Eton, and Royal Military Coll., Sandhurst. Joined King's Royal Rifles 1889, retired as Maj. 1908. Served in S. African War with mounted

171

infantry 1901-02. Served as Maj. 9th Battalion K.R.R. with Expeditionary Force in France; wounded. O.B.E. (Mil.) 1919. Lieut.-Col. Reserve of Officers, K.R. Rifles. J.P. for Midlothian. A Unionist. Unsuccessfully contested Midlothian in December 1910. Elected for Midlothian in September 1912, and for N. Midlothian in December 1918 and sat until he retired in October 1922. Died 17 April 1924.   [1922]

HOPE, John Deans. Haddington. Reform, and National Liberal. S. of James Hope, Esq., of Eastbarns, Dunbar, the eminent agriculturist, and Isabella, d. of John Deans, Esq. B. 1860 at Duddingston, Midlothian; m. 1899, d. of R.K. Holms-Kerr, Esq., of Underbank, Ayrshire. Educ. at Fettes Coll., and Edinburgh University. A member of Edinburgh Stock Exchange. A Liberal. Unsuccessfully contested W. Perthshire in 1895. Sat for W. Fife from 1900 to December 1910, when he was defeated. Elected for Haddingtonshire in April 1911; re-elected for Berwickshire and Haddingtonshire in December 1918 as a Coalition Liberal. Sat until he was defeated in November 1922, standing as an Independent Liberal with opposition from a National Liberal candidate and from an Asquithian Liberal. Died 13 December 1949.   [1922]

HOPE, Sydney. Knowles House, Handforth, Cheshire. S. of Thomas Hope, Esq., of Manchester, Publisher. B. 28 May 1905. Educ. at Glossop Grammar School, and Ellesmere Coll. Admitted a Solicitor in 1930. Member of Handforth Urban District Council. A National Conservative. Elected for the Stalybridge and Hyde division of Cheshire in October 1931 and sat until he retired in October 1935. J.P. Died 20 December 1959.   [1935]

HOPKIN, Daniel. 4 Paper Buildings, Temple, London. S. of David Hopkin, Esq., a Glamorgan farm worker. B. at Llantwit Major 1886; m. 1919, Edmée Viterbo. Educ. at South Wales Training Coll., Carmarthen, and St. Catharine's Coll., Cambridge. A Barrister-at-Law 1924. A Labour Member. Unsuccessfully contested the Carmarthen division of Carmarthenshire

in June 1928. Elected for Carmarthen in May 1929, and was defeated there in October 1931. Re-elected in November 1935 and sat until 1941 when he was appointed a Metropolitan Police Magistrate. Served in France and Gallipoli 1914-18, M.C., Maj. Died 30 August 1951.   [1941]

HOPKINS, John Wells Wainwright. 80 Regent's Park Road, London. New Place, Lingfield. Carlton, Argentine, and Constitutional. S. of John Baker Hopkins, Esq. B. 1863; m. 1894, Ethelind, d. of Charles Mackern, Esq., of Buenos Aires. Educ. privately. A Civil Engineer. A Conservative. Unsuccessfully contested E. St. Pancras in December 1910. Sat for S.E. St. Pancras from 1918-23. Defeated in 1923; re-elected there in October 1924 and sat until he retired in May 1929. Created Bart. 1929. Died 16 February 1946.   [1929]

HOPKINSON, Sir Alfred, K.C. 10 Lansdowne Crescent, London. Alpine. S. of John Hopkinson, Esq. B. 28 June 1851; m. 1873, Esther, d. of Henry Wells, Esq., of Nottingham (she died 1931). Educ. at Owens Coll., Manchester, and Lincoln Coll., Oxford; Honorary Fellow of Lincoln Coll. 1903; Honours in Lit. Hum. 1872, 1st cl. in B.C.L., Vinerian Scholar; Stowell Fellow of University Coll., Oxford 1873. Barrister-at-Law Lincolns Inn 1873; Q.C. 1892; bencher 1896; Treasurer 1921. Knighted 1910; M.A. Oxford; Honorary LL.D. Manchester, Glasgow, Aberdeen, Leeds and Bristol. Professor of Law at Owens Coll. 1875-89, Principal 1898-1904; Vice-Chancellor of Victoria University Manchester 1900-13; Adviser to Bombay University 1913-14. Chairman of many Departmental Commissions. A Unionist. Unsuccessfully contested E. Manchester in 1885, as a Liberal, and S.W. Manchester in 1892 as a Liberal Unionist. Sat for the Cricklade division of Wiltshire as a Unionist from 1895-98 when he resigned, and for the Combined English Universities from March 1926 until he retired in May 1929. Died 11 November 1939.   [1929]

HOPKINSON, Austin. 8 Westminster Mansions, Great Smith Street, London. S.

of Sir Alfred Hopkinson, MP. B. 24 June 1879. Unmarried. Served in South African War 1900 and in France 1914-18; R.N. 1939-42. J.P. for Lancashire. An Independent Member. Elected for the Prestwich division of Lancashire in October 1918, and sat for the Mossley division of Lancashire from December 1918-May 1929, when he was defeated. Re-elected for the Mossley division in October 1931 and sat until he was defeated in July 1945. Accepted the Coalition Liberal Whip in the 1918-22 Parliament but resigned it in February 1922. Supported the National Government from 1931 until November 1938. Was opposed by Conservative candidate only at the elections of 1931 and 1945. Died 2 September 1962.   [1945]

HOPKINSON, Edward. Ferns, Alderley Edge, Cheshire. 4th s. of John Hopkinson, Esq., at one time Mayor of Manchester. B. in Manchester 28 May 1859; m. Minnie, d. of John Campbell, Esq., of Co. Antrim. Educ. at Owens Coll., Manchester, and Emmanuel Coll, Cambridge. Fellow of Emmanuel Coll., Cambridge; D.Sc. (London); M.Inst. C.E. Designed the electrical plant for the first London tube railway. President of the Institution of Mechanical Engineers. Member of the Indian Industrial Commission 1916-18. A Unionist. Elected for the Clayton division of Manchester in December 1918 and sat until his death on 15 January 1922. Vice-Chairman of Mather and Platt Limited. Member of Institution of Electrical Engineers and Institution of Civil Engineers. Member of Industrial Fatigue Research Board. Died 15 January 1922.   [1922]

HORABIN, Thomas Lewis. Continued in House after 1945 : full entry in Volume IV.

HORE-BELISHA, Rt. Hon. Isaac Leslie. 16 Stafford Place, London. White's, and Reform. S. of Capt. J.I. Belisha and Lady Hore. B. 7 September 1893; m. 22 June 1944, Cynthia, d. of Gilbert Elliot, Esq., of Hull Place, Sholden. Educ. at Clifton, Paris, Heidelberg, and St. John's Coll., Oxford, M.A. President of the Oxford Union Society. Served overseas 1914-18,

Maj. Barrister-at-Law, Inner Temple 1923. Parliamentary Secretary Board of Trade November 1931-September 1932; Financial Secretary to the Treasury September 1932-July 1934; Minister of Transport July 1934-May 1937. Secretary of State for War May 1937-January 1940. PC. 1935. Sat for the Devonport division of Plymouth from December 1923 until he was defeated in July 1945, standing as a 'National' candidate. Unsuccessfully contested the Devonport division of Plymouth as a Liberal in October 1922. Sat as a Liberal from 1923 to 1931, as a Liberal Nationalist from 1931 to 1942 and as a National Independent from 1942-1945. Unsuccessfully contested S. Croydon as a Conservative in February 1950. Minister of National Insurance May-July 1945. Joined Conservative Party after the 1945 election. Member of Westminister City Council 1947. Created Baron Hore-Belisha 1954. Assumed surname of Hore-Belisha on his mother's marriage to Sir Adair Hore in 1912. Died at Rheims 16 February 1957.   [1945]

HORLICK, Lieut.-Col. James Nockells, O.B.E., M.C. 93 Eaton Place, London. Little Paddocks, Sunningdale, Berkshire. Carlton, Guards', Bucks, and Bath. S. of Sir James Horlick, 1st Bart., of Cowley Manor. B. 22 March 1886; m. 1st, 22 March 1911, Flora Macdonald, d. of Col. Cunliffe Martin, C.B., of Cheltenham (she died 1955); secondly, 1956, Joan MacGill. Educ. at Eton, and Christ Church, Oxford. Served in the Coldstream Guards 1908-20; Lieut.-Col. R. of O.; Director of Horlick's Malted Milk Company. A Conservative. Elected for the City of Gloucester in December 1923. Sat until he retired in May 1929. O.B.E. 1919. High Sheriff of Berkshire 1938. Succeeded as Bart. on the death of his nephew in 1958. Died 31 December 1972.   [1929]

HORNBY, Frank. Quarry Brook, Maghull, Liverpool. B. 1863; m. Clara, d. of W.G. Godefrey, Esq., of Liverpool. A Conservative. Elected for the Everton division of Liverpool in October 1931 and sat until he retired in October 1935. Inventor of Meccano and Hornby trains; Chairman of Meccano Limited. Died 21 September 1936.   [1935]

HORNE, Rt. Hon. Sir Robert Stevenson,
G.B.E., K.C. 69 Arlington House, London.
Carlton, Travellers', Conservative, and
Royal Thames Yacht. S. of the Rev. Robert
Stevenson Horne, of Slamannan, Stirling-
shire. B. 28 February 1871. Unmarried.
Educ. at George Watson's Coll., Edinburgh,
and at University of Glasgow. An Advocate
of the Scottish bar, called 1896; K.C. 1910.
Assistant Inspector-Gen. of Transportation;
Lieut.-Col. R.E.; Director of Materials and
Priority, Admiralty 1917; Director-Gen.
of Labour and Materials, and Third Civil
Lord of the Admiralty 1918; Minister of
Labour January 1919 to March 1920;
President of the Board of Trade March
1920-April 1921; Chancellor of the Ex-
chequer April 1921 to October 1922;
Chairman of G.W. Railway. Director of
the Suez Canal Company, of Lloyds Bank,
of the P. and O. S.N. Company, and of
other companies. Lord Rector of Aberdeen
University 1921-24. LL.D. Edinburgh 1921,
PC. January 1919. Created K.B.E. 1918,
G.B.E. 1920. A Conservative. Unsuccessfully
contested Stirlingshire in January and
December 1910. Sat for the Hillhead division
of Glasgow from 1918 until May 1937 when
he was created Visct. Horne of Slamannan.
Lecturer in Philosophy, University Coll.
of N. Wales 1895, Examiner in Philosophy,
University of Aberdeen 1896-1900. Died
3 September 1940. [1937]

HORNE, William Edgar. 110 Mount
Street, London. Hall Place, Shackleford,
Surrey. Carlton, City of London, and Arts.
S. of Edgar Horne, Esq., of The Hill,
Witley. B. 21 January 1856; m. 1886,
Margery Mary, d. of George Anderson
May, Esq. (she died 1939) Educ. at West-
minster School. President of Surveyors'
Institution, Vice-President of the National
Service League; member of Westminster
City Council, Mayor 1923-24; Dept.-Chair-
man of the Prudential Assurance Company
1917-28 and Chairman 1928-41. A Unionist.
Unsuccessfully contested the Barnstaple
division of Devon in 1906. Elected for the
Guildford division of Surrey in January
1910 and sat until he retired in October
1922. Created Bart. 1929. J.P. for London
and Dept.-Lieut. of Sutherland. Died 26
September 1941. [1922]

174

HOROBIN, Iain Macdonald. Continued
in House after 1945: full entry in Volume IV.

HORRABIN, James Francis. 72 Gower
Street, London. National Labour. S. of
James Woodhouse Horrabin, Esq., of
Sheffield, and Mary, d. of Francis Pinney,
Esq., of Stamford. B. 1 November 1884;
m. 1st, 1911, Winifred, d. of A. J. Batho,
Esq., of Sheffield (divorced 1947); secondly,
1948, Margaret McWilliams. Educ.
at Stamford Grammar School, and Sheffield
School of Art. A Journalist and Artist.
On the staff of *Daily News* and *Star* from
1911. Editor of *Plebs Magazine* from 1914.
A Labour Member. Elected for the Peter-
borough division of Northamptonshire in
May 1929 and sat until he was defeated in
October 1931. Author of many historical and
economic books and compiler of historical
atlases. Creator of many newspaper comic
cartoons. Chairman of Fabian Colonial
Bureau 1945-50. Died 2 March 1962.
[1931 2nd ed.]

HORSBRUGH Rt. Hon. Florence
Gertrude. Continued in House after 1945:
full entry in Volume IV.

HOTCHKIN, Capt. Stafford Vere. The
Manor House, Woodhall Spa, Lincolnshire.
Carlton, Naval & Military, and Cavalry.
S. of Thomas John Stafford Hotchkin,
Esq., and Mary, d. of G.V. Braithwaite,
Esq. B. at Stock Park, Windermere 1876;
m. 1906, Dorothy, youngest d. of F.H.
Arnold, Esq. Educ. at Shrewsbury. Capt.
21st (S. of I.) Lancers. M.C. A Coalition
Unionist. Elected for the Horncastle division
of Lincolnshire in February 1920 and sat
until he retired in October 1922. High
Sheriff of Rutland 1912. Alderman Lindsey
County Council. Died 8 August 1953.
[1922]

HOUFTON, John Plowright. Park Hall,
Mansfield Woodhouse, Nottinghamshire. S.
of Charles Houfton, Esq., Mining Engineer,
and Phebe Houfton. B. at Chesterfield
13 December 1857; m. 1894, Frances, d.
of George Mosley, Esq., of Garforth, near
Leeds. Educ. at the National School, Eastwood, and Nottinghamshire. A Mining

Engineer and Colliery Manager, certified 1883. Mayor of Mansfield 1912-13; Managing Director of large collieries 1910-19; President of the Midland Institute of Mining Engineers, and of the National Association of Colliery Managers. Unsuccessfully contested N.E. Derbyshire as a Liberal in 1914. Elected for E. Nottingham in June 1922 as a Conservative and sat until he was defeated in December 1923. Knighted 1929. Died 18 November 1929.   [1923]

HOUSTON, Sir Robert Paterson, Bart. 35 and 36 Park Side, Albert Gate, London. 16 Leadenhall Street, London. 10 Dale Street, Liverpool. Carlton, Royal Carlton, Royal Thames, and others. Only s. of Robert Houston, Esq. B. at Bootle 31 May 1853; m. 1924, Dame Fanny Lucy, Lady Byron, D.B.E., widow of 9th Lord Byron. Educ. at Liverpool Coll., and privately. Head of the firm of R.P. Houston and Company, Steamship Owners and Merchants, of Liverpool, London, New York, Buenos Aires, Cape Town, etc. Created Bart. 1922. A Conservative. Sat for the W. Toxteth division of Liverpool from 1892 until he resigned in April 1924. Died in Jersey 14 April 1926.   [1924 2nd ed.]

HOWARD, Capt. Hon. Donald Sterling Palmer. 1a South Audley Street, London. Carlton, Cavalry, Bucks, and Bath. S. of R.T.B. Howard, Esq., F.R.C.S., and the Baroness Strathcona and Mount Royal. B. in London 14 June 1891; m. 25 October 1922, Diana, d. of Gerald and Lady Louise Loder. Educ. at Eton, and Trinity Coll., Cambridge. Capt. 3rd Hussars 1913-19. Parliamentary Private Secretary to Mr. Betterton, Parliamentary Secretary, Ministry of Labour 1923-24, and to Mr. Bridgeman First Lord of the Admiralty 1925. A Conservative. Sat for N. Cumberland from November 1922 until August 1926 when he succeeded to the Peerage as Baron Strathcona and Mount Royal. Capt. of the Yeomen of the Guard November 1931-January 1934. Under-Secretary for War January 1934-January 1939. Member of Indian Statutory Commission 1927-30. Rejoined army in 1939; retired as Lieut.-Col. 1945. Died 22 February 1959.   [1926]

HOWARD, Hon. Geoffrey William Algernon. 75 Sussex Gardens, London. Castle Howard, Malton, Yorkshire. 5th s. of 9th Earl of Carlisle. B. 12 February 1877; m. 1915, Hon. Ethel Methuen, d. of Lord Methuen (she died 1932). Educ. at Trinity Coll., Cambridge; M.A. Vice-Chamberlain to H.M. Household 1911-15. Junior Lord of the Treasury May 1915 to December 1916, and a Liberal Whip 1911-18. Chairman of House of Commons Kitchen Committee 1917. A Liberal. Unsuccessfully contested the Richmond division of Yorkshire in 1900. Sat for the Eskdale division of Cumberland from 1906 to December 1910 when he was defeated and for the Westbury division of Wiltshire from 1911-18 when he was defeated. Unsuccessfully contested N. Cumberland in November 1922. Elected for the Luton division of Bedfordshire in December 1923 and sat until he was defeated in October 1924. Parliamentary Private Secretary to H.H. Asquith when Prime Minister 1908-10. Temporary Capt. Royal Marines 1914-15. Lord-Lieut. of N. Riding of Yorkshire 1931-35. Died 20 June 1935.
[1924 2nd ed.]

HOWARD, Stephen Goodwin, C.B.E. The Moat, Upend, Newmarket. S. of Stephen Howard, Esq., Farmer, of Kirtling. B. at Upend, Kirtling, Newmarket 1867; m. 1895, Mary Maude, d. of Henry Hailey Clare, Esq., of Suffolk. Educ. privately. J.P. for Cambridgeshire and Suffolk; Chairman of Appeal Tribunal 1914; Alderman Cambridgeshire County Council 1908; Chairman of Main Roads Committee 1903. Vice-Chairman of Cambridgeshire County Council 1919-21 and Chairman 1921-34. C.B.E. 1918. A Coalition Liberal. Elected for the Sudbury division of Suffolk in December 1918, when he defeated the 'Coupon' Conservative candidate, and sat until he was defeated in November 1922 standing as a National Liberal candidate with opposition from both Conservative and Liberal candidates. Died 13 November 1934.   [1922]

HOWARD, Tom Forrest. 8 Quernmore Road, Hornsey, London. 1912. S. of William Howard, Esq., of Lancashire. B. 23

December 1888; m. 21 December 1912, Haidie, d. of Henry Batteley, Esq., of Suffolk. Educ. at Higher Grade School, Bounds Green Road, London. An Account Book Maker. Founded Tariff Reform Scouts 1909. Member of Finsbury Borough Council 1922-25, of London County Council from 1925-28 and 1931-34. Served in France with Machine Gun Corps (D.C.M. 1917). A Conservative. Unsuccessfully contested S. Islington in October 1924 and May 1929. Elected for S. Islington in October 1931 and sat until he was defeated in November 1935. Unsuccessfully contested S. Islington in July 1945, W. Islington in September 1947 and S.W. Islington in February 1950 and October 1951. Died 12 June 1953.
[1935]

HOWARD-BURY, Lieut.-Col. Charles Kenneth, D.S.O. Belvedere House, Mullingar. Bath, Travellers'. Kildare Street, Dublin. S. of Capt. Kenneth Howard-Bury and Lady Emily, d. of the 3rd Earl of Charleville. B. 15 August 1883. Educ. at Eton, and Royal Military Coll., Sandhurst. Lieut.-Col. K.R.R.C.; Dept.-Lieut. for Co. Westmeath. Had Gold Medals of the Royal Geographical Society and of the French Geographical Society. Parliamentary Private Secretary to the Rt. Hon. Walter Guinness December 1922-24. A Conservative. Sat for the Bilston division of Wolverhampton from 1922 until he was defeated there in October 1924. Elected for the Chelmsford division of Essex in November 1926 and sat until he retired in October 1931. D.S.O. 1918. Leader of the Everest reconnaisance expedition 1921. High Sheriff of King's County 1921. Honorary Col. 85th East Anglian Brigade (T.A.) 1927-32. Died 20 September 1963.
[1931 2nd ed.]

HOWITT, Dr. Alfred Bakewell, C.V.O., M.D. 52 Warwick Square, London. Wolfhall Manor, Nr. Marlborough. Carlton. S. of Francis Howitt, Esq., M.D., of Nottingham, and of Heanor, Derbyshire. B. 1879; m. 26 May 1911, Hon. Dorothy Whiteley, d. of George, 1st Baron Marchamley (she died July 1942). Educ. at Epsom Coll., Clare Coll., Cambridge, M.A., and St. Thomas's

Hospital. Chairman of Institute of Hospital Almoners and of Parliamentary Medical Group. E.St.J.J. Capt. R.A.M.C. Served in France. A Conservative. Unsuccessfully contested Preston in May and July 1929. Elected for Reading in October 1931 and sat until he retired in June 1945. C.V.O. 1928. Knighted 1945. Fellow of Royal Society of Medicine. Died 8 December 1954. [1945]

HUBBARD, Thomas Frederick. Continued in House after 1945: full entry in Volume IV.

HUDSON, Sir Austin Uvedale Morgan, Bart. Continued in House after 1945: full entry in Volume IV.

HUDSON, James Hindle. Continued in House after 1945: full entry in Volume IV.

HUDSON, Ralph Milbanke. The Cedars, Sunderland. 116 Oakwood Court, Kensington, London. Carlton, and Constitutional. S. of Ralph Milbanke Hudson, Esq. B. at East Bolden, Co. Durham 1849; m. 1883, Eliza Westropp, d. of Graham Palliser, Esq., of Plymouth. Educ. privately in England and in France. A Shipowner; Chairman of the River Wear Commission, Sunderland from 1916; member of the Committee of Lloyd's Registry from 1906. A Unionist. Elected for Sunderland in December 1918 and sat until he retired in October 1922. Died 5 March 1938. [1922]

HUDSON, Rt. Hon. Robert Spear, C.H. Continued in House after 1945: full entry in Volume IV.

HUGHES, Collingwood James. 11 Abingdon Gardens, Kensington, London. S. of William Collingwood Hughes, Esq., of the Admiralty, and Fanny, d. of Lieut.-Col. James Fynmore, R.M.L.I. B. at Chatham 31 January 1872; m. 1899 Lilian, d. of John Crocker, Esq., head of R.N.E. Coll., Devonport. Educ. at the Plymouth Grammar School, and King's Coll., London. Paymaster Lieut.-Commander R.N.V.R. 1915-19; Admiralty Official Lecturer 1917-19. A Conservative. Unsuccessfully contested the Peckham division of Camberwell in

1918, as an Independent Conservative in opposition to the 'Coupon' Liberal candidate. Elected for the Peckham division of Camberwell in November 1922 and sat until he retired in October 1924. Principal of Civil Service Coll., Cape Town 1901-09. Gen. Secretary of Council of Retail Distributors 1943-45. Manager of Daily Express Centre of Public Opinion 1942-43. Died 25 March 1963.   [1924 2nd ed.]

HUGHES, Ronw Moelwyn. Continued in House after 1945: full entry in Volume IV.

HUGHES, Spencer Leigh. 40 Lexham Gardens, London. National Liberal, and Eighty. S. of the Rev. James Hughes. B. 21 April 1858 at Trowbridge; m. 1881, Ellen, d. of James Grove, Esq., of Newport, Isle of Wight (she died 1916). Educ. at Woodhouse School, near Leeds. A Journalist on the *Morning Leader* and *Daily News* to which he contributed the 'Sub Rosa' column. A Liberal. Unsuccessfully contested the Jarrow division of Durham Co. in 1907 and Bermondsey in 1909. Sat for Stockport from January 1910 until his death on 22 February 1920.   [1920]

HULBERT, Norman John. Continued in House after 1945: full entry in Volume IV.

HUME, Sir George Hopwood. 83 Lee Road, Blackheath, London. 5 Fig Tree Court, Temple, London. Junior Carlton. B. 24 May 1866; m. 1st, 1901, Jeanne Alice, d. of Professor Ladrierre, of Lausanne (she died 1922); secondly, 1 August 1932, Dorothy Hunt, d. of Mrs. S.J. Blundell, of Liverpool. Educ. at Coll. Galliard, Lausanne, and Finsbury Technical Coll. Barrister-at-Law, Middle Temple 1900. Member London County Council 1910-22, Alderman from 1922-46, Chairman 1926-27; Leader of M.R. Party 1918-25; Chairman of Highways Committee 1913-19 and of the London Electricity Committee 1913-26; member of London and Home Counties Joint Electricity Authority 1925-26; of the Thames Conservancy Board from 1916; Chairman of London Municipal Society. J.P. Member of Advisory Committee on Traffic of the Ministry of Transport 1924-25; Chairman of

Metropolitan division National Union of Conservative and Unionist Associations 1937; of the Mildmay Mission Hospital, of Trinitarian Bible Society, and of Rachael Macmillan Training Coll. Created Knight Bach. 1924. A Conservative. Elected for Greenwich in November 1922, defeated 1923; re-elected in 1924, again defeated May 1929; re-elected in October 1931. Sat until he retired in June 1945. Member of Greenwich Borough Council 1900. Member of Institute of Electrical Engineers. Died 13 September 1946.   [1945]

HUME-WILLIAMS, Sir Ellis William, Bart., K.B.E., K.C. 3 Hare Court, Temple, London. 59 Pall Mall, London. Carlton, and Junior Carlton. S. of J.W. Hume-Williams, Esq., Barrister-at-Law. B. 19 August 1863; m. 6 October 1886, Lucy Annette, d. of Theodor Satow, Esq., of Riga. Educ. at Trinity Hall, Cambridge, B.A., LL.B. Barrister-at-Law, Middle Temple 1881, Bencher 1906, Treasurer 1929; Q.C. 1899. Recorder of Bury St. Edmunds 1901-05, and of Norwich from 1905-1944. Author of *The Irish Parliament from 1782 to 1800, The Taking of Evidence on Commission*, and Editor of *Taylor on Evidence*. K.B.E. 1918, created Bart. 1922. A Conservative. Unsuccessfully contested N. Monmouthshire in 1895, the Frome division of Somerset in 1900, and N. Kensington in 1906. Sat for the Bassetlaw division of Nottinghamshire from January 1910 until May 1929 when he was defeated. PC. June 1929. Died 4 February 1947.   [1929]

HUNLOKE, Capt. Henry Philip. Edensor, Bakewell, Derbyshire. S. of Sir Philip Hunloke, K.C.V.O. B. 1906; m. 1st, 28 November 1929, Lady Anne Cavendish, d. of Victor, 9th Duke of Devonshire, K.G., G.C.M.G., G.C.V.O. (divorced 1945); secondly, 1945, Virginia Clive (divorced 1972); thirdly, 1972, Ruth Holdsworth. Parliamentary Private Secretary to Osbert Peake when Parliamentary Under-Secretary of State for Home Affairs April-December 1939. A Conservative. Elected for W. Derbyshire in June 1938 and sat until he resigned in January 1944. Lieut.-Col. Royal Wiltshire Yeomanry; served in Middle

East 1939-45. Died 13 January 1978.

[1944]

HUNTER, Gen. Sir Archibald, G.C.B., G.C.V.O., D.S.O. 11 Upper Grosvenor Street, London. Naval & Military, Marlborough, Royal Automobile, and Carlton. New, Edinburgh. B. in London 6 September 1856; m. 1910, Mary, d. of Hickson Fergusson, Esq., of Ayr, and widow of the 2nd Lord Inverclyde (she died 1924). Educ. at Glasgow Academy, and Royal Military Coll., Sandhurst. Obtained a commission in the army 1874. Served in the Soudan under Lord Kitchener, and was Chief of the Staff to Sir George White in the South African War. Was shut up in Ladysmith; later commanded the army victorious at Prinsloo. During the European War trained one of the new armies. Later retired from the Aldershot Command. A Coalition Unionist. Elected for the Lancaster division of Lancashire in December 1918 and sat until he retired in October 1922. D.S.O. 1886; K.C.B. 1898. G.O.C. Scottish Command 1901-03, in command of Indian Southern Army at Bombay 1903-08. Gov. and Commander-in-Chief of Gibraltar 1910-13. Fellow of Royal Geographical Society. Dept.-Lieut. for Ayrshire. Died 28 June 1936.

[1922]

HUNTER, Dr. Joseph. 33 Castle Street, Dumfries. National Liberal. B. 24 December 1875; m. 1918, Jean Augusta Hadley, M.D., d. of Dr. J.W. MacLean, of North Sydney, Nova Scotia. Educ. at Hutton Hall Academy, Royal High School, University, R.C.S. Edinburgh, and at University Coll., London. M.B., Ch.B. Edinburgh 1898, D.P.H. Cambridge 1902. Resident Physician Royal Infirmary, Edinburgh 1899-1900, Civil Surgeon South African Field Force 1900-01. Medical Officer of Health, Dumfries 1902-26. Director of Liberal Campaign Department 1927-29. National Organiser for Liberal National Party. Liberal Scottish Whip June 1929-August 1931. Parliamentary Private Secretary to the Rt. Hon. Sir A. Sinclair, Secretary of State for Scotland November 1931-September 1932. Elected for Dumfries in May 1929 as a Liberal. Supported the

National Government in 1931 and remained on the Government benches in 1933. Joined the Liberal National Party in June 1934. National Organizer of Liberal National Party 1934-35. Sat until his death on 24 July 1935.

[1935]

HUNTER, Capt. Michael John. Stoke Hall, Calver, Derbyshire. Carlton, Junior Constitutional, and 1900. S. of Michael Joseph Hunter, Esq., of Stoke Hall, Derbyshire. B. 15 July 1891; m. 1919, Clare Margaret, d. of Henry Randolph Trafford, Esq., of Michaelchurch Court, Herefordshire. Educ. at Rugby and Clare Coll., Cambridge; B.A. 1912. Served with R.F.A. 1914-18. A Conservative. Elected for the Brigg division of Lincolnshire in October 1931 and sat until he was defeated in November 1935. Killed in a hunting accident on 9 March 1951.

[1935]

HUNTER, Sir Thomas. Nimrod, 142 Glasgow Road, Perth. Constitutional. S. of Thomas Hunter, Esq., and Annabella Struthers. B. 2 October 1872; m. 1897, Janet, d. of William Harris, Esq. (she died 1938). Educ. at Perth Academy. A Newspaper Proprietor and Editor. Lord Provost of Perth 1932-35; J.P. for Co. of Perth; County Councillor for Perth 1919-32. Chairman of Perthshire Education Authority, Chairman of Perth division of Conservative Association; Director and Vice-Chairman City of Perth Royal Infirmary. Knight Bach. 1944. A Conservative. Elected for the Perth division of Perth and Kinross in November 1935 and sat until he retired in June 1945. Fellow of Institute of Journalists. Died 19 March 1953.

[1945]

HUNTER, Thomas. Castletownroche, Co. Cork. A Draper. A leader of the Sinn Fein movement who was arrested in Dublin in June 1918 for defiance of the Defence of the Realm Regulations, and interned in Gloucester prison. Released, but in 1920 again arrested. A Sinn Fein Member. Returned unopposed for N.E. Cork in December 1918 but did not take his seat. Member of Dail for N.E. Cork to 1922, as an Anti-Treaty Member.

[1922]

HUNTER-WESTON, Lieut.-Gen. Sir Aylmer Gould, K.C.B., D.S.O. 2 Culford Gardens, London. Hunterston, West Kilbridge, Ayrshire. Royal Automobile, and Carlton. Eld. s. of Lieut.-Col. Gould Hunter-Weston, 26th Laird of Hunterston. B. 23 September 1864; m. 1905, Grace, Dame of Justice, Order of St. John of Jerusalem, only d. of William Strang Steel, Esq., of Philiphaugh, Selkirkshire. Educ. at Wellington Coll., Royal Military Academy, Woolwich, and the Staff Coll. Entered army, R.E. 1884; served Miranzai 1891, Waziristan 1894-95, and Dongola 1896 Expeditions; South African War 1899-1902; Gen. Staff, Eastern Command 1904-08; Gen. Staff, Scottish Command 1908-11; Assistant Director of Military Training, Gen. Staff, War Office 1911-14; Brigadier-Gen. Commanding at Colchester February-August 1914; in command of 11th Infantry Brigade in France August 1914-February 1915; commanded 29th Division, March-May 1915; commanded 8th Army Corps, Gallipoli, May-July 1915, and in France and Flanders to November 1918. Maj.-Gen. 1914; Lieut.-Gen. 1919. Col.-Commanding R.E. G.C.St. J.; Commissioner Legion d'Honneur; Grand Officier Order of the Belgian Crown; Officer Order of the Medjidieh; D.S.O. 1900; C.B. 1911; K.C.B. 1915; Dept.-Lieut. and J.P. for Ayrshire. A Unionist. Sat for N. Ayrshire from October 1916-December 1918, and for the Buteshire and N. Ayrshire division of Ayr and Bute from December 1918 until he retired in October 1935. Died 18 March 1940. [1935]

HUNTINGFIELD, William Charles Arcedeckne Vanneck, 5th Baron (Irish Peerage). Heveningham Hall, Halesworth, Suffolk. Carlton, and Cavalry. S. of Hon. William Arcedeckne Vanneck, and Mary, d. of Dr. Armstrong, of Toowoomba, Queensland. B. 3 January 1883; m. 1st, 21 December 1912, Margaret Eleanor, d. of Judge Ernest Crosby, of New York (she died 1943); secondly, 1944, Muriel, d. of Col. J. Duke and widow of Lord Eltisley (she died 1953). Educ. at Wellington Coll. Capt. 13th Hussars. Dept.-Lieut., J.P., and County Councillor for E. Suffolk; Parliamentary Private Secretary to D. Hacking, Parliamentary Under-Secretary for Home Department from 1926-27, to Sir P. Cunliffe-Lister, President of Board of Trade from 1927-28. A Conservative. Elected for the Eye division of Suffolk in December 1923 and sat until he retired in May 1929. Succeeded to the Irish Peerage as Baron Huntingfield on the death of his uncle in 1915. Gov. of Victoria 1934-39; Acting Gov.-Gen. of Australia 1938. Appointed Gov. of S. Rhodesia 1942 but did not take up the appointment because of ill health. Died 20 November 1969. [1929]

HURD, Sir Percy Angier. Hillside, Jackson's Lane, Highgate, London. Constitutional. S. of William Hurd, Esq., Solicitor. B. 1864; m. Hannah, d. of Dr. Cox of Dundee (she died 1949). Created Knight Bach. 1932. A Conservative. Sat for the Frome division of Somerset from 1918 until December 1923, when he was defeated, and for the Devizes division of Wiltshire from October 1924 until he retired in June 1945. Journalist on *Staffordshire Sentinel* 1882, Editor of *Canadian Gazette*, London correspondent of *Montreal Gazette* and *Montreal Daily Star*. Editor of *Outlook* 1898-1904. Secretary of Tariff Commission 1917-18. President of Rural District Councils Association from 1925 to 1945. Member of Hornsey Borough Council from 1918 to 1945. Died 5 June 1950. [1945]

HURST, Sir Gerald Berkeley, K.C. 8 Old Square, Lincoln's Inn, London. 56 Ladbroke Grove, London. Athenaeum. Manchester Constitutional. S. of William Martin Hertz, Esq., of Bradford. B. 4 December 1877; m. 3 January 1905, Margaret, d. of Sir Alfred Hopkinson, K.C., MP. Educ. at Bradford Grammar School, and Lincoln Coll., Oxford (Scholar); 1st class history honours 1898; Arnold Historical Essay Prize 1900; M.A., B.C.L. Barrister-at-Law, Lincoln's Inn 1902; K.C. 1920; Bencher 1924. Practised in the Chancery division. Lieut.-Col. commanding 7th Manchesters; served in Sudan, Gallipoli, Sinai, Flanders, 1914-18. T.D. Knight Bach. 1929. A Conservative. Sat for the Moss Side division of Manchester from December 1918, until defeated in December 1923. Re-elected for the Moss Side division of

Manchester in October 1924 and sat until he retired in October 1935. County Court Judge 1937-52. Adopted the surname Hurst in lieu of Hertz in 1916. Of Jewish extraction but brought up as a Christian. Died 27 October 1957. [1935]

HUTCHINSON, Geoffrey Clegg. Continued in House after 1945: full entry in Volume IV.

HUTCHISON, Sir George Aitken Clark, K.C. 24 Hans Place, London. Island of Eriska, Argyllshire. 34 Drumsheugh Gardens, Edinburgh. Carlton, and Junior Carlton. S. of the Rev. John Hutchison, D.D. Minister of the United Free Church. B. 1873; m. 1902, Margaret, d. of John Blair, Esq., W.S., Edinburgh. Educ. at Edinburgh Academy and University. Advocate 1896; K.C. 1922; Honorary Sheriff Substitute for Argyllshire at Oban; J.P. for Argyllshire. Knighted 1928. A Conservative. Unsuccessfully contested Argyllshire in January 1906, January 1910 and December 1910. Elected for Midlothian N. in 1922, defeated there in December 1923; re-elected for Midlothian N. in October 1924 and sat until his death on 22 December 1928.
[1929]

HUTCHISON, George Ian Clark. Continued in House after 1945: full entry in Volume IV.

HUTCHISON, Maj.-Gen. Sir Robert, K.C.M.G., C.B., D.S.O. 19 Montagu Square, London. Braehead, Kirkcaldy. Reform, Marlborough, United Service, and Cavalry. New, Edinburgh. S. of Alexander Hutchison, Esq. B. 5 September 1873; m. 1st, 26 April 1905, Agnes Begbie, d. of William Drysdale, Esq., of Kilrie, Fifeshire (she died 1941); secondly, 1942, Alma, widow of James Drysdale, Esq., of Kilrie. Joined the 7th Dragoon Guards 1900; Capt. 11th Hussars 1905; Maj. 4th Dragoon Guards 1912; served in South African War and in France 1914-17; Director of Organization at the War Office in 1917-19. K.C.M.G. 1919; D.S.O. 1915; C.B. 1918; had Legion of Honour, French Croix de Guerre, Order of the Crown of Italy, and American D.S.M. Temporary Maj.-Gen. and Director of Organization, War Office, 1917-19; D.A.G. 1919; retired 1923. Chief Liberal Whip November 1926-November 1930. A Liberal until 1931, thereafter a Liberal National Member. Sat for Kirkcaldy Burghs from 1922-23, and was defeated there in December 1923. Elected for Montrose Burghs in October 1924 and sat until June 1932 when he was created Baron Hutchison of Montrose. Chairman of Liberal National Organisation 1936, Treasurer 1940. Paymaster-Gen. December 1935-June 1938. PC. 1937. Died 13 June 1950. [1932]

HUTCHISON, William. 10 University Gardens, Glasgow. Constitutional, Devonshire, St. Stephen's, and Conservative. Automobile, Glasgow. S. of William Hutchison, Esq., Printer and Publisher, of Greenock, and Margaret, d. of John Ramsay, Esq., Customs Official. B. at Greenock in about 1870; m. Agnes, d. of William Grant, Esq., of Dunoon. Educ. at Greenock Academy, and Glasgow University; M.A. and LL.B. A Solicitor with large practice in London Courts and Court of Session, Scotland. A Congregationalist. A Conservative. Unsuccessfully contested the Bridgeton division of Glasgow in December 1910. Elected for the Kelvingrove division of Glasgow in November 1922 and sat until his death on 1 May 1924. [1924 2nd ed.]

HUTCHISON, William Gordon Douglas. 40 Great Smith Street, London. Ladye Place, Hurley, Berkshire. S. of Col. K. Douglas Hutchison, R.G.A., and of Mrs. Rivers-Moore, of Ladye Place, Hurley. B. 26 September 1904. Educ. at King William's Coll., Isle of Man. A Conservative. Elected for the Romford division of Essex in October 1931 and sat until he was defeated in November 1935. An actor. Served in Royal Navy 1941-44, Lieut. 1943. Died 18 July 1975. [1935]

HYND, John Burns. Continued in House after 1945: full entry in Volume IV.

ILIFFE, Sir Edward Mauger, C.B.E. 24 Carlton House Terrace, London. Basildon

Park, Berkshire. Yattendon Court, Nr. Newbury. Carlton, Royal Thames Yacht, and Royal Automobile. S. of William I. Iliffe, Esq., J.P., of Allesley, Warwickshire. B. 17 May 1877; m. 10 June 1902, Charlotte, d. of Henry Gilding, Esq., J.P., of Rockfield, Gateacre. Chairman of Iliffe and Sons Limited, Publishers, and of the Guildhall Insurance Company. Director of Allied Newspapers Limited, of Amalgamated Press Limited, and of the Cornwall Press Limited. Joint Proprietor of *The Daily Telegraph* 1928-37. J.P. for Warwickshire. Controller of Machine Tools, Ministry of Munitions 1917-18. Knight Bach. 1922, C.B.E. 1918, Legion of Honour. A Conservative. Elected for the Tamworth division of Warwickshire in December 1923. Sat until he resigned in November 1929. President of Association of British Chambers of Commerce 1932. President of Trustees of Shakespeare Memorial Theatre 1933-58. Created Baron Iliffe 1933. Proprietor of *Birmingham Post* and *Birmingham Mail* from 1943. G.B.E. 1946. President of International Lawn Tennis Club 1945-59. Inherited the *Coventry Evening Telegraph* from his father. Died 25 July 1960. [1929 2nd ed.]

ILLINGWORTH, Rt. Hon. Albert Holden. 60 Eaton Place, London. Denton Park, Ben Rhydding, Yorkshire. Reform. S. of Henry Illingworth, Esq., of Bradford, and Mary, d. of Sir Isaac Holden, Bart., MP. B. 25 May 1865 at Bradford; m. 1st, 1895, Annie, d. of Isaac Crothers, Esq., of Le Chateau, Croix, France (divorced 1926); secondly, 1931, Margaret Mary Clare, d. of W.B. Wilberforce, Esq., of Markington Hall, Yorkshire. Educ. at London International Coll., Isleworth, and in Switzerland. Postmaster-Gen. from December 1916-April 1921. PC. 1916. President Bradford Chamber of Commerce 1910. A Liberal. Elected for the Heywood division of S.E. Lancashire in November 1915 and for the Heywood and Radcliffe division of Lancashire in December 1918. Sat until May 1921 when he was created Baron Illingworth. Joined the Conservative Party in 1930. Died 23 January 1942. [1921]

INSKIP, Rt. Hon. Sir Thomas Walker Hobart, C.B.E., K.C. 10 Eaton Square, London. Knockinaam, Stranraer. Carlton, National, and Hurlingham. S. of James Inskip, Esq., of Clifton Park House, Bristol. B. 5 March 1876; m. 30 July 1914, Lady Augusta Boyle, d. of 7th Earl of Glasgow and widow of Charles Orr Ewing, MP. Educ. at Clifton, and King's Coll., Cambridge. A Barrister-at-Law, Inner Temple 1899; K.C. 1914; Bencher 1922; Honorary LL.D. Bristol University. Chancellor of Diocese of Truro 1920-22. Admiralty Intelligence division 1915-18; Head of Naval Law Branch 1918-19. Solicitor-Gen. October 1922 to January 1924, November 1924-March 1928, and August 1931-January 1932; Attorney-Gen. March 1928-June 1929, and January 1932-March 1936; Minister for Co-ordination of Defence and Dept.-Chairman Committee of Imperial Defence with seat in the Cabinet March 1936-January 1939; Recorder of Kingston-on-Thames from 1928-1939. Knight Bach. 1922. PC. 1932. J.P. for Wigtownshire. A Conservative. Unsuccessfully contested the Berwick-on-Tweed division of Northumberland in 1906 and January 1910. Sat for central Bristol from 1918-May 1929 when he was defeated; and for the Fareham division of Hampshire from February 1931 until September 1939 when he was appointed Lord Chancellor and created Visct. Caldecote. C.B.E. 1920. Secretary of State for Dominions January 1939-September 1939 and May 1940-October 1940. Lord Chancellor September 1939-May 1940. Also Leader of the House of Lords May-October 1940. Lord Chief Justice October 1940-January 1946. Died 11 October 1947. [1939]

IRVING, David Daniel. 80 Glen View Road, Burnley. S. of Samuel and Susannah Irving. B. in Birmingham 1854; m. 1878, d. of Henry Brock, Esq., of Bristol. Educ. at Dawson's National School, Birmingham. Was in the mercantile marine from the age of 13 to 21, and a railway servant from the age of 21 to 38. Secretary to the Burnley Socialist Society for about 25 years. Member of Burnley Town Council and Education Committee for 22 years. A Labour Member. Unsuccessfully contested

Accrington in 1906, N.W. Manchester in April 1908, and Rochdale in January and December 1910. First elected for Burnley in December 1918 and sat until his death on 25 January 1924. [1922]

IRWIN, Capt. Charles Ingram Courtenay Wood, The Lord. 44 Eaton Square, London. Swynford Paddocks, Six Mile Bottom, Newmarket. Brooks's, and Buck's. S. of the Earl of Halifax, K.G. B. 3 October 1912; m. 25 April 1936, Ruth Alice Hannah Mary, d. of Capt. Rt. Hon. Neil Primrose, MP. Educ. at Eton, and Christ Church, Oxford. 2nd Lieut. Royal Horse Guards. A Conservative. Elected for York in May 1937 and sat until he was defeated in July 1945. Styled Lord Irwin from 1944 when his father was created Earl of Halifax. Succeeded to the Peerage as 2nd Earl of Halifax 1959. Lord-Lieut. of E. Riding of Yorkshire 1968-74, of Humberside from 1974. Chairman of E. Riding of Yorkshire County Council 1968-74. Pro-Chancellor of Hull University from 1974. High Steward of York Minster.* [1945]

ISAACS, George Alfred. Continued in House after 1945: full entry in Volume IV.

IVEAGH, Gwendolen Florence Mary Guinness, Countess of, C.B.E. 11 St. James's Square, London. D. of William, 4th Earl of Onslow, G.C.M.G. B. 1881; m. 8 October 1903, Rupert, 2nd Earl of Iveagh. Joint Dept. Chairman of Conservative and Unionist Party Organization 1930; Chairman of Women's Advisory Committee 1927-33. A Conservative. Sat for Southend-on-Sea from November 1927 until she retired in October 1935. Styled Viscountess Elveden from 1919 when her father-in-law was created Earl of Iveagh, until 1927 when her husband succeeded to the Earldom. C.B.E. 1920. Died 16 February 1966. [1935]

JACKSON, Rt. Hon. Francis Stanley. 33 Pont Street, London. Carlton. Youngest s. of 1st Lord Allerton. B. 21 November 1870 at Allerton Hall, Leeds; m. 5 November 1902, Julia Henrietta, d. of H. Harrison Broadley, Esq., MP. Educ. at Harrow, and Trinity Coll., Cambridge, B.A. A Director

of G.N. Railway. Raised and commanded 2/7 Battalion West Yorkshire Regiment 1914-17; Capt. 3rd Battalion Royal Lancaster Regiment; served in South Africa 1900-02. Dept.-Lieut. for the W. Riding of Yorkshire. Financial Secretary War Office October 1922-March 1923. Chairman Unionist Party Organization from March 1923-October 1926. A Conservative. Sat for the Howdenshire division of the E. Riding of Yorkshire from February 1915 until October 1926 when he resigned on appointment as Gov.-designate of Bengal. Played cricket for Yorkshire 1894-1905, President of M.C.C. 1921. PC. 1926. Gov. of Bengal 1927-32. Died 9 March 1947. [1926]

JACKSON, Sir Henry, Bart. 19 Putney Hill, London. S. of James Jackson, Esq., of Heywood. B. 22 August 1875; m. 25 August 1904, Edith, d. of Joseph Smalley, Esq. Educ. at Bury Grammar School, and the Universities of Cambridge, M.A., Edinburgh, M.B., and London B.Sc.; 1st Class Nat. Science Tripos, Parts 1 and 2. A Physician. Fellow and Tutor of Downing Coll., Cambridge 1901-11; Fellow of Cambridge Philosophical Society. Medical student at Edinburgh 1911-14. Maj. R.A.M.C. Chairman of London and Home Counties Advisory Committee on Traffic, and of Metropolitan Boroughs Standing Joint Committee 1924; Honorary Treasurer Bolingbroke Hospital, Wandsworth; Chairman of Greater London Joint Smoke Abatement Committee. Mayor of Wandsworth 1921-24. Chairman of Parliamentary Transport Committee 1931, and of Standing Committee on Mineral Transport. Trustee of London Passenger Transport Board; President of London University Conservative and Unionist Association. Created Knight Bach. 1924; Bart. 1935. A Conservative. Elected for Wandsworth central division in October 1924, and was defeated there in May 1929; re-elected for Wandsworth central division in October 1931. Sat until his death on 23 February 1937. [1937]

JACKSON, Joseph Cooksey, K.C. 99 Berkeley Court, London. Cairns Lodge, Sandbourne Road, Bournemouth. S. of George Jackson, Esq., of Lancaster. B.

12 January 1879; m. 1903, Clare, d. of George Garton, Esq., of The White House, Emsworth. Educ. at Royal Grammar School, Lancaster, and at Clare College, Cambridge; B.A., LL.B. Admitted a Solicitor 1903; Barrister-at-Law, Middle Temple 1910; K.C. 1924; Bencher 1930; Recorder of Bolton 1925-38. A Conservative. Elected for the Heywood and Radcliffe division of Lancashire in October 1931 and sat until he retired in October 1935. Died 26 April 1938.   [1935]

JACKSON, Robert Frederick. 42 Freegrove Road, London. 31 Broomhill Road, Ipswich. S. of Henry Jackson, Esq. B. at Ipswich 28 May 1880; m. 27 April 1910, Rosa Emily, d. of George Robert Garrod, Esq., of Ipswich. Educ. at St. Matthew's National School, Ipswich, and Ipswich Technical School. A Stone and marble Mason 1894-1908; organising Secretary of Ipswich I.L.P. from 1908; member of Ipswich Town Council from 1911, Mayor 1932-33 and 1940-42; Gov. of Ipswich Secondary Schools; member of Ipswich Board of Guardians from 1909-12; Ipswich Diocesan Board of Finance from 1921. A Labour Member. Unsuccessfully contested Ipswich in 1918 and 1922. Elected for Ipswich in December 1923 and sat until he was defeated in October 1924. Unsuccessfully contested Ipswich in May 1929, October 1931 and November 1935. Died 28 January 1951.   [1924 2nd ed.]

JACKSON, William Frederick. Glewstone, Herefordshire. S. of George Jackson, Esq., of Birmingham. B. 1893; m. 1923, Hope Hardy Falconer, d. of B.W. Gilmour, Esq., of Glasgow. Educ. at King Edward's High School, Birmingham. A Fruit Grower and Farmer. Sergeant 14th Loyal Warwickshire Regiment 1914-16. A Labour Member. Elected for Brecon and Radnorshires in August 1939 and sat until he retired in June 1945. Created Baron Jackson in 1945. A Liberal until 1931 when he joined the Labour Party. Member of Herefordshire County Council 1931-54. Died 2 May 1954.   [1945]

JACOB, Albert Edward. 235 St. James's Court, London. Constitutional, and 1900. Conservative, and University, Liverpool. S. of W.B. Jacob, Esq., of Ballybrack House, Co. Dublin. B. 22 January 1858; m. 1888, Mary, d. of John Buchanan, Esq., of Glasgow. Educ. at Rathmines School, and Trinity Coll., Dublin; M.A. 1883. Director of W. and R. Jacob and Company (Liverpool) Limited, and of W. and R. Jacob and Company Limited, Durham. Alderman of Liverpool City Council 1925. J.P. for Liverpool. A Conservative. Elected for the E. Toxteth division of Liverpool in October 1924 and sat until his death on 26 February 1929. Member of Liverpool City Council as a Liberal 1906-12 and as a Conservative from 1918. Vice-President of Federation of British Industries. Died 26 February 1929.   [1929]

JAGGER, John. 4 Endsleigh Gardens, London. Penn, Buckinghamshire. National Trades Union, and National Labour. S. of James Jagger, Esq., of Oldham. B. 1 October 1872; m. 1898, Martha, d. of William Southern, Esq., of Cumberbatch, Cheshire. Educ. at Elementary School. A Trades Union Official. Founder and President of Amalgamated Union of Cooperative Employees until 1920. President of National Union of Distributive and Allied Workers 1921-42. J.P. for the N. Riding of Yorkshire. Parliamentary Private Secretary to the Rt. Hon. Herbert Morrison when Minister of Supply May 1940 and when Home Secretary October 1940. A Labour Member. Elected for the Clayton division of Manchester in November 1935 and sat until his death in a road accident on 9 July 1942.   [1942]

JAMES, Wing-Commander Archibald William Henry, M.C. Brackley Grange, Brackley, Northamptonshire. Boodle's. S. of Henry James, Esq., of Hurstmonceux, Sussex. B. September 1893; m. 1st, 1919, Bridget, d. of Murray Guthrie, Esq., MP., of Torosry Castle, Isle of Mull (m. dissolved 1936 on his petition); secondly, 19 June 1940, Eugenia, d. of W. Morris, Esq., of New York, and widow of Patrick Sterling, Esq., of Kippendavie. Educ. at Eton, and

Trinity Coll., Cambridge. Joined 3rd Hussars 1914, R.A.F. 1915, retired 1926; served with B.E.F. 1914-18; in Command 60th Squadron R.A.F., India 1923-25; rejoined R.A.F. 1939. Parliamentary Private Secretary to R.A. Butler, Parliamentary Under-Secretary India Office 1936-37, when Parliamentary Secretary Ministry of Labour 1937-38, and when President of Board of Education 1943-45. Honorary First Secretary H.B.M. Embassy Madrid 1940-41. A Conservative. Unsuccessfully contested the Wellingborough division of Northamptonshire in May 1929. Elected for the Wellingborough division of Northamptonshire in October 1931 and sat until he was defeated in July 1945. K.B.E. 1945.*

[1945]

JAMES, Lieut.-Col. Hon. Cuthbert, C.B.E. (Mil.). The Dower House, Forty Hill, Enfield. Brooks's, and Beefsteak. 2nd s. of 2nd Lord Northbourne. B. 29 February 1872; m. 10 August 1905, Florence Marion, d. of Hussey Packe, Esq., of Prestwold Hall, Loughborough. Educ. at Harrow, and Magdalen Coll., Oxford. 2nd E. Surrey Regiment 1894; served in Egyptian Army, Soudan Civil Service, Egyptian Civil Service; retired in 1909. Served with 7th Battalion E. Surrey Regiment, and as Inspector, Admiralty Motor Transport 1915-19, retiring with rank of Lieut.-Col. C.B.E. 1919. A Conservative. Sat for Bromley from December 1919 until his death on 21 July 1930. [1929 2nd ed.]

JAMES, Admiral Sir William Milbourne, G.C.B. Road Farm, Churt, Surrey. S. of Maj. W.C. James. B. 22 December 1881; m. 18 January 1915, Dorothy Alexandra, d. of Admiral Sir Alexander Duff, G.C.B., G.B.E. (she died 1971). Educ. at Glenalmond, and in H.M.S. *Britannia*. Flag Capt. and Chief of the Staff to Vice-Admiral Sir Alexander Duff, China Station 1921-22; Dept. Director R.N. Staff Coll. Greenwich 1923-25, Director 1925-26; Naval Assistant to First Sea Lord 1928; Aide-de-Camp to King George V 1928-29; Chief of Staff Atlantic Fleet 1930 and Mediterranean Fleet 1931; Rear-Admiral Commanding Battle Cruiser

Squadron 1932-34; a Lord Commissioner of the Admiralty and Dept. Chief of Naval Staff 1935-38; C. in C. Portsmouth 1939-42. Admiral 1938. Chief of Naval Information 1943-44; G.C.B. 1944. Order of the Legion of Honour. A National Conservative. Elected for N. Portsmouth in February 1943 and sat until he retired in June 1945. Grand-s. of Sir John Everett Millais for whom he was the original of 'Bubbles'. C.B. 1919. Dept.-Lieut. for Surrey 1958-65. Died 17 August 1973. [1945]

JAMESON, Capt. John Gordon. 2 Mitre Court Buildings, Temple, London. S. of Andrew Jameson, Lord Ardwall (Scottish Judge). B. 13 April 1878 in Edinburgh; m. 1913, Margaret, d. of A.L. Smith, Esq., Master of Balliol. Educ. at the Edinburgh Academy, St. Andrews University, and Balliol Coll., Oxford, B.A.; Edinburgh University, LL.B. An Advocate, Scottish bar 1905; Barrister-at-Law, English bar, Lincoln's Inn 1919. Served in the South African War 1900; Queen's Medal, 2 clasps. Capt. Scottish Horse 1914; Maj. 1916. A Coalition Unionist. Unsuccessfully contested E. Edinburgh in 1912. Elected for W. Edinburgh in December 1918 and sat until he was defeated in November 1922. Unsuccessfully contested Scottish Universities as an Independent Federal Unionist in November 1946. Sheriff Substitute for the Lothians 1923-46. Died 26 February 1955. [1922]

JAMIESON, Rt. Hon. Douglas, K.C. 34 Moray Place, Edinburgh. Caledonian. S. of William Jamieson, Esq., Merchant of Glasgow. B. 14 July 1880; m. 1918, Violet, d. of H.W. Rhodes, Esq., of Stratheden House, Blackheath. Educ. at Cargilfield, Fettes Coll., Edinburgh, and Glasgow and Edinburgh Universities. Advocate Scottish bar 1911; K.C. 1926. Solicitor-Gen. for Scotland October 1933-March 1935. A Unionist. Unsuccessfully contested Stirling and Falkirk Burghs in May 1929. Elected for the Maryhill division of Glasgow in October 1931 and sat until he retired in October 1935. Lord Advocate March-October 1935. PC. May 1935. Judge of the Court of Session, with the Judicial title of Lord Jamieson 1935-52. Died 31 May 1952. [1935]

JANNER, Barnett. Continued in House after 1945: full entry in Volume IV.

JARRETT, George William Symonds. 32 Kensington Mansions, London. Princes, and 1920. S. of G.J. Jarrett, Esq. B. at Upnor, Kent 1880; m. 17 September 1912, Janet Mary, d. of Maj. P.H. Dunning, J.P., 17th Regiment, and great-grand-d. of John Dunning, Esq., 1st Lord Ashburton. Educ. in elementary schools, and privately. An Architect 1899-1908. Organizer of the National Service League 1913-14; Army (staff) 1915-17; unable to serve overseas owing to loss of right arm. Assistant Architect Devon Education Committee 1905-07; Secretary and Surveyor Lancing Coll. 1909-11. Editor of the *British Citizen* 1919-21. Author of political and economic articles, several short plays and musical numbers. Unsuccessfully contested Mansfield, Nottinghamshire in 1918 as a pro-Coalition National Democratic Party candidate. Elected for the Dartford division of Kent in November 1922, with the support of the local Conservative and National Liberal associations. Sat until he was defeated in December 1923. Joined Conservative Party in 1924 and unsuccessfully contested Edmonton in October 1924 and May 1929, and East Ham N. in April 1926. Chief Organiser of National Democratic Party 1917-20. Managing Director of Dryden Press 1924-34. Administrator of Embankment Fellowship Centre 1935-46. Member of Surrey County Council 1949-52. Died 6 December 1960. [1923]

JARVIS, Sir Joseph John, Bart. Continued in House after 1945: full entry in Volume IV.

JEFFREYS, Gen. Sir George Darell, K.C.B., K.C.V.O. Continued in House after 1945: full entry in Volume IV.

JELLETT, William Morgan, K.C. 36 Fitzwilliam Square, Dublin. Carlton, and Junior Constitutional. University, Dublin. S. of the Rev. J.H. Jellett, Provost of Trinity Coll., Dublin, and Dora, d. of James Morgan, Esq., of Tivoli, Co. Cork. B. in Dublin 19 May 1857; m. 1895, Janet, d. of H.J. Stokes, Esq., of the Indian Civil Service. Educ. at the Royal School, Armagh, and Trinity Coll., Dublin. Called to the Irish bar, Mich., 1882; Q.C. 1899. Bencher of King's Inn. Private Secretary to Lord Ashbourne, Lord Chancellor of Ireland 1888-93, and 1895. A Unionist. Unsuccessfully contested Dublin University in December 1918. Elected for Dublin University in July 1919 and sat until he retired in October 1922. Died 27 October 1936. [1922]

JENKINS, Arthur. Continued in House after 1945: full entry in Volume IV.

JENKINS, Sir William. Mount Pleasant, Cymmer, Port Talbot, Glamorganshire. S. of Miles Jenkins, Esq., of Cymmer. B. 1871; m. 1895, Mary Evans, of Cymmer. Educ. at Glyncorrwg National School. Worked in a coalmine at twelve years of age. A Miners' Agent 1906. Member of Glycorrwg School Board 1900, of the Glyncorrwg Urban District Council 1904 (Chairman 1908-16 and 1927), of Glamorgan County Council 1907 (Chairman 1920), and was Chairman of Standing Joint Committee; Vice President of County Councils Association England and Wales, and of Education Committee. J.P. Member of University Council for Wales. Chairman of County School for the Blind, Bridgend from 1924, of Federation of Education Authorities for Wales, of Petty Sessional division Aberavon January 1944, and of Technical Advisory Council South Wales and Monmouth. Knight Bach. 1931. Parliamentary Private Secretary to the Rt. Hon. V. Hartshorn when Postmaster-Gen. 1924. Temporary Chairman of House of Commons Committees 1929-34. K.(G.)St.J. Deacon in a Congregational Church. A Labour Member. Sat for the Neath division of Glamorganshire from November 1922 until his death on 8 December 1944. [1945]

JENKINS, William Albert. Tuxedo, Eaton Grove, Swansea. National Liberal. S. of Daniel and Elizabeth Anne Jenkins. B. at Swansea 9 September 1878; m. 4

June 1906, Beatrice, d. of Frederick W. Tylor, Esq., of Pirbright, Surrey (she died 1967). Educ. at Danygraig, and Swansea Higher Grade Schools. A Coal Contractor and Exporter. A Liberal. Elected for Brecon and Radnorshire in November 1922. Returned unopposed for Brecon and Radnorshire again in December 1923 and sat until he was defeated in October 1924. Unsuccessfully contested the Llanelli division of Carmarthenshire as a Liberal Nationalist in March 1936. Member of Swansea Borough Council 1927-54, Mayor 1947-49. Knighted 1938. Vice-President of Pilots Association of United Kingdom. President of Swansea Chamber of Trade. J.P. for Glamorgan. President of Royal Welsh Agricultural Society 1949. Fellow of Institute of Chartered Shipbrokers. Died 23 October 1968. [1924 2nd ed.]

JENNINGS, Roland. Continued in House after 1945: full entry in Volume IV.

JEPHCOTT, Alfred Roger. "Sandcroft", Mansel Road, Small Heath, Birmingham. Constitutional. S. of Thomas Jephcott, Esq., a member of a Coventry Quaker family. B. at Foleshill, Coventry 14 February 1853; m. 1884, Lucy, d. of William White, Esq., of Birmingham. Educ. at St. Paul's Church of England Schools, Balsall Heath. A working Engineer 1868. Member of Birmingham School Board from 1890 to 1895; local Correspondent Board of Trade from 1897-1919. Councillor City of Birmingham 1895-1912; Alderman from 1912-32. Magistrate City of Birmingham 1905. A Conservative. Unsuccessfully contested Paisley in December 1910. Sat for the Yardley division of Birmingham from December 1918 until he retired in May 1929. Died 14 March 1932. [1929]

JESSON, Charles. 15 Wenham Drive, Westcliffe-on-Sea, Essex. S. of John William and Martha Jesson. B. at Leicester 1 June 1862; m. 1889, d. of Philip Roberts, Esq., Pattern Maker. Educ. at Leicester County School. A professional musician; joined army band 1879, later Organizer, Musicians' Union. Member London County Council 1906 till 1919. Wrote on the Development of the Empire Resources. A Coalition National Democratic and Labour Party Member. Elected for W. Walthamstow in December 1918 and sat until he was defeated in November 1922 standing as the candidate of the National Democratic Party with unofficial Conservative support. Died 21 September 1926. [1922]

JESSON, Maj. Thomas Edward. Rivoli, South Drive, St. Anne's-on-Sea. S. of Thomas Jesson, Esq., of Ashby-de-la-Zouche. B. 28 July 1882; m. 1921, Beatrice Holding (she died 1941). Educ. at Charterhouse. Admitted a Solicitor 1906. A Conservative. Unsuccessfully contested Rochdale in October 1924. Elected for Rochdale in October 1931 and sat until he retired in October 1935. Served with the Leicestershire Regiment, Maj. Died 23 July 1958. [1935]

JEWSON, Dorothy. 58 Bracondale, Norwich. D. of Alderman George Jewson, J.P., Timber Merchant, Chairman of Great Yarmouth Port and Haven Commission, and Mary Jane, née Jarrold. B. at Norwich 17 August 1884; m. 1st, 1936, R. Tanner Smith, Esq. (he died 1939); secondly, 1945, Rev. Campbell Stephen, MP (he died 1947). Educ. at Norwich High School, Cheltenham, and Girton Coll., Cambridge. Trade Union Organiser 1916-22. Joint author with bro. of *The Destitute of Norwich and how they live*, an investigation into the administration of out-relief in Norwich in 1913. A Labour Member. Elected for Norwich in December 1923 and sat until she was defeated in October 1924. Unsuccessfully contested Norwich as the Labour candidate in May 1929 and as the ILP candidate in October 1931. Member of the National Council of ILP 1925-35. Member of Norwich City Council 1927-36. Died 29 February 1964. [1924 2nd ed.]

JEWSON, Percy William. Horsford Hall, Norwich. Reform, Lansdowne, and National Liberal. S. of John William Jewson, Esq., of Norwich. B. 16 February 1881; m. 29 July 1908, Ethel Marion, d. of Edward Boardman, Esq., F.R.I.B.A. Educ. privately. A Director of Jewson and Sons Limited, Timber Importers. Lord Mayor of Norwich

1934-35. J.P. for Norwich and Norfolk. President of Norwich Chamber of Commerce from 1940-46. A Liberal National. Returned unopposed for Great Yarmouth in April 1941 and sat until he was defeated in July 1945. Served with Worcestershire Regiment 1914-18. President of Westhill Training Coll. 1944-47. Died 18 April 1962.   [1945]

JODRELL, Sir Neville Paul. Stanhoe Hall, Norfolk. The Albany, Piccadilly, London. Athenaeum, Carlton, New University and Norfolk County. S. of Neville Jodrell, Esq., of Gislingham, Suffolk, and Elizabeth Charlotte, d. of the Rev. Thomas Collyer, of Gislingham. B. at Gislingham 27 May 1858; m. 1892, Mrs. R. Roudebush, of New York. Educ. at Uppingham, and Trinity Coll., Oxford; M.A. Called to the bar, Inner Temple, 1885; practised on the S.E. Circuit; travelled extensively in Europe, Egypt, Asia Minor, West Indies, and North America. Chairman of Recruiting Committee for W. Norfolk, member of Appeal Tribunal for Norfolk, and Commissioner of Food for Norfolk during the war. Was in Uppingham football team and Capt. of Oxford University Long Range Rifle Team for 3 years. Knighted 1922. A Conservative. Unsuccessfully contested N.W. Norfolk in January and December 1910 and again May 1912. Elected for the mid Norfolk division in October 1918 and for the King's Lynn division of Norfolk in December 1918. Sat until he was defeated in December 1923. Died 20 May 1932.   [1923]

JOEL, Dudley Jack Barnato. 74 Brook Street, London. Moulton Paddocks, Newmarket. S. of S.B. Joel, Esq. B. 27 April 1904; m. 1936, Esme, d. of J.M. Oldham, Esq., of Ormidale, Ascot (she died 18 May 1939). Educ. at Repton, and King's Coll., Cambridge; M.A. An Insurance Underwriter. Lieut. in R.N.V.R. A Conservative. Elected for Dudley in October 1931. Sat until he was killed in action in May/June 1941.   [1941]

JOHN, William. Continued in House after 1945: full entry in Volume IV.

JOHNSON, Sir (Louis) Stanley. 131 Clapton Common, London. Royal Automobile, and 1900. S. of Edward and Emily Rose Johnson. B. at Hackney 11 October 1869; m. 1902, Edith Emily, d. of Thomas Heather, Esq., of Adelaide House, Jersey. Educ. privately. A Solicitor (member of the firm of Downer and Johnson, 426 Salisbury House, London Wall, London). Admitted in 1899. Mayor of Hackney 1914-19. J.P. for Co. of London. Honorary Lieut.-Col. 9th Battalion County of London Volunteer Regiment. Raised the 189th Brigade R.F.A. and the 152nd Battery R.F.A. in 1915. Knighted 1920. A Conservative. Unsuccessfully contested the Walthamstow division of Essex in January and November 1910. First elected for E. Walthamstow in December 1918 and sat until he retired in October 1924. Treasurer of International Parliamentary Commercial Conference. Died 30 November 1937.   [1924 2nd ed.]

JOHNSTON, James Wellwood. 4 Heriot Row, Edinburgh. Constitutional. S. of Sir Christopher Johnston, Lord Sands, Scottish Judge. B. 5 April 1900; m. 1934, Kathleen Edith, d. of John Duncan, Esq. Educ. at Edinburgh Academy, Cargilfield, Rugby, and New Coll., Oxford. Advocate, Scotland 1924; Chairman Scottish 1924 Club. A Unionist. Elected for the Clackmannan and Eastern division of Stirling and Clackmannan in October 1931 and sat until he was defeated in November 1935. Sheriff Substitute of Lanarkshire from 1940. Advocate Depute 1935-39. Died 18 September 1958.   [1935]

JOHNSTON, Rt. Hon. Thomas. Monteviot, Kirkintilloch, Scotland. B. 1882; m. 1914, Margaret Freeland, d. of James Cochrane, Esq. Educ. at Board School, Lenzie Academy, and Glasgow University. Founder of *Forward* 1906 and Editor 1919-46. Senior magistrate, Kirkintilloch. Under-Secretary of State for Scotland June 1929-March 1931; Lord Privy Seal March-August 1931; Regional Commissioner Civil Defence for Scotland 1939-41; PC. 1931; Secretary of State for Scotland February 1941-May 1945. A Labour Member. Unsuccessfully contested W. division of Stirling and Clackmannan in 1918. Elected for the Western division of Stirling and Clackmannan in November 1922 and December 1923, defeated October 1924. Elected for Dundee in December 1924, and for the Western division of Stirling and Clackmannan in May 1929, defeated October 1931. Unsuccessfully contested Dunbartonshire in March 1932. Re-elected for the Western division of Stirling and Clackmannan in November 1935 and sat until he retired in June 1945. Chairman of Scottish National Forestry Commission 1945-48. Chairman of North of Scotland Hydro-Electric Board 1946-59. Companion of Honour 1953. Gov. of B.B.C. 1955-56. Chairman of Scottish Tourist Board 1945-55. President of British Electrical Development Association 1958-60. Fellow of Educational Institute of Scotland. Chancellor of Aberdeen University 1951-65. Died 5 September 1965. [1945]

JOHNSTONE, Rt. Hon. Harcourt. 23 Gayfere Street, London. Bachelors', White's, and St. James's. S. of the Hon. Sir Alan Johnstone, G.C.V.O. B. 19 May 1895. Educ. at Eton, and Balliol Coll., Oxford, M.A. Served with Rifle Brigade and on General Staff 1914-19. Liberal Whip November 1931-September 1932; Parliamentary Secretary for Overseas Trade May 1940-March 1945. PC. 1943. A Liberal. Unsuccessfully contested East Willesden in November 1922. Sat for East Willesden from March 1923 until 1924, when he was defeated. Unsuccessfully contested the Eastbourne division of E. Sussex in June 1925 and the Westbury division of Wiltshire in June 1927 and May 1929. Sat for South Shields from October 1931 until 1935, when he was again defeated. Returned unopposed for Middlesbrough W. in August 1940 and sat until his death on 1 March 1945. [1945]

JOHNSTONE, Joseph. Calder House, Lochwinnock, Renfrewshire. National Liberal. Liberal, Glasgow. The Club, Paisley. S. of Robert Johnstone, Esq., Cabinet Manufacturer. B. at Salford 1860; m. 1882, Jane Clerk, d. of Alexander Muir, Esq., of Gateside, Beith, Ayrshire (she died

1917). Educ. at Crummock School, Beith. A Cabinet Manufacturer. Member Renfrewshire County Council from 1889; Vice-Convenor of the County of Renfrew from 1918; Chairman Renfrewshire National Insurance Committee from 1912; Chairman Renfrewshire Tuberculosis Committee; Chairman Renfrewshire Joint Sanatorium Board; Chairman National Insurance Committees Association of Scotland; Chairman Joint Advisory Committee of the Furnishing Trade of Great Britain on the Training of Disabled Soldiers and Sailors. A Liberal. Elected for E. Renfrewshire in December 1918 and sat until he was defeated in November 1922. O.B.E. 1918. J.P. for Renfrewshire. Died 13 January 1931. [1922]

JONES, Arthur Creech. Continued in House after 1945: full entry in Volume IV.

JONES, Charles Sydney. St. James's Court, London. Eastbourne, Prince's Park, Liverpool. Reform. Eld. s. of Charles William Jones, Esq., Shipowner, of Liverpool, and Georgina, d. of Sidney Potter, Esq., of Manchester. B. at Liverpool 7 February 1872. Unmarried. Educ. at Charterhouse, and Magdalen Coll., Oxford. Entered business in 1894, later a member of firm of Alfred Holt and Company, Shipowners, of Liverpool. Member of Liverpool County Council from 1908; treasurer and Pro-Chancellor University of Liverpool; J.P. for City of Liverpool. A Liberal. Elected for the W. Derby division of Liverpool in December 1923 and sat until he was defeated in October 1924. High Sheriff of Lancashire 1929-30. Knighted 1937. Lord Mayor of Liverpool 1938-42. Died 16 February 1947. [1924 2nd ed.]

JONES, Sir Edgar Rees. Gorwel, Wattstown, Rhondda, Glamorganshire. National Liberal. S. of the Rev. M.H. Jones, Baptist Minister. B. 27 August 1878 at Cwmaman, Aberdare; m. 1919, May, d. of George Brackley, Esq., of Harringay. Educ. at University Coll., Cardiff. A Barrister, called Gray's Inn 1913. Controller Priority Department, Ministry of Munitions 1915-18. Author of *Art of the Orator, Selected English*

Speeches, Changes in the Map of Europe, etc. K.B.E. 1918. A Liberal. Elected for Merthyr Tydvil in January and December 1910, and for the Merthyr division of Merthyr Tydvil in December 1918. Sat until he retired in October 1922. Unsuccessfully contested S. Salford in December 1923 and the Gower division of Glamorganshire in October 1931. Chairman of Welsh Consultative Council of Ministry of Health 1920-22. Chairman of National Food Canning Council. President of World Trade Alliance Association. Died 16 June 1962.   [1922]

JONES, Sir Evan Davies, Bart. 6 Addison Road, London. Pentower, Fishguard, Pembrokeshire. Reform, National Liberal, and R.A.C. S. of Thomas Jones, Esq., of Pentower, Fishguard. B. at Pentower 18 April 1859; m. 1st, 1884. Cecilia, d. of Jacob Evans, Esq., of Cardiff (she died 1913); secondly, 1914, Lilly, d. of James Railton, Esq., of Malpas, Monmouthshire (she died 1945). Educ. privately, and at University Coll., Bristol. A Civil Engineer; M.I.C.E. Director of Topham, Jones and Railton Limited, Westminster. Dept.-Lieut. for Pembrokeshire; High Sheriff Pembrokeshire 1911-12; J.P. for the Co. of Pembroke and Chairman County Petty Sessions, Fishguard; Alderman Pembrokeshire County Council, Chairman 1926; member Standing Joint and Main Road Committees; member Territorial Association; member Court of Governors and Council University Coll. of Wales, and of the National Library of Wales, and Honorary Treasurer of the latter and Vice-President 1928-39. Member of War Office Committee Engineer and Railway Staff corps for Organization of Civilian Labour for London Defences 1914-18; Chairman of Road Transport Board, Board of Trade 1917-18; Dyes Commissioner, Board of Trade 1917-18. Controller of Coal Mines, Board of Trade March to October 1919. A Coalition Liberal. Elected for Pembrokeshire in December 1918 and sat until he retired in October 1922. Created Bart. 1917. President of Federation of Civil Engineering Contractors 1935-36. Died 20 April 1949.   [1922]

JONES, Sir George William Henry, K.C. 1 Essex Court, London. 22 Woodberry Down, London. S. of George Jones, Esq. B. 1874. Unmarried. Educ. at London University, LL.B. Barrister-at-law, Gray's Inn 1907. Member of London County Council 1910-19, and of Hackney Borough Council 1906-11. Knight Bach. 1928; Recorder of Colchester 1937-47. K.C. 1943. A Conservative. Unsuccessfully contested W. Leeds in December 1910. Prospective candidate for the Haggerston division of Shoreditch 1911-18. Sat for Stoke Newington from 1918 until defeated in 1923. Re-elected in October 1924 and sat until he was defeated in July 1945. Retired from the bar in 1949. Died 3 January 1956. [1945]

JONES, Sir Henry Haydn. Pantyneuadd, Towyn, Merionethshire. National Liberal. S. of Joseph David Jones, Esq., of Ruthin, and Catherine, d. of Owen Daniel, Esq., of Towyn. B. 1863; m. 1903, Gwendolen, d. of Lewis D. Jones, Esq., of Chicago. Educ. at Towyn Board School and Towyn Academy. An Iron Merchant and Quarry Owner. Member of Merioneth County Council from 1889 to 1947, Chairman 1900, Alderman 1930. Honorary Secretary Merioneth Education Committee 1903, and a Gov. of University Coll. of Wales, Aberystwyth. A J.P. for Merionethshire. Knight Bach. 1937. A Liberal. Sat for Merionethshire from January 1910 until he retired in June 1945. Died 2 July 1950.   [1945]

JONES, John Joseph. 5 Endsleigh Gardens, London. S. of John and Margaret Jones B. at Nenagh, Co. Tipperary 8 December 1873; m. 1902, Kate, d. of J.H. Holden, Esq. Educ. at Christian Brothers' Schools, Nenagh. A Builder's Labourer; became a Trade Union Organizer in 1911 for National Union of General and Municipal Workers. Member of West Ham Council 1904; West Ham Guardians 1908-11. Unsuccessfully contested Camborne for the Social Democratic Federation in January 1906 and Poplar for the British Socialist Party in February 1914. Sat for the Silvertown division of West Ham from December 1918 until he resigned in February 1940.

Elected in 1918 as the candidate of the National Socialist Party, in opposition to the official Labour candidate, but he accepted the Labour Whip and sat thereafter as a Labour Member. Died 21 November 1941. [1940]

JONES, Rev. Josiah Towyn. 12 Downing Street, London. National Liberal. S. of John Jones, Esq., of Towyn Bach, New Quay, Cardigan. B. 28 December 1858 at New Quay, Cardigan; m. 1886, Mary, d. of John Howells, Esq., of Beaufort, Morriston. Educ. at New Quay Grammar School, and Presbyterian Coll., Carmarthen. A Congregational Minister. Ordained 1880; was Minister at Dowlais 1880–84 and at Cwmaman, Carmarthenshire 1884-1906. Organizer of Central Fund of Welsh Congregationalists from 1906; Chairman of Welsh Congregational Union 1919-20. A member of Carmarthen County Council and Education Committee, and Central Welsh Board. Junior Lord of the Treasury (unpaid) from December 1916 to July 1922. A Liberal. Elected for E. Carmarthenshire in August 1912 and for the Llanelly division of Carmarthenshire in August 1912 and for the Llanelly division of Carmarthenshire in December 1918. Sat until he retired in October 1922. Died 16 November 1925. [1922]

JONES, Rt. Hon. Leifchild Stratten. 16 Bryanston Street, London. Reform. S. of the Rev. T. Jones, Chairman of the Congregational Union. B. 16 January 1862. Unmarried. Educ. at Normal Coll., Swansea, Scotch Coll., Melbourne, and at Trinity Coll., Oxford; 1st Class Maths, B.A. 1885, M.A. 1889. President of United Kingdom Alliance 1906. PC. 1916. A Liberal. Unsuccessfully contested Westminster in 1892, Central Leeds 1895, and S. Manchester in 1900. Sat for the Appleby division of Westmorland from March 1905 to January 1910 when he was defeated, and for the Rushcliffe division of Nottinghamshire from December 1910 until 1918 when he was defeated. Unsuccessfully contested the Camborne division of Cornwall in 1922. Elected for the Camborne division of Cornwall in December 1923; defeated in 1924. Re-

elected in May 1929 and sat until he was defeated in October 1931. Created Baron Rhayader 1932, when he adopted the surname of Leif-Jones in lieu of Jones. President of Liberal Council 1934-37. Died 26 September 1939. [1931 2nd ed.]

JONES, Sir Lewis. Highfield, Sketty, Swansea. S. of Evan Jones, Esq., of Tegfan, Ammanford. B. 13 February 1884; m. 1910, Alice Maude, d. of Frederick Willis, Esq., of Bath. Educ. at Ammanford School, and University Coll., Reading. Schoolmaster at Reading until 1910. Served in Ministry of Munitions 1914-17; Secretary S. Wales Siemens Steel Association from 1917 to 1961; Vice-President of Council and Court of Governors, University Coll., Swansea, and of Court of Governors, University Coll. of Wales; member of National Health Insurance Joint Committee; Parliamentary Charity Commissioner 1937-45. Knight Bach. 1944. A Liberal Nationalist. Elected for W. Swansea in October 1931. Sat until he was defeated in July 1945; again defeated in February 1950. J.P. for Swansea from 1934. Died 10 December 1968. [1945]

JONES, Morgan. Vaynor, Norrice Lea, London. S. of Elias Jones, Esq., Miner. B. 3 May 1885 at Pengam; m. 29 January 1923, Gladys, d. of John Thomas, Esq., of Merthyr. Educ. at Gelligaer and Hengoed elementary schools, Lewis School, Pengam Secondary School, and University Coll., Reading. A School-teacher 1908-16. A Labour whip 1922. Parliamentary Secretary Board of Education January-November 1924, and June 1929-August 1931. Chairman of Public Accounts Committee House of Commons from 1931 to 1938. Member of West Indies Royal Commission 1938. A Labour Member. Sat for the Caerphilly division of Glamorganshire from August 1921 until his death on 23 April 1939. Imprisoned as a conscientious objector during the Great War. Member of National Council of ILP 1920-22. Member of Executive Committee of Parliamentary Labour Party 1931-39. Chairman of Gelligaer Urban District Council 1921-22. Died 23 April 1939. [1939]

JONES, Robert Thomas. House of Commons, London. S. of David and Ellen Jones. B. at Blaenau Festiniog 1874. Unmarried. Educ. at local elementary schools. Financial Secretary to North Wales Quarrymen's Union 1908; Gen. Secretary of that Union until 1933. A Labour Member. Unsuccessfully contested Carnarvonshire in December 1918. Elected for Carnarvonshire in November 1922 and sat until he was defeated in December 1923. Defeated again in 1924 and 1929. Member of General Council of T.U.C. 1921-33. Member of Royal Commission on Licensing. Traffic Commissioner N.W. Area 1931-40. Died 15 December 1940. [1923]

JONES, Thomas Issac Mardy. 16 Llantwit Road, Pontypridd, Glamorgan. S. of Thomas and Gwen Jones. B. 1879; m. 1911, Margaret, d. of John Mordecai, Esq., of St. Hilary, Glamorgan. Educ. at the Board School, Ferndale, and Ruskin Coll., Oxford. A Parliamentary Agent of the South Wales Miners' Federation, and gave much attention to questions of local government and rating. Fellow of the Royal Economic Society. A Labour Member. Sat for the Pontypridd division of Glamorgan from July 1922 until 7 February 1931 when he resigned while under a charge of illegally allowing his wife the use of his MPs. railway travel voucher. Unsuccessfully contested the Pontypridd division of Glamorgan as an Independent Labour candidate in October 1931. Staff Officer, Ministry of Supply 1942-44. Education and Welfare Officer with British forces in Middle East 1945-46. Lecturer for National Coal Board on the economics of the coal industry. Died 26 August 1970. [1931 2nd ed.]

JONES, William Kennedy. 8 King's Bench Walk, Inner Temple, London. Royal Thames Yacht, and Constitutional. S. of Henry Jones, Esq., of Newry, Co. Down, Ireland, and Jeanie Kennedy, of Ayr, Scotland. B. in Glasgow 1865; m. 1892, Hetty, youngest d. of James Staniland, Esq., of Birmingham. Educ. at the High School, Glasgow. A Journalist, Founder, in connection with Lord Northcliffe, of the *Daily Mail, Daily Mirror,* etc. Chairman Select Committee on Transport (Metropolitan area) 1919. Published *Fleet Street and Downing Street.* A Unionist. Unsuccessfully contested the Wimbledon division of Surrey as an Independent candidate supported by the National Union of Attested Married Men in April 1916. Elected for Hornsey in December 1916 and sat until his death on 20 October 1921. Journalist on *Glasgow News, Glasgow Evening News, Birmingham Daily Mail, Sun* and *Evening News,* of which he was News Editor 1894-1900. Retired from journalism in 1912. Chairman of Waring and Gillow Limited. Director-Gen. of Food Economy, Ministry of Food 1917-19. Died 20 October 1921. [1921]

JONES, Lieut.-Col. William Nathaniel. Dyffryn, Ammanford, Carmarthenshire. S. of William Jones, Esq., of Dyffryn. B. 1858; m. Margaret, d. of Thomas Francis, Esq., of Llandeilo. A Liberal. Elected for the Carmarthen division of Carmarthenshire in June 1928 and sat until he was defeated in May 1929. Dept.-Lieut. and J.P. for Carmarthenshire, High Sheriff 1924. Died 24 May 1934. [1929]

JOWETT, Rt. Hon. Frederick William. 10 Grantham Terrace, Bradford. B. 1864 at Bradford. Worked in textile mill, later a Manufacturer's Manager. Member of Bradford Town Council from 1892-1907. Alderman 1895; J.P. 1909; PC. 1924. First Commissioner of Works January-November 1924. A Labour Member. Unsuccessfully contested W. Bradford in 1900. Sat for W. Bradford from 1906-18 when he unsuccessfully contested E. Bradford, and for E. Bradford from November 1922 until defeated in 1924. Re-elected for E. Bradford in May 1929 and sat until he was defeated in October 1931 standing as an ILP candidate. Defeated again in 1935 when he was opposed by the official Labour candidate. Chairman of ILP 1909-10 and 1914-17. Chairman of National Executive of Labour Party 1921-22. Died 1 February 1944. [1931 2nd ed.]

JOWITT, Rt. Hon. Sir William Allen, K.C. 61 Marsham Court, London. S. of the Rev. William Jowitt, Rector of Stevenage. B. 1885; m. 19 December 1913, Lesley,

d. of J.P. M'Intyre, Esq. Educ. at Marlborough, and New Coll., Oxford. Barrister-at-Law, Middle Temple 1909; K.C. 1922. Served with R.N.A.S. 1914-18. Attorney-Gen. June 1929-January 1932; Solicitor Gen. May 1940-March 1942; Paymaster Gen. March-December 1942; Minister without Portfolio December 1942; Minister of Social Insurance October-November 1944; Minister of National Insurance November 1944-May 1945. Elected for Hartlepools November 1922 and December 1923; defeated in 1924. Elected for Preston as a Liberal in May 1929, joined the Labour Party June 1929 and was re-elected in July 1929. Unsuccessfully contested the Combined English Universities in October 1931. Elected for Ashton-under-Lyne October 1939 and sat until he was appointed Lord Chancellor in July 1945. A Liberal until June 1929 when he joined the Labour Party; joined the National Labour Party in August 1931 but rejoined the Labour Party in 1936. Knighted 1929. PC. 1931. Created Baron Jowitt 1945, Visct. Jowitt 1947, and Earl Jowitt 1951. Lord Chancellor July 1945-October 1951. Treasurer of Middle Temple 1951. Trustee of National Gallery 1946-53 and of Tate Gallery 1947-53, Chairman 1951-53. Leader of Opposition in the House of Lords 1952-55. President of British Travel and Holidays Association. Died 16 August 1957. [1945]

JOYNSON-HICKS, Hon. Lancelot William. Continued in House after 1945: full entry in Volume IV.

JOYNSON-HICKS, Rt. Hon. Sir William, Bart. 70 Queen's Gate, London. Newick Park, Sussex. Carlton, Constitutional, and Royal Automobile. S. of Henry Hicks, Esq., of Abingdon House, Bromley, Kent. B. 23 June 1865 at Highbury; m. 1895, Grace Lynn, d. of R.H. Joynson, Esq., J.P., of Bowdon, Cheshire. Educ. at Merchant Taylors' School. Admitted a Solicitor 1888; Chairman of A.A. and Motor Union of Great Britain and Ireland 1908-23; served on Dept. Committee on Copyright 1909; Treasury Committee on Rating of Motor-Cars 1911; Committee on Putumayo Atrocities 1913; War Office Committee on

Motor Transport 1916, Civil Aerial Transport Committee 1917, Aerodromes Committee 1918, and Advisory Committee on Road Transport and Board of Civil Aviation. Parliamentary Secretary Overseas Trade Department October 1922-March 1923. Postmaster-Gen. and Paymaster Gen. March-May 1923; Financial Secretary to the Treasury May-August 1923; Minister of Health August 1923 to January 1924. Secretary of State for Home Affairs from November 1924-June 1929. Created Bart. 1919; PC. 1923; PC. Northern Ireland 1928. A Conservative. Unsuccessfully contested N. Manchester in 1900, and N.W. Manchester in 1906. Sat for N.W. Manchester from April 1908-January 1910, when he was defeated. Unsuccessfully contested Sunderland in December 1910. Elected for the Brentford division of Middlesex in March 1911, and for the Twickenham division of Middlesex in December 1918. Sat until June 1929 when he was created Visct. Brentford. Assumed surname of Joynson-Hicks in lieu of Hicks 1896. Member of Church Assembly. President of National Church League from 1921. Chairman of Automobile Association. Dept.-Lieut. for Norfolk. Died 8 June 1932. [1929]

KAY, Sir Robert Newbold. Poppleton Hall, Nether Poppleton, Yorkshire. National Liberal. B. 6 August 1869; m. 13 June 1899, Alice May, d. of the Rev. Thomas Lambert, of Scarborough. Educ. at Priory Street Higher Grade School, York. Admitted a Solicitor 1893; Sheriff of York City from 1913-14; member of York City Council, Lord Mayor 1924-25. A Liberal. Unsuccessfully contested the Elland division of Yorkshire in 1922. Elected for the Elland division in December 1923 and sat until he was defeated in October 1924. Knighted 1920. Died 24 February 1947. [1924 2nd ed.]

KEATINGE, Maj. Edgar Mayne. Park Road, Bury St. Edmunds. Carlton. S. of Gerald Francis Keatinge, Esq., C.I.E., I.C.S. B. 3 February 1905; m. 12 August 1930, Katharine Lucile, d. of Reginald John Burrell, Esq., J.P., of Risley Place, Bury St. Edmunds. Educ. at Rugby and at School of Agriculture, Natal. A Farmer from

1931. Member of West Suffolk County Council from 1933 to 1945. Joined R.A. 1937 served with R.W.A.F.F. 1941-43. First Commandant School of Artillery, West Africa 1942-43. A Conservative. Elected for the Bury St. Edmunds division of Suffolk in February 1944 and sat until he retired in June 1945. C.B.E. 1954. Knighted 1960. J.P. for Wiltshire from 1946. Member of Council of Royal Africa Society from 1970.*

[1945]

KEDWARD, Rev. Roderick Morris. 252 Bermondsey Street, London. Pine Tree, Hothfield Common, Ashford, Kent. National Liberal. S. of William Kedward, Esq., of Ashford. B. 14 September 1881; m. 1906, Daisy Annie, d. of J. Fedrick, Esq. Educ. at Richmond Coll. A Wesleyan Minister 1903. Chairman of Finance Committee of Bermondsey B.C. and Board of Guardians. Served in Egypt and France 1914-18 with 31st Division. A Liberal. Unsuccessfully contested Central Hull in 1918 and W. Bermondsey in 1922. Elected for W. Bermondsey in December 1923, defeated October 1924. Elected for the Ashford division of Kent in May 1929 and sat until he was defeated in October 1931. Unsuccessfully contested the Ashford division of Kent in March 1933. Superintendent of South London Mission 1918-37. President of National Tithepayers' Association. Died 5 March 1937. [1931 2nd ed.]

KEELING, Edward Herbert. Continued in House after 1945: full entry in Volume IV.

KEENS, Thomas. Warden House, New Bedford Road, Luton. S. of Thomas Keens, Esq., and Emma Hailstone. B. at Luton 1 November 1870; m. 1896, Ella, d. of Joseph Batchelor, Esq. An Accountant and senior partner in the firm of Thomas Keens, Shay and Company; member of Bedfordshire County Council 1901-52, Alderman 1919-52, Chairman 1935-52. Secretary London Chamber of Commerce. Fellow of Chartered Institute of Secretaries 1897. A Congregationalist. Dept.-Lieut. for Bedfordshire. Chairman of Lee Catchment Board. A Liberal. Unsuccessfully contested the Aylesbury division of Buckinghamshire

in November 1922. Elected for the Aylesbury division of Buckinghamshire in December 1923 and sat until he was defeated in October 1924; again defeated in May 1929. Unsuccessfully contested the Pontypool division of Monmouthshire as a Liberal National in October 1931. President of Society of Incorporated Accountants and Auditors 1926-29. Knighted 1934. Died 24 November 1953. [1924 2nd ed.]·

KEIR, Thelma Cazalet. Raspit Hill, Ivy Hatch, Sevenoaks. D. of William Cazalet, Esq., and Maud, d. of Sir John Heron Maxwell, 7th Bart., of Springhill. B. 1899; m. 3 August 1939, David Keir (he died 1969). Member of London County Council from 1925-31, Alderman 1931. Gov. of British Film Institute 1940-44. Member of Cinematograph Films Council 1940-44, and of the Council for the Encouragement of Music and Art. Parliamentary Private Secretary to Kenneth Lindsay, Parliamentary Secretary Board of Education 1937-May 1940. A Conservative. Unsuccessfully contested Islington E. in February 1931. Elected for Islington E. in October 1931 and sat until she was defeated in July 1945. Parliamentary Secretary to Ministry of Education May-July 1945. C.B.E. 1952. Gov. of B.B.C. 1956-61. President of Fawcett Society 1964. Author of *From the Wings.*★

[1945]

KELLAWAY, Rt. Hon. Frederick George. 16 Eliot Park, Lewisham Hill, London. S. of William Hamley Kellaway, Esq., of Bristol, and Elizabeth, d. of William Colley, Esq., of Bath. B. 3 December 1870 at Bishopston, Bristol; m. 1903, Sarah Ellen, d. of Henry Robinson, Esq., J.P. of Greenwich. Educ. at Bishopston, Bristol. A Journalist. A member of Lewisham Borough Council and Board of Guardians. One of the Parliamentary Secretaries to the Ministry of Munitions December 1916 January 1918; Parliamentary and Financial Secretary to that Ministry January 1918-January 1919; Parliamentary Secretary and Dept. Minister to the Ministry of Munitions January 1919 to April 1920; Parliamentary Secretary to the Department of Overseas Trade and Additional Under-Secretary to the Foreign Office April 1920 to April 1921; Postmaster-Gen. April 1921-October 1922. PC. 1920. A Liberal. Unsuccessfully contested S. Northamptonshire in January 1910. Elected for Bedford in December 1910 and for the Bedford division of Bedfordshire in December 1918. Sat until he was defeated in November 1922. Director of Marconi's Wireless Telegraph Company and one of the founders of the British Broadcasting Company. Chairman of Marconi International Marine Communication Company 1924-33. Died 13 April 1933.   [1922]

KELLETT, Col. Edward Orlando. Guards', and White's. S. of Maj.-Gen. R.O. Kellett, C.B., C.M.G., of Chonacody, Fethard, Co. Tipperary. B. 19 May 1902; m. 14 October 1926, Helen Myrtle Dorothy, d. of Arthur Atherley, Esq., of Languard Manor, Isle of Wight. Educ. at Cheltenham, and Royal Military Coll., Sandhurst. Joined Irish Guards 1922 and Nottingham Yeomanry (Sherwood Rangers) 1930; Maj. 1936. Lieut.-Col. 1940. A Conservative. Unsuccessfully contested the Carmarthen division of Carmarthenshire in November 1935. Elected for the Aston division of Birmingham in May 1939 and sat until he was killed in action while serving with the 8th Army in North Africa March 1943. D.S.O. January 1943. Fellow of Royal Geographical Society and Royal Empire Society. Died March 1943.   [1943]

KELLEY, Maj. Frederic Arthur, O.B.E. Holly Court, Harrogate. S. of Ralph and Sarah Ann Kelley. B. at Heckmondwike 6 May 1863; m. 1888, a d. of Charles Henry Pickles, Esq. Educ. at Tettenhall Coll., Wolverhampton, and Giggleswick Grammar School. Member of the Sheffield City Council for 12 years; J.P. for Sheffield, the W. Riding of Yorkshire, and Harrogate. A Conservative. Unsuccessfully contested the Hallamshire division of Yorkshire in 1906 and the Spen Valley division of Yorkshire in January and December 1910. First elected for Rotherham in December 1918 and sat until he was defeated in December 1923. O.B.E. 1919. Knighted 1923. Died 29 May 1926.   [1923]

KELLY, Edward Joseph. 12 Brighton Vale, Monkstown, Co. Dublin. S. of Peter Kelly, Esq., J.P., of Ballyshannon, Donegal. B. 31 March 1883 at Ballyshannon; m. Mollie, 2nd d. of William Hickey, Esq., of Clontarf, Dublin. Educ. at St. Vincent's Coll., Castleknock, and Royal University Dublin; M.A. A Barrister, called 1916. A Nationalist. Sat for E. Donegal from January 1910 until he retired in October 1922. K.C. 1930. Bencher of King's Inns 1937.   [1922]

KELLY, John Thomas. See O'KELLY, Sean Thomas.

KELLY, Thomas. 23 Longwood Avenue, South Circular Road, Dublin. Long known as a temperance worker in Dublin; one of the older members of the Dublin Corporation. Arrested in Dublin raid December 1919. While in Wormwood Scrubbs prison was elected Lord Mayor of Dublin; released from prison February 1920. A Sinn Fein Member. Elected for the St. Stephen's Green division of Dublin in December 1918 but did not take his seat. Member of Dail for the St. Stephen's Green division of Dublin to 1921, for S. Dublin 1921-23 as a Pro-Treaty Member.   [1922]

KELLY, William Thomas. 26 Crofton Road, London. B. 21 June 1874; m. 1896, Mary Alice, d. of Charles Gillett, Esq. (she died 1930). Chairman A.S.E. Manchester Branch; representative Manager for London Schools; Dept. Chairman of Ministry of Labour Council for Employment of Juveniles; member of County of London Advisory Committee for Selection of Justices. J.P. for London. Member of Whitley Councils for Government Departments, Chemical and other trades; Negotiator, Engineering, Shipbuilding, Civil Engineering, Lace, Net Industries. Member of Trades Board. Alderman of London County Council 1934-44; member of Farming and Mental Hospitals Committee and of Burnham Committee for Teachers' Salaries. A Labour Member. Unsuccessfully contested the Yeovil division of Somerset in 1918, 1922 and October and December 1923. Elected for Rochdale in October 1924 and May 1929; defeated there in October 1931. Re-elected for Rochdale in November 1935 and sat until he resigned in July 1940. Died 13 March 1944. [1940]

KENDALL, William Denis. Continued in House after 1945: full entry in Volume IV.

KENNEDY, Alfred Ravenscroft, K.C. 3 Brick Court, Temple, London. Abingdon Old House, Bibury, Gloucestershire. S. of Lord Justice Kennedy. B. 15 February 1879; m. 11 August 1908, Daisy, d. of Alfred Chapman, Esq., M.I.C.E. Educ. at Eton, and King's Coll., Cambridge. Barrister-at-Law, Lincoln's Inn 1903. K.C. 1919, bencher 1922. Legal Adviser to Foreign Office 1916-19. Recorder of Burnley 1925-29. A Conservative. Elected for Preston in October 1924 and sat until he was appointed a County Court Judge on 4 May 1929, 6 days before the dissolution of Parliament. Dept. Chairman of Gloucestershire Quarter Sessions from 1936. President of Corporation of Certified Secretaries 1927-37. Commissioner of Assize 1933-34. Died 10 February 1943. [1929]

KENNEDY, Myles Storr Nigel. Stone Cross, Ulverston. Windham, and Royal Automobile. S. of Myles Kennedy, Esq., Dept.-Lieut., and High Sheriff of Lancashire. B. at Ulverston 1889; m. 1946, Dorothy Emerson-Millington. Educ. at Harrow, and Trinity Coll., Cambridge. Called to the bar at the Inner Temple 1920. Capt. 3rd Border Regiment. A Conservative. Elected for the Lonsdale division of Lancashire in November 1922 and sat until he was defeated in December 1923. Member of Lancashire County Council 1922-41, Alderman from 1927. Died 19 January 1964. [1923]

KENNEDY, Rt. Hon. Thomas. 37 Westholme Avenue, Aberdeen. S. of Thomas and Ann Macdonald Kennedy. B. 25 December 1876 at Kennethmont, Aberdeenshire; m. 1919, Annie d. of George Michie, Esq., Fish-Curer, of Aberdeen. Educ. at Kennethmont Public School, and Gordon School, Huntly. Seven years Lecturer on Socialism under the auspices of the *Clarion* newspaper; Gen. Secretary of the Social Democratic Federation. Lord Commissioner of the Treasury January-November 1924; Parliamentary Secretary to the Treasury June 1929-August 1931. Chief Whip to the Labour Party 1927-31. PC. 1931. A Labour Member. Unsuccessfully contested N. Aberdeen in 1906 and January 1910. Sat for Kirkcaldy Burghs from March 1921 to November 1922, when he was defeated. Re-elected for Kirkcaldy Burghs in December 1923, and sat until defeated there in October 1931. Unsuccessfully contested Montrose Burghs in June 1932. Again re-elected for Kirkcaldy Burghs in November 1935 and sat until he resigned in January 1944. Died 3 March 1954. [1943]

KENT, David Rice. Fermoy, Co. Cork. A Farmer, in his native county of Cork, who supported the Sinn Fein movement from its early days. A Sinn Fein Member. Returned unopposed for E. Cork in December 1918 but did not take his seat. Member of Dail for E. Cork to 1927. An Anti-Treaty Member, remaining a Member of Sinn Fein after the formation of Fianna Fail. [1922]

KENWORTHY, Commander Hon. Joseph Montague. 137 Gloucester Place, London. Junior Naval & Military, and Reform. Eld. s. of 9th Baron Strabolgi. B. 7 March 1886; m. 1st, 4 December 1913, Doris, d. of Sir Frederick Whitley-Thomson (divorced 1941). secondly, 1941, Geraldine Mary Hamilton, d. of Maurice Francis, Esq. Educ. at the Royal Naval Academy, Northwood Park, Winchester, and H.M.S. *Britannia.* Joined R.N. 1903; served in China, East Indies, Mediterranean, W. Coast of Africa, etc. Commanded H.M.S. *Bullfinch* 1914-15, H.M.S. *Commonwealth* 1916; Admiralty War Staff 1917; Assistant Chief of Staff, Gibraltar, and with Mediterranean convoys 1918. A Labour Member. Unsuccessfully contested Rotherham in December 1918 as a Liberal. Sat for Central Hull from March 1919-November 1926, as a Liberal. Re-elected for Central Hull as a Labour Member November 1926. Sat until he was defeated in October 1931. President of U.K. Pilots Association 1922-25. Chairman of British Section of Inter-Parliamentary Union 1929-31. Succeeded to the Peerage as Baron Strabolgi 1934. Chief Labour Party Whip in the House of Lords 1938-42. Died 8 October 1953.

[1931 2nd ed.]

KENYON, Barnet. 3 Rosemount Avenue, North Finchley, London. 19 Shaftesbury Avenue, Chesterfield. S. of Henry Kenyon, Esq. B. 11 August 1850 at South Anston, Yorkshire; m. 1878, Elizabeth, d. of John Ramsden, Esq. Self-educated. Started work as a Miner, Checkweighman 1880-1906, President of Derbyshire Miners' Association 1896-1906; Assistant Secretary 1906-14, and Gen. Agent from 1914-1923. Member of Clowne Education Committee, Worksop Board of Guardians, Chesterfield Board of Guardians, Derbyshire Insurance and Old Age Pensions Committee, and Advisory Committee for appointment of J.Ps. for Derbyshire. Primitive Methodist local preacher for over 30 years. J.P. for Derbyshire. A Liberal. Sat for the Chesterfield division of Derbyshire from August 1913 until he retired in May 1929. Elected as a Liberal-Labour Member in 1913 but from February 1914 accepted only the Liberal Whip. Died 20 February 1930. [1929]

KENYON-SLANEY Maj. Philip Percy, M.C. 7 Chester Terrace, London. Beechwood, Plympton, Devon. S. of P.R. Kenyon Slaney, Esq., of Bratton, Clovelly. B. 12 February 1896. Unmarried. Educ. at Bradfield Coll. Joined Royal N. Devon Hussars Yeomanry 1913, and served in France, etc. 1915-18. A Conservative. Unsuccessfully contested the Tavistock division of Devon in December 1923. Elected for the Tavistock division in October 1924 and sat until his death on 9 September 1928. [1928]

KER, James Campbell, C.S.I., C.I.E. 70 Carlisle Mansions, London. Ardchattan, West Kilbride, Ayrshire. S. of the Rev. William Lee Ker, Minister of Kilwinning. B. 2 January 1878; m. 1925, Mary Katherine, d. of William Brown, Esq., of Rhuallan, Giffnock. Educ. at Irvine Academy, and Glasgow and Cambridge Universities; Scholar of Gonville and Caius Coll. In I.C.S. 1902-29. A National

Unionist. Elected for the Western division of Stirling and Clackmannan in October 1931 and sat until he retired in October 1935. Private Secretary to Gov. of Bombay 1924-29. Died 28 December 1961. [1935]

KERR, Col. Charles Iain, D.S.O., M.C. Adbury House, Newbury. Reform, and National Liberal. S. of Charles Wyndham Rudolph Kerr, Esq., and Ann Maria Olivia, d. of Admiral Sir George Elliot, K.C.B. B. 3 May 1874; m. 1st, 24 June 1911, Muriel, d. of William Gordon Canning, Esq., of Hartbury, Gloucester (marriage dissolved in 1930); secondly, 31 July 1930, Florence Angela, d. of Lieut.-Col. Charles and Lady Kathleen Villiers. Educ. at Stephen Hawtrey's School, Windsor. A Mining Engineer 1892-96; later Senior Partner of Kerr, Ware and Company, Stockbrokers. Chairman of National Liberal Federation and of Liberal Publication department 1930-31. Served with Royal Horse Guards and Machine Gun Corps 1914-18, D.S.O. 1919, M.C. J.P. for Northamptonshire. A Lord Commissioner of the Treasury May 1937-April 1939. Comptroller of H.M. Household April 1939-May 1940. Unsuccessfully contested Daventry in December 1923 and October 1924, Hull central in November 1926 and Swansea W. in May 1929 as a Liberal. Elected for Montrose Burghs as a Liberal National in June 1932 and sat until he was created Baron Teviot in June 1940. Chief Whip of Liberal National Party 1937-40. Chairman of Liberal National Party 1940-56 and Chief Whip in the House of Lords from 1945. Concluded with Lord Woolton in 1948 the 'Woolton-Teviot agreement' by which the Conservative and National Liberal Parties were amalgamated. Died 7 January 1968.

[1940]

KERR, Hamilton William. Continued in House after 1945: full entry in Volume IV.

KERR, Sir John Graham. Continued in House after 1945: full entry in Volume IV.

KERR-SMILEY, Peter Kerr. 31 Belgrave Square, London. Carlton, Marlborough, Cavalry. 2nd s. of Sir Hugh Smiley, 1st

Bart. B. 22 February 1879 at Larne; m. 1905, Maud, d. of Ernest L. Simpson, Esq., of New York. Educ. at Eton, and Trinity Hall, Cambridge. Chairman of *Northern Whig* newspaper, Belfast. A Lieut. 21st Lancers, and served on Staff in South African War 1901-02. Maj. 14th Battalion R. Irish Rifles. A Unionist. Unsuccessfully contested S. Down in 1906. Elected for N. Antrim in January 1910 and sat until he retired in October 1922. Adopted the surname of Kerr-Smiley in lieu of Smiley in 1905. Died 23 June 1943.   [1922]

KEY, Charles William. Continued in House after 1945: full entry in Volume IV.

KEYES, Admiral of the Fleet Sir Roger John Brownlow, Bart., G.C.B., K.C.V.O., C.M.G., D.S.O. 22 St. Leonards Terrace, London. Tingewick House, Buckingham. Naval & Military, and United Service. S. of Gen. Sir Charles Patton Keyes, G.C.B. B. 4 October 1872; m. 10 April 1906, Eva Mary Salvin (Red Cross Order of Queen Elizabeth of Belgium), d. of E.S. Bowlby, Esq., of Gilston Park, Hertfordshire and Knoydart, Inverness-shire. Joined R.N. 1885; Admiral of the Fleet 1930. Served in E. Africa 1890, in China 1900; Naval Attaché in Rome, Vienna, Athens and Constantinople 1905-07; Commodore Submarine Service 1910-15, Chief of Staff in Mediterranean 1915-16, with Grand Fleet 1916-17; Director of Plans 1917; Commanded Dover Patrol 1918-19, in command of Zeebrugge operation April 1918, Battle Cruiser Squadron 1919-21; Dept. Chief of Naval Staff, and a Lord Commander of the Admiralty 1921-25; C.-in-C. Mediterranean 1925-28 and at Portsmouth 1929-31; Special Liaison Officer King of the Belgians May 1940; Director of combined operations 1940-41. Honorary Col. Commandant Portsmouth division Royal Marines. Grand Officer of the Legion of Honour and Grand Cross in the Belgian Order of Leopold, the orders of St. Maurice and St. Lazarus of Italy, and D.S.M. of U.S.A., Croix de Guerre France and Belgium. Honorary D.C.L. Oxford; LL.D. Cambridge, Aberdeen, St. Andrews and Bristol Universities. A National Conserva-tive. Elected for Portsmouth N. in February 1934 and sat until 1943 when he was created Baron Keyes. Created Bart. 1919. Died 26 December 1945.   [1943]

KIDD, James. Muiredge, Carriden, Bo'ness. S. of Thomas Kidd, Esq., Blacksmith, of Bo'ness. B. 11 March 1872; m. 1899, Jessie Gardner, d. of Thomas Turnbull, Esq., of Bo'ness. Educ. at Carriden Public School, and Edinburgh University. Admitted a Solicitor 1893, B.C.L. Edinburgh 1898. Parliamentary Secretary for Health, Scotland October 1922-January 1923. A Conservative. Unsuccessfully contested Linlithgow in December 1910 and November 1913. Elected for Linlithgow in December 1918; unsuccessfully contested the same division in November 1922 and December 1923. Re-elected for Linlithgow in October 1924 and sat until his death on 2 March 1928.   [1928]

KILEY, James Daniel. 1 Whitehall Place, London. National Liberal, and Royal Automobile. B. 1865. A J.P. for the County of London; Alderman from 1913 and Mayor 1915 of the Metropolitan Borough of Stepney; member of the Metropolitan Water Board. Chairman of Messrs. Whyte, Ridsdale and Company Limited, Export Merchants, and Director of various other companies. A Liberal. Sat for the Whitechapel division of Tower Hamlets from December 1916 to December 1918 and for the Whitechapel and St. George's division of Stepney from December 1918 until he was defeated in November 1922. Defeated in the same division in February and December 1923. Died 12 September 1953.   [1922]

KIMBALL, Maj. Lawrence. Barleythorpe, Oakham. Altnaharra, Lairg, Sutherland. Carlton, and Bachelors'. S. of Marcus Morton Kimball, Esq. B. 25 October 1900; m. 1st, 22 March 1927, Kathleen Joan, d. of H.R. Ratcliff, Esq. (divorced 1946); secondly, Gillian, d. of W.S. Tresawna, Esq., of Abergavenny, and widow of Capt. J. Waterman. Educ. abroad, and at Caius Coll., Cambridge. Barrister-at-Law, Gray's Inn 1926. J.P. and High Sheriff of Rutland 1931. Dept.-Lieut., and J.P. for Sutherland.

Served with R.A. 1939-42. A Conservative. Unsuccessfully contested the central division of Hull in May 1929. Elected for the Loughborough division of Leicestershire in October 1931 and sat until he was defeated in July 1945. Died 30 December 1971.   [1945]

KINDERSLEY, Maj. Guy Molesworth, O.B.E. 1 and 2 Great Winchester Street, London. St. Paul's Walden, Welwyn, Hertfordshire. Athenaeum, Carlton, and City of London. S. of Capt. E.N.M. Kindersley. B. 28 February 1877; m. 30 July 1903, Kathleen Agnes Rhoda, d. of Sir Edmund H. Elton, 8th Bart. (she died 1950). Educ. at Marlborough. Clerk in Lord Chancellor's Office 1896; Land Registry Office 1898-1907; partner in the firm of Montagu Stanley and Company, Stockbrokers. Barrister-at-Law, Lincoln's Inn 1903; Inspector of Q.M.Gs. services France 1917-18. O.B.E. (mil.) 1918; retired 1919 with rank of Maj. A Conservative. Sat for the Hitchin division of Hertfordshire from December 1923 until he retired in October 1931. J.P. for Hertfordshire. Died 30 November 1956.

[1931 2nd ed.]

KING, Commodore Rt. Hon. Henry Douglas, C.B., C.B.E., D.S.O. 3 Hans Crescent, London. The Dales, Sheringham, Norfolk. Carlton, and Bath. S. of Capt. Henry Welchman King. B. in London 1 June 1877; m. 1900, Margaret Elizabeth, d. of W.R. Swan, Esq., of South Australia. Was in the mercantile marine 1891-99; farming 1899-1903; Barrister-at-Law, Middle Temple 1905. Served in the Royal Naval Division at Antwerp, Gallipoli (D.S.O. 1915 and 3 mentions) and France; later with R.N. siege guns in Flanders (French Croix de Guerre), and organizer of North Atlantic convoys (specially promoted Comr. and C.B.E. 1919). Commodore and C.B. 1927. Parliamentary Private Secretary to Col. Leslie Wilson 1919, to Sir Hamar Greenwood 1920. R.N.V.R. Aide-de-Camp to the King 1922-25. A Unionist Whip in the House of Commons 1921. Junior Lord of the Treasury October 1922-January 14; Financial Secretary to the War office November 1924-January 1928; Secretary for Mines January 1928-June 1929. PC. 1929. A

Conservative. Unsuccessfully contested N. Norfolk in January and December 1910. Elected for N. Norfolk in December 1918. Returned for S. Paddington in November 1922, and sat until his death on 20 August 1930, when his motor-yacht was wrecked in Lantivet Bay, Cornwall. Elected as an Independent in 1918, but rejoined the Conservative Party in 1919. Died 20 August 1930.   [1929 2nd ed.]

KING-HALL, Commander William Stephen Richard. 804 Hood House, Dolphin Square, London. Hartfield House, Headley, Bordon, Hampshire. Athenaeum, and United Service. S. of Admiral Sir George King-Hall, K.C.B. B. 21 January 1893; m. 15 April 1919, Kathleen, d. of Francis Spencer, Esq. (she died 1963). Educ. at Lausanne, and Royal Naval Colls., Osborne and Dartmouth. Served with Grand Fleet 1914-18. Adviser on Public Relations Ministry of Aircraft Production February 1942; Director of Publicity Ministry of Fuel and Power and Chairman of Fuel Economy Publicity Committee 1942-43; Founder of The National News Letter 1936, and of the Hansard Society 1944. Elected for the Ormskirk division of Lancashire in October 1939 as National Labour candidate but resigned the Whip in February 1942 and sat as an Independent National until he was defeated in July 1945. Unsuccessfully contested the Bridgwater division of Somerset in February 1950 as an Independent. Chairman of Council of Hansard Society 1944-62, President 1963-66. Knighted 1954. Created Baron King-Hall (Life peerage) 1966. Died 2 June 1966.   [1945]

KINLEY, John. Continued in House after 1945: full entry in Volume IV.

KINLOCH-COOKE, Sir Clement, Bart., K.B.E. 3 Mount Street, London. 2 Garden Court, Temple, London. Athenaeum, and Carlton. S. of R.W. Cooke, Esq., of Brighton. B. 1854; m. 1898, Florence, d. of the Rev. J.L. Errington (she died August 1944). Educ. at Brighton Coll., and St. John's Coll., Cambridge; Math. and Law Tripos, B.A., LL.M. Barrister-at-Law, Inner Temple 1883, and practised on the Oxford

Circuit. Legal Adviser to House of Lords Sweating Commission 1886-88. Private Secretary to Lord Dunraven when Under-Secretary for the Colonies. On Staff of High Commissioner for New Guinea. Member London County Council from 1907-10, member of the Committee of London Territorial Forces Association, Central Unemployed Body, and of London Higher Education Committee. Gov. Imperial Coll. of Science and Technology; Chairman of Central Emigration Board; Fellow of the Royal Colonial Institute. For many years leader writer on *Morning Post*. Edited the *Observer, Pall Mall Gazette, English Illustrated Magazine*, and *Sporting and Dramatic;* Founder and Editor of the *Empire Review.* Author of *Australian Defences and New Guinea, Official Life of the Duchess of Teck, Queen Mary* 1911, and of numerous political essays. Knighted 1905; K.B.E. 1919; Bart. 1926. A Conservative. Elected for Devonport in January and December 1910, for the Devonport division of Plymouth in December 1918 and November 1922, defeated in December 1923. sat for Cardiff E. from October 1924 until he was defeated in May 1929. Assumed the surname Kinloch-Cooke in lieu of Cooke 1905. Vice-President of Tariff Reform League. Honorary Associate of R.I.B.A. Died 4 September 1944. [1929]

KIRBY, Bertie Victor. Continued in House after 1945: full entry in Volume IV.

KIRKPATRICK, William MacColin. 9 Wedderburn Road, London. Winckley, Preston. Caledonian. S. of Colin Kirkpatrick, Esq. B. 10 December 1878; m. 23 November 1901, Marion, d. of Conrad Cooke, Esq., and grand-d. of E.W. Cooke, F.R.S., R.A. Educ. privately. An East Indian and Far Eastern Merchant. Member of Council of Asiatic Society of Bengal and of European Association of India. A Conservative National. Unsuccessfully contested Preston in 1923. Elected for Preston in October 1931 and sat until October 1936 when he was appointed Representative in China of the Export Credits Guarantee Department; subsequently Representative in Ankara and Belgrade. Honorary Magis-

trate in Delhi 1905-07. Member of Council of Zoological Society. Knight Commander of Chilean Order of Merit. Died 3 December 1953. [1936]

KIRKWOOD, David. Continued in House after 1945: full entry in Volume IV.

KNATCHBULL, Capt. Hon. Michael Herbert Rudolph, M.C. 11 Eaton Place, London. Mersham-le-Hatch, Ashford, Kent. Carlton, and Beefsteak. S. of Cecil, 4th Baron Brabourne. B. 8 May 1895; m. 22 January 1919, Lady Doreen Browne, d. of George, 6th Marq. of Sligo. Educ. at Wellington Coll., and Royal Military Academy, Woolwich. Assumed the surname of Knatchbull only in lieu of Knatchbull-Hugessen. Served with Royal Horse and Field Artillery 1914-18, and with R.A.F. 1918-20. Parliamentary Private Secretary to the Rt. Hon. Sir S. Hoare, Secretary of State for India January 1932. A Conservative. Elected for the Ashford division of Kent in October 1931 and sat until February 1933 when he succeeded to the Peerage as Baron Brabourne. Served at Gallipoli in 1915. Gov. of Bombay 1933-37, Gov. of Bengal 1937-39. Acting Viceroy of India in 1938. Knight of St. John of Jerusalem. Died in Calcutta 23 February 1939. [1933]

KNEBWORTH, Edward Anthony James Lytton, Visct. Knebworth House, Hertfordshire. Bucks, Bath, and Pratt's. S. and heir of Victor, 2nd Earl of Lytton. B. 13 May 1903. Educ. at Eton, and Magdalen Coll., Oxford. Vice-Chairman Army and Navy Cooperative Society Limited. Parliamentary Private Secretary to A. Duff Cooper, Financial Secretary War Office November 1931. Pilot Officer in Auxiliary Air Force. A Conservative. Unsuccessfully contested Shoreditch in May 1929. Elected for the Titchin division of Hertfordshire in October 1931 and sat until his death on 1 May 1933 when his aircraft crashed at Hendon. [1933]

KNIGHT, Maj. Eric Ayshford. Wolverley House, Kidderminster. Carlton, and Cavalry. S. of Capt. E.L. Knight, of Hornacott Manor, Launceston, and Henrietta Mary, d. of E.A. Sanford, Esq., of Nynehead Court, Wellington, Somerset. B. 1863 at Hampton; m. 1897, Constance Ida, d. of J.W.R. Wilson, Esq., of Winnipeg (she died 1932). Educ. at Cheltenham Coll. Was Maj. Worcestershire Yeomanry; served in South African War 1899-1902, and in late war. A J.P. for Worcestershire and Somerset. A Unionist. Unsuccessfully contested the Droitwich division of Worcestershire in 1906. Represented the borough of Kidderminster from January 1910-December 1918. Elected for the Kidderminster division of Worcestershire in December 1918 and sat until he retired in October 1922. Died 10 August 1944. [1922]

KNIGHT, George Wilfrid Holford, K.C. 2 Brick Court, Temple, London. Reform. S. of George Knight, Esq. B. 23 April 1877; m. 1908, Christine, d. of M. Logan, Esq. Educ. at London University. Barrister-at-Law, Middle Temple 1903. Counsel to Mint, Central Criminal Court 1911-30. K.C. 1930. Recorder of West Ham 1930-37. Engaged in London Municipal Government 1893-1903; a Freeman of the City of London and a member of Wheelwrights' Company. A National Labour Member. Unsuccessfully contested as a Liberal, the Wokingham division of Berkshire in January 1910, and the Bromley division of Kent in December 1918. Unsuccessfully contested S. Hackney as a Labour candidate in August and November 1922, Swindon in December 1923 and Devonport in October 1924. Elected for S. Nottingham as a National Labour candidate in October 1931 and sat until he retired in October 1935. Died 26 April 1936. [1935]

KNIGHTS, Capt. Henry Newton, M.B.E. Lake House, Dulwich Village, London. B. 1872; m. Grace, d. of Joseph Mitchell, Esq. (she died 1946). A Camberwell man who took an active part in local municipal affairs. Mayor of Camberwell; J.P. An enthusiastic Volunteer who helped to raise the Camberwell Volunteer Battalion; Second in Command. Sheriff of City of London 1920-21. In business life he was an Engineer. A Coalition Unionist. Elected for N. Camberwell in December 1918 and sat until he resigned in January 1922. Died 31 October 1959. [1922]

KNOX, Maj.-Gen. Sir Alfred William Fortescue, K.C.B., C.M.G. Binfield House, Binfield, Berkshire. Carlton, and United Service. S. of Vesey Edmund Knox, Esq., of Shimna House, Co. Down. B. 30 October 1870; m. 21 December 1915, Edith Mary, d. of Col. Halkett, and widow of Richard Boyle, Esq. (she died 1959). Educ. at St. Columba's Coll., and Royal Military Coll., Sandhurst. Joined I.A. 1893, Maj.-Gen. 1918, served on N.W. Frontier of India 1901-02, G.S. Officer War Office 1908-11; Military Attaché British Embassy, Petrograd, and Liaison Officer Russian Army 1911-18; Chief of Military Mission to Siberia 1918-20. C.B. 1917; K.C.B. 1919. A Conservative. Elected for the Wycombe division of Buckinghamshire in October 1924 and sat until he retired in June 1945. Died 9 March 1964. [1945]

LAKIN, Cyril Harry Alfred. 157 Chilton Court, London. Highlight Farm, Barry, Glamorganshire. Athenaeum. S. of Harry Lakin, Esq., of Highlight, Barry. B. 29 December 1893; m. 17 July 1926, Vera, d. of F.B. Savill, Esq. Educ. at St. John's Coll., Oxford, M.A. A Barrister-at-Law. Assistant Editor of *Daily Telegraph* and later of *The Sunday Times*. A National Conservative. Elected for the Llandaff and Barry division of Glamorganshire in June 1942 and sat until he was defeated in July 1945. Served with South Wales Borderers in France and Salonika. Died in a car accident in France 23 June 1948. [1945]

LAMB, Sir Joseph Quinton. Oaklands, Eccleshall, Staffordshire. S. of Joseph and Emily Lamb, of Hanley. B. 2 May 1873; m. 15 May 1912, Alice Mary, d. of T.V. Salt, Esq., of Derby. Educ. at Tattenhall, Cheshire. Engaged in agriculture from 1894. J.P. for Staffordshire; County Councillor 1909; Alderman 1922; Mayor of Newcastle-under-Lyme 1932. Held many agricultural offices, including Chairmanship of the National Farmers' Union, Staffordshire Branch. Member of Staffordshire Education

Committee. Knight Bach. 1929. Unsuccessfully contested the Stone division of Staffordshire as an Independent Farmers' candidate in December 1918. Elected as a Conservative for the Stone division in November 1922 and sat until he retired in June 1945. Chairman of County Councils Association 1945. Died 20 November 1949.

[1945]

LAMBERT, Rt. Hon. George. Spreyton, Crediton, Devon. Reform. S. of George Lambert, Esq. B. 25 June 1866; m. 30 August 1904, Barbara, d. of George Stavers, Esq., of Morpeth. Educ. privately. A Yeoman Farmer. A J.P., and County Alderman for Devon. Served on the Royal Committee on Agriculture 1893, and the Committee on Preferential Railway Rates on Agricultural Produce. Civil Lord of the Admiralty December 1905-May 1915. Member of Royal Commission on Fuel and Oil Engines for Navy. Foundation Chairman of Seale Hayne Agricultural Coll., Devon. Chairman Liberal Party 1919-21. PC. 1912. A Liberal until 1931, thereafter a Liberal National. Sat for the S. Molton division of Devonshire from November 1891-October 1924 when he was defeated. Re-elected for the S. Molton division in May 1929 and sat until he retired in June 1945. Created Visct. Lambert 1945. Died 17 February 1958.

[1945]

LANCASTER, Claude Granville. Continued in House after 1945: full entry in Volume IV.

LANE-FOX, Col. Rt. Hon. George Richard. 88 Eaton Square, London. Bramham Park, Boston Spa, Yorkshire. Arthur's, Turf, and Carlton. S. of Capt. J.R. Lane-Fox, of Bramham Park, Yorkshire, and Lucy, d. of H. St. John Mildmay, Esq., of Shoreham, Kent. B. 15 December 1870; m. 17 September 1903, Hon. Agnes Wood, d. of Charles, 2nd Visct. Halifax. Educ. at Eton, and New Coll., Oxford. Barrister-at-Law, Inner Temple 1895; a member of W. Riding County Council 1898-1928; J.P. and County Alderman for the W. Riding of Yorkshire; Dept.-Lieut. for Co. Leitrim. Dept.-Lieut. for the W.

Riding of Yorkshire and for City and County of City of York. Brevet-Col. Yorkshire Hussars. Served in France 1915-17. Charity Commissioner 1921. Secretary for Mines October 1922-January. 1924 and November 1924-January 1928. Member of Indian Statutory Commission 1928. PC. 1926. A Conservative. Unsuccessfully contested the Barkston Ash division of the W. Riding of Yorkshire in 1905. Elected for the Barkston Ash division in 1906 and sat until he retired in October 1931. Chairman of Pig Products Commission 1932 and Fatstock Reorganisation Commission 1933. Created Baron Bingley 1933. Died 11 December 1947. [1931 2nd ed.]

LANE-MITCHELL, Sir William. Queen Anne's Mansions, Buckingham Gate, London. Constitutional. S. of William Mitchell, Esq. B. 24 January 1861; m. 1st, 11 June 1884, Jane, d. of William Lane, Esq., of Aberdeen (she died 11 October 1925); secondly, 21 July 1926, Sarah, d. of Joseph Baker, Esq., of Formby, and former wife of Sir Edmund Vestey, 1st Bart., of Shirley (which marriage had been dissolved on her petition 1925). Mayor of Camberwell 1906-08. Created Knight Bach. 1921. A Conservative. Sat for the Streatham division of Wandsworth from December 1918 until he resigned in November 1939. Member of Cold Storage and Ice Association 1907-40. Manager of Messrs. R. and W. Davidson, Frozen Food Importers. Chairman of Lane Mitchell Limited, Produce Brokers. Adopted the surname Lane-Mitchell in lieu of Mitchell. Died 20 June 1940. [1939]

LANG, Rev. Gordon. Continued in House after 1945: full entry in Volume IV.

LANSBURY, Rt. Hon. George. 39 Bow Road, London. S. of George Lansbury, Esq., Car Contractor. B. in Suffolk 21 February 1859; m. 1880, Elizabeth Jane, d. of Isaac Brine, Esq. (she died 23 March 1933). Educ. at an elementary day school. Held all local government offices in his district of E. London. First Commissioner of Works June 1929-August 1931. PC. 1929. A Labour Member. A Liberal agent until he joined the Social Democratic Federation in 1892. Unsuccessfully contested the Walworth division of Newington as the candidate of the Social Democratic Federation in May and July 1895 and the Bow and Bromley division of Tower Hamlets in 1900; unsuccessfully contested Middlesbrough in 1906 as an Independent Socialist in opposition to the Labour candidate. Unsuccessfully contested the Bow and Bromley division of Tower Hamlets as the Labour candidate in January 1910 but was elected for the division in December 1910 and sat until November 1912 when he resigned, in order to test public opinion on the question of women's suffrage, and was defeated at the by-election. Unsuccessfully contested the Bow and Bromley division of Poplar in December 1918 but was elected there in November 1922 and sat until his death on 7 May 1940. Editor of *Daily Herald* 1913-22. Chairman of National Executive of Labour Party 1925-26. Leader of Labour Party and Leader of Opposition 1931-35. Member of Poplar Borough Council 1903-40, Mayor 1919-20 and 1936-37. Died 7 May 1940. [1940]

LARMOR, Sir Joseph. St. John's Coll., Cambridge. Athenaeum. S. of Hugh Larmor, Esq., of Magheragall, Co. Antrim. B. 11 July 1857 at Magheragall. Unmarried. Educ. at Royal Academical Institution, and Queen's Coll., Belfast, and St. John's Coll., Cambridge. Fellow of St. John's Coll. from 1880; Lucasian Professor of Mathematics Cambridge University from 1903-1932; Secretary of Royal Society 1901-12. Professor of National Philosophy Queen's Coll., Galway 1880-85; Lecturer in Mathematics Cambridge University 1885-1903. Foreign Honorary member Accademia dei Lincei of Rome and of the U.S. National Academy, of American Academy of Boston, and American Phil. Society of Philadelphia; Corr. Member Institut de France; Honorary member R. Irish Academy; F.R.S.; Honorary D.Sc. Oxford, Cambridge, and Dublin, LL.D. Glasgow, St. Andrews, Birmingham and Aberdeen, D.C.L. Durham; F.R.A.S., Honorary F.R.S. Edinburgh. Author of *Aether and Matter*, and scientific memoirs on mathematical and physical subjects. A Unionist. Elected for Cambridge University in February 1911, re-elected

there in December 1918 and sat until he retired in October 1922. Knighted 1909. Vice-President of Royal Society 1912-14. Treasurer of London Mathematical Society 1892-1913, President 1914-15. Died 19 May 1942. [1922]

LATHAM, Capt. Sir Herbert Paul, Bart. 4 Hyde Park Gardens, London. Herstmonceux Castle, Sussex. Carlton, and Marlborough. S. of Sir Thomas Latham, 1st Bart. B. 22 April 1905; m. 29 June 1933, Lady Patricia Moore, d. of Henry, 10th Earl of Drogheda (divorced 1943). Educ. at Eton, and Magdalen Coll., Oxford. Member of London County Council from 1928-34. J.P. for Sussex. Capt. 70 Sussex S/L Regiment R.E. A Conservative. Unsuccessfully contested Rotherham in May 1929. Elected for the Scarborough and Whitby division of the N. Riding of Yorkshire in May and October 1931 and sat until he resigned in August 1941 while under a charge of disgraceful conduct and attempting to commit suicide; convicted by court-martial 23 September 1941, cashiered and sentenced to 2 years imprisonment. Succeeded as Bart. 1931. Died 24 July 1955. [1941]

LATHAN, George. 24 Osidge Lane, Southgate, London. S. of G. Lathan, Esq., of Norwich. B. 5 August 1875; m. Gertrude Alice, d. of F. Everett, Esq., of Norwich. President 1906-12, Chief Assistant Secretary 1912-37, of the Railway Clerks' Association. Member of Railways National Wages Board 1921-36. President of National Federation of Professional Workers 1921-37. Member of National Executive of the Labour Party, Chairman 1931-32. National Treasurer of Labour Party 1936-42. J.P. for Middlesex. A Labour Member. Unsuccessfully contested the Watford division of Hertfordshire in December 1918, the Enfield division of Middlesex in November 1922 and the Park division of Sheffield in December 1923 and October 1924. Elected for the Park division of Sheffield in May 1929, defeated there in October 1931. Re-elected for the Park division of Sheffield in November 1935 and sat until his death on 14 June 1942. [1942]

LAVERACK, Frederick Joseph. Invergordon, 30 Redston Road, Hornsey, London. National Liberal. S. of George Laverack, Esq. B. at Leeds 1871; m. Rose, eld. d. of Robert Roberts, Esq., of Leeds. Educ. at St. George's School, Leeds, Ranmoor Coll., Sheffield, and privately. Studied law, but afterwards became a Congregational Minister, with pastorates in Yorkshire, and Fulham, London. Joined Sir Arthur Pearson in 1916 and organised the Blinded Soldiers' Children's Fund, raising £100,000. Reorganised the Chaplain's Department, National Institute for the Blind; Joint Secretary Greater London Fund for the Blind; Director of Association for the General Welfare of the Blind. A Liberal. Unsuccessfully contested the Brixton division of Lambeth in November 1922. Elected for the Brixton division of Lambeth in December 1923 and sat until he was defeated in October 1924; again defeated in June 1927. Died 11 April 1928.   [1924 2nd ed.]

LAW, Albert. 65 Starcliffe Street, Bolton. S. of John Law, Esq., Brewer. B. 1872; m. 1900, Mary Ann, d. of Samuel Jenkinson, Esq., of Bolton. Educ. at Board School, Bolton. An Operative Spinner. President of Bolton Operative Spinners 1916-18 and 1920-22; President of Bolton Trades Council and Labour Party. A Labour Member. Elected for Bolton December 1923; unsuccessfully contested the same seat in October 1924. Re-elected for Bolton in May 1929 and sat until he was defeated in October 1931. Unsuccessfully contested Bolton in November 1935. Methodist local preacher for 60 years. Died 22 October 1956.   [1931 2nd ed.]

LAW, Sir Alfred Joseph. Honresfeld, Littleborough, Manchester. Athenaeum, Carlton, Junior Carlton, and 1900. S. of John Law, Esq., of Dearnley. B. 31 May 1860. Unmarried. Educ. privately. A Director of Companies. J.P. for Lancashire; Chairman Littleborough Local Board and Urban District Council 1892-96; of Middleton division Conservative Association. Knighted 1927. A Conservative. Elected for Rochdale in December 1918, and defeated there in November 1922. Elected for the High Peak division of Derbyshire in May 1929 and sat until his death on 18 July 1939.   [1939]

LAW, Rt. Hon. Andrew Bonar. 10 Downing Street, London. Carlton. S. of the Rev. James Law, M.A., of New Brunswick, Canada, and Eliza Anne Kidston. B. 1858 in New Brunswick; m. 1891, Annie Pitcairn, d. of Harrington Robley, Esq., of Glasgow (she died 1909). Educ. in Canada, and Glasgow High School. Was Leader of the Unionist Party in the House of Commons November 1911-March 1921 and October 1922-May 1923. Was Parliamentary Secretary to the Board of Trade 1902-05. Secretary of State for the Colonies and member of War Committee May 1915 to December 1916; member of Mr. Lloyd George's War Cabinet. Chancellor of the Exchequer, and Leader of the House of Commons December 1916 to January 1919. Plenipotentiary Peace Conference 1919; Lord Privy Seal and Leader in Commons January 1919 to March 1921. First Lord of the Treasury and Prime Minister 23 October 1922- 20 May 1923. Honorary LL.D. Cambridge 1920. Iron Merchant in Glasgow, and Chairman of Scottish Iron Trade Association. J.P. for Dumbartonshire. PC. 1911. Honorary LL.D. Glasgow. Lord Rector, Glasgow University 1919. A Conservative. Sat for Glasgow Blackfriars, from 1900-06 when he was defeated, and for Dulwich from May 1906 to December 1910 when he unsuccessfully contested N.W. Manchester. Sat for Bootle 1911-18. Elected for Glasgow Central in December 1918 and again November 1922. Sat until his death on 30 October 1923.   [1923]

LAW, Arthur. 144 St. Mary's Road, Moston, Manchester. 164 Haslingden Old Road, Rawtenstall, Lancashire. S. of John Law, Esq. B. 4 January 1876; m. Lucy Ellen, d. of John Whittaker, Esq. Educ. at Centre Vale National, and Todmorden Council School. An Engine Driver. Member of Executive Committee National Union of Railwaymen 1910-12, 1918-20, 1925 and 1926. Delegate to Labour Party and Trade Union Congress. A Labour Member. Unsuccessfully contested Salford W. in November 1922. Sat for Rossendale from May 1929 until he was defeated in October 1931. Died 30 June 1933.   [1931 2nd ed.]

LAW, Rt. Hon. Richard Kidston. Continued in House after 1945: full entry in Volume IV.

LAWLESS, Francis J. Saucerstown House, Swords, Dublin. B. about 1872. A Farmer. Was deported after the rebellion but released. Re-arrested and sentenced to three months imprisonment November 1919. A Sinn Fein Member. Elected for Dublin Co. N. in December 1918 but did not take his seat. Member of Dail for Dublin Co. N. to 1921, and for Dublin Co. from 1921 until he was accidentally killed on 16 April 1922. A Pro-Treaty Member.   [1922]

LAWRENCE, Arabella Susan. 41 Grosvenor Road, London. D. of Nathaniel Tertius Lawrence, Esq., Solicitor. B. 1871. Educ. at Newnham Coll., Cambridge. Member of London County Council (Poplar) 1913-27; Dept.-Chairman 1925-26. Member of National Executive of Labour Party, Chairman 1929-30. Parliamentary Secretary Ministry of Health June 1929-August 1931. A Labour Member. Unsuccessfully contested Camberwell N.W. in 1920 and N. East Ham in 1922. Elected for N. East Ham in December 1923; defeated in 1924. Re-elected for N. East Ham in April 1926. Sat until she was defeated in October 1931. Unsuccessfully contested Stockton-on-Tees in November 1935. Organiser for National Federation of Women Workers 1912-21. Member of Poplar Borough Council 1919-24. Died 25 October 1947.
     [1931 2nd ed.]

LAWRIE, Hugh Hartley. Pontcanna, Cardiff. National Labour. S. of John Lawrie, Esq., of Rochdale. B. 1879; m. 1907, Amy Elizabeth, d. of Llewellyn Jones, Esq., of Manchester. Educ. at Board School. Worked in a Cotton Mill, and later on the staff of Manchester Newspapers. An Official of the Workers' Union (later Transport and General Workers Union) from 1910. A Labour Member. Elected for the Stalybridge

and Hyde division of Cheshire in May 1929 and sat until he retired in October 1931.   [1931 2nd ed.]

LAWSON, Hugh McDowall. 10 Gerald Road, London. 2 Otley Street, Skipton. S. of John Lawson, Esq., Pharmaceutical Chemist, of Leeds. B. 13 February 1912; m. 1 July 1937, Dorothy Louisa, d. of the Rev. T.H. Mallinson. Educ. at High School, and University Coll., Nottingham. Chartered Civil Engineer, B.Sc.Eng. London, Assoc. M. Inst. C.E. from 1932; Assoc. M.Inst. M. and Cy.E. Lieut. R.E.; joined May 1940; served at Gibraltar October 1940-May 1943. A Common Wealth Member. Elected for the Skipton division of Yorkshire in January 1944 and sat until July 1945 when he unsuccessfully contested Harrow W. as the Common Wealth candidate. Unsuccessfully contested, as the Labour candidate, the Rushcliffe division of Nottinghamshire in February 1950 and the Kings Lynn division of Norfolk in May 1955. Dept. City Engineer, Nottingham 1948-73. Director of Leisure Services, Nottingham 1973-76. Member of Council of Institution of Civil Engineers 1972-75.*   [1945]

LAWSON, John James. Continued in House after 1945: full entry in Volume IV.

LAWTHER, William. 95 Queen's Road, Finsbury Park, London. 25 Dorlinco Villas, Meadowfield, Co. Durham. S. of Edward Lawther, Esq., of Choppington, Northumberland. B. 1889; m. 1915, Lottie Laws (she died 1962). Educ. at Choppington Colliery School, and Central Labour Coll., London. A Labour Member. Unsuccessfully contested South Shields in November 1922, December 1923 and October 1924. Elected for the Barnard Castle division of Durham in May 1929 and sat until he was defeated in October 1931. Member of Durham County Council 1925-29. Member of T.U.C. General Council 1935-54, President 1949. Knighted 1949. President of Miners' Federation of Great Britain, later National Union of Mineworkers 1939-54. Died 1 February 1976.   [1931 2nd ed.]

LEACH, William. 16 Haslingden Drive, Bradford. B. 1870. Educ. at Bradford Grammar School. A Bradford Worsted Manufacturer. Chairman of the Finance Committee of the City Council 1920. Alderman 1920. Under-Secretary for Air January-November 1924. A Labour Member. Unsuccessfully contested central Bradford in 1918. Elected for central Bradford in November 1922 and December 1923, defeated there in October 1924. Re-elected for central Bradford in May 1929, defeated October 1931. Re-elected again for central Bradford in November 1935 and sat until he retired in June 1945. Member of Bradford City Council from 1907, Alderman 1920. Member of Royal Commission on Transport 1929. Died 21 November 1949. [1945]

LECKIE, Joseph Alexander. Tudor House, Walsall. Kippen, Streetly, Sutton Coldfield, Warwickshire. National Liberal. S. of John Leckie, Esq., of Glasgow and Walsall. B. 24 May 1866; m. 1889, Jean, d. of George Wightman, Esq., of Walsall. Educ. at Glasgow and Bellahouston Academies. A Leather Goods Manufacturer. Chairman of Walsall Education Committee. J.P. Member of English-speaking Union. A Liberal National. Elected for Walsall in October 1931 and sat until his death on 9 August 1938. President of West Midlands Federation of Free Church Councils. Member of Walsall Town Council 1916-37, Alderman 1930-37, Mayor 1926-27. Died 9 August 1938. [1938]

LEE, Frank. Tennyson Avenue, Chesterfield. S. of Thomas Lee, Esq., Miner. B. 1867. Worked in the mines when 13 years of age. Assistant Secretary of the Derbyshire Miners' Association from 1914. Wesleyan local preacher. A Labour Member. Unsuccessfully contested N.E. Derbyshire in December 1918. Sat for N.E. Derbyshire from November 1922 until October 1931, when he was defeated. Re-elected in November 1935 and sat until his death on 21 December 1941. [1942]

LEE, Jennie. Continued in House after 1945: full entry in Volume IV.

LEECH, Sir Joseph William. Buston Hall, Alnmouth, Northumberland. Constitutional. S. of Isaac Leech, Esq., of Cleator, Cumberland. B. 9 April 1865; m. 16 April 1903, Elfreda Louise, d. of Walter de Lancey Wilson, Esq., of Kirklinton Park, Carlisle. Educ. at Proprietary School, Egremont, Cumberland, and at University of Durham (Charlton Scholar), Berlin and Vienna. A Consulting Surgeon; M.B., B.S. 1887, M.D., M.S., F.R.C.S., Honorary D.Ch. Durham; Maj. R.A.M.C. (T.F.). Member of Middle Temple. J.P. for Northumberland. Honorary Surgeon Royal Victorian Infirmary, Newcastle for 26 years, and to Nose and Ear Hospital for 17 years. Senior Fellow Association of Surgeons of Great Britain; President Newcastle Clinical Society. Lecturer and Examiner in Clinical Surgery, University of Durham, Coll. of Medicine. President and Honorary Secretary for 4 years University of Durham Medical Graduates' Association; Honorary Secretary Newcastle Clinical Society for 4 years. Dept. Lord Mayor of Newcastle 1929-30. Lord Mayor 1932-33. Sheriff 1930-31. Member of City Council. Director of Choppington Collieries Limited, Northumberland, Elswick Building Society and other companies; member of Ecclesiastical Commission. Knight Bach. January 1938. A National Conservative. Unsuccessfully contested the W. division of Newcastle-upon-Tyne in May 1929. Elected for the W. division of Newcastle-upon-Tyne in October 1931 and sat until his death on 30 May 1940. [1940]

LEES, Jack. House of Commons, London. B. at West Rainton, Durham 1884. Worked in a Coal Mine. An Official of Northumberland Miners' Association. A Labour Member. Elected for the Belper division of Derbyshire in May 1929 and sat until he was defeated in October 1931; again defeated in November 1935. Unsuccessfully contested the Belper division of Derbyshire in October 1924. Died 11 August 1940. [1931 2nd ed.]

LEES-JONES, John. 2a Whitehall Court, London. Allandale, Bradgate Road, Altrincham. S. of Dr. J. Williams Jones, L.R.C.P.,

L.R.C.S., of Manchester. B. 25 September 1887; m. 1 June 1921, Alice May, d. of John Ryder, Esq., of Manchester. Educ. at Lymm Grammar School, and Wrekin Coll. A Company Director. Barrister-at Law, Middle Temple 1916. J.P. for Manchester 1926. Dept. President and Chairman of National Association of Discharged Prisoners Aid Societies. Served with B.E.F. Salonika 1915-19. A Conservative. Unsuccessfully contested East Ham N. in May 1929. Elected for the Blackley division of Manchester in October 1931 and sat until he was defeated in July 1945. Member of Manchester City Council. O.B.E. 1953. Chairman of J.W. Lees and Company (Brewers). Member of Advisory Council on Treatment of Offenders. Died 13 January 1966.   [1945]

LEES-SMITH, Rt. Hon. Hastings Bertrand. 77 Corringham Road, London. Athenaeum. S. of Maj. H. Lees-Smith, R.A. B. 26 January 1878; m. 5 November 1915, Joyce Eleanor, d. of S.H. Holman, Esq. Educ. at Aldenham, Royal Military Academy, Woolwich, and at Queen's Coll., Oxford. Postmaster-Gen. June 1929-March 1931; President of Board of Education March-August 1931; PC. 1931. Leader of H.M. Opposition and Acting Chairman of Parliamentary Labour Party May 1940-December 1941. A Labour Member. Sat for Northampton from January 1910 to December 1918 as a Liberal. Unsuccessfully contested the Don Valley division of the W. Riding of Yorkshire in 1918. Joined Labour Party 1919. Sat for the Keighley division of the W. Riding of Yorkshire from November 1922 to December 1923, when he was defeated. Re-elected for the Keighley division of the W. Riding of Yorkshire in October 1924 and sat until he was again defeated in October 1931. Again re-elected for the Keighley division of the W. Riding of Yorkshire in November 1935 and sat until his death on 18 December 1941. Chairman of Executive Committee of Ruskin Coll., Oxford 1907-09. Lecturer in Public Administration at London School of Economics 1906-41, Reader 1924-41. Professor of Public Administration at University of Bristol 1909-10. Died 18 December 1941.   [1942]

LEIGH, Sir John, Bart. 15 Grosvenor Square, London. Witley Park, Godalming. Carlton, and Bachelors'. S. of John Leigh, Esq., J.P., of Brooklands, Cheshire. B. 3 August 1884, m. 23 January 1908, Norah, d. of John H. New, Esq., of Melbourne (she died 1954). Educ. at Manchester Grammar School. Created Bart. 1918. J.P. for the County Palatine of Lancashire. A Conservative. Returned unopposed for the Clapham division of Wandsworth in May 1922, and November 1922 after a contest. Re-elected for the Clapham division in December 1923 and sat until he retired in June 1945. Proprietor of *Pall Mall Gazette* 1921-23. Died 28 July 1959.   [1945]

LEIGHTON, Maj. Bertie Edward Parker. Sweeny Hall, Oswestry. Carlton, and Cavalry. S. of Stanley Leighton, Esq., MP. B. 26 November 1875; m. 24 September 1936, Margaret Evelyn, d. of the Rev. Hugh Hanmer, of The Mount, Oswestry. Educ. at Eton, and Royal Military Coll., Sandhurst. Joined First Royal Dragoons 1896; served in South African War 1900-02, and in France, etc. 1914-18. Dept.-Lieut., and J.P. for Shropshire. A Conservative. Sat for the Oswestry division of Shropshire from May 1929 until he retired in June 1945. Died 15 February 1952.   [1945]

LENNON, James. Conenellan House, Borris, Co. Carlow. A Farmer. A Sinn Fein Member. Returned unopposed for Co. Carlow in December 1918 but did not take his seat. Member of Dail for Co. Carlow to 1921, for Carlow and Kilkenny 1921-22 as an Anti-Treaty Member.   [1922]

LENNOX-BOYD, Alan Tindal. Continued in House after 1945: full entry in Volume IV.

LEONARD, William. Continued in House after 1945: full entry in Volume IV.

LESLIE, John Robert. Continued in House after 1945: full entry in Volume IV.

LESSING, Edward Albert. 49 Grosvenor Square, London. Kingston House, Nr. Abingdon, Berkshire. S. of Albert Lessing,

Esq., Merchant, and Augusta Lessing. B. at 27 Park Lane, London 28 July 1890. Unmarried. Educ. at Marlborough, and University Coll., Oxford. A Barrister-at-Law; Merchant (Chairman of Strauss and Company, Grain Merchants). British Military Mission to Russia 1916-18; Capt. Grenadier Guards during the Great War. A Liberal. Unsuccessfully contested the Abingdon division of Berkshire in 1922 and 1929. Elected for the Abingdon division in December 1923 and sat until he was defeated in October 1924. Served in Royal Army Pay Corps and Pioneer Corps 1939-45. Chairman of Alexandria Trading Corporation. Director of *Contemporary Review*. O.B.E. 1918. Died 25 August 1964. [1924 2nd ed.]

LEVER, Sir Arthur Levy, Bart. 20 Hans Crescent, London. Barrow Green Court, Oxted, Surrey. Reform, National Liberal, and Ranelagh. S. of Joseph Levy, Esq., of Knighton, Leicester, and Cordelia, d. of M. Hart, Esq. B. 17 November 1860; m. 12 February 1896; Beatrice, d. of Philip Falk, Esq., when he assumed the additional surname of Lever (she died 1917). Educ. at London University Coll. School, privately, and abroad. Member of London War Pensions Committee. J.P. for Essex. A National Liberal. Sat for the Harwich division of Essex from January 1906 to January 1910 when he was defeated. Unsuccessfully contested S. Wolverhampton in December 1910. Elected for Central Hackney in November 1922 and sat until he retired in November 1923. Created Bart. 1911. Served in France with Royal Fusiliers, from 1917 Dept.-Director of Recruiting for S.E. region. Died 23 August 1924. [1923]

LEVY, Thomas. 4 Inver Court, Queensway, London. 90 Easton Way, Frinton-on-Sea. Constitutional. S. of Lewis Levy, Esq., of Denmark Hill, London. B. 1874; m. 30 January 1901, Maud, d. of Benjamin Benjamin, Esq. Educ. at City of London School. Assistant Officer of Food Control in Bournemouth 1914-18. In command of Transport during the strike 1919. Chairman of Parliamentary Textile Committee 1932-35 and of Parliamentary Tariff Policy Committee

1934-39. Director of British Celanese Limited. Chairman of British Wool Central Advisory Committee 1939-40. A Conservative. Elected for the Elland division of the W. Riding of Yorkshire in October 1931 and sat until he was defeated in July 1945. Died 14 February 1953. [1945]

LEVY-LEVER, Sir Arthur, Bart. See LEVER, Sir Arthur Levy, Bart.

LEWIS, Rt. Hon. John Herbert. 23 Grosvenor Road, London. Penucha, Caerwys, Holywell, Flintshire. Reform, and National Liberal. S. of E. Lewis, Esq., of Mostyn Quay, Shipowner. B. 1858; m. 1st, 1886, Adelaide, d. of Charles Hughes, Esq., J.P. (she died 1895); secondly, 1897, Ruth, d. of W.S. Caine, Esq., MP for Camborne. Educ. at Denbigh Grammar School, McGill University, Montreal, and Exeter Coll., Oxford; LL.D. University of Wales 1918. A Junior Lord of the Treasury and a Liberal Whip December 1905 to July 1909. Parliamentary Secretary to the Local Government Board 1909-15. Parliamentary Secretary to Board of Education from May 1915-October 1922. Constable of Flint Castle; an Alderman of Flintshire County Council; Chairman 1889-93. Dept.-Lieut. for Flintshire 1918. PC. 1913. President of the Library Association 1920-21. A Liberal. Sat for Flint district from 1892-1906 and for Flintshire from 1906 to 1918. Elected for the University of Wales in December 1918 and sat until he retired in October 1922. Admitted a Solicitor 1882. G.B.E. November 1922. President of National Library of Wales. Elected Moderator of Presbyterian Church of Wales 1925 but declined the appointment. Died 10 November 1933. [1922]

LEWIS, Oswald. Beechwood, Hampstead Lane, London. Carlton. S. of John Lewis, Esq., Founder of the firm John Lewis and Company, Oxford Street. B. 5 April 1887; m. 1928, Frances Merriman, d. of Dr. H.M. Cooper. Educ. at Westminster School, and Christ Church, Oxford, M.A. A Barrister-at-Law, Middle Temple 1912, but did not practise. F.R.G.S., F.Z.S. Served with 2nd Co. of London Yeomanry 1911-16, in

Egypt, etc. 1914-16. A Conservative. Sat for the Colchester division of Essex from May 1929 until he was defeated in July 1945. Member of St. Marylebone Borough Council 1908-12 and London County Council 1913-19. Master of Worshipful Company of Farriers. Died 12 February 1966.   [1945]

LEWIS, Thomas. Continued in House after 1945: full entry in Volume IV.

LEWIS, Thomas Arthur. Cemaes, Pontypridd. National Liberal. S. of the Rev. J.M. Lewis, Baptist Minister. B. at Nevern, Pembrokeshire 21 September 1881; m. 1919, Marjorie, d. of William Culross, Esq., of Adelaide, South Australia. Educ. at University Coll., Cardiff; Graduate in Science. A Barrister, Middle Temple 1919. Joined Inns of Court O.T.C., commissioned 1916; served Salonica 1916-18. Parliamentary Private Secretary to Capt. Hon. F.E. Guest, MP from February 1919 to July 1922. Junior Lord of the Treasury July to October 1922. A Liberal. Elected for the Pontypridd division of Glamorganshire in December 1918 and sat until defeated in July 1922 when he sought re-election on appointment to the Government. Elected for the University of Wales in November 1922 and sat until his death on 18 July 1923.   [1923]

LIDDALL, Sir Walter Sydney, C.B.E. Chequers, Scunthorpe, Lincolnshire. Constitutional. Lincoln, and County. S. of Benjamin Liddall, Esq., of Scunthorpe. B. 2 March 1884; m. 12 June 1910, Gertrude, d. of G.R. Long, Esq., of Scunthorpe. Educ. at De Aston Grammar School, Market Rasen. A Journalist. Chairman of Scunthorpe and Frodingham Urban District Council 1920-21, 1923-25; Local Manager, Scunthorpe Savings Bank; Treasurer of Scunthorpe Conservative Club. Chairman of Super Savouries Limited, Refast S.S. Company Limited, of Rumex Oil Products Limited, of British American Glass Company Limited, of North Staffordshire Pottery Company Limited, of Pressure Lubricants Limited, and of other Limited Companies. Vice-Chairman Brigg division National Unionist Association; J.P. for Parts of

Lindsey. A Conservative. Unsuccessfully contested the Don Valley division of the W. Riding of Yorkshire in May 1929. Elected for Lincoln in October 1931 and sat until he was defeated in July 1945. C.B.E. 1937. Knighted 1945. Died 24 February 1963.   [1945]

LINDLEY, Fred William. 46 St. Ann's Road, Rotherham. B. 1878. Member of the Amalgamated Society of Woodworkers, of the Sheffield Federated Trades and Labour Council, and local Unemployment Committee. A Labour Member. Elected for Rotherham in December 1923 and sat until he was defeated in October 1931. Unsuccessfully contested Central Leeds in November 1935.   [1931 2nd ed.]

LINDSAY, Kenneth Martin. Continued in House after 1945: full entry in Volume IV.

LINDSAY, Noel Ker. 60 Eaton Terrace, London. 2 Pump Court, Temple, London. Albion Chambers, Bristol. S. of John Ker Lindsay, Esq., Physician and Surgeon, of Edinburgh. B. 25 December 1904; m. 1935, June, d. of W. Clayton Mitchell, Esq. Educ. at St. Peter's School, York, and Brasenose Coll., Oxford. President O.U.D.S. 1924-25. B.A. 1926; B.C.L. 1927. Barrister-at-Law, Gray's Inn 1927, joined the Western Circuit. A National Conservative. Elected for Bristol S. in October 1931 and sat until he was defeated in November 1935. Served with R.A.S.C. and in Guards 1940-45, Lieut.-Col., Asst. Q.M.G. Director of British Non-Ferrous Metals Federation.   [1935]

LINDSAY, William Arthur. Tyrone House, Belfast. The Cottage, Goring, Oxfordshire. 16 Pall Mall, London. Devonshire, Garrick, and Kennel. Ulster, Belfast. S. of T.G. Lindsay, Esq., of Tyrone House, Belfast. B. 14 April 1866 at Belfast; m. 1892, Maud, d. of John Rabett, Esq., of Bramfield, Suffolk. Educ. at The Leys School, Cambridge, and St. Peter's Coll., Cambridge. A Unionist. Returned unopposed for S. Belfast in July 1917, in succession to Mr. Chambers, K.C., who had been Solicitor-Gen. for Ireland. Elected for the Cromac division of Belfast in December 1918 and sat until he retired in October 1922. Died 21 June 1936. [1922]

LINFIELD, Frederick Caesar. 86 Huron Road, Tooting Bec Common, London. National Liberal. S. of William Linfield, Esq. B. at Worthing 1861; m. 1884, d. of William Ayres, Esq. Educ. at Milton House. Was twice Mayor of Worthing. J.P. for Sussex. Vice-President of the Primitive Methodist Conference 1902. Served in the Ministry of Munitions during the war. A A Liberal. Unsuccessfully contested Horncastle in December 1910 and February 1911. Elected for mid Bedfordshire in November 1922 and sat until he was defeated in October 1924. Unsuccessfully contested the Howdenshire division of the E. Riding of Yorkshire in November 1926 and the Horncastle division of Lincolnshire in May 1929. M.B.E. 1918. Died 2 June 1939. [1924 2nd ed.]

LINSTEAD, Hugh Nicholas. Continued in House after 1945: full entry in Volume IV.

LIPSON, Daniel Leopold. Continued in House after 1945: full entry in Volume IV.

LISTER, Sir Robert Ashton, C.B.E. The Towers, Dursley, Gloucestershire. Reform, and National Liberal. S. of George and Louisa Lister. B. 4 February 1845 at Dursley, Gloucestershire; m. 1866, Frances Ann, d. of John Box, Esq. (she died 1911). Educ. privately, and in Germany and France. A Mechanical Engineer. Member of the Gloucestershire County Council from 1888 to 1929. Wrote *Three Months in America* and *Small Holdings in Denmark*. A Coalition Liberal. Unsuccessfully contested the Tewkesbury division of Gloucestershire in 1906, January 1910 and December 1910. Elected for the Stroud division of Gloucestershire in December 1918 and sat until he retired in October 1922. J.P. for Gloucestershire. Knighted 1911. C.B.E. 1919. Died 6 December 1929. [1922]

LITTLE, Sir Ernest Gordon Graham. See GRAHAM-LITTLE, Sir Ernest Gordon Graham. Continued in House after 1945: full entry in Volume IV.

LITTLE, Rev. James. Continued in House after 1945: full entry in Volume IV.

LIVINGSTONE, Alexander Mackenzie. The Cedars, 2 St. Alban's Road, Highgate, London. S. of Duncan Livingstone, Esq., of Applecross, Ross-shire. B. 1880; m. 1st, Mary, d. of Donald McAskill, Esq., of Skye (she died 1946); secondly, 1947, Maggie Clark, d. of Robert Murray, Esq., of Stornoway. Head of the exporting firm of Livingstone, Page and Company, London. A Liberal. Unsuccessfully contested Dover in 1918 and the Inverness division of Inverness and Ross and Cromarty in March and November 1922. Elected for the Western Isles division of Inverness and Ross and Cromarty in December 1923 and sat until he retired in May 1929. Knighted 1933. Joined Labour Party 1930 and National Labour Party 1931. Vice-Chairman of National Labour Committee from 1932. Member of Common Council of City of London 1938-46. J.P. for County of London. Died 14 September 1950. [1929]

LLEWELLIN, Col. Rt. Hon. John Jestyn, C.B.E., M.C., T.D. Upton House, Poole, Dorset. S. of William Llewellin, Esq., of Upton House, Poole. B. 6 February 1893. Unmarried. Educ. at Eton, and University Coll., Oxford. Barrister-at-Law 1921. Commanded Dorset Heavy Brigade R.A. (T.A.) 1931-38. Served in France 1915-19. Parliamentary Private Secretary to Rt. Hon. William Ormsby-Gore when Postmaster-Gen. September-October 1931, and October 1931-June 1935, when First Commissioner of Works. Assistant Government Whip June 1935-May 1937, Civil Lord of the Admiralty May 1937-July 1939; Parliamentary Secretary Ministry of Supply July 1939-May 1940, Ministry of Aircraft Production May 1940-May 1941, and Joint Parliamentary Secretary Ministry of War Transport May 1941-February 1942. President of Board of Trade February 1942; Minister of Aircraft Production February-November 1942; Minister Resident in Washington for Supply November 1942-November 1943. Minister of Food November 1943-July 1945. PC. 1941. A Conservative. Unsuccessfully contested Southwark N. in October 1924. Elected for the Uxbridge division of Middlesex in May 1929 and sat until he was defeated in July 1945. Created Baron Llewellin 1945. Gov.-Gen. of Rhodesia and Nyasaland 1953-57. G.B.E. 1953. Dept.-Lieut for Dorset; Chairman of Dorset Quarter Sessions 1950-53. President of Royal Society for Prevention of Accidents 1945-53. Died 24 January 1957. [1945]

LLEWELLYN-JONES, Frederick. Isfryn, Mold, Flintshire. National Liberal, Overseas and Royal Empire Society. S. of Humphrey Bradley Jones, Esq., Schoolmaster of Bethesda. B. 18 April 1866; m. 1892, Elizabeth, d. of Edward Roberts, Esq., of Ruthin. Educ. at Friars' School, Bangor, Bala Coll., and at University Coll. Wales, Aberystwyth; B.A. Wales and London, LL.B. London, D.Sc.Pol., Honoris Causa, University of Péco, Hungary; F.R.E.S. Admitted a Solicitor 1891. H.M. Coroner for Flintshire. Associated with administration of Education and Health in Wales. Member of Court of Governors, University of Wales, Welsh National Library and Museum; Chairman of Flint Insurance Company 1912-34; President Association of Welsh Insurance Companies and of Federation of English, Welsh and Scottish Insurance Companies; President of Welsh League of Nations Union 1933-34; member of International Law Society, of Grotius Society of London, Royal Institute of International Affairs, and of American Society of International Law. A Liberal. Elected for Flintshire in May 1929 and sat until he retired in October 1935. Joined the Liberal National group in 1931 but rejoined the Liberals in December 1932. Member of Central Council for Health Education 1923-40. Died 11 January 1941. [1935]

LLOYD, Charles Ellis. Dryburgh, Cowbridge Road, Bridgend, Glamorgan. S. of Charles Lloyd, Esq., Draper, of Newport. B. 1878. Educ. at St. Woolos Board School, Newport Bridgend National School, and Bridgend Grammar School. Entered Solicitor's Office at 14; Barrister-at-Law, Gray's Inn 1926. Practised on the S. Wales Circuit. A Journalist and Novelist. A Labour Member. Unsuccessfully contested the

Llandaff and Barry division of Glamorganshire in October 1924. Elected for the Llandaff and Barry division in May 1929 and sat until he was defeated in October 1931; again defeated in November 1935. Coroner for Ogmore district of Glamorgan. Died 7 May 1939. [1931 2nd ed.]

LLOYD, Cyril Edward. Broome, Stourbridge, Worcestershire. Carlton, and Arts. S. of Howard Lloyd, Esq., Banker. B. 21 November 1876; m. 16 June 1909, Phyllis, d. of Sir Ernest Waterlow, R.A., P.R.W.S. Educ. at Uppingham, Birmingham, and abroad. An Ironmaster and Engineer. M.Inst.C.E. Chairman of N. Hingley and Sons Limited. A Director of G.W. Railway. President of National Federation of Iron and Steel Manufacturers 1925. A Conservative. Sat for Dudley from 1922-29 when he was defeated, and from July 1941 until he retired in June 1945. Member of Sugar Industry Enquiry Committee 1934-35. High Sheriff of Worcestershire 1935. Died 19 February 1963. [1945]

LLOYD, Ernest Guy Richard. Continued in House after 1945: full entry in Volume IV.

LLOYD, Rt. Hon. Geoffrey William. Continued in House after 1945: full entry in Volume IV.

LLOYD, Sir George Ambrose, G.C.S.I., G.C.I.E., D.S.O. 24 Charles Street, London. Carlton, Bath, and St. James's. S. of Sampson Lloyd, Esq., of Dolobran, Montgomeryshire. B. 19 September 1879; m. 13 November 1911, Hon. Blanche Isabella, d. of Commander Hon. F.C. Lascelles, Maid of Honour to Queen Alexandra 1905-11. Educ. at Eton, and Trinity Coll., Cambridge. Capt. Warwickshire Yeomanry; served in Egypt, Dardanelles Expedition, in Mesopotamia and in Arabia 1914-18. Gov. of Bombay 1918-23. A Conservative. Sat for W. Staffordshire from January 1910 to November 1918 when he was appointed Gov. of Bombay, and for the Eastbourne division of E. Sussex from October 1924 until May 1925 when he was appointed High

Commissioner in Egypt and Sudan; resigned 1929. D.S.O. 1917. PC. 1924. Created Baron Lloyd November 1925. President of Navy League from 1930. Chairman of British Council from 1937. Colonial Secretary May 1940-February 1941. Leader of the House of Lords December 1940-February 1941. Fellow of Royal Geographical Society. Died 4 February 1941.

[1925]

LLOYD, George Butler. Shelton Hall, Shrewsbury. Carlton. S. of William Butler Lloyd, Esq., J.P., and Dept.-Lieut. for Shropshire. B. 8 January 1854; m. 1880, Constance, d. of Col. R. Jenkins, 1st Bengal Cavalry. Educ. at Marlborough Coll., and St. John's Coll., Cambridge. A County Councillor and J.P. for Shropshire. Alderman and J.P. for Shrewsbury; Mayor 1887 and 1889. Director of Capital and Counties Section of Lloyds Bank, Northern Assurance Company, Birmingham Branch, and Sentinel Waggon Works Limited, Shrewsbury. A Unionist. Elected for Shrewsbury in April 1913, and for the Shrewsbury division of Shropshire in December 1918 and sat until he retired in October 1922. Died 28 March 1930. [1922]

LLOYD GEORGE, Rt. Hon. David, O.M. Bron-y-de, Churt, Farnham. Ty Newydd, Llanystumdwy, North Wales. Reform, and National Liberal. S. of William George, Esq., at one time Master of the Hope Street Unitarian Schools, Liverpool, and Elizabeth, d. of David Lloyd, Esq., Baptist Minister, of Llanystumdwy, Carnarvonshire. B. 1863; m. 1st, 1888, Margaret, d. of Richard Owen, Esq., of Nynydd Ednyfed, Criccieth (she died 1941); secondly, 23 October 1943, Frances Louise, C.B.E., d. of John Stevenson, Esq., of Worthing. Educ. at Llanystumdwy Church Schools and privately. Admitted a Solicitor in June 1884. Was President of the Board of Trade December 1905 to April 1908; Chancellor of the Exchequer 1908-15; Minister of Munitions 1915-16; Secretary of State for War July to December 1916; First Lord of the Treasury and Prime Minister 7 December 1916 to 23 October 1922. PC. 1905. Awarded special war medals by the

King January 1920; Grand Cordon of the Legion of Honour 1920: Lord Rector of Edinburgh University 1920. Constable of Carnarvon Castle 1908. Chancellor for Wales of the Welsh Priory of St. J. 1918; Prior of the Priory from 1943. Honorary LL.D. University of Wales; Honorary D.C.L. Oxford. O.M. 1919. A Liberal. Sat for Carnarvon district from April 1890 to January 1945 when he was created Earl Lloyd George of Dwyfor. Leader of Liberal Party 1926-31 and of Independent Liberal Group 1931-35. Father of House of Commons 1929-45. Died 26 March 1945.

[1945]

LLOYD GEORGE, Rt. Hon. Gwilym. Continued in House after 1945: full entry in Volume IV.

LLOYD GEORGE, Lady Megan Arfon. Continued in House after 1945: full entry in Volume IV.

LLOYD-GREAME, Rt. Hon. Sir Philip, G.B.E., M.C. See CUNLIFFE-LISTER, Rt. Hon. Sir Philip, G.B.E., M.C.

LOCKER-LAMPSON, Rt. Hon. Godfrey Lampson Tennyson. 14 Southwick Crescent, London. Barlbrough Hall, Chesterfield. Marlborough. S. of Frederick Locker-Lampson, Esq. B. 19 June 1875; m. 1st, 1905, Sophy Felicité, d. of William Hatfield de Rodes, Esq., (she died 1935); secondly, 1937, Barbara Hermione, d. of O.B. Green, Esq. Educ. at Eton, and Trinity Coll., Cambridge. Served in the Foreign Office and Diplomatic Service 1898-1903. Military Service 1914-16. Charity Commissioner in House of Commons October 1922. Parliamentary Private Secretary to the Home Secretary 1916-18 and to Assistant Foreign Secretary 1918. Represented 1st Commissioner of Works in the House of Commons December 1924-December 1925. Under-Secretary of State Home Department March 1923-January 1924, and November 1924-December 1925; and for Foreign Affairs December 1925-June 1929. PC. 1928. A Conservative. Unsuccessfully contested the Chesterfield division of Derbyshire in 1906. Sat for Salisbury from January

1910-18, and for the Wood Green division of Middlesex from December 1918 until he retired in October 1935. Died 1 May 1946.

[1935]

LOCKER-LAMPSON, Oliver Stillingfleet, C.M.G., D.S.O. Roughton, Norfolk. Carlton, and Royal Automobile. S. of Frederick Locker-Lampson, Esq. B. 1880; m. 1st, 30 August 1923, Bianca Jacqueline Paget, of Pasadena, California (she died 1930); secondly, 9 December 1935, Barbara Saphira, d. of Reginald Goodall, Esq. Educ. at Cheam, Eton, and Trinity Coll., Cambridge. Barrister-at-Law, Inner Temple 1907; Commander R.N.A.S. Armoured Car Unit. Served in France, Belgium, Russia, Rumania, Turkey and Persia 1914-19. Representative for Russia, Ministry of Information; Order of Leopold of Belgium and St. Vladimir of Russia, and other Russian and Rumanian Decorations. Parliamentary Private Secretary to Sir Austen Chamberlain when Chancellor of Exchequer, Lord Privy Seal and Leader of the House of Commons 1919-22. Conductor of Victory Loan 1919. A Conservative. Elected for the Ramsey division of Huntingdonshire in January and December 1910, for Huntingdonshire in December 1918 and for the Handsworth division of Birmingham in November 1922. Sat until he retired in June 1945. C.M.G. 1917; D.S.O. 1918. Proprietor of *Peterborough Standard*, *Huntingdonshire Post* and *Empire Review*. Died 8 October 1954. [1945]

LOCKWOOD, James Horace. The Croft, Menston-in-Wharfedale, Yorkshire. Junior Carlton, and Constitutional. S. of George Lockwood, Esq., Woollen Manufacturer, of Huddersfield. B. 25 May 1888; m. Phyllis. Capt. R.F.A.; served in France 1916-18. A Solicitor 1912. President of Bradford Law Society 1929. Chairman and Director of Industrial Companies. A Conservative. Elected for the Shipley division of the W.Riding of Yorkshire in November 1930 and again in October 1931. Resigned the Conservative Whip in June 1934, after he had failed to secure readoption, and sat as an Independent Conservative until November 1935, when he unsuccessfully contested the seat in opposition to the official Conservative candidate. Died 29 November 1972.

[1935]

LOCKWOOD, John Cutts. Continued in House after 1945: full entry in Volume IV.

LODER, Capt. Hon. John de Vere. 4 Onslow Gardens, London. Carlton. S. of Gerald, 1st Baron Wakehurst. B. 5 February 1895; m. 3 June 1920, Margaret, d. of Sir Charles Tennant, 1st Bart. Educ. at Eton. Served with 4th Royal Sussex Regiment in Gallipoli, Egypt, and Palestine 1914-19; in the Foreign Office 1919-21. A Conservative. Sat for E. Leicester from October 1924 to May 1929 when he was defeated. Elected for the Lewes division of Sussex in October 1931. Sat until April 1936 when he succeeded to the Peerage as Baron Wakehurst. K.G. 1962. Gov. of New South Wales 1937-46. Gov. of Northern Ireland 1952-64. Lord Prior of Order of St. John of Jerusalem 1948-69. Died 30 October 1970. [1936]

LOFTUS, Pierse Creagh. Reydon Covert, Southwold. Carlton, and Windham. B. at Mount Loftus, Co. Kilkenny 29 November 1877; m. 1st, 1910, Dorothy, d. of T.J. Corrigan Reynolds, Esq. (she died 1943); secondly, 1945, Eileen, d. of Claude Marzetti, Esq. and widow of R.J.G. Elkington, Esq. Educ. at St. Augustine's School, Ramsgate, and Oratory School, Birmingham. Adopted the surname of Loftus in 1885. Capt. Suffolk Regiment (T.F.). Chairman of Adnams and Company Limited, Southwold. Alderman of E. Suffolk County Council from 1931; J.P. for Suffolk. A National Conservative. Elected for the Lowestoft division of Suffolk in February 1934 and sat until he was defeated in July 1945. Served in the South African War with the Maritzburg Defence Force. High Steward of Southwold from 1945. Chairman of Rural Reconstruction Association 1948. Died 20 January 1956. [1945]

LOGAN, David Gilbert. Continued in House after 1945: full entry in Volume IV.

LONG, Maj. Hon. Richard Eric Onslow. 5 Gloucester Square, London. S. of Walter,

1st Visct. Long, of Wraxall. B. 22 August 1892; m. 21 October 1916, Gwendolyn Hague, d. of Thomas Reginald Hague Cook, Esq. (she died 1959). Educ. at Harrow. Maj. Royal Wiltshire Yeomanry (T.D.). A Conservative. Elected for the Westbury division of Wiltshire in June 1927 and sat until he retired in October 1931. J.P. for Wiltshire from 1923 and Dept.-Lieut. from 1946. Succeeded to the Peerage as Visct. Long 1944. Awarded the Freedom of Athens 1947. Died 12 January 1967. [1931 2nd ed.]

LONG, Rt. Hon. Walter Hume. 46 Ebury Street, London. Rood Ashton, Trowbridge. Carlton, Cavalry, Beefsteak, Junior Constitutional, Conservative, Royal Automobile, and City Carlton. Eld. s. of Richard Penruddocke Long, Esq., of Rood Ashton, Wiltshire, by Charlotte Anna, d. of the Rt. Hon. W. Wentworth Fitzwilliam-Hume Dick, MP, of Wicklow. B. at Bath 1854; m. 1878, Lady Dorothy Blanche Boyle, d. of 9th Earl of Cork and Orrery. Educ. at Harrow, and Christ Church, Oxford. Honorary Student Christ Church, Oxford; Gov. of Harrow School. Col. commanding Wiltshire Yeomanry 1898. Parliamentary Secretary to the Local Government Board 1886-92; President Board of Agriculture 1895-1900; President of Local Government Board 1900-05 and May 1915 to December 1916. Secretary of State for the Colonies December 1916 to January 1919; First Lord of the Admiralty from January 1919-February 1921; Chief Secretary for Ireland March to December 1905. Chairman of Irish Unionist Party 1906-10; Vice-Chairman from 1910; Chairman of Cabinet Committee on Ireland 1919. Lord-Lieut. for the Co. of Wiltshire; J.P. for Somerset; F.R.S.; Honorary LL.D. Birmingham. PC. 1895. A Unionist. Sat for N. Wiltshire from 1880-85, for the Devizes division of Wiltshire 1885-92, when he was defeated, for the W. Derby division of Liverpool from January 1893 to 1900 and for Bristol S. from 1900-January 1906, when he was defeated. At the same election he was returned for Co. Dublin S. for which he sat until January 1910, when he was elected for the Strand. Sat for the Strand from January 1910 until elected for St.

George's Hanover Square in December 1918. Sat until May 1921 when he was created Visct. Long of Wraxall. Died 26 September 1924. [1921]

LONGBOTTOM, Arthur William. Celtic Hotel, Guildford Place, London. 37 Woodhall Crescent, Halifax. S. of John David Longbottom, Esq., Sexton, of Skircoat Green, Halifax, and Mary Hannah, d. of J. Firth, Esq. B. 25 May 1883; m. 4 June 1904, Beatrice, d. of William E. Kaye, Esq., of Alverthorpe, Wakefield. Educ. at All Saints' National School, and Halifax Technical Coll. A Railway Townsman from 1898. Member of Halifax County Borough Council 1912; Mayor 1923; Alderman 1924. J.P. Halifax 1924. Parliamentary Private Secretary to G.M. Gillett, Secretary of Department of Overseas Trade 1929-31. A Socialist. A Labour Member. Elected for Halifax July 1928 and sat until he was defeated in October 1931. Unsuccessfully contested Halifax in November 1935. Died 12 September 1943. [1931 2nd ed.]

LONGDEN, Fred. Continued in House after 1945: full entry in Volume IV.

LONGHURST, Capt. Henry Carpenter 22 Markham Square, London. S. of H.W. Longhurst, Esq., of Bedford. B. 18 March 1909; m. 1938, Claudine, d. of Horace E. Sier, Esq., of Dulwich. Educ. at Charterhouse, and Clare Coll., Cambridge. Author and Journalist. Capt. R.A. A Conservative. Elected for the Acton division of Middlesex in December 1943 and sat until he was defeated in July 1945. Author of several books on golf. C.B.E. 1972. Died 21 July 1978. [1945]

LONSDALE, James Rolston. 12 Sussex Square, London. Carlton, and Bachelors'. S. of James Lonsdale, Esq., Dept.-Lieut. Armagh. B. at Armagh 31 May 1865; m. September 1902, Maud, youngest d. of John Musker, Esq., of Shadwell Court, Norfolk Educ. at the Royal School, Armagh, and Trinity Coll., Dublin. High Sheriff of Co. Armagh 1907. A Unionist. First elected for mid Armagh in January 1918, re-elected in December 1918 and sat until his death on 23 May 1921. [1921]

LOOKER, Herbert William. Fen Place, Turners Hill, Sussex. Carlton, and Thatched House. S. of John Looker, Esq., of St. Ives, Huntingdonshire. B. 2 December 1871; m. 1st, Muriel, d. of Thomas Thomas, Esq., of Yokohama; secondly, Stella, d. of Basil Sharp, Esq., of Chelmsford. Admitted a Solicitor 1894, retired 1919. Practised in Hong-Kong 1895-1919. A Conservative. Unsuccessfully contested Central Hull in 1922. Elected for Essex S.E. in October 1924 and sat until he was defeated in May 1929. Member of E. Sussex County Council 1933-50. Died 13 December 1951.

[1929]

LORD, Sir Walter Greaves. See GREAVES-LORD, Sir Walter Greaves.

LORDEN, John William. Ravenswood, West Hill, Putney. Little Rattan, Willingdon, Eastbourne. Carlton, Constitutional, and St. Stephen's. S. of William Henry Lorden, Esq. B. 15 July 1862 at Colchester; m. 1st, 1883, Ellen Mary, d. of Matthew Garrod, Esq., of Wandsworth Common (she died 1923); secondly, 1924, Emma Sarah, d. of John Lord of Rochdale, widow of Robert Sawyer, Esq. Educ. privately. Governing Director of W.H. Lorden and Sons Limited, Building Contractors. Member of Wandsworth Borough Council 1900-21; Mayor 1903-04 and 1907-08; Alderman 1906; member of London County Council for Wandsworth 1910-13. Served upon the Metropolitan Water Board and Wandsworth Board of Guardians. J.P. A Conservative. Elected for N. St. Pancras in December 1918 and again in November 1922. Sat until he was defeated in December 1923. Knighted 1925. Died 21 April 1944.

[1923]

LORIMER, Henry Dubs. Old Bank Chambers, Irongate, Derby. Carlton, St. Stephen's, and Caledonian. S. of Sir William Lorimer, LL.D. B. in Renfrewshire 1879; m. 1910, Agnes Edith, d. of H. Dunsmuir, Esq. Educ. at Blair Lodge Scottish Public School. J.P. for Peebleshire. A Conservative. Elected for S. Derbyshire in November 1922 and sat until he retired in October 1924. Died 8 February 1933. [1924 2nd ed.]

LORT-WILLIAMS, John Rolleston, K.C. 1 Brick Court, Temple, London. Landale Lodge, Rotherhithe, London. Union, and 1900. S. of Charles Williams Williams, Esq., Solicitor. B. at Walsall 1881; m. 1st, 1923, Dorothy Margery Mary Russell (divorced 1949); secondly, 1950, Minnie Dorothy Margaret Lyal. Educ. at Merchant Taylors' School, and London University. A Barrister and member of Lincoln's Inn, the Inner Temple and Middle Temple; called to the bar at Lincoln's Inn 1904. Tancred Law Student 1902; K.C. 1922; Oxford Circuit. Member of London County Council (Limehouse) 1907-10; Vice-Chairman of Housing Committee; member of Central (Unemployed) Body. A Conservative. Unsuccessfully contested Pembrokeshire in 1906 and July 1908, and Stockport in December 1910. Elected for the Rotherhithe division of Bermondsey in December 1918 and sat until he was defeated in in December 1923. Recorder of West Bromwich 1923-24, of Walsall 1924-28. Puisne Judge of High Court of Bengal 1927-41. Knighted 1936. President of Hardwicke Society 1911. Served with Middlesex Imperial Yeomanry 1914-18. Adopted the surname of Lort-Williams in lieu of Williams. Died 9 June 1966. [1923]

LOSEBY, Capt. Charles Edgar, M.C. Market Bosworth. S. of Arthur John and Dorothy Loseby, of Market Bosworth, Nuneaton. B. at Market Bosworth 1 May 1881; m. 1921, Dulcibella, d. of Mr. and Mrs. Herne, of Woking. Educ. at the Grammar School, Market Bosworth, Blairlodge, London University, Transvaal University, and Gray's Inn. A Schoolmaster, a Barrister-at-Law 1914, and a soldier in the Lancashire Fusiliers. Was wounded at Cambrai November 1917; M.C. 1917. Parliamentary Secretary N.D.P. Group. A Coalition National Democratic and Labour Member. Elected for E. Bradford in December 1918 and sat until he was defeated in November 1922, standing as the N.D.P. candidate with unofficial Conservative support. Unsuccessfully contested W. Nottingham as a Constitutionalist in October 1924 and as a Conservative in May 1929. Practised at the Hong Kong bar from

1945. K.C. (Hong Kong). Retired to Guernsey where he died on 7 January 1970.
[1922]

LOUGHER, Lewis. Dan-y-Bryn, Radyr, Glamorgan. 54 Merchants' Exchange, Cardiff. Carlton, Constitutional, Royal Automobile, United, Cardiff, and County. S. of Thomas Lougher, Esq., of Llandaff, Glamorgan. B. 1 October 1871. Educ. at Cardiff High School. Chairman of Lewis Lougher and Company Limited, Bristol Channel Steamers Limited, Shipowners, of Bute Docks, Cardiff, of Redcroft Steam Navigation Company, 1921, Limited, and of Pugsley and Wakelin Limited; Director of Penarth Pontoon, Slipway and Ship Repairing Company Limited, and of Hodges and Company Limited, Barry. Member of Executive Council of Shipping Federation Limited, of Barry Pilotage Authority, and of Advisory Commission on New Lighthouse Works; Chairman of Cardiff and Bristol Channel Shipowners' Association 1919, and of Shipping Federation (Cardiff District) 1918-19; member of Council of the Chamber of Shipping of the United Kingdom, of National Trimming Board, of Court of Inquiry re Hours of Labour of Coal Tippers and Trimmers under the Industrial Courts Act 1919. Represented Cardiff Chamber of Commerce at the Conference of Chambers of Commerce of the British Empire at Toronto, Canada 1920, member of Visiting Commission of MPs. to the Baltic States 1923; member of Cape Town, South African Conference of Federation of Chambers of Commerce 1927, and of International Parliamentary Conference, Washington and Ottawa 1925, and Paris 1927; J.P. for Glamorgan. Liveryman Worshipful Company of Wheelwrights, a member Glamorganshire County Council 1922-49, High Sheriff 1931-32; Gov. of National Museum, National Library, and University Coll. of Wales, of King Edward VII Hospital (Cardiff), and of Royal Hamadryad Seamen's Hospital (Cardiff). A Conservative. Elected for the E. division of Cardiff in November 1922, unsuccessfully contested the same division in December 1923. Returned for the Central division of Cardiff in October 1924 and sat until he was

defeated in May 1929. Knighted 1929. Died 28 August 1955. [1929]

LOVAT-FRASER, James Alexander. 63 Harcourt Terrace, London. 3 King's Bench Walk, Temple, London. S. of John Fraser, Esq., of Bishopbriggs. B. 16 March 1868. Educ. at Trinity Coll., Cambridge; M.A., LL.B. A Barrister-at-Law, Inner Temple 1891, and joined the South Wales Circuit. Member of Barry Urban District Council 1905-07, and of Cardiff Corporation 1907-12. A Labour Member until August 1931, thereafter a National Labour Member. Unsuccessfully contested the Llandaff and Barry division of Glamorganshire in November 1922, and central Bristol in October 1924. Elected for the Lichfield division of Staffordshire in May 1929 as a Labour Member, and in October 1931 and November 1935 as a National Labour Member. Sat until his death on 18 March 1938. Assumed the surname Lovat-Fraser in lieu of Fraser in about 1893. Chairman of Robert Louis Stevenson Club and President of Johnson Society. Prospective Conservative candidate for the Blackfriars division of Glasgow 1914 but never contested the seat and later joined the Labour Party. Died 18 March 1938. [1938]

LOVERSEED, John Eric A.F.C. 10 Gerald Road, London. Ashfield, Helsby, Cheshire. S. of J.F. Loverseed, Esq., J.P., and MP for Sudbury. B. 4 December 1910; m. 17 April 1938, Gladys, d. of F.J. Hill-Male, Esq., of Gilfachrheda, New Quay, Cardiganshire. Educ. at Sudbury Grammar School. Joined R.A.F. 1929, served short service Commission as Pilot until 1934. Rejoined 1939 and discharged 1943. Elected for the Eddisbury division of Cheshire in April 1943 and sat until he was defeated in July 1945. Sat as Common Wealth Member until he resigned the Whip in November 1944; accepted the Labour Whip from May 1945: contested the 1945 election as a Labour candidate. Unsuccessfully contested S. Lewisham as an Independent Pacifist in May 1955.* [1945]

LOVERSEED, John Frederick. Newland, Queen's Road, Sudbury. National Liberal.

215

S. of Henry Loverseed, Esq., Builder, of Nottingham. B. at Mansfield, Nottinghamshire 22 December 1881; m. 17 November 1909, Katherine Annie, d. of William Thurman, Esq., of Birkholme House, near Grantham. Educ. at Southwell Grammar School, and Orient Coll., Skegness. Liberal Agent in S.W. Norfolk 1908-13, and in the Sudbury division of Suffolk from 1913-22. Capt. and Adjutant 5th Battalion Suffolk Volunteer Regiment T.F. 1915; West Suffolk County Councillor 1919; Sudbury Town Councillor 1919. Mayor 1921 to 1923. Chairman of Govs., Sudbury Grammar School, Girls' Secondary School, and Bury St. Edmunds Grammar School. A Liberal. Elected for the Sudbury division of Suffolk in December 1923 and sat until he was defeated in October 1924. J.P. for Suffolk. A Wesleyan Methodist. Died 14 August 1928.   [1924 2nd ed.]

LOWE, Sir Francis William, Bart. 34 Draycott Place, London. 109 Colmore Row, Birmingham. Carlton. S. of William Lowe, Esq., of Birmingham, Solicitor, and Emma, d. of William Griffiths, Esq., of Moseley, Birmingham. B. at Edgbaston 8 January 1852; m. 12 September 1883, Mary, d. of William Holden, Esq., of Scarborough. Educ. at the Birmingham (King Edward's) Grammar School, and London University. Admitted a Solicitor 1875, member of the firm of Lowe and Jolly. J.P. for Birmingham, and a Dept.-Lieut. and J.P. for Warwickshire, Chairman of the Midland Union and the National Union, and a member of the Council of the National Unionist Association. Was President of Birmingham Conservative Association from 1892 to 1918, when he became Joint President of the Birmingham Unionist Association; served for six years as a member of the City Council. Knighted 1905; created Bart. 1918. A Conservative. Unsuccessfully contested the Eastern division of Birmingham in 1885 and the Harborough division of Leicestershire in 1892. Sat for the Edgbaston division of Birmingham from February 1898 until he retired in May 1929. PC. June 1929. Died 12 November 1929.   [1929]

LOWTH, Thomas. 17 Campdale Road, Tufnell Park, London. S. of Charles Lowth, Esq. B. at Billingborough, Lincolnshire 1858; m. 1877, Eliza Davies, of Broseley, Shropshire. An official of the National Union of Railwaymen. A Labour Member. Unsuccessfully contested the Ardwick division of Manchester in November 1918. Elected for the Ardwick division of Manchester in November 1922 and sat until his death on 26 May 1931.   [1931 2nd ed.]

LOWTHER, Maj. Hon. Christopher William. Westwood, Mayfield, Sussex. Turf, Royal Automobile, Wells', and Constitutional. S. of the Rt. Hon. J.W. Lowther, Visct. Ullswater (Speaker of the House of Commons 1905-21) and Mrs. Lowther (née Miss Beresford Hope). B. in London 18 January 1887; m. 1st, 1910, Ina, d. of Canon R.P. Pelly (divorced 1920); secondly, 1921, Dorothy, d. of A. Bromley-Davenport, Esq. Educ. at Eton, and Trinity Coll., Cambridge. Honorary Attaché in the Diplomatic Service 1907; in business 1909-11. Officer H.M. Forces from 1909 (Yeomanry); invalided out with rank of Maj.; seriously wounded when serving with the Westmorland and Cumberland Yeomanry. Returned unopposed for N. Cumberland in December 1918 and sat until November 1922 when he unsuccessfully contested Wallsend. Elected as a Conservative in 1918 but in January 1921 joined Horatio Bottomley's Independent Group and sat as an Independent until 1922, when he rejoined the Conservatives. Unsuccessfully contested Wallsend again in December 1923 and the Workington division of Cumberland in October 1931. Chairman of British Dominions Land Settlement Corporation. Died 7 January 1935.   [1922]

LOWTHER, Col. Claude William Henry. Herstmonceux Castle, Sussex. 43 Catherine Street, Westminster, London. Carlton, St. James's, Garrick, Marlborough, Pratt's, and Bachelors'. S. of Capt. Francis Lowther, R.N., and cousin of the Earl of Lonsdale. B. 1872. Unmarried. Educ. at Rugby, and on the Continent. Was for several years in the Diplomatic Service, and was Attaché to Sir Henry Drummond Wolff at Madrid. Served in South African War as second in command of the Westmorland and Cumberland Yeomanry; was recommended for the V.C. for saving the life of a comrade at the battle of Faber's Spruit, and was Aide-de-Camp to Sir Charles Warren. Capt. in Cumberland Yeomanry; raised four Battalions of Sussex men 1914, which he commanded until September 1915. J.P. for Cumberland. Chairman of Anti-Socialist Union. Wrote several books under a *nom de plume*. A Coalition Unionist. Sat for the Eskdale division of Cumberland from 1900-06, when he was defeated. Unsuccessfully contested the same constituency in January 1910. Re-elected for the Eskdale division of Cumberland in December 1910, and elected for the Lonsdale division of Lancashire in December 1918 and sat until November 1922 when he unsuccessfully contested Carlisle. Withdrew his support from the Coalition Government in July 1921 and supported Horatio Bottomley's Independent Group but stood in 1922 as a Conservative. Died 17 June 1929.　　　　[1922]

LOWTHER, Maj.-Gen. Sir Henry Cecil, K.C.M.G., C.B., C.V.O., D.S.O. 19 Queen Street, Mayfair, London. Carlton, Turf, and Beefsteak. Youngest s. of Hon. W. Lowther and Mrs. Lowther. B. at Ampthill 1 January 1869; m. 1920, Dorothy, d. of John Selwyn Harvey, Esq. Educ. at Charterhouse, and the Royal Military Coll., Sandhurst. Scots Guards 1888; Adjutant 1896; South African War, Brigade-Maj. 1902-03; Staff Capt. Intelligence (War Office) 1903-05; Military Attaché, Paris Madrid and Lisbon 1905-09; Gov.-General's Secretary Canada 1911-13; Commanded 1st Battalion Scots Guards 1913-14; European War, Commanded 1st Guards Brigade 1914-15; Military Secretary to Commander-in-Chief 1915; Col. and then Maj.-Gen. on Staff in charge of training of army 1916 to end of war. Retired 1919. Author of *From Pillar to Post*. A Conservative Unionist. Sat for N. Westmorland from 1915 till the general election of 1918, when the seat was abolished. Elected for the Penrith and Cockermouth division of Cum-

berland in May 1921 and sat until he was defeated in November 1922. D.S.O. 1900. Died 1 November 1940.　　　　[1922]

LOWTHER, Rt. Hon. James William. Speaker's House, Westminster, London. Campsea Ashe, Wickham Market, Suffolk. Athenaeum, and Carlton. Eld. s. of Hon. William Lowther, MP by Hon. Alice, 3rd d. of Baron Wensleydale. B. in London 1855; m. 1886, Mary Frances, d. of the Rt. Hon. A.J.B. Beresford Hope (she died 1944). Educ. at Eton, King's Coll., London, and Trinity Coll., Cambridge; graduated LL.M. 1882; Fellow of King's Coll., London; Honorary D.C.L. Oxford 1907; Honorary LL.D. Cambridge 1910; D.C.L. Leeds 1910. Was called to the bar at the Inner Temple in 1879; Bencher 1906. Dept. Speaker and Chairman of Committee of "Ways and Means" 1895-1905. Elected Speaker of House of Commons June 1905 and remained Speaker until April 1921; was 4th Parliamentary Charity Commissioner 1887 and represented Great Britain at the Venice Conference 1892. Chairman of the Speaker's Conference on Electoral Reform 1916-17; Chairman of the Boundary Commission, England, Wales, Scotland, and Ireland 1917; Chairman of the Federal Devolution Committee 1919. Dept.-Lieut. and J.P. for Cumberland and J.P. for Suffolk. Alderman of E. Suffolk County Council 1914. Chairman of Quarter Sessions for Cumberland 1900. Parliamentary Under-Secretary for Foreign Affairs 1891-92; PC. 1898. A Unionist. Sat for Rutland from August 1883 to November 1885. Unsuccessfully contested mid Cumberland in 1885. Sat for the Penrith division of Cumberland from 1886 to 1918, and for the Penrith and Cockermouth division of Cumberland from December 1918 until he resigned in April 1921. G.C.B. 1921. Created Visct. Ullswater 1921. Chairman of Review Committee on Political Honours 1923-24. Chairman of Agricultural Wages Board 1930-40. Trustee of National Portrait Gallery 1925 and of British Museum 1922-31. Died 27 March 1949.　　　　[1921]

LOYD, Arthur Thomas. 53 Mount Street, London. Locking House, Wantage. Travellers'. 2nd s. of the Rev. L.H. Loyd. B. at Northampton 19 April 1882; m. 1911, Dorothy, d. of P.F. Willert, Esq., of Headington Hill, Oxford. Educ. at Eton, and Hertford Coll., Oxford. In the Egyptian Civil Service. A Conservative. Returned unopposed for the Abingdon division of Berkshire in May 1921 and sat until he retired in November 1923. O.B.E. 1918. Ecclesiastical Commissioner from 1923. Trustee of the Wallace Collection. High Sheriff of Berkshire 1927, Lord-Lieut. 1935-44, Chairman of County Council 1938-44. Died 8 November 1944.   [1923]

LUCAS, Sir Jocelyn Morton, Bart. Continued in House after 1945: full entry in Volume IV.

LUCAS-TOOTH, Sir Hugh Vere Huntly Duff, Bart. See MUNRO-LUCAS-TOOTH, Sir Hugh Vere Huntly Duff, Bart. Continued in House after 1945: full entry in Volume IV.

LUCE, Maj.-Gen. Sir Richard Harman, K.C.M.G., C.B. 178 Ashley Gardens, London. S. of Col. C.R. Luce, of Halcombe, Malmesbury. B. 13 July 1867; m. 11 February 1897, Mary Irene, d. of Dr. John Scott, of Bournemouth. Educ. at Clifton Coll., and at Christ's Coll., Cambridge; Scholar, 1st cl. hons. Nat. Sci. Tripos 1889, M.A., M.B., B.C. 1893; F.R.C.S. Eng. 1894. D.M.S. Egyptian Expeditionary Force 1915-18, Senior Surgeon Derbyshire Royal Infirmary. K.C.M.G. 1919. A Conservative. Sat for Derby from October 1924 until he was defeated in May 1929. C.B. 1916; C.M.G. 1918. Mayor of Romsey 1935-37. President of Hampshire Archaeological Society. Died 21 February 1952.   [1929]

LUMLEY, Lawrence Roger. 39 Eaton Square, London. Lumley Castle, Chester-le-Street. Carlton, and Cavalry. S. of Brigadier-Gen. Hon. Osbert Lumley, C.M.G. B. 27 July 1896; m. 12 July 1922, Katharine Isobel, d. of R.F. McEwen, Esq., of Bardrochat, 'Ayrshire, and Marchmont, Berwickshire. Educ. at Eton, Royal Military Coll., Sandhurst, and Magdalen Coll.,

Oxford. Served in 11th Hussars 1916-19, later Capt. Yorkshire Dragoons, Yeomanry. Parliamentary Private Secretary to the Rt. Hon. W. Ormsby-Gore, September-December 1923; to Sir Austen Chamberlain December 1924-July 1926; to Maj. Walter Elliot, Financial Secretary to the Treasury November 1931-October 1932; to the Rt. Hon. Sir John Gilmour, Bart., Home Secretary October 1932-June 1935; and to the Rt. Hon. Anthony Eden, Minister for League of Nations Affairs June-December 1935, and when Secretary of State for Foreign Affairs from December 1935-April 1937. A Conservative. Sat for E. Hull from November 1922 to May 1929, when he was defeated. Elected for York in October 1931 and sat until April 1937 when he was appointed Gov. of Bombay. Gov. of Bombay 1937-43. Succeeded to the Peerage as Earl of Scarbrough 1945. Parliamentary Under-Secretary for India and Burma May-July 1945. Lord Chamberlain 1952-63, Permanent Lord-in-Waiting 1963-69. K.G. 1948. PC. 1952. President of Royal Asiatic Society 1946-49. President of East India Association 1946-51. President of Royal Central Asian Society 1954-60. Grand Master of United Grand Lodge of Freemasons of England 1951-67. Lord-Lieut. of W. Riding of Yorkshire from 1948. Chancellor of Durham University from 1958. High Steward of York Minster from 1967. Died 29 June 1969.   [1937]

LUNN, William. "Westleigh", Rothwell, Leeds. B. at Rothwell 1 November 1872. Educ. at the Rothwell Board School, and started work in the pit at 12 years of age. A Checkweighman at the Middleton Colliery for 20 years. Member of Rothwell Urban District Council and Hunslet Board of Guardians; a School Manager for 25 years. Labour Whip November 1922. Parliamentary Secretary Department of Overseas Trade January-November 1924; Under-Secretary of State, Colonial Office June-December 1929; Under-Secretary of State, Dominions Office and Chairman of Overseas Settlement Committee December 1929-August 1931. Member of Executive Committee of Parliamentary Labour Party 1931-36. A Labour Member. Unsuccessfully contested the Holmfirth division of the W. Riding of Yorkshire in 1912. Elected for the Rothwell division of the W. Riding of Yorkshire in December 1918 and sat until his death on 17 May 1942.   [1942]

LYLE, Sir Charles Ernest Leonard, Bart. 52 Cadogan Square, London. Greystoke, Canford Cliffs, Bournemouth. Carlton, and Bath. S. of Charles Lyle, Esq., of Brooke Hall, Norwich. B. 22 July 1882; m. 14 July 1904, Edith Louise, d. of John Levy, Esq., of Rochester (she died 22 December 1942). Educ. at Harrow, and Trinity Hall, Cambridge. President of Tate and Lyle Limited. Knight Bach. 1923; Bart. 1932; Chairman of East Dorset Conservative Association 1932-40, and of Queen Mary's Hospital for the East End 1916-23; J.P. for West Ham; Parliamentary Private Secretary to the Rt. Hon. Charles McCurdy when Food Controller March 1920-March 1921. A Director of Lloyds Bank. A Conservative. MP for the Stratford division of West Ham from December 1918-November 1922 when he was defeated. Sat for the Epping division of Essex from 1923 until he retired in October 1924. Returned unopposed for Bournemouth in June 1940 and sat until August 1945 when he was created Baron Lyle of Westbourne. Died 6 March 1954.   [1945]

LYLE-SAMUEL, Alexander. Claridge's Hotel, Brook Street, London. Dower House, Sizewell-cum-Leiston, Suffolk. Devonshire, National Liberal, and Pilgrims'. S. of the Rev. George Samuel, of Aston. B. at Aston 10 August 1883; m. 1st, 1906, Eva Louisa Higgins (she died 1914); secondly, 1915, Julia G. Lyle, of Tenafly, New Jersey, U.S.A. Educ. at King Edward's School, Aston, Birmingham, and Trinity Hall, Cambridge. Assumed the name of Lyle-Samuel by Deed Poll in 1915. Two sons, one d. A Liberal. Elected for the Eye division of Suffolk in December 1918 and sat until he was defeated in December 1923. Unsuccessfully contested the Grantham division of Lincolnshire in in October 1924. Died November 1942.   [1923]

LYMINGTON, Gerard Vernon Wallop, Visct. 5a Dean's Yard, London. Farleigh House, Farleigh Wallop, Basingstoke. Carlton, and Bath. S. of Oliver, 8th Earl of Portsmouth. B. 16 May 1898; m. 1st, 31 July 1920, Mary Lawrence, d. of Waldron K. Post, Esq., of Bayport, Long Island, U.S.A. (divorced 1936). Educ. at Winchester, and Balliol Coll., Oxford. Served in France 1916-19, with Life Guards and in Guards Machine Gun Regiment. A Farmer. Member of Hampshire County Council from 1924, Alderman 1947-49. A Conservative. Elected for the Basingstoke division of Hampshire in May 1929 and sat until he resigned in February 1934. Styled Visct. Lymington from 1925 to 1943 when he succeeded to the Peerage as Earl of Portsmouth. Vice-Chairman of Hampshire War Agricultural Committee 1939-47. Chairman of Country Landowners Association 1947-48. Member of Legislative Council of Kenya 1957-60. Vice-Chairman of E. African Natural Resources Research Council from 1963. Author of a number of books on political and agricultural subjects.★
    [1934]

LYNCH, Diarmid. Was known as the Food Controller of the Sinn Feiners, having organized a seizure of pigs designed for export to this country, paying their value for them, and having them slaughtered for food. A Sinn Fein Member. Was returned unopposed for Cork S.E. in December 1918 but did not take his seat and resigned in August 1920.   [1920]

LYNCH, Finian. S. of Finian Lynch, Esq., of Kilmakerim, Co. Kerry. B. 17 March 1889; m. 1919, Brighid, d. of Thomas Slattery, Esq., of Tralee. Educ. at Rockwell and Blackrock Colleges, and National University of Ireland. A Sinn Fein Member. Returned unopposed for S. Kerry in December 1918 but did not take his seat. Member of Dail for S. Kerry to 1921, for Kerry and W. Limerick 1921-23, for Kerry 1923-37, for S. Kerry 1937-44. Dept. Speaker of Dail 1938-39. A Pro-Treaty, later Cumann na nGaedheal and Fine Gael Member. Minister without Portfolio 1922. Minister for Fisheries, later Lands and

Fisheries 1922-32. Dept. Leader of Fine Gael 1944. Circuit Judge from 1945. Died 3 June 1966.   [1922]

LYNCH, Jeremiah Christopher. See LYNCH, Diarmid.

LYNN, Sir Robert John. Atholl, King's Road, Belfast. S. of W. Lynn, Esq. B. at Antrim 1873; m. 1896, Florence, d. of William Moss, Esq., of Belfast. Educ. privately. A Journalist. Joined the *Northern Whig* in 1903, later Editor and Managing Director. Chairman of Advisory Education Council Northern Ireland. Knight Bach 1924. A Unionist. Sat for the Woodvale division of Belfast from December 1918 to November 1922 and for W. Belfast from November 1922 until he retired in May 1929. Member of the Northern Ireland Parliament for W. Belfast 1921-29, for N. Antrim 1929-45. Dept.-Speaker of Northern Ireland Parliament 1937-45. Died 5 August 1945.
[1929]

LYON, Laurance. 30 Park Lane, London. Manor House, Castle Combe, Wiltshire. Carlton, and Wellington. S. of John Laurance Lyon, Esq., of Osgoode Hall, Toronto, and Lucy, d. of the Rt. Hon. Sir Henry Strong, PC., Chief Justice of Canada. B. in Toronto 1875; m. 1901, Yvonne, d. of Sir Henri Taschereau, Chief Justice of Quebec (divorced 1923). Educ. at Trinity Coll. School, Port Hope. Called to the Ontario bar 1898; Quebec 1900. A Coalition Unionist. Elected for Hastings in December 1918 and sat until he resigned in 1921. Proprietor of *Outlook* 1916-19. Died in Montreal 12 November 1932.   [1921]

LYONS, Maj. Abraham Montagu, K.C. Constitutional. S. of R. Lyons, Esq., of West Bridgford, Nottinghamshire. B. 10 February 1894. Unmarried. Educ. at Collegiate School, Grimsby, and Old Clee Grammar School. Barrister-at-Law, Middle Temple 1922; K.C. 1933; at one time a Solicitor. Served with Durham Light Infantry as Lieut. 1914-16, and Ministry of Food Legal Department; Recorder of Great Grimsby 1936-61. Capt. and G.S.O. 3. 1940, Maj. and Dept. Assistant Director 1941.

A Conservative. Unsuccessfully contested the Clay Cross division of Derbyshire in May 1929. Elected for Leicester E. in October 1931 and sat until he was defeated in July 1945. Master of Worshipful Company of Patternmakers 1959. Leader of the Midland Circuit. Died 29 November 1961.
[1945]

LYTTELTON, Rt. Hon. Oliver. Continued in House after 1945: full entry in Volume IV.

MABANE, Rt. Hon. William. 32 Westminster Gardens, London. Pratt's, and National Liberal. Leeds. S. of Joseph Greenwood Mabane, Esq., Manufacturer, of Leeds. B. 12 January 1895; m. 1st, 1918, Louise, d. of Edward Tanton, Esq. (divorced 1926); secondly, 31 March 1944, Stella, d. of Julian Duggan, Esq., of Buenos Aires. Educ. at Woodhouse Grove School, and Gonville and Caius Coll., Cambridge, B.A. 1920, M.A. 1925. Warden of University Settlement, Liverpool 1920-23. Governing Director of T. Mabane and Sons Limited 1923-39. Served with E. Yorkshire Regiment 1914-19. Parliamentary Private Secretary to Rt. Hon. E. Brown, Parliamentary Secretary Ministry of Health November 1931-September 1932; Assistant Postmaster-Gen. June-October 1939; Parliamentary Secretary Ministry of Home Security October 1939-June 1942; Parliamentary Secretary Ministry of Food June 1942-May 1945. PC. 1944. A Liberal to 1931, a Liberal National thereafter. Unsuccessfully contested Huddersfield as a Liberal in May 1929. Elected for Huddersfield in October 1931 and sat until he was defeated in July 1945. Minister of State, Foreign Office May-June 1945. Chairman of Civil Defence Commission 1951. K.B.E. 1954. Created Baron Mabane 1962. Chairman of British Travel Association 1960-63, President 1963-66. Died 16 November 1969.   [1945]

MACANDREW, Sir Charles Glen. Continued in House after 1945: full entry in Volume IV.

MacANDREW, James Orr. South Park, Ayr. Carlton. S. of Francis Glen Mac-

Andrew, Esq., of Knock Castle, Largs. B. 22 June 1899; m. 1944, Eileen, d. of Robin Butterfield, Esq. Educ. at Trinity Coll., Glenalmond, and Trinity Hall, Cambridge. A Conservative. Elected for the S. Ayrshire division of Ayr and Bute in October 1931 and sat until he was defeated in November 1935. Served with R.A.F. in France 1918 and with Ayrshire Yeomanry 1939-45. Honorary Col. Ayrshire Yeomanry 1955-60. Dept.-Lieut. for Ayrshire.*

[1935]

McBRIDE, Joseph Michael. Kelladangan, Westport, Co. Mayo. S. of Patrick McBride, Esq., Master Mariner. B. 1860; m. 1904, Eileen, d. of Thomas Wilson, Esq., of London. Interned in Gloucester prison. A Sinn Fein Member. Elected for W. Mayo in December 1918 but did not take his seat. Member of Dail for W. Mayo to 1921, for N. and W. Mayo 1921-23. A Pro-Treaty Member. Secretary of Westport Harbour Commissioners. Fellow of Royal Society of Antiquaries. [1922]

MacCABE, Alexander. Ballymote, Co. Sligo. A School Teacher. Arrested and sentenced in 1919 for inciting to disorder. Again arrested in March 1920 and sentenced to three months imprisonment. A Sinn Fein Member. Elected for S. Sligo in December 1918 but did not take his seat. Member of Dail for S. Sligo to 1921, for Mayo E. and Sligo 1921-23, for Leitrim and Sligo 1923-24. A Pro-Treaty, later Cumann na nGaedheal Member. Managing Director of Educational Building Society. Editor of *Irish Year Book*. [1922]

McCALLUM, Duncan. Continued in House after 1945: full entry in Volume IV.

McCALLUM, Sir John Mills. Southdene, Paisley. Kingsley Hotel. National Liberal. S. of John McCallum, Esq., of Skipness and Paisley, and Janet Mills, of Ayr. B. 1847 at Paisley; m. 1875, Agnes, d. of Stephen Oates, Esq., J.P., of Grimsby. Educ. at Neilson Institute, Paisley. A Soap Manufacturer. A J.P. for Renfrewshire. A member of Paisley Town Council. Knighted 1912. A Liberal. Elected for Paisley in 1906 and

sat until his death on 10 January 1920.

[1920]

McCALMONT, Lieut.-Col. Robert Chaine Alexander, D.S.O. Inver, Larne, Co. Antrim. 92 Eaton Place, London. Carlton, and Guards'. Ulster, and Kildare Street. S. of Col. J.M. McCalmont, MP for E. Antrim from 1885-1913, and Mary, d. of Col. Romer, of Bryncemlyn, Dolgelly. B. 29 August 1881; m. 1st, 1907, Mary Caroline, d. of Andrew Skeen, Esq., I.M.S., and Lady Prinsep (she died 1941); secondly, 1950, Iris Heather, d. of J.J. Flinn, Esq. Educ. at Eton. Served in South African War 1900 with 6th Battalion R. Warwickshire Regiment. Joined Irish Guards 1900, Capt. and Adjutant 1904, Maj. 1910, half-pay 1913. Commander 1st Battalion 1915-17; Lieut.-Col. 1916; Temporary Brigadier-Gen. Commanding an Infantry Brigade 1917; half-pay 1918. Adjutant Eton Coll. O.T. Corps 1909-11. Temporary Lieut.-Col. Commanding 12th Battalion R. Irish Rifles (Central Antrim Volunteers) 1914-15; D.S.O. 1917, and despatches twice. A Unionist. First elected for E. Antrim in February 1913 and sat until he resigned in March 1919 on appointment to a command with the Irish Guards. Served with Irish Guards 1919-24, with 144th Infantry Brigade 1924-25 and with Royal Berkshire Regiment 1940-42. Exon of King's Bodyguard 1925-37, Clerk of the Cheque and Adjutant 1937-45, Lieut. 1945-51. C.B.E. 1946; K.C.V.O. 1952. Dept.-Lieut. for Gloucestershire 1936-46 and for Co. Antrim 1946-51. Member of Gloucestershire County Council 1931-46. Died 4 November 1953.

[1919]

McCANN, Pierce. Was arrested in May 1918 and interned in Gloucester prison. A Sinn Fein Member. Elected for E. Tipperary in December 1918 but did not take his seat and died of influenza in Gloucester prison on 6 March 1919. [1919]

McCARTAN, Dr. Patrick. Eskerbuoy, Carrickmore, Co. Tyrone. B. in Co. Tyrone 1883. Fellow of Royal Coll. of Surgeons in Ireland and Licentiate of Royal Coll. of Physicians in Ireland. An Ulsterman who was concerned in the rebellion of 1916 and escaped to America. There he was regarded as a Sinn Fein Ambassador. Arrested for violating American Law in connection with the war, he was admitted to bail. A Sinn Fein Member. Unsuccessfully contested S. Armagh in February 1918. In April 1918 was returned unopposed for the Tullamore division of King's Co. and was also returned unopposed for the re-formed single constituency of King's Co. in December 1918 but did not take his seat. Member of Dail for Leix and Offaly to 1923. A Pro-Treaty Member. Unsuccessful candidate for the Presidency of Irish Republic 1945 as an Independent; later joined Clann na Poblachta. Member of Senate 1948-51. Died 28 March 1963.   [1922]

M'CONNELL, Sir Joseph, Bart. Glen Dhu, Strandtown, Belfast. S. of Sir John M'Connell, Bart. B. 17 September 1877; m. 25 April 1900, Lisa, d. of Jackson McGown, Esq. Succeeded his father as Bart. in 1927. A Dept.-Lieut., and J.P. for Belfast. A Conservative. Sat for Antrim from May 1929 until his death on 27 August 1942.   [1942]

McCONNELL, Thomas Edward, C.B.E. Newlands, Deramore Park, Belfast. Constitutional. S. of Joseph and Elizabeth McConnell. B. 7 April 1868 at Clogher, Co. Antrim; m. 1891, Annie Louisa, d. of John Price, Esq., of Rosetta, Belfast. Educ. at the Royal Belfast Academical Institution. Alderman Belfast Corporation from 1917; J.P. for City of Belfast; C.B.E. 1921. Managing Director of John Robson Limited. A Conservative. Returned unopposed for the Duncairn division of Belfast in July 1921, and for N. Belfast in November 1922 and December 1923. Re-elected for N. Belfast in October 1924 and sat until he retired in May 1929. High Sheriff of Belfast 1936-37. Knighted 1937. Died 22 May 1938.   [1929]

McCORQUODALE, Malcolm Stewart. Continued in House after 1945: full entry in Volume IV.

McCRAE, Sir George, D.S.O. 17 Learmonth Terrace, Edinburgh. Tortuish, North Berwick. Reform, and National Liberal. S. of George McCrae, Esq., Merchant. B. 29 August 1860; m. 1880, Elizabeth Cameron Russell (she died 1913). Educ. at the Lancastrian School, and Heriot-Watt Coll., Edinburgh. A Merchant. Raised the 16th (S.) Battalion The Royal Scots in 1914; commanded the Battalion in France (despatches twice) and D.S.O. during the Somme push 1917. Vice-President Scottish Local Government Board 1909-19; Chairman Scottish Board of Health 1919-22; Knight Bach. 1908. Lectures on Municipal Finance and Income Tax, Old Age Pensions and Land Values. A Liberal. Sat for E. Edinburgh from 1899-1909 when he resigned on appointment as Vice-President of Scottish Local Government Board. Unsuccessfully contested Edinburgh Central in November 1922. Elected for Stirling and Falkirk Burghs in December 1923 and sat until he was defeated in October 1924. Member of Edinburgh City Council 1889, City Treasurer 1891. Dept.-Lieut. for Edinburgh. Died 27 December 1928.

                    [1924 2nd ed.]

McCURDY, Rt. Hon. Charles Albert. Lamb Building, Temple, London. Reform. Eld. s. of the Rev. A. McCurdy, a Nonconformist Minister. B. 1870 in Nottingham; m. 1893, Louise Ellen, d. of Frederick Parker, Esq., of Cambridge. Educ. at Loughborough Grammar School, and Pembroke Coll., Cambridge where he studied medicine and law. K.C. 1919, Midland Circuit. Parliamentary Secretary to the Ministry of Food January 1919 to March 1920; Minister of Food March 1920 to March 1921; Chief Coalition Liberal Whip and Joint Parliamentary Secretary to Treasury April 1921 to October 1922. Chairman Committee on Trusts and Trade Combines 1917; Chairman Central Committee Profiteering Act, 1919. PC. 1920. A National Liberal. Unsuccessfully contested Winchester in 1906. Elected for Northampton in January and December 1910. Sat until he was defeated in December 1923. Chief National Liberal Whip October-December 1922. Chairman of United Newspapers Limited 1922-27, Managing Director 1925-27. Called to the bar, Inner Temple,

1896. Died 10 November 1941.   [1923]

MacDONAGH, Joseph. 86 Mayne Road, Ranelagh, Dublin. A Sinn Fein Member. Returned unopposed for N. Tipperary in December 1918 but did not take his seat. Member of Dail for N. Tipperary to 1922, as an Anti-Treaty Member. Alderman, Dublin City Council.   [1922]

McDONALD, Dr. Bouverie Francis Primrose. Ivor Lodge, New Brighton, Cheshire. Wallasey Constitutional. S. of Commander Samuel Pendleton McDonald, of St. Kilda Trinity, Edinburgh. B. 13 April 1861; m. 1886, Elizabeth Stedman, d. of Dr. Thomas Boswell Watson, of Hong-Kong. Educ. at Edinburgh Academy, Edinburgh University, and Royal Coll. of Surgeons; L.R.C.P. and S., M.B., C.M. 1884, M.D. (Edinburgh) 1886. Acted as Assistant County Director for the British Red Cross Society for Cheshire 1914 until the end of the war. Author of various works on medical subjects. Leader of the Constitutional Party in Wallasey from 1910. J.P. for the County of Cheshire and borough of Wallasey. Chairman of Directors of the Wallasey Constitutional Association. A Coalition Unionist. Elected for Wallasey in December 1918 and sat until he retired in October 1922. Member of Cheshire County Council 1903-06. Died 8 July 1931.
     [1922]

MACDONALD, David Henderson. House of Commons, London. B. at Wishaw in about 1857. Unmarried. Chairman of N.E. Lanark Unionist Association and active in the public life of Motherwell. Chairman of Brandon Bridge Building Company Limited, of Motherwell. A Coalition Unionist. Elected for the Bothwell division of Lanarkshire in December 1918 and sat until his death on 22 June 1919.   [1919]

MACDONALD, Gordon. Orrell, Nr. Wigan. S. of Thomas and Ellen Macdonald, of Ashton-in-Makerfield. B. at Gwaensygor, Flintshire 27 May 1888; m. 1913, Mary, d. of William Lewis, Esq., of Blaenau, Ffestiniog. Educ. at elementary school, and Ruskin Coll., Oxford. A Coal Miner.

Member of the Executive Committee of Miners' Federation of Great Britain. J.P. for Lancashire. Temporary Chairman of House of Commons Committees 1934-37; Labour Party Whip 1931-34. A Labour Member. Elected for the Ince division of Lancashire in 1929 and sat until October 1942 when he was appointed Controller of the Lancashire, Cheshire and N. Wales Region of the Ministry of Fuel and Power. Gov. of Newfoundland 1946-49. K.C.M.G. 1946. Created Baron Macdonald of Gwaensygor 1949. Paymaster-Gen. April 1949-October 1951. PC. 1951. Gov. of B.B.C. 1952-60. Member of Colonial Development Corporation 1952-59. A Congregationalist and President of United Kingdom Band of Hope Union. Died 20 January 1966.   [1942]

MACDONALD, Rt. Hon. James Ramsay, F.R.S. Upper Frognal Lodge, Hampstead, London. Athenaeum. S. of John Macdonald, Esq., Farm Servant and Anne Ramsay. B. 12 October 1866 at Lossiemouth; m. 1896, Margaret, d. of Professor J. Hall Gladstone, F.R.S. (she died 1911). Educ. at Drainie Board School; Honorary LL.D. Glasgow, Edinburgh, Wales, Toronto, and McGill Universities; F.R.S. 1930. A Journalist. Secretary to the Labour Party 1900-12; Chairman 1912-14; member of London County Council 1901-04; Editor of *The Socialist Review*. Leader of the Labour Party 1922-31. Leader of the National Labour Party 1931-37. A Trustee of the Treasury, First Lord of Treasury, Prime Minister, and Foreign Secretary January-November 1924; Prime Minister and First Lord of the Treasury June 1929-35; Lord President of the Council June 1935-May 1937; PC. 1924. Elder Brother of Trinity House 1930. A National Labour Member. Unsuccessfully contested Southampton in 1895 and Leicester in 1900. Sat for Leicester from 1906-18 when he unsuccessfully contested Leicester W. Unsuccessfully contested E. Woolwich in March 1921. Sat for the Aberavon division of Glamorganshire from November 1922-May 1929. Sat for the Seaham division of Co. Durham from May 1929-October 1935 when he was defeated, and for the Scottish Universities from

January 1936 until his death on 9 November 1937. [1938]

MACDONALD, Rt. Hon. John Archibald Murray. 15 Thurlow Road, Hampstead, London. Brown's Copse, Heyshott, Midhurst, Sussex. S. of the Rev. H.F. Macdonald, D.D., and Christina McIvor. B. 9 October 1854 at Strachur, Argyllshire; m. 1885, Alice Mary, d. of Edward H. Noel, Esq. (she died 1929). Educ. at Glasgow High School, Glasgow and Edinburgh Universities. Was a member of London School Board 1897-1902. PC. 1916. A Liberal. Sat for the Bow and Bromley division of Tower Hamlets from 1892-95 when he was defeated. Unsuccessfully contested Falkirk Burghs in 1900. Sat for Falkirk Burghs 1906-18, and for Stirling and Falkirk Burghs from December 1918 until he was defeated in November 1922. Contributor to the *Nineteenth Century*. Died 16 January 1939. [1922]

MACDONALD, Rt. Hon. Malcolm John. Ottawa, Canada. Upper Frognal Lodge, Hampstead, London. Hillocks, Lossiemouth. Brooks's. S. of the Rt. Hon. J.R. MacDonald. B. 1901; m. 1946, Mrs. Audrey Fellowes Rowley, d. of Kenyon Fellows, Esq., of Ottawa and widow of Lieut.-Col. J. Rowley. Educ. at Bedales, and Queen's Coll., Oxford. Member of London County Council from 1928-31; Parliamentary Under-Secretary of State for the Dominions August 1931-June 1935; Secretary of State for the Colonies June-November 1935 and May 1938-May 1940. Secretary of State for Dominions November 1935-May 1938, and November 1938-January 1939; Minister of Health May 1940-February 1941; High Commissioner in Canada from February 1941-46. PC. 1935. A Labour Member until August 1931, thereafter a National Labour Member. Unsuccessfully contested the Bassetlaw division of Nottinghamshire in December 1923 and October 1924. Elected for the Bassetlaw division of Nottinghamshire in May 1929 and again in October 1931, defeated November 1935. Elected for the Ross and Cromarty division of Inverness, Ross and Cromarty in February 1936 and sat until he retired in June 1945. Gov.-

Gen. of Malaya and Singapore 1946-48. U.K. Commissioner-Gen. in S.E.Asia 1948-55. High Commissioner in India 1955-60. Co-Chairman of International Conference on Laos 1961-62. Gov. of Kenya 1963, Gov.-Gen. 1963-64, High Commissioner in Kenya 1964-65. U.K. Special Representative in Africa 1965-69. O.M. 1969. Honorary Fellow of Queen's Coll., Oxford. Senior Research Fellow, University of Sussex 1971-73. Chancellor of University of Malaya 1949-61, University of Durham from 1970. President of Royal Commonwealth Society from 1971.* [1945]

MACDONALD, Sir Murdoch, K.C.M.G. Continued in House after 1945: full entry in Volume IV.

MACDONALD, Sir Peter Drummond, K.B.E. Continued in House after 1945: full entry in Volume IV.

MacDONALD, Robert. Hilltop Lodge, 47 Carleton Road, Tufnell Park, London. S. of William MacDonald, Esq., Engineer and Spindle Manufacturer, of Glasgow. B. 1875. Educ. at Glasgow. A Piano Manufacturer. Member of Glasgow City Council 1914-23. J.P. for the City of Glasgow. A Conservative. Unsuccessfully contested the Cathcart division of Glasgow in 1922. Elected for the Cathcart division of Glasgow in December 1923 and again October 1924. Sat until he retired in May 1929. [1929]

McDONNELL, Lieut. Col. Hon. Angus, C.B., C.M.G. 54 Threadneedle Street, London. Darenth, Kent. Brooks's, Turf, and Bath. S. of William, 7th Earl of Antrim. B. 7 June 1881; m. 13 December 1913, Ethelwyn Sylvia, d. of Henry Arthur Jones, Esq. (she died 1948). Educ. at Eton. Served in France with Canadian Forces 1916-18. A Conservative. Elected for the Dartford division of Kent in October 1924 and sat until he retired in May 1929. A Banker with the firm of Morgan Grenfell. C.M.G. 1918; C.B. 1919. Honorary Attaché at British Embassy in Washington 1941-45. Died 22 April 1966. [1929]

McELWEE, Andrew. 44 Hollingbourne Road, London. A Labour Member. Unsuccessfully contested the Hulme division of Manchester in December 1923 and October 1924. Elected for the Hulme division of Manchester in May 1929 and sat until he was defeated in October 1931. Member of Amalgamated Society of Woodworkers from 1907 and Chairman of its Executive Council 1924-26. After a dispute over election expenses was accused of criminal libel by the Council of the Amalgamated Society of Woodworkers in February 1932, found guilty in May 1932 and bound over for 2 years. [1931 2nd ed.]

MacENTEE, John Francis. 112, Pembroke Road, Dublin. S. of James McEntee, Esq., of Belfast. B. 1889; m. Margaret, d. of Maurice Browne, Esq., of Tipperary. Educ. at St. Malachy's Coll., Belfast, and Belfast Coll. of Technology. Was arrested in May 1918 and interned in Gloucester prison. A Sinn Fein Member. Elected for S. Monaghan in December 1918 but did not take his seat. Member of Dail for S. Monaghan to 1921, for Monaghan 1921-22, for Co. Dublin 1927-37, for Dublin Townships 1937-48, for S.E. Dublin 1948-69. An Anti-Treaty, later Fianna Fail Member. Minister of Finance 1932-39, Minister of Industry and Commerce 1939-41, Minister of Local Government and Public Health 1941-46, Minister of Local Government 1946-48, Minister of Finance 1951-54, Minister of Health 1957-65, Minister of Social Welfare 1958-61, Tanaiste (Dept. Prime Minister) 1959-65.* [1922]

McENTEE, Valentine La Touche, Continued in House after 1945: full entry in Volume IV.

McEWEN, Capt. John Helias Finnie. Marchmont, Greenlaw, Berwickshire. White's. New, Edinburgh. S. of Robert F. McEwen, Esq., Dept.-Lieut., and J.P., of Marchmont. B. 21 June 1894; m. 1923, Bridget Mary, d. of Rt. Hon. Sir Francis Lindley, G.C.M.G., C.B., C.B.E. Educ. at Eton, and Trinity Coll., Cambridge. Joined Cameron Highlanders 1914, R.F.C. 1916; Diplomatic Service 1920-26. Dept.-Lieut., and J.P. for Berwickshire. Parliamentary Private Secretary to R.A. Butler, Esq., Under-Secretary of State for India March 1933-April 1936 and to the Rt. Hon. Walter Elliot when Secretary of State for Scotland November 1936-February 1938; Assistant Government Whip April 1939; Parliamentary Under-Secretary of State for Scotland September 1939-May 1940; a Lord Commissioner of the Treasury March 1942-December 1944; Chairman of Cons. Foreign Affairs Committee 1938-39. A National Conservative. Unsuccessfully contested Berwick and Haddington in May 1929. Elected for Berwick and Haddington in October 1931 and sat until he was defeated in July 1945. Chairman of Conservative Members' "1922" Committee 1944-45. Under the pseudonym 'Litotes' contributed a weekly Parliamentary column to *The Tablet*. Created Bart. 1953. President of Scottish Unionist Association 1949-50. President of Saltire Society 1957-61. Chairman of Scottish Committee of Arts Council 1957-62. Died 19 April 1962. [1945]

MACFADYEN, Eric. 1-4 Great Tower Street, London. Stake Farm, Godden Green, Sevenoaks. Youngest s. of J.A. Macfadyen, Esq., D.D., of Manchester. B. 9 February 1879; m. 27 January 1920, Violet, d. of E.H.S. Champneys, Esq., of Otterpool Manor, Sellindge. Educ. at Clifton Coll., and Wadham Coll., Oxford. Served as trooper Imperial Yeomanry, South Africa 1900-01 (Queen's Medal with 3 bars). President Oxford Union 1902. Cadet Federated Malay States Civil Service 1902-05; Contracting and Rubber Planting 1906-16; for 2 years Chairman Planters' Association of Malaya, and for 7 years an Unofficial Member of Council Federated Malay States. Joined R.G.A. 1917 (Lieut.); served in France 1918. Director Harrisons and Crosfield Limited, etc. A Liberal. Elected for the Devizes division of Wiltshire in December 1923 and sat until he was defeated in October 1924; again defeated in May 1929. Knighted 1943. President of Imperial Coll. of Tropical Agriculture, Trinidad. Died 13 July 1966. [1924 2nd ed.]

McGHEE, Henry George. Continued in House after 1945: full entry in Volume IV.

McGOVERN, John. Continued in House after 1945: full entry in Volume IV.

McGRATH, Joseph. 13 Ruttledge's Terrace, South Circular Road, Dublin. A Commercial Clerk. For his part in the rebellion, he was deported and interned in Usk prison. Escaped in January 1919. Re-arrested February 1920. A Sinn Fein Member. Elected for the St. James's division of Dublin in December 1918 but did not take his seat. Member of Dail for St. James's division of Dublin to 1921, for N.W. Dublin 1921-23, and for N. Mayo 1923-24, as a Pro-Treaty Member. Member of Dublin City Council. Minister of Labour 1922, Minister of Industry and Commerce 1922-24. [1922]

McGUFFIN, Samuel. 278 Ivydale Road, London. S. of James McGuffin, Esq. B. at Belfast 18 August 1863; m. 1894, Margaret Haire, d. of William Haire, Esq., Farmer, of Portadown. Educ. at Belfast Model School. President and Senior Trustee of No. 12 Branch, A.S.E., Belfast; Water Commissioner for Court Ward, Belfast 1915. A Labour Unionist. Elected for the Shankhill division of Belfast in December 1918 and sat until he retired in October 1922. Member of Northern Ireland Parliament for N. Belfast 1921-25. Died 21 November 1952. [1922]

McGUINNESS, Joseph. 27 Lower Dorset Street, Dublin. A Dublin Draper who, when elected, was undergoing a sentence of three years' penal servitude in Lewes Gaol for his connection with the Dublin rising in 1916. Was subsequently released. A Sinn Fein Member. Returned for S. Longford in May 1917, and for Longford Co. in December 1918 but did not take his seat and died on 31 May 1922. Member of Dail for Longford to 1921, for Longford and Westmeath 1921-22. A Pro-Treaty Member. Died 31 May 1922. [1922]

McINTEE, John Francis. See McENTEE, John Francis.

MacINTYRE, Ian. 9 Victoria Street, London. The Tower, Murrayfield, Edinburgh. Conservative. S. of Duncan MacIntyre, Esq., Shipowner, of Edinburgh. B. 27 November 1869; m. 1st, 5 September 1896, Ida, d. of Charles Vander Gucht, Esq., of Hillingdon, Uxbridge (she died 1942); secondly, 1942, Gwendoline Maude, d. of Henry Coates, Esq., of Newcastle. Educ. at Fettes Coll., and University of Edinburgh; M.A., LL.B. Writer to the Signet 1893; partner in the firm of Mackenzie and Kermack, of Edinburgh. J.P. for County of City of Edinburgh. A Conservative. Unsuccessfully contested W. Edinburgh in December 1923. Elected for W. Edinburgh in October 1924 and sat until he retired in May 1929. Member of Edinburgh City Council 1918-20. Died 29 June 1946. [1929]

McINTYRE, Robert Douglas. 11 Inverleith Place, Edinburgh. S. of Rev. John E. McIntyre, of Edinburgh. B. 1913; m. 1954, Letitia Sarah, d. of Alexander Macleod, Esq. Educ. at Hamilton Academy, Daniel Stewart's Coll., Edinburgh University, M.B., Ch.B., and Glasgow University, D.P.H. Consultant Chest Physician. A Scottish Nationalist. Elected for Motherwell in April 1945 and sat until he was defeated in July 1945. Unsuccessfully contested Motherwell in February 1950, Perthshire E. and Perth in October 1951, May 1955, October 1959 and October 1964, Stirlingshire W. in March 1966 and June 1970, Stirling and Falkirk Burghs in September 1971, and Stirling, Falkirk and Grangemouth in February and October 1974. President of Scottish National Party, formerly Secretary 1942-45 and Chairman from 1946. Honorary D. University Stirling 1976. J.P. for Stirlingshire. Provost of Stirling 1967-75.*

MACK, John David. Continued in House after 1945: full entry in Volume IV.

McKEAG, William. Glenshee, Whickham, Nr. Newcastle-upon-Tyne. National Liberal. S. of William McKeag, Esq., of Carrville, near Durham. B. 29 June 1897; m. 26 October 1922, Marie, d. of William Corn Crowe, Esq. (she died 1960). Educ. at

Belmont, and Johnston's Schools, Durham. Admitted a Solicitor 1923; Partner in the firm of Molineux, McKeag and Cooper, Newcastle-upon-Tyne. Director of various companies. Served overseas 1914-18. Russian Order of St. Stanislaus. A Liberal. Unsuccessfully contested Durham in October 1924 and again in May 1929. Elected for Durham in October 1931 and sat until he was defeated in November 1935. Unsuccessfully contested Newcastle-on-Tyne N. in July 1945 and Newcastle-on-Tyne E. in February 1950. Alderman, Newcastle-on-Tyne City Council, Lord Mayor 1951-52 and 1953-54. Served as Dept.-Assistant Adjutant Gen. 1939-45. Died 4 October 1972. [1935]

McKIE, John Hamilton. Continued in House after 1945: full entry in Volume IV.

MACKINDER, Sir Halford John. 73 Harrington Gardens, London. Carlton, Athenaeum, Alpine, and Conservative, Glasgow. S. of Draper Mackinder, Esq., M.D., of Hove, and Fanny, d. of Halford Wotton Hewitt, Esq., J.P., of Lichfield. B. 15 February 1861 at Gainsborough; m. 1889, Emilie Catherine, d. of Christian D. Ginsburg, Esq., LL.D. Educ. at Gainsborough Grammar School, Epsom Coll., and Christ Church, Oxford; M.A.; President of the Oxford Union Society; was called to the bar at the Inner Temple 1886. Reader in Geography at Oxford University 1887-1905; Student of Christ Church, 1892-1905; Principal of University Coll., Reading 1892-1903; President of Geographical Section of British Association 1895; explored in East Africa 1899; Director of London School of Economics and Political Science 1903-08; Senator of London University 1904-08; Member of the Royal Commissions on the Income Tax and on Awards to Inventors 1919; Reader in Geography in University of London 1900-23, Professor 1923-25; Member of the National War Savings Committee; Officier de I'Instruction Publique de France. British High Commissioner for South Russia October 1919. Chairman of the Imperial Shipping Committee 1920-45. Author of *Britain and British Seas, Democratic Ideals and Reality*, and other works. Knighted 1920. A Unionist. Unsuccessfully contested Warwick and Leamington as a Liberal Imperialist in 1900 and Hawick Burghs as a Liberal Unionist in 1909. First elected for the Camlachie division of Glasgow in January 1910 and sat until he was defeated in November 1922. Chairman of Imperial Economic Conference 1926-31. PC. 1926. Died 6 March 1947. [1922]

MACKINDER, William. Moorview, Hollybank Grove, Great Horton, Bradford. S. of Charles and Caroline Mackinder. B. at Hull 28 April 1880; m. 1905, Ada, d. of James Claughton, Esq. Educ. at St. Patrick's Elementary School, Bradford. A Spinner, Wool-Comber and Fisherman. A Trade Union Official; member of Bradford City Council from 1919-20. Served on Anthrax, Profiteering and Wool Control Committees. A Labour Member. Unsuccessfully contested the Shipley division of the W. Riding of Yorkshire in November 1922. Elected for the Shipley division in December 1923 and sat until his death on 8 September 1930. [1929 2nd ed.]

McKINLAY, Adam Storey. Continued in House after 1945: full entry in Volume IV.

MacLAREN, Andrew. 31 Ryfold Road, London. S. of John Maclaren, Esq., of Glasgow. B. in Glasgow 1883. Educ. at Glasgow Board School, Technical Coll., and School of Art. An Engineer. A Labour Member but resigned the Whip in March 1943 and then sat as an Independent Labour Member. Sat for the Burslem division of Stoke-on-Trent from November 1922 to December 1923, when he was defeated; from October 1924 to October 1931, when he was defeated; and from November 1935 to July 1945, when he was defeated standing as an Independent Labour candidate in opposition to the official Labour candidate. Originally a Liberal, joined the Independent Labour Party and the Union of Democratic Control in 1914. Died 11 April 1975. [1945]

McLAREN, Hon. Henry Duncan, C.B.E. 69 Eaton Place, London. Bodnant, Tal-y-Cafn, North Wales. Reform, and Brooks's. Eld. s. of Lord Aberconway. B. 1879 at Barn Elms, Surrey; m. 1910, Christabel, d.

of Sir Melville Macnaghten, C.B. Educ. at Eton (Capt. Oppidans 1897-98), and Balliol Coll., Oxford. Was called to the bar at Lincoln's Inn 1905. A Director of Bolckow Vaughan and Company Limited, Palmer's Shipbuilding and Iron Company Limited, and Tredegar Coal and Iron Company Limited. Parliamentary Private Secretary (unpaid) to Mr. Lloyd George when President of Board of Trade and Chancellor of Exchequer. Director of Area Organization at Ministry of Munitions 1916-19. C.B.E. 1917 J.P. and Chairman of Quarter Sessions for Denbighshire. A Liberal. Sat for W. Staffordshire from 1906 to January 1910, when he was defeated. First elected for the Bosworth division of Leicestershire in December 1910 and sat until he was defeated in November 1922. President of Royal Horticultural Society 1931-53. Succeeded to the Peerage as Baron Aberconway 1934. Chairman of Thomas Firth and John Brown Limited until 1951. Died 23 May 1953.   [1922]

McLAREN, Robert. Earlston, Grahamshill, Airdrie, Scotland. Caledonian, Glasgow. S. of Robert McLaren, Esq., Colliery Official. B. at Airdrie 17 December 1856; m. 1880, Margaret, d. of James Mahon, Esq. Educ. at Rawyards, Airdrie, and Gartsherrie Science and Art Coll., Coatbridge. Teacher of Mining 1876-1885; Mining Manager and Mining Engineer 1882; H.M. Inspector of Mines 1885; retired 1917. Consulting Mining Engineer; President of Mining Institute of Scotland; Vice-President of Institution of Mining Engineers. Author of *Reverse Fault in Underground Workings, Working Thick Coal by Longwall Method, New Use for Old Wire Ropes, Boring Machine for Tapping Wastes.* A Coalition Unionist. Elected for N. Lanarkshire in December 1918 and sat until he was defeated in November 1922. Unsuccessfully contested the Rutherglen division of Lanarkshire in December 1923 and October 1924. Member of Lanarkshire County Council 1924-28. Died 22 April 1940.   [1922]

MACLAY, Hon. John Scott. Continued in House after 1945: full entry in Volume IV.

MACLAY, Hon. Joseph Paton. Connaught Hotel, Carlos Place, London. Milton, Kilmacolm, Renfrewshire. S. and heir of the Rt. Hon. Lord Maclay. B. 31 May 1899; m. 24 September 1936, Nancy Margaret, d. of R.C. Greig Hall, Esq., of Caldwell, Uplowmuir, Renfrewshire. Educ. at Fettes Coll., Edinburgh, and Trinity Coll., Cambridge, M.A. Chairman of Maclay and MacIntyre, Shipowners, of Glasgow. A Liberal. Elected for Paisley in October 1931 and sat until he retired in June 1945. Remained on the Government benches after November 1933 when the Liberals went into Opposition but did not formally join the Liberal National group. Head of Convoy and Admiralty Liaison Section, Ministry of War Transport 1943-45. K.B.E. 1946. President of Chamber of Shipping of United Kingdom 1946-47. Succeeded to the Peerage as Baron Maclay 1951. Lord Dean of Guild, Glasgow 1952-54. Chairman of Clydesdale and North of Scotland Bank. Died 7 November 1969.   [1945]

McLEAN, Sir Alan, M.B.E. Burfield Hall, Wymondham, Norfolk. Littlewood Park, Alford, Aberdeenshire. Conservative, and 1900. S. of David Mclean, Esq., of Hongkong and Shanghai Bank. B. 5 July 1875; m. 17 July 1920, Elizabeth Blodwen, d. of the Rev. I. Jones. Educ. at Harrow, and Trinity Coll., Cambridge; B.A. 1898, M.A. 1905. Barrister-at-Law, Lincoln's Inn 1902; Chairman of the Lamson Paragon Supply Company Limited, and other companies. Council of the National Rifle Association. Maj. Inns of Court O.T.C.; served in France, etc. 1914-19; T.D. Created Knight Bach. 1933. A Conservative. Unsuccessfully contested the Caerphilly division of Glamorganshire in 1922. Elected for S.W. Norfolk in December 1923 and sat until defeated in May 1929. Re-elected for S.W.Norfolk in October 1931 and sat until he retired in October 1935. Member of Aberdeenshire County Council, Convenor 1950-55. Dept.-Lieut. for Aberdeenshire. Died 9 May 1959.   [1935]

McLEAN, Lieut.-Col. Charles Wesley Weldon, D.S.O., C.M.G. 9 Currie Street, London. Carlton, and Cavalry. S. of Maj.-

Gen. H.H. McLean, MP (Canadian Parliament). B. at St. John's New Brunswick August 1882. Unmarried. Educ. at the Royal Military Coll., Kingston. Maj. and Lieut.-Col. R.F.A. (Regulars). Served in South Africa 1899-1900; served in France and Flanders throughout the war; twice wounded; awarded the 1914-15 Star; D.S.O. with two bars. C.M.G. 1919. Parliamentary Private Secretary to Lieut.-Col. Amery 1919. A Unionist. Elected for the Brigg division of Lincolnshire in December 1918 and sat until he retired in October 1922. Died at Lancaster, New Brunswick 5 September 1962.   [1922]

MACLEAN, Rt. Hon. Sir Donald, K.B.E. 6 Southwick Place, London. Brooks's, Reform, Bath, National Liberal, and Eighty. S. of John Maclean, Esq., of Kilmoluag, Tiree. B. 1864; m. 2 October 1907, Gwendolen Margaret, d. of Andrew Devitt, Esq., of Coldshott. Educ. privately. Admitted a Solicitor 1887. Dept. Chairman of Ways and Means 1911-18. Chairman London Appeal Tribunal, Military Service Acts 1916; of Enemy Debts Committee; of Local Government Reconstruction Committee, and of Port Labour Enquiry 1930. PC. 1916, K.B.E. 1917. Honorary LL.D. Cambridge 1920. President Board of Education from August 1931 to June 1932. A Liberal, National Liberal from 1931. Unsuccessfully contested Bath in 1900. Sat for Bath from 1906 to January 1910 when he was defeated. Elected for Peebles and Selkirk in December 1910, and for Peebles and S. Midlothian in December 1918; was defeated there in November 1922. Unsuccessfully contested Kilmarnock in December 1923 and Cardiff E. in October 1924. Elected for N. Cornwall in May 1929 and sat until his death on 15 June 1932. Chairman of Parliamentary Liberal Party 1919-22. Acting Leader of the Liberal Party in the House of Commons from February 1919 until Mr. Asquith's election for Paisley in February 1920. President of National Liberal Federation 1922-25. J.P. for Middlesex and Peeblesshire. Died 15 June 1932.   [1932]

MACLEAN, Fitzroy Hew Royle. Continued in House after 1945: full entry in Volume IV.

MACLEAN, Neil. Continued in House after 1945: full entry in Volume IV.

McLEAN, Dr. William Hannah. Drimard, Dunoon, Argyllshire. Royal Societies. S. of William McLean, Esq., of Drimard, Dunoon. B. 1877; m. 1922, Frances Gwendoline, d. of Col. W.E. Donohue, C.B.E. (she died 1960). Educ. privately, and at University of Glasgow. Joined Sudan C.S. 1906. Planned City of Khartoum with Lord Kitchener; transferred Egyptian C.S. 1913 as Engineer-in-Chief to Minister of Interior. Prepared Protective Planning Scheme for City of Jerusalem, and National Development Plan for Egypt; retired 1926. Member of Research Committee of Empire Economic Union. M.Inst.C.E., Ph.D. Glasgow, E. St.J; Commander of the Order of Ismail and of the Order of the Nile. A Unionist. Elected for the Tradeston division of Glasgow in October 1931 and sat until he was defeated in November 1935. Engaged in information and economic work for the Colonial Office 1931-67. K.B.E. 1938. Member of Tunbridge Wells Borough Council 1936-46. Died 23 September 1967.   [1935]

MacLEOD, John Mackintosh. 4 Park Circus Place, Glasgow. Carlton. S. of the Rev. Norman MacLeod, D.D., Dean of the Thistle and Chapel Royal in Scotland, and Catherine, d. of William Mackintosh, Esq., of Geddes, Nairnshire. B. 5 May 1857 in Glasgow; m. 1888, Edith, d. of Joshua Fielden, Esq., MP of Todmorden, and Nutfield Priory, Surrey. Educ. at the Academy and Park School, Glasgow, and in Germany. A Chartered Accountant, Edinburgh Society 1880; Glasgow Society 1894; Director of Clydesdale Bank of Scotland. President of Scottish Unionist Association. A Unionist. Elected for Central Glasgow in July 1915 and for the Kelvingrove division of Glasgow in December 1918 and sat until he retired in October 1922. Created Bart. 1924. President of Glasgow Institute of Accountants and

Actuaries 1926-28. Secretary of Glasgow Society of Sons of Ministers of Church of Scotland 1887-1934. Died 6 March 1934. [1922]

MACMASTER, Sir Donald, Bart. 57 Sloane Gardens, London. Carlton, and Constitutional. S. of Donald Macmaster, Esq., of Williamstown, Ontario. B. at Williamstown, Ontario 3 September 1846; m. 1st, 1880, Janet, d. of R.S. Macdonald, Esq., of Lancaster, Ontario (she died 1883); secondly, 1890, Ella Virginia, d. of Isaac Deford, Esq., of Baltimore. Educ. at Grammar School, Williamstown, and Mc-Gill University, Montreal; Gold Medallist and Valedictorian in Law, (D.C.L.). Called to the Canadian bar in 1871; Q.C. 1882; and English bar at Lincoln's Inn in 1906. Practised for several years at the Canadian bar and was Crown Prosecutor in Canada and Arbitrator between Newfoundland Government and the Reid-Newfoundland Railway 1904-05. Was President of Montreal bar 1903-04; later mainly practised before Judicial Committee of Privy Council. A member of Ontario Legislature 1879-82, and of the Canadian House of Commons 1882-86. Member of Select Committee on Marconi Wireless Contract 1912-13, of the Speaker's Conference on Electoral Reform 1917-18, and of the Speaker's Devolution Conference 1919. Created Bart. 1921. A Unionist. Unsuccessfully contested the Leigh division of Lancashire in 1906. Elected for the Chertsey division of Surrey in January 1910. Sat until his death on 3 March 1922. [1922]

McMICKING, Maj. Gilbert, C.M.G. Miltonise, Glenwhilly, Wigtownshire. 38 Netherhall Gardens, London. Reform, and Naval & Military. S. of Gilbert McMicking, Esq., Dept.-Lieut., of Miltonise, Wigtownshire. B. 24 March 1862; m. 1st 1893, Gertrude Rosabel, d. of Nathaniel Gore, Esq. (she died 1920); secondly, 1921, Ethel, d. of Binny Douglas, Esq. Educ. at Cheltenham, Wimbledon, and Royal Military Academy, Woolwich. Hon. Maj. in the army, joined the Royal Artillery 1882 and retired 1894. Commanded the C.I.V. Battery in South African War 1900,

and was mentioned in despatches. C.M.G. 1900. Parliamentary Private Secretary (unpaid) to Mr. Haldane, Secretary of State for War 1908-10. Temporary Maj. R.F.A. October 1914; Temporary Lieut.-Col. January-October 1915. A Liberal. Sat for Kirkcudbrightshire from 1906 to January 1910, when he was defeated. Re-elected there in December 1910. Returned unopposed for Galloway in December 1918 and sat until he retired in October 1922. Died 15 November 1942. [1922]

MACMILLAN, Malcolm Kenneth. Continued in House after 1945: full entry in Volume IV.

MACMILLAN, Rt. Hon. Maurice Harold. Continued in House after 1945: full entry in Volume IV.

MACNAGHTEN, Hon. Sir Malcolm Martin, K.B.E., K.C. 21 Sheffield Terrace, London. Portballentrae. Bushmills, Co. Antrim. Carlton, and United University. S. of Lord Macnaghten (Law Lord). B. 12 Jan. 1869; m. 4 Feb. 1899, Antonia Mary d. of the Rt. Hon. Charles Booth (she died 1952) Educ. at Eton, and Trinity Coll., Cambridge. Barrister-at-Law, Lincoln's Inn 1894; Bencher 1915; K.C. 1919; K.B.E. 1920. A Conservative. Returned unopposed for N. Londonderry in June 1922. Elected for Londonderry in November 1922, and sat until December 1928 when he was appoined a High Court Judge. Judge of King's Bench Division 1928–47. Recorder of Colchester 1924-28. PC. 1948. Treasurer of Lincoln's Inn 1945. Died 24 January 1955. [1929]

MACNAMARA, Col. John Robert Jermain. 25 Palace Street, London. S. of Dr. J.R. Macnamara of Assam. B. 1905 in India. Educ. at Cheam, and Haileybury. At one time in Royal Fusiliers London Irish Rifles. Served in India with Royal Royal Fusiliers 1927-33. Served in combined operations in the Adriatic and Mediterranean with the London Irish Rifles. A Conservative. Unsuccessfully contested the Upton division of West Ham in 1934. Elected for the Chelmsford division of

Essex in November 1935 and until 22 December 1944 when he was killed in action in Italy. [1945]

MACNAMARA, Rt. Hon. Thomas James. Clontarf, Rollscourt Avenue, Herne Hill, London. National Liberal, and Eighty. S. of Sergeant Thomas Macnamara, old 47th Regiment Loyal North Lancashires. B. in Montreal 1861; m. 1886, Rachel, eld. d. of Angus Cameron, Esq., of Bristol. Educ. at St. Thomas's School, Exeter, and Borough Road Training Coll. for Teachers. A Journalist, Editor of the *Schoolmaster* 1892-1907, essayist on social questions. Fellow of Journalists' Institute; member of London School Board 1894-1903. Parliamentary Secretary to the Local Government Board January 1907 to April 1908; Parliamentary and Financial Secretary to the Admiralty April 1908-March 1920; Minister of Labour March 1920 to October 1922; Honorary LL.D. St. Andrew's 1898; Honorary M.A. Oxford 1907. PC. 1911. Author of *Schoolmaster Sketches, Schoolroom Humour, The Gentle Golfer*, and many works on educational methods. A Liberal. Unsuccessfully contested Deptford in 1895. Sat for N. Camberwell from October 1900 to December 1918 and for N.W. Camberwell from December 1918 to October 1924 when he was defeated. Unsuccessfully contested Walsall in February 1925 and May 1929. President of National Union of Teachers 1896. Died 3 December 1931. [1924 2nd ed.]

McNEIL, Hector. Continued in House after 1945: full entry in Volume IV.

MacNEILL, John. B. at Glenarm, Co. Antrim 1867; m. Agnes, d. of James Moore, Esq., of Ballymena. Educ. at St. Malachy's Coll., Belfast, and Royal University of Ireland. Professor of Early History in the University Coll. of the National University, Ireland 1909-45. An organizer of Irish Volunteers. President of the Sinn Fein organization at the time of the Easter rebellion 1916. Although taking no active part in that rebellion, was sentenced to penal servitude for association with the movement which led to it; subsequently released. Re-arrested 1920. A Sinn Fein

Member. Elected for Londonderry city and the National University of Ireland in December 1918 but did not take his seat for either constituency. Member of Dail for National University of Ireland to 1923, for Co. Clare 1923-27. A Pro-Treaty, later Cumann na nGaedheal Member. Member of Northern Ireland Parliament for Londonderry 1921-25. Speaker of Dail 1921-22. Minister for Education 1922-25. Founder of Gaelic League. Chairman of Irish Historical Manuscripts Commission 1928. Died 15 October 1945. [1922]

McNEILL, Rt. Hon. Ronald. 18 Cadogan Place, London. Cushendun, Co. Antrim. Carlton, and 1900. S. of Edmund McNeill, Esq., Dept.-Lieut. of Craigdunn, Co. Antrim, and Mary, d. of Alexander Miller, Esq., of Ballycastle, Co. Antrim. B. 30 April 1861; m. 1st, 1884, Elizabeth Maud, d. of William Bolitho, Esq., of Polwithen, Penzance (she died 1925); secondly, 1930, Catherine Louisa, d. of Sir Mortimer Margesson. Educ. at Harrow, and Christ Church, Oxford. A Barrister-at-Law, Lincoln's Inn 1887. Editor of *St. James's Gazette* 1900-04, and Assistant-Editor of *Encyclopaedia Britannica* (11th edition) 1907-11. Author of *Home Rule: Its History and Danger, Socialism (The New Order), History of Australia and New Zealand, Ulster's Stand for Union*, etc. J.P. and Dept-Lieut. for Co. Antrim 1916. Under-Secretary of State for Foreign Affairs October 1922-January 1924 and November 1924-November 1925. Financial Secretary to the Treasury from November 1925-October 1927. PC. 1924. A Conservative. Unsuccessfully contested W. Aberdeenshire in 1906, S. Aberdeen in 1907 and January 1910, and Kirkcudbrightshire in December 1910. Sat for the St. Augustine's division of Kent from July 1911 to 1918 and for the Canterbury division of Kent from December 1918 until October 1927 when he was created Baron Cushendun. Chancellor of Duchy of Lancaster October 1927-June 1929. Died 12 October 1934. [1927]

MACPHERSON, Rt. Hon. Sir James Ian, Bart. 15 Wellington Square, London. Fountain Court, Temple, London. Reform, Brooks's, and Beefsteak. S. of James

Macpherson, Esq., J.P., of Inverness. B. 1880; m. 24 September 1915, Jill, d. of Sir George Rhodes, 1st Bart. Educ. at George Watson's Coll., and Edinburgh University; M.A., LL.B., Honorary LL.D. A Barrister-at-Law, Middle Temple 1906; K.C. 1919; Bencher 1930; Recorder of Southend 1931-37. Was twice President of Edinburgh University Liberal Association and first President of University Free Trade Union. Senior President Students' Representative Council. Chairman Land Enquiry Committee (Scotland). Parliamentary Private Secretary to H.J. Tennant, Under-Secretary of State for War 1914-16. Under-Secretary of State for War December 1916-January 1919; Dept. Secretary of State for War and Vice-President of The Army Council 1918; PC. (England and Ireland) 1918. Chief Secretary for Ireland January 1919 to April 1920; Minister of Pensions, April 1920 to October 1922. Created Bart. 1933. A Liberal until 1931 thereafter a Liberal National Member. Unsuccessfully contested Wigtownshire in January 1910 and E. Renfrewshire in December 1910. Sat for the Ross and Cromarty division of Inverness and Ross and Cromarty from June 1911 until January 1936 when he was created Baron Strathcarron. Vice-President of British Empire Producers' Association. President of Tobacco Federation of British Empire 1932-37. Died 14 August 1937. [1936]

MACQUISTEN, Frederick Alexander, K.C. 35 Old Jewry, London. S. of the Rev. Alexander Macquisten, of Inverkip. B. 23 July 1870; m. 1901, Margaret, d. of John Reid, Esq. Educ. at Glasgow University. Admitted a Solicitor; Advocate 1909, Barrister-at-Law, Gray's Inn 1919. A Conservative. Unsuccessfully contested Leith Burghs as a Liberal Unionist in December 1910, and the St. Rollox division of Glasgow in 1912. Sat for the Springburn division of Glasgow from 1918-22 when he was defeated. Unsuccessfully contested Argyll in December 1923. Sat for Argyll from October 1924 until his death on 29 February 1940. Member of Glasgow City Council. K.C. (Scotland) 1919; K.C. (England) 1932. Died 29 February 1940. [1940]

MacROBERT, Rt. Hon. Alexander Munro. 28 Abercromby Place, Edinburgh. Caledonian, and Conservative. New (Edinburgh). S. of Thomas MacRobert, Esq., Solicitor, of Paisley. B. 1873; m. 1902, Emma, d. of the Rev. Thomas Gentles, D.D. Educ. at Paisley Grammar School, and Edinburgh and Glasgow Universities. A Barrister-at-Law, Scotland 1897; K.C. 1919; Admiralty 1917-18. Advocate Depute 1919-23; Sheriff of Forfar 1923-24; Solicitor-Gen. for Scotland December 1925-April 1929; Lord Advocate April-June 1929. PC. 1929. A Conservative. Unsuccessfully contested Leith in 1922. Elected for E. Renfrewshire in October 1924. Sat until his death on 18 October 1930. [1929 2nd ed.]

McSHANE, John James. House of Commons, London. S. of Philip McShane, Esq., Miner of Wishaw, Lanarkshire. B. 1 October 1882; m. 1917, Annie, d. of F.W. Bromwick, Esq. (she died 1962). Educ. at St. Ignatius School, Wishaw, Lanarkshire, and at Glasgow University Training Coll. A Schoolmaster from 1909; Headmaster, The Mount School, Walsall. Chairman Walsall Board of Guardians. A Labour Member. Elected for Walsall in May 1929 and sat until he was defeated in October 1931. J.P. for Walsall. Chairman of Midland Section of C.W.S. Director of Walsall Cooperative Society. Died 1972. [1931 2nd ed.]

MacSWINEY, Terence Joseph. B. 1883. Author of *Principles of Freedom* and of a number of poems and plays. Was prominent in the organizing and propaganda work of the Sinn Fein movement, and for this he underwent deportation. A Sinn Fein Member. Was returned unopposed for mid Cork in December 1918 but did not take his seat. Lord Mayor of Cork 1920. Died while on hunger-strike in Brixton Prison on 25 October 1920. [1920]

MacVEAGH, Jeremiah. 5 Essex Court, Temple, London. 12 Upper Bedford Place, London. S. of T. MacVeagh, Esq., of Belfast, and Jane Hughes, of Coalisland, Co. Tyrone. B. at Belfast 1870. Unmarried. Educ. at St. Malachy's Coll., Belfast.

Barrister-at-Law, Gray's Inn 1918; Journalist; Director of Dublin and South Eastern Railway; Alliance and Dublin Consumers Gas Company, and Register Publishing Company Limited. Special Irish Correspondent of the *Daily News* 1890. Author of numerous political pamphlets and leaflets. A Nationalist. First elected for S. Down in February 1902 and sat until he retired in October 1922. Unsuccessfully contested Sunderland as a Labour candidate in October 1924. Died 17 April 1932. [1922]

MADDOCKS, Sir Henry, K.C. 78 Regents Park, Road, London. 4 Brick Court, Temple, London. Garrick, St. Stephen's, and 1900. S. of William Maddocks, Esq., of Wem, Shropshire. B. 26 April 1871 at Prees, Shropshire; m. 1896, Elsie Mary, d. of John Anslow, Esq., of Coventry. Educ. at the Wem Grammar School. A Barrister-at-Law. Called by the Inner Temple 1904; K.C. February 1920. A Conservative. Contested the Nuneaton division of Warwickshire in January and December 1910. Elected for the Nuneaton division of Warwickshire in December 1918 and sat until he was defeated December 1923. Knighted June 1923. Recorder of Stamford 1924-25, of Birmingham 1925-31. Member of Imperial War Graves Commission. Died 9 June 1931. [1923]

MADEN, Henry. Rockcliffe House, Bacup. Holmhurst, Lytham. Oxford & Cambridge, and National Liberal. S. of Sir John Henry Maden, MP and Lady Maden. B. at Rockcliffe House, Bacup 31 March 1892; m. 1923, Alice, d. of J.H. Fletcher, Esq., Solicitor, of Holmfirth. Educ. at Exeter Coll., Oxford; M.A. Barrister-at-Law, Middle Temple 1916. A Liberal. Unsuccessfully contested the Lonsdale division of Lancashire in November 1922. Elected for the Lonsdale division in December 1923 and sat until he was defeated in October 1924. Defeated again in 1929, 1931 and 1935. Died 17 November 1960. [1924 2nd ed.]

MAGNAY, Thomas. Crosslands, 381 Durham Road, Gateshead. S. of George Magnay, Esq., of Newcastle-upon-Tyne. B. 14 September 1876; m. 17 September 1899, Mary, d. of John Fittes Smith, Esq.

Educ. at Elswick Works Technical School. An Accountant. J.P. for Gateshead. A Liberal National. Unsuccessfully contested the Blaydon division of Durham as a Liberal in May 1929. Elected for Gateshead in October 1931 and sat until he was defeated in July 1945. Died 3 November 1949. [1945]

MAGNUS, Sir Philip, Bart. 16 Gloucester Terrace, Hyde Park, London. Tangley Hill, Chilworth, Surrey. Athenaeum, and Carlton. S. of Jacob Magnus, Esq., and Caroline, d. of J. Barnett. B. 7 October 1842 in London; m. 1870, Katie, d. of E. Emanuel, Esq., J.P. (she died 1924). Educ. at University Coll., London, and Berlin University; B.A., B.Sc. Hons. London. A member of the Senate and Fellow of London University, Superintendent of the Technology Department of City and Guilds of London Institute; President of Council of College of Preceptors, Chairman of Secondary Schools Association; Member of Council, Royal Society of Arts; a member of Royal Commission on Technical Instruction 1881-84; and of London School Board 1890-91. J.P. for Surrey. Knighted 1886; created Bart. 1917. A Unionist. Elected for London University in 1906 and sat until he retired in October 1922. Died 29 August 1933. [1922]

MAINWARING, William Henry. Continued in House after 1945: full entry in Volume IV.

MAITLAND, Sir Adam. Beechlands, Henley-on-Thames. Carlton, and Royal Automobile. S. of Joseph Maitland, Esq., of Aberdeenshire. B. 25 May 1885; m. 6 September 1911, Nancy Helen, d. of Henry Chadwick, Esq., of Bury, Lancashire. Educ. at Manchester Central School and privately. Fellow of Society of Incorporated Accountants and Auditors; Vice-President of Association of Municipal Corporations and of National Association of Building Societies and President of National Fire Brigades Association; member of Surrey County Council; member of Select Committee on National Expenditure 1939. Knight Bach. 1939. A Conservative. Elected for the Faversham division of Kent in January 1928 and sat until he was defeated in July 1945. Chairman of board of *Pall Mall Gazette and Globe*. Died 5 October 1949.   [1945]

MAKINS, Brigadier-Gen. Sir Ernest, K.B.E., C.B., D.S.O. 180 Queen's Gate, London. Carlton, Cavalry, M.C.C., and Hurlingham. S. of Henry F. Makins, Esq. B. 14 October 1869; m. 31 January 1903, Maria Florence, d. of Sir James Mellor. Educ. at Winchester, and Christ Church, Oxford. Joined The Royal Dragoons January 1892; O.C. 1910-14; Col. 1931; served in South African War 1900-02, in France, etc. 1914-18. Staff Coll. 1905-06. F.R.G.S. Created K.B.E. 1938. A Conservative. Unsuccessfully contested S. Kensington in 1918 as the candidate of the National Party. Elected for the Knutsford division of Cheshire in November 1922 and sat until he retired in June 1945. D.S.O. 1902; C.B. 1917. Died 18 May 1959.   [1945]

MALCOLM, Ian Zachary. 5 Bryanston Square, London. Poltaloch, Lochgilphead, Argyllshire. Carlton, and Garrick. S. of Col. E.D. Malcolm, C.B., R.E., and Isabel Wyld, d. of John Brown, Esq. B. 3 September 1868 at Quebec; m. 1902, Jeanne, d. of Edward Langtry, Esq., and Lily Langtry later Lady de Bathe. Educ. at Eton, and New Coll., Oxford. Entered the Diplomatic Service in 1891, and was Attaché at Berlin 1891-93, and at Paris in 1893. Was Assistant Private Secretary to Lord Salisbury 1895-98, and Parliamentary Private Secretary to Mr. George Wyndham when Chief Secretary for Ireland 1900-03. Parliamentary Private Secretary to Mr. Balfour, Secretary of State for Foreign Affairs 1916-19. Wrote *Indian Pictures and Problems, The Calendar of Empire, War Pictures*, and other works. A Coalition Unionist. Sat for the Stowmarket division of Suffolk from 1895-1906 when he retired. Unsuccessfully contested N. Salford in January 1910. Elected for Croydon in December 1910 and for Croydon S. in December 1918 and sat until he resigned in October 1919. British Director on the Suez Canal Board 1919-39. Secretary of Union Defence League 1906-10. Died 28 December 1944.   [1919]

MALLABY-DEELEY, Sir Harry Mallaby, Bart. Mitcham Court, Surrey. Elgars, Bexhill, Sussex. Carlton, Wellington, United Empire, 1900, and Royal Automobile. Surrey Magistrates. S. of W. Clarke Deeley, Esq., of Curzon Park, Chester, and Elizabeth, d. of J. Mallaby, Esq., of Loxley Hall, Staffordshire. B. 27 October 1863; m. 1st 21 August 1890, Joan, 3rd d. of J. Parson-Smith, Esq., of Abbotsmead, near Shrewsbury (she died 1933); secondly, 1935, Edith Maud, d. of W.J.G. Shoebridge, Esq. Educ. at Shrewsbury School, and Trinity Coll., Cambridge; M.A., LL.M., Hons. Law 1885. A Director of Norwich Union Life Insurance Society, a member of the Inner Temple, a Gov. of the Royal Agricultural Society of England, patron of 5 livings, a member of the Committee of the Royal Female Orphanage Asylum, and Chairman of Conservators of Mitcham Common. J.P. for Surrey, and Lord of the Manors of Ravensbury Biggin and Tamworth. Assumed in 1922 the additional prefix surname of Mallaby. Created Bart. 1922. A Conservative. Elected for the Harrow division of Middlesex in January and December 1910, and for Willesden E. in December 1918 and November 1922. Sat until he resigned in December 1922. Died near Cannes 4 February 1937.   [1923]

MALLALIEU, Edward Lancelot. Continued in House after 1945: full entry in Volume IV.

MALLALIEU, Frederick William. Larkwood, Delph, near Oldham. National Liberal, and Reform. S. of Henry Mallalieu, Esq., J.P. for the West Riding of Yorkshire. B. at Delph, Yorkshire 1860; m. 1902, Ann, d. of Joseph Hardman, Esq., Cotton Spinner, of Oldham. Educ. at Huddersfield Coll. A Woollen Manufacturer. Member of the Saddleworth Board of Guardians 1894-09; Saddleworth District Council 1894-1911, Chairman seven years; member of the W. Riding Yorkshire County Council from 1901; Alderman from 1907; Chairman Finance Committee from 1912. J.P. for W. Riding of Yorkshire. A Liberal. Elected for the Colne Valley division of Yorkshire in August 1916 and again in

December 1918. Sat until he was defeated in November 1922. Died in South Africa 10 May 1932. [1922]

MALONE, Cecil John l'Estrange. 6 Phene Street, London. National Labour, 1917, and Royal Aero. S. of the Rev. Savile l'Estrange Malone, Rector of S. Dalton, Yorkshire. B. 7 September 1890; m. 1st, 8 June 1921, Leah, d. of Mrs. Kay (she died 1951); secondly, 1956, Dorothy Nina Cheetham, d. of E.H. Neal, Esq. Educ. at Ludgrove, New Barnet, Cordwalles, Maidenhead, and Royal Naval Coll., Dartmouth. Joined R.N. 1905; Assistant to Director of Air Department, Admiralty 1912; Air Attaché, British Embassy, Paris. Served with R.N.A.S. 1914; commanded H.M.S. *Ben-my-Chree* 1915; served with Dardanelles Expedition; commanded Seaplane Squadron in E. Indies and Egypt 1916. Fellow of Royal Aeronautical Society; Order of the Nile. Sat for E. Leyton from 1918-22 when he retired. Elected as a Coalition Liberal in December 1918 but resigned the Whip in November 1919 and transferred his allegiance to the British Socialist Party. Joined the Communist Party in July 1920 but in October 1924 unsuccessfully contested Ashton-under-Lyne as the Labour candidate. Elected as Labour Member for Northampton in January 1928 and again in May 1929. Sat until he was defeated in October 1931. Parliamentary Private Secretary to F.O. Roberts, Minister of Pensions, in 1931. Imprisoned for six months under the defence of the Realm Act 1920-21, after speaking at a meeting opposed to intervention in Russia, and was deprived of the O.B.E. which had been awarded to him in 1919. Served with City of Westminster Civil Defence 1942-43 and with the small vessels section of the Admiralty 1943-45. Died 25 February 1965. [1931 2nd ed.]

MALONE, Maj. Patrick Bernard. 40 Belmont Road, West Green, Tottenham. S. of Henry Malone, Esq., of Clifden, Co. Galway. B. 1857; m. 1st, 1881, Mary, d. of Judge Benkert of Bavaria; secondly, 1908, Anetta, d. of John Slater, Esq., of Blackburn (she died 1927). Member of Middlesex County Council to 1937. Chairman of the Tottenham War Pensions Committee; J.P.; Chairman of the Finance Committee of the Metropolitan Water Board. A Conservative. Sat for Tottenham S. from December 1918-December 1923, when he was defeated, and from October 1924 to May 1929 when he was again defeated. Knighted 1932. Member of Tottenham Urban District Council and Tottenham Borough Council. Died 31 December 1939. [1929]

MALONEY, Patrick James. Church Street, Tipperary. Arrested in 1920. A Sinn Fein Member. Elected for S. Tipperary in December 1918 but did not take his seat. Member of Dail for S. Tipperary to 1923. An Anti-Treaty Member. A Chemist. Member of Tipperary Urban District Council. [1922]

MANDER, Sir Geoffrey Le Mesurier. Wightwick Manor, Wolverhampton. Reform, Royal Air Force, and National Liberal. S. of Theodore Mander, Esq., of Wolverhampton. B. 6 March 1882; m. 1st, 10 October 1906, Rosalind Florence, d. of Col. F. Caverhill, of Montreal (m. dissolved in 1930); secondly, 18 November 1930, Rosalie, d. of A.C. Grylls, Esq. Educ. at Harrow, and Trinity Coll., Cambridge, M.A. Chairman of Mander Brothers Limited, Wolverhampton. Barrister-at-Law, Inner Temple 1921. High Sheriff of Staffordshire 1921; J.P. for Staffordshire and Wolverhampton. Parliamentary Private Secretary to Rt. Hon. Sir Archibald Sinclair, Bart., when Secretary of State for Air March 1942-May 1945. A Liberal. Unsuccessfully contested the Leominster division of Herefordshire in November 1922, the Cannock division of Staffordshire in December 1923 and the Stourbridge division of Worcestershire in October 1924. Elected for Wolverhampton E. in May 1929 and sat until he was defeated in July 1945. Member of Staffordshire County Council. Knighted January 1945. Joined Labour Party in 1948. Died 9 September 1962. [1945]

MANNING, Cecil Aubrey Gwynne. Continued in House after 1945: full entry in Volume IV.

MANNING, Elizabeth Leah. Continued in House after 1945: full entry in Volume IV.

MANNINGHAM-BULLER, Sir Mervyn Edward, Bart. Charlton Lodge, Banbury. Carlton. S. of Maj.-Gen. E.M. Manningham-Buller. B. 16 January 1876; m. 8 July 1903, Hon. Lilah Constance Cavendish, d. of 3rd Baron Chesham (she died 1944). Educ. at Eton, and Royal Military Coll., Sandhurst. Grand-s. of 1st Bart.; succeeded his uncle in 1910. Lieut.-Col. Rifle Brigade. A Conservative. Unsuccessfully contested the Heywood division of Lancashire as a Liberal Unionist in January 1906 and January 1910. Elected for the Kettering division of Northamptonshire in October 1924 and sat until he retired in May 1929. Elected for Northampton in October 1931 and sat until he resigned in November 1940. Died 22 August 1956. [1940]

MANNINGHAM-BULLER, Reginald Edward. Continued in House after 1945: full entry in Volume IV.

MANSEL, Sir Courtenay Cecil. The Manor, Maesycrugiau, Carmarthenshire. S. of Sir Richard Mansel. B. 25 February 1880; m. 2 October 1906, Mary Philippa Agnes Germaine, d. of Frederick Littlewood, Esq. Educ. at Harrow. J.P. for Cardigan and Carmarthen. A Barrister, Middle Temple 1918. Hereditary Knight of Jerusalem. A Liberal. Unsuccessfully contested Conventry in December 1918 and the Penryn and Falmouth division of Cornwall in November 1922. Elected for the Penryn and Falmouth division in December 1923 and sat until he was defeated in October 1924. Joined the Conservative Party in 1926 and unsuccessfully contested the Carmarthen division of Carmarthenshire in June 1928 and the University of Wales in May 1929. Succeeded his father as Bart. in 1892 but in 1903 resigned his claim in favour of his uncle; succeeded his uncle in the Baronetcy in 1908. From 1903 to 1908 resumed his grand-father's original surname of Phillips in lieu of Mansel. Died 4 January 1933. [1924 2nd ed.]

MANSFIELD, William Thomas. House of Commons, London. S. of Thomas Mansfield, Esq., of Staithes. B. 1884; m. 1910, Lilian, d. of William Elders, Esq. Alderman for the N. Riding of Yorkshire County Council; Gen. Secretary Ironstone Miners' Association. A Labour Member. Unsuccessfully contested the Cleveland division of the N. Riding of Yorkshire in October 1924. Elected for the Cleveland division in May 1929 and sat until he was defeated in October 1931; again defeated in November 1935. Died 19 March 1939. [1931 2nd ed.]

MANVILLE, Sir Edward. St. Stephen's House, Westminster, London. Royal Automobile, Carlton, Engineers, and Savage. S. of B.E. Manville, Esq., M.R.C.S. B. in London 1862; m. 1st, 1894, Maud Elizabeth, d. of Col. C.T. Wallis, Dept.-Lieut., of Newport, Monmouthshire; secondly, 1911, Rachel Violet, d. of John Holmes, Esq., of India. Educ. at University Coll. School, and Technical Institutions. J.P. for Coventry. A Consulting Electrical Engineer. President Association of British Chambers of Commerce. Chairman Daimler Company Limited, Coventry; Dept.-Chairman Birmingham Small Arms Company Limited; Chairman Car and General Insurance Corporation Limited; Director Royal Exchange Assurance. Knighted 1923. A Conservative. Elected for Coventry in December 1918 and sat until he was defeated in December 1923. Member of Institution of Electrical Engineers. President of Society of Motor Manufacturers and Traders. Died 17 March 1933. [1923]

MARCH, Samuel. 177 Caufield Road, East Ham, London. S. of James March, Esq., of Dagenham. B. 4 February 1861; m. 1907, d. of J.B.C. Davis, Esq., of Swansea. Educ. at Ford's Free School, Dagenham. Was Gen. Secretary of the National Union of Vehicle workers before its amalgamation with the Transport and General Workers' Union. Mayor of Poplar 1920-21. J.P. for County of London. A Labour Member. Unsuccessfully contested Poplar S. in December 1918. Elected for Poplar S. in November 1922 and sat until he retired in October 1931. Died 10 August 1935. [1931 2nd ed.]

MARCUS, Michael. House of Commons, London. S. of Nathan Marcuss, Esq. B. 9 November 1897; m. 1928, Bessie, d. of G. Morris, Esq., of Leeds. Educ. at George Heriot's School, and University of Edinburgh. A Solicitor in Edinburgh. A Labour Member. Elected for Dundee in May 1929 and sat until he was defeated in October 1931. Unsuccessfully contested Dundee in November 1935. Barrister-at-Law, Middle Temple 1935. Died November 1960.
[1931 2nd ed.]

MARDY JONES, Thomas Isaac. See JONES, Thomas Isaac Mardy.

MARGESSON, Capt. Rt. Hon. Henry David Reginald, M.C. Boddington Manor, Byfield, Northamptonshire. Carlton, and Turf. S. of Sir Mortimer Margesson. B. 26 July 1890; m. 29 April 1916, d. of Francis H. Leggett, Esq., of New York (divorced 1940). Educ. at Harrow, and Magdalene Coll., Cambridge. A Capt. in the 11th Hussars. Parliamentary Private Secretary to Sir Montague Barlow when Minister of Labour November 1922-December 1923. Assistant Whip November 1924; Junior Lord of the Treasury August 1926-June 1929 and August-November 1931; Parliamentary Secretary to the Treasury and Chief Government Whip November 1931-December 1940 (Joint Parliamentary Secretary May-December 1940). PC. 1933. Secretary of State for War December 1940-February 1942. A Conservative. Sat for the Upton division of West Ham from November 1922 until 1923 when he was defeated. Elected for the Rugby division of Warwickshire in 1924 and sat until March 1942 when he was created Visct. Margesson. Director of International Nickel Company and of Martins Bank. Died in the Bahamas 24 December 1965. [1942]

MARJORIBANKS, Edward. 1 Victoria Square, London. S. of Hon. Archibald Marjoribanks, step-s. of 1st Visct. Hailsham, and grand-s. of Dudley, 1st Baron Tweedmouth. B. 14 February 1900. Unmarried. Educ. at Eton, Capt. of School 1917-18, and at Christ Church, Oxford. President of Oxford Union 1923; 1st Class Honours Mods. 1920; 1st Class Lit. Hum. 1922. A Barrister-at-Law, Lincoln's Inn and Middle Temple 1924, and joined the S.E. Circuit. Heir Presumptive to the Barony of Tweedmouth. A Conservative. Elected for the Eastbourne division of Sussex in May 1929, Sat until he committed suicide on 2 April 1932. [1932]

MARKHAM, Sydney Frank. Continued in House after 1945: full entry in Volume IV.

MARKIEVICZ, Constance Georgine, Countess de. 10 Richmond Avenue, Fairview, Dublin. A d. of Sir Henry Gore-Booth, 5th Bart., and a sister of Sir Josslyn Gore-Booth, of Lissadell, Co. Sligo. B. 4 February 1868; m. 1900, Casimir de Markievicz, a Polish Count who fought with the Russian Army during the war. Received into Roman Catholic Church 1916. One of the leaders of the Sinn Fein movement; took part in the Irish rebellion, commanding the movement in the Royal Coll. of Surgeons. Sentenced to penal servitude, but released under the general amnesty. Arrested in Dublin in May 1918 and interned in Holloway prison. Released; again arrested, tried in Ireland, and finally sentenced to 4 months imprisonment in June 1919 for inciting to boycott. In 1920 was again arrested and sentenced to two years imprisonment with hard labour. A Sinn Fein Member. Elected for the St. Patrick's division of Dublin in December 1918 but did not take her seat. The first woman to win a parliamentary election. Member of Dail for the St. Patrick's division of Dublin to 1921, for S. Dublin 1921-27 as an Anti-Treaty Member. Joined Fianna Fail in 1926. Minister of Labour 1921-22. Died 15 July 1927. [1922]

MARKLEW, Ernest. Kia Beluro, Old Clu, Grimsby. National Trade Union. S. of William Marklew, Esq. B. 1874; m. 1912, Clara A. Bramwell. Educ. at elementary school, and Public Libraries. A Fish Merchant. Member of Grimsby Borough Council 1928. Sometime Member of Executive Committee of Social Democratic Federation. A Labour Member. Unsuccessfully contested Grimsby in May 1929 and

237

the Colne Valley division of the W. Riding of Yorkshire in 1931. Elected for the Colne Valley division of the W. Riding of Yorkshire in November 1935 and sat until his death on 14 June 1939.   [1939]

MARKS, Sir George Croydon, C.B.E. 58 Lincoln's Inn Fields, London. 99 Blackheath Park, London. Penarvor, Bude, Cornwall. Reform, and National Liberal. S. of William Marks, Esq., and Amelia, d. of Thomas Croydon, Esq. B. 9 June 1858 at Eltham; m. 1881, Margaret, d. of T.J. Maynard, Esq., of Bath. Educ. at Royal Arsenal School, Woolwich, and King's Coll., London. A Consulting Engineer and patent expert; M.Inst.Mech.E., A.M.I.C.E., senior partner of Marks and Clerk, of London, Birmingham, Manchester, and New York. Was Consulting Engineer to H.R.H. Duke of Edinburgh as Duke of Saxe-Coburg. Knighted 1911. C.B.E. 1917. A J.P. for Cornwall, Surrey, and Aberystwyth. Author of several text-books on engineering and allied subjects. Temporary Chairman of Committees, House of Commons. A Liberal. Sat for the Launceston division of Cornwall from 1906 to 1918. Returned unopposed for the N. division of Cornwall in December 1918 and November 1922, and after contest in December 1923. Sat until he was defeated in October 1924. Joined Labour Party in 1929. Created Baron Marks 1929. A Congregationalist. Died 24 September 1938.   [1924 2nd ed.]

MARLEY, James. 10 Estelle Road, Hampstead, London. S. of a Scottish Miner. B. 1893; m. 1920, Alice Louise, d. of William Pilgrim, Esq. Educ. at St. Aloysius' Coll., and St. Mungo's Academy, Glasgow, St. Mary's Coll., Hammersmith, and London School of Economics. A Schoolmaster at St.Dominic's Priory School, Haverstock Hill. Founder and Joint Secretary of Teachers' Labour League. A Labour Member. Elected for N. St. Pancras in December 1923, defeated October 1924. Re-elected for N. St. Pancras in May 1929 and sat until he was defeated in October 1931. Died 11 April 1954.   [1931 2nd ed.]

MARLOWE, Anthony Alfred Harmsworth. Continued in House after 1945: full entry in Volume IV.

MARRIOTT, Sir John Arthur Ransome. Worcester Coll., Oxford. Carlton, and Yorkshire. S. of Francis Marriott, Esq., of Bowdon, Cheshire, and Hayfield, Derbyshire, and Elizabeth, d. of Joseph Atkinson Ransome, Esq., Consulting Surgeon to Manchester Royal Infirmary. B. 17 August 1859 at Bowdon, Cheshire; m. 7 April 1891, Henrietta, d. of the Rev. W.P. Robinson, D.D., Warden of Trinity Coll., Glenalmond. Educ. at Repton School, and New Coll., Oxford. An Historian; Honorary Fellow, Fellow and Modern History Tutor of Worcester Coll., Oxford, Secretary to the University Extension Delegacy, Oxford 1895-1920. Author of many works on Historical Subjects. Knight Bach. 1924. A Conservative. Unsuccessfully contested Rochdale in 1886. Sat for Oxford City from March 1917 until he was defeated in November 1922. Sat for the City of York from 1923 until he was defeated in May 1929. Director of Great Northern Railway. Chairman of Estimates Committee 1924-26. Died 6 June 1945.   [1929]

MARSDEN, Arthur. Continued in House after 1945: full entry in Volume IV.

MARSHALL, Sir Arthur Harold, K.B.E. 19 Wimborne Road, Bournemouth. Reform, and National Liberal. S. of the Rev. H.T. Marshall, D.D., Methodist Minister, and Mary, d. of John Keats, Esq., of Hanley. B. 2 August 1870 at Ashton-under-Lyne; m. 1896, Louie, d. of J. Hepworth, Esq., J.P., of Leeds and Torquay (she died 1948). Educ. privately, and at Yorkshire Coll., Leeds. A Barrister (Gray's Inn 1904). K.B.E. 1918. Honorary Secretary of Yorkshire Liberal Federation from 1908; Chairman of Central Billeting Board 1917-19; member of National Savings Committee. A Liberal Whip 1917-18 and 1922-23. A Liberal. Sat for Wakefield from December 1910 to December 1918. Unsuccessfully contested Ashton-under-Lyne in January 1920. Elected for Huddersfield in November 1922 and sat until he was defeated in December

1923. Unsuccessfully contested Huddersfield in October 1924. Died 18 January 1956.

[1923]

MARSHALL, Fred. Continued in House after 1945: full entry in Volume IV.

MARTIN, Albert Edward. 40 Gerrard Street, London. Torville, The Cliffs, Westcliff-on-Sea. National Liberal. B. 1875; m. 1909, Edith Savory. For 20 years member of the Barking Town Council; member of Romford Board of Guardians; Overseer; Charity Trustee; Capt. Essex R.A.S.C. (V.) M.T.; Managing Director Martin's Cinematograph Film Company. J.P. for Essex. A Liberal. Elected for the Romford division of Essex in December 1918 and sat until he retired in November 1923. Charter Mayor of Barking 1931, re-elected 1932. Member of Essex County Council. Died 25 July 1936. [1923]

MARTIN, Frederick. St. Dunstan's, Mintlaw Station, Aberdeenshire. 3rd s. of William Martin, Esq., and Agnes Clark, of Peterhead. B. at Peterhead 23 October 1882; m. 1910, Flora, d. of J.C. Rennie, Esq., of Milladen, Aberdeenshire. Educ. at Peterhead Academy. Served in 1914-15 in the Territorial Battalion of the 5th Gordon Highlanders, but on becoming almost blind had to relinquish his commission. Thereafter trained at St. Dunstan's Hostel. A Liberal. Elected for E. Aberdeenshire in November 1922 and sat until he was defeated in October 1924. Unsuccessfully contested C. Aberdeenshire in May 1929 as a Liberal and E. Aberdeenshire as a Labour candidate in October 1931 and November 1935. Journalist in Aberdeen until 1914. Dept.-Lieut. for Aberdeenshire. Convenor of Aberdeenshire County Council 1949-50. C.B.E. 1942. Died 18 January 1950.

[1924 2nd ed.]

MARTIN, John Hanbury. Continued in House after 1945: full entry in Volume IV.

MARTIN, Thomas Ballantyne. 53 Romney Street, London. Naworth Keep, Brampton, Cumberland. S. of Angus Martin, Esq., F.R.C.S. (Edinburgh). B.

13 November 1901; m. 1953, Jean Elisabeth, d. of Lieut-Col. O.D. Bennett. Educ. at Giggleswick School, and at Jesus Coll., Cambridge. English Secretary to Turkish Embassy in London 1928, 1930-31. Lecturer in Germany 1929. A Conservative. Elected for the Blaydon division of Durham in October 1931 and sat until November 1935 when he unsuccessfully contested N. Camberwell. Unsuccessfully contested the Houghton-le-Spring division of Co. Durham in July 1945. Political Correspondent of *Daily Telegraph* 1937-40. Served with R.A.F.V.R., Middle East Intelligence Centre, Squadron Leader 1940-43. Public Relations Adviser to U.K. High Commissioner in Australia 1943-45. Secretary of United Europe Movement 1947-48. Member of Stock Exchange 1949-74.*

[1935]

MARTIN, William Henry Porteous. Braemar, Alexandra Street, Kirkintilloch. S. of William Martin, Esq., Colliery Company's Cashier. B. in Dunbartonshire 15 June 1886; m. 14 July 1915, Jane Isabella, d. of the Rev. Hugh Reyburn, M.A., B.D., St. David's U.F. Church, Kirkintilloch. Educ. at Uddington Higher Grade Grammar School, Lanark. A Chartered Accountant; partner in W.H. Martin and Steveley Roberts, Glasgow. Secretary Dunbartonshire Federation, I.L.P., and Chairman Scottish I.L.P. a Labour Member. Unsuccessfully contested Dunbartonshire in 1918 and 1922. Elected for Dunbartonshire in December 1923 and sat until he was defeated in October 1924. Unsuccessfully contested Dunbartonshire in January 1926, Aberdeen S. in May 1929, and Glasgow Central in October 1931. Councillor and Magistrate for Burgh of Clydebank from 1932, Provost from 1936. Died 9 January 1939. [1924 2nd ed.]

MASON, David Marshall. 34 Queens Gate Gardens, London. Reform, Bath, National Liberal, and Ranelagh. S. of Stephen Mason, Esq., at one time MP for mid Lanark. B. 7 December 1865; m. 1898, Mary, d. of Hon. G.W. Crouse, of U.S.A. Educ. at Kelvinside and Partick Academies, Craigmount, Edinburgh, in Germany, and at University of Glasgow. Merchant and Banker; Associate of Institute of Bankers. Founder and Chairman of Executive Committee of Sound Currency Association 1919. A Liberal but resigned the Whip in January 1914 and sat as an Independent anti-war Liberal until December 1918. Unsuccessfully contested the Tradeston division of Glasgow in January 1906 and January 1910. Sat for Coventry from December 1910 until, standing as an Independent Liberal, but he was defeated in December 1918. Unsuccessfully contested the Chislehurst division of Kent in November 1922, the Romford division of Essex in December 1923 and October 1924, and the Barnstaple division of Devon in May 1929. Elected for E. Edinburgh in October 1931 and sat until he was defeated in November 1935. Joined Liberal National Party in 1939. Died 19 March 1945.   [1935]

MASON, Lieut.-Col. Hon. Glyn Keith Murray, D.S.O. 4 Ennismore Gardens, London. Carlton, and R.Y.S. S. of Lord Blackford. B. 29 May 1887; m. 1918, Grace Ellinor, d. of N. Keen, Esq. Educ. at Eton, and Sandhurst. Joined 14th Hussars 1906; served in India 8 years, and in France, Macedonia and Palestine 1914-18. D.S.O. 1915; Bar to D.S.O. 1918. Director of the Midland Bank, of Guardian Assurance Company, and of several Investment Trusts. A Conservative. Sat for Croydon N. from 1922 until he resigned in June 1940. Lieut. of City of London. Succeeded to the Peerage as 2nd Baron Blackford in 1947. Dept. Speaker of the House of Lords 1949-66. Dept. Chairman of Midland Bank 1960-67. C.B.E. 1962. Chairman of Guardian Assurance Company 1950-67. Died 31 December 1972.   [1940]

MASON, Robert. Marden House, Whitley Bay, Northumberland. National Liberal. S. of John and Isabella Mason, of Belford, Northumberland. B. 1857; m. 1884, Rosa Elizabeth Thompson. Educ. at Orphan House, Wesleyan School, Newcastle-on-Tyne. A Partner in the firm of L.S. Carr and Company, Shipowners and Shipbrokers 1884; Managing Director, Tyne-Tees Steam Shipping Company Limited. A local Alder-

man who won the seat on the death of Mr. Fenwick, Miners' Representative. A Coalition Liberal. Sat for the Wansbeck division of Northumberland from May 1918, and was re-elected there in December 1918. Sat until he retired in October 1922. Died 1 August 1927.   [1922]

MASTERMAN, Rt. Hon. Charles Frederick Gurney. 46 Gillingham Street, London. National Liberal. 4th s. of Thomas William Masterman, Esq., of Rotherfield Hall, Sussex. B. 1873; m. 1908, Lucy, eld. d. of the Rt. Hon. Gen. Sir Neville Lyttelton. Educ. at Weymouth, and Christ's Coll., Cambridge. President of the Union 1896; M.A., Fellow of Christ's 1900. Wrote for *Nation, Athenaeum, Daily News*, etc. Author of *Tennyson as a Religious Teacher, The Heart of the Empire, From the Abyss, In Peril of Change, F.D. Maurice, The Condition of England*, etc. Parliamentary Secretary Local Government Board April 1908-July 1909; Under-Secretary of State Home Department July 1909-February 1912; PC. 1912; Financial Secretary to Treasury February 1912-February 1914; Chancellor Duchy of Lancaster February 1914-February 1915; Chairman of National Insurance Commission. A Liberal. Unsuccessfully contested Dulwich in 1903. Sat for West Ham N. from 1906 to June 1911 when he was unseated on petition, and for S.W. Bethnal Green from July 1911 to February 1914 when he failed to secure re-election after his appointment as Chancellor of Duchy of Lancaster. Unsuccessfully contested Ipswich in May 1914 and the Stratford division of West Ham in December 1918. Unsuccessfully contested the Claycross division of Derbyshire in 1922. Elected for the Rusholme division of Manchester in December 1923 and sat until he was defeated in October 1924. An Anglo-Catholic and member of the Christian Social Union. Director of Literature Dept. Ministry of Information 1918. Died 17 November 1927.   [1924 2nd ed.]

MATHERS, George. Continued in House after 1945: full entry in Volume IV.

MATHEW, Charles James, K.C., C.B.E. 76 Woodside, Wimbledon. 10 Old Square,

Lincoln's Inn, London. Athenaeum. Youngest s. of Lord Justice Mathew. B. 24 October 1872; m. 1896, Anna, d. of James Archbold Cassidy, Esq., of Monasterevan, Co. Kildare. Educ. at the Oratory School, Birmingham, and Trinity Hall, Cambridge. Called to the bar, Lincoln's Inn 1897; K.C. 1913; C.B.E. 1917. Member London County Council from 1910-19, when he was elected an Alderman. A Labour Member. Elected for the Whitechapel and St. George's division of Stepney in November 1922 and sat until his death on 8 January 1923. [1923]

MATTERS, Leonard Warburton. 35 Great Russell Street, London. Argentine, and 1917. S. of John Matters, Esq., of Adelaide, South Australia. B. 26 June 1881; m. 1st, 1910, Emilie Mary, d. of T. Domela; secondly, 1939, Romana Kryszek. Educ. at South Australian State School. A Journalist and Novelist from 1897. Member of Overseas Trade Development Council. A Labour Member. Elected for the Kennington division of Lambeth in May 1929 and sat until he was defeated in October 1931. Unsuccessfully contested the Kennington division of Lambeth in November 1935. Chairman of Indian and Eastern Newspaper Society. London representative of *The Hindu* of Madras. Died 31 October 1951.
[1931 2nd ed.]

MATTHEWS, David. Windsor Lodge, Swansea. S. of William and Elizabeth Matthews. B. 1868, at Morriston, Swansea; m. 1892, d. of John and Elizabeth Morris, of Swansea. Educ. at Morriston. A Tin-Plate Manufacturer and Merchant. J.P. and twice Mayor of Swansea. A Liberal. Elected for Swansea E. in July 1919 and sat until he retired in October 1922. Died 26 February 1960. [1922]

MAXTON, James. Continued in House after 1945: full entry in Volume IV.

MAXWELL, Hon. Somerset Arthur. Coneyhurst, Ewhurst, Cranleigh, Surrey. S. of Arthur, 11th Baron Farnham. B. 20 January 1905; m. 15 October 1930, Susan, d. of Capt. Marshall Roberts. Educ.

at Harrow. Capt. Middlesex Yeomanry. A Stockbroker. Parliamentary Private Secretary to the Rt. Hon. Leslie Hore-Belisha, when Secretary of State for War 1938-December 1939. A Conservative. Elected for the King's Lynn division of Norfolk in November 1935 and sat until he was killed on active service in the Middle East in December 1942. [1943]

MAXWELL FYFE, Rt. Hon. Sir David Patrick. Continued in House after 1945: full entry in Volume IV.

MAYHEW, Lieut.-Col. Sir John. 12 Chesham Street, London. Newton Hall, Dunmow, Essex. Carlton, Cavalry, and Royal Automobile. S. of Horace Mayhew, Esq., B. 2 October 1884; m. 1907, Guendolen, d. of Capt. Francis Gurney, 91st (A. and S.) Highlanders (she died 1946). Educ. at King William's Coll., Isle of Man. J.P. for Essex. An Agriculturalist and Industrialist. 2nd Lieut. Denbighshire Hussars Yeomanry 1902. Lieut.-Col. Yeomanry T.D. Served in France with Infantry 1916-17. Member of Essex T.A. and A.F. Association. A Conservative. Unsuccessfully contested the Harwich division of Essex in May 1929. Elected for East Ham N. in October 1931 and sat until he was defeated in July 1945. Defeated again in 1950. Dept.-Lieut. for Essex. Knighted June 1945. Master of Pattenmakers' Company 1944. Died 27 January 1954. [1945]

MEDLICOTT, Frank. Continued in House after 1945: full entry in Volume IV.

MELLER, Sir Richard James. Caverhill, Wallington, Surrey. S. of Richard Meller, Esq. B. 1872; m. 1896, Jeanie, d. of John Sibley, Esq. A Barrister-at-Law, Middle Temple 1904. Chairman of Croydon (County) Bench. Dept.-Lieut., and J.P. for Surrey, and Chairman of Surrey T.A. Member of Thames Conservancy. Created Knight Bach. 1933. A Conservative. Unsuccessfully contested Dartford in March 1920 and N. Camberwell in February 1922. Elected for the Mitcham division of Surrey in December 1923 and sat until his death on 24 June 1940. Secretary of Prudential

Approved Societies. Member of Surrey County Council from 1919, Alderman from 1928, Vice-Chairman 1939-40, Chairman 1940. Died 24 June 1940.   [1940]

MELLOR, Sir John Serocold Paget, Bart. Continued in House after 1945: full entry in Volume IV.

MELLOWES, Liam. Arrested and escaped from Mountjoy prison in 1919. A Sinn Fein Member. Returned unopposed for E. Galway, and also elected for N. Meath in December 1918 but did not take his seat for either constituency. Member of Dail for Co. Galway 1921-22 as an Anti-Treaty Member. Imprisoned in Mountjoy Gaol for bearing arms against the Government of Ireland and executed on 8 December 1922 by the Free State Government as a reprisal for the murder of Sean Hales.   [1922]

MELLOWES, William Joseph. See MELLOWES, Liam.

MELVILLE, Sir James Benjamin. 9 Royal Avenue, Chelsea, London. 2 Plowden Buildings, Temple, London. Author's. S. of Superintendent William Melville, M.V.O., of Scotland Yard. B. at Havre 20 April 1885; m. 1915, the former private secretary to Rt. Hon. Andrew Bonar Law. A Barrister-at-Law, Middle Temple 27 June 1906, Bencher 1929; K.C. 1927. Solicitor-Gen. June 1929-October 1930. Created Knight Bach. 1929. Served with R.A.S.C. in Gallipoli, Salonika, and Egypt, Maj. A Roman Catholic. A Labour Member. Elected for Gateshead in May 1929 and sat until his death on 1 May 1931.   [1931 2nd ed.]

MERCER, Col. Herbert. Cutedge Place, Halstead, Essex. Cavalry. Youngest s. of Richard Mercer, Esq., of Morhanger Park, Bedfordshire. B. 7 January 1862 at Sandling Place, Maidstone, Kent; m. 16 January 1907, Elizabeth, d. of Thomas Bower, Esq., of Stradishall Place, Suffolk (she died 1929). Educ. at Harrow, and Trinity Coll., Cambridge. Entered the army; gazetted 1884 to 3rd Dragoon Guards; retired Col. 1908. In command 3rd Reserve Cavalry Regiment August 1914-17; on Gen. Plumer's

Staff 1918, and at Malta 1919 with Lord Plumer. A Conservative. Elected for the Sudbury division of Suffolk in November 1922 and sat until he was defeated in December 1923. Died 8 February 1944.   [1923]

MERRIMAN, Sir Frank Boyd, O.B.E., K.C. 3 Pembroke Road, London. Farrar's Buildings, Temple, London. Carlton, Bath, and Savile. S. of Frank Merriman, Esq., of Hollingford House, Knutsford. B. 1880; m. 1st, 1907, Eva Mary, d. of the Rev. H.L. Freer (she died 1919); secondly, 1920, Olive McLaren, d. of F.W. Carver, Esq., of Oakhurst, Knutsford (she died 1952); thirdly, 1953, Jane, d. of James Stormonth, Esq., of Belfast. Educ. at Winchester. A Barrister-at-Law, Inner Temple 1904; K.C. 1919; Member of Gen. Council of the bar, and Recorder of Wigan 1920-28. Member of Lord Chancellor's Committee on Arbitration 1926. Chairman of Departmental Committee on Registration of Opticians 1927. Served in France 1915-19 with Manchester Regiment and as a D.A.A.G. Solicitor-Gen. March 1928-June 1929 and from January 1932 to September 1933. Honorary LL.D. McGill University. Knight Bach. 1928. A Conservative. Sat for the Rusholme division of Manchester from October 1924 until he was appointed a High Court Judge in September 1933. President of Probate, Divorce and Admiralty Division of High Court 1933-62. PC. 1933. Created Baron Merriman 1941. Died 18 January 1962.   [1933]

MESSER, Frederick. Continued in House after 1945: full entry in Volume IV.

MEYER, Sir Frank Cecil, Bart. 18 Lowndes Street, London. Carlton, and Bath. S. of Sir Carl Meyer, 1st Bart., of of Shortgrove. B. 7 May 1886; m. 11 February 1920, Marjorie, d. of Frederick Seeley, Esq., of Hale, Cheshire. Educ. at Eton, and New Coll., Oxford. Barrister-at-Law, Inner Temple 1910. Lieut. Essex Yeomanry. A Conservative. Unsuccessfully contested E. Norfolk in December 1910. Elected for Great Yarmouth in October 1924 and sat until he was defeated in May

1929. Succeeded as Bart. 1922. Dept.-Chairman of De Beers Consolidated Mines and Director of several mining companies. Died 19 October 1935, after being injured in a riding accident.   [1929]

MEYLER, Maj. Hugh Mowbray, C.B.E., D.S.O., M.C. 68 Victoria Street, London. National Liberal. S. of Thomas Meyler, Esq., Town Clerk of Taunton, Solicitor. B. at Pitminster, near Taunton 25 June 1875; m. 1st, 1903, Ethel, d. of Maj.-Gen. A.L. Emerson; secondly, Evelyn Margaret, d. of W.A. Faulkner, Esq. Educ. at King's Coll., Taunton, and All Hallow's, Honiton. A Solicitor, admitted 1898; Attorney (Natal) 1903; served in the army 1900-03, and 1915-19; Maj. Legal Officer in Ireland 1920-23; member of first Parliament of Union of South Africa; defeated Prime Minister of Natal in 1911 election; C.B.E. 1922, D.S.O. 1919, M.C. Belgian Order of Leopold and Croix de Guerre, with palm. A Liberal. Unsuccessfully contested S.W. Bethnal Green in December 1918 and Blackpool in November 1922. Elected for Blackpool in December 1923 and sat until he was defeated in October 1924. Lieut.-Col. 1924. Committed suicide 30 April 1929 after the financial failure of his legal practice.   [1924 2nd ed.]

MEYSEY-THOMPSON, Ernest Claude. Spellow Hill, Knaresborough, Yorkshire. Bachelors'. S. of Sir H.S. Meysey-Thompson, Bart. B. 1859; m. 1894, Alice, d. of Col. Joicey, MP. Educ. at Eton and, Trinity Coll., Cambridge. Maj. Yorkshire Hussars Yeomanry. Lieut.-Col. R.F.A. J.P. for N. and W. Riding of Yorkshire. Chairman of Yorkshire Liberal Unionist Federation. A Director of Hathorn, Davy and Company, Engineers, Leeds. Was Aide-de-Camp to Earl of Onslow when Gov. of New Zealand. A Unionist, specially interested in Agriculture and Imperial and Colonial questions. Unsuccessfully contested the Buckrose division of Yorkshire in 1900. Sat for the Handsworth division of Staffordshire from January 1906 to December 1918 and for the Handsworth division of Birmingham from December 1918 until he retired in October 1922. Died 28 February 1944.   [1922]

MIDDLEBROOK, Sir William. Holbech Hill, Scarborough. Reform, and National Liberal. S. of John Middlebrook, Esq., Woollen Manufacturer, of Birstall. B. 22 February 1851 at Birstall; m. 1880, Alma, d. of William Jackson, Esq., of Morley (she died 1925). Educ. at Huddersfield Coll. A Solicitor, admitted 1873. A member of Morley Town Council from 1892; Alderman 1894 and Mayor 1897 and 1904; Lord Mayor of Leeds 1910-11. Chairman of Local Legislation Committee House of Commons 1913-21. Knighted 1916. A Liberal. First elected for S. Leeds in February 1909 and sat until he was defeated in November 1922. Created Bart. 1930. A Wesleyan Methodist. Died 30 June 1936.   [1922]

MIDDLETON, George. 61 Kidderminster Road, West Croydon. S. of W. Middleton, Esq., of Great Linford, Newport Pagnell. B. 1876; m. 12 August 1912, Edith, d. of William Cornes, Esq., of Crewe. Educ. at the Church Elementary School, Ramsey. Editor of *The Post*, at one time Editor of the *Postal Clerks' Herald*, and later of the *Postal and Telegraph Record*. J.P. for Cheshire. Parliamentary Private Secretary to R. Richards, Under-Secretary of State for India 1924. 2nd Church Commissioner 1924 and 1929-30, 1st Commissioner 1930-38. A Labour Member. Unsuccessfully contested the Altrincham division of Cheshire in 1918. Elected for Carlisle November 1922 and December 1923, defeated October 1924. Re-elected for Carlisle in May 1929 and sat until he was defeated in October 1931. Member of Church Assembly. Knighted 1935. Died 25 October 1938.   [1931 2nd ed.]

MILDMAY, Lieut.-Col. Rt. Hon. Francis Bingham. 46 Berkeley Square, London. Shoreham Place, Kent. Flete, Ivy Bridge, and Mothecombe House, Devon. Travellers', Brooks's, Marlborough, Turf, I. Zingari, and Hurlingham. S. of Henry Bingham Mildmay, Esq., of Flete, S. Devon, by his marriage with Miss Georgina Bulteel, a grand-d. of the 2nd Earl Grey, the distinguished statesman. B. 1861; m. 1906, Alice, d. of Seymour Grenfell, Esq., of Taplow.

Educ. at Eton, and Trinity Coll., Cambridge; B.A. Lieut.-Col. West Kent Imperial Yeomanry. Served in the South African campaign; also in France throughout the war. Four times mentioned in despatches. PC. 1916. Sat for the Totnes division of Devonshire from 1885 until he retired in October 1922. Elected as a Liberal in 1885 but joined the Liberal Unionist Group in 1886 and sat as a Unionist from January 1910. Created Baron Mildmay of Flete 1922. Director of Great Western Railway. Lord-Lieut. of Devon 1928-36, J.P. and Dept.-Lieut. for Devon. Died 8 February 1947.
[1922]

MILLAR, Sir James Duncan, K.C. 18 Abercromby Place, Edinburgh. Remony Lodge, Aberfeldy. Reform, and Liberal. University, Edinburgh. S. of John Millar, Esq., M.D., of Edinburgh, and Christian, d. of James Duncan, Esq., W.S., Edinburgh. B. 1871; m. 1906, Ella, d. of Alexander P. Forrester-Paton, Esq., of Inglewood, Alloa. Educ. at Edinburgh University; M.A., LL.B. An Advocate of the Scottish bar 1896, and Barrister-at-Law, Middle Temple 1897; Senior Advocate Depute 1913-16. K.C. 1914. and Knight Bach. 1932. A Liberal until 1931, thereafter a Liberal National Member. Sat for St. Andrews Burghs from January to December 1910, when he was defeated, and for Lanarkshire N.E. from March 1911 to December 1918, when he unsuccessfully contested the Motherwell division of Lanarkshire. Sat for E. Fife from November 1922 to October 1924, when he was defeated, and from May 1929 until his death on 10 December 1932.
[1933]

MILLINGTON, Ernest Rogers. Continued in House after 1945: full entry in Volume IV.

MILLS, Sir Frederick, Bart. 18 Campden Hill Gate, London. S. of Leighton Mills, Esq., of Plymouth. B. 23 April 1865; m. 1st, 19 August 1889, Edith Mary, d. of George Topham, Esq., of Tynemouth (she died 18 November 1916); secondly, 10 April 1918, Mary Kathleen, d. of Ernest Dawkins, Esq., of St. Albans. Educ. privately,

and at Durham University. An Engineer; Chairman of Ebbw Vale Steel, Iron and Coal Company. Dept.-Lieut., and J.P. for Monmouthshire, High Sheriff 1912. A Conservative. Elected for E. Leyton in October 1931 and sat until he retired in June 1945. Created Bart. 1921. Died 31 December 1953.
[1945]

MILLS, Maj. John Digby, T.D. Bisterne, Ringwood, Hampshire. Cavalry. S. of the Rev. Cecil Mills, of Bisterne, and of Taverham Hall, Norfolk, Rector of Barford, Warwick, and Anne, d. of Capt. F.H.G. Nicolls, 4th Dragoon Guards. B. 29 September 1879; m. 16 June 1918, Carola (J.P. for Hampshire 1937), d. of Judge S.P. Tuck, of the International Court of Appeals, Egypt, and of Maryland, U.S.A. Educ. at Charterhouse, and Oriel Coll., Oxford. Dept.-Lieut. and J.P. for Hampshire; a Verderer of the New Forest 1922-38 and 1945-55. Maj. Warwickshire Yeomanry; served in Gallipoli, Egypt, and in France 1915-18 (despatches 3 times); Lieut. 8th (H.D.) Battalion Hampshire Regiment 1939-May 1940; Col. 1941. Commanded New Forest Group Home Guard May 1940-43 (Col. 1941-43); Lieut.-Col. 2nd i/c Hampshire Zone June 1943. 2nd Church Estates Commissioner 1943-45. Chairman of Hampshire Standing Joint Committee from 1928 and of New Forest and Christchurch division Conservative Association 1925-32. A Conservative. Elected for the New Forest and Christchurch division of Hampshire in February 1932 and sat until he retired in June 1945. Member of House of Laity of Church of England 1944-60. Church Commissioner 1948-58. Knighted 1958. Member of Hampshire County Council 1907-64, Alderman 1925-64. Died 2 July 1972.
[1945]

MILLS, John Edmund. 4 Lassa Road, Eltham, Kent. S. of Charles Mills, Esq., Chief Inspector Water Police, Western Australia. B. 2 September 1882 at Perth, Western Australia; m. 1903, Florence, d. of John Lashbrook, Esq. Educ. at the Higher Grade School, North Road, Plymouth. An Engineer. Chairman of the Shops Stewards' Committee, Woolwich

Arsenal, and later as Secretary; Secretary of Towns Committee. A Labour Member. Sat for Dartford division of Kent from March 1920-November 1922, when he was defeated. Re-elected for the Dartford division of Kent in December 1923. Unsuccessfully contested the same division in October 1924. Re-elected again for the Dartford division of Kent in May 1929 and sat until he was defeated in October 1931. Alderman, Woolwich Borough Council. Parliamentary Private Secretary to Rt. Hon. J. Wedgwood, Chancellor of Duchy of Lancaster 1924. President of National Housing Association 1921. Died 11 November 1951.

[1931 2nd ed.]

MILNE, Charles Black, K.C. 9 Northumberland Street, Edinburgh. S. of James Milne, Esq., M.D., L.R.C.S. Edinburgh, of Huntly, Aberdeenshire. B. 1879; m. 1957, Hilda Christian Roberts. Educ. at University of Edinburgh, M.A., LL.B. Advocate Scottish bar 1904. A Conservative. Unsuccessfully contested Edinburgh E. in October 1924 and Dumbarton Burghs in May 1929. Elected for W. Fife in October 1931 and sat until he was defeated in November 1935. K.C. 1932. Sheriff of Dumfries and Galloway 1939-60. Died 17 February 1960.   [1935]

MILNER, Rt. Hon. James. Continued in House after 1945: full entry in Volume IV.

MITCHELL, Edward Rosslyn. 20 Queensborough Gardens, and 138 West George Street, Glasgow. S. of Edward John Mitchell, Esq. B. 16 May 1879; m. 1st, 2 March 1907, Regina Constance, d. of James Taylor Bell, Esq., of Glasgow (she died 1936); secondly, Marguerite Antoinette Marie, d. of Donald Fergusson, Esq. Educ. at Hillhead High School, and University of Glasgow; M.A. 1900, LL.B. 1904. Admitted a Solicitor 1904, Notary Public 1905. Partner in the firm of Rosslyn Mitchell and Tullis Cochran. Member of Glasgow Town Council 1909-25 and from 1932; J.P. President Students Representative Council 1902; Gov. of Glasgow School of Art and of W. of Scotland Commercial Coll. A Labour Member. Unsuccessfully contested Buteshire

as a Liberal in December 1910, and Glasgow Central as a Labour candidate in November 1922 and December 1923. Elected for Paisley in October 1924 and sat until he retired in May 1929. Died 31 October 1965.   [1929]

MITCHELL, Col. Harold Paton. 12 Catherine Place, London. Tulliallan Castle, Kincardine-on-Forth. Carlton, Bath, and Alpine. New, Edinburgh. S. of Col. Alexander Mitchell. B. 21 May 1900; m. 1947, Mary, d. of William Pringle, Esq. Educ. at Eton, Royal Military Coll., Sandhurst, and University Coll., Oxford, M.A., F.R.G.S. Parliamentary Private Secretary to Lieut.-Col. D.J. Colville, Secretary of Overseas Trade Department November 1931-35, and to Ralph Assheton, Parliamentary Secretary Ministry of Labour and National Service September 1939-February 1942, and when Parliamentary Secretary Ministry of Supply February 1942. British Liaison Officer, Polish Forces 1940-41. Anti-Aircraft Command Welfare Officer. Dept.-Lieut., and J.P. for Clackmannanshire. Director of L. and N.E. Railway. Vice-Chairman Conservative and Unionist Party Organization March 1942-August 1945. A National Conservative. Unsuccessfully contested the Clackmannan and Eastern division of Stirling and Clackmannan in May 1929. Elected for the Brentford and Chiswick division of Middlesex in October 1931 and sat until he was defeated in July 1945. Created Bart. 1945. Honorary Fellow of University Coll., Oxford 1972. Author of works on ski-ing and the Caribbean. Research Professor of Latin-American Studies at Rollins Coll., Florida. Lecturer at Stanford University, California 1959-65.*   [1945]

MITCHELL, Robert Macgregor. 13 Gloucester Place, Edinburgh. 3 Atholl Place, Perth. Royal, and Ancient, St. Andrews. S. of Robert Mitchell, Esq., Solicitor, of Perth. B. at Perth 1875. Unmarried. Educ. at Perth Academy, St. Andrews University, and Edinburgh University. Advocate 1914, a Solicitor in Perth. Member of Perth Town Council. Started the Scottish County Cricket Championship. A Liberal. Elected for the

Perth division of Perth and Kinross in December 1923 and sat until he was defeated in October 1924. K.C. 1924. Chairman of Scottish Land Court, with the Judicial title of Lord Macgregor Mitchell 1934-38. Rector of St. Andrews University 1937-38. Died 25 April 1938.   [1924 2nd ed.]

MITCHELL, Stephen. Gilkerscleugh, Abington, Lanarkshire. Carlton, Caledonian, and St. Stephen's. Western, Glasgow. Stirling County. S. of Stephen Mitchell, Esq., of Boquhan, Kippen. B. 1884; m. 1910, Helen Beatrice, d. of Alexander Murdoch, Esq. Educ. at Loretto School, and Jesus Coll., Cambridge. A Tobacco Manufacturer; Director of The Imperial Tobacco Company Limited. A Conservative. Elected for the Lanark division of Lanarkshire in October 1924 and sat until he was defeated in May 1929. High Sheriff of Gloucestershire 1945-46. Died 7 June 1951.   [1929]

MITCHELL, William Foot. 186 St. James's Court, London. Quendon Hall, Quendon, Essex. Carlton, and St. Stephen's. S. of W.S. Mitchell, Esq., and Harriet Foot. B. 26 June 1859; m. 1886, Elizabeth Hannah, d. of Leonard Hadley, Esq., of Gloucester (she died 1937). Educ. privately in London and Paris. Director of Shell Transport and Trading Company Limited, and Chartered Bank of India, Australia and China. A Conservative. Sat for the Dartford division of Kent from January to December 1910, when he was defeated. Sat for the Saffron Walden division of Essex from November 1922 until he retired in May 1929. Representative in Japan of Messrs. Samuel Samuel and Company 1886-1900. Knighted 1929. J.P. for Essex. Died 31 July 1947.   [1929]

MITCHELL, Sir William Lane. See LANE-MITCHELL, Sir William.

MITCHELL-THOMSON, Rt. Hon. Sir William Lowson, Bart., K.B.E. 4 Whitehall Court, London. Carlton. S. of Sir Mitchell Mitchell-Thomson, 1st Bart., of Polmood. B. 15 April 1877; m. 1st, 6 July 1909, Madeline, d. of Sir Malcolm McEacharn, of Melbourne (divorced 1932);

secondly, 1933, Mrs. Effie Lilian Loder Johnson, d. of Lieut.-Col. C. Brennan. Educ. at Winchester, Balliol Coll., Oxford and Edinburgh Universities. British representative on Supreme Economic Council and on Blockade Council in Paris 1919. Parliamentary Secretary Ministry of Food 1920-21; Parliamentary Secretary Board of Trade 1921-22. Postmaster-Gen. from November 1924-June 1929. Chief Civil Commissioner during Gen. Strike May 1926. PC. 1924. A Conservative. Sat for N.W. Lanarkshire from January 1906 to January 1910, when he was defeated, for N. Down from April 1910 to December 1918, for the Maryhill division of Glasgow from December 1918 to November 1922, when he was defeated, and for S. Croydon from December 1923 until January 1932, when he was created Baron Selsdon. Succeeded as Bart. 1918. K.B.E. 1918. Chairman of Television Advisory Committee 1934-38. Died 24 December 1938.   [1932]

MITCHESON, Sir George Gibson. York Cottage, Green Lane, Burnham, Buckinghamshire. Carlton, and Constitutional. S. of Thomas Mitcheson, Esq., Solicitor, of Heckmondwike, Yorkshire. B. 27 June 1883; m. 1911, Eveline Anne, d. of Charles James Critchley, Esq., of Batley. Educ. privately. A Solicitor. Joint Managing Director of Standard Industrial Trust Limited; member of Worshipful Company of Gardeners. Vice-President National Temperance Hospital and National Association of Building Societies. Knight Bach. 1936. Chairman of Political Committee and Vice-Chairman of Constitutional Club; Chairman of Hosa Research Laboratories. A National Conservative. Unsuccessfully contested Bradford S. in 1923 and 1924. Elected for S.W. St. Pancras in October 1931 and sat until he retired in June 1945. Died 18 June 1955.   [1945]

MOLES, Rt. Hon. Thomas. Claremont, Ardenlee Avenue, Belfast. Constitutional. S. of Edward Moles, Esq., of Ardmore. B. November 1871; m. 20 March 1901, 1901, Charlotte, d. of M. Branigan, Esq., of Ballycastle. Educ. at the Collegiate School, Ballymena. Journalist 1893; Leader writer *Belfast Telegraph* 1909-24; Managing Editor from 1924 to 1937; member of the Secretariat, Irish Convention 1917-18, and Irish Representative British Press party's visit to Canada 1911. First Member returned to Northern Ireland Parliament 1921, of which he was Dept. Speaker. PC. (Northern Ireland) 1923. A Conservative. Sat for the Ormeau division of Belfast from 1918-22. Returned unopposed for S. Belfast from November 1922 and sat until he retired in May 1929. Sat in the Parliament of Northern Ireland for S. Belfast 1921-29 and for the Ballynafeigh division of Belfast 1929-37. Died 3 February 1937.   [1929]

MOLLOY, Maj. Leonard Greenham Star, D.S.O. 3 Brighton Parade, Blackpool. Cavalry, and 1900. S. of Richard Molloy, Esq., Civil Servant, of Rathgar, Co. Dublin. B. 22 November 1861 at Naas, Co. Kildare; m. 7 December 1922, Ethel Mary d. of James Willan, Esq., of Todmorden and Manchester. Educ. privately, and at Trinity Coll., Dublin. Entered the medical profession 1882. Kt. of Grace of St. John of Jerusalem 1921; Honorary Life Member, Examiner and Lecturer St. John Ambulance Association; District Surgeon and Chairman N.E. Lancashire Corps and Division St. John Ambulance Brigade. Served during the war with the Duke of Lancaster's Own Own Yeomanry; Maj. and second in command 1/1 Regiment. Chairman of various organizations in Blackpool; Honorary Consulting Physician Victoria Hospital, Blackpool; Medical Referee under the Workmen's Compensation Act; Consulting Physician, Rossall School; contributor to the Medical press. A Conservative. Elected for Blackpool in November 1922 and sat until he retired in December 1923. Practised in Blackpool 1891-1923 and in Monte Carlo and Harley Street 1924-36. Died 19 February 1937.   [1923]

MOLONEY, Patrick James. See MALONEY, Patrick James.

MOLSON, Arthur Hugh Elsdale. Continued in House after 1945: full entry in Volume IV.

MOLSON, Maj. John Elsdale, T.D. 21 St. James's Court, Buckingham Gate, London. Goring Hall, Worthing. Carlton, Oxford & Cambridge, and 1900. S. of Samuel Elsdale and Agnes Molson. B. at Montreal, Canada 6 August 1863; m. 1891, Mary, d. of Dr. Leeson. Educ. at Cheltenham Coll., and Emmanuel Coll., Cambridge. M.D., B.Ch. (Cambridge), qualified 1889. Maj. R.A.M.C. (T.). A Conservative. Unsuccessfully contested N.E. Bethnal Green in January and December 1910. Elected for the Gainsborough division of Lincolnshire in December 1918 and sat until he was defeated in December 1923. J.P. for W. Sussex. Died 28 November 1925.   [1923]

MOND, Rt. Hon. Sir Alfred Moritz, Bart. 35 Lowndes Square, London. Melchet Court, Nr. Romsey. Reform, Athenaeum, and Burlington Fine Arts. Bristol Channel Yacht, and Swansea County. S. of Dr. Ludwig Mond, F.R.S., of Winnington Hall, Northwich. B. 23 October 1868; m. 16 June 1894, Violet Mabel, D.B.E., d. of James Henry Goetze, Esq. Educ. at Cheltenham, St. John's Coll., Cambridge, and Edinburgh. Created Bart. 1910; PC. 1913. A Barrister-at-Law, Inner Temple 1894; First Commissioner of Works 1916-21; Minister of Health 1921-22. A Liberal until 1926, thereafter a Conservative. Unsuccessfully contested S. Salford in 1900. Sat for Chester from 1906-January 1910, for Swansea Town from January 1910-18, for Swansea W. from 1918-23. Unsuccessfully contested Swansea W. in December 1923. Elected for the Carmarthen division of Carmarthenshire in August 1924 and October 1924, as a Liberal. Joined the Conservative Party in January 1926 after a disagreement with Lloyd George's land policy. Sat until June 1928 when he was created Baron Melchett. F.R.S. 1930. Chairman of I.C.I. from 1926. Died 27 December 1930.   [1928]

MOND, Hon. Henry Ludwig. 45 Green Street, London. Woodfalls, Melchet Court, Romsey. Carlton, Wellington, Ranelagh, and Hurlingham. S. of Alfred, 1st Baron Melchett. B. 10 May 1898; m. 28 January 1920, Amy Gwen, d. of E.J. Wilson, Esq., of Johannesburg. Educ. at Winchester. Served in France 1915-18, with South Wales Borderers. A Director of Imperial Chemical Industries Limited, and of Barclay's Bank; Dept.-Chairman of the Mond Nickel Company Limited; Chairman of the London Committee of the International Nickel Company Limited, of Canada. Member of Council of National Confederation of Employers' Organizations; a Director of other Industrial undertakings. A Conservative. Sat as Liberal MP for the Isle of Ely from 1923-24 when he was defeated. Elected as Conservative MP for the E. Toxteth division of Liverpool in March and May 1929 and sat until December 1930 when he succeeded to the Peerage as Baron Melchett. Joined the Conservative Party with his father in January 1926 after a disagreement with Lloyd George's land policy. Converted to Judaism 1933. Dept.-Chairman of I.C.I. 1940-47. Died at Miami 22 January 1949.

[1929 2nd ed.]

MONSELL, Rt. Hon. Sir Bolton Meredith Eyres, G.B.E. See EYRES-MONSELL, Rt. Hon. Sir Bolton Meredith, G.B.E.

MONTAGU, Rt. Hon. Edwin Samuel. 4 Gordon Place, London. Breccles Hall, Attleborough. 2nd s. of 1st Lord Swaythling. B. 6 February 1879; m. 1915, Hon. Venetia Stanley, d. of Lord Sheffield. Educ. at Clifton Coll., City of London School, and Trinity Coll., Cambridge. Was Parliamentary Under-Secretary of State for India February 1910-February 1914; Financial Secretary to the Treasury February 1914 to February 1915 and May 1915 to July 1916. Chancellor of Duchy of Lancaster February to May 1915, and January to July 1916. Minister of Munitions July to December 1916; Vice-Chairman Reconstruction Committee till July 1917; Secretary of State for India July 1917-March 1922 when he resigned. PC. 1915. Was Parliamentary Private Secretary (unpaid) to Mr. Asquith when Chancellor of the Exchequer 1906-08 and Prime Minister 1908-10. Member of Royal Commission on Proportional Representation. A Liberal. Sat for W. Cambridgeshire 1906-18, and for Cambridgeshire from December 1918 to

November 1922 when he was defeated. Died 15 November 1924. [1922]

MONTAGUE, Frederick. Continued in House after 1945: full entry in Volume IV.

MONTAGUE-BARLOW, Rt. Hon. Sir Clement Anderson, K.B.E. See BARLOW, Rt. Hon. Sir Clement Anderson, K.B.E.

MONTAGU-DOUGLAS-SCOTT, Lord William Walter. Continued in House after 1945: full entry in Volume IV.

MOORE, Maj.-Gen. Hon. Sir Newton James, K.C.M.G., V.D. 16 Northumberland Avenue, London. Mayes Park, Warnham, Sussex. Royal Thomas Yacht, and Carlton. Weld, and South West, Western Australia. S. of James Moore, Esq., J.P., of Bunbury, Western Australia. B. 17 May 1870; m. 6 April 1897, Isabel, d. of John Lowrie, Esq., of Western Australia. Educ. in State School, and Prince Alfred Coll., Adelaide, South Australia. A Surveyor and Civil Engineer. President Institute of Surveyors, Western Australia; P. Prov. Grand Master Freemasons, Western Australia; P.G. Warden of Scotland. Sat for Bunbury, Western Australia from 1904-11. Premier of Western Australia 1906-10; in addition held the portfolios of Justice, Treasurer, Minister for Lands, and Minister for Agriculture. Agent-Gen. for Western Australia in London 1911-18. G.O.C. A.I.F. in United Kingdom 1915-18. K.C.M.G. 1910. Chairman of Standing Orders Committee 1922-23 and 1924-28. Chairman and Director of several Public Companies. Conservative. Elected for St. George's, Hanover Square in October 1918; sat for N. Islington from December 1918-23 when he retired, and for Richmond, Surrey from October 1924 until he resigned in March 1932. President of Dominion Coal and Steel Corporation of Canada 1932-36. C.M.G. 1908. Died 28 October 1936.

[1932]

MOORE, Sir Thomas Cecil Russell. Continued in House after 1945: full entry in Volume IV.

MOORE-BRABAZON, Lieut.-Col. Rt. Hon. John Theodore Cuthbert, M.C. 38 Eaton Square, London. White's, and R.Y.S. S. of Col. J. Moore-Brabazon, of Tara Hall, Co. Meath. B. 8 February 1884; m. 1906, Hilda Mary, d. of Charles Krabbe, Esq., of Colina, Buenos Ayres. Educ. at Harrow, and Trinity Coll., Cambridge. A pioneer motorist and aviator, responsible for photography in the Flying Corps during the 1914-18 war. Parliamentary Secretary Ministry of Transport October 1923-January 1924, and November 1924-January 1927. Minister of Transport October 1940-May 1941. Minister of Aircraft Production May 1941-February 1942. PC. 1940. A Conservative. Sat for the Chatham division of Rochester from December 1918 until May 1929, when he was defeated. Elected for Wallasey in October 1931 and sat until March 1942 when he was created Baron Brabazon of Tara. Member of London County Council 1931-32. President of Royal Aeronautical Society 1935. G.B.E. 1953. President of Royal Institution 1948-63. Chairman of R101 Enquiry 1930-31. Died 17 May 1964. [1942]

MORDEN, Lieut.-Col. Walter Grant Peterson. 1 and 3 Regent Street, London. Heatherden Hall, Iver Heath, Buckinghamshire. Carlton, Junior Carlton, Royal Thames Yacht, Ranelagh, Royal Automobile, and Canada. S. of Walter Henry and Sarah Anne Morden. B. in Ontario 1880; m. 1909, Doris, d. of Charles G. Henshaw, Esq., of Vancouver. Educ. at Toronto Collegiate Institute. Lieut.-Col. Canadian Overseas Forces 1915-18, Honorary Col. Royal Canadian Hussars and 4th Middlesex Battalion. J.P. for Buckinghamshire. A Conservative. Sat for the Brentford and Chiswick division of Middlesex from December 1918 until he retired in October 1931. Died 25 June 1932. [1931 2nd ed.]

MOREING, Adrian Charles. 62 London Wall, London. S. of Charles Algernon Moreing, Esq. B. 4 July 1892; m. 1934, Dorothy, d. of A.A. Haworth, Esq., of Samlesbury, Lancashire. Educ. at Winchester, and Trinity Coll., Cambridge. A Solicitor. A Partner in Bewick Moreing and Company, Mining Engineers. Member London County Council 1925-34, Chairman of Mental Hospitals Committee, Whip of the Municipal Reform Party (Conservatives) 1927-34. A Conservative. Elected for Preston in October 1931 and sat until his death on 10 July 1940. [1940]

MOREING, Capt. Algernon Henry. 52 South Eaton Place, London. Woodside, Esher, Surrey. Carlton. S. of Charles Algernon Moreing, Esq., M.Inst.C.E. B. 30 September 1889; m. 15 October 1925, Dorothy Maud, d. of J. Holman, Esq., of Roswarne, Camborne. Educ. at Winchester, and Trinity Coll., Cambridge; M.A. and Assoc. M.I.C.E. Partner in the firm of Messrs. Bewick, Moreing and Company, Mining Engineers. Served in France 1915-18. A Constitutionalist. Sat for the Buckrose division of the E. Riding of Yorkshire from 1918-22 as a Coalition Liberal. Elected for the Camborne division of Cornwall as a National Liberal with Conservative support in November 1922 and sat until December 1923 when he contested the seat as the candidate of the Conservative and Lloyd George Liberal associations but was defeated by the Asquithian Liberal candidate. Re-elected for the Camborne division of Cornwall in October 1924, as a Constitutionalist with Conservative but not Liberal support, accepted the Conservative Whip and sat until he was defeated, standing as a Conservative in May 1929. Parliamentary Private Secretary to Sir Eric Geddes, when Minister of Transport, 1920. Master of Merchant Taylors' Company. Died 22 October 1974. [1929]

MOREL, Edmund Dene. Cherry Croft, King's Langley, Hertfordshire. S. of Edmund Morel-de-Ville and Emmeline-de-Horne. B. in Paris 10 July 1873; m. 1896, Mary Richardson, d. of J.W. Richardson, Esq., of Teignmouth, South Devon. Educ. at Eastbourne, and Bedford Modern School. Author and Journalist. Secretary and part founder of the Congo Reform Association 1904-12. Secretary and part founder of the Union of Democratic Control from 1914. Author of *Affairs of West Africa, The British Case in French Congo, Great Britain and the*

Congo, Nigeria: its Peoples and its Problems, King Leopold's Rule in Africa, Truth and the War, Ten Years of Secret Diplomacy, Black Man's Burden, Africa and the Peace of Europe, and *Diplomacy Revealed.* A Labour Member. Elected for Dundee in November 1922 and sat until his death on 12 November 1924. His original name was Georges Edmond Morel-deVille but he adopted the name Edmund Dene Morel on becoming a naturalised British subject in 1896. Editor of *African Mail* 1903-15 and of *Foreign Affairs.* Prospective Liberal candidate for Birkenhead in 1914, but resigned on the outbreak of war. Sentenced to 6 months imprisonment under Defence of the Realm Act 1917. Joined ILP 1918. Vice-President of Anti-Slavery Society. Died 12 November 1924. [1924 2nd ed.]

MORGAN, Lieut.-Col. David Watts, C.B.E., D.S.O. Caemawr Hall, Porth, Glamorganshire. United Services. S. of Thomas Morgan, Esq. B. 18 December 1867 at Skewen, Neath, Glamorgan; m. secondly, Blanche Amy Morgan, Hospital Matron. Educ. at Skewen elementary school, and Glamorgan Evening School. A Mining Engineer 1900-14. Joined the army August 1914. Awarded the D.S.O. in 1918 for valuable services rendered with his "Pick and Shovel" Brigade at Cambrai in November 1917. A Miners' Agent in the Rhondda Valley from January 1898. J.P. A Labour Member. Sat for E. Rhondda from December 1918 until his death on 23 February 1933. Member of Glamorgan County Council, Chairman 1926-28. C.B.E. 1920. Chairman of Welsh Labour Party. Died 23 February 1933. [1933]

MORGAN, Hyacinth Bernard Wenceslaus. Continued in House after 1945: full entry in Volume IV.

MORGAN, John. Arkesden, Newport, Essex. B. 21 October, 1892 at Bath; m. 1921, Mary, d. of William Lord Wright of Scarborough. Educ. at Spurgeons Orphanage, London. A Farmer. *Daily Herald* Agricultural Correspondent 1930-39. Member of Lord Kirkley's Trade Mission to South Africa and Rhodesia 1930. The

B.B.C. Broadcaster "for Farmers only" talks 1933-35, "The Farmer" in Children's Hour 1935-40. Agricultural journalist with the pen-name 'John Sussex.' A Labour Member. Unsuccessfully contested the East Grinstead division of E. Sussex in October 1924, the Maidstone division of Kent in May 1929, the Rugby division of Warwickshire, where the 1929 General Election was delayed until 13 June owing to the death of the original Labour candidate, the Bosworth division of Leicestershire in 1931 and Leicester W. in 1935. Elected for the Doncaster division of the W. Riding of Yorkshire in November 1938 and sat until his death on 4 December 1940. [1941]

MORGAN, Robert Harry. Hamilton House, Mabledon Place, London. Orchard House, Woodrow, Chaddesley-Corbett. S. of Robert Henry Morgan, Esq., Draper, of Dudley. B. 25 January 1880; m. 4 November 1904, Mabel, d. of A.H. Bailey, Esq., of The Trindles, Dudley. Educ. at St. Thomas's H.G. School, Dudley, and Saltley Coll., Birmingham. Head Master of St. Thomas's School, Dudley 1904-07, and of Blue Coat School, Dudley 1907-31; for 10 years member of Dudley Education Committee, of Governing Body of Birmingham University, and of Dudley Training Coll. Director of Manbré and Garton Limited. A National Conservative. Elected for the Stourbridge division of Worcestershire in October 1931 and sat until he was defeated in July 1945. Parliamentary Secretary of National Union of Teachers. Died 28 November 1960. [1945]

MORISON, Rt. Hon. Thomas Brash, K.C. 24 Heriot Row, Edinburgh. Reform, and University. Liberal (Edinburgh). 2nd s. of P. Morison, Esq., S.S.C., Edinburgh. B. in Edinburgh 21 November 1868; m. 1st, 1899, Isabel, 2nd d. of Andrew Hendry, Esq., Solicitor (she died 1934); secondly, 1935, Georgina Morgan, d. of W. Mitchell, Esq., of Markinch. Educ. Edinburgh University, M.A., LL.B., LL.D. Called to the Scottish bar 1891, and the English bar, Middle Temple 1898; K.C. 1906; Advocate Depute 1905-08; Senior Advocate Depute 1908-10. Sheriff of Fife and Kinross 1910-

13; J.P. for Perthshire; Dept.-Chairman Fishery Board for Scotland 1910-13; Commissioner on Northern Lighthouse Board 1910-13; Solicitor-Gen. for Scotland 1913-20; Lord Advocate March 1920-February 1922; PC. and Bencher of Gray's Inn 1920. A Liberal. Unsuccessfully contested W. Perthshire in January 1910. Elected for Inverness-shire in January 1917, and for the Inverness division of Inverness-shire and and Ross and Cromarty in December 1918. Sat until February 1922 when he was appointed Judge of the Court of Session, with the Judicial title of Lord Morison; retired 1937. Treasurer of Gray's Inn 1938. Died 28 July 1945. [1922]

MORLEY, Ralph. Continued in House after 1945: full entry in Volume IV.

MORRIS, Harold Spencer, K.C. 28 Chester Square, London. Reform, and Guards. 2nd s. of Sir Malcolm Morris, K.C.V.O. B. 21 December 1876 in London; m. 26 March 1904, Olga, d. of Emil Teichmann, Esq., of Sitka, Chislehurst. Educ. at Clifton Coll., and Magdalen Coll., Oxford. A Barrister, called to the bar, Inner Temple, 26 January 1899. K.C., 25 February 1921. Recorder of Folkestone 25 February 1921-26. During the war served in France with Coldstream Guards; staff of Guards Division and staff of Royal Air Force. A National Liberal. Elected for Bristol E. in November 1922 and sat until he was defeated in December 1923. Chairman of National Wages Board for Railways 1925. President of Industrial Court 1926-45. M.B.E. 1919. Knighted 1927. Bencher of Inner Temple 1934. Died 11 November 1967. [1923]

MORRIS, John Patrick. 9 Oakhill Avenue, London. S. of Joseph Morris, Esq., of Wigan. B. 21 March 1894; m. 1937, Mary, d. of J. Egan, Esq., of Killarney. Educ. at St. Peter and St. Paul's School, Bolton. Member of London Stock Exchange. A National Conservative. Elected for N. Salford in October 1931 and sat until he retired in June 1945. Served with Royal Engineers 1914-19 and in Burma 1939-45. Died 31 July 1962. [1945]

MORRIS, Owen Temple, K.C. 4 Paper Buildings, Temple, London. Winnecowetts, Lisvane, Cardiff. S. of Frederick Temple Morris, Esq., Physician and Surgeon, of Cardiff. B. 1896; m. 1927, Vera, d. of D.H. Thompson, Esq. A Barrister-at-Law, Gray's Inn 1925, K.C. 1937, at one time a Solicitor. Member of Governing Body and Representative Body of Church in Wales; Chancellor of Diocese of Llandaff from 1935; Honorary Lay Secretary Llandaff Diocesan Conference 1928-35; Vice-President Wales and Monmouth Unionist Council; Chairman Glamorgan Provincial Unionist Council, and of Glamorgan Conservative Education Committee. Member of Governing Body A.C.C.; Chairman Wales and Monmouth Conservative Clubs Advisory Committee, and of Glamorgan Conservative Clubs Council; member of Court of Governors of Welsh University and of Wales and Welsh National Library; Chairman of Wales and Monmouthshire Conservative Education Committee; member of Cymrodorion Society; Honorary Treasury Cardiff Centre St. J., Priory of Wales; Recorder of Merthyr Tydfil 1936-42. Dept. Chairman Glamorgan County Quarter Sessions 1938-48, Pembrokeshire Quarter Sessions 1942-48. Chief Commandant (unpaid) Cardiff Volunteer Special Constabulary. A National Conservative. Unsuccessfully contested the Caerphilly division of Glamorgan in May 1929. Elected for Cardiff E. in October 1931 and sat until March 1942 when he was appointed a County Court Judge. Chairman of Carmarthenshire Quarter Sessions 1942-50. County Court Judge 1942-69. Chairman of Brecknockshire Quarter Sessions 1948-55, Monmouthshire Quarter Sessions 1950-69. Knighted 1967. Assumed surname of Temple-Morris in lieu of Morris 1948.* [1942]

MORRIS, Richard. 3 Central Buildings, Westminster, London. Royal Automobile, and Irish. B. 1869; m. 1893, Jane Jenkins, of Tregarm, Cardiganshire. Educ. as a Schoolmaster, but on coming to London turned his attention to commerce. Supporter of London County Council evening classes in commercial subjects. Was one of Mr. Burns's supporters in the undivided borough of Battersea. A Coalition Liberal. Elected for N. Battersea in December 1918 and sat until he retired in October 1922. Died 26 September 1956. [1922]

MORRIS, Rhys Hopkin. Continued in House after 1945: full entry in Volume IV.

MORRIS-JONES, Sir John Henry. Continued in House after 1945: full entry in Volume IV.

MORRISON, George Alexander. Bell Hotel, Aylesbury. National Liberal. S. of Alexander Morrison, Esq., of Dufftown, Banffshire. B. 30 October 1869; m. 1913, Rachel, d. of Malcolm Campbell, Esq., of Grantown-on-Spey. Educ. at Mortlach Public School, and Aberdeen University, Hon. LL.D. 1930. Rector of Inverness Royal Academy 1910-20; Head Master of Robert Gordon's Coll., Aberdeen 1920-33; President of Educational Institute of Scotland 1930-31. A Liberal Nationalist. Elected for Scottish Universities in March 1934 and sat until he resigned in March 1945. J.P. for City of Aberdeen. Died 8 September 1956. [1945]

MORRISON, Rt. Hon. Herbert Stanley. Continued in House after 1945: full entry in Volume IV.

MORRISON, Hugh. 9 Halkin Street, London. Fonthill House, Tisbury, Wiltshire. Islay House, Islay, N.B. Carlton. S. of Alfred Morrison, Esq. B. 8 June 1868; m. 16 August 1892, Lady (Sophia) Mary Leveson-Gower, d. of 2nd Earl Granville. Educ. at Eton, and Trinity Coll., Cambridge, B.A. High Sheriff of Wiltshire 1904; Dept.-Lieut. and J.P.; member of Wiltshire County Council, the Tisbury Rural District Council, and other bodies. A Conservative. Returned unopposed for the Wilton division of Wiltshire in November 1918. Elected for the Salisbury division of Wiltshire in December 1918 and November 1922, defeated there in December 1923. Re-elected for the Salisbury division in October 1924 and sat until he resigned in February 1931. Died 15 March 1931. [1931 2nd ed.]

MORRISON, John Granville. Continued in House after 1945: full entry in Volume IV.

MORRISON, Robert Craigmyle. 41 Talbot Road, Tottenham, London. S. of James Morrison, Esq. B. 29 October 1881 in Aberdeen; m. 1910, Grace, d. of Thomas Glossop, Esq. Chairman of Waste Food Board, Ministry of Supply from 1941. Member of Metropolitan Water Board 1937-47; Alderman Tottenham Borough Council from 1934; J.P. for Middlesex. A Co-op and Labour Member. Sat for N. Tottenham from November 1922-October 1931, when he was defeated, re-elected for N. Tottenham in November 1935 and sat until October 1945 when he was created Baron Morrison. Member of Wood Green Urban District Council 1914-19, of Middlesex County Council 1919-25. Lord-in-Waiting to the King and Government spokesman in the House of Lords January 1947-September 1948. Parliamentary Secretary to Ministry of Works September 1948-October 1951. PC. 1949. Dept.-Lieut. for Middlesex. Parliamentary Private Secretary to H. Gosling when Minister of Transport in 1924. Joint Parliamentary Private Secretary to Ramsay MacDonald when Prime Minister June 1929-August 1931. Died 25 December 1953. [1945]

MORRISON, Rt. Hon. William Shepherd. Continued in House after 1945: full entry in Volume IV.

MORRISON-BELL, Maj. Sir Arthur Clive, Bart. 7 Great Cumberland Place, London. Harpford House, Sidmouth, Devon. Carlton, Turf, Alpine, and Guards'. S. of Sir Charles Morrison-Bell, 1st Bart., of Otterburn. B. 19 April 1871; m. 21 November 1912, Hon. Lilah Wingfield, d. of 7th Visct. Powerscourt. Educ. at Eton, and Sandhurst. Joined the Scots Guards 1890; retired as Maj. 1908. Was Aide-de-Camp to Maj.-Gen. Sir E. Hutton, Commanding Militia in Canada 1898-99; served in South African War 1899-1902, with the Canadian contingent (despatches); in France 1914-15; and was Aide-de-Camp to Earl of Minto, Gov.-Gen. of Canada 1900-04. Parliamentary Private Secretary 1st Lord of the Admiralty 1919-21, to Chancellor of the Exchequer November 1924-27. Created Bart. 1923. A Conservative. Sat for the Honiton division of Devonshire from January 1910 until he retired in October 1931. Died 16 April 1956.   [1931 2nd ed.]

MORSE, William Ewart. The Croft, Swindon. National Liberal. S. of L.L. Morse, Esq., MP for S. Wiltshire. B. 23 November 1878 at Stratton, near Swindon; m. 17 July 1910, Alma, d. of Hawthorn Thornton, South Africa. Educ. at the High School, Swindon. Director of Limited Company. A Liberal. Unsuccessfully contested the Bridgwater division of Somerset in 1922. Elected for the Bridgwater division of Somerset in December 1923 and sat until he was defeated in October 1924. Unsuccessfully contested the Weston-super-Mare division of Somerset in May 1929. Member of Wiltshire County Council and Swindon Borough Council. Mayor of Swindon. Vice-President of Primitive Methodist Church 1925-26. Died 18 December 1952.   [1924 2nd ed.]

MORT, David Llewellyn. Continued in House after 1945: full entry in Volume IV.

MOSES, James John Hamlyn. House of Commons, London. S. of James Moses, Esq., Shipwright. B. 1873; m. 1897, Agnes Ferris. Educ. at Local Board School, Dartmouth. Methodist local preacher from 1891. Member of Plymouth Town Council until 1945; Mayor 1926-27. Was a Shipwright in Devonport Dockyard. A Labour Member. Unsuccessfully contested the Drake division of Plymouth in December 1923 and October 1924. Elected for the Drake division of Plymouth in May 1929 and sat until he was defeated in October 1931; again defeated in November 1935. A Liberal until 1918 when he joined the Labour Party. J.P. for Devon. Died 28 May 1946.   [1931 2nd ed.]

MOSLEY, Lady Cynthia Blanche. 8 Smith Square, London. D. of Marq. Curzon. B. 23 August 1898; m. 11 May 1920, Sir Oswald Mosley, 6th Bart., MP. Heir-presumptive to the Barony of Ravensdale. A Labour Member until February

1931 when she joined the New Party. Elected for the Stoke division of Stoke-on-Trent in May 1929 and sat until she retired in October 1931. Member of British Union of Fascists from its formation in 1932. Died 16 May 1933.   [1931 2nd ed.]

MOSLEY, Sir Oswald Ernald, Bart. 8 Smith Square, London. White's, and Cavalry. S. of Sir Oswald Mosley, 5th Bart., of Ancoats. B. 16 November 1896; m. 1st, 11 May 1920, Lady Cynthia Curzon, d. of George Nathaniel, Marq. Curzon, K.G. (she died 1933); secondly, 1936, Hon. Diana Mitford, d. of 2nd Baron Redesdale. Educ. at Winchester, and at Royal Military Coll., Sandhurst. Lieut. 16th Lancers; served in France 1914-18. Chancellor of Duchy of Lancaster June 1929-May 1930 when he resigned over the Government's Unemployment policy. Elected as a Conservative for the Harrow division of Middlesex in December 1918, resigned the Conservative Whip in October 1920 and sat as an Independent. Re-elected in November 1922 and December 1923 as an Independent, defeating the Conservative candidate, and joined the Labour Party in May 1924. Sat until October 1924 when he was the unsuccessful Labour candidate in the Ladywood division of Birmingham. Sat for Smethwick from December 1926 until October 1931. Resigned from the Labour Party in February 1931 on the formation of the New Party and unsuccessfully contested the Stoke division of Stoke-on-Trent in October 1931. Unsuccessfully contested N. Kensington in October 1959 and Shoreditch and Finsbury in March 1966 for the Union Movement. Succeeded as Bart. 1928. Founder of British Union of Fascists 1932 and of Union Movement 1948.*   [1931 2nd ed.]

MOSS, Herbert James. 81 Queen's Court, London. S. of Alfred Moss, Esq., of Glasgow. B. 22 February 1883; m. 24 February 1916, Hilda, d. of George Clark, Esq., of the Argentine (she died 1938). Educ. at Glasgow Public School, and Royal Technical Coll. Served at sea in sailing vessels and in steam 1900-17, appointed to Command 1914. Joined R.E. January 1917, retired as Capt.

1920. Head of Commercial Houses in Glasgow; member of Glasgow Corporation 1927-30. A Conservative. Unsuccessfully contested the Shettleston division of Glasgow in May 1929, and the Rutherglen division of Lanarkshire in May 1931. Elected for the Rutherglen division of Lanarkshire in October 1931 and sat until he retired in October 1935, after his constituency party had declined to readopt him. Author of *Windjammer to Westminster* (1941). [1935]

MOTT-RADCLYFFE, Charles Edward. Continued in House after 1945: full entry in Volume IV.

MOULTON, Maj. Hon. Hugh Lawrence Fletcher, M.C. 19 Gunnersbury Avenue, Ealing, London. Garrick, and Savage. S. of Lord Moulton of Bank, Lord of Appeal, and Clara, widow of R.W. Thomson, Esq., of Edinburgh. B. in London 1 April 1876; m. 1st, 30 July 1902, Ida, d. of George Boydell Houghton, Esq., (she died 1933); secondly, 1937, Marie Josephine, d. of S. Bergaentzle, Esq. Educ. at Eton, and King's Coll., Cambridge. A Barrister-at-Law, Middle Temple 1899. Author of *Life of Lord Moulton*, *Fletcher Moulton on Patents*, *Powers and Duties of Education Authorities*, *Business Man's Guides to the Peace Treaty*, *Fletcher Moulton's Abridgement for 1924*, etc. Served in the R.G.A. January 1915 to February 1919; Maj.; M.C. A Liberal. Elected for Salisbury in December 1923 and sat until he was defeated in October 1924. Fellow of Imperial Coll. of Science and Technology. Died 4 January 1962. [1924 2nd ed.]

MOUNT, Sir William Arthur, Bart., C.B.E. Wasing Place, Nr. Reading. Carlton, and Oxford & Cambridge. S. of William George Mount, Esq., MP of Wasing Place, near Reading, and Marianne Emily, d. of Robert Clutterbuck, Esq., of Watford House, Hertfordshire. B. 1866; m. 1899, Hilda, d. of Malcolm Low, Esq., MP of Clatto, Cupar, N.B. Educ. at Eton, and New Coll., Oxford (Hons. Hist.). Called to the bar at the Inner Temple 1893 and was Parliamentary Private Secretary to Sir Michael Hicks-Beach and Mr. Ritchie when Chancellor of the Exchequer. Appointed member of Council of Duchy of Lancaster 1912. Civil member of British Claims Commission in France 1916-17. 2nd Church Estates Commissioner 1919-22. Officer of the Legion of Honour. C.B.E. 1918. Dept.- Lieut. for Berkshire; created Bart. in 1921. A Unionist. Sat for the Newbury division of Berkshire from 1900 to 1906, when he was defeated. Re-elected for the Newbury division in January 1910 and sat until he resigned in May 1922. Ecclesiastical Commissioner 1923-30. Chairman of Berkshire County Council 1926-30. Died 8 December 1930. [1922]

MUFF, George. Woodhall Lane, Stanningley, Leeds. S. of George Muff, Esq., Coal Miner. B. in Bradford 1877; m. 1909, Ellen Eliza, d. of Charles Orford, Esq., of Bath. Educ. at Board School. A Textile Worker. Member of Bradford City Council. Dept.-Lieut. for W. Riding of Yorkshire; J.P. for Bradford. Army Welfare Officer from 1940. A Labour Member. Unsuccessfully contested Bradford S. as a Liberal in December 1918, and, as a Labour candidate, the City of Chester division of Cheshire in November 1922 and December 1923 and Kingston-upon-Hull E. in October 1924. Elected for Kingston-upon-Hull E. in May 1929, defeated October 1931. Re-elected for Kingston-upon-Hull E. in November 1935 and sat until he retired in June 1945. Created Baron Calverley 1945. Died 20 September 1955. [1945]

MUGGERIDGE Henry Thomas Benjamin. 22 Haling Park Road, Croydon. National Labour. B. 26 June 1864; m. 31 July 1893. Educ. at St. John's School. Secretary to Public Companies from 1907. A Writer. Member Croydon Borough Council from 1911; Croydon Education Committee from 1912; Chairman Croydon Electricity Company from 1927. J.P. for Croydon. A Labour Member. Unsuccessfully contested Croydon S. in December 1918, November 1922, December 1923 and October 1924. Elected for the Romford division of Essex in May 1929 and sat until he was defeated in October 1931. Died March 1942. [1931 2nd ed.]

MUIR, John Ramsay Bryce. Pembroke House, Richmond Green, Surrey. National Liberal. S. of the Rev. A Bryce Muir. B. at Otterburn, Northumberland 30 September 1872. Unmarried. Educ. privately, University of Liverpool, and Balliol Coll., Oxford. Professor of Modern History in the Universities of Liverpool 1906-13 and Manchester 1913-21. Author of *Short History of the British Commonwealth*, *Atlas of Modern History*, *Nationalism and Internationalism*, *Expansion of Europe*, *National Self-government*, *Making of British India*, etc. A Liberal. Unsuccessfully contested Rochdale in 1922. Elected for Rochdale in December 1923 and sat until he was defeated in October 1924. Unsuccessfully contested the Combined English Universities in March 1926, Rochdale in May 1929, the Louth division of Lincolnshire in October 1931 and the Scarborough and Whitby division of the N. Riding of Yorkshire in November 1935. Chairman of Organization Committee of Liberal Party 1930-31. Chairman of National Liberal Federation 1931-33, President 1933-36. Died 4 May 1941. [1924 2nd ed.]

MUIR, John William. 250 Cumlodden Drive, Maryhill, Glasgow. B. 1879; m. 1918, Catherine, d. of Mr. Fraser, of Govan. Engineer Co-operator. Parliamentary Secretary Ministry of Pensions January-November 1924. A Labour Member. Unsuccessfully contested the Maryhill division of Glasgow in December 1918. First elected for the Maryhill division of Glasgow in November 1922 and sat until he was defeated in October 1924. Editor of *The Worker*. Gen. Secretary of Workers' Educational Association 1928-31. Died 10 January 1931. [1924 2nd ed.]

MUIRHEAD, Lieut.-Col. Anthony John, M.C. Haseley Court, Oxford. Carlton, Constitutional, and Savile. S. of Lionel Lockhart Muirhead, Esq. B. 4 November 1890. Unmarried. Educ. at Eton, and Magdalen Coll., Oxford. A Landowner, O.C. 100th Worcestershire and Oxfordshire Field Brigade R.A. Parliamentary Private Secretary to the Rt. Hon. Sir John Gilmour August 1931-September 1932, and to the Rt. Hon.

Walter Elliot, September 1932-June 1935, Ministers of Agriculture. Parliamentary Secretary Minister of Labour June 1935-May 1937; Under-Secretary of State for Air May 1937-May 1938. Parliamentary Under-Secretary of State for India and Burma May 1938-September 1939. A Conservative. Elected for the Wells division of Somerset in May 1929 and sat until his death on 29 October 1939. Rejoined army September 1939. Member of Oxfordshire County Council 1925-37. Died 29 October 1939. [1939]

MULCAHY, Richard James. S. of Patrick Mulcahy, Esq. B. 10 May 1886 at Waterford; m. 1919, Mary Josephine, d. of John Ryan, Esq., of Tomcoole, Wexford. An old employee in the Engineering Department of the Post Office. Deported to England for his part in the Easter week rising 1916. A Sinn Fein Member. Elected for the Clontarf division of Dublin in December 1918 but did not take his seat. Member of Dail for the Clontarf division of Dublin to 1921, for N.W. Dublin 1921-23, for N. Dublin 1923-37, for N.W. Dublin in 1938-43, for Tipperary 1944-61. A Pro-Treaty, later Cumann na nGaedheal and Fine Gael Member. Commander-in-Chief of Army 1922, Minister of Defence 1922-24. Minister of Local Government and Public Health 1927-32. Leader of Fine Gael 1944-59. Minister of Education 1948-51 and 1954-57, also Minister for Gaeltacht 1956-57. Member of Senate 1937-38 and 1943-44. Died 16 December 1971. [1922]

MULVEY, Anthony. Continued in House after 1945: full entry in Volume IV.

MUNRO, Patrick. 28 Carlisle Mansions, Carlisle Place, London. Cathedine Cottage, Bwlch, Breconshire. Carlton. S. of Patrick munro, Esq., of Bonar Bridge. B. 9 October 1883; m. 2 October 1911, Jessie Margaret, d. of Edward P. Martin, Esq., of The Hill, Abergavenny. Educ. at Leeds Grammar School, and Christ Church, Oxford. Joined Sudan Political Service 1907, Gov. of Darfur 1923-24, of Khartoum Prov. 1925-29. Order of the Nile, 3rd Class. Private in the Palace of Westminster Home Guard. Parliamentary Private Secretary to Capt. D. Euan Wallace,

MP when Under-Secretary of State, Home Office June 1935 and when Secretary of Overseas Trade Department November 1935. Assistant Whip May 1937. A Junior Lord of the Treasury October 1937-March 1942. A Conservative. Elected for the Llandaff and Barry division of Glamorganshire in October 1931 and sat until his death on 3 May 1942. [1942]

MUNRO, Rt. Hon. Robert. 44 Harley House, Regent's Park, London. Reform, New, and University. Scottish Liberal, Edinburgh. S. of the Rev. Alexander Rose Munro and Margaret, d. of the Rev. John Sinclair. B. 28 May 1868 at Alness, Ross-shire; m. 1st, 1898, Edith Gwladys, d. of the Rev. Llewellyn Evans, of The Parsonage, Peebles (she died 1920); secondly, 1921, Olga Marie, d. of J.G. Grumler, Esq., of Harrogate. Educ. at Aberdeen Grammar School, and Edinburgh University. An Advocate, called to the Scottish bar 1893; Counsel to Inland Revenue 1907; Advocate Depute 1908. K.C. 1910. Lord Advocate October 1913 to December 1916; Secretary for Scotland from December 1916-October 1922. PC. 1913. LL.D. 1919. A Liberal. Sat for Wick Burghs from January 1910 to November 1918. Elected for Roxburgh and Selkirk in December 1918 and sat until October 1922 when he resigned on appointment as Lord Justice Clerk. Lord Justice Clerk, with the judicial title of Lord Alness 1922-33. Created Baron Alness 1934. Lord in Waiting and Government spokesman on Scottish affairs in the House of Lords May 1940-July 1945. Chairman of Scottish War Savings Committee 1941-45. Dept.-Lieut. for City of Edinburgh. Died 6 October 1955. [1922]

MUNRO-LUCAS-TOOTH, Sir Hugh Vere Huntly Duff, Bart. Continued in House after 1945: full entry in Volume IV.

MURCHISON, Sir Charles Kenneth. Hargrave Hall, Kimbolton, Huntingdonshire. Travellers', and Bath. S. of Charles Murchison, Esq., M.D., F.R.S. B. 1872; m. 1st, 1897, Evelyn, d. of the Rev. George Rowe, M.A. (she died 1937); secondly, 1938, Mary Lilian, d. of Rev. H.W. Richards

and widow of Dr. F.D. Crew. Educ. at Clifton, and Wiesbaden. Mayor of Hertford 1902-03; Borough Council 1900-05; London County Council 1907-10. J.P. 1912 and Alderman County Council, Northamptonshire 1927-46. Drove Red Cross Ambulance in France 1915. Attached to Military Intelligence Branch War Office 1916-18. Parliamentary Private Secretary (unpaid) to Sir John Baird, Under-Secretary of State Home Department December 1920 and to Maj. Rt. Hon. G.C. Tryon, Minister of Pensions 1922-December 1923, and from November 1924. Knight Bach. 1927. A Conservative. Prospective candidate for Stirling Burghs in January 1906 but owing to ill-health did not contest the seat and Sir Henry Campbell-Bannerman was returned unopposed. Elected for E. Hull in December 1918, and Huntingdonshire November 1922. Unsuccessfully contested Huntingdonshire in December 1923. Sat for Huntingdonshire from October 1924 until he was defeated in May 1929. Dept.-Chairman of Northamptonshire Quarter Sessions 1926-34, Chairman 1934-46. High Sheriff of Northamptonshire 1942. Died 17 December 1952. [1929]

MURNIN, Hugh. Dean Crescent, Stirling. S. of Michael Murnin, Esq., of Bathgate. B. 12 July 1865; m. 1893, Anne, d. of James McBryde, Esq., of Denny. President of Miners' Federation of Great Britain, and of National Union of Scottish Mineworkers 1920-22. A Labour Member. Sat for Stirling and Falkirk Burghs from November 1922 until he was defeated in December 1923. Re-elected for Stirling and Falkirk Burghs in October 1924 and sat until he was defeated in October 1931. J.P. for Burgh and County of Stirling. A Roman Catholic. Died 11 March 1932. [1931 2nd ed.]

MURRAY, Lieut.-Col. Hon. Arthur Cecil, C.M.G., D.S.O. Elibank, Walkerburn, Peeblesshire. Brooks's, and Bachelors'. 4th s. of 1st Visct. Elibank. B. 27 March 1879; m. 1931, Faith Celli Standing (she died 1942). Served with International Forces in China 1900 (medal); member of Royal Company of Archers. Parliamentary Private Secretary to Sir E. Grey, Secretary of State for Foreign Affairs 1910-14; former parliamentary Private Secretary to the Parliamentary Secretary to Board of Trade and to the Under-Secretary of State for India 1909. Served in 2nd King Edward's Horse with Expeditionary Force 1914-16 (despatches and D.S.O.) Employed Ministry of Munitions (Labour Disputes) 1916; Assistant Military Attaché, Washington 1917, C.M.G. 1919, Political Intelligence Department, Foreign Office 1918. Director North British Railway Company. A Liberal. Sat for Kincardineshire April 1908-December 1918, and for Kincardine and W Aberdeenshire from December 1918 until he was defeated in December 1923. Joined Liberal National Party in 1936. Succeeded to the Peerage as 3rd Visct. Elibank 1951. Died December 1962.   [1923]

MURRAY, Rt. Hon. Charles David, K.C., C.M.G. 62 Great King Street, Edinburgh. 1900. Scottish Conservative, and Northern, Edinburgh. S. of David William Murray, Esq., Silk Broker, of London. B. in London 20 October 1866; m. 1896, Annie Florence, d. of David Nicholson, Esq., of Edinburgh. Educ. at Edinburgh Academy, and Edinburgh University. Advocate at Scottish bar 1889; K.C. 1907. Maj. Forth Division R.E. (V.), resigned 1907; War Office Staff 1915-17; Lieut.-Col. (Temporary) in army July 1917; Director of National Service for Scotland 1917; Sheriff of Renfrew and Bute 1918 (resigned). Advocate Depute 1918. LL.D. Edinburgh 1919. C.M.G. (Mil.Div.) 1918. Solicitor-Gen. for Scotland March 1920-March 1922. A Unionist. Unsuccessfully contested S. Edinburgh in December 1910. Elected for S. Edinburgh in December 1918 and sat until he retired in October 1922. Dean of Faculty of Advocates 1919-20. Lord-Advocate March-October 1922. PC. March 1922. Judge of Court of Session, with judicial title of Lord Murray 1922-36. Died 9 June 1936.   [1922]

MURRAY, Hon. Charles Gideon. 6 St. James's Court, Buckingham Gate, London. Carlton, Brooks's, and Bachelors'. New, Edinburgh. Western, Glasgow. S. and heir to 1st Visct. and 10th Baron Elibank of Elibank, Co. Selkirk. B. 1877; m. 1908, Mrs. Aspinwall, widow of Lieut.-Col. Aspinwall, 3rd D.G's. and d. of Henry Robarts Madocks, Esq., of Glanywern, N. Wales. Educ. abroad, and at Blairlodge, Scotland. Colonial Civil Service 1898-1917, New Guinea and South Africa. From 1909-17 Administrator of St. Vincent and St. Lucia, West Indies; 1917-18 Food Commissioner Glasgow and West of Scotland. Author of a *United West Indies*, Silver Medal from Royal Society of Arts for paper on *Road to South African Union*. Queen's Medal (South Africa) and Coronation Medal 1911. Member of the Speaker's Parliamentary Conference on Federal Devolution 1919-20. A Coalition Unionist until February 1922 when he withdrew his support from the Coalition. Elected for the St. Rollox division of Glasgow in December 1918 and sat until he retired in October 1922. Succeeded to Peerage as 2nd Visct. Elibank 1927. Chairman of Federation of Chambers of Commerce of British Empire 1934-37. Dept.-Lieut. for Peeblesshire, Lord-Lieut. 1934-45. Died in in Capetown 12 March 1951.   [1922]

MURRAY, Dr. Donald. 4 St. Albans Road, London. National Liberal. S. of Alan Murray, Esq., of Stornoway. B. at Stornoway 21 October 1862; m. 1898, Janet Catherine Grace, d. of Alexander Macpherson, Esq., of Stornoway. Studied medicine at Glasgow University. M.B. and C.M. 1890; D.P.H. Aberdeen University 1910. Medical Officer of Health for Lewis and Burgh of Stornoway; School Medical Officer for Lewis and western portion of Ross and Cromarty. President of Glasgow University Medical Chirurgical Society 1890, and of the University Liberal Club 1889-90. Chairman of the Stornoway School Board 1905-10. J.P. for Ross and Cromarty. A Liberal. Elected for the Western Isles division of Invernessshire and Ross and Cromarty in December 1918 and sat until he was defeated in November 1922. Died 6 July 1923.
                    [1922]

MURRAY, James Dixon. Continued in House after 1945: full entry in Volume IV.

MURRAY, John. Ewelme Down, Wallingford. Reform. S. of F.R. Murray, Esq., of Fraserburgh, N.B. B. at Fraserburgh 28 February 1879; m. 1921, Ellen, widow of George Harwood, Esq., MP for Bolton, and d. of Sir Alfred Hopkinson, K.C. MP. Educ. at Robert Gordon's Coll., Aberdeen, Aberdeen University, and Christ Church, Oxford. Student and Tutor and Censor of Christ Church, Oxford and Fellow of Merton Coll., Oxford. Chairman of Central Profiteering Committee 1920-21. Parliamentary Private Secretary to Mr. Neal, Ministry of Transport. A Liberal. First elected for W. Leeds in December 1918 and sat until he was defeated in December 1923. Unsuccessfully contested Kirkcaldy Burghs in October 1924 and the Ripon division of the W. Riding of Yorkshire in December 1925. Principal of the University Coll. of South-West, Exeter 1926-51. Died 28 December 1964.

[1923]

MURRAY, Robert. 19 Arthurkie Street, Barrhead, Renfrewshire. S. of Robert Murray, Esq., of Bridgeton. B. 30 June 1869; m. 1894, Margaret McKinlay (she died 1944). A Brass-finisher, Pattern-maker, Book-seller, Journalist and Author. Sub-editor of the *Scottish Co-operator*; Editor 1924-27. A Labour Member. Unsuccessfully contested Renfrew W. in 1918. Elected for Renfrew W. in November 1922 and sat until he was defeated in October 1924. J.P. for Renfrewshire. Director of Scottish Cooperative Wholesale Society 1927-39. Member of Evangelical Union Congregational Church. Member of Neilston Parish Council 1894-1922. Died 9 August 1950.

[1924 2nd ed.]

MURRAY, Sir Thomas David King, K.C. 23 India Street, Edinburgh. Constitutional, and University. Conservative, Edinburgh. Western, Glasgow. S. of James Murray, Esq., of Bothwell, Lanarkshire. B. 29 March 1884; m. 1946, Edith Lilian Archer. Educ. at Hamilton Academy, Glasgow High School, and University of Glasgow, M.A., B.Sc., LL.B., F.R.S.E. Advocate, Scotland 1910. Lieut. R.N.V.R. 1916-18. Junior Counsel to the Treasury in Scotland 1927-28; Sheriff Substitute of Lanarkshire 1928-33; Senior Advocate Depute 1936-38; Chairman of Scottish Land Court with the Judicial Title of Lord Murray 1938-41; Solicitor-Gen. for Scotland from June 1941-July 1945. A Conservative. Unsuccessfully contested the Coatbridge division of Lanarkshire in November 1935. Elected for N. Midlothian in February 1943 and sat until he retired in June 1945. K.C. 1933. Knighted 1941. Chairman of Scottish Coalfields Committee 1942-44. Judge of Court of Session, with judicial title of Lord Birnam 1945-55. Died 5 June 1955.

[1945]

MURRAY, Maj. William, O.B.E. (Mil.) 98 Park Street, London. Murraythwaite, Ecclefechan, N.B. Carlton, and Arthur's. New, Edinburgh. Eld. s. of Capt. John Murray, R.N., of Murraythwaite. B. 1865; m. 1892, Evelyn, d. of John Bruce, Esq., of 13 Ainslie Place, Edinburgh. Educ. privately, and at Magdalen Coll., Oxford. Advocate Scottish bar 1891; A Farmer and Landowner. Capt. 5th K.O. Scottish Borderers 1899-1912. A Coalition Unionist. Unsuccessfully contested Dumfries Burghs in 1895 and 1900 and Dumfriesshire in January and December 1910. Elected for Dumfriesshire in December 1918 and sat until he retired in October 1922. Died 5 March 1923. [1922]

MURRAY-PHILIPSON, Hylton Ralph. Stobo Castle, Peebles-shire. Carlton, and R.A.F. S. of Hylton Philipson, Esq., of 6 Sussex Square, London, and the Hon. Mrs. Philipson, d. of 10th Baron Elibank. B. 12 November 1902; m. 1923, Monica, d. of W.C. Beasley-Robinson, Esq. Educ. at Eton. Chairman of North Eastern Marine Engineering Company, Wallsend; Director of other companies. J.P., and County Councillor for Peebles-shire 1925-33; member of Royal Company of Archers, King's Bodyguard for Scotland. Squadron Leader Commanding City of Edinburgh Squadron A.A.F.; Air Force Member Edinburgh T.A. Assumed the surname Murray-Philipson in lieu of Philipson in 1926. A National Conservative. Unsuccessfully contested Peebles and Southern division of Midlothian in May 1929. Elected for the Twickenham division of Middlesex in September 1932 and sat until his death on 24 May 1934.

[1934]

MURRELL, Frank Edric Joseph. Holmwood, South Wood, Weston-super-Mare. National Liberal. S. of Capt. Frederick Murrell, J.P., and Catherine Murrell, of St. Oryth, Barry, Glamorgan. B. in London 1874; m. 1906, youngest d. of James Howell, Esq., J.P., of Cardiff. Educ. at Lewisham House, Weston-super-Mare. A Master Printer 1897; member of Barry Urban District Council 1908-15; member of Executive of Master Printers; Representative for Wales on the National Joint Industrial Council of the Printing Industry. A Liberal. Unsuccessfully contested the Weston-super-Mare division of Somerset in 1922. Elected for the Weston-super-Mare division of Somerset in December 1923 and sat until he was defeated in October 1924. Liveryman of Stationers Company. Died 1 April 1931.

[1924 2nd ed.]

MYERS, Thomas. 37 Brewery Lane, Thornhill Lees, Dewsbury. S. of James and Isabella Myers. B. at Mirfield 1872; m. 1903, Sarah Eames, of Dewsbury. Educ. at an elementary school. As a youth learned glassblowing and for some years worked in a glass-bottle factory. An active Trade Unionist; wrote pamphlets on Housing and Coal Supply. Member Thornhill Urban District Council from 1904-10; member of Dewsbury County Borough Council from 1910-20 and from 1935-43. A Labour Member. Unsuccessfully contested the Spen Valley division of Yorkshire in 1918; elected there in December 1919 and sat until he was defeated in November 1922. Unsuccessfully contested the Spen Valley division of Yorkshire in December 1923 and October 1924 and the Stretford division of Lancashire in November 1935. Mayor of Dewsbury 1940-41. Died 21 December 1949.

[1922]

NALL, Col. Sir Joseph, D.S.O., T.D. 66 Queen Street, London. Hulme House, Manchester. 16 Hoveringham Hall, Nottinghamshire. Carlton, and Constitutional. S. of Joseph Nall, Esq., of Worsley. B. 24 August 1887; m. 17 August 1916, Edith Elizabeth,

d. of J.L. Francklin, Esq., of Gonalston. Educ. privately. Col. T.A. Reserves. Member of E. Lancashire County Association T.A., and President of the Institute of Transport 1925-26; a Director of Manchester Chamber of Commerce and of several Transport and Electricity Undertakings. Dept.-Lieut. for Lancashire 1931; Dept.-Lieut., 1941, J.P., and County Councillor for Nottinghamshire. Knight Bach. 1924. A Conservative. Sat for the Hulme division of Manchester from December 1918 until May 1929 when he was defeated. Re-elected for the Hulme division in October 1931 and sat until he retired in June 1945. Resigned the Government Whip in May 1935 and sat as an Independent Conservative until Parliament was dissolved in October 1935. D.S.O. 1918. Director of several transport companies. High Sheriff of Nottinghamshire 1952-53. Created Bart. 1954. Died 2 May 1958.

[1945]

NALL-CAIN, Hon. Arthur Ronald Nall. 26 Eaton Place, London. Ayot St. Lawrence, Hertfordshire. Knoydart, Mallaig, Inverness-shire. Carlton, Marlborough, and Bath. S. of Lord Brocket, of Brocket Hall. B. 4 August 1904; m. 1 November 1927, Angela Beatrix, d. of the Rev. W.G. Pennyman, Vicar of St. Mark's, North Audley Street. Educ. at Eton, and Magdalen Coll.; Oxford; M.A. 1930. A Barrister-at-Law, Inner Temple 1927. Dept. Chairman of Peter Walker and Company, (Warrington), and Robert Cain and Son Limited, and other companies. Lord of the Manor and Patron of the living of Ayot St. Lawrence; member of Hertfordshire County Council 1931-46. A Conservative. Elected for the Wavertree division of Liverpool in June 1931 and again in October 1931. Sat until November 1934 when he succeeded to the Peerage as Baron Brocket. Chairman of Land Union 1936-51. President of Association of Land and Property Owners 1960-67. Died 24 March 1967.

[1935]

NATHAN, Col. Harry Louis. 35 Wilton Crescent, London. 1 Finsbury Square, London. Old Kiln, Churt, Farnham, Surrey. Reform S. of Michael Henry Nathan, Esq. B. 1889; m. 1919, Eleanor Joan Clara, M.A.,

J.P., member of London County Council, d. of C. Stettauer, Esq. Educ. at St. Paul's School. Admitted a Solicitor 1913. Maj. London Regiment T.F. Honorary Col. 33rd (St. Pancras) A.A. Bn., R.E.; Honorary Air Commodore 906 Squadron A.A.F.; Dept.-Lieut., and J.P. for London. Chairman of Infants Hospital, Westminster; member of Board of Governors and House Committee, Westminster Hospital. A Labour Member. Unsuccessfully contested Whitechapel and St. George's as a Liberal in October 1924. Elected for N.E. Bethnal Green as a Liberal in May 1929 and October 1931; resigned the Liberal Whip in February 1933 and sat as an Independent until June 1934 when he accepted the Labour Whip Sat until November 1935 when he unsuccessfully contested S. Cardiff. Elected for Wandsworth Central in April 1937 and sat until June 1940 when he was created Baron Nathan. Under-Secretary of State for War August 1945-October 1946. Minister of Civil Aviation October 1946-May 1948. PC. 1946. President of Royal Geographical Society 1958-61. Chairman of Royal Society of Arts 1961-63. F.S.A. 1955; F.B.A. 1960. Died 23 October 1963. [1940]

NATION, Brigadier-Gen. John James Henry, C.V.O., D.S.O. 11 Manchester Square, London. Naval & Military, and Bath. S. of Gen. Sir John Nation, K.C.B. B. 5 December 1874; m. 29 October 1932, Olive, widow of Capt. Walter Rubens. Educ. abroad, and at Royal Military Academy, Woolwich. Joined R.E. 1895; served in S. African War 1899-1902, in France, etc. 1914-18, and in operations in Mesopotamia and N.W. Persia 1920 and Italian operations in Tripolitania and Cirenaica 1929-30; retired 1931. Military Attaché at Rome and at Durazzo 1927-31. A Conservative. Elected for E. Hull in October 1931 and sat until he was defeated in November 1935. Fellow of Royal Geographical Society. D.S.O. 1917; C.V.O. 1917. Member of Overseas Settlement Board 1936-37. War Correspondent with B.E.F. 1939-40. Died 5 November 1946. [1935]

NAYLOR, Thomas Ellis. Continued in House after 1945: full entry in Volume IV.

NEAL, Arthur. Ryegate, Sheffield. National Liberal. S. of John and Mary Neal. B. 23 September 1862 at Sheffield; m. 1st, 1888, Annie Elizabeth, d. of Matthias and Mrs. Scorah (she died 1917); secondly, Annie Lilian Josephine, d. of James Swift Brook, Esq. Educ. at Wesley Coll., Sheffield. A Solicitor, admitted 1883. Member of Sheffield City Council 1903-21, and of its Education Committee 1903; member, later Chairman Sheffield Insurance Committee 1912. Parliamentary Secretary to the Ministry of Transport, November 1919-October 1922. A Liberal Coalitionist. Unsuccessfully contested the Hallam division of Sheffield in January and December 1910. Elected for the Hillsborough division of Sheffield in December 1918 and sat until he was defeated in November 1922. Unsuccessfully contested the Bassetlaw division of Nottinghamshire in December 1923 and October 1924 and the Gainsborough division of Lincolnshire in May 1929. President of Sheffield Chamber of Commerce. Alderman, Sheffield City Council. Died 29 January 1933. [1922]

NEAL, Harold. Continued in House after 1945: full entry in Volume IV.

NELSON, Sir Frank. 12 Carlisle Mansions, London. Culls, Stroud. S. of Henry Ellis Hay Nelson, Esq. B. 5 August 1883; m. 1st, 14 February 1911, Jean, d. of Col. Montgomerie (she died 1952); secondly, Dorothy Moira Carling. Educ. at Bedford School, and at Heidelberg. Partner in Symons, Barlow and Company, of Bombay. Chairman of Bombay Chamber of Commerce 1922 and 1923; President of Association Chambers of Commerce, India and Ceylon. M.L.C. Bombay 1922-24; member of Council Royal Colonial Institute. Knight Bach. 1924. Served with Bombay Light Horse 1914-18. A Conservative. Elected for the Stroud division of Gloucestershire in October 1924 and sat until he resigned in May 1931. Consol in Basle 1939-40. Appointed Executive Director of Special Operations 2 in August 1940 (renamed Special Operations Executive in 1941); he retired in May 1942 due to ill-health caused by over-work. This post was secret at the time. K.C.M.G. 1942. Served in Washington and Germany with Air Intelligence Branch; retired as Air Commodore 1946. Died 11 August 1966. [1931 2nd ed.]

NELSON, Robert Frederick William Robertson. Lyndhurst, Bothwell, Lanarkshire. Carlton, St. Stephen's, and British Empire. Conservative, Glasgow. S. of A.S. Nelson, Esq., of Glasgow. B. at Stirling 29 February 1888; m. 1914, d. of James T. Tullis, Esq. Educ. at Trinity Coll., Glenalmond. A Mechanical Engineer; Managing Director of Hurst, Nelson and Company Limited; Chairman of Wagon Repairs Limited. A Unionist. Elected for the Motherwell division of Lanarkshire in December 1918 and sat until he retired in October 1922. Died 1 December 1932. [1922]

NESBITT, Robert Chancellor. Hildenborough, Kent. Athenaeum, Union, and City of London. Eld. s. of Robert Henry Nesbitt, Esq., M.A., of Oxfordshire. B. 17 November 1868; m. 1895, Lilian Mary, 4th d. of Edward Ellis, Esq., of Shadingfield Hall, Suffolk (she died 1932). Solicitor. Senior partner in Markby Stewart and Wadesons. Elected a member of the Council of the Law Society 1909-26. Chairman National Mutual Life Association of Australasia. Director Union Bank of Australia, and of the British Law Insurance Company Limited. Member of the Lord Chancellor's Committee on Supreme Court Fees 1920. Chairman Special Training Grants Committee Ministry of Labour 1921. Member Lord Chancellor's Committee on Circuit Arrangements 1922. Chairman Ministry of Labour (Irish Court Martial Officers) Committee 1922. Travelled in the Colonies and Far East. A Conservative. Elected for the Chislehurst division of Kent in November 1922 and sat until he retired in October 1924. Member of Church Assembly. Fellow of Society of Antiquaries of Scotland. Died 27 January 1944. [1924 2nd ed.]

NEVEN-SPENCE, Sir Basil Hamilton Hebden. Continued in House after 1945: full entry in Volume IV.

NEVILLE, Sir Reginald James Neville, Bart. Sloley Hall, Norwich. 7 Fig Tree Court, Temple, London. Carlton, United University, and Hurlingham. S. of Mr. Justice Sewell Neville, of the High Court of Calcutta. B. 22 February 1863; m. 1st, 1890, Ida, d. of Sir Edmund Henderson, K.C.B. (she died 1913); secondly, 1920, Violet Sophia Mary, d. of Col. C.J. Baines, of Shirehampton and widow of Capt. R.J. Hunter, Rifle Brigade. Educ. at Charterhouse, and Trinity Coll., Cambridge. Barrister-at-Law Inner Temple 1887; Recorder of Bury St. Edmunds from 1905-1943. Created Bart. 1927. A Conservative. Unsuccessfully contested S. Leeds in July and September 1892, 1895, 1900, 1908, and 1923, Wigan in January 1910 and 1918. Sat for Wigan from December 1910-18. Elected for E. Norfolk in October 1924 and sat until he was defeated in May 1929. Master of Bowyers Company 1929-30. Chairman of Quarter Sessions and J.P. for Norfolk. Died 28 April 1950. [1929]

NEWBOLD, John Turner Walton. 16 King Henry Street, Covent Garden, London. Bellscauseway, Beith, Ayrshire. S. of T. Robinson Newbold, Esq., of Buxton. B. at Newchurch, Lancashire 8 May 1888; m. 1915, Margery, d. of Alexander Wilson, Esq., of Bath. Educ. at Buxton Coll., and the University of Manchester; M.A. 1912. A Teacher of History. Author of *How Europe Armed for War 1871-1914, Capitalism and the War*, etc. Unsuccessfully contested Motherwell in 1918 as a Labour candidate. Elected for the Motherwell division of Lanarkshire as a Communist in November 1922 and sat until he was defeated in December 1923. Unsuccessfully contested the Epping division of Essex as the Labour candidate in May 1929. Joined ILP 1910, Communist Party 1921. Resigned from Communist Party 1924. Joined National Labour Party in 1931 and supported Winston Churchill in the November 1935 election at Epping. Originally a Quaker but was received into the Roman Catholic Church. F.R.S.A. 1936. Lived in Eire 1938-40 when he returned to England. Died February 1943. [1923]

NEWBOULD, Alfred Ernest. 16 Upper Cheyne Row, Chelsea, London. Stone Cross Crowborough, Sussex. Devonshire, and National Liberal. S. of John Joseph Newbould, Esq., of Tatenhill, Burton-on-Trent. B. at Walsall October 1873; m. 1909, Grace, d. of James Kirkby, of Cumberland. Educ. at Burton Grammar School. Served for five years as a private in the 1st Royal Dragoons; two African medals, eight clasps. An Independent Liberal. Unsuccessfully contested W. Leyton in December 1918. Elected for W. Leyton in March 1919 and sat until he was defeated in November 1922. Unsuccessfully contested W. Leyton in December 1923 and October 1924. Died 25 April 1952.   [1922]

NEWMAN, Lieut.-Col. John Robert Bramston Pretyman. 79 Eaton Square, London. Newberry Manor, Co. Cork. Carlton, and Royal Automobile. S. of John A.R. Newman, Esq., of Newberry Manor, Co. Cork, and Matilda, d. of Col. Brayston-Smith, of Pencraig, Angelsea. B. 22 August 1871 at Newberry Manor, Co. Cork; m. 1st, 1895, Olive, d. of Lord Plunket, Archbishop of Dublin (she died 1896); secondly, 1898, Ina, d. of Col. William Pretyman, 60th Rifles (she died 1935); thirdly, 1945, Ethel, d. of Thomas Dainty, Esq., of Geddington. Educ. at Charterhouse, and Trinity Coll., Cambridge; B.A. Was Capt. 5th Battalion Royal Munster Fusiliers 1894-99; Maj. 17th Battalion Middlesex Regiment. J.P. and Dept.-Lieut. for Co. Cork. High Sheriff 1898. A Conservative, in favour of a strong and reformed Second Chamber, a Strong Navy, Equal Rights for Parents in Elementary Schools, Imperial Preference, Fiscal Reform, etc. Unsuccessfully contested S.E. Essex in 1906. Elected for the Enfield division of Middlesex in January and December 1910, and for the Finchley division of Middlesex in December 1918 and sat until he was defeated in December 1923. Knighted 1924. Died 12 March 1947.   [1923]

NEWMAN, Sir Robert Hunt Stapylton Dudley Lydston, Bart. Mamhead Park, Exeter. Carlton, and St. Stephen's. S. of Sir Lydston Newman, 3rd Bart. B. 27 October 1871. Unmarried. Educ. privately.

An Alderman of Devon County Council; Dept.-Lieut. and J.P. for Devon. Elected for Exeter in May 1918 and sat until he retired in October 1931. A Conservative until October 1927 when, after failing to win readoption as the Conservative candidate, he announced that he would contest the seat as an Independent and the Whip was withdrawn from him. Re-elected in May 1929 as an Independent, defeating the official Conservative candidate. Succeeded as Bart. 1892. Created Baron Mamhead 1931. Member of Church Assembly. President of English Church Union. Died 2 November 1945.   [1931 2nd ed.]

NEWSON, Sir Percy Wilson, Bart. 12 Hertford Street, Mayfair, London. Carlton, and Oriental. Youngest s. of William Henry Newson, Esq., of Suffolk, and Georgina Edmunds, of Middlesex. B. in India 4 April 1874; m. 1908, Helena, eld. d. of Col. Denham Franklin of Co. Cork. Educ. privately. Partner in the firm of Jardine, Skinner and Company, East India Merchants, Calcutta. A Director of the Bengal United Tea Company Limited, the Cachar and Dooars Tea Company Limited, the Commercial Union Assurance Company Limited; the Eastern Bank Limited; and the East Indian Coal Company Limited; President of the Bank of Bengal (1920) and a Gov. of the Imperial Bank of India (1921). Knighted in 1920. A Conservative. Elected for the Tamworth division of Warwickshire in January 1922 and sat until he retired in November 1923. Created Bart. 1921. Died 17 May 1950.   [1923]

NEWTON, Sir George Douglas Cochrane, K.B.E. 105 Eaton Place, London. Croxton Park, Cambridgeshire. Carlton, and Boodle's. S. of George Onslow Newton, Esq. and Lady Alice Cochrane, d. of Thomas, 11th Earl of Dundonald. B. 14 July 1879; m. 23 August 1905, Muriel, d. of Lieut.-Col. Jemmett Duke, 17th Lancers. Educ. at Eton, and Trinity Coll., Cambridge. K.B.E. 1919. High Sheriff of Cambridgeshire and Huntingdonshire 1909-10; Dept.-Lieut., J.P., and County Councillor for Cambridgeshire (Chairman 1919-21). Director of Hours of Labour Department, etc. Ministry of Munitions Welfare and Health Department; Assistant Secretary Ministry of Reconstruction (unpaid) 1917-19. Chairman National Agricultural Council, England and Wales 1922-23. Official Adviser to the Government on Agricultural Questions at Imperial Economic Conference, Ottawa 1932, and World Monetary Conference, London 1933. Director of Public Companies. A Conservative. Unsuccessfully contested Chesterton division of Cambridgeshire in December 1910. Elected for Cambridge Borough in March 1922 and sat until January 1934 when he was created Baron Eltisley. Chairman of Water Companies Association 1923-31. Dept.-Commissioner for Civil Defence, E. Region 1939-40. Died 2 September 1942. [1934]

NEWTON, Sir Harry Kottingham, Bart. 4 Lower Sloane Street, London. Junior Carlton, Garrick, and Bath. Only s. of Sir A. Newton, Bart., at one time Lord Mayor of London. B. 2 April 1875; m. 1920, Myrtle Irene, eld. d. of Mr. and Mrs. Grantham, of 17 Cadogan Place, London, and grand-d. of Mr. Justice Grantham. Educ. at Rugby School, and New Coll., Oxford; M.A. A Barrister, called 1899, and one of H.M. Lieuts. of City of London. Was Honorary Secretary to the C.I.Vs. and accompanied the Battalion to South Africa 1900; Maj. A.S.C. 1914; appointed D.A.D. Supply and Transport, Eastern Command 1915. O.B.E. (Mil.) 1 January 1919. A Director of Harrods Stores Limited, Chairman Colchester Brewing Company. A Unionist. Unsuccessfully contested the Harwich division of Essex in 1906, but was elected there in January 1910. Sat until he retired in October 1922. Succeeded as Bart. 1921. Died 22 June 1951. [1922]

NICHOL, Robert. 34 Hillmarton Road, London. 6 Auldhouse Avenue, Pollokshaws, Glasgow. S. of James M. Nichol, Esq., Engineer. B. at Garnethill, Glasgow 12 February 1890; m. August 1920, Sallie, d. of Bailie James Alston, Esq., of Glasgow. Educ. at Shawlands Academy, and Glasgow University; M.A. 1910. A Teacher, geography master in Allan Glen's School

(Glasgow High School of Science). Wrote pamphlets on educational matters in Scotland. A Labour Member. Elected for E. Renfrewshire in November 1922 and sat until he was defeated in October 1924. Died 16 April 1925. [1924 2nd ed.]

NICHOLL, Commander Sir Edward. Littleton Park, Shepperton, Middlesex. Carlton, Constitutional, Royal Yacht, and 1900. S. of William Nicholl, Esq., of Redruth. B. at Redruth 17 June 1862; m. 1884, Frances, d. of Capt. William Garby. Educ. at Redruth Grammar School. A Shipowner. Chairman, Shipowners' Association 1913-14; officer in the R.N.R. A Unionist. Elected for the Penryn and Falmouth division of Cornwall in December 1918 and sat until he retired in October 1922. Member of Institute of Naval Architects and of Marine Engineers' Institute. Knighted 1916. K.B.E. 1928. Dept.-Lieut. for County of London and J.P. for Middlesex. Member of Cardiff City Council. President of Society of Consulting Marine Engineers and Surveyors 1934. Died 30 March 1939. [1922]

NICHOLSON, Godfrey. Continued in House after 1945: full entry in Volume IV.

NICHOLSON, Brigadier-Gen. John Sanctuary. 2 South Audley Street, London. Bordean House, Petersfield. Carlton, Naval & Military, and Cavalry. S. of William Nicholson, Esq., J.P. and Dept.-Lieut. of Basing Park, Hampshire, at one time MP for Petersfield, and Isabella Sarah, d. of John Meek, Esq. B. in London 19 May 1863. Unmarried. Educ. at Harrow, and Royal Military Coll., Sandhurst. Gazetted 7th Hussars 4 March 1884. A Conservative. Unsuccessfully contested E. Dorset in January and June 1910 and Stafford in December 1910. Elected for the Abbey division of Westminster in August 1921 as an Independent Anti-Waste Conservative. Re-elected as a Conservative in November 1922 and sat until his death on 21 February 1924. D.S.O. 1897; C.B. 1902; C.M.G. 1905. Commandant-Gen. of British South African Police 1898-1900. Inspector-Gen. of South African Constabulary 1903-05.

Served in France 1914-18, Brigadier-Gen. 1916. C.B.E. 1918. Died 21 February 1924. [1924 2nd ed.]

NICHOLSON, Otho William. 1 Ormonde Gate, London. Carlton, Oxford & Cambridge, and St. Stephen's. S. of Col. Rt. Hon. William Graham Nicholson, MP, of Basing Park, Alton. B. 30 November 1891; m. 1st, 12 January 1927, Elisabeth, d. of Frederick C. Bramwell, Esq., of Lagan, Bowmore, Isle of Islay (divorced 1932); secondly, 1976, Joan, widow of Col. K.F.W. Thomas. Educ. at Harrow, and Magdalene Coll., Cambridge. A Director of J. and W. Nicholson and Company Limited, Distillers. Served in France 1914-19; Honorary Col. 26th and 27th (London) Companies, Air Defence Brigade Signals, Royal Corps of Signals. Member London County Council 1922-25; Mayor of Finsbury 1923-24. Chairman of Finsbury Conservative Association. A Conservative. Sat for the Abbey division of Westminster from March 1924 until he resigned in July 1932. T.D. 1942. Dept.-Lieut. for Middlesex. Commander of Order of St. John of Jerusalem. Died 29 June 1978.* [1932]

NICHOLSON, Reginald. 8 Sumner Place, London. Travellers', Princes, Queen's, and Royal Automobile. S. of William Norris Nicholson, Esq., Senior Master in Lunacy. B. in Kensington 15 July 1869; m. 1915, Natalie, d. of Dr. F.S. Pearson, of New York, U.S.A. Educ. at Charterhouse. Was Assistant Traffic Manager, Bengal Nagpur Railway 1894; Manager of *The Times* 1910-15 in succession to Mr. C. Moberley Bell; resigned in 1915. A Coalition Liberal. Elected for the Doncaster division of the W. Riding of Yorkshire in December 1918 and sat until he was defeated in November 1922. M.B.E. 1918. Died 27 April 1946. [1922]

NICHOLSON, Col. Rt. Hon. William Graham. 2 South Audley Street, London. Basing Park, Alton, Hampshire. Carlton, and Oxford & Cambridge. S. of William Nicholson, Esq., of Basing Park. B. 11 March 1862; m. 19 July 1890, Alice Margaret, d. of the Rt. Hon. W.W.B. Beach,

MP (she died 1935). Educ. at Harrow, and Trinity Coll., Cambridge, B.A. A Director of J. and W. Nicholson and Company Limited, Distillers, of Clerkenwell, London; a J.P. and Dept.-Lieut. for Southampton; Alderman Hampshire County Council; Col. commanding 3rd Battalion Hampshire Regiment. Chairman of the Chairmen's Panel, and of the House of Commons Committee Selection. PC. 1925. A Conservative. Sat for the Petersfield division of Hampshire from June 1897 until he retired in October 1935. Died 29 July 1942. [1935]

NICHOLSON, Hon. Harold George, C.M.G. 4 King's Bench Walk, Temple, London. Sissinghurst Castle, Kent. S. of Arthur, 1st Baron Carnock. B. 21 November 1886; m. 1 October 1913, Hon. Victoria Sackville-West, d. of Lionel, 3rd Baron Sackville (she died 1962). Educ at Wellington Coll., and Balliol Coll., Oxford. Served in Diplomatic Service 1909-1930, at Peace Conference 1919, Lausanne Conference 1923; Counsellor at Embassy in Berlin 1928-30. Parliamentary Secretary Ministry of Information May 1940-July 1941; a Gov. of B.B.C. July 1941-46. A National Labour Member. Unsuccessfully contested Combined English Universities (New Party) in October 1931. Elected for Leicester W. in November 1935 as a National Labour candidate and sat until July 1945 when he was defeated standing as a National candidate with Conservative support. Joined the Labour Party in 1947. Unsuccessfully contested N. Croydon as the Labour candidate in March 1948. An Author and Journalist. President of Classical Association 1950-51. K.C.V.O. 1953. Fellow of Royal Society of Literature. Died 1 May 1968. [1945]

NIELD Basil Edward. Continued in House after 1945: full entry in Volume IV.

NIELD, Rt. Hon. Sir Herbert, K.C. 2 Dr. Johnson's Buildings, Temple, London. Bishop's Mead, Bishop's Avenue, East Finchley, London. St. Stephen's, 1900, and United. S. of William R. Nield, Esq., of Saddleworth, Yorkshire, and Eliza, d. of William H. Turner, Esq. B. 20 October

1862; m. 1st, 1890, Mary Catherine, d. of John Baker, Esq., of Colyton, Devon (she died 1893); secondly, 18 April 1901, Mabel, d. of Sir C.F. Cory-Wright, 1st Bart. Admitted a Solicitor 1885; Barrister-at-Law, Inner Temple 1895; K.C. 1913; practised on the N.E. Circuit. A Dept.-Lieut., J.P., and County Alderman for Middlesex. Dept.-Chairman of Middlesex Quarter Sessions from 1909; Recorder of York from April 1917. A member of Middlesex T.F. from 1909; of Lee Conservancy Board from 1901; Chairman of Council 1923-24 and member of Executive Committee National Unionist Association; Chairman of the Governing Body of Association of Conservative Clubs; Chairman of the Council of Middlesex Prov. Div. of National Conservative Union 1912-24. Knighted 1918. PC. 1924. A Conservative. Sat for the Ealing division of Middlesex from 1906 to 1918 and for the Borough of Ealing from 1918 until he retired in October 1931. Died 11 October 1932.   [1931 2nd ed.]

NIXON, Henry. Eston Nab, Frodingham Road, Scunthorpe, Lincolnshire. S. of William Nixon, Esq., of Middlesbrough. B. 1874 at Middlesbrough; m. 1896, Naomi, d. of Thomas Would, Esq., of Coningsby. Member of Eston Urban District Council, Scunthorpe Urban District Council, and Lindsey County Council. President of the Blastfurnacemen's Association. A Labour Member. Unsuccessfully contested the Newark division of Nottinghamshire in 1922. Elected for The Wrekin division of Shropshire in December 1923 and sat until he was defeated in October 1924. Unsuccessfully contested Gloucester in May 1929. Died 15 March 1939.   [1924 2nd ed.]

NOEL-BAKER, Philip John. Continued in House after 1945: full entry in Volume IV.

NOEL-BUXTON, Lucy Edith Noel-Buxton, Baroness. Continued in House after 1945: full entry in Volume IV.

NORIE-MILLER, Francis. 5 Orme Court, London. Cleeve, Perthshire. Reform. S. of Henry Miller, Esq., H.M. Customs, of London and Cheshunt. B. 11 March 1859;

m. 1st, 1884. Grace Harvey, d. of Rev. Henry Josiah Day, Vicar of Cheshunt (she died 1931); secondly, 1934, Florence Jean Belfrage, d. of William McKim, Esq., of Scone. Chairman and Managing Director of General Accident Fire and Life Assurance Corporation. Chairman of General Life Assurance Company, English Insurance Company and Scottish General Insurance Company. Chairman of Motor Traders Guarantee Corporation Limited. Unsuccessfully contested the Perth division of Perthshire as a Liberal in May 1929 and October 1931. A Liberal National Member. Elected for the Perth division of Perthshire in April 1935 and sat until he retired in October 1935. Created Bart. 1936. J.P. for Perth. Chairman of Perth School Board and of Perthshire Education Committee. Died 4 July 1947.

NORMAN, Maj. Rt. Hon. Sir Henry, Bart. The Corner House, Cowley Street, London. Honeyhanger, Hindhead, Surrey. Royal Automobile, Reform, and Ranelagh. S. of Henry and Sarah Edna Norman. B. 19 September 1858 at Leicester; m. 1st, 1891, Ménie Muriel, d. of James Muir Dowie, Esq. (divorced 1903); secondly, 1907, Hon. Priscilla McLaren (C.B.E. 1917, 1914 Star, J.P.), d. of Lord Aberconway. Educ. at Collegiate School, Leicester, privately in France and Germany, Harvard University, B.A., and University of Leipzig. Assistant Editor of *Daily Chronicle* 1895. Retired from journalism 1899 for authorship and political life. A member of council of Society of Authors; F.R.G.S. Honorary Secretary of Parliamentary Commercial Committee 1907-09, of the Budget League 1909, Assistant Postmaster-Gen. January-February 1910. Chairman of Select Committee on Patent Medicine and of War Office Committee on Wireless Telegraphy 1913, member of Second Chamber Conference 1917; Vice-Chairman Imperial Communications Committee and Chairman of Imperial Wireless Committee 1919; Chairman Industrial Paints Committee; Chairman Rent Restriction Act Committee; member of Committee National Telegraphic and Telephonic Research and British Association Committee of Radio-telegraphic Research; Vice-President of Wireless Society of London; Fellow of Amer. Inst. Radio Engineers; F. Inst.P.; member of Inventions Panel of Ministry of Munitions; Liaison Officer of Ministry of Munitions to French Ministry of Inventions, with rank of Staff Capt. 1916; Maj. 1917. Additional member of the Air Council 1918. A.I.E.E. Knighted 1906; created Bart. 1915; PC. 1918; 1914 Star. Officer of the Legion of Honour. Officer of the Order of Sts. Maurice and Lazare (Italy), and of Crown of Belgium. Commander of the Order of the Redeemer. Travelled extensively in U.S.A., Canada, Russia, Central Asia, and the Near and Far East. Author of *The Real Japan, People and Politics of the Far East, All the Russias*, etc. A Liberal. Sat for Wolverhampton S. from 1900 to January 1910, when he was defeated. Elected for Blackburn in December 1910 and sat until he retired in November 1923. J.P. for Surrey. Died 4 June 1939.   [1923]

NORMAND, Rt. Hon. Wilfrid Guild, K.C. 11 Northumberland Street, Edinburgh. Athenaeum, Carlton, and Constitutional. S. of Patrick Hill Normand, Esq., of Whitehill, Aberdour. B. 16 May 1884; m. 1st, 1913, Gertrude, d. of George Lawson, Esq., of Hill Crest, Sheringham (she died 1923); secondly, 1927, Marion, d. of David Cunningham, Esq., of Dalachy, Aberdour. Educ. at Fettes Coll., Edinburgh, Oriel Coll., Oxford, in Paris, and at the University of Edinburgh. Admitted member of Faculty of Advocates 1910; K.C. 1925. Solicitor-Gen. for Scotland April-June 1929 and November 1931-October 1933; Lord Advocate October 1933-April 1935; PC. 1933. A Trustee of National Library of Scotland from 1925-46 and 1953-62. A Unionist. Unsuccessfully contested W. Edinburgh in May 1929. Elected for W. Edinburgh in October 1931 and sat until April 1935 when he was appointed Lord President of the Court of Session. Lord Justice Gen. and Lord President of the Court of Session, with the judicial title of Lord Normand 1935-47. Created Baron Normand (Law life peerage) 1947. Lord of Appeal in Ordinary 1947-53. Trustee of British Museum 1950-53. President of Stair Society 1954. Died 5 October 1962.   [1935]

NORRIS, Col. Sir Henry (George). Lichfield House, Richmond, Surrey. Junior Carlton, and Royal Automobile. S. of John Henry Norris, Esq. B. 23 July 1865. Educ. Privately. Partner in the firm of Allen and Norris, Estate Agents. Served in the 3rd Middlesex Artillery Volunteers and 2nd Tower Hamlets Volunteers. A keen Freemason. Chairman Kinnaird Park Estates Company Limited, and Municipal Freehold Land Company Limited; Director of Municipal House Property Trust Limited. Ten times Mayor of Fulham 1909-19 During the war raised contingents of Field Artillery and assisted in recruiting. Chairman of the Fulham Football Club; Chairman of the Woolwich Arsenal Club. J.P. Knighted 1917. Dept.-Lieut. County of London. A Coalition Unionist. Elected for E. Fulham in December 1918 and sat until he retired in October 1922. Member of London County Council 1916-19. Died 30 July 1934.   [1922]

NORTH, Edward Tempest Tunstall. The Ridding, Bentham, Yorkshire. Windham. S. of Brigadier-Gen. B.N. North, C.B., M.V.O. B. 31 January 1900; m. 12 July 1928, Mary, d. of T.W. Wilkinson, Esq. Educ. at Eton, Trinity Coll., Cambridge. Capt. Yorkshire Hussars Yeomanry 1931, Maj. 1939; J.P. for Westmorland. A Conservative. Elected for the Nuneaton division of Warwickshire in October 1931 and sat until he retired in October 1935. killed on active service in January 1942. (His name appears in the casualty list in *The Times* of 10 January but *Who Was Who* gives the date of death as 20 January).   [1935]

NORTON-GRIFFITHS, Sir John Norton, Bart., K.C.B., D.S.O. 3 Central Buildings, London. Carlton, Bath, Royal Automobile, and Ranelagh. S. of John Griffiths, Esq., of Brecon. B. 13 July 1871; m. Gwladys, d. of Thomas Wood, Esq., of Browning, Wood and Fox. Director of Norton Griffiths and Company Limited, Engineers and Public Works Contractors, Commanded Scouts, Matabele-Mashona War 1896-97 (mentioned in despatches three times); Capt. Adjutant Lord Roberts's Bodyguard, South African War. In European War, raised, without cost to the public purse, 2nd King Edward's Horse; subsequently attached to Staff of Engineer-in-Chief at G.H.Q. to organize and start Tunnelling Companies, R.E. Promoted Temporary Lieut.-Col. R.E. (mentioned in despatches three times); D.S.O. January 1916; in November 1916, gazetted G.S.O. (first grade) and sent on special mission in connection with the Oil and Corn Stores in Roumania, where, for services rendered on the field of battle, he was made Commander of the Grand Star of Roumania by the King of Roumania; for the same services received the Russian Order of St. Vladimir (third class). K.C.B. January 1917; Croix d'Officier, Legion of Honour, October 1918. Created Bart. 1922. A Conservative. Elected for Wednesbury in January and December 1910, and for Central Wandsworth in December 1918 (when he defeated the 'Coupon' Liberal candidate), November 1922 and again in December 1923. Sat until he retired in October 1924. Assumed the surname of Norton-Griffiths in lieu of Griffiths 1917. Committed suicide at Alexandria 27 September 1930.

[1924 2nd ed.]

NUNN, William. Gillgrass, Gosforth, Cumberland. Thatched House. S. of Henry Nunn, Esq. B. 20 March 1879; m. 1905, Mary, d. of John Fowler, Esq. (she died). Educ. at King's Coll., London. Entered C.S. 1899. Adviser to Government of Siam on Customs and Excise 1908, retired 1924. A Conservative. Unsuccessfully contested S. Shields May 1929. Elected for the Whitehaven division of Cumberland in 1931, defeated in November 1935. Returned unopposed for Newcastle W. in July 1940 and sat until he was defeated in July 1945. Unsuccessfully contested the Whitehaven division of Cumberland in February 1950. Fellow of Royal Historical Society. Died 16 December 1971. [1945]

NUTTALL, Ellis. Middlewood, Clitheroe, Lancashire. Carlton. S. of Alfred Nuttall, Esq., of Blackburn. B. 8 December 1890; m. 2 June 1920, Muriel, d. of Sir John Allen, MP. Educ. at Rugby, and Trinity Coll.,

Oxford. Barrister-at-Law, Middle Temple 1913. Served in R.F.A. 1914-19. A Conservative. Elected for Birkenhead W. in October 1924 and sat until he was defeated in May 1929. Died 1 July 1951. [1929]

OAKLEY, Thomas. 75 Charrington Street, Oakley Square, London. B. 1879 at Prees, Shropshire. Entered L. and N.W. Railway Service 1900; President of Hearts of Oak Benefit Society; Fellow of the Faculty of Insurance; member of National Congress of Friendly Societies, of the Consultative Council of Minister of Health for National Health Insurance, and of St. Pancras Board of Guardians. A Conservative. Elected for The Wrekin division of Shropshire in October 1924 and sat until he was defeated in May 1929. Died 4 April 1936. [1929]

O BUACHALLA, Domhnall. See BUCKLEY, Donald.

O'CONNOR, Arthur John. Elm Hall, Celbridge, Co. Kildare. B. 1888. Educ. at Trinity Coll., Dublin. A Civil Engineer and Barrister. A Sinn Fein Member. Elected for S. Kildare in December 1918 but did not take his seat. Member of Dail for S. Kildare to 1921, for Kildare and Wicklow 1921-22 as an Anti-Treaty Member. Minister for Agriculture 1921-22. Circuit Judge for Cork from 1947. Chairman of Irish Army Pensions Board from 1949. Died 2 May 1950. [1922]

O'CONNOR, Sir Terence James, K.C. 4 Paper Buildings, Temple, London. Swerford Park, Oxford. Carlton, and Beefsteak. S. of James O'Connor, Esq., of Bridgnorth. B. 13 September 1891; m. 1 March 1920, Cecil, d. of Wyndham Francis Cook, Esq. A Barrister-at-Law, Inner Temple 1919, Bencher 1936; K.C. 1929; Solicitor-Gen. March 1936-May 1940. Knight Bach.1936. A Conservative. Sat for the Luton division of Bedfordshire from October 1924 until 1929 when he was defeated. Elected for Nottingham Central in May 1930 and sat until his death on 8 May 1940. Served with Highland Light Infantry and West African Frontier Force 1914-18. J.P. and Dept.-

Chairman of Quarter Sessions for Oxfordshire. Died 8 May 1940. [1940]

O'CONNOR, Rt. Hon. Thomas Power. 5 Morpeth Mansions, London. National Liberal, Garrick, and Beefsteak. S. of Thomas O'Connor, Esq., of Athlone, by Theresa, d. of Thomas Power, Esq., of the 88th Connaught Rangers. B. at Athlone 1848. Educ. at the College of the Immaculate Conception, Athlone, and Queen's Coll., Galway, and graduated M.A. in the Queen's University. Author of various works including *Lord Beaconsfield: a Biography, The Parnell Movement, Some Old Love Stories, Napoleon,* etc. Was the first Editor of the *Star* evening newspaper; later Editor of the *Sun,* the *Sunday Sun, M.A.P., T.P.'s Weekly, T.P.'s Journal* and *T.P.'s* and *Cassell's Weekly.* President of the United Irish League of Great Britain from 1883. President of the Trade Board of Film Censors December 1916. PC. 1924. A Nationalist. Sat for Galway Borough from 1880-85. Sat for the Scotland division of Liverpool from 1885 until his death on 18 November 1929. In 1885 he was elected for Galway Borough and for the Scotland division of Liverpool, but chose to sit for the latter. Father of the House of Commons 1918-29. Died 18 November 1929. [1929 2nd ed.]

O'DOHERTY, Joseph. 65 Clarendon Street, Londonderry. B. 1891. A native of Derry; interned as a suspect. A Sinn Fein Member. Elected for N. Donegal in December 1918 but did not take his seat. Member of Dail for N. Donegal to 1921, for Donegal 1921-27. An Anti-Treaty Member, joined Fianna Fail 1926. [1922]

O'DONOVAN, William James, O.B.E., M.C. 138 Harley Street, London. S. of Patrick O'Donovan, Esq., of Clonakilty. B. at Tonbridge 1886; m. Ethel K. Smith. Educ. at London University and Hospital, M.D., M.R.C.P. Medical Registrar and Physician in charge of Skin and Light Department London Hospital; Physician to Skin Department St. Paul's Hospital and Queen Mary's Hospital, Stratford; President of Dermatological Section, British Medical Association and Royal Society of Medicine;

Coroner's Pathologist for E. London. C.M.O. Ministry of Munitions 1915-18. A Conservative. Elected for the Mile End division of Stepney in October 1931 and sat until he was defeated in November 1935. Unsuccessfully contested W. Fulham in February 1950. Knight of St. Gregory the Great. Died 13 January 1955. [1935]

O'GRADY, James. 60 Cavendish Road, Balham, London. S. of John and Margaret O'Grady. B. 6 May 1866 at Bristol; m. 1887, Louisa James (she died 1929). Educ. at St. Mary's Roman Catholic School, Bristol. A Furniture Maker. President of Trade Union Congress 1898; Secretary of National Federation of General Workers; was a member of Bristol Town Council 1897-99. J.P. County of London. Undertook a mission to Russia March 1917, in the interest of Russia's support of the Allies' cause, and to Copenhagen November 1920 to arrange for exchange of prisoners of war and the repatriation of British civilians from Russia. A Labour Member. Sat for E. Leeds from 1906-1918. Sat for S.E. Leeds from December 1918 until he retired in October 1924. Gov. of Tasmania 1924-31. K.C.M.G. 1924. Gov. of Falkland Islands 1931-34. Died 10 December 1934. [1924 2nd ed.]

O'HIGGINS, Brian. O'Currey College, Kilcredann, Carrigaholt, Co. Clare. B. 1882. An Author and Journalist who was arrested in June 1918 and interned in Birmingham prison. A Sinn Fein Member. Was returned unopposed for W. Clare in December 1918 but did not take his seat. Member of Dail for W. Clare to 1921, for Clare 1921-27. An Anti-Treaty Member, remaining a Member of Sinn Fein after the formation of Fianna Fail. Dept. Speaker of Dail 1921-22. [1922]

O'HIGGINS, Kevin Christopher. Woodlands, Timogue, Stradbally. Queen's County. S. of Dr. T. Higgins, of Stradbally. B. 7 June 1892; m. 1921, Bridget Mary Cole. Educ. at Clongowes, St. Patrick's Coll., Carlow, and National University of Ireland. A Solicitor's apprentice. A Sinn Fein Member. Returned for Queen's County in December 1918 but did not take his seat.

Member of Dail for Leix and Offaly to 1923, for Co. Dublin 1923-27. A Pro-Treaty, later Cumann na nGaedheal Member. Assistant Minister of Local Government 1921-22, Minister for Economic Affairs 1922, Minister for Home Affairs, later Justice and Vice-President of Executive Council 1922-27. Minister for External Affairs June-July 1927. Assassinated on 10 July 1927. [1922]

O'KEEFE, Patrick. 21 Lower Camden Street, Dublin. One of the Secretaries of Sinn Fein. Was deported after the 1916 rising. Was also among the Sinn Feiners arrested in Dublin in June 1918, and was interned in Usk prison, for defiance of Defence of the Realm Regulations. Released 1919; re-arrested and sentenced for inciting to disorder 1919. A Sinn Fein Member. Was returned unopposed for N.Cork in December 1918 but did not take his seat. Member of Dail for N.Cork to 1922, as a Pro-Treaty Member. [1922]

O'KELLY, John Joseph. Glasnevin, Dublin. B. at Valentia Island in about 1871; m. 1904, Nora, d. of Patrick O'Sullivan, Esq., of Lisbawn. Editor of *Catholic Bulletin*. A Sinn Fein Member. Elected for Co. Louth in December 1918 but did not take his seat. Member of Dail for Co. Louth to 1921, for Louth and Meath 1921-23 as an Anti-Treaty Member. Speaker of the first Dail 1919, Minister for National Language 1919-21, Minister for Education 1921-22. Author. President of Gaelic League 1919-23, of Sinn Fein 1926-30. Secretary of Society for the Protection of the Irish Language. Died 26 March 1957. [1922]

O'KELLY, Sean Thomas. 19 Ranelagh Road, Dublin. S. of Samuel O'Kelly, Esq., of Dublin. B. in Dublin 25 August 1882; m. 1st, 1918, Mary Kate, d. of John, Esq., of Co. Wexford (she died 1934); secondly, 1936, Phyllis, younger d. of John Ryan, Esq., of Co. Wexford. Member of the Dublin Corporation from 1906; Secretary of the Gaelic League 1915-20. A Sinn Fein Member. Elected for the College Green division of Dublin in December 1918 but did not take his seat. Member of Dail for the College Green division of Dublin to 1921, for

mid Dublin 1921-23, for N. Dublin 1923-45. An Anti-Treaty Member, joined Fianna Fail 1926. Vice-President of Fianna Fail 1932-45. Minister for Local Government in the unofficial Republican Government 1922-26. Minister for Local Government and Public Health 1932-39, Minister of Finance 1939-45. President of Irish Republic 1945-1959. Speaker of Dail 1919-21. Dept. Prime Minister 1932-45. Died 23 November 1966. [1922]

OLDFIELD, John Richard Anthony. House of Commons, London. S. of Maj. H.E. Oldfield. B. 1900; m. 1953, Jonnet Elizabeth, d. of Maj. H.M. Richards. Educ. at Eton, and Trinity Coll., Cambridge. Associated with Educational and Social work. Parliamentary Private Secretary to Lord Thomson 1929-30 and to Lord Amulree 1930-31 when Secretaries of State for Air. A Labour Member. Sat for Essex S.E. from May 1929 until he was defeated in October 1931; again defeated in November 1935. Served in Coldstream Guards 1918-20 and in Royal Navy 1939-45. Member of London County Council 1931-58, Vice-Chairman 1953. Member of Kent County Council 1965.* [1931 2nd ed.]

OLDFIELD, William Henry. Continued in House after 1945: full entry in Volume IV.

OLIVER, George Harold. Continued in House after 1945: full entry in Volume IV.

OLIVER, Philip Milner, C.B.E. High Croft, Bowdon, Cheshire. S. of J.R. Oliver, Esq. B. 20 August 1884. Educ. at Bowdon Coll., Manchester Grammar School, and Corpus Christi Coll., Oxford. Barrister-at-Law, Lincoln's Inn 1908. A Liberal. Unsuccessfully contested the Blackley division of Manchester in 1918 and 1922. Elected for the Blackley division in December 1923, defeated October 1924. Re-elected in May 1929 and sat until he was defeated in October 1931. Unsuccessfully contested the Altrincham division of Cheshire in June 1933 and the Blackley division of Manchester in November 1935 and July 1945. O.B.E. 1918; C.B.E. 1920. Died 12 April 1954. [1931 2nd ed.]

O'MAHONEY, John. 32 Gardiners Place, Dublin. Interned in Lincoln prison in 1918; released 1919; re-arrested in raid on Sinn Fein offices in Dublin November 1919; sentenced to three months imprisonment. A Sinn Fein Member. Elected for S. Fermanagh in December 1918 but did not take his seat. Member of Northern Ireland Parliament for Fermanagh and Tyrone 1921-25. A Tea Merchant. Member of Dublin City Council. Died 28 November 1934. [1922]

O'MAILLE, Padraic. B. 23 February 1878. A Sinn Fein Member. Elected for the Connemara division of Galway in December 1918 but did not take his seat. Member of Dail for the Connemara division of Galway to 1921, for Galway 1921-27. A Pro-Treaty, later Cumann na nGaedheal Member, until 1926 when he joined Clann Eireann. Dept. Speaker of Dail 1922-27. Senator 1934-36 and 1938-46. Died 19 January 1946. [1922]

OMAN, Sir Charles William Chadwick, K.B.E. Frewin Hall, Oxford. Athenaeum, and Burlington. S. of Charles P.A. Oman, Esq., of Hattowrie, Bahar, Indigo Planter. B. 12 January 1860 at Mozufferpore, Bahar; m. 1892, Mary Mabel, 2nd d. of Gen. Robert Maclagan, R.E. Scholar of Winchester Coll. 1872-78 and of New Coll., Oxford 1878-82. Fellow of All Souls' Coll., Oxford 1883; Professor of Modern History, Oxford University 1905-46; President of Royal Historical Society 1917; President of Royal Numismatic Society 1919; Fellow of the British Academy 1906; LL.D. Edinburgh 1910, Cambridge 1927; D.C.L. Oxford 1925. President of Royal Archaeological Institute 1926. A Conservative. Sat for Oxford University from March 1919 until he retired in October 1935. K.B.E. 1920. Died 23 June 1946. [1935]

O'MARA, James. 10 Borough High Street, London. S. of Alderman Stephen O'Mara, MP Ossory division, Queens County 1886. B. at Limerick 1873; m. 1895, Agnes, d. of Blennerhasset Cashel. Educ. at Christian Schools, Limerick, Clongoweswood Coll., B.A. Royal University of Ireland 1898

(Exhibitions Engineering course). A Wholesale Importer and Exporter of provisions, and member of the Home and Foreign Produce Exchange, London. Sat for S. Kilkenny as a Nationalist from 1900 until he resigned in July 1907 on leaving the Nationalist Party and joining Sinn Fein. Re-elected for S. Kilkenny as a Sinn Fein Member in December 1918 but did not take his seat. Member of Dail for S. Kilkenny until 1921 and for Dublin City S. 1924-27 as a Pro-Treaty, later Cumann na nGaedheal Member. Died 21 November 1948. [1907]

O'NEILL, John Joseph. 40-43 Fleet Street, London. Engineers, National Liberal, Eccentric, and Aldwych. S. of John O'Neill, Esq., of Glasgow. B. in Glasgow 1888; m. 1908, Annie Milne, d. of John Taylor, Esq. A Director of the *Manchester Guardian* Limited, and the Guardian Newspaper Inc., New York. A Liberal. Unsuccessfully contested Preston in 1918. Elected for the Lancaster division of Lancashire in December 1923 and sat until he was defeated in October 1924. Served with Dublin Fusiliers 1916-18. Died 20 April 1953. [1924 2nd ed.]

O'NEILL, Rt. Hon. Sir (Robert William) Hugh, Bart. 28 Queen's Gate Gardens, London. Cleggan Lodge, Ballymena, Co. Antrim. Carlton, and Ulster (Belfast). S. of Edward, 2nd Baron O'Neill. B. 8 June 1883; m. 11 February 1909, Sylvia Irene, d. of Walter A. Sandeman, Esq. (she died 1942). Educ. at Eton, and New Coll., Oxford, B.A. Barrister-at-Law, Inner Temple 1909, N.E. Circuit. 2nd Lieut. N. of Ireland Yeomanry 1902-07; Capt. R. Irish Rifles 1914-16; Capt. Gen. List 1917, and Maj. 1918. Served in France 1915-17, and as D.J.A.G. in Palestine 1918. Dept.Lieut. for Co. Antrim; Honorary LL.D. and former Pro-Chancellor of Belfast University. Sat for Co. Antrim, Northern Ireland Parliament May 1921 to May 1929; Speaker of House of Commons of Northern Ireland June 1921-May 1929. PC. (Ireland) August 1921; PC. (G.B.) 1937. Created Bart. May 1929. Chairman of Conservative Party Members' "1922" Committee 1935-39. Parliamentary Under-

Secretary for India and Burma September 1939-May 1940. An Ulster Unionist. Unsuccessfully contested Stockport in 1906. Elected for mid Antrim February 1915 and December 1918. Member for Co. Antrim November 1922-February 1950, and for the N. division from February 1950 until he resigned in October 1952. Father of the House of Commons 1951-52. Created Baron Rathcavan 1953. Lord-Lieut. of Co. Antrim 1949-59.* [1952]

ONIONS, Alfred. Melrose Villa, Tredegar, Monmouthshire. S. of Jabez Onions, Esq., a Miner. B. 1858 at St. George's, Shropshire; m. 1887, S.A. Dix, d. of a Miner. Educ. at a Church of England Day School until ten and a half years old. Treasurer of the South Wales Miners' Federation; Chairman of the Monmouth County Council; was South Wales representative at the International Miners' Conference in Paris 1891. A Labour Member. Elected for the Caerphilly division of Glamorganshire in December 1918 and sat until his death on 6 July 1921. Member of Mynyddyslwyn School Board 1888, Bedwellty School Board 1899. First Chairman of Risca Urban District Council. Died 6 July 1921. [1921]

ORMISTON, Thomas, C.B.E. The Moorings, Motherwell, Lanarkshire. Constitutional. B. at Motherwell 29 September 1878; m. 11 April 1906, Louisa, d. of J.W.D. Simmons, Esq. Educ. at Hutcheson's Grammar School, Glasgow. Admitted a Solicitor 1903; F.C.I.S. 1905. A National Conservative. Elected for the Motherwell division of Lanarkshire in October 1931 and sat until he was defeated in November 1935. President of Cinematograph Exhibitors' Association 1925. C.B.E. 1929. Died 15 January 1937. [1935]

ORMSBY-GORE, Rt. Hon. William George Arthur. 5 Mansfield Street, London. Wootton House, Bedford. Carlton, and Brooks's. S. of 3rd Lord Harlech. B. 11 April 1885; m. 12 April 1913, Lady Beatrice Cecil, d of 4th Marq. of Salisbury. Educ. at Eton, and New Coll., Oxford; B.A. Served with Shropshire Yeomanry in Egypt August 1914-March 1917. Assistant Secretary War Cabinet March 1917-March 1918; with Military Intelligence Department in Egypt, March-November 1918. First British Representative on the Permanent Mandates Commission 1932. Parliamentary Under-Secretary of State for the Colonies October 1922-January 1924, and November 1924-June 1929. Postmaster-Gen. in National Government August-November 1931; First Commissioner of Works November 1931-May 1936; Secretary of State for the Colonies May 1936-May 1938. PC. 1927. Dept.-Lieut. and J.P. for Leitrim. A Trustee of the National Gallery 1927-34 and 1936, and of the Tate Gallery 1930; Vice-President National Museum of Wales. A Conservative. Elected for Denbigh district in January and December 1910. Sat for the Stafford division of Staffordshire from December 1918 until May 1938 when he succeeded to the Peerage as Baron Harlech. Lord-Lieut. of Merionethshire 1938-57. Constable of Harlech Castle 1938-64. Commissioner for Civil Defence, N.E. Region 1939-40. K.G. 1948. High Commissioner to South Africa 1941-44. Pro-Chancellor of University of Wales 1945-57. Chairman of Midland Bank 1952-57. Died 14 February 1964. [1938]

ORR-EWING, Ian Leslie. Continued in House after 1945: full entry in Volume IV.

OWEN, Maj. Sir Goronwy, D.S.O. Llwyn-y-Brain, Llanrug, Carnarvonshire. Reform. B. 1881 at Penllwyn, Aberystwyth; m. 1925, Mrs. Owen Jones, of Glanbeuno, Carnarvon. Educ. at the County School, Ardwyn Grammar School, and University Coll. of Wales, Aberystwyth. Dept.-Lieut. for Carnarvon 1936. Served in France, etc., 1914-17. Barrister-at-Law, Gray's Inn 1919. A Liberal Whip November 1926-August 1931; Liberal Chief Whip and Comptroller of the Household September-October 1931 when he resigned. Knight Bach. 1944. A Liberal. Unsuccessfully contested S. Derbyshire in 1922. Elected for Carnarvonshire in December 1923 and sat until he was defeated in July 1945. (Elected in 1931 as a member of the Lloyd George Liberal group opposed to the National Government). Alderman, Carnarvonshire County Council 1945.

Chairman of Gwynedd Police Authority 1955-56. Died 26 September 1963. [1945]

OWEN, Humphrey Frank. 25 Old Queen Street, London. Wolferlow, Hereford. National Liberal. S. of Thomas Owen, Esq., of Hereford. B. 27 September 1905; m. 1939, Grace Stewart McGillivray, of Boston, Massachusetts (she died 1968). Educ. at Monmouth School, and Sidney Sussex Coll., Cambridge. A Journalist and Author. A Liberal. Elected for the Hereford division of Herefordshire in May 1929 and sat until he was defeated in October 1931. Unsuccessfully contested the Hereford division of Herefordshire in May 1955 and February 1956. Editor of *Evening Standard* 1938-41, and of *Daily Mail* 1947-50. Served with Royal Armoured Corps and in South-East Asia, O.B.E. (Mil.). Biographer of Lloyd George.* [1931 2nd ed.]

PAGE CROFT, Brigadier-Gen. Sir Henry, Bart. See CROFT, Brigadier-Gen. Sir Henry Page, Bart.

PAGET, Maj. Thomas Guy Frederick. Sulby Hall, Rugby. Carlton, and Guards. S. of Thomas Guy Paget, Esq., of Humberstone, Leicestershire, and Edith, d. of Viscountess Forbes. B. 29 July 1886 at Humberstone Hall; m. 1907, Emma Bettine, d. of Sir William des Voeux, G.C.M.G., and Marion des Voeux, of 51 Eaton Square, London. Educ. at Eton. J.P. for Leicestershire and Northamptonshire; Leicester County Council; Dept.-Lieut. for Leicestershire. Served in the Scots Guards. Author of *History of the Raising of the 7th Northamptonshires, Chronicles of the Last Crusade* (printed for private circulation only). A Conservative. Unsuccessfully contested the mid division of Northamptonshire in January and December 1910. Elected for the Bosworth division of Leicestershire in November 1922 and sat until he was defeated in December 1923. Fellow of Royal Historical Society. Master of Company of Painter Stainers 1945-46. High Sheriff of Leicestershire 1947-48. Killed in a hunting accident 12 March 1952. [1923]

PAIN, Brigadier-Gen. Sir George William Hacket, K.B.E., C.B. United Service, and Royal Automobile. S. of George Pain, Esq. B. 5 February 1855; m. 1898, Saidie, d. of Sidney Merton, Esq., of Sydney, Australia. Entered army 1875. Served in Sudan 1888-91, in Egypt 1896-98, and in South Africa 1900-02. C.B. 1900. Commanded S. Midland district 1908-11, retired 1912. Chief of Staff to Commander in Chief of Ulster Volunteer Force 1912-14. Commanded 108th Infantry Brigade, Ulster Division 1914-16. Commanded Northern Ireland district 1916-19. Brigadier-Gen. 1919. K.B.E. 1919. Divisional Commissioner Royal Irish Constabulary 1920-21. A Unionist. Elected for S. Londonderry in January 1922 and sat until he retired in October 1922. Died 14 February 1924.

PALIN, John Henry. 121 Lower Rushton Road, Bradford. Parliamentary Labour. S. of John Palin, Esq., of Nottingham. B. 1870; m. 1895, Annie, d. of John Bettison, Esq., of Hucknall. Served with R.E. in France 1915-17. Alderman of City Council, Bradford. Lord Mayor 1924. Prominently identified with Labour movements for many years; member of Transport Workers' Union. A Labour Member. Unsuccessfully contested N. Bradford in December 1918 and November 1922. Elected for the W. division of Newcastle-on-Tyne in October 1924 and again in May 1929. Sat until he was defeated in October 1931. Active member of Church of England. Died 22 May 1934.

[1931 2nd ed.]

PALING, Rt. Hon. Wilfred. Continued in House after 1945: full entry in Volume IV.

PALMER, Charles Frederick. 21 Ridgmont Gardens, London. Constitutional, and Services. B. 9 September 1869; m. 1894, Amie Dudley Smith. Parliamentary correspondent of *The Globe* 1886-1912, Editor 1912-15. Dramatic and musical critic of *The People*. Assistant Editor of *John Bull.* An Independent and member of Horatio Bottomley's Independent Parliamentary group. Elected for The Wrekin division of Shropshire in February 1920 and sat until his death on 25 October 1920.

PALMER, Edward Timothy. 30-31 Holborn Hall, London. 74 Inverness Avenue, Westcliff-on-Sea. S. of Henry Isaac Palmer, Esq., Fruiterer. B. 1878; m. 1902, d. of Edward Gazeley, Esq., of Holloway. Educ. at local board school. A Grocer's Assistant. Agent and Supervisor, Prudential Insurance Company; Gen. Secretary Prudential Staff Union 1910-23. A Labour Member. Unsuccessfully contested Canterbury in 1918 and Greenwich in 1922. Elected for Greenwich in December 1923, unsuccessfully contested the same seat in October 1924. Re-elected for Greenwich in May 1929 and sat until he was defeated in October 1931. Member of Essex County Council 1946-47. Died 22 April 1947.

[1931 2nd ed.]

PALMER, Francis Noel. Briarpatch, Normandy, Surrey. S. of Henry Nathaniel Palmer, Esq., of Great Yarmouth. B. 20 January 1887; m. 1916, Hannah, d. of Joseph Crea, Esq. (she died 1954). Educ. at Dulwich. A National Labour Member. Unsuccessfully contested the Farnham division of Surrey as the Labour candidate in May 1929. Elected for S. Tottenham in October 1931 and sat until he was defeated in November 1935. Died 18 January 1961.

[1935]

PALMER, Brigadier-Gen. George Llewellen. Berryfield, Bradford-on-Avon, Wiltshire. Carlton, and Cavalry. S. of Michael Palmer, Esq., J.P. for Wiltshire. B. at Trowbridge 12 March 1857; m. 1881, Madeleine, d. of W. Goldsmith, Esq. (she died 1925). Educ. at Harrow, and abroad. Col. of Wiltshire Yeomanry 1910; commanded a brigade 1915-16; Hon. Brigadier-Gen. in the army 1918; C.B. 1918, T.D., Dept.-Lieut., and J.P. High Sheriff of Wiltshire 1903. A Coalition Unionist. Unsuccessfully contested the Westbury division of Wiltshire in December 1910 and February 1911. Elected for the Westbury division of Wiltshire in December 1918 and sat until he was defeated in November 1922. Died 31 March 1932.

[1922]

PALMER, Gerald Eustace Howell. Fencewood House, Hermitage, Berkshire. Bath, and Brooks's. S. of Eustace Palmer, Esq., Chairman of Huntley and Palmer's Limited, of Reading. B. 9 June 1904. Educ. at Winchester, and New Coll., Oxford. Private Secretary to Rt. Hon. Stanley Baldwin July-December 1935; Parliamentary Private Secretary to Geoffrey Lloyd, Secretary for Mines April 1939-May 1940, to Rt. Hon. Sir Stafford Cripps, Lord Privy Seal February 1942, and to Rt. Hon. Oliver Stanley, Secretary of State for the Colonies December 1942-44. A National Conservative. Elected for the Winchester division of Hampshire in November 1935 and sat until he was defeated in July 1945. Capt. in Royal Artillery, served in Italy. President of Council, University of Reading 1966-69. Verderer of New Forest 1957-66. Forestry Commissioner 1963-65. Author of books on iconography.*

[1945]

PALMER, Maj. Godfrey Mark. 5 Beaufort Gardens, London. Grinkle Park, Loftus, Yorkshire. Youngest s. of Sir Charles Mark Palmer, Bart., MP, and Gertrude, d. of James Montgomery, Esq. B. 4 August 1878; m. 1906, Elma, d. of Alexander Geddes, Esq., of Blairmore, Aberdeenshire. Educ. at Eton, and Paris. A Director of shipping and other businesses in London and on the Tyne. A J.P. for the N. Riding of Yorkshire. Maj. 4th Battalion Yorkshire Regiment. Parliamentary Private Secretary (unpaid) to Sir Eric Geddes when First Lord of the Admiralty. A Liberal. Elected for the Jarrow division of Co. Durham in January 1910 and sat until he retired in October 1922. Died 12 June 1933.

[1922]

PARKER, Herbert John Harvey. Continued in House after 1945: full entry in Volume IV.

PARKER, James. 11 Salisbury Terrace, Halifax. B. 1863 at Authorpe; m. 1887, Clara Oram, of Halifax. Educ. at Wesleyan School, Louth, Lincolnshire. Vice-Chairman Labour Party in House of Commons 1912; Whip from 1914. Junior Lord of the Treasury January 1917-October 1922. Was Secretary to Halifax branch of the Independent Labour Party, and a member of Halifax County Borough Council from

1897-1906. Companion of Honour 1918. A Labour Member. Unsuccessfully contested Halifax in 1900; elected there in 1906 and sat until 1918. Elected for the Cannock division of Staffordshire in December 1918 as a Labour supporter of the Coalition and sat until November 1922 when he unsuccessfully contested the seat as an Independent, opposed by Labour and Liberal candidates but not by a Conservative. Died 11 February 1948.   [1922]

PARKER, Myles Harper. 2 Hill Street, Sneyd Green, Hanley. S. of Henry Parker, Esq. B. 1864; m. 1888, Prudence, d. of T. Flackett, Esq., of Hanley. Began work in the mines at the age of 12. Secretary to the National Organization of Enginemen and Firemen; Alderman of Stoke-on-Trent Borough Council. A Labour Member. Unsuccessfully contested the Hanley division of Stoke-on-Trent in December 1918. Elected for the Hanley division in November 1922 and sat until he retired in October 1924. J.P. for Stoke-on-Trent. Died 14 January 1929.
[1924 2nd ed.]

PARKER, Owen. Higham Ferrers. S. of Charles Parker, Esq., J.P., of Higham Ferrers. B. 1860; m. 1887, Kate Annie, d. of George Packwood, Esq., of Rushden. Educ. at Chichele Grammar School, Higham Ferrers. Member of Northamptonshire County Council; well known for his public work in this division; seven times Mayor of Higham Ferrers. A Boot Manufacturer at Higham Ferrers; President of the Incorporated and Federated Association of Boot and Shoe Manufacturers of Great Britain and Ireland 1913-19. Organised the boot industry during the war for the supply of boots to the British and Allied Armies. A Conservative. Elected for the Kettering division of Northamptonshire in November 1922 and sat until he was defeated in December 1923. O.B.E. 1918; C.B.E. 1920. Chairman of British Boot Shoe and Allied Trades Research Association 1922-25. Died 5 November 1936.   [1923]

PARKINSON, Sir Albert Lindsay. Royal Bank, Preston Old Road, Blackpool. S. of Jacob Parkinson, Esq., of Blackpool. B. 24 February 1870; m. 1911, Margaret, d. of Robert Jackson Singleton. Mayor of Blackpool from 1916 to 1920. Principal partner in J. Parkinson and Sons Limited, Government Contractors and Builders. A Coalition Unionist. Elected for Blackpool in December 1918 and sat until he retired in October 1922. Knighted June 1922. Died 3 February 1936.   [1922]

PARKINSON, John Allen, C.B.E. Glenthorne, Orrell Mount, Nr. Wigan. B. 15 October 1870; m. 1st, Alice, d. of J. Pilkington, Esq. (she died 1904); secondly, 1905, Ida Alice, d. of W. Atkinson, Esq. Educ. at United Methodist Free Church School, Hindley Green. Miners' Agent 1917 for Lancashire and Cheshire Miners' Federation; first direct Miners' Representative on the Lancashire County Council 1915-18; J.P. for Lancaster 1908; member of Board for Mining Examinations. Member of Abram Urban District Council 1908. Comptroller of the Household January-November 1924; a Junior Lord of the Treasury June 1929-March 1931; Parliamentary Secretary Ministry of Transport March-August 1931. C.B.E. 1931. A Labour Member. Sat for Wigan from December 1918 until his death on 7 December 1941.   [1942]

PARRY, Lieut.-Col. Thomas Henry, D.S.O. 3 (North) King's Bench Walk, Temple, London. Llys Ifor, Mold, Flintshire. National Liberal. S. of Gwenllian Parry and T. Parry, Esq; J.P., of Mold. B. 21 April 1878. Unmarried. Educ. at Alyn School, Mold, University Coll., Aberystwyth, and Christ's Coll., Cambridge; B.A., LL.B. with honours. Barrister, Inner Temple 1904 and practised on the Chester and N. Wales Circuit. Lieut. in 5th R.W.F. at the outbreak of war; and commanded 5/6 Royal Welsh Fusiliers, E.E.F. Served with the Mediterranean Expeditionary Force 1915. Was in the Suvla Bay landing, wounded, then returned to Battalion, and was in the terrible storm just prior to the evacuation, and was badly frost-bitten. Returned to the Battalion September 1916; was severely wounded at Gaza March 1917 and awarded the D.S.O. Recovered and rejoined his Battalion; was through all the fighting in Palestine from September 1917 till the defeat of the Turk in 1918; mentioned in despatches. Member (mil.) Flintshire Territorial Force Association; Trustee Welsh Troops Children's Fund; member Welsh Regional Pensions Council. Order of the Nile 1918. Dept.-Lieut. for Flintshire. A Liberal. Elected for Flint district in January 1913. Returned unopposed for Flintshire in December 1918; re-elected for Flintshire in November 1922 and sat until he was defeated in October 1924. Died 8 October 1939.

[1924 2nd ed.]

PATRICK, Colin Mark. Travellers', and Bucks. S. of Colin Grant Patrick, Esq. B. 1893; m. 1st, Mary, d. of Col. H. Mulliner; secondly, 1930, Lady Evelyn King, d. of Lionel, 3rd Earl of Lovelace (who m. 1st, 1918, Miles Graham, whom she divorced). Educ. at Eton, and Christ Church, Oxford. Served with 16th Lancers 1914-19. Rejoined 16th Lancers 1939. Joined Diplomatic Service 1919; retired 1930. Parliamentary Private Secretary to the Rt. Hon. Sir Samuel Hoare, Secretary of State for India 1933-June 1935, and when Secretary of State for Foreign Affairs June-December 1935, and to Lord Cranborne Under-Secretary of State for Foreign Affairs December 1935-February 1938. A Conservative. Elected for the Tavistock division of Devonshire in October 1931 and again in November 1935 and sat until his death on 7 January 1942. [1942]

PATTINSON, Robert. Southfields, Ruskington, Nr. Sleaford. National Liberal. S. of W. Pattinson, Esq., J.P., of Ruskington, Lincolnshire, and Anne Pattinson. B. at Ruskington, near Sleaford, Lincolnshire 1872; m. 1 August 1895, Catherine Lucy, d. of Henry Pratt, Esq., of Lincoln. Educ. at Carre's Grammar School, and privately. A Director of the Railway Construction Company and several other Companies. Alderman 1905, Vice-Chairman 1920 and Chairman 1934-54 of Kesteven County Council, Lincolnshire; J.P. 1906. A Liberal. Unsuccessfully contested the Grantham division of Lincolnshire in December 1918. Elected for the Grantham division in November 1922 and sat until he was defeated

in December 1923. Unsuccessfully contested Lincoln in May 1929. Knighted 1934. High Sheriff of Lincolnshire 1941. Died 2 December 1954. [1923]

PATTINSON, Samuel. Westholme, Sleaford, Lincolnshire. Devonshire, and National Liberal. S. of William and Anne Pattinson, of Ruskington, Lincolnshire. B. at Ruskington 17 December 1870; m. 15 April 1897, d. of George Bainbridge, Esq., J.P., of Lincoln. Educ. at Abingdon House School, Northampton. A Director of private family companies. J.P. for Kesteven, Lincolnshire; Alderman of Kesteven County Council; Chairman of Finance and Rates Committee. A Liberal. Unsuccessfully contested the Horncastle division of Lincolnshire in 1918 and February 1920. Elected for the Horncastle division of Lincolnshire in November 1922 and sat until he was defeated in October 1924. Joined Conservative Party in 1929. Died 15 November 1942.

[1924 2nd ed.]

PEAKE, Rt. Hon. Osbert. Continued in House after 1945: full entry in Volume IV.

PEARCE, Sir William. 14 Park Crescent, Portland Place, London. Shepway Lodge, Walmer. Reform. S. of William Pearce, Esq., of Poplar, and Maria, d. of Capt. James Evans. B. 1853 at Poplar; m. 1885, Ethel Alexandra, d. of Edwin Neame, Esq., of Selling, Kent. Educ. at Royal College of Science. A Director of Spencer Chapman and Measel Limited, Chemical Manufacturers. A member of the London County Council from 1892-1901; a J.P. for London; Knighted 1915. Chairman of Committee on War Wealth 1920. A Liberal. Unsuccessfully contested the Limehouse division of Tower Hamlets in 1900. Sat for the Limehouse division of Tower Hamlets 1906-18 and for the Limehouse division of Stepney from December 1918 until he was defeated in November 1922. Vice-President of Federation of British Industries. Died 24 August 1932. [1922]

PEARSON, Arthur. Continued in House after 1945: full entry in Volume IV.

PEARSON, William George. 231 Albert Road, Jarrow. B. 1882. Mayor of Jarrow 1928-30. A Conservative. Unsuccessfully contested the Houghton-le-Spring division of Durham in May 1929. Elected for the Jarrow division of Durham in October 1931 and sat until he was defeated in November 1935. C.B.E. 1938. Died 4 October 1963.
[1935]

PEASE, Rt. Hon. Herbert Pike. Merrow Croft, Guildford. 65 Onslow Gardens, London. Athenaeum, Brooks's, Carlton, St. Stephen's, and Bath. S. of Arthur Pease, Esq., MP for Whitby from 1880-85, and for Darlington from 1895-98, and Mary, d. of Ebenezer Pike, Esq., of Besborough, Co. Cork (she died 1948). B. 7 May 1867; m. 1894, Alice, d. of the Very Rev. Dr. Luckock, Dean of Lichfield. Educ. at Brighton Coll., and Trinity Hall, Cambridge. A J.P. for Surrey and J.P. and Dept.-Lieut. for the N. Riding of Yorkshire; President of the Church Army 1917-49. Unionist Whip 1906-10 and January 1911 to May 1915; Assistant Postmaster-Gen. May 1915 to October 1922. PC. 1917. A Conservative. Sat for Darlington as a Liberal Unionist from September 1898 to January 1910, when he was defeated. Re-elected for Darlington in December 1910. Sat until February 1923 when he was created Baron Daryngton. Ecclesiastical Commissioner from 1923 to 1949. Church Estates Commissioner from 1926 to 1948. Joint Treasurer of Queen Anne's Bounty 1935-39. Member of Church Assembly. Died 10 May 1949.
[1923]

PEASE, William Edwin. Mowden, Darlington. Boodle's. S. of Edwin Lucas Pease, Esq., of Mowden, Darlington, and Frances Helen Edwards, of Cascob, Radnorshire. B. at Darlington 3 June 1865. Unmarried. Educ. at Clifton, and Trinity Coll., Cambridge. Director of the Cleveland Bridge and Engineering Company, Consett Steel and Iron Company, and North Brancepeth Coal Company. Alderman County Borough of Darlington. Mayor of Darlington 1924-25. A Conservative. Sat for Darlington from February 1923 until his death on 23 January 1926.
[1926]

PEAT, Charles Urie. Wycliffe Hall, Barnard Castle. Carlton, and Royal Automobile. S. of Sir William Peat, C.V.O., of Wykeham Rise, Totteridge. B. 28 February 1892; m. 1914, Ruth, d. of the Rev. Henry Pulley, of Overstrand, Norfolk. Educ. at Sedbergh, and Trinity Coll., Oxford. A Chartered Accountant, member of firm of Peat Marwick Mitchell and Company. Parliamentary Private Secretary to the Rt. Hon. Oliver Lyttelton, President of Board of Trade January-June 1941, and to Harold Macmillan, when Joint Parliamentary Secretary Ministry of Supply July 1941-March 1942; Joint Parliamentary Secretary Ministry of Supply March 1942-March 1945. A Conservative. Elected for Darlington in October 1931 and sat until he was defeated in July 1945. Parliamentary Secretary Ministry of National Insurance March-July 1945. President of Institute of Chartered Accountants in England and Wales 1959-60. Served with City of London Yeomanry 1914-18, M.C., and as a Maj. in Durham Light Infantry 1939-40.*
[1945]

PEEL, Lieut.-Col. Robert Francis. 26 Queensberry Place, London. St. Mary's, Great Bentley, Essex. Carlton, Windham, and Guards'. S. of Capt. Francis Peel and grand-s. of the Rt. Hon. William Yates Peel, MP. B. 1874; m. 1903, Alice, d. of Sir Thomas Meyrick, Bart., K.C.B. Educ. at Harrow. Joined the Coldstream Guards 1898, Capt. 1906, retired 1909, served in South African War 1899-1902, and was mentioned in despatches. Lieut.-Col. 4th (S.R.) Battalion East Surrey Regiment. A Unionist. Unsuccessfully contested mid Northamptonshire in 1906. Elected for the Woodbridge division of Suffolk in January 1910 and sat until July 1920 when he was appointed Gov. of St. Helena. Died in St. Helena 10 August 1924.
[1920]

PEEL, Lieut.-Col. Hon. Sidney, Cornwallis, D.S.O. 26 Hill Street, Berkeley Square, London. Brooks's. S. of the 1st Visct. Peel. B. in London 3 June 1870; m. 1914, Lady Delia Spencer, d. of the 6th Earl Spencer. Educ. at Eton, and New Coll., Oxford. Fellow of Trinity Coll., Oxford; Secretary of the Licensing Commission;

President of the Trust and Loan Company of Canada; Director National Bank of Egypt; Lieut.-Col. Bedfordshire Yeomanry. D.S.O. 1917. Author of *Trooper 8008 I.Y.*, and *The Binding of the Nile*. A Coalition Unionist. Elected for the Uxbridge division of Middlesex in December 1918 and sat until he retired in October 1922. Barrister-at-Law, Lincoln's Inn, 1898. Chairman of Export Credits Guarantee Department Advisory Committee 1919-38. Created Bart. 1936. C.B. 1929 Dept. Steward of Oxford University from 1922. Died 19 December 1938.

[1922]

PEMBERTON-BILLING, Noel. See BILLING, Noel Pemberton.

PENDER, Capt. John Cuthbert Denison. See DENISON-PENDER, Capt. John Cuthbert Denison.

PENNEFATHER, Sir John de Fonblanque, Bart. Lyne Place, Virginia Water, Surrey. Carlton, and St. Stephen's. S. of Maj. Kingsmill Pennefather, of Co. Tipperary. B. 29 March 1856; m. Madeline, d. of Sir R. Stewart. J.P. for Herefordshire and Hertfordshire; Master of N. Hereford Foxhounds 1901-03; wrote various pamphlets and articles on political and economic problems. Created Bart. 1924. A Conservative. Unsuccessfully contested N. Monmouthshire in 1900. Sat for the Kirkdale division of Liverpool from February 1915 until he retired in May 1929. Assumed the additional forename John in 1923. Died 8 August 1933. [1929]

PENNY, Sir Frederick George, Bart. 12 Buckingham Gate, London. The Old Rectory, Felpham, Sussex. Carlton, and Junior Carlton. S. of Frederick James Penny, Esq., of Bitterne, Hampshire. B. 1876; m. 1905, Anne Boyle, d. of Sir John Gunn, J.P., of St. Mellons, Glamorgan. Educ. at King Edward VI Grammar School, Southampton. Senior Partner of Fraser and Company (Government Brokers), Singapore. Managing Director of Eastern Smelting Company Limited, Penang. Represented Federated Malay States Government in the negotiations with the Dutch Government in regard to accumulated war tin stocks resulting in Bandoeng Agreement. A Master Mariner. Parliamentary Private Secretary to the Financial Secretary to the War Office 1923; Assistant Government Whip 1926-January 1928; Junior Lord of the Treasury January 1928-June 1929 and August-November 1931. Vice-Chamberlain to H.Ms. Household November 1931-September 1932, Comptroller September 1932-May 1935, Treasurer May 1935-May 1937. Created Knight Bach. 1929; Bart. 1933. A Conservative. Sat for Kingston-upon-Thames from November 1922 until May 1937 when he was created Baron Marchwood. Created Visct. Marchwood 1945. Treasurer of Conservative Party 1938-46. Master of Company of Master Mariners 1941-45. Died 1 January 1955.

[1937]

PERCY, Charles. House of Commons, London. S. of Hugh Percy, Esq. B. 1851. A Solicitor and Coroner for N. Northumberland. Was active in the work of local Friendly Societies and in the provision of homes for aged Miners; travelled widely. A Coalition Unionist. Unsuccessfully contested the Wansbeck division of Northumberland in January 1910 and Tynemouth in December 1910. Elected for Tynemouth in December 1918 and sat until he retired in October 1922. Died 10 September 1929. [1922]

PERCY, Rt. Hon. Lord Eustace Sutherland Campbell The Old Rectory, Albury, Nr. Guildford. S. of 7th Duke of Northumberland. B. 21 March 1887; m. 4 December 1918, Stella Katherine, d. of Maj.-Gen. Lawrence Drummond. Educ. at Eton, and Christ Church, Oxford. A Member of the Diplomatic Service. Parliamentary Secretary to the Board of Education March to May 1923; Parliamentary Secretary to the Ministry of Health May 1923 to January 1924. President of the Board of Education November 1924-June 1929; Minister without Portfolio with a seat in the Cabinet June 1935-March 1936. PC. 1924. A Conservative. Unsuccessfully contested Kingston-upon-Hull Central in March 1919. Sat for Hastings from May 1921 until he resigned in October 1937. Chairman of British Council

277

1936-37. Rector of King's Coll., Newcastle 1937-52. Vice-Chancellor of Durham University 1947-49. Created Baron Percy of Newcastle 1953. Chairman of Royal Commission on the Law relating to Mental Illness and Mental Deficiency 1954-57. Died 3 April 1958.   [1937]

PERKINS, Col. Edwin King, C.B.E., V.D. 31 Winn Road, Southampton. Carlton, 1900, St. Stephen's, and Royal Southern Yacht. S. of G.P. Perkins, Esq., J.P. B. 28 February 1855; m. 1st, 1881, Mary, d. of Thomas Forder, Esq; secondly, 1924, Eileen Isabel, d. of G.W. Nicolls, Esq., of Camberley. Educ. at King Edward's School, Southampton, and Cheltenham Coll. Dept.-Lieut. and J.P. for County of Southampton. Honorary Col. 5/7th Hampshire Regiment. A Conservative. Unsuccessfully contested Southampton in 1918. Elected for Southampton in November 1922 and sat until he retired in May 1929. Knighted June 1929. Died 8 January 1937.   [1929]

PERKINS, Walter Frank. Boldre Bridge House, Lymington, Hampshire. Carlton. S. of Walter Perkins, Esq., of Southampton. B. 3 May 1865; m. 1901, Elizabeth, d. of Robert Dempster, Esq., of Vale Royal, Cheshire. Educ. at Forest School, Essex, and Royal Agricultural Coll., Cirencester. A Consulting Surveyor. A Unionist. Elected for the New Forest division of Hampshire in January and December 1910. Returned unopposed for the New Forest and Christchurch division of Hampshire in December 1918 and sat until he retired in October 1922. Died 17 March 1946.   [1922]

PERKINS, Walter Robert Dempster. Continued in House after 1945: full entry in Volume IV.

PERRING, Sir William George. Beaulieu, Arthur Road, Wimbledon Park, London. S. of Henry Perring, Esq. B. 17 March 1866; m. 8 June 1905, Betsy, d. of John Barraball, Esq., of Saltash. Educ. at St. Pancras Wesleyan School. Mayor of Paddington 1911-12. Head of the firm of William Perring and Company Limited, House Furnishers; President of the Padding-

ton and Bayswater Chamber of Commerce. Member of various local war committees, War Aims, War Savings, V.A.D., Food Control and Red Cross. President London and Suburban Retail Traders' Federation; President National Chamber of Trade. Managing Director Crossley Bedstead Company Limited. J.P. for County of London. Alderman Paddington Borough Council, Mayor 1911-12. Knight Bach. 1926. A Conservative. Sat for Paddington N. from December 1918 until he retired in May 1929. Died 24 August 1937.   [1929]

PERRY, Samuel Frederick. 223 Pitshanger Lane, Ealing. Parliamentary Labour. S. of Samuel Perry, Esq. B. at Stockport 29 June 1877; m. 1st, 26 December 1901, d. of John Birch, Esq. (she died 8 January 1930); secondly, 1931, Olive Elizabeth Gardner, of Highgate. Father of the tennis player Fred Perry. Educ. at elementary and technical schools. Operative Cotton Spinner. Inspector Ministry of Health 1911-18. Secretary of the Co-operative Party 1918. Parliamentary Private Secretary to Rt. Hon. J. Wheatley, Minister of Health 1924 and to Rt. Hon. W. Graham, President of the Board of Trade June 1929. A Co-operative and Labour Member. Unsuccessfully contested Stockport in 1920 and 1922. Elected for the Kettering division of Northamptonshire in December 1923; defeated October 1924. Re-elected for the Kettering division in May 1929 and sat until he was defeated in October 1931. Died 19 October 1954.

[1931 2nd ed.]

PETERS, Dr. Sidney John. Hilton House, Hilton, Huntingdonshire. National Liberal, and Royal Automobile. S. of Herbert Peters, Esq. B. 2 December 1885; m. December 1912, Essie, d. of Alderman F.W. Mills, of Cambridge. Educ. at Cambridge County High School, and Cambridge and Dublin Universities. Admitted a Solicitor 1912. Practised at Cambridge, St. Ives, and Huntingdon. Commissioner for Oaths. M.A., LL.B. (Cambridge), M.A., LL.D. (Dublin). Member of Ecclesiastical Committee; President of Cambridge Society for Psychical Investigation. Parliamentary

Private Secretary to Isaac Foot, Secretary for Mines August-October 1931, to Rt. Hon. A.E. Brown when Secretary for Mines October 1932, and when Minister of Labour June 1935-May 1940. A Liberal until 1931, thereafter a Liberal National. Elected for Huntingdonshire in May 1929 and sat until he retired in June 1945. Secretary and Legal Adviser to Central Council Forage Department for Civil Supplies 1914-18. Died 9 January 1976. [1945]

PETHERICK, Maurice. 52 Westminster Mansions, Little Smith Street, London. Porthpean House, St. Austell, Cornwall. United University, and Buck's. S. of George Tallack Petherick, Esq., of Porthpean House, St. Austell. B. 5 October 1894. Educ. at Marlborough, and Trinity Coll., Cambridge. Served with 1st. Royal Devon Yeomanry 1914; Foreign Office 1916-17; with Royal Scots Greys in France 1918. Recommissioned Maj.; General List October 1939. A National Conservative. Unsuccessfully contested the Penryn and Falmouth division of Cornwall in May 1929. Elected for the Penryn and Falmouth division of Cornwall in October 1931 and sat until he was defeated in July 1945. Financial Secretary to War Office May-July 1945. High Sheriff of Cornwall 1957. Director of Prudential Assurance Company Limited 1953-71. Author of *Captain Culverin*, *Victoire* and *Restoration Rogues*.* [1945]

PETHICK-LAWRENCE, Rt. Hon. Frederick William. 11 Old Square, Lincoln's Inn, London. Fourways, Gomshall, Surrey. Royal Aero, and Queen's. S. of Alfred Lawrence, Esq. B. 28 December 1871; m. 1st, 1901, Emmeline, d. of Henry Pethick, Esq., of Weston-super-Mare (she died 1954); secondly, 1957, Helen Millar, d. of Sir John Craggs, and widow of D. McCombie, Esq. Educ. at Eton, and Trinity Coll., Cambridge. Barrister-at-Law, Inner Temple 1898. Editor of *London Echo*, *Labour Record and Review* and *Votes for Women*. Financial Secretary to the Treasury June 1929-August 1931. PC. 1937. Vice-Chairman of Parliamentary Labour Party 1942. A Labour Member. Unsuccessfully contested S. Aberdeen in April 1917 as a Peace candidate,

and S. Islington in 1922. Sat for Leicester W. from December 1923-October 1931, when he was defeated. Elected for Edinburgh E. in November 1935 and sat until August 1945 when he was created Baron Pethick-Lawrence. Fellow of Trinity Coll., Cambridge 1897. A prominent supporter of women's suffrage, imprisoned for conspiracy for nine months in 1912. Member of Union for Democratic Control, Treasurer 1916. Assumed the additional surname of of Pethick 1901. Secretary of State for India and Burma August 1945-April 1947. Member of Political Honours Scrutiny Committee 1949-61. Died 10 September 1961. [1945]

PETO, Maj. Basil Arthur John. Greenhill Brow, Farnham, Surrey. Cavalry, and Queen's. S. of Sir Basil Peto, 1st Bart., of Barnstaple. B. 13 December 1900; m. 1934, Patricia Geraldine, d. of Gerald Browne, Esq., O.B.E., and of Mrs. Riversdale Grenfell. Educ. at Harrow, and St. John's Coll., Cambridge, B.A. Maj. Kings Dragoon Guards. Retired (R.A.R.O.). Parliamentary Private Secretary to The Rt. Hon. Geoffrey Lloyd from December 1941 to July 1945. A National Conservative. Elected for the Kings Norton division of Birmingham in May 1941 and sat until he was defeated in July 1945. Died in a shooting accident 3 February 1954. [1945]

PETO, Sir Basil Edward, Bart. 99 Eaton Square, London. Tawstock Court, Nr. Barnstaple. Carlton, and Conservative. S. of Sir S. Morton Peto, 1st Bart. B. 13 August 1862; m. 30 August 1892, Mary, d. of Capt. T.C. Baird (she died 3 November 1931). Educ. at Harrow. A partner in Peto Brothers, Builders, and a Director of Morgan Crucible Company Limited. Created Bart. 1927. A Conservative. Sat for the Devizes division of Wiltshire from January 1910 to November 1918, when he retired. Elected for the Barnstaple division of Devon in November 1922, defeated there in December 1923. Re-elected for the Barnstaple division of Devon in October 1924 and sat until he retired in October 1935. Chief Commissioner for Belgian Refugees 1916. Sat as an Independent from July to November 1928 while the

Conservative Whip was withdrawn from him. Died 28 January 1945. [1935]

PETO, Geoffrey Kelsall, C.B.E. 15 Great College Street, London. Sandford Park, Sandford St. Martin, Oxford. Carlton. S. of William Herbert Peto, Esq., of Dunkinty, Elgin. B. 8 September 1878; m. 1st, 1 July 1903, Pauline, d. of William Quirin, Esq., of Boston, U.S.A., and widow of Lieut.-Col. R.C. Frith, 15th Hussars (she died 1950); secondly, 1951, Edna, d. of Edward B. Hilton, Esq. Educ. at Eton. Capt. Wiltshire Yeomanry; Director of the Morgan Crucible Company 1903-47. Parliamentary Private Secretary to Col. Lane-Fox when Secretary for Mines July 1926-January 1928, and to the Rt. Hon. Earl Winterton, Under-Secretary for India January 1928-May 1929; Parliamentary Private Secretary to the Rt. Hon. Walter Runciman, President of the Board of Trade November 1931. A Conservative. Unsuccessfully contested the Louth division of Lincolnshire in December 1923. Sat for the Frome division of Somerset from October October 1924-May 1929. when he was defeated. Elected for the Bilston division of Wolverhampton in October 1931 and sat until he retired in October 1935. Dept.-Controller of Contracts, Ministry of Munitions. C.B.E. 1919; K.B.E. 1939. Chairman of International Copyright Committee 1935. Chairman of Food Council 1936-39. Dept.-Commissioner for Civil Defence, S.W. region 1939, Commissioner 1940. Regional Controller for Southern England, Ministry of Supply 1941-45. Died 8 January 1956. [1935]

PHILIPPS, Maj.-Gen. Sir Ivor, K.Ç.B., D.S.O. Cosheston Hall, Pembroke. Chantrey House, Eccleston Street, London. United Service, and Royal Automobile. 2nd s. of the Rev. Canon Sir J.E. Philipps, Bart. B. 9 September 1861; m. 1891, Marian Isobel, d. of J.B. Mirrlees, Esq., of Glasgow. Educ. at Felsted School. Served in Militia 1881-83; entered the army as Lieut. 1883, Capt. 1894, Maj. 1901. Served in Burma Campaign 1887-89; Chin Lushai Expedition 1889; Miranzai Expedition 1891; Isazai Expedition 1895; North-West Frontier of India 1896; Tirah Campaign 1896-97;

China Expedition 1900; Relief of Pekin; D.S.O. 1900. Was Col. Commanding Pembroke Yeomanry 1908-12; Brigadier-Gen. 115th Brigade 1914; Maj.-Gen. 38th (Welsh) division 1915-16. Parliamentary Secretary (Military) Ministry of Munitions of War June-September 1915. Dept.-Lieut. and County Alderman Pembrokeshire. Vice-Chairman 1912, Chairman 1913-15, for Pembroke County Council. J.P. for Haverfordwest. Chairman Liberal War Committee. Vice-Lieut. for the County of Pembroke. K.C.B. 1917. A Knight of Justice of St. John of Jerusalem. A Liberal. Elected for Southampton in 1906 and sat until he was defeated in November 1922. Died 15 August 1940. [1922]

PHILIPPS, Sir Owen Cosby, G.C.M.G. Chelsea House, Cadogan Place, London. Amroth Castle, Pembrokeshire. Coomb, Carmarthen. Carlton, Marlborough, and Bachelors'. S. of Canon Sir James Philipps, 12th Bart., and the Hon. Lady Philipps, sister of the 5th Baron Wynford. B. 1863; m. 1902, Mai Alice Magdalene, co-heiress of Thomas Morris, Esq., Dept.-Lieut. of Coomb, Carmarthenshire. Educ. at Newton Coll., South Devon. A Shipowner; Chairman and Managing Director of the Royal Mail Steam Packet Company, the Union Castle Line, and associated shipping companies, which owned over 500 mail, passenger, and cargo steamers of a total gross register tonnage of nearly 2,000,000 tons. President of Chamber of Shipping of United Kingdom and of Federation of Chambers of Commerce of British Empire. Director of the London and South-Western Railway. M.F.H. Carmarthenshire Hounds from 1912. Served on numerous Government Committees and Inquiries. Knight of Justice of the Order of St. John; Hon. Capt. R.N.R.; member of the Executive Committee of the Imperial Institute from 1912 and Vice-President of the Royal Colonial Institute; member of the Committee of Management King Edward's Horse (Overseas Dominion Regiment) from 1913; Vice-Chairman of the Port of London Authority 1909-13; Vice-President of the Liverpool School of Tropical Medicine; Trustee of the Royal Alfred Aged Merchant Seamen's

Institute. J.P. for Carmarthenshire, Pembrokeshire, Haverfordwest, and Glasgow; High Sheriff of Pembrokeshire 1904; Dept.-Lieut. for Pembrokeshire. Owned 5,000 acres in Carmarthenshire and Pembrokeshire. Unsuccessfully contested, as a Liberal, Montgomery district in 1895 and Darlington in September 1898. Sat for Pembroke and Haverfordwest boroughs as a Liberal from January 1906 to December 1910 when he retired. Elected as a Unionist for Chester in March 1916 and for the Chester division of Cheshire in December 1918. Sat until he retired in October 1922. Created Baron Kylsant 1923. Convicted of publishing false commercial information in 1928 and sentenced to a year's imprisonment. Died 5 June 1937. [1922]

PHILIPSON, Hilton. 22 Berkeley Square, London. Broom Hill, Esher, Surrey. Guards', Bachelors', and Bath. S. of Roland Philipson, Esq., for many years a Director of the North-Eastern Railway Company. B. 5 November 1892 at Tynemouth; m. 5 June 1917, Mabel, d. of Albert Russell, Esq. Educ. at Eton, and Pembroke Coll., Oxford. A National Liberal. Elected for the Berwick-on-Tweed division of Northumberland in November 1922 and sat until May 1923 when his election was declared void on petition. (His wife was elected as Conservative Member for the division on 31 May 1923). Unsuccessfully contested, as a Conservative, the Wansbeck division of Northumberland in December 1923 and Gateshead in October 1924. Served in Scots Guards 1914-19. Died 12 April 1941. [1923]

PHILIPSON, Hylton Ralph Murray. See MURRAY-PHILIPSON, Hylton Ralph.

PHILIPSON, Mabel. Claremont Farm, Esher, Surrey. Mabel, d. of Albert Russell, Esq. B. 1887; m. 1st, 1911, Stanley Rhodes, Esq. (he died 1911); m. secondly, 5 June 1917, Capt. Hilton Philipson (he died 1941). A well-known actress. A Conservative. Elected for the Berwick-on-Tweed division of Northumberland in May 1923, in succession to her husband (unseated on petition). Re-elected for the Berwick-on-Tweed division of Northumberland in December 1923 and sat until she retired in May 1929. Died 8 January 1951. [1929]

PHILLIPPS, Henry Vivian. 14 Ashley Gardens, London. Reform, Eighty, and Scottish Liberal. S. of Henry Mitchell Phillipps, Esq., and Louise Phillipps. B. 1870; m. 1899, Agnes, d. of James Ford, Esq., of Edinburgh. Educ. at Charterhouse, Heidelberg, and Caius Coll., Cambridge. A Barrister-at-Law, Lincoln's Inn 1907. Was Mr. Asquith's Private Secretary 1917-22. Chief Liberal Whip February 1923-October 1924. A Liberal. Unsuccessfully contested Blackpool in 1906, Maidstone in January and December 1910, and Rochdale in 1918. Elected for Edinburgh W. in November 1922 and sat until he was defeated in October 1924. Unsuccessfully contested Edinburgh W. in May 1929. On the staff of Fettes Coll. 1893-1905. Private Secretary to the Rt. Hon. T. McKinnon Wood, Secretary for Scotland 1912-16. Chairman of Liberal Party Organization 1925-27. Chairman of W. Kent Quarter Sessions 1933-45, W. Kent Unemployment Appeal Tribunal 1934-40, Kent Agricultural Wages Committee 1935-40. Died 16 January 1955. [1924 2nd ed.]

PHILLIPS, Dr. Marion. 14 New Street Square, London. National Labour. B. 29 October 1881 at Melbourne. Unmarried. Educ. at the Presbyterian Ladies' Coll., Ormond Coll., Melbourne University, and at London University School of Economics; D.Sc. (Econ.) London. Secretary of Women's Labour League 1913-18. Chief Woman Officer of Labour Party from 1918. Member of Reconstruction Committee 1917-18, of Consumers' Council, of Ministry of Food 1918-19, of Central Committee of Women's Training and Employment from 1914, and of Advisory Committee of Magistrates of County of London. Editor of *The Labour Woman*. A Labour Member. Elected for Sunderland in May 1929 and sat until she was defeated in October 1931. Died 23 January 1932. [1931 2nd ed.]

PICKERING, Lieut.-Col. Emil William D.S.O. Netherton Hall, Nr. Wakefield.

St. Stephen's. S. of James and Emily Pickering, of Highcliffe, Dewsbury. B. at Dewsbury 3 January 1882; m. 1919, Evelyn Joyce Morton, eld. d. of John E. Shaw, Esq., J.P., of Brooklands, near Halifax. Educ. at Tettenhall Coll. A Woollen Manufacturer, member of the firm of Pickering, Greaves and Company, Ravensthorpe Mills, Dewsbury. From the outbreak of the war served with R.F.A., later Lieut.-Col.; D.S.O. 1917. Invalided, and seconded to the Department of Wool Textile Production. A Coalition Unionist. Sat for Dewsbury from December 1918 until he retired in October 1922. Dept-Lieut. for the W. Riding of Yorkshire. Dept. Regional Commissioner for Civil Defence 1941-42. Killed in a riding accident 14 March 1942. [1922]

PICKERING, Ernest Harold. 4 St. Albans Road, Leicester. National Liberal. S. of Aaron Pickering, Esq., of Leicester. B. 1881; m. 1st, 1910, Eleanor Maud, d. of Benjamin Sutton, Esq. (she died 1946). Classical Exhibitioner at Exeter Coll., Hebrew Prizeman at Manchester Coll., Oxford, M.A. 1916. A Unitarian Minister 1910-27. Professor of English Yamagata Koto Gakko in Japan 1927-31; a Journalist and Lecturer. Author of *A brief survey of English literature* and *Japan's place in the modern world*. A Liberal. Elected for Leicester W. in October 1931 and sat until he retired in October 1935. Unsuccessfully contested the Newark division of Nottinghamshire in February 1950. Professor of English Literature, Tokyo University of Literature and Science 1936-41 and 1945-46, Professor Emeritus 1954. Interned in Japan 1941-45. Died in Paris 31 January 1957. [1935]

PICKFORD, Hon. Mary Ada, C.B.E. 30 St. Leonard's Terrace, London. King Sterndale, Buxton. D. of Lord Sterndale. B. 1884. Unmarried. Educ. at Wycombe Abbey School, and Lady Margaret Hall, Oxford, M.A. Oxford. C.B.E. 1929. A Conservative. Unsuccessfully contested the Farnworth division of Lancashire in May 1929. Elected for Hammersmith N. in October 1931 and sat until her death on 6 March 1934. [1934]

PICKTHORN, Kenneth William Murray. Continued in House after 1945: full entry in Volume IV.

PICTON-TURBERVILL, Edith, O.B.E. 14 Gayfere Street, London. D. of Col. John Picton-Turbervill (formerly Warlow), of Emenny Priory, Glamorgan, and of Eleanor, d. of Sir Grenville Temple, of Stowe. B. 13 June 1872. Educ. at Royal School, Bath. Assumed the surname Picton-Turbervill in lieu of Warlow in 1891. An author and writer. National Vice-President Y.W.C.A. 1914-20 and 1922-28; member of Council of League of Nations Union and Women's International League; member Royal Institute for International Affairs. A Labour Member. Unsuccessfully contested N. Islington November 1922, Stroud October 1924. Elected for The Wrekin division of Shropshire in May 1929 and sat until she was defeated in October 1931. Died 31 August 1960. [1931 2nd ed.]

PIELOU, Douglas Percival. Dudley Road, Tipton, Staffordshire. S. of Percival G. Pielou, a retired civil servant. B. in Glasgow 17 October 1887; m. 5 December 1914, Nora, d. of Joseph Thomas Pitchford, Esq. Educ. privately. Registrar for Tipton 1917; member of Tipton Council; Chairman of West Midlands Area, British Legion, and Vice-Chairman of British Legion throughout the country. Served with the Cameron Highlanders in France 1915. Member of Tipton Education Committee. Chairman United Services Fund Committee. Member of Ministry of Pensions Advisory Committee. Honorary Secretary Staffordshire Training Home for Nurses. Gov. Birmingham University. Vice-President British Legion and of British Empire Service League. A Conservative. Elected for the Stourbridge division of Worcestershire in November 1922 and sat until his death on 9 January 1927. [1927]

PIKE, Cecil Frederick. 167 Retford Road, Handsworth, Sheffield. S. of William Pike, Esq., of Bromley. B. 26 February 1898; m. 22 September 1922, Elinor, d. of James Dunn, Esq., of Darlington. Educ. at elementary school, and at Owens Coll., Manchester. An Organizing Propagandist. Served with R.G.A. x6, T.M.B.R.G.A. overseas 1915-19. A Conservative. Unsuccessfully contested the Rother Valley division of Yorkshire in May 1929. Elected for the Attercliffe division of Sheffield in October 1931 and sat until he was defeated in November 1935. Unsuccessfully contested the Colne Valley division of Yorkshire in July 1939. Died 12 May 1968.   [1935]

PILCHER, GEORGE. 1 Lawrence Mansions, Chelsea, London. High Trees, St. George's Hill, Weybridge. Savile. S. of W.G. Pilcher, Esq., of Folkestone. B. 1882; m. 1910, Muriel, d. of Dr. G. Blackman, of Portsmouth. Educ. at Kent Coll., Canterbury, and at Wadham Coll., Oxford; Mod.-Hist.Hons. Joined staff of *Morning Post* 1907, Foreign Editor 1909-14, Calcutta Correspondent 1914-24, special correspondent with Turkish Army in Balkan War 1912, and with N.W. Frontier Force 1920; Assistant Editor of *Calcutta Statesman*; served with Calcutta Port Defence 1915-19. Member of Indian Imperial Assembly 1924. A Conservative. Elected for the Penryn and Falmouth division of Cornwall in October 1924 and sat until he retired in May 1929. Secretary of Royal Empire Society 1929-35. Barrister-at-Law, Inner Temple 1927. Died 8 December 1962.   [1929]

PILDITCH, Sir Philip Edward, Bart. 8 Old Bond Street, London. Bartropps, Weybridge, Surrey. Yellow Sands, Thurlestone, Devon. Carlton, Bath, and 1900. S. of Philip John Pilditch, Esq., of Plymouth. B. 12 August 1861; m. 11 July 1888, Emily Mary, eld. d. of John Lewis, Esq. Educ. at Cheveley Hall, Mannamead, and King's Coll., London. An Architect. Vice-Chairman of London County Council 1912-13. Knight Bach. 1918. Chairman Parliamentary Local Government Committees 1907-11; Delegacy of King's Coll. from 1913; Gov. of Northern Polytechnic 1913. Member of House of Commons Estimates Committee; Founder of Battalion Funds, New Army of London, Middlesex and Surrey 1915. A Conservative. Unsuccessfully contested as a Liberal Unionist the St. Ives division of Cornwall in 1906, and

E. Islington as a Unionist in December 1910. Sat for the Spelthorne division of Middlesex as a Conservative from December 1918 until he retired in October 1931. Member of London County Council 1907-19. Created Bart. 1929. J.P. for County of London. Died 17 December 1948.   [1931 2nd ed.]

PILKINGTON, Richard Antony. Continued in House after 1945: full entry in Volume IV.

PILKINGTON, Robert Rivington. 2 Langham Mansions, Earl's Court Square, London. United University. S. of Henry Mulock Pilkington, Esq., Q.C., and Dept.-Lieut., of Tore, Tyrellspass, Co. Westmeath, and Mrs. M.C. Pilkington. B. in Dublin 8 February 1870; m. 1899, Ethel, d. of Capt. Longworth Dames, of Greenhill, Edenderry, King's Co. (she died 18 May 1920). Educ. at Uppingham, and Pembroke Coll., Cambridge. A Barrister-at-Law, Lincoln's Inn 1893, admitted legal practitioner in Western Australia 1894-1921. A Liberal. Unsuccessfully contested Dundee in 1922. Elected for the Keighley division of Yorkshire in December 1923 and sat until he retired in October 1924. Member of Legislative Assembly of Western Australia 1917-21. K.C. 1906. Died 30 June 1942.   [1924 2nd ed.]

PINKHAM, Col. Charles, O.B.E. Linden Lodge, Winchester Avenue, Brondesbury, London. B. 1853; m. 1876, Margaret Mary (she died 1929). A Willesden Building Contractor. Honorary Col. Willesden Volunteers. Was for several years Chairman of the Willesden District Council; Alderman Middlesex County Council, Chairman 1927-30. J.P. and Dept.-Lieut. for Middlesex. A Coalition Unionist. Elected for Willesden W. in December 1918 and sat until he retired in October 1922. O.B.E. 1920. Knighted 1928. High Sheriff of Middlesex 1930-31. Died 7 March 1938.   [1922]

PLUGGE, Capt. Leonard Frank. 50 Portland Place, London. Franklen House, Aldwyck Bay, Sussex. Constitutional, Carlton, Authors', R.A.F., and Royal Automobile.

S. of Frank Plugge, Esq., of Brighton. B. 21 September 1889; m. 1934, Gertrude Anne, d. of F.R. Muckleston, Esq., of Muckleston, Shropshire. Educ. at Dulwich, University Coll., London, B.Sc., and University of Brussels. Served with R.N.V.R. 1917; Capt. R.A.F. 1918; Honorary Col. 29th Kent A.A. Cadet Battalion R.E.; on Interallied Aeronautical Commission of Control, Berlin 1919-20; and Paris, Chalais and Meudon 1920-21; with Royal Aircraft Establishment, Farnborough 1918, with Underground Groups of Companies 1923-30. Member of General Committee of Radio Society of Great Britain 1923-35; with National Physical Laboratory 1917, Imperial Coll. of Science 1918, with Department of Scientific Research Air Ministry 1918-19; Aeronautical Delegate Spa Conference 1919-20. A Civil Engineer. Chairman of International Broadcasting Company's Group of Companies and of Parliamentary and Scientific Committee; Honorary Secretary of Interparliamentary Union. Chevalier of the Legion of Honour. A Conservative. Elected for the Chatham division of Rochester in November 1935 and sat until he was defeated in July 1945. Fellow of Royal Aeronautical, Royal Astronomical, and Royal Meteorological Societies.* [1945]

PLUNKETT, George Noble Plunkett, Count. 26 Upper Fitzwilliam Street, Dublin. S. of P.J. Plunkett, Esq., of Rathmines. B. 1851; m. 1884, Josephine Cranny. Educ. at Jesuit Coll., Clongowes, and Trinity Coll., Dublin. A Barrister-at-Law, F.R.S.A.I., and a member of several of the principal academies of Europe. A Count of Rome 1884. Father of one of the leaders of the Sinn Fein rebellion executed in Dublin in 1916. Two other sons were imprisoned in respect of that event. Was deported to live in Oxford, but allowed by the Government to return to Ireland. Re-arrested with others in May 1918. Unsuccessfully contested, as a Parnellite Nationalist, mid Tyrone in 1892 and the St. Stephens Green division of Dublin in 1895 and 1898. A Sinn Fein Member. Elected for N. Roscommon in February 1917, and returned unopposed for that division in December 1918 but did not take his seat. Member of Dail for N. Roscommon to 1921, for Leitrim and N. Roscommon 1921-23, and for Roscommon 1923-27. An Anti-Treaty Member, remaining a Sinn Fein after the formation of Fianna Fail. Minister for Fine Arts 1921-22. Director of Science and Art Museum, Dublin 1907-16. Died 12 March 1948. [1922]

POLE, David Graham. 31 Ennismore Gardens, London. Junior Army & Navy, and National Labour. S. of Capt. John Pole. B. 11 December 1877; m. 21 March 1918, Jessie Hair, d. of G.H. Pagan, Esq. Educ. at Edinburgh School and University. Admitted a Solicitor 1900; Solicitor Supreme Courts of Scotland 1901; Notary Public 1903; Solicitor in the House of Lords and Privy Council 1913. Transferred T.A.R. 1912 as Capt.; transferred to 12th Northumberland Fusiliers August 1914, which he later commanded; served in France etc. 1914-18; retired with rank of Maj. Treasurer National Labour Club 1929-30; Vice-Chairman Machinery of Government Committee of Labour Party 1920-30; Honorary Secretary British Committee on Indian Affairs 1916-30; London Correspondent of Indian Press. Parliamentary Private Secretary to the Rt. Hon. T. Shaw, Secretary of State War January-August 1931. A Labour Member. Unsuccessfully contested East Grinstead December 1918, a by-election for N. Edinburgh April 1920, S. Cardiff November 1922, Central Cardiff October 1924. Elected for Derbyshire S. in May 1929 and sat until he was defeated in October 1931. Died 26 November 1952.
[1931 2nd ed.]

POLLOCK, Rt. Hon. Sir Ernest Murray, Bart., K.B.E. 40 Thurloe Square, London. 1 King's Bench Walk, Temple, London. Northaw, Hertfordshire. Carlton, Athenaeum, and Oxford & Cambridge. 4th s. of George Frederick Pollock, Esq., Queen's Remembrancer and Senior Master of High Court of Justice. B. 25 November 1861; m. 1887, Laura Helen, d. of Sir Thomas Salt, 1st Bart., MP of Weeping Cross, Stafford. Educ. at Charterhouse,

Scholar; and Trinity Coll., Cambridge, M.A. Was called to the bar at the Inner Temple 1885; K.C. 1905; bencher 1914, Treasurer 1936. Recorder of Kingston-on-Thames from 1911 to 1919. Gov. of Charterhouse 1913, and Wellington Coll. 1921. Chairman of the "Contraband Committee" 1915, and Controller of the Foreign Trade Department of the Foreign Office 1917. Orders of the Legion of Honour and St. Maurice and St. Lazarus, for services in the blockade. Solicitor-Gen. January 1919 to March 1922; Attorney-Gen. March to October 1922. Created Bart. 1922. K.B.E. 1917; PC. 1922. Unsuccessfully contested, as a Liberal Unionist, the Spalding division of Lincolnshire in 1900 and 1906. Elected as a Conservative for the Warwick and Leamington division of Warwickshire in January and December 1910; returned unopposed for the Warwick and Leamington division in December 1918 and sat until October 1923 when he was appointed Master of the Rolls. High Steward of Stratford-on-Avon 1924-36. Master of the Rolls 1923-35. Created Baron Hanworth 1926, Visct. Hanworth 1936. Dept. High Steward of Cambridge University 1926-36. Died 22 October 1936.   [1923]

POLSON, Col. Sir Thomas Andrew, K.B.E., C.M.G., T.D. 18 Sussex Place, Regent's Park, London. Cavalry. Royal Ulster Yacht. S. of T.A. Polson, Esq., of Dublin and Tuam. B. at Tuam 28 August 1865; m. 1st, 1887, Rachel, widow of Col. W. Denny (divorced 1898); secondly, 1918, Elizabeth Jane, d. of John Lindsay, Esq., of Edinburgh and widow of F.A. Lindsay-Smith (she died 1945). Educ. in Dublin. Chief Inspector at the Royal Army Clothing Department. Maj. City of London Yeomanry, Rough Riders. An Independent Anti-Waste Member. Elected for the Dover division of Kent in January 1921 and sat until he was defeated in November 1922. K.B.E. 1919. Personal Assistant to Visct. Rothermere, Secretary of State for Air 1917-18. Chairman of United Empire Party in 1930. Died 22 August 1946.   [1922]

PONSONBY, Arthur Augustus William Harry. Shulbrede Priory, Lynchmere,

Haslemere, Sussex. 3rd s. of the Rt. Hon. Gen. Sir Henry Posonby, Private Secretary to H.M. Queen Victoria. B. 1871; m. 1898, Dorothea, d. of Sir Hubert Parry, Bart. Educ. at Eton, and Balliol Coll., Oxford. Was a Page of Honour to H.M. Queen Victoria 1882-87; in Diplomatic Service at Constantinople, Copenhagen, and in the Foreign Office 1894-1902. Private Secretary to Sir H. Campbell-Bannerman 1905-08. Under-Secretary of State for Foreign Affairs January-November 1924; Parliamentary Under-Secretary Dominions Office June-December 1929. Unsuccessfully contested Taunton as a Liberal in 1906. Sat as a Liberal MP for Stirling Burghs from May 1908 to December 1918 when he unsuccessfully contested Dunfermline Burghs as an Independent Democrat. Labour Member for the Brightside division of Sheffield from November 1922 until January 1930 when he was created Baron Ponsonby of Shulbrede. One of the founders of Union of Democratic Control 1914. Parliamentary Secretary to Ministry of Transport December 1929-March 1931. Chancellor of Duchy of Lancaster March-August 1931. Leader of Labour Party in the House of Lords 1931-35. Author of *Falsehood in Wartime* (1927). Resigned from the Labour Party in 1940 on the formation of the National Government. Died 23 March 1946.   [1929 2nd ed.]

PONSONBY, Charles Edward. Continued in House after 1945: full entry in Volume IV.

POOLE, Cecil Charles. Continued in House after 1945: full entry in Volume IV.

PORRITT, Richard Whitaker. The Cliffe, Stubbins, Nr. Manchester. Carlton. S. of Col. Austin T. Porritt, of Grange-over-Sands. B. 4 September 1910. Unmarried. Educ. at Marlborough, and Trinity Coll., Cambridge. Capt. in Lancashire Fusiliers. Director of Porritt and Spencer Limited. A National Conservative. Elected for the Heywood and Radcliffe division of Lancashire in November 1935 and sat until he was killed in action at Sedin in France on 26 May 1940.   [1940]

POTTER, John. Olivene, Bryan Road, Blackpool. S. of Paul Potter, Esq., Police Inspector, of Kirkham. B. 9 November 1873; m. 24 March 1894, Martha Alice, d. of W. Kenyon, Esq. Educ. at Xaverian Brothers School and Catholic Coll., Preston. Incorporated Accountant and Chartered Secretary. Member of Blackpool Corporation 1911, Alderman 1926, Mayor 1928. J.P. for Blackpool. A Conservative. Unsuccessfully contested Batley and Morley in October 1922. Elected for Eccles in October 1931 and sat until he retired in October 1935. Died 5 May 1940.   [1935]

POTTS, John Samuel. 13 Victoria Road, Barnsley. S. of Robert Potts, Esq., Coal Miner, and Mary Elizabeth Kirkman. B. 12 August 1861 at Bolton. A Coal Miner from the age of 11. A Colliery Checkweighman 1890-1915; Treasurer of Yorkshire Miners' Association 1915-22. A Labour Member. Sat for Barnsley from November 1922 until October 1931 when he was defeated. Re-elected for Barnsley in November 1935 and sat until his death on 28 April 1938. Member of Hemsworth Rural District Council and W. Riding County Council. J.P. for Barnsley. Methodist local preacher. Died 28 April 1938.   [1938]

POWELL, Lieut.-Col. Evelyn George Harcourt. 28 Hyde Park Gardens, London. Guards'. S. of Capt. Harcourt Powell. B. 21 February 1883; m. 1909, d. of Robert Pryor, Esq. Educ. at Eton. Joined the Grenadier Guards in 1900, retired 1927. A Conservative. Unsuccessfully contested Southwark S.E. in May 1929. Elected for Southwark S.E. in October 1931 and sat until he was defeated in November 1935. Died 15 July 1961.   [1935]

POWER, Sir John Cecil, Bart. 18 Grosvenor Square, London. Newlands Manor, Lymington, Hampshire. Villa Fressinet, Grasse, A.M., France. Carlton, and Bath. S. of William Taylor Power, Esq., of Eldon House, Co. Down. B. 21 December 1870; m. 14 October 1902, Mabel Katherine Louisa, d. of John Hartley Perks, Esq., of Slade Hill, Wolverhampton (she died 1945).

Created Bart. 1924. A Conservative. Elected for Wimbledon in October 1924 and sat until he retired in June 1945. Honorary Treasurer of Royal Institute of International Affairs 1921-43. Benefactor of London University Institute of Historical Research and of British Council. Served on a number of committees of the League of Nations Union. Director of Royal Insurance Company 1934-49. Died in France 5 June 1950.   [1945]

POWNALL, Lieut.-Col. Sir Assheton, O.B.E., T.D. 6 Hyde Park Gate, London. Athenaeum, Carlton, and Royal Automobile. S. of C.A.W. Pownall, Esq. B. 3 October 1877; m. 8 December 1904, Florence, d. of Lieut.-Col. Clayton Cowell, Underwriter on Lloyd's (she died 1952). Educ. at Rugby. Member of Greenwich Borough Council 1904; member of London County Council for Lewisham 1907-10. Second-Lieut. 2nd V.B.R. West Kent Regiment 1897; Lieut.-Col. 20th Battalion London Regiment November 1915. Knight Bach. 1926. Dept.-Lieut. Parliamentary Private Secretary to Postmaster-Gen. 1923, and to Minister of Labour November 1924-June 1929. Member of Royal Commission on Civil Service 1929. Chairman of Public Accounts Committee 1943-45. A Conservative. Unsuccessfully contested the Rotherhithe divion of Southwark in January and December 1910. Prospective candidate for Tottenham 1911-18. Sat for E. Lewisham from December 1918 until July 1945 when he was defeated. Master of Vintners' Company 1942 and 1947. Died 29 October 1953.   [1945]

PRATT, John William. 139 Sunderland Road, Forest Hill, London. Caledonian, Junior Athenaeum, and National Liberal. Scottish Liberal, Edinburgh. Liberal, Glasgow. S. of David MacDonald Pratt, Esq., Master Mariner. B. 9 September 1873 at South Shields; m. 1895, Elizabeth, d. of Hugh Niven, Esq., of Gosforth, Newcastle-on-Tyne (she died 1945). Educ. at South Shields Public School, and Glasgow University. Was Warden of Glasgow University Settlement 1902-12; member of Glasgow Town Council from 1906, and Magistrate from 1911. A Junior Lord of the Treasury

December 1916 to August 1919; Parliamentary Under-Secretary for Health in Scotland August 1919-October 1922. A Coalition Liberal. Elected for Linlithgowshire in November 1913, and for the Cathcart division of Glasgow in December 1918. Sat until he retired in October 1922. Unsuccessfully contested, as a Liberal, Dundee in December 1923, the Kelvingrove division of Glasgow in May 1924 and Sunderland in May 1929, and, as the candidate of the New Party, the Hulme division of Manchester in October 1931. Knighted November 1922. Died 27 October 1952.   [1922]

PRESCOTT, Maj. Sir William Henry, C.B.E. Allington House, White Hart Lane, London. St. Stephen's, and Golfers. S. of John Prescott, Esq. B. 1874; m. 1898, Bessie, d. of Mark Stanley, Esq., of Ambleside (she died 1940). At one time President of the Institute of Sanitary Engineers, M.I.C.E., M.I.Mech.E., J.P. for Middlesex; member of Middlesex County Council; member London Metropolitan Water Board, Chairman 1928-40; Vice-President Urban District Councils Association; Honorary member Institution of Municipal and County Engineers. A Barrister, Gray's Inn 1909; Consulting Civil Engineer; member Middlesex Territorial Force Association; member Government Roads Advisory Committee, Ministry of Transport; Gov. Prince of Wales's General Hospital, Tottenham. Served in France with the Tottenham division Royal Engineers; invalided after a fall from a horse. C.B.E. 1920. "Medaille du Roi Albert" for war services to the Belgian cause. A Coalition Unionist. Elected for Tottenham N. at the general election in December 1918 and sat until he retired in October 1922. Unsuccessfully contested Tottenham N. in December 1923. Fellow of Royal Society of Arts. Knighted January 1922. High Sheriff of Middlesex 1929. High Sheriff of Cambridgeshire and Huntingdonshire 1938. Created Bart. 1938. Died 15 June 1945.   [1922]

PRESCOTT, William Robert Stanley. Continued in House after 1945: full entry in Volume IV.

PRESTON, Sir Walter Reuben. 125 Victoria Street, London. Ilsom Farm, Tetbury, Gloucestershire. Carlton, and Royal Yacht. S. of R.T. Preston, Esq., of Hayes Court, Kent. B. 20 September 1875; m. 18 April 1900, Ella Margaret, d. of Huson Morris, Esq. Educ. at Bedford Grammar School. Member of Army Expenditure Committee. Created Knight Bach. 1921. Largely interested in Engineering. A Conservative. Unsuccessfully contested E. St. Pancras in January 1910, and Stepney in December 1910. Elected for the Mile End division of Stepney in December 1918. and November 1922; defeated in December 1923. Elected for Cheltenham in September 1928 and sat until he resigned in May 1937. Chairman of Platt Brothers and Company Limited and Stone-Platt Engineering Company. President of Textile Machinery Makers Limited. Died 6 July 1946.
          [1937]

PRESTON, William. Bylanes, Gorway Road, Walsall. Constitutional. S. of William Preston, Esq. B. 1874; m. 1908, Lily, d. of Dr. Sanders, of Walsall. Educ. at Queen Mary's School, Walsall, and Weston School, Bath. Senior Partner in the firm of William Sanders and Company, Electrical Engineers, of Wednesbury. Member of Walsall Chamber of Commerce; Honorary Secretary of Walsall Unionist Association. A Conservative. Elected for Walsall in October 1924; unseated by disqualification, since he held a contract with the Post Office, and re-elected in February 1925. Sat until he was defeated in May 1929. J.P. for Walsall. Died 22 November 1941.   [1929]

PRETYMAN, Col. Rt. Hon. Ernest George. 2 Belgrave Square, London. Orwell Park, Ipswich. Riby Grove, Lincolnshire. Carlton, Wellington, and Turf. S. of the Rev. Frederic Pretyman, B.D., Hon. Canon of Lincoln, and Georgiana, d. of E. Knight, Esq., of Chawton House, Hampshire. B. 1859 at Great Carlton, Louth, Lincolnshire; m. 1894, Lady Beatrice Bridgeman d. of Earl of Bradford. Educ. at Eton, and Royal Military Academy, Woolwich. Entered the Royal Artillery; Capt. 1888; retired 1889. Honorary Col. 1st Suffolk Volunteer

Artillery. A J.P. for Suffolk. Dept.-Lieut. and J.P. for Lincolnshire. Was Civil Lord of the Admiralty 1900-03, and Parliamentary and Financial Secretary to the Admiralty 1903-05, in Lord Salisbury's and Mr. Balfour's ministries. Parliamentary Secretary to Board Trade May 1915 to December 1916. Civil Lord of Admiralty December 1916-January 1919. PC. 1917. Took an active interest in all questions relating to the taxation of land and the development of agriculture. A Conservative. Sat for the Woodbridge division of Suffolk from 1895 to 1906, when he was defeated. Elected for the Chelmsford division of Essex in December 1908; re-elected for the Chelmsford division of Essex at both elections in 1910 and at the general elections of December 1918 and November 1922. Sat until he was defeated in December 1923. President of Land Union. Died 26 November 1931. [1923]

PRICE, Maj. Charles William Mackay. Clareston, Haverfordwest. Constitutional. S. of James Price, Esq., of Haverfordwest. B. 22 November 1872; m. 1897, Gwyndolin, d. of Maj. Figuls, of Hove (she died 1951). Educ. at Clifton, and Haverfordwest. Admitted a Solicitor 1894; member of Middlesex County Council from 1907-11, and of Pembrokeshire County Council 1922; Maj. Queen's Royal Regiment; served in France 1914-18. A Conservative. Unsuccessfully contested Pembrokeshire in December 1923. Elected for Pembrokeshire in October 1924 and sat until he was defeated in May 1929. Unsuccessfully contested Pembrokeshire in October 1931. Forestry Commissioner from 1929. Knighted 1932. Dept.-Lieut. for Pembrokeshire. Died 6 July 1954. [1929]

PRICE, Ernest Griffith. House of Commons, London. S. of John T. Griffith Price, Esq., of Ilford. B. 13 May 1870; m. 1900, Maude Ethel, d. of Maj. W.S. Marshall, of Johannesburg (she died 1957). Head of the firm of B. Goodman and Company, Housebreakers and Contractors. A large employer of labour in Shoreditch. Warden of the Paviours' Company. A National Liberal. Elected for Shoreditch in November 1922 and sat until he was defeated in December 1923. Chairman of Goodman Price Limited. Died 5 January 1962. [1923]

PRICE, Gabriel. The Wynne, South Elmsall, Nr. Pontefract. S. of H. Price, Esq., Coalminer, of Fairburn, Castleford. B. 19 April 1879; m. 30 April 1901, Winifred, d. of F. Watson, Esq., of Hemsworth. Educ. at Hemsworth Boys' School. Started work in a coalmine when 12 years of age. Member of Hemsworth Board of Guardians 1913, Hemsworth Rural District Council 1913, W. Riding County Council 1919, County Alderman 1922; Chairman of Hemsworth Rural District Council 1919 and of Sheffield Board of Governors 1921. J.P. 1921. A Socialist. Elected for the Hemsworth division of the W. Riding of Yorkshire in October 1931 and sat until his death on 24 March 1934, when he committed suicide by drowning. [1934]

PRICE, Morgan Philips. Continued in House after 1945: full entry in Volume IV.

PRINGLE, James Alexander, K.C. Eden-a-Grena, Cranmore Park, Belfast. Constitutional. S. of Henry Pringle, Esq., of Clones, Co. Monaghan. B. 18 August 1874; m. 1898, Mary Pringle, his cousin. Educ. at Trinity Coll., Dublin. Admitted a Solicitor 1900. Barrister-at-Law 1912, K.C. Northern Ireland 1921. A Conservative. Unsuccessfully contested Fermanagh and Tyrone in November 1922 and December 1923. Elected for Fermanagh and Tyrone in October 1924 and sat until he retired in May 1929. A temperance advocate. Died 7 July 1935. [1929]

PRINGLE, William Mather Rutherford. 17 Enmore Road, Putney, London. National Liberal. S. of George and Elizabeth Pringle, of Gordon, Berwickshire and Glasgow. B. 22 January 1874 at Gordon, Berwickshire; m. 4 June 1906, Lilian Patrick, d. of Joseph Somerville, Esq., of Glasgow. Educ. at Garnethill School, Glasgow, and Glasgow University. Called to the bar 1904. A Liberal. Unsuccessfully contested the Camlachie division of Glasgow in 1906. Sat for N.W. Lanarkshire from January 1910 until December 1918, when he unsuccessfully contested the Springburn division of Glasgow. Unsuccessfully contested the Rusholme division of Manchester in October 1919 and the Penistone division of Yorkshire in March 1921. Sat for the Penistone division of Yorkshire from November 1922 until October 1924 when he was defeated. Unsuccessfully contested Ayr Burghs in June 1925. Chairman of Liberal and Radical Candidates Association 1924-28. Died 1 April 1928.

[1924 2nd ed.]

PRIOR, Commander Redvers Michael, R.N. Westwood, Bishops Avenue, London. Flansham, Bognor Regis, Sussex. B. about 1893. A Conservative. Elected for the Aston division of Birmingham in June 1943 and sat until July 1945 when he unsuccessfully contested the Stratford division of West Ham. Unsuccessfully contested West Ham N. in February 1950. D.S.C. 1940; D.S.O. 1943. Member of Kent County Council 1949. Died 4 November 1964. [1945]

PRITT, Denis Nowell. Continued in House after 1945: full entry in Volume IV.

PRIVETT, Frank John. Alresford, Craneswater Park, Southsea. Constitutional. County Club, Southsea. S. of Edward and Caroline Privett. B. at Portsmouth 28 December 1874; m. 25 August 1898, Naomi Mary, 3rd d. of George and Naomi Good, of Portsmouth. Educ. at Portsmouth. A Builder and Contractor. President Portsmouth Chamber of Commerce 1921, Master Builders 1920, and Conservative Association from 1914. Vice-President of the Employment Committee 1916-20. Member Borough Council. J.P. for Portsmouth 1919. Took an active part in Recruiting and War Pensions Committees. Chairman of the King's Fund of the latter. A Conservative. Elected for Portsmouth Central in November 1922 and sat until he was defeated in December 1923. Unsuccessfully contested Portsmouth S. in May 1929 as an Independent Conservative, supported by the South Portsmouth Constitutional Association. Mayor of Portsmouth 1926-28, Lord Mayor 1928-29 and 1934-35. Died 29 March 1937.

[1923]

PROCTER, Maj. Henry Adam. Allestree, The Drive, Sidcup. Constitutional. S. of William Procter, Esq., of Liverpool. B. 15 November 1883; m. 1 January 1907, Amy Bedford, d. of Richard Kelley, Esq. Educ. at Bethany Coll., and Universities of Melbourne and Edinburgh, M.A., LL.D. An Engineer and Inventor. Barrister-at-Law, Middle Temple 1931. Served with Australian Forces 1916-20, with English army 1920-22, Assistant Brigadier-Maj. 1921. A Conservative. Unsuccessfully contested the Stratford division of West Ham in May 1929. Elected for Accrington in October 1931 and sat until he was defeated in July 1945. Unsuccessfully contested Accrington in February 1950. Died 26 March 1955. [1945]

PROFUMO, John Dennis. Continued in House after 1945: full entry in Volume IV.

PROTHERO, Rt. Hon. Rowland Edmund, M.V.O. 3 Cheyne Walk, Chelsea, London. Oakley House, Oakley, Bedfordshire. Athenaeum, Carlton, and New University. S. of the Rev. G. Prothero, Canon of Westminster. B. 6 September 1851 at Clifton-on-Teme; m. 1st, 1891, Beatrice, d. of John Bailward, Esq., of Horsington Manor, Somerset (she died 1899); secondly, 1902, Barbara, d. of Lieut.-Col. Charles Hamley (she died 1930). Educ. at Marlborough Coll. and Balliol Coll., Oxford; Fellow of All Souls' Coll., Oxford 1875-91. Called to the bar, Middle Temple 1878. Editor of *Quarterly Review* 1894-99. Agent-in-Chief to Duke of Bedford from 1898. Member of Royal Commission on Railways 1913, J.P. for London and Bedfordshire, Alderman of Bedfordshire County Council. M.V.O. 1901. President of the Board of Agriculture from December 1916 to August 1919. PC. 1916. Author of *Life and Letters of Dean Stanley*, *Letters of Edward Gibbon*, *Letters and Journal of Lord Byron*, *Psalms in Human Life*, *Pleasant Land of France*, *English Farming, Past and Present*, etc. etc. Unsuccessfully contested the Biggleswade division of Bedfordshire as a Liberal Unionist in January 1910. Elected for Oxford University as a Conservative in June 1914, re-elected in December 1918 and sat until January 1919 when he was created Baron Ernle. Fellow of Royal Historical Society. Proctor of Oxford University 1883-84. President of English Association 1921-22. Died 1 July 1937.   [1918]

PULLEY, Charles Thornton. Lower Eaton, Hereford. 20 Park Lane, London. Junior Carlton, and Devonshire. S. of Charles Oldaker Pulley, Esq. B. 24 July 1864; m. 1906, Irva, d. of Peter M. Keenan, Esq., of Washington, U.S.A. (she died 1942). Educ. at King's Coll. School, and King's Coll., London. Member of the London Stock Exchange. High Sheriff for Herefordshire 1912-13; Dept.-Lieut. and J.P. Presented an Art Gallery to the city of Hereford. Was well known as a breeder of thoroughbred pedigree Hereford cattle and Shropshire sheep. A Coalition Unionist. Elected for the Ross division of Herefordshire in May 1918 and for the Hereford division of Herefordshire in December 1918 and sat until he resigned in December 1920. Knighted 1922. Died 5 April 1947.   [1920]

PURBRICK, Reginald. The Kennels, Wooburn Green, Buckinghamshire. Carlton. S. of Frederick Purbrick, Esq., of Melbourne, Australia. B. 2 February 1877; m. 1st, September 1902, Dorothy, d. of John Stevens, Esq., of Melbourne (m. dissolved in 1931); secondly, 2 November 1939, Mme. Gisele Melanie Camille Mouton, formerly Baronne de Vivario (she died 21 January 1942). Educ. at St. Kilda Grammar School, Melbourne. Member of Parliamentary Delegation to Australia and New Zealand 1944. A Conservative. Elected for the Walton division of Liverpool in May 1929 and sat until he was defeated in July 1945. Died 6 November 1950.   [1945]

PURCELL, Albert Arthur. 1 Brook Terrace, Davyhulme, Urmston, Manchester. S. of Albert Duncan and Charlotte Purcell. B. in London 3 November 1872; m. August 1895, d. of G.T. Fidler, Esq. Educ. at Keighley, Yorkshire Elementary School. Was a half-timer in Keighley Mills; became French Polisher. Chairman French Polish-ers' Union 1894, and Secretary 1895; Organizer of Furnishing Trades Association 1910; member of Labour Delegation to Soviet Russia 1920. A Labour Member. Unsuccessfully contested W. Salford in January 1910 as an Independent Labour candidate. Elected for Coventry in December 1923. Unsuccessfully contested Coventry in October 1924. Sat for the Forest of Dean division of Gloucestershire from July 1925 until May 1929 when he unsuccessfully contested the Moss Side division of Manchester. Member of Salford Borough Council 1907-12. Member of General Council of T.U.C. from 1919, President 1924. President of International Federation of Trade Unions 1924-27. Died 24 December 1935.   [1929]

PURCHASE, Henry George. 35 Queen Anne Street, Cavendish Square, London. 3 Paper Buildings, Temple, London. National Liberal. Surrey County Cricket. Eld. s. of George Henry Purchase, Esq. B. 1873 in London; m. 1902, Kathleen, youngest d. of Charles Roberts, Esq., J.P., of Hollybrook, Co. Cork (she died 1910). Educ. at St. Mark's Coll., University Tutorial Coll., and King's Coll., London; LL.B. (Hons.) London. Honorary Secretary Cromwell Tercentenary Celebration 1899. Took an active part in the formation of the New Reform Club as Assistant Honorary Secretary; called to the bar, Middle Temple 1913; Joined the Northern Circuit. Sent on a special mission to France for the purpose of re-organizing an English and American Hospital at Neuilly 1915. Assisted (1918) in the establishment of the Enforcement Branch of the Ministry of Food, and was subsequently made an Assistant Director of the Ministry. Appointed Parliamentary Secretary (unpaid) to the Chairman of the National Insurance Joint Committee January 1919. Member of Select Parliamentary Committee on Telephone Charges 1920. Honorary Secretary of Committee of London Liberal MPs., and of the Parliamentary Committee dealing with coastwise traffic. A Coalition Liberal. Elected for the Kennington division of Lambeth in December 1918 and sat until he was defeated in November 1922. Unsuccessfully contested the Kidderminster division of Worcestershire in December 1923 and October 1924, S. Leicester in May 1929, the Gainsborough division of Lincolnshire in October 1931 and Blackpool in November 1935. Senior Legal Assistant, Ministry of Food 1942-43. Died September 1945. [1922]

PYBUS, Sir Percy John, Bart., C.B.E. 4 Whitehall Court, London. Reform, and Beefsteak. S. of Alderman John Pybus, of Kingston-upon-Hull. B. 25 January 1880. Unmarried. An Engineer. Director of the *Times* Publishing Company; of Associated Portland Cement Company; Chairman of Phoenix Assurance Company. M.I.E.E. C.B.E. 1917. Served on Royal Commission on Civil Service, Unemployment Grants Committee, the Advisory Committee of Department of Overseas Trade (Board of Trade) and Balfour Commission of Industry and Trade. Minister of Transport September 1931-February 1933. Created Bart. January 1934. A Liberal until 1931, thereafter a Liberal Nationalist. Unsuccessfully contested the Shipley division of the W. Riding of Yorkshire in December 1923 and October 1924. Elected for the Harwich division of Essex in May 1929 and sat until his death on 23 October 1935, 2 days before Parliament was dissolved. [1935]

PYM, Leslie Ruthven. 2 Halkin Place, London. Penpergwm Lodge, Abergavenny. Carlton, and Travellers'. S. of the Rt. Rev. Walter Ruthven Pym, Bishop of Bombay. B. 24 May 1884; m. 1 January 1914, Iris, d. of Charles Orde, Esq., of Hopton House, Great Yarmouth. Educ. at Bedford, and Magdalene Coll., Cambridge. President of Land Agent's Society 1936. Parliamentary Private Secretary to A.T. Lennox-Boyd, later to Robert Boothby, and to Maj. Rt. Hon. G. Lloyd George, Parliamentary Secretary to Ministry of Food 1940-42. A Lord Commissioner of the Treasury March 1942-May 1945. J.P. and Dept.-Lieut. for Monmouthshire. Comptroller of H.M. Household May-July 1945. A Conservative. Elected for the Monmouth division of Monmouthshire in July 1939 and sat until his death on 17 July 1945, after the comple-

tion of polling for the General Election but before the result was announced. He was posthumously returned at the head of the poll. [1945]

QUIBELL, David John Kinsley. 17 Henry Street, Scunthorpe. B. 21 December 1879; m. 1st, 1900, Edith Foster (she died 1953); secondly, 1954, Catherine Cameron Rae. A Builder and Contractor at Scunthorpe. J.P. for Flintshire and J.P., and County Councillor for Lincolnshire. Member of Forestry Commission 1942-45; Chairman of Scunthorpe and Frodingham Urban District Council 1914-15 and 1934-35. A Labour Member. Unsuccessfully contested the Brigg division of Lincoln and Rutland in December 1918, November 1922, December 1923 and October 1924. Elected for the Brigg division of Lincoln and Rutland in May 1929, defeated October 1931; re-elected there in November 1935 and sat until he retired in June 1945. Created Baron Quibell 1945. Mayor of Scunthorpe 1953. Died 16 April 1962. [1945]

RADFORD, Edmund Ashworth. White Gables, Wilmslow, Cheshire. St. Stephen's, Royal Automobile, and Constitutional. Engineers', Manchester. S. of George Radford, Esq., of Manchester. B. February 1881; m. 1912, Beatrice, d. of William Hay, Esq., of Manchester. Educ. at Buxton Coll. A Chartered Accountant, practised in Manchester. Honorary Secretary Manchester and Salford Street Children's Mission, and Honorary Treasurer of Charter Street Ragged School, Manchester; Honorary Treasurer Manchester and District Branch of Working Men's Club and Institute Union. A Conservative. Sat for S. Salford from October 1924-May 1929, and unsuccessfully contested S. Salford in May 1929. Elected for the Rusholme division of Manchester in November 1933 and sat until his death on 27 May 1944. [1944]

RAE, Sir Henry Norman. Rossett Green, Harrogate. Reform. S. of Rev. James Rae, of Harrogate. B. 1860; m. 1883, Emily, d. of Joshua Cass, Esq., of Mirfield (she died 1927). Educ. at Batley Grammar School. A Wool Merchant. Member of the Wool

Council and of the Board of Trade Committee which reported on the Textile Trades after the war. Knighted 1922. A Liberal. Unsuccessfully contested the Ripon division of Yorkshire in December 1910. Sat for the Shipley division of the W. Riding of Yorkshire from December 1918 until he retired in November 1923. Died 31 December 1928. [1923]

RAEBURN, Sir William Hannay, Bart. Woodend, Helensburgh. 86 Northgate, Regent's Park, London. Constitutional, City, and Caledonian. S. of William Raeburn, Esq., Merchant, and Grace Raeburn. B. at Glasgow 11 August 1850; m. 1st, 1876, Sarah, d. of John T. Manifold (she died 1882); secondly, 1888, Ellinor Martha, d. of Rev. Archibald Weir (she died 1915); thirdly, 1917, Olga Lucia, d. of Dr. Peel-Yates of Jersey, and widow of Capt. E. Hatton. Educ. at Rothesay Academy and Dollar Academy. A Shipowner. Chairman Clyde Trust; Chairman Clyde Lighthouse Trust; Vice-Chairman British Corporation Registry of Shipping; President of the Chamber of Shipping of the United Kingdom 1916-18, and on many important Committees. A Conservative. Elected for Dumbartonshire in December 1918 and sat until he retired in November 1923. Knighted 1918. Created Bart. June 1923. Died 12 February 1934. [1923]

RAFFAN, Peter Wilson. 22 Denbigh Place, London. National Liberal. S. of James Raffan, Esq., of Aberdeen. B. at Aberdeen 1863; m. September 1890, Margaret, d. of Joseph Weir, Esq., of Dumfries. Educ. at Aberdeen Public Schools. A Printer and Publisher. Chairman of the Monmouthshire County Council from 1909-10; J.P. for Monmouthshire from 1907. Wrote several pamphlets on the land question; President English League for the Taxation of Land Values. A Liberal. Sat for the Leigh division of Lancashire from January 1910 to December 1918 and for the Borough of Leigh from December 1918 to November 1922. Unsuccessfully contested Ayr Burghs in 1922. Elected for Edinburgh N. in December 1923 and sat until he was defeated in October 1924. Chairman of S.

Wales Workers' Educational Association. Editor and Proprietor of *South Wales Gazette*. Secretary of Band of Hope Union. Died 23 June 1940. [1924 2nd ed.]

RAFFETY, Frank Walter. 30 Belsize Avenue, Hampstead, London. Eighty, and National Liberal. S. of C.W. Raffety, Esq., J.P., of High Wycombe. B. at High Wycombe 1875; m. 1912, Jessie, d. of W.H. Brown, Esq., of Hart, Woodford Green. A Barrister-at-Law, Middle Temple 1898. Recorder of High Wycombe 1905-46; member of London County Council for West Islington 1922-25. Edited Burke's Works (World's Classics); author of *The Future of Party Government, Modern Business Practice*, etc. A Liberal. Unsuccessfully contested W. Lewisham in September 1921 and W. Bristol in November 1922. Elected for Bath in December 1923 and sat until he was defeated in October 1924. Unsuccessfully contested Cheltenham in May 1929 and E. Dorset in November 1935. Secretary of Social and Political Education League. Chairman of Industrial Co-partnership Association. O.B.E. 1945. Died 8 September 1946. [1924 2nd ed.]

RAIKES, Henry Victor Alpin MacKinnon. Continued in House after 1945: full entry in Volume IV.

RAINE, Sir Walter. 5 Esplanade, Sunderland. Constitutional. S. of John and Elizabeth Raine. B. at Sunderland May 1874; m. 1st, 1899, Rosa, d. of H. Barnes, Esq. (she died 1929); secondly, 1930, Violet, d. of E.C. Evans, Esq. Educ. at the North Eastern County School, Barnard Castle. Active in municipal work at Sunderland; member of the Town Council from 1902; Mayor for 2 years 1920-22. Member of a local firm of Coal Exporters and Shipowners. Vice-Chairman of the Sunderland Football Club. River Wear Commissioner; J.P.; President Sunderland Chamber of Commerce; Dept.-President Associated Chambers of Commerce. Knight Bach. 1927. A Conservative. Sat for Sunderland from November 1922 until he was defeated in May 1929. Chairman of Coal Exporters Federation of Great Britain. A Methodist.

Died 19 December 1938.   [1929]

RAMAGE, Capt. Cecil Beresford. Blyth-wood, Barker's Lane, Ashton-on-Mersey, Manchester. S. of John Walker Ramage, Esq., of Edinburgh. B. 1895 at Edinburgh; m. 1921, the actress Cathleen Nesbitt. Educ. at Edinburgh Academy, and Pembroke Coll., Oxford. Was President of the Oxford Union Society. A Barrister-at-Law, Middle Temple 1921. Served in the Royal Scots during the war 1914-18, M.C. A Liberal. Unsuccessfully contested W. Newcastle-upon-Tyne in 1922 as a National Liberal with unofficial Conservative support. Elected for W. Newcastle-upon-Tyne in December 1923 and sat until he was defeated in October 1924. Unsuccessfully contested Southport in May 1929.*
                                   [1924 2nd ed.]

RAMSAY, Alexander. 4 Amphion Road, Edgbaston. Phoenix Chambers, Colmore Row, Birmingham. Constitutional. S. of Alexander Ramsay, Esq., of Perth. B. 1887; m. 1913, Mary, d. of Richard Callan, Esq. (she died 1964). Educ. at Hamilton Academy and privately. An Engineer. Chairman of Birmingham Employers' Association and of F.B.I. in Midlands; Director of Enfield Cycle Company; member of Lincoln Corporation 1916-19. A Conservative. Elected for West Bromwich in October 1931 and sat until he retired in October 1935. O.B.E. 1920. Knighted 1938. Director of Engineering and Allied Employers' National Federation. Died 17 October 1969.   [1935]

RAMSAY, Capt. Archibald Henry Maule. 24 Onslow Square, London. Kellie Castle, Arbroath. Carlton. S. of Lieut.-Col. Henry Ramsay, Indian Political Department. B. 4 May 1894; m. 30 April 1917, Hon. Ismay Lucretia Mary Preston, d. of Jenico 14th Visct. Gormanston, and widow of Lord Ninian Crichton-Stuart, MP. Educ. at Eton, and Royal Military Coll., Sandhurst. Joined Coldstream Guards 1913, served in France 1914-16, at War Office 1917-18; with British War Mission, Paris 1918, retired 1920. Parliamentary member of Potato Marketing Board 1936. A Unionist. Elected

for the Peebles and Southern division of Midlothian and Peebles in October 1931 and sat until he retired in June 1945 but from 23 May 1940 to 26 September 1944 was detained in Brixton Prison under Defence Regulation 18b as a result of expressing anti-semitic opinions. Died 11 March 1955.   [1945]

RAMSAY, Thomas Bridgehill Wilson. 10 King's Bench Walk, Temple, London. 88 Ebury Street, London. S. of A.W. Ramsay, Esq., of Sleaford, Ayr. B. 2 July 1877. Unmarried. Educ. at Edinburgh University, M.A., LL.B. Barrister-at-Law, Gray's Inn, 1910. Specialist in Privy Council and Scottish Appeals. Trustee, Elder and Session Clerk of St. Columbas Church, Pont Street. Convener of Aged and Infirm Ministers Fund (also Smaller Livings Fund of Presbytery of Synod in England of Church of Scotland); President of Gray's Inn Debating Society; Chief of Scottish Clans Association; Secretary, Treasurer and Chairman of Indian Gymkhana Club. Contested the Shettleston division of Glasgow in 1922 as a Coalition Liberal. Returned as a Liberal for the Western Isles division of Ross and Cromarty in 1929 and sat until defeated in 1935. (National Liberal from 1931). Died 20 October 1956.   [1935]

RAMSAY-STEEL-MAITLAND, Rt. Hon. Sir Arthur Herbert Drummond, Bart. See STEEL-MAITLAND, Rt. Hon. Sir Arthur Herbert Drummond Ramsay, Bart.

RAMSBOTHAM, Rt. Hon. Herwald, O.B.E., M.C. 47 Hyde Park Gate, London. Kingswood House, Heath, Leighton Buzzard. Carlton. S. of Herwald Ramsbotham, Esq., J.P., and Ethel, d. of T. Bevan, Esq., of Stone Park, Greenhithe. B. 6 March 1887; m. 1st, 14 November 1911, Violet Doris, d. of S. de Stein, Esq. (she died 1954); secondly, 1962, Ursula, d. of Armand Jerome, Esq., and widow of Frederick Wakeham, Esq (she died 1964). Educ. at Uppingham School, and University Coll., Oxford; double first in Honours School Oxford, First Class Hon. Mods., First Class Lit. Hum. A Barrister-at-Law 1910-14. A Merchant from 1919. Parliamentary

Secretary to the Board of Education November 1931-November 1935, and to the Ministry of Agriculture November 1935-July 36; Minister of Pensions July 1936-June 1939. First Commissioner of Works June 1939-April 1940; President of the Board of Education April 1940-July 1941. PC. 1939. A Conservative. Unsuccessfully contested the Lancaster division of Lancashire in December 1910 and February 1928. Elected for the seat in May 1929 and sat until July 1941 when he was created Baron Soulbury. O.B.E. 1919. Chairman of Assistance Board 1941-48. Gov.-Gen. of Ceylon 1949-54. G.C.M.G. 1949. Created Visct. 1954. Honorary Fellow University Coll., Oxford. President of Classical Association 1948. Died 30 January 1971.

[1942]

RAMSDEN, Sir Eugene Joseph Squire Hargreaves, Bart., O.B.E. The Wheatleys, Gomersal, Leeds. Trem-y-Mor, St. Davids. Carlton, Union, and Yorkshire. S. of James Ramsden, Esq., of Leeds. B. 2 February 1883; m. 22 May 1919, Margaret, M.D., d. of F.E. Withey, Esq., of Michigan, and widow of Maj. Farwell, U.S. Army. Educ. in France and Germany. Chairman and Director of a number of Limited Liability Companies. Served overseas 1915-19. J.P. for the W. Riding of Yorkshire. Created Knight Bach. 1933; Bart. 1938; Chairman of U.K. Trade Mission to Poland 1934 and of Departmental Committee on Education and Training of Overseas Students 1933-34; Chairman of Executive Committee of National Union of Conservative and Unionist Associations 1938-43. A Conservative. Unsuccessfully contested the Spen Valley division of the W. Riding of Yorkshire in December 1923. Elected for Bradford N. in in October 1924, defeated May 1929. Re-elected in October 1931 and sat until he retired in June 1945. Created Baron Ramsden 1945. Died 9 August 1955. [1945]

RAMSDEN, Capt. George Taylor. Colebrook Lodge, West Hill, Putney Heath, London. 1900. S. of John Taylor Ramsden, Esq., of King's Lynn. B. at Illingworth, near Halifax 6 April 1879, m. 1915, Elizabeth Juel, d. of Niels Juel Hansen, Esq. Educ. at

Eton, and Trinity Hall, Cambridge, M.A. Chairman and Managing Director of Messrs. Thomas Ramsden and Son Limited, Brewers, of Halifax. Mayor of Halifax from 1911-12, and four years Dept.-Mayor; Alderman 1910-19. J.P. of the borough. Joined army 8 August 1914, and obtained the rank of Capt. 1919. Parliamentary Private Secretary to Sir Auckland Geddes, November 1919. A Coalition Unionist. Unsuccessfully contested the Elland division of Yorkshire in January and December 1910; was elected there at the general election in 1918 and sat until he was defeated in November 1922. Died 9 October 1936. [1922]

RANDLES, Sir John Scurrah. Bristowe Hill, Keswick. Carlton, and Constitutional. S. of the Rev. M. Randles, D.D. Wesleyan Minister. B. 1857 at Boston, Lincolnshire; m. 1883, Elizabeth Hartley, d. of R. Spencer, Esq., of Bolton. Educ. at Woodhouse Grove School, near Leeds. An Iron-Master, Director of Furness Railway Company, Cleator and Workington Railway Company, and Cockermouth, Keswick and Penrith Railway Company. A member of Cumberland County Council. J.P. for Cumberland. Knighted 1905. Honorary President International Parliamentary Commercial Conference; Commander of the Order of the Crown of Belgium; Order of the Rising Sun (Japan) 2nd class. A Unionist. Sat for the Cockermouth division of Cumberland from 1900-06. Defeated at the general election of January 1906; re-elected in August 1906 and sat until December 1910 when he was again defeated. Elected for N.W. Manchester in August 1912 and for the Exchange division of Manchester in December 1918 and sat until he retired in October 1922. Member of the Executive Committee of National Trust. Died 11 February 1945. [1922]

RANKIN, James Stuart. 10 North Street, Westminster, London. Boodle's. 2nd s. of John Rankin, Esq., of St. Michael's Hamlet, Liverpool. B. 1880. Educ. at Sedbergh, and University Coll., Oxford. A Conservative. Was serving with the Royal Field Artillery when returned unopposed for the E. Toxteth division of Liverpool in February 1916; again returned unopposed during absence on service in Mesopotamia and Persia, at the general election in December 1918. Sat until he retired in October 1924. Died 20 October 1960. [1924 2nd ed.]

RANKIN, Sir Robert, Bart. Broughton Tower, Broughton-in-Furness. Athenaeum, and Oxford & Cambridge. S. of John Rankin, Esq., of Liverpool. B. 18 October 1877; m. 1st, 17 July 1907, Renee Helen Mary, d. of Edmund Baker, Esq., Government Medical Service, Teheran (she died 13 March 1932); secondly, 2 August 1940, Rachel, d. of Charles Dupin Drayson, Esq., of Melton Court, London. Educ. at Sedbergh, and Clare Coll., Cambridge. Chairman of Rankin, Gilmour and Company Limited, Shipowners, Liverpool. J.P. for Lancashire. Councillor of Royal Empire Society. Enlisted in 18th Battalion (Public School Brigade) Royal Fusiliers 1914, Capt. Horse Transport, R.A.S.C.; served in France 1915-18. Created Bart. 1937. A Conservative. Unsuccessfully contested the Kirkdale division of Liverpool in May 1929. Returned for the seat in October 1931 and sat until he retired in June 1945. High Sheriff of Lancashire 1948-49. Died 11 October 1960. [1945]

RAPER, Lieut. Alfred Baldwin. 12 Park Lane, 24-28 Lombard Street, London. Bachelors', Bucks, City Carlton, and Royal Automobile. S. of Walter Raper, Esq., of Gerrard's Cross, Buckinghamshire. B. in London 8 May 1889; m. 1st, 1922, Bessie Alice, Marchioness Conyngham, d. of W.A. Tobin, Esq., of Australia, former wife of 6th Marq. Conyngham (divorced 1925); secondly, 1928, Renée Angêle Rosalie, d. of Hector Benoist, Esq., of Lille. Educ. at Merchant Taylors School, and Brussels. A Timber Merchant, partner in the firm of C. Peto Bennett, 24-28 Lombard Street, London. Served as a pilot in the Royal Air Force during the war. A Coalition Unionist. Elected for E. Islington in December 1918 and sat until he retired in October 1922. Died 30 April 1941. [1922]

RATCLIFFE, Arthur. Burnfields, Spenser Avenue, Leek. The Hillocks, Ecton, Wetton, Ashbourne. S. of Joseph Ratcliffe, Esq., of Leek. B. 17 February 1882; m. 13 July 1901, Ellen, d. of G.H. Horrobin, Esq. (she died 1946). Educ. at Leek British School. A Plumber and Decorator. Member of Leek Urban District Council 1923-34; President of National Federation of Master Painters and Decorators of England and Wales 1931-32. A Conservative. Elected for the Leek division of Staffordshire in October 1931 and sat until he retired in October 1935. Chairman of Leek United and Midlands Building Society 1959. Died 3 May 1963. [1935]

RATCLIFFE, Henry Butler. 13 Lindum Terrace, Bradford. B. in about 1844; m. 1871, Miss Knight of Bradford (she died 1927). Educ. at Bradford Grammar School. A retired Bradford Butcher. President of the Yorkshire Federation of Butchers; member of Bradford City Council. Closely identified with church, adult school, and Sunday School work. A Coalition Unionist. Elected for the Central division of Bradford in December 1918 and sat until he retired in October 1922. President of Bradford Third Equitable Benefit Building Society to 1928. Died 9 April 1929. [1922]

RATHBONE, Beatrice Frederika. See WRIGHT, Beatrice Frederika.

RATHBONE, Eleanor Florence. Continued in House after 1945: full entry in Volume IV.

RATHBONE, Hugh Reynolds. Greenbank, Liverpool. Red House, Nr. Keswick. Reform, and Albemarle. S. of Richard R. Rathbone, Esq., and Frances Rathbone. B. at Liverpool 4 April 1862; m. 20 October 1888, Evelyn, d. of William Rathbone, Esq. Educ. at Eton, and Trinity Coll., Cambridge. A Merchant; admitted partner of Ross, Smyth and Company, Liverpool, London, etc. 1889. J.P. for Co. of Lancaster; member of Mersey Docks and Harbour Board from 1905-1933; Treasurer University of Liverpool 1903-18; President of Council and Pro-Chancellor of University 1918-24; member of Royal Commission on Wheat Supplies 1916-20; member of Departmental Committee on Superannuation of Teachers 1922-23. A Liberal and Free Trader. Un-

295

successfully contested the E. Toxteth division of Liverpool in November 1902. Elected for the Wavertree division of Liverpool in December 1923 and sat until he was defeated in October 1924. Defeated for the same seat in May 1929. Honorary LL.D. Liverpool University 1925. Died 19 January 1940.

[1924 2nd ed.]

RATHBONE, John Rankin. 4B Dean's Yard, London. Elmsleigh Par, Cornwall. Carlton. S. of Maj. W. Rathbone, R.E. B. 5 February 1910; m. 1932, Beatrice, d. of F. Roland Clough, Esq., of Boston, U.S.A. Educ. at Eton, and Christ Church, Oxford. Parliamentary Private Secretary to Lieut.-Col. J. Llewellin, Civil Lord of the Admiralty May 1937-July 1939, and when Parliamentary Secretary Ministry of Supply July-September 1939. Joined R.A.F. September 1939. A National Conservative. Elected for the Bodmin division of Cornwall in November 1935 and sat until December 1940 when he was reported missing and presumed killed on active service. His widow was elected for Bodmin on 11 March 1941.

[1941]

RAW, Leiut.-Col. Nathan, C.M.G. 45 Weymouth Street, London. Carlton, Authors', and Royal Societies. Liverpool. S. of William Raw, Esq. B. 1866, at Durham; m. 1897, Annie Louisa, d. of Charles Strong, Esq. (she died 1940). Educ. at Newcastle-on-Tyne Royal Grammar School, and University of Durham, and London. M.D., M.R.C.P. (London), F.R.C.S.E., F.R.S. (Edinburgh), D.P.H. Physician Mill Road Infirmary, Liverpool from 1897, and to Haydock Lodge Asylum. Specialized in tuberculosis. Lieut.-Col. O.C. and Senior Physician Liverpool Hospital, France, Saw much service on the Western front; mentioned in despatches. Wrote many works on Tuberculosis. A Coalition Unionist. Elected for the Wavertree division of Liverpool in December 1918 and sat until he retired in October 1922. Died 28 August 1940.

[1922]

RAWLINSON, Rt. Hon. John Frederick Peel, K.C. 5 Crown Office Row, Temple, London. Carlton, United University, and Travellers'. S. of Sir C. Rawlinson, Chief Justice of Madras. B. 1860. Unmarried. Educ. at Eton, and Trinity Coll., Cambridge; Honorary LL.D., Cambridge, 1st Class Law Tripos 1882; Prizeman, Common Law, Inner Temple. Was called to the bar at the Inner Temple 1884; Q.C. 1897; Bencher 1907. Lecturer in Law at Pembroke Coll., Cambridge 1885-87, later Honorary Fellow. Recorder of Cambridge from 1898; Commissary of Cambridge University from 1900; Dept. High Steward of Cambridge University from 1918; Fellow of Eton Coll. 1919; represented the Treasury in South Africa in investigating the causes of the Jameson Raid 1896; a J.P. for Cambridgeshire; member of General Council of the Bar from its formation, later Vice-Chairman; member of Governing Bodies of Eton, Malvern, Brighton and Selwyn Colleges; Editor of *Rawlinson's Municipal Corporation Acts*. One of the Temporary Chairman in Committee of the whole House from 1916. PC. 1923. A Conservative. Unsuccessfully contested Ipswich in 1900. Sat for Cambridge University from 1906 until his death on 14 January 1926. [1926]

RAWSON, Sir Alfred Cooper. 11 Upper Drive, Hove, Sussex. Carlton, and Constitutional. B. 26 July 1876; m. 19 July 1902, Elizabeth, d. of J. Robson, Esq. Sub-Lieut. R.N.D. 1915; R.N.V.R. 1916-18; Honorary Capt. R.N.V.R. Awarded Legion d'-Honneur. Honorary British Government Delegate International Road Congress, Seville 1923 and Milan 1926. Member of London County Council from 1913-22, of Wandsworth Borough Council from 1911-22, Mayor 1918 and 1919. Knight Bach. 1926. President of Granite Guild 1930. President Institute of Quarrying 1931; Honorary Capt. R.N.V.R. January 1940. A Conservative. Sat for Brighton from November 1922 until he accepted Chiltern Hundreds in January 1944. Died 11 January 1946.

[1944]

RAY, Sir William. 21 Downage, Hendon, London. Constitutional, and Junior Constitutional. S. of John Marr Ray, Esq., of Lancaster. B. 17 February 1876; m. 1st, 1902, Ada, d. of Charles Cornish, Esq. (she died 1931); secondly, 1935, Eileen, d. of Dr. Foden Wilson. Educ. at St. Thomas' School, Lancaster, and St. John's Coll., Battersea. Created Knight Bach. 1929; member London County Council from 1913-34 and leader of the Municipal Reform Party 1925-34, when he retired. Chairman of Electrical Development Association 1933-36. Served with Remount Service 1916-18. A Conservative. Unsuccessfully contested Finsbury in May 1929. Returned unopposed for Richmond, Surrey in April 1932, and sat until he resigned in January 1937. Died 30 September 1937.   [1937]

RAYNER, Ralph Herbert. Continued in House after 1945: full entry in Volume IV.

RAYNES, William Robert. 13 Commerce Street, Derby. S. of Henry Eley Raynes, Esq., Blacksmith. B. 26 January 1871; m. 3 April 1893, Alice Elizabeth Foster. Educ. in elementary schools. An Organizing Secretary. Member of Derby County Borough Council from 1911, Alderman 1923-66, Mayor 1921-22. A Labour Member. Unsuccessfully contested Derby in November 1922; but elected in 1923. Defeated October 1924 and re-elected for Derby in May 1929. Sat until he was defeated in October 1931. Died 30 January 1966.   [1931 2nd ed.]

REA, Walter Russell. 6 Barton Street, London. Reform, Bath, and National Liberal. S. of the Rt. Hon. Russell Rea, MP. B. 1873; m. 1st, 1896, Evelyn, d. of J.J. Muirhead, Esq., J.P. of Edinburgh (she died 1930); secondly, 1931, Jemima, d. of the Rev. A. Ewing. Educ. at Liverpool, University Coll. School, and abroad. Junior Lord of the Treasury February 1915-December 1916; a Liberal Whip 1924. Comptroller of H.M.'s Household November 1931-September 1932. A Liberal. Sat for Scarborough from 1906-18. Unsuccessfully contested Oldham in 1918, Nelson and Colne in 1920, and Bradford N. in 1922. Elected for Bradford N. in December 1923, defeated there in October 1924. Unsuccessfully contested the Taunton division of Somerset in May 1929. Elected for Dewsbury in October 1931 and sat until he was defeated in November 1935. Liberal

Chief Whip November 1931-November 1935. Created Bart. 1935. Created Baron Rea 1937. Chairman of Rea Brothers, Merchants Bankers. Died 26 May 1948.
                         [1935]

REAKES, George Leonard. 11 Hoseside Road, Wallasey. S. of J.H. Reakes, Esq., of Bath. B. 31 July 1889. Educ. at Bath Secondary School. A Journalist. Author of Educational Works. Served with Artist's Rifles O.T.C. 1916-18. Postal Censorship 1939-42; Volunteer Air Raid Warden 1939-43. Member of Wallasey Town Council 1922-50; Mayor 1936-37. J.P. 1939. Director of *Wallasey News.* An Independent Member. Elected for Wallasey in April 1942 and sat until he was defeated in July 1945. Died 15 April 1961.   [1945]

REDMOND, William Archer, D.S.O. Aughavanagh, Aughrim, Co. Wicklow. Bath. Stephen's Green, Dublin. S. of John Redmond, Esq., MP, Leader of the Irish Party. B. 1886; m. 1930, Bridget Mary, d. of John Mallick, Esq., of The Curragh, Co. Kildare. Educ. at Clongowes Wood Coll., and University Coll., Dublin; B.A., R. University, Ireland. A Barrister, called to the Irish bar 1910 and to English bar, Gray's Inn 1921. Capt. Irish Guards Special Reserve; D.S.O. France 1917. A Nationalist. Sat for E. Tyrone from December 1910 to March 1918 when he resigned and was elected for Waterford City. Re-elected for Waterford City in December 1918 and sat until he retired in October 1922. Member of Dail for Waterford City to 1921, for Co. Waterford 1923-32, as an Independent until 1926, thereafter as a member of the National League until 1932 when he joined Cumann na nGaedheal. Died 17 April 1932.
                         [1922]

REED, Arthur Conrad. 157 Queen Victoria Street, London. Thornlea, Exeter. Carlton, and Constitutional. S. of William Henry Reed, Esq., of Bathford, Somerset. B. 1881; m. 1905, Emily Ward, d. of John Berry, Esq., of Bondleigh, Devon (she died 1947). Educ. at Queen's Coll., Taunton. Member of Exeter County Borough Council from 1922. Alderman 1940; J.P., member of

Devon County Council from 1925. Chairman of Reed and Smith Limited, and of Wansbrough Paper Company Limited, and Director of other companies; President of Paper Makers' Association of Great Britain and Northern Ireland 1934-37. A Conservative. Elected for Exeter in October 1931 and sat until he retired in June 1945. Knighted 1945. Died 15 January 1961.

[1945]

REED, Sir Herbert Stanley, K.B.E. Continued in House after 1945: full entry in Volume IV.

REES, Sir John David, Bart., K.C.I.E., C.V.O. 9 Chesham Place, London. Thames House, Queen Street Place, London. 5 Burton Street, Nottingham. Carlton, Hurlingham, and Bachelors'. S. of Lodowick William Rees, Esq. B. December 1854; m. 1891, Hon. Mary Dormer, sister of 14th Baron Dormer. Educ. at Cheltenham Coll. Was in the Indian Civil Service 1875-1901; Under-Secretary to Madras Government, District Magistrate, Collector, Civil and Sessions Judge, Dept. Registrar, High Court, British Resident in Travancore and Cochin; Additional Member of Gov.-General's Council 1895-97 and 1898-1900; Private Secretary to Sir M. Grant Duff, Lord Connemara, and Lord Wenlock, Governors of Madras; Government Translater in Persian, Tamil, Telugu, and Hindustani; H.S. Arabic, and Russian Interpreter; C.I.E. 1890. C.V.O. 1908; K.C.I.E. 1910; Russian Order of St. Stanislaus. Chairman of British Central Africa Company; Director of S. Indian Railway Company, Bengal Dooars Railway Company, Consolidated Tea and Lands Company, Mysore Gold Mining Company, and other companies; member of Council East India Association; Fellow of University of Madras. Author of *Tours in India, The Mahomedans, The Real India, Modern India, Current Political Problems,* etc. Director of Prisoners of War Information Bureau 1915 to 1920. Created Bart. 1919. Author of several political works on Indian and English politics. Silver medallist, Society of Arts. A Unionist. Sat as a Liberal Imperialist for Montgomery District from 1906-December 10 when he retired. Resigned the

Liberal Whip and joined the Unionists November 1910. Unsuccessfully contested Kilmarnock Burghs as a Unionist in September 1911. Prospective candidate for Walworth from 1911-12. Elected for E. Nottingham in April 1912 and sat until his death on 2 June 1922, after falling from the London-Glasgow express train at Chesterfield.   [1922]

REES, Capt. John Thomas Tudor. 2 Hare Court, Temple, London. Fairlawn, Banstead, Surrey. S. of I.J. Ress, Esq., of Maesteg, Glamorgan. B. 1880; m. 1918, Dorothy, d. of E.J. Sidebotham, Esq., M.A., of Erlesdene, Bowdon. Educ. privately, and at the University of Wales. Barrister-at-Law, Gray's Inn 1922; J.P. for Surrey; Freeman City of London. Served during the war in the Welsh Regiment (Capt.) and Machine Gun Corps. A Liberal. Sat for the Barnstaple division of Devonshire from 1918-22 when he was defeated. Re-elected for Barnstaple in December 1923 and sat until he was defeated in October 1924. Dept.-Lieut. for Surrey. Chairman of Surrey Quarter Sessions 1941-55. County Court Judge from 1939 to 1955. Lay Assessor of Dioceses of Canterbury and Southwark. Died 27 February 1956.

[1924 2nd ed.]

REES, Sir William Beddoe. 72 Ashley Gardens, London. Ty Mynydd, Radyr, Glamorgan. Reform, and National Liberal. S. of Isaac Rees, Esq., of Maesteg. B. 1877; m. 29 January 1925, Elizabeth, d. of R.J. Griffith, Esq., of Dolgelly. Educ. privately, and at the University of Wales. Shipowner and Colliery Proprietor. Joint Treasurer and President of National Free Church Council. Chairman of Directors of the Ashburnham Steamship and Coal Company Limited; Ashburnham Collieries Limited, and The North Amman Collieries Limited, Cardiff; United Kingdom and Overseas Development Limited, Welsh Anthracite Collieries Limited and Berry Hinge Limited, London, etc. Took a prominent interest in the Housing Question and was Chairman of Welsh Garden Cities Limited. Knighted 1917. A Liberal. Unsuccessfully contested the Cannock division of Staffordshire in December 1918. Sat for

Bristol S. from November 1922 until he was defeated in May 1929. Adjudicated a bankrupt July 1930. Died 12 May 1931.

[1929]

REID, Sir David Douglas, Bart. Rademon, Crossgar, Co. Down. Carlton. Ulster. S. of Joseph and Elizabeth Reid. B. 24 August 1872; m. 28 December 1904, Florence, d. of D.C. Stiebel, Esq. Educ. at Royal Belfast Academical Institution, Queen's Coll., Belfast, and New Coll., Oxford. A Barrister-at-Law, Inner Temple 1898. Dept.-Lieut. and J.P. for Co. Down. Chairman of Ulster Unionist Parliamentary Party 1923-39. Created Bart. 1936. A Conservative. Unsuccessfully contested E. Tyrone in December 1910. Elected for E. Down in December 1918. Sat for Down from November 1922 until his death on 23 March 1939. [1939]

REID, Rt. Hon. James Scott Cumberland. Continued in House after 1945: full entry in Volume IV.

REID, William Allan. Bank Chambers, Iron Gate, Derby. Carlton, Constitutional, and United. S. of John Reid, Esq., of Ockbrook House, Derbyshire, Civil Engineer, and Agnes, d. of Alan Roberts, Esq. B. 11 October 1865; m. 14 February 1917, Ethel Walker, d. of William Walker Smith, Esq., and widow of Dr. H. Boam (she died 6 June 1943). Educ. privately. Admitted a Solicitor 1895. Chairman of Derbyshire Children's Hospital 1920-31. A Conservative. Elected for Derby in October 1931 and sat until he retired in June 1945. Died 17 March 1952. [1945]

REITH, Rt. Hon. Sir John Charles Walsham, G.C.V.O., G.B.E. Athenaeum, Brooks's. S. of Very Rev. George Reith. B. 1889; m. 1921, Muriel Katharine, d. of John Lynch Odhams, Esq. Educ. at Glasgow Academy, Gresham's School, Holt and Royal Technical Coll., Glasgow. An Engineer in Glasgow and London. Served in France 1914, later with Admiralty and Ministry of Munitions. Gen. Manager William Beardmore and Company Limited, Coatbridge 1920-22. Gen. Manager of

B.B.C. 1922, Managing Director 1923, Director-Gen. 1927-38. Chairman of Imperial Airways 1938-39 and of British Overseas Airways Corporation 1939-40. A National Member. Sat for Southampton from February 1940 until October 1940 when he was created Baron Reith. Minister of Information January-May 1940. Minister of Transport May-October 1940. Minister of Works and Buildings October 1940-February 1942. Knighted 1927; G.B.E. 1934; G.C.V.O. 1939; C.B. (Mil.) 1945; PC. 1940. Joined R.N.V.R. 1942, Director of Combined Operations, Material Department, Admiralty 1943-45. Chairman of Commonwealth Telecommunications Conference 1945, of Commonwealth Telecommunications Board 1946-50, of Hemel Hempstead Development Corporation 1947-50, of National Film Finance Corporation 1948-50, of Colonial Development Corporation 1950-59, of State Building Society 1960-64. Lord High Commissioner of Church of Scotland 1967 and 1968. Honorary Fellow of Worcester Coll., Oxford; Lord Rector of Glasgow University 1965-68. K.T. 1969. Died 16 June 1971.

REMER, John Rumney. 25 Victoria Street, London. Carlton. S. of John Sutton and Mary Bertha Remer. B. at Waterloo, Liverpool 2 July 1883; m. 1913, Beatrice, d. of Henry Crummack, Esq., of St. Annes-on-Sea (she died 1921). Educ. privately. A Timber Merchant and Saw-Mill Proprietor 1900. A Conservative. Elected for the Macclesfield division of Cheshire in December 1918 and sat until he resigned in November 1939. Died 12 March 1948.

[1939]

REMNANT, Sir James Farquharson, Bart. The Grange, Twyford, Berkshire. Carlton, Constitutional, and United. S. of Frederick William Remnant, Esq., J.P., of Southwold, Suffolk. B. 13 February 1863; m. 30 August 1892, Frances Emily, d. of Robert Gosling, Esq., of Hassobury, Bishop's Stortford. Educ. at Harrow, and Magdalen Coll., Oxford, B.A. A Barrister-at-Law, Lincoln's Inn 1886. Held a commission in the 3rd Royal Sussex Regiment 1884-88; Lieut.-Col. in R.A.S.C. 1914-18. Represented the Holborn division of Finsbury on the County Council from 1892-1901, Whip of Conservative Party London County Council 1895-98. Member of Royal Commission on Canals and Waterways 1906, of the Select Committee on Taxation of Land Values in Scotland Bill 1906, of the Select Committee on the Weekly Rest Day for Metropolitan Police Force 1908-09, and Select Committee on the Police Service 1919. Was a member of the Thames Conservancy 1897-1901. Created Bart. 1917. A Conservative. Sat for the Holborn division of Finsbury from March 1900 to December 1918 and for Holborn from December 1918 until June 1928 when he was created Baron Remnant. Died 30 January 1933.   [1928]

RENDALL, Athelstan. Redlands, Branksome Park, Bournemouth. Reform, and Bristol Liberal. S. of Henry Rendall, Esq., J.P., of Bridport, and Julia, d. of Edward Pratt, Esq., of Northover, Glastonbury. B. 16 November 1871 at Bridport; m. 1st, 1897, Amy, d. of J.J. Young, Esq., J.P., of Portsmouth (she died 1945); secondly, 1946, Beatrice Sophia, d. of Capt. A.W. Brooke Smith. Educ. at University Coll. School, London. A Solicitor, admitted 1894, and practised at Bournemouth, Yeovil, etc.; mainly concerned in development of building estates. Member House of Commons Committee Debtors' Imprisonment and drafted report. Member of House of Commons Chairmen's Panel and Selection Committee. Wrote articles on Magistrates, Divorce Reform, etc. An Advanced Radical, member of the Fabian Society. Sat for the Thornbury division of Gloucestershire as a Liberal from 1906-22 when he was defeated. Re-elected for Thornbury in December 1923 and sat until he was defeated in October 1924. Joined Labour Party 1925. Died 12 July 1948.   [1924 2nd ed.]

RENTOUL, Sir Gervais Squire Chittick, K.C. 76 Greencroft Gardens, London. 2 Harcourt Buildings, Temple, London. Conservative, and United. Royal Norfolk & Suffolk Yacht. S. of Judge Rentoul, K.C., MP for E. Down from 1890-1902. B. 1 August 1884; m. 30 March 1912, Muriel, d. of Harold Smart, Esq., Banker. Educ. at

the City of London School, Royal University, Ireland (Scholar), and Christ Church, Oxford, (President of Union 1906); M.A. 1907, (1st Honours in Jurisprudence). Barrister-at-Law, Gray's Inn and Middle Temple 1907. Recorder of Sandwich 1929-34. Chairman of Conservative Private Members "1922" Committee 1922-32. Legal Adviser to Headquarters Staff, Eastern Command 1916-20; Capt. General List 1915. Parliamentary Private Secretary to the Rt. Hon. Sir Douglas Hogg, Attorney-Gen. 1925-28. Knight Bach. 1929. A Conservative. Sat for the Lowestoft division of Suffolk from November 1922 until January 1934 when he was appointed a Metropolitan Police Magistrate. Held this post from 1934-46. K.C. 1930. Member of Kensington Borough Council 1941-46. Died 7 March 1946.   [1934]

RENWICK, Sir George, Bart. Abbey, Newminster, Morpeth. Carlton, and Junior Constitutional. S. of John Nixon Renwick, Esq., of Newcastle. B. at Newcastle-on-Tyne 8 March 1850; m. 1877, Mary Jane, d. of William Thompson, Esq., of Jubblepore, India. Educ. at Commercial Schools in Newcastle. A Shipowner who was very active in war work. Dept.-Lieut. for Northumberland; Chevalier of the Legion of Honour. Bart. 1921. A Conservative. Sat for Newcastle-on-Tyne from 1900-06 when he was defeated, and from September 1908 to January 1910, when he was again defeated. Elected for Central division of Newcastle-on-Tyne in 1918 and sat until he was defeated in 1922. Chairman of Manchester Dry Docks Limited. Joint Managing Director of Fisher Renwick Steamers Limited. J.P. for Newcastle-on-Tyne and Tynemouth. Died 19 June 1931.   [1922]

RENWICK, Maj. Gustav Adolph. 34 Westminster Mansions, Great Smith Street, London. Sandicroft, Great Budworth, Cheshire. Holystone Grange, Hepple, Morpeth. S. of Sir George Renwick, 1st Bart. B. 17 December 1883; m. 1907, Mabel, d. of James Deuchar, Esq., of Stichill, Kelso. Educ. at Giggleswick School. Managing Director of Fisher Renwick, Manchester. London Steamers Limited; Chairman of

Manchester Dry Docks Company Limited and of Shipping Federation, Manchester; Director of Scammel Lorries Limited and of Anglian Insurance Company; member of Executive Council of Shipping Federation and of Council of Chamber of Shipping. A Conservative. Elected for the Stretford division of Lancashire in October 1931 and sat until he retired in October 1935. Died 10 September 1956.   [1935]

REYNOLDS, Col. Sir James Philip, Bart., D.S.O. 48 Hans Place, London. 12 Abercromby Square, Liverpool. Carlton, and Royal Automobile. S. of Francis William Reynolds, Esq., of Hillside, Woolton, Liverpool. B. 17 February 1865; m. 13 January 1892, Elizabeth Emilia, d. of Nicholas Robert Roskell, Esq. Educ. at Ushaw, and Fort Augustus. President of Liverpool Cotton Association 1903. Dept.-Lieut. and J.P., of Lancashire; High Sheriff 1927. Lieut.-Col. R.F.A., T.F.R. Served with 2nd Canadian Division and 55th Division 1915-16. D.S.O. 1917. A Director of Public Companies. Created Knight Bach. 1920; Bart. 1923. Privy Chamberlain to the Pope 1929. A Conservative. Elected for the Exchange division of Liverpool in May 1929 and sat until his death on 12 December 1932.   [1933]

REYNOLDS, William George Waterhouse. The Holt, Birstall, Nr. Leicester. Junior Carlton, Constitutional, and British Empire. S. of Thomas Leethem and Ruth Augusta Reynolds. B. in Australia 1862; m. 1887, Ida Maud, d. of Joseph Roberts, Esq., of Leicester (she died 1927). Educ. privately, and at Vicary's School, Southsea. A Manufacture; Income Tax Commissioner and J.P for Leicestershire. A Conservative. Elected for S. Leicester in November 1922 and sat until he was defeated in December 1923. Master of Worshipful Company of Framework Knitters. Died 3 September 1928.   [1923]

RHODES, Lieut.-Col. John Phillips, D.S.O. 5a Stanhope Gardens, London. Marlborough, and Wellington. S. of Sir George Wood Rhodes, Bart. B. in Manchester 19 July 1884; m. 1st, 1913, Elsie,

d. of Lieut.-Col. G.A. Maclean Buckley, C.I.E., D.S.O., of Dorking (divorced 1925); secondly, 1926, Doris Mary, d. of W.H. Adams, Esq. Educ. at Harrow, and Royal Military Coll., Woolwich. Served in the Royal Engineers March 1904-June 1920. Lieut.-Col. D.S.O. 1918; Director of Thomas Rhodes Limited, Cotton Spinners and Manufacturers, Hollingworth, Cheshire. A Conservative. Elected for the Stalybridge and Hyde division of Cheshire in November 1922 and sat until he was defeated in December 1923. Succeeded as Bart. 1924. Fellow of Royal Geographical Society. Died at Monte Carlo 14 November 1955.   [1923]

RHYS, Hon. Charles Arthur Uryan, M.C. 2 Wellington Square, London. Carlton, Guards', and Pratt's. S. of Walter, 7th Baron Dynevor. B. 21 September 1899; m. 29 September 1934, Hope Mary Woodbine Soames, d. of C.W. Parish, Esq. Educ. at Eton, and at Royal Military Coll., Sandhurst. R. of O. Grenadier Guards; served in Russia 1919, Order of St. Anne of Russia. M.C. 1919. Dept.-Lieut. and J.P. for Carmarthenshire. Parliamentary Private Secretary to the Rt. Hon. Stanley Baldwin 1927-29. A Conservative. Elected for the Romford division of Essex in December 1923, and October 1924; unsuccessfully contested the same division in May 1929. Returned unopposed for the Guildford division of Surrey in August 1931; re-elected in the General Election and sat until he retired in 1935. Unsuccessfully contested N. Islington in July 1945. President of University Coll. of S. Wales 1960-62. Succeeded as 8th Baron Dynevor 1956. C.B.E. 1962. Died 15 December 1962.   [1935]

RHYS-WILLIAMS, Col. Sir Rhys, Bart., K.C., D.S.O. See WILLIAMS, Col. Sir Rhys, Bart., K.C., D.S.O.

RICE, Sir Frederick Gill. 15 Stockwell Road, London. Great Bromley Lodge, Colchester. Carlton, and Junior Athenaeum. S. of D.S. Rice, Esq., of Tavistock. B. 6 August 1866; m. 2 September 1893, Rose, d. of James Baker, Esq., of Kennington.

Lieut.-Col. 1st Cadet Battalion Royal Fusiliers; member of Board of Trade Commission on War Contracts; member of Council of London Chamber of Commerce; President London Master Builders' Association and of Institute of Public Builders. Created Knight Bach. 1921. A Conservative. Unsuccessfully contested the Harwich division of Essex in December 1923. Elected for the Harwich division of Essex in October 1924 and sat until he retired in May 1929. Died 30 June 1935. [1929]

RICHARDS, Robert. Continued in House after 1945: full entry in Volume IV.

RICHARDS, Rt. Hon. Thomas. Ninian Road, Cardiff. S. of Thomas and Mary Richards. B. 1859 at Beaufort, Ebbw Vale; m. Elizabeth, d. of David Thomas, Esq. Educ. at Beaufort British School. Gen. Secretary to the South Wales Miners' Federation, appointed 1887; Alderman of Monmouthshire County Council from 1904, Chairman 1924-31. J.P. for Breconshire and Monmouthshire; PC. 1918; Knight of Grace of St. John of Jerusalem 1918. Director of Ambulances for Wales. A Labour Member. Sat for W. Monmouthshire from November 1904 until December 1918. Returned unopposed for the Ebbw Vale division of Monmouthshire in December 1918 and sat until he resigned in July 1920. Member of Gen. Council of T.U.C. from 1925. President of Miners' Federation of Great Britain 1929-30. Died 7 November 1931. [1920]

RICHARDSON, Sir Albion Henry Herbert. 5 Portman Mansions, York Place, London. Junior Athenaeum, and Eighty. S. of James Henry Richardson, Esq. B. 2 October 1874 at Hendon. Unmarried. Educ. at Herne House School, and in France and Germany. A Solicitor and later Barrister, called Gray's Inn 1912. Chairman of United Law Society 1904. A Liberal. Unsuccessfully contested the Peckham division of Camberwell in January 1910. Elected for the Peckham division in December 1910 and sat until he retired in October 1922. C.B.E. 1918. Knighted 1919. K.C. 1930. Recorder of Warwick 1931-36, of

Nottingham 1936-50. Treasurer of Gray's Inn 1944. Died 7 July 1950. [1922]

RICHARDSON, Sir Alexander. Garshake, Clarence Road, Clapham Park, London. Carlton, Junior Carlton, Constitutional, and Authors'. S. of James Richardson, Esq., of Dumbarton. B. 27 March 1864; m. 1886, Georgina, d. of Capt. George Fleming. Member of the Council of the Institution of Naval Architects; Vice-President of the Junior Institution of Engineers; joint Editor of *Engineering* and of *Brassey's Naval and Shipping Annual*. Wrote much on naval, shipbuilding, engineering and economic subjects. Knighted 1922. A Conservative. Returned for the old borough of Gravesend in June 1918. Sat for the Gravesend division of Kent from December 1918 until he was defeated in December 1923. Assistant Commercial Editor of *Glasgow Herald*. Died 30 March 1928. [1923]

RICHARDSON, Lieut.-Col. Sir Philip Wigham, Bart., O.B.E., V.D. Aldenholme, Ellesmere Road, Weybridge. Carlton, Constitutional, and Royal Automobile. S. of John Wigham Richardson, Esq., Shipbuilder and Engineer, and Marian Henrietta Richardson. B. 26 January 1865; m. 1st, 1891, Rosa, d. of Gen. C. Colorado, of Barcelona; secondly, 27 November 1909, Bertha Anne, d. of J.E. Greenley, Esq., of Dulwich. Educ. at Rugby, and King's Coll., Cambridge. Knight Bach. 1921. A Shipbuilder 1891; Ship and Insurance Broker. Created Bart. 1929. A Conservative. Sat for the Chertsey division of Surrey from March 1922 until he retired in October 1931. O.B.E. 1919. Member of Council of National Rifle Association from 1901, Chairman 1939-46. Director of Swan Hunter and Wigham Richardson Limited, Shipbuilders of Wallsend. Died 23 November 1953. [1931 2nd ed.]

RICHARDSON, Robert. Roseville, St. Aidan's Terrace, New Herrington, Durham. B. 1862; m. 1886, Elizabeth Fletcher. Educ. at Ryhope National School. An Alderman of Durham County Council 1917-25; Chairman of the County Education Committee. Member of Durham Miners' Association

Executive Committee 1897-1919. J.P. for Durham. Parliamentary Charity Commissioner January-November 1924 and June 1929-August 1931. A Labour Member. Sat for the Houghton-le-Spring division of Durham from December 1918 until he was defeated in October 1931. A Coal Miner from 1871, Checkweighman 1900-18. Member of Ryhope Board of Guardians 1904-22. Member of Durham County Council 1901-25. Member of Sunderland Rural District Council 1904-22, Chairman 1910-13. An active member of the Church of England. Died 28 December 1943. [1931 2nd ed.]

RICKARDS, George William. 6 Relton Mews, London. S. of Charles Ayscough Rickards, Esq. B. 16 December 1877; m. 1904, Katharine, d. of William Rigby, Esq., of Bowdon, Cheshire. Educ. at Sedbergh School. A Silk Manufacturer. Member of W. Riding of Yorkshire County Council from 1929-33. Served with Cheshire Regiment 1915-20. Chairman of Proportional Representation Society. A National Conservative. Elected for the Skipton division of the W. Riding of Yorkshire in November 1933 and sat until his death on 27 November 1943. [1944]

RICKETT, Rt. Hon. Sir Joseph Compton. See COMPTON-RICKETT, Rt. Hon. Sir Joseph Compton.

RIDLEY, George. 6 Winscombe Crescent, London. Trade Union. S. of George Ridley, Esq., of Holt, Norfolk. B. 29 November 1886; m. 6 May 1919, Ethel Winifred, d. of William Sporne, Esq., of King's Lynn. Educ. at elementary schools. A Railway Clerk 1901; Trade Union Secretary 1920. Chairman of National Executive of Labour Party 1943-44. Parliamentary Private Secretary to the Rt. Hon. Arthur Greenwood, when Minister Without Portfolio May 1940-February 1942. Editor of *Railway Services Journal*. A Labour Member. Elected for the Clay Cross division of Derbyshire in November 1936 and sat until his death on 4 January 1944. [1944]

RILEY, Benjamin 28 Westfield Avenue, Huddersfield. S. of Samuel Riley, Esq. B. 1866; m. Lucy, d. of J. Rushworth, Esq., of Halifax. Educ. at Elementary School. A Bookbinder. Member of Huddersfield Town Council and Education Committee; represented Yorkshire on National Council of Independent Labour Party; a founder of National Labour Press in Manchester 1910. Parliamentary Private Secretary to Rt. Hon. Noel Buxton, Minister of Agriculture, June 1929. A Labour Member. Unsuccessfully contested Dewsbury in December 1918. Sat for Dewsbury from November 1922 to December 1923 when he was defeated; re-elected for Dewsbury in October 1924 and sat until he was defeated in October 1931; re-elected for Dewsbury in November 1935 and sat until he retired in June 1945. Died 6 January 1946. [1945]

RILEY, Frederick Fox. Milton, Wraysbury, Staines. B. at Hinckley, Leicestershire 1869. Acting Gen. Secretary Postal Clerks' Association. A Labour Member. Unsuccessfully contested S. Leicester in December 1918 and Bedford in April 1921. Unsuccessfully contested Stockton-on-Tees November 1922, December 1923 and October 1924. Elected for Stockton-on-Tees May 1929 and sat until he was defeated in October 1931. Member of Leicester City Council for 9 years. Died 3 February 1934. [1931 2nd ed.]

RITSON, Joshua. 21 Dale Terrace, Fulwell, Sunderland. S. of Joshua Ritson, Esq., of Bampton, Cumberland. B. 1874; m. 1900, Elizabeth, d. of Irvin Dinning, Esq., of Cambois, Northumberland. A Checkweighman at Monkwearmouth Colliery. Member of Sunderland Town Council from 1912, Mayor 1945; J.P. for Sunderland. A Labour Member. Unsuccessfully contested the Durham division of Co. Durham in December 1918. Sat for the Durham division of Durham Co. from November 1922-October 1931 when he was defeated. Re-elected in November 1935 and sat until he retired in June 1945. C.B.E. 1949. Died 5 February 1955. [1945]

ROBERTS, Aled Owen. Alton House, Aigburth, Liverpool. National Liberal. S. of Robert Roberts, Esq., of Liverpool. B. 17 July 1889; m. 1918, Ione Ruth, d. of Henry Irwin, Esq., of Stone, Staffordshire (she died 1940). Educ. at Liverpool Coll. An Insurance Broker and Underwriter. Principal of Aled O. Roberts and Company, Insurance Brokers, of Liverpool. Capt. Royal Welsh Fusiliers; served overseas 1916. A Liberal. Unsuccessfully contested E. Toxteth division of Liverpool in March and May 1929. Elected for the Wrexham division of Denbighshire in October 1931 and sat until he was defeated in November 1935. Unsuccessfully contested the Kirkdale division of Liverpool as a Conservative in July 1945. Member of Liverpool City Council from 1936. Member of Presbyterian Church of Wales. Died 25 August 1949. [1935]

ROBERTS, Charles Henry. 10 Holland Park, London. Brooks's, and National Liberal. S. of the Rev. A.J. Roberts, Vicar of Tidebrook, Sussex. B. 22 August 1865 at Tidebrook; m. 1891, Lady Cecilia Howard, d. of 9th Earl of Carlisle, a Fellow and Tutor at Balliol (she died 1947). Educ. at Marlborough, and Balliol Coll., Oxford; scholar. Fellow of Exeter Coll., Oxford 1889. Was a Commissioner of Lunacy (unpaid). J.P. for Cumberland. Under-Secretary for India February 1914-May 1915. Comptroller of the Household May 1915 to December 1916. Chairman National Health Insurance Joint Committee 1915-16. A Liberal. Unsuccessfully contested Wednesbury in 1895, the Osgoldcross division of Yorkshire in 1899, and Lincoln in 1900. Sat for Lincoln from 1906-18 when he was defeated. Unsuccessfully contested S. Norfolk in July 1920. Sat for Derby from November 1922 until defeated in December 1923. Unsuccessfully contested Central Nottingham in October 1924. Chairman of Cumberland County Council 1938-58. Dept.-Chairman of Cumberland Quarter Sessions to 1950. Died 25 June 1959. [1923]

ROBERTS, Ernest Handforth Goodman. 1 Brick Court, Temple, London. The Cottage, Mold, Wales. Bath, and Cavendish. S. of Hugh Goodman Roberts, Esq., Solicitor, of Mold. B. 20 April 1890. Unmarried. Educ. at Malvern, and Trinity Coll., Oxford. Barrister-at-Law, Inner Temple 1916; President of Oxford Union 1914; Capt. Royal Welsh Fusiliers; served in France 1916-17; member of Governing Body of Church in Wales 1916-36 and 1947-59. A Conservative. Unsuccessfully contested Flintshire in December 1923. Elected for Flintshire in October 1924 and sat until defeated in May 1929. Chief Justice of High Court at Rangoon 1936-48. Knighted 1936. Chancellor of Diocese of Bangor 1947-59, Diocese of Chelmsford 1950-69. K.C. 1949. Dept.-Chairman of Flint Quarter Sessions 1949-61. Died 14 February 1969. [1929]

ROBERTS, Rt. Hon. Frederick Owen. Sanbree, Broadway Corner, Northampton. S. of Thomas Andrew Roberts, Esq., of East Haddon. B. 2 July 1876; m. 27 February 1899, Celia Dorothea, d. of Francis Sexton, Esq., of Northampton. Educ. at National School. J.P., and County Councillor for Northampton. A Member of Committee of Management of Royal National Lifeboat Institution; Member of National Executive Labour Party (Chairman 1926-27). Minister of Pensions January-November 1924, and June 1929-August 1931. PC. 1924. A Labour Member. Sat for West Bromwich from December 1918-October 1931, when he was defeated. Re-elected for West Bromwich in November 1935 and sat until he resigned in April 1941. Organising Secretary of the Midlands Branch of Typographical Association. Died 23 October 1941. [1941]

ROBERTS, Rt. Hon. George Henry. Westminster House, 104 Earlham Road, Norwich. 6 Buckingham Street, London. S. of George Henry and Anne Roberts. B. 27 July 1868 at Chedgrave, Norfolk; m. 1895, Annie, d. of Horace Marshall, Esq. Educ. at St. Stephen's School, and evening classes, Norwich. A Printer and Compositor; member of Norwich School Board 1898-1903. J.P. for Norwich. Chief Whip to the Labour Party 1908-14. Chairman of National Executive of Labour Party 1912-13. Junior Lord of the Treasury May 1915 to December 1916. Parliamentary Secretary to Board of Trade December 1916 to August 1917; Minister of Labour August 1917 to January 1919; Food Controller January 1919 to February 1920. PC. 1917. Unsuccessfully contested Norwich in 1904. Elected for Norwich in 1906 and sat until he was defeated in December 1923. A Labour Member until 1918 when he was returned for the National Democratic Party. These ex-Labour Coalitionists renamed themselves the National Liberal Party at the general election of 1922, in which Roberts alone survived. He accepted the Conservative Whip in October 1923 and unsuccessfully contested the general election in December 1923 as a Conservative candidate. Died 25 April 1928.   [1923]

ROBERTS, Rt. Hon. Sir Samuel, Bart. Queen's Tower, Sheffield. 4 Whitehall Court, London. Carlton, and Oxford & Cambridge. S. of Samuel Roberts, Esq., J.P., of Sheffield, and Sarah Anne, d. of Robert Sorby, Esq., J.P., of Sheffield. B. at Sheffield 30 April 1852; m. 1880, Martha Susan, d. of Ven. Archdeacon Blakeney, D.D. Educ. at Repton School, and Trinity Coll., Cambridge, M.A. (Math. Tripos). A Barrister-at-Law, Inner Temple; called 1877. A Director of Cammell Laird and Company, and of National Provincial Bank of England; Chairman of Wright, Bindley and Company, Birmingham. A J.P. and Dept.-Lieut. for the W. Riding of Yorkshire; Dept.-Chairman of W. Riding Quarter Sessions; a J.P. for Sheffield. Lord Mayor of Sheffield 1900; member of Royal Commission on King's Bench Division 1913; Knighted 1917; created Bart. 1919. Member of Chairman's Panel for Grand Committee, Chairman of Selection Committee, House of Commons. PC. 1922. A Conservative. Unsuccessfully contested the High Peak division of Derbyshire in 1900. Sat for the Ecclesall division of Sheffield from February 1902 until he retired in November 1923. Died 19 June 1926.   [1923]

ROBERTS, Sir Samuel, Bart. 405 St. Ermius, London. Queen's Tower, Sheffield. Cockley, Cley Hall, Swaffham, Norfolk. Carlton. S. of the Rt. Hon. Sir Samuel Roberts, 1st Bart., MP, of Ecclesall. B. 2

Sept. 1882; m. 5 July 1906, Gladys Mary, d. of W.E. Dring, Esq., M.D., of Tenterden, Kent. Educ. at Harrow, and Trinity Coll., Cambridge, M.A., LL.B. Admitted a Solicitor 1906, retired 1921. J.P. for the W. Riding of Yorkshire 1913; J.P. for Sheffield 1920; Lord Mayor of Sheffield 1919-20; Chairman Panel from 1924. A Conservative. Sat for the Hereford division of Herefordshire from January 1921-May 1929. Elected for the Ecclesall division of Sheffield in May 1929, and was returned unopposed in October 1931. Sat until he retired in October 1935. Succeeded as 2nd Bart. 1926. Master Cutler 1935-36. Died 13 December 1955.   [1935]

ROBERTS, Wilfrid Hugh Wace. Continued in House after 1945: full entry in Volume IV.

ROBERTSON, Sir David. Continued in House after 1945: full entry in Volume IV.

ROBERTSON, John. Cadzowburn House, Union Street, Hamilton. B. 1867; m. 1893, Helen, d. of J. Nimmo, Esq. Chairman of the Scottish Miners' Union and a strong advocate of nationalization of mines. M.B.E. 1918. A Labour Whip 1922-25. Junior Lord of the Treasury January-November 1924. A Labour Member. Unsuccessfully contested N.E. Lanarkshire in August 1904, January 1906 and March 1911. Unsuccessfully contested the Bothwell division of Lanarkshire in December 1918. Elected for the Bothwell division of Lanarkshire in July 1919 and sat until his death on 14 February 1926.   [1926]

ROBERTSON, Rt. Hon. Sir Malcolm Arnold, G.C.M.G., K.B.E. Hoewyck Farm, Fernhurst, Haslemere, Surrey. St. James's, and Beefsteak. S. of Charles Boyd Robertson, Esq. B. 2 September 1877; m. 24 March 1917, Gladys, d. of Melville E. Ingalls, Esq., of Washington D.C. Educ. at Marlborough, and abroad, Fellow of St. Catharine's Coll., Cambridge 1940. Joined the Foreign Office 1898, served in Berlin, Pekin, Madrid, Bucharest, Monte Video, Rio de Janeiro, Washington, and The Hague. High Commissioner Rhineland High

Commission 1920; British Agent and Consul-Gen. Tangier 1921; Minister at Buenos Aires 1925, Ambassador 1927-29; retired 1930. Chairman of Spillers Limited 1930-47. PC. 1927. Chairman of the British Council 1941-45. Director of British Oak Insurance Company Limited. A Conservative. Returned unopposed for the Mitcham division of Surrey in August 1940 and sat until he was defeated in July 1945. Died 23 April 1951.   [1945]

ROBERTSON, Thomas Atholl. Inver Atholl, Palmer's Green, Middlesex. National Liberal. Eld. s. of John Robertson, Esq., of Snaigow, Dunkeid, and Margaret Morrison, of Bowmore, Islay, Argyll. B. in Glasgow 27 October 1874; m. 1st, 1905, Flora, d. of James Cumming, Esq., L.D.S., of Chester, a Sales Director and Fine Art Publisher (she died 1943); secondly, 1948, Agnes Christie, d. of James Paterson, Esq., of Redgorton, Perthshire. Educ. at Clunie Public School, Blairgowrie. Chief of the Scottish Clans Assocation of London 1920-21; Gov. of the Royal Caledonian Schools, Bushey; F.R.G.S.; President English League for Taxation of Land Values; travelled widely. A Liberal. Unsuccessfully contested S. Hammersmith in 1918, and the Finchley division of Middlesex in December 1922. Elected for the Finchley division of Middlesex in December 1923 and sat until he was defeated in October 1924. Unsuccessfully contested the Finchley division of Middlesex in May 1929, Kinross and W. Perthshire in October 1931 and the Aylesbury division of Buckinghamshire in May 1938. F.S.A. (Scot.). Died 14 December 1955.
[1924 2nd ed.]

ROBINSON, John Roland. Continued in House after 1945: full entry in Volume IV.

ROBINSON, Sidney. Lansdown Croft, Bath. Reform, and National Liberal. S. of John Robinson, Esq., of Backwell House, Somerset. B. 1863 at Wotton Lodge, Gloucestershire; m. 1887, Catherine d. of John Grant, Esq. (she died 1935). Educ. at Mill Hill School. A J.P. for Glamorgan, Somerset, and Wiltshire. A Liberal. Sat for Breconshire from 1906 to 1918. Returned unopposed for

Brecon and Radnor in December 1918 and sat until he retired in October 1922. Member of Cardiff City Council 1895. Died 6 December 1956.   [1922]

ROBINSON, Sydney Walter. 77 Orford Road, Walthamstow, London. S. of Alfred and Georgina Robinson, of Walthamstow. B. 1876; m. 1898, Gwendolene Edith King. Educ. at Walthamstow, and Metropolitan Coll., Chicago. An Alderman of Essex County Council. Engaged in farming in the constituency. A Liberal. Unsuccessfully contested S.E. Essex in 1918 and the Chelmsford division of Essex in 1922. Elected for Chelmsford in December 1923 and sat until he was defeated in October 1924. Defeated when contesting the same seat in November 1926 and in May 1929, also in W. Walthamstow in October 1931 and the Epping division of Essex in July 1945. Knighted 1934. Died 17 November 1950.
[1924 2nd ed.]

ROBINSON, Sir Thomas, O.B.E. The Hawthorns, Edge Lane, Stretford. S. of Peter Robinson, Esq., of Stretford, Lancashire. B. 2 January 1864; m. 1st, 19 January 1887, Emma, d. of William Lowe, Esq., of Chorlton (she died 6 May 1928); secondly, 1936, Mrs. Emmeline Mary Standring. Chairman of Stretford Urban District Council. J.P. for Lancashire; Chairman County Licensing Committee, Salford Hundred, of Manchester Port Sanitary Authority; Stretford British Red Cross Society; of Stretford Civic League of Help; and of Local Legislation Committee of House of Commons. Chairman of Legal Parliamentary Committee. Dept.-Chairman Bradford Dyers' Association Limited. Knighted 1920. O.B.E. 1919. Sat for the Stretford division of Lancashire as a National Liberal from December 1918-October 1924. Returned as an Independent (with Conservative and Liberal support) for the same seat in October 1924 and sat until he retired in October 1931. Charter Mayor of Stretford 1933-34, again Mayor 1944-45. K.B.E. 1934. Died 30 December 1953.   [1931 2nd ed.]

ROBINSON, William Albert. York House, Walton Breck Road, Liverpool.

B. 1877. Gen. Secretary of National Union of Distributive and Allied Workers. A Labour Member. Unsuccessfully contested the W. Toxteth division of Liverpool in 1918, the Wavertree division of Liverpool in 1924, the Exchange division of Liverpool in 1929, and the Shipley division of the W. Riding of Yorkshire in November 1930 and October 1931. Elected for St. Helens in November 1935 and sat until he retired in June 1945. Member of Liverpool City Council. Chairman of National Executive of Labour Party 1934-35. Died 31 December 1949.   [1945]

ROBINSON, William Cornforth, O.B.E. Spring Bank, 239 Manchester Road, Bury. S. of William C. Robinson, Esq., of Oldham. B. 12 July 1861; m. 1885, Martha, d. of Dennis Booth, Esq., of Burnley (she died March 1931). Secretary of Amalgamated Association of Beamers, Twisters and Drawers 1894-1931. President of the National Labour Party. Representative from British Labour to American Federation of Labour 1923. A Labour Member. Unsuccessfully contested Oldham in November 1911 and December 1918, and Ashton-under-Lyne January 1920. Elected for the Elland division of Yorkshire in November 1922, defeated in December 1923, and was re-elected for the same seat in October 1924. Sat until he retired in May 1929. Chairman of National Executive of Labour Party 1910-11. O.B.E. 1917. Died 11 June 1931.   [1929]

ROBINSON, William Edward. House of Commons, London. S. of William Robinson, Esq., of Stoke-on-Trent. B. at Burslem 1863; m. 1892, d. of Thomas Cope, Esq. A Potter's Merchant. Alderman of Stoke-on-Trent Town Council; Mayor for three years 1917-20; active in housing and transport questions. A Liberal. Elected for the Burslem division of Stoke-on-Trent in December 1923 and sat until he retired in October 1924. Died 10 May 1927.   [1924 2nd ed.]

ROCHE, William. See DE ROISTE, Liam.

RODD, Rt. Hon. Sir James Rennell, G.C.B., G.C.M.G., G.C.V.O. 39 Bryanston Square, London. Ardath, Shamley Green, Guildford. Athenaeum, Travellers', Carlton, and R.Y.S. S. of Maj. James Rennell Rodd. B. 9 November 1858; m. 27 October 1894, Lilias Georgina, d. of James Alexander Guthrie, Esq., of Craigie. Educ. at Haileybury, and Balliol Coll., Oxford; B.A. Entered Diplomatic Service 1883; served at Berlin, Athens, Rome, Paris, Zanzibar, Abyssinia, Cairo; Minister to Sweden 1904-08, Ambassador at Rome 1908-19; with Lord Milner's Mission to Egypt 1920; British delegate, League of Nations 1921 and 1923; retired 1921. PC. 1908. A Conservative. Elected for St. Marylebone in April 1928 and sat until he resigned in April 1932. Created Baron Rennell 1933. Died 26 July 1941.   [1932]

RODGER, Adam Keir. Avonholm, Rutherglen, Lanarkshire. S. of William Rodger, Esq., of Glasgow. B. at Greenock 1855; m. 1888, Amy Jane Lawton, of Ceylon. Educ. at the High School, Glasgow. Founder in 1883 of Scottish Temperance Life Assurance Company and was its Manager from 1883. Chairman Scottish Temperance League; Honorary Secretary Victoria Infirmary, Glasgow; Provost of Royal Burgh of Rutherglen. J.P. for Lanarkshire; J.P. for County of City of Glasgow. A Coalition Liberal. Elected for the Rutherglen division of Lanarkshire in December 1918 and sat until he retired in October 1922. Died 17 February 1946.   [1922]

ROGERS, Sir Hallewell. Greville Lodge, Edgbaston. Carlton, St. Stephen's, and Automobile. Union, Birmingham. S. of George Rogers, Esq., of Hampstead. B. in London 1864; m. 1st, 1885, Lydia Watton (she died 1908); secondly, 1927, Phyllis, d. of W.H. Burton, Esq., and widow of J.L. Reeve, Esq. Educ. privately. Chairman of the Birmingham Small Arms Company Limited; Director of Barclays Bank Limited; Lord Mayor of Birmingham 1902-04. Knighted 1904. Honorary Col. 3rd South Midland Brigade, Royal Field Artillery. A Coalition Unionist. Elected for the Moseley division of Birmingham in December 1918 and sat until he resigned in February 1921. Dept.-Lieut. for Warwickshire. Died

16 November 1931. [1921]

ROGERSON, Capt. John Edwin. Mount Oswald, Durham. 19 South Street, Park Lane, London. Carlton, and Brooks's. S. of John Rogerson, Esq., C.E. B. at Tynemouth 8 January 1865; m. 1892, Frances Mary, youngest d. of Pierce Creagh, Esq., of Mount Elva, Co. Clare. Educ. at Durham, and Trinity Coll., Cambridge. A Civil Engineer. A Conservative. Unsuccessfully contested the Barnard Castle division of Durham in 1918. Elected for the Barnard Castle division of Durham in November 1922 and sat until he was defeated in December 1923. O.B.E. 1919. Dept.-Lieut. for Co. Durham, High Sheriff 1905-06. Alderman, Durham County Council. Died 23 March 1925. [1923]

ROISTE, Liam de. See DE ROISTE, Liam.

ROMERIL, Herbert George. 78 Brunswick Crescent, London. B. 1881. Member of the Railway Clerks' Association, and was employed at the Railway Clearing House. Chairman of the Metropolitan Branch Independent Labour Party. A Labour Member. Unsuccessfully contested S.E. St. Pancras in 1918 and 1922. Elected for S.E. St. Pancras in December 1923, defeated October 1924. Re-elected for S.E. St. Pancras in May 1929 and sat until he was defeated in October 1931. Unsuccessfully contested S. Battersea in November 1935. Chairman of Estimates Committee 1930-31. J.P. for Middlesex. Died 2 October 1963. [1931 2nd ed.]

ROPNER, Leonard. Continued in House after 1945: full entry in Volume IV.

ROSBOTHAM, Sir Samuel Thomas. 45 Forest Road, Southport. S. of Samuel Rosbotham, Esq., of Stanley Farm, Bickerstaffe. B. 26 June 1864; m. 1st, 23 November 1887, Jane, d. of John Heyes, Esq. (she died 1945); secondly, 1946, Joan, d. of Rev. A.E. Dearden, Vicar of Waterfoot. Educ. at Ormskirk Grammar School. Member of Lancashire County Council from 1905; J.P. for Lancashire 1917; Knight Bach. 1933. A Labour Member until 1931, thereafter a

National Labour Member. Elected for the Ormskirk division of Lancashire in May 1929 and sat until he resigned in October 1939. Died 12 March 1950. [1939]

ROSE, Frank Herbert. Dumbarton. 192 Brixton Hill, London. S. of Thomas Rose, Esq. B. 5 July 1857; m. 1880, Ellen Mary, d. of Noah Bishop, Esq., of Lambeth. Educ. at the George Street Lambeth (British) School. Worked at the bench as an Operative Engineer till 1899, when he entered journalism. Wrote *The Coming Force* (official history of the Labour Party). A Labour Member. Often acted as an Independent Labour Member in defiance of the Labour Whip. Unsuccessfully contested Stockton in 1906 and Crewe in January 1910. Elected for N. Aberdeen in December 1918 and sat until his death on 10 July 1928. [1928]

ROSS, Sir Ronald Deane, Bart. Continued in House after 1945: full entry in Volume IV.

ROSS TAYLOR, Walter, C.B.E. The Castle House, Orford, Suffolk. Travellers'. S. of the Rev. Walter Ross Taylor, D.D. B. 1877; m. 1910, Frances, d. of Robert Orr, Esq., of Kinnaird (she died 1957). Educ. at the Leys, Cambridge, and Universities of Glasgow and Edinburgh, M.A., LL.B. Admitted Advocate Scotland 1902; in Egyptian Government Service 1905-23. J.P. for Suffolk. A Conservative. Elected for the Woodbridge division of Suffolk in October 1931 and sat until he retired in June 1945. Died 12 July 1958. [1945]

ROTHSCHILD, James Armand Edmond de. 23 St. James's Place, London. Waddesdon, Buckinghamshire. St. James's, Reform, Turf, and Jockey. S. of Baron Edmond de Rothschild. B. 1 December 1878; m. 1913, Dorothy, d. of Eugene Pinto, Esq. Educ. at Lycée Louis le Grand, Paris, and Trinity Coll., Cambridge, M.A. J.P., Dept.-Lieut. for the City and County of London and Buckinghamshire. Served in France and Palestine 1914-18; D.C.M. 1916; Maj. Royal Fusiliers 1918; Chairman Palestine Jewish Colonisation Association. A Trustee of the Wallace Collection 1941-55.

A Liberal. Elected for the Isle of Ely in May 1929 and sat until he was defeated in July 1945. Parliamentary Secretary to Ministry of Supply March-May 1945. Died 7 May 1957. [1945]

ROTHSCHILD, Lionel Nathan de, O.B.E. 46 Park Street, London. Exbury House, Exbury, Hampshire. Marlborough, and Carlton. S. of Leopold de Rothschild, C.V.O., and Marie, d. of A. Perugia, of Trieste. B. 1882; m. 1912, Marie Louise, d. of M. Edmond Beer, of Paris. Educ. at Harrow, and Trinity Coll., Cambridge. A Banker and J.P. for Buckinghamshire. O.B.E. 1917. A Conservative. Sat for the Aylesbury division of Buckinghamshire from January 1910 until he retired in November 1923. Died 28 January 1942. [1923]

ROUNDELL, Lieut.-Col. Richard Foulis. Gledstone. Skipton-in-Craven. Carlton, Travellers', Bachelors', and Garrick. S. of William Roundell, Esq. B. at Leamington 4 November 1872; m. 1898, Beatrice Maud, 2nd d. of Sir Mathew Wilson, 3rd Bart. Educ. at Harrow. Lieut.-Col. 3rd Battalion Northumberland Fusiliers. Assistant Whip (unpaid) November 1922 to January 1924. A Conservative. Unsuccessfully contested the Skipton division of the W. Riding of Yorkshire in 1906, January 1910, and again in December 1910. Elected for Skipton in December 1918 and sat until he retired in October 1924. Fellow of Royal Geographical Society. Died 5 January 1940. [1924 2nd ed.]

ROWLANDS, Sir Gwilym, C.B.E. 19 Llanfair Road, Penygraig, Rhondda, Glamorgan. S. of Rowland Rowlands, Esq., of Penygraig, Colliery Manager. B. 2 December 1878; m. 1908, Elizabeth Ann, d. of John Mason, Esq., of Tonypandy. Educ. at Penycraig Elementary School, and at Heath School, Pontypridd. J.P. Chairman of National Union of Conservative and Unionist Associations. C.B.E. 1928. A Conservative. Unsuccessfully contested W. Rhondda in December 1920 and November 1922, the Caerphilly division of Glamorgan in December 1923 and October 1924, and the Pontypool division of Monmouthshire in

May 1929. Elected for Flintshire in November 1935 and sat until he retired in June 1945. Knighted 1945. Died 16 January 1949. [1945]

ROWLANDS, James. 119 Mercer's Road, Tufnell Park, London. 8 Buckingham Street, Strand, London. National Liberal. S. of William Bull Rowlands, Esq. B. 1 October 1851 in Finsbury; m. 1879, Kate, d. of Joseph Boyden, Esq. (she died 1905). Educ. at Working Men's Coll. Was apprenticed to Watch Case-making, and was a freeman of the Goldsmiths' Company. A member of the London School Board. Honorary Secretary of the Land Law Reform Association. A Liberal. Unsuccessfully contested E. Finsbury in 1885. Sat for E. Finsbury from 1886 to 1895, when he was defeated. Sat for the Dartford division of Kent from 1906 to January 1910, when he was again defeated; re-elected for the Dartford division of Kent in December 1910 and December 1918 and sat until his death on 1 March 1920. [1920]

ROWSON, Guy. 7 Beechfield Avenue, Hindley Green, Wigan. S. of Joseph Rowson, Esq., Coal Miner. B. 1883 at Ellenbrook, Lancashire; m. Miss Gregory, of Tyldesley. A Coal Miner; Miners' Agent in the Lancashire and Cheshire Miners' Federation 1923. J.P. for Lancashire 1932. Member of Tyldesley with Shakerly Urban District Council 1919-22; of Lancashire County Council from 1919-25. Parliamentary Private Secretary to the Rt. Hon. C.R. Attlee 1935. A Labour Member. Elected for the Farnworth division of Lancaster in May 1929, and was defeated in October 1931. Re-elected for the same seat in November 1935 and sat until his death on 16 November 1937. [1938]

ROYCE, William Stapleton. The Hall, Pinchbeck, Spalding. B. 1857; m. 1882, Emma Louisa, d. of O.L. Broedelet, Esq., of Rotterdam. Educ. at Pretty's Preparatory School, Spalding. In early life worked as a Joiner. J.P., Holland 1911. President of the Holland-with-Boston United Association. A Landowner in the constituency; was concerned in large railway and building contracts in South Africa. A Labour Member. Unsuccessfully contested the Spalding division of Lincolnshire in January 1910 and December 1910, as a Unionist. Elected for the Holland-with-Boston division of Lincolnshire in December 1918 and sat until his death on 23 June 1924. He accepted the post of Gov. of Tasmania in June 1924 but died before an official appointment could be made. [1924 2nd ed.]

ROYDEN, Sir Thomas, Bart., C.H. 34 Dover Street, London. Frankby Hall, Frankby, Cheshire. Marlborough, Carlton, and Bath. S. of Sir Thomas Bland Royden, Bart., at one time MP for W. Toxteth. B. at Mossley Hill, Aigburth, near Liverpool 1871; m. 1922, Quenelda Mary d. of H. Clegg, Esq., of Anglesey, widow of C. Williamson, Esq. Educ. at Winchester Coll., and Magdalen Coll., Oxford. A Shipowner from 1902. Chairman of the Liverpool Steamship Owners' Association and President of the Chamber of Shipping of the United Kingdom. High Sheriff for Cheshire 1917-18; Dept.-Lieut. and J.P. for Cheshire. Appointed to represent the Shipping Controller at the Peace Conference discussions in Paris January 1919. Companion of Honour 1919 and Commandeur de la Legion d'Honneur. A Coalition Unionist. Elected for Bootle in December 1918 and sat until he retired in October 1922. Succeeded as Bart. 1917. Chairman of Cunard Steamship Company. Created Baron Royden 1944. Died 6 November 1950. [1922]

ROYDS, Edmund, O.B.E. (Mil.) 46 Bedford Square, London. Stubton Hall, Newark. Carlton, and Union. S. of the Rev. Francis Coulman Royds, Hon. Canon of Chester, and Cornelia Frances, d. of Canon G.B. Blomfield, of Mollington Hall, Cheshire. B. 6 July 1860 at Coddington, Cheshire; m. 1889, Rachel Louisa, d. of Col. Francis Fane, of Fulbeck (she died 1943). Educ. at Haileybury Coll. A Solicitor, admitted 1882, a Director of Life Association of Scotland. Maj. Lincolnshire Yeomanry. Lieut.-Col. and County Commandant Lincolnshire Volunteer Force. A Unionist. Returned for the Sleaford division of Lincolnshire in January and December 1910, and for the Grantham division of Lincolnshire in December 1918. Sat until he was defeated in November 1922. O.B.E. 1919. Dept.-Lieut. for Lincolnshire, High Sheriff 1931. Knighted 1939. Died 31 March 1946. [1922]

ROYDS, Admiral Sir Percy Molyneux Rawson, C.B., C.M.G. Highcoombe, Warren Road, Kingston Hill. United Service. S. of Ernest E.M. Royds, Esq., Banker, of Rochdale, and Blanche, d. of Christopher Rawson, Esq. B. 5 April 1874; m. 5 November 1898, Florence, d. of Sir Alfred Yarrow, Bart. (she died 1948). Educ. at Eastman's Royal Naval Academy, Southsea, and in H.M.S. *Britannia*. Director of Physical Training of the Navy 1920; Admiral Superintendent Chatham Dockyard 1923-25; Chairman of Conservative Association, Kingston-upon-Thames 1928-37; President of Rugby Union 1927-28. Served in Boxer Rising, in China War and 1914-18. Created Knight Bach. January 1938. Legion of Honour, The Russian Order of St. Anne and the Danish Order of Dannebrog. A Conservative. Elected for Kingston-upon-Thames in July 1937 and sat until he retired in June 1945. C.M.G. 1917; C.B. 1924. Vice-Admiral 1927, Admiral 1932. Died 25 March 1955. [1945]

ROYLE, Charles. House of Commons, London. S. of Samuel Royle, Esq. B. 17 January 1872; m. Maria, d. of Oliver Wolfe, Esq. Educ. at Portwood Wesleyan Higher Grade School, Stockport. Engaged in the meat trade at Stockport. Member of Stockport Town Council for 44 years; Mayor four times. President of the Free Church Brotherhood movement. A Liberal. Elected for Stockport in December 1923 and sat until he was defeated in October 1924. Unsuccessfully contested Stockport as an Independent Liberal in May 1929. President of National Federation of Meat Traders 1929 and 1942. Died 3 November 1963. [1924 2nd ed.]

RUDKIN, Lieut.-Col. Charles Mark Clement, D.S.O. 15 Old Square, Lincoln's Inn, London. Royal Automobile, and National Liberal. S. of Maj. H.W. Rudkin, 85th

Regiment. B. at Collon House, Co. Louth 12 November 1872; m. 1st, 1906, Margaret Gordon, grand-d. of Lord Cecil Gordon; secondly, Marie, d. of Thomas Russell, Esq. Served in South African War; on Lord Methuen's Staff; and finally commanded a composite Brigade of Artillery 1899-1902 (Queen's Medal, 4 clasps; King's Medal, 2 clasps). Commanded the Royal Artillery Reserve at the Coronation 1911. Coronation Medals 1902 and 1911. Served European War 1914-18, in France, Belgium and Italy; commanded an Artillery Division at Ypres, the Somme and on the Piave, Italy (wounded); despatches twice; D.S.O. 1919; 1914 Star. Barrister-at-Law 1912, Lincoln's Inn; travelled and shot in Africa, Australia and Canada, and travelled in America, New Zealand, Tasmania and Ceylon, and extensively in Europe, including Russia. Instructed himself in the progress of agriculture in Holland, Sweden, Norway, Belgium, France, Canada, America, Australia, and New Zealand, by travel and inspection. A Freeman of the City of London. A Liberal. Elected for the Chichester division of Sussex in December 1923 and sat until he was defeated in October 1924. Unsuccessfully contested S. Portsmouth in May 1929. Died at Umtali, Southern Rhodesia 30 December 1957.

[1924 2nd ed.]

RUGGLES-BRISE, Sir Edward Archibald, Bart., M.C. Spains Hall, Finchingfield, Braintree, Essex. Carlton. S. of A.W. Ruggles-Brise, Esq. B. 9 September 1882; m. 1st, 1906, Agatha, d. of J.H. Gurney, Esq., Dept.-Lieut., and J.P., of Keswick Hall, Norfolk (she died 2 April 1937); secondly, 14 March 1939, Lucy Barbara, d. of the Rt. Rev. W.R. Pym, Bishop of Bombay. Educ. at Eton, and Trinity Coll., Cambridge. A Landowner and Land Agent. Fellow of Land Agents' Society. Maj. Essex Yeomanry 1903-22; Lieut.-Col. 104th Essex Yeomanry Field Brigade R.A. (T.A.) 1927-34; Brevet-Col. 1931; served in France, etc. 1914-19. Vice-Lieut., Dept.-Lieut., and J.P. for Essex. Member of the Agricultural Committee of Essex County Council. T.D. Created Bart. 1935. A Conservative. Elected for the Maldon division of Essex in

November 1922, but defeated in December 1923. Re-elected for Maldon in October 1924 and sat until his death on 12 May 1942. [1942]

RUNCIMAN, Hilda. 8 Barton Street, London. Doxford Hall, Chathill, Northumberland. D. of J.C. Stevenson, Esq., MP, of Westoe, South Shields. B. 1869; m. 23 August 1898, Walter Runciman, subsequently MP, created Visct. Runciman 1937 (he died 1949). Educ. at Notting Hill High School, and Girton Coll., Cambridge. A Liberal. Elected for the St. Ives division of Cornwall in March 1928 and sat until May 1929 when she unsuccessfully contested the Tavistock division of Devon. Died 28 October 1956. [1929]

RUNCIMAN, Rt. Hon. Walter. 8 Barton Street, London. Doxford Hall, Chathill, Northumberland. Isle of Eigg, Invernessshire. Royal Yacht Squadron, Brooks's, and Reform. S. of Sir Walter Runciman, Bart., MP., 1st Baron Runciman B. 19 November 1870; m. 23 August 1898, Hilda (MP for the St. Ives division of Cornwall 1928-29), d. of J.C. Stevenson, Esq., MP, of Westoe, South Shields. Educ. at Trinity Coll., Cambridge, M.A.; Honorary LL.D. Manchester 1910, and Bristol 1929; Honorary D.C.L. Oxford 1932. J.P. for Northumberland. Chairman of United Kingdom Provident Institution 1920-31; Vice-Chairman of the Moor line of Cargo Steamers; President of Chamber of Shipping of the U.K. 1926-27; Chairman of International Shipping Conference 1926; Master of the Shipwrights Company 1926-27. Director of the Westminster Bank and of L.M. and S. Railway to November 1931; Dept. Chairman and Voting Trustee R.M.S.P.C. and its Associated Companies 1930-31. PC. 1908. Parliamentary Secretary to Local Government Board 1905-07; Financial Secretary to the Treasury 1907-08; President of Board of Education 1908-11, of Board of Agriculture 1911-14. President of Board of Trade 1914-16 and November 1931-May 1937. A Liberal until 1931, thereafter a National Liberal. Unsuccessfully contested Gravesend in 1898. Sat for Oldham from 1899-1900, when he was defeated. Sat for

Dewsbury from 1902-18, when he was again defeated. Unsuccessfully contested N. Edinburgh in April 1920, Berwick-upon-Tweed in November 1922 and Brighton in December 1923. Elected for Swansea W. in October 1924, and for St. Ives in May 1929. Returned unopposed for the St. Ives division of Cornwall in October 1931 and again in November 1935. Sat until June 1937 when he was created Visct. Runciman of Doxford. Succeeded his father as Baron Runciman August 1937. Lord President of the Council October 1938-September 1939. Died 14 November 1949.   [1937]

RUNGE, Norah Cecil, O.B.E. St. John's House, Smith Square, London. Kipperton Court, Sevenoaks. Ladies' Carlton. D. of Lawrence Hasluck, Esq. B. 1884; m. 1st. 1906, J.J. Runge, Esq. (he died 1935); secondly, 1939, Dr. T.A. Ross (he died 1941). Superintendent of Soldiers' and Sailors' Free Buffet, Paddington Station 1915-19; Chairman of Women's Branch of Rotherhithe Conservative Association 1927-32. A Conservative. Elected for the Rotherhithe division of Bermondsey in October 1931 and sat until she was defeated in November 1935. Unsuccessfully contested the Rotherhithe division of Bermondsey in July 1945. O.B.E. 1918. Member of London County Council 1937-61, Dept. Chairman 1951-52. Chairman of London Area Women's Advisory Committee of Conservative and Unionist Associations 1938-43, President 1943-45. Died 6 June 1978.
                                   [1935]

RUSSELL, Albert, K.C. 16 Moray Place, Edinburgh. Constitutional, and Caledonian. S. of Sir William Russell, Merchant, of Glasgow. B. 1884; m. 1913, Florence Muir, d. of Thomas Galloway, Esq., of Auchendrane, Ayrshire. Educ. at Glasgow Academy and University. Served with Royal Engineers 1915-18. Advocate, admitted to Scottish bar 1908; K.C. 1931. A Conservative. Elected for Kirkcaldy Burghs in October 1931 and sat until he was defeated in November 1935. Advocate Depute 1928-29. Solicitor-Gen. for Scotland November 1935-June 1936. Judge of the Court of Session, with the judicial title of Lord Russell 1936-

60. Died 12 May 1975.   [1935]

RUSSELL, Sir Alexander West. 76 Hamilton Terrace, London. Athenaeum, Carlton, and Royal Automobile. S. of William Russell, Esq., of Grayshall, Bathgate. B. 27 November 1879; m. 24 September 1914, Agnes Bunten, d. of David Sturrock, Esq., of Glasgow (she died December 1930). Educ. at Bathgate Academy, and Edinburgh University, M.A. Barrister-at-Law, Middle Temple 1920. Served in France 1915-18. Knight Bach. 1937. A Conservative. Sat for Tynemouth from November 1922 until he was defeated in July 1945. Died 22 April 1961.   [1945]

RUSSELL, Hamer Field. 23 Palace Street, London. Crabtree Bank, Pitsmoor, Sheffield. Constitutional. S. of J.T. Russell, Esq., of Hull. B. 1876; m. 8 December 1904, Florence, d. of John Marshall, Esq., of Halifax. Educ. at Eton House School, Hull. A Timber and Builders' Merchant. Unsuccessfully contested the Ecclesall division of Sheffield as a Liberal in December 1923. Unsuccessfully contested the Brightside division of Sheffield as a Conservative in 1930. Elected for that division in October 1931 and sat until he was defeated in November 1935. Commander of Order of St. John of Jerusalem; Superintendent of the Sheffield Corps. Died 6 June 1941.   [1935]

RUSSELL, Richard John. 19 Balls Road, Birkenhead. Blea Busk, Askrigg, Yorkshire. S. of R.J. Russell, Esq., Engineer, of Birkenhead. B. 12 April 1872; m. Ellen, d. of William Atkinson, Esq., of Skell Gill, Wensleydale (she died 3 June 1942). Educ. at St. Ann's School, Birkenhead, and the University of Liverpool. A Dental Surgeon. Alderman of Birkenhead County Borough Council from 1901; J.P. for Birkenhead. A Liberal, and National Liberal from 1931. Unsuccessfully contested the Eddisbury division of Cheshire in December 1923 and October 1924. Returned for the Eddisbury division in March 1929 and sat until his death on 5 February 1943.   [1943]

RUSSELL, Stuart Hugh Minto. Crooksbury Hurst, Farnham, Surrey. Carlton,

Brooks's, and Pratt's. S. of Sir Lennox Russell. B. 18 January 1909. Educ. at Rugby, and Trinity Coll., Cambridge. Capt. Coldstream Guards. Parliamentary Private Secretary to Sir Philip Sassoon when Under-Secretary of State for Air November 1936-May 1937, and to the Rt. Hon. Sir John Simon, Chancellor of the Exchequer May 1937-November 1938. A Conservative. Elected for the Darwen division of Lancashire in November 1935 and sat until he died on active service in October 1943 after contracting fever in Sicily.   [1943]

RUSSELL, William. House of Commons, London. S. of George Russell, Esq., of Bolton. B. 28 August 1859; m. Mary, d. of Thomas Taylor, Esq., of Bolton. Educ. at Booth's Academy, and privately. A Bolton Solicitor. Mayor of Bolton November 1921-November 1922. A Conservative. Sat for Bolton from November 1922 until he retired in November 1923. Died 31 October 1937.   [1923]

RUSSELL-WELLS, Sir Sydney Russell. 126 Wigmore Street, London. The Shoals, Irstead Neatishead, Norfolk. Athenaeum. S. of Benjamin Weston Wells, Esq., and Mary Elizabeth, née Russell. B. at Kensington 25 September 1869; m. 1895, Harriett, 3rd d. of Stephen Smith, Esq. Educ. at various schools, the Royal Coll. of Science, South Kensington; B.Sc. 1889, and St. George's Hospital; A Physician, M.D., F.R.C.P., M.R.C.S., M.B., 1893; M.R.C.P. 1895; M.D. 1895. Senior Physician Seamen's Hospital, Greenwich; Physician National Hospital for Diseases of the Heart. Senator University of London from 1903; Chairman Council for External Students 1907-19; Vice-Chancellor 1919-22. Knighted 1921, when he assumed the surname Russell-Wells in lieu of Wells. Made various contributions to scientific and medical journals. A Conservative. First elected for the University of London in November 1922 and sat until his death on 14 July 1924.   [1924 2nd ed.]

RUTHERFORD, Sir John, Bart. Beardwood, Blackburn. Rutherford Lodge, Roxburghshire. Carlton, Cavalry, and Boodle's.

S. of John Rutherford, Esq., J.P., of Blackburn. B. 1854 at Blackburn. Unmarried. Educ. at Royal Grammar School, Lancaster, and Glasgow University. Col. commanding Duke of Lancaster's Own Yeomanry; T.D. (1909); a J.P. for Blackburn and Dumfries-shire, and a Dept.-Lieut. for Lancaster. Was Mayor of Blackburn 1888-89. President of the Blackburn and East Lancashire Royal Infirmary. Created Bart. 1916. A Unionist. Sat for the Darwen division of Lancashire from 1895-January 1910, when he was defeated. Re-elected for the Darwen division of Lancashire in December 1910 and sat until he retired in October 1922. Died 26 February 1932.   [1922]

RUTHERFORD, Sir John Hugo, Bart. Woodlands, Gateacre, Liverpool. S. of Sir (William) Watson Rutherford, 1st Bart., MP. B. 31 October 1887. His birth was registered under the name of John Hughes Rutherford but in 1928 he assumed the name Hugo in lieu of Hughes; m. 5 June 1913, Isabel, d. of J.T. Smith, Esq., of Liverpool. Partner in the firm of Mayo, Elder and Rutherford, Solicitors. A Conservative. Unsuccessfully contested the Edge Hill division of Liverpool in May 1929. Elected for the division in October 1931 and sat until he retired in October 1935. Member of Liverpool City Council. Succeeded as Bart. 1927. Died 28 December 1942.   [1935]

RUTHERFORD, John Rutherford. 5 Elm Court, Temple, London. Weir Lodge, Aylesbury. Rutherford Lodge, Roxburghshire. Carlton, and Constitutional. New, Edinburgh. S. of John Rutherford Chalmers, Esq., Banker. B. 27 August 1904; m. 1937, Doreen, d. of C.F. Hilton, Esq. (divorced 1947). Educ. at Repton, and Worcester Coll., Oxford. Barrister-at-Law, Inner Temple 1928. Assumed by Royal Licence in 1933 the surname of Rutherford in lieu of Chalmers, under the will of Sir John Rutherford. A Conservative. Elected for Edmonton in October 1931 and sat until he was defeated in November 1935. Died 5 July 1957.   [1935]

RUTHERFORD, Sir William Watson.
48 Cannon Street, London. 28 Brunswick
Square, Hove, Sussex. Carlton. S. of William
Rutherford, Esq., of Liverpool. B. in Liverpool 1853; m. 1878, Elspeth, d. of Capt.
Alexander Strachan (she died 1914). Educ.
at Merchant Taylors' School, Great Crosby. A Solicitor, admitted 1875. Member
of the Liverpool City Council 1895-1912,
Lord Mayor 1903. J.P. for Liverpool.
Knighted 1918. A Conservative. Unsuccessfully contested the Scotland division of
Liverpool in 1900. Sat for the W. Derby
division of Liverpool from January 1903,
and for the Edge Hill division of Liverpool
from December 1918 until he resigned in
February 1923. Created Bart. June 1923.
Died 3 December 1927.   [1923]

RYAN, Dr. James. Selskar Street, Wexford. B. in Co. Wexford 1892; m. 1919,
Mairin Cregan. Educ. at University Coll.,
Dublin. A Physician and Surgeon of Wexford. A Sinn Fein Member. Elected for
the S. division of Wexford in December
1918 but did not take his seat. Member of
Dail for S. Wexford to 1921, for Wexford
1921-22 and 1923-65. An Anti-Treaty
Member, joined Fianna Fail 1926. Minister
of Agriculture 1932-47, Minister of Health
1947-48 and 1951-54. Minister of Finance
1957-65. Member of Senate 1965-69. Died
25 September 1970.   [1922]

RYE, Frank Gibbs. 13 Golden Square,
London. Basing House, Thames Ditton.
Carlton, and Union. S. of Walter Rye,
Esq., Solicitor, of Westminster. B. 12 August
1874; m. 1st, 18 April 1901, Ethel Mary, d.
of E.M. Beloe, Esq., Solicitor, of Kings
Lynn (she died 1938); secondly, 1947,
Nora, widow of G. Gayford, Esq., of Rayn-
ham. Educ. at Fauconberg Grammar
School, Beccles, and St. Paul's Schools.
Admitted a Solicitor 1901. Alderman West-
minster City Council, Mayor 1922-23; Vice-
Chairman Abbey division of Westminster
Constitutional Association; member of Exe-
cutive Committee London Municipal Socie-
ty. Director of County Fire Office Limited.
A Conservative. Unsuccessfully contested the
Loughborough division of Leicestershire in
December 1923. Elected for the division

in October 1924 and sat until he was
defeated in May 1929. Member of London
County Council 1937-48, Dept.-Chairman
1946-47. Died 18 October 1948.   [1929]

SAKLATVALA, Shapurji. 2 St. Albans
Villas, Highgate Road, London. S. of
Dorabji Saklatvala, Esq. B. in Bombay
28 March 1874; m. 1907, Sehri, d, of
Henry Marsh, Esq., of Tansley, Derby-
shire. Educ. at St. Xavier's School and
Coll., Bombay. Served as Private Secretary
to Sir Ratan Tata, and afterwards Departmental Manager Tata Limited, London. An
Independent Member. Elected for Battersea N. in November 1922, defeated in
1923. Re-elected for Battersea N. in
October 1924 and sat until he was defeated
in 1929. Unsuccessfully contested the
Shettleston division of Glasgow in June
1930 and Battersea N. in October 1931.
Contested elections as a Member of the
Communist Party. Received the support
of the Labour Party in 1922 and 1923;
but was opposed by Labour candidates in
1929, 1930 and 1931. Died 16 January
1936.   [1929]

SALMON, Sir Isidore, C.B.E. 51 Mount
Street, London. Carlton, and Junior Carlton. S. of Barnett Salmon, Esq. B. 10
February 1876; m. 10 December 1899,
Kate Abrahams. Chairman and Manag-
ing Director of J. Lyons and Company
Limited; member London County Council
from 1907-25, Vice-Chairman 1924-25;
Chairman London War Pensions Committee
1918-22, and of City of London Employ-
ment Committee from 1922, of Special Re-
organisation Committee London County
Council 1921; of Home Office Committee for
Employment of Prisoners 1932-34; Member
of House of Commons Select Committee on
Public Accounts from 1925, and of Estimates
Committee from 1931, Chairman from 1936
to 1939; of Ministry of Health Committee
on Prices of Building Materials; member of
Central Housing Advisory Committee, of
Royal Commission on Transport 1928-30;
President of Decimal Association; member
of Governing Body of Regent Street Poly-
technic; Chairman of National Training
Coll. of Domestic Subjects; Honorary Advis-

er on Catering to British Army. Dept.-Lieut., and J.P. C.B.E. 1920. Created Knight Bach. 1933. Vice-President of Board of Deputies of British Jews. A Conservative. Elected for the Harrow division of Middlesex in 1924 and sat until his death on 16 September 1941. [1941]

SALT, Sir Edward William. Avon Hurst, Tiddington, Stratford-on-Avon. Constitutional. S. of Ashton Trow Salt, Esq., of Birmingham. B. 18 May 1881; m. 30 March 1910, Alice Elizabeth, d. of J.J.P. Edmunds, Esq., of Hawkesley Hall, Kings Norton (she died 1945). Educ. at King Edward's Grammar School, Birmingham. Managing Director of Salt and Son Limited from 1904. Member of Birmingham City Council from 1924. Chairman of British Artificial Limb Association 1923-25, and of Parliamentary and Scientific Committee. A Unionist. Unsuccessfully contested the Yardley division of Birmingham in May 1929. Elected for the division in October 1931 and sat until he was defeated in July 1945. Knighted June 1945. High Sheriff of Warwickshire 1952. Died 8 September 1970. [1945]

SALTER, Dr. Alfred. 75a Balham Park Road, London. S. of W.H. Salter, Esq., of Bromley. B. 1873; m. 1900, Ada, d. of Samuel Brown, Esq., of Thorpe House, Northamptonshire (she died 1942). Educ. at Roan School, Greenwich and Guy's Hospital. M.D. London, B.S., M.R.C.S., L.R.C.P., D.P.H.; member London County Council from 1905-10; J.P. for London; Alderman of Bermondsey Borough Council from 1919, and member of Board of Guardians 1909-18; Treasurer of London Labour Party from 1909; Chairman of Bermondsey I.L.P. and President of West Bermondsey Labour Party. A Labour Member. Unsuccessfully contested the Bermondsey division of Southwark in October 1909, and Bermondsey W. in 1918. Elected for Bermondsey W. in November 1922, defeated December 1923. Re-elected in October 1924 and sat until he retired in June 1945. Died 24 August 1945. [1945]

SALTER, Rt. Hon. Sir James Arthur, G.B.E., K.C.B. Continued in House after 1945: full entry in Volume IV.

SAMUEL, Sir Arthur Michael, Bart. 48 Montagu Square, London. Carlton. S. of Benjamin and Rosetta Samuel, of Norwich. B. 6 December 1872; m. 1912, Phoebe, d. of Dr. Alfred Fletcher, of Charterhouse. Educ. at King Edward VI Grammar School, Norwich. A Manufacturer, retired. Lord Mayor of Norwich 1912. Parliamentary Under-Secretary for Foreign Affairs, Parliamentary Secretary Board of Trade and Secretary Overseas Trade Department November 1924-November 1927; Financial Secretary to the Treasury November 1927-June 1929. Chairman of Public Accounts Committee 1929-31. Created Bart. January 1932. A Conservative. Unsuccessfully contested the Stretford division of Lancashire in January and December 1910. Sat for the Farnham division of Surrey from December 1918 until February 1937 when he was created Baron Mancroft. Died 17 August 1942. [1937]

SAMUEL, Rt. Hon. Sir Harry Simon. The Crossways, Sunningdale, Berkshire. Carlton, and Junior Carlton. S. of Horatio S. Samuel and Henrietta, niece of Sir Moses Montefiore. B. 1853 at 40 Gloucester Place, Portman Square, London; m. 1878, Rose, d. of E.H. Beddington, Esq. Educ. at Eastbourne Coll., and St. John's Coll., Cambridge; B.A. Knighted 1903. PC. 1916; J.P. for the County of London. A Unionist. Unsuccessfully contested Limehouse in 1892. Sat for Limehouse from 1895 to 1906, when he was defeated. Elected for Norwood division of Lambeth in January and December 1910 and sat until he retired in October 1922. Died at Monte Carlo 26 April 1934. [1922]

SAMUEL, Rt. Hon. Sir Herbert Louis, G.C.B., G.B.E. 36 Porchester Terrace, London. S. of Edwin Louis Samuel, Esq. B. 6 November 1870; m. 17 November 1897, Beatrice Miriam, d. of Ellis A. Franklin, Esq. (she died 1959). Educ. at University Coll. School, and Balliol Coll., Oxford, M.A. Parliamentary Under-Secretary of

State for Home Department 1905-09; PC. 1908; Chancellor of Duchy of Lancaster 1909-10; Postmaster-Gen. 1910-14; President Local Government Board 1914-15; Postmaster-Gen. May 1915-January 1916, Chancellor of the Duchy of Lancaster November 1915-January 1916; Home Secretary January-December 1916 and August 1931-September 1932; Chairman of House of Commons National Expenditure Committee 1917-18; High Commissioner for Palestine 1920-25; President of British Institute of Philosophy from 1931 to 1959. A Liberal. Unsuccessfully contested the Henley division of Oxfordshire in 1895 and 1900. Sat for the Cleveland division of the N. Riding of Yorkshire from 1902 to 1918, when he was defeated. Elected for the Darwen division of Lancashire in May 1929 and sat until he was defeated in November 1935. Leader of Liberal Party in the House of Commons 1931-35 and in the House of Lords 1944-55. Created Visct. Samuel 1937. Honorary Fellow of Balliol Coll., Oxford 1935, Visitor 1946-57 Chairman of Royal Commission on the Coal Industry 1925. Chairman of Liberal Party Organisation 1927-29. President of Royal Asiatic Society 1940-43. Died 5 February 1963.   [1935]

SAMUEL, Howel Walter. 46 Lynette Avenue, London. S. of Thomas Samuel, Esq., of Swansea. B. 1881; m. 1st, 1911, Harriot Sawyer Polkinghorne (she died died 1939); secondly, 1941, Annie Gladys, Lady Gregg, widow of Sir Henry Gregg. In early life was engaged in mining and other industries in Swansea. Barrister-at-Law, Middle Temple 1915, S. Wales Circuit. A Labour Member. Unsuccessfully contested Swansea W. in November 1922. Elected in 1923, and defeated in 1924. Re-elected for W. Swansea in May 1929 and sat until he was defeated in October 1931. K.C. 1931. Recorder of Merthyr Tydfil 1930-33. County Court Judge 1933-53. Chairman of Radnorshire Quarter Sessions. Died 5 April 1953.   [1931 2nd ed.]

SAMUEL, Marcus Reginald Anthony. 21 South Street, London. Carlton, and Constitutional. S. of Joseph Samuel, Esq.

B. 7 September 1873; m. 1903, Adelaide Esther, d. of Charles Johnson, Esq. Educ. at University Coll. School, and abroad. An East India Merchant. A Conservative. Unsuccessfully contested N. Southwark in May 1929. Elected for the Putney division of Wandsworth in November 1934 and again in November 1935 and sat until his death on 3 March 1942.   [1942]

SAMUEL, Samuel. Berkeley House, Berkeley Square, London. Carlton, Royal Automobile, and Portland. S. of Marcus Samuel, Esq. B. 7 April 1855. Unmarried. Educ. in London and Paris. Senior partner in the firm of M. Samuel and Company, Bankers and Merchants; Director of Shell Transport and Trading Company, Lloyds Bank, Capital and Counties Bank, and other companies. Lieut. of City of London. Associate Officer St. J. A Conservative. Unsuccessfully contested W. Leeds in 1906 and January 1910, and Sunderland in December 1910. Elected for Wandsworth in June 1913 and sat for the Putney division of Wandsworth from December 1918 until his death on 23 October 1934.   [1934]

SAMUELS, Rt. Hon. Arthur Warren, K.C. 13 Ely Place, Dublin. Cloghereen, Howth. 2nd s. of Arthur Samuels, Esq., M.A., of Langad, Kingstown, and Katharine, d. of Owen Daly, Esq., of Mornington, Co. Westmeath, J.P. B. 19 May 1852; m. 1881, Emma Margaret, 2nd d. of the Rev. James Irwin, M.A., of Sharon, Co. Donegal, and Florine Griffiths-Lloyd, only sister of Sir Herbert Edwardes, K.C.B. (she died 1904); two daughters, one s. (Arthur P.I., Capt. R. Irish Rifles, killed in action in France September 1916). Educ. at the Royal School, Dungannon and Trinity Coll., Dublin. Called to the Irish bar 1877; Q.C. 1894; called to the English bar, Gray's Inn 1896. K.C. Ireland; Bencher of King's Inn; was Permanent Counsel and Crown Prosecutor for G.P.O., Ireland; Solicitor-Gen. for Ireland September 1917-April 1918; Attorney-Gen. for Ireland April 1918-July 1919; President of the Social and Statistical Society of Ireland 1906-08. Chancellor of the United Dioceses of Down, Connor, and Dromore, and of the United Dioceses of

Limerick, Ardfert, and Aghadoe. Published works on Irish Social and Financial Questions, the Fiscal Question, and Home Rule; articles in quarterly and other periodicals. Was Capt. of the Dublin University Rowing Club. PC. (Ireland) 1918. A Unionist. Unsuccessfully contested Dublin University in March 1903. Elected for the University in February 1917; re-elected there in December 1918 and sat until he was appointed a Judge of the Irish High Court in July 1919. Judge of King's Bench Division of High Court of Ireland 1919-25. Bencher of Gray's Inn 1919. Died 11 May 1925.
[1919]

SANDEMAN, Sir Alexander Nairne Stewart, Bart. See STEWART-SANDEMAN, Sir Alexander Nairne Stewart, Bart.

SANDERS, Rt. Hon. Sir Robert Arthur, Bart. 3 Eaton Square, London. Bayford Lodge, Wincanton, Somerset. Carlton, Arthur's, and Garrick. S. of Arthur Sanders, Esq., of Fernhill, Isle of Wight. B. 20 June 1867; m. 1893, Lucy, d. of W.H. Halliday, Esq., of Glenthorne, N. Devon. Educ. at Harrow, and Balliol Coll., Oxford. Barrister-at-Law, Inner Temple 1892; Alderman of Somerset County Council, Chairman from 1937; Commanded Royal North Devon Hussars in Gallipoli, Egypt, and Palestine 1915-18. Dept.-Lieut., and J.P. for Somerset; J.P. for Devon. Master of Devon and Somerset Staghounds 1895-1907. A Unionist Whip 1911-15, and 1918-21. Treasurer of the Household 1918-19; Junior Lord of the Treasury 1919-21; Under-Secretary for War 1921-22; Minister of Agriculture 1922-24. Bart. 1920. PC. 1922. A Conservative. Unsuccessfully contested E. Bristol in 1900 and the Bridgwater division of Somerset in 1906. Sat for the Bridgwater division of Somerset from January 1910-December 1923, when he was defeated. Sat for the Wells division of Somerset from October 1924 until he retired in May 1929. Created Baron Bayford 1929. Died 24 February 1940.
[1929]

SANDERS, Capt. William Stephen, C.B.E. 3 Baskerville Road, Wandsworth Common, London. S. of Stephen Sanders,

Esq., Saddler. B. 2 January 1871; m. 1899, Beatrice Helen, d. of Leonard Martin, Esq. (she died 1932). Educ. at elementary schools, Polytechnics and the Universities of Berlin and Jena. Lecturer at Ruskin Coll. in English Working Class History. An Official of International Labour Office of the League of Nations 1920-29. Financial Secretary to the War Office 1930-31. A Labour Member. Elected for N. Battersea in May 1929, and defeated there in October 1931. Re-elected for N. Battersea in November 1935 and sat until he resigned in April 1940. C.B.E. 1918. Secretary of Fabian Society 1914-20. Alderman, London County Council 1904-10. Died 6 February 1941.
[1940]

SANDERSON, Sir Frank Bernard, Bart. Continued in House after 1945: full entry in Volume IV.

SANDHAM, Elijah. House of Commons, London. B. at Chorley 1875. Member of Chorley Borough Council from 1906; joined ILP 1907. A Labour Member. Unsuccessfully contested the Chorley division of Lancashire in December 1918 and the Kirkdale division of Liverpool in October 1924. Elected for the Kirkdale division of Liverpool in May 1929 and sat until he was defeated in October 1931, standing as the ILP candidate. Resigned from ILP in 1934 and became President of Independent Socialist Party. Died 7 May 1944.
[1931 2nd ed.]

SANDON, Dudley Ryder, Visct. Sandon Hall, Stafford. Burnt Norton, Campden, Gloucestershire. Carlton, and Travellers'. S. of John, 5th Earl of Harrowby. B. 11 October 1892; m. 31 January 1922, Hon. Helena Coventry, d. of Visct. Deerhurst (she died 1974). Educ. at Eton, and Christ Church, Oxford; B.A. Dept.-Lieut. and J.P. for Staffordshire. Maj. R.F.A.; T.A. Res. Parliamentary Private Secretary to Sir Samuel Hoare December 1922-23. A Conservative. Sat for the Shrewsbury division of Shropshire from November 1922-December 1923, when he was defeated. Re-elected for the Shrewsbury division of Shropshire in October 1924 and sat until he retired in May 1929. Styled Visct. Sandon 1900-56. Succeeded to Peerage as Earl of Harrowby 1956. Assistant Private Secretary to Visct. Milner when Colonial Secretary 1919-20. Member of London County Council 1932-40. Member of Royal Commission on Historical Manuscripts 1935-66. Author of *England at Worship* (1928).★   [1929]

SANDYS, Rt. Hon. Duncan Edwin. Continued in House after 1945: full entry in Volume IV.

SASSOON, Rt. Hon. Sir Philip Albert Gustave David, Bart., G.B.E., C.M.G. 45 Park Lane, London. S. of Sir Edward Sassoon, 2nd Bart. B. 4 December 1888. Unmarried. Educ. at Eton, and Christ Church, Oxford. Served with Royal East Kent Yeomanry, Private Secretary to Sir Douglas Haig in France 1915-18. Succeeded as Bart. 1912. Parliamentary Private Secretary to Rt. Hon. D. Lloyd George when Prime Minister 1920-22. Trustee of the National Gallery (Chairman 1933), Wallace Collection and Tate Gallery. Honorary Air Commodore No. 601, Company of London (Bomber) Squadron A.A.F., R.A.F. Under-Secretary of State for Air November 1924-June 1929, and August 1931-May 1937; First Commissioner of Works May 1937-June 1939. PC. 1929. A Conservative. Sat for Hythe from June 1912 until his death on 3 June 1939.   [1939]

SAVERY, Sir Samuel Servington. 11 The Boltons, London. Carlton. S. of the Rev. George Savery, of Oxford. B. 1861. Unmarried. Educ. at Kingswood, Bath, and Christ Church, Oxford; M.A. Founder of Bramcote, Scarborough 1893; J.P. for Scarborough; Vice-President of Scarborough and Whitby Conservative Association. Member of N. Riding County Council. Knight Bach. 1937. A Conservative. Sat for the Holderness division of Yorkshire from December 1923 until his death on 27 December 1938.   [1939]

SAVORY, Professor Douglas Lloyd. Continued in House after 1945: full entry in Volume IV.

SAWYER, George Francis. House of Commons, London. S. of James Sawyer, Esq., of Cuddesdon, Oxfordshire. B. 1871; m. 1899, Minnie Tadbrooke, of Broadway. A Railway Guard. Member National Union of Railwaymen, and of Birmingham County Borough Council. A Labour Member. Unsuccessfully contested the Duddeston division of Birmingham in December 1923 and October 1924. Elected for the Duddeston division of Birmingham in May 1929 and sat until he was defeated in October 1931. Unsuccessfully contested the Duddeston division of Birmingham in November 1935. Died 27 August 1960.
                          [1931 2nd ed.]

SCHUSTER, Sir George Ernest, K.C.S.I., K.C.M.G., C.B.E., M.C. 179 City Road, London. Nether Worton House, Middle Barton, Oxfordshire. Athenaeum, Brooks's, and City of London. S. of Ernest Schuster, Esq., K.C. B. 25 April 1881; m. 12 December 1908, Hon. Gwendolen Parker, d. of Lord Parker of Waddington. Educ. at Charterhouse, and New Coll., Oxford. Barrister-at-Law, Lincoln's Inn 1905. Partner in the firm of Schuster, Son and Company. Lieut.-Col. T.F. Reserves. Served overseas with Oxfordshire Hussars 1914-19, M.C. Chairman of Allied Suppliers, of Maypole Dairy Company, of Home and Colonial Stores Limited, and of Liptons Limited. A Director of Westminster Bank, and of Bank of New Zealand, of the Southern Railway, Commercial Union Assurance, etc. Financial Secretary to Sudan Government 1922-27; Financial Adviser Colonial Office 1927-28; finance member of Executive Council of Viceroy of India 1928-34. Grand Cordon of the Order of the Nile and the Order of St. Vladimir. A Liberal National. Elected for Walsall in November 1938 and sat until he was defeated in July 1945. C.B.E 1918; K.C.M.G. 1926; K.C.S.I. 1931. Member of Colonial Development Advisory Committee 1936-38. Member of Medical Research Council 1947-51. Chairman of Oxford Regional Hospital Board 1951-63. Member of Oxfordshire County Council 1952-74. Honorary D.C.L. Oxford. Author of *India and Democracy*, and *Christianity and*

Human Relations in Industry.★   [1945]

SCONE, Mungo David Malcolm Murray, Lord. Balboughty, Old Scone, Perthshire. Carlton, and Pratt's. S. of Alan, 6th Earl of Mansfield and Mansfield. B. 9 August 1900; m. 19 July 1928, Dorothea Helen, d. of the Rt. Hon. Sir Lancelot Carnegie, G.C.V.O., K.C.M.G. Educ. privately, and at Christ Church, Oxford, B.A. Director of Highland Agricultural Society 1928-32. Gov. of Edinburgh and E. of Scotland Agricultural Coll., 1925-30; member of Perthshire Educational Authority 1925-30; F.Z.S., F.Z.S. (Scotland). Lieut. 6/7 The Black Watch; Joint Honorary Secretary British Group Inter-parliamentary Union; J.P. for Perthshire and Dumfriesshire. A Unionist. Unsuccessfully contested Lanarkshire N. in March and May 1929. Elected for the Perth division of Perth and Kinross in October 1931 and sat until March 1935 when he succeeded to the Peerage as Earl of Mansfield and Mansfield. Member of Perthshire County Council from 1935. Fellow of Linnaean Society and Royal Horticultural Society. Chairman of British Trust for Ornithology 1933-39. Lord-Lieut. of Perthshire 1960-71. Lord High Commissioner to Church of Scotland 1961-62. Died 2 September 1971.   [1935]

SCOTT, Alexander MacCallum. 110 Cheyne Walk, Chelsea, London. National Liberal. S. of John Scott, Esq., of Millhill, Polmont, and Rebecca MacCallum. B. 16 June 1874 at Boathouse, Blantyre; m. 1910, Jessie, d. of Dr. John Hutchison, Rector of Glasgow High School. Educ. at Polmont Public School, Falkirk High School, and Glasgow University. A Barrister, Middle Temple 1908, on the Western Circuit. A member of Lewisham Borough Council 1903-06. Private Secretary to Lord Pentland, Secretary for Scotland 1909; Parliamentary Private Secretary to Mr. Winston Churchill, Ministry of Munitions and Secretary for War 1917-1919. Author of *The Truth About Tibet, Through Finland to St. Petersburg, Winston Churchill in Peace and War, Barbary, the Romance of the Nearest East,* and other works. A Liberal. Sat for the Bridgeton division of Glasgow from December 1910

until he was defeated in November 1922. Unsuccessfully contested the Patrick division of Glasgow in December 1923. Coalition Liberal Scottish Whip 1922. Joined Labour Party in 1924. Prospective Labour candidate for E. Aberdeenshire 1926-28. Killed 25 August 1928 in an aeroplane accident, along with his wife, while flying from Victoria, British Columbia to Seattle.   [1922]

SCOTT, James. 1 Glencairn Crescent, Edinburgh. National Liberal. S. of James Scott, Esq., Railway Superintendent, of Forres. B. 8 March 1876; m. 28 September 1910, Georgina Geddes, of Buckhaven, Fife. Educ. at Forres Academy, and at Edinburgh University. Admitted a Solicitor, Supreme Courts of Scotland, Notary Public. Member Game and Heather Burning Committee 1921; Dept.-Chairman of Trade Boards for Jute, Flax and Made-up Textiles 1921-24. An author. A Liberal. Unsuccessfully contested Moray and Nairn November 1922, West Renfrewshire December 1923, and Kincardine and West Aberdeenshire October 1924. Elected for the Kincardine and Western division of Aberdeen and Kincardine in May 1929 and sat until he was defeated in October 1931. Parliamentary Private Secretary to Sir Archibald Sinclair, Secretary of State for Scotland 1931. Died 30 October 1939.

   [1931 2nd ed.]

SCOTT, Rt. Hon. Sir Leslie Frederic, K.C. 20 Egerton Terrace, London, Carlton. S. of Sir John Scott, K.C.M.G., at one time Judicial Adviser to H.H. Khedive of Egypt, and Nora, d. of Frederic Hill, Esq. B. 29 October 1869; m. 1898, Ethel, d. of H.A. James, Esq. Educ. at Rugby, and New Coll., Oxford. Barrister-at-Law, Inner Temple 1894, Northern Circuit. K.C. 1909. Official delegate of Great Britian at International Conferences on Maritime Law at Brussels 1909 and 1910, 1922 and 1923. Chairman during the war of various committees. Was for several years head of the Agricultural Co-operative Movement. Chairman from 1913 of the Central Association for Mental Welfare. Grand Cross of Belgian Order of Leopold II. Solicitor-Gen.

March to October 1922. Knight Bach. 1922. PC. 1927. A Unionist. Unsuccessfully contested the Exchange division of Liverpool in January 1910. Sat for the Exchange division from December 1910 until he retired in May 1929. Lord Justice of Appeal 1935-48. President of National Association of Parish Councils. Died 19 May 1950. [1929]

SCOTT, Robert Donald. Continued in House after 1945: full entry in Volume IV.

SCOTT, Sir Samuel Edward, Bart. 78 Mount Street, London. Westbury Manor, Nr. Brackley, Northamptonshire. North Harris, Inverness-shire. Turf, and White's. S. of Sir E.H. Scott, 5th Bart., by Emilie, d. of Col. H. Packe, of Twyford Hall, Norfolk (she m. secondly, 1895, Sir Horace (later Visct.) Farquhar). B. 1873; m. 1896, Sophie, d. of Earl Cadogan (she died 1937). Educ. at Eton, and Royal Military Coll., Sandhurst. Succeeded as 6th Bart. 1883; Lieut. Royal Horse Guards 1893; retired 1897. Served in South Africa 1900-01; Maj. W. Kent Yeomanry. Served in the Great War 1914-18; Gallipoli and Egypt 1915-17; later Maj. Royal Horse Guards. Dept.-Lieut. for Inverness. A Unionist. Sat for W. Marylebone from 1898, and for St. Marylebone from December 1918 until he retired in October 1922. President of International Association for the Promotion and Protection of Trade. Died 21 February 1943. [1922]

SCOTT, Lord William Walter Montagu Douglas. See MONTAGU-DOUGLAS-SCOTT, Lord William Walter. Continued in House after 1945: full entry in Volume IV.

SCRYMGEOUR, Edwin. 92 Victoria Road, Dundee. S. of James Scrymgeour, Esq. B. 28 July 1866; m. 14 June 1892, Margaret Croston, d. of Thomas and Bridget Lyon Croston, of Dundee. Educ. at West End Academy, Dundee. Organizing Secretary of the Scottish Prohibition Party from 1901; Town and Parish Councillor for Dundee at periods ranging over 25 years. An Independent Member with un-

official Labour support. Unsuccessfully contested Dundee in May 1908, January and December 1910, July 1917 and December 1918. Elected for Dundee in November 1922 and sat until he was defeated in October 1931. Chaplain at East House and Maryfield Hospital, Dundee from 1932. Died 1 February 1947. [1931 2nd ed.]

SCRYMGEOUR-WEDDERBURN, Capt. Henry James. Birkhill, Cupar, Fife. Carlton, and Travellers'. S. of Col. Henry Scrymgeour-Wedderburn, of Wedderburn. B. 3 May 1902; m. 1946, Patricia Katherine, d. of Lord Herbert Montagu-Douglas-Scott and widow of Lieut.-Col. David Scrymgeour-Wedderburn. Educ. at Winchester, and Balliol Coll., Oxford; President of Union 1924. Dept.-Lieut., and J.P. for Fifeshire. Hereditary Royal Standard Bearer of Scotland. Parliamentary Under-Secretary of State for Scotland October 1936-September 1939, and Joint Parliamentary Under-Secretary of State for Scotland February 1941-March 1942. A Unionist. Unsuccessfully contested Kirkcaldy Burghs in May 1929. Elected for Renfrew W. in October 1931 and sat until he was defeated in July 1945. Unsuccessfully contested Dundee W. in February 1950. His claim to have succeeded to the Peerage as Visct. Dudhope admitted by the House of Lords Committee of Privileges in 1952 and as Earl of Dundee in 1953. Created Baron Glassary 1954. Minister without Portfolio October 1958-October 1961. Minister of State, Foreign Office October 1961-October 1964. PC. 1959. Dept.-Leader of House of Lords 1962-64. Honorary LL.D. University of St. Andrews.* [1945]

SCURR, John. 46 Hornsey Lane Gardens, London. S. of L.J. Rennie, Esq., of Poplar-adopted by uncle, Capt. John Scurr, and took his surname. B. at Brisbane 6 April 1876; m. 4 August 1900, Julia, d. of John O'Sullivan, Esq. (she died 10 April 1927). Educ. at George Green's Schools, Poplar. Clerk, Accountant, Secretary and Journalist. Alderman Poplar Borough Council 1919; Chairman and Vice-Chairman Metropolitan Boroughs Standing Joint

Committee 1919-22. Imprisoned in 1921 with the other Poplar Councillors over the question of the Metropolitan Boroughs' financial Contributions to the London County Council. Mayor of Poplar 1922-23; Alderman London County Council 1925-29; member of Central Unemployment Body. A Labour Member. Unsuccessfully contested S.W. Bethnal Green in July 1911 and February 1914, the Chesterfield division of Derbyshire in August 1913 and Ipswich May 1914 as an Independent Socialist. Unsuccessfully contested the Buckingham division of Buckinghamshire in 1918, and the Mile End division of Stepney in November 1922. Sat for the Mile End division of Stepney from December 1923 until he was defeated in October 1931. Resigned from ILP 1928. A Roman Catholic. Died 10 July 1932.   [1931 2nd ed.]

SEAGER, Sir William Henry. Lynwood, Newport Road, Cardiff. Reform, and National Liberal. Eld. s. of William Seager, Esq., of Cardiff. B. at Cardiff 1862; m. 1890, Margaret Annie, 2nd d. of John Elliot, Esq., of Woodfield House, Cardiff. Educ. at the Wesleyan School, Cardiff. Chairman of the Ropner Shipbuilding Company, Stockton-on-Tees, and the Garforth Colliery Company, Leeds; Vice-Chairman of the Cardiff Ship Store Merchants' Association; Director of the North of England P. and I. Association, of Messrs. James Howell and Company Limited, and a member of the Executive Council of the Shipping Federation. Managing Director of the Tempus Shipping Company Limited, W.H. Seager and Company Limited, Seager's Shipping Supplies Limited, and associated with many commercial enterprises in the Bristol Channel. Gov. of the King Edward VII Hospital and the Royal Hamadryad Seamen's Hospital; Chairman of the Cardiff Institute for the Blind, Treasurer of "John Cory" Soldiers' and Sailors' Rest, Vice-President of the Cardiff Liberal Association, and Vice-President of the Cardiff Naval Brigade. Knighted 1918. A Coalition Liberal. Elected for E. Cardiff in December 1918 and sat until he retired in October 1922. Dept.-Lieut. for Glamorgan and J.P. for Cardiff. President of

Chamber of Shipping of United Kingdom 1928. High Sheriff of Monmouthshire 1932-33. Died 10 March 1941.   [1922]

SEARS, William. 74 Leinster Road, Rathmines, Dublin. B. 1868; m. Gretta, d. of William Morris, Esq., of Wexford. Sentenced at Dublin 7 January 1919 to six months imprisonment for inciting to shoot military, police, and Government officials. A Sinn Fein Member. Returned unopposed for S. Mayo in December 1918 but did not take his seat. Member of Dail for S. Mayo to 1921, for S. Mayo and S. Roscommon 1921-23, for S. Mayo 1923-27. A Pro-Treaty, later Cumann na nGaedheal member. A Journalist, Founder and Editor of *Enniscorthy Echo*. Senator, Irish Free State December 1928-March 1929. Died 23 March 1929.   [1922]

SEDDON, James Andrew. 12 Woodberry Gardens, North Finchley, London. S. of Thomas Seddon, Esq., of Prescot. B. 7 May 1868 at Prescot, Lancashire; m. 1891, Ellen, d. of George Brown, Esq., of Prescot. Educ. at Huyton and Prescot. A Trade Union Organizer. Vice-Chairman National Democratic Party February 1919. C.H. 1918. Sat as Labour Member for the Newton division of Lancashire from 1906 until defeated in December 1910. Elected as a Coalition National Democratic Party Member for the Hanley division of Stoke-on-Trent in December 1918 and sat until he was defeated in November 1922 standing as an Independent with unofficial Conservative support. Unsuccessfully contested the Hanley division of Stoke-on-Trent as a Conservative in December 1923. President of T.U.C. 1914. Chairman of British Workers' League. Secretary of Church Association from 1929. Died 31 May 1939.   [1922]

SEELY, Sir Hugh Michael, Bart. 55 Curzon Street, London. Sherwood Lodge, Arnold, Nottinghamshire. Brooke House, Isle of Wight. S. of Sir Charles Seely, 2nd Bart. B. 2 October 1898; m. 1st, 1942, Hon. Patricia Chetwode, d. of 1st Visct. Camrose and widow of Roger Chetwode, Esq. (divorced 1948); secondly, 1970, Katherine

Thornton. Succeeded as Bart. 1926. Lieut. Grenadier Guards and South Nottinghamshire Hussars. J.P. for Nottinghamshire, High Sheriff 1925. Squadron Leader A.A.F. September 1939. Parliamentary Private Secretary to The Rt. Hon. Sir Archibald Sinclair, Bart. when Secretary of State for Air from May 1940. A Liberal. Unsuccessfully contested Norfolk E. in November 1922 and Kensington S. in May 1929. Sat for Norfolk E. from December 1923 to October 1924, when he was defeated. Elected for the Berwick-on-Tweed division of Northumberland in November 1935 and sat until July 1941 when he was created Baron Sherwood. Under-Secretary of State for Air July 1941-May 1945. Died 1 April 1970.   [1941]

SEELY, Maj.-Gen. Rt. Hon. John Edward Bernard, P.C., C.B., C.M.G., D.S.O. 11 Smith Square, Westminster, London. Brooke House, Isle of Wight. Marlborough, and Reform. Youngest s. of Sir Charles Seely, 1st Bart., MP for Nottingham, and Emily, d. of William Evans, Esq. B. 1868; m. 1st, 1895, Emily Florence, d. of the Hon. Sir H.G.L. Crichton (she died 1913); secondly, 1917, Hon. Evelyn Izmé Nicholson, widow of Capt. George C.N. Nicholson, R.F.C., and youngest d. of the 1st Visct. and 10th Baron Elibank. Educ. at Harrow, and Trinity Coll., Cambridge. Was called to the bar at the Inner Temple 1897. A Col. in the Hampshire Yeomanry; commanded 41st Co. Imperial Yeomanry in South Africa 1900-01, D.S.O.; on special service with Expeditionary Force 1914; Brigadier Gen. Commanding Canadian Cavalry Brigade 1915-18. Alderman of Isle of Wight County Council; Lord-Lieut. of Hampshire and the Isle of Wight 1917-47; Maj.-Gen. 1918. C. Crown (Belgium); C. Legion of Honour and Croix de Guerre (France). Was Under-Secretary for the Colonies 1908-11, and Under-Secretary of State for War 1911-12. Secretary of State for War June 1912-March 1914 when he resigned. Parliamentary Secretary Ministry of Munitions and Dept. Minister of Munitions June 1918-January 1919; Under-Secretary of State for Air and President of Air Council January-November 1919 when he resigned. PC. 1909. C.B. 1916. Elected for the Isle of Wight division as a

Conservative in May 1900. In March 1904, having disagreed with the Government on the fiscal question and Chinese labour, he resigned his seat, but was returned unopposed in April and accepted the Liberal Whip in May 1904. Sat as a Liberal for the Abercromby division of Liverpool from 1906-10 when he was defeated at the general election in January. Elected for the Ilkeston division of Derbyshire in March 1910; re-elected there in December 1910 and December 1918 as a Coalition Liberal, defeated 1922. Elected for the Isle of Wight in December 1923 and sat until he was defeated in October 1924. Chairman of National Savings Committee 1926-43. Created Baron Mottistone 1933. Died 7 November 1947.
                                            [1924 2nd ed.]

SELLEY, Sir Harry Ralph. 2 West Drive, Streatham Park, London. Constitutional. B. 9 December 1871; m. 1st, 26 December 1896, Eleanor Kate, d. of Thomas Westcott, Esq., of Newton St. Cyres, Devon (she died February 1935); secondly, 7 September 1939, Margaret Avelyn, widow of Joseph Hendrick, Esq. Educ. privately. J.P. for London. In business of Estate development. Member London County Council from 1925-37. Knight Bach. 1944. A Conservative. Unsuccessfully contested S. Battersea in February and May 1929. Elected for S. Battersea in October 1931 and sat until he retired in June 1945. President of Federation of Master Builders. Died 24 February 1960.
                                            [1945]

SEXTON, Sir James, C.B.E. Homefield, Huyton, Liverpool. B. 1856; m. 1882 Christine, d. of W. Boyle, Esq. Educ. at Low House School, St. Helens. Was for some years at sea; author and playwright. J.P. Secretary of the National Union of Dock Labourers from 1890 to 1926. Knight Bach. 1931. A Labour Member. Unsuccessfully contested Ashton-under-Lyne in 1895, the West Toxteth division of Liverpool in 1906 and January 1910. Elected for St. Helens in December 1918 and sat until he was defeated in October 1931. Member of Parliamentary Committee of T.U.C. 1899-1923, of Gen. Council from 1923. President of T.U.C. 1905. C.B.E. 1917. Member of Liverpool

City Council from 1905, Alderman from 1930. A Roman Catholic. Died 27 December 1938.   [1931 2nd ed.]

SEXTON, Thomas Miles. Waverley Hotel, Southampton Row, London. Dales Terrace, Stanhope, Co. Durham. B. 1879; m. 1902, Edith Longstaff. Educ. at Bede Coll., Durham. J.P. for Durham. Head Teacher at Stanhope County School 1909-35. A Labour Member. Elected for the Barnard Castle division of Durham in November 1935 and sat until he retired in June 1945. Died 11 July 1946.   [1945]

SHAKESPEARE, Rt. Hon. Sir Geoffrey Hithersay, Bart. 69 Westminster Gardens, London. S. of the Rev. J.H. Shakespeare, M.A., D.D., Secretary of the Baptist Union, and Amy Goodman. B. September 1893; m. 1st, 16 September 1926, Aimée, d. of Walter Loveridge, Esq., and widow of Commander Sir Thomas Fisher, K.B.E. (she died 1950); secondly, 1952, Elizabeth, d. of Brigadier-Gen. R.W. Hare. Educ. at Highgate School, and Emmanual Coll., Cambridge, M.A., LL.B., President of the Union Society. A Journalist. Barrister-at-Law, Middle Temple 1922. Private Secretary to the Rt. Hon. D. Lloyd George, March 1921-23; Parliamentary Private Secretary to J. Pybus, Minister of Transport August-October 1931. A Lord Commissioner of the Treasury and Chief Liberal Nationals Whip November 1931-September 1932; Parliamentary Secretary Ministry of Health September 1932-July 1936, to Board of Education July 1936-May 1937; Parliamentary and Financial Secretary to the Admiralty May 1937-April 1940. Parliamentary Secretary of Overseas Trade April-May 1940; Parliamentary Under-Secretary of State for Dominions May 1940-March 1942, and Chairman of Children's Overseas Reception Board June 1940-March 1942. Created Bart. 1942. A Liberal National. Elected for the Wellingborough division of Northamptonshire as a National Liberal in November 1922, defeated December 1923. Elected for Norwich in May 1929 as a Liberal, joined the Liberal National group in 1931 and sat until he was defeated in July 1945. PC. June 1945. Chairman of Standing Council of Barone-

tage 1972-75. Director of Abbey National Building Society 1943-77, Dept. Chairman 1965-69. President of Society of British Gas Industries 1953-54. Chairman of Industrial Co-Partnership Association 1958-68. Author of *Let candles be brought in.*★   [1945]

SHANAHAN, Philip. 134 Foley Street, Dublin. A Licensed Victualler in the City of Dublin. Arrested April 1920. A Sinn Fein Member. Elected for the Harbour division of Dublin in December 1918 but did not take his seat. Member of Dail for Dublin Harbour to 1921, for mid Dublin 1921-22, as an Anti-Treaty Member.   [1922]

SHARMAN-CRAWFORD, Col. Rt. Hon. Robert Gordon, C.B.E. Crawfordsburn, Co. Down. Carlton, Royal Thames Yacht, and Constitutional. S. of Arthur and Louisa Sharman-Crawford. B. at Dublin 8 September 1853; m. 1882, Annie Helen, d. of Ernest Arbouirn, Esq., of Cuckfield. Educ. at Elstree Hill; M.A. Dublin University. Joined 15th Hussars 1876; Col., Privy Councillor (Ireland) 1919; Senator Northern Parliament of Ireland 1921-34; C.B.E. 1919. A Conservative. Sat for E. Belfast from April 1914. Until he retired in 1918. Returned unopposed for mid Down in July 1921 and sat until he retired in October 1922. Member of Down County Council. Died in New York 20 March 1934.

[1922]

SHAW, Hon. Alexander. 24 Prince's Gate, London. Craigmyle, Torphins, Aberdeenshire. National Liberal, and Royal Automobile. S. of Thomas Shaw, Lord Shaw of Dunfermline and Baron Craigmyle. B. 28 February 1883 in Edinburgh; m. 1913, Hon. Margaret Cargill Mackay, d. of Lord Inchcape, G.C.M.G. Educ. at George Watson's Coll., and the University, Edinburgh, and Trinity Coll., Oxford, M.A. Was called to the bar at the Inner Temple 1908; President of the Oxford Union 1905. Lieut. Royal Marines 1915; Chairman 1917-18 of Special Arbitration Tribunal on Women's Wages. Member of various Departmental and Select Committees. A Liberal, in favour of Home Rule for Scotland. Unsuccessfully contested Midlothian in 1912. Elected for

323

Kilmarnock Burghs in May 1915 and for the Kilmarnock division of Ayr and Bute in in December 1918 and sat until he resigned on 10 November 1923, 6 days before the dissolution of Parliament. Director of Bank of England 1923-43. Director of P. and O. Steam Navigation Company from 1920, Managing Director from 1927. Chairman 1932-38. High Sheriff of County of London 1931. Dept.-Lieut. for Selkirkshire and City of London. Succeeded to the Peerage as Baron Craigmyle 1937. Died 29 September 1944. [1923]

SHAW, Col. Archibald Douglas MacInnes. Ballochmyle, Mauchline, Ayrshire. Carlton. S. of Col. Sir Archibald MacInnes Shaw, C.B. B. 15 March 1895; m. 5 November 1920, Dorothy Ada, d. of Peter MacLellan, Esq., of Cormiston Towers, Biggar. Educ. at St. Ninians, Moffat, and at Charterhouse. D.S.O. 1918. Dept.-Lieut. for Glasgow. A Conservative. Unsuccessfully contested Paisley in 1923. Elected for Renfrew W. in October 1924 and sat until he retired in May 1929. Unsuccessfully contested the Bridgeton division of Glasgow in November 1935 and the Springburn division of Glasgow in September 1937. Member of Glasgow City Council 1921. Convenor of Ayrshire County Council 1955-57. Knighted 1953. Died 10 June 1957. [1929]

SHAW, Geoffrey Reginald Devereux. 18 Lennox Gardens, London. Carlton. S. of James Edward Shaw, Esq., of Welburn Hall, Kirbymoorside. B. 29 May 1896; m. 1924, Elizabeth Mary Margaret, d. of Admiral Sir Cyril Fuller. Educ. at Cheltenham, and King's Coll., Cambridge. Served with K.O.Y.L.I. and East Riding Yeomanry 1914-18. Barrister-at-Law, Inner Temple 1923. A Conservative. Elected for the Sowerby division of the W. Riding of Yorkshire in October 1924 and sat until he retired in May 1929. High Sheriff of Northamptonshire 1938. Died 8 September 1960.

[1929]

SHAW, Helen Brown, M.B.E. Merchiston, Uddingston, Lanarkshire. D. of David Graham, Esq., of Glasgow. B. in about 1879. Widow of Maj. D.P. Shaw, 6th Camero-

nians. Educ. privately. J.P. for Lanarkshire. M.B.E. 1920. A Unionist. Unsuccessfully contested the Bothwell division of Lanarkshire in October 1924 and May 1929. Elected for the Bothwell division of Lanarkshire in October 1931 and sat until she was defeated in November 1935. Unsuccessfully contested the Bothwell division of Lanarkshire in July 1945. Member of Lanarkshire County Council. Vice-Chairman of W.V.S. 1938-43. Died 20 April 1964. [1935]

SHAW, Maj. Peter Stapleton, O.B.E. Nodes, Hailsham, Sussex. Carlton. S. of Henry Shaw, Esq., J.P., of Ashton-under-Lyne. B. 6 July 1888. Educ. at Loretto, and Royal Military Coll., Sandhurst. Queen's Bays and Royal Tank Corps. Served overseas 1915-19; Chief Gunnery Instructor, Royal Tank Corps; commanded Sharpshooters. A Conservative. Elected for the Wavertree division of Liverpool in November 1935 and sat until he retired in June 1945. O.B.E. 1918. Director of Walker Cain Limited. Died 3 August 1953. [1945]

SHAW, Rt. Hon. Thomas, C.B.E. 12 Cardinal Mansions, Carlisle Place, London. Savage. S. of Ellis Shaw, Esq. B. 9 April 1872. Educ. at an elementary school. Half-time worker at 10, full-time at 13. Was 18 years Secretary Colne Weavers; Secretary of International Textile Workers Federation 1911-29, and 1931-38 and Labour and Socialist International 1922-24. Minister of Labour January-November 1924; Secretary of State for War June 1929-August 1931. PC. 1924. A Labour Member. Sat for Preston from December 1918 until he was defeated in October 1931. Director of National Service in W. Midland Region during the war. C.B.E. 1919. Died 26 September 1938. [1931 2nd ed.]

SHAW, Capt. Walter William. Rood Ashton, Trowbridge, Wiltshire. Carlton, Royal Automobile, Pilgrims, and Ranalagh. S. of Edward Dethick Shaw, Esq., of Oaklands, Wolverhampton. B. 1868; m. 1893, Mary Louise, d. of W.W. Wakeman, Esq., of New York. Educ. at Private School, and at Jesus Coll., Cambridge. Served with 3rd N. Staffordshire Regiment; Capt. Royal

W. Surrey Regiment; County Councillor for Dorset; Sheriff for Town and County of Poole 1913. A Conservative. Unsuccessfully contested Houghton-le-Spring division of Durham in 1922, and the Westbury division of Wiltshire in 1923. Elected for Westbury in October 1924 and sat until his death on 10 May 1927.   [1927]

SHAW, William Thomas. 17 Lindfield Gardens, London. Killicrankie Cottage, Killicrankie, Perthshire. Carlton. S. of William Shaw, Esq., Landowner and Farmer. B. 26 February 1879; m. 1908, Margaret, d. of Charles Maclean, Esq., of Victoria, B.C. (she died 1949). Educ. at Dundee High School. Member of London Stock Exchange from 1901. Served with R.A.S.C. 1914-18. A Unionist. Unsuccessfully contested Dumbartonshire in December 1910. Sat for Forfarshire from December 1918-November 1922 when he was defeated. Defeated again in December 1923. Re-elected for Forfarshire in October 1931 and sat until he retired in June 1945. Died 20 October 1965.   [1945]

SHEFFIELD, Sir Berkeley Digby George, Bart. 8 South Audley Street, London. Turf, Jockey, Orleans, and Beefsteak. S. of Sir Robert Sheffield, 5th Bart., of Normanby. B. in London 19 January 1876; m. 19 July 1904, Baroness Julia de Tuyll, O.B.E., Lady of Grace of St. John of Jerusalem, d. of Baron de Tuyll. Educ. at Eton, and in France and Germany. Served in the Lincolnshire Regiment and Yeomanry, Diplomatic Service, and the Foreign Office. High Sheriff of Lincolnshire 1905. A Conservative. Elected for the Brigg division of Lincolnshire in February 1907; defeated in January 1910. Re-elected for the Brigg division in 1922 and sat until he was defeated in May 1929. Succeeded as Bart. 1886. Member of Lindsey County Council from 1902 to 1906, Alderman 1908 to 1915. Charter Mayor of Scunthorpe 1936. Died 26 November 1946.   [1929]

SHEPHARD, Sidney. Continued in House after 1945: full entry in Volume IV.

SHEPHERD, Arthur Lewis. 18 Wilson House, Larkhill Rise, London. S. of Herbert Shepherd, Esq. B. at King's Norton, Worcestershire 7 February 1884. Educ. at Birmingham University. A School-teacher. A Socialist. Unsuccessfully contested Darlington in 1924. Elected for Darlington in February 1926 and sat until he was defeated in October 1931. Unsuccessfully contested Darlington in November 1935. Died 14 April 1951.   [1931 2nd ed.]

SHEPPERSON, Sir Ernest Whittome, Bart. 6 Fig Tree Court, Temple, London. Upwood House, Huntingdonshire. Keyworth House, Benwick, March. Carlton, 1900, and Constitutional. S. of Joseph William Shepperson, Esq., of Benwick, March. B. 4 October 1874; m. 19 July 1916, Doris, d. of Cole Ambrose, Esq., of Stuntney Hall, Ely. Educ. at Christ's Coll., Cambridge, B.A., (Science Tripos 1901), LL.B. (Law Tripos 1902), M.A. 1909. Barrister-at-Law, Gray's Inn 1908, S.E. Circuit. A Landowner. National Diploma in Agriculture and Agricultural Diploma, Cambridge. J.P. for Isle of Ely 1910, County Councillor 1914; J.P. for Huntingdonshire. Dept. Chairman Isle of Ely Quarter Sessions. Served with Cambridgeshire Regiment 1914-18. Director of various agricultural undertakings. Knighted 1929. A Conservative. Elected for the Leominster division of Herefordshire in November 1922 and sat until he retired in June 1945. Created Bart. June 1945. Member of Church Assembly. Died 22 August 1949.   [1945]

SHERWOOD, George Henry. Oak Villa, Sandal, Wakefield. B. 1877 at Barnsley; m. 1898, Esther Annie, d. of John Cobb, Esq., of Hayton. Engaged in Railway Clearing House. Alderman Wakefield City Council; J.P. for Wakefield. A Labour Member. Elected for Wakefield in December 1923, defeated October 1924. Re-elected for Wakefield in May 1929 and sat until he was defeated in October 1931. Mayor of Wakefield 1926-27. Died 10 October 1935.
                    [1931 2nd ed.]

SHIELD, George William. Sievehill, Throckley, Newcastle-upon-Tyne. B. 24

March 1876 at Coanwood, Northumberland; m. 3 February 1900, Alice, d. of John Dickinson, Esq. Educ. at Elementary School, Featherstone. A Miners' Checkweighman. J.P. and County Councillor for Northumberland. A Labour Member. Unsuccessfully contested the Hexham division of Northumberland in 1922. Elected for the Wansbeck division of Northumberland in February 1929 and sat until he was defeated in October 1931. Died 1 December 1935.
[1931 2nd ed.]

SHIELS, Dr. Thomas Drummond, M.C. 159 Kent House Road, Beckenham, London. S. of James Drummond Shiels, Esq., of Edinburgh. B. 7 August 1881; m. 1st, 11 August 1904, Christian Blair, d. of Alexander Young, Esq., of Edinburgh (she died 1948); secondly, 1950, Gladys Buhler. Educ. at Board School, and Edinburgh University; M.B., Ch.B. Was a professional photographer before studying medicine. President Edinburgh Fabian Society, and of Edinburgh "Parliament". Fellow and President Royal Medical Society. Served in France and Belgium 1914-18, with Royal Scots; commanded Trench Mortar Battery; Belgian Croix de Guerre. Member of Edinburgh Town Council; member of Empire Parliamentary Association Delegation to Canada and Australia 1926, and of Special Commission on Ceylon Constitution 1927. Under-Secretary of State for India June-December 1929, Parliamentary Under-Secretary of State, Colonial Office from December 1929 to August 1931. A Labour Member. Elected for E. Edinburgh October 1924 and sat until he was defeated in October 1931. Member of Colonial Economic and Development Council 1946. Public Relations Officer for General Post Office 1946-49. Knighted 1939. Died 1 January 1953.
[1931 2nd ed.]

SHILLAKER, James Frederick, M.B.E. 31 Rustic Avenue, London. National Labour. S. of James Shillaker, Esq., of Rutland, and Mary, d. of J. Bunn, Esq., of Knowle. B. 28 January 1870; m. 21 December 1891, Caroline Jane, d. of Harry Heaton, Esq. Educ. at Taplow Grammar School, and City of London Coll. A Jour-

nalist. Assistant Editor *T.P.'s Weekly* 1903-17. Dept.-Regional Director Northern Region Ministry of Pensions 1919-23; on Advisory and Research Staff Parliamentary Labour Party 1923. A Labour Member. Sat for the Acton division of Middlesex from 1929 until he was defeated in October 1931. Died 20 July 1943.
[1931 2nd ed.]

SHINWELL, Emanuel. Continued in House after 1945: full entry in Volume IV.

SHIPWRIGHT, Capt. Denis Ewart Bernard Kingston. Mortimer House, Egerton Gardens, London. Treloyhan, St. Ives, Cornwall. United, Constitutional, Queen's, Ranelagh, and Royal Automobile. S. of T.J. Shipwright, Esq. B. in London 20 May 1898; m. 1st, 20 March 1918, Kate, only d. of Sir Edward Hain, MP (divorced 1926); secondly, 1927, Christabel, d. of Henry Parkes, Esq. (she died 1929); thirdly, 1934, Joy Walter, of Houston, Texas (divorced 1946); fourthly, 1947, Margaret, d. of R.E. Haynes, Esq., of Woking (she died 1977). Educ. at Lille University and University Coll., Oxford. Entered the army as a private in 1914; Capt. R.F.C. 1918; Capt. Royal 1st Devon Yeomanry 1920. A Conservative. Sat for the Penryn and Falmouth division of Cornwall from November 1922 until he was defeated in December 1923. Served in R.A.F. 1939-45. Fellow of Royal Society of Arts. Knight of St. John of Jerusalem. Employed in film industry and in civil service, Post Office and Ministry of Agriculture.*
[1923]

SHORT, Alfred. 11 King's Bench Walk, Temple, London. The Triangle, 1 Hooking Green, Harrow. B. at Gloucester 24 November 1882; m. 1912, Mary, d. of Henry Mellors, Esq., of Norton Cuckney. A Boilersmith; official of the Transport and General Workers' Union. Member of Sheffield City Council 1913-19, and was a specialist on Housing and Public Health. A Barrister-at-Law, Gray's Inn 1923. Under-Secretary of State for Home Affairs June 1929-August 1931. A Labour Member. Sat for Wednesbury from December 1918-October 1931 when he was defeated. Elected for the Doncaster division of the W. Riding of

Yorkshire in November 1935 and sat until his death on 24 August 1938. [1938]

SHORTT, Rt. Hon. Edward. 220 St. James's Court, Buckingham Gate, London. 3 Hare Court, Temple, London. Reform. S. of the Rev. Edward Shortt, Vicar of Woodhorn, Northumberland. B. 1862 in Newcastle; m. 1890, Isabella, d. of A.G. Scott, Esq., of Valparaiso. Educ. at Durham School, and Durham University. A Barrister, called to the bar, Middle Temple 1890. K.C. 1910, and joined the N.E. Circuit. Member of the Flying Corps Committee 1916; member of the Defence of the Realm (Losses) Royal Commission; Chairman of the Select Committee of the House of Commons on Medical Re-examinations. Chief Secretary for Ireland May 1918 to January 1919; Home Secretary January 1919-October 1922. A Liberal. Unsuccessfully contested Newcastle in 1908. Elected for Newcastle in January and December 1910, and for Newcastle W. in December 1918. Sat until he retired in October 1922. Recorder of Sunderland 1907-18, PC. 1918. Honorary D.C.L. Durham 1920. Bencher of Middle Temple 1919. President of British Board of Film Censors 1929-35. Died 10 November 1935. [1922]

SHUTE, Col. Sir John (Joseph), C.M.G., D.S.O. Rivacre, Hooton, Cheshire. Ramona, Derwent Square, Stoneycroft, Liverpool. Carlton, Constitutional, and Travellers'. S. of John Shute, Esq., of Liverpool. B. 1873. Unmarried. Educ. privately, and at Catholic Institute, Liverpool. Partner in the firm of Reynolds and Gibson, Liverpool, Manchester, and London, Cotton and General Produce Brokers. President of Liverpool Cotton Association 1920-21. Dept.-Lieut. for Lancashire; J.P. for Liverpool; Chairman of Combined Egyptian Mills Limited. Trustee and Executive of Empire Cotton Corporation and of executive British Cotton Growing Association; member of Council of Liverpool Royal Infirmary, and Chairman of Nursing Committee; Chairman and Honorary Treasurer of Open Air Hospital for Children, Leasowe, Cheshire, and of Liverpool Metropolitan Cathedral Fund; Chairman of Liverpool Re-

pertory Theatre, of Liverpool Boys' Association, of Playing Fields (Boys' Association) Committee, of British Legion, City of Liverpool Branch, of Youth Organisations Committee, and of Liverpool United Trades Association. Served in France with 5th Liverpool Regiment 1915-18 (despatches 5 times). Honorary Col. 2nd Cavalry division R.A.S.C. A Conservative. Elected for the Exchange division of Liverpool in January 1933 and sat until he was defeated in July 1945. Member of Imperial War Graves Commission. Knighted 1935. Died 13 September 1948. [1945]

SIDNEY, Capt. Hon. William Philip, V.C. c/o Barclays Bank, 1 Pall Mall East, London. Turf. S. of the Hon. William Sidney. Esq., who succeeded to the Peerage as 5th Baron De L'Isle and Dudley in April 1945. B. 23 May 1909; m. 1st, 8 June 1940, Hon. Jaqueline Corinne Yvonne Vereker, d. of Field-Marshal Visct. Gort, V.C., G.C.B. (she died 1962); secondly, 1966, Margaret, widow of 3rd Baron Glanusk and d. of Maj.-Gen. T.H. Shoubridge. Educ. at Eton, and Magdalene Coll., Cambridge. A Chartered Accountant. Member of Chelsea Borough Council. Capt. Grenadier Guards; served in France and Belgium 1939-40 and in Italy 1943-44. A National Conservative. Returned unopposed for Chelsea in October 1944 and sat until Parliament was dissolved on 15 June 1945. Succeeded to the Peerage as 6th Baron De L'Isle and Dudley 18 June 1945. Honorary Fellow of Magdalene Coll., Cambridge 1955. V.C. 1944. Parliamentary Secretary to Ministry of Pensions May-July 1945. Secretary of State for Air October 1951-December 1955. PC. 1951. Dept.-Lieut. for Kent. Chairman of Phoenix Assurance Company from 1966. Chancellor of Order of St. Michael and St. George from 1968. Created Visct. De L'Isle 1956. Honorary LL.D. University of Sydney 1963. Gov.-Gen. of Australia 1961-65. G.C.M.G. 1961; G.C.V.O. 1963; K.C. 1968.* [1945]

SILKIN, Lewis. Continued in House after 1945: full entry in Volume IV.

SILVERMAN, Samuel Sydney. Continued in House after 1945 : full entry in Volume IV.

SIMM, Matthew Turnbull. 29 Otterburn Avenue, Gosforth, Newcastle-on-Tyne. S. of Frank Simm, Esq., Miner. B. 4 January 1869 at Cramlington, Northumberland; m. 1895, Elizabeth Emma, d. of George Dodds, Esq., of Cramlington. Educ. at the local colliery school. A Merchant Tailor. Appointed National Democratic Party Whip February 1919. A National Democratic Party Member Elected for Wallsend in December 1918 and sat until he was defeated in November 1922. Died 8 October 1928. [1922]

SIMMONDS, Sir Oliver Edwin. Great West Road, Brentford. Dunsborough House, Ripley. Carlton, and Royal Aero. S. of the Rev. Frederick Thomas Simmonds, of King's Lynn. B. 1897; m. 1922, Gladys Evelyn Hewitt (she died 1977). Educ. at Taunton, and Magdalene Coll., Cambridge. Governing Director of Simmonds Development Corporation Limited; Managing Director of Simmonds Aerocessories Limited, and of Simmonds Products Limited; a Director of Aerocessories Simmonds of Paris; Vice-President Simmonds Aerocessories Incorporated, New York. Chairman of Parliamentary Air Raid Precautions Committee; of Conservative Civil Defence Committee; and of Joint Air Transport Committee; F.R.Ae.S. President of Institute of Civil Defence 1938-40, and of Committee of Brick Industry 1941. Knight Bach. 1944. A National Unionist. Elected for the Duddeston division of Birmingham in October 1931 and sat until he was defeated in July 1945. Emigrated to the Bahamas 1948. President of Bahamas Employers Confederation 1966-68.* [1945]

SIMMONS, Charles James. Continued in House after 1945: full entry in Volume IV.

SIMMS, Very Rev. Dr. John Morrow, C.B., C.M.G. Scrabo Isles, Newtownards, Co. Down. Naval & Military, Royal Automobile, and Ulster. S. of John Simms, Esq., of Holywood, Co. Down, and Elizabeth Alexander, of Newtownards. B. at Newtownards 23 November 1854. Educ. at the Old Academy, Belfast, Coleraine Academical Institution, Queen's, Edinburgh and Leipzig Universities. Ordained 16 May 1882. Chaplain to the Forces 29 March 1887. Principal Chaplain to the Armies in France August 1914 to 6 March 1920. C.M.G. 1915 and C.B. 1918. with the rank of Maj.-Gen. D.D., LL.D.; Honorary Chaplain to the King. A Conservative. Returned unopposed for N. Down July 1922 and for Down in November 1922 and December 1923. Re-elected in October 1924 and sat until he retired in October 1931. Moderator of Presbyterian Church of Ireland 1919-20. Died 29 April 1934. [1931 2nd ed.]

SIMON, Ernest Emil Darwin. Broomcroft, Didsbury. S. of Henry Simon, Esq., Engineer, of Didsbury. B. 9 October 1879; m. 22 November 1912, Shena Dorothy, d. of J.W. Potter, Esq., of Westminster. Educ. at Rugby, and Pembroke Coll., Cambridge. M.I.C.E. and M.I.M.E. Lord Mayor of Manchester 1921-22. A Liberal. Unsuccessfully contested the Withington division of Manchester in November 1922. Elected for the Withington division of Manchester in December 1923; unsuccessfully contested the same division in October 1924 and Dundee in December 1924. Elected for the Withington division of Manchester in May 1929 and sat until October 1931 when he unsuccessfully contested the Penryn and Falmouth division of Cornwall. Unsuccessfully contested the Combined English Universities as an Independent in March 1946. Parliamentary Secretary to Ministry of Health September-November 1931. Knighted 1932. Joined Labour Party 1946. Created Baron Simon of Wythenshawe 1947. Treasurer of Manchester University 1932-41, Chairman of Council 1941-57, Honorary LL.D. 1944. Chairman of B.B.C. 1947-52. Died 3 October 1960. [1931 2nd ed.]

SIMON, Rt. Hon. Sir John Allsebrook, G.C.S.I., G.C.V.O., O.B.E., K.C. 11 Downing Street, London. 3 Central Buildings,

London. Dowding, Walton-on-the-Hill. Reform, Garrick, National Liberal, and Royal Automobile. S. of the Rev. Edwin Simon, Congregational Minister. B. 28 February 1873; m. 1st, 1899, Mary Ethel, d. of Gilbert Venables, Esq. (she died 1902); secondly, 17 December 1917, Kathleen Manning, D.B.E., D.(G.) St. J., d. of Francis Eugene Harvey, Esq., of Wexford. Educ. at Fettes Coll., Classical Scholar and Fellow of Wadham Coll., Oxford; Honorary D.C.L. Oxford, Honorary LL.D. Cambridge, Edinburgh, Manchester, Leeds, Sheffield, St. Andrews, Toronto, McGill and Columbia, Fellow of All Souls. A Barrister-at-Law, Inner Temple 1899; K.C. 1908; Bencher 1910; Solicitor Gen. 1910-13; Knighted 1910; PC. 1912; Attorney-Gen. with a seat in the Cabinet 1913-15; Home Secretary May 1915-January 1916, when he resigned, and June 1935-May 1937; Secretary of State for Foreign Affairs November 1931-June 1935; Dept. Leader of House of Commons June 1935; Leader of Liberal National Party 1931-40; Chancellor of the Exchequer May 1937-May 1940. Member of War Cabinet September 1939-May 1940. Maj. R.A.F. Served in France 1917-18. Chairman of Indian Statutory Commission 1927; President of R. 101 Court of Enquiry 1930. G.C.S.I. 1930; G.C.V.O. 1937. A Liberal until 1931, thereafter a Liberal National. Sat for the Walthamstow division of Essex from 1906-18, defeated in E. Walthamstow December 1918. Unsuccessfully contested the Spen Valley division of Yorkshire in December 1919; elected for the Spen Valley division of Yorkshire in November 1922 and sat until May 1940 when he was appointed Lord Chancellor and created Visct. Simon. K.C.V.O. 1911; O.B.E. 1919. Lord Chancellor May 1940-July 1945. High Steward of Oxford University 1948-54. Died 11 January 1954. [1940]

SIMPSON, Fred Brown. 25 Euston Road, London. S. of George Henry Simpson, Esq., of Nottingham. B. 6 November 1886; m. 26 June 1914, Anne Stirling, d. of William Smith, Esq. Educ. at Mundella Higher Grade School. Chief Assistant Secretary Railway Clerks' Association, President 1932-37; Alderman Leeds City Council; Lord Mayor of Leeds 1931-32. A Labour Member. Sat for Ashton-under-Lyne from November 1935 until his death on 23 September 1939. [1939]

SIMPSON, John Hope, C.I.E. Blagroves Farm, Oake, Taunton. Farmers', and National Liberal. S. of John Hope Simpson, Esq., General Manager Bank of Liverpool, and Margaret. d. of the Rev. Thomas Swan, of Birmingham. B. at Liverpool 23 July 1868; m. 1st, 1900, Quita, d. of Robert Barclay, Esq., J.P., of Sedgley New Hall, Prestwich, Manchester (she died 1939); secondly, 1941, Evelyn, d. of J. Forster Hamilton, Esq., and widow of W.H. Brookes, Esq. Educ. at Liverpool Coll., and in Germany, Switzerland, France, and Balliol Coll., Oxford. Was in the Indian Civil Service from 1889-1916. Assistant Magistrate and Collector, U.P. 1889-95. Sessions Judge 1896. District Magistrate 1895-1902. Secretary to Board of Revenue, U.P. 1902-04. Registrar of Co-operative Credit Societies 1904-07. Commissioner 1912-14. Chief Commissioner of Andaman and Nicobar Islands 1914 and 1916. C.I.E. 1913. A Liberal. Elected for the Taunton division of Somerset in November 1922 and sat until he was defeated in October 1924. Knighted 1925. Director-Gen. of National Flood Relief Commission for China 1931-33. Commissioner for Natural Resources, Newfoundland 1934-36. K.B.E. 1937. Died 10 April 1961. [1924 2nd ed.]

SIMPSON-HINCHLIFFE, William Algernon. House of Commons, London. S. of William Simpson, Esq., of Aberford, Yorkshire. B. 1880; m. 1902, Helen, d. of Hinchliffe Hinchliffe, Esq. A Cotton Spinner and Landowner. President of Halifax Royal Infirmary; J.P. for the W. Riding of Yorkshire. A Conservative. Unsuccessfully contested the Sowerby division of Yorkshire in July 1904, January 1906 and January 1910. Sat for Sowerby from November 1922 until he was defeated in December 1923. Assumed the surname Simpson-Hinchliffe in lieu of Simpson. Died 8 June 1963. [1923]

SINCLAIR, Rt. Hon. Sir Archibald Henry Macdonald, Bart., K.T., C.M.G. 23 Gayfere Street, London. Thurso Castle, Thurso, Caithness. Travellers', and Brooks's. S. of Col. Clarence G. Sinclair, and grand-s. of Sir Tollemache Sinclair, 3rd Bart., of Ulbster. B. 22 October 1890; m. 18 May 1918, Marigold, d. of Lady Angela Forbes and Col. J. Forbes. Educ. at Eton, and Sandhurst. Succeeded as Bart. 1912. Lord-Lieut. of Caithness 1919-64. Personal Military Secretary to Rt. Hon. Winston Churchill when Secretary of State for War 1919-21; Assistant Secretary to Rt. Hon. Winston Churchill at the Colonial Office, 1921-22. Temporary Chairman of Committees, House of Commons 1925-30; member of Empire Marketing Board 1927-30. Chief Liberal Whip November 1930-August 1931; Secretary of State for Scotland August 1931-September 1932. Secretary of State for Air May 1940-May 1945. Honorary LL.D. Edinburgh University 1932 and Glasgow University 1940; Leader of Liberal Parliamentary Party November 1935-July 1945. Honorary Air Commodore A.A.F. 1942. Lord Rector of Glasgow University October 1938 and 1941. PC. 1931. A Liberal. Elected for Caithness and Sutherland in November 1922 and sat until he was defeated in July 1945. Unsuccessfully contested Caithness and Sutherland in February 1950. Created Visct. Thurso 1952. Member of Political Honours Scrutiny Committee 1954-61. President of Air League of British Empire 1956-58. Died 15 June 1970. [1945]

SINCLAIR, Col. Thomas, C.B. 22 University Square, Belfast. St. Stephen's. S. of Samuel Sinclair, Esq., of Belfast. B. 1857. Educ. at private schools, on the Continent, Queen's University, Belfast, London Hospital, Vienna and Berlin; M.D., M.Ch., L.M., Queen's University; F.R.C.S. England. Member of General Medical Council. Emeritus Professor of Surgery, and Pro-Chancellor of Queen's University, Belfast; Consulting Surgeon of Royal Victoria Hospital; Consulting Surgeon, B.E.F.; Senator, Parliament of Northern Ireland 1921-40. A Conservative. Returned unopposed for Queen's University in December 1923 and

sat until he resigned in September 1940. C.B. 1917. Died 25 November 1940. [1940]

SINGLETON, John Edward, K.C. Horwich House, Nr. Preston, Lancashire. Oxford & Cambridge. S. of George Singleton, Esq., J.P., of Garstang. B. 18 January 1885 at St. Michaels-on-Wyre, Garstang, Lancashire. Unmarried. Educ. at Lancaster School, and Pembroke Coll., Cambridge, Honorary Fellow 1938. A Barrister-at-Law, Inner Temple 1906. K.C. 1922. Honorary Capt. R.F.A. A Conservative. Elected for the Lancaster division of Lancashire in November 1922 and sat until he was defeated in December 1923. Judge of Appeal, Isle of Man 1928-33. Recorder of Preston 1928-34. Knighted 1934. Judge of Kings Bench Division 1934-48. PC. 1948. Lord Justice of Appeal 1948-57. Died 6 January 1957. [1923]

SINKINSON, George. 36 Howard Place, Edinburgh. S. of Hamilton and Mary Sinkinson. B. 25 November 1874 at Kendal; m. 1896, Lily Kendall, of Barrow-in-Furness. Chairman of East of Scotland Independent Labour Party Federation; member of Edinburgh Trades Council. A Labour Member. Elected for Berwick and Haddington in May 1929 and sat until he was defeated in October 1931. Died 14 January 1939. [1931 2nd ed.]

SITCH, Charles Henry. 1 Whitehall Road, Cradley Heath, Staffordshire. S. of Thomas Sitch, Esq., J.P. and County Councillor, Chainmaker, of Cradley Heath. B. at Saltney, Cheshire 4 May 1887; m. 1913, Mabel, d. of Edward Jackson, Esq., of Goole. Educ. at the Rowley Regis Council Schools, and Ruskin Coll., Oxford. Secretary to Workers' Organizations. A Labour Member. Sat for the Kingswinford division of Staffordshire from December 1918 until he was defeated in October 1931. Resigned from the Liberal Party 1916. Member of Rowley Regis Urban District Council 1913. President of S. Staffordshire and Worcestershire Federation of Trades Councils 1914-18. Secretary of Chainmakers and Strikers Association 1923-33.

Convicted of fraudulent conversion of trade union funds in 1933 and sentenced to 9 months imprisonment. Employed by *Reynolds News* and *Sunday Citizen* in Leeds 1937-52. Died 13 June 1960.   [1931 2nd ed.]

SKELTON, Archibald Noel. 21 Northumberland Street, Edinburgh. Conservative. S. of Sir John Skelton, K.C.B. B. 1880. Unmarried. Educ. at Trinity Coll., Glenalmond, and Universities of Oxford and Edinburgh, Scholar of Christ Church. Advocate 1906. Capt. Scottish Horse Yeomanry. Parliamentary Under-Secretary of State for Scotland September 1931-November 1935. A Conservative. Unsuccessfully contested E. Perthshire in December 1910. Sat for Perth from 1922, was defeated there in December 1923, then re-elected in October 1924 and May 1929. Returned unopposed for the Scottish Universities in October 1931 and sat until his death on 22 November 1935 before the declaration of the result of the general election for the Scottish Universities, for which he was returned posthumously.   [1936]

SLANEY, Maj. Philip Percy Kenyon, M.C. See KENYON-SLANEY, Maj. Philip Percy, M.C.

SLATER, John. 8 Vigo Street, London. Stelvio Court, Eastbourne. Carlton. S. of William Slater, Esq., of Adlington, Lancashire. B. 6 April 1889; m. 1910, Elizabeth Ann, d. of William Crompton, Esq., of Bolton. Educ. by Mr. Bond privately. Chairman of Berry Hill Collieries Limited, Stoke-on-Trent; of John Slater (Stoke) Limited, Sanitary Potters and Engineers; of John Bright and Brothers, Rochdale, Spinners, Weavers and Bleachers; of Aux Classes Laborieuses Limited. Director of Keramag Keramische Werke A.G., Bonn, Sanitary Potters and Engineers; of Tritonwerke Bamberger Leroi A.G., Hamburg, Sanitary Engineers; and of De Forenede Isvaerker A/S, Copenhagen; also Settle, Speakman and Company Limited, Colliery Proprietors. A Presbyterian. Member of Staffordshire County Council, 1919-21. A Conservative. Returned unopposed for the Eastbourne division of Sussex in April 1932 and sat until his death on 15 February 1935.   [1935]

SLESSER, Sir Henry Herman, K.C. 7 Crown Office Row, Temple, London. Cornerways, Bourne End, Buckinghamshire. Parliamentary Labour. S. of Ernest Slesser (formerly Schloesser), Esq., of Bourne End, Buckinghamshire. B. 12 July 1883; m. 1910, Margaret, d. of Corrie Grant, Esq., MP, K.C. Educ. at Oundle, and St. Paul's Schools. Barrister-at-Law, Inner Temple 1906, K.C. 1924, Bencher 1924. A Lecturer on Industrial Law and Member of Faculty of Laws, University of London; Solicitor-Gen. January-November 1924. Knight Bach. 1924. J.P. for Buckinghamshire. A Labour Member. Unsuccessfully contested Central Leeds in November 1922 and July and December 1923. Elected for S.E. Leeds in October 1924 and sat until June 1929 when he was appointed a Lord Justice of Appeal. PC. 1929. Lord Justice of Appeal 1929-40. Member of Devon County Council 1946-68, Alderman 1956-68. Chairman of Dartmoor National Park Committee 1948-64. Honorary LL.D. Exeter 1963. Oblate of Order of St. Benedict. Author of a number of works on the law, politics and ecclesiastical history and several volumes of verse. Adopted the surname Slesser in lieu of Schloesser in 1914.*   [1929]

SLOAN, Alexander. Kerse Cottage, Rankinston, Ayrshire. S. of John Sloan, Esq., Ironstone Miner, of Rankinston, Ayrshire. B. 2 November 1879. Conscientious objector in First World War. Member of Ayrshire. County Council 1919. Secretary of Ayrshire Miners' Union and from 1936 to 1940 of National Union of Scottish Mineworkers. A Labour Member. Unsuccessfully contested Ayrshire N. and Bute in May 1929 and October 1931. Elected for S. Ayrshire 20 April 1939 and sat until his death on 16 November 1945.   [1945]

SMILES, Sir Walter Dorling. Continued in House after 1945: full entry in Volume IV.

SMILEY, Peter Kerr. See KERR-SMILEY, Peter Kerr.

SMILLIE, Robert. Miller Street, Lark-hall, Lanark. B. in Belfast 1857; m. 1879, Anne Hamilton, of Larkhall, Lanarkshire. President of Scottish Miners' Federation 1894-1918, and 1922-28. President of Miners' Federation of Great Britain 1912-21. A Labour Member. Unsuccessfully contested mid Lanark April 1894, January 1910 and December 1910, the Camlachie division of Glasgow in 1895, N.E. Lanarkshire in September 1901, Paisley in January 1906, and the Cockermouth division of Cumberland in August 1906. Elected for Morpeth in June 1923 and sat until he retired in May 1929. Chairman of Parliamentary Labour Party during the period of the first Labour Government 1924. Until his early manhood used the spelling 'Smellie'. Chairman of Parliamentary Committee of Scottish T.U.C. 1897-99. Member of Parliamentary Committee of T.U.C. from 1917, Member of Gen. Council 1920-26. Member of the Sankey Commission on the Coal Industry 1919. Author of *My life for Labour* (1924). Died 16 February 1940.   [1929]

SMITH, Capt. Albert. 41 Hibson Road, Nelson, Lancashire. S. of Leeming Smith, Esq. B. 15 June 1867 at Cowling, Yorkshire; m. 1890, Elizabeth Ann, d. of John Towler, Esq. Educ. at Colne Wesleyan School. Mayor of Nelson 1908-10. A Labour Member. Elected for the Clitheroe division of Lancashire in December 1910, and for Nelson and Colne in December 1918. Sat until he resigned in June 1920. O.B.E. 1919. Secretary of Colne Overlookers' Association in 1898. President of Gen. Union of Loom Overlookers in 1902 and 1920-27. J.P. and Dept.-Lieut. for Lancashire. Served with Royal Lancaster Regiment 1914-15, when he was invalided home, and 1917-18. Died 7 April 1942.   [1920]

SMITH, Alfred. 71 Burns Road, London. S. of William Smith, Esq. B. 1860; m. 1914, d. of I. Collins, Esq., of Brighton. Was variously employed. A National Official of the Transport and General Workers' Union and formerly of the Cab Drivers' Union. A member of Middlesex County Council; J.P. for Middlesex. A Labour Member. Unsuccessfully contested E. Dorset in December 1918 and W. Leyton in November 1922, December 1923 and October 1924. Elected for Sunderland in May 1929 and sat until his death on 12 February 1931. Member of Willesden Borough Council. A Roman Catholic. President of London Cabdrivers' Union 1906-13. Died 12 February 1931.   [1931 2nd ed.]

SMITH, Sir Allan Macgregor, K.B.E. 9 Oakhill Avenue, London. B. in about 1870; m. Isabella Clow (she died 1933). Educ. at Glasgow University, M.A., LL.B. Chairman of the Engineering and National Employers Federations and of the Employers section of the Joint Committee of the Industrial Conference. A Solicitor; K.B.E. 1918. A Conservative. Sat for Croydon S. from November 1919 until December 1923 when he unsuccessfully contested the Patrick division of Glasgow. Died 21 February 1941.   [1923]

SMITH, Rt. Hon. Sir Benjamin, K.B.E. Continued in House after 1945: full entry in Volume IV.

SMITH, Bracewell. Park Lane Hotel, Piccadilly, London. Carlton, Constitutional, and Royal Automobile. S. of Samuel Smith, Esq., of Keighley. B. 29 June 1884; m. 29 December 1909, Edith, d. of George Whitaker, Esq., of Keighley (she died 1953). Educ. at University of Leeds, B.Sc. Member of Finsbury and Holborn Board of Guardians 1919-22, of Holborn Borough Council 1922-37, and of London County Council 1925-28. Mayor of Holborn 1931-32; a Lieut. of City of London; Alderman of City of London for Ward of Lime Street from 1938; Sheriff 1943-44; Lord Mayor 1946-47; Chairman of House of Commons Kitchen Committee from January 1938. A Conservative. Sat for the Dulwich division of Camberwell from June 1932 until he was defeated in July 1945. Knighted January 1945. Created Bart. 1947. Died 12 January 1966.   [1945]

SMITH, Edward Percy. Continued in House after 1945: full entry in Volume IV.

SMITH, Ellis. Continued in House after after 1945: full entry in Volume IV.

SMITH, Francis Samuel. 67 Longley Road, London. 36 Stewart Street, Nuneaton. National Liberal, and Emerson. S. of Alfred Smith, Esq. B. 1854; m. 1875, Elizabeth, d. of George Hall, Esq. Educ. at Oxford House, Chelsea. In the Upholstery Trade 1870, subsequently Salvation Army Commissioner; London Correspondent of *Eastern Morning News* and Editor of *Weekly Dispatch.* Parliamentary Private Secretary to the Rt. Hon. George Lansbury when 1st Commissioner of Works October 1930. A Labour Member. Unsuccessfully contested Hammersmith in 1892, the Attercliffe division of Sheffield 5 July 1894, the Tradeston division of Glasgow in 1895, Taunton 23 February 1909, Croydon 29 March 1909, Chatham December 1910, the Balham and Tooting division of Wandsworth in 1918, W. Birmingham in 1922 and 1923, and the Nuneaton division of Warwickshire in 1924. Elected for the Nuneaton division of Warwickshire in May 1929 and sat until he was defeated in October 1931. Member of London County Council 1892-1910. Secretary of Confederation of Engineering and Shipbuilding Trades for 20 years. Died 26 December 1940.   [1931 2nd ed.]

SMITH, Rt. Hon. Sir Frederick Edwin, Bart. 32 Grosvenor Gardens, London. 4 Elm Court, Temple, London. The Cottage, Charlton, Banbury. Carlton, and Union. S. of Frederick Smith, Esq., Barrister. B. 12 July 1872 at Birkenhead; m. 1901, Margaret Eleanor, d. of the Rev. H. Furneaux. Educ. at Birkenhead School, and Wadham Coll., Oxford; Class-Sch., 1st Class Final Hons. Jurisprudence, Vinerian Law School 1895. A Barrister, called 1889. K.C. 1908. Bencher of Gray's Inn 1908. Treasurer of Gray's Inn 1917 and 1918. Fellow and Lecturer, Merton Coll. 1896; Lecturer Oriel Coll. 1897; University Extension Lecturer in Modern History 1898; examiner in Final Schools, Oxford 1899-1900; on special duty with Expeditionary Force with temporary rank of Maj. 1914. Knighted 1915. Solicitor-Gen. May to October 1915; Attorney-Gen. from October 1915 to January 1919. Proceeded on a mission to the U.S. in December 1917. Created Bart. 1918. Author of *International Law, Newfoundland, The Case for Tariff Reform, International Law, as interpreted during Russo-Japanese War*, and other works. PC. 1911. A Unionist. Sat for the Walton division of Liverpool from 1906 to 1918 and for the West Derby division of Liverpool from December 1918 to January 1919 when he was appointed Lord Chancellor and created Baron Birkenhead. Lord Chancellor January 1919-October 1922. Secretary of State for India November 1924-October 1928. Created Visct. Birkenhead 1921 and Earl 1922. High Steward of Oxford University from 1922. Rector of Glasgow University 1922, Aberdeen University 1926. Director of I.C.I. Limited and of Tate and Lyle Limited 1928-30. Died 30 September 1930.   [1918]

SMITH, Sir Harold. 68 St. James's Court, London. Middleton House, Middleton Cheney, Nr. Banbury. Carlton. S. of Frederick Smith, Esq., Barrister. B. 18 April 1876 at Birkenhead; m. 1914, Joan, d. of the Rev. H. Furneaux. Educ. at Birkenhead School. A Barrister, called to the bar 1911; bencher Gray's Inn 1920. A Surveyor and Valuer. Member of Birkenhead Town Council. First Secretary Press Bureau. Honorary Lieut. in R.N.V.R. 1914. Knighted 1921. A Conservative. Unsuccessfully contested Huddersfield in January 1910. Elected for Warrington December 1910 and December 1918, and for the Wavertree division of Liverpool in November 1922. Sat until he was defeated in December 1923. J.P. for Northamptonshire. K.C. 1923. Recorder of Blackburn 1922-24. Died 10 September 1924.   [1923]

SMITH, Rt. Hon. Hastings Bertrand Lees. See LEES-SMITH, Rt. Hon. Hastings Bertrand.

SMITH, Sir Jonah Walker. See WALKER-SMITH, Sir Jonah Walker.

SMITH, Sir Louis William. 23 Marsham Court, London. Carlton Scroop Hall, Nr. Grantham. Constitutional. S. of John Higson Smith, Esq., of Grimsby. B. 21 March 1879; m. 1906, Clare Ellina, d. of Felix Levy, Esq., of Berlin. Educ. at Harrogate Coll. An Engineer, M.I.Mech.E. Chairman of

333

Clarke's Crank and Forge Company Limited, Lincoln, of Farrar Boilerworks Limited, Newark, of Doughty Richardson Fertilisers Limited, Lincoln, and of Ambrose Shardlow and Company Limited, of Sheffield. Director of Fison, Packard and Prentice Limited of Ipswich. Knight Bach. 1938. A Conservative. Elected for the Hallam division of Sheffield in July 1928 and sat until his death on 15 March 1939.   [1939]

SMITH, Sir Malcolm. Clifton Lodge, Leith, Midlothian. S. of Peter Halcrow Smith and Agnes Henderson Smith. B. at Hoswick, Shetland 1 December 1856; m. 1883, Jane, d. of Thomas Dickson, Esq., of Granton, Edinburgh. Educ. at the Parish School, and Anderson Institute, Lerwick. A Merchant. Member of Leith Town Council for 19 years; Provost of Leith 1909-17. A Coalition Liberal. Unsuccessfully contested Leith Burghs in February 1914. Returned unopposed for Orkney and Shetland in May 1921 and sat until he was defeated in November 1922. K.B.E. 1920. Master of Edinburgh Merchant Company 1921-22. Chairman of North British Cold Storage and Ice Company Limited. Died 12 March 1935.   [1922]

SMITH, Rennie. 28 Melrose Road, Merton Park, London. S. of Ben Smith, Esq., of Nelson. B. 14 April 1888; m. 1922, d. of Otto Peemüller, Esq. Educ. at Nelson Schools; Graduate in Economics and Political Science, London University. W.E.A. Tutor, Sheffield University; Joint Principal of International People's Coll. 1922-23; Lecturer under Miners' Welfare Scheme and Tutor for Iron and Steel Trades Confederation. Secretary British Group Inter Parliamentary Union. Parliamentary Private Secretary to Hugh Dalton, Under-Secretary of State for Foreign Affairs June 1929. A Labour Member. Unsuccessfully contested the Penistone division of the W. Riding of Yorkshire in December 1923. Elected for the Penistone division of the W. Riding of Yorkshire in October 1924 and sat until he was defeated in October 1931. Secretary of Friends of Europe 1933. Joint Editor of *Central Europe an Observer* 1940-46. Died 25 May 1962.   [1931 2nd ed.]

SMITH, Sir Robert Workman, Bart. Crowmallie, Pitcaple, Aberdeenshire. Carlton, and Bath. New, Edinburgh. S. of George Smith, Esq., of the City Line, Glasgow. B. 7 December 1880; m. 6 December 1911, Jessie Hill, d. of William Workman, Esq., of Belfast. Educ. at Glasgow Academy, and Trinity Coll., Cambridge, B.A. Barrister-at-Law, Inner Temple 1908. J.P. for Aberdeenshire. Knight Bach. 1934. A Conservative. Unsuccessfully contested central Aberdeenshire division of Aberdeen and Kincardine in 1922 and 1923. Elected for the division in October 1924 and sat until he retired in June 1945. Served with R.A.S.C. 1917-19. Created Bart. 1945. Died 6 December 1957.   [1945]

SMITH, Tom. Continued in House after 1945: full entry in Volume IV.

SMITH, Walter Robert. 33 Thorpe Road, Norwich. B. 7 May 1872. Educ. at Elementary Schools. An Organizer of the National Union of Boot and Shoe Operatives until 1935; President of the Rural Workers' and Agricultural Labourers' Union. J.P. for Norwich; many years member of Norwich County Council. Parliamentary Secretary Ministry of Agriculture January-November 1924; Parliamentary Secretary Board of Trade June 1929-August 1931. Member of the Royal Commission on Transport 1929. A Labour Member. Sat for the Wellingborough division of Northamptonshire from 1918-22 when he was defeated. Elected for Norwich December 1923, defeated October 1924. Re-elected for Norwich in May 1929 and sat until he was defeated in October 1931. Member of Forestry Commission. Died 25 February 1942.   [1931 2nd ed.]

SMITH-CARINGTON, Neville Woodford. 26 Harrington Gardens, London. Ashby Folville, Melton Mowbray. Carlton, and National. County, Leicester. 2nd s. of H.H. Smith-Carington, Esq., of Ashby Folville Manor, Melton Mowbray. B. 1878; m. 1915, Ethel Wemyss, d. of Col. W.J.W. Muir. Educ. at Harrow, and Exeter Coll., Oxford; M.A., B.C.L. A Barrister-at-Law, Inner Temple 1903. President of Shire Horse Society 1931. A Conservative. Unsuccessfully contested Loughborough in January and December 1910. Sat for the Rutland and Stamford division of Lincolnshire from October 1923 until his death on 7 October 1933. [1933]

SMITHERS, Sir Alfred Waldron, Kt. Knockholt, Kent. City of London, and Devonshire. S. of William Henry Smithers, Esq., of the Bank of England. B. at Brixton 4 October 1850; m. 1880, Emma Roberta, d. of Dr. Theobald, of Blackheath. Educ. at Lewisham Grammar School. Dept.-Chairman South Eastern and Chatham Railway Company 1911; Chairman English Association of American Bond and Shareholders 1905. A Liberal Unionist. Elected for the Chislehurst division of Kent in December 1918 and sat until he retired in October 1922. Knighted 1919. Died 22 August 1924. [1922]

SMITHERS, Sir Waldron. Continued in House after 1945: full entry in Volume IV.

SNADDEN, William McNair. Continued in House after 1945: full entry in Volume IV.

SNELL, Henry, C.B.E. 12 Palmer Street, London. Emerson, and Connaught. S. of an Agricultural Labourer. B. 1865 at Sutton-on-Trent, Nottinghamshire. Unmarried. Educ. at a village school, Nottingham University Coll., London School of Economics, and Heidelberg University. Charity Organisation Society Agent in London 1890; Hutchinson Trust Lecturer to the Fabian Society; Lecturer to the British and American Ethical Societies. Chairman of the British Ethical Union. Member London County Council from 1919-25 and Chairman 1934-38. Temporary Chairman of Committees. A Labour Member. Unsuccessfully contested Huddersfield in January and December 1910 and December 1918. Sat for Woolwich E. from November 1922 until March 1931 when he was created Baron Snell. Chairman of Parliamentary Labour Party Consultative Committee May 1929-March 1931. Under-Secretary of State for India March-August 1931. Leader of the Labour Party in the House of Lords 1935-40.

PC. 1937. Capt. of Gentlemen-at-Arms and Dept. Leader of the House of Lords May 1940-April 1944. Vice-President of Royal Empire Society and Royal Institute of International Affairs 1940-43. President of National Council of Social Service 1938. Vice-Chairman of British Council. Died 21 April 1944. [1931 2nd ed.]

SNOWDEN, Rt. Hon. Philip. 11 Downing Street, London. Eden Lodge, Tilford, Surrey. S. of John Snowden, Esq., of Cowling, Yorkshire. B. 18 July 1864; m. 13 March 1905, Ethel, d. of Richard Annakin, Esq., of Harrogate. Educ. at Board School, and privately. At one time in the Civil Service. Member of Keighley Town Council and Honorary Freeman of the borough. Chairman I.L.P. 1904-07 and 1917-20. Resigned from ILP 1927. Honorary LL.D. Leeds, Bristol and Manchester Universities; a Freeman of City of London and of Leeds. Chancellor of the Exchequer January-November 1924, and from June 1929-November 1931. PC. 1924. A Labour Member, National Labour from August 1931 when he remained in office with Ramsay MacDonald. Unsuccessfully contested Blackburn in 1900 and Wakefield in 1902. Sat for Blackburn from 1906-18, when he was defeated. Sat for the Colne Valley division of Yorkshire from November 1922 until he retired in October 1931. Created Visct. Snowden November 1931. Lord Privy Seal from November 1931 to September 1932 when he resigned. Died 15 May 1937. [1931 2nd ed.]

SNOWDEN, Tom. House of Commons, London. B. 1875 at Cowling, Yorkshire; m. 1st, 1894, Alice Stephenson; secondly, 1939, Dorothy Carlisle. Worked as a Weaver; later a Worsted Manufacturer at Bingley, Yorkshire. Member of W. Riding County Council 1913-19 and 1925-28. A Labour Member. Unsuccessfully contested the Shipley division of the W. Riding of Yorkshire in December 1918, the Skipton division of the W. Riding of Yorkshire in November 1922, and the Central division of Sheffield in December 1923 and October 1924. Elected for Accrington in May 1929 and sat until he was defeated in October 1931. Member of

Bingley Urban District Council, Chairman 1921-22. Member of Keighley Borough Council, Mayor 1942-43. C.B.E. 1949. Died 27 November 1949. [1931 2nd ed.]

SOMERSET, Sir Thomas. Malone, Belfast. Carlton, and Constitutional. Ulster Reform. S. of James Somerset, Esq., Engineer, of Belfast. B. 14 December 1870; m. 25 September 1906, Ethel, d. of Thomas Parker, Esq., of Baguley House, Cheshire. Educ. at Largymore, and Belfast Model School. Dept.-Lieut. for Belfast; Knight Bach. 1944. A Conservative. Sat for N. Belfast from May 1929 until he retired in June 1945. A Linen Manufacturer. Member of Belfast City Council. Died 16 June 1947. [1945]

SOMERVELL, Rt. Hon. Sir Donald Bradley, K.C., O.B.E. The Old Rectory, Ewelme, Oxford. Brooks's, and Beefsteak. S. of Robert Somervell, Esq., at one time Assistant Master at Harrow. B. 24 August 1889; m. 29 July 1933, Laelia Helen, d. of Sir Archibald Buchan-Hepburn, 4th Bart. (she died 1945). Educ. at Harrow, and Magdalen Coll., Oxford. Fellow of All Souls' Coll, Oxford. Barrister-at-Law, Inner Temple 1916; K.C. 1929; Solicitor-Gen. October 1933-March 1936; Attorney-Gen. March 1936-May 1945. Knight Bach. 1933. PC. 1938. Recorder of Kingston-upon-Thames 1940-46; a Trustee of the Tate Gallery. A Conservative. Unsuccessfully contested the Crewe division of Cheshire in May 1929. Elected for Crewe in October 1931 and sat until he was defeated in July 1945. Home Secretary May-July 1945. O.B.E. 1919. Lord Justice of Appeal 1946-54. Created Baron Somervell of Harrow (Law life peerage) 1954. Lord of Appeal in Ordinary from 1954 until he retired in January 1960. Honorary Fellow of Magdalen Coll., Oxford. Died 18 November 1960. [1945]

SOMERVILLE, Sir Annesley Ashworth, K.B.E. 4 Courthope Road, Wimbledon, London. United University. S. of D.A. Somerville, Esq., of Ballincollig, Co. Cork. B. 1858; m. Ethel Elizabeth, d. of Dr. William Orange, C.B. Educ. at Queen's Coll., Cork, and Trinity Coll., Cambridge; Scholar and Wrangler. Senior Assistant Master 1885-1922 and Head of the army class at Eton; Housemaster 1892-1917. Chairman of the Eton Tribunal, and of the Eton Food Control Committee 1914-18. Lieut.-Col. in the 1st Battalion Bucks Volunteers. Chairman Eton Urban District Council. President of Independent Schools' Association from 1927. K.B.E. 1939. A Conservative. Unsuccessfully contested London University in December 1918 as an Independent Teachers candidate. Sat for the Windsor division of Berkshire from November 1922 until his death on 15 May 1942. [1942]

SOMERVILLE, Daniel Gerald. 35 Grosvenor Place, London. Carlton. S. of Dr. A.T. Somerville, F.R.G.S., of Edinburgh. B. 26 October 1879; m. 1908, Dora Wentworth, d. of Thomas Ekin, Esq. Educ. at George Watson's Coll., and Heriot Watt Technical Coll., Edinburgh. An Engineer. Managing Director of Somerville-Barnard Construction Company Limited, New Cross, London, and of D.G. Somerville and Company Limited. A Conservative. Elected for Barrow-in-Furness in November 1922 and December 1923, and was defeated there in October 1924. Elected for Willesden E. in May 1929 and sat until his death on 1 July 1938. [1938]

SOPER, Richard John. Ridge House, Bond Road, Barnsley. National Liberal. S. of William Soper, Esq. B. at Bishop Auckland 13 June 1878; m. 1st, 14 October 1903, Laura, d. of J. Pinder, Esq. (she died 1951); secondly, 1953, Margaret Shaw, of Middlewich. Educ. at Board School. A Timber Merchant. Member of Barnsley Town Council 1924, Mayor 1930, Alderman 1933. J.P. for Barnsley. A Liberal Nationalist. Elected for Barnsley in October 1931 and sat until he was defeated in November 1935. Unsuccessfully contested Barnsley in July 1945. Vice-President of Methodist Conference 1945. Died 23 January 1954. [1935]

SORENSON, Reginald William. Continued in House after 1945: full entry in Volume IV.

SOTHERON-ESTCOURT, Capt. Thomas Edmund. Darrington Hall, Pontefract. Estcourt, Tetbury, Gloucestershire. Cavalry, and Royal Yacht Squadron. S. of the Rev. E.W. Southeron-Estcourt (formerly Estcourt), of Newnton, Wiltshire. B. 27 April 1881; m. 10 October 1912, Anne Evelyn, d. of Frederick Anson, Esq. Educ. at Harrow, and New Coll., Oxford. Joined Scots Greys 1904, retired 1919. J.P. for W. Riding of Yorkshire. A National Conservative. Elected for the Pontefract division of the W. Riding of Yorkshire in October 1931 and sat until he retired in October 1935. Assumed name of Southeron-Estcourt in lieu of Estcourt. Died 25 January 1958. [1935]

SOUTHBY, Sir Archibald Richard James, Bart. Continued in House after 1945: full entry in Volume IV.

SPARKES, Herbert Weston Sheppard. House of Commons, London. S. of Rev. Weston Joseph Sparkes, of Dawlish. B. at Crediton 1859; m. 1890, Emily Marianne, d. of Col. F.T. Lyster. Educ. at Crediton Grammar School. A Solicitor who practised in India. A Conservative. Unsuccessfully contested the S. Molton division of Devon in 1918. Elected for the Tiverton division of Devon in November 1922 and sat until his death on 22 May 1923. [1923]

SPEARMAN, Alexander Cadwallader Mainwaring. Continued in House after 1945: full entry in Volume IV.

SPEARS, Maj.-Gen. Sir Edward Louis, K.B.E., C.B., M.C. Burnt Lebanon, Damascus, Syria. 12 Strathearn Place, London. St. Stephen's House, London. Carlton, and Cavalry. S. of Charles McCarthy Spiers, Esq. B. 7 August 1886; m. 1st, 31 March 1918, Mary, d. of William Borden, Esq., of Chicago, U.S.A. (she died 1968); secondly, 1969, Nancy, d. of Sir Frederick Maurice. Capt. and Brevet Lieut.-Col. 11th Hussars, served overseas 1914-18. Head of British Military Mission, Paris 1917-20; retired as Brigadier-Gen. 1920. Commander of Legion of Honour and French Croix de Guerre with Palms. H.B.M.

Minister in Syria and Lebanon February 1942. Sat for the Loughborough division of Leicestershire as a National Liberal from November 1922-October 1924 when he was defeated. Joined Conservative Party in 1925. Unsuccessfully contested, as a Conservative, the Bosworth division of Leicestershire in May 1927 and Carlisle in May 1929. Sat for Carlisle as a National Conservative from October 1931 until he was defeated in July 1945. Adopted the surname Spears in lieu of Spiers in 1918. C.B.E. 1919; C.B. 1921; K.B.E. 1942. Prime Minister's Representative in France 1940 and Head of British Mission to Gen. de Gaulle. Created Bart. 1953. President of Institute of Directors 1953-54. Died 27 January 1974. [1945]

SPENCE, Robert. 29 Thomson Street, Clydebank, Dumbartonshire. S. of Thomas Spence, Esq. B. 1879 at Airdrie; m. 1899, Jane Mossman Niven. Educ. at McIntyre's School, Glasgow, and Scottish Labour Coll. A Clydebank Engineer. Secretary and Parliamentary Agent of Scottish Temperance Alliance. President of National Association of Temperance Officials. A Labour Member. Unsuccessfully contested E. Renfrewshire in 1918 and Berwick and Haddington in 1922. Elected for Berwick and Haddington in December 1923 and sat until he was defeated in October 1924. Died February 1965. [1924 2nd ed.]

SPENCER, George Alfred. Miners' Offices, New Basford, Nottingham. B. 13 December 1872; m. 1896, Emma, d. of Richard Carlin, Esq., of Sutton-in-Ashfield. A Checkweighman. Member of Sutton-in-Ashfield Urban District Council and of the Education Committee; member of the Military Tribunal. President of the Nottinghamshire Miners' Association 1912-26. A Labour Member. Sat for the Broxtowe division of Nottinghamshire as a Labour Member from December 1918. Seceded from the Labour Party in 1927 and sat as an Independent Labour Member until he retired in May 1929. Founder of Nottinghamshire and District Miners' Industrial Union 1926. President of Nottinghamshire Miners' Federated Union 1937-45. Member of National Coal Board. J.P. and Dept.-Lieut.

for Nottinghamshire. Wesleyan local preacher. President of Nottinghamshire County Cricket Club 1949-50. Died 21 November 1957. [1929]

SPENCER, Herbert Harvey. 114 Sunbridge Road, Bradford. National Liberal. S. of John Spencer, Esq. B. 1869; m. 1895, Marion, d. of F.W. Hill, Esq., of Bradford. Educ. at Bradford Grammar School. Was connected with a Bradford firm of stuff manufacturers and merchants. J.P. for Bradford. Member of Bradford City Council 1901-04. A Liberal. Elected for S. Bradford in November 1922 and sat until he was defeated in October 1924. Died 23 February 1926. [1924 2nd ed.]

SPENCER, Capt. Richard Austin. 22 Westgate, Hale, Cheshire. S. of T.W. Spencer, Esq., of Urmston. B. 8 August 1892. Unmarried. Educ. at Salford Grammar School, and University of London; M.A. A Schoolmaster. Chairman of Hale Urban District Council. Served overseas with Manchester Regiment and R.F.C. 1914-18. A Conservative. Unsuccessfully contested St. Helens in May 1929. Elected for St. Helens in October 1931 and sat until he was defeated in November 1935. Barrister-at-Law, Gray's Inn 1937. Secretary of Royal Society of Teachers 1936-53. Died 8 December 1956. [1935]

SPENDER-CLAY, Lieut.-Col. Rt. Hon. Herbert Henry, C.M.G., M.C. 2 Hyde Park Street, London. Ford Manor, Lingfield, Surrey. Carlton, and Turf. S. of J.Spender-Clay, Esq., of Ford Manor, Lingfield. B. 1875; m. 29 October 1904, Pauline, d. of 1st Visct. Astor. Educ. at Eton, and Sandhurst. Lieut. 2nd Life Guards 1896-1902; served in South Africa 1899-1900, and in France and Belgium 1914-18. Dept.-Lieut., and J.P. for Surrey. PC. 1929. Parliamentary Commissioner to Charity Commission April 1923-January 1924 and December 1924-June 1929. A Conservative. Sat for the Tonbridge division of Kent from January 1910 until his death on 15 February 1937. [1937]

SPENS, Sir William Patrick. Continued in House after 1945: full entry in Volume IV.

SPERO, Dr. George Ernest. 10 Lancaster Gate Terrace, London. West Indian. S. of Isidore Spero, Esq., Dentist, of Beaufield, Co. Durham. B. 2 March 1894 at Dover; m. September 1922, Rina Eileen, d. of Henry Ansley, Esq. Educ. privately, and at London University. A Physician and Surgeon, also a Wireless Manufacturer; Honorary Secretary Parliamentary Medical Committee 1923-24. A Labour Member. Unsuccessfully contested W. Leicester as a Liberal in November 1922. Elected as Liberal MP for Stoke Newington in December 1923, and was defeated there in October 1924. Joined the Labour Party in 1925. Elected for Fulham W. as a Labour Member in May 1929 and sat until he resigned in April 1930. Member of Royal Coll. of Surgeons. Served as Surgeon-Lieut. in Royal Navy 1915-17. Declared bankrupt 1930. [1929 2nd ed.]

SPOOR, Rt. Hon. Benjamin Charles. House of Commons, London. S. of John Joseph Spoor, Esq., of Bishop Auckland. B. 2 June 1878 at Witton Park; m. 1st, 1900, Annie Louisa, d. of William Leyburn, Esq., of Bishop Auckland (she died 1920); secondly, 1923, Anne Mary, d. of James Fraser, Esq., of Wrexham. Educ. at Barrington School, Bishop Auckland. Member of Bishop Auckland Urban District Council from 1906. Acting Chief Whip of Labour Party November 1922. Parliamentary Secretary to the Treasury January-November 1924 and Chief Whip 1924-25. PC. 1924. A Labour Member. Sat for the Bishop Auckland division of Durham from December 1918 until his death on 22 December 1928. Wesleyan lay preacher. Served with Mediterranean Expeditionary Force as a Y.M.C.A. Commissioner in Salonika. O.B.E. 1918. Died 22 December 1928. [1929]

SPROT, Sir Alexander, Bart., C.M.G. Stravithie, Fife. Carlton, and Junior Constitutional. New (Edinburgh). S. of Alexander Sprot, Esq., of Garnkirk. B. 24 April 1853; m. 11 September 1879, Ethel Florence, d. of

Surgeon-Gen. E.C. Thorp, I.M.S. Educ. at Harrow, and Trinity Coll., Cambridge; B.A. 1874, Col. 6th Dragoon Guards; served in Afghan War 1879-80, in S. African War 1899-1902, in France 1914-18. C.M.G. 1917. Created Bart. 1918. A Conservative. Unsuccessfully contested Montrose Burghs in 1906 and E. Fife in January and December 1910. Sat for E. Fife from December 1918 until November 1922, when he was defeated. Unsuccessfully contested the seat again in December 1923. Elected for N. Lanarkshire in October 1924 and sat until his death on 8 February 1929.   [1929]

STACK, Austin. Tralee, Co. Kerry. S. of William Stack, Esq., of Tralee. B. 1880; m. 1925, Miss Cassidy. A Solicitor's Managing Clerk. Was imprisoned in Belfast Gaol in 1918 for his part in the Sinn Fein movement of that year. Escaped from Strangways Gaol October 1919. A Sinn Fein Member. Returned unopposed for W. Kerry in December 1918 but did not take his seat. Member of Dail for W. Kerry to 1921, for Kerry and W. Limerick 1921-23, for Kerry 1923-27. An Anti-Treaty Member, remaining a Member of Sinn Fein after the formation of Fianna Fail. Minister for Home Affairs 1921-22. Died 28 April 1929.
                    [1922]

STAINES, Michael. 56 Lower O'Connell Street, Dublin. B. 1885 at Newport, Co. Mayo; m. 1922, Sheila Cullen, of Ashford, Co. Wicklow. Educ. at Castlerea Grammar School. Member of Dublin City Council. A Director of the New Ireland Insurance Company. Arrested for complicity in the rebellion. A Sinn Fein Member. Elected for the St. Michan's division of Dublin in December 1918 but did not take his seat. Member of Dail for the St. Michan's division of Dublin to 1921, for N.W. Dublin 1921-23 as a Pro-Treaty Member. Alderman, Dublin City Council 1919-52. Member of the Senate 1930-36. First Commissioner of Garda Siochana. Died 26 October 1955.   [1922]

STAMFORD, Thomas William. Continued in House after 1945: full entry in Volume IV.

STANIER, Sir Beville, Bart. The Citadel, Preston, Brockhurst, Shrewsbury. 21 Buckingham Gate, London. Carlton. S. of Francis Stanier, Esq., Dept.-Lieut. of Peplow. B. 12 June 1867; m. 1894, Constance, d. of the Rev. B. Gibbons, of Waresley House, Hartlebury. Educ. privately, and at the Royal Agricultural Coll., Cirencester, M.R.A.C. A J.P. and Dept.-Lieut. for Shropshire, and Dept.-Chairman of N. Staffordshire Railway. Gov. of Harper Adams Agricultural Coll. Secretary to Shropshire Territorial Force Association 1914 to 1918. Capt. (T. Reserve); Commandant of Shropshire Regiment V.T.C. Member of Shropshire County Council and Rural District Council of Market Drayton. Chairman British Sugar Beet Growers' Society of England; Chairman Central Chamber of Agriculture 1917; Chairman Rural League. Created Bart. in 1917. A Conservative. Sat for the Newport division of Shropshire from May 1908-December 1918. Returned unopposed for the Ludlow division of Shropshire in December 1918 and sat until his death on 15 December 1921.   [1922]

STANLEY, Rt. Hon. Sir Albert Henry. 43 South Street, Mayfair, London. Reform, Garrick, Royal Automobile. Walton Heath, and Coombe Hill Golf Clubs. S. of Henry Stanley, Esq., of Detroit. B. at Derby 8 November 1874; m. 1904, Grace Lowry, d. of Edward L. Woodruff, Esq. Educ. at the American Coll. and Technical Schools. For twelve years was General Manager of the American Electric Railways, chiefly the Detroit United Railways and the Public Service Railways of New Jersey. Chairman and Managing Director of the Underground Electric Railway Company, Central London, City and South London, and London Electric Railways, the London General Omnibus, and the Associated Equipment Company. Knighted in 1914. President of the Board of Trade December 1916 to May 1919. A Unionist. Elected for Ashton-under-Lyne in December 1916 as a member of Mr. Lloyd George's War Ministry. Re-elected for Ashton-under-Lyne in December 1918 and sat until January 1920 when he was created Baron Ashfield. Chairman and Managing Director of Underground Group of Companies 1919-33. Chairman of London Passenger Transport Board 1933-47. Member of British Transport Commission 1947-48. Died 4 November 1948.   [1920]

STANLEY, Rt. Hon. Edward Montagu Cavendish Stanley, Lord, M.C. 43 Belgrave Square, London. Holwood, Keston, Kent. Carlton, Turf, and Guards'. S. of Edward 17th Earl of Derby, K.G. B. 9 July 1894; m. 17 July 1917, Hon. Sibyl Cadogan, d. of Lord Chelsea and Lady Charles Montagu. Educ. at Eton, and Magdalen Coll., Oxford. Capt. Grenadier Guards R. of O.; Honorary Col. 9th Manchester Regiment. Dept.-Lieut. for Lancashire; member of Imperial War Graves Commission 1928; Chairman of Junior Imperial League 1928-33, President from 1933. Parliamentary Private Secretary to the Earl of Derby November 1922; Junior Lord of the Treasury November 1924-November 1927; Dept. Chairman of Conservative and Unionist Party November 1927-July 1929; Parliamentary and Financial Secretary to the Admiralty November 1931-June 1935 and November 1935-May 1937; Parliamentary Under-Secretary of State for Dominions June-November 1935 and for India May 1937-May 1938. PC. 1934. A Conservative. Sat for the Abercromby division of Liverpool from June 1917 to December 1918 when he retired. Sat for the Fylde division of Lancashire from November 1922 until his death on 16 October 1938. Secretary of State for Dominions May-October 1938. Styled Lord Stanley from 1908, when his father succeeded to the Peerage as Earl of Derby. Died 16 October 1938.   [1938]

STANLEY, Lieut.-Col. Rt. Hon. George Frederick, C.M.G. 9 Cadogan Square, London. Sibertoft Manor, Market Harborough. Carlton. S. of Frederick, 16th Earl of Derby, K.G. B. 14 October 1872; m. 26 November 1903, Lady Beatrix Taylour, d. of Thomas, 3rd Marq. of Headfort. Educ. at Wellington Coll., and at the Royal Military Academy, Woolwich. Joined R.H.A. 1893; Lieut.-Col. 1915. Served in South African War 1899-1900 and in France 1914-18. Comptroller of the Household

1919-21; Financial Secretary to the War Office 1921-22; Under-Secretary for Home Affairs November 1922-March 1923 when he resigned after his defeat in the E. Willesden by-election; Parliamentary Secretary Ministry of Pensions November 1924-April 1929. PC. 1927. A Conservative. Sat for Preston from January 1910 to November 1922 when he was defeated. Unsuccessfully contested Willesden E. in March and December 1923. Elected for Willesden E. in October 1924 and sat until April 1929 when he was appointed Gov. of Madras 1929-34. Died 1 July 1938.   [1929]

STANLEY, Rt. Hon. Oliver Frederick George. Continued in House after 1945: full entry in Volume IV.

STANTON, Charles Butt. Tydraw House, Aberdare, South Wales. Tavistock Hotel, London. B. Aberaman, South Wales 1873; m. 1893, Alice Maud Thomas, of Aberdare. Educ. at the Aberaman British Schools. Vice-President of the British Workers National League; Gov. of Cardiff and Aberystwyth Universities. A Miner and Docker; Miners' Agent, Journalist. Socialist speaker of the National League. Author of *Facts for Federationists, Maxims for Miners, Why We Should Agitate*, etc. C.B.E. and J.P. 1920. Unsuccessfully contested E. Glamorgan in December 1910 as a Labour candidate. Elected for Merthyr Tydvil in November 1915 as an Independent Labour candidate. Elected for the Aberdare division of Merthyr Tydvil as the Coalition National Democratic Party candidate in December 1918 and sat until he was defeated in November 1922. Member of Executive of Miners' Federation of Great Britain 1911-12. Joined Liberal Party in 1928. Died 6 December 1946.   [1922]

STARKEY, John Ralph. Norwood Park, Southwell, Nottinghamshire. Carlton. Eld. s. Lewis R. Starkey, Esq., of Norwood Park, Southwell. B. 1859; m. 1888, Emily, d. of Sir Charles Seely, Bart. Educ. at Eton, and Christ Church, Oxford. A Dept.-Lieut. and J.P. for Nottinghamshire. Capt. in South Nottinghamshire Yeomanry, rejoined 1915. A Unionist. Sat for the Newark division of

Nottinghamshire from 1906 until he retired in October 1922. Chairman of Nottinghamshire Quarter Sessions until 1937. Created Bart. 1935. Died 13 November 1940.

[1922]

STARMER, Sir Charles Walter. Danby Lodge, Darlington. National Liberal. S. of C. William Starmer, Esq., of Haltham, Horncastle. B. at Haltham 12 July 1870; m. 1st, 7 June 1893, Ada, d. of Capt. Cornforth, of West Hartlepool (she died 1923); secondly, 1929, Cecily, d. of Very Rev. J.W. Willink, Dean of Norwich. Managing Director of *Westminster Gazette* and several provincial newspapers. Member of Darlington Town Council 1903; Mayor 1907-08 and in 1933; Alderman from 1915. Knighted 1917. A Liberal. Unsuccessfully contested the Sedgefield division of Durham in 1918, and the Cleveland division of Yorkshire in 1922. Elected for the division in December 1923 and sat until he was defeated in October 1924. Unsuccessfully contested the Cleveland division in May 1929. Died 27 June 1933. [1924 2nd ed.]

STEEL, Maj. Samuel Strang. 39 Portman Square, London. Philiphaugh, Selkirk, Scotland. Carlton, and Arthur's. New, Edinburgh. S. of W. Strang Steel, Esq., of Philiphaugh, Selkirk. B. 1882; m. 3 August 1910, Hon. Vere Cornwallis, d. of Fiennes, 1st Baron Cornwallis, of Linton. Educ. at Eton, and Trinity Coll., Cambridge. Maj. Lothians and Border Horse. Parliamentary Private Secretary to Sir Robert Sanders when Minister of Agriculture 1923 and to R. McNeill when Financial Secretary to the Treasury 1926-27. A Conservative. Unsuccessfully contested Peebles and Selkirk as a Liberal Unionist in January and December 1910. Sat for the Ashford division of Kent from December 1918 until May 1929 when he was defeated. Barrister-at-Law, Middle Temple 1906. Created Bart. 1938. Member of Forestry Commission 1933-49. Lord-Lieut. of Selkirkshire 1948-58. Convenor of Selkirkshire County Council. Died 14 August 1961. [1929]

STEEL-MAITLAND, Rt. Hon. Sir Arthur Herbert Drummond Ramsay, **Bart.** 72 Cadogan Square, London. Sauchieburn, Stirling. Carlton, and Travellers'. S. of Col. E.H. Steel, R.A., and Emmeline, d. of Gen. Henry Drummond. B. 5 July 1876; m. 10 July 1901, Mary, d. of Sir James Ramsay Gibson-Maitland, 4th Bart., of Clifton. Educ. at Rugby, and Balliol Coll., Oxford. Assumed the names of Ramsay-Steel-Maitland by Royal Licence in lieu of Steel on his marriage. A Fellow of All Souls Coll. 1900. Private Secretary (unpaid) to the Rt. Hon. C.T. Ritchie and Rt. Hon. A. Chamberlain when Chancellors of the Exchequer 1902-05, and Assistant Commissioner of Poor Law Commission 1907. Head of the Central Conservative Organization 1911 to December 1916. Under-Secretary for the Colonies May 1915 to September 1917; Joint Under-Secretary of State for Foreign Affairs and Parliamentary Secretary to the Board of Trade, as head of Department of Overseas Trade September. 1917-July 1919. Minister of Labour November 1924-June 1929. PC. 1924. Created Bart. 1917. A Conservative. Unsuccessfully contested the Rugby division of Warwickshire in 1906. Elected for E. Birmingham in January and December 1910, and for the Erdington division of Birmingham in 1918. Returned unopposed for the same seat in November 1922; re-elected for that seat in December 1923 and October 1924, defeated there in May 1929 and elected for the Tamworth division of Warwickshire in December 1929 and again in October 1931. Sat until his death on 30 March 1935. [1935]

STEPHEN, Rev. Campbell. Continued in House after 1945: full entry in Volume IV.

STEPHENSON, Lieut.-Col. Henry Kenyon, D.S.O. Hassop Hall, Hassop, Derbyshire. Reform, Wellington, and Royal Automobile. S. of Sir Henry Stephenson and Lady Stephenson. B. at Sheffield 16 August 1865; m. 1894, Frances, eld. d. of Maj. William Greaves Blake, Dept.-Lieut., and J.P. Educ. at Rugby. Chairman and Managing Director of Stephenson, Blake and Company Limited, Type-Founders; Chairman of the Sheffield Gas Company, and Thomas Turton and Sons Limited; member of the Advisory Board of Williams Deacons

Bank, Sheffield. Lieut.-Col. R.F.A., T.F.; served as Lieut.-Col. in European War from August 1914 to January 1918; mentioned in despatches three times and awarded the D.S.O. 1918. Pro-Chancellor of the University of Sheffield from 1910; LL.D. (Hon.); Lord Mayor of Sheffield 1908-09 and 1910-11; Master Cutler 1919-20; Dept.-Lieut. and J.P. for the W. Riding of Yorkshire 1900 and J.P. City of Sheffield 1905. A Liberal. Elected for the Park division of Sheffield in December 1918 and sat until he was defeated in December 1923. High Sheriff of Derbyshire 1931. Created Bart. 1936. Died 20 September 1947. [1923]

STEVENS, Marshall. 59 Northgate, Regent's Park, London. Trafford Hall, Manchester. Caledonian, St. Stephen's and Constitutional. Brasenose, Manchester. S. of Sanders Stevens, Esq., well known in shipping circles. B. at Plymouth 1852; m. 1873, d. of Philip Blamey, Esq., of Cusgarne, Cornwall. Educ. privately at Exeter. Chairman of Trafford Park Estates Limited, Port of Manchester Warehousing, and five other companies. Director of Manchester Chamber of Commerce; Member of Council Federation of British Industries. A Coalition Conservative. Elected for Eccles December 1918 and sat until he was defeated in November 1922. Unsuccessfully contested Eccles in December 1923. Gen. Manager of Manchester Ship Canal Company 1885-96. Died 12 August 1936. [1922]

STEVENSON, James, O.B.E. 20 Heriot Row, Edinburgh. Caledonian. S. of William Stevenson, Esq., Writer to the *Signet*, of Glasgow. B. 2 February 1883; m. 1919, Sophronia Reynolds Gleeson, of Lower Canada. Educ. at Kelvinside Academy, and University of Glasgow. Admitted Advocate 1908; K.C. 1931. Served with Royal Corps of Signals in France 1914-18, retired with rank of Lieut.-Col. A Unionist. Unsuccessfully contested the Camlachie division of Glasgow in May 1929. Elected for the Camlachie division of Glasgow in October 1931 and sat until he was defeated in November 1935. O.B.E. 1919. Advocate Depute 1929. Judge of the Court of Session, with the judicial title of Lord Stevenson

1936-48. Died 3 March 1963. [1935]

STEWART, Gershom. Whiteholme, Hoylake, Cheshire. Carlton, and Conservative. B. at Greenock 1857; m. 1904, Henrietta Ellen, 2nd d. of Maj. W.H. Gresson. Educ. at Bishop Vesey's Grammar School, Sutton Coldfield. Engaged in business in Hong-Kong 1882-1906 and was a member of the Legislative Council, and held various offices in the Colony. A Conservative. Sat for the Wirral division of Cheshire from January 1910 until he was defeated in December 1923. K.B.E. 1924. Dept.-Lieut. for Cheshire. Died 5 December 1929. [1923]

STEWART, James. 312 Cumbernauld Road, Glasgow. B. 1863; m. 1885, Margaret, d. of J. Fyfe, Esq. Educ. at St. Enoch's, and Normal School, Glasgow. A Hairdresser in Glasgow from the age of 14. Member of Glasgow City Council 1909-22. Under-Secretary of Health for Scotland January to November 1924. A Labour Member. Unsuccessfully contested the St. Rollox division of Glasgow in December 1918. Sat for the Rollox division from November 1922 until his death on 17 March 1931.

[1931 2nd ed.]

STEWART, James Henderson, See HENDERSON-STEWART, Sir James Henderson, Bart. Continued in House after 1945: full entry in Volume IV.

STEWART, Joseph Francis. House of Commons, London. S. of Robert Stewart, Esq. B. 1889; m. 1st, 1915, Jane, d. of J. Corr, Esq., of Coalisland; secondly, 1941, Sheelagh. Educ. at Christian Brothers School, Dungannon. A Nationalist. Elected for Fermanagh and Tyrone in June 1934 and sat until he retired in October 1935. Member of Dungannon Urban District Council until 1961. Member of Northern Ireland Parliament for Tyrone E. 1929-64; Leader of the Nationalist Party at Stormont. Died 6 May 1964. [1935]

STEWART, Maj. Robert Strother. 7 Leazes Terrace, Newcastle-upon-Tyne. National Liberal. S. of the Rev. Robert Stewart, M.A., Presbyterian Minister, of

Newcastle-on-Tyne, and May Collingwood Stewart (née Strother). B. at Gateshead 16 May 1878; m. 3 December 1913, Ida Lillie Taylor, d. of George Green Taylor, Esq., of Newcastle-on-Tyne. Educ. privately, and at Durham University; B.A. 1899, M.A. and B.Litt. 1902, B.C.L. 1905; Gladstone Prize Essayist; President of the Union. A Solicitor, admitted 1905; Barrister-at-Law, Inner Temple 1919, N.E. Circuit. Member Newcastle Board of Guardians 1909-12; member Newcastle County Borough Council from 1912 to 1924. Gov. Royal Victoria Infirmary; Director Newcastle United Football Club; President North Eastern Council, and member of National Executive of National League of Young Liberals. Maj. R.M.A., T.F. Reserve; Aide to G.O.C. Tyne Marines 1914-15; Assistant competent Military Authority, Tyne Garrison 1919-20. A Liberal. Unsuccessfully contested Workington in 1918, and Stockton-on-Tees in 1922. Elected for Stockton-on-Tees in December 1923 and sat until he was defeated in October 1924. Magistrate in Trinidad 1927-29. Assistant Legal Adviser to Colonial Office 1929-30. Legal Adviser to Gov. of Malta 1930-33. Judge of the Supreme Court of Gold Coast 1933-42. Died 15 November 1954.   [1924 2nd ed.]

STEWART, William John. 105 Baker Street, London. 2 Templewood Avenue, London. Crawfordsburn House, Co. Down. Devonshire, and Royal Automobile. S. of John Stewart, Esq., of Belfast. B. 1868; m. Caroline Margaret, d. of Jason Law, Esq., of Enniskillen. Educ. privately, and at Queen's Coll., Belfast. Governing Director of Stewart and Partners Limited, Civil Engineering and Public Works Contractors, London and Belfast. A Conservative. Unsuccessfully contested the Ormean division of Belfast as an Independent Unionist in December 1918. Sat for S. Belfast from May 1929 until he retired in June 1945. Founder of Progressive Unionist Association which unsuccessfully contested seats in the 1938 Northern Ireland election. Member of Institute of Structural Engineers. Member of Belfast City Council 1936-39. Died 14 May 1946.   [1945]

STEWART, William Joseph. B. in about 1878. Member of Durham County Council from 1922. A Labour Member. Sat for the Houghton-le-Spring division of Durham from November 1935 until he retired in June 1945. Died 5 March 1960.   [1945]

STEWART-SANDEMAN, Sir Alexander Nairne Stewart, Bart. 9 Westminster Gardens, London. Kenlygreen, St. Andrews, Fife. Carlton. S. of Frank Stewart-Sandeman, Esq. B. 12 October 1876 at Stanley, Perthshire; m. 2 April 1902, Evelyn, d. of Thomas Bell, Esq., of Hazlewood, Broughty Ferry. Educ. at Trinity Coll., Glenalmond. Director of Dawney Day and Company. Assumed the surname Stewart-Sandeman in lieu of Sandeman 1929. Created Bart. 1929. A Conservative. Elected for the Middleton and Prestwich division of Lancashire in December 1923 and sat until his death on 23 April 1940.   [1940]

STOCKTON, Sir Edwin Forsyth. Holly Grange, Bowdon, Cheshire. Constitutional. S. of Edwin Stockton, Esq., of Sale, Cheshire, and Sarah, d. of John Forsyth, Esq. B. 18 March 1873; m. 1st, 4 October 1899, Jessie, d. of James Lowe, Esq., of Sale, Cheshire (she died 1922); secondly, 1923, Alice Marion Armitage, of Hale. Educ. privately. A Cotton Merchant and Manufacturer; President of Manchester Chamber of Commerce 1919-20 and 1921. Director of the Manchester Ship Canal. J.P. for Cheshire; Gov. of Manchester University; member of Cotton Control Board and of Cotton Reconstruction Board. Knighted 1921. A Conservative. Sat for the Exchange division of Manchester from November 1922 until he was defeated in December 1923. Chairman of Lancashire County Cricket Club 1927-32. Died 4 December 1939.   [1923]

STOKER, Robert Burdon. House of Commons, London. S. of Robert Stoker, Esq. B. at South Shields 1859. Educ. at Liverpool Coll. Managing Director of Manchester Liners Limited; a Director of the Manchester Ship Canal; and President of the Manchester Chamber of Commerce. A Coalition Unionist. Returned unopposed for

343

S. Manchester in March 1918. Elected for the Rusholme division of Manchester in December 1918 and sat until his death on 4 September 1919.   [1919]

STOKES, Richard Rapier. Continued in House after 1945: full entry in Volume IV.

STONES, James. 34 Penn Road, Holloway, London. Sunnyside, Highfield Road, Farnworth, Lancashire. S. of Thomas Stones, Esq. B. 6 April 1868; m. September 1890, Betsy, d. of J. Young, Esq., Farmer. Educ. at St. James's School, Farnworth. A Railway Clerk 1882-1920; Cashier and Paymaster 1920-28. Chairman of Farnworth Urban District Council 1915-19; J.P. 1919. A Conservative. Elected for the Farnworth division of Lancashire in October 1931 and sat until his death on 17 September 1935.   [1935]

STOREY, Samuel. Continued in House after 1945: full entry in Volume IV.

STORRY DEANS, Richard. See DEANS, Richard Storry.

STOTT, Lieut.-Col. William Henry, C.B. Mapledene, Egerton Park, Roch Ferry, Cheshire. Constitutional. S. of William Henry Stott, Esq., Shipowner, of Liverpool. B. 1863; m. 1893, Christine Brunfeldt, d. of John Martin, Esq. Educ. at Southport, Fairfield Coll., Manchester, and on the Continent. Managing Director of W.H. Stott and Company, Shipowners. Lieut.-Col. 7th Battalion (T.F.) Liverpool Regiment; served in France 1916-18. Dept-Lieut. A Conservative. Sat for W. Birkenhead from November 1922-December 1923, when he was defeated. Sat for Birkenhead E. from October 1924 until he retired in May 1929. Died 30 December 1930.   [1929]

STOURTON, Hon. John Joseph. Camden Hill, Wadhurst, Sussex. Carlton. S. of Charles, 24th Lord Mowbray. B. 5 March 1899; m. 1st, 1923, Kathleen Alice, d. of Robert Louis George Gunther, Esq. (divorced 1933); secondly, 14 May 1934, Gladys Leila, d. of Col. Sir William Waldron, of

Ascot Cottage, Winkfield, Berkshire (divorced 1947). Educ. at Downside School. Lieut. 10th Hussars; Maj. 5th Battalion Royal Norfolk Regiment (T.A.). Served in N. Russia with N. Russian Relief Force 1919. A Conservative. Elected for S. Salford in October 1931 and sat until he retired in June 1945.*   [1945]

STRACHEY, Evelyn John St. Loe. Continued in House after 1945: full entry in Volume IV.

STRANGER, Innes Harold. 2 Paper Buildings, Temple, London. National Liberal. S. of Innes Thomas and Mary Stranger. B. 21 June 1879; m. 31 August 1907, Millicent Norah, d. of J.B. Tunbridge, Esq., J.P., of Hythe. Educ. privately. A Barrister-at-Law, Middle Temple 1909. A Liberal. Unsuccessfully contested the Newbury division of Berkshire in 1922. Elected for the Newbury division in December 1923 and sat until he was defeated in October 1924. K.C. 1933. Recorder of Sunderland January-July 1936. Died 28 July 1936.   [1924 2nd ed.]

STRAUSS, Edward Anthony. 68 Borough High Street, London. Reform, Bath, Royal Automobile, and National Liberal. S. of Joseph Strauss, Esq., of Southwark. B. 7 December 1862. Unmarried. Educ. at King's Coll., London. Managing Director of Strauss and Company, Merchants, Southwark. J.P. for London and Berkshire. Liberal MP for the Abingdon division of Berkshire from January 1906-January 1910, when he was defeated. Sat for W. Southwark as a Liberal from December 1910-1918; for Southwark N. from December 1918-December 1923. Unsuccessfully contested Southwark N. in December 1923 and October 1924. Re-elected for Southwark N. in March 1927; unsuccessfully contested the same seat in May 1929. Re-elected as a Liberal National in October 1931 and sat until his death on 25 March 1939.   [1939]

STRAUSS, George Russell. Continued in House after 1945: full entry in Volume IV.

STRAUSS, Henry George. Continued in House after 1945: full entry in Volume IV.

STREATFEILD, Capt. Sidney Richard. Barlay, Balmaclellan, Kirkcudbrightshire. S. of Maj. H.S. Streatfeild, R.F.A., of Barlay, Balmaclellan. B. 27 June 1894; m. 1st, 4 March 1916, Muriel Mary, d. of C.S. Bristowe, Esq., of Craig, Balmaclellan, Kirkcudbrightshire (divorced 1928); secondly, 1934, Doris Marion, d. of Herbert Wimbledon Gibbs, Esq., of Bristol. Educ. at Rugby. Served in France etc. 1914-19. A Conservative. Unsuccessfully contested the Durham division of Co. Durham in October 1924. Sat for Galloway from November 1925 until he was defeated in May 1929. Died 2 December 1966. [1929]

STRICKLAND, Sir Gerald, G.C.M.G. 5 Holland Park, London. Sizergh Castle, Kendal. Villa Bologna, Malta. Carlton, and St. Stephen's. Count della Catena in Malta. S. of Capt. Walter Strickland, R.N. and Louise Bonici, niece and heiress of 5th Maltese Count della Catena. B. 24 May 1861; m. 1st, 26 August 1890, Lady Edeline Sackville, d. of Reginald, 7th Earl de la Warr (she died 1918); secondly, 31 August 1926, Margaret, d. of Edward Hulton, Esq., of Manchester. Educ. at Oscott Coll. in Birmingham and at Trinity Coll., Cambridge; B.A., LL.B., honours on Law 1887; President of Union Society 1887. A Barrister-at-Law, Inner Temple 1887. Member of Council of Malta 1887, Assistant Colonial Secretary 1888, Chief Secretary 1889-1902, Gov. and C.-in-C. Leeward Islands 1902-04, of Tasmania 1904-09, of Western Australia 1909-13, of New South Wales 1913-17. M.L.A. Malta 1921 and Leader of British Opposition; Prime Minister and Minister for Justice 1927-32. Maj. Royal Malta Regiment and Col, West Australian Infantry. Member of Committee of Privileges of Malta Nobles recognized by the Crown. Vice-President Royal Colonial Institute. Owner of *The Times of Malta* and Progress Newspapers. G.C.M.G. 1913; K.C.M.G. 1897. A Conservative. Elected for the Lancaster division of Lancashire in October 1924 and sat until January 1928 when he was created Baron Strickland. Died in Malta 22 August 1940. [1928]

STRICKLAND, Capt. William Frederick. The Manor, Cubbington, Leamington Spa. Constitutional. S. of W.F. Strickland, Esq., of Northampton. B. 1 February 1880; m. 5 September 1908, Anne Lucretia, d. of George Storton, Esq. Educ. at Waterloo Coll. Member of House of Laity in Church Assembly 1935-46. Served in Egypt and Palestine with 4th Northamptonshire Regiment and Imperial Camel Corps 1914-19; Chairman of Cornercroft Limited, and of Thames Plywood Manufacturers Limited, Director of John Morton and Son Limited, and of E. and H.P. Smith Limited. A National Unionist. Elected for Coventry in October 1931 and again in November 1935. Sat until July 1945 when he unsuccessfully contested W. Coventry. Died 29 November 1954. [1945]

STROTHER STEWART, Maj. Robert. See STEWART, Maj. Robert Strother.

STUART, Rt. Hon. James Gray. Continued in House after 1945: full entry in Volume IV.

STUDHOLME, Henry Gray. Continued in House after 1945: full entry in Volume IV.

STURROCK, John Leng. Newport, Fife. Reform, and Liberal. S. of James Sturrock, Esq., of Dundee. B. at Newport, Fife 1878; m. 1925, Winifred Mary, d. of William Anning, Esq. Educ. at the High School, Dundee, and University Coll. Interested in John Leng and Company Limited, Newspaper Proprietors, of Dundee. Parliamentary Private Secretary to Rt. Hon. Edward Shortt, Home Secretary 1918-22. Assistant Whip to National Liberal Party 1923. A Liberal. First elected for Montrose Burghs in December 1918 and sat until October 1924 when he unsuccessfully contested N. Tottenham as a Constitutionalist with Liberal and Conservative support. Died 22 July 1943. [1924 2nd ed.]

STYLES, Herbert Walter. Blackmoor, Edenbridge, Kent. Carlton, and St. James's. S. of Frederick Styles, Esq. B. 4 April 1889; m. 19 September 1922, Violet, d. of Maj. H. Hawkins, of Everdon, Northampton-shire. Educ. at Eton, and Exeter Coll., Oxford. Capt. T.A. (Res.). A Conservative. Elected for the Sevenoaks division of Kent in October 1924 and sat until he retired in May 1929. Died 5 October 1965.   [1929]

SUETER, Rear-Admiral Sir Murray Fraser, C.B. The Howe, Howe Hill, Watlington, Oxfordshire. S. of Fleet-Pay-master J.T. Suter, R.N. B. 1872; m. 1903, Elinor Mary, d. of Lieut.-Gen. Hon. Sir Andrew Clarke, G.C.M.G., R.E. (she died 1948). Joined Royal Navy 1886; Rear-Ad-miral 1920. Assistant to Director of Naval Ordance at the Admiralty; assisted Capt. Bacon in introducing Submarines into the navy. Inspecting Capt. of Airships; Direc-tor of Air Department Admiralty, and member of 1st War Air Committee; initiated Anti-Aircraft Corps for London, and the Armoured Car Force; Superintendent of Aircraft Construction, and member of Ad-visory Committee on Aeronautics. Received gratitude and appreciative thanks of Army Council for his contribution towards the evolution of the Tank; member of Post Office Advisory Council and Air Mail Panel from 1934. Commanded R.N.A.S. units in S. Italy 1917-18. Created Knight Bach. January 1934. Sat for the Hertford division of Hertfordshire from June 1921 until he retired in June 1945. Elected in 1921 as the candidate of the Anti-Waste League and of Horatio Bottomley's Independent Parlia-mentary Group, defeating the Coalition Conservative candidate. Re-elected as the official Conservative from 1922 onwards. Died 3 February 1960.   [1945]

SUGDEN, Sir Wilfrid Hart. 2 Dr. John-son's Buildings, Temple, London. 206 Waterloo Street, Oldham. Carlton. S. of W.A. Sugden, Esq., of Oldham. B. 1889. Unmarried. Educ. at Waterloo School, and London University. A Steel and Con-structional Engineer; R.E. War Service Overseas 1914-19; Temporary Capt. Special Brigade (Oil Flame R.E.). Member of Oldham Town Council 1912-18. Gov. of Waterloo and Oldham Municipal Techni-cal Schools. Barrister-at-Law 1928, Middle Temple and Gray's Inn. Parliamentary Private Secretary to Sir Hamar Greenwood when Chief Secretary for Ireland 1921-22. Knighted 1922. A Conservative. Elected for the Royton division of Lancashire in December 1918 and November 1922. Un-successfully contested the Royton division Lancashire in December 1923. Sat for the Hartlepools from 1924-May 1929 when he unsuccessfully contested Rossendale. Elected for Leyton W. in October 1931 and sat until he was defeated in November 1935. Unsuccessfully contested N. Islington in October 1937, the Platting division of Manchester in July 1945 and Barrow-in-Furness in February 1950. Died 27 April 1960.   [1935]

SUIRDALE, John Michael Henry Hely-Hutchinson, Visct. 1 Chesham Street, London. Carlton, and Buck's. S. of 6th Earl of Donoughmore. B. 12 November 1902; m. 27 July 1925, Dorothy Jean, d. of John Beaumont Hotham, Esq. Educ. at Winchester, and Magdalen Coll., Oxford. Maj. Royal Armoured Corps (T.A.). A Conservative. Elected for the Peterborough division of Northamptonshire in October 1943 and sat until he was defeated in July 1945. Styled Visct. Suirdale 1902-48. Suc-ceeded to the Peerage as Earl of Donough-more 1948. Grand-Master of Freemasons Lodge of Ireland 1964.*   [1945]

SULLIVAN, Joseph, M.B.E. 523 Main Street, Mossend, Lanarkshire. 33 Chester Street, Kennington Road, London. S. of Bernard Sullivan, Esq., of Cambuslang. B. 8 September 1866; m. 1st, 1888, d. of Thomas Winter, Esq. (she died 6 August 1923); secondly, 1929, Anne, d. of Michael Murphy, Esq. Educ. at Bellshill and New-ton Elementary Schools. J.P. for Lanark-shire; Miners' Agent and President of Lanarkshire Miners' Association. A Labour Member. Unsuccessfully contested N.W. Lanarkshire in 1906, N.E. division of Lanarkshire in January 1910, and the N. division of Lanarkshire in 1918. Elected for N. Lanarkshire in November 1922 and again in December 1923, unsuccessfully contested the same seat in October 1924. Elected for the Bothwell division of Lanarkshire in March 1926 and sat until he was defeated in October 1931. A Roman Catholic. Died 13 February 1935. [1931 2nd ed.]

SUMMERS, Gerard Spencer. Continued in House after 1945: full entry in Volume IV.

SUMMERSBY, Charles Harold. 46 Queens Avenue, London. Burwood, Peppard Common, Henley-on-Thames. S. of the Rev. B.J. Summersby, of Peppard Common, Oxfordshire. B. 1882. Educ. at Peppard School. Proprietor and Director of Textile businesses. Mayor of Hornsey 1930-31. A Liberal Nationalist. Elected for Shoreditch in October 1931 and sat until he retired in October 1935. Died 13 August 1961. [1935]

SUMMERSKILL, Edith Clara. Continued in House after 1945: full entry in Volume IV.

SUNLIGHT, Joseph. 14 Victoria Square, London. Hillside, Knutsford, Cheshire. Belmont, Shrewsbury. S. of Israel and Minnie Sunlight. B. in Russia 2 January 1889. Unmarried. Educ. at Gordon House School, Kingston. An Architect 1906, of 4 St. Ann's Square, Manchester; exhibited 1919, 1920 and 1921 at the Royal Academy. A Liberal. Unsuccessfully contested the Shrewsbury division of Shropshire in November 1922. Elected for the Shrewsbury division in December 1923 and sat until he was defeated in October 1924. Unsuccessfully contested the Shrewsbury division of Shropshire in May 1929.* [1924 2nd ed.]

SURTEES, Brigadier-Gen. Herbert Conyers, C.B., C.M.G., D.S.O., M.V.O. Mainsforth Hall, Ferryhill. Carlton, and 1900. S. of Col. Charles Freville Surtees, J.P., Dept.-Lieut., MP for S. Durham 1865-68. B. 13 January 1858; m. 1887, Madeleine, d. of E. Crabbe, Esq. Educ. at Harrow, and Sandhurst. Entered the Coldstream Guards 1876; Military Attaché Constantinople and Athens 1905-09; Brigadier-Gen. commanding 52nd Infantry Brigade, Western Front

1915-16; Honorary Col. 4th Battalion D.L.I.; Inspector of Infantry. Author of *Campaign in Italy 1796*, and Histories of Brancepeth Castle and Church. A Coalition Unionist. Unsuccessfully contested Gateshead in December 1910. Elected for Gateshead in December 1918 and sat until he was defeated in November 1922. Unsuccessfully contested the Spennymoor division of Co. Durham in October 1924. High Sheriff of Co. Durham 1927-28. Knighted 1932. F.S.A. and F.R.G.S. J.P. for Co. Durham. Served in Egypt 1884-86, South Africa 1899-1902 (D.S.O. 1900). Died 18 April 1933. [1922]

SUTCLIFFE, Harold. Continued in House after 1945: full entry in Volume IV.

SUTCLIFFE, Tom. Stallingborough Manor, Lincolnshire. Conservative, Empire, and St. Stephen's. S. of John and Isabella Sutcliffe. B. at Stallingborough 2 July 1865. Unmarried. Educ. at Haileybury, and Pembroke Coll., Oxford. A Shipping Agent and Merchant at Grimsby, Manchester, Liverpool, Bradford, Sheffield, Birmingham, and London. A Conservative. First elected for Grimsby in November 1922 and sat until he retired in October 1924. Vice-Chairman of Humber Conservancy Board. High Sheriff of Lincolnshire 1929. Died 8 January 1931.
[1924 2nd ed.]

SUTHERLAND, Rt. Hon. Sir William, K.C.B. 51 Westminster Palace Gardens, London. Birthwaite Hall, Darton, Yorkshire. S. of Alan Sutherland, Esq., of Glasgow. B. at Glasgow 4 March 1880; m. 1921, Anne Christine Fountain, of Birthwaite Hall, Darton, Yorkshire (she died July 1949). Educ. at Glasgow High School, and Glasgow University; M.A. Aided in preparing and putting into operation the Old Age Pensions Act and National Insurance Act. Wrote *Old Age Pensions*, 1907. Made a special study of the land question; wrote *The Call of the Land*, 1909, *The Land Question*, 1910, *Rural Regeneration in England*, 1913. Worked with Secretary for Scotland in preparing the Small Landholders Act. Assisted Mr. Lloyd George in preparing his land policy before the war. Secretary to the Cabinet Committee on the Supply of Munitions 1915. Private Secretary to Mr. Lloyd George as Minister of Munitions, Secretary of State for War, and Prime Minister 1915-18. Parliamentary Private Secretary to Mr. Lloyd George January 1919-February 1920, K.C.B. January 1919; Junior Lord of the Treasury February 1920 to April 1922; Chancellor of the Duchy of Lancaster April to October 1922; Commander of the Order of Leopold 1919. PC. 1922. A Liberal. Elected for Argyllshire in December 1918; re-elected there March 1920 on joining the Government, and sat until he was defeated in October 1924. Unsuccessfully contested Barnsley in May 1929. Died 19 September 1949.

[1924 2nd ed.]

SUTTON, John Edward. 115 Egerton Road South, Chorlton-cum-Hardy, Manchester. S. of Edward Sutton, Esq., Carter. B. at Manchester 23 December 1862; m. 6 November 1880, eld. d. of William and Elizabeth Etchells (she died 1925). Educ. at St. Luke's School, Manchester. Worked in cotton mill and in a mine. A Miners' Agent from 1910 to 1933; first Labour Councillor for Manchester 1894; J.P. for Manchester 1905. A Labour Member. Sat for E. Manchester from January 1910 to December 1918, when he unsuccessfully contested the Clayton division of Manchester. Sat for the Clayton division of Manchester from February to November 1922, when he was defeated. Re-elected for the Clayton division of Manchester in December 1923 and sat until he was defeated in October 1931. Advocate of temperance reform and member of the Rechabites Friendly Society. Died 29 November 1945.　　[1931 2nd ed.]

SWAN, John Edmund. Dipton S.O., Co. Durham. S. of George Swan, Esq., Engineer, of Tanfield, Co. Durham. B. 1877; m. 1st, 1902, Alice, d. of Henry Beatham, Esq., of Dipton; secondly, Mrs. Jack Foster. Educ. at Colliery Board School, Dipton, Co. Durham. A Miner, later Checkweighman and one of the mining leaders in Durham. A Labour Member. Elected for the Barnard Castle division of Durham in December

1918 and sat until he was defeated in November 1922. Gen. Secretary of Durham Miners' Association 1935-45. Member of National Executive of Labour Party 1932-41. Member of Annfield Plain Urban District Council and Lanchester Board of Guardians. Author of two novels, *The Mad Miner* and *People of the Night*, and a play, *On the Minimum*. Died 9 February 1956.　　[1922]

SWEENEY, Joseph Aloysius. Burtonport, Co. Donegal. S. of John Sweeney, Esq. B. 13 June 1897. Was sentenced to ten years' penal servitude for his part in the Sinn Fein rebellion; reduced to two years; afterwards released. Re-arrested April 1920. A Sinn Fein Member. Elected for W. Donegal in December 1918 but did not take his seat. Member of Dail for W. Donegal to 1921, for Donegal 1921-23 as a Pro-Treaty Member. Served with Irish Army until 1940, retired as Maj.-Gen. Gen. Secretary of Irish Red Cross Society 1956-62.★

[1922]

SWEETMAN, Roger Mary. Derrybawn, Glendalough, Co. Wicklow. B. 15 August 1874; m. 1904, Kathleen Mary, d. of Thomas Kelly, Esq., of Dublin. A Barrister, King's Inns 1898. A Sinn Fein Member. Elected for N. Wexford in December 1918 but did not take his seat and resigned in January 1921. Died 20 May 1954.

[1921]

SYKES, Col. Sir Alan John, Bart. South View, Cheadle, Cheshire. 2 Down Street, London. Carlton, and Royal Automobile. S. of Thomas Hardcastle Sykes, Esq., Dept.-Lieut., and J.P., and Mary, d. of John Platt, Esq., MP for Oldham. B. 11 April 1868 at Cheadle, Cheshire. Unmarried. Educ. at Rugby, and Oriel Coll., Oxford. Chairman of Bleachers' Association Limited, and Director of Alliance Mortgage and Investment Company Limited, and Colwyn Bay and Pwllycrochan Estate Company. J.P. and Dept.-Lieut. for Cheshire. Mayor of Stockport 1910-11. Lieut.-Col. commanding 6th Battalion Cheshire Regiment 1911-14. Group Commandant and Honorary Secretary Cheshire Volunteer Regiment. Dept. Commander Cheshire Division Comrades of the Great War. Created Bart. 1917. A Coalition Unionist. Elected for the Knutsford division of Cheshire in January 1910 and sat until he retired in October 1922. Died 21 May 1950. [1922]

SYKES, Sir Charles, Bart. Kingsknowes, Galashiels, Scotland. National Liberal. S. of Benjamin and Rachel Sykes. B. at Spa Green, Lyston, near Huddersfield 31 December 1867; m. 1892, Mary, d. of Benjamin Newsome, Esq., of Huddersfield (she died 1944). Educ. privately. A Woollen Manufacturer. Resigned his connection with John Crowther and Sons, Milnsbridge, Huddersfield, in the early part of 1917, when he took over the Government position of Director of Wool Textile Production at the War Office, Bradford, to provide cloth for the British Army and Navy and the Allies. Later Chief Director of Sir Charles Sykes and Sons Limited, Scottish Woollen Manufacturers, Netherdale Mills, Galashiels. Bart. 1921. A Coalition Liberal. Elected for Huddersfield in December 1918 and sat until he was defeated in November 1922. K.B.E. 1918. Died 16 November 1950. [1922]

SYKES, Maj.-Gen. Rt. Hon. Sir Frederick Hugh, G.C.S.I., G.C.I.E., G.B.E., K.C.B., C.M.G. 50 Egerton Gardens, London. Carlton, and United Service. S. of Henry Sykes, Esq., of Addiscombe. B. 23 July 1877; m. 3 June 1920, Isabel, d. of Rt. Hon. A. Bonar Law. Joined 15th Hussars 1901; Maj.-Gen. 1918; served in South African War 1900-01 and in France 1914-15; commanded R.F.C. 1912-14; commanded R.N.A.S. in E. Mediterranean 1915-16; A.A.G. at War Office 1916; Dept. Director of Organization at War Office 1917; Brigadier-Gen. General Staff Supreme War Air Council at Versailles 1917-18; Maj.-Gen. Chief of the Air Staff, Air Ministry 1918-19; Chief of British Section Peace Conference, Paris 1919; Controller Gen. of Civil Aviation and member of Air Council 1919-22; member of Council of R.G.S., Chairman of Government Broadcasting Board 1923-27; Gov. of Bombay 1928-33; Chairman of Council of Royal Empire Society 1938-41, and of Miners

Welfare Commission from 1934 to 1946; President of East India Association, Vice-President of Royal India Society, and of many Government Committees. PC. 1928. Commander of Legion of Honour, the D.S.O. of U.S.A., Orders of Leopold of Belgium, of St. Vladimir of Russia, of the Rising Sun of Japan, and of the Cross of the Lion and Sun of Persia. A Conservative. Sat for the Hallam division of Sheffield from November 1922 to June 1928 when he was appointed Gov. of Bombay. Returned unopposed for Nottingham Central in July 1940 and sat until he was defeated in July 1945. Died 30 September 1954. [1945]

SYKES, Sir Mark, Bart. Sledmere House, Malton, Yorkshire. Carlton, Marlborough, Beefsteak, Princes, and 1900. Yorkshire (York). Only s. of Sir Tatton Sykes, 5th Bart., and Jessica, d. of the Rt. Hon. George Cavendish-Bentinck, MP. B. 16 March 1879; m. 1903, Edith Violet, d. of the Rt. Hon. Sir John Gorst. Educ. at Institut St. Louis, Brussels, and Jesus Coll., Cambridge. Succeeded as Bart. 1913. Lieut.-Col. 5th Battalion Yorkshire Regiment; served in South African War 1902, and was mentioned in despatches; Lieut.-Col. G.S.O.Q. from June 1915. Honorary Attaché to the British Embassy at Constantinople 1905-07. Assistant Secretary of the War Cabinet 1917. County Councillor for the E. Riding of Yorkshire. A Unionist. Unsuccessfully contested the Buckrose division of the E. Riding of Yorkshire in January and December 1910. Elected for Central Hull in July 1911 and sat until his death in Paris on 16 February 1919. J.P. for the E. Riding of Yorkshire. Fellow of Royal Geographical Society. Died 16 February 1919. [1918]

TALBOT, Rt. Hon. Lord Edmund Bernard, G.C.V.O., D.S.O. 1 Buckingham Palace Gardens, London. Carlton, and Naval & Military. S. of 14th Duke of Norfolk. Only bro. of the 15th Duke of Norfolk. B. 1 June 1855; m. 1879, Mary Caroline Bertie, d. of the 7th Earl of Abingdon (she died 1938). Educ. at the Oratory School, Edgbaston. He took the name of Talbot in lieu of Fitzalan-Howard in 1876 by Royal Licence under the will of the late Earl of

Shrewsbury. Lieut.-Col. (later retired) 11th Hussars; joined 20 November 1875; served in South Africa 1899-1901, D.S.O. 1900, M.V.O. 1902. Dept. Earl Marshal of England 1917-29. Was a Junior Lord of the Treasury May to December 1905. A Unionist Whip from 1905, and Chief Whip from 1913. Joint Parliamentary Secretary to the Treasury from May 1915 to April 1921. PC. 1918. A Unionist. Unsuccessfully contested Burnley in 1880, and the Brightside division of Sheffield in 1885 and 1886. Elected for the Chichester division of Sussex in 1894 and sat until April 1921 when he was appointed Lord-Lieut. of Ireland. Lord-Lieut. of Ireland 1921-22. Created Visct. Fitzalan of Derwent 1921. K.G. 1925. President of Catholic Record Society and Catholic Union of Great Britain. Died 18 May 1947. [1921]

TALBOT, Gustavus Arthur. Hemel Hempstead. Carlton, and City of London. S. of the Hon. and Rev. G.G. Chetwynd Talbot. B. at Withington, Gloucestershire 24 December 1848; m. 1880, Susan, d. of Robert Elwes, Esq. Educ. at Wellington Coll. An Owner of coffee, tea and rubber plantations in Ceylon and Straits Settlements. Member of the Legislative Council of Ceylon; member of Hertfordshire County Council; J.P. for Hertfordshire; Mayor of Hemel Hempstead 1914-20. A Coalition Unionist. Elected for the Hemel Hempstead division of Hertfordshire in December 1918 and sat until his death on 16 October 1920. [1920]

TASKER, Sir Robert Inigo. 7 Gray's Inn Square, London. Oakfield, Lyonsdown Road, New Barnet. Carlton, and Magistrates'. S. of G.R. Tasker, Esq., of Shillingstone. B. 1868; m. 1900 Elizabeth Emma, d. of E. Lange, Esq. Educ. at Ardingly Coll. President 1929-30, Vice-President I.A.A.S.; Dept.-Lieut., and J.P. for London. Member London County Council 1910-37; Chairman 1930-31; Master of the Gardeners' Company 1908-09 and 1939-40; member of the Paviors' and of the Fanmakers' Companies; F.R.S.L. 1897; Chairman of London Old Age Pensions Committee 1922-37 and of London

County Council Building Committee 1924-30. Raised and commanded 3/11th London Battalion 1915; retired 1920. Knight Bach. 1931. A Conservative. Unsuccessfully contested N.E. Bethnal Green in December 1923. Sat for Islington E. from October 1924-May 1929 when he was defeated. Elected for Holborn in November 1935 and sat until he retired in June 1945. Died 28 February 1959. [1945]

TATE, Mavis Constance. 6 Bloomfield Terrace, London. D. of Guy Weir Hogg, Esq. B. 17 August 1893 (her birth was registered under the name of Maybird Constance Hogg but she adopted the name of Mavis in lieu of Maybird in 1930); m. 1st, 1915, Capt. G.E. Gott (divorced); secondly, 22 August 1925, Henry Burton Tate (whom she divorced in 1944). Educ. privately, and at St. Paul's Girls' School. J.P. for Middlesex. A National Conservative. Sat for W. Willesden from October 1931-35. Returned for the Frome division of Somerset in November 1935 and sat until she was defeated in July 1945. Died 5 June 1947. [1945]

TATTERSALL, John Lincoln. Woodeaves, Linden Road, Dibsbury, Manchester. National Liberal. S. of Cornelius Tattersall, Esq., of Manchester. B. 1865; m. 1893, Lizzie, d. of R.T. Harland, Esq. A Cotton Spinner. A Liberal. Unsuccessfully contested the Stalybridge and Hyde division of Cheshire in November 1922. Elected for the division in December 1923 and sat until he was defeated in October 1924. Died 6 June 1942. [1924 2nd ed.]

TAYLOR, Charles Stuart. Continued in House after 1945: full entry in Volume IV.

TAYLOR, Vice-Admiral Ernest Augustus. Continued in House after 1945: full entry in Volume IV.

TAYLOR, Harry Bernard. Continued in House after 1945: full entry in Volume IV.

TAYLOR, John, O.B.E. Craigforth, 29 Baskerville Road, Wandsworth Common, London. Liberal, Glasgow. S. of Robert

Taylor, Esq., and Janet McNab. B. 23 December 1857 at Whiteburn, Linlithgowshire; m. 1891, Agnes Gordon, d. of William Wood, Esq. Educ. at Cambusbarran Public School, and Stirling Art School. Was in business as a Painter and Decorator. Councillor in Clydebank for 25 years; Provost of Clydebank from 1904 to 1919; Chairman of Water Trust from 1906 to 1919; Chairman Licensing Court from 1904 to 1919; Member of Clyde Trust from 1905 to 1919; Chairman of Insurance Committee, War Pensions Committee, Military Tribunal, War Savings, Old-Age Pensions, and Food Control Committees. J.P. for the Co. of Dumbartonshire from 1906. A Liberal Coalition Member. Elected for Dumbarton Burghs in December 1918 and sat until he was defeated in November 1922. O.B.E. 1918. Died 19 September 1936. [1922]

TAYLOR, John Wilkinson. The Avenue, Durham. B. 1855; m. d. of J. Mason, Esq. Started work when 9 years old, was apprenticed to a Blacksmith at 12, and afterwards worked in Dipton Colliery. Secretary of Durham Colliery Mechanics' Association and member of Co. Durham Mining Federated Board. President of Durham Aged Mineworkers' Homes Association. J.P. for Co. Durham. A Labour Member. Sat for the Chester-le-Street division of Durham from 1906 until he resigned in October 1919. Died 26 June 1934. [1919]

TAYLOR, Robert Arthur. House of Commons, London. S. of John Taylor, Esq., of Metheringham, Lincolnshire. B. 17 October 1886; m. 1909, Laura Webber, of Sleaford. Educ. at Ruskin Coll., Oxford. A Tailor in Lincoln. Member of Lincoln City Council from 1914, Mayor 1924-25. A Labour Member. Unsuccessfully contested Lincoln in 1918, 1922 and again in 1923. Elected for Lincoln October 1924 and sat until he was defeated in October 1931. Organiser of Shop Assistants' Union 1933-34. Died 5 April 1934. [1931 2nd ed.]

TAYLOR, Robert John. Continued in House after 1945: full entry in Volume IV.

TAYLOR, Walter Ross. See ROSS TAYLOR, Walter.

TAYLOR, William Benjamin. Tottington Old Hall, Thetford, Norfolk. National Labour. S. of Robert Taylor, Esq. B. 22 May 1875; m. 1900, Rose Kate, d. of William Meek, Esq. Educ. at Watton National School. A Farmer. J.P., and County Councillor for Norfolk. A Labour Member. Unsuccessfully contested the E. division of Norfolk in December 1918 as an Agricultural candidate. Unsuccessfully contested the S.W. division of Norfolk in November 1922, December 1923 and October 1924. Elected for S.W. division of Norfolk in May 1929 and sat until he was defeated in October 1931. Congregationalist lay preacher. C.B.E. 1931. Died 29 July 1932. [1931 2nd ed.]

TEELING, Luke William Burke. Continued in House after 1945: full entry in Volume IV.

TEMPLETON, William Paterson. 16 Glen Avenue, Springboig, Glasgow. Scottish Constitutional. B. 1876. A Wood Turner. Organizing Secretary Unionist Workers' League from 1909. F.R.S.A. A Conservative. Unsuccessfully contested Ross and Cromarty as a Liberal Unionist in 1911. Sat for Banff from October 1924-May 1929, when he was defeated. Unsuccessfully contested the Shettleston division of Glasgow in June 1930. Elected for the Coatbridge division of Lanarkshire in October 1931 and sat until he retired in October 1935. Died 4 July 1938. [1935]

TERRELL, George. 45 Wilton Crescent, London. Carlton, St. Stephen's and Royal Thames. S. of Thomas Terrell, Esq., County Court Judge. B. 1862; m. Grace, d. of J.J. Hawkins, Esq. (she died 1939). Managing Director of Tyer and Company Limited. A Unionist. Elected for the Chippenham division of Wiltshire in January 1910 and sat until he was defeated in November 1922. Unsuccessfully contested the Attercliffe division of Sheffield in December 1923. President of National Union of Manufacturers from 1916 to 1932. Treasurer of National League for Freedom. Died 7 November 1952.

[1922]

TERRELL, Capt. Reginald. 12 Suffolk Street, Pall Mall, London. S. of George Terrell, Esq., MP for the Chippenham division of Wiltshire. B. at Mortlake 1889; m. 16 July 1923, Marjorie Ethel, d. of Mr. and Mrs. O'Connor, of Hampstead. Educ. at Harrow. Served in the Grenadier Guards, wounded on the Somme. Director of many large business undertakings. A Conservative. Elected for the Henley division of Oxfordshire in December 1918 and sat until he retired in October 1924. Knighted 1959.*

[1924 2nd ed.]

TERRINGTON, Vera Florence Annie Woodhouse, Lady. 11 Clarges Street, Street, London. D. of H.G. Bousher, Esq. B. 1889; m. 1st, Ivo Guy Sebright, Esq. (he died 1912); secondly, 8 May 1918 Lord Terrington (divorced 1927); thirdly, 1949, Max W. Lensvelt, of Johannesburg. A Liberal. Unsuccessfully contested the Wycombe division of Buckinghamshire in 1922. Elected for the Wycombe division of Buckinghamshire in December 1923 and sat until she was defeated in October 1924.

[1924 2nd ed.]

THOM, Lieut.-Col. John Gibb, D.S.O., M.C. 83 Great King Street, Edinburgh. Constitutional. Caledonian. S. of John Thom, Esq., Solicitor, of Linlithgow. B. 1 August 1891; m. 1932, Anna Elizabeth Taylor, d. of Robert Brown, Esq. Educ. at Linlithgow Academy, and University of Edinburgh, M.A., LL.B. A Barrister-at-Law, Scotland 1919. Served in France, etc. 1914-18. Commanded 8/10th and 6th Battalion of Gordon Highlanders. A Conservative. Sat for Dumbartonshire from January 1926 to May 1929, when he was defeated. Re-elected for Dumbartonshire in October 1931 and sat until February 1932 when he was appointed a Judge of the High Court of India. Judge of Allahabad High Court 1932-41, Chief Justice 1937-41. D.S.O. 1917. Knighted 1937. Advocate Depute 1931-32. Died 19 February 1941.

[1932]

THOMAS, Ivor. Continued in House after 1945: full entry in Volume IV.

THOMAS, Rt. Hon. James Henry. 12 Thurlow Park Road, Dulwich, London. B. 3 October 1874 at Newport; m. 1898, 3 October 1874 at Newport; m. 1898, Agnes Hill. Educ. at Board School. Was Gen. Secretary of National Union of Railwaymen 1918-24 and 1925-31; President 1910. A member of Swindon Town Council. PC. 1917. Honorary LL.D. Cambridge 1920. J.P. for Kent. Secretary of State for the Colonies January-November 1924; Lord Privy Seal June 1929-June 1930. Secretary of State for the Dominions June 1930-August 1931; and for Dominions and Colonies in 1st National Government August-November 1931, for the Dominions November 1931-November 1935; Secretary of State for Colonies November 1935 to May 1936, when he resigned as a result of a budget leak. A Labour Member until August 1931, thereafter a National Labour Member. Sat for Derby from January 1910 until he resigned in May 1936. Honorary D.C.L. Oxford 1926. President of International Federation of Trade Unions 1920-24. President of T.U.C. 1920. Died 21 January 1949.

[1936]

THOMAS, James Purdon Lewes. Continued in House after 1945: full entry in Volume IV.

THOMAS, Maj. Lionel Beaumont, M.C. 23 Newton Court, Church Street, London. Brampton House, Madley, Hereford. Carlton, Cavalry, Royal Automobile, and Royal Motor Yacht. S. of Richard Beaumont Thomas, Esq., of Alvington Court, Gloucestershire, Chairman and Managing Director of Messrs. Richard Thomas and Company, and Nora, d. of J. Anderson, Esq. B. 1 August 1893; m. 1st, 29 May 1913, Pauline Grace, d. of Sidney Marriott, Esq. (divorced 1934); secondly, 1934, Iseult Margery Hazlehurst, d. of O.T. Bland, Esq. Educ. at Rugby. Maj. R.H.A. and R.F.A. Served in France 1914-18. J.P. for Herefordshire and County Councillor 1925. A Freeman of the City of London. A Director of Richard Thomas and Company, and Vice-Chairman and Director of other companies. A Livery-man of Haberdashers' Company. A Conservative. Unsuccessfully contested Llanelly in December 1923, and Pontypool October 1924. Elected for the King's Norton division of Birmingham in May 1929 and again in October 1931 and sat until he retired in October 1935. Died December 1942.

[1935]

THOMAS, Brigadier-Gen. Sir Owen. Carlton House, Regent Street, London. 178 Ashley Gardens, London. S. of Owen Thomas, Esq., of Anglesey. B. 18 December 1858; m. 1887, Frederica, d. of Frederick Pershouse, Esq. Served in South African War; raised and commanded Prince of Wales Light Horse in the South African War; mentioned in despatches twice, King's and Queen's Medals. Raised several Battalions R.W.F. in European War; commanded the 113th Infantry Brigade and the 14th Reserve Infantry Brigade; later Brigadier-Gen. commanding N. Wales Brigade, 38th Welsh Division. A noted breeder of farm stock; Chief Officer, Life-Saving Apparatus at Sea under Board of Trade 1876-99; High Sheriff for Anglesey 1890; Dept.-Lieut., J.P., County Councillor, and Alderman for the County of Anglesey. Knighted 1917. Unsuccessfully contested the Oswestry division of Shropshire as a Liberal in 1895. Elected as an Independent Labour candidate in 1918 and afterwards accepted the Labour Whip but resigned it in October 1920 and sat as an Independent; re-elected as an Independent in 1922. Elected for Anglesey in December 1918 and sat until his death on 6 March 1923. [1923]

THOMAS, Sir Robert John, Bart. Garreglwyd, Holyhead. Reform, and National Liberal. S. of William Thomas, Esq., of Bootle. B. 23 April 1873; m. 18 February 1908, Marie Rose, d. of Arthur Burrows, Esq. (she died 1948). Educ. at Bootle Coll., Liverpool Institute, and Tettenhall Coll. A Ship and Insurance Broker and Underwriter at Lloyd's. Honorary Secretary North Wales Heroes Memorial Fund, inaugurated by himself with a donation of £20,000. Member of Anglesey County Council; High Sheriff of Anglesey 1912.

Member of Council of University Coll. of North Wales, Bangor. Honorary Treasurer of Anglesey Eisteddfod Association for 15 years. Created Bart. 1918. A Liberal. Sat for the Wrexham division of Denbighshire from 1918-22. Unsuccessfully contested Anglesey in November 1922. Elected for Anglesey in April 1923, returned unopposed December 1923. Re-elected for Anglesey in October 1924 and sat until he retired in May 1929. Died 27 September 1951. [1929]

THOMAS, Dr. William Stanley Russell. 1 Tanfield Court, Temple, London. Bramley House, Warlingham, Surrey. S. of David Thomas, Esq. B. 5 February 1896; m. 1922, Kathleen, d. of R.C. Bennett, Esq., of Hampstead. Educ. at Christ's Coll., Brecon, at Queens Coll., Cambridge, and Guy's Hospital, M.A., M.B., B.Ch. Cambridge, M.R.C.S., L.R.C.P. Treasurers Gold Medallist in Medicine, Guy's Hospital. Barrister-at-Law, Lincoln's Inn 1930. Dept. Chairman of London Liberal National Party. A Liberal National. Unsuccessfully contested as a Liberal, Ilford in October 1931, Aberdeen and Kincardineshire Central in November 1935, and the Ross and Cromarty division of Inverness-shire, Ross and Cromarty in February 1936. Joined Liberal National Party 1936. Returned unopposed for Southampton in November 1940 and sat until he was defeated in July 1945. Unsuccessfully contested, as a Liberal, Middlesbrough E. in February 1950 and Brecon and Radnor in May 1955. Member of Council of R.S.P.C.A. 1943-54, Chairman 1951-52. Member of Caterham and Warlingham Urban District Council 1926-32. Died 21 March 1957. [1945]

THOMAS-STANFORD, Charles. Preston Manor, Brighton. Carlton, and Brooks's. S. of D.C. Thomas, Esq., J.P., of Hove. B. 1858 in London; m. 1897, Ellen, d. of William Stanford, Esq., of Preston Manor, Brighton, and widow of V.F. Benet-Stanford, Esq., MP. Educ. at Highgate School, and Oriel Coll., Oxford; M.A. Assumed the name and arms of Stanford by Royal Licence 1897. Was called to the bar at the Inner Temple, but did not practise. Mayor of Brighton 1910-13. President of Library Association

1907. J.P. for Sussex. F.S.A. Author of *A River of Norway, Leaves from a Madeira Garden, About Algeria, The Ace of Hearts, a Romance, Sussex in the Great Civil War*, etc. A Unionist. Elected for Brighton in June 1914; re-elected there in December 1918 and sat until he retired in October 1922. Honorary D.Litt. University of Wales. Created Bart. 1929. Chairman of Council of Sussex Archaeological Society. Died 7 March 1932.
[1922]

THOMPSON, Ernest Claude Meysey. See MEYSEY-THOMPSON, Ernest Claude.

THOMPSON, Sir Luke. Thornhill, Beresford Park, Sunderland. Fell End, Slaggyford, Northumberland. Constitutional, and Overseas. S. of John Thompson, Esq., of Sunderland. B. 13 July 1867; m. 1895, Annie Trobe, d. of Cuthbert Potts, Esq., of Sunderland. Educ. at the Grange School, Sunderland. A Coal Merchant and Director of various industrial undertakings. Knight Bach. January 1934. A Conservative. Sat for Sunderland from November 1922-May 1929, when he was defeated. Re-elected for Sunderland in March and again in October 1931 and sat until he retired in October 1935. Died 15 January 1941. [1935]

THOMPSON, Piers Gilchrist. 69 Romney Street, London. S. of the Rev. Canon Henry Percy Thompson, M.A., Rector of Hayes, Kent, and Rural Dean of Beckenham, and Lilian Gilchrist, d. of Melicent Gilchrist and William Thomas, Esq., Solicitor's Department, Somerset House. B. at Battersea 10 May 1893; m. 1932, Hester M. Barnes. Educ. at Winchester, and Brasenose Coll., Oxford. Publisher with the firm of Jonathan Cape of 11 Gower Street, London 1923-32. A Liberal. Unsuccessfully contested the Torquay division of Devonshire in 1922. Elected for the Torquay division of Devonshire in December 1923 and sat until he was defeated in October 1924. Managing Director of Lovat, Dickson and Thompson 1933-36. Served with Royal West Kent Regiment 1914-18 and 1939-45. Died 7 February 1969. [1924 2nd ed.]

THOMSON, Sir Frederick Charles, Bart., K.C. 8 Egerton Place, London. Carlton, and Athenaeum. S. of James Wishart Thomson, Esq., Shipowner, of Leith. B. 27 May 1875; m. 1904, Constance Margaret, d. of Hamilton A. Hotson, Esq., General Manager of the British Linen Bank. Educ. at Edinburgh Academy and University, and at University Coll., Oxford. An Advocate of the Scottish Bar 1901; Barrister-at-Law, Inner Temple 1904; K.C. 1923. Lieut. Scottish Horse, and Lovat Scouts; served in Egypt and Salonika 1916-18. Parliamentary Private Secretary to Sir Robert Horne 1919-22; Junior Lord of the Treasury February to April 1923; Solicitor-Gen. for Scotland April 1923-January 1924; Junior Lord of the Treasury November 1924-January 1928; Vice-Chamberlain of H.Ms. Household January 1928-June 1929 and September-November 1931; Treasurer of H.Ms. Household November 1931-April 1935. Scottish Unionist Whip February to April 1923, and from 1924 to 1935. Created Bart. 1929. A Conservative. Sat for S. Aberdeen from December 1918 until his death on 21 April 1935. [1935]

THOMSON, Sir James Douglas Wishart, Bart. Continued in House after 1945: full entry in Volume IV.

THOMSON, Walter Trevelyan. 17 Albert Road, Middlesbrough. The Corner, Old Battersby, Nr. Great Ayton, Yorkshire. S. of Thomas James Thomson, Esq., Ironfounder, of Stockton-on-Tees. B. 30 April 1875 at Stockton-on-Tees; m. 1907, Hilda Mary, d. of the Rev. J.G. Tolley, of London. Educ. at Ackworth School, and Bootham School, Yorkshire. An Iron and Steel Merchant. Member of Middlesbrough Borough Council from 1904; J.P. for Middlesbrough 1912. Served in the ranks with the Expeditionary Force 1917-19. A Liberal. Sat for Middlesbrough W. from December 1918 until his death on 8 February 1928. [1928]

THOMSON, Rt. Hon. Sir William Lowson Mitchell, Bart. See MITCHELL-THOMSON, Rt. Hon. Sir William Lowson, Bart.

THORNE, George Rennie. 11 Great James Street, Bedford Row, London. Coalway Road, Wolverhampton. National Liberal. S. of George Thorne, Esq., Collector of Inland Revenue. B. 12 October 1853 at Longside, near Peterhead, N.B.; m. 1881, Susan Mary, d. of Thomas Jones, Esq., J.P., of Newtown. Educ. at Tettenhall Coll. Admitted a Solicitor 1876; took Hons. Final Exam.; received Law Society Prize. An Alderman of Wolverhampton; Mayor 1902-03, and Chairman of the S. Staffordshire Joint Smallpox Hospital Board. Chief Non-Coalition Liberal Whip February 1919-February 1923. A Liberal. Unsuccessfully contested W. Wolverhampton in 1895 and S. Wolverhampton in 1898. Sat for E. Wolverhampton from May 1908 until he retired in May 1929. Vice-Chairman of Parliamentary Liberal Party 1923. A Baptist. President of W. Midland Federation of Evangelical Free Church Councils 1933-34. Died 20 February 1934.   [1929]

THORNE, Rt. Hon. William James, C.B.E. 5 Endsleigh Gardens, London. S. of Thomas and Emma Thorn. B. 8 October 1857 (his birth was registered under the name of Thorn but he always used the spelling Thorne); m. 1st, 9 February 1879, Harriet, d. of John Hallam, Esq.; secondly, 1895, Emily, d. of William Byford Esq.; thirdly, 1925, Rebecca Cecilia, d. of Thomas Sinclair, Esq. (she died 1926); fourthly, 26 April 1930, Beatrice, d. of J. Collins, Esq. Founder and Gen. Secretary of the National Union of General and Municipal Workers 1889-1934; a member of West Ham Town Council from 1890; Dept. Mayor 1898; Mayor 1917-18; member of the Trade Union Congress Parliamentary Committee 1894-1934. J.P. A Labour Member. Unsuccessfully contested West Ham S. in 1900. Sat for West Ham S. from January 1906-December 1918. Elected for the Plaistow division of West Ham in December 1918 and sat until he retired in June 1945. President of T.U.C. 1912. PC. 1945. C.B.E. 1930. Chairman of Social Democratic Federation 1930. Died 2 January 1946.   [1945]

THORNEYCROFT, George Edward Peter. Continued in House after 1945: full entry in Volume IV.

THORNEYCROFT, Harry. Continued in House after 1945: full entry in Volume IV.

THORNTON, Maxwell Ruthven. 2. Lyall Street, Belgrave Square, London. Wellington, Reform, and National Liberal. S. of George Ruthven Thornton, Esq., M.A., Vicar of St. Barnabas, Addison Road, Kensington, and Teresa, d. of John Labouchere, Esq. B. at Bengeo, Hertfordshire 11 July 1878; m. 9 December 1909, Katharine, d. of Edward Yates, Esq. Educ. at St. Paul's. A Solicitor 1901; Advocate and Solicitor Straits Settlements 1903; acting member of the Legislative Council of the Straits Settlements April to October 1908. A Liberal. Elected for the Tavistock division of Devon in November 1922 and sat until he was defeated in October 1924. Died 30 August 1950.   [1924 2nd ed.]

THORNTON-KEMSLEY, Colin Norman. Continued in House after 1945: full entry in Volume IV.

THORP, Linton Theodore, K.C. 3 Hare Court, Temple, London. Wisby, Burtons Lane, Chalfont St. Giles, Buckinghamshire. Carlton. S. of F.W.T. Thorp, Esq., Solicitor, of Roseneath, Marlow. B. 21 February 1884; m. 25 July 1912, Stella, d. of J.F.W. Silk, Esq., M.D., M.R.C.S., of Dartmouth. Educ. at Manchester Grammar School, University Coll., London, and London University, LL.B. A Barrister-at-Law, Lincoln's Inn 1906; Judge of Supreme Court, Egypt 1919-21, of Ottoman Porte 1921-24. K.C. 1932. Recorder of Saffron Walden and Maldon 1932-50. Maj. R.A., R. of O.; served overseas 1914-19. A National Conservative. Unsuccessfully contested Nelson and Colne in May 1929. Elected for that seat in October 1931 and sat until he was defeated in November 1935. Resigned the Conservative Whip in May 1935 and sat as an Independent Conservative until November 1935. Bencher of Lincoln's Inn 1936. Unsuccessfully contested the Farnham division of Surrey in March

1937 as an Independent Conservative supported by the Liberty Restoration League. Chancellor of Diocese of Chelmsford 1948-50. Chairman of Essex Quarter Sessions 1946-50, Dept.-Chairman 1936-46. Died 6 July 1950. [1935]

THORPE, Capt. John Henry, O.B.E. Farrar's Buildings, Temple, London. St. George's Vicarage, Stockport. Carlton. S. of John Henry Thorpe, Esq., Archdeacon of Macclesfield, and Vicar of St. George's, Stockport. B. at Cork 7 August 1887; m. 1922, Ursula, d. of Sir J. Norton-Griffiths, MP. Educ. at Leatherhead, and Trinity Coll., Oxford. Barrister-at-Law, called Inner Temple Michaelmas 1911, Bencher 1941. Capt. 7th Battalion Manchester Regiment. Served in the European War; mentioned in despatches; O.B.E. 1919. A Conservative. Elected for the Rusholme division of Manchester in October 1919 and sat until he was defeated in December 1923. Recorder of Blackburn 1925-44. K.C. 1935. Dept.-Chairman of Middlesex Quarter Sessions 1941-44. Chairman of Central Price Regulation Committee 1942-44. Died 31 October 1944. [1923]

THURTLE, Ernest. Continued in House after 1945: full entry in Volume IV.

TICKLER, Thomas George. Shirley Lodge, Langley, Buckinghamshire. Constitutional, St. Stephen's, and Royal Automobile. S. of George Tickler, Esq., of Withern, Lincolnshire. B. 1852 at Withern; m. 1878, Fanny Louisa, d. of W.T. Wells, Esq., of The Hall, Withern. Educ. at Louth Grammar School. Was articled as an Engineer in Hull 1872-77. A Jam Manufacturer at Grimsby and Southall. Member of Grimsby Town Council 1896-1911; Mayor 1907. J.P. for Lincolnshire. A Unionist. Elected for Grimsby in May 1914; re-elected there in December 1918 and sat until he retired in October 1922. Died 19 January 1938. [1922]

TILLETT, Benjamin. Transport House, Smith Square, London. S. of Benjamin Tillett, Esq., Labourer, of Bristol. B. at Bristol 1860; m. 1882, Jane Tompkins

(she died 1936). Was variously employed until he joined the Royal Navy; later joined the Merchant Service. Settled at the docks and organized the Dockers' Union, of which he was Gen. Secretary from its inception in 1887 until it became part of the Transport and General Workers' Union in 1922. Secretary to the Political and International Department of the latter Union. Alderman London County Council 1892-98. A Labour Member. Unsuccessfully contested W. Bradford in 1892 and 1895, Eccles in 1906, and Swansea Town in January 1910. Elected for N. Salford in November 1917 as a 'Pro-War Labour' candidate. Returned for N. Salford from December 1918 until defeated in October 1924. Re-elected again in May 1929 and sat until he was defeated in October 1931. Member of General Council of T.U.C. 1921-31, President of T.U.C. 1929. Congregationalist lay preacher. Died 27 January 1943.

[1931 2nd ed.]

TINKER, John Joseph. 30 Wolseley Road, St. Helens. B. at Little Hulton 1875. Began work at the pithead at the age of 10. Miners' Agent for St. Helens from 1913. Joined the army 1915. Member of St. Helens Town Council 1919. Parliamentary Private Secretary to the Rt. Hon. S. Walsh January-October 1924, and to the Rt. Hon. A.V. Alexander, 1st Lord of the Admiralty June 1929-August 1931. A Labour Member. Sat for Leigh from December 1923 until he retired in June 1945. Died 30 July 1957. [1945]

TINNÉ, John Abraham. Daresbury Hall, Warrington. Union. S. of John Ernest Tinné, Esq., Sugar Planter and Shipowner, of Liverpool. B. 27 November 1877; m. 1906, Kathleen Heron, d. of Hon. A.P.P. Mackey, M.C.P., of Demerara. Educ. at Eton, and University Coll., Oxford; M.A. Partner in the firms of Sandbach Tinné and Company, of Liverpool, and of Sandbach Parker and Company, of Demerara, from 1902. Director of West India Company Limited, of Montreal; of Sandbach's (Trinidad) Limited; and of Demerara Company Limited. J.P. for Cheshire. Capt. R.F.A. 1916-19. Parliamentary Private Secretary to Sir Burton Chadwick 1927-January 1928, and to H.G. Williams January 1928-June 1929 when Parliamentary Secretary to Board of Trade. A Conservative. Elected for the Wavertree division of Liverpool in October 1924 and sat until he resigned in June 1931. Died 22 September 1933.   [1931 2nd ed.]

TITCHFIELD, William Arthur Henry Cavendish-Bentinck, Marq. of. 15 Eaton Square, London. Welbeck Woodhouse, Workshop, Nottinghamshire. S. of 6th Duke of Portland, B. 16 March 1893; m. 12 August 1915, Ivy, d. of Lord Algernon Gordon Lennox. Educ. at Eton, and Royal Military Coll., Sandhurst. Capt. Royal Horse Guards; served in France with R.H.G. August 1914-15 and 1916-18; Aide-de-Camp to Lieut.-Gen. Sir Graham Byng, March 1915-June 1916. Lord-Lieut. of Nottinghamshire 1939-62. Assistant Government Whip 1927-January 1928; a Junior Lord of the Treasury January 1928-June 1929, and in the National Government September–November 1931. A Conservative. Sat for the Newark division of Nottinghamshire from November 1922 until April 1943, when he succeeded to the Peerage as Duke of Portland. K.G. 1948. Chancellor of Nottingham University 1954-71. Died 21 March 1977.   [1943]

TODD, Alan Livesey Stuart. 33 Rossetti Gardens Mansions, London. Woodstock House, Woodstock, Oxfordshire. S. of Richard Stuart Todd, Esq., of Birmingham. B. 3 June 1900; m. Cynthia, d. of H. Sanders, Esq., of Paignton. Educ. at Wellington, and Magdalen Coll., Oxford. A Barrister-at-Law, Inner Temple 1924. Member of Chelsea Borough Council 1928-37. A Conservative. Elected for the Kingswinford division of Staffordshire in October 1931 and sat until he was defeated in November 1935. Member of Worcestershire County Council 1938-76, Alderman from 1953. C.B.E. 1958. J.P. for Staffordshire. Executive Director of National Association of Drop Forgers and Stampers 1948-69. Died 14 August 1976.   [1935]

TODD, Lieut.-Col. Alfred John Kennett. 109 St. George's Square, London. Little-houghton Hall, Alnwick, Northumberland. Cavalry. S. of George Todd, Esq. B. 13 April 1890; m. 26 January 1920, Edith Mary, d. of William Ernest Gray, Esq., of Blackheath. Educ. at Rugby. Capt. Queen's Bays; served in France 1915-18; Lieut.-Col. Commanding 7th Northumberland Fusiliers from 1933. Conservative Agent for Berwick-upon-Tweed from 1925. J.P. for Northumberland. A Conservative. Elected for Berwick-upon-Tweed in May 1929; returned unopposed in October 1931 and sat until he was defeated in November 1935. Resigned the Conservative Whip in May 1935 and sat as an Independent Conservative until the dissolution. Member of Hampshire County Council 1949-53 and Bath City Council 1957-63. Died 27 August 1970.   [1935]

TOMLINSON, George. Continued in House after 1945: full entry in Volume IV.

TOMLINSON, Robert Parkinson. Poulton-le-Fylde, Preston. National Liberal. S. of William Ormond Tomlinson, Esq., of Poulton-le-Fylde, Preston, B. 20 May 1881. Unmarried. Educ. at Barnes's Grammar School, Poulton-le-Fylde, and at Claremont Coll., Blackpool. A Corn Merchant. J.P. for Lancaster; member of Poulton-le-Fylde Urban District Council 1905-43. Chairman of Finance Company and of Rating and Valuation Company. A Liberal. Unsuccessfully contested the Fylde division of Lancashire in December 1923. Sat for the Lancaster division of Lancashire from February 1928 until he was defeated in May 1929. Unsuccessfully contested Lancaster in November 1935. Vice-President of Methodist Conference 1938. Died 3 June 1943.   [1929]

TOOLE, Joseph. Longford House, Victoria Park, Manchester. B. at Salford 1887; m. 1908, Margaret Dearden. Educ. at Mount Carmel Roman Catholic School, Salford. Began life as a newspaper boy; worked in foundry. Member of Manchester City Council from 1919, Lord Mayor 1936-37; J.P. for Manchester. A Labour Member. Unsuccessfully contested the Everton division of Liverpool in 1922. Elected for Sal-

357

ford S. in December 1923, defeated October 1924. Re-elected for Salford S. in May 1929 and sat until he was defeated in October 1931. Unsuccessfully contested Salford S. in November 1935 and, as an Independent Labour candidate, the Skipton division of the W. Riding of Yorkshire in January 1944, when he was expelled from the Labour Party for breaking the wartime electoral truce. Died 4 June 1945.

[1931 2nd ed.]

TOOTILL, Robert, C.B.E. Westfield, South Shore, Blackpool. S. of James Tootell, Esq. B. 23 October 1850 at Chorley, Lancashire (his birth was registered under the name Tootell but he used the spelling Tootill); m. 1875, Jane, d. of James Smith, Esq. Self-Educ. Was Labour Correspondent to Board of Trade. Member of Bolton Town Council for 26 years from 1888. Registrar of Births and Deaths, and for 20 years Secretary of Bolton Trades Council. C.B.E. 1918. A Labour Member. Elected for Bolton in September 1914, and returned unopposed for that division in December 1918. Sat until he retired in October 1922. Methodist local preacher. Secretary of Machine and Labourers' Union. J.P. for Bolton and Blackpool. Vice-President of British Workers' League 1916-18. Died 2 July 1934. [1922]

TOUCHE, Gordon Cosmo. Continued in House after 1945: full entry in Volume IV.

TOUT, William John. 18 Hare Hill Street, Todmorden. B. 1870. A Weaver at Todmorden; officially connected with the Weavers' Amalgamation. A Labour Member. Unsuccessfully contested the Fylde division of Lancashire in 1918. Elected for Oldham November 1922 and again in December 1923, defeated October 1924. Unsuccessfully contested Oldham in June 1925. Elected for the Sowerby division of the W. Riding of Yorkshire in May 1929 and sat until he was defeated in October 1931. Unsuccessfully contested the same division in November 1935. Died 24 February 1946. [1931 2nd ed.]

TOWNEND, Arnold Ernest. 25 Euston Road, London. Edale, Norman Road, Sale, Cheshire. S. of John Townend, Esq., of Salford. B. 1880; m. 1904, Florrie, d. of W.E. Parrish, Esq., of Sale. Educ. at Woodhouses Church School. A Railway Clerk from 1896. A Labour Member. Unsuccessfully contested the Blackley division of Manchester in 1918 and 1922. Unsuccessfully contested Stockport in December 1923 and October 1924. Elected for Stockport in September 1925 and sat until he was defeated in October 1931. Unsuccessfully contested Carlisle in November 1935. J.P. for Lancashire. Mayor of Southport 1955-56. Died 1968.

[1931 2nd ed.]

TOWNLEY, Maximilian Gowran. Melchbourne, Sharnbrook, Bedfordshire. Carlton. S. of Charles Watson Townley, Esq., Lord-Lieut. of Cambridgeshire from 1874-93. B. 22 June 1864 at Fulbourn, Cambridgeshire; m. 1902, Hon. Ellen Sydney St. John, eld. d. of the 15th Baron St. John of Bletsoe. Educ. at Eton, and Trinity Coll., Cambridge; M.A. A Land Agent; J.P. for Bedfordshire 1908. A Coalition Unionist. Elected for mid Bedfordshire in December 1918 and sat until he was defeated in November 1922. Unsuccessfully contested the Isle of Ely in December 1923. Died 12 December 1942. [1922]

TOWNSHEND, Maj.-Gen. Sir Charles Vere Ferrers, K.C.B., D.S.O. Vere Lodge, Raynham, Norfolk. Bachelors', Naval & Military, Brooks's, and White's. Union, Paris. A cousin of the 6th Marq. Townshend, and grand-s. of Lord George Townshend. B. 21 February 1861; m. 1898, Alice, d. of Comte Cahen d'Anvers. Entered the army in 1881, and had a distinguished career, becoming Maj.-Gen. in 1911. Served in the Soudan Expedition with the Mounted Infantry, in the Nile Expedition with the Guards Camel Corps, in the Hunza Nagar Expedition, and as Commander of the garrison at Chitral Fort during the siege (thanked by the Government of India). Was in the Dongola and Nile Expeditions of 1898 and in South Africa 1899-1900. In the European war became famous for his work in Mesopotamia; taken prisoner at

Kut; K.C.B. 1916. An Independent Conservative. Elected for The Wrekin division of Shropshire in November 1920 as a supporter of Horatio Bottomley's Independent Parliamentary Group but accepted the Conservative Whip from February 1922 until he retired in October 1922. D.S.O. 1898. Died in Paris 18 May 1924.   [1922]

TRAIN, Sir John. Cathkin, Carmunnock, Lanarkshire. Carlton, Constitutional, Royal Automobile, and Conservative. Conservative (Edinburgh), and Royal Scots Automobile, (Glasgow). S. of James Train, Esq. B. 8 May 1873; m. March 1898, Sarah, d. of Charles Wark, Esq. A Building Contractor. Vice-Convener of the County of Lanark 1923-30, County Councillor 1916-30; Deacon-Convener of the Trades of Glasgow 1927-29; Dept.-Lieut., and J.P. Glasgow, and J.P. for Lanark. Knight Bach. 1936. Unsuccessfully contested the Rutherglen division of Lanarkshire as a Coalition Liberal in November 1922. Elected for the Cathcart division of Glasgow as a Conservative in May 1929 and sat until his death on 18 March 1942.   [1942]

TREE, Arthur Ronald Lambert Field. Ditchley Park, Enstone, Oxfordshire. Buck's, Turf, and White's. S. of Arthur Tree, Esq., and Countess Beatty. B. 26 September 1897; m. 1st, 4 May 1920, Nancy, widow of Henry Field, Esq., of Chicago and d. of Moncure Perkins, Esq., of Richmond, Virginia; secondly, 1947, Mary Endicott Fitzgerald, d. of Rt. Rev. Malcolm Peabody, of Syracuse, N.Y. Educ. at Winchester. A Journalist, 1921-27; Managing Editor of *The Forum*, New York 1923-27. Parliamentary Private Secretary to R.S. Hudson, Esq., Minister of Pensions 1936, when Parliamentary Secretary Ministry of Health 1936, and when Secretary of Overseas Trade Department May 1937-November 1938, to Sir John Reith January-May 1940, to the Rt. Hon. Alfred Duff Cooper May 1940, and to the Rt. Hon. Brendan Bracken July 1941-January 1943, successively Ministers of Information. A Trustee of the Wallace Collection 1941. A National Conservative. Elected for the Harborough division of Leicestershire in November 1933 and sat

until he was defeated in July 1945. As a security measure in 1940-43 the Prime Minister frequently used his house in Ditchley as an alternative to Chequers. Parliamentary Secretary to Ministry of Town and County Planning May-July 1945. Died 14 July 1976.   [1945]

TREVELYAN, Rt. Hon. Sir Charles Philips, Bart. 14 Great College Street, London. Wallington, Cambo, Morpeth. 1917. S. of the Rt. Hon. Sir George O. Trevelyan, 2nd Bart., O.M., MP. B. 28 October 1870; m. 6 January 1904, Mary Katharine, d. of Sir Hugh Bell, 2nd Bart. Educ. at Harrow, and Trinity Coll., Cambridge; D.C.L. Durham University. Lord-Lieut. of Northumberland 1930-49. Private Secretary to Lord Houghton when Lord-Lieut. of Ireland 1892-93. Succeeded as Bart. 1928. Charity Commissioner 1906-08; Parliamentary Secretary to Board of Education 1908-14, resigned as protest against the Great War. President of Board of Education January-November 1924, and from June 1929 to March 1931 when he resigned. PC. 1924. Unsuccessfully contested N. Lambeth as a Liberal in 1895. Sat for the Elland division of Yorkshire from 1899-1918 as a Liberal. Unsuccessfully contested the same division as an Independent in December 1918 Elected as Labour Member for Newcastle-upon-Tyne Central division in November 1922 and sat until he was defeated in October 1931 standing as an Independent Labour candidate. Died 24 January 1958.   [1931 2nd ed.]

TROYTE, Lieut.-Col. Sir Gilbert John Acland, C.M.G., D.S.O. Huntsham Court, Bampton, Devon. Army & Navy. S. of Col. C.A.W. Troyte, of Huntsham Court, Bampton. B. 4 September 1876; m. 1909, Gwladys Eleanor, d. of E.H. Quicke, Esq., of Newton St. Cyres, Exeter. Educ. at Eton, and Trinity Hall, Cambridge. Joined K.R.R.C. 1899; served in South African War 1900-02, in Somaliland 1903-04, in France 1914-18. J.P., and County Alderman for Devon. A Conservative. Unsuccessfully contested the Tiverton division of Devon in June and December 1923. Sat for the Tiverton division of Devon from October 1924 until he retired in June 1945. President of Central Land-owners' Association 1937-39. Knighted January 1945. Died 27 April 1964.

[1945]

TRYON, Maj. Rt. Hon. George Clement. 19 Eaton Square, London. Manor House, Great Durnford, Salisbury. Only s. of Vice-Admiral Sir George Tryon, K.C.B., and Hon. Clementina Charlotte Heathcote, sister of 1st Earl of Ancaster. B. 15 May 1871; m. 28 February 1905, Hon. Averil Vivian, d. of 1st Baron Swansea. Educ. at Eton, and Royal Military Coll., Sandhurst. Joined Grena-dier Guards 1890, and retired as Capt. 1902, rejoined 1914; Brevet Maj 1917; served in South African War 1899-1900. Under-Secretary for Air December 1919 April 1920; Parliamentary Secretary Ministry of Pensions April 1920-October 1922; Minister of Pensions October 1922-January 1924, November 1924-June 1929 and September 1931-June 1935; Post-master-Gen. June 1935-April 1940. PC. 1922. A Conservative. Unsuccessfully contes-ted Brighton in January 1906. Sat for Brighton from January 1910 until April 1940 when he was created Baron Tryon. Chancellor of Duchy of Lancaster April-May 1940. First Commissioner of Works May-October 1940. Parliamentary Secre-tary to Ministry of Pensions October-November 1940. Died 24 November 1940.

[1940]

TUBBS, Stanley William. 9 Hanover Terrace, Regent's Park, London. Ulern-croft, Wotton-under-Edge, Gloucester-shire. Junior Carlton, St. Stephen's, 1900, and Royal Automobile. S. of Henry Thomas Tubbs, Esq., J.P., of Lether Court, Church End, Finchley, and Littlestone-on-Sea, Kent. B. 22 March 1871 at Finchley; m. 1st, 1901, Ellen Emma, d. of Compton Prescott, Esq. (she died 1918); secondly, 1921, Evelyn Sherbrook, 2nd d. of C.A. Crane, Esq., of the Reddings, Cheltenham. Educ. privately. A member of Gloucester-shire County Council from 1904-08; J.P. for Gloucestershire 1905. A Conservative. Sat for the Stroud division of Gloucestershire from November 1922 until he was defeated in December 1923. Member of Executive

Committee of National Union of Conser-vative and Unionist Associations 1925-30. Created Bart. 1929. High Sheriff of Gloucestershire 1931. President of Gloucestershire County Cricket Club. Died 11 December 1941.

[1923]

TUFNELL, Lieut. Commander Richard Lionel, R.N. 46 Eaton Square, London. Manor House, Calmsden, Cirencester. 4 Park Terrace, Cambridge. S. of Lieut.-Col. Edward Tufnell, at one time Conservative MP for S.E. Essex, and Ellen Bertha, d. of the Rev. E.E. Gubbins, Rector of Upham, Hampshire. B. 10 December 1896; m. 8 June 1922, Eleanor Dorothy, d. of J.A.K. Falconer, Esq., of Calmsden Manor, Cirencester. Educ. at Osborne, at Dart-mouth, and Trinity Coll., Cambridge, M.A. Joined R.N. 1909, retired 1921. Served in Grand Fleet 1914-19. Member of Board of Guardians and Public Assistance for St. George's, Westminster 1928-31. A National Conservative. Elected for Cam-bridge in February 1934 and sat until he was defeated in July 1945. Died in Spain 1 October 1956.

[1945]

TURNER, Sir Ben, C.B.E. The Homes-tead, Carlton Avenue, Batley. 1917. S. of Jonathan Turner, Esq. B. 25 August 1863; m. October 1884, Elizabeth, d. of J. Hop-kinson Esq. (she died 1939). Educ. at Dame and National Schools. A Trade Union Official. Town Councillor, Alderman, Mayor, and Freeman of Batley; County Alderman and J.P. for the W. Riding of Yorkshire. Secretary for Mines June 1929-June 1930. A Labour Member. Unsuccess-fully contested Dewsbury in January 1906 and April 1908 and Batley and Morley in December 1918. Elected for Batley and Morley in November 1922 and again in December 1923, defeated October 1924. Re-elected for Batley and Morley in May 1929 and sat until he was defeated in October 1931. President of National Union of Textile Workers 1922-29. Chairman of T.U.C. 1928. O.B.E. 1917; C.B.E. 1930. Knighted June 1931. Chairman of National Executive Committee of Labour Party 1911-12. Died 30 September 1942. [1931 2nd ed.]

TURNER-SAMUELS, Moss. Continued in House after 1945 : full entry in Volume IV.

TURTON, Sir Edmund Russborough, Bart. Upsall Castle, Thirsk. Russborough, Blessington, Co. Wicklow. Brooks's, Carlton, St. Stephen's, and Baldwin. Kildare Street, Dublin. Yorkshire, York. S. of Maj. Edmund Henry Turton, 3rd Dragoon Guards, and Lady Cecilia, d. of 4th Earl of Milltown. B. 1 November 1857; m. 9 August 1888, Clementina, d. of the Rt. Hon. Sir Spencer Ponsonby Fane, G.C.B. Educ. at Eton, and Brasenose Coll., Oxford. Was called to the bar at the Inner Temple 1882; Under-Secretary to Royal Commission on Industrial Schools and Reformatories 1881 ; Chairman of North Riding Quarter Sessions from 1898; Chairman County Licensing Committee; Director London Joint City and Midland Bank and Yorkshire Insurance Company; Chairman Railway Clearing House; J.P. and Dept.-Lieut. for the N. Riding of Yorkshire; member of London County Council from 1892-97. Master of the Bilsdale Hounds. Member of N. Riding of Yorkshire County Council from 1898, Alderman from 1919. Chairman of Standing Committees and a Referee of Private Bills. Member of the Speaker's Conference on Electoral Reform 1916-17, of the Royal Commission on London 1923. Bart. 1926. Unsuccessfully contested the Thirsk and Malton division of the N. Riding of Yorkshire as a Liberal in 1885, and the Richmond division of Yorkshire as a Gladstonian Liberal in 1886, 1892 and 1895. Returned as a Unionist for Thirsk and Malton from February 1915 until his death on 9 May 1929, the day before Parliament was dissolved. [1929]

TURTON, Robert Hugh. Continued in House after 1945: full entry in Volume IV.

TWIST, Henry. House of Commons, London. S. of Henry Twist, Esq., Miner. B. 30 January 1870 at Platt Bridge, Lancashire. Educ. at Platt Bridge Wesleyan School. A Miner from the age of 11, Checkweighman at Bamfurlong 1900. Agent of Lancashire and Cheshire Miners' Federation from 1906. A Labour Member. Sat for Wigan from Janurary to December 1910 when he was defeated. Elected for Leigh in November 1922 and sat until he retired in November 1923. Vice-President of Lancashire and Cheshire Miners' Federation 1929-34. Member of Abram Urban District Council 1905-08. A Congregationalist. J.P. for Lancashire. Died 16 May 1934. [1923]

UA BUACHALLA, Domhnall. See BUCKLEY, Donald.

VARLEY, Frank Bradley. 4 Caledon Road, Nottingham. S. of Thomas Henry Varley, Esq., of Alfreton, Miner. B. 18 June 1885; m. 1907, Alice, d. of Walter Maycock, Esq. Educ. part-time at Sheffield University. A Checkweighman, and Financial Secretary of the Nottinghamshire Miners' Association from 1921. Member of Executive of the Miners' Federation of Great Britain. A Labour Member. Elected for the Mansfield division of Nottinghamshire in December 1923 and October 1924. Sat until his death on 17 March 1929. Member of Derbyshire County Council 1913-19. Member of National Executive of Labour Party 1921-22. died 17 March 1929. [1929]

VAUGHAN, David John. The Ridgeway, Newport, Monmouthshire. Labour. S. of David Vaughan, Esq., of Tredegar, Monmouthshire. B. 15 November 1873; m. 17 September 1906, Kathleen, d. of J.E. Martin, Esq., of Dromore, Co. Down. Educ. at Council School, Tredegar. A Builder and Contractor. Member of Monmouth County Council from 1918 and Chairman Monmouth Standing Joint and other Committees. A Labour Member. Unsuccessfully contested Bristol S. in November 1922, December 1923 and October 1924. Elected for the Forest of Dean division of Gloucestershire in May 1929 and sat until he was defeated in October 1931. Wesleyan local preacher. Died 23 November 1938. [1931 2nd ed.]

VAUGHAN DAVIES, Matthew Lewis. 17 Hyde Park Gardens, London. Tan-y-Bwlch, Aberystwyth. Brooks's. S. of Matthew Davies, Esq., J.P. and Dept.-Lieut. B. at Tan-y-Bwlch 1840; m. 1889, Minnie, d. of

Thomas Powell, Esq., and widow of Alexander Jenkins, Esq. (she died 1926). Educ. at Harrow School. A J.P. and Dept.-Lieut. for Cardiganshire and High Sheriff 1875. Unsuccessfully contested Cardiganshire as a Conservative in 1885. Represented Cardiganshire as a Liberal from 1895 until January 1921 when he was created Baron Ystwyth. Died 21 August 1935. [1920]

VAUGHAN-MORGAN, Lieut.-Col. Sir Kenyon Pascoe, O.B.E. 1 Hans Place, London. West Clandon, Surrey. Carlton, Orleans, and Ranelagh. S. of Edward Vaughan-Morgan, Esq. B. 27 October 1873; m. 28 April 1897, Muriel, d. of John Collett, Esq. Educ. at Charterhouse, and in France and Germany. A Director and Vice-Chairman of the Morgan-Crucible Company Limited, London. Chairman of London Municipal Society, and of London and Greater London Playing Fields Association. Gov. of St. Thomas' and of other hospitals; Gen. Commissioner of Income Tax. Served with R.A.S.C. 1915-19; on Gen. Staff 1917; retired with rank of Lieut.-Col., Honorary Col. 64th (7th London Field Brigade, R.A., T.A.); O.B.E. 1919; Dept.-Lieut. London 1928. Knight Bach. 1929. A Conservative. Sat for E. Fulham from November 1922 until his death on 21 August 1933. [1933]

VIANT, Samuel Philip. Continued in House after 1945: full entry in Volume IV.

VICKERS, Douglas. Chapel House, Charles Street, Mayfair, London. Temple Dinsley, Hitchin, Hertfordshire. Tulloch Castle, Dingwall. Carlton, Wellington, St. Stephen's, and Prince's Racquet and Tennis. S. of Col. T.E. Vickers, C.B., and Frances Mary Vickers, d. of John Douglas, Esq. B. at Sheffield 1861; m. 1893, Katharine Adelaide, d. of Capt. Hon. H.W. Chetwynd, R.N., and sister of Visct. Chetwynd. Educ. at Marlborough. Chairman of Vickers Limited 1918-26, Director of Midland Railway, etc. Served 1880-94 in 1st (Hallamshire) Volunteer Battalion York and Lancaster Regiment retiring as Capt. J.P. for Derbyshire. A Conservative. Unsuccessfully con-

tested the Brightside division of Sheffield in both 1910 elections. Elected for the Hallam division of Sheffield in December 1918 and sat until he retired in October 1922. Treasurer of Sheffield University 1917-26. Died 23 November 1937. [1922]

VIVIAN, Henry Harvey. The Limes, Crouch End Hill, London. National Liberal. S. of William Henry and Mary Norris Vivian. B. 20 April 1868 at Cornwood, Devon. Educ. at Cornwood National School. A Garden Suburb and Town Planning Adviser. J.P. for Middlesex. A Liberal. Unsuccessfully contested S. Somerset in November 1911, Edmonton in December 1918 and Northampton in November 1922. Sat for Birkenhead from 1906 to December 1910 when he was defeated. Elected for the Totnes division of Devonshire in December 1923 and sat until he was defeated in October 1924. Secretary of Labour Co-partnership Association from 1890. A pioneer of co-pertnership housing schemes. Died 30 May 1930. [1924 2nd ed.]

WADDINGTON, Robert. Springfield, Haslingden, Rossendale, Lancashire. Constitutional. S. of William Waddington, Esq., of Rawtenstall. B. 13 December 1868; m. 1896, Pollie, d. of James Rothwell, Esq., of Haslingden, Managing Director of James Rothwell Limited, Cotton Spinners and Manufacturers. Educ. at St. Mary's School, Rawtenstall. Chairman of Hoyle and Company Limited, Shoe and Slipper Manufacturers, Rawtenstall; member of Empire Cotton Growing Corporation and of Dye Stuffs Advisory Licensing Commission. Member of Lancashire County Council and Haslingden Town Council; Chairman of Tramways and Electricity Committee 1911-20; Chairman of Higher Education Committee 1898-1911; Chairman of Finance Committee, Bury and District Joint Water Board 1910-16. A Conservative. Sat for Rossendale from 1918 to October 1922 when he retired; re-elected for Rossendale in December 1923 and again in October 1924 and sat until he retired in May 1929. Knighted 1937. Controller of Dyestuffs 1939-41. Died 25 June 1941. [1929]

WAKEFIELD, Sir William Wavell. Continued in House after 1945: full entry in Volume IV.

WALKDEN, Alexander George. 25 Euston Road, London. Meadowside, Great Bookham, Surrey. Labour Party. S. of Charles Henry Walkden, Esq., and Harriet, d. of T. Rogers, Esq. B. 11 May 1873; m. December 1898, Jennie, d. of Jessie Wilson, Esq. (she died 1934). Educ. at Merchant Taylors' School, Ashwell, Hertfordshire. Employed as a Clerk in Great Northern Railway; Gen. Secretary to the Railway Clerks' Association 1906-36; President of Trade Union Congress 1933. A Labour Member. Unsuccessfully contested W. Wolverhampton in December 1918 and March and November 1922, and Heywood and Radcliffe in October 1924. Elected for Bristol S. in May 1929, defeated October 1931. Re-elected for Bristol S. in November 1935 and sat until he retired in June 1945. Created Baron Walkden 1945. Capt. of the Yeoman of the Guard August 1945-July 1949. Died 25 April 1951. [1945]

WALKDEN, Evelyn. Continued in House after 1945: full entry in Volume IV.

WALKER, James. 99 Briar Avenue, Norbury, London. S. of John Walker, Esq., of Glasgow. B. 1883 at Glasgow; m. 1910, Ada, d. of John Chivers, Esq., of Oxford. Educ. at Ruskin Coll. Member of Glasgow City Council from 1914. J.P. for Lanarkshire. Chairman of Scottish T.U.C.; for 18 years Organizer of Iron and Steels Trades Association. Chairman of the National Executive Committee of the Labour Party 1940-41. A Labour Member. Unsuccessfully contested Rotherham in December 1918 and November 1922. Sat for Newport, Monmouthshire from May 1929-October 1931 when he was defeated. Elected for the Motherwell division of Lanarkshire in November 1935 and sat until his death in a road accident on 5 January 1945. [1945]

WALKER, Col. William Hall. Horsley Hall, Gresford. Sandy Brow, Tarporley, Cheshire. Sussex Lodge, Regent's Park, London. Carlton, Marlborough, Arthur's,

Hurlingham, and Coaching. S. of Sir Andrew Barclay Walker, Bart., of Osmaston, Derbyshire, and Eliza, d. of Capt. Reid, of Dunfermline, Fifeshire. B. 1856; m. 1896, Sophie Florence Lothrop, 2nd d. of A. Brinsley Sheridan, Esq., of Frampton, Dorset, and great-grand-d. of Richard Brinsley Sheridan, the statesman and orator. Educ. at Harrow. Managing Director of the firm of Peter Walker and Son Limited, Brewers; Honorary Col. of the Lancashire Artillery; Honorary Col. (T.D.) of 9th King's Liverpool; a Dept.-Lieut. for Lancashire; founder and donor of "The National Stud." A Unionist. Elected for the Widnes division of Lancashire in 1900 and sat until August 1919 when he was created Baron Wavertree. Member of Liverpool City Council. Died 2 February 1933. [1919]

WALKER-SMITH, Sir Jonah Walker. 22 Mansfield Street, London. Carlton. University, Edinburgh. S. of John Jonah Smith, Esq., Engineer and Manufacturer, of Watford. B. 22 November 1874; m. 27 April 1905, Maud Coulton, d. of Coulton Walker Hunter, Esq., of Barton Hall, Yorkshire. Educ. privately, and at King's Coll. (Engineering) London. Controller of Housing and Town Planning Local Government Board for Scotland 1910-19. Director of Housing, Ministry of Health 1919-25. M.-Inst.C.E., M.Inst.Mech.E., F.S.I., and Barrister-at-Law, Grays' Inn 1922. A Conservative. Elected for Barrow-in-Furness in October 1931 and sat until he was defeated in July 1945. Borough Engineer, Barrow-in-Furness 1902-08. City Engineer, Edinburgh 1908-10. Knighted 1925. Adopted the surname of Walker-Smith in lieu of Smith in 1934. Died 23 February 1964. [1945]

WALLACE, Capt. Rt. Hon. David Euan, M.C. 15 Grosvenor Square, London. Lavington Park, Petworth. Turf, Carlton, and Beefsteak. S. of John Wallace, Esq., of Glassingall, Dunblane. B. 20 April 1892; m. 1st, 1913, Lady Idina Sackville, d. of Gilbert, 8th Earl de la Warr (marriage dissolved in 1919); secondly, 1920, Barbara, d. of Sir Edwin Lutyens, R.A. Educ. at Harrow, and Royal Military Coll., Sandhurst. Joined 2nd Life Guards 1911. Served in France 1914-18; on staff of Military Attaché, British Embassy, Washington 1919; Aide-de-Camp to Gov.-Gen. of Canada 1920; Parliamentary Private Secretary (unpaid) to Rt. Hon. L.S.Amery when 1st Lord of the Admiralty 1922-23, and as Secretary of State for the Colonies November 1924-January 1928. Assistant Government Whip January 1928-January 1929. Junior Lord of the Treasury January-June 1929, and in 1st National Government September-November 1931. Civil Lord of the Admiralty November 1931. Parliamentary Under-Secretary of State, Home Office June 1935; Secretary of Overseas Trade Department November 1935; Parliamentary Secretary Board of Trade May 1937; Financial Secretary to the Treasury May 1938; Minister of Transport April 1939-May 1940. Senior Regional Commissioner for Civil Defence, London Region May 1940-January 1941. PC. 1936. A Conservative. Elected for the Rugby division of Warwickshire in November 1922, and defeated there in December 1923. Elected for Hornsey in October 1924 and sat until his death on 9 February 1941. [1941]

WALLACE, Harry Wright. Continued in House after 1945: full entry in Volume IV.

WALLACE, Sir John. St. Oswalds, Stormont Road, Highgate, London. Reform. S. of John Wallace, Esq., of Kirkcaldy. B. 1 July 1868; m. 1913, Mary, d. of James Graham Temple, Esq. Educ. at Kirkcaldy Public School. A Director of Michael Nairn and Company Limited, London and Kirkcaldy. Sat for Dunfermline Burghs from 1918-22 as a Coalition Liberal. Unsuccessfully contested Dunfermline in 1922 and 1923. Re-elected for Dunfermline in October 1931 as a Liberal Nationalist and sat until he was defeated in November 1935. Knighted 1935. Died 12 April 1949. [1935]

WALLACE, Thomas Browne. Regent House, Dromore, Co. Down. Constitutional. S. of Robert Smyth Wallace, Esq., Merchant. B. at Dromore, Co. Down 28 January 1865; m. 1891, Margaret, d. of James C. Patterson, Esq., of Aughnaskeagh House, Dromore. Educ. at Belfast Royal Academical

Institution, and Queen's Coll., Belfast. A Solicitor from 1887. A Unionist. Returned unopposed for W. Down in July 1921 and sat until January 1922 when he was appointed Chief Clerk of the High Court of Northern Ireland. Chief Clerk in Chancery and Registrar in Lunacy, High Court of Northern Ireland 1922-50. Died 28 April 1951. [1922]

WALLHEAD, Richard Collingham. 15 Valley Road, Welwyn Garden City, Hertfordshire. S. of Richard Wallhead, Esq. B. 28 December 1869 (his birth was registered under the name Richard Christopher but he adopted the name Collingham in lieu of Christopher); m. 1891, Ellen, d. of J. Staines, Esq. Educ. at St. Edward's Elementary School, Romford. A Decorator and Designer, Journalist, and Lecturer. Chairman of the ILP from 1920-23; member Bureau International Union of Socialist Parties (Vienna Union). Member of Manchester City Council 1919-21. A Labour Member. Unsuccessfully contested Coventry in 1918. Sat for the Merthyr division of Merthyr Tydvil from November 1922 until his death on 27 April 1934. Imprisoned for 2 months under the Defence of the Realm Act in 1917. Elected as an ILP member in 1931 but rejoined the Parliamentary Labour Party in September 1933, after resigning from the ILP. Died 27 April 1934. [1934]

WALSH, James Joseph. S. of James J. Walsh, Esq., of Bandon. B. 1880; m. Jennie Turner, of Cork. Educ. at Cork Christian Brothers School, and King's Coll., London. An employee in the telegraph service of the Cork Post Office. Was sentenced to death for complicity in the Irish Rebellion, but that sentence was commuted to one of penal servitude for life, and later he was released. Re-arrested 1919; escaped from Mountjoy Gaol. A Sinn Fein Member. Elected for Cork City in December 1918 but did not take his seat. Member of Dail for Cork City to 1927. A Pro-Treaty, later Cumann na nGaedheal Member. Alderman, Cork City Council 1918-26. Postmaster-Gen., later Minister for Posts and Telegraphs 1922-27. Died 3 February 1948. [1922]

WALSH, Rt. Hon. Stephen. 8 Swinley Road, Wigan. S. of John Walsh, Esq., of Kirkdale, Liverpool. B. 1859; m. 1885, Anne Adamson. Educ. at Kirkdale Schools, Liverpool. Started work in Coal Mine at the age of 14; Agent at Wigan for Lancashire and Cheshire Miners' Federation from 1901; Vice-Chairman of Miners' Conciliation Board; President of Wigan and District Trades Council. Dept.-Lieut. for Lancashire, and J.P. for Wigan and Lancashire. Parliamentary Secretary to Ministry of National Service March-July 1917, and to Local Government Board July 1917 to January 1919. Senior Vice-Chairman of the Labour Party November 1922. Secretary of State for War January-November 1924. PC. 1924. A Labour Member. Sat for the Ince division of S.W. Lancashire from 1906 until his death on 16 March 1929. Brought up as a Roman Catholic but joined the Church of England in early manhood. Member of Ashton-in-Makerfield Urban District Council 1894-1901. Supported the Coalition Government at the 1918 general election but resigned from the Government and withdrew his support in January 1919. Vice-President of Miners' Federation of Great Britain 1922-24. Died 16 March 1929. [1929]

WALTERS, Rt. Hon. Sir John Tudor. 26 Prince's Gate, London. Reform, Wellington, Royal Automobile, and Ranelagh. S. of John Tudor Walters, Esq. B. 1866; m. Mary, d. of William Hill, Esq., of Leicester. Educ. at Clitheroe Grammar School. J.P. for Leicestershire. Knighted 1912; PC. 1919. Paymaster-Gen. October 1919-October 1922 and September-November 1931; First President of Education Association of England and Wales; Chairman of Committee appointed to consider Post-War Housing, which reported in 1918; Chairman of London Housing Board. Founded the Industrial Housing Association Limited. Published *The Building of 12,000 Houses.* A Liberal. Sat for the Brightside division of Sheffield from 1906-22 when he was defeated. Unsuccessfully contested the Pudsey and Otley division of Yorkshire in December 1923. Elected for the Penryn and Falmouth division of Cornwall in May 1929 and sat until

he retired in October 1931. President of Housing and Town Planning Trust. Died 16 July 1933. [1931 2nd ed.]

WALTON, James. 101 Avenue Road, Wath-on-Dearne, Nr. Rotherham. S. of James and Sarah Walton. B. at Broomhill, near Barnsley 7 September 1867; m. 1889, d. of William Jackson, Esq., Educ. at Broomhill Board Schools. A Coal Miner employed at the Manners Main collieries till 28 December 1918. Member of Mexbro Trades Council; Secretary from 1908. Member Wath Urban District Council from 1912-15. Member of Food Control Committee. Labour Agent in recruiting campaign. Organizer for the N.D. and L.P. A Coalition National Democratic Party Member. Elected for the Don Valley division of the W. Riding of Yorkshire in December 1918 and sat until he was defeated in November 1922, standing as a Constitutional Labour candidate with the support of the National Democratic Party and unofficial Conservative support. Died January 1924. [1922]

WALTON, Sir Joseph, Bart. Rushpool Hall, Saltburn-by-the-Sea. Reform, Ranelagh, Royal Automobile, and National Liberal. S. of Joseph Walton, Esq., of Frosterley, Lead-Mine owner and Smelter. B. at Bollihope, Weardale 1849; m. 1880, Faith, d. of Robert Gill, Esq., Solicitor, of Middlesbrough. Educ. privately. A Colliery-Owner, etc. Commenced business at Middlesbrough in 1870, in coal and allied trades. A J.P. and Dept.-Lieut. for the N. Riding of Yorkshire and J.P. for Middlesbrough. Author of *China and the present Crisis,* 1900. He travelled much in America and the Colonies, Persia, India and Burma, and in China, Japan and Africa with a view to the promotion of British trade. Created Bart. 1910. A Liberal, in favour of Home Rule all round, and the Radical programme generally, and of an extension of British trade by means of Colonial development. Unsuccessfully contested the Doncaster division of Yorkshire in 1895. First elected for the Barnsley division of Yorkshire in 1897 and sat until 1918; returned unopposed for the new borough of Barnsley in December 1918 and sat until he retired in October 1922. A Wesleyan

365

Methodist. Died 8 February 1923.   [1922]

WARD, Col. Sir Albert Lambert, Bart., C.V.O., D.S.O. 12a Collingham Gardens, London. Carlton. S. of A.B. Ward, Esq., J.P. B. 7 November 1875; m. 1920, Constance, only d. of J.B. Tidmas, Esq., of Normanton-on-Soar and Sutton Bonington. Educ. at St. Paul's School, in Paris and Darmstadt. Commanded 2nd Battalion H.A.C. in France 1916-17. D.S.O. 1915. Parliamentary Private Secretary to W.C. Bridgeman, when Home Secretary 1922-23, and when First Lord of the Admiralty November 1924-26, to Sir Laming Worthington-Evans when Secretary of State for War April 1928-June 1929. A Lord Commissioner of the Treasury November 1931-May 1935; Vice-Chamberlain of H.M's. Household May-December 1935, Comptroller December 1935-May 1937, Treasurer May-October 1937. Created Bart. 1929. Col. Commanding Home Guard Zone 1940-42. A Conservative. Unsuccessfully contested W. Hull in December 1910. Sat for N.W. Hull from December 1918 until he was defeated in July 1945. Dept.-Lieut. for County of London. Died 21 October 1956.   [1945]

WARD, George. House of Commons, London. S. of William Ward, Esq., of Barwell, Leicestershire. B. 1878; m. 1906, Emily J. Haydon. J.P. for Leicestershire. A Boot Manufacturer at Barwell. Member of Leicestershire County Council. A Liberal. Elected for the Bosworth division of Leicestershire in December 1923 and sat until he was defeated in October 1924. Died 3 December 1951.   [1924 2nd ed.]

WARD, Irene Mary Bewick. Continued in House after 1945: full entry in Volume IV.

WARD, Peter Joseph. 11 Molesworth Street, Dublin. A Solicitor, practised in Donegal Town. Arrested in April 1920. A Sinn Fein Member. Elected for S. Donegal in December 1918 but did not take his seat. Member of Dail for S. Donegal to 1921, for Donegal 1921-24. A Pro-Treaty, later Cumann na nGaedheal Member.   [1922]

WARD, Lieut.-Col. John, C.B., C.M.G. Omsk, Weyhill, Andover. S. of Robert Ward, Esq., Journeyman Plasterer, of Weybridge. B. 1866; m. 1892, Lilian Elizabeth, d. of George Gibbs, Esq. (she died 1926). Worked as a navvy on the Manchester Ship Canal; a member of Social Democratic Federation; served in the Soudan 1885; founded the Navvies' Union 1889. J.P. for Co. of London, member of London Territorial Forces Association and of the Lord-Lieut.'s Advisory Committee for Co. London for the appointment of J.Ps. Lieut.-Col. P.W.P. Battalion Middlesex Regiment; served in Siberia 1918-19. Croix de Guerre 1919 of France, Czechoslovakia, and Italy; Japanese Order of the Sacred Treasure 3rd class 1920. A Constitutionalist. Sat for Stoke-on-Trent as a Liberal and Labour Member from 1906-18. Sat for the Stoke division of Stoke-on-Trent from December 1918 as an 'Independent Labour' Member with Liberal and Conservative, but not Labour support until he was defeated in May 1929. Died 19 December 1934.   [1929]

WARD, Sarah Adelaide. Grange Farm, Walsall Wood, Walsall. Century. D. of John Ainsworth, Esq., of Meaford, Stone, Staffordshire. B. 25 December 1895; m. 1921, William John Ward, Esq., a School Teacher. Educ. at Orme Girls' School. V.A.D. 9th Staffordshire detachment 1914-18. A Conservative. Elected for the Cannock division of Staffordshire in October 1931 and sat until she was defeated in November 1935. Unsuccessfully contested Lichfield and Tamworth in February 1950 and the Perry Barr division of Birmingham in October 1951. Member of Staffordshire County Council from 1950. Died 9 April 1969.   [1935]

WARD, Rt. Hon. William Dudley. 62 Portland Place, London. Windham. S. of W.H. Dudley Ward, Esq., and Hon. Eugénie Violet Brett, d. of 1st Lord Esher. B. 1877; m. 1913, Winifred, d. of Col. C. Birkin (divorced 1931). Educ. at Eton, and Trinity Coll., Cambridge; B.A. A Barrister, called Inner Temple 1904; was Assistant Private Secretary (unpaid) to Mr. Lewis Harcourt when First Commissioner of Works. Treasurer of H.M. Household and Liberal Whip December 1909-February 1912. Vice-Chamberlain of the Household and Liberal Whip from December 1917-October 1922. A Liberal. Elected for Southampton in 1906 and sat until he was defeated in November 1922. PC. 1922. Died at Calgary 11 November 1946. [1922]

WARD-JACKSON, Maj. Charles Lionel Atkins. Street Court, Kingsland, Herefordshire. Normanby Hall, North Riding of Yorkshire. Carlton, White's, Boodle's, and Cavalry. Yorkshire, York. S. of Rev. William Ward-Jackson, of Normanby Hall. B. 31 January 1869; m. 1908, Florence Olga, d. of J. Bennett, Esq., and Mrs. Onslow Traherne, of Bourne End. Educ. at Eton. Served with Yorkshire Hussars in South African War 1900-01, and in the European War with the Yorkshire Hussars and on the staff. A Coalition Unionist. Unsuccessfully contested S. Manchester in January 1910; elected for the Leominister division of Herefordshire in December 1918 and sat until November 1922 when he unsuccessfully contested the Harrow division of Middlesex. Died 28 April 1930. [1922]

WARDLAW-MILNE, Sir John Sydney, K.B.E. 311 Carrington House, Hertford Street, London. Grayswood Place, Haslemere. Carlton, Oriental, City of London, and Royal Cruising. S. of James Milne, Esq., Banker, of Helensburgh, N.B., and Elizabeth, d. of James Fleming Wardlaw, Esq., W.S. B. 1879; m. 1st, 1907, Aimée Margaret, d. of William Garden, Esq., of Uttershill, Penicuik, N.B. (she died 15 May 1933); secondly, 20 June 1935, Vyvien Mary, d. of E. St. Clair Bolton, Esq., and widow of Lieut.-Col. Montague Headland-Pike, O.B.E., M.C. (she died 1965). Educ. privately. Director of Turner, Morrison and Company, of Calcutta and Bombay until 1917. Ten years member Bombay Municipal Corporation; Additional member Government of Bombay's Legislative Council (twice); Viceroy's Council; Chairman Bombay Chamber of Commerce; Trustee of the Port of Bombay; Trustee of the City of Bombay Improvement Trust; J.P. and Honorary Magistrate, Bombay;

Director Bank of Bombay, etc.; President Government of India Shipping Advisory Board. Commanded 4th (Bombay) Artillery, Indian Defence Force 1916-19. Official Lecturer in U.S.A. for British Government upon Mesopotamia and Near Eastern questions 1918. Member of Imperial Economic Committee 1927-29, and of Joint Committee on Indian Reform 1934-35; Chairman of Select Committee on National Expenditure from 1939 to 1945 and of House of Commons Conservative Foreign Affairs Committee. K.B.E. 1932. A Conservative. Sat for the Kidderminster division of Worcestershire from November 1922 until he was defeated in July 1945. Assumed surname of Wardlaw-Milne in lieu of Milne in 1922. Died 11 July 1967. [1945]

WARDLE, George James. 107 Brownlow Road, New Southgate, London. S. of George and Ella Wardle. B. 15 May 1865 at Newhall, Derbyshire; m. 1889, Atla Matilda, d. of John Terry, Esq., of Keighley. Educ. at private schools and Wesleyan day-schools. A Journalist; Fellow of the Institute of Journalists. Started work as a factory lad, then became a Railway Clerk; Editor of the *Railway Review* 1898 to 1917. Acting Chairman of Labour Party 1916. Companion of Honour 1917. Parliamentary Secretary to Board of Trade August 1917-January 1919; Parliamentary Secretary to Ministry of Labour January 1919-March 1920. A Labour Member who continued to support the Coalition after 1918. Sat for Stockport from 1906 until he resigned in March 1920. J.P. for Hove 1928. Died 18 June 1947. [1920]

WARING, Maj. Walter. 23 Catherine Street, Westminster, London. The Mount, Salcombe, South Devon. Lennel, Coldstream, Scotland. Brooks's, and Guards'. S. of Charles Waring, Esq., MP for Poole, and Eliza, d. of Sir George Denys, Bart., of Draycott, Yorkshire. B. 11 August 1876; m. 1901, Lady Clementine Hay, d. of 10th Marq. of Tweeddale, and had two daughters. Educ. at Eton. Joined 1st Life Guards 1897; served in South Africa 1899-1900; mentioned in despatches; retired (Capt.) 1906; Master of the Horse to Lord-

Lieut. of Ireland 1906-07; Parliamentary Private Secretary (unpaid) to Sir E. Strachey, when Parliamentary Secretary to Board of Agriculture. Served in Yeomanry (Maj. 1914) in France 1915; Macedonia 1916-17; in N.I.D. 1918 (Legion of Honour). J.P. and Dept.-Lieut. for Berwickshire. Parliamentary Private Secretary to Mr. Churchill November 1919. A National Liberal. Unsuccessfully contested Wigtownshire in 1906. Sat for Banffshire from February 1907 to December 1918, for the Blaydon division of Durham from December 1918, and for Berwick and Haddington from November 1922 until he was defeated in December 1923. Unsuccessfully contested Wallsend as a Conservative in May 1929. Member of London County Council 1925-28. Died in Munich 16 November 1930.

[1923]

WARNE, George Henry. 18 The Drive, Gosforth, Newcastle-upon-Tyne. S. of William Warne, Esq., of Cramlington, Northumberland. B. 1881; m. 1904, Dorothy Isabel Fenwick. Educ. at Cramlington Elementary School. Entered the mines at 12 years of age. Trustee of the Northumberland Miners' Association; President of Northumberland and Durham Miners Approved Society; Junior Lord of the Treasury January-November 1924. Labour Whip. A Labour Member. Sat for the Wansbeck division of Northumberland from November 1922 until his death on 24 December 1928. Member of Ashington Urban District Council 1907-22, Chairman 1919-21. Member of Northumberland County Council 1919-24. Died 24 December 1928.

[1929]

WARNER, Sir Thomas Courtenay Theydon, Bart., C.B. 34 Grosvenor Gardens, London. Brettenham Park, Suffolk. Reform, and Bachelors'. S. of Edward Warner, Esq., MP for Norwich, of Highams, Woodford, Essex, and Maria, d. of Thomas Carr, Esq., of New Ross. B. in London 19 July 1857; m. 1883, Lady Leucha Diana Maude, d. of Earl of Montalt. Educ. at Eton, and Brasenose Coll., Oxford. Chairman of Warner Estate Company, and Law Land Company. J.P. for Somerset and Lord-Lieut. of Suffolk 1910-34. Alderman W. Suffolk County Council. A County Councillor for Essex 1889-1901; Col. 3rd Oxfordshire Light Infantry. President of Central Chamber of Agriculture 1906. Sheriff of Essex 1891; C.B. 1909. Director of National Service Eastern Regions 1917-18. Created Bart. 1910. A Radical. Unsuccessfully contested Coventry in 1885. Sat for N. Somerset from 1892-95 when he was defeated. First elected for the Lichfield division of Staffordshire in 1896 and sat until he retired in November 1923. President of Rural District Councils Association. Died 15 December 1934.

[1923]

WARNER, Brigadier-Gen. William Ward, C.M.G. 45B, Chester Square, London. Burwell House, Cambridgeshire. Carlton, and Cavalry. S. of Capt. George Augustus Alves Warner, I.C.S. B. 14 March 1867; m. 6 December 1899, Hon. Clarice May, d. of Robert, 1st Baron Borwick of Hawkshead. Joined Warwickshire Regiment 1887, 30th Lancers I.A. 1888-1907, Royal Air Force 1914-18. Director of Air Personal Service and of General Hydraulic Company Limited 1909; member London County Council from 1919-22. A Conservative. Unsuccessfully contested mid Bedfordshire in December 1923. Sat for mid Bedfordshire from October 1924 until he was defeated in May 1929. Died 21 March 1950.

[1929]

WARREN, Sir Alfred Haman, O.B.E. Mountain Ash, Wansted. S. of Richard Sambell Warren, Esq., of Callington. B. at Poplar 6 February 1856; m. 1896, Jane Blacey, d. of George William Castle, Esq., of Deal (she died 1926). Educ. at the local Wesleyan School. An Accountant and Secretary. Five years Mayor of Poplar 1913-18. Grand Master, Manchester Unity of Oddfellows 1911-12; President National Conference of Friendly Societies 1913. A Coalition Unionist. Elected for Edmonton in December 1918 and sat until he was defeated in November 1922. O.B.E. 1918. Knighted 1918. Died 1 August 1927.

[1922]

WARRENDER, Sir Victor Alexander George Anthony, Bart., M.C. 32 Charles

Street, London. Turf, Bucks, Beefsteak, and R.Y.S. S. of Vice-Admiral George Warrender, 7th Bart., K.C.V.O., C.B., and Lady Maud Ashley, d. of the 8th Earl of Shaftesbury. B. 23 June 1899; m. 1st, 1 June 1920, Dorothy, d. of Col. R.H. Rawson, MP (divorced 1945); secondly, 1948, Tania, d. of Dr. Michael Kolin, of Dubrovnik. Educ. at Eton. Lieut. R. of O.; Grenadier Guards; M.C. 1918. Succeeded as Bart. 1917. Parliamentary Private Secretary to Earl Winterton November 1924-January 1928; Assistant Whip Japan 1928-31; a Lord Commissioner of the Treasury November 1931-September 1932; Vice-Chamberlain of H.Ms. Household September 1932-May 1935, Comptroller May-June 1935; Parliamentary and Financial Secretary to the Admiralty June-November 1935 and April 1940-July 1945, to War Office November 1935-April 1940. A Conservative. Elected for the Grantham division of Lincolnshire and Rutland in December 1923 and sat until February 1942 when he was created Baron Bruntisfield.*   [1942]

WASON, John Cathcart. 40 Grosvenor Road, London. Pinlan, Pinwherry, Ayrshire. Reform. S. of Rigby Wason, Esq., MP for Ipswich, by Euphemia, d. of Peter McTier, Esq., of Galloway. B. 1848 at Corwar, Ayrshire; m. 1874, Alice Seymour, d. of Edward Bell. Esq., C.E. Educ. at Laleham and Rugby. A Farmer in New Zealand and Ayrshire; a Fellow of the Royal Geographical Society; was for a number of years member of the New Zealand House of Representatives. Was called to the bar at the Middle Temple 1887. Was elected for Orkney and Shetland in 1900 as a Liberal Unionist, but resigned, and was re-elected for Orkney and Shetland again in 1902 as an Independent Liberal in opposition to both Liberal and Liberal Unionist candidates. Later accepted the Liberal Whip, was re-elected as a Liberal in 1906 and sat until his death on 19 April 1921.   [1921]

WATERHOUSE, Rt. Hon. Charles. Continued in House after 1945: full entry in Volume IV.

WATERSON, Alfred Edward. 34 Harcourt Road, Wood Green, London. B. 5 August 1880; m. 1904, Gertrude, d. of Mr. and Mrs. Jesse Panter, of Derby. Educ. at Derby elementary school. A Co-operative and Labour Member. Elected for the Kettering division of Northamptonshire in December 1918 and sat until he was defeated in November 1922. Unsuccessfully contested Nottingham Central in May 1930 and October 1931. National organizer of Co-operative Party 1922-45. Died 25 November 1964.   [1922]

WATKINS, Frederick Charles. Parham, Woodbridge, Suffolk. S. of Frank Watkins, Esq., of Hampstead. B. 24 February 1883; m. 1908, Enid, d. of William Hall, Esq., of Rochester. President of the Railway Clerks' Association. J.P. for Buckinghamshire 1923. Parliamentary Private Secretary to the Rt. Hon. Herbert Morrison Secretary of State Home Office July 1942-May 1945. A Labour Member. Unsuccessfully contested the Aylesbury division of Buckinghamshire in December 1923 and October 1924. Elected for central Hackney in May 1929, defeated October 1931. Re-elected for Central Hackney in November 1935 and sat until he retired in June 1945. Died 31 January 1954.   [1945]

WATSON, Sir Francis. 91 Victoria Street, London. Torrack's Hill, Pool-in-Wharfedale. Carlton. S. of Thomas Adam Watson, Esq., of Beulah, Idle. B. 7 January 1864; m. 10 August 1892, Maude, d. of William Glossop, Esq., of Endsleigh, Hull. Educ. at Bradford Grammar School, and in France. A Solicitor admitted 1886; head of the firm of Watson, Son and Smith, Bradford. Member of Bradford City Council 1899-1907. Chairman of Bradford Conservative Association. J.P. Knighted 1919. A Conservative. Elected for the Pudsey and Otley division of Yorkshire in December 1923 and again October 1924 and sat until he retired in May 1929. Died 27 August 1947.   [1929]

WATSON, Capt. John Bertrand. Taunton, The Park, Hampstead, London. Woodlands, Stockton-on-Tees. Reform. S. of

John Wilson Watson, Esq., J.P., and Emma Watson. B. at Stockton-on-Tees 16 May 1878; m. 1909, Ethelwynne Gladys d. of Ralph Jameson, Esq., of West Bank, Stockton-on-Tees. Educ. at Harrogate Coll. A Solicitor, admitted 1900. A Barrister-at-Law of Gray's Inn for Durham and North Eastern Circuit. Dept. County Coroner for Durham 1902-11; Mayor of Stockton-on-Tees 1915-16. Parliamentary Private Secretary (unpaid) to Mr. Shortt, Home Secretary 1919. A Liberal. Sat for Stockton-on-Tees from 20 March 1917 until he retired in November 1923. Metropolitan Police Magistrate 1928-36 and 1938-41. Chief Metropolitan Magistrate 1941-48. Knighted 1942. Member of Durham County Council 1912-19. Died 16 February 1948. [1923]

WATSON, Rt. Hon. William, K.C. 8 Heriot Row, Edinburgh. Carlton, and National. S. of Lord Watson, Lord of Appeal in Ordinary. B. 8 December 1873; m. 26 July 1902, Sophia Marjorie, d. of J.J. Cowan, Esq., of Wester Lea, Murray-field. Educ. at Winchester, and Jesus Coll., Cambridge. Advocate 1899, K.C. 1914; Honorary Bencher of Gray's Inn 1928. Procurator of the Church of Scotland 1918-22; Advocate Depute 1919-22; Solicitor-Gen. for Scotland June-October 1922, Lord Advocate October 1922-January 1924, and from November 1924-April 1929. PC. 1922. A Conservative. Sat for S. Lanark from 1913-18 when he retired. Unsuccessfully contested Galloway in November 1922 and Carlisle in December 1923. Sat for Carlisle from October 1924 until April 1929 when he was appointed Lord of Appeal in Ordinary and created Baron Thankerton (Life Peerage). Lord of Appeal in Ordinary 1929-48. Honorary Fellow of Jesus Coll., Cambridge 1929. Died 13 June 1948. [1929]

WATSON, William McLean. Continued in House after 1945: full entry in Volume IV.

WATT, Francis Clifford. 27 Nelson Street, Edinburgh. Constitutional. New, Edinburgh. S. of the Rev. Charles James Watt, of Polwarth Manse, Greenlaw, Berwickshire. B. 20 July 1896: m. 1945, Theresa Dorothy, d. of John M'Quaker, Esq., of Edinburgh. Educ. at Berwickshire High School, and University of Edinburgh. Served overseas 1914-18. Advocate June 1925. Junior Counsel to Treasury in Scotland 1940-46. A Conservative. Elected for Central Edinburgh in December 1941 and sat until he was defeated in July 1945. Unsuccessfully contested Central Edinburgh in February 1950. K.C. 1946. Sheriff of Caithness, Sutherland, Orkney and Shetland 1952-61. Sheriff of Stirling, Dunbarton and Clackmannan 1961-71. Died 8 April 1971.

[1945]

WATTS, Sir Thomas. "Illovo", 15 Sandringham Road, Birkdale. 27 King Street, Manchester. Constitutional, Manchester. S. of John Taylor Watts, Esq., J.P. for Cheshire. B. 1 July 1868; m. 1922, Dorothy Dudley Ryder, d. of Alfred Ryder, Esq., of Faylands, Durban, Natal. Educ. at Bolton Grammar School, Owens Coll., Manchester, and University of Durham. A Physician, M.D., M.B., B.S. (Durham), B.Sc. (Manchester), M.R.C.S. (Eng.), L.R.C.P. (London) 1889. President Ashton Division British Medical Association and Treasurer of the Incorporated Association of Factory Surgeons. Member of Cheshire Insurance Company; Vice-President Lancashire and Cheshire Branch of British Medical Association. Knight Bach. 1928. A Conservative Member. Elected for the Withington division of Manchester in November 1922, defeated December 1923. Re-elected for the Withington division in October 1924 and sat until he was defeated in May 1929. Died 3 June 1951. [1929]

WAYLAND, Lieut.-Col. Sir William Abraham. Hempton Lodge, Monks Horton, Sellindge, Ashford, Kent. Carlton, Authors', Royal Automobile, Farmers', and Constitutional. S. of William Robinson Wayland, Esq., Civil Service. B. 1 September 1869; m. 1st, 1889, Bessie, d. of William Wynn, Esq.; secondly, 9 August 1944, Kathleen Browne, M.B.E. Educ. at Marlowes Coll. A Farmer and Chemical Manufacturer. F.C.S., F.S.A. Mayor of Deptford 1914-20; J.P. Chairman of Empire Day movement 1927-48. A Conservative.

Elected for the Canterbury division of Kent in November 1927 and sat until he retired in June 1945. Knighted 1920. The Conservative Whip was withdrawn from him March-April 1931 as a result of his support for the Independent Conservative candidate in the St. George's Westminster by-election, who attacked Baldwin's leadership. Died 15 July 1950. [1945]

WEBB, Sir Henry, Bart. Llynarthan, Castleton, Cardiff. Reform, Bath, Ranelagh, and National Liberal. S. of Henry Webb, Esq., of Bristol. B. 28 July 1866; m. 1st, 8 November 1894, Ellen, M.B.E., d. of W.P. Williams, Esq., of Cardiff (she died 4 January 1919); secondly, 22 July 1919, Helena Kate de Paula, d. of Mrs. de Paula, of Netherdale, Finchley. Educ. privately in England, Lausanne, and Paris. A Mining Engineer; Director of the Ocean Coal Company Limited, of Wilson, Son and Company Limited, and Deep Navigation Coal Company Limited. Dept.-Lieut. for Gloucestershire; J.P. for Monmouth, Hereford and Gloucestershire. Junior Lord of the Treasury 1912-15; a Proprietor of the *Westminster Gazette*. Raised and commanded 13th Pioneer Battalion Gloucestershire Regiment and 14th Pioneer Battalion Worcester Regiment; Commander Labour Centre Western Command. A Liberal. Unsuccessfully contested the Ross division of Herefordshire in January and December 1910. Sat for the Forest of Dean division of Gloucestershire from 1911-18 when he was defeated. Unsuccessfully contested Cardiff E. in November 1922. Elected for Cardiff E. in December 1923 and sat until he retired in October 1924. Created Bart. 1916. High Sheriff of Monmouthshire 1921. Died 29 October 1940. [1924 2nd ed.]

WEBB, Rt. Hon. Sidney James. 41 Grosvenor Road, London. Passfield Corner, Liphook. S. of Charles Webb, Esq. B. 13 July 1859; m. 1892, Beatrice, d. of Richard Potter, Esq. (she died 1943). Educ. privately in Switzerland, and Mecklenburg Schwerin; Barrister-at-Law, Gray's Inn 1885; LL.B. For 13 years successively in the War Office, Inland Revenue and Colonial Office. Author, Lecturer, Barrister,

Professor (unpaid) of Public Administration in the University of London. Served on various Royal Commissions; member of London County Council for Deptford 1892-1910; member of the Senate University of London 1900-09. A Gov. of London School of Economics. Author of many works on Labour, Social and Economic subjects. President of Board of Trade January-November 1924. PC. 1924. A Labour Member. Unsuccessfully contested London University in 1918. Sat for the Seaham division of Durham from November 1922 until he retired in May 1929. Created Baron Passfield 1929. Secretary of State for the Colonies June 1929-August 1931 and for the Dominions June 1929-June 1930. O.M. 1944. Died 13 October 1947. [1929]

WEBBE, Sir William Harold. Continued in House after 1945: full entry in Volume IV.

WEDGWOOD, Col. Rt. Hon. Josiah Clement, D.S.O. 903 Howard House, Dolphin Square, London. Moddershall, Stone, Staffordshire. S. of Clement F. Wedgwood, Esq. B. 16 March 1872; m. 1st, 3 July 1894, Ethel, d. of the Rt. Hon. Lord Bowen (marriage dissolved in 1919); secondly, 25 June 1919, Florence, d. of Edward Willett, Esq. Educ. at Clifton Coll., and Royal Naval Coll., Greenwich. Assistant Constructor Royal Corps of Naval Constructors 1894; naval Architect with Sir W.G. Armstrong and Company 1895-1900; Capt. of Elswick Battery in South African War 1900-01. Resident Magistrate at Ermelo, Transvaal 1902-04. Lieut.-Commander R.N.A.S. 1914; Commander 1915; commanded squadron of armoured motor-cars in Flanders 1914, and Gallipoli 1915, D.S.O. 1915; Maj. on Gen. Smuts' Staff, East Africa 1916. Assistant-Director in the Trench Warfare Department November 1917. Col (Temporary) Gen. Service in Siberia 1918. President of the English League for the Taxation of Land Values. Vice-Chairman Parliamentary Labour Party 1922-24; member of National Executive of the Labour Party 1924. Member of Staffordshire County Council from 1910-18; Dept.-Lieut., and J.P. for Staffordshire.

Mayor of Newcastle-under-Lyme 1930-32. Chairman of Committee on House of Commons Records 1929. Chancellor Duchy of Lancaster January-November 1924. PC. 1924. A Liberal until April 1919 when he resigned the Whip; accepted the Labour Whip in May 1919 but from 1931 sat as an Independent Labour Member, remaining a member of the Labour Party but not acknowledging the authority of the Parliamentary Whip. Sat for Newcastle-under-Lyme from 1906 until January 1942 when he was created Baron Wedgwood. Died 26 July 1943. [1942]

WEIGALL, Lieut.-Col. William Ernest George Archibald. Petwood, Woodhall Spa, Lincolnshire. Carlton, Junior Carlton, and Boodle's. 5th s. of Henry Weigall, Esq., Dept.-Lieut., of Southwood House, St. Lawrence, Isle of Thanet, and Lady Rose Weigall, d. of 11th Earl of Westmorland. B. 8 December 1874; m. 1910, Grace Emily, only d. of Sir J. Blundell Maple, Bart., MP (she died 1950). Educ. at Wellington Coll. and Royal Agricultural Coll., Cirencester, Gold Medallist. Resident Agent for Apethorpe Estate, Northamptonshire, and Blankney Estate, Lincolnshire 1902-10. Maj. 3rd Battalion Northamptonshire Regiment, retired; served in South Africa 1902, retired 1913; Inspector Quarter Master General's Service 1914-17. Member of Royal Agricultural Society; representative member National Agricultural Council. J.P. for Kent and Lincolnshire. Surveyor of Food Consumption in Public Services for Ministry of Food January 1918. A Unionist. Unsuccessfully contested the Gainsborough division of Lincolnshire in December 1910 Elected for the Horncastle division of Lincolnshire in February 1911 and sat until February 1920 when he was appointed Gov. of South Australia. Gov. of South Australia 1920-22. Chairman of Royal Empire Society 1932-36. Created Bart. 1938. President of Land Agents Society 1934. President of Royal Agricultural Society 1946. Died 3 June 1952. [1920]

WEIR, Lauchlan MacNeill. 4 Woodside Avenue, Highgate, London. Traigh Bheag, Port Ellen, Isle of Islay, Argyllshire. S. of Robert Weir, Esq., of Isle of Islay. B. 1877; m. 1913, Margaret Gillison, d. of James Smith, Esq., of Milngavie. Educ. at Highland Society School, and University of Glasgow. A Journalist. Parliamentary Private Secretary to the Rt. Hon. J.R. MacDonald when Prime Minister January-November 1924 and June 1929-August 1931. Author of *The Tragedy of Ramsay MacDonald*. A Labour Member. Unsuccessfully contested Argyllshire in November 1918 as the candidate of the Highland Land League. Sat for the Clackmannan and Eastern division of Stirling and Clackmannan from November 1922-October 1931 when he was defeated; re-elected for the division in November 1935 and sat until his death on 18 August 1939. [1939]

WELLOCK, Wilfred. Victoria Avenue, Quinton, Birmingham. S. of John Wellock, Esq., of Nelson, Lancashire. B. 1879; m. 24 July 1913, Frances, d. of James Wilson, Esq., of Colne, Lancashire. Educ. at University of Edinburgh. Author and Lecturer. Junior President of Edinburgh University Historical Society. A Labour Member. Unsuccessfully contested the Stourbridge division of Worcestershire in December 1923 and October 1924. Elected for the Stourbridge division of Worcestershire in February 1927 and sat until he was defeated in October 1931. Unsuccessfully contested the Stourbridge division of Worcestershire in November 1935. Died 22 July 1972.

[1931 2nd ed.]

WELLS, Sir (Sydney) Richard, Bart. Felmersham Grange, Nr. Bedford. Carlton. S. of Charles Wells, Esq., Brewer, of Bedford. B. 1879; m. 1907, Mary Dorothy, d. of C.J. Maltby, Esq (she died May 1956). Educ. at Bedford School. Knight Bach. 1938. Dept.-Lieut. for Bedfordshire; created Bart. 1944. A Conservative. Sat for the Bedford division of Bedfordshire from November 1922 until he was defeated in July 1945. Chairman of Brewers' Society 1940-42. Died 26 November 1956. [1945]

WELSH, James. House of Commons, London. B. 29 January 1881 at Paisley; m. 1910, Nell Greig (she died 1945). A

Cinema Proprietor in Glasgow. Member of Glasgow Corporation for many years. A Labour Member. Elected for Paisley in May 1929 and sat until he was defeated in October 1931. J.P. and Dept.-Lieut. for Lanarkshire. Lord Provost of Glasgow 1943-45. Chairman of Scottish Committee of Arts Council 1946-51. Died 16 December 1969.   [1931 2nd ed.]

WELSH, James C. Tinto View, Douglas Water, Lanarkshire. S. of William Welsh, Esq., Miner, of Haywood, Lanarkshire. B. 1880; m. 1905, Elizabeth. d. of John Hunter, Esq. (she died 1951). Was a working Miner and Miners' Agent; Vice-President of the Lanarkshire Miners' County Union. A Labour Member. Unsuccessfully contested the Lanark division of Lanarkshire in December 1918. Sat for the Coatbridge division of Lanarkshire from November 1922-October 1931 when he was defeated. Elected for the Bothwell division of Lanarkshire in November 1935 and sat until he retired in June 1945. Member of Executive of Miners' Federation of Great Britain 1923. Parliamentary Private Secretary to Rt. Hon. W. Adamson when Secretary of State for Scotland 1931. Author of a number of novels, short stories and volumes of poetry. Adopted the initial C when he started writing and used it during his parliamentary career to distinguish him from James Welsh, MP for Paisley. Died 4 November 1954.
[1945]

WEST, Fielding Reginald. 42 Sedgeford Road, London. B. at Huddersfield 1892. Educ. at the Polytechnic, Regent Street, London. A Schoolmaster. Member of Hammersmith Borough Council 1923-25. Parliamentary Private Secretary to H.B. Lees Smith, Esq., when Postmaster Gen. and Minister of Education 1929-31. A Labour Member. Unsuccessfully contested Kensington N. in October 1924. Returned for the seat in 1929; defeated in 1931. Elected for Hammersmith N. in April 1934 and sat until his death on 6 October 1935.
[1935]

WESTON, Col. John Wakefield. Enyeat, Erdmoor, Kendal. Carlton, and Arts. S. of Canon G.F. Weston and Mary, d. of John Wakefield, Esq. B. 13 June 1852 at Crosby Ravensworth; m. 1890, Kate, d. of J.R. Brougham, Esq., Registrar in Bankruptcy. Educ. at Rugby, and University Coll., Oxford. A Director of W.H. Wakefield and Company, Explosives Manufacturers, of Kendal, and Nobel's Industries Limited. Chairman of Westmorland County Council 1908-26. Chairman Cumberland and Westmorland Territorial Association; Col. 4th Battalion Border Regiment. J.P. and Dept.-Lieut. for Westmorland. A Conservative. Elected for the Kendal division of Westmorland as a Unionist Free Trader in March 1913; returned unopposed for Westmorland in December 1918, November 1922 and again in December 1923. Sat until he retired in October 1924. Created Bart. July 1926. Died 19 September 1926.   [1924 2nd ed.]

WESTON, Willard Garfield. 40 Berkeley Square, London. Wittington, Marlow, Buckinghamshire. S. of George Weston, Esq., of Toronto. B. 1898; m. 1st, 1921, Reta Lila, d. of S. Howard, Esq., of British Columbia (she died 1967); secondly, 1972, Marguerita Martin de Montoya. Educ. at Harbord Collegiate Institute, Toronto. President of George Weston Limited, Toronto; Chairman of George Weston Holdings Limited, of Allied Bakeries and of Weston Foods Limited. A Manufacturer. A Conservative. Elected for the Macclesfield division of Cheshire in November 1939 and sat until he retired in June 1945. President of Associated British Foods Limited. Chairman of Fortnum and Mason Limited. Died in Toronto 22 October 1978.   [1945]

WESTWOOD, Rt. Hon. Joseph. Continued in House after 1945: full entry in Volume IV.

WEYMOUTH, Henry Frederick Thynne, Visct. 8 Tite Street, London. Greenway House, Warminster. S. of Thomas, 5th Marq. of Bath. B. 26 January 1905; m. 1st, 27 October 1927, Hon. Daphne Vivian, d. of George, 4th Baron Vivian (divorced 1953); secondly, 1953, Mrs. Virginia Penelope Tennant, d. of A.L.R. Parsons, Esq. Educ. at Harrow, and Christ Church,

373

Oxford. Lieut. Royal Wiltshire Yeomanry. A Conservative. Elected for the Frome division of Somerset in October 1931 and sat until he retired in October 1935. Styled Visct. Weymouth from his elder brother's death in 1916 until his father's death in 1946. Succeeded to the Peerage as Marq. of Bath 1946. J.P. for Wiltshire. Member of Wiltshire County Council.*   [1935]

WHEATLEY, Rt. Hon. John. Braehead House, Sandyhills Road, Tollcross, Glasgow. S. of Thomas Wheatley, Esq. B. 1869; m. 1896, Mary, d. of B. Meechan, Esq. Member of Lanark County Council from 1910-12, and Glasgow Town Council from 1912-22. Minister of Health from January-November 1924. PC. 1924. A Labour Member Unsuccessfully contested the Shettleston division of Glasgow in December 1918. Sat for the Shettleston division from November 1922 until his death on 12 May 1930.
[1929 2nd ed.]

WHELER, Lieut.-Col. Sir Granville Charles Hastings, Bart., C.B.E. Otterden, Faversham, Kent. Ledston Hall, Yorkshire. Carlton, and Royal Automobile. S. of Charles Wheler Wheler, Esq., of Otterden Place, Faversham. B. 2 October 1872; m. 6 June 1905, Faith Florence, d. of Capt. E.T. Clarke, of Alcombe, Somerset. Educ. at Eton, and Christ Church, Oxford. A Barrister-at-Law, Middle Temple 1898. Member of the County Council for the W. Riding of Yorkshire from 1907-10. Dept.-Lieut., and J.P. for Kent, J.P. for the W. Riding of Yorkshire. D.A.Q.M.G. Western Command 1915-18; Lieut.-Col. 1918. C.B.E. 1919. Created Bart. 1925. Chairman Central Chamber of Agriculture 1919. A Conservative. Unsuccessfully contested the Osgoldcross division of the W. Riding of Yorkshire in 1906, and the Colne Valley division of the W. Riding of Yorkshire in 1907. Sat for the Faversham division of Kent from January 1910 until his death on 14 December 1927.   [1928]

WHITE, Charles Frederick, (I). The Woodlands, Matlock. S. of Frederick White, Esq., Farmer and Market Gardener. B. 11 March 1863 at Tetbury, Gloucester-shire; m. 1881, Alice, 2nd d. of William and Jemima Charlesworth, of Bonsall, Matlock. Educ. at a private school at Tetbury. Registration Agent and Secretary of Political Association 1905-18. Chairman of Matlock Bath Urban District Council 1909-14; member of Derbyshire County Council 1909-14. Member Executive Committee League of Nations Union (Co. of Derby). A Liberal. Unsuccessfully contested W. Derbyshire in December 1910. Sat for W. Derbyshire from December 1918 until his death on 4 December 1923 during the campaign for the general election for which he was a candidate. (Polling was delayed and another Liberal candidate was nominated).
[1923]

WHITE, Charles Frederick, (II). Continued in House after 1945: full entry in Volume IV.

WHITE, Lieut.-Col. Sir Godfrey Dalrymple, Bart. See DALRYMPLE-WHITE, Lieut.-Col. Sir Godfrey Dalrymple. Bart.

WHITE, Henry. Continued in House after 1945: full entry in Volume IV.

WHITE, Henry Graham. Mere Cottage, Birkenhead. Reform, National Liberal, and Eighty. University, Liverpool. S. of John Arnold White, Esq., of Birkenhead and Annie, d. of Capt. John Graham, of Birkenhead. B. 26 August 1880; m. 1910, Mary Irene, d. of the Rev. Charles Heath, of Nether Stowey, Somerset (she died 1962). Educ. at Birkenhead School, and University of Liverpool. Chairman of Birkenhead and District Ministry of Labour and Employment Committee; Fellow of Royal Statistical Society. Member of Birkenhead Town Council 1917-23, of Dept. Committee on Private Schools 1930-31, of Chancel Repairs Committee 1930; member of Council of Royal Institute of International Affairs; Chairman of British Association for Labour Legislation and of War Risk Insurance (Restriction of Advertisement Committee); member of Council on Aliens 1940 and of Select Committee on National Expediture 1940. A Stockbroker. Assistant Postmaster-Gen.

September 1931-September 1932. Member of Indian Round Table Conference, of Lord Ullswater's Broadcasting Committee 1936, of Executive Committee League of Nations Union and of Rent Restriction Acts Enquiry Committee 1937. Executive Committee of British Council; Chairman of Committee on Seamen's Welfare in Ports 1943-44. A Liberal. Unsuccessfully contested E. Birkenhead in December 1918. Elected for E. Birkenhead in November 1922 and December 1923, defeated October 1924. Re-elected for E. Birkenhead in May 1929 and sat until he was defeated in July 1945. Unsuccessfully contested Bebington in February 1950. PC. 1945. President of Liberal Party 1954-55. Died in France 19 February 1965. [1945]

WHITE, Sir Rudolph Dymoke, Bart. Continued in House after 1945: full entry in Volume IV.

WHITELEY, Lieut.-Col. John Percival, O.B.E. The Grange, Bletchley, Buckinghamshire. Carlton, Cavalry, and Naval & Military. S. of Frank Whiteley, Esq., C.M.G., of Ilkley, Yorkshire, and Sarah Emily, d. of John Walker, Esq., of Dewsbury. B. at Mafeking 7 January 1898; m. 3 November 1925, Amy Beatrice, d. of H.G. Tetley, Esq., of Cranleigh. Educ. at Shrewsbury School, and Royal Military Academy, Woolwich. Served with R.A. 1916-26, with Life Guards 1926-28, and with Bucks Yeomanry from 1928. O.B.E. 1940. A County Councillor and J.P. for Buckinghamshire. A Conservative. Unsuccessfully contested the Aston division of Birmingham in 1929. Elected for the Buckingham division of Buckinghamshire in June 1937 and sat until 4 July 1943 when he was killed on active service in an air crash while travelling with Gen. Sikorski. [1943]

WHITELEY, Wilfrid. 3 Hallewell Road, Edgbaston, Birmingham. S. of Joe Whiteley, Esq., of Huddersfield. B. 3 February 1882; m. 2 April 1904, Alice Maud, d. of Frank Slade, Esq., of Hillhouse, Huddersfield. Educ. at Paddock Council School. Political Registration Agent from 1921. A Labour Member. Unsuccessfully contested the Colne Valley division of the W. Riding of Yorkshire in December 1918. Elected for the Ladywood division of Birmingham in May 1929 and sat until he was defeated in October 1931. Labour Party Agent in Huddersfield 1921-26, the Ladywood division of Birmingham 1926-29, W. Birmingham 1932-36, and Elland 1936-47. C.B.E. 1950. Mayor of Brighouse 1947-50. Member W. Riding County Council. Died 4 April 1970. [1931 2nd ed.]

WHITELEY, Rt. Hon. William. Continued in House after 1945: full entry in Volume IV.

WHITESIDE, Borras Noel Hamilton. 28 Lower Belgrave Street, London. Carlton, and United. S. of Capt. R. Borras Whiteside, R.A.S.C., and Leonore, d. of 9th Lord Belhaven and Stenton. B. 12 December 1903; m. 1935, Dorothy Mai, d. of John Farrington, Esq. Educ. at Wellington Coll., and University Coll., London. West End Local Director of London and Scottish Association Company 1925. A Nationalist Conservative. Elected for Leeds S. in October 1931 and sat until he was defeated in November 1935. Unsuccessfully contested Wembley S. in July 1945. Assistant Divisional Food Officer, London 1939-41; Principal, Board of Trade 1941-42; Dept. Director of Salvage and Recovery, Ministry of Supply 1942-45. Died 13 June 1948. [1935]

WHITLA, Sir William. Lennox Vale House, Belfast. St. Stephen's, and Authors'. S. of Robert and Ann Whitla. B. at Monaghan September 1851; m. 1876, Ada, d. of George Bourne, Esq., of The Draconage, Staffordshire. Educ. at Queen's University, Belfast. M.D., R.U.I. 1878; M.D. *Hon. Causa*, T.C.D.; LL.D. *Hon. Causa*, Glasgow University; M.A. R.U.I., *Hon. Causa*, D.Sc., *Hon Causa* Queen's University, etc., Consulting Physician to Royal Victoria Hospital; Professor Materia Medica Q.U.B. 1890; member G.M. Council; Physician to H.M. George V. 1917; member of Irish Convention 1917; President of British Medical Association 1909; Consulting Physician to various hospitals; Senator Q.U.B.

Author of textbook on *Materia Medica* (11th Ed.); *Dictionary of Treatment* (7th Ed.); and 5th Chinese Edition *Practice of Medicine* (2 volumes). A Conservative. Elected for Queen's University, Belfast in December 1918. Returned unopposed for Queen's University, Belfast in November 1922 and sat until he retired in November 1923. Knighted 1902. Pro-Chancellor of Queen's University, Belfast 1924. Died 11 December 1933. [1923]

WHITLEY, Rt. Hon. John Henry. The Speaker's House, Westminster, London. Brantwood, Halifax. S. of Nathan Whitley, Esq., of Halifax. B. 8 February 1866; m. 1st, 29 June 1892, Marguerita Virginia, d. of G. Marchetti, Esq., of Halifax (she died 6 November 1925); secondly, 1928, Helen, d. of J.A. Clarke, Esq., of Hunstanton. Educ. at Clifton Coll. and London University, B.A. J.P. for the W. Riding of Yorkshire. A Cotton Spinner. Junior Lord of the Treasury (unpaid) and a Liberal Whip 1907-10; Dept.-Chairman of Ways and Means 1910-11. Dept. Speaker and Chairman of Ways and Means 1911-21. Chairman of Committee on the Relations of Employers and Employed 1917-18, the forerunner of the Whitley Councils. PC. 1911. A Liberal. Sat for Halifax from 1900 until he resigned in June 1928. Member of Halifax Borough Council 1893-1900. Speaker of the House of Commons April 1921-June 1928. Chairman of Royal Commission on Labour in India 1929-31. Chairman of B.B.C. 1930-35. President of National Council of Social Service from 1921. Kaisar-i-Hind medal 1932. Died 3 February 1935. [1928]

WHITTAKER, Rt. Hon. Sir Thomas Palmer. 2 Wetherby Gardens, Kensington, London. Reform. S. of Thomas Whittaker, Esq., J.P., of Scarborough, and Louisa Palmer, of London. B. 1850 at Scarborough; m. 1874, Emma Mary, d. of Capt. Charles Theedam. Educ. at Huddersfield Coll. Chairman and Managing Director of a Life Assurance Institution, and was a member of the Royal Commission on the Licensing Laws 1896-99. Was in the hardware trade. A Newspaper Proprietor and editor; Knighted 1906; PC. 1908. Chairman and member of numerous Parliamentary Select Committees; a member of the Joint Conference of the two Houses on the reconstruction of the Second Chamber; Chairman of the Royal Commission on paper. Member of Scarborough Corporation, and author of articles on economic and social questions in leading reviews. A Liberal. Represented the Spen Valley division of the W. Riding of Yorkshire from 1892 until his death on 9 November 1919. [1919]

WHYTE, Jardine Bell. 4 Cumberland Terrace, London. Canmore, Braemar, Aberdeenshire. Carlton, and Caledonian. Scottish Conservative, Edinburgh. S. of Robert Whyte, Esq., of Lauchope House, Lanarkshire, and 111 St. Vincent Street, Glasgow. B. 5 March 1880; m. 24 November 1923, d. of Ralph Shainwald, Esq., of New York. Educ. at Royal High School, and University of Edinburgh. M.I.Mech.E., Consulting Engineer and Naval Architect, San Francisco 1907-14. Chief Engineer H.M.T. *Nile* 1915-17, and personal assistant to Sir William Rowen Thompson, D.A.S.E., Admiralty 1917; Assistant Director and Manager, British Ministry of Shipping in U.S.A. and Canada 1917-18; Chief Technical Adviser and Director to British Ministry of Shipping in U.S.A. and Canada 1918-21. J.P. for Aberdeen. A Nationalist Conservative. Elected for N.E. Derbyshire in October 1931 and sat until he retired in October 1935. Died 8 July 1954. [1935]

WICKHAM, Lieut.-Col. Edward Thomas Ruscombe, M.V.O. 121 Whitehall Court, London. Lynchfield House, Bishops Lydeard, Taunton. Carlton, and East India United Service. S. of Col. W.J.R. Wickham, C.B., I.A., and Mary Rose, d. of J. Ruscombe Poole, Esq., of Clevedon, Somerset. B. 4 May 1890; m. 5 August 1929, Rachel Marguerite, d. of W.G. Alexander, Esq., of Warley Lodge, Essex (she died 1955). Educ. at Oratory School, and Royal Military Coll., Sandhurst. Joined I.A. 1910; Indian Political Department 1919-35. Parliamentary Private Secretary to Miss Florence Horsburgh, when Parliamentary Secretary Ministry of Health July-December 1939, and to Rt. Hon. Leslie Hore-Belisha, Secretary of State for War December 1939-January 1940, to Sir Victor Warrender, Bart., Financial Secretary to the War Office February-May 1940, and when Financial Secretary to the Admiralty May 1940, to Rt. Hon. David Margesson, Secretary of State for War January 1941-February 1942; Leader of Empire Parliamentary Delegation to Australia and New Zealand June 1944. A National Conservative. Elected for the Taunton division of Somerset in November 1935 and sat until he was defeated in July 1945. Died 25 August 1957.   [1945]

WIGAN, Brigadier-Gen. John Tyson, C.B., C.M.G., D.S.O. Danbury Park, Chelmsford, Essex. Carlton, and Cavalry. S. of C. Wigan, Esq., and his wife Louise, d. of Henry Tyson, Esq., of Steelfield Hall, Gosforth. B. at West Hartlepool 31 July 1877; m. 1911, Aline, eld. d. of H.W. Henderson, Esq. Educ. at Rugby. Served in the South African War, King and Queen's medals with four clasps. Commanded Berkshire Yeomanry at Gallipoli (wounded at Suvla Bay), on the Western Frontier of Egypt (D.S.O. 1916). and in Palestine (wounded at Gaza). Commanded Cavalry Brigade 1917-19. Dept.-Lieut. for Essex. A Coalition Unionist. Returned unopposed for the Abingdon division of Berkshire in December 1918 and sat until he resigned in May 1921. J.P. for Essex. Honorary Col. 1st/4th Battalion Essex Regiment 1922-45. High Sheriff of Essex 1930. Died 23 November 1952.   [1921]

WIGGINS, William Martin. The Cottage, Hollingworth, Manchester. National Liberal, and 1920. S. of the Rev. William Wiggins. B. 4 August 1870; m. 1st, 31 July 1896, Flora Isabel, d. of G.A. Coleman, Esq., of Oldham; secondly, 12 July 1917, Elizabeth, d. of Stephen Hayhurst, Esq., of Hellifield. Educ. privately. Mayor of Middleton 1914-19, Honorary Freeman of the borough 1919. A Liberal. Unsuccessfully contested Oldham in December 1923. Elected for Oldham in June 1925 and sat until he retired in May 1929. President of International Federation of Cotton Spinners and Manufacturers. Died 4 October 1950.   [1929]

WIGNALL, James. Newnham, 17 Fawnbrake Avenue, Herne Hill, London. Effingham House, Arundel Street, Strand, London. S. of George Wignall, Esq., soldier. B. at Swansea 21 July 1856; m. 1875, Mary, d. of George and Jane Rees, of Carmarthen (she died 1924). Educ. at the Swansea National School. Trade Union Organizer for the Docker's Union and the Transport and General Workers' Union 1890; at one time employed as a Copper Sheet Roller. Member of Swansea School Board 1899-1906. Baptist lay preacher. J.P. for Swansea 1907. A Labour Member. Sat for the Forest of Dean division of Gloucestershire from December 1918 until his death on 10 June 1925.   [1925]

WILD, Sir Ernest Edward. 25 Albert Hall Mansions, Kensington Gore, London. 1 Garden Court, Temple, London. Carlton, Garrick, and St. Stephen's. S. of Edward Wild, Esq., J.P., of Norwich. B. at Norwich 1 January 1869; m. 1894, Myra, d. of William Barnard, Esq., of Caistor, near Great Yarmouth. Educ. at Norwich School, and Jesus Coll., Cambridge. Barrister Middle Temple 1893; K.C. 1912. Judge of Norwich Guildhall Court of Record 1897-1922. Published lectures on Spenser's *Faerie Queene*, *The Lamp of Destiny*, and other poems. A Coalition Unionist Unsuccessfully contested Norwich in 1904 and 1906, and N. West Ham in December 1910 and 1911. Elected for the Upton division of West Ham in December 1918 and sat until he retired in October 1922. Member of London County Council 1907-10. Knighted 1918. Recorder of City of London 1922-34. High Steward of Southwark 1922-34. Died 13 September 1934.   [1922]

WILKIE, Alexander. Leven House, 36 Lesbury Road, Heaton, Newcastle-on-Tyne. B. 30 September 1850 at Leven, Fife; m. 1872, Mary, d. of James Smillie, Esq. (she died 1921). Educ. at Fife Public School. After some seagoing experience, apprenticed to a Ship Constructor. Became Secretary, afterwards President, of the Glasgow Shipwrights' Society, and for 17 years represented it on the Glasgow Trades Council. In 1882 reconstituted the local self-contained societies into the Ship-Constructors' and Ship-wrights' Association, of which he was Gen. Secretary. Represented that Association on the Trades Union Congress; was for a number of years member of the Congress Parliamentary Committee; represented the British Congress at the Detroit Convention of the American Federation of Labour in 1899; member of the Mosely Industrial Commission to America 1902. On removal to Newcastle, was member of the School Board till its dissolution. Member of Newcastle Town Council for a number of years; elected Alderman; J.P. for Newcastle-on-Tyne; Companion of Honour 1917. A Labour Member. Unsuccessfully contested Sunderland in 1900, and was first elected for Dundee in 1906. Sat until he retired in October 1922. Died 2 September 1928. [1922]

WILKINSON, Ellen Cecily. Continued in House after 1945: full entry in Volume IV.

WILLEY, Arthur Wellesley. House of Commons, London. S. of Thomas Willey, Esq., of Leeds. B. 1868 at Leeds; m. 1895, Maud Ellicott, of Calcutta. Educ. at Trinity Coll., Harrogate, and Leeds Grammar School. Admitted a Solicitor in 1890. An Alderman of Leeds. A Conservative. Elected for Central Leeds in November 1922 and sat until his death on 2 July 1923. [1923]

WILLEY, Lieut.-Col. Hon. Francis Vernon, C.M.G., C.B.E., M.V.O., T.D. Blyth Hall, via Rotherham, Nottinghamshire. Carlton, St. Stephen's, Bath, Cavalry, and Hurlingham. S. of Francis Willey, Esq J.P., of Blyth Hall, Nottinghamshire who was created Baron Barnby in 1922. B. at Bradford 1884; m. 1940, Banning, d. of William Drayton Grange, Esq., of Bryn Mawr, Pennsylvania. Educ. at Eton, and Magdalen Coll., Oxford; M.A., Law (Oxon) 1908. Lieut.-Col. Commanding Sherwood Rangers (T.F.); Temporary Lieut.-Col. R.A.O.C.; Assistant-Director of Equipment and Ordnance Services. Controller of Wool Supplies, Ministry of Munitions (Supply). Partner in Messrs. Francis Willey and Company, Wool Merchants, Bradford, and Boston, U.S.A. M.F.H. Blankney Hounds 1919. A Coalition Unionist. Elected for S.

Bradford in December 1918 and sat until he was defeated in November 1922. C.B.E. 1919. Succeeded to the Peerage as Baron Barnby in 1929, President of Federation of British Industries 1925-26. Member of Central Electricity Board 1927-46. Member of Overseas Settlement Board 1937. President of Textile Institute 1961-62.* [1922]

WILLIAMS, Alfred Martyn. Werrington Park, Launceston, Cornwall. S. of John Charles Williams, Esq., of Caerhays Castle, Cornwall. B. 1897; m. 1st, 1920, Audrey, d. of C. Rogers, Esq., of Stanage Park, Radnorshire (she died 1943); secondly, 1945, Dorothea Veronica, widow of Maj. F.F. Robins, and d. of Col. W.H. Carver, MP. Educ. at Osborne, and Dartmouth Colls. Lieut.-Commander, D.S.C. A Conservative. Elected for N. Cornwall in October 1924 and sat until he was defeated in May 1929. Unsuccessfully contested N. Cornwall in October 1931 and July 1932. Served in Royal Navy 1939-45. Dept.-Lieut. for Cornwall, High Sheriff 1938. C.B.E. 1957.* [1929]

WILLIAMS, Aneurin. 26 Cheyne Walk, London. Reform, National Liberal, and Eighty. S. of Edward Williams, Esq., C.E., of Middlesbrough. B. 11 October 1859 at Dowlais, Glamorgan; m. 1888, Helen Elizabeth, d. of John Pattinson, Esq., J.P., of Shipcote House, Gateshead (she died 1922). Educ at private school, and St. John's Coll., Cambridge; M.A. Was called to the bar at the Inner Temple 1884; Acting Partner in Linthorpe Ironworks 1886-90. Chairman Public Accounts Committee of House of Commons 1921-22. Honorary Treasurer Proportional Representation Society; Chairman British Armenia Committee; President Urban District Councils Association; Joint Honorary Secretary Labour Co-Partnership Association. Was first editor of *Co-partnership;* wrote on Co-operative Societies and Profit Sharing in *Encyclopaedia Britannica*, etc. A Liberal. Unsuccessfully contested mid Kent in 1906. Sat for Plymouth from January to December 1910 when he was defeated. Elected for N.W. Durham in January 1914, and for the Consett division of Durham in December

1918 and sat until he was defeated in November 1922. Died 20 January 1924.

[1922]

WILLIAMS, Arnold. 54 Portland Court, Great Portland Street, London. Charnwood House, Higher Crumpsall, Manchester. Reform, National Liberal, Manchester Reform, and Old Colony. S. of S.W. Williams, Esq., C.A., of Manchester, and Annie Williams, née Collins. B. at Rochdale 30 September 1890; m. 12 August 1915, Bessie Clarke, d. of J.R. Morland, Esq., of Manchester. Educ. privately, and at Manchester University. Associate Institute Chartered Accountants 1915; Fellow 1921. Member of Ecumenical Methodist Committee, Federal Council Evangelical Free Churches, and International and Industrial Relationship Committee of the Wesleyan Methodist Church. Chairman of Joseph Byrom and Sons Limited, Saunders Garage and Motor Car Company Limited, Dalton Investment Corporation Limited, the D.I.C. House (Cross Street) Limited, and the General Estates and Insurance (Manchester) Limited; Director of Fred W. Millington Limited, Hepworth Picture Plays Limited, Mills Brothers Limited, J. and T. Alexander Limit`d, Henry Reid and Sons Limited, Dalton Property Company Limited, Minerva (Roumania) Oil Company Limited, and the Midland Merino Spinning Company Limited. A Liberal. Unsuccessfully contested the Sowerby division of Yorkshire in 1922. Elected for the Sowerby division of Yorkshire in December 1923 and sat until he was defeated in October 1924. Fellow of Royal Economic Society. Died 1 January 1958. [1924 2nd ed.]

WILLIAMS, Charles. Continued in House after 1945: full entry in Volume IV.

WILLIAMS, Christmas Price. 42B Courtfield Gardens, London. S. of Peter Williams, Esq., Managing Director of Brymbo Steel Company. B. 1881; m. 1909, Marion, d. of Thomas Davies, Esq., of Brymbo. Educ. at Wrexham, Mold and at Victoria University, Manchester; B.Sc. A Liberal. Sat for the Wrexham division of Denbighshire from October 1924 until he

was defeated in May 1929. Died 18 August 1965. [1929]

WILLIAMS, David. 25 Windmill Terrace, Swansea. S. of David Williams, Esq. B. 8 September 1865; m. 1889, Elizabeth, d. of George Colwill, Esq. A Boiler-Maker. Member for 24 years of Swansea Town Council. A Labour Member. Unsuccessfully contested Swansea E. in December 1918 and July 1919. Sat for Swansea E. from November 1922 until he resigned in January 1940. Mayor of Swansea 1912-13. Chairman of Swansea Cooperative Society 1900-41. Died 22 January 1941. [1940]

WILLIAMS, David James. Continued in House after 1945: full entry in Volume IV.

WILLIAMS, Edward John. Continued in House after 1945: full entry in Volume IV.

WILLIAMS, Sir Herbert Geraint. Continued in House after 1945: full entry in Volume IV.

WILLIAMS, John. Godre'r Bryn, Sketty, Swansea. S. of David Williams, Esq., Collier. B. 1861 at Aberaman; m. 1884, Lizzie, d. Daniel Jones, Esq., of Aberaman. Educ. at British School, Aberaman. Commenced work in a colliery when 12 years old. Miner for 8 years; Checkweigher for 12 years. Miners' Agent and Advisory Agent Western Miners' Association for 20 years. Baptist Minister; Lecturer on Economics; Welsh poet; J.P. for Glamorganshire. A Labour Member. Elected for the Gower division of Glamorganshire in 1906 and sat until his death on 20 June 1922. Member of Mountain Ash Urban District Council. Gov. of University of Wales. Died 20 June 1922.

[1922]

WILLIAMS, Dr. John Henry. Snowdon House, Burry Port, Carmarthen. S. of Capt. Evan Williams, of Pwll. B. 1870; m. 1892, Ann, d. of William Thomas, Esq., of Pwll, Llanelly. Educ. at Cardiff, Oxford, and London Hospital. In practice at Burry Port, Carmarthenshire. Chairman of Carmarthenshire County Council. J.P.

379

Licenciate of Society of Apothecaries 1902. A Labour Member. Unsuccessfully contested E. Carmarthenshire in December 1910 and August 1912, and the Llanelly division of Carmarthenshire in December 1918. Sat for the Llanelly division of Carmarthenshire from November 1922 until his death on 7 February 1936. [1936]

WILLIAMS, Lieut.-Col. Penry. Pinchinthorpe Hall, Guisborough, Yorkshire. Reform, and National Liberal. S. of Edward Williams, Esq., C.E., of Middlesbrough. B. at Middlesbrough 5 September 1866; m. 1st, Alexandra Octavia, d. of William Jenkins, Esq., J.P., of Consett Hall, Co. Durham; secondly, Edith Martha, d. of William Petherick, Esq., of London. Educ. privately. Managing Director of the Linthorpe, Dinsdale Smelting Company Limited; J.P. for the N. Riding of Yorkshire, and Middlesbrough. Lieut.-Col. 1st N. Riding Yorkshire Volunteer Artillery; Lieut.-Col. Commanding 2-4th Battalion Yorkshire Regiment (T.) 1915. A Liberal. Sat for Middlesbrough from January 1910 to 1918, and for Middlesbrough E. from December 1918 to November 1922 when he was defeated. Re-elected for Middlesbrough E. in December 1923 and sat until he was defeated in October 1924. Unsuccessfully contested the Berwick-upon-Tweed division of Northumberland in May 1929. Died 26 June 1945.

[1924 2nd ed.]

WILLIAMS, Col. Sir Rhys, Bart., K.C., D.S.O. 6 Charles Street, Berkeley Square, London. Miskin Manor, Ponyclun, Glamorgan. Brooks's, White's, and Guards. S. of Gwilym Williams, Esq., Judge of County Courts. B. 1865; m. 1921, Juliet, youngest d. of Clayton Glyn, Esq., of Durrington House, Harlow. Educ. at Eton, and Oriel Coll., Oxford. Called to the bar at the Inner Temple 1890; K.C. 1913. Obtained a commission in the Grenadier Guards August 1914; transferred to the Welsh Guards; Capt. 1915; Lieut.-Col. on Staff August 1917. Dept.-Lieut. for Glamorgan. Vice-Chairman of Quarter Sessions for Glamorgan 1906-17; Chairman 1917. Assistant Director-Gen. of Movements and

Railways War Office July 1917-February 1918. Dept.-Director Staff Duties Admiralty February 1918-December 1918. Parliamentary Secretary to the Ministry of Transport September to November 1919. A Coalition Liberal. First elected for the Banbury division of Oxfordshire in September 1918, re-elected in December 1918 and June 1922, on appointment as Recorder of Cardiff, and sat until November 1922 when he unsuccessfully contested the Pontypridd division of Glamorgan. D.S.O. 1915. Created Bart. 1918. Recorder of Cardiff 1922-30. Joined Conservative Party. Assumed the surname Rhys-Williams in lieu of Williams 1938. Died 29 January 1955. [1922]

WILLIAMS, Sir Robert, Bart. Bridehead, Dorchester. Carlton, British Empire, and National. Eld. s. of Robert Williams, Esq., of Bridehead, Dorchester, by his 1st wife, Mary Anne, d. of the Rev. J.W. Cunningham. B. 1848 in London; m. 1869, Rosa, d. of N.P. Simes, Esq., of Strood Park, Sussex (she died in 1916). Educ. at Eton, and Christ Church, Oxford. A Director of Williams Deacon's Bank. Honorary Col. 4th Battalion Dorsetshire Regiment. C.A., J.P., and Dept.-Lieut. for Dorset; Lieut. of City of London, a Director of the London and S. Western Railway, etc. A Unionist, strongly opposed to the dismemberment of the Church, the Empire, or the Constitution, but in favour of amendments to the Liquor Laws. First elected for W. Dorset in May 1895 and sat until he retired in October 1922. Created Bart. 1915. President of Church Missionary Society. Died 15 April 1943. [1922]

WILLIAMS, Maj. Ronald Samuel Ainslie. 5 Linnell Close, London. Junior United Service. S. of Frank Williams, Esq., of Brasted Hall, near Sevenoaks. B. at Streatham 2 April 1890; m. 28 December 1918, Cicely, d. of H.T. Monro, Esq. Educ. at Repton, and Royal Military Academy, Woolwich. R.F.A. December 1910. A Liberal. Elected for the Sevenoaks division of Kent in December 1923 and sat until he was defeated in October 1924. J.P. for Wiltshire. County Alderman for Wiltshire

1945-52. Died 10 December 1971.
[1924 2nd ed.]

WILLIAMS, Rt. Hon. Thomas. Continued in House after 1945: full entry in Volume IV.

WILLIAMS, Thomas Jeremiah. Maes-y-gwenen Hall, Nr. Swansea. Royal Automobile. S. of William Williams, Esq., MP for the Swansea district. B. 1872 at Morriston; m. 1912, Laura Alice, d. of Thomas Marlow, Esq., of Southport. Educ. at Swansea Grammar School, University Coll. School, London, and Firth Coll., Sheffield. Was called to the bar at Gray's Inn 1902. Chairman of Beaufort Works Limited, Swansea and Mumbles Railway, etc. A Liberal. Unsuccessfully contested W. Glamorgan in 1906. Elected for Swansea District in February 1915 and for Swansea E. in December 1918 and sat until his death on 12 June 1919. [1919]

WILLIAMS, Lieut.-Col. Thomas Samuel Beauchamp. Imperial Chambers, 3 Cursitor Street, Chancery Lane, London. S. of Archdeacon Williams, of Merioneth. B. at Bangor 1877. Unmarried. Educ. on H.M.S. *Conway* and at Edinburgh University, M.B., Ch. B. Was in the Indian Medical Service for 20 years; served in the medical service during the war on the N.W. Frontier and Mesopotamia. After the fall of Kut was engaged in transporting wounded to the base. A Labour Member. Unsuccessfully contested the Bridgwater division of Somerset in 1922. Elected for the Kennington division of Lambeth in December 1923 and sat until he was defeated in October 1924. Unsuccessfully contested the Eastbourne division of E. Sussex in June 1925. Parliamentary Private Secretary to Rt. Hon. Sidney Webb, President of Board of Trade 1924. Committed suicide July 1927.
[1924 2nd ed.]

WILLIAMSON, Rt. Hon. Sir Archibald, Bart. Glenogil, Kirriemuir, Forfarshire. 36 Belgrave Square, London. Brooks's, Reform, Bath, City of London, and Automobile. S. of Stephen Williamson, Esq., MP, and Annie, d. of the Rev. Dr. T. Guthrie, of Edinburgh. B. 13 September 1860; m. 1st, 1887, Caroline Maria, d. of J.C. Hayne, Esq. (she died 1911); secondly, 1912, Hon. Agnes Freda Herschell, d. of 1st Baron Herschell. Educ. at Craigmount School and Edinburgh University. A partner in Balfour, Williamson and Company, Merchants, a Director of Central Argentine Railway, Lobitos Oilfields Limited, and other companies. J.P. for Liverpool, member of Liverpool City Council 1890-94; on the Council of Jubilee Institute for Nurses, and of the Royal National Pension Institute for Nurses; Chairman of Committees on Taxi-Cabs 1911, on Derelicts 1913, on Short Weights 1914, and on Telegraph Organization 1914. Member of Mesopotamia Commission 1916. Chairman of the Electric Power Supply Committee 1917. PC. 1918. Financial Secretary to the War Office December 1919-April 1921. Chairman of Committee on Artificial Limbs 1921. A Liberal. Unsuccessfully contested Elgin and Nairn in 1900. Sat for Elgin and Nairn from 1906 to 1918. Returned unopposed for Moray and Nairn in December 1918 and sat until June 1922 when he was Created Baron Forres. Created Bart. 1909. Died 29 October 1931. [1922]

WILLINK, Rt. Hon. Henry Urmston. Continued in House after 1945: full entry in Volume IV.

WILLISON, Herbert. Watford House, Middleton Hall Road, King's Norton. B. 1872 at Cosgrove, Northamptonshire; m. Frances Mary, d. of G. Pearson, Esq. A Solicitor at Birmingham. A Liberal. Unsuccessfully contested the Deritend division of Birmingham in 1922. Elected for the Nuneaton division of Warwickshire in December 1923 and sat until he was defeated in October 1924. Unsuccessfully contested Nuneaton division in May 1929 and, as a Liberal National, in October 1931. Died 30 November 1943. [1924 2nd ed.]

WILLOUGHBY, Hon. Claud Heathcote-Drummond-. 20 Gloucester Square, London. Carlton, Guards', and Turf. 3rd s. of 1st Earl of Ancaster. B. 15 October 1872; m. 1905, Lady Florence Astley, d. of 3rd Marq. Conyngham and widow of B.F.

Russell Astley, Esq. (she died 1946). Joined the Coldstream Guards 1891, Capt. 1900, Maj. 1908; served in South African War 1899-1902; served in the European War 1914-18; Lieut.-Col. A Unionist. Elected for the Stamford division of Lincolnshire in Januray and December 1910, and for the Rutland and Stamford division of Lincolnshire in December 1918. Sat until he retired in October 1922. Died 24 February 1950.
[1922]

WILLOUGHBY DE ERESBY, Gilbert James Heathcote-Drummond-Willoughby, Lord. Continued in House after 1945: full entry in Volume IV.

WILLS, Lieut.-Col. Sir Gilbert Alan Hamilton, Bart. Northmoor, Dulverton, Somerest. Carlton, Junior, and Cavalry. S. of Sir Frederick Wills, 1st Bart. B. 28 March 1880 at Clifton; m. 1914, Victoria May, d. of Rear-Admiral Sir Edward Chichester. Educ. privately, and at Magdalen Coll., Oxford; M.A. A Director of Imperial Tobacco Company, Maj. Royal North Devon Hussars; Lieut.-Col. Machine Gun Corps; served in the European War, Gallipoli 1915, France 1917-18; mentioned in despatches; extra Aide-de-Camp to Lord-Lieut. of Ireland 1908-12; J.P. for Somerset and Gloucestershire. A Unionist. Elected for Taunton in November 1912, and for the Weston-super-Mare division of Somerset in December 1918. Sat until he retired in October 1922. O.B.E. 1919. Succeeded as Bart. 1909. Chairman of Imperial Tobacco Company 1924-47, President 1947-56. Created Baron Dulverton 1929. High Sheriff of Gloucestershire 1928. Died 1 December 1956.
[1922]

WILLS, Wilfrid Dewhurst. 2 Whitehall Court, London. Carlton. S. of Arthur Stanley Wills, Esq., Barrister-at-Law. B. 15 October 1898. Unmarried. Educ. at Cheltenham, and Royal Military Coll., Sandhurst. Joined 5th Dragoon Guards 1917, retired 1919. Student of agriculture at Royal Agricultural Coll., Cirencester. A Conservative. Elected for Batley and Morley in October 1931 and sat until he was defeated in November 1935. Unsuccessfully contested

Batley and Morley in March 1939. Lieut.-Commander R.N.V.R. 1939-45. Died 20 April 1954.
[1935]

WILMOT, John Charles. Continued in House after 1945: full entry in Volume IV.

WILSON, Lieut.-Col. Sir Arnold Talbot, K.C.I.E., C.S.I., C.M.G., D.S.O. S. of James Wilson, Esq., D.D., Canon of Worcester. B. 18 July 1884; m. 29 July 1922, Rose, d. of C.H. Ashton, Esq., of Ellesmere, and widow of Lieut. Robin Carver, R.A.F. Educ. at Clifton, and Royal Military Coll., Sandhurst. Joined Indian Army 1903; Political Department, Government of India 1909-20; H.B.M. Consul, Mohammerah 1909-11; on Turco-Persian Frontier Commission 1913-14. Served in Mesopotamia Civil Commission 1918-20; with Anglo-Persian Oil Company 1921-32; Chairman of Industrial Health Research Board 1929-33; Chairman of Board of Trade Advisory Committee on Cinematograph Films Act 1935, and of Home Office Committee on Structural Precautions against Air Raids 1936. Joined R.A.F. as Air Gunner with the rank of Pilot Officer in November 1939. A Conservative. Elected for the Hitchin division of Hertfordshire in June 1933 and sat until 31 May 1940 when he was reported missing, presumed killed on active service. His decision to volunteer for active service at the age of 56 was all the more remarkable in the light of his long record of support for the fascist regimes in Germany and Italy.
[1941]

WILSON, Arthur Stanley. Raywell, Hull. Carlton, Marlborough, and Bachelors'. Eld. s. of Arthur Wilson, Esq., of Tranby Croft. B. 1868; m. 1892, Alice Cecil Agnes, d. of Sir Edmund A. Filmer, 9th Bart, MP Educ. at Eton, and Magdalene Coll., Cambridge. A Temporary Capt. (was a prisoner of war); threw his despatches overboard when the s.s. *Spezzia* was captured by an Austrian submarine; liberated August 1917. A J.P. for the E. Riding of Yorkshire. A Unionist. Elected for the Holderness division of the E. Riding of Yorkshire in 1900 and sat until he was defeated in November 1922. Died 12 April 1938.
[1922]

WILSON, Cecil Henry. 7 Vincent Square Mansions, London. S. of Henry Joseph Wilson, Esq., for 27 years MP for the Holmfirth division of Yorkshire. B. 8 September 1862; m. 1st, 11 June 1890, Sarah Catherine, d. of E.L. Turner, Esq., of Sheffield (she died 1909); secondly, 2 August 1912, Grace, d. of the Rev. W. Satchwell, of Nuneaton. Educ. at Friends' School, Kendal, Wesley Coll., Sheffield, and Victoria University, Manchester. A Freeman of Sheffield; Chairman of Executive of National Anti-gambling League; City Councillor for Darnall Ward, Sheffield 1903-24; J.P. for Sheffield 1907; Chairman of Licensing Justices 1932-40. Leader of Labour Group in City Council 1919-22. A Labour Member. Sat for the Attercliffe division of Sheffield from November 1922-October 1931 when he was defeated. Re-elected for the Attercliffe division in November 1935 and sat until he resigned in February 1944. Died 7 November 1945. [1944]

WILSON, Sir Charles Henry. Osgodby House, Yorkshire. The Bungalow, Nawton, Yorkshire. Constitutional, and St. Stephen's. S. of John Wilson, Esq., of Skipwith Hall, Yorkshire. B. 13 January 1859; m. 1st, Victoria, d. of Joseph Renton, Esq., of Harrogate; secondly, 24 June 1920, Elizabeth Parvin, d. of J.P. Garnett, Esq., of Nawton, Yorkshire, and widow of Joshua Hill. Incorporated Accountant 1895; LL.D. University of Leeds March 1923. Freeman of the City of London 1917 and of Leeds 1923; French Consular Agent for Leeds. Transcribed for publication the Registers of the Parish of Skipwith, E. Riding of Yorkshire. Member of Leeds City Council 1890-1926; Alderman and J.P. for Leeds for 20 years. Knighted 1923. A Conservative. Elected for Central Leeds in July and December 1923 and sat until he was defeated in May 1929. Died 30 December 1930. [1929]

WILSON, Clyde Tabor. 2 Harcourt Buildings, Temple, London. Carlton, Constitutional, and Royal Automobile. S. of Foden Wilson, Esq., M.R.C.S., L.R.C.P., of Birkenhead. B. 21 September 1889. Unmarried. Educ. at Rugby, and Trinity Coll., Cambridge, B.A., LL.B. A Barrister-at-Law, Inner Temple 1913. Recorder of Birkenhead 1934-35. Member of London County Council from 1925 to 1935. A Conservative. Unsuccessfully contested N. Lambeth in May 1929. Elected for the W. Toxteth division of Liverpool in October 1931 and sat until May 1935 when he was appointed a Metropolitan Police Magistrate. Metropolitan Police Magistrate 1935-62. Served with 5th London Brigade R.F.A. 1914-18. Died 13 November 1971. [1935]

WILSON, Daniel Martin. 15 Fitzwilliam Place, Dublin. Constitutional, and Junior Constitutional. S. of the Rev. David Wilson, D.D., a Moderator of the Presbyterian General Assembly. B. at Limerick 1862; m. 14 August 1894, Eleanor, d. of the Rev. Robert Black, of Dundalk. Educ. at the Royal Academical Institution, Belfast, and Trinity Coll., Dublin, B.A. Barrister, Michaelmas 1885; K.C. (Ireland) 1908; Gray's Inn 1919; Bencher King's Inn 1911; Solicitor-Gen. for Ireland July 1919-June 1921. 2nd Lieut. Royal Inniskillen Fusiliers 1914; Capt. July 1915; resigned owing to ill-health with honorary rank of Capt. 1916. A Unionist. Elected for W. Down in December 1918 and sat until he was appointed Recorder of Belfast in June 1921. Recorder of Belfast and County Court Judge, Co. Antrim June-October 1921. Judge of High Court of Northern Ireland October 1921-January 1932. Died 5 January 1932. [1921]

WILSON, Godfrey Harold Alfred. Clare College, Cambridge. Athenaeum, and Oxford & Cambridge. S. of Daniel Wilson, Esq. B. 29 October 1871; m. 1899, Margaret Mabel, d. of the Rev. J. Bartlett. Educ. at Melbourne Grammar School, Trinity Coll., University of Melbourne, and Clare Coll., Cambridge. Master of Clare Coll., Cambridge 1929-39; Treasurer of Cambridge University 1926-29. A Conservative. Elected for Cambridge University in May 1929, returned unopposed for Cambridge University in October 1931 and sat until he resigned in January 1935. Vice-Chancellor of Cambridge University 1935-37. O.B.E. Secretary of Financial Board, Cambridge

University 1920-26. Died 13 July 1958.
[1935]

WILSON, Field Marshal Sir Henry Hughes, Bart., G.C.B., D.S.O. 36 Eaton Place, London. Grove End, Bagshot, Surrey. Currygrane, Edgeworthstown, Co. Longford, Ireland. White's, Travellers', and Royal Yacht Squadron. S. of James Wilson, Esq., Dept.-Lieut., and J.P., of Edgeworthstown, Co. Longford. B. 5 May 1864; m. 1891, Cecil Mary, d. of George Cecil Gore Wray, Esq., of Ardnamona, Co. Donegal. Educ. at Marlborough Coll. Entered army 1884, Royal Irish Regiment, Rifle Brigade. Served in Burma 1885-89. Brigade-Maj. 2nd Brigade, Aldershot 1897-99. Served in South Africa 1899-1901. D.S.O. 1900. Commandant, Staff Coll. 1907-10. C.B. 1908. Director of Military Operations, War Office 1910-14. K.C.B. 1915. G.O.C. Eastern Command 1917-18. Chief of Imperial General Staff 1918-22. G.C.B. 1918. Created Bart. 1919. Col. Commandant Rifle Brigade 1920. Croix de Guerre, Legion of Honour, Grand Cross of Russian White Eagle. Field Marshal 1919. A Unionist. Elected for N. Down in February 1922 and sat until 22 June 1922 when he was murdered on the steps of his London home.

WILSON, James. 40 Lynwood Terrace, Newcastle-upon-Tyne. S. of William Wilson, Esq., Farmer, of Aberdeenshire. B. 1879; m. 4 November 1899, Marjorie Ann, d. of William Park, Esq., of Belhelvie. Educ. at Oldmeldrum Public School. A Railwayman. Member of Newcastle Council 1914-21; Executive National Union Railwaymen 1916-19. A Labour Member. Elected for Dudley March 1921, defeated November 1922. Unsuccessfully contested the Rushcliffe division of Nottinghamshire in December 1923, and Oldham October 1924. Elected for Oldham in May 1929 and sat until he was defeated in October 1931. Died 15 August 1943. [1931 2nd ed.]

WILSON, Rt. Hon. John William. 4 Whitehall Court, London. Perrycroft, Malvern. National Liberal, Reform, and Bath. Eld. s. of John E. Wilson, Esq., of Wyddrington, Edgbaston, J.P., and Catharine, d. of George Stacey, Esq., of Tottenham. B. 1858 at Edgbaston; m. 1st, 1883, Florence Jane, d. of Smith Harrison, Esq., of Woodford, Essex (she died 1911); secondly, 1919, Isabella, d. of Andrew Bannatyne, Esq., of Hamilton. Educ. at Grove House, Tottenham, and in Germany. A Partner in the firm of Albright and Wilson Limited, Chemical Manufacturers, of Oldbury; a J.P. for Worcestershire and Herefordshire; a Director of Great Western Railway. A Liberal Unionist until April 1903 when he joined the Liberals. Represented N. Worcestershire from 1895 to 1918; elected for the Stourbridge division of Worcestershire in December 1918 and sat until he was defeated in November 1922. PC. 1911. Died 18 June 1932. [1922]

WILSON, Joseph Havelock. St. George's Hall, Westminster Bridge Road, London. National Liberal. S. of John Wilson, Esq. B. at Sunderland 16 August 1858; m. 1879, Jane Anne Watham. Educ. at the Sunderland Boys' British School. President of the National Sailors and Firemen's Union; Secretary of the Merchant Seamen's League. Unsuccessfully contested Bristol E. in 1890 as an Independent Socialist. Returned for Middlesbrough in 1892 as a Labour Member, being the first Labour candidate to defeat a Liberal. From 1895 to 1910 he enjoyed Liberal support. He was defeated only in 1900 and retired in January 1910. Unsuccessfully contested Wandsworth in 1913 as Independent Labour candidate with unofficial Liberal support. Elected for South Shields in October and December 1918 and sat until defeated in 1922 standing as a National Liberal. He kept his Union out of the General Strike of 1926. C.B.E. 1917. Companion of Honour 1922. Died 16 April 1929. [1922]

WILSON, Lieut.-Col. Rt. Hon. Leslie Orme. 3 Buckingham Gate, London. Tithe Barn, Wokingham, Berkshire. Carlton, and Bath. S. of H. Wilson, Esq. B. 1 August 1876 in London; m. 1909, Winifred, d. of Capt. C. Smith, of New South Wales. Educ. at St. Michael's, Westgate, and St. Paul's School. Entered Royal Marines 1895; Capt. 1901, retired 1909. Capt. Berkshire

R.H.A. (T.). Served in South African War 1900, mentioned in despatches. D.S.O. 1900. Aide-de-Camp to Gov. of New South Wales 1903-09. Lieut.-Col. (temporary) Hawke Battalion R.N. Division; mentioned in despatches; C.M.G. 1916; wounded in the left lung 13 November 1916; Lieut.Col. Reserve of Officers, Royal Marines. Parliamentary Assistant Secretary to the War Cabinet 1918; Parliamentary Secretary to the Ministry of Shipping January 1919-March 1921; Joint Parliamentary Secretary to the Treasury and Chief Conservative Whip April 1921-October 1922. Parliamentary Secretary to the Treasury and Chief Whip October 1922-July 1923. A Conservative. Unsuccessfully contested Poplar in January 1910 and Reading in December 1910. Elected for Reading in November 1913, and re-elected there in December 1918. Unsuccessfully contested the St. George's division of Westminster in November 1922. Elected for Portsmouth S. in December 1922 and sat until July 1923 when he was appointed Gov. of Bombay. PC. 1922. Gov. of Bombay 1923-28. Gov. of Queensland 1932-46. Died 29 September 1955. [1923]

WILSON, Sir Mathew Richard Henry, Bart., C.S.I., D.S.O. Eshton Hall, Gargrave, Yorkshire. Hill House, Stanmore, Middlesex. Carlton, Turf, Pratt's, St. James's, and Bath. Eld. s. of Sir Mathew Wilson, 4th Bart. B. 25 August 1875; m. 1905, Hon. Barbara Lister, d. of 4th Baron Ribblesdale (she died 1943). Educ. at Harrow, and Sandhurst. Joined 10th Hussars 1897, Capt. 1902, Maj. 1908, later commanded Middlesex Hussars Yeomanry. Served in South Africa 1899-1902. Instructor at Royal Military Coll., Sandhurst 1907-09. Military Secretary to Commander-in Chief in India 1909. C.S.I. 1911; D.S.O. 1918. A Unionist. Elected for S.W. Bethnal Green in February 1914 and sat until he was defeated in November 1922. Succeeded as Bart. 1914. Died 17 May 1958. [1922]

WILSON, Col. Sir Murrough John, K.B.E. Cliffe Hall, Darlington. Carlton. S. of Lieut.-Col. J.G. Wilson, C.B., of Cliffe Hall, Darlington. B. 14 September 1875; m. 1st, 16 February 1904, Sybil May, d. of Sir Powlett Milbank, 2nd Bart., MP (she died 1930); secondly, 1934, Gladys Rhoda, widow of Hon. A.P. Henderson. Educ. at Marlborough. Landowner; Lieut.-Col. T.F. Reserve. Created K.B.E. 1927. A Conservative. Elected for the Richmond division of the N. Riding of Yorkshire in December 1918. Returned unopposed for the Richmond division in November 1922, and sat until he retired in May 1929. County Councillor and Dept.-Lieut. for N. Riding of Yorkshire. Dept. Chairman of London and North Eastern Railway Company 1934-46. Died 30 April 1946. [1929]

WILSON, Robert John. The Cleveland Hotel, 27 Montagu Street, London. 4 Side Cliff Road, Sunderland. S. of Robert Simpson Wilson, Esq., Grocer. B. at Gateshead 14 July 1865; m. 1887, Catherine Soulsby, d. of Robert and Kate Soulsby. Educ. privately at Durham. Drapery Manager 1888-1912. Member of Sunderland Borough Council 1907-22. J.P. 1916. Chairman of Electricity Committee and Governors of Traning Coll. A Labour Member. Unsuccessfully contested N. Newcastle-on-Tyne in 1918. Sat for the Jarrow division of Durham from November 1922 until he was defeated in October 1931. Parliamentary Private Secretary to W. Leach when Under Secretary for Air 1924. Died 5 November 1946. [1931 2nd ed.]

WILSON, Roderick Roy. 11A, St. James's Court, Buckingham Gate, London. Wood End, Pyrford, Woking. Constitutional. S. of Dr. Thomas Wilson, of Alton, Hampshire. B. 10 August 1876; m. 3 June 1908, Florence Emily, d. of George Garratt, Esq., of Runcorn. Educ. privately. Assistant Gen. Manager of Bank of British West Africa Limited until 1924; Chairman of British Guiana Parliamentary Commission 1926. A Conservative. Unsuccessfully contested the Lichfield division of Staffordshire in December 1923. Elected for Lichfield in October 1924 and sat until he retired in May 1929. Knighted June 1929. Director of Bank of British West Africa Limited from 1929, Vice-Chairman from 1937. Died 27 August 1942. [1929]

WILSON, William Tyson. 98 Mornington Road, Bolton. S. of Edward Wilson, Esq., Master Tailor, of Undermillbeck. B. 1855 in Westmorland; m. 1882, Frances, d. of George Tyrrell, Esq., of Lancaster. Was apprenticed as a Carpenter. Chairman of the General and Executive Councils of the Amalgamated Society of Carpenters and Joiners 1898-1906; one of the Founders of Bolton Building Trades Federation, and took a leading part in establishing Central and National Conciliation Boards for settlement of disputes in the building trade. Whip to Labour Party 1915; Chief Labour Whip January 1919. J.P. for Lancashire. A Labour Member. Elected for the Westhoughton division of Lancashire in 1906 and sat until his death on 14 August 1921.   [1921]

WILSON-FOX, Henry. 20 Lowndes Square, London. Carlton, Junior Carlton, and St. Stephen's. S. of Wilson Fox, Esq., M.D., F.R.S., and Emily Anne Doyle. B. in London 18 August 1863; m. 1898, the Hon. Eleanor Birch Sclater-Booth, 5th d. of the 1st Baron Basing. Educ. at Charterhouse, Marlborough Coll., University Coll., London, and Trinity Coll., Cambridge. Was called to the bar at Lincoln's Inn 1888; Manager of British South Africa Company from 1897 and Director and member of the Executive Committee from 1913. A Unionist. Elected unopposed for the Tamworth division of Warwickshire in February 1917; re-elected there in December 1918 and sat until his death on 22 November 1921. On the staff of Consolidated Gold Fields, South Africa 1889. Editor of *South African Mining Journal* 1892. Public Prosecutor of Rhodesia 1894. Fellow of Royal Statistical Society and Royal Colonial Institute. Vice-President of Royal Geographical Society. Died 22 November 1921.   [1921]

WINBY, Lieut.-Col. Lewis Phillips. 11 Trevor Square, London. Carlton, Cavalry, Oxford & Cambridge, and Ranelagh. S. of F.C. Winby, Esq. B. 17 January 1874. Educ. at Brighton Coll., and Trinity Coll., Cambridge; M.A. A Civil Engineer; served with R.E. in South African War 1900-02; Lieut.-Col. Westminster Dragoons 1914-18. A Conservative. Elected for the Harborough division of Leicestershire in October 1924 and sat until he retired in May 1929. Died 27 January 1956.   [1929]

WINDSOR, Ivor Miles Windsor-Clive, Visct. 24 Oxford Square, London. Carlton, Bachelors', Turf, and Beefsteak, S. of Earl and Countess of Plymouth. B. at Hewell Grange, Redditch 4 February 1889; m. 14 July 1921, Lady Irene Charteris, d. of Earl and Countess of Wemyss. Educ. at Eton, and Trinity Coll., Cambridge. Parliamentary Private Secretary to Mr. W.C. Bridgeman (unpaid) November 1922. A Conservative. Returned unopposed for the Ludlow division of Shropshire in January 1922 and sat until March 1923 when he succeeded to the Peerage as Earl of Plymouth. Lord-Lieut. of Glamorgan from 1923. Government Chief Whip in the House of Lords June 1925-January 1929. Under-Secretary for the Dominions January-June 1929. Parliamentary Secretary to Ministry of Transport November 1931-September 1932. Under-Secretary for the Colonies September 1932-July 1936. Under-Secretary for Foreign Affairs July 1936-May 1939. PC. 1929. Styled Visct. Windsor from the death of his elder brother in 1908 until his father's death in 1923. Pro-Chancellor of University of Wales 1941. Dept.-Lieut. for Worcestershire and Shropshire. Sub-Prior, Order of St. John of Jerusalem 1943. Died 1 October 1943.   [1923]

WINDSOR, Walter. 8 Willow Road, London. Labour. S. of James Windsor, Esq., Dock Labourer, of Bethnal Green. B. 18 July 1884; m. 1910. Educ. at Elementary School. Member of London County Council 1934-37. A Labour Member. Unsuccessfully contested N.E. Bethnal Green in November 1922 as a Communist with unofficial Labour support. Sat for N.E. Bethnal Green from December 1923 to May 1929 when he was defeated. Unsuccessfully contested E. Nottingham in October 1931. Elected for Hull central in November 1935 and sat until his death on 29 June 1945 during the campaign for the general election for which he was a candidate. (Polling was delayed and another Labour candidate was nominated).   [1945]

WINDSOR-CLIVE, Lieut.-Col. George, C.M.G. 35 Cadogan Square, London. Guards', and Carlton. S. of Lieut.-Col. Hon. G.H.W. Windsor Clive, (2nd s. of Hon. R.H. Clive and Harriet Baroness Windsor) and Hon. Gertrude Trefusis, d. of 19th Baron Clinton. B. 6 April 1878; m. 19 November 1912, Sidney, d. of Charles Lacaita, Esq., MP of Selham House, Petworth (she died 5 July 1935). Educ. at Eton, and Royal Military Coll., Sandhurst. Joined the Coldstream Guards September 1897. Served in the South African War 1899-1901; Staff Coll. 1906-07; France, etc. 1914-18. C.M.G. 1919. Retired March 1923. A Conservative. Elected for the Ludlow division of Shropshire in April 1923 and sat until he retired in June 1945. Died 25 June 1968.   [1945]

WINFREY, Sir Richard. Castor House, Nr. Peterborough. Reform, and National Liberal. S. of Richard F. Winfrey, Esq., J.P., of Long Sutton, Lincolnshire. B. 8 August 1858; m. 1897, Annie Lucy, d. of William Pattinson, Esq., of Ruskington, Lincolnshire. A Newspaper Proprietor; J.P. for Norfolk and the Liberty of Peterborough. Chairman of Lincolnshire and Norfolk Small Holdings Association. Private Secretary (unpaid) to Lord Carrington when President of Board of Agriculture. Parliamentary Secretary to the Board of Agriculture December 1916 to January 1919. Knighted 1914. A Liberal. Unsuccessfully contested S.W. Norfolk in 1895 and 1900. Represented S.W. Norfolk from 1906 to 1923. Elected for the Gainsborough division of Lindsey in December 1923 and sat until he was defeated in October 1924. A Pharmaceutical Chemist. Election Agent in Spalding and Wisbech from 1885. Member of Holland County Council from 1889. Member of Peterborough City Council 1898-1918, Mayor 1914. Died 18 April 1944.   [1924 2nd ed.]

WINGFIELD DIGBY, Kenelm Simon Digby. See DIGBY, Kenelm Simon Digby Wingfield. Continued in House after 1945: full entry in Volume IV.

WINTERTON, Edward Turnour, Rt. Hon. Earl. 61 Eccleston Square, London. Shillinglee Park, Chiddingfold. Carlton, Turf, and Beefsteak. S. of 5th Earl Winterton and Lady Georgiana Hamilton, d. of 1st Duke of Abercorn. B. 4 April 1883; m. 28 February 1924, Hon. Cecilia Monica Wilson, d. of Charles, 2nd Baron Nunburnholme. Educ. at Eton, and New Coll., Oxford. Succeeded his father as 6th Earl Winterton in the Peerage of Ireland 1907. Served in Gallipoli and Palestine 1915, with Sussex Yeomanry, and afterwards with Imperial Camel Corps. T.D. Had Orders of the Nile and El Nahda. Under-Secretary of State for India March 1922-January 1924, and November 1924-June 1929. Parliamentary Private Secretary to Rt. Hon. George Pretyman when Financial Secretary to the Admiralty 1903-05. Chancellor of Duchy of Lancaster May 1937-January 1939. Dept. to Secretary of State for Air and Vice-President of Air Council March-May 1938. Member of the Cabinet March 1938-January 1939; Assistant to Home Secretary June 1938. Chairman of Intergovernmental Committee 1938-45. Paymaster-Gen. January-November 1939. Dept.-Lieut. and J.P. for Sussex. PC. 1924. Member of Sussex T.A. A Conservative. Member for Horsham division November 1904-December 1918, for Horsham and Worthing division December 1918-July 1945, and for Horsham division from July 1945 until he retired in October 1951. Father of the House of Commons 1945-51. Styled Visct. Turnour until he succeeded to the Earldom in 1907. Created Baron Turnour in the U.K. Peerage 1952. Author of *Pre-War*, *Fifty Tumultuous* and *Orders of the Day*. Died 26 August 1962.   [1951]

WINTERTON, George Ernest. Gracedieu, Warlingham, Surrey. S. of George Winterton, Esq., and Martha Mary, d. of J. Horsley, Esq. B. 17 May 1873; m. September 1902, Ethel, d. of William Clarke, Esq., of Oadby, Leicester. Educ. at Charnwood Street Elementary School, Leicester and Borough Road Coll., Isleworth, London. A Schoolmaster. Interested in Temperance Work and Police Problems. On the staff of the *Daily Herald* 1920-29. A Labour Member. Unsuccessfully contested the Loughborough division of Leicestershire in December 1923 and October 1924. Elected for the Lough-borough division of Leicestershire in May 1929 and sat until he was defeated in October 1931. Unsuccessfully contested the Lough-borough division of Leicestershire in November 1935. Died 15 May 1942.

[1931 2nd ed.]

WINTRINGHAM, Margaret. Little Grimsby Hall, Louth. Forum. D. of David Longbottom, Esq., of Silsden, Yorkshire. B. at Oldfield, Yorkshire 4 August 1879; m. 1903, Tom Wintringham, MP for the Louth division of Lincolnshire from June 1920 until his death in August 1921. Educ. at Keighley Girls' Grammar School, and Bed-ford Coll. Among many other activities was V.A.D. at the Louth Auxiliary Hospital during the war; Chairman of the Women's War Agriculture Committee; member of the County Agriculture Committee for con-serving and increasing food supplies; Presi-dent of the Louth Women's Liberal Associa-tion. J.P. for Lindsey. A Liberal. Elected for the Louth division of Lincolnshire in succes-sion to her husband in September 1921-the second woman MP to take her seat. Sat until she was defeated in October 1924. Un-successfully contested Louth in May 1929 and the Aylesbury division of Buckingham-shire in November 1935. President of Women's National Liberal Federation. Member of Lindsey County Council 1933. Died 10 March 1955.   [1924 2nd ed.]

WINTRINGHAM, Thomas. Little Grims-by Hall, Louth. National Liberal. S. of John and Mary Wintringham. B. 22 August 1867 at The Abbey, Grimsby; m. 1903, Margaret, d. of David Longbottom, Esq., of Silsden, Yorkshire. Educ. at Mill Hill School. A Timber Inspector. A Liberal. Unsuccessfully contested Grimsby in 1898. Elected for the Louth division of Lincoln-shire in June 1920 and sat until his death on 8 August 1921. His widow was elected for Louth in September 1921.   [1921]

WISE, Alfred Roy. Continued in House after 1945: full entry in Volume IV.

WISE, Edward Frank, C.B. 13 John Street, London. Hazledene, Wendover,

Buckinghamshire. National Labour. S. of Edward Wise, Esq., of Bury St. Edmunds. B. 3 July 1885; m. 1912, Dorothy Lilian Owen, M.A. Educ. at Guildhall Feoffment Elementary School, King Edward VI School, Bury St. Edmunds, and Sidney Sussex Coll., Cambridge, M.A. Barrister-at-Law, Middle Temple 1911. Higher division of Civil Service 1908-23; Junior Clerk House of Commons 1908-12; National Health Insurance Committee 1912-14; Assistant Director Army Contracts 1915; Second Secretary to Ministry of Food 1918; British representative on Inter-allied Supreme Economic Council 1919; Acting Assistant Secretary Board of Trade 1922; Economic Adviser on Foreign Trade to Russian Co-operative Movement 1923-29. A Labour Member. Unsuccessfully contes-ted Bradford N. October 1924. Elected for Leicester E. in May 1929 and sat until he was defeated in October 1931. C.B. 1919. Sub-Warden of Toynbee Hall 1911. Died 5 November 1933.   [1931 2nd ed.]

WISE, Sir Fredric. Holwell Court, Hat-field, Hertfordshire. Carlton, and Oriental. S. of Alexander J.P. Wise, Dept.-Lieut. and J.P. of Belleville Park, Cappoquin, Co. Waterford. B. 1871; m. 16 June 1904, Lucy, d. of Sir Thomas Wrightson, 1st Bart., MP of Neasham Hall, Darlington. Educ. at Marlborough Coll. Founded in 1903 the firm of Wise, Speke and Company, Stockbrokers, of Newcastle-on-Tyne. Dept.-Lieut. and J.P. for Northumberland. Knighted 1924. Charter Mayor of Ilford 1926. A Director of *Daily Express*. A Conser-vative. Sat for Ilford from September 1920 until his death on 26 January 1928.

[1928]

WITHERS, Sir John James, C.B.E. 77 South Lodge, Circus Road, London. 4 Arundel Street, London. Carlton, Oxford & Cambridge, and Alpine. S. of James Tuck Withers, Esq. B. 21 December 1863; m. 1893, Caroline, d. of Dr. Gifford Rans-ford. Educ. at Eton, and King's Coll., Cambridge; M.A., Fellow of St. Catharine's Coll., Cambridge 1920. Founded the firm of Withers and Company. Admitted a Solicitor in 1890; President of the Alpine

Club 1932; in the Propaganda Department of Ministry of Information 1916-18. Created Knight Bach. 1929; C.B.E. 1918. A Conservative. Sat for Cambridge University from February 1926 until his death on 29 December 1939. [1940]

WOLMER, Rt. Hon. Roundell Cecil Palmer, Visct. 3 Chester Gate, Regent's Park, London. Temple Manor, Selborne, Alton, Hampshire. Carlton. S. of 2nd Earl of Selborne. B. 15 April 1887; m. 1st, 9 June 1910, Hon. Grace Ridley, d. of 1st Visct. Ridley (she died 1959); secondly, 1966, Valerie Irene de Thomka de Tomkahaza et Folkusfalva (she died 1968). Educ. at Winchester, and University Coll., Oxford. Parliamentary Private Secretary to Lord Robert Cecil, Under-Secretary for Foreign Affairs November 1916 to November 1918; Assistant Director of the War Trade Department January 1917-18; Parliamentary Secretary to the Board of Trade October 1922-January 1924; Assistant Postmaster-Gen. November 1924-June 1929. PC. 1929. A Director of National Provincial Bank 1937, Chairman 1951-54; Chairman of Cement Makers' Federation 1934-42 and 1945-51; Vice-Chairman of Boot's Pure Drug Company Limited 1936-63. A Conservative. Unsuccessfully contested the Newton division of Lancashire in January 1910. Elected for the Newton division in December 1910, and for the Aldershot division of Hampshire in December 1918. Sat until November 1940 when he resigned. Called up to the House of Lords as Baron Selborne January 1941. Director of Cement, Ministry of Works and Buildings 1940-42. Succeeded his father as Earl of Selborne in March 1942. Minister of Economic Warfare and Minister responsible for the secret Special Operations Executive February 1942-May 1945. President of Church Army 1949-61. Chairman of House of Laity, Church Assembly 1955-59. Styled Visct. Wolmer from his father's succession to the Earldom in 1895 until his father's death in 1942. Died 3 September 1971. [1940]

WOMERSLEY, Rt. Hon. Sir Walter James. St. Brelades, Seacroft Road, Cleethorpes. Constitutional. S. of William Womersley, Esq., of Bradford. B. 5 February 1878; m. 20 January 1905, Annie, d. of John Stamp, Esq. (she died 1952). Educ. at Bradford Board School. Partner in the firm of Womersley and Stamp, House Furnishers, Jewellers and General Merchants. Vice-President of Association of Municipal Corporations; Honorary Vice-President National Chamber of Trade. Mayor of Grimsby 1922-23; member of Grimsby Town Council from 1911; Alderman 1931; J.P.; Knight Bach. June 1934. Parliamentary Private Secretary to Sir Kingsley Wood when Parliamentary Secretary Board of Education August-October 1931. A Lord Commissioner of the Treasury November 1931-December 1935; Assistant Postmaster-Gen. December 1935-June 1939. Minister of Pensions June 1939-July 1945. PC 1941. A Conservative. Elected for Grimsby in October 1924 and sat until he was defeated in July 1945. Created Bart. August 1945. Died 15 March 1961.
[1945]

WOOD, Brooks Crompton, C.B.E. Holnicote House, Allerford, Taunton. Bruern Abbey, Kingham, Oxfordshire. Carlton, Albemarle, and Royal Automobile. S. of Charles Manby Wood, Esq., of Swansea. B. 27 March 1870; m. 24 October 1900, Mary Elizabeth Margaret, d. of Sir Alfred Billson, MP, of Rowton Castle, Shrewsbury. Educ. at Birkenhead School, and University Coll., Liverpool. Senior partner of Smith, Rathbone and Company, Cotton Merchants, of Liverpool; Director of State Fire Insurance Company; Master of Exmoor Fox Hounds 1920-23. Raw Cotton Adviser to the War Office and Chairman of Board of Trade Commission for the Control of Egyptian Cotton 1915-18. A Conservative. Elected for the Bridgwater division of Somerset in October 1924 and sat until he retired in May 1929. Died 29 July 1946. [1929]

WOOD, Capt. Hon. Charles Ingram Courtenay. See IRWIN, Capt. Charles Ingram Courtenay Wood, The Lord.

WOOD, Edmund Walter Hanbury. 57 Eaton Square, London. Carlton. S. of Sir John Wood, 1st Bart. MP, of Hengrave. B. 16 November 1898; m. 17 January 1920,

Margaret, d. of George Coles Walton, Esq. Educ. at Eton, and Royal Military Coll., Sandhurst. Joined 2nd Life Guards 1917; resigned 1920. Served in France 1918. A Conservative. Elected for Stalybridge and Hyde in October 1924 and sat until he was defeated in May 1929. Member of London County Council 1932-46. J.P. for County of London. Chairman of London Municipal Society. Died 12 December 1947.   [1929]

WOOD, Rt. Hon. Edward Frederick Lindley. 88 Eaton Square, London. Garrowby, Yorkshire. Carlton. S. of 2nd Visct. Halifax. B. 1881 at Powderham Castle, Devon; m. 1909, Lady Dorothy Onslow, d. of 4th Earl of Onslow. Educ. at Eton, and Christ Church, Oxford; M.A., Fellow of All Souls Coll., Oxford 1903. J.P. for West and East Riding of Yorkshire. Maj. Yorkshire Dragoons Yeomanry; served with Expeditionary Force 1915-17. Author of biography of John Keble in Leaders of the Church Series. Under-Secretary for the Colonies April 1921 to October 1922; President of Board of Education October 1922-January 1924 and June 1932-June 1935. Minister of Agriculture and Fisheries November 1924-October 1925. PC. 1922. A Conservative. Sat for the Ripon division of the W. Riding of Yorkshire from January 1910 until October 1925 when he was appointed Viceroy of India. Viceroy of India 1925-31. Created Baron Irwin 1925. K.G. 1931. Succeeded his father as Visct. Halifax 1934; created Earl of Halifax 1944. Secretary of State for War June-November 1935. Lord Privy Seal November 1935-May 1937. Lord President May 1937-February 1938. Foreign Secretary February 1938-December 1940. Leader of the House of Lords November 1935-October 1938 and October-December 1940. Ambassador to United States 1940-46. Chancellor of Oxford University 1933-59, of Sheffield University 1948-59. High Steward of Westminster 1947-59. Died 23 December 1959.   [1925]

WOOD, Rt. Hon. Sir Howard Kingsley. 15 Walbrook, London. Broomhill Bank, Tunbridge Wells. Carlton. S. of the Rev. Arthur Wood, Wesleyan; Minister. B. 1881; m. 1908, Agnes, d. of Henry Fawcett, Esq.

Admitted a Solicitor 1903. Senior partner of Kingsley Wood and Company, Solicitors. Parliamentary Private Secretary to Minister of Health 1918-22; Secretary of Parliamentary Allotments Committee 1923; member of London County Council for Woolwich 1911-18; Chairman of Old Age Pensions Committee 1915, and London Insurance Committee 1916. Master of Worshipful Company of Wheelwrights 1924. Parliamentary Secretary to Ministry of Health November 1924-June 1929, to Ministry of Education September-November 1931; Postmaster-Gen. November 1931-June 1935; Minister of Health June 1935-May 1938; Secretary of State for Air May 1938-April 1940. Lord Privy Seal and Chairman of Home and Food Policy Committee April-May 1940; Chancellor of the Exchequer May 1940-September 1943; member of the War Cabinet October 1940-February 1942. Chairman of Executive Committee National Union of Conservative and Unionist Organisations 1930-32. Grand Master of the Primrose League 1938. Created Knight Bach. 1918. PC. 1928. J.P. for Brighton. Joined the Cabinet December 1933. A Conservative. Sat for Woolwich W. from December 1918 until his death on 21 September 1943.   [1943]

WOOD, Col. Sir John, Bart. Hengrave Hall, Bury St. Edmunds. Whitfield House, Glossop. Forrest Lodge, Dalry Galloway, N.B. Carlton, Constitutional, Bachelors', and New University. S. of J.H. Wood, Esq., J.P., of Whitfield, Derbyshire. B. 8 September 1857; m. 1st, 1883, Estelle, d. of Henry Benham, Esq. (divorced 1889); secondly, 1892, Hon. Gertrude Emily Bateman-Hanbury, d. of 2nd Baron Bateman (she died 1927). Educ. at Rugby, and Magdalen Coll., Oxford; M.A. Was called to the bar at the Inner Temple 1883. A J.P. and Dept.-Lieut. for Herefordshire; Sheriff 1900, and a J.P. for Derbyshire and Suffolk. Lieut.-Col. and Honorary Col. late 4th V.B. Cheshire Regiment V.D.; Commandant late 5th V.B. Cheshire Regiment. Created Bart. 1918. A Unionist. Elected for Stalybridge in January and December 1910 and for the Stalybridge and Hyde division of Cheshire in December 1918. Sat until he retired in October 1922. Died 28 January 1951. [1922]

WOOD, Maj. Sir Murdoch McKenzie, O.B.E. 51 South Street, London. Mayfield, Cullen, Banffshire. Reform, National Liberal, and Scottish Liberal. S. of James Wood, Esq., of Cullen, Banffshire. B. 1881; m. 1924, Muriel, d. of Moss Davis, Esq. Educ. at Fordyce Academy, Banffshire, Edinburgh University, and London School of Economics, M.A. Barrister-at-Law, Gray's Inn 1910. Sub-editor of the *Daily Mail*. Served in 6th Battalion Gordon Highlanders 1914-18; and on Staff of R.A.F. 1918-19. Knight Bach. 1932. Scottish Liberal Whip 1923-24 and Assistant Government Whip August 1931-September 1932. A Liberal. Unsuccessfully contested Ayr Burghs in December 1918. Sat for central Aberdeenshire from April 1919-October 1924 when he was defeated Elected for Banffshire in May 1929; returned unopposed in October 1931 and sat until he was defeated in November 1935. O.B.E. 1919. Dept.-Lieut. for Banffshire. Liberal Whip 1932-34. Died 11 October 1949. [1935]

WOOD, Sir Samuel Hill, Bart. See HILL-WOOD, Sir Samuel Hill, Bart.

WOODBURN, Arthur. Continued in House after 1945: full entry in Volume IV.

WOODCOCK, Col. Herbert Charles. Clifton, Bristol. Carlton, Conservative, and Royal Automobile. Constitutional, Bristol. S. of Alderman Charles Woodcock, J.P. B. 2 June 1871; m. Annie, d. of William Saint Lyddon, Esq., of Clifton. Member of Bristol Stock Exchange 1898. Alderman of City and Co. of Bristol. Member of Gloucestershire T.F.A. Served on active service 1914-18. Commanded 6th Battalion Gloucester Regiment 1911 and mobilized Unit 1914. T.D. Commanding-Brigadier. First Chairman of Junior Conservative Association. President Bristol and Wessex Aeroplane Club; President of Society of Bristolians in London; J.P. for Bristol. Member of Parliamentary Commercial Commission and of Select Committee on Estimates. Author of numerous financial contributions.

Dept.-Lieut. for Gloucestershire and Bristol. A Conservative. Elected for the Thornbury division of Gloucestershire in November 1922, defeated December 1923. Sat for the Everton division of Liverpool from October 1924 until retired in May 1929. Died 18 January 1950. [1929]

WOODS, Rev. George Saville. Continued in House after 1945: full entry in Volume IV.

WOODS, Sir Robert Henry. 39 Merrion Square, Dublin. Rathleigh, Killiney, Co. Dublin. Constitutional, St. Stephen's, and University. Royal Irish Yacht. S. of Christopher Woods, Esq., and Dorothy (née Lowe). B. at Tullamore 1865; m. 1894, Margaret, d. of James J. Shaw, Esq., K.C., Recorder of Belfast. Educ. at Wesley Coll., Dublin, Trinity Coll., Dublin, and Vienna. Graduated in Medicine 1889, M.B., etc., M.Ch. *Hon. Causa* Dub. 1913. President Royal College Surgeons in Ireland 1910-11. Professor of Laryngology and Otology, Trinity Coll., Dublin. Numerous contributions to surgical literature. An Independent Unionist. Unsuccessfully contested Dublin University 1917. Elected for Dublin University in December 1918 and sat until he retired in October 1922. Knighted 1913. Died 8 September 1938. [1922]

WOODWARK, Lieut.-Col. George Graham, C.B.E. Croylands, King's Lynn. National Liberal. 2nd s. of Alderman George Smith Woodwark, J.P., Mayor of King's Lynn 1887. B. at King's Lynn 1 July 1874; m. 1930, Isabel, d. of Hunter Palmer, Esq. Educ. at Grammar School, King's Lynn. Long engaged as a Territorial Officer during the war in the training of troops; member of the Lynn Town Council 1908-38, Mayor 1926, 1932 and 1938. Author of *Great Britain for Democracy*, 1918. A Liberal. Unsuccessfully contested King's Lynn in 1922. Elected for the King's Lynn division of Norfolk in December 1923 and sat until he was defeated in October 1924. Died 26 December 1938. [1924 2nd.ed.]

WOOLCOCK, William James Uglow, C.B.E. 36 Glebe Road, Barnes, London.

Reform, and Chemical Industry S. of the Rev. James Woolcock. B. at Plymouth 1878; m. 1903, Katherine Maud, d. of J.T Horner, Esq., of Witchampton. Educ. privately. Secretary of the Pharmaceutical Society and Registrar under the Pharmacy Act 1913-18. Assistant Director of Army contracts 1917-18; Chairman of Committee on Medical Supplies, Surveyor-Gen. of Supplies Department War Office 1918; Parliamentary Private Secretary to Minister of Supply 1919-20, and to Postmaster-Gen. 1921. Gen. Manager of the Association of British Chemical Manufacturers from 1918-28. A Coalition Liberal. Returned unopposed for the central division of Hackney in December 1918 and sat until he retired in October 1922. C.B.E. 1920. President of Society of the Chemical Industry 1924-26. C.M.G. 1933. Died 13 November 1947.

[1922]

WOOLLEY, William Edward. Brae Crest, Meins Road, Blackburn. National Liberal. S. of William Woolley, Esq., of Blackburn. B. 17 March 1901; m. 1929, Marion Elizabeth, d. of Edgar Aspinall, Esq. Educ. at Woodhouse Grove School, Apperley Bridge, and at University of Edinburgh. A Manufacturing Chemist. Member of the Pharmaceutical Society. J.P. 1935. A Gov. of Woodhouse Grove School. Parliamentary Private Secretary to Rt. Hon. Ernest Brown when Minister of Health 1943 and when Minister of Aircraft Production 1945. A Liberal National. Returned unopposed for the Spen Valley division of the W. Riding of Yorkshire in June 1940 and sat until he was defeated in July 1945. Unsuccessfully contested Brighouse and Spenborough in February 1950, May 1950 and October 1951. Dept.-Lieut. for Lancashire. Chairman of Blackburn and District Hospital Management Committee 1952-74. President of Blackburn and District Council of Social Service. Chairman of Cupal Limited from 1947. C.B.E. 1974.* [1945]

WOOTTON-DAVIES, James Henry. Bronwylfa Hall, Wrexham. Starling Castle, Bronygarth, Oswestry. Carlton, and Constitutional. S. of James Davies, Esq., of Chester. B. 1884; m. 1937, Shirley Gertrude Mabel,

d. of Professor William Bale Wootton. Educ. at Chester Technical School. A Soap and Chemical Manufacturer. Fellow of Institute of Chemistry; J.P. for Lancashire. Chairman of Peter Lunt and Company Limited. A Director of many companies. A Conservative. Returned unopposed for the Heywood and Radcliffe division of Lancashire in August 1940 and sat until he was defeated in July 1945. Assumed the surname of Wootton-Davies in lieu of Davies after his marriage. Died 21 December 1964.

[1945]

WORSFOLD, Dr. Thomas Cato. 9 Staple Inn, London. The Hall Place, Mitcham, Surrey. Savage, and Authors'. Surrey Conservative. S. of William and Eliza Worsfold, of The Hall Place, Mitcham. B. in London, c. 1861; m. 1900, Louise, d. of John Jeffree, Esq., F.R.C.S. Educ. at Trinity Coll., Dublin. M.A. and Doctor of Laws; F.R. Hist.S., F.R.S.L. J.P. for Surrey. Admitted a Solicitor 1883. Commissioner in Great Britain for the Supreme Courts of the British Colonies and Empire of India etc., also Commissioner in Great Britain for the High Courts of the United States of America. Author of *A Concise Text-Book on the Law of Repairs and Dilapidations*, *The French Stonehenge* (second edition), *Staple Inn and its Story* (third edition), *The Serpent Column of the Delphic Oracle*, and of various encyclopaedic and archaeological articles. Member of many public and local bodies. Chairman of Eastwoods Limited. A Conservative. Sat for the Mitcham division of Surrey from December 1918 until he resigned in February 1923. Created Bart 1924. Died 11 July 1936. [1923]

WORTHINGTON, Sir John Vigers. House of Commons, London. S. of James C. Worthington, Esq., Surgeon, of Lowestoft. B. 1872; m. 8 June 1904, Agnes Janet, d. of E.J. Edwards, Esq. Educ. at Woodbridge, Haileybury, and London Hospital. Parliamentary Private Secretary to the Rt. Hon. J.R. MacDonald, Prime Minister December 1931-June 1935. A Nationalist Labour Member. Elected for the Forest of Dean division of Gloucestershire in October 1931 and sat until he was defeated in

November 1935. Knighted June 1935. Died 16 June 1951. [1935]

WORTHINGTON-EVANS, Rt. Hon. Sir Worthington Laming, Bart., G.B.E. 6 Eaton Place, London. Doghurst, Limpsfield, Surrey. Carlton, City Carlton, 1900, and United. S. of Worthington Evans and Susannah, d. of James Laming, Esq., of Birchington Hall, Kent. B. 23 August 1868; m. 5 November 1898, Gertrude, d. of William Hale, Esq. Educ. at Eastbourne Coll., and privately. Admitted a Solicitor 1890, Hons. and Mackrell Prizeman; retired 1910. Member of Board of Trade Committee for the Reform of Company Law 1905. Author of *Notes on the Companies Acts.* Capt. 2nd Middlesex Volunteer Artillery. Inspector of Administrative Services, Northern Command, York 1914-15; temporary Maj. Parliamentary Private Secretary to Mr. H.W. Forster, Financial Secretary to War Office 1915-16. Controller Foreign Trade Department of the Foreign Office 1916. Parliamentary and Financial Secretary to Ministry of Munitions 1916-18. Minister of Blockade and Parliamentary Under-Secretary Foreign Office 1918-19; Minister of Pensions January 1919-April 1920; Minister without Portfolio with seat in Cabinet April 1920-February 1921; Secretary of State for War February 1921 to October 1922, and November 1924-June 1929; Postmaster-Gen. May 1923-January 1924. Created Bart. 1916; PC. 1918; G.B.E. 1922. A Conservative. Unsuccessfully contested Colchester in 1906. Sat for Colchester from January 1910 to December 1918; and for the Colchester division of Essex from December 1918 to May 1929. Elected for the St. George's division of Westminster in May 1929 and sat until his death on 14 February 1931. Editor-in-Chief of *Financial News* 1924. Assumed the surname Worthington-Evans in lieu of Evans in 1916. Died 14 February 1931. [1931 2nd ed.]

WRAGG, Sir Herbert. Bretby House, Burton-on-Trent. Carlton, and St. Stephen's. County, Derby. S. of Alderman J.D. Wragg, of Swadlincote, Derbyshire. B. 1880; m. 1st, 1905, Fanny, d. of Thomas Sutcliffe, Esq. (she died 1918); secondly, 1919, her sister Marion, d. of Thomas Sutcliffe, Esq. Educ. at Uppingham. Chairman of Thomas Wragg and Sons Limited, Stoneware and Brickmakers, Swadlincote. J.P. for Derbyshire. Alderman County Council. Director of Granville Colliery Company Limited; Chairman of South Leicestershire Colliery Company Limited. Knight Bach. 1944. A Conservative. Elected for the Belper division of Derbyshire in December 1923 and October 1924, defeated May 1929. Re-elected for the Belper division of Derbyshire in October 1931 and sat until he retired in June 1945. President of Ceramic Society. President of National Federation of Clay Industries. Died 13 February 1956. [1945]

WRIGHT, Beatrice Frederika. 4b, Deans Yard, London. D. of F. Roland Clough, Esq., of Boston, U.S.A. B. 1910, at New Haven, Connecticut; m. 1st, 1932, Flight-Lieut. J.R. Rathbone, MP, Conservative Member for the Bodmin division of Cornwall 1935-40 (who was reported missing, presumed killed on active service in December 1940); secondly, 23 May 1942, Capt. P.H.G. Wright, K.R.R.C. (subsequently Sir Paul Wright, K.C.M.G.). Educ. at Radcliffe Coll., Oxford. A National Conservative. Returned unopposed for the Bodmin division of Cornwall in March 1941 and sat until she retired in June 1945.* [1945]

WRIGHT, Group Capt. John Allan Cecil 50 Sloane Street, London. Rectory Lane, Castle Bromwich. Carlton, Royal Air Force, Royal Aero, Kennel, R.A.F., and Yacht. Conservative, Birmingham. S. of Alfred Cecil Wright, Esq. B. 1886; m. 1st, 1910, Irene, d. of A.C. Auster, Esq., of Barnt Green (marriage dissolved in 1919); secondly, 1920, Lillian Annie May, d. of R.B.P. Dolman, Esq., 3rdly, 1946, Ethne Monica, d. of Dr. W.E. Falconar. Educ. at Winchester. Joined 1st Volunteer Battalion Royal Warwickshire Regiment 1905; served with B.E.F. 1914-19; joined R.F.C. 1916; Squadron Leader No. 605 (Co. of Warwick) Bomber Squadron 1926-36; recalled to active duty August 1939. Dept.-Lieut. for Warwickshire; member of Birmingham City Council

1934-40. A Conservative. Elected for the Erdington division of Birmingham in October 1936 and sat until he was defeated in July 1945. Unsuccessfully contested the Erdington division of Birmingham in February 1950. Assumed name of Cecil-Wright in lieu of Wright in 1957. Chairman of Warne Wright and Rowland Limited 1920-63. Member of Warwickshire County Council 1958-61. President of Kennel Club and Cruft's Dog Show. A.F.C.* [1945]

WRIGHT, Brigadier-Gen. Wallace Duffield, V.C., C.B., C.M.G., D.S.O. Army & Navy, Royal Automobile, and Ranelagh. S. of J.S. Wright, Esq. B. 1875 in Gibraltar; m. 1919, Flora, d. of Richard Bewick, Esq., of Atlanta, U.S.A. Educ. at Royal Military Coll., Sandhurst. Joined the Queen's Regiment 1896. Served on N.W. Frontier of India 1897-98, in Nigeria 1902-03, in the Cameroons 1915, in France 1916-19, and in German Occupied Territory 1923-25. Retired 1927. A Conservative. Elected for the the Tavistock division of Devon in October 1928 and again in May 1929 and sat until he retired in October 1931. C.M.G. 1916; D.S.O. 1918; V.C. 1903; C.B. 1926. Member of Honourable Corps of Gentlemen-at-Arms 1932-50. Dept.-Lieut. for Surrey. Died 25 March 1953. [1931 2nd ed.]

WRIGHT, William. 96 Rosslyn Avenue, Rutherglen. B. near Lincoln 1862. Educ. at a Council School. Well known in Scotland for work on behalf of the Co-operative movement. A Labour Member. Sat for the Rutherglen division of Lanarkshire from November 1922 until his death on 9 April 1931. ILP Organiser in S. Wales 1898. Anglican lay reader. Author of *Down Under*, a volume of poetry, and *Agriculture and the Unemployed*. Died 9 April 1931.

[1931 2nd ed.]

WRIGHTSON, Lieut.-Col. Harry. 94 Ashley Gardens, Westminster. S. of Rev. W.G. Wrightson, of Hurworth-on-Tees. B. at Bromley 1874. Underwriter at Lloyd's. Lieut.-Col. Essex Royal Army Service Corps. A Conservative. Elected for W. Leyton in December 1918 but died on 29 January 1919 before the first meeting of the new Parliament.

394

YATE, Col. Sir Charles Edward, Bart., C.S.I., C.M.G. 17 Prince of Wales Terrace, Kensington, London. Ashfordby House, Melton Mowbray. Madeley Hall, Shropshire. Carlton, and Junior United Service. Eld. s. of the Rev. Charles Yate, B.D., Vicar of Holme-on-Spalding Moor, Yorkshire. B. 28 August 1849; m. 1899, Charlotte Heath, d. of J. Hume Burnley, Esq., of H.M. Diplomatic Service (she died 1936). Educ at Shrewsbury. Appointed Ensign 49th (Royal Berkshire) Regiment 1867, became Capt. in Indian Army 1879 and Col. 1901. Served in Afghan War 1880-81 as political officer at Kalat-i-Ghilzai and on march to and at battle of Kandahar (despatches, medal and clasp and bronze star); Afghan Boundary Commission 1884-86. Was British Representative at Panjdeh at time of Russian attack on Afghan troops 1885. Appointed British Commissioner to complete demarcation of Russio-Afghan Frontier 1887; H.M. Consul at Muscat, Arabia 1889; political Agent at Baluchistan and acting Revenue Commissioner 1890-93. H.M. Commissioner for settlement of Kushk Canal Question on Russian-Afghan Frontier 1893; British Consul-Gen. and Agent to Gov.-Gen. of India for Khorassan and Siestan at Meshed, Persia 1893-98; Resident at Jodhpur; Acting Agent to Gov.-gen. for Rajputana, and Resident at Udaipur 1899; Chief Commissioner of Baluschistan 1900-04. Clock tower erected to his memory at Quetta by the chiefs and people on his departure. Present at assault and capture of Nodiz Fort in Mekran 1902. A Knight of Grace of St. John of Jerusalem. Member of Committee of British Ophthalmic Hospital, Jerusalem; member of council Royal Geographical Society and Central Asian Society; of Indian Section Royal Society of Arts; and of East Indian Association. Author of *Northern Afghanistan, Khorassan and Siestan*, and Gazetteers of Mewar, Banswara and Partabgarh in Rajputana and various papers on Herat, etc.; member of Afghan Order of Hurmat. Dept.-Lieut. for Leicestershire. Created Bart. 1921. A Conservative. Unsuccessfully contested Pontefract in 1906 and the Melton division of Leicestershire in January 1910. Sat for the Melton division of Leicestershire from December 1910 until he retired in October

1924. Died 29 February 1940.

[1924 2nd ed.]

YEO, Sir Alfred William. 86-88 St. Leonard's Road, Poplar, London. Leamington, Chalkwell Avenue, Westcliff-on-Sea. National Liberal. S. of George R.J. Yeo, Esq., of Devon. B. 13 October 1963; m. 1st, 1886, Mary Ann Brown (she died 1911), d. of Mrs. Stevens; one s.; secondly, 1911, Florence J. Stevens, of Poplar. Educ. at Marner Street and High Street Schools, Bromley. Started work in an Iron Foundry; thirty years in business in music trade. Member of Poplar Vestry, Board of Works and Borough Council for 25 years; member of Poplar Board of Guardians 10 years, Chairman 6 years; Chairman Poplar Distress Committee 10 years; Mayor Poplar 1903-04; Chairman over 20 years under L.B.S. of Managers of Local Schools in St. Leonard's Road, Hay Currie, and Bromley Hall Road Groups; Chairman of Lord Buxton's Committee dealing with distress during great Dock Strike. Member of London County Council for seven years; J.P. (Tower Bench). Knighted 1918. Published *Trade after the War.* A Liberal. Elected for Poplar in February 1914 and S. Poplar in December 1918 and sat until he was defeated in November 1922. Unsuccessfully contested the Kettering division of Northamptonshire in December 1923. Died 14 April 1928. [1922]

YERBURGH, Maj. Robert Daniel Thwaites. 34 Cadogan Square, London. Carlton, and Bachelors'. S. of Robert Armstrong Yerburgh, Esq., MP for Chester, and Elma Amy Yerburgh, d. of D. Thwaites, Esq., MP for Blackburn. B. 10 December 1889; m. 1st, 16 December 1911, Dorothea, d. of J. Eardley Yerburgh (she died 10 February 1927); secondly, 1936, Mrs. Maud Lytton Grey Bright, d. of Charles Lytton Grey Morgan, Esq. Educ. at Harrow, and University Coll., Oxford. Served in the army February 1915 to July 1919; retired with the rank of Brevet-Maj. A Conservative. Sat for S. Dorset from November 1922 until he retired in May 1929. Created Baron Alvingham 1929. Died 27 November 1955. [1929]

YORK, Christopher. Continued in House after 1945: full entry in Volume IV.

YOUNG, Andrew. 13 Gayfield Square, Edinburgh. S. of David Young, Esq., Soldier, and Jessie Young. B. in Edinburgh 6 November 1858; m. 1 January 1885, Alexandrina, d. of Alexander Leggett, Esq., Artist, of Edinburgh. Educ. at Heriot and Dr. Bell's Schools, Edinburgh Church of Scotland Training Coll., and Edinburgh University. A Teacher December 1881; Headmaster from 1895 to 1922. Chairman of Scot Company of Convalescent Homes from 1906. Wrote numerous pamphlets on social subjects. A Labour Member. Elected for the Partick division of Glasgow in December 1923 and sat until he was defeated in October 1924. Bailie of City of Edinburgh. Fellow of Educational Institute of Scotland, President 1923. Died 9 February 1943.

[1924 2nd ed.]

YOUNG, Sir Arthur Stewart Leslie, Bart. Continued in House after 1945: full entry in Volume IV.

YOUNG, Rt. Hon. Sir Edward Hilton, G.B.E., D.S.O., D.S.C. Leinster Corner, Lancaster Gate, London. Brooks's. S. of Sir George Young, 3rd Bart. B. 20 March 1879; m. 3 March 1922, Kathleen, d. of Canon L.S. Bruce, and widow of Capt. R.F. Scott, R.N. (she died 1947). Educ. at Eton, and Trinity Coll., Cambridge, M.A., Honorary D.C.L. Durham. Barrister-at-Law, Inner Temple 1904. Served as Lieut.-Commander R.N.V.R., at sea and in Serbia, Flanders and Russia 1914-19. Had Grand Cordon of Order of Polonia; Order of Karageorge and Croix de Guerre. Parliamentary Private Secretary to the Rt. Hon. H.A.L. Fisher February 1919; Financial Secretary to the Treasury April 1921 to October 1922. Secretary of Overseas Trade Department September.-November 1931; Minister of Health November 1931-June 1935. PC. 1922; G.B.E. 1927. Chairman of Royal Commission on Indian Currency 1926, and other Missions and Inquiries. British Representative at The Hague Conference 1922, and League of Nations 1926-28 and 1932. A Liberal until 1926, thereafter a

Conservative. Unsuccessfully contested E. Worcestershire in January 1910 and Preston in December 1910. Elected for Norwich in February 1915; sat until he was defeated in December 1923; re-elected for Norwich in October 1924 and sat until May 1929. Joined Conservative Party in June 1926. Elected for the Sevenoaks division of Kent in May 1929; returned unopposed for the Sevenoaks division of Kent in October 1931 and sat until June 1935 when he was created Baron Kennet. Chief National Liberal Whip 1922-23. Resigned Liberal Whip February 1926. Assistant Editor of *The Economist* 1908-10, City Editor of *Morning Post* from 1910. President of Royal Statistical Society 1936-38. Died 11 July 1960. [1935]

YOUNG, Ernest James. 56 Erroll Road, Hove, Sussex. S. of Trayton Young, Esq., of Hove, Sussex. B. 28 July 1882; m. 1908, Phoebe, d. of James Terry, Esq., of Portslade. Educ. privately. A Journalist and Lecturer. Member of Portslade Urban District Council. Served overseas with Royal Engineers 1914-18. A Liberal. Unsuccessfully contested the Jarrow division of Durham 1922, Rossendale in 1923 and 1924, the Bothwell division of Lanarkshire in 1926, and Middlesbrough E. in May 1929. Elected for Middlesbrough E. in October 1931 and sat until he was defeated in November 1935. [1935]

YOUNG, Sir Frederick William. 63 Portland Place, London. S. of John Young, Esq., of Mount Templeton, South Australia. B. 5 January 1876; m. 1904, Florence, d. of John Darling, Esq., of Adelaide (she died 1947). Educ. at Prince Alfred Coll., and Adelaide University. A Member of the South Australian Parliament, in which he held office as Commissioner of Crown Lands and Immigration 1912-14, and assisted in passing Acts dealing with Land Settlement and Boy Immigrants. Was Agent-Gen. in London for South Australia 1915-18. A Coalition Unionist. Elected for the Swindon division of Wiltshire in December 1918 and sat until he retired in October 1922. Member of the Bar of South Australia and of Commonwealth of Australia. Knighted 1918. Chairman of Australian Estates Company Limited. Chairman of English Scottish and Australian Bank 1946-48. Died 26 August 1948. [1922]

YOUNG, Sir Robert. Continued in House after 1945: full entry in Volume IV.

YOUNG, Robert Stanley. 3 Walden House, High Street, London. S. of Alexander Young, Esq., Director of Brookfield, Aitchison, Limited, of Manchester, and of Elizabeth, d. of T. Stephenson, Esq. B. 28 May 1891; m. 1923, Doris Littel White, d. of Percival Hill, Esq., of Portsmouth. Educ. at Manchester Grammar School. A Play Producer and Critic. A Labour Member. Elected for Islington N. in May 1929 and sat until he was defeated in October 1931. Unsuccessfully contested Islington N. in November 1935. Author of *Cricket on the Green*. Served with Anzacs at Gallipoli and in France 1914-18.* [1931 2nd ed.]

YOUNG, William. 4 Albemarle Street, London. Reform, and Royal Automobile. S. of James Young, Esq., of Glenmuick, Aberdeenshire. B. 1863; m. 1919, Stephanie, youngest d. of Dr. S. MacSwiney, M.D., of Dublin. Educ. at Ballater Public School. A Director of William Young and Company Limited, Foreign Merchants and Bankers, London and Mexico City. A Liberal. Sat E. Perthshire from January 1910 to December 1918. Returned unopposed for the Perth division of Perth and Kinross in December 1918 and sat until he retired in October 1922. Died 7 June 1942. [1922]

YOUNGER, Sir George, Bart. Leckie, Gargunnock, Stirlingshire. Alloa, N.B. Carlton, and Conservative. S. of J. Younger, Esq., of Alloa. B. 1851; m. 1879, Lucy, d. of Edward Smith, Esq., M.D. (she died May 1921). Educ. at Edinburgh Academy. Chairman of George Younger and Son, Brewers, of Alloa. A Director of National Bank of Scotland, of Lloyds Banks, and of the N. British and Mercantile Insurance Company; a member of Royal Commission on Licensing 1896. President of National Union of Conservative Associations in Scotland 1904. Chairman of the Unionist Party Organization from 1 January 1917 to March 1923. A J.P. and Dept.-Lieut. for Clackmannan, of which Co. he was Convener 1895-1906. A J.P. and Dept.-Lieut. for Stirlingshire. Created Bart. 1911. A Unionist. Unsuccessfully contested Clackmannan and Kinross in 1895, 1899 and 1900, and Ayr Burghs in 1904. Elected for Ayr Burghs in 1906 and sat until he retired in October 1922. President of County Councils Association of Scotland 1902-04. Created Visct. Younger of Leckie 1923. Treasurer of Unionist Party 1923-29. Lord-Lieut. of Stirlingshire 1925-29. Vice-Lieut. of Clackmannan 1922-29. Died 29 April 1929.

[1922]

Index of Names

Index of Names

This index lists all Members of Parliament who sat in the House of Commons between 1919 and 1945. Cross references are given where necessary. All names appear in the same order as in the text. Members who continued to sit after 1945, and whose full entries appear in Volume IV, are marked with an asterisk. Members who have full entries in both Volumes II and III are marked with a dagger; in the majority of cases some further information has been added to the entry in Volume III.

A

†Abraham, Rt. Hon. W.
Ackroyd, T.R.
Acland, Rt. Hon. Sir F.D., Bart.
*Acland, Sir R.T.D., Bart.
Acland-Troyte, Lieut.-Col. Sir G.J.A. *see* Troyte, Lieut.-Col. Sir G.J.A.
Adair, Rear-Admiral T.B.S.
Adams, D.
Adams, D.M.
Adams, Maj. S.V.T.
*Adamson, J.L.
Adamson, Rt. Hon. W.
Adamson, W.M.
Addison, Rt. Hon. C.
Adkins, Sir W.R.D.
Agg-Gardner, Rt. Hon. Sir J.T.
*Agnew, P.G.
Ainsworth, Lieut.-Col. C.
Aitchison, Rt. Hon. C.M.
Albery, Sir I.J.
Alden, P.
*Alexander, Rt. Hon. A.V.
Alexander, E.E.
Alexander, Lieut.-Col. M.
Alexander, Brigadier-Gen. Sir W.
Allen, Col. J.S.
Allen, Sir J.S.
Allen, R.W.
Allen, W.
Allen, W.E.D.
Allen, Lieut.-Col. Sir W.J.
*Alpass, J.H.
Alstead, R.
Amery, Lieut.-Col. Rt. Hon. L.C.M.S.
Ammon, C.G.
Anderson, Sir A.G.
*Anderson, F.
Anderson, H.A.
*Anderson, Rt. Hon. Sir J.
Angell, Sir R.N.
*Anstruther-Gray, W.J.
Applin, Lieut.-Col. R.V.K.

Apsley, Lieut.-Col. A.A.B., The Lord
Apsley, V.E.M.B., The Lady
Archdale, Rt. Hon E.M.
Archer-Shee, Lieut.-Col. M.
Armitage, R.
Armstrong, H.B.
Arnold, S.
Arnott, J.
Ashley, Lieut.-Col. Rt. Hon. W.W.
Ashmead-Bartlett, Capt. E.
Aske, Sir R.W., Bart.
†Asquith, Rt. Hon. H.H.
*Assheton, Rt. Hon. R.
Astbury, Lieut.-Commander F.W.
Astor, Lieut.-Col. Hon. J.J.
Astor, N.W. A., The Viscountess
Astor, Hon. W.
*Astor, Hon. W.W.
Atholl, K.M.S.M., Duchess of
Atkey, A.R.
Atkinson, C.
*Attlee, Rt. Hon. C.R.
Austin, Sir H.
*Ayles, W.H.

B

Bagley, Capt. E.A.A.
Bailey, E.A.G.S.
Baillie, Sir A.W.M., Bart.
Baillie-Hamilton, Hon. C.W.
Baird, Rt. Hon. Sir J.L., Bart.
Baker, J.
Baker, W.J.
*Baldwin, O.R. *see* Corvedale, O.R.B., Visct.
†Baldwin, Rt. Hon. S.
Baldwin-Webb, Col. J.
†Balfour, Rt. Hon. Sir A.J.
Balfour, G.
Balfour, Capt. Rt. Hon. H.H.
Balfour, Sir R., Bart.
Balniel, D.R.A.L., Lord

Banbury, Rt. Hon. Sir F.G., Bart.
Banfield, J.W.
Banks, Sir R.M.
Banner, Sir J.S.H. *see* Harmood-Banner, Sir J.S.
Banton, G.
Barclay, R.N.
Barclay-Harvey, Sir C.M.
Barker, G.
Barker, Maj. R.H.
Barlow, Rt. Hon. Sir C.A.
*Barnes, A.J.
Barnes, Rt. Hon. G.N.
Barnes, Maj. H.
Barnett, Maj. Sir R.W.
Barnston, Sir H., Bart.
Barr, Rev. J.
Barrand, A.R.
Barrie, Sir C.C.
Barrie, Rt. Hon. H.T.
*Barstow, P.G.
*Bartlett, C.V.O.
Bartley-Denniss, Sir E.R.B.
Barton, Sir A.W.
Barton, Capt. B.K.
Barton, R.C.
Bateman, A.L.
Batey, J.
*Baxter, A.B.
Beamish, Rear-Admiral T.P.H.
Beasley, P.
Beattie, F.
*Beattie, J.
Beauchamp, Sir B.C., Bart.
Beauchamp, Sir E., Bart.
*Beaumont, H.
Beaumont, M.W.
Beaumont, Hon. R.E.B.
Beaumont-Thomas, Maj. L. *see* Thomas, Maj. L.B.
Beck, Sir A.C.T.
Becker, H.T.A.
Beckett, J.W.
Beckett, Hon. Sir W.G., Bart.
Beech, Maj. F.W.
*Beechman, N.A.
Beit, Sir A.L., Bart.

INDEX OF NAMES

E

Eady, G.H.
Eales, J.F.
Eastwood, J.F.
* Eccles, D.M.
Eckersley, P.T.
* Ede, Rt. Hon. J.C.
* Eden, Rt. Hon. R.A.
Edgar, C.B.
Edge, Sir W., Bart.
Edmonds, G.
Edmondson, Maj. Sir A.J.
Edmunds, J.E.
Ednam, W.H.E.W., Visct.
* Edwards, A.
Edwards, A.C.
* Edwards, Rt. Hon. Sir C.
Edwards, E.
Edwards, G.
Edwards, Lieut.-Col. J.
Edwards, J.H.
* Edwards, N.
* Edwards, W.J.
Egan, W.H.
* Elliot, Rt. Hon W.E.
Elliott, Sir G.S.
Ellis, Sir R.G., Bart.
Ellis, W.C.
    see Craven-Ellis, W.C.
Ellis-Griffith, Rt. Hon. Sir
    E.J., Bart.
Elliston, Capt. Sir G.S.
Emley, W.L., Visct.
Elveden, R.E.C.L.G., Visct.
Emery, J.F.
Emlyn-Jones, J.E.
Emmott, C.E.G.C.
Emrys-Evans, P.V.
England, Col. A.
Entwistle, Sir C.F.
* Errington, E.
Erskine, J.M.M.
Erskine, J.F.A.E., The Lord
Erskine-Bolst, Capt. C.C.A.L.
Erskine-Hill, Sir A.G.E., Bart.
Essenhigh, R.C.
Etchingham, J.R.
Etherton, R.H.
Evans, D.O.
Evans, E.
Evans, Col. Sir H.A.
Evans, H.
Evans, Capt. R.T.
Evans, Rt. Hon. Sir W.L., Bart.
    see Worthington-Evans, Rt.
    Hon. Sir W.L., Bart.
Everard, Sir W.L.
Eyres-Monsell, Rt. Hon.
    Sir B.M.

F

Fahy, F.P.
Fairbairn, R.R.
Fairfax, Capt. J.G.
Falcon, Capt. M.
Falconer, J.
Falle, Sir B.G., Bart.
Falls, Maj. Sir C.F.
Fanshawe, Commander G.D.
Farquharson, Maj. A.C.
Fawkes, Maj. F.H.
Fell, Sir A.
Fenby, T.D.
Ferguson, H.
Ferguson, Sir J.
Fermor-Hesketh, Maj. T.
Fermoy, E.M.R.
Fielden, F.B.
Fildes, Sir H.
Finburgh, S.
Findlay, Sir J.E.R., Bart.
Finney, S.
Finney, V.H.
Fisher, Rt. Hon. H.A.L.
Fison, F.G.C.
Fitzgerald, T.D.
Fitzroy, Capt. Rt. Hon. E.A.
Flanagan, W.H.
Flannery, Sir J.F., Bart.
Fleming, D.P.
* Fleming, E.L.
Fletcher, R.T.H.
Flint, A.J.
* Foot, D.M.
Foot, I.
Ford, Sir P.J., Bart.
Foreman, Sir H.
Forestier-Walker, Sir C.L.,
    Bart.
Forgan, Dr. R.
Forrest, W.
†Forster, Rt. Hon. H.W.
Foster, Sir H.S.
* Foster, W.
* Fox, Sir G.W.G., Bart.
Fox, H.W.
    see Wilson-Fox, H.
Foxcroft, Capt. C.T.
France, G.A.
Frankel, D.
Franklin, L.B.
Fraser, Maj. Sir K.A., Bart.
* Fraser, T.
* Fraser, Sir W.J.I.
* Freeman, P.
Fremantle, Sir F.E.
Fuller, Capt. A.G.H.
Furness, G.J.
Furness, S.N.

* Fyfe, Rt. Hon. Sir D.P.M.
    see Maxwell Fyfe, Rt. Hon.
    Sir D.P.

G

Gadie, Lieut.-Col. A.
Galbraith, J.F.W.
Galbraith, S.
* Galbraith, T.D.
* Gallacher, W.
Galligan, P.P.
* Gammans, L.D.
* Gander Dower, A.V.
    see Dower, A.V.G.
Gange, E.S.
Ganzoni, Capt. Sir F.J.C.,
    Bart.
Gardiner, J.
Gardner, B.W.
Gardner, E.
Gardner, J.P.
Gardner, Rt. Hon. Sir J.T.A.
    see Agg-Gardner, Rt. Hon.
    Sir J.T.
Garland, C.S.
Garro-Jones, G.M.
* Gates, E.E.
Gates, P.G.
Gault, Lieut.-Col. A.H.
Gaunt, Vice-Admiral Sir
    G.R.A.
Gavan Duffy, G.
    see Duffy, G.G.
Gavan-Duffy T.
    see Duffy, T.G.
Geddes, Rt. Hon. Sir A.C.
Geddes, Maj.-Gen. Rt. Hon.
    Sir E.C.
Gee, Capt. R.
* Gibbins, J.
Gibbons, Lieut.-Col. W.E.
Gibbs, Col. Rt. Hon. G.A.
Gibson, Sir C.G.
Gibson, H.M.
Gibson, R.
Gilbert, J.D.
Gill, T.H.
Gillett, Sir G.M.
Gillis, W.
Gilmour, Lieut.-Col. Rt. Hon.
    Sir J., Bart.
Ginnell, L.
Glanville, H.J.
* Glanville, J.E.
Glassey, A.E.
Gledhill, G.
* Glossop, C.W.H.

Other
Works of Reference

ANNUAL BIBLIOGRAPHY OF BRITISH AND IRISH HISTORY

Edited by G.R. ELTON

This major new reference book is under the editorial direction of Professor G.R. Elton, the Cambridge historian whose works include *The Tudor Revolution in Government, England Under the Tudors, Reformation Europe* and *The Practice of History.*

It is published annually in association with the Royal Historical Society. Important features of this new work are that it is written by a team of eleven experts, co-ordinated by Professor Elton, it is absolutely up-to-date, with less than a six-month gap between final copy and finished books, it is the only work of its kind, and it is as comprehensive as possible.

Each Autumn a volume appears covering the previous year's publications. As well as books and articles published in Great Britain the book covers publications produced in the U.S.A., Canada, and elsewhere. The aim is to be as comprehensive as possible without attempting the impossible ambition of exhaustiveness. However, provision is made for picking up omissions and oversights in the following year.

The subject matter is defined as the history of England, Scotland, Wales and Ireland but not that of the British Empire overseas except where imperial matters are treated primarily as domestic concerns, from the point of view of the mother-country's history.

The sections are mainly chronological though medieval Wales, pre-Union Scotland, and Ireland are treated separately: each section is sub-divided into topically defined subsections. An index of authors, of editors, and a subject index is provided.

This is conceived as a reference work which any historian of Britain in any period will not wish to be without; to libraries it will be absolutely essential.

"This bibliography will be indispensable for scholars of British and Irish history. As a reference book, it will be essential to academic and large public libraries." CHOICE.

The Annual Bibliography...*is highly recommended for university libraries."* LIBRARY JOURNAL.

BIBLIOGRAPHY OF THE CHARTIST MOVEMENT, 1837-1976

J.F.C. Harrison and Dorothy Thompson

This new reference book brings together a large body of material located as the result of several years of research. It includes all known primary and secondary works, and constitutes an unparalleled source record both of contemporary pamphlets, periodicals, memoirs, articles and archives as well as listing all modern work.

Chartism continues to fascinate successive generations of students and historians. No adequate bibliography of Chartism has ever been produced before. This new work will give authoritative guidance.

This extensive bibliography covers the greatest of all working-class movements in Britain before the rise of modern socialism. It has been prepared by two leading scholars both of whom are internationally-known for their scholarship in this field.

ELECTORAL FACTS, FROM 1832-1853, IMPARTIALLY STATED. A COMPLETE POLITICAL GAZETTEER

CHARLES R. DOD

Edited, with a new 20,000 word introduction and bibliographical guide to electoral sources, by H.J. Hanham.

Dod's *Electoral Facts* is a famous rare book, better known by reputation than by use. A pioneer work of electoral analysis, it is a frank account of British constituency politics for the twenty years after the Great Reform Act of 1832. The second edition—an entire revisal of the first—deals with the local position and nature of each constituency, the prevailing influence, registered electors, annual value of real property paying income tax, amount of assessed taxes, population, prevailing trades, noted members, noted elections, together with polls for seats returning members to parliament.

Professor Hanham's new introduction is a substantial analysis of early and mid-Victorian electoral politics: here, and in his extensive bibliography for the years 1832-85, are the most up-to-date materials available on the electoral system after 1832.

"*This is a most valuable reprint, which every serious student of 19th century British politics ought to possess....This reissue can be highly recommended, the presentation being in every way fully worthy of the subject.*" BRITISH BOOK NEWS.

THE WARWICK GUIDE TO BRITISH LABOUR PERIODICALS, 1790-1970

Edited by ROYDEN HARRISON, GILLIAN WOOLVEN and ROBERT DUNCAN

This *Guide* fills one of the greatest gaps in the basic information available to historians of British Labour and of modern Britain. No such bibliography as this exists, and it is the result of an extensive co-operative effort by Professor Harrison and his colleagues at the Centre for the Study of Social History at Warwick University.

There are over 4,000 entries, and the new *Guide* entirely overtakes the few earlier attempts to cover small sections of the ground. For scholars who have previously sought to locate bibliographical data, information about locations, etc., Britain has compared very unfavourably with France and even more so with the U.S.A. and Canada.

This new work is a landmark in Labour studies. When the general history of Labour in Britain comes to be rewritten it may well be around the history of the Labour periodical press that this is done. For this is the one great institution of the Labour world which has still to find its historian and it is the institution which, in many ways affords best access to the non-institutional world of the workman.

The Warwick Guide to British Labour Periodicals is a standard tool of the trade, of exceptional value not only to historians of Labour but to historians generally and also to students of related disciplines like industrial relations.

"An indispensable reference work, it is solidly constructed in the publisher's probable expectation of its repeated use." CHOICE.

"This is a highly informative compendium of information which will be indispensable to the serious student of Labour history. If the authors modestly describe it as a provisional list, it actually goes a very long way towards being a comprehensive guide." BRITISH BOOK NEWS.

"The Guide far surpasses any tools currently available. Its usefulness is greatly enhanced by the inclusion of both a date index and a subject index. A necessary purchase for large research collections." LIBRARY JOURNAL.

"...we have long wanted the Labour equivalent of BUCOP (British Union Catalogue of Periodicals); and this we now have with the publication of the Warwick Guide. *It is a considerable event in the history of labour studies in this country."* SOCIETY FOR STUDY OF LABOUR HISTORY BULLETIN.

F.H. McCALMONT'S PARLIAMENTARY POLL BOOK OF ALL ELECTIONS, 1832-1918

Edited by J.R. Vincent and M. Stenton.

This new, eighth enlarged edition is a unique reference work with complete electoral facts and figures for more than 12,000 British election results 1832-1918.

Here in convenient easily-used form is the political history of the constituencies of the U.K. from the great Reform Act to the end of World War I.

For a general guide to electoral fortunes—and the specific detail to test and develop historical explanations—McCalmont stands alone as the essential starting point.

'McCalmont has its stern puritan joys. It allows the man on the Walsall omnibus to speak as well as the man on the Clapham omnibus. It is democratic in allowing the inarticulate and inaudible to command as much of a hearing as they can ever command. It raises questions, rather than gives answers: but if it pre-selects the questions in any obvious way (which is doubtful) it does not do so for anyone's convenience. It serves no theory, while on the other hand any theory one may choose about the opinions of the man in the street, must at least not be countermanded by what is here.' (From the new Introduction by Professor J.R. Vincent.)

New features of this eighth edition include its extension from 1910 to 1918 with a complete chronological table of by-elections (unavailable elsewhere) giving reasons for vacancies, party affiliation of candidates, polls etc. More familiar features are full results of all General and by-elections from 1832, government majorities, tabulated numerical strength of parties, registered electors and population, relative size and wealth of constituencies, 'moral' history of seats with boroughs of disfranchised etc., etc.

McCalmont is a rich feast of specimens of British life in Victorian and Edwardian England—a reference work of wide scope for the historian, sociologist and political scientist.

"It is to be hoped that as many pleasure seekers as scholars will find McCalmont in their hands, as it is now produced in facsimile by Harvester Press: a fat, small book, blue bound, with a wonderfully Victorian seriousness of air about it." TIMES LITERARY SUPPLEMENT.

THE HISTORY OF THE BOROUGHS AND MUNICIPAL CORPORATIONS OF THE UNITED KINGDOM. FROM THE EARLIEST TO THE PRESENT TIME

HENRY ALWORTH MEREWETHER and JOHN ARCHIBALD STEPHENS

With a new introduction and select bibliography by Geoffrey Martin.

First published in 1835, Merewether and Stephens' three-volumed *History of the Boroughs*, a book of commanding authority, was regarded throughout the nineteenth century as the chief work on British municipal history. It retains its historical importance in quite different circumstances and remains one of the most comprehensive and detailed surveys.

The debate on the best form of municipal government continues today in an age still consciously refining nineteenth century techniques. This work, by two distinguished lawyers, combines substantial learning with an immediate political purpose as a contribution to the contemporary debate on administrative reform and the development of the institutions of urban government. It first appeared in a period that determined the patterns of British town government for a half-century of extraordinary growth.

A 130-page index provides easy reference to all boroughs in England, Scotland, Wales and Ireland and to the records, charters, and other documents brought together in more than 2,400 pages.

Dr. Martin's new introduction assesses the authors' conclusions and arguments in the light of subsequent revision and research. A select bibliography of relevant literature is also supplied.

SOUTH ASIAN BIBLIOGRAPHY. A HANDBOOK AND GUIDE

South Asia Library Group
Edited by J.D. PEARSON

THIS NEW, extensive guide, edited by the distinguished professor of bibliography, J.D. Pearson, is a major achievement in area bibliography which will speedily become the essential handbook of scholars, students and librarians working in this large field.

South Asian Bibliography was produced, under the auspices of the South Asia Library Group, by an assemblage of leading scholars and librarians with expert knowledge of, and experience of working in South Asia—India, Pakistan, Bangladesh, Sri Lanka, Afghanistan, Burma, Tibet and the Maldives.

The plan of the work is a series of documents ranging in style from the discursive bibliographical essay to the annotated list.

Part I covers unpublished materials (manuscripts in Oriental and Western languages, archives, theses) followed by maps, periodicals and newspapers, and official publications of the pre- and post-partition eras. Other parts are concerned with bibliographies and reference books relating to the area as a whole and its constituent countries, and to individual subjects: the religions and philosophical systems, art, archaeology, music, history, languages and literatures, the social sciences, and the natural sciences both traditional and modern.

ARAB ISLAMIC BIBLIOGRAPHY
The Middle East Library Committee Guide
Edited by DIANA GRIMWOOD-JONES, DEREK HOPWOOD and J.D. PEARSON

This is the new reference guide to the literature of Arab Islamic Studies in all languages. It is a major achievement of modern bibliography and must immediately become the definitive work. It is alone in its field.

This *Arab Islamic Bibliography* is the collective work of a group of experts co-ordinated by the Middle East Library Committee in response to a very evident need in libraries and among scholars for such a modern and comprehensive work of reference. It will be an essential tool for scholars, librarians and bibliographers—especially so for those interested in Near and Middle East Studies.

A new reference guide—modern, authoritative, and comprehensive—has been much wanted for most of this century. Guiseppe Gabrieli's *Manuale* is the only attempt to cover the ground. The first part was published (and in Italian only) in 1916. It is the only work of its kind in Islamic Studies. For all its great qualities it has long needed to be re-done, extended and brought forward to the present day.

The plan of the work is that of a series of bibliographical essays which vary in format depending on the nature of the material dealt with in each section. The work deals with reference books in general, bibliographics, periodicals, manuscripts (including archives and papyri), *Festschriften* and the publications of expeditions. Other chapters discuss the history of Islamic Studies, their present cultivation and the libraries which serve them, as well as the history of printing in Arabic and the question of Middle Eastern geographical names. It forms an essential reference tool for the librarian and bibliographer, as well as an indispensable *vade mecum* for the Arabist and the student of Middle Eastern affairs.

"Seldom in this wonderful world of bibliographies does one come across one as skillfully done as this: it is the work of many fine scholars and is thoughtfully planned and expertly accomplished." CHOICE.

". . . an indispensable reference source for all concerned with Islamic studies. It will be of great use not only to librarians, but to serious students and scholars as well." LIBRARY JOURNAL.

"It is in all respects a new creation and will be a most valuable work of reference for students, teachers and librarians. The editors have been able to persuade a number of specialists to write chapters on their own fields, and themselves have ensured a high level of consistency in editing. . . . This work of reference has many excellent features and tries to provide basic guidance over the whole field of Arabic language and the related culture. It will surely become the standard handbook that Gabrieli's Manuale *was for previous generations."* BRITISH BOOK NEWS.

A CUMULATIVE ANALYTICAL INDEX TO 'THE DICKENSIAN', 1905-1974

Compiled by FRANK DUNN

The 70-year run of *The Dickensian* represents the biggest and best Dickens encyclopaedia in existence. This new analytical index gives immediate and easy access to the wealth of material on Dickens and his times that has appeared in *The Dickensian* since 1905. It is published simultaneously with The Harvester Press microfiche edition of *The Dickensian*. Here will be found information on a host of critical problems and on every aspect of Dickens's crowded life, together with a wealth of background material—historical, topographical, bibliographical, biographical—to his novels and other writings.

This new, fully analysed, index is as detailed and exhaustive as possible. It will be invaluable to scholars of the Victorian period and to students of Dickens and of English Literature generally.

"...*Frank Dunn's admirably comprehensive and discriminating index (which includes a most useful index to the illustrations: one of the great attractions of* The Dickensian*) is the essential guide to it. An immense amount of material, invaluable to all Dickensians, has been compressed into less than 200 pages.*" TIMES LITERARY SUPPLEMENT.

"...*locates an immense range of information on Dickens and Dickens scholarship.*" NINETEENTH-CENTURY FICTION.